THE OXFORD READER

THE OXFORD READER

Varieties of Contemporary Discourse

Edited by
FRANK KERMODE
and
RICHARD POIRIER

New York   OXFORD UNIVERSITY PRESS   1971

Copyright © 1971 by Oxford University Press, Inc.
Library of Congress Catalogue Card Number: 78-141846

Since this page cannot legibly accommodate all the copyright notices, the three pages following constitute an extention of the copyright page.

Printed in the United States of America

A. Alvarez: from *Beyond All This Fiddle*. Copyright © 1968 by A. Alvarez. Reprinted by permission of Random House, Inc.
James Baldwin: from *The Fire Next Time*. Copyright © 1963, 1962 by James Baldwin. Reprinted by permission of The Dial Press.
Donald Barthelme: from *Esquire,* April 1969. Copyright © 1969 by Donald Barthelme. Reprinted by permission of Donald Barthelme c/o International Famous Agency, Inc.
Eric Bentley: from *The Life of the Drama*. Copyright © 1964 by Eric Bentley. Reprinted by permission of Atheneum Publishers, Inc.
Bruno Bettelheim: from *The Children of the Dream*. Copyright © 1969 by The Macmillan Company. Reprinted by permission of the publisher.
Leonard Bloomfield: from *American Speech,* 1927. Reprinted by permission of Columbia University Press.
William Burroughs: from *The Ticket That Exploded*. Copyright © 1962, 1964, 1967 by William S. Burroughs. Reprinted by permission of Grove Press, Inc.
Angus Calder: from *The People's War*. Copyright © 1969 by Angus Calder. Reprinted by permission of Pantheon Books, a Division of Random House, Inc.
Stuart Chase: from *The Most Probable World*. Copyright © 1968 by Stuart Chase. Reprinted by permission of Harper & Row, Publishers, Inc.
Noam Chomsky: from *The Dissenting Academy,* ed. by Theodore Roszak. Copyright © 1967 by Random House, Inc. Reprinted by permission of Pantheon Books, a Division of Random House, Inc.
Marshall Cohen: from *The Massachusetts Review*. Copyright © 1969 by The Massachusetts Review, Inc. Reprinted by permission of the publisher.
Robert Coles: from *The American Scholar,* Autumn 1968. Copyright © 1968 by the United Chapters of Phi Beta Kappa. Reprinted by permission of the publisher.
Cyril Connolly: from *Enemies of Promise*. Copyright © 1938, 1946, 1948, 1960 by Cyril Connolly. Reprinted by permission of Deborah Rogers Ltd.
Frank Conroy: from *Stop-Time*. Copyright © 1965, 1966, 1967 by Frank Conroy. Reprinted by permission of The Viking Press, Inc.
Edwin Denby: from *Dancers, Buildings and People in the Streets*. Copyright © 1965 by Horizon Press. Reprinted by permission of the publisher.
John Donat: from *The Listener,* September 26, 1968. Reprinted by permission of the publisher and the author.

René Dubos: from *So Human an Animal.* Copyright © 1968 by René Dubos. Reprinted by permission of Charles Scribner's Sons.
F. W. Dupee: from *The New York Review of Books,* September 26, 1968. Copyright © 1968 by The New York Review. Reprinted by permission of the publisher.
Erik H. Erikson: from *Daedalus,* Summer 1967. Reprinted by permission of the American Academy of Arts and Sciences.
Leslie Fiedler: from *Partisan Review,* Fall 1965. © 1965 by Partisan Review. Reprinted by permission of the publisher.
Philip French: from *Encounter,* November 1966. Reprinted by permission of the author.
Edgar Friedenberg: from *Dissent,* Spring 1963. Reprinted by permission of the publisher and the author.
Buckminster Fuller: from *Saturday Review,* March 2, 1968. Copyright 1968 by Saturday Review, Inc. Reprinted by permission of the publisher.
John Kenneth Galbraith: from *Harper's Magazine,* November 1969. Copyright © 1969 by Harper's Magazine, Inc. Reprinted by permission of the author.
Paul Goodman: from *The New York Review of Books,* November 20, 1969. Reprinted by permission of the author.
Gerald S. Hawkins and John B. White: from *Stonehenge Decoded.* Copyright © 1965 by Gerald S. Hawkins and John B. White. Reprinted by permission of Doubleday & Company, Inc.
Lillian Hellman: from *Unfinished Woman.* Copyright © 1969 by Lillian Hellman. Reprinted by permission of Little, Brown and Co.
Ernest Hemingway: from *A Moveable Feast.* Copyright © 1964 by Ernest Hemingway, Ltd. Reprinted by permission of Charles Scribner's Sons.
Richard Hoggart: from *The Uses of Literacy: Aspects of Working-Class Life with Special Reference to Publications and Entertainments.* Oxford University Press, 1957. Reprinted by permission of the publisher.
John Hollander: from *Harper's Magazine,* April 1969. Reprinted by permission of the author.
Alfred Kazin: from *A Walker in the City.* Copyright 1951 by Alfred Kazin. Reprinted by permission of Harcourt Brace Jovanovich, Inc.
Murray Kempton: from *The New York Review of Books,* September 4, 1969. Copyright © 1969 by The New York Review. Reprinted by permission of the publisher.
Kenneth Keniston: from *The New York Times Magazine,* April 27, 1969. Copyright © 1969 by The New York Times Company. Reprinted by permission of the publisher.
Frank Kermode: from *The Month,* April 1969. Reprinted by permission of The Month.
Herbert Kohl: from *36 Children.* Copyright © 1967 by Herbert Kohl. Reprinted by permission of The World Publishing Company.
Elinor Langer: from *The New York Review of Books,* March 26, 1970. Copyright © 1970 by The New York Review. Reprinted by permission of Elinor Langer c/o International Famous Agency, Inc.

Susanne K. Langer: from *Feeling and Form*. Copyright 1953 by Charles Scribner's Sons. Reprinted by permission of the publisher.

Robert Lowell: from *Life Studies*. Copyright © 1956, 1959 by Robert Lowell. Reprinted by permission of Farrar, Straus & Giroux, Inc.

John Lyons: from *Noam Chomsky*. Copyright © 1970 by John Lyons. Reprinted by permission of The Viking Press, Inc.

Dwight Macdonald: from *Against the American Grain*, Random House, 1962. © 1962 by Dwight Macdonald. Originally in *The New Yorker*. Reprinted by permission.

James Alan McPherson: from *The Atlantic Monthly*, June 1969. Copyright © 1969 by The Atlantic Monthly Company. Reprinted by permission of the publisher and the author.

Norman Mailer: from *The Armies of the Night*. Copyright © 1968 by Norman Mailer. Reprinted by permission of The World Publishing Company.

Peter Manso: from *Vroom!! Conversations with Grand Prix Champions*. Copyright © 1969 by Peter Manso. Reprinted by permission of Funk & Wagnalls.

Herbert Marcuse: from *One Dimensional Man*. Copyright © 1964 by Herbert Marcuse. Reprinted by permission of Beacon Press.

P. B. Medawar: from *Encounter*, December 1966. Reprinted by permission of the author.

Jonathan Miller: from *The New York Review of Books*, October 6, 1966. Copyright © 1966 by The New York Review. Reprinted by permission of the publisher.

Lewis Mumford: from *Diogenes*, Fall 1966. Reprinted by permission of the Conseil international de la philosophie et des sciences humaines.

Frank Norman: from *Encounter*, March 1967. Reprinted by permission of the author.

Robert Oppenheimer: from *Listen to Leaders in Science*, ed. by Albert Love and James Saxon Childers. Copyright © 1965 by Tupper and Love, Inc. Reprinted by permission of David McKay Company, Inc.

George Orwell: from *Nineteen Eighty-four*. Copyright 1949 by Harcourt Brace Jovanovich, Inc. Reprinted by permission of Brandt & Brandt.

George Plimpton: from *Paper Lion*. Copyright © 1964, 1965, 1966 by George Plimpton. Reprinted by permission of Harper & Row, Publishers, Inc.

Richard Poirier: from *Writers at Work: The Paris Review Interviews*, Second Series. Copyright © 1963 by The Paris Review, Inc. Reprinted by permission of The Viking Press, Inc.

Editors of *Rolling Stone:* from *Rolling Stone*. Copyright © by Straight Arrow Publishers, Inc. Reprinted by permission of the publisher.

Pierre Schneider: from *Louvre Dialogues*. Copyright © 1967, 1971 by Pierre Schneider. Reprinted by permission of Atheneum Publishers and the author. Appeared originally in *Art in America*.

Stephen Spender: from *The New York Review of Books*, July 11, 1968. Copyright © 1968 by The New York Review. Reprinted by permission of the publisher.

Gertrude Stein: from *The Autobiography of Alice B. Toklas*. Copyright 1933 and renewed 1961 by Alice B. Toklas. Reprinted by permission of Random House, Inc.

Igor Stravinsky and Robert Craft: from *Restrospectives and Conclusions*. Copyright © 1969 by Igor Stravinsky and Robert Craft. Reprinted by permission of Alfred A. Knopf, Inc.

G. Rattray Taylor: from *The Biological Time Bomb*. Copyright © 1968 by Gordon Rattray Taylor. Reprinted by permission of The World Publishing Company.

Studs Terkel: from *Division Street: America*. Copyright © 1967 by Studs Terkel. Reprinted by permission of Pantheon Books, a Division of Random House, Inc.

Hugh Trevor-Roper: from *The Last Days of Hitler*. Copyright 1947 by H. R. Trevor-Roper. Reprinted by permission of The Macmillan Company.

John Wain: from *Sprightly Running*. Copyright © 1962 by John Wain. Reprinted by permission of Curtis Brown Ltd.

Paul West: from *The New American Review*, #3. Copyright © 1968 by Paul West. Reprinted by permission of Paul West c/o International Famous Agency, Inc.

T. H. White: from *The Goshawk*. Copyright 1951 by Jonathan Cape Ltd. Reprinted by permission of David Higham Associates, Ltd.

Norbert Wiener: from *The Human Beings—Cybernetics and Society*. Copyright 1950, 1954 by Norbert Wiener. Reprinted by permission of the Houghton Mifflin Company.

Edmund Wilson: from *Apologies to the Iroquois*. Copyright 1959, 1960 by Edmund Wilson. Reprinted by permission of the author.

Tom Wolfe: from *The Pump House Gang*. Copyright © 1968 by Tom Wolfe, copyright © 1966 by the World Journal Tribune Corporation, copyright © 1964, 1965, 1966 by the New York Herald Tribune, Inc. Reprinted by permission of Farrar, Straus & Giroux, Inc.

Richard Wright: from *Black Boy*. Copyright 1937, 1942, 1944, 1945 by Richard Wright. Reprinted by permission of Harper & Row Publishers, Inc.

PREFACE

Anthologies devoted to the best writings of a period, anthologies meant to display a variety of rhetorical modes, anthologies representing a range of political or social or philosophical views on some urgent matter of contemporary interest —these are familiar enough and are numerously available. This anthology is all of these, each strengthened by an uncustomary combination with the others and given some further originality of appeal by the larger intentions of the whole book. *The Oxford Reader* is special because it refuses to be specialized. Either through a topicality that can become dated or because of pedagogical organization that however initially useful proves eventually constricting, most anthologies end up in the second-hand bookstore, the attic, or the home library where they more frequently require dusting than invite rereading. So that while the editors have been guided by such factors as topical interest and representativeness, they have been especially anxious to select materials which will attract a first reading and encourage a second or third one, a continuing interest and a renewable enjoyment.

It is hoped that the pieces assembled here are alive now in what they express and will remain alive because of the way they are written. Looking for both contemporaneity and longevity has meant that in deciding between two pieces on the same subject, preference has gone to the one where the author's concern for writing is as evident as a concern for the event or issue being written about. In many collections the essays become moribund even before the topics to which they are addressed have ceased to matter very much; the editors have tried here to ensure that the reverse will be true, though it is not of course in the nature of things that they should have succeeded in every case. It is impossible that everything in a book of this kind will remain of enduring interest. The passage of time can diminish the power of even some very revered literary forms almost as surely as it eventually makes most social and historical issues altogether less pressing than they were originally thought to be. Precisely because issues do deteriorate even faster than literary forms or styles, it has seemed best to favor those pieces where the predictable limit to the life-span of a given subject has been measurably increased by the power of presentation.

Preface

In each section of this book there should be, ideally, some vital and discoverable relationship between the subject and the shapes it assumes in the written or, in the many taped interviews, the spoken style. The enormous expansion in the modes of contemporary expression, of which the tape machine alone is a significant illustration, is important for more than merely instrumental or technical reasons, however. The study of media is a subject in its own right. It is as crucial to an understanding of the modern world as are any of the problems, political, personal, or other, which get expressed through the burgeoning varieties of forms, instruments, and styles by which contemporary peoples express themselves. To be concerned with the importance of modes of expression with respect to the subject of any particular essay is not, therefore, a matter simply of caring in the usual way about good writing or about the intricate identity of form with content. What might normally function as no more than conventional criteria for selection have here been given the status also of a historical phenomenon. The *ways* structure is given to the world through uses of language are among the most important available evidences of the kind of world we populate and of who and where we are, both as individuals and as participants in the different kinds of corporate life. This is a fact of importance in any piece of expression, whether its ostensible subject be the concerns of childhood, the communities, investigations, skilled performances of later life, or the nature of language itself, to mention some of the several divisions into which the material has been divided.

The Prologue is a kind of capsule form of the design of the whole. The three pieces included in it offer testimony not simply about important events in recent history, but also about the different ways in which particular people have witnessed and reported them. History is no longer located in the places where it once found itself, and people even recently ignored are now vocally at the center of history, as any attention to the shifts of political and social lines of force will reveal. One aspect of this fluid situation is that no one can any longer be dogmatic about the relative importance of one inquiry as against another; no one can be sure just where the most telling and eloquent voices are to be heard. Some of these selections discuss this situation directly, others by implication, and all of them, in one way or another, respond to its challenge. The editors hope that much of what is given here will illuminate the way we live now and will in addition offer an experience of some of the movements of contemporary thinking and feeling, as these exist in the language and structures of prose.

F. K.
R. P.

January 1971

CONTENTS

PROLOGUE: EVENTS AND THEIR AFTER-LIFE   3

     * The Editors of "Rolling Stone"/Let It Bleed   4
     * Norman Mailer/The Liberal Party   51
     * Angus Calder/The Blitz   62

I.   IMAGES OF CHILDHOOD   93

     * Frank Norman/Banana Boy: Footnotes to a Dossier   94
     * Richard Wright/Black Boy   104
     Frank Conroy/White Days and Red Nights   112
     * Alfred Kazin/From the Subway to the Synagogue   127
     Robert Lowell/91 Revere Street   137
     * Bruno Bettelheim/Results of Kibbutz Education   165

II.   SCHOOL   181

     * Paul West/A Passion To Learn   182
     * Herbert Kohl/Teaching   193
     * Cyril Connolly/A Georgian Boyhood   211

III.   YOUTH   221

     Kenneth Keniston/You Have To Grow Up in Scarsdale To Know How Bad Things Really Are   222
     * Edgar Friedenberg/The Image of the Adolescent Minority   234
     Leslie Fiedler/The New Mutants   246
     F. W. Dupee/The Uprising at Columbia   264
     * Stephen Spender/Paris in the Spring   291
     * Tom Wolfe/The Pump House Gang   304

* Selections that appear in the shorter edition.

xii   Contents

IV.   PERSONS   319

      * Peter Manso/An Interview with Jackie Stewart   320
      * Studs Terkel/Bob and Therese Carter   345
      * Lillian Hellman/Helen   355
      * Jonathan Miller/On Lenny Bruce (1926–1966)   370
        John Wain/E. H. W. Meyerstein   375
      * Gertrude Stein/Hemingway   395
      * Ernest Hemingway/Gertrude Stein   395

V.   COMMUNITIES   407

      * Richard Hoggart/Mother and Father   408
      * James Alan McPherson/Chicago's Blackstone Rangers   421
      * Robert Coles/Whose Strengths, Whose Weaknesses   434
        Edmund Wilson/The Iroquois Resurgence   444
        James Baldwin/Letter from a Region of My Mind   453

VI.   LANGUAGE   461

      * Philip French/The Stammerer as Hero   462
        Dwight Macdonald/The String Untuned   475
      * George Orwell/Newspeak   493
      * John Lyons/Chomsky   503
      * Leonard Bloomfield/Literate and Illiterate Speech   512
        Herbert Marcuse/The Closing of the Universe of Discourse   521
      * William Burroughs/The Invisible Generation   535

VII.   PERFORMANCES   543

      * A. Alvarez/Shiprock   544
        T. H. White/The Goshawk   550
      * George Plimpton/Paper Lion   559
        Edwin Denby/Dancers, Buildings, and People in the Street   567
      * Susanne Langer/A Note on the Film   575
      * Donald Barthelme/And Now Let's Hear It for the Ed Sullivan Show!   580
      * Richard Poirier/Robert Frost Interviewed   585
        Eric Bentley/Actor and Playwright   605
        Pierre Schneider/At the Louvre with Steinberg   609
        Igor Stravinsky/Interview: Side Effects   625

VIII.   INVESTIGATIONS   635

      * John Hollander/From Beyond the Cigarette: Notes of a Redeemed Smoker   637

Gerald S. Hawkins/Stonehenge and the Computer   646
* Murray Kempton/Crime Does Not Pay   663
* John Kenneth Galbraith/Financial Genius Is Before the Fall: How Fools and Their Money Are Still Being Parted   675
Hugh Trevor-Roper/The Last Days of Hitler   691
* Marshall Cohen/Civil Disobedience in a Constitutional Democracy   699
* Frank Kermode/Marshall McLuhan Interviewed   711
* Noam Chomsky/The Responsibility of the Intellectuals   723

IX. SCIENCE AND TECHNOLOGY   753

Lewis Mumford/The First Megamachine   754
Norbert Wiener/Cybernetics   767
* P. B. Medawar/Science and the Sanctity of Life   777
* G. Rattray Taylor/Genetic Surgery: The New Eugenics   788
* René Dubos/The Pursuit of Significance   797
* Stuart Chase/Our Shrinking Living Space   812
Robert Oppenheimer/Physics   823
* Paul Goodman/Can Technology Be Humane?   834
* Elinor Langer/The Women of the Telephone Company   848

EPILOGUE   865

* Buckminster Fuller/What I Am Trying To Do   866
* John Donat/Buckminster Fuller   867
* Erik H. Erikson/Youth Today and the Year 2000   879

THE OXFORD READER

Prologue   EVENTS AND THEIR AFTER-LIFE

Each of these selections is a report on an event or series of events. The first is by several hands, and was compiled almost on the scene and at the time of the occurrences it describes. The second is by a participant in the events it describes, himself a famous writer; but it stands back somewhat, is more ruminative, and even refers to the writer himself in the third person. The third selection describes events that occurred before the writer was born, in a war that ended more than a quarter of a century ago.

The first selection has a vivid immediacy that derives from the speech of witnesses, full of the slang of the moment yet extremely serious because the event itself seemed of the utmost cultural and personal significance. Here the distance between what happened, and the linguistic and rhetorical reactions of observers to what happened, is reduced to something like the minimum possible. There is almost no "art" save in the assembly of the testimony; the article is as near to being a verbal equivalent of a photograph as we can imagine, yet it is interesting that there remain in the piece quite strong moral elements—shock, despair, betrayal. In the second piece the distance is of course much greater, though the writer is still close to the events, and part of his rhetorical technique is to use a vocabulary which despite its breadth contains many colloquial elements. What we notice is that the increase in the distance between event and account allows Mailer to deploy ironical and other devices not available to the reporters who compiled the first piece, and to include material about his personal and professional lives that is not obviously germane to the account of the protest. The third essay is more conventionally historical; the writer consulted documents and eye-witnesses, and though motivated by a strong concern for social justice is cut off by a generation from the events he describes; he does not know the feeling of an air raid at first hand. One step further would be into history written of events which survive only as documents because all the participants are dead. Such events still have an after-life.

The Editors of "Rolling Stone" / Let it Bleed

This piece, a report on the Altamont Rock Festival of December 6, 1969, and of the violence that accompanied it, is the only one in the collection written by a group rather than by a single person. While we see it in prose, its reality is much more nearly like that of a radio or television report of an event than like a piece of writing. The repetitions, the overlapping accounts, the clumsy transitions are those of the media, and like reports of events such as conventions or parades, where dullness yields haphazardly to high drama, the sudden shifts from bookkeeping details to theatrical and mythic metaphors give the piece an impersonality which seems to have been that of the event itself, where no one would or could take responsibility. Depersonalized by the shade of the events, those who write and those who are quoted agree that a disaster did occur, but they disagree on emphases and on where to place the blame.

Yet the reports have been grouped in an order which indicates an editorial intention worth tracing out. In nearly every case we learn not only how a witness reacted after the festival but what he had expected of it before he got there; the kind of performance, the sort of event which each witness had in mind before the experience is a frequent issue in the report. The editors seem to have intended a collage effect of "instant history," where elements oddly juxtaposed are made to yield an effect which has a unity its method should deny, yet the heightened language of the retrospective accounts placed here makes it obvious that, at this distance, history resides in the preconceptions of the beholder.

The writers of this special on the Altamont disaster were, alphabetically, Lester Bangs, Reny Brown, John Burks, Sammy Egan, Michael Goodwin, Geoffrey Link, Greil Marcus, John Morthland, Eugene Schoenfeld, Patrick Thomas, and Langdon Winner. It was assembled from their combined reports, and the firsthand accounts of dozens of others, by the editorial staff of *Rolling Stone*.

I didn't know his name or anything, but he was standing along side of me. You know, we were both watching Mick Jagger, and a Hell's Angel, the fat one. I don't know his name or anything, he reached over—he didn't like us being so close or something, you know, we were seeing Mick Jagger too well, or some-

Beth Bagby

thing. He was just being uptight. He reached over and grabbed the guy beside me by the ear and hair, and yanked on it, thinking it was funny, you know, kind of laughing. And so, this guy shook loose; he yanked away from him.

ROLLING STONE: Now this guy that you're talking about, is this the black guy that got killed?

Yeah, right. He shook loose, and the Hell's Angel hit him in the mouth and he fell back into the crowd and he jumped off stage and jumped at him. And he tried to scramble, you know, through the crowd, to run from the Hell's Angel, and four other Hell's Angels jumped on him. They started mugging him and,

R.S.: This is when they claim he had the gun?

No, no, he didn't pull out the gun yet. See, and they started, they were mugging him, and then he started running . . . and he was running straight into the crowd, you know, pushing people away, you know, to run from the Hell's Angels.

R.S.: What was this guy's condition? Had he been smoking, had he been drinking, or do you know?

He was really straight, he was really . . . Feeling really weird about being pushed around and stuff, but he was really pretty straight.

R.S.: When the cat started grabbing him, what did he say? What did this black guy say?

He just gave him a weird look, kind of a mean look, and yanked away. He didn't give him any verbal provocation or anything. So they're chasing through the crowd. And they're hitting him and one Hell's Angel pulled out a knife and stabbed him in the back.

R.S.: What kind of knife?

I couldn't tell. I just saw the flash of the blade. Everything was happening too fast. And he hit him in the back and he pulled out a gun and held it up in the air you know . . . like that was kind of his last resort, you know . . . and . . .

R.S.: Could you tell what kind of a gun?

It was a long . . . long barrel, really long. Looked like a six shooter or something . . . I've never seen . . . it was really . . . like the barrel was about six inches or so . . .

R.S.: Like a service revolver or something?

Yeah . . . it was really a fancy gun . . . really shiny . . . He had it in the air, and he was still running, and people were telling him—I remember this chick screaming "Don't shoot anyone." And he was too scared to shoot because he could have shot anyone in the crowd or anything. So he didn't shoot. And one of the Hell's Angels grabbed the gun from him . . . and then stabbed him again in the back.

R.S.: They grabbed the gun from him, and then stabbed him again in the back?

Yeah, yeah.

R.S.: What did the cat who stabbed him look like?

I think there was two people that stabbed him. One had his hair straight. It was straight and thick, and it was straight back, combed straight back. The front of his . . . you know . . . he combed it back so much that the front of his head was kind of bald . . . getting thin. I know what he looks like, but I can't describe him.

R.S.: But you'd know him if you saw him, right?

Yeah, yeah. I've seen him before.

R.S.: Would you be willing to testify?

No. I don't want to get killed.

They hit him . . . I couldn't tell whether it was a knife or not . . . but on the side of the head. And then he kind of stumbled and he fell down on his knees. He came running toward me. I grabbed onto the scaffold, held onto the scaffold, you know, and then he came running kind of toward me and then he fell down on his knees, and then the Hell's Angel, the same one I was talking about, grabbed onto both of his shoulders and started kicking him in the face about five times or so and then he fell down on his face, you know. He let go and he fell down on his face. And then one of them kicked him on the side and he rolled over, and he muttered some words. He said, "I wasn't going to shoot you." That was the last words he muttered.

R.S.: How close were you to all of this?

About three feet away.

R.S.: You kept right up with them. You could have gotten hurt.

I just stayed as close . . . like, I wanted to jump into it but I couldn't so I stayed close so that as soon as they were done mugging him I could help him.

R.S.: That's a real question there: why 300,000—well 299,900—people would allow themselves to be dominated by a hundred Angels?

Yeah, well I couldn't see it either. If some other people had jumped in I would have jumped in. But nobody jumped in and after he said "I wasn't going to shoot you," one of the Hell's Angels said, "Why did you have a gun?" He didn't give him time to say anything. He grabbed one of those garbage cans, you know, one of those cardboard garbage cans with the metal rimming, and he smashed him over the head with it, and then he kicked the garbage can out of the way and started kicking his head in. Five of them started kicking his head in. Kicked him all over the place. And then the guy that started the whole thing, the fat guy, stood on his head for a minute or so and then walked off. And then the one I was talking about, described to you, he wouldn't let us touch him for about two or three minutes. Like, "Don't touch him, he's going to die anyway, let him die, he's going to die."

R.S.: So what did everybody do? Did anybody say anything?

Chicks were just screaming. It was all confusion. I jumped down anyway to grab him and some other dude jumped down and grabbed him, and then the Hell's Angel just stood over him for a little bit and then walked away. We turned him over and ripped off his shirt.

R.S.: You turned him over so he was face up?

No, so he was face down.

R.S.: So you could see his back?

We rubbed his back up and down to get the blood off so we could see, and there was a big hole on his spine and a big hole on the side and there was a big hole in his temple. A big open slice. You could see all the way in. You could see inside. You could see at least an inch down and stuff, you know. And then there was a big hole right where there's no ribs on his back . . . and then the side of his head was just sliced open . . . you couldn't see so far in . . . it was bleeding quite heavy . . . but his back wasn't bleeding too heavy after that . . . there . . . all of us were drenched in blood.

R.S.: Did you stick with him after that?

Yeah. I picked up his legs and someone else . . . this guy said he was a doctor or something . . . I don't know who he was . . . he picked up his arms and he said, "Got to get him some help because he's going to die. We've got 15 or 20 minutes, if we can get him some help . . ." And so we tried to carry him on the stage. Tell Mick Jagger to stop playing so we could get him on the stage and get some attention for him.

R.S.: Who told Jagger that?

No one told Jagger that, but someone was trying to tell him to stop and he kept leaning over and looking out at the crowd like he was paying attention and trying to figure out what was happening.

R.S.: This is while he's singing?

Yeah. He kept leaning over with his ear trying to hear what somebody was telling him, but he couldn't hear. So they kept on playing and the Hell's Angels wouldn't let us through . . . get on the stage . . . They kept blocking us saying go around . . . go through some other way. They wouldn't let us through. They knew he was going to die in a matter of minutes. They wanted him to die probably so he wouldn't talk or something, you know. And so we carried . . . we turned around and went the other way. It took about 15 minutes to get him behind the stage. We went around that whole thing and got behind where there was a Red Cross truck . . . something like that. And someone brought out a metal stretcher and laid him on that. Well first we laid him on the ground. And then we felt his pulse and it was just barely doing it . . .

R.S.: Real slow or real fast or what?

Real slow and real weak. His whole mouth and stuff is bashed up into his nose and stuff and he couldn't breathe out of his nose. He was trying to breathe out of his mouth. There really wasn't anything you could do. We carried him over to some station wagon and then whoever owned the car hopped in and some other people hopped in and I stayed there. I went over and they had this thing of coffee and I had it . . . poured it all over to wipe off all the blood.

R.S.: Hot coffee?

Yeah, because there was nothing else. Then I walked away feeling, wanting to do something, wanting to tell somebody what happened so they could get the Hell's Angels. It scared me so much I couldn't do anything . . . it really put me on such a big bummer . . . really, for days. For the last couple of days I've been really brought down about it.

R.S.: Do you intend to go to any more of these mass concerts?

If there's no Hell's Angels there. No violence. I don't know, I enjoyed it until that happened. I did get bummed out . . . I got a little depressed about . . . the way I was feeling from being pushed around and stuff by the crowd. But the Hell's Angels were responsible. They're really the whole thing.

Robert Hiatt, a medical resident at the Public Health Hospital in San Francisco, was the first doctor to reach 18-year-old Meredith Hunter after the fatal wounds. He was behind the stage and responded to Jagger's call from the stage for a doctor. When Hiatt got to the scene, people were trying to get Hunter up on the stage, apparently in the hope that the Stones would stop playing and help could get through quicker.

"I carried him myself back to the first aid area," Hiatt said. "He was limp in my hands and unconscious. He was still breathing then, though quite shallowly, and he had a very weak pulse. It was obvious he wasn't going to make it, but if anything could be done, he would have to get to a hospital quickly.

"He had very serious wounds. He had a wound in the lower back which could have gone into the lungs, a wound in the back near the spine which could have severed a major vessel, and a fairly large wound in the left temple. You couldn't tell how deep the wounds were, but each was about three-fourths of an inch long, so they would have been fairly deep.

"It was just obvious he wasn't going to make it. There was no equipment there to treat him. He needed to be operated on immediately, to have a couple large vessels repaired. Treatment immediately would have been intravenous fluids, none of which were available."

Dr. Richard Baldwin, the general practitioner from Point Reyes who supervised and coordinated the various medical units, agreed: "He got a bad injury in that they got him in the back and it went in between the ribs and the side of the spine, and there's nothing but big arteries in there, the aorta, the main artery in the body, and a couple kidney arteries. And if you hit one of those you're dead. You're dead in less than a minute and there's nothing anyone can do. In other words, if you're standing in front of the hospital, or even if he was stabbed in an operating room, there's nothing they could have done to save him. That's one of those injuries that's just irreparable."

Roland W. Prahl, senior coroner's investigator for Alameda County, said Hunter's official cause of death was "shock and hemorrhage due to multiple wounds in the back, a wound on the left side of the forehead, and another on the right side of the neck."

Prahl said that as far as he knew, Hunter was taken from the scene on a stretcher to the racetrack offices area. Fearing further mutilation to the body, sheriff's deputies then apparently transported him to another location on the grounds in their van. He was brought by deputies to the coroner's office at 10:50 that night, and an autopsy was performed Sunday.

"I don't know if doctors treated him at any time at the site," Prahl added. "But I do know he was never in a hospital. They pronounced him dead at the site; if anyone had thought he was alive, they'd have helped him." Prahl, however, didn't know who "they" were.

Three others had died: two in a hit-and-run accident, another by drowning; countless more were injured and wounded, during the course of this day-long "free" concert. It was such a bad trip that it was almost perfect. All it lacked was mass rioting and the murder of one or more *musicians*. These things *could* have happened, with just a little more (bad) luck. It was as if Altamont's organizers had worked out a blueprint for disaster. Like:

1. Promise a free concert by a popular rock group which rarely appears in this country. Announce the site only four days in advance.
2. Change the location 20 hours before the concert.
3. The new concert site should be as close as possible to a giant freeway.
4. Make sure the grounds are barren, treeless, desolate.
5. Don't warn neighboring landowners that hundreds of thousands of people are expected. Be unaware of their out-front hostility toward long hair and rock music.
6. Provide one-sixtieth the required toilet facilities to insure that people will use nearby fields, the sides of cars, etc.
7. The stage should be located in an area likely to be completely surrounded by people and their vehicles.
8. Build the stage low enough to be easily hurdled. Don't secure a clear area between stage and audience.
9. Provide an unreliable barely audible low fidelity sound system.
10. Ask the Hell's Angels to act as "security" guards.

All these things happened, and worse. Altamont was the product of diabolical egotism, hype, ineptitude, money manipulation, and, at base, a fundamental lack of concern for humanity.

"Jagger was very, very shattered," according to an associate who was with the Stones post-Altamont. "I cannot overemphasize how depressed and down he was with the way it turned out. They'd like to just be able to blink and make it go away. When they knew about the murder—it shook them."

Jagger had been so eager to do the gig that when he learned, in Muscle Shoals, that his San Francisco advance people were having trouble coming up with a site, he kept saying: "Well, man, we'll play in the streets if we have to." He was almost prepared to pick a street corner in downtown Market Street in San Francisco and play there.

But then, after Altamont had been set up and all the people were there, and the violence had begun, and Angels were menacing everybody in sight, the reports started coming in to the Huntington Hotel, and the Stones did *not* want to complete the gig. Well, they couldn't do that . . . So they thought about going straight out there, playing immediately, and closing the concert down as quick as possible. In the end, they decided to play it according to the original plan.

But they knew early in the day that it was grim and getting grimmer.

Mick Taylor, the newest Rolling Stone, was still aghast at what had happened when contacted in London shortly after his return home from Altamont.

"I was really scared," he said. "I was frightened for all of us, particularly for Mick because he had to be very careful what he said all the time, very careful. He had to pick and choose his words. When you read about a thing this size—like 300,000 people, four people born, four people killed—you don't think of it as a violent thing. But that's all I saw: violence all the time. I've always heard about the incredible violence in America, but I'd never actually seen it. They're so used to it over there, it's a commonplace thing. They find it easier to accept. I've just never seen anything like that before.

"It was just completely barbaric, like there was so much violence there it completely took the enjoyment out of it for me . . . it was impossible . . . to enjoy the music, or anything, because most of the violence was going on right in front of the stage, right in front of our eyes, and like I've never seen anything like it before. I just couldn't believe it.

"About five minutes after we arrived, just after we got out of the helicopter, I was with Mick and there were a couple of security guards with us, and a guy broke through and punched Mick in the face. That put me off a bit, but even after that had happened I didn't expect all those other things.

"It got so bad at one point that we just had to stop playing, we had to keep stopping in the middle of numbers. Mick did his best to cool the people out. He was doing everything in his power to cool them out. We were speechless for a little while afterwards . . . We didn't enjoy it.

"I think at one point we might have walked off stage, but that would have been a disaster. We just had to carry on and play the best we could. We played longer than we would have done because we had to keep stopping all the time. We still did a complete show. We must have been on stage for about an hour-and-a-half. It seemed like ages.

"The Hell's Angels had a lot to do with it. The people that were working with us getting the concert together thought it would be a good idea to have them as a security force. But I got the impression that because they were a security force they were using it as an excuse. They're just very, very violent people.

"I think we expected probably something like the Hell's Angels that were our security force at Hyde Park, but of course they're not the real Hell's Angels, they're completely phony. These guys in California are the real thing—they're very violent.

"I had expected a nice sort of peaceful concert. I didn't expect anything like that in San Francisco because they are so used to having nice things there. That's where free concerts started, and I thought a society like San Francisco could have done much better.

"We were on the road when it was being organized, we weren't involved at all. We would have liked to have been. Perhaps the only thing we needed security for was the Hell's Angels.

"I really don't know what caused it but it just depressed me because it could have been so beautiful that day."

According to Keith Richard, it *did* go pretty well. On his arrival in London, he told a United Press reporter that Altamont "was basically well-handled, but lots of people were tired and a few tempers got frayed."

It is impossible to speak of the music that went down without placing it in the context of the violence, the fear and the anxiety, which, during the course of the day, peaked to higher and higher points of refinement and climax.

As Santana was setting up, a chick toward the front of the stage was telling her old man: "It's weird. They consulted the astrologers before setting the dates for Woodstock, but they couldn't have consulted an astrologer about today. Anyone can see that with the moon in Scorpio, today's an *awful* day to do this concert. There's a strong possibility of violence and chaos and any astrologer could have told them so. Oh well, maybe the Stones know something I don't know."

The violence was not long to follow. (It had already begun earlier, of course, but to have it going on while the bands were playing was a new twist.) Between the first song and the second, one young-looking fellow tried to pass nearby to get on stage. He was wearing a blue and yellow sports shirt, jeans and had long straight blond hair over his ears. As he tried to get by some Hell's Angels he was kicked in the face by an Angel's booted feet and pulverized with punches and lay spread out on the ground unable to move or be moved, there were so many people jammed up to the stage.

A lot of photographers kept right on taking their photos through the worst of it, right up close, without getting hassled. So did the movie crews—but then they had Angels for bodyguards.

Not every photographer was so lucky, though. John Young, 24, who moved in with his Leica to capture some of the bashing, wound up with 13 stitches in his head. The Angels were beating a couple of naked people to the ground during Santana's set. In moments, the nudies were up again, and Young started taking pictures, when the Angels resumed bashing them.

An Angel spotted him—out of some ten or twelve photogs immediately surrounding him—and demanded: "I want your film or you get hit." Young kept shooting, and the Angel leapt at him, smashing the camera into Young's face. Down he went. When several Angels began pounding him, Young rolled into a protective ball. "It felt like they were hitting me with a hammer and a broken bottle," Young said later. Observers said they were pool cues.

The Angels, many of them, were carrying—and applying to a lot of non-Angel heads—loaded pool cues, sawed-off (usually) to a length somewhat longer than a billy club. About the length, in fact, of the cattle prods that we've all seen in photographs of red-neck brutality against black people in the South.

Eventually they got around to removing the film from his camera. Drenched in blood—hair, face, neck, shirt back and front—Young ran 50 yards into the crowd, then sort of collapsed until the Red Cross took him to their tent, where they cleaned him up, administered novocaine, and stitched him up.

"I'd never seen a Hell's Angel before," explained Young, who's from a small town in Maine, "and I didn't really know they could *do* that." After the patchwork, he was able to watch the rest of the concert. He took no more photos.

Santana began their next song, but were interrupted by the Angels' running across stage to the right to beat someone up. Santana finished their set amidst very uptight vibes around the stage.

The next group up was the Airplane and by the time they came on it was standing room only for about seventy-five yards from the stage but everyone slowly sat down when the people seventy-six yards from the stage yelled.

Sam Cutler announced that a woman had given birth and clean sheets and diapers were needed and within minutes the stage was beseiged with them. Then Cutler introduced the Jefferson Airplane and they began their set with "We Can Be Together" and ended the set with "Volunteers of America." In between there was a disturbance with some Hell's Angels and members of the audience and Marty Balin was knocked out by a punch from one of the Angels when he tried to intercede in the disturbance. Paul Kantner began to make a speech about the event and was challenged by a Hell's Angel who grabbed a microphone and the people began to boo. Another Hell's Angel came up to Kantner and a fight almost broke out between them but was cooled down before any punches were thrown on stage and they went into a song. When it ended, Grace Slick was rapping softly into the microphone about what was going down with the Hell's Angels and everyone else. It was almost too much to take in. An Instant Re-Play would have been useful, the action was so thick and heavy. Consider the symbolism alone:

With all the grandeur of Bert Parks inviting last year's Miss America to step forward, the Airplane had asked, "Will the Hell's Angels please take the stage."

Then came that "up against the wall motherfucker" song, with its soaring (old-fashioned) harmonies, Marty Balin's voice riding high and clear over the ensemble, the Jefferson Airplane celebrating the forces of chaos and anarchy, proud to be part of that trip. Very, very proud.

Then Marty saw a black man getting swallowed up by the forces of chaos and anarchy—in the form of the Angels, half a dozen of whom were thumping the shit out of him. At some point near the start of "Somebody to Love," Balin jumped in to break it up. He at least laid a hand on an Angel. It is said he threw a punch, and maybe said, "Fuck you!"

During the second half of "Somebody to Love," Marty Balin lay unconscious, having gotten himself blasted by an Angel. The rest of the band played on. Balin's absence, in musical terms, scarcely mattered. The sound was so bad you couldn't tell the difference.

It was at just about this point that the Angels' position became clear. They were in charge of the stage. They had taken it that morning. It was *theirs,* musicians or no musicians. What the fuck, wasn't nobody tough enough to *take* it from them, was there? The Stones? Not likely. It had become, to a disturbing degree, a Hell's Angels Festival.

Nothing profound happened musically, during the Flying Burrito Brothers set. It seldom does. But somehow the simple verities of their countrified electric music soothed the warriors. There were no fights. As luck would have it, Mick Jagger and Keith Richard chose to emerge from the backstage trailer where they'd been holed up to have a look at the stage and the audience during this period of calm. They strolled about, wound up onstage, smiling, for a bit. Then back to the trailer, where, in true super-star fashion, Jagger was signing autographs (on album jackets, and even draft cards). Whenever they ventured any distance from the smallish white trailer, it was behind three or four burly Angels.

The scene back there was dense with groupies (most dazzling: Miss Mercy behind her raccoon-ring eye makeup), and celebrities (a toss-up between Tim Leary, who went forth, gamely flashing smiles and peace signs in the direction of violence; and manager/promoter/entrepreneur Steve Paul, gloomy in his blue bathrobe, muttering dire presentiments), not to mention writers and photographers.

Out front, the battle was rejoined during Crosby, Stills, Nash and Young's desultory performance (the rest of the band had played only after David Crosby had urged them to in the strongest terms). The Angels, at one point, amassed a fairly spectacular charge, pool cues flailing whoever got in their way. At the end of their set, several stretchers were sent into the audience and bodies were passed overhead and across the stage to the Red Cross area. Those who were carried out and those who departed under their own steam were quickly replaced, as it became obvious that the next set was going to be the Stones.

Despite balloons and pennants and a few other picturesque touches (like the big polyethylene walk-in bubble/dome some co-freaks had set up), the physical atmosphere at Altamont was singularly ominous and depressing. The more people arrived, the more clear it was that this was nowhere in particular; just a patch of land, covered with bleached-out long grass and sticker burrs. Nothing had been done to make it the least bit festive. And the later it got, the worse the air became—filled with a rancid combination of fog, dust, smoke and glare. A squinty grey light made everything hard to look at.

The 300,000 anonymous bodies huddled together on the little dirt hills were indeed an instant city—a decaying urban slum complete with its own air pollution. By the time the Stones finally came on, dozens of garbage fires had been set all over the place. Flickering silhouettes of people trying to find warmth around the blazing trash reminded one of the medieval paintings of tortured souls in the Dance of Death. The stench of the smoke from tens of thousands of potato chip packages and half-eaten sandwiches brought vomiting to many. It was in this atmosphere that Mick sang his song about how groovy it is to be Satan. Never has it been sung in a more appropriate setting.

The hill on the concert side of the west fence was packed almost as tight with people as center stage area. People tended to fade into one another after awhile —unless there was something especially strange or loud about them that made you remember they were real and not just part of a huge movie set.

There was the young mother in blue blouse with Peter Pan collar and pleated skirt, looking like she'd just stepped out of a Hayward model home, who pushed ahead of her husband. In one hand she carried a baby only a few months old. She'd nudge the person ahead of her with the baby, smile and look wide-eyed at them as they turned to see who was pushing—and then she'd push right through.

Just a few feet from the fence and about 100 yards from the stage was a freak cat about 25, wearing wire-rimmed glasses, trim black goatee, T-shirt and jeans. With him was a big cat, blond, with mustache.

They were drinking from a gallon of Red Mountain Vin Rose. "It's got two tabs of mescaline in it," the blond guy told someone who asked for a drink. "Organic. Good stuff, too. We put it in this morning."

"Good thing these people ain't on reds and wine," Goatee guffawed at about 4:45 when Cutler came to the stage and announced:

"The Rolling Stones won't come out till everyone gets off the stage."

"If they'd been on reds and wine, you bet he wouldn't been sayin' it like that."

Then about a dozen Angels, mostly officers, some carrying double, ploughed through the crowd on their bikes. An admirer in the crowd offered a shaggy Angel a swig from his wine bottle. The Angel, sporting clean new colors, stopped, dismounted, grabbed the gallon in both hands and put it to his lips for just a moment, handed it back and putted on off—a lotta show for a little sip of wine.

"We come down on our bikes," said Sonny Barger later, "because we were told we were supposed to park in front of the stage, and so like when we started coming down through the crowd everybody was outa sight got up and moved and we come down in low gear and didn't try to run into anybody or do any of that kind of thing. Everybody got up really nice, some people offered us drinks on the way down and like . . . we must have come into approximate contact with at least a thousand people and outa them thousand people we had trouble with one person . . . one broad jumped up and said something that pertained to a four letter word and then one of the Angels stopped his bike and he had his old lady on the back and he said, 'Are you gonna let them talk about Angels like that?' and she jumped off the bike and slapped the other broad that said that that was in the crowd and got back on the bike and we proceeded down with no problem. We pulled up in front of the stage and parked where we were told we were supposed to park."

The flaw in this story, according to Sam Cutler and Rock Scully, is no one told the Angels to put their bikes down in front of the stage.

It got cold. Then it got colder. Time passed. More time. The Stones were waiting, like they always wait. Tuning up, they said. But really, there was something else going on, and it tied in with the whole super-star sensibility in which the Stones increasingly enwrap themselves. They were waiting for it to get really dark out, so the banks of spotlights would set them off to the most dramatic effect possible.

Suddenly, the lights glowed on, a cold-fire red gleaming on the Stones, as they wedged between the Angels onstage to their places. Jagger's demonic orange and black satin cape/robe gleamed wickedly. Into "Jumpin' Jack Flash," rather haltingly. To open up a little dancing room for himself, Jagger had to ask the Angels to step back a few paces. There must have been a hundred people—who knows? maybe 200—on that stage, and Jagger was performing in a small pocket at center stage, like it or not.

"Carol" was a little better, but stiff.

"Sympathy for the Devil." They stopped in the middle. A skirmish had broken out at stage left. This was the knifing/stomping of Meredith Hunter, perhaps 25 feet from where Jagger pranced and sang, then stopped. To one observer 20 feet to Jagger's rear, the glint of the long knives was clearly visible. So, if the Stones were looking, they saw it too. The same observer spoke with several others who were onstage (as did *Rolling Stone*), and none, except for the onstage Angels, claim to have seen a gun.

One Angel later told it this way to KSAN-FM: This black guy had come toward the stage and been pushed off by Angels. "He flipped over and he's got this revolver—it looked like a cannon. It was pointed right at me. I hit the deck and this gun was pointed right at Jagger." And then, according to this account, "everybody was on him and that was the last I seen of him. . . . When it was all over, man, Jagger looks at me and says, 'why?' I says: 'I dunno, man, that's just the way people are.' "

Whether Jagger had time for this game of eye contact is dubious. He was busy telling the audience—"brothers and sisters, come on now! That means everybody just cool out! We can cool out, everybody! Everybody be cool, now. Come on."

Turning toward side of stage: "How are we doing over there? Everybody all right? Can we still collect ourselves? I don't know what happened, I couldn't see, I hope you're all right. Are you all right? Okay, let's just give ourselves another half a minute before we get our breath back. Everyone just cool down. Is there anyone there who's hurt? Okay, I think we're cool, we can groove. We always have something very funny happen when we start that number."

"Sympathy" started again, but not too convincingly. Somebody tried to climb onstage. Angels tossed him back.

Jagger: "Why are we fighting? Why are we fighting? We don't want to fight at all. Who wants to fight, who is it? Every other scene has been cool. We gotta stop right now. You know, if we can't there's no point. . . ."

The fight scene got worse. Long silence at the mike. Dense uncertainty crowded the night chill. Amazingly, Jagger seemed to lose control of his audience. A rare moment.

Keith Richard stepped forward: "Either those cats cool it, man, or we don't play. . . ."

Pause. More nastiness in the audience immediately in front of the stage. Of 300,000 people, only a few thousand can see the trouble.

Jagger, with something like a sob: "If he doesn't stop it, man. . . ."

Richard: "Keep it cool! Hey, if you don't cool it, you ain't gonna hear no music!"

An Angel commandeered the mike to shout: "Fuck you!"

The goring had ended by now, and Jagger took the mike again to say, "We need a doctor here, now! Look, can you let the doctor get through, please. We're trying to get to someone who's hurt."

People who were trying to help Meredith Hunter were raising bloody hands to show Mick how bad it was.

A doctor got through, the man was carried off, eventually.

Next a blues, an instrumental to ease the tension. When it's over, Jagger says: "That's to cool out with."

Then, "Stray Cat Blues."

"Love in Vain." Jagger again urges the crowd to sit down. They do, as he watches. "Now, boys and girls, are you sitting comfortably? When we get to the end and we all want to go absolutely crazy and jump on each other, well, then we'll stand up again. I mean, we can't seem to keep together standing up."

"Under My Thumb." A bad fight this time: a body sails across the stage. "We're splitting; we're splitting if those cats don't stop!" Jagger shouts. "I want them out of the way! I don't like doing it to them. . . ." The people onstage crowd in to surround him. An extremely menacing moment.

What an enormous thrill it would be for an Angel to kick Mick Jagger's teeth down his throat. They have been watching his dancing and wild gesticulations with disgusted scowls, derisive laughter, elbows in each other's ribs. The looks on their faces read: "So easy—I could stomp shit outa this fuckin' sissy *so easy* —I could snuff this motherfucker!" Several of the Angels who have parked their bikes in front of the stage gun their engines defiantly.

From the stage, it is difficult to hear the shouts from the middle and outer reaches of the huge crowd, which extends a quarter of a mile out into the night. Some are shouting: "Music, music, music. . . ." Others chanting: "Get off the fucking stage, get off the fucking stage. . . ."

Jagger follows the long onstage silence with: "Please relax and sit down. If you move back and sit down, we *can* continue and we *will* continue. We need a doctor as soon as possible, please."

Stones road manager Sam Cutler, who has MC'd all day long, takes the mike to try to clear the stage. "First of all, everyone is going to get to the side of the stage who's on it now, aside from the Stones. Please, everyone. We need a doctor and ambulance, right away. Just sit down and keep calm and relax. We can get it together."

They finish "Under My Thumb." Then get into a new song they've never performed in public before: "Brown Sugar." It goes well. Beautifully, in fact. The Stones are making miraculous music, despite everything.

"Midnight Rambler" comes next, and, ooh, it is funky; but too late. The damage has been done. It's later and later by the minute. Many are leaving.

Jagger takes a hit of Jack Daniels bourbon and makes a toast of it. "One more drink to you all."

"Live With Me" is driving, vibrant.

It's just amazing. There could be no worse circumstance for making music, and the Stones are playing their asses off. Jagger is incredible. They all look like they'd rather be *anyplace* else. But it's getting better and better. Driving, powerhouse waves of rhythm roll on and on. Jagger is opening up. At first, when he really was trying to cool everybody out, his performance was the epitomy of cool: restrained, distanced, but still—even with fear welling in his throat—deeply *inside* each song, laying it on us.

Now, as he feels himself taking command again, the passion is building song by song. It is hard to imagine that "Gimmie Shelter" ever got a more burning treatment. "Queenie" is a bitch. During "Satisfaction," long-stem roses shower off him from the audience (and where did *they* get them? Must have been laid on them by Stones' management). He changes the line in "Honky Tonky Woman" to say "I laid a divorcee right here in Frisco . . ." (some think he said "in Tracy . . ." which is the small town on the highway from Altamont; same difference, really) and gets a big laugh from everybody.

It ends with "Street Fighting Man," a great performance of it, an unfortunate selection, considering what kind of day it's been.

It has been an awful day. One of the worst in memory. The tendency was to blame it on the Angels, and, fundamentally, on the Stones, since they had paid the Angels to come and act as security. Sam Cutler, acting on behalf of the band, had paid the Hell's Angels $500 worth of beer to come and act as a security force.

When San Francisco rock station KSAN-FM did a four-hour news special on the festival, Sunday evening, just a little over 24 hours after Altamont had ended, Sam Cutler was asked what he thought in retrospect about using the Angels.

"I myself," said Cutler, "feel that the Hell's Angels were as helpful as they saw that they could be in a situation which most people found very confusing including the Hell's Angels. Everybody found last night very confusing so everybody acted on their own initiative. If you want to ask me what the Hell's Angels were doing last night then I'm not qualified to speak for the Hell's Angels, you'll have to talk to the Hell's Angels yourself."

KSAN: "Well, what I'm speaking to, and what I'm sure you saw because you were right on the stage . . ."

Cutler: "I was right on the stage all the time."

KSAN: ". . . where they treated various incidents of people standing up and so forth, and what do you think about that? I understand that even the members of the Airplane were roughed up a little bit."

Cutler: "If you're asking me to issue a general put down of the Angels, which I imagine a lot of people would be only too happy to do, I'm not prepared to do that. The Angels did as they saw best in a difficult situation as I have said before. Now 50 per cent of the people will dig what they did and 50 per cent not dig what they did. I don't need to get into a kind of positive-anti kind of thing. As far as I'm concerned they were people who were here, who tried to help in their own way. . . . You know . . . these people didn't dig it. I'm sorry. I didn't dig in fact what a lot of people did yesterday."

Why did the Stones require any security force at all? According to a Hell's Angel caller (unidentified) to KSAN, "What Cutler was afraid of is that the Stones was gonna get ripped off by a hundred thousand little girls." Cutler later described this as "complete bullshit."

More damning is a quote two on-stage sources separately attribute to Cutler, when discussions of how to handle the crowd arose between him and the Angels. "We don't give a fuck," he reportedly told them. "Just keep these people away."

Whatever the case, people were comparing the Angels with regular cops in confrontation situations, and nobody said they liked Angels better. Said one person who'd been on the streets during the People's Park demonstrations in Berkeley: "Not one of those policemen conducted themselves in a manner that even could be compared with what the Angels were doing. It was just impossible—imposing their will with over three hundred thousand people!" Said another: "They acted just like pigs."

A photographer who'd taken part in the Chicago demonstrations during the Democratic Party Convention felt the Chicago cops had been both more together when it came to applying force, and more reasonable.

During the worst of the Angels' outrages, a few of the braver non-Angels had suggested (quietly) to the friends that with enough men they could put the Angels down, and maybe they ought to. But cats like Marty Balin, who actually leapt in to fight the Angels, were exceedingly rare. They usually got bloody fast.

Asked by KSAN what if the crowd had turned on them, Pete of the Frisco Angels hardly batted an eye. "The way I feel about that," he said, "is if it happens, everybody will really see what we *can* take care of. We ain't gonna go down with no kind of scene, and the closest ones to it are gonna get it. I'm not tryin' to be on no trip, but there ain't nobody gonna be whippin' on us. And get away with it."

Wavy Gravy (or Hugh Romney, take your choice), leader, in his way, of the Hugh Farm, the non-violent commune that policed Woodstock, was at Altamont. Like the vast majority of freaks, he felt it would have gone better without *any* security, instead of the Angels. And he thinks the Angels could have been disposed of easily—though not by force.

"The Angels were together and the people weren't together—they didn't have *time* to get together, you know? If they had wanted to get rid of the Angels, honorably, they could have taken up another collection and laid another five hundred dollars on them to split, which they would have done, man."

To all complaints that they had been over-zealous—too rough—in keeping the stage clear, the Angels simply replied that they was just doin' their thing. Which is violence.

"Rough?" said Frisco Pete. "What I feel the roughness is if we say we're gonna do somethin', we do it. Do you understand that? That's our whole thing. Now if these people asked us to do this thing, we did it. What are we supposed to do? We ain't cops. We're not into that thing. When we decide to do somethin', it's done, no matter how far we have to go to do it."

But it was Angels' chief Sonny Barger who laid down the single most fascinating (if not illuminating) rap on KSAN's entire special.

He was "bum kicked" by the whole thing because he felt "this here hysterical Englishman," Cutler, had laid an impossible job of security on them.

Two or three of the Angels' bikes had gotten kicked, Barger said, and that had called for mashing some heads. "Ain't nobody gonna get my bike," he said, matter-of-factly. "Anybody tries that is gonna get *got*. And they GOT got."

All in all, Barger thought the Stones had misrepresented the trip to the Angels. "Mick Jagger used us for dupes, man," he said. He made it pretty clear that the Angels don't dig being duped. "We were the biggest suckers for that idiot that I ever can see."

As to the violence, Barger said the Angels had *tried* not to be overly violent, but, shit, non-violence has its limits. Like, there was this fat naked broad who'd tried to climb onstage. Five Angels had held her off, but after awhile it got to be a pain in the ass. "So finally we backed off and one of the cats let her have it. That took care of *that*."

Repeatedly, Barger spelled it out on the Angels' terms. "I don't wanna do it, man, but I'm a violent cat. I ain't no cop. I ain't never gonna police nothin'. I just went there to sit on the front of the stage and drink beer and have a good time, like we was told. But when they started kickin' our bikes, man, that started it. I ain't no peace creep, man, but if a cat don't wanna fight me, I wanna be his friend."

Barger was especially irate that people refused to move out of the way fast enough when an Angel bike caught fire. Those people were moved away, and quickly, by the Angels: "Now I ain't saying anything about no Angel hit anybody. I *know* some of them hit people. But they moved them people back out of the way of the bike. And we got the fire put out. In the process, you know what, some people got hit.

"And you know what, some of them people were like maybe them Friday nighters that got that front row, I don't know, but they didn't want to give up that spot even to put that fire out. And they come back fightin'. And when they come back fightin' they got thumped. And a lot of times there were six or seven Angels on one guy, and a lot of times there wasn't. After that happened, we got the fire out. And everything was cool. The people moved back in again," he explained.

Barger also had a few words for people who "call themselves flower children. There is some of them lousy people ain't a bit better than the worst of us, and it's about time they realized it. They can call us all kinds of lousy dogs, and say that we shouldn't be there. But you know what, when they started messing with our bikes, they started it."

The night before it started, Altamont felt great. There were campfires all over the place (many of them the product of the race track's fence, which is now being replaced), and people were engaged in a range of worthy activities, like smoking dope or sharing it, drinking beer or sharing it, playing tapes of the Stones, or playing guitars and singing their own, playing touch football under the stage lights Chip Monck's work crews were using to set up a stage.

Monck had gotten all the necessary goods—lumber and wiring and speakers and tools and scaffolding—to the Altamont site at Friday afternoon. By 9 o'clock, he had erected a thoroughly serviceable stage, and well before midnight it would be basically set.

Two diesel generators, already raging to supply power for the lights, were the only noise. Huge derricks lifted scaffolds, then speakers and lights into place in the island of light. Everyone was remarking how much it was like a Fellini movie. To heighten the effect, there were three dozen or so wrecked cars from the raceway's normal activity: destruction derbies. As the hour grew later, freaks were to be seen sleeping in their front seats. At least one couple balled in the back seat of a crunched old Plymouth.

Down the service road, gleaming by the floodlight glare came eight ancient trucks, each loaded with about a dozen porta-toilets. A weird sight. They were applauded all along the way. Tall, shiny green shitters. We needed about five times as many as we got.

Dealers were among the first to show—spacey madmen with their dazzling raps. "Our goal," one was saying, "is to smuggle five tons of dope to London, but you don't print shit like that, man, it's like a war. Twice been in Mexico in drag, to make buys. Oh, man, the way hash gets smuggled into this country . . .

Most smack smugglers are in it for the bucks. I mean, I'm in it for the bucks, but it's a trip, too, and it makes things like *this* happen, and it helps the trip . . ." etc.

The dealers were more than mildly disconcerted to see so much shit being given away on Friday night. Maybe there'd be nobody buying come Saturday. But they had nothing to fear: it got a lot greedier when there were 300,000 instead of 30,000, and finally when it got really bad, when the music was on and the Angels were wailing, all deals were cash on the line. Merchants and consumers.

The layout at the raceway is easy enough to visualize without a map. It consists of an 80-acre plot of land with an auto raceway carved into its central plateau. This has got high rolling ground on three sides—these sides were where the earliest autos parked—and a low bowl-like fourth area on the side nearest the highway. The latter was where the stage was set up, since it afforded the greatest line-of-sight, line-of-hearing potential for the greatest number of people. By night, with only some 5,000 people milling around the interior section, it seemed to stretch on forever. It was hard to imagine that it could ever be totally filled with people, as far as the eye could see looking out from the stage.

Up at the racetrack office building, Dick Carter, the manager-promoter of Altamont Raceway, was taking care of all the arrangements he could think of. Mainly this seemed to consist of talking with the local cops when they dropped by on their rounds, and chatting with his hot dog concession lady about what to expect.

The attorney for the Stones (and friends), Melvin Belli, was handling all his legal arrangements, he said.

He had parking for 80,000, though the largest crowd Carter, who, with his thin little mustache and snazzy black and white checkered sportcoat, looks rather like a used car salesman, had ever had at the raceway was 6,500, for demolition derbies.

Totally without experience in the rock and roll game, it seemed odd that Carter had offered his facilities on such short order—let alone for free.

To understand the chain of events that finally put the Stones on Dick Carter's patch of land, it is necessary to understand the big-money negotiations that were going on concerning the movie the Stones were making of their tour.

The possibility of a film had been no spontaneous afterthought. Arrangements were underway at the very outset of the tour. Haskell Wexler, who directed the motion picture *Medium Cool,* was the first considered by the Stones to shoot the American tour. Then some disagreements over the form and content of the film ended in Wexler's disassociating himself from the enterprise. There were apparently no ill feelings.

Wexler had in mind something with a little more craft and depth than, say, a movie like *Monterey Pop.* He was interested in doing a behind-the-scenes chronicle of the tour, perhaps involving other bands and other countries. Wexler claims that it was perhaps the Stones' disenchantment with Godard's *Sympathy for the Devil* that made them skeptical of his plans.

It was the movie, as a latent source of revenue, that spawned the hassles over the concert site.

Craig Murray, president of the Sears Point Raceway, had offered his land at no cost on the following conditions: that the proper health and safety clearances be obtained from the cities of Marin and Vallejo, and from the Highway Patrol; that the Stones provide some 100 security officers who had had experience at Woodstock; that the raceway be re-imbursed for any costs incurred in the preparation of the site (earth-moving, construction, etc.); and finally, that any profits derived from the event go to a Vietnamese orphans' fund. According to Murray, John Jaymes, of Young American Productions, who claimed to represent the Stones, had agreed to all these terms. In addition, said Murray, it was they who made the formidable offer to fly out the 100 security officers from the East Coast.

Sears Point Raceway is owned by a large holding company in LA that goes by the name "Filmways." If the graciousness of the raceway seemed a bit unbelievable, it all became clearer when Filmways, the parent company, attached the following last-minute rider to the agreement: that Filmways be given exclusive distributing rights to any film that might come out of the concert. In lieu of distribution rights, Filmways would agree to accept $100,000 in cash. Furthermore, the Stones were to put up an additional $100,000 in escrow for any damage that might be done to the raceway.

The final dose of irony was injected into the negotiations when it was learned that Filmways also owned Concert Associates, a promotional subsidiary, which one month before had been under the thumb of the Stones.

Concert Associates, the promoters of the Rolling Stones concert at the Inglewood Forum, outside of LA, had accepted, as did sponsors in each of the other tour cities, some unusually demanding contract terms, for the privilege of promoting the event. These included coming up with a cash guarantee of 60% of the anticipated gate receipts, months in advance. Outside of the outrageous cash advance, most of the conditions were for the ego gratification of the Stones.

Concert Associates went along with every contract clause without a whimper. It wasn't until the Stones reneged on an unwritten promise to make a return appearance at the Forum, two or three weeks later, that tensions began to tell. The unexpected opportunity to turn tables on the Stones came with the Sears Point package.

According to Richard St. John, president of Filmways, Sam Cutler (the Stones' road manager) and Rock Scully (manager of the Grateful Dead) failed to meet any of the requirements that had been set down for the use of the Sears Point Raceway. Foremost in the ultimate breakdown of negotiations was the sticky matter of the film rights.

At noon on Friday, 24 hours from the start of the concert, the Stones retained

Melvin Belli to untangle their commitments to Filmways. Belli worked quickly. In a few hours, the Sears Point site was dropped, and a new contract with Dick Carter of the Altamont Raceway near Livermore was signed.

The Stones' representatives had been working out of Alembic, the sound studio which houses the offices of the Grateful Dead, in Marin County, a half hour drive north of San Francisco, near Hamilton Air Force Base. Dozens of people were involved. At various times one saw Chip Monck, the man who designed and executed the Woodstock sets, later to do the same for Altamont; Sam Cutler; Rock Scully; Jerry Garcia and Phil Lesh of the Dead; Lenny Hart, part of the Dead management (he was heard telling Taj Mahal over the phone that they didn't think there'd be time for him on the program, though, in retrospect, it is clear that Taj, or somebody, could have done much to cool out the crowd during the one hour fifteen minute wait for the Stones to appear); Chet Helms of the Family Dog; Emmet Grogan of the Diggers; David Crosby; Owsley Stanley, the wizard of acid; Jo Bergman of the Stones' London office; John James, who'd served as transportation and security man for the Stones' tour; Ron Schneider, who'd run the tour on behalf, more or less, of their manager, Allen Klein; and hordes of newsmen and other hangers-on.

The telephones were in constant use. Meetings of two-three-ten-fifteen people took place in side offices, broke up in confusion. Everyone seemingly was trying to find a new concert site, and there was an air of frantic activity about the place. But in fact, nothing was happening. It looked like the Sears Point cancellation had ended the trip. Nobody was coming up with anything.

A complicated business. But, anyway, after having miraculously built a stage at one raceway, Chip Monck had miraculously disassembled it, moved it via truck to another site 65 miles away and set up anew, in a miraculously short time span. A miracle of logistics. Now, the question was, how had they gotten Altamont so amazingly quickly?

Dick Carter had an answer for that one, all right. "Stanford Business School has been working with me on ideas for management and promotion of the track so we can build it up again. The track has gone broke three times. It was about to be turned into a housing development when I took over. And the Stanford people came to me, no charge, with their business school, advising me what to do. Last night they called me and kiddingly said, 'Are you having the Rolling Stones out at Altamont?' I said, 'Yeah,' you know? They said, 'Seriously, it's off at Sears Point and don't you wish you had it?' I said, 'If you're not kidding, we'll get it.' So I made a few phone calls and here we are."

And he was doing it entirely for free? "Right. They're paying the basic expenses, we're donating the use of the track. We feel that it's good publicity for us, and it's good for the area. We want to put Altamont on the map.

"By the way, young fella, we're trying to give this place a kinda new image, if you see what I mean. The old management hasn't been so good, so we want to try to identify it a little differently. So when you write about the place, I'd appreciate it if you called it *Dick Carter's* Altamont Raceway."

The Altamont contract called for these things: that the site be used for the concert without charge to the Stones or to the spectators; that the Stones pay $5000 for clean-up after the event; and that a $1,000,000 insurance policy be taken out to protect the facilities from any damages incurred. Interestingly enough, there has been no subsequent mention of this insurance policy, even though a several hundred thousand dollar suit has been lodged by ranch owners in the area. There was no mention of a film, potential profits, or any charity.

Carter was reminded of Woodstock, he said, though he hadn't been there. He could be excused that. A lot of other people who *had* been there were reminded of Woodstock themselves. What a surprise they were in for.

Late in the evening Mick Jagger arrived by helicopter to have a look. He strode about and talked with the people some. A chick gave him her long yellow scarf to ward off the cold, he smiled and walked on. Another chick planted a huge kiss on him, then promptly freaked out.

A radio interviewer asked him questions like:

"Have you seen all the preparations that are going on here?"

MICK JAGGER: "Yeh man. It's great."

and

"Do you know who's going to play with you tomorrow?"

M.J.: "No, not yet. Not everybody."

Mick Jagger dressed in a red velvet cape and red velvet cap which hung over the side of his head to one side and then some tv lights went on and the interviewer asked a few more questions and then a joint was passed up to Jagger and he asked for the tv lights to be shut off and then took a hit and passed the joint on.

He split later to helicopter back to the plush Huntington Hotel in San Francisco.

As usual, the Stones trip included the best of everything. The best of hotels, limousines, cuisine. Maybe it was a free concert, but there was no good reason not to do it in style.

By 7:30, Saturday morning, the hills were solidly packed with people, and it was clear that those who expected only 100,000 or so had miscalculated. For as far as you could see in any direction, the army of rock freaks was advancing over rises and hillocks, through valleys, along the road and the railroad tracks, converging on Altamont. Whatever else it would be, it would be *big*.

From the air, it was an incredible scene. From six to eight miles from the site, cars lined the highway like the traffic jam in *Weekend*. Nothing on wheels except motorcycles could move, so people just left their cars and started the long hot trek to the racetrack. The air was alive with aircraft.

As the helicopter nears the site, the pilot says, "See that big brown spot off to the right? Those are people."

He's right. The huge, brown mass now appears to be moving. It no longer just looks like a burnt out field. From every direction, people are converging on the scene. It looks like the peons following Marlon Brando to the town where he's killed in *Viva Zapata!*

We circle the area once for pictures and swoop toward the asphalt racetrack where another copter is hovering to land. Faces become distinct now and we set down, causing a whirlwind. Bystanders look interested momentarily until they see we aren't from a band and then turn away.

Jan Vinson, who piloted the Stones helicopter, swore he would never work a rock festival again, because of the "mass confusion and because I was put in a position which was dangerous to both me and the machine and the crowd. Those people were messed up on everything—dope, wine, needles. They were higher than any altitude I've ever flown at. I wasn't about to get out of the chopper and talk to any of them. If the Hell's Angels hadn't been there, it would have been worse. They did a good job of keeping the way cleared when crowds surged around us, and didn't bother me at all."

Some people—mainly news crews and film crews, but also some civilians—paid up to $250 an hour to be airlifted to the concert site by helicopter, 45 minutes each way. Traffic congestion on the roads was bad enough that helicopter was the only way to be certain that all the bands and equipment would get there on time.

Crosby, Stills, Nash and Young, who were to fly in and out in time to be in Los Angeles for a gig at UCLA that evening, had arranged to go out on a 9-passenger chopper leaving from Marin Heliport in Sausalito.

David Crosby, first to arrive with the band's road crew, was enthusiastic, hopeful about the day. A broad smile creased his face, even after he heard the helicopter pilot had refused to land because of fog and they would have to drive 20 miles through and beyond San Francisco to catch another helicopter at International Airport.

"We'll make it," he said. But be back in time for the gig?

He smiled again. "We've got till 8 o'clock."

It was nearly noon already.

It was quarter to three on Saturday when the first helicopter carrying the Stones and their entourage touched down on the asphalt pit area of the Altamont racetrack. Immediately, a minor mob scene formed as about 500 people jumped off the nearby fence they were sitting on or rushed from the hill toward the copter, almost crushing a smiling Stone and his escorts.

"Who is it? Who is it?" rasped a blonde chick to her black-garbed girlfriend.

"It's Mick Jagger! It's Mick Jagger!" And, mouth wide with joy, she bent over slightly, arms pressed tightly to her sides, her hands clenched as if in religious fervor—the way only 16-year-old chicks can do to show just how excited they are.

They were both soon lost in the sea that seemed to swallow the Stones.

Shortly thereafter, a crazed freak broke through shouting, "I hate you, I hate you!" and punched Mick smack in the chops. It was a foretaste of delights to come.

Mid-morning on Saturday, Berkeley people laid what looked like a thousand tabs of sunshine acid on the Angels—not good sunshine: it had a lot of speed in it—and this was being dispersed both at the Angels' bus thirty yards uphill and on the stage. At one point, 500 reds were scattered on the front portion of the stage. The Angels were downing tabs of acid/speed and reds in huge gulps of Red Mountain wine. The more they took, the more fighting there was. The usual thing was to pick off non-Angels, but they were seen to turn on their own prospects (non-members who were trying to gain full status into the club). One prospect was soundly kicked—they were jumping on him—after Santana's set. He took a terrible beating, and, amazingly, was back on his feet ten minutes later, telling the full-fledged Angels he was their brother and everything was cool.

Meredith Hunter wasn't the only one who never made it home from Altamont. Three others died that day, two in a hit-and-run auto case, one by jumping into an irrigation canal where the fast-moving waters overpowered him.

The two killed by the car were Mark Feiger and Richard Savlov, both 22, of Berkeley. They had recently moved to the Bay Area from New Jersey. They were killed around midnight Saturday when a 1964 Plymouth sedan plowed into them and several others as they sat around their camp fire by the side of the speedway road. The official cause of death was listed by the coroner as "multiple blunt crushing injuries." The wheels of the hit-and-run car went across their chests, and they were dead on arrival at Valley Memorial Hospital in Livermore at 12:20 a.m. Sunday. The driver of the car has not yet been found.

Candy Sue Johnson, 22, of Oakland and James McDonald, 21, of Santa Cruz both suffered head and internal injuries in that hit-and-run. Both were hospitalized, and Candy's infant child, who was with her but not injured, was put in the custody of Candy's parents in Oakland.

The fourth death was listed by the coroner as "John Doe," who died of asphyxiation due to drowning. Sheriff's deputies said he slid down an irrigation canal after being warned not to, and drowned almost immediately. By Wednesday, his identity had not been established. He was in his early 20's, and wearing a white metal cross in his pierced right ear. He had long dark brown hair, a moustache, sideburns below the ears, and was wearing black levis with a sash brown cloth belt and brown buckle shoes. He was 5'10", 155 pounds, and had brown eyes. An attempt is being made to identify him through FBI fingerprint files.

As for the number injured seriously, there are no precise figures. The confusion which reigned over the affair made it impossible for medics to keep records, local hospitals were generally uncooperative in dealing with the media, and the injured seem to be spread out in hospitals all over the Bay Area.

One thing is most certain: Even the most incomplete medical reports show that this was a festival dominated by violence. The volunteer medics treated more than just the usual bad trips and cut feet. They also treated dozens of lacerations and skull fractures. On top of those, they had an extraordinary number of bad trips—so many that they ran out of thorazine even though they didn't

William Owens for GIOS

start using it until late in the day. They came to the four medical tents in waves after each escalation by the Angels, many of them having bad trips on good acid —bad trips seemingly induced by the violence going on around them. People sitting near the stage said they could feel the wave of paranoia spreading through the stoned crowd with each beating. Acid plus muggings equalled terror and revulsion.

Understandably, there was a bad aftertaste in the mouths of medical volunteers along with just about everybody else at the festival. Richard Fine, chairman of the Medical Committee for Human Rights, labeled the concert promoters "morally irresponsible" for the manner in which the festival was staged.

"We had one day to mobilize medical personnel and supplies. We got shitty support from the people running the thing who didn't realize what was crucial from a medical standpoint, and wouldn't give us the authority to do such things as set up a workable evacuation procedure. And we had no time to mobilize community people for help with bad trips. It was just piss-poor planning. A lot of the bad trips were violent because there was so much violence in the air. There were a lot of beatings. Girls were beaten—I sewed up a lot of girls. It was like the fucking [police] Tac[tical] Squad ran around. We feel that we as well as everyone else in the crowd were exploited by the promoters," Fine fumed.

According to Fine, the medical people had been promised telephone communications. It never happened. They'd been promised a helicopter. None materialized. And when it turned dark—during the hour and a quarter wait for the Stones—and dozens of people lay injured in the medical area, Stones representatives refused to turn on the backstage lights so the medics could tend to them. The lights would just damn well have to wait until the Stones came out to play. (To turn them on before might rob some impact from the Stones' entry. People were injured? Well . . . tough shit . . . the Stones were more important.)

The MCHR is an all-volunteer group which provides medical aid at almost all Bay Area demonstrations and festivals. They're an irreplaceable part of the scene. They were assisted at Altamont by four Red Cross chapters, Langley Porter Neuropsychiatric Institute staff members, and dozens of volunteers. The medical aid was coordinated primarily by Dr. Richard Baldwin of Point Reyes, who said the main problem was "all those freak-outs."

"With all our units, we treated probably about 700 freak-outs," he guessed, "plus all those we never saw, that were handled by friends in the crowd. That's a lot. They came in waves. We got one big wave early in the morning, and then another one when the violence broke out with the Airplane. Then it was back to 'normal' again. The biggest wave we got was near the end, when the Angels started picking up again. They were leading each other in twos and threes, totally confused and totally freaked-out by it," Baldwin said.

The standard procedure for dealing with bum trips was to assign a person experienced in drug crises to each person who came in. They would try to "talk down" anyone in trouble on a one-to-one personal basis. But as the day wore on, and the violence increased, personnel were unable to keep up with the massive numbers seeking help, and doctors had to start relying solely on thorazine. Although none had any idea how much thorazine was finally used, doctors had to have an emergency supply flown in later in the day as bad trips increased. Aside from thorazine, though, first aid tents were well stocked with everything they needed.

Some of the bad trips were the result of yellow pills given away in the crowd and said to be organic acid. "It was very crude stuff," according to Baldwin. Most of the dope being sold at the festival, though, was of about standard street quality. Several bummed out when they drank wine without knowing it had acid in it. Only two drug cases had to be evacuated, though, both because of too many reds. The extraordinary amount of wine consumed posed another problem for Baldwin's crews.

Aside from the bad trips, doctors treated a large number of victims of the Angel rampages. The number of violence-induced injuries was "unusually high," according to Fine. Doctors at one tent said they treated 12—one skull fracture, one fractured facial bones, and 10 skull lacerations. And that wasn't even the tent behind the stage, which was the first aid station closest to the danger zone and thus presumably the one most of the injured would go to.

Both doctors seemed certain that, despite reports, there were no births at the festival. First reports had four babies being born, two before, two during the music. There were cases of false labor, but none of the medical staff at the site delivered a baby, and no one showed up at any of the medical tents with a newborn child. The same was true of local hospitals. "I think somebody just picked up on that story because it sounded groovy and the promoters could use the story about births to try to balance out the deaths," Fine charged.

The frustration of trying to provide adequate medical service at an affair where the sponsors didn't seem to give a shit about the injured apparently got to some of the doctors. "Wavy Gravy" (Hugh Romney) of the Hog Farm, who spent most of his time at the medical tent, gave this report: "The medics were squaring off against each other. It was really funny, man. This other medic wasn't working hard enough, so they were punching away at each other. It seemed like a pretty convenient place, in the hospital and all." That's some idea of how high tensions were running.

Medics weren't the only ones pissed off by a complete lack of cooperation from the Stones' management. Another man with a medical problem related his run-in with the promoters: "I went up on the stage to make an announcement to find the father that was stoned on acid and got separated from his wife and baby, because the baby had been stepped on by an Angel and they thought the baby was dead. The Stones' manager said, 'We're not making any personal announcements; we've told people where lost and found is, we've told people where the Red Cross is. There will be no personal announcements. I don't care if you die; there's not going to be an announcement.' He was the most uptight dude anybody ever saw."

Photographer Jim Marshall, who's been to perhaps 200 festivals in the past ten years, including about a dozen during 1969, said he'd seen more violence at Altamont than all others this year combined. "The sound was crappy and everybody felt bummed by that. There was no community feeling here at all. There was more violence at this festival than all the other ones I've attended this year. And somehow it relates to the hysteria over the Stones, though I can't really make the connection."

Frank Morin, administrator of Valley Memorial Hospital in Livermore, said that between Friday night and Sunday night his staff treated "about 45" people from the festival. Ten were for drugs (all bum trips, no needle O.D.'s), 24 were for auto accidents, and eight were for "other traumas." By Wednesday, only one person was still at the hospital. That was James McDonald of Santa Cruz, who was injured in the hit-and-run that killed two. He suffered head and internal injuries, and fractured ribs and left leg. By Wednesday, he was no longer in the intensive care unit, and was able to talk.

"I don't remember a thing except where I am right now and what they told me about the guy who ran into us. But I remember about the festival. I'd hitched down from Capitola [near Santa Cruz] and I just wanted to hear the music. But lots of people weren't there for the same reason. They didn't really dig what was going on. They were there so they could say they had been there, and they wanted to get as close as possible. I just wanted to have a good time, and I was trying to be pretty cool about all the other stuff going on. I don't even know now if it was worth it, and I can't say because this might never have happened."

Eden Hospital in Castro Valley still had two casualties on Wednesday. One was Candy Sue Johnson, who suffered head injuries as a result of the same accident as McDonald. The other was Steven Vitali, 19, who also suffered head injuries in an accident of still-undetermined origin. By Wednesday, Steve was in satisfactory condition, and Candy in fair condition, but both were still in the intensive care unit and unable to speak. Highland Hospital in Oakland reported treating one person.

At least one casualty was admitted to Mt. Zion Hospital in San Francisco—Denise Jewkes of the Ace of Cups. She had a fractured skull.

She had undergone emergency surgery to have a jagged chunk of skull (about the size of a quarter) removed. This was over her left eye, in her forehead, below her hairline. Because of the position, nothing more than a local anesthetic was possible. The doctors told her she could have died from the injury.

"Somebody threw a beer bottle way up in the air and it came down on me and knocked me unconscious," she said. "There were lots of beer cans still full being thrown around, and that was the stupidest thing going on. I was between the stage and the bus to the right, and the vibes weren't very good at all around there. It was very packed, and more people were always walking through, stepping on us and trying to find a place to sit when there obviously wasn't one. There was no way. It seemed kind of cool early in the morning, like it was going to be a nice day and was going to get a lot better, but as the day went on it just wasn't there at all."

The other serious injury reported immediately was that of Arnold Hull, 21, of Oakland. Hull supposedly told an ambulance driver to take him to a maternity ward, that he was about to have a baby. He then undressed and jumped off a freeway overpass, and was taken to Valley Memorial in critical condition.

David Crosby put most of the blame for the whole sordid mess on sloppy planning due to lack of time, but had some scathing remarks for the Stones as well.

"You can't have that big a gathering that sloppily, and it wasn't sloppy for lack of effort, but for lack of time," he said. "The people made a heroic effort. But doing it that sloppily, we could have paid much heavier dues. We could have dumped a helicopter full of two or three good rock bands into a crowd of about a thousand people and killed them all; we could have paid *much* heavier dues.

"There were several big mistakes. They weren't necessarily mistakes of intent, but people just didn't really know certain things. The Rolling Stones are still a little bit in 1965. They didn't really know that security isn't a part of anybody's concert anywhere anymore. I mean, our road managers could have covered it. Nobody would have gotten on that stage, nobody would have hassled anybody. We didn't need the Angels. I'm not downgrading the Angels, because it's not healthy and because they only did what they were expected to do. I don't know why anyone would expect them to do anything other than exactly what they did. The mistake that was made was in thinking security was needed, and that the Angels should do it. The Stones don't know about Angels. To them an Angel is something in between Peter Fonda and Dennis Hopper. That's not real, and they just found out the reality of it. Unfortunately, we all had to pay some dues for that.

"Another level of this is that I don't think gatherings that big is where it's at. I don't think it's conducive to making magic. The Airplane and the Dead have done this kind of thing right before. They've taken a sunny afternoon and a beautiful field and put a few thousand people on the best possible state of consciousness that a few thousand people can reach on this planet that I know of. Full-out brotherhood and a full-out really happy feeling. That kind of trip you can proveably do and you can proveably control how many people come to it and what kind of people by how you disseminate the information. Our own band is kind of like that, and this big trip thing is not for me, since this one went down. I've talked to my friends in the Airplane and they're kind of the same way, and the Dead, too, and we're three of the bands you'd call if you want to do that kind of hugeness, and we won't go now. We won't play this kind any more," Crosby stated emphatically.

The rest of his own band feels pretty much the same way, he noted. "They were all bummed out by this; they did it mostly for me, because I asked them to. When you're trying to do something that's as fragile as making music, to have a couple cats pick some dude off, fire on him with blows that are out of his order of magnitude entirely, lay him out cold and then kick him for 15 minutes right in front of you, you just can't do it."

Crosby felt the Angels were not entirely to blame for what went down. "They have an absolutely definable code, and they stick to it very carefully. They are, in their own way, intensely moralistic; they have a very definite rigid set. That's how they work, and it's very definite and very committed; they are not kidding. There's another mistake that was made. Nobody knew that there was an Angels officers' meeting in Oakland that afternoon. And the Angels that came were all people like Hayward Angels, Berdoo Angels, cats that I did not know, that I could not talk to. Had Sonny Barger been there, Terry the Tramp, Magoo, these are cats I can talk to. I say it's a better trip if they don't do that, and they say cool it and they don't do it. It's that simple, but those guys weren't there."

Barger *was* there, but arrived too late to alter the tide of violence.

"Remember, the Angels were asked there. If it's not that kind of scene, they don't get into that kind of bag. I've been around the Angels dozens of times . . . remember the Magic Mountain festival on Mt. Tamalpais, or all the times you've ever been at the Avalon? I don't think the Angels seek it out; I've never seen the Angels deliberately seek large scale trouble. They've always showed up at gatherings, but they were not asked to guard a stage. This time they were and they did it. In their mind, guard a stage means guard it. That means if anyone comes near it, you do them in, and in the Angels' style if you do them in, you *do* them in. I don't dig everybody blaming the Angels. Blame is the dumbest trip there is; there isn't any blame.

"The overall point to be taken is that we have proven as a subculture, and they are not part of it, that we can get together and have a set of values that does not include beating each other up, and get along conspicuously well with it. And do it for a period of time, with huge numbers, and we've done it beyond the capacity of the straight world or anybody else to equal, in history. Those cats are on a different trip, and I think that people who don't understand what trip they're on should not judge so quickly what went down. I ain't trying to justify it at all, you don't see me hanging out with the Angels, because at any point you can break what they think are the rules and get dead. I can't live with that; that's not my kind of way to live, that's their way, that's the trip they're on. I ain't going to put them down, I'm not going to put them up. I understand it, I know how to deal with it, and that's to stay the hell away from it and respect it for what it is—pure unadulterated danger. Don't mess with them, but I don't think they were the major mistake. I think they were just the most obvious mistake."

And, finally, some harsh words for the Stones themselves. "I think the major mistakes were taking what was essentially a party and turning it into an ego game and a star trip. An ego trip of 'look how many of us there are' and a star trip of the Rolling Stones, who are on a star trip, and who qualify in my book as snobs. I've talked with them many times and I still think they're snobs. I didn't want to talk to them at all Saturday, once I saw what was going on. I'm sure they don't understand what they did, and I'm sure they won't understand my thinking they're snobs, but they are in my book. I don't like them. I think they have an exaggerated view of their own importance; I think they're on a grotesque ego trip. I think they're out of touch with the people to whom they're trying to speak. I think they are on negative trips intensely, especially the two leaders."

Carlos Santana, lead guitarist for Santana, the afternoon's first band, watched the fighting breaking out in front of him during Santana's set.

"There was bad vibes from the beginning. The fights started because the Hell's Angels were pushing people around. There was no provocation; the Angels started the whole violence thing and there's no fucking doubt about that.

"It all happened so fast, it just went right on before us and we didn't even know what was going on. There were lots of people just fucking freaked out. During our set I could see a guy from the stage who had a knife and just wanted to stab somebody, I mean, he really wanted a fight. Anybody getting in the way of anybody had himself a fight, whether he wanted it or not. There were kids being stabbed and heads cracking the whole time. We tried to stop it the best we could by not playing, but by the time we got to our fourth song, the more we got into it, the more people got into their fighting thing."

Santana said that besides the Angels, "you could blame reds and liquor for the whole fucking mess. People just got themselves fucked up and wanted to fuck up everybody. You lose control of respect for yourself, and you lose control of respect for anybody else. That's what happened—reds and liquor did it."

But the big mistake, he felt, was having the Angels act as security guards. "I mean, the stage has to be guarded by somebody, but you don't need cops and you don't need Hell's Angels. At Woodstock, they had all kinds of cats keeping the stage clear who were all wearing colored jackets and you knew who they were and you didn't need cops or Angels."

As a musician there to play for the people, he was also disappointed in the audience. "The bands played good," Santana said, "And then at the end of their sets, people who just have the attitude, oh well, they're finished now. There was no energy there, nobody wanted to get it on or the bands would have played that much better. The vibrations were really strange. Everybody was trying to have a good time, but there just wasn't any energy from them. It was all a big ego thing. They wanted another Woodstock, but they didn't want to make one, they wanted it to just happen to them. We made a nice try, but maybe next time we'll be better. As long as we're alive we deserve another chance and we'll try it again," he added.

Several of the musicians who were there placed the blame directly on Jagger. "If I ever get that asshole up against the wall," promised one San Francisco musician, "he ain't never gonna walk away."

Told of this, Sam Cutler exploded: "That's bullshit! Mick didn't make the arrangements. I did. Put it on me."

Asked for his comments on the festival, Marty Balin declined. Paul Kantner was the lone member of the Airplane willing to speak, and his basic point was to make clear the fact that the Angels would not be asked to provide security at any more concerts involving the Airplane. Members of the Grateful Dead refused to discuss it at all, at least not for the record.

The Dead were scheduled to play just before—and then, as the day wore on, just after—the Stones. But by the time the Stones had finished their set, the scene was too tense to risk stretching the day out any longer. That's the way things went at Altamont—so badly that the Grateful Dead, prime organizers and movers of the festival, didn't even get to play.

Getting there had been half the fun, just like Woodstock. Except not as bad as Woodstock. Only suckers parked ten miles away, and there were no serious traffic jams—never mind the Top 40 radio hype—to speak of.

True, some people had parked six or eight miles away. But hustlers from the nearby town of Livermore were giving rides to Altamont for $5 per customer. Just hop in the back of this pickup, pal, I'll get you there. Twenty minutes worth of back road and you're there.

At first—before people settled in on the rolling pasture land—there was a nice kind of communal spirit on the hike. At least half the crowd was from the San Francisco Bay Area, but lots of them had come from afar. There was one red-headed longhair in Bermuda shorts who'd driven up in three and a half days from Florida. People from Denver, Los Angeles, Orange County ("everybody we know is coming up," says one VW busload full), San Diego, Seattle, Vancouver, even New York and Pennsylvania.

"We cheated," said Tom Frieberg, of Beaver Falls, Pennsylvania, who'd driven to Altamont with his old lady, "We were already in Chicago when we heard about it."

In the early morning hours of that disastrous Saturday, several thousand persons took their micro-buses up a wrong turn in the road and wound up stranded on Altamont Pass five to ten miles from the concert site. Apparently convinced that they were reliving the wonderful Woodstock experience, all of them happily abandoned their cars in the middle of the road (just like they'd read in *Life*) and began the long trek to the promised land. The absurdity of it all was compounded by the fact that many left the winding asphalt road and began climbing the dusty hills. "I think it's just over the next ridge," they shouted as they waded through the cow dung eight miles from their destination. Hundreds of others decided to beat the crowd by walking on the railroad tracks which cut right through the pass—right through the pass and into the countryside in the wrong direction. As they all walked blindly in several erroneous beelines, the California Highway Patrol (CHP), which had directed them to the *cul de sac* in the first place, was busy having their cars towed away.

That new freeway, still under construction, was converted by the California Highway Patrol into a parking lot, and had cars parked across all four lanes for six miles. Even that wasn't enough.

One CHP who refused to identify himself said the main problem was just too many people. "Those roads are only designed for about 15,000 cars at the most, and there were thousands more than that. It wouldn't have even mattered if the new freeway was finished; it couldn't have handled it either."

Those people who had cars towed away had incredible hassles. When they returned to their cars that night, it was pitch black, and many thought they were lost, or that their cars had been stolen. Most of them either had to find another way home or sleep there overnight, sleeping bag or no sleeping bag.

The next morning they had to find out where their cars were, lay out $30–$40, and pay a traffic fine. And towers were none too concerned about how they got the cars out. No safety catches on the axles. There were several cases where the tow truck would go around a corner, and the car it was towing would swing out and smash into other cars along the roadside. The primary concern of the towers seemed to be to move as many as cars as possible. One bragged of making $500 in just five hours.

Art Gilbertson, manager of G and H Garage in Livermore, said the traffic jams were to blame for the jacked-up towing fees. He said he went in at 9 a.m. Saturday and it was 9 p.m. before he was able to move a car because he had to clear the roads first. Even when the roads were clear, traffic turned what is normally a one hour round trip into a two or two and one-half hour trip. He felt the extra charge was justified, as did a tower from Groth Bros. Oldsmobile, also in Livermore.

Both denied doing any damage to cars, though the obvious physical condition of some of the cars showed otherwise. In all, about 200 cars were towed off, and some are still sitting in the yards of garages in Livermore and Tracy.

Capt. William Bradshaw of the CHP's San Leandro station complained that the CHP hadn't been given enough time to plan for the event, and vowed to oppose any future festivals in that area.

"I was contacted at 11 Friday morning by my zone commander in San Francisco, who had just been told himself. That gave us 20 hours and at the time we had nobody there but the regular beat patrol. For the rest of the time, we had to have two forty-man shifts there, and had to get help from the Tracy and Concord stations."

"So I had to direct the whole thing from a helicopter. Traffic was backed up at least 10 miles both ways all day, but people didn't have much trouble leaving because they were parked so far away they couldn't all get out at once. The people who had parked far away and were walking to the Speedway on foot generally didn't know where they were going."

It was Bradshaw who ordered cars blocking the roads to be towed away. He said it was necessary to keep one lane open at all times for emergency vehicles, and those who parked in the middle of the road came back to find their cars towed away.

Bradshaw said that because he was in the helicopter, he didn't get to speak with any of the rock audience. Many of his officers did, he said, with mixed results. "Some found the people cooperative, others found them uncooperative. Lots of those people were intoxicated on one thing or another. And there were lots of complaints from neighbors about cars parked on their property, fences torn down for firewood, frightening the livestock, vulgarities, obscenities, and you name it."

The CHP made three arrests, all for public drunkenness. Alameda County Sheriffs, who policed the festival periphery, refused to disclose the number of arrests they made, or any information about the murder investigation.

It is authoritatively reported (by an intimate of the higher echelons of the Sheriff's department) that there were four, possibly five, plainclothesmen from the department near the stage, close to the action, on duty—which means that they were carrying their firearms. Their exact instructions are unknown, but, generally, it is a law enforcement officer's duty to stop any crime he sees being committed, especially murder. (In fairness, it is not certain they were present during the Hunter murder.)

The sheriffs are said to have attempted to intercede in some of the fighting, but there were, according to our source, more Angels than they were prepared to handle. So the lawmen backed off.

A number of sheriff's officers are beginning to confide that they feel the department is somehow at fault; that they should have prevented the Angels from taking over. Whether or not the *Stones* wanted cops to handle security for the concert, the decision ultimately rested with the cops themselves.

Though they have nothing to say about it publicly, the Alameda County Sheriff's office is pressing very hard on an investigation of the entire event— one of the prime reasons being that the department has been getting so much heat from county officials for "mishandling" it in the first place. The investigation has not gone especially well so far. Sheriff's sleuths are "surprised and frustrated" to discover that hardly any witnesses to the violence are willing to talk with them.

It may surprise many of the people who suffered Altamont to discover that they were, in effect, unpaid extras in a full production color motion picture.

The fact of the matter seems to be that the real reason for the free concert was to make a sort of *Woodstock West* movie. Jagger was eager for the movie to be rush-processed, edited as quickly as possible, and hurried into release to beat the real Woodstock film to the punch. A March 15th release date was guaranteed Jagger as part of the deal whereby the Stones and the movie-makers own the film 50-50, according to Maysles representative Porter Bibb. According to Stones manager Allen Klein, however, no such 50-50 deal exists. "The Stones own the film," says Klein. "The Maysles own nothing. They were paid a fee to shoot it and to make it. That's all."

They knew what kind of movie they were after before they started. They wanted it groovy. Good vibes. One big happy party. Even on Saturday, after it obviously was not that kind of a trip, David Maysles, one of the Maysles Brothers that's doing the movie, noticed one of his cameramen shooting footage of a naked, porcine young lady who was freaking out backstage. A fairly typical scene, definitely worth recording as part of any *true* motion picture account of what happened at Altamont.

Maysles tapped the cameraman on the shoulder and said: "Don't shoot that. That's ugly. We only want beautiful things." The cameraman's response was quick: "How can you possibly say that? Everything here is so ugly."

There were camera crews everywhere, identifiable not only by the equipment but by their khaki hats with the painted yellow stripes down the middle. The Maysles used 17 film crews for the day, each of them with Hell's Angels for security. Three different camera men were aimed, they think, at the murder. It is not yet known what, if anything, they got.

Asked about David Maysles' on-site censoring of his cameramen, Porter Bibb acknowledged that some of this may have occurred. They had not been emotionally set (who had?) for the way the thing had developed.

Bibb described them as being emotionally and psychically shattered by the violence they'd seen.

"We really didn't even want to make this film when we sat down Saturday night back at the hotel. Mick didn't want to make it. He said, 'I don't want— it's not that it didn't happen, I don't want to try to muzzle it, but I don't see any sense in trying to exploit what happened.'

"His first reaction about the concert was, he said: 'Man, I wish—I didn't want it to be like this.' And now he's saying: 'Well, look, there's a lotta shit, but it was a concert, it was free, the kids did come out fantastically, and . . .'"

The Stones figure they spent something like $80,000 on the Altamont affair, including helicopters, which isn't bad at all—when you consider the cost of a movie set.

Any proceeds from the film, Schneider said, would be used first to pay back neighboring ranchers who had property damaged (they're filing the lawsuit anyhow), to recoup the costs of the film, and to pay back those persons who made donations to the festival so it could be set up in the first place.

Proceeds beyond that (if any) would be split up equally among the participating bands. This in itself is a shuck, because the word at first was that all proceeds from the film would go to charity. "It'd be presumptuous of us to decide what the other bands want to do, so we're just going to let them have their own share and decide for themselves," Schneider explained.

The Stones themselves, however, have definitely committed *their* share to some as yet undecided cause, according to Schneider. "Anything we get out of this will either go to a charity or else directly back to the kids in San Francisco, so they can buy some land out there and have lots of free concerts without the hassles we've had. That was Mick's idea, that's the best idea because we want the people there to have their own piece of land. The trouble with giving it to some organizational charity is that by the time they take off their fee and everything, the money doesn't get to the people you wanted to have it. But we don't want any money from this, we never wanted to make a profit and we were never trying to like people said."

A full week after the event, the legal hassles still hadn't been straightened out. The murder investigation was continuing, several lawsuits were being prepared, and the only thing that was certain was that someone is responsible for something, and eventually will have to pay the price.

The Stones' New York management apparently felt pressed to say *something*. But they were unable to get it together. A press conference planned for Friday following the concert (which attorney Melvin Belli was scheduled to attend, having booked a San Francisco-New York flight) was cancelled.

Belli, who represented Jack Ruby during his trial for offing Lee Harvey Oswald, and is one of the nation's gaudier torts lawyers—also one of the best— was representing just about everybody who'd been involved in organizing the concert—the Stones and all their management and retinue, the Dead, even the race track. This may explain why he was playing his cards so close to the vest.

He acknowledged, on one hand, that it was "like a hurricane went through Altamont." He said, on the other hand, that "you've got to anticipate, with this number of people, that this would happen." Basically, Belli thought it had gone pretty smoothly—though lots of questions "remained unresolved," and if he'd "had more time to arrange things, it could have gone smooth as clockwork."

Asked who was responsible for the deaths and the damage, Belli said it was a "foolish" question.

Ron Schneider had told Ralph Gleason that the event was covered by a $5 million Lloyd's of London insurance policy.

Asked about the amount of the Stones' insurance for the event—reports ranged from $100,000 to Schneider's $5 million—Belli called it "ample." What did that mean? "I mean *ample*," he said. Might it include some recompense for the family of the young man who had been murdered?

The question summoned forth Belli's most contemptuous voice. "I think," he declared, "that you're over your head in a legal story like this, when you're asking whether there's going to be recompense for the man that died when it hasn't been established whether he was at fault."

Is it possible, then, that everybody who'd been at Altamont might *somehow* have been at fault, and therefore the Stones (et al.) bore no responsibility for the injured, the wounded and the maimed? That was a question Belli had no time to hear. Busy man. Didn't have all day. Lotta phone calls. Don't know what you're talking about anyway. Good day.

Well, fuck Mel Belli. We don't need to hear from the Stones via a middle-aged jet-set attorney. We need to hear them directly. Who *really* cares whether they're going to lay some bread on Meredith Hunter's family? It isn't going to bring him back to life.

But some display—however restrained—of compassion hardly seems too much to expect. A man died before their eyes. Do they give a shit? Yes or no?

No, according to Gwen, the 17-year-old sister of the dead man. "No one has contacted us. The Stones should have. But I didn't expect them to, because I know they don't care. The Stones should have called my mother, but they didn't, because it doesn't matter to them. They'll just go off somewhere and have another 'rock festival.'"

No one has offered even the slightest condolences to the family. No one even told the family their son was dead. They found out when a friend called the family at 2:30 Sunday morning. Gwen then called the Livermore hospital, the Alameda County Sheriff's Department at Santa Rita and several other locations before she was able to determine that her brother was at the morgue in Oakland. At 8 that morning, she left to identify the body.

"We were sure it was somebody else, and nobody knew anything," she remembered bitterly. "He was a very highly educated boy. He almost never raised his voice; he talked very quietly. That would make people mad when they wanted to fight; he'd talk very quietly, and he was so educated in the way he spoke. His job just came through . . . his job at the Post Office."

Meredith had never been in any trouble. He had only been involved in one fight in his life, that one to defend his sister. Gwen said he did have a gun. "It was almost always in the house; he had it for his own protection. He only took it with him when he'd go out to big affairs. I know he took it with him to the festival. He pulled it out and showed it to them, but only to make them stop and think when they were beating him. I know he would never have used it. The Angels have the gun now. Patty saw them take it."

Patty is Meredith's girl-friend. She attended the concert with him. She is white, and Gwen implied that that might have had something to do with the killing. "I don't know if their being a mixed couple had anything to do with it; it may have had quite a lot to do with it. The Hell's Angels are just white men with badges on their backs," she said.

Meredith liked all kinds of music, his sister said. He'd gone to the Monterey Jazz Festival, had a good time, and went to this one thinking it would be much the same. He went to see the Stones, "just like everyone else."

"They don't care, they don't care," Miss Hunter kept repeating in the family's apartment, an older four-plex off Ashby Avenue in Berkeley. Pictures of Jesus hang in the window; the apartment is neat, small, and dark. "The Rolling Stones are responsible, because they hired the Hell's Angels as police and paid them. But they don't care."

To this day, the Hunter family has not been contacted by anyone—the Stones personally, any representative of their offices, by the police, or by anyone connected in any way with the family. Gwen doesn't expect "any investigation." Mrs. Hunter has been in Herrick Hospital in Berkeley since December 11th, having become hysterical after her son's funeral. A friend, Mr. Charles Talbot, has been staying with the family.

"I don't care if he is just a name," Gwen concluded. "My brother was a very respectable person, and I was closer to him than to anyone in my family."

One prominent San Francisco attorney told *Rolling Stone* that the Hunters have an excellent case for a wrongful death suit against the Rolling Stones for criminal negligence. He indicated that given the past record and reputation of Angels and the fact that the Stones did in fact hire them, it's doubtful that any jury would fail to return a judgement in excess of $100,000. Several attorneys have indicated a willingness to handle the suit for no fee unless there was a settlement.

Stones representative Ron Schneider suggested that his office would offer some kind of compensation to the Hunter family. "We haven't talked to the family yet, but we'll have to do something about that. If we come up and say we're going to give $500,000 to the family, it all sounds so tacky. As far as I'm concerned, if we gave the family $50 million it still doesn't make up for the kid being killed. So whatever you give it doesn't matter, you're just giving something to them. What could I say to them? I don't know what to say to them, that's the problem."

Perhaps Schneider will eventually think of something to say. For now, Gwen and the family are still waiting.

The murder investigation itself was not proceeding very quickly, mostly because no one will talk with detectives from the Alameda County Sheriff's Office. Thus, witnesses are hard to come by. The cops, however, did have several plainclothesmen around the stage area, and presumably they witnessed the killing. Their very presence, though, raises another serious question, namely, why didn't they come to Hunter's aid? Their instructions were to act "with discretion" (in other words, don't start a riot), but does discretion include standing by idly while a single young man is being viciously knifed and beaten to death by a pack of thugs?

It's impossible to say what sheriff's investigators will come up with. They stopped listening . . . when one eyewitness said he wasn't sure he could positively identify the killers.

At any rate, the cops have no suspects in the murder, or they haven't announced any. Detectives seem most interested in determining exactly who hired the Angels, which raises the possibility that if some Angels do eventually stand trial for murder, Cutler and Scully will share the guilt as accessories.

And then there's the law suits, none filed, all imminent.

Neighboring ranchers are preparing to file suit for what they say is extensive damage to their property. They claim fences were torn down for firewood, water lines were broken, cattle lost, and they and their families threatened.

The ranchers, headed by C. W. Tripp, whose property borders the raceway, confronted Carter at a meeting that was as chaotic as the actual event. One said vandals tried unsuccessfully to burn down his barn, a rancher's wife said she held off would-be rapists with a gun, and another collapsed and had to be helped out of the hall when she spoke directly to Carter. Several expressed fear that "hippies" were still back in the hills around their property, and that they might pull a Sharon Tate-type number. The dominant tone of the meeting was full-blown rage and paranoia, but it was on both sides.

For his side, Carter called the whole thing "a rotten political trick" play-acted by the ranchers' attorney, Robert Hannon. There may be substance in that charge, too. Hannon is an Alameda County supervisor, and the Board of Supervisors was planning to file a suit of its own. The ranchers dropped Hannon as attorney after a week due to "possible conflict of interest."

That's part of the reason for the delay in filing the suit. The other is that they are unable to decide exactly how much they want to sue for. They started out with a figure of $10,000, and at one point were talking about a million. The figure they've been bandying about most is $500,000.

The Board of Supervisors' own suit, if they go ahead and file, will be for something over $100,000. This would get them back the money they spent to pay county employees forced to work on the day of the festival, most prominently 160 deputy sheriffs who worked a total of 5000 hours overtime.

The supervisors, to a man, expressed outrage over the whole affair, and immediately began taking steps to lift Carter's license. In their first meeting after the weekend, chairman John D. Murphy requested that county planner William Fraley initiate action to revoke the permit. The County Planning Commission set an open hearing on the matter for December 22nd, and will decide whether or not to revoke the permit on the basis of that hearing.

Fraley told *Rolling Stone* that the festival was not the only reason that Carter's permit was jeopardized, but that "certainly had something to do with it." The permit, he said, was granted in 1966 for races, rodeos, and "limited spectator events," which doesn't include a free rock festival of unlimited numbers. Fraley also pointed out that his office had found further violations of Carter's permit even before the festival happened, including destruction of derby autos at the track, inadequate parking, and failure to carry out required landscaping. With all these charges against him as well as those stemming from the actual festival, it seems pretty safe to assume that Carter will lose his permit. A weekly motorcycle magazine has offered him the services of San Francisco attorney Ted Long, but this aspect of the legal affairs is also pretty much Belli's trip.

There's even a bit of black humor in the story, for a week after Altamont, two Monterey disc jockeys and a Newark businessman announced plans for "the biggest rock festival of them all" in March. They're shooting for a half-million people to gather on a 462-acre site near Prunedale, on Highway 101, eight miles north of Salinas, near the site of the original Monterey Pop Festival in 1967.

These three—their names are Lawrence A. Lee, Dean Brown, and Robert DeCelee—are already counting their money. They expect to gross $2,695,000 and net $2,343,000, with $24,000 going to charity. The festival would be March 20–22nd, and the site would be enclosed in a barb-wire topped fence. That's one of the ways they figure they can avoid the problems of Altamont. The other is through nine months of planning that has been going on.

They're crazy. At this point, the best thing we can do is pray for rain, or hope that bands will refuse to play, as David Crosby has said Crosby, Stills, Nash and Young have promised to do. The promoters have so many dollar signs in their eyes they can't see that size alone does not a festival make.

Anyhow, the Monterey County supervisors are taking steps to stop the project before it ever gets going. Since the 1968 Monterey Pop Festival was shot down before it ever got off, the chances are good this one can be headed off too. In the wake of Altamont, what is needed is not "bigger" festivals, but a serious reappraisal of what the word "festival" really means.

Contacted in New York, Ron Schneider of Stone Promotions Ltd. (promoters of the American tour) did a fancy job of fence-straddling, on the one hand condemning the Angels for excesses, on the other trying to justify them. His primary concern seemed to be to get his office off the hook.

"We're denying that we had the Angels kill anybody or do anything unfair," Schneider said. "As far as I understand, at all the San Francisco free concerts, like for the Grateful Dead, they come up and provide security, they keep people off the stage. That's what they tried to do here, they tried to protect everybody. Mainly because one person died, which is extremely regrettable, it's all been blown up.

"I'd like to mention that a few times I saw the Angels picking up children that were being squashed in the crowd, they picked up a man and his baby and carried them out. Even though they had this incident with the Airplane, you can't control every single thing. They came—we really didn't want them there, with the harshness and violence, because it affected all of us. During the show the Stones stopped and tried to get them out of there, but it was a little too late to have any kind of control."

Responsibility for hiring the Angels belongs to Cutler, as well as Rock Scully and the Grateful Dead, according to Schneider. "Sam's from England, and isn't familiar with the Hell's Angels. He used a branch of the Angels in England at the Hyde Park festival and it went off quite well. The Angels provided security and everything was nice and pleasant. When he came here, he thought he had the same kind of situation and wanted to use the Angels if they were available. He didn't know they were a different chapter of Angels. He just asked Rock Scully to get him the Angels. They weren't supposed to get on the stage, but they thought their place was on the stage and that's where they went."

(Quite the contrary, according to two witnesses on the stage. They said Cutler was well aware of what the Angels were doing then, and that he told them to do whatever they had to do to keep people off the stage.)

"I feel that we gave a free concert for the kids to enjoy, there should never have been any violence or any of that, and it sickens me to know that somebody died at something we gave for everybody so they could have a good time. It bothers the Stones that something like this could happen.

"Even if nobody died, even if just three kids got punched in the nose, there's just no excuse for it. The Angels were there the entire morning and what happened is they just got completely out of their heads on acid and everything. There was nothing you could do, it just became a violent thing with them; we tried to get them off the stage once we saw what was happening. But the people who asked the Angels to come were the people organizing from that end—Sam Cutler, Rock Scully, the Dead. Not our office."

Aside from that, Schneider felt there had not been enough talk about the good things. "If you were 50 feet away from the stage, you thought you were at a fantastic concert, because nobody there knew what was happening; the kids who were on the outskirts thought it was the best, everybody raved about it, it was really good."

Bullshit.

Schneider would not blame the Angels for the killing. "At first I thought it would have been better if there were no Angels, but now I say I don't know. What if the police had been there when the guy pulled the gun? Keith saw him pull it. The guy would probably have been shot to death by the police instead of being stabbed. That's the only difference. And the kids would probably have immediately attacked the police thinking it was their fault.

"My position is, it happened, there's nothing else I could say about it. It just happened like it did, and that's how come we have to accept it, as much as it disgusts us. How can we disavow a death? I mean, the man died, it's regrettable. The man shouldn't have pulled a gun like he did, but that's no reason to die. We were trying to have a good time and entertain people."

Ralph J. Gleason was not entertained. He saw Altamont, in his newspaper column, as a sort of culmination of the worst trends in the rock and roll. Gleason raised the real questions about Altamont more forcefully than anyone else had dared.

"Why," wrote Gleason, "did Jagger and Cutler put the Angels with a truck load of free beer in charge of stage security? Why did the Grateful Dead people and the other locals involved (Grogan, Chet Helms, etc.) go along with the idea?

"Why Saturday's episode? I suspect it is because, just as their parents 25 years ago thought America was full of Comanches scalping stagecoach riders and Capone gangsters shooting passersby on Chicago streets, Jagger and Cutler think San Francisco is the Hell's Angels and the Pranksters since those are the ones who went to London last year and first broached the idea of the Stones playing free here.

"Now it has ended in murder. And that was a murder, not just a 'death' like the drowning or the hit-and-run victims. Somebody stabbed that man five times in the back. Overkill, like Pinkville. Like a Chicago cop's reaction to long hair.

"Is this the new community? Is this what Woodstock promised? Gathered together *as* a tribe, what happened? Brutality, murder, despoliation, you name it. . . .

"The name of the game is money, power and ego, and money is first and it brings power. The Stones didn't do it for free, they did it for money, only the tab was paid in a different way. Whoever goes to see that movie paid for the Altamont religious assembly.

"All right, let me ask the question. Are Mick Jagger, Sam Cutler, Emmet Grogan and Rock Scully any less guilty of that black man's death than Sheriff Madigan is of the death of James Rector?"

It was one of Sheriff Madigan's men who killed James Rector in the People's Park uprising in Berkeley this Spring. Gleason's implication was that it was one of Jagger's/Cutler's/Grogan's/Scully's boys who'd offed Meredith Hunter. The air was dense with *blame*.

Bill Graham, an interested observer of the whole fiasco, had plenty to say after it was all over but the shouting. Graham had loaned out a sound man and an electrician, but only after it was obvious that unless he did so, the thing would have to be called off. He had his own ideas about who was to blame.

"I would offer Mr. Jagger $50,000 to go on coast-to-coast television or radio with me, not stoned, not copping out, but sit down, mister, and rap, open, for an hour. I'll ask you what right you had, Mr. Jagger, to walk out on stage every night with your Uncle Sam hat, throw it down with complete disdain, and leave this country with $1.2 million? And what right did you have in going through with this free festival? And you couldn't tell me you didn't know the way it would have come off. What right did you have to leave the way you did, thanking everybody for a wonderful time, and the Angels for helping out? He's now in his home country somewhere—what did he leave behind throughout the country? Every gig he was late. Every fucking gig he made the promoter and the people bleed. What right does this god have to descend on this country this way?

"It will give me great pleasure to tell the public that Mick Jagger is not God, Jr. And it's worth it to me. I am not trying to blast at someone that is 10,000 miles away, but you know what is a great tragedy to me? That cunt is a great entertainer," Graham thundered.

Next in line for the verbal thrashing was Chip Monck. "There were certain local people who are good people, but who were very stupid in agreeing to this. Without realizing it, they were accessories to the crime. I blame two or three people who could've stopped the festival regardless of what anybody did. Mr. Jagger could've realized what he was doing; his ego wouldn't allow it. Mr. Chip Monck is the best stage manager that I know; I respect him as a man. But the man knew what he was doing, and I can't think that anything but his ego got him to do this. He was one of the engineers of Woodstock; it took him months to build Woodstock, and how could he think that in one day . . .

"Once they took Sears Point from him, which would have only given them three or four days, and he had to move to this location, he must have, as a man, as a logician, known. You cannot tell me that this same person thought, not that he couldn't put up the stage and the lights, but that this person thought it could come off right. And I don't mean just the Angels, because even if the Angels weren't there, peace isn't enough anymore. Where was it held, what did it do the surrounding areas, where were the first aid kits, where were the sanitation facilities, the emergency crews, who stopped the people from climbing the scaffolding? The stage was four feet high. This one person had the power to stop the whole thing, and he didn't, and I must accuse him of that."

As Graham sees it, about the only good thing that could possibly have come out of this festival is that it means the end of festivals. "The strange thing that went on this past weekend is that in the long run, it may help to eliminate festivals, which I think is one of the best things that can happen to rock and roll. *Woodstock*—the film that is coming out of Woodstock—is a masterpiece; I've seen it, but the aftereffects of Woodstock and the aftereffects of this one and the aftereffects of many of the others. . . . The question that I've asked after every one and that hasn't been answered by anyone justifiably is: Who gains? Other than the people in the 50-foot perimeter of the stage? 290,000 others can't see or hear anything. But I think that we are losing the major groups because they're becoming as guilty as anyone else . . . the big dollar very quickly. It's not for me to speak for any of the groups, but if you speak to the Airplane, Crosby, Stills, Nash and Young, any of the heavy groups who have tremendous integrity, they've gone sour. They went sour before this weekend, but this weekend, I think, blew their minds. I knew it blew mine," he added.

"But the guiltiest one of all is the law. The law had the greatest power to avert this. The law is most responsible whenever there's a danger and they don't stop it. To me, anytime the law sees anything like this coming, which is a holocaust, when the law realizes the citizenry of an area is in danger, they can stop anything at any time. You can block a highway, you could force them by injunction, or by force—sometimes force is valid. They should have taken Mr. Jagger, twisted his fucking arms behind his back, put him in front of a radio, and said, 'Mr. Jagger, if we have to break your arm, call if off.' Mr. Monck, the minute he put up one platform, they stop him. If there was no stage, no sound, no lights, and if there was no Rolling Stones, the kids wouldn't have left their homes. Once the kids started, once the ants come down the hill, watch out, make way . . . they're going to eat you. My point is, the law *knew* what was coming," Graham concluded.

Emmet Grogan told how he'd gone with Rock Scully, manager of the Grateful Dead, down to see Jagger when the Stones had first set foot in Los Angeles nine weeks earlier. Grogan, best known as a Digger during the Haight's flowering a couple of years back, says Jagger and Richard agreed to do a free concert then, and were eager that Scully and Grogan start working right then to get it together.

The way Scully tells it now, the concert would have been geared for something like 50,000–75,000 in San Francisco's lush, green Golden Gate Park. The secret here was that a full-scale festival would be organized, with all sorts of theater groups and performing troupes in addition to the rock bands. The Stones would not even have been announced until perhaps two or three hours beforehand.

All was cool, Scully and Grogan say, between them and Jagger. The hangup was with the Stones' New York management: the Allen Klein axis which includes lieutenants John Jaymes and Ron Schneider. "They kept stringing us along," says Grogan. "The New York people. They wanted control over it."

So, on one hand, they could get no go-ahead for the groundwork that needed to be done: getting a permit for the park, lining up other performers, and all the details of putting on a free rock and roll festival. On the other hand, there was a series of publicity leaks about the affair, and these, Scully says, could only have come from the Stones' people in New York. No one else knew so many specifics to leak to the press.

"They started building up a hype," says Scully, "to be certain they'd get a lot of people, big numbers."

More and more time passed, and eventually it all came down to a big last-minute crisis. Scully and Grogan had been made to look foolish repeatedly, by starting to enter negotiations with San Francisco park and recreation people on various occasions, four, three and two weeks ahead of the scheduled December 7th concert date—only to withdraw without explanation.

They did manage to rap with an aide to the Mayor, and at one point, ten days before the concert, got themselves on the Park and Recreation commission meeting agenda. The day that meeting was to have taken place, they withdrew their request for a park permit, under what then appeared to be mysterious circumstances.

Now they say it was just another no-go from the Stones' New York people.

Stones' manager Allen Klein, belatedly worried about what had gone down, phoned *Rolling Stone*'s San Francisco offices to try to get specific details as to who, in the Stones contingent, had been responsible for making which arrangements. Specifically, Klein was asking for almost a blow-by-blow account of the planning, because he felt assured he'd need that for the legal difficulties that loom for the Stones.

He made a particular point of stressing that the "Stones management" had not been involved in setting up the free concert.

Ah, but Stones management had been involved, he was told. Sam Cutler most prominently, and all those other people (Schneider, Jaymes, Bergman, Monck).

"Yes, but not the real Stones management," he said. By that he meant that *he* directly had had nothing to do with it—"and now they want to pass the blame on the Stones."

The San Francisco people who'd worked in advance trying to line up Golden Gate Park said that a huge stumbling block was the lack of response from the Stones' New York office—meaning Klein and his man Schneider. "All I can say," said Klein, "is nobody contacted me."

Klein thought only the people who set it up were responsible. And they did not include any of the Stones, nor Allen Klein. Sam Cutler? "Well, he's the guy they hired to help on the road and with this Altamont thing because he did a good job on their free concert in Hyde Park. But he's not part of the Stones management."

But he had been hired to help the Stones manage their tour. He was part of their management at the time of the Altamont "party."

Klein's response was that he would have done it in Los Angeles. "The climate is better."

What about Sam Cutler?

"I'm not," said Klein, "copping a plea. But let's be clear about this: I did not hire Sam Cutler."

There's a saying somewhere about abandoning sinking ships. . . .

While charges and recriminations were flying, there were some people trying to see what we can learn from the Altamont disaster.

Wavy Gravy, of Hog Farm fame and notoriety, and who had been there, working mainly with the medical aid people, saw plenty that was wrong with Altamont—and more importantly, has much to say about how those things can be done right in the future.

For one thing, Wavy feels people had a whole wrong set of expectations about what it was going to be. What it *was,* as compared with what it might have been, is sad to ponder.

"It was," says Wavy, "the Rolling Stones, which is a real super-commercial rock group, doing their thing, and to expect anything more is a mistake that a lot of people made. The whole hip community got co-opted into helping to put this thing on to the point that they should have saw that it wasn't gonna work. I mean, just in the sensible things like sound reproduction, it wasn't gonna work. There wasn't time. At this thing, there were only certain areas where there was fidelity in terms of listening to what was going on.

"How you *can* do it is you don't make it a one-day thing. You make it, say, three days, and in a place that's ecologically sound, I mean as far as groovy grass and water's available and stuff like that. And there's facilities for medical stuff and food. What I think is, to avoid the hype, you have more than one stage to start with. The pressure keeps moving. If there was like three stages, and a band didn't have to go on according to schedule, but anybody could play when they felt like it, that would be a real festival.

"You don't have all the stages going at once, maybe. You don't say where it's going to happen next. You run up a flag or shoot off a rocket or somethin'. Like in Shakespeare's time, they ran up a flag. Or you could have them all go at once all playing the same song. There's all kinda combinations. There's an old Prankster adage: do it all. And that didn't happen at Altamont.

"You need a day to sorta settle in. It has to be at least like a week-end thing. And then, there's not all that hype that you gotta get there, because if you don't get there you're missin' everything. And after the second day, you sorta been there. You slept together and you figured out how to eat breakfast together, and the crowd is pretty much amalgamated into a one sorta thing. Sorta there to do *whatever* it is. It gets sorta logical.

"The one-day thing sets up the fact that you gotta enjoy yourself, you know? Like you're there and gettin' sorta hard-pressed and it's gettin' later and later, and you gotta go home—and we can't hear anything—well, let's push our way up there and may be we can hear a little bit and maybe see somebody and——"

Dick Carter (of *Dick Carter's* Altamont Raceway fame) is charging recklessly full speed ahead. He has gotten a taste of the Big Time, now, and it sure as hell beats the 40-lap main event. Rock and roll has a new promoter. Carter wants to bring the Beatles out to Altamont for a three-day freebie in the Spring. That's right: the Beatles, for free, at Altamont.

"Of course nothing's definite yet," he says modestly, "but if all things go right, the will of the people will win out. They want the Beatles; we'll give them the Beatles." Carter spoke with Young American Enterprises to that effect last week.

In his conversation, Carter seemed totally out of touch with anything real. For example: "Now I've just been reading this book called *Naked City,* from around 1945, and about when Frank Sinatra was at Coney Island. It's all the same, the exact same complaints—a few bad guys getting all the headlines, the security problems. These are all very minor. I was just reading in the paper where Shirley Temple says you have a good person if you have a happy person. And, you know, she's trying to make people happy. She's for the Indians, and she wants to let 18-year-olds vote, and we think she's right and we want to make everyone happy so they'll be good. Maybe we can get Shirley to help us out on future festivals." Honest, he *really* said that!

His plan is to have smaller pay concerts at places like the Oakland Coliseum or the Cow Palace. The money from these will pay for the costs of the all-weekend free concerts at Altamont. Since Carter believes that if you start charging people money, there'll be "real trouble," the idea is to make nothing off the Altamont concerts except from concessions and film proceeds. That means he has absolutely nothing to gain from the free concerts.

"That is, we have nothing to gain except the good will of the people," he noted.

A full nine days later, the Altamont Raceway area looked more than anything else like a picture of Hiroshima the day after—not a person to be seen, the whole area still piled high with the litter and refuse that were the last remnants of what had been. A couple fences in the area had been mended, but the fence around the racetrack was still down. The thousands of wine bottles and tons of litter were stacked in piles around the grounds, but none of it had been removed. A lone man walked about the huge field, stooping over occasionally to pick up a scrap of paper.

Cutler had made an appeal over the radio the day after the concert for the "beautiful people of San Francisco" to come back and help clean up the some tons of litter which they had left there "by their very presence." Also to help dismantle the stage, the scaffolding, and the other construction which had a lifetime of one day.

Oh, there was a little help. Ralph Haley, 23, of Washington, and his wife Sandy (they had been married December 4th) were in San Jose visiting friends Thursday when they heard about the festival. They went Friday to help set things up, and Sunday started heading the clean-up detail. They got some help from George Cooper of Spokane, fresh out of the service, Steve Mercier of San Francisco, and Mike and Susan Metcalf of Berkeley, members of Ecology Action. And 30, may be 40, others of the original 300,000. They figured they had at least another week of work ahead of them.

"The land itself is OK," Haley said, "It's mostly just debris. There must be a million Red Mountain bottles here, and about half of them are broken. Spirits are really good; we're doing it because we want to. There's pretty good vibrations here while we're working, but it gets pretty cold at night." They planned to clean the land of the neighboring ranchers when they finished around the speedway, "if the ranchers will let us." Fat chance the ranchers will let them. They're pretty leery about longhairs these days. Remember what happened to Sharon Tate. One local rancher went so far as to quite seriously and quite openly propose genocide as the solution to the whole concert problem. Try to tell that man you want to mend his fence.

That lesson was learned by program director Tom Swift and the staff of KMPX-FM in San Francisco. The jocks there had started a project to help clean the place up. They got several hundred volunteers, plus the support of the CHP, the San Francisco police, and Mayor Joseph Alioto. The Livermore Herald News was going to co-sponsor the project. Then, when the dust was starting to settle, Swift got this letter from Herald News managing editor Fred Dickey:

"After talking with several ranchers, we discovered they're too skittish to even think about importing San Francisco kids for clean-up.

"So after hearing that and weighing other factors, Mr. Sparks decided the risk is too great for the possible gains in such a joint venture.

"Accordingly, I must withdraw from the project we discussed.

"Thank you for your interest."

Meanwhile, scavengers are combing over the grounds for pop bottles they can turn in for deposit, and several have taken geiger counters out to the raceway to find change and valuables that were left behind.

Who knows, maybe for them the festival will have been worth it.

Norman Mailer / The Liberal Party

In *Armies of the Night,* for which this is the fourth chapter of the section entitled "History as a Novel," Mailer is writing, as are the authors and speakers of "Let It Bleed," about his participation in a mass public event —the march on the Pentagon of October 21, 1967, to protest the war in Vietnam. If "Let It Bleed" exhibits the effects of composite authorship trying to encompass a shared public occasion, "The Liberal Party" is emphatically the expression of a strongly personal voice. The voice claims as much historical dimension for itself—for its difficulties and triumphs in social badinage with Robert Lowell, for its capacity to infuse details of personal behavior, even of home furnishing, with large political and moral significance—as it allows to any group or crowd or to the March itself. Yet the Mailer who writes is extraordinarily more self-measuring, more skeptical, less gregarious than the man who marches. He is indeed a kind of odd man out even in so small a gathering as the party. A careful look at his characterization of the party in the third paragraph, for example, reveals that his "deepest detestation" is probably more easily excited by the people he is with than by those he is marching against. There is somehow a similarity between the décor of the liberals who helped initiate the march and the Pentagon which is its destination.

There was a party first, however, given by an attractive liberal couple. Mailer's heart, never buoyant at best, and in fact once with justice called "sodden" by a critic, now collected into a leaden little ball and sank, not to his feet but his stomach. He was aware for the first time this day of a healthy desire to have a drink for the party gave every promise of being dreadful. Mailer was a snob of the worst sort. New York had not spoiled him, because it had not chosen to, but

New York had certainly wrecked his tolerance for any party but a very good one. Like most snobs he professed to believe in the aristocracy of achieved quality—"Just give me a hovel with a few young artists, bright-eyed and bold" —in fact, a party lacked flavor for him unless someone very rich or social was present. An evening without a wicked lady in the room was like an opera company without a large voice. Of course there were no wicked ladies when he entered this room. Some reasonably attractive wives to be certain, and a couple of young girls, too young for him, they were still in the late stages of some sort of extraordinary progressive school, and were innocent, decent-spirited, merry, red-cheeked, idealistic, and utterly lobotomized away from the sense of sin. Mailer would not have known what to do with such young ladies—he had spent the first forty-four years of his life in an intimate dialogue, a veritable dialectic with the swoops, spooks, starts, the masks and snarls, the calm lucid abilities of sin, sin was his favorite fellow, his tonic, his jailer, his horse, his sword, say he was not inclined to flirt for an hour with one bright seventeen-year-old or another when they conceived of lust as no more than the gymnasium of love. Mailer had a diatribe against LSD, hippies, and the generation of love, but he was keeping it to himself. (The young girls, incidentally, had been brought by de Grazia. Not for nothing did de Grazia * bear a resemblance to Sinatra.)

But we are back with the wives, and the room has not yet been described. It was the sort of room one can see at many a faculty party in places like Berkeley, the University of Chicago, Columbia—the ground of common being is that the faculty man is a liberal. Conservative professors tend to have a private income, so their homes show the flowering of their taste, the articulation of their hobbies, collections adhere to their cabinets and odd statements of whim stand up in the nooks; but liberal instructors, liberal assistant professors, and liberal associate professors are usually poor and programmatic, so secretly they despise the arts of home adornment. Their houses look one like the other, for the wives gave up herculean careers as doctors, analysts, sociologists, anthropologists, labor relations experts—great servants of the Social Program were lost when the women got married and relinquished all for hubber and kids. So the furnishings are functional, the prevailing hues of wall and carpet and cloth are institutional brown and library gray, the paintings and sculpture are stylized abstract, hopeless imitation I. Rice Pereira, Leonard Baskin, Ben Shahn, but bet your twenty-five dollars to win an assured ten dollars that the artist on the wall is a friend of the host, has the right political ideas, and will talk about literature so well, you might think you were being addressed by Maxim Gorky.

Such were the sour and near to unprintable views of the semi-distinguished and semi-notorious author as he entered the room. His deepest detestation was often reserved for the nicest of liberal academics, as if their lives were his own life but a step escaped. Like the scent of the void which comes off the

* de Grazia: leading lawyer for the Mobilization's Legal Defense Committee.

pages of a Xerox copy, so was he always depressed in such homes by their hint of oversecurity. If the republic was now managing to convert the citizenry to a plastic mass, ready to be attached to any manipulative gung ho, the author was ready to cast much of the blame for such success into the undernourished lap, the overpsychologized loins, of the liberal academic intelligentsia. They were of course politically opposed to the present programs and movements of the republic in Asian foreign policy, but this political difference seemed no more than a quarrel among engineers. Liberal academics had no root of a real war with technology land itself, no, in all likelihood, they were the natural managers of that future air-conditioned vault where the last of human life would still exist. Their only quarrel with the Great Society was that they thought it temporarily deranged, since the Great Society seemed to be serving as instrument to the Goldwater wing of the Republican party, a course of action so very irrational to these liberal technologues that they were faced with bitter necessity to desert all their hard-earned positions of leverage on real power in the Democratic party, a considerable loss to suffer merely because of an irrational development in the design of the Great Society's supermachine. Well, the liberal technologues were not without character or principle. If their living rooms had little to keep them apart from the look of waiting rooms of doctors with a modern practice, it was exactly because the private loves of the ideologues were attached to no gold standard of the psyche. Those true powers of interior decoration—greed, guilt, compassion and trust—were hardly the cornerstones of their family furnishings. No, just as money was a concept, no more, to the liberal academic, and needed no ballast of gold to be considered real, for nothing is more real to the intellectual than a concept! so position or power in society was, to the liberal technologue, also a concept, desirable, but always to be relinquished for a better concept. They were servants of that social machine of the future in which all irrational human conflict would be resolved, all conflict of interest negotiated, and nature's resonance condensed into frequencies which could comfortably phase nature in or out as you please. So they were servants of the moon. Their living rooms looked like offices precisely because they were ready to move to the moon and build Utope cities there— Utope being, one may well suppose, the only appropriate name for pilot models of Utopia in Non-Terrestrial Ecologically Sub-Dependent Non-Charged Staging Areas, that's to say dead planets where the food must be flown in, but the chances for good civil rights and all-out social engineering are one hundred percent zap!

As is invariably the case with sociological ruminations the individual guests at this party disproved the general thesis, at least in part. The hostess was small, for example, almost tiny, but vivid, bright-eyed, suggestive of a fiery temper and a childlike glee. It was to pain Mailer later to refuse her cooking (she had prepared a buffet to be eaten before the move to the theater) but he was drinking with some devotion by then, and mixing seemed fair neither to the food nor the bourbon. It was of course directly unfair to the hostess: Mailer priding himself on his good manners precisely because the legend of his bad manners was so prevalent, hated to cause pain to a hostess, but he had learned from years of speaking in public that an entertainer's first duty was to deliver himself to the stage with the maximum of energy, high focus, and wit—a good heavy dinner on half a pint of bourbon was likely to produce torpor, undue search for the functional phrase, and dry-mouthed maunderings after a little spit. So he apologized to the lady, dared the look of rejection in her eye which was almost balanced on a tear—she was indeed surprisingly adorable and childlike to be found in such a liberal academic coven—tried to cover the general sense of loss by marshaling what he assumed his most radiant look, next assuring her that he would take a rain check on the meal.

"Promise?"

"Next time I'm in Washington," he lied like a psychopath. The arbiter of nicety in him had observed with horror over many a similar occasion that he was absolutely without character for any social situation in which a pause could become the mood's abyss, and so he always filled the moment with the most extravagant amalgams of possibility. Particularly he did this at the home of liberal academics. They were brusque to the world of manners, they had built their hope of heaven on the binary system and the computer, 1 and 0, Yes and No—they had little to do therefore with the spectrum of grace in acceptance and refusal; if you did not do what they wished, you had simply denied them. Now Mailer was often brusque himself, famous for that, but the architecture of his personality bore resemblance to some provincial cathedral which warring orders of the church might have designed separately over several centuries, the particular cathedral falling into the hands of one architect, then his enemy. (Mailer had not been married four times for nothing.) If he was on many an occasion brusque, he was also to himself at least so supersensitive to nuances of manner he sometimes suspected when in no modest mood that Proust * had lost a cell mate the day they were born in different bags. (Bag is of course used here to specify milieu and not the exceptional character of the mothers, Mme. Proust and Mrs. I. B. Mailer.) At any rate, boldness, attacks of shyness, rude assertion, and circumlocutions tortured as arthritic fingers working at lace, all took their turn with him, and these shuttlings of mood became most pronounced in their resemblance to the banging and shunting of freight cars when he was with liberal academics. Since he—you are in on the secret—disapproved of them far more than he could afford to reveal (their enmity could be venomous) he therefore exerted himself to push up a synthetic exaggerated sweetness of manner, and his conversations with liberal ideologues on the consequence consisted almost entirely of overcorrections of the previous error.

* Marcel Proust: (1871–1922), French novelist famous for supersensitivity to nuances of manner; author of *A la Recherche du temps perdu* (Eng. trans., *Remembrance of Things Past*).

"I know a friend of yours," says the ideologue. A nervous voice from the novelist for answer. "Yes? Who?" Now the name is given: it is X.

Mailer: I don't know X.

The ideologue proceeds to specify a conversation which M held with X. M recollects. "Oh, yes!" he says; "of course! X!" Burbles of conversation about the merits of X, and his great ebullience. Actually X is close to flat seltzer.

There had been just this sort of dialogue with a stranger at the beginning of the party. So Mailer gave up quickly any thought of circulation. Rather, he huddled first with Dwight Macdonald,* but Macdonald was the operative definition of the gregarious and could talk with equal facility and equal lack of personal observation to an Eskimo, a collector from the New York Department of Sanitation, or a UN diplomat—therefore was chatting happily with the world fifteen minutes after his entrance. Hence Mailer and Robert Lowell * got into what was by all appearances a deep conversation at the dinner table sometime before food was laid out, Mailer thus doubly wounding the hostess with his later refusal.

We find, therefore, Lowell and Mailer ostensibly locked in converse. In fact, out of the thousand separate enclaves of their very separate personalities, they sensed quickly that they now shared one enclave to the hilt: their secret detestation of liberal academic parties to accompany worthy causes. Yes, their snobbery was on this mountainous face close to identical—each had a delight in exactly the other kind of party, a posh evil social affair, they even supported a similar vein of vanity (Lowell with considerably more justice) that if they were doomed to be revolutionaries, rebels, dissenters, anarchists, protesters, and general champions of one Left cause or another, they were also, in private, *grands conservateurs*,* and if the truth be told, poor damn émigré princes. They were willing if necessary (probably) to die for the cause—one could hope the cause might finally at the end have an unexpected hint of wit, a touch of the Lord's last grace —but wit or no, grace or grace failing, it was bitter rue to have to root up one's occupations of the day, the week, and the weekend and trot down to Washington for idiot mass manifestations which could only drench one in the most ineradicable kind of mucked-up publicity and have for compensation nothing at this party which might be representative for some of the Devil's better creations. So Robert Lowell and Norman Mailer feigned deep conversation. They turned their heads to one another at the empty table, ignoring the potentially acolytic drinkers at either elbow, they projected their elbows out in fact like flying buttresses or old Republicans, they exuded waves of Interruption Repellent from the posture of their backs, and concentrated on their conversation, for indeed they

---

* Dwight Macdonald: (1906–), American critic and journalist. Some of his important pieces are collected in *Memoirs of a Revolutionist: Essays in Political Criticism* (New York: Farrar, Straus, 1957) and *Against the American Grain* (New York: Random House, 1962). His article "The String Untuned" appears in Section VI.
* Robert Lowell: (1917–), American poet.
* *grands conservateurs*: great conservatives.

were the only two men of remotely similar status in the room. (Explanations about the position of Paul Goodman * will follow later.)

Lowell, whose personal attractiveness was immense (since his features were at once virile and patrician and his characteristic manner turned up facets of the grim, the gallant, the tender and the solicitous as if he were the nicest Boston banker one had ever hoped to meet) was not concerned too much about the evening at the theater. "I'm just going to read some poems," he said. "I suppose you're going to speak, Norman."

"Well, I will."

"Yes, you're awfully good at that."

"Not really." Harumphs, modifications, protestations and denials of the virtue of the ability to speak.

"I'm no good at all at public speaking," said Lowell in the kindest voice. He had indisputably won the first round. Mailer the younger, presumptive, and self-elected prince was left to his great surprise—for he had been exercised this way many times before—with the unmistakable feeling that there was some faint strain of the second-rate in this ability to speak on your feet.

Then they moved on to talk of what concerned them more. It was the subject first introduced to Mailer by Mitch Goodman. Tomorrow, a group of draft resisters, led by William Sloane Coffin, Jr., Chaplain at Yale, were going to march from their meeting place at a church basement, to the Department of Justice, and there a considerable number of draft cards would be deposited in a bag by individual students representing themselves, or their groups at different colleges, at which point Coffin and a selected few would walk into the Department of Justice, turn the cards over the Attorney General, and await his reply.

"I don't think there'll be much trouble at this, do you?" asked Lowell.

"No, I think it'll be dull, and there'll be a lot of speeches."

"Oh, no," said Lowell with genuine pain, "Coffin's not that kind of fool."

"It's hard to keep people from making speeches."

"Well, you know what they want us to do?" Lowell explained. He had been asked to accompany a draft resister up to the bag in which the draft cards were being dropped. "It seems," said Lowell, with a glint of the oldest Yankee light winging off like a mad laser from his eye, "that they want us to be *big buddy.*"

It was agreed this was unsuitable. No, Lowell suggested, it would be better if they each just made a few remarks. "I mean," said Lowell, beginning to stammer a little, "we could just get up and say we respect their action and support it, just to establish, I suppose, that we're there and behind them and so forth."

Mailer nodded. He felt no ease for any of these suggestions. He did not even know if he truly supported the turning in of draft cards. It seemed to him at times that the students who disliked the war most should perhaps be the first to

---

* Paul Goodman: (1911–), American educator and writer, utopian of anarchist sympathies; one of his best-known books is *Growing Up Absurd* (1961). A sample of his writing may be found in Section IX.

volunteer for the Army in order that their ideas have currency in the Army as well. Without them, the armed forces could more easily become Glamour State for the more mindless regions of the proletariat if indeed the proletariat was not halfway to Storm Troop Junction already. The military could make an elite corps best when the troops were homogenized. On the other hand, no soldier could go into combat with the secret idea that he would not fire a gun. If nothing else, it was unfair to friends in his outfit; besides it suggested the suicidal. No, the iron of the logic doubtless demanded that if you disapproved of the war too much to shoot Vietcong, then your draft card was for burning. But Mailer arrived at this conclusion somewhat used up as we have learned from the number of decisions he had to make at various moral crossroads en route and so felt no enthusiasm whatsoever for the preliminary demonstration at the Department of Justice tomorrow in which he would take part. To the contrary, he wondered if he would burn or surrender his own draft card if he were young enough to own one, and he did not really know the answer. How then could he advise others to take the action, or even associate his name? Still, he was going to be there.

He started to talk of these doubts with Lowell, but he could hear the sound of his own voice, and it offended him. It seemed weak, plaintive, as if his case were —no less incriminating word—phony, he did not quite know why. So he shut up.

A silence.

"You know, Norman," said Lowell in his fondest voice, "Elizabeth and I really think you're the finest journalist in America."

Mailer knew Lowell thought this—Lowell had even sent him a postcard once to state the enthusiasm. But the novelist had been shrewd enough to judge that Lowell sent many postcards to many people—it did not matter that Lowell was by overwhelming consensus judged to be the best, most talented, and most distinguished poet in America—it was still necessary to keep the defense lines in good working order. A good word on a card could keep many a dangerous recalcitrant in the ranks.

Therefore, this practice annoyed Mailer. The first card he'd ever received from Lowell was on a book of poems, *Deaths for the Ladies and other disasters* it had been called, and many people had thought the book a joke which whatever its endless demerits, it was not. Not to the novice poet at least. When Lowell had written that he liked the book, Mailer next waited for some word in print to canonize his thin tome; of course it never came. If Lowell were to begin to award living American poets in critical print, two hundred starving worthies could with fairness hold out their bowl before the escaped Novelist would deserve his turn. Still Mailer was irked. He felt he had been part of a literary game. When the second card came a few years later telling him he was the best journalist in America, he did not answer. Elizabeth Hardwick, Lowell's wife, had just published a review of *An American Dream* in *Partisan Review* which had done its best to disembowel the novel. Lowell's card might have arrived with the best of motives, but its timing suggested to Mailer an exercise in neutralsmanship—neutralize the maximum of possible future risks. Mailer was not critically equipped for the task, but there was always the distant danger that some bright and not unauthoritative voice, irked at Lowell's enduring hegemony, might come along with a long lance and presume to tell America that posterity would judge Allen Ginsberg the greater poet.

This was all doubtless desperately unfair to Lowell who, on the basis of two kind cards, was now judged by Mailer to possess an undue unchristian talent for literary logrolling. But then Mailer was prickly. Let us hope it was not because he had been beaten a little too often by book reviewers, since the fruit of specific brutality is general suspicion.

Still Lowell now made the mistake of repeating his remark. "Yes, Norman, I really think you are the best journalist in America."

The pen may be mightier than the sword, yet at their best, each belong to extravagant men. "Well, Cal," said Mailer, using Lowell's nickname for the first time, "there are days when I think of myself as being the best writer in America."

The effect was equal to walloping a roundhouse right into the heart of an English boxer who has been hitherto right up on his toes. Consternation, not Britannia, now ruled the waves. Perhaps Lowell had a moment when he wondered who was guilty of declaring war on the minuet. "Oh, Norman, oh, certainly," he said, "I didn't mean to imply, heavens no, it's just I have such *respect* for good journalism."

"Well, I don't know that I do," said Mailer. "It's much harder to write"—the next said with great and false graciousness—"a good poem."

"Yes, of course."

Chuckles. Headmastermanship.

Chuckles. Fellow headmastermanship.

They were both now somewhat spoiled for each other. Mailer got up abruptly to get a drink. He was shrewd enough to know that Lowell, like many another aristocrat before him, respected abrupt departures. The pain of unexpected rejection is the last sweet vice left to an aristocrat (unless they should happen to be not aristocrats, but secret monarchs—then watch for your head!).

Next, Mailer ran into Paul Goodman at the bar—a short sentence which contains two errors and a misrepresentation. The assumption is that Goodman was drinking alcohol but he was not; by report, Goodman never took a drink. The bar, so-called, was a table with a white tablecloth, set up near the archway between the dining room where Lowell and Mailer had been talking and the living room where most of the party was being enacted—to the tune of ten couples perhaps—so the bar did not qualify as a bar, just a poor table with a cloth to support Mailer's irritated eye. Finally he did not run into Goodman.

Goodman and Mailer had no particular love for one another—they tended to slide about each other at a party. In fact, they hardly knew each other.

Their lack of cordiality had begun on the occasion of a piece written by Goodman for *Dissent* which had discussed Washington in the early days of the Kennedy Administration. Goodman had found much to displease him then, and kept referring to the "wargasms" of this Kennedy Administration which wargasms he attached with no excessive intellectual jugglery to the existential and Reichian notions of the orgasm which Mailer had promulgated in his piece *The White Negro* (Goodman was a sexologue—that is, an ideologue about sex— Mailer was then also a sexologue; no war so rich without quarter as the war between two sexologues.) Goodman, at any rate, had scored off Mailer almost at will, something to the general effect that the false prophet of the orgasm was naturally attached to the false hero of Washington who went in for wargasms. Writing for a scholarly Socialist quarterly like *Dissent,* it was hard to miss. The magnetic field of *Dissent*—hostile to Kennedy at the time—bent every wild shot to the target. So Mailer wrote a letter in reply. It was short, sought to be urbane, and was delivered exactly to the jugular, for it began by asserting that he could not judge the merits of Goodman's intellectual points since the other had made a cardinal point of emphasizing Mailer's own incapacity to reason and Goodman was doubtless correct, but Mailer did nonetheless feel competent to comment on the literary experience of encountering Goodman's style and that was not unrelated to the journeys one undertook in the company of a laundry bag. . . . Great ferment in scholarly Socialist quarters! A small delegation of the Editors assured Mailer they would print his letter if he insisted, but the hope was that he would not. Mailer had always thought it senseless to undertake an attack unless you made certain it was printed, for otherwise you were left with a determined enemy who was an unmarked man, and therefore able to repay you at leisure and by the lift of an eyebrow. Mailer acceded however. He was fond of the Editors of *Dissent,* although his private mixture of Marxism, conservatism, nihilism, and large parts of existentialism could no longer produce any polemical gravies for the digestive apparatus of scholarly Socialist minds; nonetheless Mailer had never been asked to leave the Board, and would not have resigned on his own since that would have suggested a public attack on the ideas of people with whom he had no intellectual accord but of whom he was personally fond.

Nonetheless, from that day, Mailer and Goodman slid around one another at parties and waved languid hands in greeting. It was just as well. Each seemed to have the instinct a discussion would use up intellectual ordnance best reserved for articles. Besides, they had each doubtless read very little of the other.

Mailer, of course, was not without respect for Goodman. He thought Goodman had had an enormous influence in the colleges and much of it had been, from his own point of view, very much to the good. Paul Goodman had been the first to talk of the absurd and empty nature of work and education in America, and a generation of college students had formed around the core of his militancy. But, oh, the style! It set Mailer's teeth on edge to read it; he was inclined to think that the body of students who followed Goodman must have something de-animalized to put up with the style or at least such was Mailer's bigoted view. His fundamental animus to Goodman was still, unhappily, on sex. Goodman's ideas tended to declare in rough that heterosexuality, homosexuality, and onanism were equally valid forms of activity, best denuded of guilt. Mailer, with his neo-Victorianism, thought that if there was anything worse than homosexuality and masturbation, it was putting the two together. The super-hygiene of all this mental prophylaxis offended him profoundly. Super-hygiene impregnated the air with medicated Vaseline—there was nothing dirty in the damn stuff; and sex to Mailer's idea of it was better off dirty, damned, even slavish! than clean, and without guilt. For guilt was the existential edge of sex. Without guilt, sex was meaningless. One advanced into sex against one's sense of guilt, and each time guilt was successfully defied, one had learned a little more about the contractual relation of one's own existence to the unheard thunders of the deep—each time guilt herded one back with its authority, some primitive awe—hence some creative clue to the rages of the deep—was left to brood about. Onanism and homosexuality were not, to Mailer, light vices—to him it sometimes seemed that much of life and most of society were designed precisely to drive men deep into onanism and homosexuality; one defied such a fate by sweeping up the psychic profit which derived from the existential assertion of yourself—which was a way of saying that nobody was born a man; you earned manhood provided you were good enough, bold enough.

This most conservative and warlike credo could hardly have meaning to a scientific humanist like Goodman for whom all obstacles to the good life derived precisely from guilt: guilt which was invariably so irrational—for it derived from the warped burden of the past. Goodman therefore said hello mildly to Mailer, who answered in as mild a voice, and that was all they had to say. Lowell, following, expressed his condolences to Goodman on the recent death of his son, and Mailer after depressing the hostess by his refusal to eat, went on to talk to Macdonald.

That was most brief. They were old friends, who had a somewhat comic relation, for Macdonald—at least as Mailer saw it—was forever disapproving of the younger author until the moment they came together at one or another party or meeting. Then Macdonald would discover he was glad to see Mailer. In fact, Macdonald could hardly help himself. Of all the younger American writers, Mailer was the one who had probably been influenced most by Macdonald, not so much from the contents of Macdonald's ideas which were always going in and out of phase with Mailer's, but rather by the style of Macdonald's attack. Macdonald was forever referring the act of writing to his sense of personal standards which demanded craft, care, devotion, lack of humbug, and simple *a fortiori* *

* *a fortiori:* with stronger reason, still more conclusively. Apparently misused in text.

honesty of sentiment. All this was a little too simple for Mailer's temper. Nonetheless, Macdonald had given him an essential clue which was: look to the feel of the phenomenon. If it feels bad, it *is* bad. Mailer could have learned this as easily from Hemingway, as many another novelist had, but he had begun as a young ideologue—his mind had been militant with positions fixed in concrete, and Macdonald's method had worked like Zen for him—at the least it had helped to get his guns loose. Macdonald had given the hint that the clue to discovery was not in the substance of one's idea, but in what was learned from the style of one's attack. (Which was one reason Mailer's style changed for every project.) So, the younger author was unquenchably fond of Macdonald, and it showed. Not a minute would go by before he would be poking Macdonald's massive belly with a finger.

But for now, they were ill at ease. Macdonald was in the process of reviewing Mailer's new novel *Why Are We In Vietnam?* for *The New Yorker,* and there was an empty space in the presence of the mood. Mailer was certain Macdonald did not like the new novel, and was going to do a negative review. He had seemed professionally unfriendly these past few weeks. The Novelist would have liked to assure the Critic that the review could not possibly affect their good feeling for one another, but he did not dare, for such a remark would break a rule, since it would encourage Macdonald to talk about what was in his review, or at worst trick him into an unwilling but revealing reply. Besides, Mailer did not trust himself to speak calmly about the matter. Although Macdonald would not admit it, he was in secret carrying on a passionate love affair with *The New Yorker*—Disraeli on his knees before Victoria. But the Novelist did not share Macdonald's infatuation at all—*The New Yorker* had not printed a line in review of *The Presidential Papers, An American Dream,* or *Cannibals and Christians,* and *that,* Mailer had long ago decided, was an indication of some of the worst things to be said about the magazine. He had once had a correspondence with Lillian Ross who asked him why he did not do a piece for *The New Yorker.* "Because they would not let me use the word 'shit,' " he had written back. Miss Ross suggested that all liberty was his if only he understood where liberty resided. True liberty, Mailer had responded, consisted of his right to say shit in *The New Yorker.* So there was old rage behind the arms-length bantering about Dwight's review of Norman's book, and Mailer finally left the conversation. Macdonald was beginning to like him again, and that was dangerous. Macdonald was so full of the very beans of that old-time Wasp integrity, that he would certainly bend over much too far backward if for a moment while reviewing the book he might have the thought he was sufficiently fond of Norman to conceivably be giving him too-gentle treatment. "No," thought the Novelist, "let him keep thinking he disapproves of me until the review is written."

Among his acquaintances at the party, this now left de Grazia. As has been indicated, they were old friends of the most superficial sort, which is to say that they hardly knew each other, and yet always felt like old friends when they met.

Perhaps it was no more than the ability of each man to inspire an odd sense of intimacy. At any rate they never wasted time in needless conversation, since they were each too clever about the other to be penned in position by an evasion.

"How would you like to be the first speaker of the evening?" de Grazia asked.

"There'll be nothing interesting to follow me."

De Grazia's eyes showed pleasure. "Then I thought of starting with Macdonald."

"Dwight is conceivably the world's worst speaker." It was true. Macdonald's authority left him at the entrance to the aura of the podium. In that light he gesticulated awkwardly, squinted at his text, laughed at his own jokes, looked like a giant stork, whinnied, shrilled, and was often inaudible. When he spoke extempore, he was sometimes better, often worse.

"Well," said de Grazia, "I can't start with Lowell."

"No, no, no, you must save him."

"That leaves Goodman."

They nodded wisely. "Yes, let's get rid of Goodman first," said Mailer. But then the thought of that captive audience tuned to their first awareness of the evening by the pious drone of Goodman's voice injured every showman's instinct for the opening. "Who is going to be M.C.?" Mailer asked.

"Unless you want to, I thought I might be."

"I've never been an M.C.," said Mailer, "but maybe I should be. I could warm the audience up before Goodman drops them." De Grazia looked uneasily at Mailer's bourbon. "For Christ's sake, Ed," said Mailer.

"Well, all right," said de Grazia.

Mailer was already composing his introductory remarks, percolating along on thoughts of the subtle annoyance his role as Master of Ceremonies would cause the other speakers.

Angus Calder / The Blitz

Mr. Calder was born in 1942, a year or so after the "blitz," so this account of it is a historical reconstruction, offering a good deal of detail, but naturally not seeking the immediacy of personal reaction notable in the opening piece on the Rolling Stones' concert, and necessarily lacking the personal involvement of Mr. Mailer in the events and personalities upon which he ruminates. Furthermore, Mr. Calder is not trying to write the general history of the great air attack on London in 1940–41, but to focus attention on the way in which it affected the eight million or so civilians who had to live and work under it for many months.

Cecil Beaton

After the fall of France the Germans planned an invasion of Britain, for which they required control of the air over the Channel. The first assault was therefore on British fighter airfields, and it continued from early July to early September 1940, by which time British Fighter Command was nearing the end of its resources; the Battle of Britain, as this phase of the conflict was called, was almost lost. By what is now regarded as a bad strategic error, the Germans then switched their attack from the airfields to London, first in great daylight raids on the docks, then in seventy-six consecutive night raids, one night of very bad weather excepted. The night blitz on London continued until the raid of May 10, 1941, the last and worst of the series; it destroyed the House of Commons, damaged the Law Courts, Westminster Abbey, and the British Museum, with a loss of a quarter of a million books. It also killed 1436 people, injured 1792 seriously, and made thousands homeless.

Although civilians performed the duties of air-raid wardens and fire-watchers, most of the population could do little except endure the onslaught passively and try to go on working. Such precautions as could be taken for their safety were a mixture of forethought and improvisation; nobody knew what it was going to be like. There were many mistakes, some forgivable and some not; and in the midst of all this, as Mr. Calder shows, there was still time to think about social injustice and the democratic prospects for the future.

This extract should be read as a careful, documented, in some ways committed, account of a great crisis not only in the war but in the history of a society. There is enough detail of the course of military events to keep the line of the story clear; Calder astutely borrows from good writers such as Graham Greene and John Strachey when he needs graphic detail—the sound of a raid or the smell of an "incident"; and he is capable himself of reconstructing a typical incident in the concluding pages of this extract. But his main concern, in accordance with the title of his book (*The People's War*) is to show how ordinary citizens conducted their lives, to describe their morale, to note, for example, that even in circumstances of great common danger there can be differences between the comfort, and the chances, of rich and poor. He achieves his ends by accuracy of reporting and the employment of a very efficient, occasionally lively, prose.

In the nature of the case Mr. Calder quotes from official sources, from the reports of journalists and diarists, and from many other works relating to the period. We have not thought it necessary to annotate all of these sources, nor to explain who all the writers were. Their importance in this case arises entirely from their having witnessed and recorded extraordinary scenes; they speak, as it were, for all the people of London.

It so happens that this war, whether those at present in authority like it or not, has to be fought as a citizen's war. There is no way out of that because in order to defend and protect this island, not only against possible invasion but also against all the disasters of aerial bombardment, it has been found necessary to bring into existence a new network of voluntary associations such as the Home Guard, the Observer Corps, all the A.R.P. and fire-fighting services, and the like. . . . They are a new type, what might be called the organized militant citizen. And the whole circumstances of their wartime life favour a sharply democratic outlook. Men and women with a gift for leadership now turn up in unexpected places. The new ordeals blast away the old shams. Britain, which in the years immediately before this war was rapidly losing such democratic virtues as it possessed, is now being bombed and burned into democracy.

J. B. Priestley, Out of the People

THE EVEN TENOR OF THE BLITZ

> *Medals? We don't want no —— medals. The whole —— borough deserves a —— medal."*
> Heavy rescue workers of Bermondsey, asked to nominate some of their number for decorations, May 1941.

A great provincial city like Sheffield could erect a dummy town in the neighbouring hills to attract and deceive the Luftwaffe, but the sprawling size of London made it impossible to disguise, and the U-shaped bend of the Thames round the Isle of Dogs, in the heart of Dockland, was unmistakable from the air.

Ten or a dozen miles from the centre of the capital, to north, south, west and east, lay the outer suburbs, from which office workers surged towards the centre in the morning, and to which they swarmed out again in the evenings. Harrow and Hornsey, Ealing and Richmond, Woodford, Wimbledon, Croydon and Bromley were the heartland of the English middle class, zones of tidy gardens, extensive green playing fields, quiet and propriety. Now tired commuters struggled home somehow on slow trains (when there were any) and went straight to their Andersons * for the night, perhaps to read Trollope,* whose pictures of the croquet lawns and country houses of the mid-Victorian age of equipoise were enjoying a marked but easily explained boom. Few footsteps, after darkness, echoed in the avenues. The warden's post was the liveliest social centre which the blacked-out, owner-occupied acres could afford. Within this outer ring of

---

* Andersons: domestic air-raid shelters; for details, see below, p. 81.
* Trollope: Anthony Trollope (1815–82), prolific Victorian novelist best known for his series of novels about the cathedral town of "Barchester"; he enjoyed a revival during the war.

pebble dash, red brick and ornamental trees lay intermediate suburbs, shabbier genteel; then, to the north and west, older suburbs which gave flats and mansions to the well-to-do. Some, like Chelsea, were battered remorselessly. Others, like Hampstead, came off relatively lightly. Incendiaries would lodge in the rafters of mansions deserted by their owners, and burn them out. At the hub of the wheel lay the twin cities of London and Westminster. With Whitehall, Bloomsbury, Fleet Street, St. Paul's, the Bank of England, the central area still concentrated within its few square miles Britain's cultural past, its commercial present and its legislative future. The raider could be sure that whatever he struck there was of objective or sentimental importance, and later this would become the most heavily blitzed area of all.

But on September 7th and the days which followed the bombs poured chiefly on Stepney, with its inimitable mixture of races, where nearly two hundred thousand people lived at an average of twelve per dwelling; on the tailors of Whitechapel; the factories, warehouses and gasworks of Poplar; the woodworking firms of Shoreditch; the docks of West Ham and Bermondsey. They poured on the sweated clothing trade, on the casual labour of the docks, on petty businesses Jewish and Gentile, on jerry-built Victorian slums, on marshy land which had made it hard to provide decent shelters. They poured on Cockneys * who often knew little of the world beyond their immediate neighborhood, who found their shops, their entertainments and their marriages near at home, who often spent their lives in the streets in which they had grown up, where two or three generations of the same family would commonly be found living in adjacent houses, where poverty and community flourished on the same stalk.

Here communism had found its best base in Britain outside a few mining districts. Here, in the mid-'thirties, Mosley had sought a foundation for his British Union of Fascists. The monotonous sequence of small bankruptcies in the tailoring and furnishing trades had given him his chance. Jews whose fathers had fled from the pogroms of eastern Europe had had their shop windows smashed and their lives threatened. When Mosley had limped through the narrow streets, thickets of arms had shot up on each side, though strong socialist feeling had thwarted the breakthrough he had needed.

"Everybody is worried about the feeling in the East End," wrote Harold Nicolson in his diary on September 17th. ". . . There is much bitterness. It is said that even the King and Queen were booed the other day when they visited the destroyed areas." Had the East End lost all heart, the chain reaction might have crippled London's morale. This nearly happened, but not quite, and after a few days the attack shifted noticeably westwards. But dockland witnessed frightful scenes, not all by any means of the Luftwaffe's making.

The authorities, drawing up and implementing the plans for civil defence, had based them on the expectation of a swift, gigantic assault, probably by daylight.

* Cockney: Londoner, especially East Ender.

So the blitz caught A.R.P.* on the wrong foot when it came. The elaborate precautions against gas and the proposals for mass burial in quick-lime were mercifully redundant. But the attacks took place at night, thanks to Fighter Command, and they might last for twelve or fourteen hours. This at once exposed the inconvenience of the private and public shelters; that people would have to sleep, eat and excrete in them night after night had not been allowed for.

Because the casualties were relatively light, and because the squalid dwellings of the East End were easily ravaged by blast, people who should, according to plan, have been dead, were flooding the rest centres. While there were too many stretcher parties for carrying off casualties, the men of the Heavy Rescue Service —the Demolition Squads as they were loosely called—were on duty for twenty-four-hour shifts, extricating the living and the dead, shifting and loading debris, shoring up buildings and salvaging personal belongings. Troops soon had to be called in to assist with demolition.

Aggravating every difficulty, there was another unexpected factor, the unexploded bomb, or "U.X.B." Perhaps one in ten of the bombs dropped on London were duds; but others were equipped with delayed action fuses and all "U.X.B.s" had to be treated as if they were "D.A." At first, all premises were evacuated and all roads closed within a six hundred yard radius of each bomb. Only a handful of troops, Royal Engineers, were present to deal with them, and by the end of October, though a special organization had been created, there were three thousand U.X.B.s waiting for treatment. Hundreds, even thousands, of people might be made homeless by one dud bomb. The cold courage of the bomb disposal squads was one of the marvels of the period. It was spectacularly in evidence when the most famous U.X.B. of all entered the ground at an angle, very close to St. Paul's, on September 12th, and began to creep towards the foundations of the cathedral. With great bravery, it was finally extricated on the 15th, was driven in a lorry at headlong speed through the East End, and exploded in Hackney Marshes, where it made a crater one hundred feet in diameter.

Fairly or unfairly, the reaction of the East Enders to the failure of the authorities to plan for the real nature of the blitz was first bewilderment, then anger. Yet they did not revolt nor, truly speaking, panic. Explaining this phenomenon, some journalists of the period created a myth of the Cockney wisecracking over the ruins of his world, which is as famous as the myth of the Few soaring into battle with laughter on their lips, and equally misleading. Other journalists, running the risk of censorship and suppression, did visit the battlefronts of Stepney and West Ham to report what they saw in cold, angry terms, and to spearhead the storm of protest which swept westwards to Whitehall.

The reasons, so far as they can be analysed, why morale in the East End did not collapse, may help to explain, *mutatis mutandis,** why morale in Berlin was not shattered by its still more destructive raids later in the war.

* A.R.P.: Air Raid Precautions.
* *mutatis mutandis:* if you change the details that need changing.

In the first place, those who wanted to, or thought they had to, fled. From the East End, the homeless and the fearful trekked out in the mornings, pushing their chattels in prams or hand carts. Such towns to the west as Reading, Windsor and Oxford coped with a sizable influx of helpless refugees. Vera Brittain, who visited Oxford in the early days of the blitz, found babies' nappies * drying in the august Tom Quad * of Christ Church; the colleges acted for a while as clearing houses while the authorities found billets for the refugees. Five hundred to a thousand people were put up for nearly two months in the Majestic cinema on the city's outskirts:

> Covering the floor beneath the upturned velveteen seats of the cinema chairs [wrote Miss Brittain], disorderly piles of mattresses, pillows, rugs and cushions indicate the "pitches" staked out by each evacuated family. Many of the women, too dispirited to move, still lie wearily on the floor with their children beside them in the foetid air, though the hour is eleven a.m. and a warm sun is shining cheerfully on the city streets. Between the mattresses and cushions, the customary collection of soiled newspapers and ancient applecores is contributing noticeably to the odoriferous atmosphere.

Other frightened or homeless people trekked out to the open spaces in or near London. Several thousand, as Richard Titmuss puts it, "trudged off to Epping and sat down in the forest," where camps were set up for them. It was in this area of suburban Essex that an influential local dignitary, confronted with the idea that the homeless should be compulsorily billeted there, said flatly, "I will not have these people billeted on our people." Even now, when the need for evacuation was obvious enough, some of the well-to-do people of the suburbs and countryside still revealed the bleak class hatred which had underlain the first response to evacuation a year before.

It follows that those who remained in the blitzed areas, night by night, were those who preferred to stay, or felt they had to stay. Their work or their business lay in the East End. They were, perhaps, wardens or Home Guard,* who felt the call of duty (though in London and elsewhere, there were wardens amongst those who fled). In this case, they had to adapt themselves to danger. As they did so, they set an example of calm and courage which others, in their turn, felt constrained to follow. Local leaders—parsons, doctors, social workers —stuck to their posts and tried to bring order to the hideous chaos. Others, fearful at first, found themselves drawn to assist in various more or less spontaneous activities designed to alleviate conditions.

Political agitation was bound to fail. Anti-semitism persisted, and was inflamed to some extent when better-off Jews (like better-off Gentiles) bought their

---

* nappies: diapers.
* Tom Quad: the main quadrangle of Christ Church, Oxford college and cathedral.
* Home Guard: originally L.D.V. (Local Defense Volunteers); defense force raised from civilian population to repel invasion.

way out of London. Fascists still scrawled "This is a Jewish War" on some of the walls which still stood, and anti-semitic feeling in the shelters was always a problem. But what could have been more ludicrous than to smash up Jewish homes when the Luftwaffe was smashing up Jewish homes? What rescue worker asked himself, as he burrowed into a shattered building, whether the girl trapped inside was Gentile, Jewish, or, as was likely enough in Stepney, Indian or Chinese?

For the Communists, also, the immediate physical enemy was bound to distract attention from the theoretical class enemy. Communists remained faithful to their long-standing interest in A.R.P. as a potential revolutionary flashpoint. They agitated more than ever now for deep shelters, while the public simply equipped itself with deep shelters—the tubes. Fearful Communists, clearly, did not wish to agitate during air raids. Fearless ones were conspicuous enough; one would see girls standing in the raids selling the *Daily Worker* * from their familiar pitches. The story is told of a young cripple who was so distressed when the breakdown of public transport meant that he did not get his big parcel of *Workers* regularly, that he would cycle with his one leg each night to the office (which was in one of the hardest hit quarters), take three heavy rucksacks of papers, and make his way back as best he could along the blazing Thames waterfront. Such courage did not spread defeatism, it set an example of defiance.

There seems to have been only one significant left-wing demonstration. Detailed descriptions, with photographs, of the revelling which continued in the West End had appeared in the newspapers. The Savoy Hotel had equipped its underground banqueting hall as a restaurant-dormitory. On September 15th, about a hundred East Enders, under Communist leadership, rushed on the hotel when the alert sounded in the evening and insisted on occupying the restaurant. The demonstration was frustrated by a freak; the siren, exceptionally, sounded the all clear soon afterwards. The invaders retreated. According to one somewhat unlikely version, they passed a hat round and poured a pile of coppers into the hand of the head porter on the way out. It was, in any case, a polite enough occasion on both sides.

Even if the Luftwaffe had realized that raids concentrated solely on the East End might have been their most effective tactic, the bombers were not accurate enough to ensure such a concentration. From the first, other areas of inner and outer London suffered considerable damage. In a less intense way, morale was endangered throughout the metropolis. The feeling that the bombers were allowed to roam the skies unimpeded was not a happy one from the Government's point of view. The British night fighters remained ineffective until near the end of the blitz, but they complicated life for the anti-aircraft gunners. The A.A. barrage was in any case far from formidable. Thanks to an ineffectual system of sound locators, firing was sporadic, almost inaudible, and almost useless. On Sep-

---

* *Daily Worker:* Communist Party daily paper, suppressed later in the war.

tember 11th, the night fighters were withdrawn. London's "Ack Ack" * had been reinforced from the provinces and the redoubtable General Pile * ordered his troops to blaze away with every ounce of energy they could muster. The resulting, hideous noise kept most Londoners awake for most of the night, but they loved it. Shelterers laughed for joy, "even at three a.m.," reports Barbara Nixon. The barrage, in strictly military terms, remained quite ineffectual, though it forced the raiders to fly higher. Falling shell fragments added to the perils of the streets, and Pile's men killed far more British civilians than German pilots. One borough asked Ack Ack to remove itself on the grounds that its thunders were cracking the lavatory pans in council houses. But few people took up the Government's offer of ear plugs, and many were ready to stand free drinks to the soldiers of the Royal Artillery—who thoroughly deserved them, for they lived in crude dugouts and for the first eight days got almost no sleep themselves.

Another boost for morale came somewhat paradoxically on the morning of September 13th. A lone German raider was foolish enough to attack Buckingham Palace. Nothing was more calculated to arouse a feeling of solidarity across the classes. The Queen remarked, "I'm glad we've been bombed. It makes me feel I can look the East End in the face." The palace was hit twice more, once in November and once in March.

After the first wave of terror, workers began to return to their daily jobs, from the rest centres and the forest, and from billets as far away as Bishop's Stortford, thirty miles to the north. The attack was extended to the central and western boroughs, and remained general for the rest of the long first phase of the blitz. Up to November 13th, an average of 160 bombers dropped an average of 200 tons of high explosive and 182 canisters of incendiaries nightly. The average was much exceeded on nights of full moon, "Bombers' Moon," and Londoners came to expect a particularly heavy attack in the middle of the month. On October 15th, there were 410 raiders over London, and they dropped 538 tons of high explosive—sufficient, by pre-war estimates, to cause more than 25,000 casualties. As it was, more than 400 civilians were killed, nearly 900 seriously injured, over 900 fires were started and nearly all rail travel in and out of London was shut off. But the Port of London was never knocked out completely. Chaos never became ungovernable. The effect of two months of continuous blitz was to spread the habit of adaptation from those who were brave and active to those who were not, so that increasing proportions of the population became brave and active. In the immensity of Greater London, with its peacetime population of nearly nine million, three or four hundred bombers would waste their efforts.

On October 8th, Churchill exercised his wit in parliament at the Luftwaffe's expense. Announcing that casualties were less than one-tenth, on a typical night, of those expected, he proceeded, "Statisticians may amuse themselves by calcu-

* Ack Ack: Anti-Aircraft (a World War I term).
* General Pile: General Sir Frederick Albert Pile, Baronet (1884–), General Officer Commander-in-Chief Anti-Aircraft Command, 1939–45.

lating that after making allowance for the working of the law of diminishing returns, through the same house being struck twice or three times over, it would take ten years at the present rate, for half the houses of London to be demolished. After that, of course, progress would be much slower."

Even after the R.A.F. had consolidated its control of the daylight skies, minor day raids continued to be frequent. Churchill records that at the approach of half a dozen aeroplanes, or only one, or even at the sounding of a false alarm, "all the occupants of a score of ministries were promptly collected and led down to the basements, for what these were worth. Pride, even, was being taken in the efficiency and thoroughness with which this evolution was performed." Factory workers were spending more time in the shelters than at their benches; where only damp crowded trenches were available, men might be found calmly playing cards on the deserted shop floor rather than using them, but in any case, no work was done. Churchill, whose vagrant intelligence fastened on this problem, called, on September 17th, for the training of workers as "Jim Crows or lookout men," who would watch from the roofs of factories and office buildings and would give an alarm when danger was truly imminent. As this system was slowly adopted, the problem was solved. The important Ford's factory, in east London, lost nearly 380 hours of work through alerts in September. In October, when the spotters were at work, only 145 hours were lost, though the area had been under alert for 350.

Those caught in the streets while raids were in progress rapidly adjusted to what seemed a minor enough danger when they compared the random carnage of the day to the wholesale slaughter of the nights. At first, buses had drawn up and disgorged their passengers into the nearest shelter, post offices and shops had shut, tradesmen had unharnessed their horses and tied them to the rears of their carts. But soon such behaviour ceased, and Londoners began to continue casually with their business. A visiting American journalist was shocked by their calm. In a police station, registering as an alien, he did not hear the siren.

> A policeman from the street simply stuck his head in the door and blew loudly on a police whistle. I jumped a mile. The room was suddenly still. The sergeant in the middle of the counter chanted in a monotonous voice without looking up:
> "An air raid alarm has been sounded. There is a shelter underneath this building. The man at the door will show you the way to it. If you do not choose to go to the shelter we will carry on."
> Nobody went. The buzz of conversation resumed.

But at night, no pretence of normality was possible. Except in the depths of the tube, no one escaped the noises of the blitz, and even there those with their bodies against the walls felt its vibrations.

First, there was the alert, a wail rising and falling for two minutes, "warbling" as the official handbook somewhat inexactly put it. There was not one siren but a series, as the note was taken up by borough after borough. Then, there was the heavy, uneven throb of the bombers. "Where are you? Where are you?" Graham Greene imagined them saying. Then there were many noises. The howling of dogs; the sound of a high explosive bomb falling, like a tearing sheet; the clatter of little incendiaries on roofs and pavements; the dull thud of walls collapsing; the burglar alarms which destruction had set ringing; the crackle of flames, a relishing, licking noise, and the bells of the fire engines. Each individual A.A. gun, to the increasingly sensitive ears of Londoners, had its own voice. One set near John Strachey's warden's post in Chelsea was called "the tennis racket" because it made "a staccato, and yet plangent, wang, wang; wang, wang." The shells shrieked and their splinters pattered on the pavements. A bomb falling half a mile away gave you ten seconds' warning by its swish and rush through the air, but the one "with your number on it," the one which killed you or buried you alive, was heard only when it was almost upon you, because the sound waves caught up with themselves.

Outside, if bravado or duty sent the citizen outside, there was a world of beauty; Charlotte Haldane has said that for her, the "aesthetic pleasure" which the fires provoked "banished all sense of fear." "The sky over London," as Evelyn Waugh saw it, "was glorious, ochre and madder, as though a dozen tropic suns were simultaneously setting round the horizon. . . . Everywhere the shells sparkled like Christmas baubles." Searchlights crossed and recrossed in stiff and awkward arcs, plunging thousands of feet into the sky, each terminating in a "mist area" which reminded Harold Nicolson of "a swab of cotton wool." The raiders, to begin with, would drop parachute flares, magnificent fireworks which drifted slowly down in a constellation, illuminating earth and sky with an amber or greenish light and casting exotic shadows over grubby and familiar townscapes. Suddenly, a street would be carpeted with brilliant incendiaries, hissing and sparkling with a whitish green glare. A high explosive bomb, by comparison, was disappointing; its upward streaks of yellow or red were as crude as a little boy's painting of Guy Fawkes' Night (a fixture which few citizens found it hard to forgo on November 5th). Once, in October, a bomb struck a gasholder in the south. Five thousand cubic feet of gas burnt in a couple of seconds, and "an enormous uprush of white light, like a gigantic mushroom with a huge black cap" suddenly towered over London.

But there were other colours, those of the injured in bombed buildings, white with plaster dust and streaked with black blood. J. L. Hodson wrote, after the office of his own newspaper had been hit, "What strikes me so forcibly is the tawdry look, the cheap and nasty look this sort of thing wears after the explosion. . . . So often it exposes, or seems to, that everything is jerrybuilt—makes it seem so even if it wasn't. One is humiliated by it."

And the smells were evil. On September 10th, the Luftwaffe breached the northern outfall sewer, which discharged its contents into the River Lea. Early in October, London's main sewage outfall was destroyed. The Thames stank first of excrement, then of the chemicals poured into it. Blitzed or burning warehouses filled the air with disconcerting odours, the familiar suddenly made strange, the devil's Christmas dinner. The sickly, bitter-sweet smell of a blitzed chemist's shop might make a warden reach hurriedly for his gasmask.

Above all, there was what John Strachey called the "harsh, rank, raw smell" of an "incident," of a bombed street.

> Its basis certainly came from the torn, wounded, dismembered houses; from the gritty dust of dissolved brickwork, masonry and joinery. But there was more to it than that. For several hours there was an acrid overtone from the high explosive which the bomb itself had contained; a fiery constituent of the smell. Almost invariably, too, there was the mean little stink of domestic gas, seeping up from broken pipes and leads. But the whole of the smell was greater than the sum of its parts. It was the smell of violent death itself.

There were comic, or superficially comic "incidents." A lady hurled out into a Mayfair street in her bath; a man blown clean out of his bedroom who risked his life to go back for a clothesbrush. Some people were caught on the lavatory when the bomb dropped. But if people were not trapped in the debris or torn apart so that no trace was found of them, they were likely to be stabbed by splinters of flying glass. Graham Greene, then a warden in Bloomsbury, looking back on a major "incident," remembered chiefly, "the squalor of the night, the purgatorial throng of men and women in dirty torn pyjamas with little blood splashes standing in doorways. . . ." When Barbara Nixon saw her first casualty, she was "not let down lightly. In the middle of the street lay the remains of a baby. It had been blown clean through the window and had burst on striking the roadway. To my intense relief, pitiful and horrible as it was, I was not nauseated, and found a torn piece of curtain in which to wrap it."

Most of the high explosive bombs which fell on Britain up to May 1941 were relatively light—fifty or two hundred and fifty kilograms—though later in the war the proportion of heavier bombs, up to two thousand, five hundred kilograms, increased greatly. The blast from any bomb could tear a man to shreds, or it could kill him without an obvious wound. Houses well away from the explosion would pitch like ships and appear to shift on their foundations, and their windows would shatter. Within ten days of the start of the blitz, the Luftwaffe began to drop sea mines by parachute, and these were known as land mines; huge cylinders, eight feet long and two feet in diameter, which swung silently down at about forty miles per hour, but seemed to float like sycamore seeds. They did not penetrate the earth and their blast, which was not muffled by the soil, could blow a man a quarter of a mile and throw thirty-five ton train cars into the air like shoe-boxes, or, such were its freaks, tweak the slippers from a man's feet several streets away.

The thermite incendiaries, by contrast, weighed only a couple of pounds. They were eighteen inches long and were shaped like hock bottles. They were dropped in containers of various sizes—seventy-two incendiaries was an average "breadbasket." A man could easily smother one with a sandbag, and if that were lacking could cope with tongs or heavy gloves. But unless they were dealt with swiftly and thoroughly incendiaries were the most destructive of all bombs. In December, the sport of "I.B." hunting which was popular with London's doughtier citizens was spoilt when the Germans began to drop a proportion of incendiaries with explosive charges; thereafter, far greater caution had to be used.

The all clear was a steady two-minute blast on the siren. At night, the noise and fires made it seem that large areas must be completely devastated. Next morning, the damage was surprisingly small. "Ow! Don't it look as if the mice 'ad been at it," one Cockney girl exclaimed as she stood in a small crowd staring at the B.B.C.'s headquarters the morning after the news had been interrupted by a crash and listeners had heard a voice whisper to the announcer that it was "all right." In the suburbs, one saw housewives busy with their brooms each morning, making neat little piles of debris for the borough workmen, and heard the broken glass grating on the pavements. Boys searched the ruins, still occasional enough, for shrapnel, prizing pieces of German bomb more highly than the splinters of A.A. shells.

There would be many streets barred where the police had set up a yellow board marked Diversion. Behind these, the grim mingled with the normal. John Lehmann recorded the scene when a U.X.B. drove him from his Bloomsbury home:

> Mecklenburgh Square was a pretty sight when I left it. Broken glass everywhere, half the garden scorched with incendiary bombs, and two houses of Byron Court on the east side nothing but a pile of rubble. Clouds of steam were pouring out of one side, firemen still clambering over it and ambulances and blood transfusion units standing by with A.R.P. workers and police. The road was filled with a mass of rubble muddied by the firemen's hoses, but the light grey powder that had covered the bushes at dawn had been washed off by the drizzle. The time bomb in the Square garden sat in its earth crater, coyly waiting. The tabby Persian cat from No. 40 picked her way daintily and dishevelledly among the splinters of glass on her favourite porch.

At first, such vistas seemed marvellous, bizarre, but the eye grew accustomed to their like. Freaks would still catch it—two beautiful porcelain vases standing undamaged behind the shattered plate glass windows of an elegant furniture shop, "corpses" from Madame Tussaud's waxworks scattered beside the road. Walking through a park, Inez Holden saw "the highest branches of a tree draped with bits of marabout, with some sort of silk, with two or three odd stockings and, wrapped round the top of the tree, like a cloak quick-thrown over the shoulder of some high-born hidalgo, some purple damask. Below it, balanced on a twig as if twirled round a finger, was a brand new bowler hat." What never palled, above all, was the sudden, curious insight which a bomb might give into the lives of "those people across the way," the Londoners' usually unknown neighbours. Their taste in wallpaper and bedlinen was mercilessly exposed to the autumn sunshine.

In that sunshine, the day became, in the words of Elizabeth Bowen, "a pure and curious holiday from fear." It appeared to her that "The very soil of the city at this time seemed to generate more strength; in parks the outsize dahlias, velvet and wine, and the trees on which each vein in each yellow leaf stretched out perfect against the sun blazoned out the idea of the finest hour." But she adds that people were soon "disembodied" by tiredness. "The night behind and the night to come met across every noon in an arch of strain. To work or think was to ache."

The manufacturers of Horlicks found a new focus for the invocation in their advertisements of "deep, healing sleep." After a time, nervous people grew used to the noise and slept somehow through the raids, but even then the swish of a bomb falling especially near would shake them awake. John Strachey remarks that for the air raid warden, whose work kept him awake and about night after night in those early days, "Sleep replaced food as the simplest, most everyday, object of desire. Whenever he had anything over half an hour to spare during the day, he had not the slightest doubt as to what to do with the time. He slept."

In the same way, people adapted themselves to the fear which returned night after night. "The individual's reaction to the sound of falling bombs," Ed Murrow told his American audience, "cannot be described. The moan of stark terror and suspense cannot be encompassed by words, no more can the sense of relief when you realize that you weren't where that one fell." The luckiest, as well as the bravest, were those whose jobs took them out into the raids, where danger was visible and visibly limited. A writer in the Hampstead *Warden's Bulletin* noted laconically early in December, "Not all, of course, were able to stand firm against the new conditions, but it is noteworthy that our resignations have been offset by new enrolments. . . ." To many, Civil Defence work acquired a new attraction, if only because it quenched curiosities both sensational and sociological.

Others found less prestigious techniques of adaptation. We learn of one woman who had laid in a remarkable stock of brandy and "simply drank herself stupid every night. . . . One night she fell down the whole flight of stairs when a heavy bomb fell, but she simply lay at the bottom dead to the world and quite unharmed."

Fear found its antidote both in relief and fatigue. ". . . Every morning one is pleased to see one's friends appearing again," wrote Harold Nicolson in his diary twelve days after the start of the blitz. "I am nerveless, and yet I am conscious that when I hear a motor in the empty streets I tauten myself lest it be a bomb screaming towards me." ". . . As time goes on," wrote the film director Paul Rotha, early in November, "you get experienced. A plane overhead, a scream, you count one-two-three-four, they either get closer or get distant. If closer, you seek handy shelter—a doorway usually. If distant, you go on doing what you are doing. . . . It's remarkable how sensitive your ears get."

A man from Hampshire who visited London on the third week-end of the blitz went to the cinema with friends. "The performance began nightly at about eight o'clock, with the first bomb five minutes later, I was told, and so it was." He found among those he stayed with "an indefinable light-heartedness, springing perhaps from the feeling, 'why take care for tomorrow, for tomorrow may never come?' " The prosperous classes settled down to "the even tenor of the blitz," as one lady called it. Danger became boring rather than harrowing. London, in the slogan of the day, was "taking it," and self-respecting citizens resolved to "take it."

Shops became a favourite symbol of defiance. Big and small, they had their windows blown out. The West End stores would erect painted wooden fronts with only tiny panes of glass to replace them; the little fruiterers and grocers would often do without any glass at all. The impromptu signs became favourite blitz jokes. "MORE OPEN THAN USUAL" was a common one. "BLAST!" was the most laconic. One pub advertised, "OUR WINDOWS ARE GONE BUT OUR SPIRITS ARE EXCELLENT. COME IN AND TRY THEM."

But the machinery set up by the Government to cope with the new calls for evacuation was never swamped, and demand grew less as the weeks went by. The Government meditated compulsory evacuation of schoolchildren, but quite soon realized that there was no possible method of compelling parents to send them away. "Assisted private evacuation," whereby the Government gave free travel vouchers and billeting certificates to those who found their own accommodation in the countryside, was offered to many groups—mothers with small children, pregnant women, old, blind or sick people, and those made homeless by bombs. But, as Richard Titmuss points out, "fewer people left London during the first nine months of air attack than the number who went away either just before or just after the declaration of war."

By the end of November, the population of central London had dropped by a quarter, but most of the workers remained at their posts. Very few firms or organizations removed their headquarters from London unless they were bombed out. Mark Benney, who was working in an aircraft factory, has recorded that

> There was very little absenteeism caused by the raids; in part because we all felt that the raids gave an added importance to our work, but much more because we knew that if we didn't turn up our mates would be worrying. You would see men staggering at their work from lack of sleep, snatching a ten minutes' doze in the canteen over their food, and still, when knocking off time came, going off with a cheerful, "See yer in the morning, boys!"

It became a sort of war cry, a common affirmation of faith pregnant with unstated defiances and resolutions, that phrase. We threw it at each other gaily, but always with the implication very near the surface, "If I don't see yer, it means they'll be digging me out."

There were perhaps half a million munitions workers living within a fifteen-mile radius of London. Nothing showed the stubbornness which set in better than the dogged fashion in which these, and the workers in important offices, strove to get to work on time.

Several train services out of London were blocked for months at a time, though railway employees would work valiantly to try to clear a line before the first of the morning's trains was due. By October 17th, so many buses were "blitzed" that London Transport had to appeal for reinforcements from the provinces, and black, white, brown, green and blue buses from places as far away as Exeter and Inverness joined the familiar red double-deckers in the streets. Trolleybuses, with their overhead electric wires, were especially vulnerable to cut lines and craters in their path, and "linesmen" sometimes struggled with repairs standing on their tower wagons while the blitz proceeded around them. A special boat service on the Thames was laid on for a period of six weeks after most of central and southern London had been deprived of trams and trolleybuses by U.X.B.s.

Queues stretching back a hundred yards from the bus stops were a common sight. What buses ran were forced to take uncouth, circuitous routes. Letters from one London postal district to another might take a week or more to arrive. Telegrams, unless they were official, were subject to unlimited delay. Telephone lines were cut with monotonous frequency, and it was a matter for congratulation if someone with an urgent call found that the exchange which he was phoning was actually in business that day.

Every time a bomb pierced a road it tore through the mass of pipes, cables and conduits which lay like a nervous system under the city. Repair went on as the bombs still fell. Where a gas main had been broken, a man from the gas company had to plug its end, working in scorching, poisoned air, or force his way through blazing debris to cut off the supply. Men were properly given decorations for repairing flaming splinter holes sixty feet up on the crowns of gasholders. When a telephone cable was severed, as many as two thousand, eight hundred wires might be broken, each requiring reconnection. Men did this finicky work night after night; thanks to them, and their counterparts working with water conduits, electricity cables and sewage pipes, the trappings of civilization, somewhat erratically, persisted.

Food remained relatively plentiful. The meat ration, during the last quarter of 1940, was at its highest level of the war, because of a glut of slaughtering. But when gas and electricity were cut off, it was not always easy to cook it, and after-raid feeding was a major problem for the authorities. Women would improvise field-kitchens in the gardens or the roads, and burn shattered woodwork or furniture to give their husbands something hot to eat. Water spurted one day from the gas stoves of Pimlico, and all the cooking at the Ritz Hotel was done, for several days, on two up-ended electric radiators.

Eating out in expensive West End restaurants continued; besides the Savoy, several other well-known establishments offered all-night shelter as part of the service. There was only one serious incident in a West End resort. In March 1941 the fashionable Café de Paris, crowded with young officers on leave, was blitzed as the clients danced to the music of "Snakehips" Johnson. The macabre scenes which followed were among the most indelibly horrifying of the period. One woman had her broken leg washed in champagne, while looters plundered rings from the fingers of the dead and wounded.

Theatres rapidly shut their doors; after ten days of blitz, only the Windmill kept open with its blend, now doubly defiant, of bare flesh and comedy. Many London cinemas "took it" in their stride, though sixty were totally destroyed by bombing over the period of the war. Of those of the small Granada chain, based in London, one was destroyed, and nine others closed for longer or shorter periods; but "the remaining ten cinemas never missed a day nor curtailed a performance."

The absence of panic in the many incidents which occurred in cinemas was one of the most remarkable features of the blitz. Granada offered shelter and entertainment throughout the night for their clients, and those who stayed might enjoy five feature films in succession, together with impromptu sing-songs and amateur variety. People took to bringing their blankets to the last house. Though the strain on the staffs soon ended this experiment, the historian of the chain is surely right to suggest that the cinemas in this phase were confirming themselves as the new centres of communal life.

One morning when a score of fire engines were still busy in Leicester Square, the usual long queue was seen to form outside the cinema which was showing *Gone With the Wind*. Granada's figures suggest that total attendances fell by about five-sixths in some hard hit boroughs in September, but they soon picked up and were actually above normal in Christmas week. By the beginning of 1941, most other places of entertainment had reopened, and the pubs had recovered their appeal.

Certain younger cinema patrons preferred to take their girl-friends to the empty, because perilous, dress circles. Individual public shelters were monopolized by courting couples, to the concern of moralists. Barbara Nixon was standing outside a surface shelter one night when a couple emerged. "The gunfire was getting heavy, and the girl was anxious—'I can't stop now, Tom, really. I must get down the shelter. Mum will be worrying. But I'll meet you tomorrow, same time, same sandbag.' "

A sensible fatalism made risks in pursuit of pleasure acceptable. "If your number's on it, the bomb'll get you" was the philosophy of the poor; and the rich accepted it too. "When my time is due it will come," said Winston Churchill to his "shadow," exposing himself to danger, as was his joy and his habit, on the roof of the bomb-proof "annexe" to No. 10 Downing Street which he had been persuaded, with some difficulty, to occupy at nights.

Superstitions, taboos and rituals flourished. One Nigerian air raid warden in an inner suburb was regarded as a lucky omen by the shelterers; when they saw his dark face they felt safe for the night. It was clearly religion, not reason, which now prompted an enthusiastic, and sometimes violent, defence of the rituals of blackout. It was absurdly, but very widely believed that a German bomber a couple of miles up would see the light from a cigarette in the street, or from the dim torches which A.R.P. workers used at incidents, and would aim deliberately at it. A belief which was quite as illogical but equally current was that "they" never hit the same building twice, so you were safe enough in a bombed house. There was also a prevalent rumour that "they" had developed a bomb which could chase you round corners.

But Miss Leaky Mouth and Mr. Glumpot,* those staunch adherents of Rumour in the Silent Column days, could now content themselves with facts. The crowds of sightseers, often well dressed for the day out, who would inquire at railway stations where the worst damage might be found, naturally infuriated rescue workers. But it was probably good for those who were apprehensive that they should stare at destruction rather than imagine it; this, too, was a method of adaptation.

So was the freedom with which people now conversed with total strangers. By the time a shaken citizen had told a dozen people in buses or pubs about "his" bomb or "his" near-miss, it didn't seem so bad after all. It was, rather, a matter for pride. Little boys fought over whose bomb had been worst. In self-defence, some people took to wearing badges, "I'VE GOT A BOMB STORY TOO." One of the best was Willie Gallacher's.* One lovely day, he was walking down a main London thoroughfare just after lunch. The all clear had sounded, but a bomb hit the side of the road a few yards from him, dug in and hit a water main. "The bursting of the water main synchronized with the exploding of the bomb, and the force of the water was so strong [he relates] that it sent everything, blast and rubble, straight up into the air, like a great oil gusher. Although it was just outside, not a pane of glass was broken in Unity House." Fortunately, no doubt, for his reputation for veracity, Gallacher was a total abstainer.

War had already weakened the famous English reserve; the blitz swept it away. The shift of values which Priestley had exhorted was implicit in shared disaster and danger. A grocer excavating the ruins of his store, handing tins of soup and milk to those who wanted them, and saying quite solemnly, "Put it on the account"; a pub standing drinks out of hours to the local raid victims; a

---

* Miss Leaky Mouth and Mr. Glumpot: characters used in government propaganda against careless talk and despondency.
* Willie Gallacher: (1881–1965), Communist leader and Member of Parliament.

manager staying on late at the factory so as to give a lift in his car to weary workmen—such things were unknown before September 1940; and after June 1945. Neighbours forgot their censorious rivalries and joined together in impromptu parties to fight fires, to repair each other's houses, to look after children, to cook meals. Life, briefly, seemed more important than money. Ed Murrow observed that no one talked about the cash value of the damage, even when their own homes and offices had gone. ". . . It's much more important that the bomb missed you; that there's still plenty of food to eat—and there is."

This new attitude should be considered in relation to the looting which undoubtedly occurred in many places. Some of it seems to have been organized by gangs, and was callous and inexcusable. But what of the A.F.S. men—"selfless heroes" one moment, "criminals" the next—who were quite often convicted of looting? As Murrow pointed out, most of those citizens who came before the courts for this offence were not "criminal" types. Trivial things like books and ribbons and coal were carried away or pocketed. "One has a strange feeling, or at least I have," said Murrow, "in looking at the contents of a bombed house or shop, that the things scattered about don't belong to anyone. . . . Picking up a book or a pipe that's been blown into the street is almost like picking an apple in a deserted and overgrown orchard far from any road or house."

But there were many people in London who had never had much property to speak of, anyway. These could not refresh themselves with week-ends away from "town," nor retreat to their country cottages or the houses of well provided friends when bombs blasted their streets; nor could they eat out in comfortable restaurants when the gas failed. In the public shelters, another American journalist, Negley Farson, recorded the comments of the poor:

> "We didn't ask for the blinking war, *did* we?"
> "No wonder Germany's not fed up—they've *got* some blinking air raid shelters!"
> "My man's in the Army. At Dunkirk, he was. And I'm *here!*"
> "We're prisoners of war: that's what we are."
> "The official attitude is horrible!"
> "No use looking to Labour. They let us in for this war, they did."
> "Bloody L.C.C. red tape!"

As Farson saw it, "these people were beginning to lose faith—faith in all degrees of people higher up."

To pre-war Governments, it had seemed that the knockout blow from the air would mean huge "incidents" in great numbers if the public was assembled in large public shelters—unless, of course, these were so deep underground that they were impregnable, in which case the craven populace invented by the official imagination would contract out of the war effort and immerse itself more or less permanently in the womb-like security they would provide.

So the Chamberlain Government,* intent on dispersing the population as widely and evenly as possible, had made the Anderson shelter the spearhead of its policy, and had otherwise recommended that householders should strengthen basements and ground-floor rooms for use as shelters. Not until a few days before the outbreak of war had the local authorities been asked to build structures specifically designed as public shelters. The Anderson had first been planned as a shelter for erection inside a small working-class home, but technical objections had ensured that it became an outdoor shelter. Unfortunately, under a quarter of the public, Mass Observation * pointed out, had gardens.

The Anderson was a masterpiece of cheap and simple engineering, and the two and a quarter million Andersons which the Government had given away free by the start of the blitz represented a formidable investment for the security of the more fortunate sections of the working class. Two curved walls of corrugated steel met in a ridge at the top and were bolted to stout rails. The Anderson was sunk three feet into the ground, and covered with eighteen inches of earth (in which many proud owners grew flowers or vegetables). The entrance was protected by a steel shield and an earthen blast wall. The Anderson would protect up to six people against practically anything but a direct hit, and many were grateful for it when the blitz came. There is no doubt that it was well worth the £6 14s. to £10 18s. which was charged for it when, in October 1939, it was put on sale to those earning over two hundred and fifty pounds a year, who did not qualify for the free issue. However, less than a thousand were sold.

The Anderson at once revealed snags which might well deter a prospective buyer. Many flooded as soon as they were installed and continued to flood in spite of repeated bailings out. Most of those delivered after the start of the war were, for reasons of economy, somewhat too small to sleep in. There was a further, pre-eminent disadvantage which ensured that many never used their free Andersons after the raids started; they did not shut out the din.

As the steel shortage led to the falling off and then to the cessation of the production of Andersons, the Government turned in March 1940 to a new type of brick and concrete surface shelter—a "communal" rather than "public" shelter designed to protect some fifty residents from a single street or block of dwellings. This policy in turn ran headlong into another shortage, that of cement. An unfortunate ambiguity in a Ministry of Home Security circular of the spring of 1940 persuaded some borough engineers and local builders that these shelters might be constructed without any cement in the mortar at all. (In fact, the Government was only suggesting dilution with lime.) In the London region alone,

---

* Chamberlain Government: Neville Chamberlain (1869–1940), became Prime Minister in 1937, concluded the Munich Agreement 30 September 1938 and, after British withdrawal from Norway, was succeeded by Churchill on 10 May 1940, as the Battle of France began.
* Mass Observation: an organization with volunteer helpers which produced regular sociological reports on public opinion and reactions to events.

well over five thousand shelters were built without cement; besides this, unscrupulous contractors were quite often guilty of faulty workmanship.

These squat erections were the common type of shelter in many working-class districts. Their ventilation was limited; they were cold, dark and damp; even where chemical closets were provided, they stank and sometimes overflowed. Not surprisingly, the surface shelters were generally unpopular, especially when they showed a disconcerting propensity to collapse, through poor construction, when bombs fell near by.

There were also many trench shelters in public gardens and parks. Authorities had been told to make permanent those dug during the Munich crisis, by lining and covering them with concrete or steel. But trenches had fallen out of official favour well before the blitz began; the supplies of lining materials were erratic, and they were often impossible to keep waterproof. A typical trench, also, would hold some fifty people, who were liable to find themselves sitting out an all-night raid with stinking water lapping over their shoes. But they were more popular than the surface shelters; people felt safer even a few feet underground.

This did not by any means exhaust the variety of shelters. Strong buildings of any sort lent themselves to this function, and many public or communal shelters were improvised in basements by the local authorities. The case of the London borough of Paddington, socially a very mixed area, will provide an example, not necessarily representative, of the balance of various types. Some 76,000 people could take shelter within the borough on any one night; 21,000 of these could go to Andersons; 39,000 to other types of domestic or communal shelter. Forty public shelters had been adapted from existing buildings; eleven were surface shelters specially constructed, and there were four trenches.

The public and communal shelters rapidly developed individual characters. There were quiet, genteel ones; noisy ones, where people brought beer in after the pubs closed; shelters on main roads which served drunks and casual passers by; shelters favoured by taxi-drivers or prostitutes. Specialized shelters developed where people had to work late or be on call all night; hospitals turned their underground vaults into nurses' sleeping quarters and casualty wards. Dignity and privacy went by the board. In one block of flats in a well-to-do suburb, where there was no shelter but the corridors might be slept in quite safely because the building was steel framed, "it was really extraordinary," one resident relates, "to see all these people who had spent so much time avoiding each other in the past now giving each other cups of tea or handing over chocolate, which was then unrationed and very scarce. It was the first—and last—time that big block of flats ever came near to having a soul and individuality of its own."

Indeed, by November most Londoners were not using specially created shelters. The first "Shelter Census," early that month, suggested that in the central area only 9 per cent slept in public shelters; 4 per cent in the underground railway system (though some accounts of the blitz make it sound as if almost everyone took to the tubes); and 27 per cent in domestic shelters. In the outer suburbs, these proportions were even lower. The rest were in most cases either on duty or sleeping in their own homes; if not in their bedrooms, at least in ground floor rooms, under the stairs or in cupboards. Though these figures are for only one night, at a stage when adaptation to the blitz had reached its peak, they should put the somewhat lurid stories which follow into perspective. However, London's population was so vast that a smallish proportion of it was sufficient to produce some impressive social phenomena.

Early in the blitz, some enterprising Londoners discovered the existence of a fine set of caves in the sandy hills at Chislehurst in Kent. These were ancient workings, pleasant, airy and equable in temperature. Families took over individual caves and set up homes—sometimes with double beds, armchairs and tables. Special trains were run from London every night, and the caves eventually came to have their own barber's shop, concerts and church services. Several thousand people might dwell there in great safety.

There was, among some, an urge to congregate in familiar centres. Father Wilson of Haggerston found that his church hall, though it was far from safe, was regularly used by between seventy and two hundred people. "I continued to impress on all and sundry," he wrote, "that the hall was not an official shelter; but the few such things in the neighbourhood were filled to capacity; the hall was warm, airy and well lit; it gave its temporary inhabitants both a sense of security and the companionship of their friends and neighbours. They liked to be there. I had not the heart to turn them away." The mayor of the borough gave a radio; the local wardens provided impromptu concerts; refreshment was purchased at the pub; there were card games and dances, and the East Enders had a good time. When the wireless packed up as the raiders approached, somebody would thump away at the piano, louder and louder as the bombs crashed nearer and nearer. The assistant curate sat among the shelterers reading the letters of Madame de Sévigné.*

Railway arches were chosen by many for shelter. They looked secure enough, but the authorities knew that they could be death traps. The most famous, or notorious, of all London's shelters was found under the Tilbury railway arches in Stepney. Part of a complex of cellars and vaults had been taken over by the borough council as a public shelter for three thousand people. The other part was the loading yard of a huge warehouse. The shelter was famous as a popular refuge in the raids of the First World War, and people flocked to it from a wide area. Communists encouraged the shelterers to overflow into the "unofficial" part of the arches, where massive steel girders maintained an illusion of safety. This became the largest, and perhaps the most unspeakable of all London's shelters; as many as fourteen or sixteen thousand were estimated to use it on certain nights.

* Madame de Sévigné: Marie de Rabutin-Chantal, marquise de Sévigné (1626–96), French writer, noted for correspondence on personal, literary, and social subjects; about 15,000 letters survive.

Great stocks of margarine were stored in the "unofficial" section. There was sanitation only for the handful of workmen usually employed there. Children slept among trodden feces and soiled margarine; so did Indians, Lascars, Negroes, spivs, prostitutes and Jewish refugees. Parties of sightseers from the West End would make the Tilbury Arches the highlight of their tour of black spots. American journalists were taken there to shudder; though Negley Farson found its "vital, impulsive life" oddly "inspiring," and when Harold Scott visited it, "A girl in a scarlet cloak danced wildly to the cheers of an enthusiastic audience; a party of Negro sailors sang spirituals while someone played the accordion. . . ." "Tilbury" became the spearhead of the agitation for a general improvement in public shelters which journalists and social workers began to conduct as soon as the blitz settled in.

Another big shelter in Stepney, "Mickey's Shelter," rivalled the "Tilbury"; indeed the Minister of Health referred to it as the worst in London. Mickey Davis, who soon gave his name to it, was an East End optician, three feet, three inches tall and hunchbacked. On the first night of blitz he found himself in a cellar, designated a shelter but not yet made safe, which had accommodation for five thousand people; more than twice that number had crowded their way into it. "The heat of that cellar," Davis wrote, "became literally hardly bearable. A steady stream of semi-conscious or unconscious people was passed towards the doorway. . . ." One Red Cross nurse, with one man helping her, was trying to cope with the sick.

Davis inspired his fellow shelterers to create their own order out of something which it seems polite to call chaos. A shelter committee was democratically elected; and when Davis was replaced as leader by a "shelter marshal" officially appointed from outside, the committee insisted on his reinstatement. As the state of the shelter became known, voluntary help came from outside. A gleaming canteen was installed by Marks and Spencer's chain stores. From its profits, free milk was given each day to the children. When Wendell Willkie, Roosevelt's Republican rival, visited London that autumn, he was taken to "Mickey's Shelter" as a showplace of British democracy.

Official policy had rejected the use of the Tubes as shelters. Apart from the fear that "deep shelter mentality" would develop there, the railways should be kept clear for troop movements. The public overruled the authorities very simply, and without much disorder. People bought platform tickets for a penny halfpenny, quite legally, and camped on the platforms.

Mercifully, one danger had been thoroughly provided against. If the tunnels under the Thames had been breached without due precaution having been taken, a very large area of the Tube would have been flooded. Such a breach did occur, very early in the blitz, but well before then a system of floodgates had been constructed, at huge cost. Even so, many Tube platforms seemed much safer than they really were. The deepest were more or less invulnerable, but a high explosive bomb could penetrate up to fifty feet through solid ground. When a small bomb scored a direct hit on the Marble Arch subway, filled with shelterers, on September 17th, its blast ripped the white tiles off the walls as it burst and made them deadly projectiles. Twenty people died. In October, four Tube stations were hit in three nights. The most terrible incident, at Balham, involved six hundred shelterers. A bomb tore through the road above the platform, smashing through mains, cables and conduits so that water, sand and rubble cascaded down on the platforms. A similar incident at Bank station in January 1941 killed a hundred and eleven shelterers and travellers.

Yet confidence in the Tubes survived these horrors. They were dry, they were warm, they were well lit and the raids were inaudible. The authorities beat a retreat. A short branch line to Aldwych station was closed and largely given over to shelterers. ("Pray let me have more information about this, and what has happened to supersede the former decisive arguments," Churchill, who favoured this development, minuted huffily; his colleagues had recently insisted when he had raised the matter at the cabinet that the use of the Tubes as shelters was "most undesirable.") Three disused stations were specially opened to the public. An uncompleted extension running from Liverpool Street under the East End became one vast shelter holding about ten thousand people, where a visiting American walked for half a mile "literally after each step having to find a place to put the next foot down without stepping on something human." Some seventy-nine stations in Greater London became *de facto* shelters, and at a peak near the end of September, 177,000 people were sleeping in the Underground system.

Sefton Delmer calls it "the panic slum on the Underground"; the sight of it filled this hardened war correspondent with "shame." "For the first time in many hundreds of years," Mass Observation pointed out, "civilized families conducted the whole of their leisure and domestic lives in full view of each other. . . . Most of these people were not merely sheltering in the Tubes; they were living there." Queues began to form outside the stations as early as six in the morning. Children or servicemen on leave would be sent to establish priority for their families—"The constant worry," writes Bernard Kops, "was whether we would find a space for that night. We lived only for four o'clock when they let us down. . . ." Spivs joined in, to reserve places on the platform for which they would charge half a crown or more when the raid "hotted up." Rain, wind, and even daylight bombing did not shift the queues. Two white lines had been painted on the platforms. Until seven thirty in the evening, shelterers must keep within the one drawn eight feet from the edge, leaving the rest for passengers. From eight until ten thirty, they might encroach as far as the second line four feet from the edge. Then the Tubes stopped running; the light was dimmed; the current was cut off in the rail. People would sling hammocks over the rails, and would walk a little way down the dark tunnel to relieve themselves. In the early days, the platforms were packed tight, and people slept on the escalators or even on the bannisters between them. The snoring rose and fell like a loud wind.

In the Liverpool Street extension, where there was no compulsion to leave, some people stayed down for weeks on end; this, and the queues, did justify to some extent the fears of a "deep shelter mentality," but those who acquired it were a minority within a small minority, no more significant to the life of the city as a whole than the rich, idle women who had fled to luxury hotels in the Lake District. And many of the Tube dwellers were homeless; looking at the rows of unrepaired houses, the squalid rest centres, the chaos of billeting arrangements, which characterized some parts of London, could anyone blame them? Bernard Kops, with other children, adapted gaily to life in the dusty stations. ". . . I got bars and bars of chocolate out of the chocolate machines and weighed myself incessantly. Here was a new life, a whole network, a whole city under the world. We rode up and down the escalators . . . and I used to ride backwards and forwards in the trains to see the other stations of underground people."

But where the Tubes lay below the level of the sewage mains, there were no sanitation or washing facilities on the platforms. Winds, now hot, now cold, howled through the tunnels. Mosquitoes flourished in the fug; lice crawled from head to head. In the mornings, people shook the dust and germs from their blankets over the line. One witness remarks that "The stench was frightful, urine and excrement mixed with strong carbolic, sweat, and dirty, unwashed humanity."

Ignoring the East End, the progress of a Tube shelter can be charted from the *Swiss Cottager,* organ of the self-appointed "shelterers' committee" at Swiss Cottage station in the wealthy and cosmopolitan suburb of Hampstead, where a motley gathering of thirteen to eighteen hundred English, Austrians, Czechs, Poles, Hungarians, French, Dutch, Belgians, Swiss and Spaniards, many of them refugees, assembled every night.

The Committee began as a somewhat matronly group of "busybodies" who tried to ensure hygiene, order and co-operation with the London Transport staff —organizing voluntary collections to pay for first aid equipment and to give something to the transport workers who had to clean up each morning; laying on a nightly cup of tea for the shelterers; spraying (or at least proposing to spray) the throat of each shelterer with disinfectant. In the second issue of their magazine, they warn against agitators who "have endeavoured to instil dissatisfaction where none existed."

But the committee members themselves turned agitators. The fourth issue, published in November, reveals that they took part in an "Inter Station Conference of Tube Shelterers"—though they later withdrew protesting about Communist interference. The bulletin inveighs "against shameful apathy, indifference amounting almost to callousness, neglect, soulless contempt for elementary human decencies, against red tape, authority, and officialdom, and against practised experts in the time-honoured game of 'passed-to-you-please.' " The Ministry of Health had promised that the first aid post, which was in any case inadequately equipped, would at least be open from the moment the shelterers were admitted each afternoon, and this promise had not been fulfilled. Two cases of infectious disease had been found, not by the medical staff sent in by the local council, but by the committee, and a child had died of meningitis. The buck appeared to have been passed between the ministry, the local authority and London Transport, and meanwhile the nurse worked in a space "little larger than a telephone booth."

It was the anger and concern of sensible, moderate people like these which brought immediate improvement in the shelter situation, always anticipating action by the authorities. Clearly, such action had to be taken. The steel-framed buildings in the West End notoriously provided much better protection than the nineteenth-century slums to the east. The contrast between the arches and the Tubes and the shelter provided for the occupants of the Dorchester Hotel in Park Lane was one which might well make the most myopic bureaucrat feel uncomfortable. The Dorchester had converted its Turkish baths, and there was "a neat row of cots, spaced about two feet apart, each one covered with a lovely fluffy eiderdown. Its silks billowed and shone in the dim light in pale pinks and blues. Behind each cot hung the negligee, the dressing gown. . . . The pillows on which the heads lay were large and full and white. . . . There was a little sign pinned to one of the Turkish-bath curtains. It said, 'Reserved for Lord Halifax.' " * There was, furthermore, the factor which had prompted social reforms in the nineteenth century; the health of Whitehall itself was endangered if epidemics broke out in Whitechapel.

A week after the blitz began, the Government set up an expert committee under Lord Horder to investigate conditions in the shelters. It reported, verbally, within four days, and formally before the end of September. It stressed the dangers to health from overcrowding and urged the importance of proper medical facilities and supervision. Its recommendations were followed, but not always rapidly, and some areas did not feel the full force of the improvements till after the blitz had ended in May 1941.

Between early in December and the end of April six hundred thousand bunks were provided in the shelters. (This improvement was not always welcomed; it meant that fewer people could use a favourite shelter, and restricted the space available for card games and dancing.) Small coal stoves or electric fires had been introduced. Food was usually available in the larger shelters, provided by private caterers, local authorities or voluntary bodies like the Salvation Army and the W.V.S. In some big shelters, full-time "shelter wardens" had been installed, with power to expel undesirables. The social life of the shelters was developed, with official support; gramophones, concerts, play readings, discussions on current affairs, religious services, film shows, libraries, even play centres for the children, were provided by outside bodies or improvised by the shelterers themselves. One close observer notes that, as quiet nights became more frequent

---

* Lord Halifax: (1881–1959), Conservative statesman, Viceroy of India (1938–40), Foreign Secretary in Chamberlain's government (1938–40), Ambassador to U.S. (1941–46).

towards the end of 1940, "The shelter crawl became almost as popular a pastime as the old-time pub crawl. The advantages of this and that shelter were compared, and thus there set in a remarkable redistribution of the shelter population."

Thanks partly to the installation of first aid posts, and partly to sheer good fortune, there were no epidemics. Hospitals observed a serious increase in scabies, impetigo and lice. The Anglican Pacifist Fellowship set up the famous "Hungerford Club" in arches near Charing Cross station, and segregated some four thousand, five hundred down-and-outs from the rest of London's shelterers. Through the club's agency, a good number of pathetic vagrants were resuscitated.

The Government also rethought the question of deep shelters. The outward motives for its change of policy were technical—the Germans were using heavier bombs, and the fact that people were spending all night in the shelters ruled out the objection that big deep caverns would have to be so widely spaced that most citizens could not reach them in time. But it is likely that the invasion of the Tubes really carried more weight. Eight enormous shelters, eighty to a hundred and five feet underground, each of them to hold eight thousand people, were constructed; work on the first of them started in November. Had they ever been fully used, the cost would have amounted to thirty-five pounds per shelterer. None were ready until long after the blitz had ended, but Londoners found shelter of unsurpassed comfort and safety there during the flying bomb attacks, and they provided General Eisenhower with his D Day invasion offices.

Meanwhile, the authorities embarked on the structural improvement of existing shelters and the provision of more. (In February it was announced that public shelters were available for 1,400,000 people in the London region, and domestic shelters for 4,500,000; this still left about one Londoner in five "unprotected," but since so many people insisted on sleeping in their beds, the deficiency was purely theoretical.) In March 1941 it was decided that all the brick surface shelters made without cement should be demolished at Government expense. By the autumn of that year, most of the dampness in the remaining shelters had been countered. A further improvement was the invention and introduction of the "Morrison," named after the new Minister of Home Security. This, like the Anderson, was a family shelter, free for most people, but it could be erected indoors. It had a steel plate on top which could be used as a table in the daytime, and sides of wire mesh, two feet, nine inches high. Though few were in use by the end of the blitz, over half a million had been distributed by November 1941, and they gave good service in later attacks.

● ● ●

A mine exploded. The nearest warden raced towards the sound, assessed the extent and character of the damage, and ran to his post to report to the control centre, a bomb-proof fastness in the borough town hall. From there, messages went to the police, to the public utilities, and to the fire, rescue and casualty services in their various depots. If the borough was especially hard pressed, a call for help might go to the group control centre which served several boroughs. Word would go also to the regional headquarters. This was located, oddly enough, in a museum in South Kensington, with walls mainly of glass, barely a pane of which was shattered during the war.

There were twelve regions in all. Everywhere except London, they were presided over by one regional commissioner, a man of national, rather than local standing, who was expected to coordinate, and if necessary overrule, the squabbling county councils and borough councils and to assume quasi-dictatorial control if and when circumstances seemed to him to warrant it.

London was unique. Its area embraced an unusual number of authorities. The L.C.C.* was almost a state within the state, and besides the metropolitan boroughs which existed subordinately but autonomously, there were the county boroughs of West Ham and Croydon, with major powers of their own. London region had a senior Regional Commissioner, who was, when the blitz began, a Conservative M.P. (Captain Euran Wallace). Beneath him, it was not clear who overruled whom among the two lesser commissioners and Harold Scott, the region's Chief Administrative Officer. But these three men were all imaginative appointments, and they worked together effectively. Scott was an unusually warm civil servant, whose own theory was that he had been chosen "because they suspected that I was a bit slapdash and unorthodox." One of the commissioners was Sir Ernest Gowers, a distinguished civil servant who was known as a deadly opponent of Whitehall jargon. The other was the cheerful Admiral Evans, "Evans of the Broke," a veteran of Scott's Antarctic expedition and a hero of the First World War, who had been told that his job was to keep up the Londoners' spirits. To this end, he "literally visited thousands of incidents" and made himself a familiar figure in the shelters, where his immaculate naval uniform, complete with white kid gloves, raised laughter and cheers.

At the top of the whole structure was the Minister of Home Security. The replacement of Anderson with Herbert Morrison in October 1940 was hailed as a victory for the multifarious protests against conditions in the shelters and rest centres, and was duly followed by the improvements already mentioned; but cause and effect in this episode were more complex than the public supposed. Psychologically, however, it was important that the energetic Morrison, with his democratic manner and his rubbery London voice, was now in charge. His junior minister was Ellen Wilkinson, M.P. for Jarrow, a tiny, passionate woman who had once led her constituents on a celebrated "hunger march" from Durham to Whitehall. Even more than Morrison, "Red Ellen," with her unsparing energy, convinced hard-pressed social workers and civil defenders that the Government was on their side.

The communications upon which the whole system depended were bombed, of

---

* L.C.C.: London County Council.

course, as haphazardly as everything else. The girls who manned the telephones in the control rooms, and the messenger boys who took over when the lines were knocked out, had plenty of hair-raising stories of their own to tell. But the purpose for which the machine was run was the saving of life; the "incidents" were the front line.

At the incident, the wardens would be alone for perhaps half an hour with the cries of casualties, the debris and the noise of the raid. They would begin the tasks of fire fighting and rescue, assisted by those residents who were still able to help, and perhaps by passing Home Guards and even casual pedestrians. When the first and least serious casualties, shaken but cheerful, were led from the ruins, W.V.S. housewives would provide cups of tea, sofas and blankets in their houses near by while they waited for the ambulance to arrive.

Let us say this was a big incident. Several houses had been destroyed and more than a score of people had been killed. When one warden shouted to another, dust would seem to fill his mouth and muffle the sound. Because of the blackout, only screened hand torches could be used to penetrate the murk, though the fire which had broken out among the ruins gave some assistance. Drivers searching for the spot would find the whole geography of a familiar area transformed.

The firemen and the rescue team would quite soon appear, and the heavy rescue men would begin at once to negotiate the wreckage with care and yet with amazing speed. The stretcher party, according to the pre-war scheme, was supposed to stand by until the casualties were brought out or the ruins were safe to enter, but its members were normally disinclined to remain idle and would help their more expert colleagues.

If the police appeared, there would be an unedifying argument between the officer of the law and the senior warden over who had the right to control the incident. The policeman would say that the ultimate responsibility was his; the warden would argue that the police knew nothing of Civil Defence; while the effective leader of the operation might well be the chief man of the rescue team. (Still less edifying demarcation disputes would occur when bombs fell on the boundaries between post areas or boroughs, and two teams of wardens disputed jealously over whose they were.) The policeman would probably have his way. It was over two years before this problem was settled.

Every so often, the clatter of activity would stop, and the leader of the rescue team would call for silence as his men listened for the faint moaning or the muffled cry which would lead them to a trapped casualty. A grey auxiliary ambulance, a high-powered saloon car with a square van back, would have arrived; and its woman driver might well be smoking to calm her nerves after a tortuous trip through craters and explosions. There would also be a mobile first aid post, a car with three nurses and a doctor.

At this point, we may let one such nurse bring us back from typicality to actuality. What follows is a report written by a fully trained nurse who, with two untrained assistants, helped at such an incident. She calls the rescue men, "demolition men."

"On arrival we were told that there were a number of trapped people and several dead. Four of these we saw, but they had been certified by a private doctor as dead before arrival. We stood by and then found a man who was suffering very severely from shock. A. helped to put him into a bed in a basement nearby; he was given hot tea, hot water bottles, and generally treated for shock. Dr. S. saw and ordered 1 gr Phenobarbitone. I gave this and was able to obtain particulars. MPC 46 given. We also found slight cuts over several parts of his body, and Dr. S. queried embedded glass. The casualty was told to see his own doctor in the morning (later sent for treatment to Post "C" first aid post). Demolition Squad asked doctor and me to stand by as they were trying to reach a woman (trapped by legs) in a lavatory. She was quite cheerful, and kept up a conversation with the men and also spoke to me. I did not see her, and she had not been rescued when I left at 0700 hours. Screams were also coming from debris nearby; men were working to release trapped people. These also were still trapped at 0700 hours. We were then called to a heap of debris (No. 16 was on the gatepost) where a girl was trapped. While taking a short cut with A. and S., S. tripped over a body; this was a female who was decapitated and disembowelled. We helped to put her on a stretcher and then went on to the trapped girl —who was too ill to give her name. Dr. S. ordered ½ gr. morphine (we checked this and I gave it. Given at 5:43 a.m.). Hot tea was also given her. The demolition men got debris away as far as her feet and I was able to give her hot water bottles (provided by neighbours). At 0634 hours, Dr. S. ordered another quarter of a grain of morphine (checked by Dr. S. and given by me). The girl remained conscious, but was in pain and was very brave. As I came out of the hole I noticed the back part of a body in a green skirt under the above girl's trapped legs and told demolition men. The demolition men then unearthed a girl's hand (not the girl in the green skirt). The men made a hole and the girl made noises—I gave them a rubber tube which the girl was able to put into her mouth to help her to breathe. Fires started to break out under this debris and the firemen were ordered to keep it down with a gentle flow of water. We stood by until 0700 hours when I was relieved by Sister S. . . . Both A. and S. were excellent in helping us and looking after me. A. pulled aside a man when a beam fell and S. shouted to me and I was able to fall over backwards out of its way. Thanks to them, a nasty accident was avoided."

As morning cast a pale light through the dust, the rescue workers could at last see what they were doing. Sightseers would stand vacantly about in clusters; tearful relatives would tug at the rescuers' sleeves and beg for information; a yellow diversion sign would advertise another blocked thoroughfare. In exceptional cases, the work would carry on into the following night's raid, even for several days. At some stage, the leader of the rescue team must decide that he could no longer risk several lives, and keep his men back from other incidents, for the sake of just possibly saving one life. It was not a decision which could be taken lightly. Later in the blitz, one girl on Merseyside was buried for a hundred and six hours, with a dead child in her arms, and brought out alive.

But in some cases, even the remains of the dead would not be found. They might come to light in the final work of demolition, perhaps a year later. They might perhaps figure in the basket of "unidentified flesh" which wardens were expected to collect. If enough remained recognizable, a body would be taken to the mortuary, where attendants and volunteers would work on it. One volunteer, useful because she was an artist trained in anatomy, has written: "We had somehow to form a body for burial so that the relatives (without seeing it) could imagine that their loved one was more or less intact for that purpose. But it was a very difficult task—there were so many pieces missing and, as one of the mortuary attendants said, 'Proper jigsaw puzzle, ain't it, Miss?' The stench was the worst thing about it. . . ." She adds, "It became a grim and ghastly satisfaction when a body was fairly constructed—but if one was too lavish in making one body almost whole, then another one would have sad gaps. . . . I think that this task dispelled for me the idea that human life is valuable. . . ."

I IMAGES OF CHILDHOOD

We move now into a group of studies in which writers try to communicate the sense of their own childhood. There is of course no limit to the variety of backgrounds which might be remembered and evoked in exercises of this kind; but the reader may like to consider whether there exists any direct relationship between a man's childhood and the style in which he describes it. Frank Norman and Richard Wright describe underprivileged childhoods; Alfred Kazin remembers times that were perhaps poor in material terms though not in other respects; Frank Conroy speaks of a situation to which such terms may hardly seem relevant; Robert Lowell recalls the pride and eccentricities of a great New England family.

With all their differences one could say that these pieces have one thing in common: the presence or absence, the kindness or unkindness of parents, are all-important. But it is not impossible now to envisage a wholly different kind of society, in which parents are important only genetically because the children, removed from their mothers at the age of seven days, are brought up in the kind of community foreshadowed by the *kibbutzim* of Israel, and so taken out of the context of family love and strife. We might well find it difficult even to imagine the social and psychological implications of such a change, or to guess how it would alter the stories men tell of their childhood lives. So far as we know, no *kibbutz* child has yet provided such an account. But Dr. Bettelheim's careful study provides ample material for discussing the point.

Julia Trevelyan Oman

Frank Norman / Banana Boy: Footnotes to a Dossier

Dr. Barnardo's homes are English charity schools which provide for orphans and other underprivileged children, including those born into the kind of situation outlined in the dossier which Mr. Norman cites at the beginning of his essay. After leaving the home, Mr. Norman spent some time in prison, and then began his present successful career as a writer by publishing an article on his experiences there. Here again he is recording an actual experience, though his work has included non-autobiographical books and a successful musical.

If you compare this with Mr. Connolly's reminiscences of Eton in the next section, you will see that the differences are not only of milieu but of tone. There is little obvious "art" in Norman's prose; delicate elegiac writing would hardly have suited the material anyway, but the plainness is also a matter of temperament. We invite the comparison with Connolly's more "mandarin" writing not only because there is an interesting, even shocking, contrast between the two modes of education described, but because the difference of tone is obviously not of the kind that would justify our saying that Norman is not a good writer. In his own way he is. He has the kind of accuracy that is necessary to this particular task, an accuracy that calls for a measure of moral as well as intellectual toughness. He includes anecdotes that are sometimes concerned with painful or miserable experiences over long periods during childhood; but in speaking, for instance, of his kitchen work, or of his running away (note that he doesn't dwell on the decision—you have to sense why he did it), he maintains a matter-of-fact tone. Thus, too, he mentions only in passing that nobody ever called him by his first name, and he speculates quite calmly on his mother's shady motives in trying to re-enter his life. To make such privations and childish suffering easy to imagine without sentimentalizing them is a genuine stylistic achievement.

Apart from the omission of several names, this is the first page of my Dr. Barnardo's dossier:

> John Frank Norman. (Illegitimate.) Admitted 24.3.1937.
> Born: 9.6.1930 at Whiteladies Road, Bristol.

This article formed the basis of Frank Norman's autobiography *Banana Boy* published in 1969 by Secker & Warberg.

Baptised: C. of E.* No particulars. Mother C. of E.
Last six months address: c/o Mrs. A., Prittlewell, Southend-on-Sea.
Last school attended: Barnes Private School, Church Road, Barnes.
Payment: See Below.
Period: Six Months probation.
Agreement: None.
Information: from: Report (Kim)
Applicant: Lady W., Onslow Square, South Kensington.
Mother: Beatrice Spence Smith née Norman (30); health was good; character indifferent, separated from her husband; last known address—Hudds Vale, St. George's, Bristol.
Father: (Putative): Frank Charles Booth (35); Engineer; £800 per annum; M.; "Netherleigh," Highfield, Llandaff, Cardiff. Not affiliated.
Mother's husband: Vernon Leslie Smith; married the mother 24.1.31 at Bristol Register Office; no other particulars.
Half-brother or sister: Child of the mother's marriage, no other particulars.

The mother is described as an adventuress. At the time she met the putative father, she was a secretary at some works.* She married in 1931, and her present address is unknown. When last heard of, two years ago, she had separated from her husband, and the child of the marriage was boarded out.

The putative father is the son of a managing director of an Engineering Works, and is very well-off financially. After John was born, the putative father paid the mother through a solicitor the sum of £300 in order to clear his name. Later the mother made herself a nuisance, and in June 1933, Mr. Buttle, of the Church of England Adoption Society, was asked by the putative father's mother to get John adopted. For a short time the putative father paid £1 per week, while John was in the Society's Home at Kingsbury. John was sent to several people, with a view to adoption, but each time he was returned with such excuses as being untruthful, dishonest, and unintelligent.

Two years ago, applicant, who is Roman Catholic, made herself responsible, through the Adoption Society, for the maintenance of John, but did not legally adopt him. He was boarded out by applicant with a Mrs. A., at Prittlewell, Southend, for about eighteen months prior to last September. He was then brought to London and handed over to the care of a Mr. and Mrs. M., White Hart Lane, Barnes, who contemplated adopting him. On 12.2.37 Mr. M. took him back to applicant, as not being suitable. He has remained in her care ever since. Applicant states she cannot afford to keep John, and there are reasons why she cannot keep him, but she wishes to keep in touch with him. When our officer called, the conditions in applicant's home were not at all

* C. of E.: Church of England.
* works: factory.

good, and it was reported that John should not be allowed to remain there a day longer than necessary.

John is a weak-looking child, and mentally backward, but he has never had a chance, being pushed about from pillar to post. At school he was said to be quite docile and friendly. The putative father should be persuaded to contribute regularly towards John's maintenance....

I remember the day that I was delivered to Barnardo's. I cried my heart out. For a small boy of seven years it seemed like the final straw.

As far as I know Lady W. did not keep in touch, and there is no record of Mr. Booth contributing to my maintenance.

So, life in the Homes began and so did the dossier. An extract from my medical record dated the same day as admission reads:

Height: 45½ inches. Weight: 48¾ lbs. Measles: No. Scarlet Fever: No. Diphtheria: No. Whooping Cough: Yes. Teeth: F/G. General Physique: F/G. Lymphatic Gland. Mental Condition: Backward (does not know letters). Disposition: ? GRADE B.2.

On 3 April 1937 I was transferred from Barnardo's headquarters in Stepney to their home for "Backward" children at Bedford. It had the rather austere name of Cardington Abbey. I was accompanied on the journey by a frightening matron, dressed from head to toe in black. I remember boarding the train but nothing of the journey, until we reached our destination, where we were met by another matron dressed from head to toe in black. The second one took over responsibility for my delivery to the Home; the other one took the next train back to London.

My first impression of Cardington Abbey was a mixture of awe and curiosity. What manner of place was this that I had been brought to, against my will, and why? The reception hall was vast. As I came through the front door, I was faced with a huge stained glass window, depicting Jesus and several apostles. The floor was tiled and a great oak stair-case led up to a gallery, off which were several rooms (serving as the children's dormitories). Several idiot-looking children (boys and girls) appeared in the gallery and stared down at me over the banister rail.

The head mistress was a Scots lady named Miss Duke, who owned a vicious Pekingese dog which she wore over her shoulder like a mink stole. When any of the children attempted to stroke it, it snapped and snarled frantically.

Life at Cardington Abbey was uneventful. There were classes every day, at which I learned the alphabet parrot fashion, chanting it over and over in a high pitched soprano voice. "A B C D E F G (*change of key*) H I J K L M N O P (*repeat last five letters*) L M N O P Q (*change of key*) R S T U-V-W-X-Y-Z!!" "Once more, children," the mistress would say, as she conducted us with a pencil as baton. I was slow to learn my three *R*'s, but was good at history and could reel off the names of the Kings and Queens of England, also the clergy, statesmen, soldiers and sailors after only a glance at their pictures in the history books: "Henry VIII. Captain Cook. Thomas Abecket. Bonny Prince Charley. The Venerable Bede. The Iron Duke. The Black Prince. Robert the Bruce. King Arthur. Oliver Cromwell. . . ." It was a game I loved to play.

During the next five years I had Schick and Dick Immunisations, caught measles and chicken pox, trod on a rusty nail which pierced the instep of my left foot, and had to be immunised against typhoid and tetanus. I fell in love with a girl called Irene and became the best fighter in the school.

I was well aware that the Bedford Home was for "Backward" children and in protest I would, on occasions, run around the lawn outside Miss Duke's window *backwards*. This infuriated her greatly and she regularly applied the hair brush to my bare bottom. This was not a punishment for running backwards; the reason given was that I was out of bounds. I also had quite a lot of trouble over not eating the food, which was wholesome but nasty. The day I dreaded most was Thursdays, for that was the day we had tripe for lunch. I have since learned to consider this dish as at best an acquired taste but in those days I thought it absolutely revolting, indeed the very sight of it made me retch. There was a rule that whatever one did not eat at one meal was given back to you for the next. The guilty child was also made to stand, in the cold stone passage outside the head mistress's office, holding the uneaten meal in his hand until the next meal time. He would then be made to take his plate into the dining room, and sit with it in front of him, whilst the other children ate something delicious, like bread and jam or fish cakes. I spent every Thursday afternoon standing in the passage, holding my uneaten dish of congealed tripe in my hand. There was one little boy who could not eat the porridge that we were given for breakfast every morning and as far as I can remember he spent his entire life standing in the passage. I was once so hungry that I stalked into the kitchen and stole a handful of raisins. Unfortunately the cook appeared and caught me red-handed as I forced them into my mouth. As a punishment for this, I was brought before the assembled school at evening prayers, and was made to drink salt water until I vomited.

Empire Day was the best day of the year. There were no classes, a pageant was organised by the games mistress, and a fete was held on the front lawn. The boys and girls dressed up in cardboard armour and period dresses, singing: "And did those feet in ancient time, walk upon England's mountains green. And was the Holy Lamb of God . . . etc," *at the tops of our voices. We walked in procession around the rose-beds, bearing the standard of St. George, and delighted the visitors from the outside world.

Christmas Day was also nice. There were presents (donated by charitable organisations), we sang carols lustily, and there was no standing in the passage for not eating your Christmas dinner.

* "And did those feet . . .": poem from William Blake's *Jerusalem;* sung in England as a kind of national song.

When the war broke out in 1939, there was a lot of activity at Cardington Aerodrome just up the road. Tanks lumbered past the gates of the Abbey, and for days on end envoys of lorries roared by full of soldiers, who threw us pennies, and we waved at them and wished them luck. I was convinced that the war was going on just up the road at the Aerodrome.

As the battle raged in Europe, our classes took an interesting turn. A large map of the Continent was pinned to the wall, and each day the mistress stuck little flags on it, black for the Germans and red for the Allies, to denote the progress of each. I was quite sure the Germans would win the war, as the Axis forces advanced into one European country after another. The map became a mass of black flags and not a red one in sight. On days when I felt that I was being particularly badly treated, I wished the Germans would hurry, for I felt sure they would release me from my torment. We listened to Churchill's speeches, and were told by Miss Duke that all would be well, so long as he was running things. She was, at least, right in that.

My report to the General Superintendent of Barnardo's from Miss Duke reads: "Behaviour: Good. Progress at school: Fair. Habits: Clean. Improving very slowly." When I was eleven a decision had to be made on my progress at the Abbey. If satisfactory I would be sent to a Boys Home, if not to a Senior School for Educationally Subnormal Boys. On 21 August 1941 I was sent to Barnardo's Home at Kingston which would indicate that I was no longer thought to be mentally backward, though a note states: "Educationally still some way to go."

Though there were many things that I did not like about Cardington Abbey, I was sorry to leave it. I had been there for some five years and had long been used to the place and the staff. It was like being uprooted all over again. At Kingston I was a "new boy" again; where at Bedford I had been the oldest I was now the youngest and the weakest.

The biggest difference between the two homes was that at Kingston the boys went to an outside school. It was at this school that the stigma of being brought up in an orphanage was made clear to me. There were many fights with the outside boys, who also went to the school. Particularly when they referred to us as: "Dr. Banana boys!" We were also rather looked down on by the teachers and the parents. If there was ever any trouble we invariably got the blame for it. During my three years there I was caned on my hands so often, my arithmetic was never good enough to keep count.

The war was at a critical stage: the sirens wailed almost every day warning us of the arrival of enemy aircraft overhead. To be caught without your gas mask was a punishable offence, and fire drill was as regular as going to church on Sundays. We learnt how to use a "stirrup-pump" * and spent a good deal of our time in air-raid shelters. Any progress that I might have made at Bedford was soon lost, I came at the bottom of the class in just about every subject in the

---

* stirrup-pump: a foot pump for extinguishing incendiary bombs.

curriculum. But things were to improve. Few, if any, bombs fell on Kingston, but in 1943 and after we really came under attack from the Doodle Bugs and V.2 rockets, both of which gave eager schoolboy truants no warning of their arrival.

Mr. Gardener was the name of the Governor of the Home. Of all the people I met in the Homes, he remains the most difficult to fathom. He was tall, smoked voraciously, and seemed only interested in the band. He left the running of the place to the rest of the staff and I saw him rarely. One of my greatest ambitions was to join his band, and learn to play the bagpipes; I applied several times but was turned down flat. Instead I got all the terrible jobs. I built flower-bed walls with clinkers * from the furnace and then white-washed them. For a time I was put to work in the lavatory: every day I washed the urinal and scrubbed the floor with a yard broom. One morning I found one of the lavatory pans blocked with excrement, and full to the brim with foul water. The master in charge took one look at it and then at me: "Come on, lad! don't just stand there!" he said. "Get your hand down there and fish it out! It's all your own!" It was my command performance of the war.

The Governor was also interested in boxing. It was more or less compulsory to volunteer to fight, for refusal meant being branded a coward by the rest of the boys and petty victimisation by the staff. I was once matched against a boy with a bright red face, who had high blood pressure and was absolutely useless in the ring. Neither of us were keen on having the bout, but there was no help for it. The gloves were put on and we entered the ring. The bell clanged and there we were facing each other, the boys cheered us on and the Governer bellowed: "Show us what you can do!" More by luck than from good judgment I took a blind swipe at the boy and the blow landed squarely on the end of his nose, which exploded and blood spurted in all directions drenching us both. The bell rang indicating the end of the round, and I thought the end of the match. Mr. Gardener went to the other boy's corner, inspected the damage and declared him fit to continue. The second round went much the same as the first, and by the end of it I was sure that the fight would be stopped. But we were made to go the final round, making three in all. The boy was a pitiful sight and I hero for the first time, and most reluctantly.

A report on my progress from Kingston to head office dated 30 April 1943 reads: "Behaviour: F/G. Progress at school: Fair. Habits: Clean. Relatives who keep in touch: No." This was followed by several comments. "A peculiar boy mentally. Making little progress. Very sullen."

On 15 November 1943 my mother wrote the following letter to the head office at Stepney.

* clinkers: cinders, burnt-out coals.

Dear Sir,
 I am writing in asking if I could have my Son John Norman Home or as he got to stay untill the War is over been as he is on National Importance work I expect he feels it now as hes 2 Brothers are at home or if not could he come home for Xmas on a Holiday for a week or tow if you would write & let me know I should be very gratefull
 I am your faithful

MRS. NORMAN

Whether this was a belated act of motherly love or because I was approaching school-leaving age (and could go to work), I will never know. She was at the time living in Birmingham where a Barnardo's enquiry officer visited her and recommended to the General Superintendent that I should spend the following Christmas with her. Leave was granted. But I think she must have got cold feet at the last minute, for I did not get to go, nor have I heard a word from her since, or the two aforementioned brothers.

From time to time we were visited by contingents of the U.S. army and air force who were stationed in Richmond Park, just down the hill. They were the kind Americans armed to the teeth with chewing gum, peanuts, toys, sweets, and of course Coca Cola. They were also the funny Americans who could improvise a show and make children laugh.

One day a Doodle Bug came "pop-pop-popping" across the sky and the engine stopped directly overhead. We stood there gorping up at it, as it glided softly down towards us, just missing the bell tower of the Home. It crashed in a field less than a mile away and exploded, like a mighty clap of thunder, blowing every window out of the Home and me off my feet. Later we were allowed to go and see the crater, which to me at the time seemed to be the size of a football pitch. Later several rockets came down around and about, but no one was seriously hurt.

When I turned fourteen, it was decided that since I was so far behind at school, it would not be wise to find me "a situation." Instead, I was sent to a Barnardo's Technical School in Hertfordshire called Goldings. I arrived there on 8 July 1944, and what a fearsome place it was! Though the Head Master was a mild clergyman named MacDonald, the institution was run with a rod of iron. Drill, marching, physical training and cold showers were the order of the day. You had to be tough or you went under. Indeed one boy died whilst I was there; it was said to have been from natural causes, but then some causes are more natural than others.

I absconded several times but was always caught or gave myself up after spending a night in a freezing ditch or hay stack. I would be returned to the Home by the police (who incidentally were always kind to me and gave me tea and cakes). I was thrashed soundly and put back to whatever work I had been allocated. "He has problems and I am anxious about his future," states the Head

Master in a letter to head office about me. Which comes as no surprise to me whatever.

I spent my first few months there being a "spare boy," *i.e.* a boy they could find nothing to do with. After a time they tried me in the Carpenters' Shop, in the hope that I would learn a trade. It was useless. I could not handle such things as planes, chisels and tenon saws. I ruined every exercise I was given, and was eventually taken out of the course, before I could destroy every last plank of wood they had in the place.

They tried me then in the Bootmakers' Shop. This too ended in desperation and disaster. They told me that I was not trying (I certainly was). It did not occur to them that perhaps I was not cut out to be a craftsman or a tradesman. Their attitude seems to have been: if you can't learn to be a Carpenter or a Bootmaker you can learn nothing. So they put me in the kitchen washing dishes and peeling potatoes. The cockroaches in the kitchen outnumbered the boys ten to one. During the day they hid behind the steam coppers, but at night they ventured forth for a bit of exercise. If anyone walked across the kitchen floor at night when the lights were out, they would leave a trail of mangled corpses behind them, for the cockroaches covered the floor from wall to wall like a thick pile carpet in a Mayfair penthouse. An attempt or two was made to put them down, but to no avail; they were hardy creatures and defied every insecticide on the market, indeed I think they thrived on them.

At least working in the kitchen meant that I got out of the incessant marching about and being bullied by prefects. I spent so much of my time in there I began to smell and even look like a kitchen. The cook was a hard task-master, inspecting my washing-up as closely as a sergeant-major might inspect a squad of recruits. He warned me that every saucepan that I washed was to be wiped *dry*. He would then choose one at random and tell me to hold it upside down. For every drop of water that dripped out he would strike me on the head with a wooden spoon. This tended to leave me somewhat dazed at times, depending upon how many drops of water fell out of the saucepan.

The highest honour that could be bestowed on a boy at Goldings was to be made a prefect: a boy would have to "excel at sports" or be "of exemplary character." For prefects there were many perks * (being allowed to stay later than the rest of the boys, use of the prefects' room, in which there was a billiards table and dart board; they were also permitted to smoke, though I do not think that this was official). It was also the prefects who were usually chosen to go to Wimbledon each year, to act as ball boys at the famous tennis tournaments. But their greatest privilege was that they could report any boy they saw breaking one of the hundred-and-one rules. They could also, within reason, inflict the punishment themselves. It was no joke if a prefect had it in for you, particularly if it

---

* perks: perquisites, privileges.

was the school captain who, like the other great dictators of our day, had absolute power.

In November 1945 I ran away again, this time with another boy whose name I have long since forgotten and would not print here if I had not. As usual we had no destination in mind. To get away from the frightful place was the only object. We walked for miles across the ploughed fields and pastures where cattle grazed. By late afternoon we were tired, hungry, freezing cold, and wet all through. Then as we turned a bend in a country lane, we saw a farm wagon parked by the wayside and decided to investigate. Our hope was to find some food. As we clambered into the back of the wagon, we noticed a man working in the fields some way off. He was absorbed in whatever it was he was doing and did not see us. I do not remember which one of us it was that found the man's jacket, but suddenly there it was in our hands. We wasted no time in searching the pockets. We found a packet of cigarettes and a wallet which contained some papers, a few photographs and a ten shilling note. Without hesitating we pocketed the money and cigarettes and ran away.

Later that night we were stopped by a policeman who questioned us about what we were doing and where we lived. We told him and were taken to the police station. The farm hand must have reported the theft to the police. No sooner had we entered the police station than we were searched by a sergeant, who found the note in our pockets. We grudgingly confessed to the crime, were charged, and appeared in court the following morning. After the reading of the evidence, etc., the Magistrate adjourned the case for three months for a "Report on the Conduct and Progress of the Boys." The other boy was hastily transferred to another Home, and I was given my very last chance.

I was summoned to the headmaster's office, who for the first time talked to me kindly, and told me that the incident was now closed, but that it really was my last chance. Much to my amazement he then asked me what I would like to do. I immediately said that I would like to go to work in the gardens; I had had enough of the kitchen. He agreed that I should, but warned me again about the consequences of failure. What could they be? How could I know? He must have thought I was laughing up my sleeve.

Though we had little or no contact with girls at Goldings, there was very little, if any, homosexuality. But there was a good deal of masturbation. In fact there were masturbation competitions amongst the elder boys as to who could ejaculate quickest and farthest. Though those sporting affairs had to do with our latent sexual frustration, the boys looked upon it only as a mild joke.

My first real sexual experience was with a Girl Guide * when, one year, we went to a summer camp. I think she might have been slightly older than I, but we

---

* Girl Guide: Girl Scout.

were both young and inexperienced. It was, anyway, something to boast about to the other boys. I remember their reaction was one of disgust, with just a slight tinge of envy.

On 17 October 1946 I was released from Barnardo's care, though they remained my legal guardians until I came of age. I was found a place to live at Waltham Cross and a situation with a tomato grower near by. My final report to head office from Goldings documented their continuing anxiety about their difficulty in getting any co-operation from me and that I was very unsettled.

Time has passed, things have changed. Looking back, I cannot ever remember being called by my Christian name; today the children are not called by anything else. And the old tradition of calling the governor or headmistress "Sir" or "Madam" has been dropped. It is now "Mum" and "Dad" and even "Pop."

Richard Wright / Black Boy

This section of Richard Wright's autobiography of childhood and youth seems at first glance relatively unambitious, not more than an anecdote about the way two black boys were tricked by their white employers into a fight, disguised as a boxing match. The possibilities of some larger significance are subtly proposed throughout, however. They can be felt initially in the evoked sense of threat whereby the very dullness of the routine of a summer morning in the factory probably means that the black boy will have to compensate for the white man's boredom; and it is evident at the end, where Wright feels that he has done something "for which I could never properly atone."

The story is about the exploitation and domination of the precarious manhood of blacks by economic and psychological intimidation. It is clear by the end that Harrison, the black who becomes Wright's antagonist, will feel nothing of Wright's guilt or any need for atonement. He nowhere chooses to imagine himself as more than what his white oppressors imagine him to be. The different ways in which the blacks respond to the power of the whites and of the fact that they are eventually forced to fight and to distrust one another has political implications that are understated and, for the time, predictive. The reader might want to remember that Wright had been a member of the Communist Party in the 1930's and though he left it disheartened in the 1940's, he had meanwhile learned to see the structure of social conflict through the writings of Marx and other social theorists. *Black Boy* was published in 1945.

One summer morning I stood at a sink in the rear of the factory washing a pair of eyeglasses that had just come from the polishing machines whose throbbing shook the floor upon which I stood. At each machine a white man was bent forward, working intently. To my left sunshine poured through a window, lighting up the rouge smears and making the factory look garish, violent, dangerous. It was nearing noon and my mind was drifting toward my daily lunch of a hamburger and a bag of peanuts. It had been a routine day, a day more or less like the other days I had spent on the job as errand boy and washer of eyeglasses. I was at peace with the world, that is, at peace in the only way in which a black boy in the South can be at peace with a world of white men.

Perhaps it was the mere sameness of the day that soon made it different from the other days; maybe the white men who operated the machines felt bored with their dull, automatic tasks and hankered for some kind of excitement. Anyway, I presently heard footsteps behind me and turned my head. At my elbow stood a young white man, Mr. Olin, the immediate foreman under whom I worked. He was smiling and observing me as I cleaned emery dust from the eyeglasses.

"Boy, how's it going?" he asked.

"Oh, fine, sir!" I answered with false heartiness, falling quickly into that nigger-being-a-good-natured-boy-in-the-presence-of-a-white-man pattern, a pattern into which I could now slide easily; although I was wondering if he had any criticism to make of my work.

He continued to hover wordlessly at my side. What did he want? It was unusual for him to stand there and watch me; I wanted to look at him, but was afraid to.

"Say, Richard, do you believe that I'm your friend?" he asked me.

The question was so loaded with danger that I could not reply at once. I scarcely knew Mr. Olin. My relationship to him had been the typical relationship of Negroes to southern whites. He gave me orders and I said, "Yes, sir," and obeyed them. Now, without warning, he was asking me if I thought that he was my friend; and I knew that all southern white men fancied themselves as friends of niggers. While fishing for an answer that would say nothing, I smiled.

"I mean," he persisted, "do you think I'm your friend?"

"Well," I answered, skirting the vast racial chasm between us, "I hope you are."

"I am," he said emphatically.

I continued to work, wondering what motives were prompting him. Already apprehension was rising in me.

"I want to tell you something," he said.

"Yes, sir," I said.

"We don't want you to get hurt," he explained. "We like you round here. You act like a good boy."

"Yes, sir," I said. "What's wrong?"

"You don't deserve to get into trouble," he went on.

"Have I done something that somebody doesn't like?" I asked, my mind frantically sweeping over all my past actions, weighing them in the light of the way southern white men thought Negroes should act.

"Well, I don't know," he said and paused, letting his words sink meaningfully into my mind. He lit a cigarette. "Do you know Harrison?"

He was referring to a Negro boy of about my own age who worked across the street for a rival optical house. Harrison and I knew each other casually, but there had never been the slightest trouble between us.

"Yes, sir," I said. "I know him."

"Well, be careful," Mr. Olin said. "He's after you."

"After me? For what?"

"He's got a terrific grudge against you," the white man explained. "What have you done to him?"

The eyeglasses I was washing were forgotten. My eyes were upon Mr. Olin's face, trying to make out what he meant. Was this something serious? I did not trust the white man, and neither did I trust Harrison. Negroes who worked on jobs in the South were usually loyal to their white bosses; they felt that that was the best way to ensure their jobs. Had Harrison felt that I had in some way jeopardized his job? Who was my friend: the white man or the black boy?

"I haven't done anything to Harrison," I said.

"Well, you better watch that nigger Harrison," Mr. Olin said in a low, confidential tone. "A little while ago I went down to get a Coca-Cola and Harrison was waiting for you at the door of the building with a knife. He asked me when you were coming down. Said he was going to get you. Said you called him a dirty name. Now, we don't want any fighting or bloodshed on the job."

I still doubted the white man, yet thought that perhaps Harrison had really interpreted something I had said as an insult.

"I've got to see that boy and talk to him," I said, thinking out loud.

"No, you'd better not," Mr. Olin said. "You'd better let some of us white boys talk to him."

"But how did this start?" I asked, still doubting but half believing.

"He just told me that he was going to get even with you, going to cut you and teach you a lesson," he said. "But don't you worry. Let me handle this."

He patted my shoulder and went back to his machine. He was an important man in the factory and I had always respected his word. He had the authority to order me to do this or that. Now, why would he joke with me? White men did not often joke with Negroes, therefore what he had said was serious. I was upset. We black boys worked long hard hours for what few pennies we earned and we were edgy and tense. Perhaps that crazy Harrison was really after me. My appetite was gone. I had to settle this thing. A white man had walked into my delicately balanced world and had tipped it and I had to right it before I could feel safe. Yes, I would go directly to Harrison and ask what was the matter, what I had said that he resented. Harrison was black and so was I; I would ignore the warning of the white man and talk face to face with a boy of my own color.

At noon I went across the street and found Harrison sitting on a box in the basement. He was eating lunch and reading a pulp magazine. As I approached him, he ran his hand into his pocket and looked at me with cold, watchful eyes.

"Say, Harrison, what's this all about?" I asked, standing cautiously four feet from him.

He looked at me a long time and did not answer.

"I haven't done anything to you," I said.

"And I ain't got nothing against you," he mumbled, still watchful. "I don't bother nobody."

"But Mr. Olin said that you came over to the factory this morning, looking for me with a knife."

"Aw, naw," he said, more at ease now. "I ain't been in your factory all day." He had not looked at me as he spoke.

"Then what did Mr. Olin mean?" I asked. "I'm not angry with you."

"Shucks, I thought *you* was looking for me to cut me," Harrison explained. "Mr. Olin, he came over here this morning and said you was going to kill me with a knife the moment you saw me. He said you was mad at me because I had insulted you. But I ain't said nothing about you." He still had not looked at me. He rose.

"And I haven't said anything about you," I said.

Finally he looked at me and I felt better. We two black boys, each working for ten dollars a week, stood staring at each other, thinking, comparing the motives of the absent white man, each asking himself if he could believe the other.

"But why would Mr. Olin tell me things like that?" I asked.

Harrison dropped his head; he laid his sandwich aside.

"I . . . I . . ." he stammered and pulled from his pocket a long, gleaming knife; it was already open. "I was just waiting to see what you was gonna do to me. . . ."

I leaned weakly against a wall, feeling sick, my eyes upon the sharp steel blade of the knife.

"You were going to cut me?" I asked.

"If you had cut me, I was gonna cut you first," he said. "I ain't taking no chances."

"Are you angry with me about something?" I asked.

"Man, I ain't mad at nobody," Harrison said uneasily.

I felt how close I had come to being slashed. Had I come suddenly upon Harrison, he would have thought I was trying to kill him and he would have stabbed me, perhaps killed me. And what did it matter if one nigger killed another?

"Look here," I said. "Don't believe what Mr. Olin says."

"I see now," Harrison said. "He's playing a dirty trick on us."

"He's trying to make us kill each other for nothing."

"How come he wanna do that?" Harrison asked.

I shook my head. Harrison sat, but still played with the open knife. I began to doubt. Was he really angry with me? Was he waiting until I turned my back to stab me? I was in torture.

"I suppose it's fun for white men to see niggers fight," I said, forcing a laugh.

"But you might've killed me," Harrison said.

"To white men we're like dogs or cocks," I said.

"I don't want to cut you," Harrison said.

"And I don't want to cut you," I said.

Standing well out of each other's reach, we discussed the problem and decided that we would keep silent about our conference. We would not let Mr. Olin know that we knew that he was egging us to fight. We agreed to ignore any further provocations. At one o'clock I went back to the factory. Mr. Olin was waiting for me, his manner grave, his face serious.

"Did you see that Harrison nigger?" he asked.

"No, sir," I lied.

"Well, he still has that knife for you," he said.

Hate tightened in me. But I kept a dead face.

"Did you buy a knife yet?" he asked me.

"No, sir," I answered.

"Do you want to use mine?" he asked. "You've got to protect yourself, you know."

"No, sir. I'm not afraid," I said.

"Nigger, you're a fool," he spluttered. "I thought you had some sense! Are you going to just let that nigger cut your heart out? His boss gave *him* a knife to use against *you!* Take this knife, nigger, and stop acting crazy!"

I was afraid to look at him; if I had looked at him I would have had to tell him to leave me alone, that I knew he was lying, that I knew he was no friend of mine, that I knew if anyone had thrust a knife through my heart he would simply have laughed. But I said nothing. He was the boss and he could fire me if he did not like me. He laid an open knife on the edge of his workbench, about a foot from my hand, I had a fleeting urge to pick it up and give it to him, point first into his chest. But I did nothing of the kind. I picked up the knife and put it into my pocket.

"Now, you're acting like a nigger with some sense," he said.

As I worked Mr. Olin watched me from his machine. Later when I passed him he called me.

"Now, look here, boy," he began. "We told that Harrison nigger to stay out of this building and leave you alone, see? But I can't protect you when you go home. If that nigger starts at you when you are on your way home, you stab him before he gets a chance to stab you, see?"

I avoided looking at him and remained silent.

"Suit yourself, nigger," Mr. Olin said. "But don't say I didn't warn you."

I had to make my round of errands to deliver eyeglasses and I stole a few minutes to run across the street to talk to Harrison. Harrison was sullen and bashful, wanting to trust me, but afraid. He told me that Mr. Olin had telephoned his boss and had told him to tell Harrison that I had planned to wait for him at the back entrance of the building at six o'clock and stab him. Harrison and I found it difficult to look at each other; we were upset and distrustful. We were not really angry at each other; we knew that the idea of murder had been planted in each of us by the white men who employed us. We told ourselves again and again that we did not agree with the white men; we urged ourselves to keep faith in each other. Yet there lingered deep down in each of us a suspicion that maybe one of us was trying to kill the other.

"I'm not angry with you, Harrison," I said.

"I don't wanna fight nobody," Harrison said bashfully, but he kept his hand in his pocket on his knife.

Each of us felt the same shame, felt how foolish and weak we were in the face of the domination of the whites.

"I wish they'd leave us alone," I said.

"Me too," Harrison said.

"There are a million black boys like us to run errands," I said. "They wouldn't care if we killed each other."

"I know it," Harrison said.

Was he acting? I could not believe in him. We were toying with the idea of death for no reason that stemmed from our own lives, but because the men who ruled us had thrust the idea into our minds. Each of us depended upon the whites for the bread we ate, and we actually trusted the whites more than we did each other. Yet there existed in us a longing to trust men of our own color. Again Harrison and I parted, vowing not to be influenced by what our white boss men said to us.

The game of egging Harrison and me to fight, to cut each other, kept up for a week. We were afraid to tell the white men that we did not believe them, for that would have been tantamount to calling them liars or risking an argument that might have ended in violence being directed against us.

One morning a few days later Mr. Olin and a group of white men came to me and asked me if I was willing to settle my grudge with Harrison with gloves, according to boxing rules. I told them that, though I was not afraid of Harrison, I did not want to fight him and that I did not know how to box. I could feel now that they knew I no longer believed them.

When I left the factory that evening, Harrison yelled at me from down the block. I waited and he ran toward me. Did he want to cut me? I backed away as he approached. We smiled uneasily and sheepishly at each other. We spoke haltingly, weighing our words.

"Did they ask you to fight me with gloves?" Harrison asked.

"Yes," I told him. "But I didn't agree."

Harrison's face became eager.

"They want us to fight four rounds for five dollars apiece," he said. "Man, if I had five dollars, I could pay down on a suit. Five dollars is almost half a week's wages for me."

"I don't want to," I said.

"We won't hurt each other," he said.

"But why do a thing like that for white men?"

"To get that five dollars."

"I don't need five dollars that much."

"Aw, you're a fool," he said. Then he smiled quickly.

"Now, look here," I said. "Maybe you *are* angry with me. . . ."

"Naw, I'm not." He shook his head vigorously.

"I don't want to fight for white men. I'm no dog or rooster."

I was watching Harrison closely and he was watching me closely. Did he really want to fight me for some reason of his own? Or was it the money? Harrison stared at me with puzzled eyes. He stepped toward me and I stepped away. He smiled nervously.

"I need that money," he said.

"Nothing doing," I said.

He walked off wordlessly, with an air of anger. Maybe he will stab me now, I thought. I got to watch that fool. . . .

For another week the white men of both factories begged us to fight. They made up stories about what Harrison had said about me; and when they saw Harrison they lied to him in the same way. Harrison and I were wary of each other whenever we met. We smiled and kept out of arm's reach, ashamed of ourselves and of each other.

Again Harrison called to me one evening as I was on my way home.

"Come on and fight," he begged.

"I don't want to and quit asking me," I said in a voice louder and harder than I had intended.

Harrison looked at me and I watched him. Both of us still carried the knives that the white men had given us.

"I wanna make a payment on a suit of clothes with that five dollars," Harrison said.

"But those white men will be looking at us, laughing at us," I said.

"What the hell," Harrison said. "They look at you and laugh at you every day, nigger."

It was true. But I hated him for saying it. I ached to hit him in his mouth, to hurt him.

"What have we got to lose?" Harrison asked.

"I don't suppose we have anything to lose," I said.

"Sure," he said. "Let's get the money. We don't care."

"And now they know that we know what they tried to do to us," I said, hating myself for saying it. "And they hate us for it."

"Sure," Harrison said. "So let's get the money. You can use five dollars, can't you?"

"Yes."

"Then let's fight for 'em."

"I'd feel like a dog."

"To them, both of us are dogs," he said.

"Yes," I admitted. But again I wanted to hit him.

"Look, let's fool them white men," Harrison said. "We won't hurt each other. We'll just pretend, see? We'll show 'em we ain't dumb as they think, see?"

"I don't know."

"It's just exercise. Four rounds for five dollars. You scared?"

"No."

"Then come on and fight."

"All right," I said. "It's just exercise. I'll fight."

Harrison was happy. I felt that it was all very foolish. But what the hell. I would go through with it and that would be the end of it. But I still felt a vague anger that would not leave.

When the white men in the factory heard that we had agreed to fight, their excitement knew no bounds. They offered to teach me new punches. Each morning they would tell me in whispers that Harrison was eating raw onions for strength. And—from Harrison—I heard that they told him I was eating raw meat for strength. They offered to buy me my meals each day, but I refused. I grew ashamed of what I had agreed to do and wanted to back out of the fight, but I was afraid that they would be angry if I tried to. I felt that if white men tried to persuade two black boys to stab each other for no other reason save their own pleasure, then it would not be difficult for them to aim a wanton blow at a black boy in a fit of anger, in a passing mood of frustration.

The fight took place one Saturday afternoon in the basement of a Main Street building. Each white man who attended the fight dropped his share of the pot into a hat that sat on the concrete floor. Only white men were allowed in the basement; no women or Negroes were admitted. Harrison and I were stripped to the waist. A bright electric bulb glowed above our heads. As the gloves were tied on my hands, I looked at Harrison and saw his eyes watching me. Would he keep his promise? Doubt made me nervous.

We squared off and at once I knew that I had not thought sufficiently about what I had bargained for. I could not pretend to fight. Neither Harrison nor I knew enough about boxing to deceive even a child for a moment. Now shame filled me. The white men were smokng and yelling obscenities at us.

"Crush that nigger's nuts, nigger!"

"Hit that nigger!"

"Aw, fight, you goddamn niggers!"

"Sock 'im in his f--k--g piece!"

"Make 'im bleed!"

I lashed out with a timid left. Harrison landed high on my head and, before I knew it, I had landed a hard right on Harrison's mouth and blood came. Harrison shot a blow to my nose. The fight was on, was on against our will. I felt trapped and ashamed. I lashed out even harder, and the harder I fought the harder Harrison fought. Our plans and promises now meant nothing. We fought four hard rounds, stabbing, slugging, grunting, spitting, cursing, crying, bleeding. The shame and anger we felt for having allowed ourselves to be duped crept into our blows and blood ran into our eyes, half blinding us. The hate we felt for the men whom we had tried to cheat went into the blows we threw at each other. The white men made the rounds last as long as five minutes and each of us was afraid to stop and ask for time for fear of receiving a blow that would knock us out. When we were on the point of collapsing from exhaustion, they pulled us apart.

I could not look at Harrison. I hated him and I hated myself. I clutched my five dollars in my fist and walked home. Harrison and I avoided each other after that and we rarely spoke. The white men attempted to arrange other fights for us, but we had sense enough to refuse. I heard of other fights being staged between other black boys, and each time I heard those plans falling from the lips of the white men in the factory I eased out of earshot. I felt that I had done something unclean, something for which I could never properly atone.

Frank Conroy / White Days and Red Nights

The special attribute of Frank Conroy's account of his experiences is that he is able to show how being left alone can fill ordinary hours with as many horrors as are to be found among the inmates of the terror-filled world that is the Southbury Training School for the feeble minded. Alone all night while his parents are at work, he animates his world—and his writing about it—with fantasies of terror nearly as compelling as those he will eventually encounter in the flesh. Enduring the "overbearing, undeniable reality of those empty days" of winter, either alone in the cabin or sitting for hours silently while his parents sleep, he becomes as nearly lost to himself as the unfortunate patient to whom, as he later discovers, he bears a physical resemblance. His confrontations at the school make him aware that his solitary fantasies of terror are after all a "lower order of reality." But they are reality nonetheless. Indeed to compare the style of his conversations with his parents—open, direct, a bit aggressive in a comradely way even when they are mistreating him—with the style of his recollected responses to sights and sounds is to see with what remarkable distinctness Conroy can hold together in his mind the various worlds of his childhood and communicate the fearful coherence of one with the other.

Jean and my mother had weekend jobs as wardens at the Southbury Training School, a Connecticut state institution for the feeble-minded. Every Friday afternoon we drove out deep in the hills to an old cabin they had bought for a few hundred dollars on the installment plan.

The first dirt road was always plowed for the milk truck, but never the second, and in the snow you could see the tracks of wagon wheels and two narrow trails where the horses had walked. A mile down the road was the Greens' farm. Every morning they hauled milk to the pick-up station, a full silent load up to the hill, and then back, the empty returns from the previous day clanging raucously behind the horses as if in melancholic celebration. No one else ever used the road. If it was passable we drove to the cabin, if not, we walked, single file, in the horses' tracks, our arms full of food.

Every Friday the cheap padlock was opened, every Friday I stepped inside. A room so dim my blood turned gray, so cold I knew no human heart had ever beaten there—every line, every article of furniture, every scrap of paper on the floor, every burned-out match in a saucer filling me with desolation, depopulating me. A single room, twelve feet by eighteen. A double bed, a bureau, a round table to eat on, and against the wall a counter with a kerosene cooker. In the exact center of the room, a pot-bellied coal stove. All these objects had been watched by me in a state of advanced terror, watched so many long nights that even in the daytime they seemed to be whispering bad messages.

My mother would make a quick meal out of cans. Corned-beef hash or chile. Conversation was usually sparse.

"I have a good cottage tonight."

"I can't remember where I am. We'd better stop at the administration building."

Outside, the lead-gray afternoon slipped almost imperceptibly into twilight. Very gradually the earth moved toward night and as I sat eating I noted every darkening shadow. Jean sipped his coffee and lighted a Pall Mall. My mother arranged the kerosene lamp so she could see to do the dishes.

"Frank, get me some water."

Through the door and into the twilight, the bucket against my thigh. There was a path beaten through the snow, a dark line curving through the drifts to the well. The low sky was empty, uniformly leaden. Stands of trees spread pools of darkness, as if night came up from their sunken roots. At the well I tied a rope to the handle of the bucket and dropped it into the darkness upside down, holding the line. The trick was not to hit the sides. I heard a muffled splash.

Leaning over the deep hole, with the faintest hint of warmer air rising against my face, I hauled the bucket hand over hand until it rose suddenly into view, the dim sky shimmering within like some luminous oil. Back to the house with the water. Absolute silence except for the sounds of my own movement, absolute stillness except for a wavering line of smoke from the stovepipe.

While Mother did the dishes Jean and I sat at the table. He sipped at his second cup of coffee. I fished a dime out of my pocket. "Could you get me a couple of Baby Ruth bars?"

Jean sucked his teeth and reached for a wooden pick. "The stuff is poison. It rots your teeth."

"Oh Jean, I know. It won't take you a second. There's a stand in the administration building."

"You're so finicky about food and you go and eat that stuff. Can you imagine the crap in those mass-produced candy bars? Dead roaches and mouse shit and somebody's nose-pickings."

"Jean, for heaven's sake!" My mother laughed.

"Well, he won't touch a piece of perfectly good meat and then he'll eat that junk."

"It'll only take you a second." I pushed the dime across the table.

"I know the trouble with you. You're too lazy to chew your food. You wash everything down with milk." He glanced at the coin, his eyes flicking away. "All right. If you want to kill yourself. Keep the dime." He finished his coffee and cigarette slowly, savoring the mixed flavors and the moment of rest. Since he'd stopped using the holder his smoking style had changed. He'd take a quick drag, blow out about a third of the smoke immediately, inhale the rest, and let it come out as he talked. I often made it a point to sit in such a way that a strong light source behind him showed up the smoke. It was amazing how long it came out, a fine, almost invisible blue stream, phrase after phrase, changing direction smoothly as he clipped off the words. For some reason I admired this phenomenon tremendously. I could sit watching for hours.

Jean pushed back his chair and stood up, stretching his arms and yawning exaggeratedly. Even this he did gracefully. Like a cat, he was incapable of making an awkward move. Looking out the window he sucked his teeth noisily. "Well," he said slowly, "the lions and tigers seem to be under control tonight."

I felt my face flush and quickly turned away. It was a complicated moment. My fear of staying alone in the house had been totally ignored for weeks. For Jean to mention it at all was somehow promising, and I was grateful despite the unfairness of his phrasing. He knew of course that it wasn't lions and tigers I was afraid of—by using that image he was attempting to simplify my fear into the realm of childishness (which he could then ignore in good conscience) as well as to shame me out of it. Jean was telling me, with a smile, that my behavior was irrational and therefore he could do nothing to help me, something I would never have expected in any case. I knew perfectly well that no one could help me. The only possible solution would have been for me to stay in the city on weekends with Alison, but that battle had been lost. Jean and Mother wanted me with them. Not because they felt they had to look after me but because I was useful. I drew the water. I tended the fire so the house would be warm in the morning when they returned.

"We'd better go," Mother said, lifting the last dripping dish from the plastic basin. "Frank, you dry the dishes and put them away."

I watched their preparations with a sense of remoteness. It was as if they were already gone. Mother dried her hands carefully and put on her heavy coat. Jean bent over the row of paperback books and pulled out an Erskine Caldwell. "I won't be able to read tonight but I'll take it anyway."

"All right?" Mother asked. They stood for a last moment, waiting, making sure they hadn't forgotten anything, sensing in each other the precise moment to leave. Then they were through the door and away. I followed a few moments later, stepping in their footprints to the road. I watched them walk into the darkness underneath the trees. My mother turned at the top of a rise and called back to me over the snow. "Don't forget to set the alarm!" She hurried to catch up with Jean. As they moved down the hill it was as if they sank deeper and deeper into the snow. Dimly I could make out the top halves of their bodies, then only their shoulders, their heads, and they were gone.

I went back to the house. After an initial surge of panic my mind turned itself off. Thinking was dangerous. By not thinking I attained a kind of inner invisibility. I knew that fear attracted evil, that the uncontrolled sound of my own mind would in some way delineate me to the forces threatening me, as the thrashing of a fish in shallow water draws the gull. I tried to keep still, but every now and then the fear escalated up into consciousness and my mind would stir, readjusting itself like the body of a man trying to sleep in an uncomfortable position. In those moments I felt most vulnerable, my eyes widening and my ears straining to catch the sound of approaching danger.

I dried the dishes slowly and put them away, attempting to do the whole job without making a sound. Occasionally a floorboard creaked under my weight, sending a long, lingering charge up my spine, a white thrill at once delicious and ominous. I approached the stove nervously. The coal rattled and the cast-iron grate invariably banged loudly despite my precautions. I had to do it quickly, holding my breath, or I wouldn't do it at all. Once finished I checked the window latches. There was nothing to be done about the door; it couldn't be locked from the inside and mother refused to lock it from the outside because of the danger of my getting trapped in a fire.

By the yellow light of the kerosene lamp I sat on the edge of the bed and removed my shoes, placing them carefully on the floor. The Big Ben alarm clock ticked off the seconds on a shelf above my head, and every now and then a puff of coal gas popped in the stove as the fuel shifted. I got under the covers fully clothed and surveyed the stillness of the room, trying to slow my breathing. For an hour or more I lay motionless in a self-induced trance, my eyes open but seldom moving, my ears listening to the sounds of the house and the faint, inexplicable, continuous noises from outside. (In this state my ears seemed rather far away. I was burrowed somewhere deep in my skull, my ears advance outposts sending back reports to headquarters.) As I remember it the trance must have been close to the real thing. It was an attempt to reach an equipoise of fear, a state in which the incoming fear signals balanced with some internal process of dissimulation. At best it worked only temporarily, since fear held a slight edge. But for an hour or two I avoided what I hated most, the great noisy swings up and down. The panic and the hilarity.

At the first flashing thought of the Southbury Training School I sat up and took a book from the shelf. Escaped inmates were rare, and supposedly harmless, but I knew that a runaway had ripped the teats from one of the Greens' cows with a penknife, and that another had strangled four cats in a barnyard. I read quickly, skimming the pages for action and dialogue while most of my mind stood on guard. Book after book came down from the shelf, piling up on the bed beside me as I waited for sleep. I knew that if I left the lamp on I would stay awake most of the night, so when the pages began to go out of focus I set the alarm clock, cupped my hand over the mouth of the lamp chimney and blew myself into darkness.

Being sleepy and being scared do not cancel each other out. After hours of waiting the mind insists and slips under itself into unconsciousness. The sleeping body remains tense, the limbs bent as if poised for flight, adrenalin oozing steadily into the blood. Every few minutes the mind awakens, listens, and goes back to sleep. Fantastic dreams attempt to absorb the terror, explaining away the inexplicable with lunatic logic, twisting thought to a mad, private vision so that sleep can go on for another few seconds.

I wake up in the dark, a giant hand squeezing my heart. All around me a tremendous noise is splitting the air, exploding like a continuous chain of fireworks. The alarm clock! My God, the clock! Ringing all this time, calling, calling, bringing everything evil. I reach out and shut it off. The vibrations die out under my fingers and I listen to the silence, wondering if anything has approached under the cover of the ringing bell. (Remember a children's game called Giant Steps?)

I sit up cautiously. My body freezes. Rising before me over the foot of the bed is a bright, glowing, cherry-red circle in the darkness, a floating globe pulsating with energy, wavering in the air like the incandescent heart of some dissected monster, dripping sparks and blood. I throw myself backward against the wall behind the bed. Books tumble around me from the shelves, an ashtray falls and smashes on the floor. My hands go out, palms extended, towards the floating apparition, my voice whispering "Please . . ." Impossibly a voice answers, a big voice from all around me. "FRANK! FRANK!" My knees give out and I fall off the bed to the floor. I can feel the pieces of broken ashtray under my hands.

From the corner of my eye I see the red circle. I keep quite still, and the circle doesn't move. If I turn my head I seem to sense a corresponding movement, but I can't be sure. In the blackness there is nothing to relate to. Step by step I begin to understand. My body grows calmer and it's as if a series of veils were being whisked away from my eyes. I see clearly that the circle is only the red-hot bottom of the stove—a glowing bowl, its surface rippling with color changes from draughts of cool air. The last veil lifts and reveals an image of magic beauty, a sudden miracle in the night. I fall asleep watching it, my shoulder against the bed.

Hours later the cold wakes me and I climb up under the covers. When dawn comes my limbs relax. I can tell when the dawn has come even though I'm asleep.

I woke up when the wagon went by, creaking like a ship, passing close, just on the other side of the wall by my head. Chip would be driving, I knew, with Toad in back watching the cans. They never spoke as they went by. Sometimes Chip would murmur to the horses, "Haw, gee-aw." The traces rang quietly and the tall iron-rimmed wheels splintered rocks under the snow.

It was hard to get out of bed. The air was cold. Water froze in the bucket and the windows were coated with ice. The light was gray, exactly the same quality as the twilight of the night before, devoid of meaning. I cleaned out the stove, laid paper, a few sticks of kindling and some coal, splashed kerosene over everything, and struck a match. With a great whoosh the stove filled with flames. My teeth chattering, I rushed back under the covers. I fell asleep waiting to get warm.

When Jean and my mother came through the door I woke up. They seemed tremendously alive, busting with energy, their voices strangely loud.

"It's freezing in here. What happened to the fire?" I sat up in bed. The fire had gone out, or more likely had never caught after the kerosene had burned.

"You forgot to set the alarm," my mother said.

"No I didn't."

She knelt and relit the fire. Jean stood in the open doorway, knocking snow off his galoshes. He closed the door and sat on the edge of the bed, bending over to open the buckles. "My God, it's cold. We should have stayed in Florida."

"I vote for that," I said.

"Just get your ass out of that bed." He rubbed his stocking feet and twisted up his face. "How about some coffee?"

"Just a second," my mother said, still fussing with the stove.

Jean stood up and undid his belt. "Okay. Let's go." He waited till I was out of bed, took off his trousers, and climbed in. The heavy black and red flannel shirt he wore in cold weather was left on, buttoned tight over his narrow chest. He ran a finger over his mustache and waited for his cup of coffee.

Mother made it for him while I fixed a bowl of cornflakes.

"It's not very much to ask to keep the stove going," my mother said. "I never ask you to do anything."

I ate my cornflakes. The stove was beginning to give off a little heat and I pulled my chair closer, arranging it so my back was to the bed. I heard Mother undressing, and then the creak of the rusty springs as she got in beside Jean. From that moment on I was supposed to keep quiet so they could sleep.

There was no place else to go. Outside the land was hidden under two and a half feet of snow. The wind was sharp and bitter (I found out later that locals considered it the worst winter in forty years) and in any case I didn't have the proper clothes. Even indoors, sitting in the chair with the stove going, I kept a blanket wrapped around me Indian style. The time dragged slowly. There was nothing to do. I tried to save the few books for nighttime, when my need of them was greater. I drew things with a pencil—objects in the room, my hand, imaginary scenes—but I was no good and quickly lost interest. Usually I simply sat in the chair for six or seven hours. Jean snored softly, but after the first hour or so I stopped hearing it.

Midway through the morning I remembered the candy bars. Certain Jean had forgotten them, I looked anyway, getting up from the chair carefully, tiptoeing to his clothes and searching through the pockets. Nothing. I watched him in bed, his face gray with sleep, his open mouth twitching at the top of each gentle snore. My mother turned to the wall. Jean closed his mouth and rolled over. The room was absolutely silent. I went back to the chair.

They awoke in the early afternoon and stayed in bed. Although the small stove was working it was still the warmest place. Freed from the necessity of keeping quiet, I walked around the room aimlessly, getting a drink of water, rubbing the haze off the windows to look outside. My mother raised her voice and I realized she was talking to me.

"Take some money from my purse and go down to the Greens' and get a dozen eggs."

The trip to the Greens' would take an hour each way. Outside the temperature was five or ten degrees above zero and it was windy. I didn't want to go. My heart sank because I knew I had to.

Children are in the curious position of having to do what people tell them, whether they want to or not. A child knows that he must do what he's told. It matters little whether a command is just or unjust since the child has no confidence in his ability to distinguish the difference. Justice for children is not the same as justice for adults. In effect all commands are morally neutral to a child. Yet because almost every child is consistently bullied by older people he quickly learns that if in some higher frame of reference all commands are equally just, they are not equally easy to carry out. Some fill him with joy, others, so obviously unfair that he must paralyze himself to keep from recognizing their quality, strike him instantly deaf, blind, and dumb. Faced with an order they sense is unfair children simply stall. They wait for more information, for some elaboration that will take away the seeming unfairness. It's a stupid way of defending oneself, but children are stupid compared to adults, who know how to get what they want.

"Couldn't we wait until they come up with the wagon?"

"No. The walk will do you good. You can't sit around all day, it's unhealthy."

"Oh Mother, it'll take hours."

Suddenly Jean sat up, his voice trembling with anger. "Look, this time just go. No arguments this time."

I looked at him in amazement. He'd never even raised his voice to me before. It was against the unwritten rules—my mother was the disciplinarian. I could see he was angry and I had no idea why. Even my mother was surprised. "Take it easy," she said to him softly. "He's going."

Jean's anger should have tipped me off, but it didn't. Wearing his galoshes and his overcoat I went to the Greens' without realizing why they had sent me.

It was no secret that I wanted to go along to the training school at night, to sleep on an extra bed somewhere. For months Mother put me off, but when she realized I would never get accustomed to staying alone she gave in. She was tired of dealing with me, tired of my complaints and my silences. (Alternative unconscious motivations for her change of heart: one, she felt guilty about me; two, she decided to show me something that was worth being afraid of—namely, the worst men's cottage, to which Jean was assigned the night I tagged along.)

We drove slowly down the steep, twisting road to Southbury, our headlight beams traversing back and forth across the snow. Jean leaned over the wheel, craning his neck to watch for the cutoff through the black truncated trees. "It's along here somewhere."

"We have to pass that boarded-up farmhouse," my mother said.

"Here it is." He applied the brakes slowly and the tires pulled against the sanded road. We were entering the grounds through the back, saving a mile. The car bumped along through the woods for a few hundred yards and then emerged at the top of a hill.

The Southbury Training School spread below us like a toy village in a Christmas display. Small dormitories disguised to look like suburban homes were spread evenly over a square mile of stripped and graded hillside. Halfway down, the two administrative buildings rose into the air, their white cupolas lighted by floodlights. Weaving across the hillside in every direction were the lines and curves of a network of private roads, described in the darkness by chains of street lights winking on slender poles.

Jean edged the Ford over the lip of the hill and the bumpy dirt road changed immediately to a smooth, carefully plowed asphalt ribbon. We rolled along silently, watching the powdered snow drift across the surface of the road under the headlights.

"There it is," my mother said as we approached one of the dormitories. "Number Twelve."

Jean pulled up in the driveway. There was a brass knocker on the front door, and a mailbox, and a green metal tube on a stand with *"Danbury Times"* written in elaborate lettering. I caught some movement out of the corner of my eye. The blinds were raised in one of the ground-floor windows and a girl stood combing her hair with long, even strokes. She saw the lights of the car and smiled. Half her teeth were gone. I looked away quickly.

My mother rang the bell and stood close to the door to be out of the wind. Almost immediately it swung open, spilling a long bar of yellow light across the snow. She lifted her hand in a signal that could just as easily have meant we should wait a moment as to wave goodbye, and was gone.

We drove slowly across the hill toward the boys' side of the school. In the bad weather the roads were empty.

"It looks deserted," I said.

"It isn't. Wait till you get inside."

The tires spun on a patch of ice as we climbed the driveway to Cottage Eight. We stopped next to a black Chevy, the only car in the parking area. Its windshield was coated with snow.

"That's Olsen's car. He has the shift before mine."

"It's brand new."

"Some of these guys work two shifts. They make a lot of money."

"Why don't you?"

He laughed. We sat for a moment, watching the building. Jean took out a cigarette. "The smell is pretty bad at first but after a couple of hours you don't notice it."

I could see small ways in which the building differed from the one my mother had entered. There was no box for the newspaper, no potted evergreens at the edge of the drive. Even in the darkness one could see that the front door needed painting. Some of the shutters were closed.

"None of these people are dangerous, are they?"

Jean finished his cigarette. "They're just feeble-minded. They can't take care of themselves."

We stepped out of the car. The air was cold and gusts of wind seemed to pass uninterrupted through my clothes. After a few steps the smell began, like a tangible line in space. Smells are hard to describe. This was a combination of pine, vomit, licorice, old urine, sweat, soap, and wet hair. Jean rang the bell and after a few moments the door opened.

I was prepared, of course, but prepared through my imagination, and I couldn't possibly have imagined the reality. First of all it was hot, really hot, like a furnace room. I began to sweat immediately. The smell was overpowering. It was useless to breathe carefully as I'd done outside; here the smell was so pungent and thick it seemed to have taken the place of air—a hot substitute filling my lungs, seeping into my blood, and making me its own creature. With the first deep breath I was no longer an air breather. I'd changed to another species.

It was noisy. A noise that raised the hair on the back of my neck. Far-out throats, tongues, and lips forming sounds that wound their independent way up and down the scale with no relation to anything. Whispering, mumbling, fake laughter and true laughter, bubbling sounds, short screams, bored humming, weeping, long roller-coaster yells—all of it in random dynamic waves like some futuristic orchestra. In this meaningless music were sudden cries of such intense human significance that I stood paralyzed.

It was as if all the saints, martyrs, and mystics of human history were gathered into a single building, each one crying out at the moment of revelation, each one truly *there* at his extreme of joy or pain, crying out with the purity of total selflessness. There was no arguing with these sudden voices above the general clamor, they rang true. All around me were men in a paroxysm of discovery, seeing lands I had never known existed, calling me with a strength I had never known existed. But they called from every direction with equal power, so I couldn't answer. I stood balanced on the pinpoint of my own sanity, a small, cracked tile on the floor.

"They're a little noisy now. It's just before bedtime and we let them blow off some steam."

I looked up and discovered a huge man standing in front of me, smiling. Involuntarily I took a step backward. He was all eyes, immense white eyes impossibly out of his head, rushing at me. No, he was wearing his eyes like glasses. Two bulbous eyes in steel frames. He turned his head and the illusion disappeared. Thick lenses, that was all. His bald head gleamed with sweat. His arm was as big as my leg.

"I'm Olsen," he said.

"Where's Jean?"

"He'll be back in a minute."

There was movement behind his back. I watched from the corner of my eye, afraid to look directly. A naked man slipping into the room, hunched over like a beaten dog, a shiny thread of spittle hanging from his jaw. He cruised silently along the wall, limp fingers touching the plaster, turned, and stopped, his shaggy head facing the blank wall one inch away. Without even looking Olsen raised his voice and said, "Back to bed."

The creature lifted one leg and touched his toes to the surface of the wall as if it was a ladder he was about to climb. Below the tangle of black hair in his crotch, his veined penis and scrotum hung limply almost halfway to the knee, against the inside of his thigh. It was as if they'd been grabbed and stretched like soft taffy. His toes scratched the wall. Olsen took a step toward him, leaning over slightly, and clapped his hands smartly. "Back to bed!" The creature scurried along the wall and disappeared through an open doorway. For the first time I noticed there were no doors. Doorways without doors. From each darkened passageway the noises rushed at us. Suddenly, the sound of a crash. Olsen knew just where it came from. "Back in a second," he said.

Alone in the room, I stood by the door, my hand touching the knob. I could hear Olsen shouting in another part of the building. Far back in the corridors half-visible figures were moving in the dim light. I supposed that Jean was with them.

An old man appeared, hesitating at the edge of the room. When he saw me he froze instantly, like a highly trained hunting animal. His watery blue eyes were fuzzy spirals and his cheeks sank into his head, making hollows the size of pingpong balls. He wore a kind of diaper from which his skinny legs, all tendon and finely wrinkled skin, emerged, half bent with age. He took a step forward.

"Back to bed!" I said. "Back to bed!" For a moment he didn't move, then, leaning his head back, he opened his mouth and revealed two gleaming pink gums, toothless, looking like wet rubber. His thin shoulders shook with laughter. When his fuzzy eyes found me he shouted across the room.

"Sonny, I've been here since before you were born. I don't even belong here. I belong in a mental hospital. Everybody knows that." He turned and left the room.

I wanted to wait outside until Jean came back. There was a large brass lock high on the door. I turned what seemed to be the appropriate knob but the bolt didn't move. Examining the mechanism more closely, I heard a noise behind me.

Something was rushing down one of the corridors, something low and fast. No bullfighter ever waited for his foe more apprehensively. To my amazement I found myself giving a short, nervous laugh, a desperate guffaw in the teeth of my predicament. Zooming into the room was a flash of chrome-man, a monstrous human machine blurred with speed, bearing down on me like a homicidal hot-rodder. A man in a wheelchair, but what kind of man? His body was tiny, like a child's, his head impossibly huge, the size of a watermelon. Flailing at the wheels of his chair like a beserk rowboat enthusiast, he backed me into a corner and threw his hands into my face.

"See my pretty 'racelet?" he said in a high voice. "See my pretty 'racelet?"

Flinching, twisting to avoid the touch of his wild hands, I tried to slip past. He slammed his chair into the wall and trapped me.

"See my pretty 'racelet?"

"What? What do you want? What?" Reluctantly I looked him in the eye. His bland idiot's features seemed small in the gargantuan hydrocephalic head. All scrunched together in the cavity that was his face they stared out at me like a fish from a goldfish bowl.

"See my pretty 'racelet?" he said, still holding his arms up. In a tantrum of infantile frustration he drummed his heels against the bottom of the chair. "See! See!"

"He wants you to look at his bracelet," Jean said, grabbing the back of the chair and pulling him away. "This is Freddie. His nickname is pinhead."

"Pinhead, pinhead! See!"

"Go ahead," Jean said. "Just look at it."

Around the creature's wrist was a cheap chrome I.D. bracelet. He held his hand motionless when he realized I was looking at it. The word FREDDIE was engraved in block letters. I touched it with my index finger. "It's very pretty. Very nice."

"Pretty 'racelet?" Freddie said, calmer now.

"Yes. Very pretty."

"Pretty 'racelet?"

Olsen appeared from one of the corridors. His big feet clomped noisily on the tile floor. "Time for lights out?"

"Okay," Jean answered, rolling Freddie away. "Frank, you can go in the office." He pointed to an open doorway.

Freddie rocked back and forth in the chair. "Lice-out. Lice-out. Lice-out."

Olsen reached out and slapped his immense dome with an open hand. "Shut up, idiot." They rolled him down one of the corridors.

The office was a small room with a desk, a chair, and a cot. There was no door to close. I sat on the cot and watched the blank wall. As Jean and Olsen progressed through the building turning out lights, the screaming gradually subsided, falling to a steady murmur like the crowd noises in a movie. It was less nerve-wracking, but somehow more ominous. The mood in the building was changing from wildness to slyness. Plans were beginning to cook in countless heads, and as a novelty, a break in the routine, it seemed to me that I would be the focus. I jumped up nervously as Olsen came in. He looked down at me, his big white eyes embedded in their surrealistic lenses. "I'm going off now. I want to show you something."

I followed him out of the office, sticking close behind. We took a few steps into a hallway and stopped. In the gloom stray rays of light collected in his glasses like fireflies.

"The boys are harmless. They're scareder of you than you are of them, so you got nothing to worry about. I want to show you this guy so you know what he looks like. A couple of times he's grabbed a broom and snuck up behind somebody and belted them. If he ever tries anything all you got to do is look him in the eye and he backs down."

"Maybe it's better if he doesn't see me."

"He won't. He can't see past the light."

There was a snapping sound and a powerful flashlight beam showed us a glowing circle of green wall. We took a few steps and the beam spilled into a small room. With a flick of his wrist Olsen found the occupant, sitting on his bed, knees drawn up to his chest, rocking slowly back and forth. (In the South they call it hunkering.) He looked young, and strong—completely normal except for his nakedness and the fixed expression of anger on his face. His eyes blinked in the strong light but he didn't look away. The creaking of the bedsprings stopped as he held himself rigid. He seemed to be looking directly into my eyes in a contest of wills. Suddenly his head jerked forward and a glob of spittle curved through the air and fell at my feet.

"Tough guy," said Olsen. "Once he threw his own shit at me. But he'll never do that again."

My eyes were locked with the inmate's. "Did you punish him?"

"Punish him!" Olsen laughed. "I beat the living daylights out of him. He was in the infirmary for three days."

"Did he understand?"

"What?"

"Did he understand why you hit him?"

"He didn't throw no more shit so I guess he did."

"What's his name?"

"Gregory."

"Can we go back now?"

"He doesn't know how lucky he is. He's the only one in the building with a room of his own. Look." He flashed his light up the hall. Beds were set up along the walls of the corridor. People were sitting up in them watching us silently. Most of them fell back as the light struck them, like dominoes in a row. To the rest Olsen yelled "Lights out! Bedtime!"

"Can we go back now?"

Olsen had gone off duty and Jean and I were in the office.

"Lovely, isn't it," Jean said sitting on the edge of the desk.

"Is there any place with a door? I'd feel better with a door."

"No, but you'll be all right."

"What about that guy named Gregory?"

"He won't do anything. He's probably asleep. They go to sleep like *that*." He snapped his fingers. After a moment he raised his head and stared out the doorway. "Isn't it incredible the way some of them are hung? They've got equipment a horse would be proud of."

"Jean, I don't think I can make it."

"It's perfectly safe." He stood up. "I've got to make the rounds."

"I can't stay here."

"Well I can't take you back. You'll just have to."

"I'll sleep in the car."

"It's freezing out there."

"I'll take some blankets. It'll be all right."

He stood for a moment without answering.

"Please, Jean."

"Okay. Suit yourself. I've got to make the rounds." He started out, then looked back. "If it gets too cold out there you'd better come back in."

"I will. Yes. Thanks." Quickly I began to strip the blankets from the cot. Then, remembering, I rushed after him. "Jean! The lock! How do you work the lock?"

So for the rest of the winter I stayed in the cabin at night. I never got used to it, but in some ways the nights were better than the days. The nights were warm fantasies of terror, Technicolor nightmares. I recognized somehow that everything happening to me alone at night in the cabin was of a low order of reality. My hallucinations, the fear itself, the entire drama came from inside my own head. I was *making* it all, and although it was terrifying, it was not, as were the days, cosmically threatening.

The days were emptiness, a vast, spacious emptiness in which the fact of being alive became almost meaningless. The first fragile beginnings of a personality starting to collect in my twelve-year-old soul were immediately sucked up into the silence and the featureless winter sky. The overbearing, undeniable reality of those empty days! The inescapable fact that everything around me was nonhuman, that in terms of snow and sky and rocks and dormant trees I didn't exist, these things rendered me invisible even to myself. I wasn't conscious of what was happening, I lived it. I became invisible. I lost myself.

At night I materialized. The outlines of my body were hot, flushed, sharply defined. My senses were heightened. I knew I was real as I animated the darkness with extensions of myself. If the sky was more real than I was, than I was more real than my phantoms.

But the days predominated. The flat sky. As the winter passed a sense of desolation invaded my mind. I wasn't afraid, it was too nebulous for that, but I was profoundly uneasy. Perhaps in the back of my mind was the fear that everything would go blank, that I would become the sky, without a body, without thought. I remembered the peculiarly impersonal quality of some of the screams in Cottage Eight.

In the spring I started going down to the school just to hang around, walking the four miles with a quarter in my pocket to get a milkshake at the soda fountain in the administration building. I roamed freely through the public rooms. In a scaled-down bowling alley I used to set up the pins for myself after each frame. Sometimes there were movies in the auditorium. I'd wait for a group of boys to come across the lawn behind their counselor and tag along at the end. I remember a conversation I had one day before a Gene Autry picture with a boy who attracted my attention because I thought he looked exactly like me.

"Who're you?" he asked. "Are you new?"

"No. I'm Mr. Fouchet's son."

"He takes our cottage at night sometimes. He's okay. He never hits you."

"Do the others?"

"Some of them."

(Whistles and applause as Mr. Miller, the director of the school, climbs on stage to make a few announcements before the picture. I laugh at the wildness of the audience. They're having a great time.)

"I'm going home next week," the boy says. "If you're around you'll see the car. It's a red Buick."

"We have a Ford."

"My pop's a policeman. He carries a gun."

(More whistles and cheers as the house lights go down and the picture begins. I watch the boy. There's no way to tell anything is wrong with him.)

The Southbury school affected me more deeply than I realized at the time. Most immediately it was a place in which being different was a good thing—I was different only because I wasn't feeble-minded. My general loneliness in the world was dramatized microcosmically, in terms favorable to myself.

I believed I was intelligent. For a long time that thought had been important to me. At the school I felt for the first time that my intelligence was worth something to someone else besides myself. Here was a huge organization, an immense, powerful world existing for the inmate, but existing for me as well. I was the other extreme! At last I'd found someplace where my only possession would be relevant! To picture myself as being aware of all this would be a misrepresentation. I wasn't vain. I didn't look down on the boys. In some ways I needed the school as much as they did, and I certainly felt closer to them than to the children at conventional schools.

But of course the Southbury school, except for one incident, was as uninterested in me as the world it represented. Which is as it should be. While I passed through the attenuated agonies of growing up, trying to get through to a psychologist in the library of the administration building, there were boys next door who were never going to grow up at all, boys who would starve to death without someone to feed them.

I was alone in the library reading *Life* magazine. A man stopped in the hallway and looked at me through the double glass doors. I watched him come in without raising my head.

"Hi," he said casually. "What are you reading?"

"Just this magazine."

"It's a good issue. I've read it myself." He spoke to me as if we were old friends. "You remember me, don't you?"

It came to me in a flash. He'd mistaken me for one of the boys. Perhaps the boy from the movies who looked so much like me. A bewildering array of emotions exploded simultaneously—confusion, embarrassment, a kind of childish love, apprehensiveness, but behind it all, as steady as the solid bar of sunlight across the polished table, triumph. The moment was at hand.

"Of course you're not really reading it, are you?" he said. "You mean you're looking at the pictures."

"No. I'm reading it."

"Don't you remember me? I'm Dr. Janetello."

I hesitated, trying to think up an answer, but he went on.

"Would you mind reading something for me?"

I looked down at the page. "Members of the Eighty-second airborne reserves bail out over Colorado. Four thousand men took part in a mock attack . . ."

"That's enough," he said. On the table were two books I'd taken from the shelves. He picked them up. *"The Short Stories of de Maupassant* and *Pickwick Papers.* Do you read this too?"

"Yes. I liked *David Copperfield* so I thought I'd try this."

"How did you get in here?" he asked quickly. "Are you from Southbury?"

"My stepfather works here."

"You think it's clever to play me along like that?"

I didn't answer. It was going wrong. I looked up at his round face. A few beads of sweat were collected along his upper lip and his eyes suddenly seemed very small.

"Do you have permission to use the library?"

"No. I guess not."

He stood for a moment without saying anything, as if undecided whether to continue. Then he dropped the books on the table with a bang, turned quickly, and left the room. The double doors continued swinging long after he was gone.

Alfred Kazin / From the Subway to the Synagogue

Alfred Kazin's career as a critic of American literature began early, with the publication at age twenty-five of *On Native Ground,* his influential study of American literature. It may then be surprising, initially at least, to be told how much he feared the "tests" of childhood, how awed he felt about his teachers, about even the atmosphere of the school in Brownsville. But the reader will also notice that many of the elements of schooling and childhood that still can give him "the shivers" are made distant and special by being put into quotation marks, as with such words as "tests," "good impression," or "speaking nicely." We soon learn that for Kazin these words refer not merely to an educational standard but to a social and ethnic one and that the account being offered deals not simply with a "typical" boy but with a very special one who felt acutely that he carried at school a racial and familial as well as an individual responsibility. To do well was to liberate his parents "from the shame of being what they were," Jews who did not speak at home the "refined" "correct" or "nice" English spoken by the educated.

Images of Childhood

Like Philip French (Section VI), Kazin was a stammerer, but he scarcely enjoys anything like French's amused sense of the stammerer as a "hero." His account of childhood alienation and of old-style classroom exercises in learning is made possible only because the later Kazin, who is doing the writing, manages to surmount their possible crippling effects. But the signs of survival are not asserted. They are implied in a style that gives evidence of a highly receptive mind. It holds its recollections not as one usually holds what has been learned at school but rather as one retains sensuous and sensual associations. Such a mind is more than usually vulnerable, yet more than usually resilient as well. Consider the configuration of impressions in his account of a visit to the speech clinic or his fused recollections about posters of the Black Forest, smells of the classrooms, open toilets, and early sexual stirrings.

All my early life lies open to my eye within five city blocks. When I passed the school, I went sick with all my old fear of it. With its standard New York public-school brown brick courtyard shut in on three sides of the square and the pretentious battlements overlooking that cockpit in which I can still smell the fiery sheen of the rubber ball, it looks like a factory over which has been imposed the façade of a castle. It gave me the shivers to stand up in that courtyard again; I felt as if I had been mustered back into the service of those Friday morning "tests" that were the terror of my childhood.

It was never learning I associated with that school: only the necessity to succeed, to get ahead of the others in the daily struggle to "make a good impression" on our teachers, who grimly, wearily, and often with ill-concealed distaste watched against our relapsing into the natural savagery they expected of Brownsville boys. The white, cool, thinly ruled record book sat over us from their desks all day long, and had remorselessly entered into it each day—in blue ink if we had passed, in red ink if we had not—our attendance, our conduct, our "effort," our merits and demerits; and to the last possible decimal point in calculation, our standing in an unending series of "tests"—surprise tests, daily tests, weekly tests, formal midterm tests, final tests. They never stopped trying to dig out of us whatever small morsel of fact we had managed to get down the night before. We had to prove that we were really alert, ready for anything, always in the race. That white thinly ruled record book figured in my mind as the judgment seat; the very thinness and remote blue lightness of its lines instantly showed its cold authority over me; so much space had been left on each page, columns and columns in which to note down everything about us, implacably and forever. As it lay there on a teacher's desk, I stared at it all day long with such fear and anxious propriety that I had no trouble believing that God, too, did nothing but keep such record books, and that on the final day He would face me with an account in Hebrew letters whose phonetic dots and dashes looked strangely like decimal points counting up my every sinful thought on earth.

All teachers were to be respected like gods, and God Himself was the greatest of all school superintendents. Long after I had ceased to believe that our teachers could see with the back of their heads, it was still understood, by me, that they knew everything. They were the delegates of all visible and invisible power on earth—of the mothers who waited on the stoops every day after three for us to bring home tales of our daily triumphs; of the glacially remote Anglo-Saxon principal, whose very name was King; of the incalculably important Superintendent of Schools who would someday rubberstamp his name to the bottom of our diplomas in grim acknowledgment that we had, at last, given satisfaction to him, to the Board of Superintendents, and to our benefactor the City of New York—and so up and up, to the government of the United States and to the great Lord Jehovah Himself. My belief in teachers' unlimited wisdom and power rested not so much on what I saw in them—how impatient most of them looked, how wary—but on our abysmal humility, at least in those of us who were "good" boys, who proved by our ready compliance and "manners" that we wanted to get on. The road to a professional future would be shown us only as we pleased *them. Make a good impression the first day of the term, and they'll help you out. Make a bad impression, and you might as well cut your throat.* This was the first article of school folklore, whispered around the classroom the opening day of each term. You made the "good impression" by sitting firmly at your wooden desk, hands clasped; by silence for the greatest part of the live-long day; by standing up obsequiously when it was so expected of you; by sitting down noiselessly when you had answered a question; "speaking nicely," which meant reproducing their painfully exact enunciation; by "showing manners," or an ecstatic submissiveness in all things; by outrageous flattery; by bringing little gifts at Christmas, on their birthdays, and at the end of the term—the well-known significance of these gifts being that they came not from us, but from our parents, whose eagerness in this matter showed a high level of social consideration, and thus raised our standing in turn.

It was not just our quickness and memory that were always being tested. Above all, in the word I could never hear without automatically seeing it raised before me in gold-plated letters, it was our *character*. I always felt anxious when I heard the word pronounced. Satisfactory as my "character" was, on the whole, except when I stayed too long in the playground reading; outrageously satisfactory, as I can see now, the very sound of the word as our teachers coldly gave it out from the end of their teeth, with a solemn weight on each dark syllable, immediately struck my heart cold with fear—they could not believe I really had it. Character was never something you had; it had to be trained in you, like a technique. I was never very clear about it. On our side *character* meant demonstrative obedience; but teachers already had it—how else could they have become teachers? They had it; the aloof Anglo-Saxon principal whom we remotely saw only on ceremonial occasions in the assembly was positively encased in it; it glittered off his bald head in spokes of triumphant light; the President of the United States had the greatest conceivable amount of it. Character belonged to great adults. Yet we were constantly being driven onto it; it was the great threshold we had to cross. *Alfred Kazin, having shown proficiency in his course of studies and having displayed satisfactory marks of character. . . .* Thus someday the hallowed diploma, passport to my further advancement in high school. But there —I could already feel it in my bones—they would put me through even more doubting tests of character; and after that, if I should be good enough and bright enough, there would be still more. *Character* was a bitter thing, racked with my endless striving to please. The school—from every last stone in the courtyard to the battlements frowning down at me from the walls—was only the stage for a trial. I felt that the very atmosphere of learning that surrounded us was fake— that every lesson, every book, every approving smile was only a pretext for the constant probing and watching of me, that there was not a secret in me that would not be decimally measured into that white record book. All week long I lived for the blessed sound of the dismissal gong at three o'clock on Friday afternoon.

I was awed by this system, I believed in it, I respected its force. The alternative was "going bad." The school was notoriously the toughest in our tough neighborhood, and the dangers of "going bad" were constantly impressed upon me at home and in school in dark whispers of the "reform school" and in examples of boys who had been picked up for petty thievery, rape, or flinging a heavy inkwell straight into a teacher's face. Behind any failure in school yawned the great abyss of a criminal career. Every refractory attitude doomed you with the sound "Sing Sing." Anything less than absolute perfection in school always suggested to my mind that I might fall out of the daily race, be kept back in the working class forever, or—dared I think of it?—fall into the criminal class itself.

I worked on a hairline between triumph and catastrophe. Why the odds should always have felt so narrow I understood only when I realized how little my parents thought of their own lives. It was not for myself alone that I was expected to shine, but for them—to redeem the constant anxiety of their existence. I was the first American child, their offering to the strange new God; I was to be the monument of their liberation from the shame of being—what they were. And that there was shame in this was a fact that everyone seemed to believe as a matter of course. It was in the gleeful discounting of themselves—what do we know?—with which our parents greeted every fresh victory in our savage competition for "high averages," for prizes, for a few condescending words of official praise from the principal at assembly. It was in the sickening invocation of "Americanism"—the word itself accusing us of everything we apparently were not. Our families and teachers seemed tacitly agreed that we were somehow to be a little ashamed of what we were. Yet it was always hard to say why this should be so. It was certainly not—in Brownsville!—because we were Jews, or simply because we spoke another language at home, or were absent on our holy days. It was rather that a "refined," "correct," "nice" English was required of us at school that we did not naturally speak, and that our teachers could never be quite sure we would keep. This English was peculiarly the ladder of advancement. Every future young lawyer was known by it. Even the Communists and Socialists on Pitkin Avenue spoke it. It was bright and clean and polished. We were expected to show it off like a new pair of shoes. When the teacher sharply called a question out, then your name, you were expected to leap up, face the class, and eject those new words fluently off the tongue.

There was my secret ordeal: I could never say anything except in the most roundabout way; I was a stammerer. Although I knew all those new words from my private reading—I read walking in the street, to and from the Children's Library on Stone Avenue; on the fire escape and the roof; at every meal when they would let me; read even when I dressed in the morning, propping my book up against the drawers of the bureau as I pulled on my long black stockings—I could never seem to get the easiest words out with the right dispatch, and would often miserably signal from my desk that I did not know the answer rather than get up to stumble and fall and crash on every word. If, angry at always being put down as lazy or stupid, I did get up to speak, the black wooden floor would roll away under my feet, the teacher would frown at me in amazement, and in unbearable loneliness I would hear behind me the groans and laughter: *tuh-tuh-tuh-tuh.*

The word was my agony. The word that for others was so effortless and so neutral, so unburdened, so simple, so exact, I had first to meditate in advance, to see if I could make it, like a plumber fitting together odd lengths and shapes of pipe. I was always preparing words I could speak, storing them away, choosing between them. And often, when the word did come from my mouth in its great and terrible birth, quailing and bleeding as if forced through a thornbush, I would not be able to look the others in the face, and would walk out in the silence, the infinitely echoing silence behind my back, to say it all cleanly back to myself as I walked in the streets. Only when I was alone in the open air, pacing the roof with pebbles in my mouth, as I had read Demosthenes had done to cure himself of stammering; or in the street, where all words seemed to flow from the length of my stride and the color of the houses as I remembered the perfect tranquillity of a phrase in Beethoven's *Romance in F* I could sing back to myself as I walked—only then was it possible for me to speak without the infinite premeditations and strangled silences I toiled through whenever I got up at school to respond with the expected, the exact answer.

It troubled me that I could speak in the fullness of my own voice only when I was alone on the streets, walking about. There was something unnatural about it; unbearably isolated. I was not like the others! I was not like the others! At midday, every freshly shocking Monday noon, they sent me away to a speech clinic in a school in East New York, where I sat in a circle of lispers and cleft palates and foreign accents holding a mirror before my lips and rolling difficult sounds over and over. To be sent there in the full light of the opening week, when everyone else was at school or going about his business, made me feel as if I had been expelled from the great normal body of humanity. I would gobble down my lunch on my way to the speech clinic and rush back to the school in time to make up for the classes I had lost. One day, one unforgettable dread day, I stopped to catch my breath on a corner of Sutter Avenue, near the wholesale fruit markets, where an old drugstore rose up over a great flight of steps. In the window were dusty urns of colored water floating off iron chains; cardboard placards advertising hairnets, Ex-Lax; a great illustrated medical chart headed The Human Factory, which showed the exact course a mouthful of food follows as it falls from chamber to chamber of the body. I hadn't meant to stop there at all, only to catch my breath; but I so hated the speech clinic that I thought I would delay my arrival for a few minutes by eating my lunch on the steps. When I took the sandwich out of my bag, two bitterly hard pieces of hard salami slipped out of my hand and fell through a grate onto a hill of dust below the steps. I remember how sickeningly vivid an odd thread of hair looked on the salami, as if my lunch were turning stiff with death. The factory whistles called their short, sharp blasts stark through the middle of noon, beating at me where I sat outside the city's magnetic circle. I had never known, I knew instantly I would never in my heart again submit to, such wild passive despair as I felt at that moment, sitting on the steps before The Human Factory, where little robots gathered and shoveled the food from chamber to chamber of the body. They had put me out into the streets, I thought to myself; with their mirrors and their everlasting pulling at me to imitate their effortless bright speech and their stupefaction that a boy could stammer and stumble on every other English word he carried in his head, they had put me out into the streets, had left me high and dry on the steps of that drugstore staring at the remains of my lunch turning black and grimy in the dust.

In the great cool assembly hall, dominated by the gold sign above the stage Knowledge Is Power, the windowsills were lined with Dutch bulbs, each wedged into a mound of pebbles massed in a stone dish. Above them hung a giant photograph of Theodore Roosevelt. Whenever I walked in to see the empty assembly hall for myself, the shiny waxed floor of the stage dangled in the middle of the air like a crescent. On one side was a great silk American flag, the staff crowned by a gilt eagle. Across the dry rattling of varnish-smelling empty seats bowing to the American flag, I saw in the play of the sun on those pebbles wildly sudden images of peace. *There* was the other land, crowned by the severe and questioning face of Theodore Roosevelt, his eyes above the curiously endearing straw-dry mustache, behind the pince-nez glittering with light, staring and staring me through as if he were uncertain whether he fully approved of me.

The light pouring through window after window in that great empty varnished assembly hall seemed to me the most wonderful thing I had ever seen. It was that thorough varnished cleanness that was of the new land, that light dancing off the glasses of Theodore Roosevelt, those green and white roots of the still raw onion-brown bulbs delicately flaring up from the hill of pebbles into which they were wedged. The pebbles moved me in themselves, there were so many of them. They rose up around the bulbs in delicately strong masses of colored stone, and as the sun fell between them, each pebble shone in its own light. Looking across the great rows of empty seats to those pebbles lining the windowsills, I could still smell summer from some long veranda surrounded by trees. On that veranda sat the family and friends of Theodore Roosevelt. I knew the name: Oyster Bay. Because of that picture, I had read *The Boy's Life of Theodore Roosevelt;* knew he had walked New York streets night after night as Police Commissioner, unafraid of the Tenderloin gangsters;* had looked into *Theodore Roosevelt's Letters to His Children,* pretending that those hilarious drawings on almost every page were for me. *There* was America, I thought, the real America, *his* America, where from behind the glass on the wall of our assembly hall he watched over us to make sure we did right, thought right, lived right.

"Up, boys! Up San Juan Hill!" I still hear our roguish old civics teacher, a little white-haired Irishman who was supposed to have been with Teddy in Cuba, driving us through our Friday morning tests with these shouts and cries. He called them "Army Navy" tests, to make us feel big, and dividing the class between Army and Navy, got us to compete with each other for a coveted blue star. Civics was city government, state government, federal government; each government had functions; you had to get them out fast in order to win for the Army or the Navy. Sometimes this required filling in three or four words, line by line, down one side of the grimly official yellow foolscap that was brought out for tests. (In the tense silence just before the test began, he looked at us sharply, the watch in his hand ticking as violently as the sound of my heart, and on command, fifty boys simultaneously folded their yellow test paper and evened the fold with their thumbnails in a single dry sigh down the middle of the paper.) At other times it meant true-or-false tests; then he stood behind us to make sure we did not signal the right answers to each other in the usual way—for true, nodding your head; for false, holding your nose. You could hear his voice barking from the rear. *"Come on now, you Army boys! On your toes like West Point cadets! All ready now? Get set! Go! Three powers of the legislative branch? The judiciary? The executive? The subject of the fifteenth amendment? The capital of Wyoming? Come on, Navy! Shoot those landlubbers down! Give 'em a blast from your big guns right through the middle! The third article of the Bill of Rights? The thirteenth amendment? The sixteenth? True or false, Philadelphia is*

---

* the Tenderloin gangsters: in New York City the Tenderloin was a vice area, a police precinct west of Broadway between 23rd and 42nd streets, where a flourishing trade in gambling and prostitution afforded police officers rich opportunities for graft.

the capital of Pennsylvania. Up and at 'em, Navy! Mow them down! COME ON!!!" Our "average" was calculated each week, and the boys who scored 90 percent or over were rewarded by seeing *their own names* lettered on the great blue chart over the blackboard. Each time I entered that room for a test, I looked for my name on the blue chart as if the sight of it would decide my happiness for all time.

Down we go, down the school corridors of the past smelling of chalk, lysol out of the open toilets, and girl sweat. The staircases were a gray stone I saw nowhere else in the school, and they were shut in on both sides by some thick unreflecting glass on which were pasted travel posters inviting us to spend the summer in the Black Forest. Those staircases created a spell in me that I had found my way to some distant, cool, neutral passageway deep in the body of the school. There, enclosed within the thick, green boughs of a classic summer in Germany, I could still smell the tense probing chalk smells from every classroom, the tickling high surgical odor of lysol from the open toilets, could still hear that continuous babble, babble of water dripping into the bowls. Sex was instantly connected in my mind with the cruel openness of those toilets, and in the never-ending sound of the bowls being flushed I could detect, as I did in the maddeningly elusive fragrance of cologne brought into the classroom by Mrs. B., the imminence of something severe, frightening, obscene. Sex, as they said in the "Coney Island" dives outside the school, was like going to the toilet; there was a great contempt in this that made me think of the wet rings left by our sneakers as we ran down the gray stone steps after school.

Outside the women teachers' washroom on the third floor, the tough guys would wait for the possible appearance of Mrs. B., whose large goiterous eyes seemed to bulge wearily with mischief, who always looked tired and cynical, and who wore thin chiffon dresses that affected us much more than she seemed to realize. Mrs. B. often went about the corridors in the company of a trim little teacher of mathematics who was a head shorter than she and had a mustache. Her chiffon dresses billowed around him like a sail; she seemed to have him in tow. It was understood by us as a matter of course that she wore those dresses to inflame us; that she *was* tired and cynical, from much practice in obscene lovemaking; that she was a "bad one" like the young Polish blondes from East New York I occasionally saw in the "Coney Island" dives sitting on someone's lap and smoking a cigarette. How wonderful and unbelievable it was to find this in a teacher; to realize that the two of them, after we had left the school, probably met to rub up against each other in the faculty toilet. Sex was a grim test where sooner or later you would have to prove yourself doing things to women. In the smell of chalk and sweat and the unending smirky babble of the water as it came to me on the staircase through my summer's dream of old Germany, I could feel myself being called to still another duty—to conquer Mrs. B., to rise to the challenge she had whispered to us in her slyness. I had seen pictures of it on the block—they were always passing them around between handball games—the man's face furious, ecstatic with lewdness as he proudly looked down at himself; the woman sniggering as she teased him with droplets from the contraceptive someone had just shown me in the gutter—its crushed, filmy slyness the very sign of the forbidden.

They had never said anything about this at home, and I thought I knew why. Sex was the opposite of books, of pictures, of music, of the open air, even of kindness. They would not let you have both. Something always lingered to the sound of those toilets to test you. In and out of the classroom they were always testing you. *Come on, Army! Come on, Navy!* As I stood up in that school courtyard and smelled again the familiar sweat, heard again the unending babble from the open toilets, I suddenly remembered how sure I had always been that even my failures in there would be entered in a white, thinly ruled, official record book.

On Belmont Avenue, Brownsville's great open street market, the pushcarts are still lined on each other for blocks, and the din is as deafening, marvelous, and appetizing as ever. They have tried to tone it down; the pushcarts are now confined to one side of the street. When I was a boy, they clogged both sides, reached halfway up the curb to the open stands of the stores; walking down the street was like being whirled around and around in a game of blind man's buff. But Belmont Avenue is still the merriest street in Brownsville. As soon as I walked into it from Rockaway, caught my first whiff of the herrings and pickles in their great black barrels, heard the familiarly harsh, mocking cries and shouts from the market women—*"Oh you darlings! Oh you sweet ones, oh you pretty ones! Storm us! Tear us apart! Devour us!"*—I laughed right out loud, it was so good to be back among *them.* Nowhere but on Belmont Avenue did I ever see in Brownsville such open, hearty people as those market women. Their shrewd open-weather eyes missed nothing. The street was their native element; they seemed to hold it together with their hands, mouths, fists, and knees; they stood up in it behind their stands all day long, and in every weather; they stood up for themselves. In winter they would bundle themselves into five or six sweaters, then putting long white aprons over their overcoats, would warm themselves at fires lit in black oil drums between the pushcarts, their figures bulging as if to meet the rain and cold head-on in defiance.

I could hear them laughing and mock-crying all the way to Stone Avenue, still imploring and pulling at every woman on the street—*"Vayber! Vayber! sheyne gute vayber! Oh you lovelies! Oh you good ones! Oh you pretty ones! See how cheap and good! Just come over! Just taste! Just a little look! What will it cost you to taste? How can you walk on without looking? How can you resist us? Oh! Oh! Come over! Come over! Devour us! Storm us! Tear us apart! BARGAINS BARGAINS!!"* I especially loved watching them at dusk, an hour before supper, when the women would walk through to get the food at its freshest.

Then, in those late winter afternoons, when there was that deep grayness on the streets and that spicy smell from the open stands at dusk I was later to connect with my first great walks inside the New York crowd at the rush hour—then there would arise from behind the great flaming oil drums and the pushcarts loaded with their separate mounds of shoelaces, corsets, pots and pans, stockings, kosher kitchen soap, memorial candles in their wax-filled tumblers and glassware, "chiney" oranges, beet roots and soup greens, that deep and good odor of lox, of salami, of herrings and half-sour pickles, that told me I was truly home.

As I went down Belmont Avenue, the copper-shining herrings in the tall black barrels made me think of the veneration of food in Brownsville families. I can still see the kids pinned down to the tenement stoops, their feet helplessly kicking at the pots and pans lined up before them, their mouths pressed open with a spoon while the great meals are rammed down their throats. *"Eat! Eat! May you be destroyed if you don't eat! What sin have I committed that God should punish me with you! Eat! What will become of you if you don't eat! Imp of darkness, may you sink ten fathoms into the earth if you don't eat! Eat!"*

We never had a chance to know what hunger meant. At home we nibbled all day long as a matter of course. On the block we gorged ourselves continually on "Nessels," Hersheys, gumdrops, polly seeds, nuts, chocolate-covered cherries, charlotte russe, and ice cream. A warm and sticky ooze of chocolate ran through everything we touched; the street always smelled faintly like the candy wholesaler's windows on the way back from school. The hunger for sweets, jellies, and soda water raged in us like a disease; during the grimmest punchball game, in the middle of a fist fight, we would dash to the candy store to get down two-cent blocks of chocolate and "small"—three-cent—glasses of cherry soda; or calling "upstairs" from the street, would have flung to us, or carefully hoisted down at the end of a clothesline, thick slices of rye bread smeared with chicken fat. No meal at home was complete without cream soda, root beer, ginger ale, "celery tonic." We poured jelly on bread; we poured it into the tea; we often ate chocolate marshmallows before breakfast. At school during the recess hour Syrian vendors who all looked alike in their alpaca jackets and black velours hats came after us with their white enameled trays, from which we took *Halvah,* Turkish Delight, and three different kinds of greasy nut-brown pastry sticks. From the Jewish vendors, who went around the streets in every season wheeling their little tin stoves, we bought roasted potatoes either in the quarter or the half—the skins were hard as bark and still smelled of the smoke pouring out of the stoves; apples you ate off a stick that were encrusted with a thick glaze of baked jelly you never entirely got down your throat or off your fingers, so that you seemed to be with it all day; *knishes;* paper spills of hot yellow chick peas. I still hear those peddlers crying up and down the street—*Árbes! Árbes! Hayse gute árbes! Kinder! Kinder! Hayse gute árbes!* From the "Big" Italians, whom we saw only in summer, we bought watermelons as they drove their great horse-smelling wagons down the street calling up to every window—"Hey you ladies!

Hey ladies! Freschi and good!"—and from the "small" ones, who pushed carts through the streets, paper cups of shaved ice sprinkled before our eyes with drops of lemon or orange or raspberry syrup from a narrow water bottle.

But our greatest delight in all seasons was "delicatessen"—hot spiced corned beef, pastrami, rolled beef, hard salami, soft salami, chicken salami, bologna, frankfurter "specials" and the thinner, wrinkled hot dogs always taken with mustard and relish and sauerkraut, and whenever possible, to make the treat fully real, with potato salad, baked beans, and french fries which had been bubbling in the black wire fryer deep in the iron pot. At Saturday twilight, as soon as the delicatessen store reopened after the Sabbath rest, we raced into it panting for the hot dogs sizzling on the gas plate just inside the window. The look of that blackened empty gas plate had driven us wild all through the wearisome Sabbath day. And now, as the electric sign blazed up again, lighting up the words Jewish National Delicatessen, it was as if we had entered into our rightful heritage. Yet *Wurst* carried associations with the forbidden, the adulterated, the excessive; with spices that teased and maddened the senses to demand more, still more. This was food that only on Saturday nights could be eaten with a good conscience. Generally, we bought it on the sly; it was supposed to be bad for us; I thought it was made in dark cellars. Still, our parents could not have disapproved of it altogether. Each new mouthful of food we took in was an advantage stolen in the battle. The favorite injunction was to *fix yourself,* by which I understood we needed to do a repair job on ourselves. In the swelling and thickening of a boy's body was the poor family's earliest success. "Fix yourself!" a mother cried indignantly to the child on the stoop. "Fix yourself!" The word for a fat boy was *solid*.

Robert Lowell / 91 Revere Street

Oblivious to the possibility that anyone will question the importance of, or be unfamiliar with, his reference to various family members, the types who passed through the household, and the privileged educational and social geography of Boston, Robert Lowell, the descendant of the famous literary family, gives little sign that he needs to *make* his life interesting. Perhaps he felt that the poems which accompanied this piece, in his collection *Life Studies,* were effort enough. The style is without tenseness, either in the life being reported or in the reporting of it. One *has* style, he seems to suggest.

An interesting comparison can be made between Lowell's autobiographical meandering and the compulsive struggle for recognition that informs Alfred Kazin's account of his childhood. Consider how each piece alludes to

Theodore Roosevelt. In Kazin's recollection the portrait hangs in the school assembly hall—"the severe and questioning face of Theodore Roosevelt, his eyes above the endearing straw-dry mustache, behind the pince-nez glittering with light, staring and staring me through as if he were uncertain whether he fully approved of me." Lowell, on the other hand, reports of his father and his father's friends that "a man they had to take their hats off to was Theodore Roosevelt."

The quiet assurance of Lowell's account depends, however, not on social complacency so much as on a stylistic gentleness. It's as if he doesn't dare ask too much of any of the people he is characterizing, and he thereby at once embraces and surpasses any styles displayed by the other Lowells. There is a becalmed but still quirky juxtaposition of terms whenever he describes them: "platitudinous, worldly, and fond," said of early ancestors, or "fumbling languor," said of his father, or "childish, disloyal, romantic," said of himself as a little boy. The assessments are, under a surface ease, precise, qualified but nicely blurred, showing an aristocratic disdain for any sorting out of impressions into neat, merely explanatory categories.

The account of him is platitudinous, worldly and fond, but he has no Christian name and is entitled merely Major *M.* Myers in my Cousin Cassie Mason Myers Julian-James's privately printed *Biographical Sketches: A Key to a Cabinet of Heirlooms in the Smithsonian Museum.* The name-plate under his portrait used to spell out his name bravely enough: he was Mordecai Myers. The artist painted Major Myers in his sanguine War of 1812 uniform with epaulets, white breeches, and a scarlet frogged waistcoat. His right hand played with the sword "now to be seen in the Smithsonian cabinet of heirlooms." The pose was routine and gallant. The full-lipped smile was good-humoredly pompous and embarrassed.

Mordecai's father, given neither name nor initial, is described with an air of hurried self-congratulation by Cousin Cassie as "a friend of the Reverend Ezra Styles, afterward President of Yale College." As a very young man the son, Mordecai, studied military tactics under a French émigré, "the Bourbons' celebrated Colonel De la Croix." Later he was "matured" by six years' practical experience in a New York militia regiment organized by Colonel Martin Van Buren. After "the successful engagement against the British at Chrysler's Field, thirty shrapnel splinters were extracted from his shoulder." During convalescence, he wooed and won Miss Charlotte Bailey, "thus proving himself a better man than his rivals, the united forces of Plattsburg." He fathered ten children, sponsored an enlightened law exempting Quakers from military service in New York State, and died in 1870 at the age of ninety-four, "a Grand Old Man, who impressed strangers with the poise of his old-time manners."

Undoubtedly Major Mordecai had lived in a more ritualistic, gaudy, and animal world than twentieth-century Boston. There was something undecided, Mediterranean, versatile, almost double-faced about his bearing which suggested that, even to his contemporaries, he must have seemed gratuitously both *ci-devant* * and *parvenu*.* He was a dark man, a German Jew—no downright Yankee, but maybe such a fellow as Napoleon's mad, pomaded son-of-an-innkeeper-general, Junot, Duc D'Abrantes; a man like mad George III's pomaded, disreputable son, "Prinny," the Prince Regent. Or he was one of those Moorish-looking dons painted by his contemporary, Goya—some leader of Spanish guerrillas against Bonaparte's occupation, who fled to South America. Our Major's suffering almond eye rested on his luxurious dawn-colored fingers ruffling an off-white glove.

Bailey-Mason-Myers! Easy-going, Empire State patricians, these relatives of my Grandmother Lowell seemed to have given my father his character. For he likewise lacked that granite *back-countriness* which Grandfather Arthur Winslow * attributed to his own ancestors, the iconoclastic, mulish Dunbarton New Hampshire Starks. On the joint Mason-Myers bookplate, there are two merry and naked mermaids—lovely marshmallowy, boneless, Rubenesque butterballs, all burlesque-show bosoms and Flemish smiles. Their motto, *malo frangere quam flectere,* reads "I prefer to bend than to break."

Mordecai Myers was my Grandmother Lowell's grandfather. His life was tame and honorable. He was a leisured squire and merchant, a member of the state legislature, a mayor of Schenectady, a "president" of Kinderhook village. Disappointingly, his famous "blazing brown eye" seems in all things to have shunned the outrageous. After his death he was remembered soberly as a New York State gentleman, the friend and host of worldly men and politicians with Dutch names: De Witt Clinton, Vanderpoel, Hoes, and Schuyler. My mother was roused to warmth by the Major's scarlet vest and exotic eye. She always insisted that he was the one properly dressed and dieted ancestor in the lot we had inherited from my father's Cousin Cassie. Great-great-Grandfather Mordecai! Poor sheepdog in wolf's clothing! In the anarchy of my adolescent war on my parents, I tried to make him a true wolf, the wandering Jew! *Homo lupus homini!* *

Major Mordecai Myers' portrait has been mislaid past finding, but out of my memories I often come on it in the setting our Revere Street house, a setting now fixed in the mind, where it survives all the distortions of fantasy, all the

---

* *ci-devant:* during the French Revolution, someone who had been a noble before titles were abolished; a person of the past.
* *parvenu:* "arrived"; a derogatory term for someone who has risen from a low station to wealth or social position; an upstart.
* Grandfather Arthur Winslow: the Winslows have been a prominent New England family ever since Edward Winslow (1595–1655), an English-born Puritan, came to America on the *Mayflower;* he served three times as governor of the Plymouth Colony.
* *Homo lupus homini:* man is a wolf to man.

blank befogging of forgetfulness. There, the vast number of remembered *things* remains rocklike. Each is in its place, each has its function, its history, its drama. There, all is preserved by that motherly care that one either ignored or resented in his youth. The things and their owners come back urgent with life and meaning—because finished, they are endurable and perfect.

Cousin Cassie only became a close relation in 1922. In that year she died. After some unpleasantness between Mother and a co-heiress, Helen Bailey, the estate was divided. Mother used to return frozen and thrilled from her property disputes, and I, knowing nothing of the rights and wrongs, would half-perversely confuse Helen Bailey with Helen of Troy and harden my mind against the monotonous *parti pris* * of Mother's voice. Shortly after our move to Boston in 1924, a score of unwanted Myers portraits was delivered to our new house on Revere Street. These were later followed by "their dowry"—four moving vans groaning with heavy Edwardian furniture. My father began to receive his first quarterly payments from the Mason-Myers Julian-James Trust Fund, sums "not grand enough to corrupt us," Mother explained, "but sufficient to prevent Daddy from being entirely at the mercy of his salary." The Trust sufficed: our lives became tantalized with possibilities, and my father felt encouraged to take the risk —a small one in those boom years—of resigning from the Navy on the gamble of doubling his income in business.

I was in the third grade and for the first time becoming a little more popular at school. I was afraid Father's leaving the Navy would destroy my standing. I was a churlish, disloyal, romantic boy, and quite without hero worship for my father, whose actuality seemed so inferior to the photographs in uniform he once mailed to us from the Golden Gate. My real *love,* as Mother used to insist to all new visitors, was toy soldiers. For a few months at the flood tide of this infatuation, people were ciphers to me—valueless except as chances for increasing my armies of soldiers. Roger Crosby, a child in the second grade of my Brimmer Street School, had thousands—not mass-produced American stereotypes, but hand-painted solid lead soldiers made to order in Dijon, France. Roger's father had a still more artistic and adult collection; its ranks—each man at least six inches tall—marched in glass cases under the eyes of recognizable replicas of mounted Napoleonic captains: Kleber, Marshal Ney, Murat, King of Naples. One delirious afternoon Mr. Crosby showed me his toys and was perhaps the first grownup to talk to me not as a child but as an equal when he discovered how feverishly I followed his anecdotes on uniforms and the evolution of tactical surprise. Afterwards, full of high thoughts, I ran up to Roger's play room and hoodwinked him into believing that his own soldiers were "ballast turned out by central European sweatshops." He agreed I was being sweetly generous when I traded twenty-four worthless Jordan Marsh papier-mâché doughboys for

---

* *parti pris:* obstinate bias, set prejudice.

whole companies of his gorgeous, imported Old Guards, Second Empire "redlegs," and modern *chasseurs d'Alpine* * with sky-blue berets. The haul was so huge that I had to take a child's wheelbarrow to Roger's house at the top of Pinckney Street. When I reached home with my last load, Mr. Crosby was talking with my father on our front steps. Roger's soldiers were all returned; I had only the presence of mind to hide a single soldier, a peely-nosed black sepoy wearing a Shriner's fez.

Nothing consoled me for my loss, but I enjoyed being allowed to draw Father's blunt dress sword, and I was proud of our Major Mordecai. I used to stand dangerously out in the middle of Revere Street in order to see through our windows and gloat on this portrait's scarlet waistcoat blazing in the bare, Spartan whiteness of our den-parlor. Mordecai Myers lost his glory when I learned from my father that he was only a "major *pro tem*." * On a civilian, even a civilian soldier, the flamboyant waistcoat was stuffy and no more martial than officers' costumes in our elementary school musicals.

In 1924 people still lived in cities. Late that summer, we bought the 91 Revere Street house, looking out on an unbuttoned part of Beacon Hill bounded by the North End slums, though reassuringly only four blocks away from my Grandfather Winslow's brown pillared house at 18 Chestnut Street. In the decades preceding and following the First World War, old Yankee families had upset expectation by regaining this section of the Hill from the vanguards of the lace-curtain Irish. This was bracing news for my parents in that topsy-turvy era when the Republican Party and what were called "people of the right sort" were no longer dominant in city elections. Still, even in the palmy, laissez-faire '20s, Revere Street refused to be a straightforward, immutable residential fact. From one end to the other, houses kept being sanded down, repainted, or abandoned to the flaking of decay. Houses, changing hands, changed their language and nationality. A few doors to our south the householders spoke "Beacon Hill British" or the flat *nay nay* of the Boston Brahmin.* The parents of the children a few doors north spoke mostly in Italian.

My mother felt a horrified giddiness about the adventure of our address. She once said, "We are barely perched on the outer rim of the hub of decency." We were less than fifty yards from Louisburg Square, the cynosure of old historic Boston's plain-spoken, cold roast elite—the Hub of the Hub of the Universe. Fifty yards!

As a naval ensign, Father had done postgraduate work at Harvard. He had

---
* *chasseurs alpins:* a special French regiment.
* *pro tem: pro tempore,* for the time being.
* Boston Brahmin: upper-class New Englander; derived from the name of the Hindu priestly caste. In *Elsie Venner* (1861), Oliver Wendell Holmes speaks of "the harmless, inoffensive, untitled aristocracy" of New England, and specifically of Boston, "which has grown to be a caste by the repetition of the same influences generation after generation." (See *The Oxford Companion to American Literature*.)

also done postgraduate work at M.I.T., preferred the purely scientific college, and condescended to both. In 1924, however, his tone began to change; he now began to speak warmly of Harvard as his second alma mater. We went to football games at the Harvard Stadium, and one had the feeling that our lives were now being lived in the brutal, fashionable expectancy of the stadium: we had so many downs, so many minutes, and so many yards to go for a winning touchdown. It was just such a winning financial and social advance that my parents promised themselves would follow Father's resignation from the Navy and his acceptance of a sensible job offered him at the Cambridge branch of Lever Brothers' Soap.

The advance was never to come. Father resigned from the service in 1927, but he never had a civilian *career;* he instead had merely twenty-two years of the civilian *life*. Almost immediately he bought a larger and more stylish house; he sold his ascetic, stove-black Hudson and bought a plump brown Buick; later the Buick was exchanged for a high-toned, as-good-as-new Packard with a custom-designed royal blue and mahogany body. Without drama, his earnings more or less decreased from year to year.

But so long as we were on Revere Street, Father tried to come to terms with it and must have often wondered whether he on the whole liked or disliked the neighborhood's lack of side. He was still at this time rather truculently democratic in what might be described as an upper middle-class, naval, and Masonic fashion. He was a mumbler. His opinions were almost morbidly hesitant, but he considered himself a matter-of-fact man of science and had an unspoiled faith in the superior efficiency of northern nations. He modeled his allegiances and humor on the cockney imperialism of Rudyard Kipling's swearing Tommies, who did their job. Autochthonous Boston snobs, such as the Winslows or members of Mother's reading club, were alarmed by the brassy callousness of our naval visitors, who labeled the Italians they met on Revere Street as "grade-A" and "grade-B wops." The Revere Street "grade-B's" were Sicilian Catholics and peddled crummy second-hand furniture on Cambridge Street, not far from the site of Great-great-Grandfather Charles Lowell's disused West Church, praised in an old family folder as "a haven from the Sodom and Gomorrah of Trinitarian orthodoxy and the tyranny of the letter." Revere Street "grade-A's," good North Italians, sold fancy groceries and Colonial heirlooms in their shops near the Public Garden. Still other Italians were Father's familiars; they sold him bootleg Scotch and *vino rosso* * in teacups.

The outside of our Revere Street house was a flat red brick surface unvaried by the slightest suggestion of purple panes, delicate bay, or triangular window-cornice—a sheer wall formed by the seamless conjunction of four inseparable façades, all of the same commercial and purgatorial design. Though placed in the heart of Old Boston, it was ageless and artless, an epitome of those "leveler"

---

* *vino rosso:* red wine.

qualities Mother found most grueling about the naval service. 91 Revere Street was mass-produced, *regulation-issue,* and yet struck Boston society as stupidly out of the ordinary, like those white elephants—a mother-of-pearl scout knife or a tea-kettle barometer—which my father used to pick up on sale at an Army-Navy store.

The walls of Father's minute Revere Street den-parlor were bare and white. His bookshelves were bare and white. The den's one adornment was a ten-tube home-assembled battery radio set, whose loudspeaker had the shape and color of a Mexican sombrero. The radio's specialty was getting programs from Australia and New Zealand in the early hours of the morning.

My father's favorite piece of den furniture was his oak and "rhinoceros hide" armchair. It was ostentatiously a masculine, or rather a bachelor's, chair. It had a notched, adjustable back; it was black, cracked, hacked, scratched, splintered, gouged, initialed, gunpowder-charred and tumbler-ringed. It looked like pale tobacco leaves laid on dark tobacco leaves. I doubt if Father, a considerate man, was responsible for any of the marring. The chair dated from his plebe days at the Naval Academy, and had been bought from a shady, shadowy, roaring character, midshipmen "Beauty" Burford. Father loved each disfigured inch.

My father had been born two months after his own father's death. At each stage of his life, he was to be forlornly fatherless. He was a deep boy brought up entirely by a mild widowed mother and an intense widowed grandmother. When he was fourteen and a half, he became a deep young midshipman. By the time he graduated from Annapolis, he had a high sense of abstract form, which he beclouded with his humor. He had reached, perhaps, his final mental possibilities. He was deep—not with profundity, but with the dumb depth of one who trusted in statistics and was dubious of personal experience. In his forties, Father's soul went underground: as a civilian he kept his high sense of form, his humor, his accuracy, but this accuracy was henceforth unimportant, recreational, *hors de combat.** His debunking grew myopic; his shyness grew evasive; he argued with a fumbling languor. In the twenty-two years Father lived after he resigned from the Navy, he never again deserted Boston and never became Bostonian. He survived to drift from job to job, to be displaced, to be grimly and literally that old cliché, a fish out of water. He gasped and wheezed with impotent optimism, took on new ideals with each new job, never ingeniously enjoyed his leisure, never even hid his head in the sand.

Mother hated the Navy, hated naval society, naval pay, and the trip-hammer rote of settling and unsettling a house every other year when Father was transferred to a new station or ship. She had been married nine or ten years and still suspected that her husband was savorless, unmasterful, merely considerate. Unmasterful—Father's specialized efficiency lacked utterly the flattering bossi-

---

* *hors de combat:* out of the fight, disabled from combat.

ness she so counted on from her father, my Grandfather Winslow. It was not Father's absence on sea-duty that mattered; it was the eroding necessity of moving *with* him, of keeping in step. When he was far away on the Pacific, she had her friends, her parents, a house to herself—Boston! Fully conscious of her uniqueness and normality she basked in the refreshing stimulation of dreams in which she imagined Father as suitably sublimed. She used to describe such a sublime man to me over tea and English muffins. He was Siegfried carried lifeless through the shining air by Brunnhilde to Valhalla,* and accompanied by the throb of my Great Aunt Sarah playing his leitmotif in the released manner taught her by the Abbé Liszt.* Or Mother's hero dove through the grottoes of the Rhine and slaughtered the homicidal and vulgar dragon coiled about the golden hoard. Mother seemed almost light-headed when she retold the romance of Sarah Bernhardt * in *L'Aiglon,* the Eaglet, the weakling! She would speak the word *weakling* with such amused vehemence that I formed a grandiose and false image of L'Aiglon's Father, the *big* Napoleon: he was a strong man who scratched under his paunchy little white vest a torso all hair, muscle, and manliness. Instead of the dreams, Mother now had the insipid fatigue of keeping house. Instead of the *Eagle,* she had a twentieth-century naval commander interested in steam, radio, and "the fellows." To avoid naval yards, steam, and "the fellows," Mother had impulsively bought the squalid, impractical Revere Street house. Her marriage daily forced her to squander her subconsciously hoarded energies.

"*Weelawaugh, we-ee-eeelawaugh, weelawaugh,*" shrilled Mother's high voice. "*But-and, but-and, but-and!*" Father's low mumble would drone in answer. Though I couldn't be sure that I had caught the meaning of the words, I followed the sounds as though they were a movie. I felt drenched in my parents' passions.

91 Revere Street was the setting for those arthritic spiritual pains that troubled us for the two years my mother spent in trying to argue my father into resigning from the Navy. When the majestic, hollow boredom of the second year's autumn dwindled to the mean boredom of a second winter, I grew less willing to open my mouth. I bored my parents, they bored me.

"Weelawaugh, we-ee-eeelawaugh, weelawaugh!" "But-and, but-and, but-and!"

During the week ends I was at home much of the time. All day I used to look forward to the nights when my bedroom walls would once again vibrate, when I

---

* Siegfried, Brunnhilde, Valhalla: Lowell is thinking (inaccurately) of Wagner's opera *Die Götterdämmerung,* in which Brunnhilde rides into the funeral pyre of her husband Siegfried, and Valhalla, the abode of the gods and of dead warriors, is seen burning in the distance.
* the Abbé Liszt: Franz Liszt (1811–86), Hungarian pianist and composer, and closely associated with Wagner; during the last years of his life, a brilliant teacher of piano.
* Sarah Bernhardt (1844–1923), the great French tragedienne. *L'Aiglon* was specially written for her in 1900 by the playwright Edmond Rostand.

would awake with rapture to the rhythm of my parents arguing, arguing one another to exhaustion. Sometimes, without bathrobe or slippers, I would wriggle out into the cold hall on my belly and ambuscade myself behind the banister. I could often hear actual words. "Yes, yes, yes," Father would mumble. He was "backsliding" and "living in the fool's paradise of habitual retarding and retarded do-nothing inertia." Mother had violently set her heart on the resignation. She was hysterical even in her calm, but like a patient and forbearing strategist, she tried to pretend her neutrality. One night she said with murderous coolness, "Bobby and I are leaving for Papá's." This was an ultimatum to force Father to sign a deed placing the Revere Street house in Mother's name.

I writhed with disappointment on the nights when Mother and Father only lowed harmoniously together like cows, as they criticized Helen Bailey or Admiral De Stahl. Once I heard my mother say, "A *man* must make up his *own* mind. Oh Bob, if you are going to resign, do it *now* so I can at least plan for your son's *survival* and education on a single continent."

About this time I was being sent for my *survival* to Dr. Dane, a Quaker chiropractor with an office on Marlborough Street. Dr. Dane wore an old-fashioned light tan druggist's smock; he smelled like a healthy old-fashioned drugstore. His laboratory was free of intimidating technical equipment, and had only the conservative lay roughness and toughness that was so familiar and disarming to us in my Grandfather Winslow's country study or bedroom. Dr. Dane's rosy hands wrenched my shoulders with tremendous éclat and made me feel a hero; I felt unspeakable joy whenever an awry muscle fell back into serenity. My mother, who had no curiosity or imagination for cranky occultism, trusted Dr. Dane's clean, undrugged manliness—so like home. She believed that chiropractic had cured me of my undiagnosed asthma, which had defeated the expensive specialists.

"A penny for your thoughts, Schopenhauer," my mother would say.
"I am thinking about pennies," I'd answer.
"When *I* was a child I used to love telling Mamá everything I had done," Mother would say.
"But you're not a child," I would answer.
I used to enjoy dawdling and humming "Anchors Aweigh" up Revere Street after a day at school. "Anchors Aweigh," the official Navy song, had originally been the song composed for my father's class. And yet my mind always blanked and seemed to fill with a clammy hollowness when Mother asked prying questions. Like other tongue-tied, difficult children, I dreamed I was a master of cool, stoical repartee. "What have you been doing, Bobby?" Mother would ask. "I haven't," I'd answer. At home I thus saved myself from emotional exhaustion.

At school, however, I was extreme only in my conventional mediocrity, my colorless, distracted manner, which came from restless dreams of being admired. My closest friend was Eric Burckhard, the son of a professor of architecture at

Harvard. The Burckhards came from Zurich and were very German, not like Ludendorff,* but in the kindly, comical, nineteenth-century manner of Jo's German husband in *Little Men,* or in the manner of the crusading *sturm und drang* * liberal scholars in second year German novels. "Eric's mother and father are *both* called Dr. Burckhard," my mother once said, and indeed there was something endearingly repellent about Mrs. Burckhard with her doctor's degree, her long, unstylish skirts, and her dramatic, dulling blond braids. Strangely the Burckhards' sober continental bourgeois house was without golden mean—everything was either hilariously old Swiss or madly modern. The Frau Doctor Burckhard used to serve mid-morning hot chocolate with rosettes of whipped cream, and receive her friends in a long, uncarpeted hall-drawing room with lethal ferns and a yellow beeswaxed hardwood floor shining under a central skylight. On the wall there were large expert photographs of what at a distance appeared to be Mont Blanc *—they were in reality views of Frank Lloyd Wright's * Japanese hotel.

I admired the Burckhards and felt at home in their house, and these feelings were only intensified when I discovered that my mother was always ill at ease with them. The heartiness, the enlightenment, and the bright, ferny greenhouse atmosphere were too much for her.

Eric and I were too young to care for books or athletics. Neither of our houses had absorbing toys or an elevator to go up and down in. We were inseparable, but I cannot imagine what we talked about. I loved Eric because he was more popular than I and yet absolutely *sui generis* * at the Brimmer School. He had a chalk-white face and limp, fine, white-blond hair. He was frail, elbowy, started talking with an enthusiastic Mont Blanc chirp and would flush with bewilderment if interrupted. All the other boys at Brimmer wore little tweed golf suits with knickerbockers, but Eric always arrived in a black suit coat, a Byronic collar, and cuffless gray flannel trousers that almost hid his shoes. The long trousers were replaced on warm days by gray flannel shorts, such as were worn by children still in kindergarten. Eric's unenviable and freakish costumes were too old or too young. He accepted the whims of his parents with a buoyant tranquillity that I found unnatural.

My first and terminating quarrel with Eric was my fault. Eventually almost our whole class at Brimmer had whooping cough, but Eric's seizure was like his long trousers—untimely: he was sick a month too early. For a whole month he was in quarantine and forced to play by himself in a removed corner of the Pub-

---

* Erich von Ludendorff: (1865–1937), German general; a leader of Hitler's Munich putsch in 1923; fanatically opposed to Jews, Jesuits, and freemasons.
* *sturm und drang:* storm and stress; term referring to the revolutionary movement in German literature that flourished between 1770 and 1784.
* Mont Blanc: highest peak in the Swiss Alps.
* Frank Lloyd Wright: (1869–1959), innovatory American architect; the earthquake-proof Imperial Hotel in Tokyo is one of his largest works.
* *sui generis:* unique, in a class by himself.

lic Garden. He was certainly conspicuous as he skiproped with his Swiss nurse under the out-of-the-way Ether Memorial Fountain far from the pond and the swan boats. His parents had decided that this was an excellent opportunity for Eric to brush up on his German, and so the absoluteness of his quarantine was monstrously exaggerated by the fact that child and nurse spoke no English but only a guttural, British-sounding, Swiss German. Round and round and round the Fountain, he played intensely, frailly, obediently, until I began to tease him. Though motioned away by him, I came close. I had attracted some of the most popular Brimmer School boys. For the first time I had gotten favorable attention from several little girls. I came close. I shouted. Was Eric afraid of girls? I imitated his German. *Ein, swei, drei, BEER.* I imitated Eric's coughing. "He is afraid he will give you whooping cough if he talks or lets you come nearer," the nurse said in her musical Swiss-English voice. I came nearer. Eric flushed, grew white, bent double with coughing. He began to cry, and had to be led away from the Public Garden. For a whole week I routed Eric from the Garden daily, and for two or three days I was a center of interest. "Come see the Lake Geneva spider monkey!" I would shout. I don't know why I couldn't stop. Eric never told his father, I think, but when he recovered we no longer spoke. The breach was so unspoken and intense that our classmates were actually horrified. They even devised a solemn ritual for our reconciliation. We crossed our hearts, mixed spit, mixed blood. The reconciliation was hollow.

My parents' confidences and quarrels stopped each night at ten or eleven o'clock, when my father would hang up his tuxedo, put on his commander's uniform, and take a trolley back to the naval yard at Charlestown. He had just broken in a new car. Like a chauffeur, he watched this car, a Hudson, with an informed vigilance, always giving its engine hair-trigger little tinkerings of adjustment or friendship, always fearful lest the black body, unbeautiful as his boiled shirts, should lose its outline and gloss. He drove with flawless, almost instrumental, monotony. Mother, nevertheless, was forever encouraging him to walk or take taxis. She would tell him that his legs were growing vestigial from disuse and remind him of the time a jack had slipped and he had broken his leg while shifting a tire. "Alone and at night," she would say, "an amateur driver is unsafe in a car." Father sighed and obeyed—only, putting on a martyred and penny-saving face, he would keep his self-respect by taking the trolley rather than a taxi. Each night he shifted back into his uniform, but his departures from Revere Street were so furtive that several months passed before I realized what was happening—we had *two* houses! Our second house was the residence in the Naval Yard assigned to the third in command. It was large, had its own flagpole, and screen porches on three levels—yet it was something to be ashamed of. Whatever pomp or distinction its possession might have had for us was destroyed by an eccentric humiliation inflicted on Father by his superior, Admiral De Stahl, the commandant at Charlestown. De Stahl had not been consulted about our buying the 91 Revere Street house. He was outraged, stormed about "flaunting private fortunes in the face of naval tradition," and ordered my father to sleep on bounds at the Yard in the house provided for that purpose.

On our first Revere Street Christmas Eve, the telephone rang in the middle of dinner; it was Admiral De Stahl demanding Father's instant return to the Navy Yard. Soon Father was back in his uniform. In taking leave of my mother and grandparents he was, as was usual with him under pressure, a little evasive and magniloquent. "A woman works from sun to sun," he said, "but a sailor's watch is never done." He compared a naval officer's hours with a doctor's, hinted at surprise maneuvers, and explained away the uncommunicative arrogance of Admiral De Stahl: "The Old Man has to be hush-hush." Later that night, I lay in bed and tried to imagine that my father was leading his engineering force on a surprise maneuver through arctic wastes. A forlorn hope! "Hush-hush, hush-hush," whispered the snowflakes as big as street lamps as they broke on Father —broke and buried. Outside, I heard real people singing carols, shuffling snow off their shoes, opening and shutting doors. I worried at the meaning of a sentence I had heard quoted from the *Boston Evening Transcript:* "On this Christmas Eve, as usual, the whole of Beacon Hill can be expected to become a single old-fashioned open house—the names of mine host the Hill, and her guests will read like the contents of the Social Register." I imagined Beacon Hill changed to the snow queen's palace, as vast as the north pole. My father pressed a cold finger to his lip: "hush-hush," and led his surprised squad of sailors around an altar, but the altar was a tremendous cash register, whose roughened nickel surface was cheaply decorated with trowels, pyramids, and Arabic swirls. A great drawer helplessly chopped back and forth, unable to shut because choked with greenbacks. "Hush-hush!" My father's engineers wound about me with their eye-patches, orange sashes, and curtain-ring earrings, like the Gilbert and Sullivan pirates' chorus. . . . Outside on the streets of Beacon Hill, it was night, it was dismal, it was raining. Something disturbing had befallen the familiar and honorable Salvation Army band; its big drum and accordion were now accompanied by drunken voices howling: *The Old Gray Mare, she ain't what she used to be, when Mary went to milk the cow.* A sound of a bosun's whistle. Women laughing. Someone repeatedly rang our doorbell. I heard my mother talking on the telephone. "Your inebriated sailors have littered my doorstep with the dregs of Scollay Square." There was a gloating panic in her voice that showed she enjoyed the drama of talking to Admiral De Stahl. "Sir," she shrilled, "you have compelled my husband to leave me alone and defenseless on Christmas Eve!" She ran into my bedroom. She hugged me. She said, "Oh Bobby, it's such a comfort to have a man in the house." "I am not a man," I said, "I am a boy."

Boy—at that time this word had private associations for me; it meant weakness, outlawry, and yet was a status to be held onto. Boys were a sideline at my Brimmer School. The eight superior grades were limited to girls. In these grades, moreover, scholarship was made subservient to discipline, as if in contempt of the male's two idols: career and earning power. The school's tone, its *ton,* was a blend of the feminine and the military, a bulky reality governed in turn by stridency, smartness, and steadiness. The girls wore white jumpers, black skirts, stockings, and rectangular low-heeled shoes. An ex-West Pointer had been appointed to teach drill; and, at the moment of my enrollment in Brimmer, our principal, the hitherto staid Miss Manice, was rumored to be showing signs of age and of undermining her position with the school trustees by girlish, quite out of character, rhapsodies on the varsity basketball team, winner of two consecutive championships. The lower four grades, peaceful and lackadaisical, were, on the other hand, almost a separate establishment. Miss Manice regarded these "coeducated" classes with amused carelessness, allowed them to wear their ordinary clothes, and . . . carelessness, however, is incorrect—Miss Manice, in her administration of the lower school, showed the inconsistency and euphoria of a dual personality. Here she mysteriously shed all her Prussianism. She quoted Emerson and Mencken,* disparaged the English, threatened to break with the past, and boldly coquetted with the non-military American genius by displaying movies illustrating the careers of Edison and Ford. Favored lower school teachers were permitted to use us as guinea pigs for mildly radical experiments. At Brimmer I *un*learned writing. The script that I had mastered with much agony at my first school was denounced as illegible: I was taught to print according to the Dalton Plan—to this day, as a result, I have to print even my two middle names and can only really *write* two words: "Robert" and "Lowell." Our instruction was subject to bewildering leaps. The usual fall performance by the Venetian glass-blowers was followed by a tour of the Riverside Press. We heard Rudy Vallee,* then heard spirituals sung by the Hampton Institute choir. We studied grammar from a formidable, unreconstructed textbook written by Miss Manice's father. There, I battled with figures of speech and Greek terminology: *Chiásmus,* the arrangement of corresponding words in opposite order; *Brachyology,* the failure to repeat an element that is supplied in more or less modified form. Then all this pedantry was nullified by the introduction of a new textbook which proposed to lift the face of syntax by using game techniques and drawings.

Physical instruction in the lower school was irregular, spontaneous, and had nothing of that swept and garnished barrack-room camaraderie of the older girls' gymnasium exercises. On the roof of our school building, there was an ugly concrete area that looked as if it had been intended for the top floor of a garage. Here we played tag, drew lines with chalk, and chose up sides for a kind of kids' soccer. On bright spring days, Mr. Newell, a submerged young man from Boston University, took us on botanical hikes through the Arboretum. He had an eye for inessentials—read us Martha Washington's poems at the Old State House,

* H. L. Mencken: (1880–1956), American philologist, editor, and satirist; Miss Manice would have been quoting Emerson and Mencken in their roles as propagandists for American culture and for a break with the European cultural past.
* Rudy Vallee: one of the first crooners, especially popular during the 1930's and 1940's.

pointed out the roof of Brimmer School from the top of the Custom House, made us count the steps of the Bunker Hill Monument, and one rainy afternoon broke all rules by herding us into the South Boston Aquarium in order to give an unhealthy, eager, little lecture on the sewage-consumption of the conger eel. At last Miss Manice seemed to have gotten wind of Mr. Newell's moods. For an afternoon or two she herself served as his substitute. We were walked briskly past the houses of Parkman * and Dana,* and assigned themes on the spunk of great persons who had overcome physical handicaps and risen to the top of the ladder. She talked about Elizabeth Barrett, Helen Keller; her pet theory, however, was that "women simply are not the equals of men." I can hear Miss Manice browbeating my white and sheepish father, "How can we stand up to you? Where are our Archimedeses, our Wagners, our Admiral Simses?" * Miss Manice adored "Sir Walter Scott's *big bow-wow,*" wished "Boston had banned the tubercular novels of the Brontës," and found nothing in the world "so simpatico" as the "strenuous life" lived by President Roosevelt. Yet the extravagant hysteria of Miss Manice's philanthropy meant nothing; Brimmer was entirely a woman's world—*dumkopf,** perhaps, but not in the least Quixotic, Brimmer was ruled by a woman's obvious aims and by her naive pragmatism. The quality of this regime, an extension of my mother's, shone out in full glory at general assemblies or when I sat with a handful of other boys on the bleachers of Brimmer's new Manice Hall. In unison our big girls sang "America"; back and forth our amazons tramped—their brows were wooden, their dress was black and white, and their columns followed standard-bearers holding up an American flag, the white flag of the Commonwealth of Massachusetts, and the green flag of Brimmer. At basketball games against Miss Lee's or Miss Winsor's, it was our upper-school champions who rushed onto the floor, as feline and fateful in their pace as lions. This was our own immediate and daily spectacle; in comparison such masculine displays as trips to battle cruisers commanded by comrades of my father seemed eyewash—the Navy moved in a realm as ghostlike and removed from my life as the elfin acrobatics of Douglas Fairbanks * or Peter Pan. I wished I were an older girl. I wrote Santa Claus for a field hockey stick. To be a boy at Brimmer was to be small, denied, and weak.

I was promised an improved future and taken on Sunday afternoon drives through the suburbs to inspect the boys' schools: Rivers, Dexter, Country Day. These expeditions were stratagems designed to give me a chance to know my fa-

* Francis Parkman: (1823–93), American historian; among his works are *The Oregon Trail* (1849) and *La Salle and the Discovery of the Great West* (1879).
* Richard Henry Dana: (1815–82), sailor, lawyer, writer; author of *Two Years Before the Mast* (1840).
* Admiral Sims: (1858–1936), American naval officer; during World War I, he was in command of American naval operations in European waters; co-author of *Victory at Sea* (1920).
* *dumkopf:* blockheaded, simple-minded.
* Douglas Fairbanks: (1883–1939), American movie star; famous for his swashbuckling-hero roles (e.g. *The Mark of Zorro; Robin Hood*).

ther; Mother noisily stayed behind and amazed me by pretending that I had forbidden her to embark on "men's work." Father, however, seldom insisted, as he should have, on seeing the headmasters in person, yet he made an astonishing number of friends; his trust begat trust, and something about his silences encouraged junior masters and even school janitors to pour out small talk that was detrimental to rival institutions. At each new school, however, all this gossip was easily refuted; worse still Mother was always ready to cross-examine Father in a manner that showed that she was asking questions for the purpose of giving, not of receiving, instruction; she expressed astonishment that a wishy-washy desire to be everything to everybody had robbed a naval man of any reliable concern for his son's welfare. Mother regarded the suburban schools as "gerrymandered" and middle-class; after Father had completed his round of inspections, she made her own follow-up visits and told Mr. Dexter and Mr. Rivers to their faces that she was looking for a "respectable stop-gap" for her son's "three years between Brimmer and Saint Mark's." Saint Mark's was the boarding school for which I had been enrolled at birth, and was due to enter in 1930. I distrusted change, knew each school since kindergarten had been more constraining and punitive than its predecessor, and believed the suburban country day schools were flimsily disguised fronts for reformatories. With the egotistic, slightly paranoid apprehensions of an only child, I wondered what became of boys graduating from Brimmer's fourth grade, feared the worst—we were darkly imperiled, like some annual bevy of Athenian youths destined for the Minotaur.* And to judge from my father, men between the ages of six and sixty did nothing but meet new challenges, take on heavier responsibilities, and lose all freedom to explode. A ray of hope in the far future was my white-haired Grandfather Winslow, whose unchecked commands and demands were always upsetting people for their own good—he was all I could ever want to be: the bad boy, the problem child, the commodore of his household.

When I entered Brimmer I was eight and a half. I was distracted in my studies, assented to whatever I was told, picked my nose whenever no one was watching, and worried our third-grade teacher by organizing creepy little gangs of boys at recess. I was girl-shy. Thick-witted, narcissistic, thuggish, I had the conventional prepuberty character of my age; whenever a girl came near me, my whole person cringed like a sponge wrung dry by a clenching fist. I was less rather than more bookish than most children, but the girl I dreamed about continually had wheel-spoke black and gold eyelashes, double-length page-boy blond hair, a little apron, a bold, blunt face, a saucy, shivery way of talking, and . . . a paper body—she was the girl in John Tenniel's illustrations to *Alice in Wonderland*. The invigorating and symmetrical aplomb of my ideal Alice was soon

---

* the Minotaur: in Greek mythology, the monster confined in a labyrinth built by Daedalus for the Cretan king Minos; Minos forced Athens to pay him a yearly tribute of seven youths and seven maidens who were then shut up in the labyrinth to be devoured by the Minotaur.

enriched and nullified by a second face, when my father took me to the movies on the afternoon of one of Mother's headaches. An innocuous child's movie, the bloody, all-male *Beau Geste* had been chosen, but instead my father preferred a nostalgic tour of places he had enjoyed on shore leave. We went to the Majestic Theater where he had first seen Pola Negri—where we too saw Pola Negri,* sloppy-haired, slack, yawning, ravaged, unwashed . . . an Anti-Alice.

Our class belles, the Norton twins, Elie and Lindy, fell far short of the Nordic Alice and the foreign Pola. Their prettiness, rather fluffy, freckled, bashful, might have escaped notice if they had been one instead of two, and if their manners had been less goodhumored, entertaining, and reliable. What mattered more than sex, athletics, or studies to us at Brimmer was our popularity; each child had an unwritten class-popularity poll inside his head. Everyone was ranked, and all day each of us mooned profoundly on his place, as it quivered like our blood or a compass needle with a thousand revisions. At nine character is, perhaps, too much *in ovo* * for a child to be strongly disliked, but sitting next to Elie Norton, I glanced at her and gulped prestige from her popularity. We were not close at first; then nearness made us closer friends, for Elie had a gracious gift, the gift of gifts, I suppose, in a child: she forgot all about the popularity-rank of the classmate she was talking to. No moron could have seemed so uncritical as this airy, chatty, intelligent child, the belle of our grade. She noticed my habit of cocking my head on one side, shutting my eyes, and driving like a bull through opposition at soccer—wishing to amuse without wounding, she called me Buffalo Bull. At general assembly she would giggle with contented admiration at the upper-school girls in their penal black and white. "What bruisers, what beef-eaters! Dear girls," she would sigh, parroting her sophisticated mother, "we shall all become fodder for the governess classes before graduating from Brimmer." I felt that Elie Norton understood me better than anyone except my playful little Grandmother Winslow.

One morning there was a disaster. The boy behind me, no friend, had been tapping at my elbow for over a minute to catch my attention before I consented to look up and see a great golden puddle spreading toward me from under Elie's chair. I dared not speak, smile, or flicker an eyelash in her direction. She ran bawling from the classroom. Trying to catch every eye, yet avoid commitment, I gave sidelong and involuntary smirks at space. I began to feel manic with superiority to Elie Norton and struggled to swallow down a feeling of goaded hollowness—was I deserting her? Our teacher left us on our honor and ran down the hall. The class milled about in a hesitant hush. The girls blushed. The boys smirked. Miss Manice, the principal, appeared. She wore her whitish-brown dress with darker brown spots. Shimmering in the sunlight and chilling us, she stood mothlike in the middle of the classroom. We rushed to our seats. Miss Manice talked about how there was "nothing laughable about a malaise." She broke

* Pola Negri: famous vamp of the silent screen.
* *in ovo:* in the egg, undeveloped.

off. Her face took on an expression of invidious disgust. She was staring at me. . . . In the absentmindedness of my guilt and excitement, I had taken the nearest chair, the chair that Elie Norton had just left. "Lowell," Miss Manice shrieked, "are you going to soak there all morning like a bump on a log?"

When Elie Norton came back, there was really no break in her friendliness toward me, but there was something caved in, something crippled in the way I stood up to her and tried to answer her disengaged chatter. I thought about her all the time; seldom meeting her eyes now, I felt rich and raw in her nearness. I wanted passionately to stay on at Brimmer, and told my mother a fib one afternoon late in May of my last year. "Miss Manice has begged me to stay on," I said, "and enter the fifth grade." Mother pointed out that there had never been a boy in the fifth grade. Contradicted, I grew excited. "If Miss Manice has begged me to stay," I said, "why can't I stay?" My voice rose, I beat on the floor with my open hands. Bored and bewildered, my mother went upstairs with a headache. "If you won't believe me," I shouted after her, "why don't you telephone Miss Manice or Mrs. Norton?"

Brimmer School was thrown open on sunny March and April afternoons and our teachers took us for strolls on the polite, landscaped walks of the Public Garden. There I'd loiter by the old iron fence and gape longingly across Charles Street at the historic Boston Common, a now largely wrong-side-of-the-tracks park. On the Common there were mossy bronze reliefs of Union soldiers, and a captured German tank filled with smelly wads of newspaper. Everywhere there were grit, litter, gangs of Irish, Negroes, Latins. On Sunday afternoons orators harangued about Sacco and Vanzetti,* while others stood about heckling and blocking the sidewalks. Keen young policemen, looking for trouble, lolled on the benches. At nightfall a police lieutenant on horseback inspected the Common. In the Garden, however, there was only Officer Lever, a single white-haired and mustached dignitary, who had once been the doorman at the Union Club. He now looked more like a member of the club. "Lever's a man about town," my Grandfather Winslow would say. "Give him Harris tweeds and a glass of Scotch, and I'd take him for Cousin Herbert." Officer Lever was without thoughts or deeds, but Back Bay and Beacon Hill parents loved him just for being. No one asked this hollow and leonine King Log to be clairvoyant about children.

One day when the saucer magnolias were in bloom, I bloodied Bull-dog Binney's nose against the pedestal of George Washington's statue in full view of Commonwealth Avenue; then I bloodied Dopey Dan Parker's nose; then I stood in the center of a sundial tulip bed and pelted a little enemy ring of third-graders

* Sacco and Vanzetti: Italian-born philosophical anarchists convicted of murder in Massachusetts, July 1921. Because of irregularities in the evidence and suspicion that they had been tried not for the crime but for their radical views, there was popular demand for a retrial; but the men were executed in 1927 to the accompaniment of many demonstrations of protest all over the world.

with wet fertilizer. Officer Lever was telephoned. Officer Lever telephoned my mother. In the presence of my mother and some thirty nurses and children, I was expelled from the Public Garden. I was such a bad boy, I was told, "that *even* Officer Lever had been forced to put his foot down."

New England winters are long. Sunday mornings are long. Ours were often made tedious by preparations for dinner guests. Mother would start airing at nine. Whenever the air grew so cold that it hurt, she closed the den windows; then we were attacked by sour kitchen odors winding up a clumsily rebuilt dumb-waiter shaft. The windows were again thrown open. We sat in an atmosphere of glacial purity and sacrifice. Our breath puffed whitely. Father and I wore sleeveless cashmere jerseys Mother had bought at Filene's Basement. A do-it-yourself book containing diagrams for the correct carving of roasts lay on the arm of Father's chair. At hand were Big Bill Tilden on tennis, Capablanca on chess, newspaper clippings from Sidney Lenz's bridge column, and a magnificent tome with photographs and some American's nationalist sketch of Sir Thomas Lipton's errors in the Cup Defender races. Father made little progress in these diversions, and yet one of the authors assured him that mastery demanded only willing readers who understood the meaning of English words. Throughout the winter a gray-whiteness glared through the single den window. In the apoplectic brick alley, a fire escape stood out against our sooty plank fence. Father believed that churchgoing was undignified for a naval man; his Sunday mornings were given to useful acts such as lettering his three new galvanized garbage cans: R.T.S. Lowell—U.S.N.

Our Sunday dinner guests were often naval officers. Naval officers were not Mother's sort; very few people *were* her sort in those days, and that was her trouble—a very authentic, human, and plausible difficulty, which made Mother's life one of much suffering. She did not have the self-assurance for wide human experience; she needed to feel liked, admired, surrounded by the approved and familiar. Her haughtiness and chilliness came from apprehension. She would start talking like a *grande dame* and then stand back rigid and faltering, as if she feared being crushed by her own massively intimidating offensive.

Father's old Annapolis roommate, Commander Billy "Battleship Bilge" Harkness, was a frequent guest at Revere Street and one that always threw Mother off balance. Billy was a rough diamond. He made jokes about his "all-American family tree," and insisted that his name, pronounced H*a*rkness, should be spelled H*e*rkness. He came from Louisville, Kentucky, drank whisky to "renew his Bourbon blood," and still spoke with an accent that sounded—so his colleagues said—"like a bran-fed stallion." Like my father, however, Commander Billy had entered the Naval Academy when he was a boy of fourteen; his Southernisms had been thoroughly rubbed away. He was teased for knowing nothing about race horses, mountaineers, folk ballads, hams, sour mash, tobacco . . . Kentucky Colonels. Though hardly an officer and a gentleman in the old Virginian style, he was an unusual combination of clashing virtues: he had led his class in the sciences and yet was what his superiors called "a *mathmaddition* with the habit of command." He and my father, the youngest men in their class, had often been shipmates. Bilge's executive genius had given color and direction to Father's submissive tenacity. He drank like a fish at parties, but was a total abstainer on duty. With reason Commander Harkness had been voted the man most likely to make a four-star admiral in the class of '07.

Billy called his wife *Jimmy* or *Jeems,* and had a rough friendly way of saying, "Oh, Jimmy's bright as a penny." Mrs. Harkness was an unpleasant rarity: she was the only naval officer's wife we knew who was also a college graduate. She had a flat flapper's figure, and hid her intelligence behind a nervous twitter of vulgarity and toadyism. "Charlotte," she would almost scream at Mother, "is this mirAGE, this MIRAcle your *own* dining room!"

Then Mother might smile and answer in a distant, though cosy and amused, voice, "I usually manage to make myself pretty comfortable."

Mother's comfort was chic, romantic, impulsive. If her silver service shone, it shone with hectic perfection to rebuke the functional domesticity of naval wives. She had determined to make her *ambiance* beautiful and luxurious, but wanted neither her beauty nor her luxury unaccompanied. Beauty pursued too exclusively meant artistic fatuity of a kind made farcical by her Aunt Sarah Stark Winslow, a beauty too lofty and original ever to marry, a prima donna on the piano, too high-strung ever to give a public recital. Beauty alone meant the maudlin ignominy of having one's investments managed by interfering relatives. Luxury alone, on the other hand, meant for Mother the "paste and fool's-gold polish" that one met with in the foyer of the new Statler Hotel. She loathed the "undernourishment" of Professor Burckhard's Bauhaus * modernism, yet in moments of pique she denounced our pompous Myers mahoganies as "suitable for politicians at the Bellevue Hotel." She kept a middle-of-the-road position, and much admired Italian pottery with its fresh peasant colors and puritanical, clean-cut lines. She was fond of saying, "The French *do* have taste," but spoke with a double-edged irony which implied the French, with no moral standards to support their finish, were really no better than naval yahoos. Mother's beautiful house was dignified by a rich veneer of the useful.

"I have always believed carving to be *the* gentlemanly talent," mother used to proclaim. Father, faced with this opinion, pored over his book of instructions or read the section on table carving in the Encyclopaedia Britannica. Eventually he discovered among the innumerable small, specialized Boston "colleges" an establishment known as a carving school. Each Sunday from then on he would sit silent and erudite before his roast. He blinked, grew white, looked winded, and

---

* Bauhaus: German art school, founded in 1919, which revolutionized art training by combining the teaching of the pure arts with the study of crafts; Bauhaus "modernism" laid great stress on functionalism in design.

wiped beads of perspiration from his eyebrows. His purpose was to reproduce stroke by stroke his last carving lesson, and he worked with all the formal rightness and particular error of some shaky experiment in remote control. He enjoyed quiet witticisms at the expense of his carving master—"a philosopher who gave himself all the airs of a Mahan!" * He liked to pretend that the carving master had stated that "No two cuts are identical," *ergo:* "each offers original problems for the *executioner*." Guests were appeased by Father's saying, "I am just a plebe at this guillotine. Have a hunk of my roast beef hash."

What angered Father was Mrs. Harkness's voice grown merciless with excitement, as she studied his hewing and hacking. She was sure to say something tactless about how Commander Billy was "a stingy artist at carving who could shave General Washington off the dollar bill."

Nothing could stop Commander Billy, that born carver, from reciting verses:

> "By carving my way
> I lived on my pay;
> This *reeward*, though small,
> Beats none at all. . . .
>
> My carving paper-thin
> Can make a guinea *hin*,
> All giblets, bones, and skin,
> Canteen a party of *tin*."

And I, furious for no immediate reason, blurted out, "Mother, how much does Grandfather Winslow have to fork up to pay for Daddy's carving school?"

These Sunday dinners with the Harknesses were always woundingly boisterous affairs. Father, unnaturally outgoing, would lead me forward and say, "Bilge, I want you to meet my first coupon from the bond of matrimony."

Commander Billy would answer, "So this is the range-finder you are raising for future wars!" They would make me salute, stand at attention, stand at ease. "Angel-face," Billy would say to me, "you'll skipper a flivver."

"Jimmy" Harkness, of course, knew that Father was anxiously negotiating with Lever Brothers' Soap, and arranging for his resignation from the service, but nothing could prevent her from proposing time and again her "hens' toast to the drakes." Dragging Mother to her feet, Jimmy would scream, "To Bob and Bilgy's next battleship together!"

What Father and Commander Billy enjoyed talking about most was their class of '07. After dinner, the ladies would retire to the upstairs sitting room. As a special privilege I was allowed to remain at the table with the men. Over and over, they would talk about their ensigns' cruise around the world, escaping the "reeport," gun-boating on the upper Yangtse during the Chinese War,

---

* A. T. Mahan: (1840–1914), American naval officer, lecturer, and historian; his works on the historical significance of sea power were extremely influential and had an important effect on subsequent naval strategy.

keeping sane and sanitary at Guantanamo, patroling the Golfo del Papayo during the two-bit Nicaraguan Revolution, when water to wash in cost a dollar a barrel and was mostly "alkali and wrigglers." There were the class casualties: Holden and Holcomb drowned in a foundered launch off Hampton Roads; "Count" Bowditch, killed by the Moros and famous for his dying words to Commander Harkness: "I'm all right. Get on the job, Bilge."

They would speak about the terrible 1918 influenza epidemic, which had killed more of their classmates than all the skirmishes or even the World War. It was an honor, however, to belong to a class which included "Chips" Carpender, whose destroyer, the *Fanning,* was the only British or American warship to force a German submarine to break water and surrender. It was a feather in their caps that three of their classmates, Bellinger, Reade, and another, should have made the first trans-Atlantic seaplane flight. They put their faith in teamwork, and Lindbergh's solo hop to Paris struck them as unprofessional, a newspaper trick. What made Father and Commander Billy mad as hornets was the mare's-nest made of naval administration by "deserving Democrats." Hadn't Secretary of State Bryan ordered their old battlewagon the *Idaho* to sail on a goodwill mission to Switzerland? "Bryan, Bryan, Bryan," * Commander Billy would boom, "the pious swab had been told that Lake Geneva had annexed the Adriatic." Another "guy with false gills," Josephus Daniels, "ordained by Divine Providence Secretary of the Navy," had refused to send Father and Billy to the war zone. "You are looking," Billy would declaim, "at martyrs in the famous victory of red tape. Our names are rubric." A man they had to take their hats off to was Theodore Roosevelt; Billy had been one of the lucky ensigns who had helped "escort the redoubtable Teddy to Panama." Perhaps because of his viciously inappropriate nickname, "Bilge," Commander Harkness always spoke with brutal facetiousness against the class *bilgers,* officers whose services were no longer required by the service. In more Epicurean moods, Bilge would announce that he "meant to accumulate a lot of dough from complacent, well-meaning, although misguided West Point officers gullible enough to bet their shirts on the Army football team."

"Let's have a squint at your *figger* and waterline, Bob," Billy would say. He'd admire Father's trim girth and smile familiarly at his bald spot. "Bob," he'd say, "you've maintained your displacement and silhouette unmodified, except for somewhat thinner top chafing gear."

Commander Billy's drinking was a "pain in the neck." He would take possession of Father's sacred "rhino" armchair, sprawl legs astraddle, make the tried and true framework groan, and crucify Mother by roaring out verbose toasts in what he called "me boozy cockney-h'Irish." He would drink to our cocktail shaker. " 'Ere's to the 'older of the Lowelldom nectar," he would bellow. "Hip, hip, hooray for senor Martino, h'our h'old hipmate, 'elpmate, and hhonorary

---

* Bryan: Commander Billy is alluding to Vachel Lindsay's poem "Bryan Bryan Bryan Bryan" in which William Jennings Bryan is treated as a folk hero.

member of '07—h'always h'able to navigate and never says dry." We never got through a visit without one of Billy's "Bottoms up to the 'ead of the Nation. 'Ere's to herb-garden 'Erb." This was a swaggering dig at Herbert Hoover's notoriously correct, but insular, refusal to "imbibe anything more potent than Bromo-Seltzer" at a war-relief banquet in Brussels. Commander Billy's bulbous, water-on-the-brain forehead would glow and trickle with fury. Thinking on Herbert Hoover and Prohibition, he was unable to contain himself. "What a hick! We haven't been steered by a gentleman of parts since the redoubtable Teddy." He recited *wet* verses, such as the following inserted in Father's class book:

> "I tread the bridge with measured pace;
> Proud, yet anguish marks my face—
> What worries me like crushing sin
> Is where on the sea can I buy dry gin?"

In his cups, Commander Bilge acted as though he owned us. He looked like a human ash-heap. Cigar ashes buried the heraldic hedgehog on the ash tray beside him; cigar ashes spilled over and tarnished the golden stork embroidered on the table-cover; cigar ashes littered his own shiny blue-black uniform. Greedily Mother's eyes would brighten, drop and brighten. She would say darkly, "I was brought up by Papá to be like a naval officer, to be ruthlessly neat."

Once Commander Billy sprawled back so recklessly that the armchair began to come apart. "You see, Charlotte," he said to Mother, "at the height of my *climacteric* I am breaking Bob's chair."

Harkness went in for tiresome, tasteless harangues against Amy Lowell,* which he seemed to believe necessary for the enjoyment of his after-dinner cigar. He would point a stinking baby stogie at Mother. " 'Ave a peteeto cigareeto, Charlotte," he would crow. "Puff on this whacking black cheroot, and you'll be a match for any reeking senorita *femme fatale* in the spiggotty republics, where blindness from Bob's bathtub hooch is still unknown. When you go up in smoke, Charlotte, remember the *Maine*.* Remember Amy Lowell, that cigar-chawing, guffawing, senseless and meterless, multimillionheiress, heavyweight mascot on a floating fortress. Damn the *Patterns!* Full speed ahead on a cigareeto!"

Amy Lowell was never a welcome subject in our household. Of course, no one spoke disrespectfully of Miss Lowell. She had been so plucky, so *formidable, so beautifully and unblushingly immense,* as Henry James * might have said. And

---

* Amy Lowell: (1874–1925), descendant of the poet James Russell Lowell and kin to Robert Lowell; a poet and a leader of the Imagist movement. "Patterns" is her most widely anthologized poem.
* the *Maine:* U.S. battleship exploded in Havana harbor in 1898; American public opinion attributed this event to the Spanish and "Remember the *Maine!*" became a catchword that fed American patriotism during the Spanish-American War.
* Henry James: (1843–1916), American novelist; his convoluted prose style is a favorite subject for parodists.

yet, though irreproachably decent herself apparently, like Mae West * she seemed to provoke indecorum in others. There was an anecdote which I was too young to understand: it was about Amy's getting migraine headaches from being kept awake by the exercises of honeymooners in an adjacent New York hotel room. Amy's relatives would have liked to have honored her as a *personage,* a personage a little *outrée* * perhaps, but perfectly within the natural order, like Amy's girlhood idol, the Duse.* Or at least she might have been unambiguously tragic, short-lived, and a classic, like her last idol, John Keats. My parents piously made out a case for Miss Lowell's *Life of Keats,* which had killed its author and was so much more manly and intelligible than her poetry. Her poetry! But was *poetry* what one could call Amy's loud, bossy, unladylike *chinoiserie* *— her free verse! For those that could understand it, her matter was, no doubt, blameless, but the effrontery of her manner made my parents relish Robert Frost's remark that "writing free verse was like playing tennis without a net."

Whenever Amy Lowell was mentioned Mother bridled. Not distinguishing, not caring whether her relative were praised or criticized, she would say, "Amy had the courage of her convictions. She worked like a horse." Mother would conclude characteristically, "Amy did insist on doing everything the *hard* way. I think, perhaps, that her brother, the President of Harvard, did more for *other* people."

Often Father seemed to pay little attention to the conversation of his guests. He would smack his lips, and beam absentmindedly and sensuously, as if he were anticipating the comforts of civilian life—a perpetual shore leave in Hawaii. The Harknesses, however, cowed him. He would begin to feel out the subject of his resignation and observe in a wheedle obscurely loaded with significance that "certain *cits* * no brighter than you or I, pay income taxes as large as a captain's yearly salary."

Commander Harkness, unfortunately, was inclined to draw improper conclusions from such remarks. Disregarding the "romance of commerce," he would break out into ungentlemanly tirades against capital. "Yiss, old Bob," he would splutter, "when I consider the ungodly hoards garnered in by the insurance and broking gangs, it breaks my heart. Riches, reaches, overreaches! If Bob and I had half the swag that Harkness of Yale has just given Lowell of Harvard to build Georgian houses for Boston quee-eers with British accents!" He rumbled on morosely about retired naval officers "forced to live like coolies on their half-

---

* Mae West: (1892–), American stage and film personality; she began her career as a burlesque artist and is famous for her broadly humourous and suggestive treatment of sex.
* *outrée:* extravagant, exaggerated, bizarre.
* the Duse: Eleonora Duse (1859–1924), famous Italian actress, excelling in roles demanding strong emotional effects.
* *chinoiserie:* imitation Chinese art or decoration.
* a *cit:* military and naval slang for someone not in the army or navy.

pay. Hurrah for the Bull Moose Party!" * he'd shout. "Hurrah for Boss Curley! * Hurrah for the Bolshies!" *

Nothing prevented Commander Billy from telling about his diplomatic mission in 1918, when "his eyes had seen the Bolshie on his native heath." He had been in Budapest "during the brief sway of Béla Kun-Whon.* Béla was giving those Hunkyland money-bags and educators the boot into the arms of American philanthropy!"

Then Mother would say, hopefully, "Mamá always said that the *old* Hungarians *did* have taste. Billy, your reference to Budapest makes me heartsick for Europe. I am dying for Bob and Bobby's permission to spend next summer at Etretat."

Commander Billy Harkness specialized in verses like "The Croix de Guerre":

> "I toast the guy, who, crossing over,
>   Abode in London for a year,
> The guy who to his wife and lover
>   Returned with conscience clean and clear,
> Who nightly prowling Piccadilly
>   Gave icy stares to floozies wild,
> And when approached said, 'Bilgy Billy
>   Is mama's darling angel child—'
> Now he's the guy who rates the croy dee geer!"

Mother, however, smiled mildly. "Billy," she would say, "my cousin, Admiral Ledyard Atkinson, always has a twinkle in his eye when he asks after your *vers de société*." *

"'Tommy' Atkins!" snorted Commander Billy. "I know Tommy better than my own mother. He's the first chapter in a book I'm secretly writing and leaving to the archives called *Wild Admirals I Have Known*. And now my bodily presence may no longer grace the inner sanctum of the Somerset Club, for fear Admiral Tommy'll assault me with five new chapters of his *Who Won the Battle of Jutland?*"

After the heat and push of Commander Billy, it was pleasant to sit in the shade of the Atkinsons. Cousin Ledyard wasn't exactly an admiral: he had been promoted to this rank during the World War and had soon reverted back to his

---

* the Bull Moose Party: familiar name for the Progressive party organized in 1912 to support ex-President Theodore Roosevelt for re-election in opposition to William Howard Taft (President 1909–13); however Woodrow Wilson (Democrat) won the election.

* Boss Curley: James Michael Curley (1874–1958), big power in the Democratic party of Boston; three times Mayor of Boston, once Governor of Massachusetts.

* Bolshies: Bolsheviks.

* Béla Kun: (1886–1939?), Hungarian Communist who presided over a tough Communist regime in Hungary, 1919, and was defeated the same year by counterrevolutionists.

* *vers de société*: light social verse of the kind illustrated.

old rank of captain. In 1926 he was approaching the retiring age and was still a captain. He was in charge of a big, stately, comfortable, but anomalous warship, which seldom sailed further than hailing distance from its Charlestown drydock. He was himself stately and anomalous. Serene, silver-maned, and Spanish-looking, Cousin Ledyard liked full-dress receptions and crowed like a rooster in his cabin crowded with liveried Filipinos, Cuban trophies, and racks of experimental firearms, such as pepper-box pistols and a machine gun worked by electric batteries. He rattled off Spanish phrases, told first-hand adventure stories about service with Admiral Schley, and reminded one of some landsman and diplomat commanding a galleon in Philip II's Armada. With his wife's money he had bought a motor launch which had a teak deck and a newfangled diesel engine. While his warship perpetually rode at anchor, Cousin Ledyard was forever hurrying about the harbor in his launch. "Oh, Led Atkinson has dash and his own speedboat!" This was about the best my father could bring himself to say for his relative. Commander Billy, himself a man of action, was more sympathetic: "Tommy's about a hundred horse and buggy power." Such a dinosaur, however, had little to offer an '07 Annapolis graduate. Billy's final judgment was that Cousin Ledyard knew less *trig* than a schoolgirl, had been promoted through mistaken identity or merely as "window-dressing," and "was really plotting to put airplane carriers in square sails to stem the tide of our declining Yankee seamanship." Mother lost her enthusiasm for Captain Atkinson's stately chatter—he was "unable to tell one woman from another."

Cousin Ledyard's wife, a Schenectady Hoes distantly related to my still living Great-Grandmother Myers, was twenty years younger than her husband. This made her a trying companion; with the energy of youth she demanded the homage due to age. Once while playing in the Mattapoisett tennis tournament, she had said to her opponent, a woman her own age but married to a young husband, "I believe I'll call you Ruth; you can call me Mrs. Atkinson." She was a radiant Christian Scientist, darted about in smart serge suits and blouses frothing with lace. She filled her purse with Science literature and boasted without irony of "Boston's greatest grand organ" in the Christian Science mother temple on Huntington Avenue. As a girl, she had grown up with our Myers furniture. We dreaded Mrs. Atkinson's descents on Revere Street. She pooh-poohed Mother's taste, snorted at our ignorance of Myers family history, treated us as mere custodians of the Myers furniture, resented alterations, and had the memory of a mastodon for Cousin Cassie's associations with each piece. She wouldn't hear of my mother's distress from neuralgia, dismissed my asthma as "growing-pains," and sought to rally us by gossiping about healers. She talked a prim, sprightly babble. Like many Christian Scientists, she had a bloodless, euphoric, inexhaustible interest in her own body. In a discourse which lasted from her first helping of roast beef through her second demitasse, Mrs. Atkinson held us spellbound by telling how her healer had "surprised and evaporated a cyst inside a sac" inside her "major intestine."

I can hear my father trying to explain his resignation from the Navy to Cousin Ledyard or Commander Billy. Talking with an unnatural and importunate jocularity, he would say, "Billy Boy, it's a darned shame, but this State of Massachusetts doesn't approve of the service using its franchise and voting by mail. I haven't had a chance to establish residence since our graduation in '07. I think I'll put my blues in mothballs and become a *cit* just to prove I still belong to the country. The directors of Lever Brothers' Soap in Cambridge . . . I guess for *cits,* Billy, they've really got something on the ball, because they tell me they want me on their team."

Or Father, Cousin Ledyard, Commander Billy, and I would be sitting on after dinner at the dining-room table and talking man to man. Father would say, "I'm afraid I'll grow dull and drab with all this goldbricking ashore. I am too old for tennis singles, but too young for that confirmed state of senility known as golf."

Cousin Ledyard and Commander Billy would puff silently on their cigars. Then Father would try again and say pitifully, "I don't think a naval man can ever on the *outside* replace the friends he made during his years of wearing the blue."

Then Cousin Ledyard would give Father a polite, funereal look and say, "Speaking of golf, Bob, you've hit me below the belt. I've been flubbing away at the game for thirty years without breaking ninety."

Commander Billy was blunter. He would chaff Father about becoming a "beachcomber" or "purser for the Republican junior chamber of commerce." He would pretend that Father was in danger of being jailed for evading taxes to support "Uncle Sam's circus." *Circus* was Commander Billy's slang for the Navy. The word reminded him of a comparison, and once he stood up from the table and bellowed solemnly: "Oyez, oyez! Bob Lowell, our bright boy, our class baby, is now on a par with 'Rattle-Ass Rats' Richardson, who resigned from us to become press agent for Sells-Floto Circus, and who writes me: 'Bilgy Dear—Beating the drum ahead of the elephants and the spangled folk, I often wonder why I run into so few of my classmates.' "

Those dinners, those apologies! Perhaps I exaggerate their embarrassment because they hover so grayly in recollection and seem to anticipate ominously my father's downhill progress as a civilian and Bostonian. It was to be expected, I suppose, that Father should be in irons for a year or two, while becoming detached from his old comrades and interests, while waiting for the new life.

I used to sit through the Sunday dinners absorbing cold and anxiety from the table. I imagined myself hemmed in by our new, inherited Victorian Myers furniture. In the bleak Revere Street dining room, none of these pieces had at all that air of unhurried condescension that had been theirs behind the summery veils of tissue paper in Cousin Cassie Julian-James's memorial volume. Here, table, highboy, chairs, and screen—mahogany, cherry, teak—looked nervous and disproportioned. They seemed to wince, touch elbows, shift from foot to foot. High above the highboy, our gold National Eagle stooped forward, plastery and doddering. The Sheffield silver-plate urns, more precious than solid sterling, peeled; the bodies of the heraldic mermaids on the Mason-Myers crest blushed a metallic copper tan. In the harsh New England light, the bronze sphinxes supporting our sideboard looked as though manufactured in Grand Rapids. All too clearly no one had worried about synchronizing the grandfather clock's minutes, days, and months with its mellow old Dutch seascape-painted discs for showing the phases of the moon. The stricken, but still striking gong made sounds like steam banging through pipes. Colonel Myers' monumental Tibetan screen had been impiously shortened to fit it for a low Yankee ceiling. And now, rough and gawky, like some Hindu water buffalo killed in mid-rush but still alive with mad momentum, the screen hulked over us . . . and hid the pantry sink.

Our real blue-ribbon-winning *bête noire* * was of course the portrait of Cousin Cassie's father, Mordecai Myers' fourth and most illustrious son: Colonel Theodorus Bailey Myers. The Colonel, like half of our new portraits, was merely a collateral relation; though really as close to us as James Russell Lowell, no one called the Colonel "Great Grand Uncle," and Mother playfully pretended that her mind was overstrained by having to remember his full name, rank, and connection. In the portrait, Colonel Theodorus wore a black coat and gray trousers, an obsequiously conservative costume which one associated with undertakers and the musicians at Symphony Hall. His spats were pearl gray plush with pearl buttons. His mustache might have been modeled on the mustache of a bartender in a Western. The majestic Tibetan screen enclosed him as though he were an ancestor-god from Lhasa, a blasphemous yet bogus attitude. Mr. Myers' colonel's tabs were crudely stitched to a civilian coat; his New York Yacht Club button glowed like a carnation; his vainglorious picture frame was a foot and a half wide. Forever, his right hand hovered over a glass dome that covered a model locomotive. He was vaguely Middle-Eastern and waiting. A lady in Mother's sewing circle had pertly interpreted this portrait as, "King Solomon about to receive the Queen of Sheba's shares in the Boston and Albany Railroad." Gone now was the Colonel's place of honor at Cousin Cassie's Washington mansion; gone was his charming satire on the belles of 1850, entitled, *Nothing to Wear,* which had once been quoted "throughout the length and breadth of the land as generally as was Bret Harte's * *Heathen Chinee";* gone was his priceless collection of autographed letters of *all* the Signers of the Declaration of Independence —he had said once, "my letters will be my tombstone." Colonel Theodorus Bailey Myers had never been a New Englander. His family tree reached to no obscure Somersetshire yeoman named Winslowe or Lowle. He had never even, like

---

* *bête noire:* person or object of special aversion (literally, "black beast").
* Bret Harte: (1836–1902), American writer; his famous comic ballad *Plain Language from Truthful James* (1870) was sometimes called *The Heathen Chinee.*

his father, Mordecai, gloried in a scarlet War of 1812 waistcoat. His portrait was an indifferent example from a dull, bad period. The Colonel's only son had sheepishly changed his name from Mason-Myers to Myers-Mason.

Waiting for dinner to end and for the guests to leave, I used to lean forward on my elbows, support each cheekbone with a thumb, and make my fingers meet in a clumsy Gothic arch across my forehead. I would stare through this arch and try to make life stop. Out in the alley the sun shone irreverently on our three garbage cans lettered: R.T.S. LOWELL—U.S.N. When I shut my eyes to stop the sun, I saw first an orange disc, then a red disc, then the portrait of Major Myers apotheosized, as it were, by the sunlight lighting the blood smear of his scarlet waistcoat. Still there was no *coup de théâtre* * about the Major as he looked down on us with his portly young man's face of a comfortable upper New York State patroon and the friend of Robert Livingston * and Martin Van Buren. Great-great-Grandfather Myers had never frowned down in judgment on a Salem witch. There was no allegory in his eyes, no *Mayflower*. Instead he looked peacefully at his sideboard, his cut-glass decanters, his cellaret—the worldly bosom of the Mason-Myers mermaid engraved on a silver-plated urn. If he could have spoken, Mordecai would have said, "My children, my blood, accept graciously the loot of your inheritance. We are all dealers in used furniture."

The man who seems in my memory to sit under old Mordecai's portrait is not my father, but Commander Billy—*the* Commander after Father had thrown in his commission. There Billy would sit glowing, perspiring, bragging. Despite his rowdiness, he even then breathed the power that would make him a vice-admiral and hero in World War II. I can hear him boasting in lofty language of how he had stood up for democracy in the day of Lenin and Béla Kun; of how he "practiced the sport of kings" (i.e., commanded a destroyer) and combed the Mediterranean, Adriatic, and Black Seas like gypsies—seldom knowing what admiral he served under or where his next meal or load of fuel oil was coming from.

It always vexed the Commander, however, to think of the strings that had been pulled to have Father transferred from Washington to Boston. He would ask Mother, "Why in God's name should a man with Bob's brilliant cerebellum go and mess up his record by actually *begging* for that impotent field nigger's job of second in command at the defunct Boston Yard!"

I would squirm. I dared not look up because I knew that the Commander abhorred Mother's dominion over my father, thought my asthma, supposedly brought on by the miasmal damp of Washington, a myth, and considered our final flight to Boston a scandal.

My mother, on the other hand, would talk back sharply and explain to Billy that there was nothing second-string about the Boston Yard except its comman-

---

* *coup de théâtre:* sudden and sensational turn in a play; a theatrical "act."
* Robert Livingston: (1746–1813), New York lawyer and political figure; one of the five men who drew up the Declaration of Independence.

dant, Admiral De Stahl, who had gone into a frenzy when he learned that my parents, supposed to live at the naval yard, had set themselves up without his permission at 91 Revere Street. The Admiral had *commanded* Father to reside at the yard, but Mother had bravely and stubbornly held on at Revere Street.

"A really great person," she would say, "knows how to be courteous to his superiors."

Then Commander Harkness would throw up his hands in despair and make a long buffoonish speech. "Would you believe it?" he'd say. "De Stahl, the anile slob, would make Bob Lowell sleep seven nights a week and twice on Sundays in that venerable twenty-room pile provided for his third in command at the yard. 'Bobby me boy,' the Man says, 'henceforth I will that you sleep wifeless. You're to push your beauteous mug into me boudoir each night at ten-thirty and each morn at six. And don't mind me laying to alongside the Missus De Stahl,' the old boy squeaks; 'we're just two oldsters as weak as babies. But Robbie Boy,' he says, 'don't let me hear of you hanging on your telephone wire and bending off the ear of that forsaken frau of yours sojourning on Revere Street. I might have to phone you in a hurry, if I should happen to have me stroke.' "

Taking hold of the table with both hands, the Commander tilted his chair backwards and gaped down at me with sorrowing Gargantuan wonder: "I know why Young Bob is an only child."

Bruno Bettelheim / Results of Kibbutz Education

Dr. Bettelheim's interest in the new social situation created by the kibbutz system of rearing children in isolation from their parents gave rise to his book *The Children of the Dream,* from which this chapter is excerpted. Here we have a summary account of Dr. Bettelheim's findings and the implications arising from them. He points out the ways in which first-generation kibbutzniks differ from their ghetto-born parents and how the second generation of kibbutzniks differs from the first. This second generation escapes many of the conflicts undergone by the first; it is "a new generation in a new land." This lofty vision has produced a down-to-earth generation, which is at least suited to the life of the kibbutz.

Whether the system would be valid for the world in general is—as Dr. Bettelheim says—a harder question. Among other points, made with exemplary care and clarity, the author notes that kibbutzniks tend to form a static society of their own and have little contact with the larger society on which they ultimately depend. They do not, so far as present knowledge goes, tend to move out into scientific, intellectual, or aesthetic careers; their upbringing prevents even those who might have done so from wishing such a change. Their personalities are in this sense depleted. On the other hand, there are great advantages on the side of the kibbutzniks—mutual support, the abolition of antisocial behavior, the absence of deprived children.

Note, in this chapter, the caution with which the scientific observer qualifies his opinions, states the facts, and allows for possibilities of error (i.e. in the educational tests employed, which reflect values foreign to those of the kibbutz).

Any system of education can be judged in a number of ways but at least two of them seem specially important. The first is: How well does the system achieve what it was designed for? The second: How viable are its results for the individual, for his society, and for mankind in general?

The first question is much easier to answer because one need only compare results with expressed goals. The second is impossible to answer while we lack for a universal consensus on what is the ultimate good for individual or society.

Either way, there is one count on which kibbutz education is an unqualified success, though I doubt that its founders gave it a thought: It has disproved the critics. Much as some economists were convinced, a few decades ago, that the soviet system would have to break down because of inner contradictions, so did psychologists and psychiatrists predict that a system that removed the infant from his family, particularly from his mother, and raised him in institutions would have to result in total failure. Kibbutz education has conformed as little to these predictions as did communism. More important, it has clearly reached its own goal: to create a radically new personality in a single generation.

A NEW KIND OF JEW

Both as idea and ethic, the kibbutz originated with men and women who were born to a way of life as different from kibbutz ways as one can imagine. Among its founders—mainly Jews of Eastern Europe—the two highest aspirations were intellectual achievement and the acquisition of property. Ghetto life was utterly remote from any livelihood wrested from the earth. Its redeeming virtues were extremely close kinship ties; deep feelings openly shown, often histrionically displayed; strong emotional attachments between parents and children; and a deep commitment to religious custom. The founders' defensive rejection of these parental mores shows up in almost every aspect of their life and behavior.

A total absence of such defensiveness—or indeed of any interest in ghetto values and attitudes, pro or con—is the clearest sign of how different is the kibbutz-born generation from their parents.

It could be argued that this is because they were not born in a ghetto but in a country that wanted them for its own; that it therefore has little to do with kibbutz education. But my impression is that children who were born and raised in Israel outside the kibbutz, while they differ from their parents, still show clearly many of those features that marked Eastern Jewry. They show the same desire for intellectual achievement and the acquisition of property, for close family ties and more open emotionality, though the show of feeling is more subdued.

While I have known many children whose personalities differed radically from their parents', partly because of an entirely different education, I have never seen an entire generation so unlike their own parents. Not only do their personalities differ from their parents', but their ideas and the nature of their commitment (because there are puritanical parents whose radical children are as puritanical in devotion to their radical ideas as their parents ever were about religion). In fact, this very difference from their parents welds the second generation together and makes for a relative disinterest in their parents. In many ways they embrace the ideas their parents hoped to instill in them much more ardently than their parents, but in wholly different ways. At least this is so for the ones who remain in the kibbutz.

The founding generation (like the non-puritanical children of puritans) were and still are as emotional about their new kibbutz values as their parents were about old ghetto values. While the two creeds differ radically, the emotional stance is the same. Kibbutz life, to its founders, is as much holy scripture as the religious life was to their parents. To them, as the other was to their parents, it is the only good life, permitting no deviation, and invested with deepest emotions.

The kibbutz-born generation is committed to an entirely different *Sachlichkeit,* a literalness, a matter-of-fact objectivity which has no place for emotions. On the contrary, those emotions their parents show seem a bit ridiculous to them, unbefitting the new kibbutz generation. As an educator of the founding generation put it: "It's not only the minute we get romantic about our values that they say in disgust, 'Oh, come on! That's Zionism!' It's also in other matters. For example in my own field, biology, they approach it with dispassion. We had real feeling for our animals because of our humanism. They are only interested in the usefulness of the animal. We've had heated discussions, for example, about the artificial insemination of cows—whether we should do that to our animals. But the reactions of our youngsters are quite realistic, and they have no feeling for our qualms. Their attitude is 'that's how things are!' "

And this rationality, this unemotional attitude is not restricted to animals. It extends to human beings, even their own children. For example, I was told that the kibbutz-born generation felt that nurses, metapelets,* and teachers used to be much too involved in their work with the children; that theirs should have been a work assignment like any other.

As another of the founding generation told me: "We brought up our children with such careful consideration for them as human beings, but when they grow

---

* metapelets: substitute mothers.

up and work as nurses, even those who have children of their own, they are much less concerned. Let's say they're more realistic, mechanistic, objective, than we are; less humanistic, less involved. They are much quicker to do things, even those things that might hurt the children, because they see it in a framework of necessities and reasons, of rational work. They've lost some of the consideration we had all the time."

Georges Friedmann, the French sociologist (*The End of the Jewish People?*, 1967), writes that though he was told (of this new generation of kibbutzniks) that "they have lost the defects of their parents and also their qualities," it took him "weeks or months to explore the implications of those few words." Eventually Friedmann came to accept J. Ben David's conclusions (1964) that "in fact . . . there was nothing idealistic for them in living and working in the settlements where they were born; it was just part of their inherited way of life." Friedmann also comments on the changing image of the kibbutz in Israel. During the thirties, he writes, the kibbutz-born generation

> became an ideal image, closely linked with the older ideal image of the Halutz, the altruistic pioneer. . . . Thanks to their real qualities, but also aided by the image that floated around them, [they] had meteoric careers in Israeli society. . . . After the [1948] war of independence this splendid image deteriorated and rapidly gave place to another. J. Ben David gives an ingenious explanation of the process. This ideal image, of the Israeli-born generation as a rejuvenated version of the Halutz image . . . was based on a mistake. Altruism and devotion to duty are always displayed in wars of national or social liberation. During the period of the heroic fraternity of wartime they had shared the collectivist ideals of the first generation only in appearance. The return to settled conditions brought to the surface the moral discontinuity between the generations that had been temporarily papered over. . . . Parallel with this, the collective principles of Israeli society propagated in the schools and by the youth movements, the press, the radio and the army implied a critical image of the Sabra * that is a revised version of that of the thirties. According to this image, the Israeli [non-kibbutz born and raised] Sabra thinks only of himself; Halutz ideals are alien to him, indeed in his "egoism" all ideals are alien to him. In short, he is a materialist. His manners are not just offhand, they are positively discourteous and rude.

To which I would like to add that the kibbutz-born and raised Sabra has retained many of the Halutz ideals, but he, too, is otherwise a materialist, kibbutz-egocentric, offhand, and often discourteous.

At the same time I was deeply impressed by the lengths the kibbutzniks go to in taking care of the few children who are mentally retarded, brain damaged, etc. The whole kibbutz makes these children its concern. Metapelets and teach-

---

* Sabra: a native-born Jewish Israeli.

ers make all necessary allowances and go out of their way to help them adjust to kibbutz life. I saw some of these children as grown-ups, and although one or the other of them was most difficult to live with and work with—obstinate, cantankerous, etc.—the kibbutz felt they had to be accepted and special allowances made, not only because they were children of the kibbutz, but because one must make their parents (who are also kibbutzniks) feel their children are being well taken care of. I state this very forcefully, because it was most moving to see how wonderful they were about keeping such defectives within their society.

I have spoken of the kibbutznik's love for the land. In the founding generation this was and remains very much a romantic idea, a love intellectually cherished, but by no means strongly felt. Though many love their flowers, they love them as many a suburbanite does. The opposite is true for their children. Their love is deep, unquestioning, unromantic, not for the flowers in their little gardens, but for the very terrain. The same is true for their attitude toward private possessions. The founding generation has slowly acquired some private property, usually just a handful of things, some of them presents from relatives outside the kibbutz. But owning them makes quite a difference. And though they try to restrict and regulate such gifts, the wish for possessions seems so strong that there are many infractions of the principle of common property. The reason, I believe, is that the abolition of property was an idea defensively embraced in revolt against the old ways of parents and society; hence the ambivalence about it continues to seethe.

Things are very different for the second generation, those raised in the kibbutz. Rarely do they leave because of any wish for property. To be with their children, yes; or to have greater freedom to develop emotionally or otherwise. But to own things, hardly ever, or for only a very few. Even those who leave are much less ambivalent about property than their parents, while those who stay are universally critical of their elders for the concessions they make. For them, communal property is not an idea defensively or consciously embraced, but the only normal way to live.

The same goes for having their children raised by the community. I have said that mothers of the first generation were conflicted about their femininity— feared they would not make good as mothers, showed strong tendencies toward "masculine protest," etc.—and that all this was reflected in how their infants reacted to them and to communal rearing. I found little of all this among mothers who were born in the kibbutz. Many of them are quite secure in their femininity. True, they hold on to all the gains their mothers have won toward equality of the sexes; but these, too, they take for granted and hence are very casual about.

For the same reason they are much more casual about having their children live in the children's houses. It does not disturb them to have their children as emotionally distant from them as they are from their children. To them it is not a deliberate means of creating a better society, not even so much the right or the natural way, but the most convenient order of things. Since they are much less ambivalent about it than their parents were, their own children, the third generation, accept it more easily in turn.

The founding generation complains that their pre-teen or adolescent children are cool or indifferent to them, even rude; that they are too engrossed in their peer group. Behind it is the old ambivalence: "I expected you to love me, as I loved (or wanted to love) my parents. But I wanted you to love me, and not also hate me as I hated my parents (and hated hating them). That's why I gave you up to the children's house. It is wrong of you to repay me for this sacrifice with indifference." And behind it lies the greater fear: "Maybe I gave you up to the children's house for selfish reasons: because I wanted to live my own life with my comrades, without the burden of taking care of you all day long. Love me, to prove that my reasons were not selfish; to prove that I sacrificed much to make a better world for you than the one I grew up in."

None of these involuted fears and desires can bedevil the second generation. They are indeed a new generation in a new land. The founding generation tore the messianic idea from its religious matrix and turned hope into fact. They did not wait for the Messiah, as did all the generations before them. But in bringing a lofty vision to earth, they brought forth an earthy generation—the price of transforming ideals into everyday life. This second generation expects nothing more of its children than that they live out this everyday reality, and is well content with things as they are.

Hence I feel there is good reason to accept that kibbutz education has achieved its major purpose: to create a personality type that is not only different from, but more suited to kibbutz life than that of the parents who devised it.

WORLD OF KIBBUTZIM?

This brings me to my second set of criteria about kibbutz education; one that is much harder, if not impossible to answer: the question of how successful a system it is, for the individual and for his society? But this will depend on whether or not we believe that kibbutz life makes for a more successful individual, and whether a society composed of kibbutzim would make for a better world. That the vast majority of Israelis opt against this idea, and quite a few kibbutz-born also opt against it, by leaving, hardly settles the question.

Does Israel, even in kibbutz eyes, need an entire population that is satisfied with living in small, self-contained agricultural communities, even with small industries attached? If the kibbutz answer were yes, it could only be yes with many reservations, since they realize that Israel is not self-sufficient in providing the modern war machinery she feels she must have for her security. But even if the kibbutz answer were yes, I could not accept it. Because even the most cursory inspection convinces one that kibbutz society could not survive economically without drawing on the highly developed technology of surrounding Israel.

The kibbutz could never provide itself with the farm machinery it needs, nor with enough of experimental science and its findings. Yet these alone permit its farms to survive, even to flourish, as do the low interest loans and special tax advantages they enjoy. Nor could a society based on small groups create the complex machinery they need for even the small industries they have.

All efforts to create kibbutzim among urban groups who work in large-scale production have failed. Kibbutzim can exist only (it seems) if the group life is not interfered with by meeting non-group members at every step. They may even need the emotional replenishment that comes of a love for and contact with nature.

Kibbutzniks, or at least nearly all those I talked with, are quite aware that, while they wish the kibbutz were the universal image of the good life, as it is for them and many others, it is not so for all. They are also very concerned about the number of persons who leave the kibbutz. They are well aware that the kibbutz movement has so far survived, has even grown in population, not so much by keeping or increasing its own, but by attracting new blood from the outside. And a great deal of effort goes into recruiting through the youth movement, both in Israel and abroad.

Thus the kibbutz, somewhat like our farming communities, represents a process of self-selection. Kibbutzniks of the second generation are those who remained behind on the farm or, depending on how one looks at it, those who stayed in the forefront of the struggle for a more just society. It is impossible to say what the kibbutz would be like today if no one had ever left. What divisive, even disruptive influence might its leavers have exerted, had they stayed? Or what reforms might they have pressed for and gotten through? This question is important because kibbutz educators wish very much to feed Israeli society with future leaders for the good life.

Now it is nothing unusual in history for yesterday's radicals, once the new religion or society is safely rooted, to become its staunchest defenders against further change. The question is: Does kibbutz education *of necessity* lead to a status quo society? And related to this: What are the educational goals of this system as to the individual's role in society?

Here I found the system strangely contradictory, in which it resembles our own. Its goal is to have the next generation carry on kibbutz life exactly like their parents, and also wield moral leadership in Israel (if not the world), preferably as political leaders. I have mentioned the feeling of many thoughtful Israelis: that were it not for the kibbutz, the creation of a new state simply to harbor a persecuted religious minority would by now be of limited appeal. The more so, since the persecution of Jews—at least in the free world—is no longer imminent, and religion not too vital anymore in the life of the people.

There can be no doubt that the kibbutz provides a new secular religion for its members, along with a moral and emotional focus for Israel. It represents the new Jewish covenant—no longer now between a stern God and his children, but between equals; a covenant resting not on obedience to a supernatural power, but on individual freedom and a rational ordering of things. In a fashion it replaces the old religion as the link binding Jewry together. The kibbutz—international in its basic tenets, though also nationalistic—tries to weld the Jewish people into a nation by becoming its new collective conscience. (Of course, the Arab threat too, ties Israeli Jews together, and world Jewry to Israel. But this has little to do with the role of the kibbutz within Israel.)

Here too, we see a strange difference between the founding generation and its children. The first generation provided political and moral leadership for Israel, and to some degree still does, both through an active role in politics, and through the living example of the kibbutz. Things have shifted radically for the second generation, which is still looked to for moral leadership, but no longer in actual politics. For that they are far too estranged from the world of ideas, including political ideas; are too unused to extending themselves in a world at large, where they feel out of place. Theirs is a kind of monasticism that provides spiritual leadership by its sheer existence, not by any actual inducement to change.

Thus to the question of whether kibbutz education can and does provide leadership in Israel one can tentatively answer that indeed it can, but of a very unique kind: by setting an example rather than by actual doings for the nation; by a modern monasticism rather than the kind of intellectual, scientific, and social advances we associate with leadership and change.

Once again we find the second generation extremely different from the first. In the founding generation was an inordinately high percentage of imaginative persons given to innovation, deep thought, and strong convictions, at the heart of whose commitments stood social problems. Given these and related characteristics in such high degree, one cannot help expecting to find them in the children, to whose rearing they devoted so much planning and thought. But this one does not.

Somehow these dynamic people managed to create a static society. This does not mean that the kibbutz is not changing. But it resists change, worries about innovations rather than rising to the challenge of the new with alacrity. Behind this is no lack of concern or sensitivity, but a fear of what it may do to the integrity of the kibbutz idea. For example, while they are very much concerned about a social problem that has long been central for Israel—namely the assimilation of North African Jews and groups like them—they do almost nothing about it. Kibbutzniks make token efforts, halfhearted at best, because they are convinced that these Jews cannot fit themselves into kibbutz life. They feel that an influx of people so variant in background, holding values so radically different, would seriously hinder their comradely life. Therefore, and much as they would like to help, kibbutzniks feel they cannot afford to. They act in self-protection. And the self-protection, by drawing them inward, has become more alluring than to meet crisis with daring new solutions. This is why I feel that despite inner change, as in the sleeping arrangements of children, the kibbutz has become a static society.

As for these African newcomers, the kibbutz relies on the state of Israel to do the job. Not just economically now, but morally too, though they recognize and accept the Jewish obligation to take them in. At the same time they continue with active efforts to recruit members elsewhere: from Europe, our own continent, South America, South Africa.

But modern science and technology, along with poetry and the arts, require a dynamic, an open society. If Israel is to survive, even to keep and improve a living standard that is already far superior to that of neighboring countries, she will have to stay in the forefront of scientific and cultural development. To these it is doubtful that kibbutzniks will contribute importantly. Here, of course, one might ask: But how many great scientists or artists are apt to be born to a group numbering less than 100,000 who live in small, scattered, farming communities? In short, is my question valid?

The answer is probably both: yes and no. It is valid insofar as this small group does indeed produce men and women who make significant contributions to Israeli life. It is invalid because to make their contributions, nearly all such persons feel they must leave the kibbutz either officially or *de facto.** Some of them remain members out of sentiment, or for the high prestige that membership still confers. But in fact they live in the cities and only visit their kibbutz for a few days a year on the High Holidays.

As one of them told me, "I'm a good kibbutznik by virtue of my wife," meaning that his wife took part in all kibbutz affairs while he was busy outside the kibbutz. And another who holds a high government position confided, "Most of this is foolishness in modern Israel. But they're the ones who made Israel possible; they built it; they did such wonderful things in the past; they are the friends of my youth. So as long as I don't have to spend more than the holidays with them, I stay a member and thoroughly enjoy it."

Even more significant is what seemed like an emotional flatness in the second generation. To this question, when I raised it with kibbutz educators, I was told again and again—so much so, that one got the feeling it had become a pat answer—that these young people are very shy of strangers. That they turn inward so very much that they cannot reveal themselves to any but those persons most intimate with them, but they are possessed of great depth. Which brings us back to their own age group, the only ones who respond to them instantly with deep understanding based on a common life experience. But a depth that cannot reveal itself in varied intercourse is a solipsistic virtue, at best. I failed to evoke any such depth in the younger generation, though I found it often enough in the founding generation and in those who were kibbutz-born but had left.

Or is this again posing an unfair question? Because how many "deep feeling" persons are we apt to find among 100,000 farmers? And who, in this day and age, are the ones who stay on the farm? A relative emotional flatness may be

---

* *de facto:* in fact (even if not officially).

just the selective factor that determines who stays on, in this relatively simple, undemanding environment.

Still another strange factor is involved here. What the world has labeled typically Jewish has fallen away from the second generation, and in many ways they are like those others who peopled the non-Jewish world their parents once had to contend with. So another question is: What, of all this, is the consequence of this second generation's having been born and raised in a farming community, out in the country, in rather small settlements? And what is the consequence of their having been born, not as members of a small and discriminated-against minority, but as those of the dominant in-group?

But why have I felt compelled at all to ask questions that seem unanswerable, or ones that I then call unfair because of the small numbers involved and the fact that these people live a rather remote life?

My reason has to do with a final and fundamental difficulty in evaluating this system of education: that one's estimate of the kibbutz population depends on who and what one is mentally comparing them with.

THE MIDDLE REACHES

The results of a nationwide study of scholastic achievement in Israel highlight this problem. It is a study in which five groups of Israeli youngsters were compared; those attending (1) urban schools with high academic standards, serving mainly upper-middle-class families; (2) urban schools of middle standards, used mainly by the middle-class population; (3) urban schools of relatively low standards, used mainly by lower class families; (4) rural schools serving rural families and including the cooperative settlements called moshavim; and finally (5) kibbutz schools.

Without detailing all findings, but looking at how the five groups scored percentage-wise on the tests, the kibbutz appears to rank second in achievement, whether one looks at those who scored highest or lowest. For example, looking at those who scored in the upper quarter of the test (scores of 75 and above), the distribution was 42.8 percent for the high-standard urban schools, 29.9 percent for the kibbutz, 24.5 percent for the rural and moshav, 18.2 percent for the middle-urban group, and 10.2 percent for the low-urban group. Thus the kibbutz students did considerably less well than the highest urban group, but otherwise better than all the rest, and considerably so.

If we look at the low performers on these tests (scores of 64 or lower) we find parallel results. The smallest number falls in the upper urban group (27.6 percent) and the next smallest number in the kibbutz (38.2 percent). The rural and moshav again take a position between the kibbutz and the middle-urban group with 52.7 percent, compared to 56.4 percent in the middle-urban, and 75.7 percent in the lower urban group.

A very interesting subfinding was the distribution of top achievers (scores of 85 and above) among the five groups.[1] In the urban high-level schools 5.2 percent of the group were top achievers. This percentage drops to 2.3 percent for the rural and moshav group; 1.6 percent for the middle-urban group; and 0.7 percent for the lower urban group. For the kibbutz the figure for these top achievers is only 2.1 percent, which is slightly below the rural and moshav groups.

The leveling impact of kibbutz education is quite apparent from these scores. In over-all achievement, the spread is narrower than one might expect, because both ends of the distribution are smaller while the middle is larger. If, on the other hand, we look at top performers alone, the story differs. Then the leveling influence seems to have reduced to a respectable middle level those students who (we must assume from their high over-all performance) had the potential to be top performers. At the same time, it also leveled up (if one may use the term), the low performers. Again the educational system shows up as favoring the middle reaches, or the group. In statistical terms, kibbutz educational achievement shows that both ends of the distribution curve are radically reduced, while the middle is expanded.

That is why—if one views the kibbutz as populated by children who would otherwise be living in a good middle-class home, one of education and culture —it is doubtful if kibbutz education is superior to other systems we know of, in helping students toward intellectual, aesthetic, and scientific achievements. The question is: Are such achievements more important than setting an example of moral leadership? And even this consideration holds only if such a cultivated, middle-class home is the kind that many (though by no means all) of the first generation would have provided for their children. If, on the other hand, one looks at them as children who would otherwise have grown up in a lower working-class environment, then the picture is entirely different—and a few of the first generation would probably have belonged to this group.

Also, while a sizable segment of the founding generation can be considered well educated and essentially middle-class in origin, the story is entirely different if we go by the work they perform. By kibbutz claims, most of its members would have been factory workers or done other lower class work, had they not joined the kibbutz. Therefore (they claim) the comparison should be with lower class families, whose children, unless very gifted, would have enjoyed only limited schooling. But my observation of the founding generation does not bear out this claim.

Most of them, I believe, though not all, would have risen in any society, edu-

---

1. These data were taken from a tabulation showing educational level according to national origin of the parent: e.g., Israeli-born, European or Middle-Eastern. Of these, the Middle-Eastern subdivision was omitted here, since that population is nearly absent in most kibbutzim.

cationally and socially. As a matter of fact, there are many for whom it was only their having joined the kibbutz at an early age that pegged them to a limited educational level, while their brothers or sisters who bypassed the kibbutz movement typically advanced to higher social and educational levels. Had the founding generation striven as hard in society at large as they strove in and for the kibbutz, they could not have failed, in their majority, to rise to professional or upper-middle-class levels. And if some few had not made it that far for themselves, they would certainly have secured it for their children.

I believe it is myth to claim—as do kibbutzniks—that most of them would have lived a lower class life. But they wish to believe it because, if true, kibbutz achievements for its members would be even greater. If I could agree with them, my task would be easy and the findings clear.

That is, were this an average population of small agricultural communities, the results of kibbutz child rearing would be close to miraculous—so well educated, for such an assumed background, are most of its younger generation. That they would be a static, conservative, provincial group, one would take for granted, because what else could one expect of the children of such a community? And if they were not, who would stay and tend the farm? Certainly they are puritanical in their way of life and outlook. But what else would one expect of people, born and raised in a small rural community, who have chosen to remain there for the rest of their lives?

Much more important is the question of whether kibbutz education does not produce exactly the personality type the kibbutz needs—though a type not too acceptable to American middle-class parents, nor to those who (like the first kibbutz generation) put a high value on leadership.

Here it should be added that the test results, noted earlier, reflect an essentially non-kibbutz outlook on life and on what constitutes academic achievement. Results might have been radically different had these tests been constructed by kibbutz educators. That is, they were designed to measure the kind of achievement the test constructors valued: an intellectual development that prepares well for ever higher (competitive) academic achievement, without regard for what effect it has on the student's personality and social relations. But the kibbutz youngster spends a vast amount of his emotional energy on becoming a highly socialized person, in terms of kibbutz standards. And this achievement none of the tests measure.

In many ways the second generation of kibbutzniks are farmers in a true and real sense, though not peasants in the style of Eastern Europe. They are very modern farmers, but farmers nonetheless, concerned chiefly with kibbutz goings on, uninvolved in the broader society, save for Israel, and even then only with aspects that concern them.

Political life, for example, is highly diversified and active in Israel, and the literature of politics abounds. But the second generation in their vast majority are well satisfied with arrangements that provide them with only the party newspaper. There is little desire to read the press of other parties, even if the kibbutz did not frown on its distribution. Most are satisfied to read what their own party organ has to say about the politics of others.

While they probably read more (and more widely) than the average farmer, they shy away from material that differs in viewpoint from theirs. Partly this is for lack of interest, but largely because it might inspire disagreement with their peers. They do read those professional publications that advance knowledge in their own field of work. That is, they try to educate themselves in ways that will help them do better at work they are already doing.

Quite a few kibbutzniks follow serious intellectual pursuits. Several kibbutzim have archeological museums, others have folklore collections and so forth. Interest is particularly avid for anything pertaining to Israel, for her archeology and history, biblical and otherwise. But more often than not these come about through individual efforts—and in all cases I could observe, that of non-kibbutz born persons—which then carry others along. For the most part kibbutzniks try very hard to keep from growing boorish. Though dead tired, they read "serious" literature, listen to "good" music. But the way they do it I found moving, even pathetic, given the heavy odds against them. Because their efforts spring from a defensive need not to slip into boorishness, rather than a spontaneous delight in the pleasures of literature and the arts. For too many their enjoyment of the "finer" things in life is very hard labor indeed: something they owe to themselves, or feel they owe the kibbutz movement, to show it is not incompatible with the higher things in life. But with rare exceptions what else can it be, given the long hours and hard work they put into the kibbutz economy, the hours spent on kibbutz affairs, and the relative lack of privacy. In their vast majority, they read little out of intellectual curiosity, and their aesthetic interest in art, music, and letters is standard rather than original. So far as I could observe, they read nothing controversial or experimental, see no movies or theater that would throw their values in question.

In this respect, too, the personality of the kibbutz-born generation seems depleted, compared to a complexity and richness in some of the first generation. On the other hand, compared with the often severe neuroses of that first generation, these young people seem much less neurotic than their parents, secure within their limitations, though these are often marked.

Perhaps the assets and liabilities of kibbutz education may best be summarized by the deep peer attachments felt by the second generation. On the one hand, their reluctance to contemplate a life apart from each other, the way each one, alone, seems to feel things only half as acutely as when all function together as a unit—all these seem to speak more of bondage than attachment. (Though what is bondage in one society may be experienced very differently in another.) On the other hand, if intense group ties discourage individuation, neither do they breed human isolation, asocial behavior or other forms of social disorganizations that plague modern man in competitive society.

What I have said here about the results of kibbutz rearing may sound quite critical. But let us consider for a moment how many people in our society, or anywhere, grow up to be full individuals? How many, if they had a choice, would prefer to live with their own mistakes? How many would wish to suffer their own personal grief sooner than be supported by the group, when distressed, even if that means casting their feelings into a mold the community provides? We have no idea how many, among us, reach the individuation that some hoped to reach when they left the kibbutz. But until we know that, we are in no position to judge how many are denied it by kibbutz education.

Much, too, has been said here about the reluctance of kibbutz-reared persons to have opinions of their own in the face of group disapproval. This, too, may have sounded quite critical. But how large a percentage in our society are very different? Or I speak of the inability to form truly intimate relations. But how many in our society can?

On the other hand, and in favor of kibbutz education, how many in our society form ties as meaningful and rewarding as those between the kibbutz-born and his group? Or how many in our society are able, as grown-ups, to break away from all values instilled by home and society in order to strike out on their own against greatest odds? How many can as radically shed a viewpoint and way of life that no longer tally with inner convictions? Because this a percentage of kibbutz-reared persons do when they leave the kibbutz.

Perhaps to leave takes less strength because of the lesser attachments to parents. Estimates vary incredibly, and some claim that up to half or more of all kibbutz-raised children leave the kibbutz. Others, like Professor Talmon, put the percentage at less than 15 percent. Friedmann (1967) reports that "only 5 percent of young people leave the kibbutzim of the left wing movement annually, according to Darin-Drabkin." He adds that according to Shlomo Rosen, joint secretary of the seventy-two kibbutzim of this movement, their population includes 2,080 who were kibbutz-born, of whom 93 percent have remained. Clearly the kibbutz offers to some of those it educates the freedom to follow their convictions, however radical.

The exceptions here would be those very few who are so stunted by communal rearing that they cannot use the opportunity. My impression is that while a few are thus penalized, percentage-wise their number is considerably smaller than in most social systems.

A FINE WAY FOR SOME

Since in psychology, unlike ethics or religion, we are not dealing with absolute values, I think it would be very wrong to pass judgment on kibbutz education on grounds of individuation. Any educational system has to be judged not by what it attains for a very few, but for the vast majority—and without preventing the very few from going far beyond it. In regard to the latter, kibbutzniks are specially fortunate. If all Israel were composed of kibbutzim this would not be so, and then I might worry more, and so might they. But Israel is an open society, unusually so for such a very new nation. Hence nothing worse than economic and psychological barriers keep anyone from leaving the closed kibbutz society for the open society of Israel.

No doubt the system prevents some from developing as fully as they might, witness the data I have quoted on scholastic achievement. But in sheer number they are more than offset by those who (based again on these data) would have achieved much lower were it not for ample support from the group and the educational system. Moreover, there are no children in the kibbutz who, because of economic and social deprivation, never attain even that minimum of human development the kibbutz assures to all whom it educates.

There are, for example, no neglected children in the kibbutz, none whose physical needs in sickness and health are not well taken care of, none who could not learn in school because they had no decent place to sleep, or enough to eat. There is no child there who fails because of too much pressure to compete and perform. There are no drunken parents in the kibbutz, nor any who beat their children. I could go on but I think my point is clear. These protections the kibbutz can offer precisely because, in return for protection, its members grant it so much control of their lives.

To sum up with a truism: The more egalitarian a society, the more all are equal. Given the personal variations of history and endowment, there will always be differences from person to person, but they will always be the smaller, the more egalitarian the system. An egalitarian system of education will both lift up the bottom group and lower the top group toward the middle. And it will do so the more, the more egalitarian the system.

What this leveling could mean for the future of society, if it became universal, is an open question. How one evaluates it will again depend on whether one cares more about raising up the lower groups, or about lifting the top toward still higher achievement. I personally believe that at this stage of our knowledge the issue can be argued either way: that society benefits most if the lowest group is raised to the middle level and there is not too much difference between groups; but also that the top group should be given every chance to lift itself higher, and grow in number, because only this group through its intellectual achievement can best improve the welfare of all.

At least kibbutz education seems free of the contradiction that presently bedevils much of the American educational scene: the wish, at one and the same time, to lift our lowest achievers to considerably higher levels, and to speed and push upward our highest achievers. That this contradiction has not torn apart our educational system is thanks only to the fact that we operate two separate and different educational systems: the public one, where the avowed concentration is on the first task, and a widespread private and suburban educational system where we concentrate on the second. Only this division into two (or, considering the parochial schools, three or more) different educational systems has so far prevented our running head on into stresses that would otherwise tear education to pieces, with disastrous results for what it can do for all students.

Certainly kibbutz education turns out a majority of persons well content with themselves and their lives. For others it is stifling. But as long as they can escape, leave and join, with some effort, a world beyond the kibbutz, I personally would not worry about them. On the other hand, I am confronted daily in my life's work with children whose anguish is the tragic result of their parents' alienation, but for whom no community stands ready to shield them. I am not sure that it wouldn't be nice to have a few kibbutzim around for those who long to escape the anonymity, selfishness, competitiveness, social disorganization and widespread feeling of purposelessness which are so often found in modern mass society. The more so since fate has denied them individuation anyway, whether because of low native ability or the conditions they were born to.

Such a suggestion bespeaks my preference for an open society which, by its very pluralism, invites kibbutz and non-kibbutz alike to exist. Unhappily, pluralism and the open society are anathema to the kibbutz; which leaves my problem and theirs insoluble, as are many key problems of human existence.

Fortunately my task is not to judge the kibbutz, nor even kibbutz education, but to try to understand it. Moreover, with only the second generation to go by, so far as results in maturity are concerned, final answers will have to wait till their children are grown. Only this third generation will have been raised without the pressures of parental ambivalence, without desires strongly felt and just as strongly controlled or repressed. Since this third generation has not yet matured, everything further I might say, or have said, about kibbutz education, is tentative, very open to question, beset by uncertainties.

I have tried to suggest why I believe this system of education came into being, what some of its roots may have been, and some of its results as I saw them. My visit convinced me that, as a system of rearing, the kibbutz way is as viable as any other and could become more so in time, if the kibbutz should survive. It is a fine system for some and not for others. Like all educational systems it shapes the human personality in ways that differ importantly from those our own system produces. I conclude, therefore, with an effort to see how well fact and speculation fit into a theoretical system. This, it is hoped, may shed further light on the question: What is essentially different about personality formation between the kibbutz system of rearing and ours?

II SCHOOL

This section includes three versions of educational experience. Mr. Connolly's is apparently very different from the others, since, on any ordinary view, his education was intensely overprivileged; but it may be inferred from his account that there are disadvantages as well as advantages in this kind of education, since he himself, though permanently molded by it, cannot regard it as unequivocally beneficial. Mr. West's contribution is also quite plainly the work of a self-conscious and highly educated writer, but is concerned with the education of a retarded child by her parents, who must live in her world rather than fit her into theirs. Mr. Kohl is working on new lines in the desperate contemporary educational worlds of New York and California; his creative classroom experimentation is very far from the ethos of Connolly's Eton, and concerns a situation in which society rather than nature has retarded the development of the child.

Together the pieces are intended to offer a glimpse of the huge problems of modern education, problems in which privilege, underprivilege, and natural obstacles all have a part, which involve deep issues of social justice, and which require in ever-increasing measure the attention of creative intelligence.

Paul West / A Passion To Learn

This is a father's account of his backward child. He begins with an impression of her extraordinary behavior, then describes the experts' examinations. The child is mistress of her family; she "quickens in you the sense of life." Her father shares her kind of life with her, even while standing apart and considering her in relation to "Nature's" other characteristic errors. This double process—of "ignorant" sympathy with the child's world and a sophisticated explanation, on his own account, of how she fits into the "real" world—determines the tone and structure of the essay. Notice that the author never speaks outright of his love for the child; that he nevertheless makes that emotion the one that is most powerfully expressed. He hints at, but does not stress, the unhappiness and destruction her defect must often cause. Although one senses an intelligent and explicit mind at work, much of the effect is gained in this way, by omission and underemphasis. Consider the passage about the doll in the airplane. Is it there simply because it happened, or are we expected to infer from it something relevant to the meaning and tone of the whole piece? Perhaps such restraint and underemphasis not only reflects the strategies he uses in his dealings with the child, but also invites the reader to feel himself into a situation where great imagination and energy are required to be under strict control. The essay reflects, both in its reticence and in its display of literary and imaginative energy, something of the conflict between a natural force and a cultural situation which the child precipitates in a civilized household.

I

Exceptional children come in two kinds, advanced and retarded. Both, like jugglers and mystics and astronauts, are astounding, especially the second kind, of which I've had a close view for six years. Amanda West, the daughter who is my theme, didn't seem unusual—not to mention exceptional—until she was two. Slow to speak, she was cautious about starting to walk; but once she had walked she ran like a bird preparing to take off. She fell in love, as well, with water and umbrellas, and in the presence of either orated vehemently (although nonverbally) to herself. Water she preferred in puddles on the livingroom floor or in baths, but she also liked it in rainspouts, saucepans, and lavatory basins. Umbrellas—which, I think, exerted the stronger spell—she collected with casual relentlessness. She never had fewer than a dozen. They were her trees, really: a plastic-

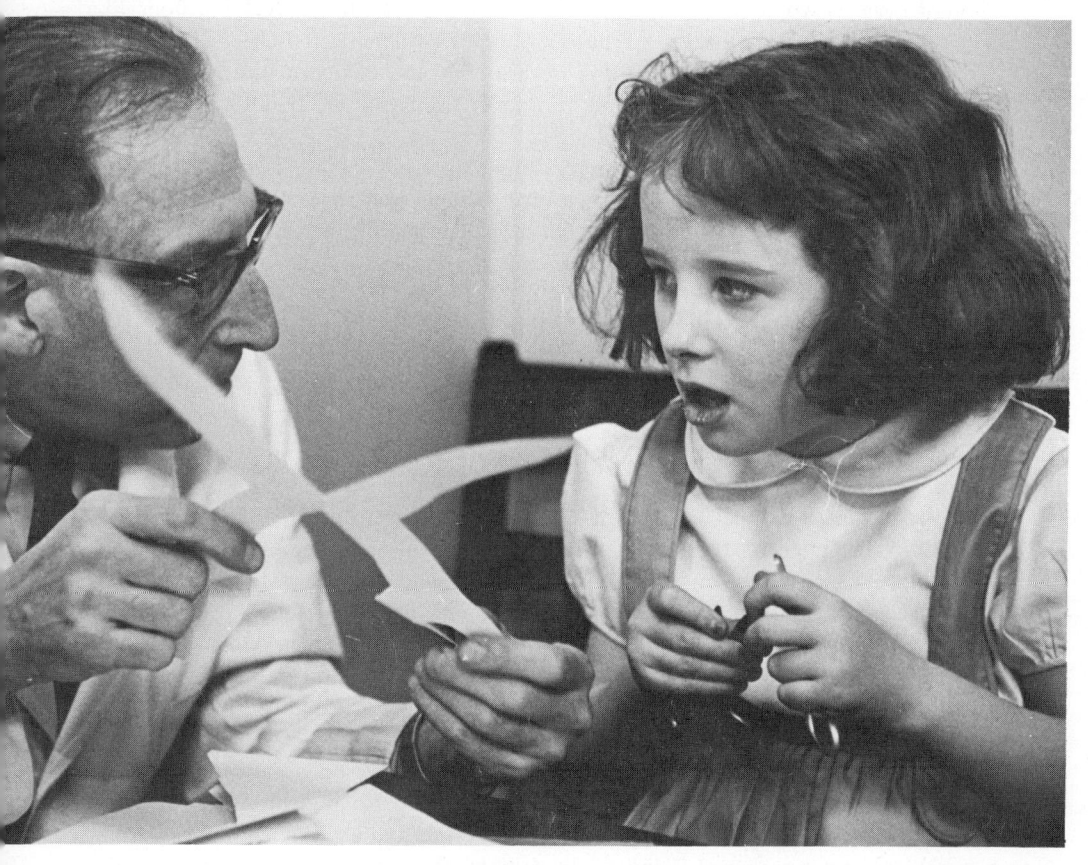
Cornell Capa, Magnum

leaved, tin-branched orchard of them, which every night had to be rolled up firm and laid across her bed, and every morning landed in a cascade on ours when she came heavy-footedly in, hooting for them to be opened. Then, with half-blind eyes, down to the living room where we spread them over the floor like Pan and Company afforesting a bare mountain while she, red-cheeked with elation, danced among them, catching occasionally the beads on the rib-ends and skimming the canopies half-around, but never trampling the handles or ramming a fist through the fabric.

She would stand, do a preliminary skip to get her timing right—a one-two-three with her big toes creased downward as if to scratch earth—and then flow into a joyous high-kneed pounding, her long hair a flash, her arms providing her with a tightrope-walker's balance, her eyes unobtainably fixed on an upper corner of the room, where she saw what no one else saw. She looked and smiled, and danced the more wildly for it, fueling her semi-tarantella from the presence in the vacancy.

Fred, we began to say, domesticating the ghost: *it's Fred again.* And so, each morning, with flim and a flam, and a flim again, followed by a swift series of flim-flams, she danced spread-eagled, lithe, and bony, chirping on an empty stomach.

We began to wonder, hard as it was even to begin to do it, if she wasn't deaf or autistic. Or both. To think a thing is to make it so, whereas to deny it is to abolish it—especially on the Isle of Man, Amanda's home, island of witches, banshees, and temperamental goblins. But being not altogether pagan, we kept on wondering until the day we took her to the mainland, to the Manchester University Audiology Clinic. It was winter, the sea heaving and pumice-gray; so we flew in a BEA Viscount, lurching through the rain, and Amanda, at each plunge or sideslip, let out a birdcall of delight.

Born on the island, she had never been off it—never been Across to England—and now, leaving it for the first time, she seemed isolated in a new way. Her three words—"baba," "more," and "ish-ish"—she had used heroically, intending meanings we missed and being credited with others that we invented. I listened to the lax, feathered whine of the engines, wondering what noise they made to her as she sat smiling into the clouds. I'd heard, I told myself, on humid days, the squeak of my sinuses filling, and then a pop of contraction on a day of high pressure, with all the sinews and membranes tugging and fluctuating in a mucous orchestration. But that was nothing to what I imagined for Amanda's head: a tinnitus of bad bells, a frying noise, which in combination drove her to cup a hand over her right ear and rock heavily to that side as if trying to shake something loose or back into place or—thought ended: the two-foot doll that bathed with Amanda in the teeth-chattering English bathroom and that we brought with us on the plane, slipped sideways from my casual hug, and a cache of bathwater spilled into my lap. My fault, I said; you can't blame a stark-naked doll.

When we landed, Amanda whooped down the steps from the plane. It was still raining, but we had two umbrellas, both hers. The only trouble was that she didn't want them open or up; they had to be carried before us like totems, one red, the other green, every loose fold clamped tight by a rubber band. Two umbrellas, kept from getting wet, made good folk stare; but good folk knew nothing of umbrellas, water, and Amanda. In the taxi, however, she opened up the red umbrella and sat in an indifferent silence, an erect-sitting being of utter trustfulness, heedless of the roof-lining she might puncture, and with no more idea of where she was going than of where she had come from. Out of the taxi, she insisted, with a plangent squeak, on the umbrella's being folded again and rebound in its rubber band. Then she was ready to march with us past the porter's lodge (empty), wrongly up steps to the Department of Law and down again, and finally into a waiting room stocked with heavy, ridable toys, and equipped with tiny toilets whose still water she inspected and approved.

Called for, we went left into the laboratory (one wall of which was a one-way window facing a lecture room). Amanda stared at the people, the things, and, it seemed, at Fred, whom she has always been able to find anywhere. She grew busy and began to chirp. When, to her exact satisfaction, she had arranged the umbrellas and the doll on a low table, she turned to the experts with a patronizing smile. We sat and watched—her mother at one end of the room, myself (still feeling damp) at the other—helpless on the perimeter and unable to smoke. There was some tinkering with a green box, all dials, and a chart. The door snicked open, admitting an authoritative-looking face which beamed and vanished. Then testing began with overtures of friendship from the studious-mannered man whose trousers looked as if he kneeled a lot. The calm woman in patent-leather high heels clicked a tiny clicker, but Amanda did not turn. They gave her a doll then and tried her from behind with a duck quack, a whistle of low pitch, several rattles, then a small tom-tom. Abruptly, not having turned, she ran to the table, slammed one doll alongside the other and hooted, with finger pointed, for the red umbrella to be opened. There were nods; the umbrella opened, sprang taut, was set in her hands, and she squatted, drawing it down over her as if sheltering under a thin, frail mushroom, slipping out a hand to adjust a downslid sock, and beginning to make again the birdcall (as if a curlew tried to bleat) which had driven countless local dogs into emulative frenzy, provoked birds into surpassing themselves (searching for a bird, they never saw *her*), and scared all the cats away.

Private under the panels of vinyl, she sang with mounting fervor, the umbrella stem between her legs. No one moved. It was clear that she was going to be given her leisure, allowed to collect herself. In succession she fluted her voice upward in an ecstatic trill, twirled the umbrella like a color disc without once catching the rim or the plastic against her face (a perfect, sheltering fit it was), peeped out to giggle just a bit fearfully, hoisted the umbrella up and away behind her in a pose from *The Mikado,* and then hid again beneath it. We had seen her face shining with heat, seen her only long enough for that.

Now they tapped on her roof, flicked middle finger hard off thumb against the fabric, and brought their mouths close to the surface, calling her name. Out she came, astounded at something heard: not her name, because she didn't know it, but something—a retaliating and envious dog, a curlew weary of being competed with, a cat returning to venture a duet—amplified and vibrating in the umbrella above her, but only faces and maneuvering mouths to make it. Us. Us only; so she concealed herself again, tilting the canopy forward.

What brought her out again and kept her out was the xylophone. She abandoned the umbrella for it, fondled it a while, then beat the living decibels out of it, a Lionel Hampton Lilliputian who struck away and then canted her ear close to the trembling bars, her eyes widening in half-piqued recognition that *this* was what we'd flown her across the sea for. She banged on it with her wooden hammer a few times more and let it fall the two-and-a-half feet to the parquet, wincing once in the wrong direction as it hit.

After calls, hums, hisses, pops, buzzes, barks, bays, and several indeterminate ululations, all from behind her, they did the left side while she smiled at a distracting monkey puppet over on the right. My hands were holding each other too tightly; her mother, twelve yards down the room, looked pale, her maternality shut painfully off and her own hand beginning gestures that ended halfway, the fingers tongue-tied.

"Now," said the studious, kneeling man, his kindly face tense, and snapped two wooden bars together. A slapstick, I thought; like the split lath of the harlequin. But whatever was going on, it wasn't low comedy. What he said next, after a fractional shake of his head to the woman in heels—the professional pair's exchange of glances crossing the parental one—sounded like:

"Right down the track." The headshake was a zero in mime.

Amanda smiled at the puppet, offering her hand to put inside it. They let her, working through all the modes of sound, but not to a crescendo, only to a punctuational drum-tap which she ignored. And then, as the light waned—that legendary dank Manchester light swollen with soot and rain and absorbed by tons on tons of Victorian brick and tile—they switched sides, this time beguiling her with a model farm at which she sat, cantankerously checking the cows for udders (as a country girl should) and stationing Clydesdale horses at the water trough. Brilliants of wet formed along her narrow nose, and she heard not the snap-crack of the wooden bars: not the first time, anyway. But when it came from a yard closer—these testers gliding about the room like prankish Druids— she flinched, directed an offended stare in a vaguely right-hand direction, and went back to her farm. Again and again they worked from the right, varying the angle and the sound. Again and again, with just a few moments of preoccupied indifference, she jerked her head sideways, beginning to be cheerful as she discovered the routine: beginning to play.

Suddenly there was no farm. It went into a gray steel cabinet against which Amanda kicked and at which she took a running kick as her eyes began to pour (tears whopping enough, I thought, to merit nostrils for conduits) and her bird-call harshened. As she swung, both-handed, the xylophone at the locked handle of the door, I got up, stuck out a hand as I half-fell in a skid on the polish. I took a tonic sol-fa smack in the forehead as she swung the instrument backward again, farther than before, the better to mangle the steel between her and the authentic cows, the horses a-thirsting.

"Ap," I sort of said through the plong and the blank crash, not seeing well. "You might as well get it out again."

"Naughty girl," her mother said unconvincedly as Amanda laugh-cried, pitching the xylophone over her shoulder without so much as a look. I have seen her dispose in the same way of bus tickets, mail, money, books, food, scissors, and plates. The oubliette is anywhere behind her.

"She'll soon——" I heard, but the rest was drowned by a scream of unmitigated anger while Amanda pounded the cabinet with both fists.

"Strong!" called the man who kneeled a lot, busying himself with earphones attached to the many-dialed machine. "She's a grand temper."

"You've seen nothing," I told him. "Yet." I knew how, in the Cleopatra-Clytemnestra rages to which she entitled herself, she could butt her head through a firm window (one so far, without bloodshed, but there were long blond hairs on the splinters of glass). Or pound her uncallused hand down through the crisp and warm pulp of a loaf not long out of the oven, once burying her hand and bringing her arm up with a bread mallet wedged on her wrist, crying "Ish! Ish!" which is anthem, plea, and threat in one.

But it wasn't "Ish" she came out with this time; it was the first of her calls, "Baba—babababba," uttered with pauses only long enough for everyone present to shout the same phonemes back at her. If you didn't, she increased the volume, blustering and raucous. It was the most comprehensive aural version of herself. So the clinic-room, soundproof of course (there is even a sign just inside the entrance requesting silence), became a barnyard for a while. Turning wet-eyed, grime-faced, to each of us in turn, she babbled at us, coercing, commanding, appealing; and in turn and sometimes in unison we babbled and brayed back, short only of a cock-a-doodle-doo, the hymn of a pig wallowing or even farrowing in hot lava, and a moose drowning in a swamp of caviar. This, so that the testing could go on; one farmyard for another.

In the beginning is the test, and in the end comes a remedy of sorts. But how, I wondered, can they even begin—overworked but obliged not to rush; never short of children to work with, one in six being somehow deaf and usually not deaf only—until they too have run their fingers across the crowns of her blunt, curiously thick teeth, have seen her dance a full hour among the umbrellas, have night after night studied her fanatical attention to the placing of her slippers within an invisible outline which is there and symmetrical for her beneath the chest of drawers in her bedroom.

"You haven't——" I began to say on our third trip to the clinic, seen her do the living things; give Creation a run for its money. Not at home. They hadn't seen her, like a gross Ophelia, distribute around the house—on the window ledges, in the wardrobe between two decent suits or dresses, on the rim of the letter box, on the Christmas tree itself—pork sausages on butcher's hooks or threaded on wire coat-hangers. Or eat the sausage raw, oblivious of worms. Or, in hydrodynamic delight, rip off shoes and socks to plant her bare feet on the TV screen whenever it showed water. Or (I stopped: they were calling her name again and she wasn't ever going to answer) sit naked and warbling for an hour in a washbasin of cold water. Or green her face with eye-shadow, eat nail-varnish, coat the windows with lavender furniture polish, jump down five stairs fearlessly, mimic (by waving a stiffened arm) men carrying umbrellas, chant into a toilet pedestal after choking it with a whole roll of tissue, chew cigarettes, cover herself with Band-Aids when there wasn't a scratch in sight, climb any ladder and refuse to descend, slide pencils up her nose, use a rubber hammer on the doctor's private parts, drink from her potty, wade into a sewer-inspection chamber the plumber had opened, eat six bananas in six minutes, wind and play an alarm clock at her right ear time and again, shave her face and arms and legs with instant lather and bladeless razor, threaten enormous dogs by advancing upon them with a reed in hand, cut her own hair at random, dissolve soap in a tin basin, rock so hard that her hair touched the floor on either side, sit motionless and rapt in front of a mirror, voluminously autograph walls, tear samples from the dictionary or a book of Picasso prints, stare unblinking into 150-watt bulbs, run, run, run everywhere, heedless of gesticulating and half-felled adults and the sanity of drivers.

"Mandy . . . *Mandy* . . . MANDY," they said, upping the decibels as she gazed from them to the red finger spinning across the dial and back again. When she heard them, her expression changed, fixing in atavistic wonder. Funny, it was as if we were watching the face of sound itself while she, flushed and nervous, heard something visible. After an interval they let her use the microphone herself, and she began to boom and call in an almost continuous orgy of sound, confronted for the first time with her own share of the missing continent: a Columbus of euphony dumbfoundedly exclaiming at the glories of exclamation itself, every bit like the man in Xenophon who kept shouting *thalassa!* * when he saw the sea. I myself felt a bit like shouting; I'd never heard anyone hearing before. And since then I've known a good many firsts with her—things which, up to then, I'd done without really experiencing them, or which she herself thought up and I myself had never dreamed of doing. Some of the latter are grotesque and sometimes rather revolting as well; I try not to do them, but usually Amanda prevails, imperious queen with her dithering court. I do as I am told. Most people would. You have to; that's where the education begins.

* *thalassa!:* the sea!

II

She quickens in you the sense of life; makes you grateful for what's granted, what's *taken* for granted. A handicap so severe drives you through fury, then through an empty, vengeful indignation, to two points: first, when, in the absence of explanations medical and reasons cosmic, you ignore the handicap to make it go away; second, nearer to common sense, when you welcome it in as her special gift and, while trying to eliminate it, learn its nature by heart as a caution to yourself, and study the voracious subtlety of her compensations—as when she, unlike most of us, smells at a pencil newly sharpened, inhaling from the beechwood its own soot-sour bouquet, or traces with addicted fingers the corrugations on the flat of a halved cabbage before eating it raw with the same naturalness with which she drinks vinegar, steak sauce, and mayonnaise, and sniffs glue. I too, now, have tasted ink (a flavor of charred toenail), coal (a rotted iron-and-yeast pill), bark (woolly and raw, suggesting vulcanized crabmeat), leather (a taste here not of the meat or fat next the hide but of the fur once outside it and of seaweed-iodine).

Tasting—testing—with her, I have found new ways into the world. She discovers what she discovers because she has lost what she's lost. I tag along on her voyages, and together we sneak into the randomness, the arbitrariness, of the universe as distinct from its patterns. Without her—although I have in my time delighted in *The Compleat Angler's* * bald and bland arcana, in insect and fungus books, in Jean Rostand's reports on tadpoles and toads—I don't think I would be delving, as I now am, with strangely relevant irrelevance, into the behavior of slugs, mushrooms, cicadas, and flesh-eating plants, or into a way of death called atherosclerosis, the result not (I learn) of saturated fats yielding cholesterol but of unsaturated fats—much used in the paint and varnish industry—varnishing our insides with lipofuscin. Because she brandished it at a big dog, I found out about Great Reed Mace (*Typha latifolia*), often wrongly called the bulrush, but rightly, I reckon, thought sexy. The black six-foot stem is a long cheroot, topped by a yellow spike, and, as my *Observer's Book of Wild Flowers* says, "the closely packed pistillate flowers forming the 'mace' consist of a stalked ovary, with a slender style and a one-sided, narrow stigma, and enveloped in tufts of soft, brownish hairs."

I keep two books, one for what Amanda does, one for what I find out while waiting for our first conversation. She ate a dandelion flower some time back; one day I'll try her with the leaves in oil and vinegar, that good salad. I have a lot to tell her which, thank goodness, I've been late in learning: the hyena isn't quite the scavenger he's supposed to be, whereas the almost extinct American

---

* *The Compleat Angler:* a discourse on the art of fishing by the English writer Izaak Walton (1593–1683).

Bald Eagle is a scavenger out and out. And so on; it's a question, really, of finding a life-style, of opening up for myself a universe into which she fits. So I try to devise for her the biggest memberships possible, now and then blundering from wishful thinking into wishful biology, but at other times enrolling her in majestic clans we'd stare at if knew about them, just as some of the inhumanly ordinary on the earth have stared at her.

Take the shark, created perpetually with two inexplicable handicaps: it has no swim bladder, so must keep on the move or sink; its fixed, paired fins have hardly any braking effect and no motive power, which means that it finds difficulty stopping or reversing. A shark, therefore, is compulsive and a bit helpless; no one knows why. But all sharks are handicapped thus, whereas what I am casting around for is a handicap not just inexplicable but also affecting a minority only. Trying again, I come up with such samples of a partly mismanaged universe as so-called "waltzing" mice, which have an abnormality of that part of the inner ear concerned with balance; the hereditary deafness found in white dogs like Dalmatians and Bull Terriers; *Gentian acaulis,* which for reasons unknown refuses to flower in good soil but does well where the acid and lime counts are high; holly, whose greenish flowers are sometimes bisexual, although sometimes male and female flowers exist on *separate* plants (which is why they tell you to plant hollies in groups); uranium 235, old faithful of an unstable and vulnerable isotope which is as it is because it isn't otherwise; the particle for which, it seems, there is no anti-particle; flawed crystals in which one atom is where another should be or where no atom ought to be at all; the so-called incoherence of natural light, traveling as it does in brief packets of energy in random directions at uncorrelated times, compared with the light from an optical maser; acridines, believed to produce mutations which consist in the deletion or addition of a base or bases from the DNA chain. Such is the beginning of my list: Amanda's alibi, not so much an excuse (the popular sense) as her being genuinely elsewhere while the universe put a foot wrong with that mouse or this crystal, but suffering a similar misadministration that relates her more closely than most people to Nature; a Nature I never really noticed until it bungled.

As a factory, Nature—the more familiar end of the universe—is more reliable than the best baseball pitcher ever, but less reliable than the London Underground. To be sure, where it falters it sometimes lowers its guard usefully: U 235 gives us the chain reaction, or at least the possibility of it; the misbehaving particle may teach us something about the "elementariness" of particles (e.g., are two different particles equally fundamental or is one merely an "excited" state of the other?). The imperfect crystal tells physicists a great deal about the mechanical properties of solids. And the deaf—also, perhaps, in this case, the autistic and/or brain-damaged—child, from whom I have wandered briefly only to hunt out some of her peers and analogues, is equally instructive, preparing you for the next phase, in which you find what I will call the superior intricacy of one child at the deaf-blind unit at Condover in England: a child born without eyes or ears and with all internal organs so garbled that sex cannot be determined. Yet he/she knows how to get angry, is eager to sniff at things and people alike. Something on the lines of "Age 6—80 decibel hearing loss—IQ 120" says nothing much if you are willing to learn something more; neither does "Age 7— hearing nil—sight nil—sex?—IQ minimal" if you have a passion to learn (I intend the ambiguity). How you proceed from the statistics depends on who and what you are, how much of Nature you're willing to look at; but, pretty certainly, there will be some desperation in your proceeding. Which, given such standard desirables as warmth, light, and some health, may not be a bad thing. It's a bit like writing the prospective novel—being a prospector for fiction in uncharted areas—inasmuch as you don't know where you will end up or how.

To put it topically, locally: you run the home around the child. You learn her ignorances until they are yours. You steal her condition from her by risky analogies, like the mystic borrowing the lover's terms, like the lover borrowing the mystic's. You give your Amanda a glut of olibles, tangibles, edibles, and visibles: all the perfumes of Arabia; all the grades of sandpaper, leading up to a feel at an elephant; all the fluents from goat's milk to mercury; all the spices from cinnamon to chili; all the zoos, parades, Dufys, flags, unwanted *National Geographics,* French colonial stamps, travel posters, and rainbows you can muster. Always a color camera: preferably Polaroid, because she doesn't like to wait.

Against all this—the stark handicap and any voluptuously zany sharing in it —set a thought neither apocalyptic nor original. The years after the atomic explosion on Bikini Atoll, birds were sitting on sterile eggs; turtles, instead of going back to the sea after laying their own eggs, pressed on to the island's interior where they died of thirst. Their skeletons remain, thousands of them, evidence of a gratuitous handicap we might have had the brains to do without.

III

It is three years since that first visit to the clinic when powerlessness hit home to us. The strain told on Amanda too. She fetched a shovel from the garden to destroy with: lighting fixtures, windows, crockery, clocks. Strong always, she lifted and swung it with ease, pouting with birdcall. It took her two years to reject the shovel, to change from indefatigable and destructive hobgoblin into a girl who, gaining a word a month only to lose it the month after, developed luminously beautiful, big, Nordic features. Capable, without warning, of histrionic graciousness of manner (as if all the pressures lifted at once and the noises in her head stopped), she enjoyed her increasingly frequent visits to the clinic (toys, earphones, EEG apparatus), ate mightily, hardly ever caught a cold, thumped obliviously past staring or derisive children, and rebaffled the experts. Deaf, yes; "stone" deaf (in that melodramatic inversion of the pathetic fallacy) in the left ear; autistic, perhaps, but that's a vague word like "romantic"; brain damage not ruled out; amblyopia mentioned, with an ophthalmologist joining her team.

At five she left the island for the last time, blasé by now about Viscounts, to live near the clinic and the school associated with it. I signed out a speech-trainer, donated by the Variety Artists' Federation, on which she had a daily lesson, dealing sometimes in words, sometimes in sheer noise. She did her jigsaws like an impatient robot, began to lip-read, and gradually built up and kept a tiny vocabulary enunciated with almost coy preciosity, intoning "more" like an aria, raising "hair" into "har," curtailing "mouth" into "mou," lengthening "nose" into a three-second sound, but all the same *talking* although she still didn't know her name. Nicknames accumulated: Moo, from Mandy-Moo; Birdie, from her call; Tish from "ish-ish"; Lulu (developed cunningly from the two-syllable, high-pitched call with which her mother called her in); Yee (which sound she herself had substituted for Baba); Proof, from the condition called Manda-proof, she being the only thing or person invulnerable to herself, or so we said; and, strangest of all to strangers, Boat (her word for water—until she got *worbar*—shouted while paddling her feet on the TV screen). Epic formulae, these, while she went incognito.

During one spell, she averaged only three hours' sleep a night, erupting at midnight with umbrellas and jigsaws, then fetching a guitar, one mechanical top, several model baths, a dish brimming with soap dissolved, a length of iron piping, and a purloined fruit-knife, with all of which to while the night away until she could go out. And always wet. She became frenetic, twitched more than ever, during this waiting period: all that soothed her was running water, the swing in the garden, and ghoulish faces I pulled while pursuing her up the stairs. She partnered everyone at the lavatory, exclaiming "Oh" in exaggerative dismay at anyone's being under the vile necessity and then seeking to examine the deposit. But, we noticed, her "Yee" was less strident, less insistent; a month later, it had become a delicate, diffident greeting to be answered just as quietly, and she became drier, banged her head less, was less obsessed by the grotesque or the effluvial, gave up rending the day's newspaper, lost her passion for knives, began to draw faces and bodies that had two eyes, not one, with two legs instead of a barbed-wire entanglement of blue ball-point. She even drew a bath—always the long throne of her joy—with a Mandy in it.

She took the intelligence test and passed it before, after forty minutes' concentration, she flung the next puzzle across the room and mounted a full-size tantrum. The children's hospital lost her file, and two starch-bosomed nurses lost their cool when she screamed twenty minutes solid because they took from her the model jet kept to calm little boys during EEG tests. She thought it was a present.

"I'll buy it," I said against the screams. "It's worth it." No, that was out of the question; it was part of the equipment—it was government property. She vanished into the pathology lab, and was there found admiring fetuses, tumors, and cysts in their quiet jars, a true humanist explaining to her what was what. We got her a jet at the airport, and, later, a helicopter, a new swing, a miniature cooking set in Bavarian iron, building blocks, and card games, a thousand candy cigarettes, as many lollipops and ices: a surplus for purposes of habilitation.

Out of the clutter has come a girl who can make beds, bake bread, fry bacon, iron and fold clothes, hoover the carpets, mow the lawn (she calls escalators "bo" now), set a table, adjust the TV, fell apples from the tree by swatting it with a tennis racquet, tune her own hearing-aid, on her best days say "roundabout" as "rounabou" and "elephant" as almost that (it's otherwise known as "NO-o-se"), and on most days recite her own name. She cried and shuffled not at all when she began at the school for the deaf, a day-girl, almost six. She dotes on baths, Scotch tape (which she calls *yap*), steaks, and tenon saws, has become unoffendably gregarious, has learned to spit, looks through illustrated magazines with an anthropologist's gravity, has discovered how "No" doubles her range of concepts, and, I realize, sees Fred less and less. The Martian, we call her, or Miss Rabelais. Photogenic, long and agile, she has about forty words all told, a schoolbag and a homework book, which is all penumbra to the darkness of Amanda invading the house with a big shovel, sometimes a coal hammer, and that unfailing drooped-eyelid leer.

One special thing left a new light shining. Her class of nine children, working by the loop that amplifies sound identically for them whichever way they turn, was told to draw a spider's web. All drew but Amanda, who sat abstractedly apart, aloof from this planet. No one saw her move—and, being ambidextrous, she could have done it with either hand—but when the teacher got to her, Amanda was *yee*-ing gently beside a perfectly delineated web, all done in one unbroken line, with a spider at center. It's a prized school exhibit now, which she can bring home at year's end, when, presumably, she will bury it unsentimentally in her crate of junk in which, I once thought, she meant to bury us all, outclassed by her energy, thwarted by her privacy, heartsick at Nature's misbehavior, and as short of new expedients as of sleep.

One day, home from school with her homework book in which the teacher uses the special alphabet ("home" is "hoem"), she will extend *yee* into what I think it is, what it has been all along. I mean *yes,* and so will she, even if she's as incoherent as daily light, as vulnerable as uranium 235, and has an atom where an atom shouldn't be.

Herbert Kohl / Teaching

At the end of this essay Herbert Kohl is joined, as an author, by some of the thirty-six black children of the sixth-grade class he taught at a Harlem school. Such communal effort at composition illustrates nicely the attempt

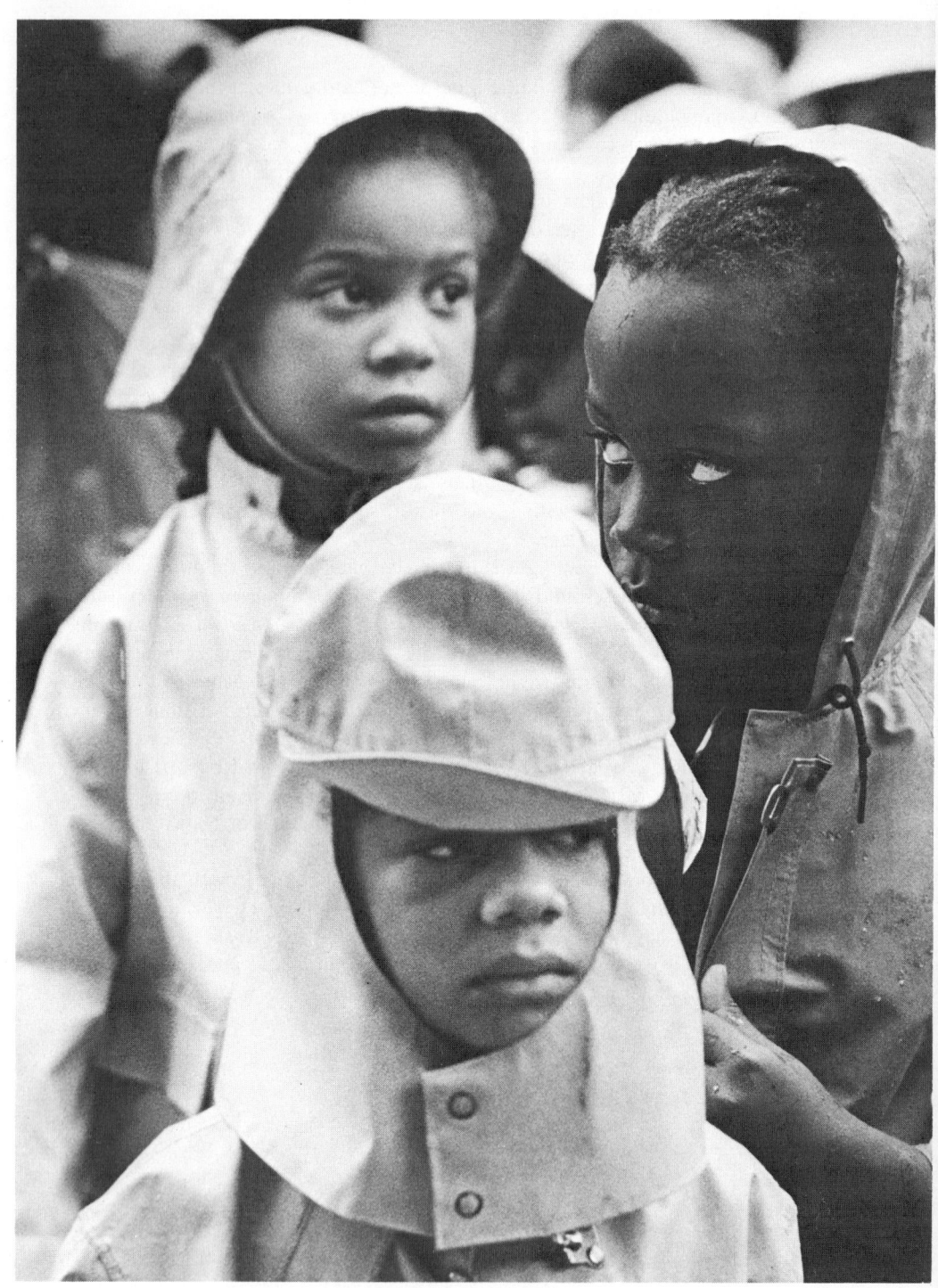

Jim Kappes

in the class to find a language which will join the world of the teacher, a graduate of Harvard, where he majored in philosophy, with the world of the twenty boys and sixteen girls, a world quite different, more frightening, and altogether less hospitable than his of the "humanities" in any sense of that term. Such a difference makes most teachers the more insistent on their own superiority and on the necessity of control. Kohl tries instead to do away as much as possible with authoritarianism even while keeping his authority, his grasp of certain subjects, available in an open and spontaneous way to his class. He teaches them what he knows about the language they innocently use even while being eager to learn what they might be thinking of his language.

The children's study of their vocabulary, of the music they like to dance to or listen to becomes mixed with equivalent elements from Kohl's own life and leads to quite another kind of exchange among them: first talk and then writing from the students about the nature of their daily lives, about the environment wherein they have developed an interest in some things and a nearly total indifference to others, wherein their fears and also their courage are given constant exercise. These testimonies suggest the pain of trying to place any kind of schooling in the context of living conditions so harsh and hurtful. But the student writings indicate some success in this venture, a gesture, at least, toward giving shape to a world that is sometimes as chaotic to the children as to their teachers.

One day Ralph cursed at Michael and unexpectedly things came together for me. Michael was reading and stumbled several times. Ralph scornfully called out, "What's the matter, psyches, going to pieces again?" The class broke up and I jumped on that word "psyches."

"Ralph, what does *psyches* mean?"

An embarrassed silence.

"Do you know how to spell it?"

Alvin volunteered. "S-i-k-e-s."

"Where do you think the word came from? Why did everybody laugh when you said it, Ralph?"

"You know, Mr. Kohl, it means, like crazy or something."

"Why? How do words get to mean what they do?"

Samuel looked up at me and said: "Mr. Kohl, now you're asking questions like Alvin. There aren't any answers, you know that."

"But there are. Sometimes by asking Alvin's kind of questions you discover the most unexpected things. Look."

I wrote *Psyche,* then *Cupid,* on the blackboard.

"That's how *psyche* is spelled. It looks strange in English, but the word doesn't come from English. It's Greek. There's a letter in the Greek alphabet that comes out *psi* in English. This is the way *psyche* looks in Greek."

Some of the children spontaneously took out their notebooks and copied the Greek.

"The word *psyche* has a long history. *Psyche* means mind or soul for the Greeks, but it was also the name of a lovely woman who had the misfortune to fall in love with Cupid, the son of Venus, the jealous Greek goddess of love. . . ."

The children listened, enchanted by the myth, fascinated by the weaving of the meaning of *psyche* into the fabric of the story, and the character, Mind, playing tricks on itself, almost destroying its most valuable possessions through its perverse curiosity. Grace said in amazement:

"Mr. Kohl, they told the story and said things about the mind at the same time. What do you call that?"

"*Myth* is what the Greeks called it."

Sam was roused.

"Then what happened? What about the history of the word?"

"I don't know too much, but look at the words in English that come from *Cupid* and *Psyche*."

I cited *psychological, psychic, psychotic, psychodrama, psychosomatic, cupidity*—the children copied them unasked, demanded the meanings. They were obviously excited.

Leaping ahead, Alvin shouted: "You mean words change? People didn't always speak this way? Then how come the reader says there's a right way to talk and a wrong way?"

"There's a right way now, and that only means that's how most people would like to talk now, and how people write now."

Charles jumped out of his desk and spoke for the first time during the year.

"You mean one day the way we talk—you know, with words like *cool* and *dig* and *sound*—may be all right?"

"Uh huh. Language is alive, it's always changing, only sometimes it changes so slowly that we can't tell."

Neomia caught on.

"Mr. Kohl, is that why our reader sounds so old-fashioned?"

And Ralph.

"Mr. Kohl, when I called Michael *psyches,* was I creating something new?"

Someone spoke for the class.

"Mr. Kohl, can't we study the language we're talking about instead of spelling and grammar? They won't be any good when language changes anyway."

We could and did. That day we began what had to be called for my conservative plan book "vocabulary," and "an enrichment activity." Actually it was the study of language and myth, of the origins and history of words, of their changing uses and functions in human life. We began simply with the words *language* and *alphabet,* the former from the Latin for tongue and the latter from the first two letters of the Greek alphabet. Seeing the origin of *alphabet* and the relationship of *cupidity* to Cupid and *psychological* to Psyche had a particularly magical effect upon the children. They found it easy to master and acquire words that would have seemed senseless and tedious to memorize. Words like *psychic* and *psychosomatic* didn't seem arbitrary and impenetrable, capable of being learned only painfully by rote. Rather they existed in a context, through a striking tale that easily accrued associations and depth. After a week the children learned the new words, asked to be tested on them, and demanded more.

"Vocabulary" became a fixed point in each week's work as we went from Cupid and Psyche to Tantalus, the Sirens, and the Odyssey and the linguistic riches that it contains. We talked of Venus and Adonis and spent a week on first *Pan* and *panic, pan-American,* then *pandemonium,* and finally on *demonic* and *demons* and *devils.* We studied *logos, philos, anthropos, pathos,* and their derivatives. I spun the web of *mythos* about language and its origins. I went to German (*kindergarten*), Polynesian (*taboo*), or Arabic (*assassin*), showing what a motley open-ended fabric English (and for that matter any living language) is. The range of times and peoples that contributed to the growth of today's American English impressed me no less than it did the class. It drove me to research language and its origins; to reexplore myth and the dim origins of man's culture; and to invent ways of sharing my discoveries with the children.

The children took my words seriously and went a step further. Not content to be fed solely words that grew from sources that I, the teacher, presented, they asked for words that fitted unnamed and partially articulated concepts they had, or situations they couldn't adequately describe.

"Mr. Kohl, what do you call it when a person repeats the same thing over and over again and can't stop?"

"What is it called when something is funny and serious at the same time?"

"What do you call a person who brags and thinks he's big but is really weak inside?"

"Mr. Kohl, is there a word that says that something has more than one meaning?"

The class became word-hungry and concept-hungry, concerned with discovering the "right" word to use at a given time to express a specific thought. I was struck by the difference of this notion of rightness and "the right way" to speak and write from the way children are supposed to be taught in school. They are supposed to acquire correct usage, right grammar and spelling, the right meaning of a word, and the right way to write a sentence. Achievement and I.Q. tests give incomplete sentences and the child is instructed to fill in the "right" word. Many teachers correct children's writing on the basis of a canon of formal rightness without bothering to ask what the children's words mean. I did the same thing myself.

I noticed that the children frequently said that they were bad at their friends, or their parents, or some teacher who angered them. They insisted upon describing a certain type of anger as "being bad at," and I kept telling them that it was wrong because "to be bad at" someone doesn't exist in English. And in a way I was "right"; it didn't exist, nor did the concept it was trying to express exist in English as I spoke and wrote it. But the children did mean "to be bad at," and meant something very specific by it. "To be bad" is a way of defying authority and expressing anger at the same time, as indicating one's own strength and independence. The use of "bad" here is ironical and often admiring. One child explained to me that down South a "bad nigger" was one who was strong enough and brave enough to be defiant of the white man's demands no matter how much everyone else gave in. Only later did I discover Bessie Smith * in J. C. Johnson's "Black Mountain Blues," using "bad" in the same way as the kids:

> Back on Black Mountain a child would smack your face
> Back on Black Mountain a child would smack your face
> Babies cry for liquor and all the birds sing bass.
>
> Black Mountain people are bad as they can be
> Black Mountain people are bad as they can be
> They uses gun powder just to sweeten their tea [1]

I think that before we talked about language and myth the children, if they thought about it at all, felt that most words were either arbitrary labels pinned on things and concepts the way names seem to be pinned onto babies, or indicators of connections amongst these labels. These "labels" probably represented the way the adult world capriciously decided to name things. I doubt whether the children ever thought of adults as having received language from yet other adults even more remote in time. My pupils must have found the language of their teachers strange and arbitrary indeed. The "right" language of school texts and middle-class teachers must have seemed threatening and totalitarian, especially since the only living words the children knew and used were the words they used on the streets, words teachers continually told them were "wrong" and "incorrect."

The idea that words were complex phenomena with long and compelling histories was never presented to the children. I doubt many teachers entertained it. The canons of the schools pretend that a small preselected segment of the language of the moment is an eternally correct and all-inclusive form. This form is embodied in basic word lists and controlled vocabulary readers, as if the mastering of language consists of learning a list of fifty or a hundred words by rote. The use of language in human life is continually avoided or ignored, as if it

---

1. Lines from "Black Mountain Blues," words and music by J. C. Johnson, Copyright © 1931, 1958 by J. C. Johnson. All rights reserved. Reproduced by special permission.

* Bessie Smith: (1898?–1937), blues singer from Chattanooga, Tennessee; known in the 1920's as the "Empress of the Blues."

poses too great a threat to "correctness" and "rightness." No wonder then that the children showed so persistently and ingeniously how much they feared and avoided the language of the schools.

Later in the semester I taught the class a lesson on naming, a topic that seems deceptively simple yet minimally encompasses history, psychology, sociology, and anthropology. I put everybody's full name on the blackboard, including my own, and asked the class how people got names. The answer was, naturally, from their parents who made the choice—but not the full choice, it emerged, when Michael remembered that his parents' surnames came from their parents. Then how far back can you go? The children thought and Grace raised a delicate question. If the names go back through the generations how come her name wasn't African since her ancestors must have been? In answer I told the class about my own name—Kohl, changed from Cohen, changed from Okun, changed from something lost in the darkness of history; one change to identify the family as Jewish, one change to deny it. Then I returned to the question of slave names and the destruction of part of the children's African heritage that the withholding of African names implied.

Neomia said that she knew of someone who changed his name because he wanted to start a new life, and Sam told the class that his brother called himself John X because X meant unknown and his original African name was unknown. We talked of people who named their children after famous men and of others who gave exotic names. From there the discussion went on to the naming of animals—pets, wild animals, racehorses; things—boats, houses, dolls; and places. The class knew by that time in the school year that one doesn't talk of words in isolation from human lives and history, and by then I had begun to know what to teach.

The emphasis on language and words opened the children to the whole process of verbal communication. Things that they had been struggling to express, or worse, had felt only they in their isolation thought about, became social, shareable. Speaking of things, of inferiority and ambiguity, or irony and obsession, brought relief, and perhaps for the first time gave the children a sense that there were meaningful human creations that one could discover in a classroom.

Yet not all concepts have been verbalized, and the children frequently talked of having feelings and desires that no words I gave them expressed adequately. They had to create new words, or develop new forms of expression to communicate, and that can neither be taught nor done upon command. We could go to the frontier, however, and speak about the blues, about being bad or hip or cool —about how certain ways of living or historical times created the need for new words. We talked about the nuclear age, the smallness of the modern world, the jargon of democracy and communism, integration and segregation. The children looked in awe at *Finnegans Wake* and Joyce's monumental attempt to forge a new language; they listened to Bob Dylan, recorded the words of soul songs and classical blues, read poetry. We started out talking about words and ended up with life itself. The children opened up and began to display a fearless curiosity about the world.

I sense that I've jumped ahead too quickly, for the whole thing happened slowly, almost imperceptibly. There were days of despair throughout the whole year, and I never learned how to line the class up at three o'clock. There were days when Alvin was a brilliant inspiring pupil at ten and the most unbearable, uncontrollable nuisance at eleven thirty; when after a good lesson some children would turn angry and hostile, or lose interest in everything. There were small fights and hostilities, adjustments and readjustments in the children's relationships to each other and to me. I had to enlarge my vision as a human being, learn that if the complex and contradictory nature of life is allowed to come forth in the classroom there are times when it will do so with a vengeance.

I still stuck to the curriculum as much as possible. The social studies was impossible so I collected the books and returned them to the bookroom. It was too painful to see the children twist their faces into stupid indifference and hear their pained dull answers accompanied by nervous drumming on the desks.

"New York is a large modern country."

"The Hudson is an important ocean."

"The Industrial Revolution was a benefit to all."

Better drop it altogether, try anything so long as it didn't humiliate the children. These answers were not a function of the children's lack of experience, as the hopelessly respectable anti-poverty program believes; rather they were a direct response to the institutionalized hypocrisy that is characteristic of schools in the United States today.

I brought part of my library to school and temporarily substituted it for social studies. The children were curious about those Greeks and Latins who contributed so many words and concepts to our language. I brought in books on Greek and Roman architecture and art, as well as Robert Graves's version of the *Iliad*, a paperback translation of Apuleius' *Cupid and Psyche*, the *Larousse Encyclopedia of Mythology*, and anything else that seemed relevant or interesting. I showed the books to the children and let them disappear into their desks. It was made clear that the books were to be read, the pages to be turned. If someone reads a book so intensely that the book is bruised it is flattering to the book.

For three-quarters of an hour a day the Pantheon * circulated along with Floyd Patterson * and J. D. Salinger,* Partridge's dictionary of word origins made its way through the class with Langston Hughes * and the Bobbsey twins.*

* the Pantheon: assemblage of all the gods.
* Floyd Patterson: (1935–), heavyweight champion boxer; he held the heavyweight title from 1956 to 1959, when he lost it to Ingemar Johansson; a year later he became the first man ever to regain the heavyweight title, but in 1962 he lost the championship to Sonny Liston; Mr. Kohl's students were reading his autobiography, *Victory Over Myself* (1962).
* J. D. Salinger: (1919–), author of *The Catcher in the Rye* (1951).
* Langston Hughes: (1902–67), American Negro writer best known for his poetry which frequently makes use of Negro folk and jazz rhythms.
* the Bobbsey twins: heroes of a long series of children's books by L. L. Hope.

Anything I could get my hands on was brought to class—a great deal remained unread, and some books I hadn't read myself shocked and surprised the class. They were sexy and popular. Later that year my supervisor told me I was running a very effective individualized reading program. That may have been it, but the truth seemed simpler and less structured. I overwhelmed the class with books, many of which I loved, and let them discover for themselves what they liked. There were no reports to be written, no requirements about numbers of pages to be read. Some children hardly read at all, others devoured whatever was in the room. The same is true of my friends.

Robert Jackson grabbed a book on Greek architecture, copied floor plans and perspective drawings, and finally, leaping out of the book, created a reasonably accurate scale model of the Parthenon. Alvin and Michael built a clay volcano, asked for and got a chemistry book which showed them how to simulate an eruption. Sam, Thomas, and Dennis fought their way through war books; through the Navy, the Seabees, the Marines, and the Paratroops. The girls started with the Bobbsey twins and worked through to romantic novels and, in the case of a few, Thurber * and O. Henry.* I learned that there were no books to fear, and having been divested of my fear of idleness, I also wasn't worried if some children went through periods of being unable to do anything at all.

People entering my classroom during those forty-five minutes of "social" studies usually experienced an initial sense of disorder followed by surprise at the relative calm of the room. If they bothered to look more closely or ask they would find that most of the children were working.

I remember once a supervisor from the District Office visited my class in late October. She entered the room unannounced, said nothing to me, but proceeded to ask the children what they were doing. In small groups or individually they showed her. She was pleased until she came to Ralph, who boldly told her that he was spending the morning ripping up pieces of paper—which is precisely what he had been doing all morning. Her whole impression of the classroom changed. I was a failure, allowing a child not to work, the thought of it . . . shocking. She took the situation into her own hands and spoke to Ralph. He merely turned a dumb face to her, rolled his eyes, and went back to his paper. She left, muttering something about discipline and emotional disturbance.

Ralph wasn't the only one who couldn't do anything for a while. When I started bringing books to school and opening the supply closets to the class, most children demurred from any change in routine. They wanted the social studies books even though they learned nothing from them; they enjoyed copying the mindless exercises that kept them dull and secure in class. It was just that I, as a teacher, couldn't pretend they were learning just to make our life together quieter and easier. So, with the textbooks gone many children stuck to chess and

---

* James Thurber: (1894–1961), American humorous writer and artist.
* O. Henry: pseudonym of W. S. Porter (1862–1910), American short-story writer skilled in the technique of the "surprise ending."

checkers. The girls started playing jacks, and with my encouragement created a vocabulary to describe the jack fever that seized them.

For days, until they got bored or became bold enough to explore new books, strange personal books they had never seen before, the girls lived in the throes of jackomania. The jack contagion spread until almost every girl cultivated jackophilia. As a reaction to this the boys in the class became jackophobes and misjackophiles. I managed in this way to keep the children talking about what they were doing, and to push them to explore their actions. Little by little groups of girls formed to read together and talk about books. I remember the stir caused by *Mary Jane,* Dorothy Sterling's book about a Negro girl who helped desegregate a Southern junior high school. I read the class a selection on Mary Jane's first day in the previously all-white school. The demand for the book was so great that I got four copies and let them circulate.

Because the children began choosing their work slowly I could follow the many directions pursued during "social" studies, could sometimes jump ahead, and getting a sense of the children's tastes and preferences, make sure material was there. Also I had time to listen and even participate in some of the projects. Alvin and Michael were joined by Charles, Franklin, and Thomas C. in their volcanic endeavors. After the first successful eruption created by Alvin's mother-er's vinegar poured over Michael's mother's baking soda, the volcano became less interesting. The five boys sat poring over the book of experiments I gave them, planning and plotting how to steal the equipment.

I asked the assistant principal for equipment for the kids, and he replied that the school hadn't received any. When I told that to the boys they laughed and said they knew where it was, only they'd never see it because their school was in Harlem. I was incredulous, but have since learned how often the children are acutely aware of what the staff attempts to conceal from them. Instead of becoming moralistic and telling the children that they couldn't possibly know about such things as hidden science materials I challenged them and they led me into the hall and up to a locked supply closet. The next day I managed to get the key and found just what I'd been told, several years' untouched, packaged science supplies—batteries in sealed boxes dating as much as five years back, bells, buzzers, chemicals, aquariums, terrariums—enough for a whole elementary school.

It was useless trying to fight the administration over their irresponsibility. I had done that before in another public school in New York City, had been given thoroughly evasive answers, and found myself transferred to Harlem at the end of the year. The principal may have thought that was a deserving punishment for defiance. At any rate it sobered me—I wanted to teach, and after a few months did not want to leave Harlem and the kids. Grade 6-1 had become a part of me. So I learned to keep quiet, keep the door of my classroom shut, and make believe that the class and I functioned in a vacuum, that the school around us didn't exist. It was difficult not to feel the general chaos—to observe the classes without teachers, the children wandering aimlessly, sometimes wantonly through the halls, disrupting classes, intimidating, extorting, yet being courted by the administration: "Please don't make trouble, anything you want, but no trouble." I kept quiet that year anyway, and tried not to make trouble for them either. I wasn't a good enough teacher yet, or confident enough to accuse others of failing with the children when I wasn't sure of my own work. But I had to get that science equipment, so I volunteered to take care of science supplies for the school, mentioning casually that I noticed that there were some in the closet. The principal gave me the closet key with a smile that said, "Anytime you want to do more work, come to me. Who knows what you could find hidden in the other closets. . . ." Then he asked, truly puzzled, "Do you think those children will get anything out of it?"

We had the equipment, and that was the important thing at the moment. The boys went through many experiments, put together elaborate combinations of bells, buzzers, and lights, and contrived a burglar-alarm system for the classroom. They made a fire extinguisher and invisible ink. After a week they were joined by several girls who took over the equipment as the boys broke away to help Robert with the Parthenon. The groups formed and re-formed as projects developed and were abandoned. It was good to see the children, once so wild over a simple game of chess, move freely about the room, exploring socially and intellectually. Still there were moments of doubt and anxiety; it was difficult to see where this classroom of mine was going.

As usual the children led me. I have found one of the most valuable qualities a teacher can have is the ability to perceive and build upon the needs his pupils struggle to articulate through their every reaction. For this he needs antennae and must constantly work upon attuning himself to the ambience of the classroom. To the mastery of observation of children must be added the more difficult skill of observing his own effect upon the class, something only partially done at best. But if the easy guides of a standard curriculum and authoritarian stance are to be discarded any clues arising from actual experience in the classroom are welcome.

I had brought many things from home for the children; now they brought things for me to learn from. Sam brought in a Moms Mabley record and from the other children's reaction it was obvious that she was "in." I had never heard of her and asked the class who she was. They all volunteered information: that she was ancient, funny, and nice, that she liked young boys and kids, that people lined up on 125th Street whenever she was at the Apollo Theater, that she sounded on people in the audience.

Sam shyly suggested that we listen to the record instead of doing reading, and I reluctantly agreed. It was still difficult for me to discard my schedule with confidence. There was another problem—I explained to the class that there was no phonograph in the room or, as far as I knew, in the school.

Thomas S. and Dennis jumped up, asked me to write a note saying I wanted to borrow a record player, and disappeared with the note, only to reappear in five minutes with a machine. They knew the exact distribution of all the hidden and hoarded supplies in the school, and I learned to trust their knowledge over official statements of what was available.

We listened to Moms, the class explaining the jokes, translating some of her dialect for me. It pleased them to be listened to. After that we kept a phonograph in the room, and the children brought in the latest records. We listened to them together at the end of the morning or the afternoon. I transcribed the words and every once in a while put them on the blackboard and discussed what the songs were all about. One particularly interesting song was "Do You Love Me?" by Barry Gordy, Jr.

> You broke my heart because I couldn't dance
> You didn't even want me around.
> And now I'm back to let you know
> I can really shake 'em down.
>
> Do you love me? I can really move.
> Do you love me? I'm in the groove.
> Do you love me? Do you love me
> Now that I can dance? [2]

I asked the kids if it really was that important to be able to dance. They replied in veiled terms that I couldn't understand. I pushed them. Why couldn't I understand? Dancing is a simple social phenomenon, it has to do with parties and popularity, not the soul. . . .

That hit something direct. One of the boys said, just loud enough for me to hear, that dancing *was* a soul thing. Others took up the argument, it was a way of being together, of expressing yourself when you were alone, of feeling strong when everything was wrong, of feeling alive in a dead world.

"Besides, Mr. Kohl, they don't only mean dancing. That's a way of saying you can't do nothing, that you're weak. Dancing is kind of, you know, like a symbol."

Alvin explained it to me. It was only a step from there to letting the kids actually dance in class. I started on Friday afternoons, and later let the kids dance when the afternoon work was done. At first only the girls were interested. Half of them would dance (it was the Wobble at that time), while the others would read or talk, or even begin their homework. The boys would hover about the dancers, joking, moving ever so slightly with the music, pushing Michael and Maurice into the Wobble line, urging them to continue the satire of the girls' movement that they were performing in a corner. Once in a while everyone danced—I even tried to overcome my leaden-footed self-consciousness and take a few steps, but my soul wasn't free enough.

2. 1962 Jobete Music Company, Inc. Quoted by permission.

Music became an integral part of the classroom. The children brought in their records; I responded with my own. One morning I put twenty-five records ranging from blues and Fats Waller through Thelonius Monk and Coltrane to Mozart and Beethoven on top of the phonograph. During the morning breaks the kids explored freely, and when the music began to interest some individuals enough, I brought in biographies of the composers, pictures of the musicians. We talked in small groups during social studies of chain gangs, field music, modern jazz, rock and roll, child prodigies, anything that came up. A dialogue between the children and myself was developing.

It deepened quickly. Alvin and Ralph decided to wait for me at eight o'clock and spend an hour in the classroom before the class arrived. They were soon joined by Maurice, Michael, Reginald, Pamela, and Brenda W. At one time or another during the year every child went through a phase of coming early. The only limitations I had to impose on this were forced upon me by other teachers who didn't want to be bothered by children so early in the morning and complained to the administration.

I would arrive at the school at eight. Several of the children would be waiting and we would walk the five flights up to the room. One of the boys would take my briefcase, another the keys. Once in the room the children went their own ways. Maurice and Michael went to the phonograph, Alvin to his latest project with Robert Jackson. The girls would play jacks or wash the boards. Grace explored the books on my desk. Every once in a while one of the children would come up to my desk and ask a question or tell me something. The room warmed up to the children, got ready for the day. At first the questions were simple, irrelevant.

"Mr. Kohl, what's today's date?"

"Where is Charles this morning?"

Then there was some testing.

"Mr. Kohl, when are you going to be absent?"

"Will you come back here next year?"

By the end of October a few children were coming to my desk in the morning and saying things that nothing in my life prepared me to understand or respond to.

"Mr. Kohl, the junkies had a fight last night. They cut this girl up bad."

"Mr. Kohl, I couldn't sleep last night, they was shouting and screaming until four o'clock."

"I don't go down to the streets to play, it's not safe."

"Mr. Kohl, those cops are no good. They beat up on this kid for nothing last night."

I listened, hurt, bruised by the harshness of the children's world. There was no response, no indignation or anger of mine, commensurate to what the children felt. Besides, it was relief they wanted, pronouncement of the truth, acceptance of it in a classroom which had become important to them. I could do nothing about the facts, therefore my words were useless. But through listening, the facts remained open and therefore placed school in the context of the children's real world.

At eight o'clock on October 22, Alvin pushed Ralph up to my desk. Ralph handed me "The Rob-Killing of Liebowitz," and retreated.

> Last night on 17 St. Liebowitz collected the rent. They told him not to come himself but he came for many years. The junkies got him last night. He wouldn't give them the money so they shot him and took it. They was cops and people runny all over the roofs and the streets.
>
> There were people from the news and an ambulance took Liebowitz.

I read Ralph's article to the class and asked them if it were true. There was an awkward silence, then Neomia said with bitterness:

"If you don't believe it you can look in the *Daily News*."

"Mr. Kohl, you don't know what it's like around here."

The others agreed, but when I pressed the class to tell me, silence returned. The more I tried to get the class to talk the dumber the children acted, until they finally denied that there was any truth in Robert's article whatever. The topic was too charged for public discussion; it somehow had to be made private, between each individual child and myself. After all, not everybody saw the same things, and worse perhaps, if things were so bad it would be natural for some of the children to be afraid. So I asked the class to write, as homework in the privacy of their apartments, and tell me what their block was like, what they felt about it. The papers were not to be marked or shown to anybody else in the class. If anybody objected, he didn't have to do the assignment. This was probably the first time in their school lives that the children wrote to communicate, and the first sense they had of the possibilities of their own writing.

The next evening I read the responses.

NEOMIA, "WHAT A BLOCK!"

"My block is the most terrible block I've ever seen. There are at lease 25 or 30 narcartic people in my block. The cops come around there and tries to act bad but I bet inside of them they are as scared as can be. They even had in the papers that this block is the worst block, not in Manhattan but in New York City. In the summer they don't do nothing except shooting, stabbing, and fighting. They hang all over the stoops and when you say excuse me to them they hear you but they just don't feel like moving. Some times they make me so mad that I feel like slaping them and stuffing and bag of garbage down their throats. Theres only one policeman who can handle these people and we all call him "Sunny." When he come around in his cop car the people run around the corners, and he wont let anyone sit on the stoops. If you don't believe this story come around some time and you'll find out."

MARIE

"My block is the worse block you ever saw people getting killed or stabbed men and women in building's taking dope. And when the police come around the block the block be so clean that nobody will get hurt. There's especially one police you even beat woman you can't even stand on your own stoop he'll chase you off. And sometime the patrol wagon comes around and pick up al the dope addicts and one day they picked up this man and when his wife saw him and when she went to tell the police that that's her husband they just left so she went to the police station and they let him go. You can never trust anyone around my block you even get robbed when the children in my building ask me to come down stairs I say no because you don't know what would happen. Only sometimes I come down stairs not all the time."

SONIA, "THE STORY ABOUT MY BLOCK"

"My block is dirty and it smell terrible

"The children picks fights. And it hardly have room to play. its not a very long thing to write about, but if you were living there you won't want to stay there no longer. it have doopedics and gabbage pan is spill on the side walk and food is on the ground not everyday but sometimes children make fire in the backyard. on the stoop is dirty. I go out to play that the End about My block."

PHYLLIS, "MY BLOCK"

"My block has a lot of kids who thing that the can beat everybody (like a lot of blocks) They pick on children that they know they can beat. There trouble makers and blabbers mouths."

CHARISSE, "MY BLOCK"

"I live 62 E 120st My neighborhood is not so bad. Everyone has children in the block. Many of the children are Spanish. Some of them run around nude and dirty. Some of the house are so dirty you would be sacre to come in the door. Sometime the drunks come out and fight. Some of the house are nice and clean. The block is not to dirty its the people inside of it. At night it's very quite. But if you come in my building at about 10:00 you would be surprise to see some naked children running around like animals. The mothers don't even seem to care about them. Many of the children ages run from 1 to 4 years of age. Many of the people in the block drink so much they don't have time for the children. The children have no place to play they have the park but the parents don't care enough to take them. Now you have a idea of what my block is like."

RALPH, "MY NEIGHBORHOOD"

"I live on 117 street, between Madison and 5th avenue. All the bums live around here. But the truth is they don't live here they just hang around the street. All the kids call it 'Junky's Paradise.' Because there is no cops to stop them. I wish that the cops would come around and put all the bums out of the block and put them in jail all their life. I would really like it very much if they would improve my neighborhood. I don't even go outside to play because of them. I just play at the center or someplace else."

GAIL, "MY BLOCK"

"My block is sometimes noisy and sometimes quiet when its noisy children and grownups are out side listening to the boys playing the steel drums or there's a boy who got hit by a car or something. When the block is quiet, there is a storm, raining or snowing and people don't come out side. Farther down the block near Park Avenue, some of the houses are not kept clean.

"There's a lot right next to a building and there's a lot of trash, you can see rats running back and forth. The Sanitation Department cleans it every week, but it just gets dirty again because people throw garbage out the windows. From Madison Ave. to about the middle of the block the houses are kept clean. The back yards are keep swept and the stoops are clean. I like my building and block."

CAROL

"Around my block all you can see is drug addits. The other day the Cops came and took over 15 men in the cops wagon and they came out the next day but one man shim they kept him beated him from 7 in the morning until 1:30 in the afternoon because they thought he had something to do with the Rob Killing of Lebrowize."

RONNIE

"I think my block is not as lively as it use to be cause all the jive time people are moving out. I think my block is nice compare to 117 St. were people be getting kill."

CHARLES

"My block is a dirty crumby block."

THOMAS S.

"Ounce their was a gang fight around my block and the police came and a man got shot. And their was detives around my block and junkies shot at a copes and a lady curse out the copes and they broke in a lady house. Around 119 street a cop was bricked and kill and junkies took dop and needles."

KATHLEEN, "ABOUT MY BLOCK"

"Around my block theirs no trees on the side walks like the Park on the outside but of course theres not going to be any trees on the side walks but there are some trees on the side walks mabe in brooklyn or long island. New Jersey and Queens but I know there are some in long island I know that because thats like a little country in some parts of it. And around my block I have nice friends and nice neighbors of my mother, people are nice around my block I go to Church with my friends and we all go together and learn more and more about God and I like it very much Because when I grow up to be a lady (if I live to see and if gods willing) and know all about God and understand the facts I want to be a nice mannered lady and go to church as long as I live to see."

The day after we talked about them. I had asked for the truth, and it presented its ugly head in the classroom, yet I didn't know what to do about it. That was all I could say to the children—that I was moved, angry, yet as powerless to change things as they were. I remembered How We Became Modern America, the books I couldn't use, and felt dumb, expressionless—how else can one put up with such lies of progress, prosperity, and cheerful cooperation when we do face problems. The next day the children wrote of how they would change things if they could.

THOMAS S., "IF I COULD CHANGE MY BLOCK"

"If I could change my block, I would first get read of all of the wine heads and clean up the gobash and then try to improve the buildings and paint the apartments. That's what I would do."

NEOMIA

"If I could change my block I would stand on Madison Ave and throw nothing but Teargas in it. I would have all the people I liked to get out of the block and then I would become very tall and have big hands and with my big hands I would take all of the narcartic people and pick them up with my hand and throw them in the nearest river and Oceans. I would go to some of those old smart alic cops and throw them in the Oceans and Rivers too. I would let the people I like move into the projects so they could tell their friends that they live in a decent block. If I could do this you would never see 117 st again."

KATHLEEN, "MY BLOCK"

"If I could change my block I would have new house but in it I would have all the bums take out of it. There would be garden where I live. There would be some white people live there we would have all colors not just Negro. There would be 7 room apt. There be low rent for the poor family. The poor family would have the same thing as the average or rich family have. There would be club for the boys and girls. There would be place where the Old could come. Where the young can share there problem"

BRENDA T.

"If I could change my block I would put all the bums on an Island where they can work there. I would give them lots of food. But I wouldn't let no whiskey be brought to them. After a year I would ship them to new York and make them clean up junk in these back yard and make them maybe make a baseball diamond and put swings basketball courts etc. When I get thought they'll never want whiskey or dope cause If I catch them I'll make a them work day and night with little food. Lunch would be at 5:00 super 10:00 bed 1:00 (If caught 2 times) breakfast 8:30. Get up at 3.00"

MARIE, "HOW I WOULD CHANGE MY BLOCK"

"If I could change my block I would take out all of the junkies and I would take out all of the old building and put in new ones and give hot water every day and make a play street out of my block.

"That's what I would do if I could"

THOMAS C.

"Well I would like to change my block into a play street, first I'd take all the junkies out the block and take the parking cars out the block and make whaw that everyman put their cars in a garage at nights. Because too many children get hit by cars and make all the buildings neat and clean with stream and hot and cold water."

ANASTASIA

"The very first thing that I would like to do to change my block if I could, put up a no litering sign to keep away stange people who hang aroung the steps. Nexs I would have less garbage containers on the sidewalks, expecially those that are uncovered because they are unsightly and unhealthy, and last bus at least. I would make a carfew at least 5 p.m. for ander age children to be upt the corners, sidewalks, and if they are not, hold their parents severly responsible for any harm that befails them."

CHARLES

"If I could do anything to chang my block tear down the buildings on both sides. And have a school on one side and a center on the other. Inside the center there would be a swimming pool inside and also a gym. And outside a softball field and also four baskball courts."

SONIA

"If I could of change my block I would make it cleaner no gabbage pans open and falling down and not so many fights and don't let it have dead animals in the street."

How we became modern America, how we became modern man—that was our problem, my problem to teach, but where to start, at what moment in history does one say, "Ah, here's where it all began"? How could the children get some saving perspective on the mad chaotic world they existed in, some sense of the universality of struggle, the possibility of revolution and change, and the strength to persist? That, if anything, was my challenge as a teacher—it was spelled out before me unambiguously. Could I find anything in human history and the human soul that would strengthen the children and save them from despair?

Cyril Connolly / A Georgian Boyhood

Mr. Connolly went to Eton, a school unlike any other, even the other English public schools (preparatory schools). For five hundred years the usual nursery of the aristocracy, Eton is a very large, very complex society, related to the world outside in a most obscure way, yet traditionally filling most of its great offices. Eton does not make all boys happy, but in its way it offers extraordinary, almost premature fulfillment to others. At the time of this essay Latin and Greek still predominated in class; the highest ambition one might have out of class was to become a member of "Pop," a hugely privileged society or club which was the top rank of the top school. Balliol, an Oxford College once noted for its austere humane learning, was regarded as simply another step in a career that could not fail.

Connolly speaks of the environment of Eton as one he dreaded to leave, and gives us the sense of its privacy by using its slang. His purpose is to stress the isolation and intimacy of the society, and he does not explain the slang; if we can guess its meaning, so much the better; if not, we feel—as we are—"outside." As he writes, Connolly delicately, morbidly, expresses the sense of his disappointment in the rest of what life has to offer him. Were we, as he felt in 1938, at the end of the civilized world as he suggests both at the beginning, in the quotation from Sir Thomas Browne, and in the affected Latinate conclusion? Or should he blame himself, rather than the world or the school? The case for the school is put by "the voice of Henry's holy shade" (Henry VI was the founder of Eton).

Connolly's book is called *Enemies of Promise*. Eton is one of them; but though he tells us much about the school (none too explicitly, however) his chief interest is in the state of his own life and his readiness for the age of conflict, darkness, and courage that is about to begin.

Of all the passages in the book this is the most artificially written, the most complex and allusive. The manner is what the education described

Henri Cartier-Bresson, Magnum

produced in this boy, at this moment in time; it fully illustrates what he is saying, even when it may seem unsatisfactory. It criticizes itself. It also gives, in little, a convincing picture of one of the most secure bastions of privilege in the world. Eighty or so miles away, in Bristol, was Frank Norman's charity school.

I was now entering the third hot room of English education; from St. Wulfric's I had got a scholarship to Eton, from Eton to Balliol and from thence there would, I supposed, be other scholarships awaiting me; I could not imagine a moment when I should not be receiving marks for something, when "poor" or "very fair" or "Beta plus" was not being scrawled across my conduct-sheet by the Great Examiner. And yet already I was a defeatist, I remembered Teddy Jessel saying to me by the fives courts, in my hour of triumph: "Well, you've got a Balliol scholarship and you've got into Pop—you know I shouldn't be at all surprised if you never did anything else the rest of your life. After all, what happens to old tugs? If they're clever they become dons * or civil servants, if not they come back here as ushers *; when they're about forty they go to bed with someone, if it's a boy they get sacked, if it's a woman they marry them. The pi * ones go into the church and may become bishops. There goes Connolly, K.S., a brilliant fellow, an alpha mind, he got the Rosebery and the Brackenbury, and all the other berries, and passed top into the Office of Rears!"

There was much truth in this, in fact were I to deduce any system from my feelings on leaving Eton, it might be called *The Theory of Permanent Adolescence*. It is the theory that the experiences undergone by boys at the great public schools, their glories and disappointments, are so intense as to dominate their lives and to arrest their development. From these it results that the greater part of the ruling class remains adolescent, school-minded, self-conscious, cowardly, sentimental and in the last analysis homosexual. Early laurels weigh like lead and of many of the boys whom I knew at Eton, I can say that their lives are over. Those who knew them then knew them at their best and fullest; now, in their early thirties, they are haunted ruins. When we meet we look at each other, there is a pause of recognition, which gives way to a moment of guilt and fear. "I won't tell on you," our eyes say, "if you won't tell on me"—and when we do speak, it is to discover peculiar evidence of this obsession. For a nightmare I have often had has been that of finding myself back; I am still a boy at Eton, still in Pop, still in my old room in Sixth Form * Passage but nobody remembers me, nobody tells me where to go. I am worse than a newboy, I am a new oldboy. I go into Hall and search for a place to eat, I wander in schoolrooms trying

* dons: university teachers.
* ushers: schoolmasters.
* pi: contemptuous abbreviation of "pious."
* Sixth Form: the graduating class.

to find a class where I am expected. When I first used to have this dream I had only just left Eton, I knew most of the boys and the masters and the nightmare then took the form of everyone, after my place had been filled, my gap closed over, having to pretend they were glad I had come back. As time went on nobody remembered me and the dream ended with my ignominious ejection. I have found other old Etonians who have had the same experience; some dream they are back in their old rooms while their wives and children hang about outside to disgrace them.

Once again romanticism with its deathwish is to blame for it lays an emphasis on childhood, on a fall from grace which is not compensated for by any doctrine of future redemption; we enter the world, trailing clouds of glory, childhood and boyhood follow and we are damned. Certainly growing up seems a hurdle which most of us are unable to take and the lot of the artist is unpleasant in England because he is one of the few who, bending but not breaking, is able to throw off these early experiences, for maturity is the quality that the English dislike most and the fault of artists is that, like certain foreigners, they are mature.[1] For my own part I was long dominated by impressions of school. The plopping of gas mantles in the class-rooms, the refrain of psalm tunes, the smell of plaster on the stairs, the walk through the fields to the bathing places or to chapel across the cobbles of School Yard, evoked a vanished Eden of grace and security; the intimate noises of College, the striking of the clock at night from Agar's plough, the showers running after games of football, the housemaster's squeak, the rattle of tea-things, the poking of fires as I sat talking with Denis or Charles or Freddie on some evening when everybody else was away at a lecture, were recollected with anguish and College, after I left, seemed to me like one of those humming fortified paradises in an Italian primitive outside which the angry Master in College stood with his flaming sword. . . .

Since I was unable to write in any living language when I left Eton I was already on the way to becoming a critic. My ambition was to be a poet but I could not succeed when poetry was immersed in the Georgian or Neo-Tennysonian tradition. I could but have imitated Housman, Flecker, Brooke, de la Mare or Ralph Hodgson. By the time Eliot and Valéry came to save my generation from the romantic dragon it had already devoured me. I was however well grounded enough to become a critic and drifted into it through unemployability.

In other respects I had been more deeply scarred. The true religion I had learnt at Eton and St. Wulfric's had not been Christianity nor even Imperialism but the primitive gospel of the Jealous God, of τo $\phi\theta o\nu\epsilon\rho o\nu$ *—a gospel which emerged as much from the old Testament as from Greek tragedy and was confirmed by experience. Human beings, it taught, are perpetually getting above

---

1. Even the Jews in England are boyish, like Disraeli, and not the creators of adult philosophies like Marx or Freud.

* to phthoneron: the jealous, grudging, envious.

themselves and presuming to rise superior to the limitations of their nature; when they reach this state of insolence or ὕβρις,* they are visited with some catastrophe, the destruction of Sodom or the Sicilian expedition, the fate of Œdipus or Agamemnon, the Fall of Troy or the Tower of Babel. The happiness, to which we aspire, is not well thought of and is visited with retribution; though some accounts are allowed to run on longer than others, everything in life has to be paid for.

Even when we say "I am happy" we mean "I was" for the moment is past; besides, when we are enjoying ourselves most, when we feel secure of our strength and beloved by our friends, we are intolerable and our punishment—a beating for generality, a yellow ticket, a blackball or a summons from the Headmaster, is in preparation. All we can do is to walk delicately, to live modestly and obscurely like the Greek chorus and to pay a careful attention to omens—counting our paces, observing all conventions, taking quotations at random from Homer or the Bible, and acting on them while doing our best to "keep in favour"—for misfortunes never come alone.

Consider Jacky; playing fives with me one afternoon he said "Damn and blast" when he missed a ball. The Headmaster, who was passing, heard him and told Sixth Form. That night he was beaten. In the excitement of the game he had forgotten to prepare his construe.* Others had prepared theirs but after the silence before boys are put on to construe, when all diversions have been tried in vain, it was he who was called upon. He was ploughed * and given a "ticket" "Failed in Construe" to get signed by his tutor. He had not the courage to show it him, forged his tutor's initials on the bottom and handed it back. By chance the two masters met, the ticket was mentioned and the fraud discovered. Within three days of the game of fives the Praepostor came with the terrible summons. "Is O'Dwyer K.S. in this division? He is to go to the Headmaster at a quarter to twelve." The wide doors are open which means a birching will take place. The block is put out. Two boys in Sixth Form are there to see the Headmaster does not raise his arm above the shoulder, and an old College servant to lower his trousers and hold him down. "Call no man happy till he's dead. Next time it may be me."

Morally I was not in advance of this abject religion; I rejected Christian ethics yet was not enough of a stoic to adopt pagan standards in their place. I was a *vierge folle* * full of neurotic pride and this gave to my thinking a morbid tinge.

Politically I was a liberal individualist with a passion for freedom and justice and a hatred of power and authority but I disliked politics and wished for nothing better than to talk to my friends, travel abroad, look at Old Masters and ro-

---

* hubris: human overconfidence that provokes divine retribution.
* his construe: his translation.
* ploughed: flunked.
* *vierge folle:* foolish virgin; an allusion to the New Testament parable of the Foolish Virgins.

manesque cathedrals, read old books and devote myself to lost causes and controversies of the Past.

The cause of the unhappiness I had come across I put down as Competition. It was Competition that turned friends into enemies, that exhausted the scholars in heart-breaking sprints and rendered the athletes disappointed and bitter. "Never compete" was my new commandment, never again to go in for things, to be put up and blackballed, to score off anyone; only in that way could the sin of Worldliness be combated, the Splendid Failure be prepared which was the ultimate "gesture." Otherwise when free from guilt and fear I was gay, with evening high spirits hardly distinguishable from intoxication and which rose and rose until the shutter fell, a glass which cut me off from loving friends and imagined enemies and behind which I prepared for that interview with the moment, that sacred breathless confrontation from which so little always results, and so much is vainly expected. I was also an affected lover of sensations which I often faked, a satirist in self-defence, a sceptical believer in the Heraclitan flux, an introspective romantic-sensitive, conceited, affectionate, gregarious and, at the time of leaving Eton, the outstanding moral coward of my generation.

Sometimes I imagine Eton replying to these criticisms, the voice of "Henry's holy shade" * answering me with the serenity of a dowager.

"Yes. Very interesting. It was one of my masters, I think, who said, 'Connolly has a vulgar streak'—but we won't discuss that. As I understand, you blame us because our teaching encouraged æstheticism and the vices that are found with it and then punished them when they occurred. Has it ever occurred to you to blame yourself? You say winning a scholarship and getting into Pop turned your head, and set you back ten years. Well, I'm sorry for you. Other boys achieved this and more and were not harmed by it. Look at Robert Longden. The same age as you are and Headmaster of Wellington and Lord Dufferin, almost in the Cabinet. You complain that my teaching is cynical and concentrates on success. Don't forget what Jowett said. 'There are few ways in which a young man can be more harmlessly employed than in making money.' Not that I altogether approve of Pop myself, but since your time its morals have improved and its powers been restricted. The state of College has improved too, that Bolshy epoch, when some of the post-war unrest reached our little backwater, is a thing of the past.

"I think if you had been less vain, less full of the wrong sort of pride and with a little more stuffing, you would not have been attracted to the 'primrose path.' You would not have let a little success get the better of you. Don't forget we put you in a strong position. The great world is not unlike the Eton Society. Their values are the same. You could have made lasting friendships with people who will govern the country—not flashy people but those from whose lodges, in a Scotch deer-forest, great decisions are taken. You Bolshies keep on thinking the things we stand for—cricket, shooting, Ascot, Lords, the Guards, the House of

---

* "Henry's holy shade": see the headnote. The phrase is from Thomas Gray's "Ode on a Distant Prospect of Eton College" (1742).

Commons and the Empire—are dead. But you all want to put your sons down for Eton. It's twenty years now since you came here. Even then people talked about this world being dead but what is more alive to-day? your Bolshevism or the English governing class, the Tory Party?

"But let's leave Pop, let's suppose it is no good in after life to a boy—excuse me—with your income. There was always a Balliol scholarship. Why didn't you follow that up? I see you show a tendency to sneer at the government offices and the diplomatic service. And yet they rule the country more than ever. If 'Pop' leads to the Cabinet, 'College' leads to the Permanent Under Secretaryships, the plums of the administration. It was the old Colleger type, prelate, judge or civil servant who turned out the late king (not an old Etonian) with such absence of friction. They decide who's to be given a visa or permitted to land; they open the mail and tap the telephones. I shouldn't sneer at them. You imply our education is of no use to you in after life. But no education is. We are not an employment agency; all we can do is to give you a grounding in the art of mixing with your fellow men, to tell you what to expect from life and give you an outward manner and inward poise, an old prescription from the eighteenth century which we call a classical education, an education which confers the infrequent virtues of good sense and good taste and the benefit of dual nationality, English and Mediterranean and which, taking into account the difficulties of modern life, we find the philosophy best able to overcome them.

"You complain that Ruskin's cult of beauty and Tennyson's imagery of water and summer still predominate; but we can't help our buildings being beautiful or our elms stately. If you think boys are happier for a retarded development in unfriendly surroundings, you should have gone to Wellington. You say we are sterile and encourage composition only in dead languages. Shelley and Swinburne and Dr. Bridges * wouldn't agree with you. And what matter, if the spirit is alive. . . .

". . . You were never a very good classical scholar. Too lazy. You would not grasp that, as one of my masters writes, 'No education is worth having that does not teach the lesson of concentration on a task, however unattractive. These lessons, if not learnt early, will be learnt, if at all, with pain and grief in later life.' Now I expect you have found that out, as you will one day find out about character, too.

"About the civilisation of the lilies,* Percy Lubbock * and Santayana * say

---

* The poets Percy Bysshe Shelley, Algernon Charles Swinburne, and Robert Bridges were Etonians.
* the civilisation of the lilies: the traditional and over-sophisticated Etonian culture; the lilies of Henry VI form the Eton crest.
* Percy Lubbock: (1879–1965), historian, biographer, critic (*The Craft of Fiction,* 1921) and typical Old Etonian writer of precious prose (*Shades of Eton,* 1929).
* George Santayana: (1863–1952), Spanish-born American philosopher and man of letters; here Connolly is alluding to the highly Platonic aspects of his philosophy of essences. Lubbock and Santayana became friends while they were both living as expatriates in Italy.

very different things from you. However, we bear no ill-will. We shall be here when you have gone. Come down and see us some time. I admit we have been disappointed in you. We hoped that you would conquer your faults but we can't all be Pitt * or J. K. Stephen * and, in spite of what you say, we have since turned out a writer * who has been able to reconcile being a 'live wire,' with loyalty to the school tradition, even on the Amazon."

I have concluded at this point, for it marks the end of my unconscious absorption of ideas, besides there was now nothing new which could happen to me. Although to the world I appeared a young man going up to Oxford "with the ball at his feet," I was, in fact, as promising as the Emperor Tiberius retiring to Capri. I knew all about power and popularity, success and failure, beauty and time, I was familiar with the sadness of the lover and the bleak ultimatums of the beloved. I had formed my ideas and made my friends and it was to be years before I could change them. I lived entirely in the past, exhausted by the emotions of adolescence, of understanding, loving and learning. Denis' fearless intellectual justice, Robert's seventeenth-century face, mysterious in its conventionality, the scorn of Nigel, the gaiety of Freddie, the languor of Charles, were permanent symbols which would confront me fortunately for many years afterwards, unlike the old red-brick box and elmy landscape which contained them. I was to continue on my useless assignment, falling in love, going to Spain and being promising indefinitely.

Somewhere in the facts I have recorded lurk the causes of that sloth by which I have been disabled, somewhere lies the sin whose guilt is at my door, increasing by compound interest faster than promise (for promise is guilt—promise is the capacity for letting people down); and through them run those romantic ideas and fallacies, those errors of judgment against which the validity of my criticism must be measured.

For the critic's role was implicit in this Georgian boyhood.

> Beneath the hot incurious sun,
> Past stronger beats and fairer,
> He picks his way, a living gun,
> With gun and lens and Bible
> A militant enquirer;

* William Pitt: (1708–1778), Eton-educated statesman and orator whose portrait hangs in the Provost's Lodge along with those of other Etonian political worthies.
* J. K. Stephen: (1859–92), known as "J.K.S."; writer of sentimental poetry and highly polished light verse (*Lapsus Calami* and *Quo Musa Tendis,* 1891), who had his volumes bound in pale blue; an epitome of esoteric Etonian culture.
* "a writer": i.e. Peter Fleming whose *Brazilian Adventure* (1933), an account of an expedition to look for the lost explorer Colonel Fawcett, adopts a tone, classically Etonian, of disillusioned amusement and facetious understatement; his younger brother Ian Fleming (author of the James Bond stories) was considered by Etonians to be vulgar in comparison.

> The friend, the rash, the enemy,
> The essayist, the able,
> Able at times to cry.*

It is too early to tell if he has been misled by the instinct for survival. It may be that, having laid the ghost of his past, he will be able to declare himself and come out in the open—or it may be that, having discarded the alibi of promise, it will only be to end up in the trenches or the concentration camp.

> Determined on Time's honest shield
> The lamb must face the Tigress,*

and the Tigress may win for in spite of the slow conversion of progressive ideas into the fact of history, the Dark Ages have a way of coming back. Civilisation —the world of affection and reason and freedom and justice—is a luxury which must be fought for, as dangerous to possess as an oil-field or an unlucky diamond.

Or so now I think; whom ill-famed Coventry * bore, a mother of bicycles, whom England enlightened and Ireland deluded, round-faced, irritable, sun-loving, a man as old as his Redeemer, meditating at this time of year when wars break out, when Europe trembles and dictators thunder, inglorious under the plane.

* W. H. Auden, "As He Is" in *Look, Stranger* (1935).
* "As He Is."
* Coventry: center of British automobile and bicycle manufacturing.

III YOUTH

It is hardly necessary to explain the presence of this section, which deals with a social problem so acute that it is now a major political issue: the condition of "disenfranchised" youth, and its relations with age. The development of the situation is explained in a brilliant conjecture by the young psychologist Kenneth Keniston, and the sociologist Edgar Z. Friedenberg with equally convincing ingenuity characterizes the image of youth in the mind of the elders as having much in common with that of other feared minorities such as the blacks. The outcome of these tensions is the subject of Mr. Fiedler's apocalyptic guesses; he believes that we are undergoing a cultural mutation, that not only is the widening generation gap larger than it has ever been, but it represents a definitive rift in our cultural history. These essays will, we trust, serve as a basis for well-informed discussion of the sociological, political, and psychological aspects of the situation; all, even Mr. Fiedler's, which is more excited and in tone more provocative than the others, exhibit a beneficial willingness to look at the facts as well as the theories. Mr. Wolfe's essay describes a fantastic extreme of the youthful subculture.

The remaining two essays are by extremely cultivated, politically alert men in their sixties, both notable for their intelligent sympathy with the movements of youthful thought, and both caught up in the chaos of revolutionary student movements. They are self-conscious, observing themselves as well as the extraordinary events; yet each is, by some aspects of them, bewildered and even alarmed. To the most generous of the elders there is—or at any rate there was, until the events of 1970 broke down a few barriers—some difficulty in identifying more than partially with student aspirations. These reports, by Professors Dupee and Spender, admirably render the reactions of the intelligent elders to the first major demonstration of youthful protest.

Kenneth Keniston / You Have To Grow Up in Scarsdale To Know How Bad Things Really Are

The Scarsdale of Mr. Keniston's title is a town within commuting distance of New York City. It is typical of certain American suburbs, with "their affluence, their upper-middle-class security and abundance, their well-fed, well-heeled children and their excellent schools." In short, Scarsdale is a most unlikely breeding ground for young radical dissenters. Keniston sets himself the task of showing why, nonetheless, the existence of Scarsdales, and of the colleges and universities which their young people attend, is a symptom both of the enormous success and the revealed limitations and failures of the American social, economic, and political systems.

Keniston's emphasis, indeed a kind of discovery, is that youthful dissenters are very often not alienated from their families at all. They are often the relatively assured offspring of prosperous and harmonious homes. Their radicalism is the result of their having experienced the unfulfilling satisfactions offered within even the most affluent areas of American society. They feel on the one hand that everyone should enjoy the benefits they do and, on the other, that there should also be a qualitative change in the nature of American life. Keniston argues that "student unrest is a reflection not only of the failures, but of the extraordinary success of the liberal-industrial revolution." Although he is thereby sympathetic to youthful dissenters, he is hardly as militant or dismissive as they in his characterizations of contemporary society. His is a historical overview which commits him to a tone of impartiality. He is not interested in put-downs of any kind, and however he may differ with other commentators he is never abrasive. Since he wants to contribute to social exchanges of useful energy, to social unities, his mode of argument is appropriately generous, expansive, and impatient only of constrictive or mean-spirited theory.

The recent events at Harvard are the culmination of a long year of unprecedented student unrest in the advanced nations of the world. We have learned to expect students in underdeveloped countries to lead unruly demonstrations against the status quo, but what is new, unexpected and upsetting to many is that an apparently similar mood is sweeping across America, France, Germany, Italy and even Eastern European nations like Czechoslovakia and Poland. Furthermore, the revolts occur, not at the most backward universities, but at the most distinguished, liberal and enlightened—Berkeley, the Sorbonne, Tokyo, Columbia, the Free University of Berlin, Rome and now Harvard.

This development has taken almost everyone by surprise. The American public is clearly puzzled, frightened and often outraged by the behavior of its most privileged youth. The scholarly world, including many who have devoted their lives to the study of student protest, has been caught off guard as well. For many years, American analysts of student movements have been busy demonstrating that "it can't happen here." Student political activity abroad has been seen as a reaction to modernization, industrialization and the demise of traditional or tribal societies. In an already modern, industrialized, detribalized and "stable" nation like America, it was argued, student protests are naturally absent.

Another explanation had tied student protests abroad to bad living conditions in some universities and to the unemployability of their graduates. Student revolts, it was argued, spring partly from the misery of student life in countries like India and Indonesia. Students who must live in penury and squalor naturally turn against their universities and societies. And if, as in many developing nations, hundreds of thousands of university graduates can find no work commensurate with their skills, the chances for student militancy are further increased.

These arguments helped explain the "silent generation" of the nineteen-fifties and the absence of protest, during that period, in American universities, where students are often "indulged" with good living conditions, close student-faculty contact and considerable freedom of speech. And they helped explain why "super-employable" American college graduates, especially the much-sought-after ones from colleges like Columbia and Harvard, seemed so contented with their lot.

But such arguments do not help us understand today's noisy, angry and militant students in the advanced countries. Nor do they explain why students who enjoy the greatest advantages—those at the leading universities—are often found in the revolts. As a result, several new interpretations of student protest are currently being put forward, interpretations that ultimately form part of what Richard Poirier has termed "the war against the young."

Many reactions to student unrest, of course, spring primarily from fear, anger, confusion or envy, rather than from theoretical analysis. Governor Wallace's attacks on student "anarchists" and other "pinheaded intellectuals," for example, were hardly coherent explanations of protest. Many of the bills aimed at punishing student protestors being proposed in Congress and state legislatures reflect similar feelings of anger and outrage. Similarly, the presumption that student unrest *must* be part of an international conspiracy is based on emotion rather than fact. Even George F. Kennan's recent discussion * of the American student left is essentially a moral condemnation of "revolting students," rather than an effort to explain their behavior.

* Kennan's recent discussion . . . : see *Democracy and the Student Left,* ed. George F. Kennan, students, and teachers (Boston: Little Brown, 1968).

If we turn to more thoughtful analyses of the current student mood we find two general theories gaining widespread acceptance. The first, articulately expressed by Lewis S. Feuer in his recent book on student movements, *The Conflict of Generations,* might be termed the "Oedipal Rebellion" interpretation. The second, cogently stated by Zbigniew Brzezinski* and Daniel Bell,* can be called the theory of "Historical Irrelevance."

The explanation of Oedipal Rebellion sees the underlying force in all student revolts as blind, unconscious Oedipal hatred of fathers and the older generation. Feuer, for example, finds in all student movements an inevitable tendency toward violence and a combination of "regicide, parricide and suicide." A decline in respect for the authority of the older generation is needed to trigger a student movement, but the force behind it comes from "obscure" and "unconscious" forces in the child's early life, including both intense death wishes against his father and the enormous guilt and self-hatred that such wishes inspire in the child.

The idealism of student movements is thus, in many respects, only a "front" for the latent unconscious destructiveness and self-destructiveness of underlying motivations. Even the expressed desire of these movements to help the poor and exploited is explained psychoanalytically by Feuer: Empathy for the disadvantaged is traced to "traumatic" encounters with parental bigotry in the students' childhoods, when their parents forbade them to play with children of other races or lower social classes. The identification of today's new left with blacks is thus interpreted as an unconscious effort to "abreact and undo this original trauma."

There are two basic problems with the Oedipal Rebellion theory, however. First, although it uses psychoanalytic terms, it is bad psychoanalysis. The real psychoanalytic account insists that the Oedipus complex is universal in all normally developing children. To point to this complex in explaining student rebellion is, therefore, like pointing to the fact that all children learn to walk. Since both characteristics are said to be universal, neither helps us understand why, at some historical moments, students are restive and rebellious, while at others they are not. Second, the theory does not help us explain why some students (especially those from middle-class, affluent and idealistic families) are most inclined to rebel, while others (especially those from working-class and deprived families) are less so.

In order really to explain anything, the Oedipal Rebellion hypothesis would have to be modified to point to an unusually *severe* Oedipus complex, involving especially *intense* and unresolved feelings of father-hatred in student rebels. But much is now known about the lives and backgrounds of these rebels—at least those in the United States—and this evidence does not support even the modified theory. On the contrary, it indicates that most student protesters are rela-

---

* Zbigniew Brzezinski: see "Revolution and Counter-revolution" in *The New Republic,* June 1968.
* Daniel Bell: see "Columbia and the New Left" in *Confrontations,* ed. Irving Kristol and Daniel Bell (New York: Basic Books, 1969).

tively *close* to their parents, that the values they profess are usually the ones they learned at the family dinner table, and that their parents tend to be highly educated, liberal or left-wing and politically active.

Furthermore, psychological studies of student radicals indicate that they are no more neurotic, suicidal, enraged or disturbed than are nonradicals. Indeed, most studies find them to be rather more integrated, self-accepting and "advanced," in a psychological sense, than their politically inactive contemporaries. In general, research on American student rebels supports a "Generational Solidarity" (or chip-off-the-old-block) theory, rather than one of Oedipal Rebellion.

The second theory of student revolts now being advanced asserts that they are a reaction against "historical irrelevance." Rebellion springs from the unconscious awareness of some students that society has left them and their values behind. According to this view, the ultimate causes of student dissent are sociological rather than psychological. They lie in fundamental changes in the nature of the advanced societies—especially, in the change from industrial to post-industrial society. The student revolution is seen not as a true revolution, but as a counterrevolution—what Daniel Bell has called "the guttering last gasp of a romanticism soured by rancor and impotence."

This theory assumes that we are moving rapidly into a new age in which technology will dominate, an age whose real rulers will be men like computer experts, systems analysts and technobureaucrats. Students who are attached to outmoded and obsolescent values like humanism and romanticism unconsciously feel they have no place in this post-industrial world. When they rebel they are like the Luddites * of the past—workers who smashed machines to protest the inevitable industrial revolution. Today's student revolt reflects what Brzezinski terms "an unconscious realization that they [the rebels] are themselves becoming historically obsolete"; it is nothing but the "death rattle of the historical irrelevants."

This theory is also inadequate. It assumes that the shape of the future is already technologically determined, and that protesting students unconsciously "know" that it will offer them no real reward, honor or power. But the idea that the future can be accurately predicted is open to fundamental objection. Every past attempt at prophecy has turned out to be grievously incorrect. Extrapolations from the past, while sometimes useful in the short run, are usually fundamentally wrong in the long run, especially when they attempt to predict the quality of human life, the nature of political and social organization, international relations or the shape of future culture.

The future is, of course, made by men. Technology is not an inevitable master of man and history, but merely provides the possibility of applying scientific

---

* the Luddites: workingmen from the great industrial towns of England who rioted from 1811 to 1816, systematically destroying the machinery they thought responsible for low wages and unemployment.

knowledge to specific problems. Men may identify with it or refuse to, use it or be used by it for good or evil, apply it humanely or destructively. Thus, there is no real evidence that student protest will emerge as the "death rattle of the historical irrelevants." It could equally well be the "first spark of a new historical era." No one today can be sure of the outcome, and people who feel certain that the future will bring the obsolescence and death of those whom they dislike are often merely expressing their fond hope.

The fact that today's students invoke "old" humanistic and romantic ideas in no way proves that student protests are a "last gasp" of a dying order. Quite the contrary: *All* revolutions draw upon older values and visions. Many of the ideals of the French Revolution, for example, originated in Periclean Athens. Revolutions do not occur because new ideas suddenly develop, but because a new generation begins to take *old* ideas seriously—not merely as interesting theoretical views, but as the basis for political action and social change. Until recently, the humanistic vision of human fulfillment and the romantic vision of an expressive, imaginative and passionate life were taken seriously only by small aristocratic or Bohemian groups. The fact that they are today taken as real goals by millions of students in many nations does not mean that these students are "counterrevolutionaries," but merely that their ideas follow the pattern of every major revolution.

Indeed, today's student rebels are rarely opposed to technology *per se*. On the contrary, they take the high technology of their societies completely for granted, and concern themselves with it very little. What they *are* opposed to is, in essence, the worship of Technology, the tendency to treat people as "inputs" or "outputs" of a technological system, the subordination of human needs to technological programs. The essential conflict between the minority of students who make up the student revolt and the existing order is a conflict over the future direction of technological society, not a counterrevolutionary protest against technology.

In short, both the Oedipal Rebellion and the Historical Irrelevance theories are what students would call "put-downs." If we accept either, we are encouraged not to listen to protests, or to explain them away or reject them as either the "acting out" of destructive Oedipal feelings or the blind reaction of an obsolescent group to the awareness of its obsolescence. But if, as I have argued, neither of these theories is adequate to explain the current "wave" of student protest here and abroad, how can we understand it?

One factor often cited to explain student unrest is the large number of people in the world under 30—today the critical dividing line between generations. But this explanation alone, like the theories just discussed, is not adequate, for in all historical eras the vast portion of the population has always been under 30. Indeed, in primitive societies most people die before they reach that age. If chronological youth alone was enough to insure rebellion, the advanced societies—where a greater proportion of the population reaches old age than ever before in history—should be the *least* revolutionary, and primitive societies the *most*. This is not the case.

More relevant factors are the relationship of those under 30 to the established institutions of society (that is, whether they are engaged in them or not); and the opportunities that society provides for their continuing intellectual, ethical and emotional development. In both cases the present situation in the advanced nations is without precedent.

Philippe Aries, in his remarkable book, *Centuries of Childhood,* points out that, until the end of the Middle Ages, no separate stage of childhood was recognized in Western societies. Infancy ended at approximately 6 or 7, whereupon most children were integrated into adult life, treated as small men and women and expected to work as junior partners of the adult world. Only later was childhood recognized as a separate stage of life, and our own century is the first to "guarantee" it by requiring universal primary education.

The recognition of adolescence as a stage of life is of even more recent origin, the product of the 19th and 20th centuries. Only as industrial societies became prosperous enough to defer adult work until after puberty could they create institutions—like widespread secondary-school education—that would extend adolescence to virtually all young people. Recognition of adolescence also arose from the vocational and psychological requirements of these societies, which needed much higher levels of training and psychological development than could be guaranteed through primary education alone. There is, in general, an intimate relationship between the way a society defines the stages of life and its economic, political and social characteristics.

Today, in more developed nations, we are beginning to witness the recognition of still another stage of life. Like childhood and adolescence, it was initially granted only to a small minority, but is now being rapidly extended to an ever-larger group. I will call this the stage of "youth," and by that I mean both a further phase of disengagement from society and the period of psychological development that intervenes between adolescence and adulthood. This stage, which continues into the 20's and sometimes into the 30's, provides opportunities for intellectual, emotional and moral development that were never afforded to any other large group in history. In the student revolts we are seeing one result of this advance.

I call the extension of youth an advance advisedly. Attendance at a college or university is a major part of this extension, and there is growing evidence that this is, other things being equal, a good thing for the student. Put in an oversimplified phrase, it tends to free him—to free him from swallowing unexamined the assumptions of the past, to free him from the superstitions of his childhood, to free him to express his feelings more openly and to free him from irrational bondage to authority.

I do not mean to suggest, of course, that all college graduates are free and liberated spirits, unencumbered by irrationality, superstition, authoritarianism or blind adherence to tradition. But these findings do indicate that our colleges, far from cranking out only machinelike robots who will provide skilled manpower for the economy, are also producing an increasing number of highly critical citizens—young men and women who have the opportunity, the leisure, the affluence and the educational resources to continue their development beyond the point where most people in the past were required to stop it.

So, one part of what we are seeing on campuses throughout the world is not a reflection of how bad higher education is, but rather of its extraordinary accomplishments. Even the moral righteousness of the student rebels, a quality both endearing and infuriating to their elders, must be judged at least partially a consequence of the privilege of an extended youth; for a prolonged development, we know, encourages the individual to elaborate a more personal, less purely conventional sense of ethics.

What the advanced nations have done is to create their own critics on a mass basis—that is, to create an ever-larger group of young people who take the highest values of their societies as their own, who internalize these values and identify them with their own best selves, and who are willing to struggle to implement them. At the same time, the extension of youth has lessened the personal risks of dissent: These young people have been freed from the requirements of work, gainful employment and even marriage, which permits them to criticize their society from a protected position of disengagement.

But the mere prolongation of development need not automatically lead to unrest. To be sure, we have granted to millions the opportunity to examine their societies, to compare them with their values and to come to a reasoned judgment of the existing order. But why should their judgment today be so unenthusiastic?

What protesting students throughout the world share is a mood more than an ideology or a program, a mood that says the existing system—the power structure—is hypocritical, unworthy of respect, outmoded and in urgent need of reform. In addition, students everywhere speak of repression, manipulation and authoritarianism. (This is paradoxical, considering the apparently great freedoms given them in many nations. In America, for example, those who complain most loudly about being suffocated by the subtle tyranny of the Establishment usually attend the institutions where student freedom is greatest.) Around this general mood, specific complaints arrange themselves as symptoms of what students often call the "exhaustion of the existing society."

To understand this phenomenon we must recognize that, since the Second World War, some societies have indeed begun to move past the industrial era into a new world that is post-industrial, technological, post-modern, post-historic or, in Brzezinski's term, "technectronic." In Western Europe, the United States, Canada and Japan, the first contours of this new society are already apparent. And, in many other less-developed countries, middle-class professionals (whose children become activists) often live in post-industrial enclaves within pre-industrial societies. Whatever we call the post-industrial world, it has demonstrated that, for the first time, man can produce more than enough to meet his material needs.

This accomplishment is admittedly blemished by enormous problems of economic distribution in the advanced nations, and it is in terrifying contrast to the overwhelming poverty of the Third World. Nevertheless, it is clear that what might be called "the problem of production" *can,* in principle, be solved. If all members of American society, for example, do not have enough material goods, it is because the system of distribution is flawed. The same is true, or will soon be true, in many other nations that are approaching advanced states of industrialization. Characteristically, these nations, along with the most technological, are those where student unrest has recently been most prominent.

The transition from industrial to post-industrial society brings with it a major shift in social emphases and values. Industrializing and industrial societies tend to be oriented toward solving the problem of production. An industrial ethic—sometimes Protestant, sometimes Socialist, sometimes Communist—tends to emphasize psychological qualities like self-discipline, delay of gratification, achievement-orientation and a strong emphasis on economic success and productivity. The social, political and economic institutions of these societies tend to be organized in a way that is consistent with the goal of increasing production. And industrial societies tend to apply relatively uniform standards, to reward achievement rather than status acquired by birth, to emphasize emotional neutrality ("coolness") and rationality in work and public life.

The emergence of post-industrial societies, however, means that growing numbers of the young are brought up in family environments where abundance, relative economic security, political freedom and affluence are simply facts of life, not goals to be striven for. To such people the psychological imperatives, social institutions and cultural values of the industrial ethic seem largely outdated and irrelevant to their own lives.

Once it has been demonstrated that a society *can* produce enough for all of its members, at least some of the young turn to other goals: for example, trying to make sure that society *does* produce enough and distributes it fairly, or searching for ways to live meaningfully with the goods and the leisure they *already* have. The problem is that our society has, in some realms, exceeded its earlier targets. Lacking new ones, it has become exhausted by its success.

When the values of industrial society become devitalized, the élite sectors of youth—the most affluent, intelligent, privileged and so on—come to feel that they live in institutions whose demands lack moral authority or, in the current jargon, "credibility." Today, the moral imperative and urgency behind production, acquisition, materialism and abundance has been lost.

Furthermore, with the lack of moral legitimacy felt in "the System," the least request for loyalty, restraint or conformity by its representatives—for example, by college presidents and deans—can easily be seen as a moral outrage, an authoritarian repression, a manipulative effort to "co-opt" students into joining the

Establishment and an exercise in "illegitimate authority" that must be resisted. From this conception springs at least part of the students' vague sense of oppression. And, indeed, perhaps their peculiar feeling of suffocation arises ultimately from living in societies without vital ethical claims.

Given such a situation, it does not take a clear-cut issue to trigger a major protest. I doubt, for example, that college and university administrators are in fact *more* hypocritical and dishonest than they were in the past. American intervention in Vietnam, while many of us find it unjust and cruel, is not inherently *more* outrageous than other similar imperialistic interventions by America and other nations within the last century. And the position of blacks in this country, although disastrously and unjustifiably disadvantaged, is, in some economic and legal respects, better than ever before. Similarly, the conditions for students in America have never been as good, especially, as I have noted, at those élite colleges where student protests are most common.

But this is *precisely* the point: It is *because* so many of the *other* problems of American society seem to have been resolved, or to be resolvable in principle, that students now react with new indignation to old problems, turn to new goals and propose radical reforms.

So far I have emphasized the moral exhaustion of the old order and the fact that, for the children of post-industrial affluence, the once-revolutionary claims of the industrial society have lost much of their validity. I now want to argue that we are witnessing on the campuses of the world a fusion of *two revolutions* with distinct historical origins. One is a continuation of the old and familiar revolution of the industrial society, the liberal-democratic-egalitarian revolution that started in America and France at the turn of the 18th century and spread to virtually every nation in the world. (Not completed in any of them, its contemporary American form is, above all, to be found in the increased militancy of blacks.) The other is the new revolution, the post-industrial one, which seeks to define new goals relevant to the 20th and 21st centuries.

In its social and political aspects, the first revolution has been one of universalization, to use the sociologist's awkward term. It has involved the progressive extension to more and more people of economic, political and social rights, privileges and opportunities originally available only to the aristocracy, then to the middle class, and now in America to the relatively affluent white working class. It is, in many respects, a *quantitative* revolution. That is, it concerns itself less with the quality of life than with the amount of political freedom, the quantity and distribution of goods or the amount and level of injustice.

As the United States approaches the targets of the first revolution, on which this society was built, to be poor shifts from being an unfortunate fact of life to being an outrage. And, for the many who have never experienced poverty, discrimination, exploitation or oppression, even to *witness* the existence of these evils in the lives of others suddenly becomes intolerable. In our own time the impatience to complete the first revolution has grown apace, and we find less willingness to compromise, wait and forgive among the young, especially among those who now take the values of the old revolution for granted—seeing them not as goals, but as *rights*.

A subtle change has thus occurred. What used to be utopian ideals—like equality, abundance and freedom from discrimination—have now become demands, inalienable rights upon which one can insist without brooking any compromise. It is noteworthy that, in today's student confrontations, no one requests anything. Students present their "demands."

So, on the one hand, we see a growing impatience to complete the first revolution. But, on the other, there is a newer revolution concerned with newer issues, a revolution that is less social, economic or political than psychological, historical and cultural. It is less concerned with the quantities of things than with their qualities, and it judges the virtually complete liberal revolution and finds it still wanting.

"You have to have grown up in Scarsdale to know how bad things really are," said one radical student. This comment would probably sound arrogant, heartless and insensitive to a poor black, much less to a citizen of the Third World. But he meant something important by it. He meant that *even* in the Scarsdales of America, with their affluence, their upper-middle-class security and abundance, their well-fed, well-heeled children and their excellent schools, something is wrong. Economic affluence does not guarantee a feeling of personal fulfillment; political freedom docs not always yield an inner sense of liberation and cultural freedom; social justice and equality may leave one with a feeling that something else is missing in life. "No to the consumer society!" shouted the bourgeois students of the Sorbonne * during May and June of 1968—a cry that understandably alienated French workers, for whom affluence and the consumer society are still central goals.

What, then, are the targets of the new revolution? As is often noted, students themselves don't know. They speak vaguely of "a society that has never existed," of "new values," of a "more humane world," of "liberation" in some psychological, cultural and historical sense. Their rhetoric is largely negative; they are stronger in opposition than in proposals for reform; their diagnoses often seem accurate, but their prescriptions are vague; and they are far more articulate in urging the immediate completion of the first revolution than in defining the goals of the second. Thus, we can only indirectly discern trends that point to the still-undefined targets of the new revolution.

What are these trends and targets?

First, there is a revulsion against the notion of quantity, particularly economic quantity and materialism, and a turn toward concepts of quality. One of the most delightful slogans of the French student revolt was, "Long live the passionate revolution of creative intelligence!" In a sense, the achievement of abun-

---

* students of the Sorbonne: see Stephen Spender's "Paris in the Spring." pp. 291–304.

dance may allow millions of contemporary men and women to examine, as only a few artists and madmen have examined in the past, the quality, joyfulness and zestfulness of experience. The "expansion of consciousness"; the stress on the expressive, the aesthetic and the creative; the emphasis on imagination, direct perception and fantasy—all are part of the effort to enhance the quality of this experience.

Another goal of the new revolution involves a revolt against uniformity, equalization, standardization and homogenization—not against technology itself, but against the "technologization of man." At times, this revolt approaches anarchic quaintness, but it has a positive core as well—the demand that individuals be appreciated, not because of their similarities or despite their differences, but because they *are* different, diverse, unique and noninterchangeable. This attitude is evident in many areas: for example, the insistence upon a cultivation of personal idiosyncrasy, mannerism and unique aptitude. Intellectually, it is expressed in the rejection of the melting-pot and consensus-politics view of American life in favor of a post-homogeneous America in which cultural diversity and conflict are underlined rather than denied.

The new revolution also involves a continuing struggle against psychological or institutional closure or rigidity in any form, even the rigidity of a definite adult role. Positively, it extols the virtues of openness, motion and continuing human development. What Robert J. Lifton * has termed the protean style is clearly in evidence. There is emerging a concept of a lifetime of personal change, of an adulthood of continuing self-transformation, of an adaptability and an openness to the revolutionary modern world that will enable the individual to remain "with it"—psychologically youthful and on top of the present.

Another characteristic is the revolt against centralized power and the complementary demand for participation. What is demanded is not merely the consent of the governed, but the involvement of the governed. "Participatory democracy" summarizes this aspiration, but it extends far beyond the phrase and the rudimentary social forms that have sprung up around it. It extends to the demand for relevance in education—that is, for a chance for the student to participate in his own educational experience in a way that involves all of his faculties, emotional and moral as well as intellectual. The demand for "student power" (or, in Europe, "co-determination") is an aspect of the same theme: At Nanterre, Columbia, Frankfurt and Harvard, students increasingly seek to participate in making the policies of their universities.

This demand for participation is also embodied in the new ethic of "meaningful human relationships," in which individuals confront each other without masks, pretenses and games. They "relate" to each other as unique and irreplaceable human beings, and develop new forms of relationships from which all participants will grow.

* Robert J. Lifton: see "Protean Man" in his book *History and Human Survival* (New York: Random House, 1969).

In distinguishing between the old and the new revolutions, and in attempting to define the targets of the new, I am, of course, making distinctions that students themselves rarely make. In any one situation the two revolutions are joined and fused, if not confused. For example, the Harvard students' demand for "restructuring the university" is essentially the second revolution's demand for participation; but their demand for an end to university "exploitation" of the surrounding community is tied to the more traditional goals of the first revolution. In most radical groups there is a range of opinion that starts with the issues of the first (racism, imperialism, exploitation, war) and runs to the concerns of the second (experiential education, new life styles, meaningful participation, consciousness-expansion, relatedness, encounter and community). The first revolution is personified by Maoist-oriented Progressive Labor party factions within the student left, while the second is represented by hippies, the "acid left," and the Yippies. In any individual, and in all student movements, these revolutions coexist in uneasy and often abrasive tension.

Furthermore, one of the central problems for student movements today is the absence of any theory of society that does justice to the new world in which we of the most industrialized nations live. In their search for rational critiques of present societies, students turn to theories like Marxism that are intricately bound up with the old revolution.

Such theories make the ending of economic exploitation, the achievement of social justice, the abolition of racial discrimination and the development of political participation and freedom central, but they rarely deal adequately with the issues of the second revolution. Students inevitably try to adapt the rhetoric of the first to the problems of the second, using concepts that are often blatantly inadequate to today's world.

Even the concept of "revolution" itself is so heavily laden with images of political, economic and social upheaval that it hardly seems to characterize the equally radical but more social-psychological and cultural transformations involved in the new revolution. One student, recognizing this, called the changes occurring in his California student group, "too radical to be called a revolution." Students are thus often misled by their borrowed vocabulary, but most adults are even more confused, and many are quickly led to the mistaken conclusion that today's student revolt is nothing more than a repetition of Communism's in the past.

Failure to distinguish between the old and new revolutions also makes it impossible to consider the critical question of how compatible they are with each other. Does it make sense—or is it morally right—for today's affluent American students to seek imagination, self-actualization, individuality, openness and relevance when most of the world and many in America live in deprivation, oppression and misery?

The fact that the first revolution is "completed" in Scarsdale does not mean that it is (or soon will be) in Harlem or Appalachia—to say nothing of Bogotá or Calcutta. For many children of the second revolution, the meaning of life may be found in completing the first—that is, in extending to others the "rights" they have always taken for granted.

For others the second revolution will not wait; the question, "What lies beyond affluence?" demands an answer now. Thus, although we may deem it self-indulgent to pursue the goals of the new revolution in a world where so much misery exists, the fact is that in the advanced nations it is upon us, and we must at least learn to recognize it.

Finally, beneath my analysis lies an assumption I had best make explicit. Many student critics argue that their societies have failed miserably. My argument, a more historical one perhaps, suggests that our problem is not only that industrial societies have failed to keep all their promises, but that they have succeeded in some ways beyond all expectations. Abundance was once a distant dream, to be postponed to a hereafter of milk and honey; today, most Americans are affluent. Universal mass education was once a Utopian goal; today in America almost the entire population completes high school, and almost half enters colleges and universities.

The notion that individuals might be free, en masse, to continue their psychological, intellectual, moral and cognitive development through their teens and into their 20's would have been laughed out of court in any century other than our own; today, that opportunity is open to millions of young Americans. Student unrest is a reflection not only of the failures, but of the extraordinary successes of the liberal-industrial revolution. It therefore occurs in the nations and in the colleges where, according to traditional standards, conditions are best.

But for many of today's students who have never experienced anything but affluence, political freedom and social equality, the old vision is dead or dying. It may inspire bitterness and outrage when it is not achieved, but it no longer animates or guides. In place of it, students (and many who are not students) are searching for a new vision, a new set of values, a new set of targets appropriate to the post-industrial era—a myth, an ideology or a set of goals that will concern itself with the quality of life and answer the question, "Beyond freedom and affluence, what?"

What characterizes student unrest in the developed nations is this peculiar mixture of the old and the new, the urgent need to fulfill the promises of the past and, at the same time, to define the possibilities of the future.

Edgar Friedenberg / The Image of the Adolescent Minority

Mr. Friedenberg's discussion of the "adolescent minority" might seem in some of its particulars like Mr. Fiedler's discussion of what he calls the

Wayne Miller, Magnum

"new mutants." Both writers make use of types and archetypes drawn from literature and film in their effort to explain the styles of contemporary youth and adolescents. But there the similarity ends. Friedenberg's essay is altogether a more sympathetic treatment of the subject of youth. Unlike Fiedler he does not see the mores he discusses as either aberrant or mutant. Instead, he thinks they are an expression of certain social and sexual powers that belong to the species but that get lost in most adults as they become what is considered "mature" and accommodate themselves to the "adult" world. There is evidence of a tone in this essay all but missing from Fiedler's and also from the judicious historical view of Keniston: some sharp, pointed, salty, slangy intrusions of personality. It is as if Friedenberg, justifiably it would appear, is trying to show the persistence in him of some of the good "adolescent" characteristics that society at large finds hard to accommodate.

Readers might want to place Friedenberg's "adolescence" in a framework proposed by Keniston, who suggests that adolescence is followed now by a new period of prolonged "youth" that can last into the thirties. What, one might ask, is the difference in the kind of dissent expected from Keniston's youth and the kind expected from Friedenberg's adolescents? And are both somehow different from Fiedler's mutants? Obviously, generational differences tend to become a subject for fictional speculation in these essays, despite their socio-scientific presumptions.

Friedenberg's contention that adolescents are notably free of political interests doesn't seem to be true any more (the essay was written in 1966). In any case, the state of affairs he postulates—a division of adolescents into "hot-blooded" and "long-suffering" minorities (the first boys, the second girls)—has political implications obvious to everybody, including presumably the adolescents themselves, in this period of agitation for women's liberation. Friedenberg's essay is provocative in its implications that minorities have not only a common economic or social cause, but a common sexual cause as well. Of the essays in this collection, this is perhaps the one which makes the most direct inquiries about the relation of sex to the nature of social institutions and to the various guilts and impulses that determine them.

In our society there are two kinds of minority status. One of these I will call the "hot-blooded" minorities, whose archetypical image is that of the Negro or Latin. *In the United States, "Teen-agers" are treated as a "hot-blooded" minority*. Then, there are the "long-suffering minorities," whose archetype is the Jew, but which also, I should say, includes women. Try, for a second, to picture a Jewish "teenager," and you may sense a tendency for the image to grate. "Teen-agers" err on the hot side; they talk jive, drive hot-rods and become juvenile delinquents. Young Jews talk volubly, play the violin, and go to medical school, though never on Saturday.

The minority group is a special American institution, created by the interaction between a history and an ideology which are not to be duplicated elsewhere. Minority status has little to do with size or proportion. In a democracy, a dominant social group is called a majority and a part of its dominance consists in the power to arrange appropriate manifestations of public support; while a subordinate group is, by the logic of political morality, a minority. The minority stereotype, though affected by the actual characteristics of the minority group, develops to fit the purposes and expresses the anxieties of the dominant social group. It serves as a slimy coating over the sharp realities of cultural difference, protecting the social organism until the irritant can be absorbed.

Now, when one is dealing with a group that actually is genetically or culturally different from the dominant social group, this is perhaps to be expected. It is neither desirable nor inevitable, for xenophobia is neither desirable nor inevitable; but it is not surprising.

What is surprising is that the sons and daughters of the *dominant* adult group should be treated as a minority group merely because of their age. Their papers are in order and they speak the language adequately. In any society, to be sure, the young occupy a subordinate or probationary status while under tutelage for adult life. But a minority group is not merely subordinate; it is not under tutelage. It is in the process of being denatured; of becoming, under social stress, something more acceptable to the dominant society, but essentially different from what its own growth and experience would lead to. Most beasts recognize their own kind. Primitive peoples may initiate their youth; we insist that ours be naturalized, though it is what is most natural about them that disturbs adults most.

The court of naturalization is the public school. A high school diploma is a certificate of legitimacy, not of competence. A youth needs one today in order to hold a job that will permit even minimal participation in the dominant society. Yet our laws governing school attendance do not deal with education. They are not *licensing* laws, requiring attendance until a certain defined minimum competence, presumed essential for adult life, has been demonstrated. They are not *contractual,* they offer no remedy for failure of the school to provide services of a minimum quality. A juvenile may not legally withdraw from school even if he can establish that it is substandard or that he is being ill-treated there. If he does, as many do, for just these reasons, he becomes *prima facie* * an offender; for, in cold fact, the compulsory attendance law guarantees him nothing, not even the services of qualified teachers. It merely defines, in terms of age alone, a particular group as subject to legal restrictions not applicable to other persons.

* *prima facie:* constituting evidence sufficient to raise a presumption of fact.

SECOND-CLASS CITIZEN

Legally, the adolescent comes pretty close to having no basic rights at all. The state generally retains the final right even to strip him of his minority status. He has no right to *demand* the particular protection of *either* due process or the juvenile administrative procedure—the state decides. We have had several cases in the past few years of boys sixteen and under being sentenced to death by the full apparatus of formal criminal law, who would not have been permitted to claim its protection had they been accused of theft or disorderly conduct. Each of these executions has so far been forestalled by various legal procedures, but none in such a way as to establish the right of a juvenile to be tried as a juvenile; though he long ago lost his claim to be treated as an adult.

In the most formal sense, then, the adolescent is one of our second class citizens. But the informal aspects of minority status are also imputed to him. The "teen-ager," like the Latin or Negro, is seen as joyous, playful, lazy, and irresponsible, with brutality lurking just below the surface and ready to break out into violence.[1] All these groups are seen as childish and excitable, imprudent and improvident, sexually aggressive, and dangerous, but possessed of superb and sustained power to satisfy sexual demands. *West Side Story* is not much like *Romeo and Juliet;* but it is a great deal like *Porgy and Bess.*

The fantasy underlying this stereotype, then, is erotic; and its subject is male. The "hot-blooded" minorities are always represented by a masculine stereotype; nobody asks "Would you want your *son* to marry a Negro?" In each case, also, little counter-stereotypes, repulsively pallid in contrast to the alluring violence and conflict of the central scene, are held out enticingly by the dominant culture; the conscientious "teener" sold by Pat Boone * to soothe adults while the kids themselves buy *Mad* and *Catcher;* the boy whose Italian immigrant mother sees to it that he wears a clean shirt to school every day on his way to the Governor's mansion; *Uncle Tom.* In the rectilinear planning of Jonesville these are set aside conspicuously as Public Squares, but at dusk they are little frequented.

---

1. A very bad—indeed, vicious—but remarkably ambivalent reenactment of the entire fantasy on which the minority-status of the teen-ager is based can be seen in the recent movie *13 West St.* Here, the legal impotence of the "teen-ager" is taken absolutely for granted, and sadistic hostility of adults against him, though deplored, is condoned and accepted as natural. Occasional efforts are made to counterbalance the, in my judgment, pornographic picture of a brutal teen-age gang by presenting "good" teen-agers unjustly suspected, and decent police trying to resist sadistic pressure from the gang's victim, who drives one of its members to suicide. But despite this, the picture ends with a scene of the gang's victim—a virile-type rocket scientist—beating the leader of the gang with his cane and attempting to drown the boy in a swimming pool—which the police dismiss as excusable under the circumstances. A Honolulu paper, at least, described this scene of attempted murder as "an old-fashioned caning that had the audience cheering in its seats."

* Pat Boone: clean-cut all-American-boy-type popular singer whose career flourished in the late 1950's.

One need hardly labor the point that what the dominant society seeks to control by imposing "hot-blooded" minority status is not the actual aggressiveness and sexuality of the Negro, the Latin, or the JD, but its own wish for what the British working classes used to call "a nice game of slap and tickle," on the unimpeachable assumption that a little of what you fancy does you good. This, the well-lighted Public Squares cannot afford; the community is proud of them, but they are such stuff as only the driest dreams are made of. These are not the dreams that are wanted. In my experience, it is just not possible to discuss adolescence with a group of American adults without being forced onto the topic of juvenile delinquency. Partly this is an expression of legitimate concern, but partly it is because only the JD has any emotional vividness for them.

I would ascribe the success of *West Side Story* to the functional equivalence in the minds of adults between adolescence, delinquency, and aggressive sexuality. Many who saw the show must have wondered, as I did, why there were no Negroes in it—one of the best things about Juvenile Delinquency is that, at least, it is integrated. Hollywood, doubtless, was as usual reluctant to show a member of an enfranchised minority group in an unfavorable light. But there was also a rather sound artistic reason. Putting a real Negro boy in *West Side Story* would have been like scoring the second movement of the *Pastorale* for an eagle rather than flute. The provocative, surly, sexy dancing kids who come to a bad end are not meant realistically. Efforts to use real street-adolescents in *West Side Story* had to be abandoned; they didn't know how to act. What was depicted here was neither Negro nor white nor really delinquent, but a comfortably vulgar middle-class dream of a "hot-blooded" minority. In dreams a single symbolic boy can represent them all; let the symbol turn real and the dreamer wakes up screaming.

Adolescents are treated as a "hot-blooded" minority, then, because they seem so good at slap-and-tickle. But a number of interesting implications flow from this. Slap-and-tickle implies sexual vigor and attractiveness, warmth and aggression, salted with enough conventional perversity to lend spice to a long dull existence. Such perversity is a kind of exuberant overflow from the mainstream of sexuality, not a diversion of it. It is joyous excess and bounty; extravagant foreplay in the well-worn marriage-bed; the generosity of impulse that leads the champion lover of the high school to prance around the shower-room snapping a towel on the buttocks of his team-mates three hours before a hot date, just to remind them that life can be beautiful.

EXPERIENCE REPRESSED

When a society sees impulsiveness and sexual exuberance as minority characteristics which unsuit the individual for membership until he is successfully naturalized, it is in pretty bad shape. Adolescents, loved, respected, taught to accept, enjoy, and discipline their feelings, grow up. "Teen-agers" don't; they pass. Then, in middle-age, they have the same trouble with their former self that many ethnics do. They hate and fear the kinds of spontaneity that remind them of what they have abandoned, and they hate themselves for having joined forces with and having come to resemble their oppressors.[2] This is the vicious spiral by which "hot-blooded" minority status maintains itself. I am convinced that it is also the source of the specific hostility—and sometimes sentimentality—that adolesdents arouse in adults. The processes involved have been dealt with in detail by Daniel Boorstin, Leslie Fiedler, Paul Goodman, and especially Ernest Schachtel.[3] Their effect is to starve out, through silence and misrepresentation, the capacity to have genuine and strongly felt experience, and to replace it by the conventional symbols that serve at the common currency of daily life.

Experience repressed in adolescence does not, of course, result in amnesia, as does the repression of childhood experience; it leaves no temporal gaps in the memory. This makes it more dangerous, because the adult is then quite unaware that his memory is incomplete, that the most significant components of feeling have been lost or driven out. We at least know that we no longer know what we felt as children. But an adolescent boy who asks his father how he felt on the first night he spent in barracks or with a woman will be told what the father now thinks he felt because he ought to have; and this is very dangerous nonsense indeed.

Whether in childhood or in adolescence, the same quality of experience is starved out or repressed. It is still the spontaneous, vivid and immediate that is most feared, and feared the more because so much is desired. But there is a difference in focus and emphasis because in adolescence spontaneity can lead to much more serious consequences.

This, perhaps, is the crux of the matter; since it begins to explain why our kind of society should be so easily plunged into conflict by "hot-blooded" minorities in general and adolescent boys in particular. We are consequence-oriented and future-oriented. Among us, to prefer present delights is a sign of either low or high status, and both are feared. Schachtel makes it clear how we go about building this kind of character in the child—by making it difficult for him to notice his delights when he has them, and obliterating the language in which he might recall them joyfully later. This prepares the ground against the subsequent assault of adolescence. But it is a strong assault, and if adolescence wins, the future hangs in the balance.

2. Cf. Abraham Kardiner and Lionel Ovesey's classic, *The Mark of Oppression* (New York: Norton, 1951), for a fascinating study of these dynamics among American Negroes.
3. Daniel Boorstin, *The Image*. New York: Atheneum, 1962; Leslie Fiedler, "The Fear of the Impulsive Life." *WFMT Perspective,* October, 1961, pp. 4–9; Paul Goodman, *Growing Up Absurd*. New York: Random House, 1960, p. 38; Ernest Schachtel, "On Memory and Childhood Amnesia." Widely anthologized, cf. the author's *Metamorphosis*. New York: Basic Books, 1959, pp. 279–322.

THE ADOLESCENT GIRL

In this assault, adolescent boys play a very different role from adolescent girls; and are dealt with unconsciously by totally different dynamics. Adolescent girls are not seen as members of a "hot-blooded" minority, and to this fact may be traced some interesting paradoxes in our perception of the total phenomenon of adolescence.

Many critics of the current literature on adolescence—Bruno Bettelheim [4] perhaps most cogently—have pointed out that most contemporary writing about adolescents ignores the adolescent girl almost completely. Bettelheim specifically mentions Goodman and myself; the best novels about adolescents of the past decade or so have been, I think there would be fair agreement, Salinger's *The Catcher in the Rye,* John Knowles' *A Separate Peace,* and Colin MacInnes' less well known but superb *Absolute Beginners.* All these have adolescent boys as heroes. Yet, as Bettelheim points out, the adolescent girl is as important as the adolescent boy, and her actual plight in society is just as severe; her opportunities are even more limited and her growth into a mature woman as effectively discouraged. Why has she not aroused more interest?

There are demonstrable reasons for the prominence of the adolescent boy in our culture. Conventionally, it is he who threatens the virtue of our daughters and the integrity of our automobiles. There are so many more ways to get hung up on a boy. "Teen-agers," too, may be all right; but would you want your daughter to marry one? When she doesn't know anything about him except how she feels—and what does that matter when they are both too young to know what they are doing; when he may never have the makings of an executive, or she of an executive's wife?

For this last consideration, paradoxically, also makes the *boy,* rather than the girl, the focus of anxiety. He alone bears the terrible burden of parental aspirations; it is his capacity for spontaneous commitment that endangers the opportunity of adults to live vicariously the life they never managed to live personally.

Holden, Finny, and the unnamed narrator of *Absolute Beginners,* are adolescent boys who do not pass; who retain their minority status, their spontaneous feelings, their power to act out and act up. They go prancing to their destinies. But what destiny can we imagine for them? We leave Holden in a mental hospital, being adjusted to reality; and Finny dead of the horror of learning that his best friend, Gene, had unconsciously contrived the accident that broke up his beautifully articulated body. The Absolute Beginner, a happier boy in a less tense society, fares better; he has had more real contact with other human beings, including a very satisfactory father, and by his time there is such a thing as a "teen-ager," little as it is, for him to be. On this basis the Beginner can

---

4. In "Adolescence and the Conflict of Generations," *Daedalus,* Winter, 1962, p. 68.

identify himself; the marvelous book ends as he rushes out onto the tarmac at London Airport, bursting through the customs barrier, to stand at the foot of the gangway and greet a planeload of astonished immigrants by crying, "Here I am! Meet your first teen-ager."

POLITICAL DISINTEREST

There are still enough Finnys and Holdens running around free to give me much joy and some hope, and they are flexible enough to come to their own terms with reality. But the system is against them, and they know it well. Why then, do they not try to change it? Why are none of these novels of adolescence political novels? Why have their heroes no political interests at all? In this respect, fiction is true to American life; American adolescents are notably free from political interests. I must maintain this despite the recent advances of SANE * kids and Freedom Riders; * for, though I love and honor them for their courage and devotion, the causes they fight for are not what I would call political. No controversy over basic policy is involved, because nobody advocates atomic disaster or racial persecution. The kids' opponents are merely in favor of the kind of American society that these evils flourish in, and the youngsters do not challenge the system itself, though they are appalled by its consequences.

Yet could they, as adolescents, be political? I don't think so; and I don't know that I would be pleased if they were. American politics is a cold-blooded business indeed. Personal clarity and commitment are not wanted in it and not furthered by it. I do not think this is necessarily true of all politics; but it becomes true when the basic economic and social assumptions are as irrational as ours.

Political effectiveness in our time requires just the kind of caginess, pseudo-realism, and stereotyping of thought and feeling; the same submergence of spontaneity to the exigencies of collective action, that mark the ruin of adolescence. Adolescents are, inherently, anti-mass; they take things personally. Sexuality, itself, has this power to resolve relationships into the immediate and interpersonal. As a symbol the cocky adolescent boy stands, a little like Luther, an obstacle to compromise and accommodation. Such symbols stick in the mind, though the reality can usually be handled. With occasional spectacular failures we do manage to assimilate the "teen-age" minority; the kids learn not to get fresh; they get smart, they dry up. We are left then, like the Macbeths, with the memory of an earlier fidelity. But Lady Macbeth was less resourceful than ourselves; she knew next to nothing about industrial solvents. Where she had only perfume we have oil.

* SANE: National Committee for a Sane Nuclear Policy.
* Freedom Riders: the Freedom Rides of 1961 continued the sit-in movement of the previous year; small groups of civil rights activists traveled through the South, sitting in at segregated public places such as lunch counters and waiting rooms.

THE GIRL AS WOMAN

This is how we use the boy, but what about the girl? I have already asserted that, since she is not perceived as a member of the "hot-blooded" minority she cannot take his place in the unconscious, which is apt to turn very nasty if it is fobbed off with the wrong sex. Is she then simply not much involved by our psychodynamics, or is she actively repressed? Is she omitted from our fantasies or excluded from them?

It may seem very strange that I should find her so inconspicuous. Her image gets so much publicity. Drum-majorettes and cheerleaders are ubiquitous; *Playboy* provides businessmen with a new *playmate* each month. Nymphets are a public institution.

Exactly, and they serve a useful public function. American males are certainly anxious to project a heterosexual public image, and even more anxious to believe in it themselves. None of us, surely, wishes to feel obligated to hang himself out of respect for the United States Senate; it is, as Yum-Yum * remarked to Nanki-Poo, such a stuffy death. I am not questioning our sincerity; the essence of my point is that in what we call maturity we feel what we are supposed to feel, and nothing else. But I am questioning the depth and significance of our interest in the cover or pin-up girl. Her patrons are concerned to experience their own masculinity; they are not much interested in her: I reject the celebration of "babes" in song and story as evidence that we have adolescent girls much on our minds; if we did we wouldn't think of them as "babes." I think, indeed, that in contrast to the boy, of whom we are hyperaware, we repress our awareness of the girl. She is not just omitted, she is excluded.

The adolescent heroine in current fiction is not interpreted in the same way as the adolescent hero, even when the parallel is quite close. Her adolescence is treated as less crucial; she is off-handedly accepted as a woman already. This is true even when the author struggles against it. Lolita,* for example, is every bit as much a tragic heroine of adolescence as Holden is a hero—she isn't as nice a girl as he is a boy, but they are both victims of the same kind of corruption in adult society and the same absence of any real opportunity to grow up to be themselves. Lolita's failure is the classic failure of identity in adolescence; and Humbert knows this and accepts responsibility for it; this is the crime he expiates. But this is not the way Lolita—the character, not the book—is generally received. Unlike Holden, she has no cult and is not vouchsafed any dignity. It is thought to be comical that, at fourteen, she is already a whore.

A parallel example is to be found in Rumer Godden's *The Greengage Summer*. Here the story is explicitly about Joss's growing up. The author's emphasis

---

* Yum-Yum, Nanki-Poo: characters in Gilbert and Sullivan's comic opera *The Mikado* (1885).
* *Lolita:* novel by Vladimir Nabokov (Paris, 1955; U.S., 1958).

is on the way her angry betrayal of her lover marks the end of her childhood; her feelings are now too strong and confused, and too serious in their consequences, to be handled with childish irresponsibility; she can no longer claim the exemptions of childhood. But what the movie presented, it seemed to me, was almost entirely an account of her rise to sexual power; Joss had become a Babe at last.

One reason that we do not take adolescent growth seriously in girls is that we do not much care what happens to people unless it has economic consequences: what would Holden ever be, since he never even graduates from high school; who would hire him? He has a problem; Lolita could always be a waitress or something, what more could she expect? Since we define adulthood almost exclusively in economic terms, we obviously cannot concern ourselves as much about the growth of those members of society who are subject from birth to restricted economic opportunity. But so, of course, are the members of the "hot-blooded" minorities; though we find their hot-bloodedness so exciting that we remain aware of them anyway.

But girls, like Jews, are not supposed to fight back; we expect them, instead, to insinuate themselves coyly into the roles available. In our society, there are such lovely things for them to be. They can take care of other people and clean up after them. Women can become wives and mothers; Jews can become kindly old Rabbis and philosophers and even psychoanalysts and lovable comic essayists. They can become powers behind the power; a fine old law firm runs on the brains of its anonymous young Jews just as a husband's best asset is his loyal and unobtrusive wife. A Jewish girl can become a Jewish Mother, and this is a role which even Plato would have called essential.

EFFECTS OF DISCRIMINATION

Clearly, this kind of discrimination is quite different from that experienced by the "hot-blooded" minorities; and must be based on a very different image in the minds of those who practice it and must have a different impact upon them. Particularly, in the case of the adolescent, the effect on the adult of practicing these two kinds of discrimination will be different. The adolescent boy must be altered to fit middle-class adult roles, and when he has been he becomes a much less vital creature. But the girl is merely squandered, and this wastage will continue all her life. Since adolescence is, for boy and girl alike, the time of life in which the self must be established, the girl suffers as much from being wasted as the boy does from being cut down; there has recently been, for example, a number of tragic suicides reported among adolescent girls, though suicide generally is far less common among females. But from the point of view of the dominant society nothing special is done to the female in adolescence—the same squeeze continues throughout life, even though this is when it hurts most.

The guilts we retain for our treatments of "hot-blooded" and "long-suffering" minorities therefore affect us in contrasting ways. For the boy we suffer angry, paranoid remorse, as if he were Billy the Kid, or Budd. We had to do our duty, but how can we ever forget him? But we do not attack the girl; we only neglect her and leave her to wither gradually through an unfulfilled life; and the best defense against this sort of guilt is selective inattention. We just don't see her; instead, we see a caricature, not brutalized as in the case of the boy, to justify our own brutality; but sentimentalized, roseate, to reassure us that we have done her no harm, and that she is well contented. Look: she even has her own telephone, with what is left of the boy dangling from the other end of the line.

A LONELY RIDE

This is the fantasy; the reality is very different, but it is bad enough to be a "Teen-ager." The adolescent is now the only totally disfranchised minority group in the country. In America, no minority has ever gotten any respect or consistently decent treatment until it began to acquire political power. The vote comes before anything else. This is obviously true of the Negro at the present time; his recent advances have all been made under—sometimes reluctant—Federal auspices because, nationally, Negroes vote, and Northern Negroes are able to cast a ballot on which their buffeted Southern rural fellows may be pulled to firmer political ground. This is what makes it impossible to stop Freedom Rides; just as the comparative militance of the Catholic Church in proceeding toward integration in Louisiana may have less to do with Louisiana than Nigeria, which is in grave danger of falling into the hands of Black Muslims. People generally sympathetic with adolescents sometimes say, "Well, it really isn't fair; if they're old enough to be drafted, they're old enough to vote," which is about as naive as it is possible to get.

Can the status of the "teen-ager" be improved? Only, presumably, through increased political effectiveness. Yet, it is precisely here that a crucial dilemma arises. For the aspirations of the adolescent minority are completely different from those of other minorities. All the others are struggling to obtain what the adolescent is struggling to avoid. They seek and welcome the conventional American middle-class status that has been partially or totally barred to them. But this is what the adolescent is left with if he gives in and goes along.

In the recent and very moving CORE * film, *Freedom Ride,* one of the heroic group who suffered beatings and imprisonment for their efforts to end segregation says, as nearly as I can recall, "If the road to freedom leads through the jails of the South, then that's the road I'll take." It may be the road to freedom; but it is the road to suburbia too. You can't tell which the people are headed for until they are nearly there; but all our past ethnic groups have settled for suburbia, and the people who live there bear witness that freedom is somewhere else.

I am not sure there *is* a road to freedom in America. Not enough people want to go there; the last I can recall was H. D. Thoreau, and he went on foot,

---

* CORE: Congress of Racial Equality.

through the woods, alone. This still may be the only way to get there. For those with plenty of guts, compassion, and dedication to social justice, who nevertheless dislike walking alone through the woods, or feel it to be a Quixotic extravagance, a freedom ride is a noble enterprise. Compared to them, the individual boy or girl on a solitary journey must seem an anachronism. Such a youngster has very little place in our way of life. And of all the criticisms that might be directed against that way of life, this is the harshest.

Leslie Fiedler / The New Mutants

Mr. Fiedler's characterization of the " 'mutants' among us" begins as an essay in literary history and ends with a quotation from William Burroughs, the "laureate of that new conquest" of inner space which is among the ambitions, as Fiedler would have it, of the children of the future. Fiedler is trying to come to terms with the "prophetic content" common to science fiction and post-modernist literature. The prophecy spells out the end of man as he has been created and defined in literature of the past, and his transformation into the kind of man already implicit in some current literary, social, and psychological styles.

The reader will probably have to remind himself at many points that Fiedler *is* talking about literary myths rather than social history and that the young to whom he is referring are meant to be a "mythologically representative minority." Fiedler passes rather too easily from literary mythology into a sort of hectoring reportage more appropriate to socially concerned editorials. If "only fiction and verse . . . have dealt with the conjunction of homosexuality, drugs and civil rights," he himself comes close to dealing with the conjunction as a mere threat to the good old days: "the new barbarians join the old homosexuals in reviling, seeking to replace Mom, Pop, and the kids with a new-Whitmanian gaggle of giggling *camerados.*" The tensions in the piece between such rhetoric and the claims to "objective" mythological and anthropological inquiry make it possible that Fiedler is himself sometimes guilty here of the mistake he ascribes to Arthur C. Clarke's *Childhood's End:* taking metaphor for fact. Is he reading the young, if not the authors he discusses, through terminologies and categories so outmoded as to prove his contention that the young are indeed in a different time period from his own even though they are not yet in the future?

The work of demonstrating a major change in consciousness, a break in cultural tradition, obviously requires of the author that he demonstrate familiarity with the old consciousness and the old traditions. This explains a good deal of rapid theorizing, the use of undeveloped allusions to many different bodies of knowledge. There is also an epigrammatic quality, a desire to shock the reader into dispute or acquiescence. (Has the schizophrenic really replaced the sage as the ideal of youth?) Yet the piece has substance; it was written in 1965 and it still sounds cogent. These are arguments on which the views of the young are especially valuable.

A realization that the legitimate functions of literature are bewilderingly, almost inexhaustibly various has always exhilarated poets and dismayed critics. And critics, therefore, have sought age after age to legislate limits to literature—legitimizing certain of its functions and disavowing others—in hope of insuring to themselves the exhilaration of which they have felt unjustly deprived, and providing for poets the dismay which the critics at least have thought good for them.

Such shifting and exclusive emphasis is not, however, purely the product of critical malice, or even of critical principle. Somehow every period is, to begin with, especially aware of certain functions of literature and especially oblivious to others: endowed with a special sensitivity and a complementary obtuseness, which, indeed, give to that period its characteristic flavor and feel. So, for instance, the Augustan Era is marked by sensitivity in regard to the uses of diction, obtuseness in regard to those of imagery.

What the peculiar obtuseness of the present age may be I find it difficult to say (being its victim as well as its recorder), perhaps toward the didactic or certain modes of the sentimental. I am reasonably sure, however, that our period is acutely aware of the sense in which literature if not invents, at least collaborates in the invention of time. The beginnings of that awareness go back certainly to the beginnings of the Renaissance, to Humanism as a self-conscious movement; though a critical development occurred toward the end of the eighteenth century with the dawning of the Age of Revolution. And we may have reached a second critical point right now.

At any rate, we have long been aware (in the last decades uncomfortably aware) that a chief function of literature is to express and in part to create not only theories of time but also attitudes toward time. Such attitudes constitute, however, a politics as well as an esthetics; or, more properly perhaps, a necessary mythological substratum of politics—as, in fact, the conventional terms reactionary, conservative, revolutionary indicate: all involving stances toward the past.

It is with the past, then, that we must start, since the invention of the past seems to have preceded that of the present and the future; and since we are gathered in a university at whose heart stands a library [1]—the latter, like the

1. "The New Mutants" is a written version of a talk given by Mr. Fiedler at the Conference on the Idea of The Future held at Rutgers, in June, 1965. The conference was sponsored by Partisan Review and the Congress for Cultural Freedom, with the cooperation of Rutgers, The State University.

former, a visible monument to the theory that a chief responsibility of literature is to preserve and perpetuate the past. Few universities are explicitly (and none with any real degree of confidence) dedicated to this venerable goal any longer. The Great Books idea * (which once transformed the University of Chicago and lives on now in provincial study groups) was perhaps its last desperate expression. Yet the shaky continuing existence of the universities and the building of new college libraries (with matching Federal funds) remind us not only of that tradition but of the literature created in its name: the neo-epic, for instance, all the way from Dante to Milton; and even the frantically nostalgic Historical Romance, out of the counting house by Sir Walter Scott.

Obviously, however, literature has a contemporary as well as a traditional function. That is to say, it may be dedicated to illuminating the present and the meaning of the present, which is, after all, no more given than the past. Certainly the modern or bourgeois novel was thus contemporary in the hands of its great inventors, Richardson, Fielding, Smollett and Sterne; and it became contemporary again—with, as it were, a sigh of relief—when Flaubert, having plunged deep into the Historical Romance, emerged once more into the present of Emma Bovary. But the second function of the novel tends to transform itself into a third: a revolutionary or prophetic or futurist function; and it is with the latter that I am here concerned.

Especially important for our own time is the sense in which literature first conceived the possibility of the future (rather than an End of Time or an Eternal Return, an Apocalypse or Second Coming); and then furnished that future in joyous or terrified anticipation, thus preparing all of us to inhabit it. Men have dreamed and even written down utopias from ancient times; but such utopias were at first typically allegories rather than projections: nonexistent models against which to measure the real world, exploitations of the impossible (as the traditional name declares) rather than explorations or anticipations or programs of the possible. And, in any event, only recently have such works occupied a position anywhere near the center of literature.

Indeed, the movement of futurist literature from the periphery to the center of culture provides a clue to certain essential meanings of our times and of the art which best reflects it. If we make a brief excursion from the lofty reaches of High Art to the humbler levels of Pop Culture—where radical transformations in literature are reflected in simplified form—the extent and nature of the futurist revolution will become immediately evident. Certainly, we have seen in recent years the purveyors of Pop Culture transfer their energies from the Western and the Dracula-type thriller (last heirs of the Romantic and Gothic concern

---

* The Great Books idea: educational approach advocated by Robert M. Hutchins (president of the University of Chicago, 1929–45; chancellor, 1945–51); he was suspicious of specialized learning and believed in the study of basic abstractions as transmitted through those texts "which have given the Western tradition its life and light." Encyclopedia Britannica has published his selection of 443 works by 74 authors, *Great Books of the Western World.*

with the past) to the Detective Story especially in its hard-boiled form (final vulgarization of the realists' dedication to the present) to Science Fiction (a new genre based on hints in E. A. Poe and committed to "extrapolating" the future). This development is based in part on the tendency to rapid exhaustion inherent in popular forms; but in part reflects a growing sense of the irrelevance of the past and even of the present to 1965. Surely, there has never been a moment in which the most naïve as well as the most sophisticated have been so acutely aware of how the past threatens momentarily to disappear from the present, which itself seems on the verge of disappearing into the future.

And this awareness functions, therefore, on the level of art as well as entertainment, persuading quite serious writers to emulate the modes of Science Fiction. The novel is most amenable to this sort of adaptation, whose traces we can find in writers as various as William Golding and Anthony Burgess, William Burroughs and Kurt Vonnegut, Jr., Harry Matthews and John Barth—to all of whom young readers tend to respond with a sympathy they do not feel even toward such forerunners of the mode (still more allegorical than prophetic) as Aldous Huxley, H. G. Wells and George Orwell. But the influence of Science Fiction can be discerned in poetry as well, and even in the polemical essays of such polymath prophets as Wilhelm Reich, Buckminster Fuller, Marshall McLuhan, perhaps also Norman O. Brown. Indeed, in Fuller the prophetic-Science-Fiction view of man is always at the point of fragmenting into verse:

> men are known as being six feet tall
> because that is their tactile limit;
> they are not known by how far we can hear them,
> e.g., as a one-half mile man
> and only to dogs are men known
> by their gigantic olfactoral dimensions. . . .

I am not now interested in analyzing, however, the diction and imagery which have passed from Science Fiction into post-Modernist literature, but rather in coming to terms with the prophetic content common to both: with the myth rather than the modes of Science Fiction. But that myth is quite simply the myth of the end of man, of the transcendence or transformation of the human —a vision quite different from that of the extinction of our species by the Bomb, which seems stereotype rather than archetype and consequently the source of editorials rather than poems. More fruitful artistically is the prospect of the radical transformation (under the impact of advanced technology and the transfer of traditional human functions to machines) of *homo sapiens* into something else: the emergence—to use the language of Science Fiction itself—of "mutants" among us.

A simpleminded prevision of this event is to be found in Arthur C. Clarke's *Childhood's End,* at the conclusion of which the mutated offspring of parents much like us are about to take off under their own power into outer space. Mr. Clarke believes that he is talking about a time still to come because he takes metaphor for fact; though simply translating "outer space" into "inner space" reveals to us that what he is up to is less prediction than description; since the post-human future is now, and if not we, at least our children, are what it would be comfortable to pretend we still only foresee. But what, in fact, are they: these mutants who are likely to sit before us in class, or across from us at the dinner table, or who stare at us with hostility from street corners as we pass?

Beatniks or hipsters, layabouts and drop-outs we are likely to call them with corresponding hostility—or more elegantly, but still without sympathy, passive onlookers, abstentionists, spiritual catatonics. There resides in all of these terms an element of truth, at least about the relationship of the young to what we have defined as the tradition, the world we have made for them; and if we turn to the books in which they see their own destiny best represented (*The Clockwork Orange,** say, or *On the Road* * or *Temple of Gold* *), we will find nothing to contradict that truth. Nor will we find anything to expand it, since the young and their laureates avoid on principle the kind of definition (even of themselves) for which we necessarily seek.

Let us begin then with the negative definition our own hostility suggests, since this is all that is available to us, and say that the "mutants" in our midst are non-participants in the past (though our wisdom assures us this is impossible), drop-outs from history. The withdrawal from school, so typical of their generation and so inscrutable to ours, is best understood as a lived symbol of their rejection of the notion of cultural continuity and progress, which our graded educational system represents in institutional form. It is not merely a matter of their rejecting what happens to have happened just before them, as the young do, after all, in every age; but of their attempting to disavow the very idea of the past, of their seeking to avoid recapitulating it step by step—up to the point of graduation into the present.

Specifically, the tradition from which they strive to disengage is the tradition of the human, as the West (understanding the West to extend from the United States to Russia) has defined it, Humanism itself, both in its bourgeois and Marxist forms; and more especially, the cult of reason—that dream of Socrates, redreamed by the Renaissance and surviving all travesties down to only yesterday. To be sure, there have long been anti-rational forces at work in the West, including primitive Christianity itself; but the very notion of literary culture is a product of Humanism, as the early Christians knew (setting fire to libraries), so that the Church in order to sponsor poets had first to come to terms with reason itself by way of Aquinas and Aristotle.

Only with Dada * was the notion of an anti-rational anti-literature born; and

---

* *The Clockwork Orange:* Anthony Burgess (1962).
* *On the Road:* Jack Kerouac (1957).
* *Temple of Gold:* William Goldman (1957).
* Dada: extremist and nihilistic movement in art and literature initiated in Zurich during World War I; dedicated to disorder, irrationality, and instinctive expression, it rebelled against all previous aesthetic systems; "sense through nonsense" was one of its favorite slogans.

Dada became Surrealism,* i.e., submitted to the influence of those last neo-Humanists, those desperate Socratic Cabalists, Freud and Marx—dedicated respectively to contriving a rationale of violence and a rationale of impulse. The new irrationalists, however, deny all the apostles of reason, Freud as well as Socrates; and if they seem to exempt Marx, this is because they know less about him, have heard him evoked less often by the teachers they are driven to deny. Not only do they reject the Socratic adage that the unexamined life is not worth living, since for them precisely the unexamined life is the only one worth enduring at all. But they also abjure the Freudian one: "Where id was, ego shall be," since for them the true rallying cry is, "Let id prevail over ego, impulse over order," or—in negative terms—"Freud is a fink!"

The first time I heard this irreverent charge from the mouth of a student some five or six years ago (I who had grown up thinking of Freud as a revolutionary, a pioneer), I knew that I was already in the future; though I did not yet suspect that there would be no room in that future for the university system to which I had devoted my life. Kerouac might have told me so, or Ginsberg, or even so polite and genteel a spokesman for youth as J. D. Salinger, but I was too aware of what was wrong with such writers (their faults more readily apparent to my taste than their virtues) to be sensitive to the truths they told. It took, therefore, certain public events to illuminate (for me) the literature which might have illuminated them.

I am thinking, of course, of the recent demonstrations at Berkeley and elsewhere, whose ostensible causes were civil rights or freedom of speech or Vietnam, but whose not so secret slogan was all the time: *The Professor is a Fink!* And what an array of bad anti-academic novels, I cannot help reminding myself, written by disgruntled professors, created the mythology out of which that slogan grew. Each generation of students is invented by the generation of teachers just before them; but how different they are in dream and fact—as different as self-hatred and its reflection in another. How different the professors in Jeremy Larner's *Drive, He Said* from those even in Randall Jarrell's *Pictures from an Institution* or Mary McCarthy's *Groves of Academe.*

To be sure, many motives operated to set the students in action, some of them imagined in no book, however good or bad. Many of the thousands who resisted or shouted on campuses did so in the name of naïve or disingenuous or even nostalgic politics (be careful what you wish for in your middle age, or your children will parody it forthwith!); and sheer ennui doubtless played a role along with a justified rage against the hypocrisies of academic life. Universities have long rivaled the churches in their devotion to institutionalizing hypocrisy; and more recently they have outstripped television itself (which most professors af-

---

* Surrealism: art movement founded in 1924 by André Breton. Its program was to eliminate the checks placed on expression by conscious reason; dreams and reality were to merge into a "surreality" achieved by the spontaneous or automatic functioning of the subconscious. Probably the best known examples of surrealism are the paintings of Salvador Dali.

fect to despise even more than they despise organized religion) in the institutionalization of boredom.

But what the students were protesting in large part, I have come to believe, was the very notion of man which the universities sought to impose upon them: that bourgeois-Protestant version of Humanism, with its view of man as justified by rationality, work, duty, vocation, maturity, success; and its concomitant understanding of childhood and adolescence as a temporarily privileged time of preparation for assuming those burdens. The new irrationalists, however, are prepared to advocate prolonging adolescence to the grave, and are ready to dispense with school as an outlived excuse for leisure. To them work is as obsolete as reason, a vestige (already dispensable for large numbers) of an economically marginal, pre-automated world; and the obsolescence of the two adds up to the obsolescence of everything our society understands by maturity.

Nor is it in the name of an older more valid Humanistic view of man that the new irrationalists would reject the WASP version; Rabelais * is as alien to them as Benjamin Franklin. Disinterested scholarship, reflection, the life of reason, a respect for tradition stir (however dimly and confusedly) chiefly their contempt; and the Abbey of Theleme would seem as sterile to them as Robinson Crusoe's Island. To the classroom, the library, the laboratory, the office conference and the meeting of scholars, they prefer the demonstration, the sit-in, the riot: the mindless unity of an impassioned crowd (with guitars beating out the rhythm in the background), whose immediate cause is felt rather than thought out, whose ultimate cause is itself. In light of this, the Teach-in, often ill understood because of an emphasis on its declared political ends, can be seen as implicitly a parody and mockery of the real classroom: related to the actual business of the university, to real teaching only as the Demonstration Trial (of Dimitrov,* of the Soviet Doctors,* of Eichmann *) to real justice or Demonstration Voting (for one party or a token two) to real suffrage.

* François Rabelais: (1494?–1553), French satirist and humanist; in his *Gargantua*, the Abbey of Theleme is a utopian monastic institution whose code of rules consists only of the clause; "Do what thou wilt"; Rabelais believed that among free, wellborn, and well-educated people, the human instincts led naturally to virtuous behavior.
* Georgi Dimitrov: (1882–1949), Bulgarian Communist leader; he was in Berlin as leader of the central European section of Comintern at the time of the Reichstag fire in 1933. Hitler accused the Communists of arson; Dimitrov was greatly admired for his courageous defense against the charge that he was responsible.
* the Soviet Doctors: in January 1953 Pravda announced that a group of distinguished Soviet doctors (the majority of whom were Jewish) had plotted to kill certain leading army officers in order to weaken the country's defense; this was the excuse for another purge, primarily of Jews. Shortly after Stalin's death (April 1953) the doctors were released from prison and it was officially admitted that the charges had been false and that the doctors had "confessed" under torture.
* Adolf Eichmann: (1906–62), German war criminal hanged by the state of Israel for his part in the extermination of the Jews in World War II; his trial, which lasted from April 11 to December 15, 1961, was the focus of world-wide attention and controversy.

At least, since Berkeley (or perhaps since Martin Luther King provided students with new paradigms for action) the choice has been extended beyond what the earlier laureates of the new youth could imagine in the novel: the nervous breakdown at home rather than the return to "sanity" and school, which was the best Salinger could invent for Franny * and Holden; * or Kerouac's way out for his "saintly" vagrants, that "road" from nowhere to noplace with homemade gurus at the way stations. The structure of those fictional vaudevilles between hard covers that currently please the young (*Catch 22*,* *V.*,* *A Mother's Kisses* *), suggest in their brutality and discontinuity, their politics of mockery something of the spirit of the student demonstrations; but only Jeremy Larner, as far as I know, has dealt explicitly with the abandonment of the classroom in favor of the dionysiac pack, the turning from *polis* * to *thiasos*,* from forms of social organization traditionally thought of as male to the sort of passionate community attributed by the ancients to females out of control.

Conventional slogans in favor of "Good Works" (pious emendations of existing social structures, or extensions of accepted "rights" to excluded groups) though they provide the motive power of such protests are irrelevant to their form and their final significance. They become their essential selves, i.e., genuine new forms of rebellion, when the demonstrators hoist (as they did in the final stages of the Berkeley protests) the sort of slogan which embarasses not only fellow-travelers but even the bureaucrats who direct the initial stages of the revolt: at the University of California, the single four-letter word no family newspaper would reprint, though no member of a family who could read was likely not to know it.

It is possible to argue on the basis of the political facts themselves that the word "fuck" entered the whole scene accidentally (there were only four students behind the "Dirty Speech Movement," only fifteen hundred kids could be persuaded to demonstrate for it, etc., etc.). But the prophetic literature which anticipates the movement indicates otherwise, suggesting that the logic of their illogical course eventually sets the young against language itself, against the very counters of logical discourse. They seek an anti-language of protest as inevitably as they seek anti-poems and anti-novels, end with the ultimate anti-word, which the demonstrators at Berkeley disingenuously claimed stood for FREEDOM UNDER CLARK KERR.*

Esthetics, however, had already anticipated politics in this regard; porno-po-

* Franny: character in J. D. Salinger's *Franny and Zooey* (1961).
* Holden: hero of Salinger's *The Catcher in the Rye* (1951).
* *Catch 22:* novel by Joseph Heller (1961).
* *V.:* novel by Thomas Pynchon (1963).
* *A Mother's Kisses:* novel by Bruce Jay Friedman (1964).
* *polis:* the city as a political unit; a commonwealth or state.
* *thiasos:* a religious community organized for the worship of some deity, especially Dionysus; also a procession of such a company, marching through the streets with dance and song.
* Clark Kerr: president of the University of California at Berkeley, 1958–67.

etry preceding and preparing the way for what Lewis Feuer has aptly called porno-politics. Already in 1963, in an essay entitled *"Phi Upsilon Kappa,"* the young poet Michael McClure was writing: "Gregory Corso has asked me join with him in a project to free the word FUCK from its chains and strictures. I leap to make some new freedom. . . ." And McClure's own "Fuck Ode" is a product of this collaboration, as the very name of Ed Saunders' journal, *Fuck You,* is the creation of an analogous impulse. The aging critics of the young who have dealt with the Berkeley demonstrations in such journals as *Commentary* and the *New Leader* do not, however, read either Saunders' porno-pacifist magazine or *Kulchur,* in which McClure's manifesto was first printed—the age barrier separating readership in the United States more effectively than class, political affiliation or anything else.

Their sense of porno-esthetics is likely to come from deserters from their own camp, chiefly Norman Mailer, and especially his recent *An American Dream,* which represents the entry of anti-language (extending the tentative explorations of "The Time of Her Time") into the world of the middle-aged, both on the level of mass culture and that of yesterday's ex-Marxist, post-Freudian avantgarde. Characteristically enough, Mailer's book has occasioned in the latter quarters reviews as irrelevant, incoherent, misleading and fundamentally scared as the most philistine responses to the Berkeley demonstrations, Philip Rahv and Stanley Edgar Hyman providing two egregious examples. Yet elsewhere (in sectors held by those more at ease with their own conservatism, i.e., without defunct radicalisms to uphold) the most obscene forays of the young are being met with a disheartening kind of tolerance and even an attempt to adapt them to the conditions of commodity art.

But precisely here, of course, a disconcerting irony is involved; for after a while, there will be no Rahvs and Hymans left to shock—anti-language becoming mere language with repeated use and in the face of acceptance; so that all sense of exhilaration will be lost along with the possibility of offense. What to do then except to choose silence, since raising the ante of violence is ultimately self-defeating; and the way of obscenity in any case leads as naturally to silence as to further excess? Moreover, to the talkative heirs of Socrates, silence is the one offense that never wears out, the radicalism that can never become fashionable; which is why, after the obscene slogan has been hauled down, a blank placard is raised in its place.

There are difficulties, to be sure, when one attempts to move from the politics of silence to an analogous sort of poetry. The opposite number to the silent picketer would be the silent poet, which is a contradiction in terms; yet there are these days non-singers of (perhaps) great talent who shrug off the temptation to song with the muttered comment, "Creativity is out." Some, however, make literature of a kind precisely at the point of maximum tension between the tug toward silence and the pull toward publication. Music is a better language really for saying what one would prefer not to say at all—and all the way from certain sorts of sufficiently cool jazz to Rock'n'Roll (with its minimal lyrics that defy understanding on a first hearing), music is the preferred art of the irrationalists.

But some varieties of skinny poetry seem apt, too (as practised, say, by Robert Creeley after the example of W. C. Williams), since their lines are three parts silence to one part speech:

> My lady
> fair with
> soft
> arms, what
> can I say to
> you—words, words . . .

And, of course, fiction aspiring to become Pop Art, say, *An American Dream* (with the experiments of Hemingway and Nathanael West behind it), works approximately as well, since clichés are almost as inaudible as silence itself. The point is not to shout, not to insist, but to hang cool, to baffle all mothers, cultural and spiritual as well as actual.

When the Town Council in Venice, California was about to close down a particularly notorious beatnik cafe, a lady asked to testify before them, presumably to clinch the case against the offenders. What she reported, however, was that each day as she walked by the cafe and looked in its windows, she saw the unsavory types who inhabited it "just standing there, looking—nonchalant." And, in a way, her improbable adjective does describe a crime against her world; for nonchaleur ("cool", the futurists themselves would prefer to call it) is the essence of their life-style as well as of the literary styles to which they respond: the offensive style of those who are not so much *for* anything in particular, as "with it" in general.

But such an attitude is as remote from traditional "alienation," with its profound longing to end disconnection, as it is from ordinary forms of allegiance, with their desperate resolve not to admit disconnection. The new young celebrate disconnection—accept it as one of the necessary consequences of the industrial system which has delivered them from work and duty, of that welfare state which makes disengagement the last possible virtue, whether it call itself Capitalist, Socialist or Communist. "Detachment" is the traditional name for the stance the futurists assume; but "detachment" carries with it irrelevant religious, even specifically Christian overtones. The post-modernists are surely in some sense "mystics," religious at least in a way they do not ordinarily know how to confess, but they are not Christians.

Indeed, they regard Christianity, quite as the Black Muslim (with whom they have certain affinities) do, as a white ideology: merely one more method—along with Humanism, technology, Marxism—of imposing "White" or Western values on the colored rest of the world. To the new barbarian, however, that would-be-post-Humanist (who is in most cases the white offspring of Christian forebears) his whiteness is likely to seem if not a stigma and symbol of shame, at least the outward sign of his exclusion from all that his Christian Humanist ancestors rejected in themselves and projected mythologically upon the colored man. For such reasons, his religion, when it becomes explicit, claims to be derived from Tibet or Japan or the ceremonies of the Plains Indians, or is composed out of the non-Christian sub-mythology that has grown up among Negro jazz musicians and in the civil rights movement. When the new barbarian speaks of "soul," for instance, he means not "soul" as in Heaven, but as in "soul music" or even "soul food."

It is all part of the attempt of the generation under twenty-five, not exclusively in its most sensitive members but especially in them, to become Negro, even as they attempt to become poor or pre-rational. About this particular form of psychic assimilation I have written sufficiently in the past (summing up what I had been long saying in chapters seven and eight of *Waiting for the End*), neglecting only the sense in which what starts as a specifically American movement becomes an international one, spreading to the *yé-yé* girls of France or the working-class entertainers of Liverpool with astonishing swiftness and ease.

What interests me more particularly right now is a parallel assimilationist attempt, which may, indeed, be more parochial and is certainly most marked at the moment in the Anglo-Saxon world, i.e., in those cultural communities most totally committed to bourgeois-Protestant values and surest that they are unequivocally "white." I am thinking of the effort of young men in England and the United States to assimilate into themselves (or even to assimilate themselves into) that otherness, that sum total of rejected psychic elements which the middle-class heirs of the Renaissance have identified with "woman." To become new men, these children of the future seem to feel, they must not only become more Black than White but more female than male. And it is natural that the need to make such an adjustment be felt with especial acuteness in post-Protestant highly industrialized societies, where the functions regarded as specifically male for some three hundred years tend most rapidly to become obsolete.

Surely, in America, machines already perform better than humans a large number of those aggressive-productive activities which our ancestors considered man's special province, even his *raison d'être*. Not only has the male's prerogative of making things and money (which is to say, of working) been preempted, but also his time-honored privilege of dealing out death by hand, which until quite recently was regarded as a supreme mark of masculine valor. While it seems theoretically possible, even in the heart of Anglo-Saxondom, to imagine a leisurely, pacific male, in fact the losses in secondary functions sustained by men appear to have shaken their faith in their primary masculine function as well, in their ability to achieve the conquest (as the traditional metaphor has it) of women. Earlier, advances in technology had detached the wooing and winning of women from the begetting of children; and though the invention of the condom had at least left the decision to inhibit fatherhood in the power of males, its replacement by the "loop" and the "pill" has placed paternity at the mercy of the whims of women.

Writers of fiction and verse registered the technological obsolescence of masculinity long before it was felt even by the representative minority who give to the present younger generation its character and significance. And literary critics have talked a good deal during the past couple of decades about the conversion of the literary hero into the non-hero or the anti-hero; but they have in general failed to notice his simultaneous conversion into the non- or anti-male. Yet ever since Hemingway at least, certain male protagonists of American literature have not only fled rather than sought out combat but have also fled rather than sought out women. From Jake Barnes * to Holden Caulfield they have continued to run from the threat of female sexuality; and, indeed, there are models for such evasion in our classic books, where heroes still eager for the fight (Natty Bumppo * comes to mind) are already shy of wives and sweethearts and mothers.

It is not absolutely required that the anti-male anti-hero be impotent or homosexual or both (though this helps, as we remember remembering Walt Whitman), merely that he be more seduced than seducing, more passive than active. Consider, for instance, the oddly "womanish" Herzog of Bellow's current best seller, that Jewish Emma Bovary with a Ph.D., whose chief flaw is physical vanity and a taste for fancy clothes. Bellow, however, is more interested in summing up the past than in evoking the future; and *Herzog* therefore seems an end rather than a beginning, the product of nostalgia (remember when there were real Jews once, and the "Jewish Novel" had not yet been discovered!) rather than prophecy. No, the post-humanist, post-male, post-white, post-heroic world is a post-Jewish world by the same token, anti-Semitism as inextricably woven into it as into the movement for Negro rights; and its scriptural books are necessarily *goyish,* not least of all William Burroughs' *The Naked Lunch.*

Burroughs is the chief prophet of the post-male post-heroic world; and it is his emulators who move into the center of the relevant literary scene, for *The Naked Lunch* (the later novels are less successful, less exciting but relevant still) is more than it seems: no mere essay in heroin-hallucinated homosexual pornography—but a nightmare anticipation (in Science Fiction form) of post-Humanist sexuality. Here, as in Alexander Trocchi, John Rechy, Harry Matthews (even an occasional Jew like Allen Ginsberg, who has begun by inscribing properly anti-Jewish obscenities on the walls of the world), are clues to the new attitudes toward sex that will continue to inform our improbable novels of passion and our even more improbable love songs.

The young to whom I have been referring, the mythologically representative minority (who, by a process that infuriates the mythologically inert majority out

---

* Jake Barnes: hero of Ernest Hemingway's novel *The Sun Also Rises* (1926).
* Natty Bumppo: hero of James Fenimore Cooper's series of five novels collectively known as the Leather-Stocking Tales (1823–41).

of which they come, "stand for" their times), live in a community in which what used to be called the "Sexual Revolution," the Freudian-Laurentian revolt of their grandparents and parents, has triumphed as imperfectly and unsatisfactorily as all revolutions always triumph. They confront, therefore, the necessity of determining not only what meanings "love" can have in their new world, but—even more disturbingly—what significance, if any, "male" and "female" now possess. For a while, they (or at least their literary spokesmen recruited from the generation just before them) seemed content to celebrate a kind of *reductio* or *exaltatio ad absurdum* * of their parents' once revolutionary sexual goals: The Reichian-inspired * Cult of the Orgasm.

Young men and women eager to be delivered of traditional ideologies of love find especially congenial the belief that not union or relationship (much less offspring) but physical release is the end of the sexual act; and that, therefore, it is a matter of indifference with whom or by what method one pursues the therapeutic climax, so long as that climax is total and repeated frequently. And Wilhelm Reich happily detaches this belief from the vestiges of Freudian rationalism, setting it instead in a context of Science Fiction and witchcraft; but his emphasis upon "full genitality," upon growing up and away from infantile pleasures, strikes the young as a disguised plea for the "maturity" they have learned to despise. In a time when the duties associated with adulthood promise to become irrelevant, there seems little reason for denying oneself the joys of babyhood—even if these are associated with such regressive fantasies as escaping it all in the arms of little sister (in the Gospel according to J. D. Salinger) or flirting with the possibility of getting into bed with papa (in the Gospel according to Norman Mailer).

Only Norman O. Brown in *Life Against Death* has come to terms on the level of theory with the aspiration to take the final evolutionary leap and cast off adulthood completely, at least in the area of sex. His post-Freudian program for pan-sexual, non-orgasmic love rejects "full genitality" in favor of a species of indiscriminate bundling, a dream of unlimited sub-coital intimacy which Brown calls (in his vocabulary the term is an honorific) "polymorphous perverse." And here finally is an essential clue to the nature of the second sexual revolution, the post-sexual revolution, first evoked in literature by Brother Antoninus more than a decade ago, in a verse prayer addressed somewhat improbably to the Christian God:

> Annul in me my manhood, Lord, and make
> Me woman sexed and weak . . .
>   Make me then
> Girl-hearted, virgin-souled, woman-docile, maiden-meek . . .

* *reductio* or *exaltatio ad absurdum:* reduction or elevation to absurdity.
* Reichian-inspired: refers to Wilhelm Reich (1897–1957), Austrian psychiatrist and biophysicist; author of *The Function of the Orgasm* (1948).

Despite the accents of this invocation, however, what is at work is not essentially a homosexual revolt or even a rebellion against women, though its advocates seek to wrest from women their ancient privileges of receiving the Holy Ghost and pleasuring men; and though the attitudes of the movement can be adapted to the anti-female bias of, say, Edward Albee. If in *Who's Afraid of Virginia Woolf* Albee can portray the relationship of two homosexuals (one in drag) as the model of contemporary marriage, this must be because contemporary marriage has in fact turned into something much like that parody. And it is true that what survives of bourgeois marriage and the bourgeois family is a target which the new barbarians join the old homosexuals in reviling, seeking to replace Mom, Pop and the kids with a neo-Whitmanian gaggle of giggling *camerados*. Such groups are, in fact, whether gathered in coffee houses, university cafeterias or around the literature tables on campuses, the peace-time equivalents, as it were, to the demonstrating crowd. But even their program of displacing Dick-Jane-Spot-Baby, etc., the WASP family of grade school primers, is not the fundamental motive of the post-sexual revolution.

What is at stake from Burroughs to Bellow, Ginsberg to Albee, Salinger to Gregory Corso is a more personal transformation: a radical metamorphosis of the Western male—utterly unforeseen in the decades before us, but visible now in every high school and college classroom, as well as on the paperback racks in airports and supermarkets. All around us, young males are beginning to retrieve for themselves the cavalier role once piously and class-consciously surrendered to women: *that of being beautiful and being loved.* Here once more the example of the Negro—the feckless and adorned Negro male with the blood of Cavaliers in his veins—has served as a model. And what else is left to young men, in any case, after the devaluation of the grim duties they had arrogated to themselves in place of the pursuit of loveliness?

All of us who are middle-aged and were Marxists, which is to say, who once numbered ourselves among the last assured Puritans, have surely noticed in ourselves a vestigial roundhead rage at the new hair styles of the advanced or—if you please—delinquent young. Watching young men titivate their locks (the comb, the pocket mirror and the bobby pin having replaced the jackknife, catcher's mitt and brass knuckles), we feel the same baffled resentment that stirs in us when we realize that they have rejected work. A job and unequivocal maleness—these are two sides of the same Calvinist coin, which in the future buys nothing.

Few of us, however, have really understood how the Beatle hairdo is part of a syndrome, of which high heels, jeans tight over the buttocks, etc., are other aspects, symptomatic of a larger retreat from masculine aggressiveness to female allure—in literature and the arts to the style called "camp." And fewer still have realized how that style, though the invention of homosexuals, is now the possession of basically heterosexual males as well, a strategy in their campaign to establish a new relationship not only with women but with their own masculinity.

In the course of that campaign, they have embraced certain kinds of gesture and garb, certain accents and tones traditionally associated with females or female impersonators; which is why we have been observing recently (in life as well as fiction and verse) young boys, quite unequivocally male, playing all the traditional roles of women: the vamp, the coquette, the whore, the icy tease, the pure young virgin.

Not only oldsters, who had envisioned and despaired of quite another future, are bewildered by this turn of events, but young girls, too, seem scarcely to know what is happening—looking on with that new, schizoid stare which itself has become a hallmark of our times. And the crop-headed jocks, those crew-cut athletes who represent an obsolescent masculine style based on quite other values, have tended to strike back blindly; beating the hell out of some poor kid whose hair is too long or whose pants are too tight—quite as they once beat up young Communists for revealing that their politics had become obsolete. Even heterosexual writers, however, have been slow to catch up, the revolution in sensibility running ahead of that in expression; and they have perforce permitted homosexuals to speak for them (Burroughs and Genet and Baldwin and Ginsberg and Albee and a score of others), even to invent the forms in which the future will have to speak.

The revolt against masculinity is not limited, however, to simple matters of coiffure and costume, visible even to athletes; or to the adaptation of certain campy styles and modes to new uses. There is also a sense in which two large social movements that have set the young in motion and furnished images of action for their books—movements as important in their own right as porno-politics and the pursuit of the polymorphous perverse—are connected analogically to the abdication from traditional maleness. The first of these is nonviolent or passive resistance, so oddly come back to the land of its inventor, that icy Thoreau who dreamed a love which ". . . has not much human blood in it, but consists with a certain disregard for men and their erections. . . ."

The civil rights movement, however, in which nonviolence has found a home, has been hospitable not only to the sort of post-humanist I have been describing; so that at a demonstration (Selma, Alabama will do as an example) the true hippie will be found side by side with backwoods Baptists, nuns on a spiritual spree, boy bureaucrats practicing to take power, resurrected socialists, Unitarians in search of a God, and just plain tourists, gathered, as once at the Battle of Bull Run, to see the fun. For each of these, nonviolence will have a different sort of fundamental meaning—as a tactic, a camouflage, a passing fad, a pious gesture —but for each in part, and for the post-humanist especially, it will signify the possibility of heroism without aggression, effective action without guilt.

There have always been two contradictory American ideals: to be the occasion of maximum violence, and to remain absolutely innocent. Once, however, these were thought hopelessly incompatible for males (except, perhaps, as embodied in works of art), reserved strictly for women: the spouse of the wife-beater, for instance, or the victim of rape. But males have now assumed these classic roles; and just as a particularly beleaguered wife occasionally slipped over the dividing line into violence, so do the new passive protestors—leaving us to confront (or resign to the courts) such homey female questions as: *Did Mario Savio* * *really bite that cop in the leg as he sagged limply toward the ground?*

The second social movement is the drug cult, more widespread among youth, from its squarest limits to its most beat, than anyone seems prepared to admit in public; and at its beat limit at least inextricably involved with the civil rights movement, as the recent arrests of Peter DeLissovoy and Susan Ryerson revealed even to the ordinary newspaper reader. "Police said that most of the recipients [of marijuana] were college students," the U.P. story runs. "They quoted Miss Ryerson and DeLissovoy as saying that many of the letter packets were sent to civil rights workers." Only fiction and verse, however, has dealt with the conjunction of homosexuality, drugs and civil rights, eschewing the general piety of the press which has been unwilling to compromise "good works" on behalf of the Negro by associating it with the deep radicalism of a way of life based on the ritual consumption of "pot."

The widespread use of such hallucinogens as peyote, marijuana, the "mexican mushroom," LSD, etc., as well as pep pills, goof balls, airplane glue, certain kinds of cough syrups and even, though in many fewer cases, heroin, is not merely a matter of a changing taste in stimulants but of the programmatic espousal of an anti-puritanical mode of existence—hedonistic and detached—one more strategy in the war on time and work. But it is also (to pursue my analogy once more) an attempt to arrogate to the male certain traditional privileges of the female. What could be more womanly, as Elémire Zolla was already pointing out some years ago, then permitting the penetration of the body by a foreign object which not only stirs delight but even (possibly) creates new life?

In any case, with drugs we have come to the crux of the futurist revolt, the hinge of everything else, as the young tell us over and over in their writing. When the movement was first finding a voice, Allen Ginsberg set this aspect of it in proper context in an immensely comic, utterly serious poem called "America," in which "pot" is associated with earlier forms of rebellion, a commitment to catatonia, and a rejection of conventional male potency:

> America I used to be a communist when I was a kid I'm not sorry.
> I smoke marijuana every chance I get.
> I sit in my house for days on end and stare at the roses in the closet.
> When I go to Chinatown I . . . never get laid . . .

Similarly, Michael McClure reveals in his essay, *"Phi Upsilon Kappa,"* that before penetrating the "cavern of Anglo-Saxon," whence he emerged with the

---

* Mario Savio: leader of the student rebellion at Berkeley in 1964.

slogan of the ultimate Berkeley demonstrators, he had been on mescalin. "I have emerged from a dark night of the soul; I entered it by Peyote." And by now, drug-taking has become as standard a feature of the literature of the young as oral-genital love-making. I flip open the first issue of yet another ephemeral San Francisco little magazine quite at random and read: "I tie up and the main pipe [the ante-cobital vein, for the clinically inclined] swells like a prideful beggar beneath the skin. Just before I get on it is always the worst." Worse than the experience, however, is its literary rendering; and the badness of such confessional fiction, flawed by the sentimentality of those who desire to live "like a cunning vegetable," is a badness we older readers find it only too easy to perceive, as our sons and daughters find it only too easy to overlook. Yet precisely here the age and the mode define themselves; for not in the master but in the hacks new forms are established, new lines drawn.

Here, at any rate, is where the young lose us in literature as well as life, since here they pass over into real revolt, i.e., what we really cannot abide, hard as we try. The mother who has sent her son to private schools and on to Harvard to keep him out of classrooms overcrowded with poor Negroes, rejoices when he sets out for Mississippi with his comrades in SNCC,* but shudders when he turns on with LSD; just as the ex-Marxist father, who has earlier proved radicalism impossible, rejoices to see his son stand up, piously and pompously, for CORE * or SDS,* but trembles to hear him quote Alpert and Leary * or praise Burroughs. Just as certainly as liberalism is the LSD of the aging, LSD is the radicalism of the young.

If whiskey long served as an appropriate symbolic excess for those who chafed against Puritan restraint without finally challenging it—temporarily releasing them to socially harmful aggression and (hopefully) sexual self-indulgence, the new popular drugs provide an excess quite as satisfactorily symbolic to the post-Puritans—releasing them from sanity to madness by destroying in them the inner restrictive order which has somehow survived the dissolution of the outer. It is finally insanity, then, that the futurists learn to admire and emulate, quite as they learn to pursue vision instead of learning, hallucination rather than logic. The schizophrenic replaces the sage as their ideal, their new culture hero, figured forth as a giant schizoid Indian (his madness modeled in part on the author's own experiences with LSD) in Ken Kesey's *One Flew Over the Cuckoo's Nest*.

The hippier young are not alone, however, in their taste for the insane; we live in a time when readers in general respond sympathetically to madness in literature wherever it is found, in established writers as well as in those trying to establish new modes. Surely it is not the lucidity and logic of Robert Lowell or

---

* SNCC: Student Non-violent Co-ordinating Committee.
* CORE: Congress of Racial Equality.
* SDS: Students for a Democratic Society.
* Richard Alpert and Timothy Leary: proselytizers of the psychedelic "revolution"; dismissed from the faculty of Harvard University in 1963 for testing drugs on students without proper authorization.

Theodore Roethke or John Berryman which we admire, but their flirtation with incoherence and disorder. And certainly it is Mailer at his most nearly psychotic, Mailer the creature rather than the master of his fantasies who moves us to admiration; while in the case of Saul Bellow, we endure the theoretical optimism and acceptance for the sake of the delightful melancholia, the fertile paranoia which he cannot disavow any more than the talent at whose root they lie. Even essayists and analysts recommend themselves to us these days by a certain redemptive nuttiness; at any rate, we do not love, say, Marshall McLuhan less because he continually risks sounding like the body-fluids man in *Dr. Strangelove*.

We have, moreover, recently been witnessing the development of a new form of social psychiatry [2] (a psychiatry of the future already anticipated by the literature of the future) which considers some varieties of "schizophrenia" not diseases to be cured but forays into an unknown psychic world: random penetrations by bewildered internal cosmonauts of a realm that it will be the task of the next generations to explore. And if the accounts which the returning schizophrenics give (the argument of the apologists runs) of the "places" they have been are fantastic and garbled, surely they are no more so than, for example, Columbus' reports of the world he had claimed for Spain, a world bounded—according to his newly drawn maps—by Cathay on the north and Paradise on the south.

In any case, poets and junkies have been suggesting to us that the new world appropriate to the new men of the latter twentieth century is to be discovered only by the conquest of inner space: by an adventure of the spirit, an extension of psychic possibility, of which the flights into outer space—moonshots and expeditions to Mars—are precisely such unwitting metaphors and analogues as the voyages of exploration were of the earlier breakthrough into the Renaissance, from whose consequences the young seek now so desperately to escape. The laureate of that new conquest is William Burroughs; and it is fitting that the final word be his:

> "This war will be won in the air. In the Silent Air with Image Rays. You were a pilot remember? Tracer bullets cutting the right wing you were free in space a few seconds before in blue space between eyes. Go back to Silence. Keep Silence. Keep Silence. K.S. K.S. . . . From Silence re-write the message that is you. You are the message I send to The Enemy. My Silent Message.
> The Naked Astronauts were free in space. . . ." *

2. Described in an article in the *New Left Review* of November-December 1964, by R. D. Laing who advocates "ex-patients helping future patients go mad."
* *The Naked Lunch* (Paris, 1959; New York, 1962).

F. W. Dupee / The Uprising at Columbia

At the end of "You Have To Grow Up in Scarsdale To Know How Bad Things Really Are," Kenneth Keniston remarks, speaking of the kind of young people who might eventually go to Columbia or Berkeley or Harvard, that because of their feelings about the general failures of American society it "does not take a clear cut issue to trigger a major protest." The troubles at Columbia in 1968 in which F. W. Dupee found himself involved are a case in point. His writing manages to encompass the possible multiplicity of convergent causes. He does so without moralistically insisting, as others have done, that without any specifically academic cause for rebellion, the damage caused is unacceptable. He is able to show here something of the strange chemistry of events by which a university crisis of major proportions manages to involve itself with most of the important issues that divide and disturb the nation as a whole.

This larger dimension is not allowed, however, to obscure the aspect of family quarrel in the Columbia crisis. By finely managed shifts of focus we are shown many details (the appearance of the SDS, the manners of the faculty) but made aware at the same time of their representative value. Dupee here and Mailer in "The Liberal Party" both show a capacity to personalize public issues and trends, though their ways of doing so are quite different. Dupee is at first chiefly desirous of continuing his classes in Shakespeare, but he is gradually politicized (he had been active on the Left in the 1930's and 1940's) by events and by the students. Eventually, he finds himself standing as part of a human barrier between the police and the student occupiers of a university building. His action separates him from that kind of academic for whom, as he wryly observes at one point, "only the arguable was the possible."

Here are some impressions of, and reflections upon, the *first phase* of the Columbia crisis of 1968 as it was experienced by a member of the faculty. That phase began with the student demonstrations of Tuesday, April 23 [1968] and ended with the big police raid during the early hours of Tuesday, April 30. The crisis still continued for several more weeks in the form of a student strike; ending with an uneasy peace with the close of the spring semester on June 4. The impressions reported in this article are peculiarly, although I think not uniquely, my own. For if the Columbia ordeal was primarily a collective shake-up, it has also amounted to an individual shake-up for most of us who participated in the experience—an experience which, in its duration and its bitterness, its capacity to absorb every major issue dividing the nation, was probably without precedent in the history of American universities at that time.

I

During the early hours of Wednesday, April 24th, 1968, I was preparing for my Shakespeare class at 11 a.m. The subject that day was *The Winter's Tale; Coriolanus* had gotten its final touches at the preceding session—"Just in time for the *local* mob scenes," a student remarked later. I wasn't happy about meeting any class that day. The show must go on, but I wished it could go on without me. For there was trouble on campus and I was by self-election a teacher and not a campus politician or a "trouble shooter."

It was one of Columbia's great virtues that it allowed its teachers this freedom of election, together with plenty of intellectual and social freedom and plenty of good students. It is true that my habitual detachment from campus politics had recently broken down as I saw the students growing more and more desperate under the pressures of the Vietnam war. The war's large evil was written small in the misery with whicn they pondered hour by hour the pitiful little list of *their* options: Vietnam or Canada or graduate school or jail! Naturally they were edgy, staying away from classes in droves and staging noisy demonstrations on campus. To all this, the Columbia Administration added further tension. Increasingly capricious in the exercise of its authority, it alternated, in the familiar American way, between the permissive gesture and the threatened crackdown.

So little unchallenged authority survives anywhere at present, even in the Vatican, that those who think they have authority tend to get "hung up" on it. Many of my fellow teachers shared the Administration's "hang-up." One of them said to me of the defiant students, "As with children, there comes a time when you have to say no to them." But the defiant students weren't children, and saying no meant exposing them to much more than "a good spanking." The War was doing far more violence to the University than they were. Altogether, Columbia (especially the College where I teach and where the big April disturbances began) had been grim throughout the school year. And while nobody—not even the student radicals—expected any such explosion as actually occurred, I would not have been surprised if the year had ended with an epidemic of nervous breakdowns. On that Wednesday morning I was tired of the routines of teaching. I wanted neither to lecture on *The Winter's Tale* nor cope with a student riot.

But I must go back a day. The troubles began at noon on Tuesday, April 23. That morning a College dean phoned and asked me, in a slightly anxious voice, to join him and others at a noonday rally called by the Students for a Democratic Society (SDS) at the Sundial. It was hoped, the dean said, that the demonstrators might be persuaded to adjourn to McMillin Theatre where they could discuss their grievances peacefully with David Truman, the former dean of Columbia College, now the University's Vice-President. If persuasion worked, would I sit on the McMillin stage with other senior professors? I said I would attend the rally and see what happened.

It seemed doubtful that persuasion *would* work in this case. On March 27 the SDS had staged an indoor demonstration in open defiance of a ban on such demonstrations issued by President Grayson Kirk still earlier in the year. In itself the ban was acceptable to a majority of students and faculty, including myself—indoor demonstrations *are* disruptive—even though many of us thought it impolitic of the President (to put it mildly) to have made this important move without consulting formally any faculty or student body. Six student leaders who had participated in the March event were now subject to University discipline. The SDS claimed, first, that the six had been invidiously singled out; and second, that only a public trial conducted with due process could properly dispense justice in such cases. The Administration had denied both claims, in particular the second. The demand for a public trial challenged the right of this private university to conduct its disciplinary affairs by the *in loco parentis* principle that governed most of its relations with its students. Thus the issues behind the present rally combined, just as the issues presented by the demonstrators in the coming crisis were to do, a relatively superficial one (the disciplining of the six) with an absolutely fundamental one: the theory and practice of the University *vis-à-vis* its student body. "The University is *not* a democracy," one of its officials announced, with a candor which, in the present state of unrest, was the opposite of disarming.

I went to the rally: access to the campus is quick and easy from my apartment on West 116th Street, a short half block from the Amsterdam Avenue gate to College Walk. The rally, I found, was already in progress on and around the Sundial. Columbia's chief landmark, this squat cylinder of granite is capable of seating a dozen or so persons around its rim. It can also serve as a rostrum for a speaker and several associates if they all cling together. As rostrum, the Sundial was now occupied by a speaker and three or four associates, including (briefly) a couple of what I guessed were Barnard girls. The boys tended to be quite tall with hair wild, eyes haunted, lower jaws protruded, shoulders hunched: the SDS look; while the girls were short, dark, stern-faced, and had their hair pulled tight into knots at the back. The group didn't look as scary to me as they were reputed to be, perhaps because a couple of them were students of mine—the family quarrel aspect of the coming crisis was already present. In the bright Spring sunlight, squinting watchfully across the expanses of the campus, the SDSers made a familiar, disarming, storybook or TV Western impression—that of an embattled cluster of frontiersmen and their women in Indian country. This image fitted in—too conveniently, I was to find—with what I knew of their ideology (or anti-ideology) which, despite its debts to Marcuse,* Sorel, * Camus,* Mao,* etc., seemed to me in essence radically American and populist, with Cuba as the latest frontier and the great Guevara * as the tragic hero.

Now one of the taller youths—probably Mark Rudd, the SDS chairman—was making a speech to a crowd thickly gathered around the Sundial. Farther off, on Low Plaza, where I was standing, the crowd was more fluid. Unaffiliated students, faculty members, University officials, we moved around easily, exchanging campus pleasantries while keeping eyes and ears on the Sundial speaker. Beyond us, at the foot of the Low Library steps, was a line of picketers shouting "Stop SDS!" They were some of the Students for a Free Campus, an anti-SDS faction whose numbers were soon to multiply, and with them its potential for violence.

Something now went on at the Sundial which I couldn't follow at that distance but learned about later. A College dean handed the speaker David Truman's letter inviting the group to McMillin. The speaker read the letter aloud, went into a huddle with his associates, and then told the dean that they would go to McMillin if the meeting there were converted into a public trial of the six students under discipline. To this demand the dean replied, "Unthinkable." A famous last word if there ever was one.

With that, the Sundial crowd broke and ran for the Security Entrance. One of the four smallish ground floor entrances to the bulky granite pile of Low Memorial Library, this entrance owes its name to the presence just inside of the campus police headquarters. The Security Entrance was locked. So, I believe, were the rest of the building's doors. The SDSers were being thwarted in their attempt to stage an indoor demonstration and thus provoke a confrontation which the Administration couldn't overlook, as it had overlooked others on various pretexts, hesitating to enforce a ban which it had imposed too rashly. What the authorities expected to accomplish by the present maneuver, at once so provocative and so petty, remains obscure. But for a few moments the lockout looked effective. The SDSers paused, consulted; and Mark Rudd, less impulsive than many of his followers, continued to ponder Truman's letter as if hoping to find in it some negotiable item. Finally, without Rudd, the others rushed off in the direction of

---

* Herbert Marcuse: (1898–), German-born social philosopher (now U.S. citizen); his books include *Eros and Civilization* (1954) and *One-Dimensional Man* (1965). See pp. 522–34.
* Georges Sorel: (1857–1922), French social philosopher; *Reflections on Violence* (1908), is his best-known book.
* Albert Camus: (1913–60), French writer and social philosopher; the ideological debt mentioned here is especially to his essay *L'Homme révolté* (1951; Eng. trans., *The Rebel*, 1954).
* Mao Tse-tung: (1893–), leader of the Chinese Communists and influential theoretician; his "little red book" *The Thoughts of Chairman Mao* is frequently referred to by students of the radical left.
* Ernesto Che Guevara: (1928–67), Cuban revolutionary and guerrilla leader; killed in Bolivia while attempting to lead a peasant revolution.

Morningside Park. There, ominously overlooking Harlem, construction of a gymnasium was under way in defiance of opinion not only in City Hall but in the University and among the militant elements of Harlem itself. At the gymnasium site, the demonstrators tore down a section of fence and briefly battled some patrolmen, who arrested one demonstrator.

I saw the start of the rush to the Park and later in the day, when I went to Hamilton Hall, headquarters of Columbia College, for a 2 p.m. office hour, a sort of sit-in seemed to be developing in the lobby. At that moment the affair looked insignificant. However, coming down about 3:30 I found the crowd much larger and louder. Its spirit was still festive, though: there were guitars, far-out costumes, acrobatics. The walls were hung with posters of Che Guevara, etc. This quick transformation of the lobby's drab expanses was remarkable. Compared to the radicals of the Thirties, so stodgy and uninventive, these youths seemed to unite the politics of a guerrilla chieftain with the aesthetic flair of a costumer and an interior decorator. Of course they could draw, as Depression radicals could not, on an affluent and elaborate popular culture which was more or less the exclusive property of their generation. Further transformation scenes, involving persons as well as properties, were in store for us in dizzying abundance as the crisis grew.

In the lobby crowd were students I knew. They were excited, talkative, unapologetic, even rather proud of the show. About one feature of it they were, nevertheless, somewhat uneasy. This was the confinement of Dean Harry Coleman in his office about an hour earlier. One of the students maintained that Coleman had been forcibly detained, a bad deal. Another disputed this, saying that Coleman was free to leave at any time and that if he chose to stay that was his business. As it turned out, he was soon declared a hostage for the students arrested earlier at the gym site.

Once out of Hamilton Hall I didn't go back till the following day (Wednesday the 24th). But the radio had brought news of Hamilton's occupation by the blacks and of the seizure of President Kirk's offices in Low Library by the whites. Hence my reluctance to go to the Shakespeare class. Nevertheless I went, found about a third of the students present, asked some questions about *The Winter's Tale* and got some answers, collected the term papers, which were due on that date, called the class off early, and on my way to Hamilton walked past the west wall of Low Library. Several large windows form a stately row along the second story of that wall. An incredible number of rebel students stood or sat in those windows, while others were climbing up to them, or down from them, by the wrought iron grilles conveniently fixed to the smaller windows on the ground floor. Some of the students, again, I recognized. All of them looked fatigued, bedraggled, and a little ghostly, as if they might be washed away by the rain that was beginning to fall. So that's where Kirk's office is, I thought, and only later wondered why, after some twenty-five years on the Columbia faculty,

I had never known this before, or ever cared enough to inquire. A while later, I learned that some patrolmen had entered the President's office earlier, not to remove the rebel students, as might have been expected, but to salvage a Rembrandt painting that hung in those offices. So it turned out that our art-impoverished University secreted a Rembrandt. The things one didn't know!

I went on to the entrance of Hamilton Hall, where much of my academic existence has centered. The life-size bronze of the youthful Alexander Hamilton in front of the building had had his shoes painted red several days earlier—possibly a portent. They were still red; and he now supported a red flag, a placard, and an empty coke bottle. The three glass doors that form the entrance to Hamilton were blocked from within by benches, tables, stacks of mailboxes—familiar schoolhouse objects now converted to the uses of a barricade. Two very young, very serious blacks perched on this uncomfortable pile behind the center door. They were guards.

What was going on farther inside could be seen by cupping one's hands to the glass of the doors and unabashedly spying on one's former domain. The lobby swarmed with busy blacks. Our entire schoolhouse was now definitely their hive. While I watched, several more were let in: mostly adults, evidently members of the Harlem community. Loaded with shopping bags, blankets, towels, and bulky packages intended for the occupants, they were as casual about this traffic as if delivering provisions to the victims of a flood or fire, or helping a friend to stock his new home.

Rumors multiplied in the circle of watching whites. These packages might hold guns. grenades, ammunition, cans of gasoline! But the calm presence of all these blacks might, I thought, argue something different from "Burn, baby, burn." It could mean that Columbia's student blacks had completed their self-taught course in racial separatism and now, with the aid of Harlem brothers and sisters, were settling in, not for good, but for long enough to set the precedent for some lasting take-over in the future. It wouldn't necessarily, or even probably, be a *violent* take-over. It was conceivable that Columbia, half or more of whose income derives from public funds of one kind or another, *could* have its charter revoked by the State of New York, in which case it *could* become the Harlem branch of the State University system. In such a transformation there would be a certain rough justice. But would a preponderantly black Columbia be any better, educationally, humanly, than the present preponderantly white Columbia? I didn't think so.

Watching outside Hamilton I saw a professor approach the two guards with a grin and a "Hello!" He probably needed something in his office. Luckily I didn't urgently need anything in mine: classes had been officially suspended for the rest of the week. The guards ignored the professor. No campus pleasantries or amenities for them. No visible reaction of any kind. And was it that day or later that a banner appeared over the entrance saying MALCOLM X UNIVERSITY? This message seemed a mixture of put-on and—again—portent, especially if one remembered that angry shouts of "To Columbia!" had been heard during the disturbances in Harlem following Dr. Martin Luther King's assassination three weeks earlier.

It was clear that the blacks completely dominated the situation at Columbia. There were only about seventy active student blacks at the University. But, organized into the Students Afro-American Society (SAS), and supported by Harlem CORE, SNCC, and the Mau Mau Society, the strength of each was as the strength of, say, a hundred whites. This weird imbalance of forces had been dramatized the night before in the muted power struggle between the SAS and the SDS-oriented whites in Hamilton. Some of the story of this struggle was in Wednesday's *Spectator,* the undergraduate-edited newspaper; and the rest of it could be heard over WKCR, the student-run radio station. (These two local media were more reliable than the City dailies, and they continued to function admirably throughout the crisis.) What happened in Hamilton during the long, hot, sleepless night of Tuesday-Wednesday was, in its political essence, very much what had happened the year before at the Chicago Conference for a New Politics—a decisive black-white split engineered by the blacks, greatly to their advantage. But this time the split occurred, not only on the parliamentary level as at Chicago, but also on the level of *action,* intense, confused, beset by immediate perils for both factions. I doubt that American students had ever before, even at Berkeley, found themselves engaged in decisions and actions of such moment, locally and nationally.

The all-white demonstration in Hamilton had been gradually infiltrated by blacks, including the professional outside organizers. "The black community is taking over," a SNCC man announced. Two separate caucuses developed. Those in the white caucus debated whether they should leave the building or stay and risk involvement with the blacks, some of them reportedly armed, in an action of indeterminate magnitude and violence. Those whites who wanted to stay hoped for some limited form of action carried out on the basis of black-white solidarity. At dawn, the blacks settled the matter by asking—ordering—the divided whites to leave in a body. They did, very unhappily, their dreams of interracial solidarity disappointed.

There they were, some 300 of them, outside in the dawn light, shaken, exhausted, confused, the doors of Hamilton barricaded behind them. What then came into play among them was a kind of "challenge and response" psychology which was to operate throughout the entire crisis of the next few weeks. Some people have dismissed this mental state as the low-grade "chicken" psychology of gang warfare. But I think it is more accurately described as a system of competitive militancy. Their militancy challenged by that of the blacks, the whites could only respond as militantly as possible. They were soon streaking across campus to the formidable bulk of Low Library, the University's administrative and ceremonial center from which they had been locked out the day before. There they smashed through the Security Entrance and occupied the President's suite. In doing so they incurred large temporary losses. About half of them fled at the noise of the door being smashed; a lot more leapt from the windows when the police arrived for the Rembrandt. But some forty-seven stayed and many others returned later. Why did their occupancy of Low survive the removal of the Rembrandt? Because, as I understand it, the Administration feared that to evacuate the whites in Low would have been to invite reprisals from Hamilton and from a Harlem still smouldering in the aftermath of the King murder. Besides, Dean Coleman was still a Hamilton hostage.

By Wednesday afternoon the group in Low felt secure enough to act as if this were no mere sit-in demonstration but a take-over demonstration. So, by way of making themselves at home, they went about doing all those things—daring, ingenious, outrageous—that everybody in the world was soon to hear about. They re-connected lights and phones, explored the President's files for tell-tale documents, found his Xerox machine out of order and repaired it to copy the documents, discovered (so they claimed) his World War II draft card and sent it back to his draft board, smoked his cigars, drank his sherry, worked at his desk, lined up to use his bathroom, inspected the books on his shelves, vacuumed the rugs, slept wherever a surface offered, held interminable meetings, climbed in and out of windows, and received guests. The guests included a distinguished professor of history. Wearing the academic robe in which he, uniquely at Columbia, conducts his classes, he arrived "like Batman" (as somebody said) by the grille-and-windowsill route to urge their departure. But it was the brave, conscientious professor who did the departing.

They had—in their word—"liberated" the President's office and everything usable in it. By doing so they had also released in themselves latent energies of all kinds, from the creative to the euphoric to the malicious. Euphoric, it seemed to me, was the impulse that led them to read, copy, and publicize portions of the President's correspondence. In the long run this procedure was self-defeating. It indulged the revolutionary delusions of the fanatical few in their own ranks, while submitting too many others to a test of political sophistication which they were glad to flunk.

The euphoria, I must add, was no overnight phenomenon. It persisted beyond the first dramatic hours in Low, consolidated itself as a political force on campus, became a contagion, spread to large numbers of students and younger teachers who, I would guess, by normal temper and conviction, were scarcely to be identified with the fanatical few. In other words, what had originated as a demonstration began to assume in their minds the stature of a revolution—a power seizure effected within a single institution which they regarded as a microcosm of the whole society. True, this delusion—as I fear it must be called—was unwittingly encouraged by the grim intransigence of the central Administration, which, becoming virtually invisible, refusing to negotiate with the rebels "under coercion," threatening police action, was like an embattled government-in-exile. Their fear of the consequences of the demonstration seems to have amounted to sheer physical repugnance toward meeting its leaders in person. David Truman confided to a *Newsweek* interviewer that it made him "uncomfortable to be in the same room with" Mark Rudd. (It is reported, however, that David Truman did on at least one occasion try, without success, to make personal contact with the rebels in the President's office.)

Still, the delusion remained a delusion, whatever its causes. And although industrious rebel researchers were able to come up with historical precedents for their "liberation" of the President's letters (for example, Benjamin Franklin's interception of the Governor Hutcheson letters in 1775), these precedents had the effect of further confusing the issue. The issue as I saw it, was the precise function of demonstrations in the realm of radical politics. The leftist English critic, John Berger, writing in *New Society* (May 28, 1968), observes that "the aims of a demonstration are symbolic." They are "rehearsals . . . of revolutionary awareness. . . . The demonstrators' view of the city surrounding their stage changes. By demonstrating, they manifest a greater freedom and independence—a greater creativity even, although the product is only symbolic—than they can ever achieve individually or collectively when pursuing their regular lives. In their regular pursuits they only modify circumstances; by demonstrating they symbolically oppose their very existence to circumstances." Up to a point "the rehearsal of revolutionary awareness" at Columbia was the more effective in its symbolic character, the richer in "creativity," because, unlike average street demonstrations—which, as Berger says, symbolize the revolutionary seizure of whole cities—the Columbia event took place almost entirely on the confined territory formed by the University's walled-in Morningside campus. This territory became a kind of artificial city, but *only* an artificial one. To assume, as the far-outers assumed, that the University could be subverted, as a city state or a national state can be subverted by large-scale revolutionary action, was to mistake the symbol for the reality, and thus to threaten the future of the University under any conceivable management. To my mind, the rifling and publicizing of the letters was a symbol of revolutionary hubris, not of revolutionary consciousness.

For the rest, the inventive zeal let loose by the Low demonstrators was, as I said, to be a powerful force on campus for many days and nights. Columbia became the setting for a continuous "Happening" in which the political content was fused with the generally antic form and the meaning of the whole act was —or seemed to be—in the act itself. Reporters and photographers flocked to Morningside to record the scandalous comedy of it all. With raggle-taggle students draped all over its classic façades, the University's austere campus had never before been so photogenic. But the actions were not *always* antic and their meaning was not *wholly* in the actions themselves. On the contrary they attracted many uncommitted students to the cause of the demonstrators.

Being "where the action is" had acquired political status. Meanwhile many other students were driven to extremes of opposition, an opposition which soon consolidated itself in the quasi-vigilante group known as the Majority Coalition (or "Jocks" since a number of them were athletes). By Wednesday afternoon, moreover, the demonstrators were ready with a list of demands, duly mimeographed and distributed on campus. The demands boiled down to three: no gym in Morningside Park, no ties with the Pentagon-related Institute for Defense Analysis, and amnesty for all the demonstrators in the present action as well as in that of March 27. But the amnesty demand was declared to be non-negotiable: acceptance of it by the Administration was a condition for any transactions at all. Similarly, the Administration had announced itself to be opposed to amnesty as firmly as the demonstrators were for it. So the list of demands looked like a bid for further confrontations from both parties, culminating sooner or later in the supreme confrontation of a police raid.

It was, however, only the fearsome presence of the Hamilton blacks that enabled the whites to hold out in Low, at least through the first day (Wednesday) of their occupancy. After Wednesday—since nothing succeeds like success or, in political terms, nothing makes for *de facto* legitimacy like staying put—they collected, as I said, enough moderate support to survive in Low more or less on their own, and presently to add three more buildings to their empire. With three entire buildings and a presidential suite for whites, and one entire building for blacks, the rebels had, one sardonic professor noted, the makings of an independent "university complex," duly separatist, and lacking nothing toward the inauguration of intramural sports except a gymnasium. Something like this possibility was to occur retrospectively to Archibald Cox of the Harvard Law School, who became the chairman of a fact-finding commission set up after the April 30 police raid. Questioning a witness, Cox asked: "Did it ever occur to the Administration to just *leave* the demonstrators in the buildings and go on with the university's business?" "No," replied the witness, "that was unthinkable."

So a tenuous solidarity did actually exist between the two racial groups until the police raid. The declared demands of the blacks coincided with those of the whites. After the raid the blacks, making their own deal with the Administration, agreed to a peaceful evacuation of Hamilton under the auspices of the police, a couple of watchful city officials, and an elder statesman of the black movement, Kenneth Clark. In the month-long student strike that ensued, the blacks took no active part, and as a large-scale campus force they have seldom been visible since. Presumably, they decided—or it was decided for them—that their point had been sufficiently made by their occupying Hamilton for a week and leaving it neat as a pin. I mention the neatness because the University authorities made so much of it in their propaganda, possibly by way of trying to justify their separate treatment of the blacks. If so, their defense was, logically, rather vulnerable. It was as if the illegal occupation of buildings were somehow less illegal if the occupiers were good housekeepers. In any case, there was to be no special treatment for the whites, and no guard of honor to preside over their final dragging-out on April 30. If the authorities were less afraid of the whites, they were also, it seems, more determined to punish them, or at least to make certain of punishing their leaders. "Whatever happens, *you'll* be expelled!" one high official impulsively shouted at Mark Rudd on a public occasion.

II

The official propaganda was one thing. The tightness of the spot the officials were on was another: fearful, pitiable, grotesque. Physically they were confined to substitute quarters on the ground floor of Low where they communed endlessly with representatives of the Trustees, of City Hall, of Harlem, of the police. Emotionally and politically they were confined by less tangible but more serious considerations. Among these *may* have been: personal anger, understandable but unstatesmanly, at the invasion of presidential privacy by the demonstrators upstairs; belief that the rebellion was merely an extreme symptom of a debilitated and overly permissive society against which President Kirk had inveighed in certain public addresses; inefficient operation of the complex Trustees-Kirk-Truman chain of command (three days notice was required by statute to convene a meeting of the Trustees); refusal to appoint an emergency committee of faculty and students to advise Administration members, mediate between them and the demonstrators, keep them posted on campus affairs, above all on the rapidly swelling ranks of student protestors. The authorities' lack of information on this last point, their persistence in the belief that only "a small disruptive minority" was involved, made great trouble for all, including the undermanned police contingent, when the April 30 raid occurred. Testifying weeks later to the Cox Commission, the Dean of the Graduate Faculties, who is third in command among Administration members, admitted that he had been "flabbergasted" at the multitude of demonstrators found in the buildings by the police. Instead of the estimated total of 350, he said, there had been 300 in Fayerweather alone.

Contributing crucially to the tightness of the spot the Administration was on was the urgency of the time element. This element, however, the Administration itself clearly introduced into the situation from the start. Early Wednesday, one official said, "There's going to be a limit" on the time allowed the demonstrators; while another made the situation still clearer by saying, "We are making every effort to reach a solution without *resorting to police action*" (my italics). Only as the end approached did the active faculty—and, I think, many of the demonstrators—suspect that it had been more or less predetermined, both as to the date and to the means (i.e., police action). Meanwhile, faculty members and demonstrators had been consulting together in mediation sessions and, seemingly, in good faith, as if the end were *not* fully determined, as to either date or means.

What few people outside the Administration quite knew at the time, however, was the exact extent and nature of the outside pressure being exerted upon it to act quickly and firmly. The authorities did, it is true, make a great deal of the numerous letters and phone calls they received from other schools urging upon Columbia the kind of prompt and decisive action which would keep the infection of student revolt from spreading to their own premises. Out of these appeals, which no one doubts were many and impassioned, the authorities constructed for Columbia a messianic role. Columbia alone could save academic America! This was a terrible error. Columbia could best have helped to save academic America by first saving itself. Doing this required that the authorities move with all *deliberate* speed. They did the opposite, and by resorting to speed without sufficient deliberation they imperiled Columbia's own future.

The severest pressure on the Administration probably came from the alumni —or rather from four members of the Board of Directors of the College Alumni Association who evidently delegated to themselves the privilege of speaking for a total membership of about 25,000.

This point can be documented. Copies of a letter of April 27 addressed to President Kirk by the four alumni have circulated widely on campus. The letter formed a part of a document issued several weeks later, during the student strikes that followed the police raid of April 30, by a group of sixteen athletes, including the all-star basketball players, David Newmark and James McMillian. The sixteen had been invited to attend an official alumni dinner to receive awards. But they were subsequently *disinvited* when the athletes asked permission to read at the dinner a statement of their own position on the crisis. The letter of April 27 to President Kirk from the four alumni read, in part:

> The take-over of Hamilton Hall and other University buildings, students ransacking and vandalizing your office, the complete disruption of the University—this is anarchy and mob rule and cannot and must not be tolerated.
> Accordingly, we urge upon you the following considerations:
> 1. The ultimatum of the demonstrators must be rejected;
> 2. The Administration must retain the right to discipline and that right should not be surrendered or delegated in this situation;
> 3. Discipline must be invoked and it must be swift, strong and appropriate to the circumstances.
> We commend you and Dr. Truman for the firmness which you have shown in not capitulating to mob rule. We urge you to remain steadfast.
> Any action short of the foregoing will, in our view, result in an invitation for further trouble of a higher order; further, the affection and *support* [my italics] which you have from the alumni will be lost.

It was only natural and decent for the alumni to express solidarity with the President in his distress. But to mingle threats with the sentiments of solidarity, and actually to specify, in their three points, the precise procedures he should use in settling the crisis, was to stage a "confrontation" of their own, and one which, as the word "support" probably implies, had important financial implications. But the fact is that the President, resentful though he may well have been at this rude intrusion into University affairs, accepted, for whatever reasons of his own, the alumni ultimatum. He acted in a manner that was "appropriate to the circumstances," namely, called in the police.

The sixteen athletes refused to be excluded from the alumni dinner. While the alumni were dining inside the Columbia Club, in midtown New York, the sixteen picketed the building outside, wearing their C jackets, *in a rainstorm*—to be grudgingly admitted after a couple of hours on the insistence of younger alumni at the dinner. Another lockout of students had been enacted, this time not of radical students but of just ordinary ones. A *New York Times* sportswriter made a fine ironic little story out of the incident; Dickens couldn't have done it better.

But the sixteen were not a band of helpless Dickensian waifs shut out in a storm by a lot of Mr. Podsnaps.* They had had a Columbia education!—and on top of that a month-long extra-curricular course in crisis politics (a few, I am told, were "reformed Jocks"). The statement they had prepared for the alumni is headed WHY WE ARE HERE and is better formulated than were most such documents issued during the troubles by other groups, student or faculty or Administration. It has the further advantage, for me as the author of this article, that it documents fully the general state of opinion prevailing among those many students whom I have vaguely called the "moderates." For these reasons I include the important part of their statement in full.

> 1. The "fundamental rights of free speech and assembly" were abrogated by the University Administration. President Kirk had issued an arbitrary ban on indoor demonstrations. But far more important than this, free speech is meaningless at Columbia when it exists in a vacuum and is unheeded by Administration officials.
>
> 2. One cannot divorce the issues from the events at Columbia. The issues here *are* the Institute for Defense Analysis, the gymnasium, and the restructuring of the University. The occupation of buildings by the demonstrators came after many attempts by students, faculty, and community members to oppose I.D.A. and the gym through legitimate channels. The Administration was repeatedly unresponsive to the demands of these groups.
>
> 3. The Administration must *now* delegate disciplinary powers to the students and faculty. Those most involved in student life are the most qualified to pass judgment on disciplinary affairs.
>
> 4. An overwhelming majority of students supported the demands of the demonstrators in a university-wide referendum conducted by the

---

* Mr. Podsnap: a complacent, self-righteous character in Charles Dickens's *Our Mutual Friend*.

Ted Kremer Society and the Van Am Society [two undergraduate honor societies]. The Strike Committee now represents 5,000 students. The demonstrators and their supporters were never a "small militant minority."

5. We find it deplorable that in the [administration's] statement issued directly after the police action on campus, there was *no* mention whatsoever of the brutal and terrifying violence committed by the police who were called onto this campus by the Columbia Administration. By resorting to this police action the University once again displayed its intransigence and unwillingness to negotiate. This action inevitably resulted in the aggravation of the situation. In addition, many people, including faculty and innocent bystanders, were injured by the police. Do the members of the Alumni Association actually support police intervention on campus?

6. The Board of Directors of the Alumni Association has claimed to speak for 25,000 alumni. Do they represent your views accurately enough to threaten the Administration with loss of alumni support? This coercion may well have contributed to President Kirk's decision to bring the police on campus.

OUR PROPOSALS

1. We believe that the University exists for its faculty and its students. The University also exists within a community. These groups must play a *significant role* in the decision-making process of the University. The ultimate role of the Administration should be to implement and co-ordinate the will of students, faculty, and community.

2. Civil and criminal charges must be dropped against all demonstrators; discipline should be handled within the University by faculty and students.

3. The gym and I.D.A. are urgent and pressing considerations and action must be taken on them immediately. We do not want these issues to be submerged in committees for yet another year.

Considering the powerful and unique position occupied by the Alumni, we strongly urge you to help us to implement the necessary reforms in our University.

The sixteen signatures that follow I omit.

III

Because the Administration refused to negotiate "under coercion"—while, that is, the rebels remained in the buildings—the only other permanent University body with any claims to authority, and hence with any grounds for attempting negotiations, was the faculty. But the authority of the Columbia faculty is clearly defined only in respect to academic affairs. It is particularly amorphous in respect to administrative affairs. Moreover, the total Columbia faculty is actually made up of a number of individual and quite separate faculties (of Medicine,

Law, Business, Engineering, etc.) which until the crisis had never been convened as a single body. Further, these several faculties have widely divergent interests and include members with differing ideas of their roles and responsibilities as teachers. In addition, the members of Columbia's faculty system have recently been subjected to a complication of loyalties which if not peculiar to Columbia has become exceptionally acute here. On the one hand, our Vietnam-fevered students have been expecting—and getting—more sympathetic attention from us individually and as a body than ever before—attention which, on the war issue, can amount to outright identification. On the other hand, we have—or had—equally personal affinities with the Administration which, from the Vice President down to the local deans, is now packed with men who recently belonged to the faculty and who, as in the prime case of David Truman—elevated to his present rank only last year—we think of as colleagues still. Finally, as I have said, Columbia has had no faculty-administration committee or all-University senate, such as exists in certain other universities, to act in emergencies.[1]

In the present Columbia emergency, the gap was filled by a self-appointed body that came to be known as the Ad Hoc Faculty Group (AHFG). The nucleus of what was to be the AHFG met informally on Wednesday morning the 24th. Those present were greatly alarmed by the possibilities of destruction and bloodshed which seemed to be implicit in the blacks' occupation of Hamilton and the confinement of Dean Coleman. The discussion was agitated. Out of it emerged, in embryonic form, two considerations that were to become major issues in the later deliberations of the AHFG. One was the strongly felt necessity of forestalling police action. The other was the necessity of setting up some kind of body—students, faculty, administrators—to decide methods of disciplining the offenders in the present demonstration. Without such a body, disciplinary action would rest in the hands of the President and the Trustees, in whom all final powers—legislative, executive, *and* judicial—are vested by our 150-year-old statutes.

Both of these concerns were embodied in a resolution introduced by professor of sociology Daniel Bell to an emergency meeting of the *College* faculty Wednesday afternoon. The meeting was a curiously casual affair. At the start, more than a half hour was spent debating the first clause of the Bell resolution, which of necessity had been composed in haste. The first clause read: "A university exists as a community dedicated to rational discourse, and the use of communication and persuasion as the means of furthering discourse."

Such an abstract appeal to first principles would be a luxury at any time. It was an absurdity just then, when the necessary corollary to it—the recognition

---

1. An all-University senate composed of faculty, student, and Administration representatives was established in 1969. This, like other reforms demanded by various groups during the 1968 crisis—the abandonment of the Morningside gyms, the disengagement of the University from IDA and from uncontrolled Defense contracts in general—soon ceased to be the concern of the radicals alone.

that a university is also a *social institution*—was being luridly dramatized in several ways: by the fact that we were meeting in a science classroom instead of in our usual quarters, the elegant Faculty Room adjacent to the President's now "liberated" offices; by the shouts of mutually hostile student groups outside; by the sudden arrival of Dean Coleman, just released from his round-the-clock confinement in a Hamilton Hall threatened—as it appeared—by an outbreak of fires and gun battles. Some "community"! Some "discourse"! The meeting did nonetheless pass the Bell resolution with several modifications. These represented compromises appropriate to a faculty now clearly divided into, roughly, right, left, and center contingents. In the resolution the demonstrators were condemned; amnesty was tacitly refused them; opposition to police action was cautiously affirmed; suspension of further work on the present gym site was urged pending the approval of "a group of community spokesmen to be appointed by the Mayor"; and the disciplinary body proposed at the morning meeting was voted in, having acquired the name of a "tripartite committee."

President Kirk, who briefly chaired the meeting, took occasion to remind us that "under the present statutes of the University, its role [that of the tripartite committee] would be purely advisory." He made no mention at this time of any disposition to have the statutes changed by the Trustees, whose "property" they are; although later on, when the general situation was much worse, he did give vague indications of such a disposition. When, however, the tripartite committee was finally established (as the Joint Committee on Disciplinary Affairs), after the April 30 police raid, the President harassed its feeble infant existence to such an extent that the committee members made reluctant concessions which proved unfortunate all round.

Indeed, I have come to think that the whole triparite committee issue as developed by the AHFG, which took it over from the College faculty meeting, was a mistake. For one thing, the motives behind it were mixed, or at least confused, in our minds at the time. On the one hand, the motives were both humane and politic. We wanted to make it as certain as possible that the disciplining of the demonstrators would not be so severe as to make for further strife on campus. On the other hand, we capitalized on the general emergency to attempt a cautious power play of our own by way of the proposed Tripartite Committee. It didn't work, owing to Kirk's stubborn shrewdness in defending the prerogatives of his office. Meanwhile the President's qualified acceptance of the committee bred illusions among the membership concerning the reality of our little power. Further, those members of the AHFG who set about holding mediation sessions with the demonstrators were in the awkward position of using, however cautiously, this and other merely *projected* reforms as a bargaining point.

On Thursday, April 25, the AHFG acquired its name, together with a steering committee of sixteen professors, many of them specialists in the relevant disciplines of government, law, history, and sociology. The AHFG also acquired a general membership composed of the approximately 200 professors (junior staff was later admitted) who signed the AHFG statement Wednesday afternoon. The statement's contents approximated those of the College faculty resolution voted Wednesday afternoon, but the severity of the crisis was described in terms far more emphatic and authoritative. Point 4 read: "Until this crisis is settled, we will stand before the occupied buildings to prevent forcible entry by the police or others." Finally, the AHFG acquired a regular place of meeting: the Graduate Students Lounge in 301 Philosophy Hall where the students are normally served tea and cookies and provided with other much needed forms of assistance. With its comfortable chairs and sofas in green leather, its immensely tall, heavily draped, windows extending around three sides, 301 Philosophy became our political clubroom throughout the April days. It was the scene of crowded gatherings; of reports from the members of the steering committee who were carrying on mediation sessions with the demonstrators; of endless speeches; of disputes which in a few cases (extreme left and extreme right) resulted in walkouts; of rumors; of excited announcements of sudden emergencies on campus. In the long run, the AHFG's efforts toward conciliation were a failure—or, as an original member of the Group, professor of anthropology Marvin Harris, has asserted in a brilliant and indispensable article (*Nation*, June 10, 1968), in effect a sell-out and a disaster because the faculty as a whole failed to act independently and decisively. In any case, mediation between the intransigent Administration and the intransigent "hard core" demonstrators proved futile in the circumstances. Amnesty remained non-negotiable for both sides. Hostility toward the mediators increased on both sides. On Saturday the 27th Mark Rudd rushed panting into 301 Philosophy to shout that the whole procedure was "bullshit."

For me, however, the Group meetings were vastly instructive. While Marvin Harris's drastic conclusions seem to rest on the assumption that Columbia's faculty was capable of instant "politicalization," my own reaction was the opposite. I was amazed at the extent to which we *were* "politicalized," and within a single week. With this in mind, I believed that concerted and independent faculty action would be an achievement of the future.

Listening to the chief speakers of the AHFG, I occasionally asked myself if they constituted any kind of an intellectually cohesive group which might be said to form a Columbia "elite." Elite, yes, I decided, but without the overtones of exclusiveness attached to that word. No faculty group is so cohesive at Columbia as to constitute itself a ruling circle, even if it wanted to. Indeed, it is not unusual for an exceptional individual, such as the late professor of English Andrew Chiappe, to be thought of as an elite of one. Still, most of the Ad Hoc leaders shared enough intellectual common ground to cause, not the deliberate exclusion of others, but the necessity on the part of certain others to exclude themselves, to go their own way. One of these was the great mathematician and pioneer Columbia reformer, the lean gentle quixotic Serge Lang. Another was Marvin Harris, a powerful speaker, whose logic never lapsed, whose syntax never wavered, even when his face went literally black with passion. No, in the leaders' eyes Lang and Harris were not politically "reliable." From the start they were for granting amnesty or some rhetorical simulacrum of it. So was I (and so were many others) after about the third day. In the past my own differences with the "elite" had been a matter more of temperament than of fully formulated or expressed dissent on my part. From their point of view amnesty wasn't a reliable position, politically; it was too simple to be arguable in an intellectual milieu where only the conventionally arguable position was the possible. The mere thought of amnesty annihilated that universe of logics, structures, processes, continuities, compromises, pragmatic realism, anti-ideology, "discourse," and "dialogue" which most of the leaders inhabited by reason partly of the subjects they taught, partly of the generation they belonged to.

So I have, after all, characterized the Ad Hoc leaders, or a majority of them, as an intellectually cohesive group: the post New Deal, post World War II intelligentsia. Naturally, their own talents and good will, with a little help from the *Zeitgeist*,* had made them influential—but, again, not wholly dominant—at Columbia. And naturally they chose to exercise their special talents and temperaments in those strenuous, and well-meaning, efforts at mediation with the radical students, even at the risk of their turning out to be—as in fact they were—as quixotic as Serge Lang. In any case it was a pleasure to study their several styles as speakers, together with their efforts, in some cases, to *preserve* their styles amid the terrible identity-devouring convulsions of the crisis: Allan Westin (public law and government), with his man-of-destiny manner, his powerful compact figure, an artist of parliamentary procedure to the extent of audaciously violating procedure when he saw fit; Immanuel Wallerstein (sociology), with his affecting wailing-wall rhetoric and gesticulation; Allen Silver (sociology), quiet, concentrated, intense, suffering, his considerable wit sounding as if it, too, were wrung from his world anguish; and Robert Belknap (Russian) whose perfect logic and selfless adherence to principle make him a one-man vindicator of liberalism.

If the mediation efforts were quixotic, so was another specialty of the AHFG: the patrols we organized, partly to keep the peace between the demonstrators and the Majority Coalitionists, or "Jocks," partly to manifest our opposition to the use of police in the crisis. This passionate opposition to the police was, I think, the one great stabilizing and unifying element in the AHFG. The impulse behind it would probably bear extensive analysis—legal, psychological, and phenomenological. On our parts, however, it was just a matter of instinct. But the instinct proved right. The police action resorted to by the authorities on April 30—and again, on a smaller scale but with more vicious effects on May 22–23—was catastrophic for the cause of enlightened peace and unity at Columbia for months to come.

* the *Zeitgeist:* the spirit of the age.

IV

When, as a patrol member, you weren't attending meetings in 301 Philosophy you were on the patrol line alongside some occupied building, wearing a white armband made out of a rolled up handkerchief like an improvised tourniquet. You worked in daily and nightly shifts. And, between your attendance at meetings and your presence on the patrol line, there was little time for sleep, reading, food, reflection. Memory failed; all happenings seemed somehow simultaneous in the mind. The passing days added up to a single unit of time, unbroken and seemingly endless.

The increasingly hallucinatory atmosphere of our lives was intensified by the unpredictableness of happenings on campus. There were continual emergencies that required your hasty departure from your apartment or from 301 Philosophy to the scene of action. Once it is the sudden arrival at the Broadway gate of some fifty members of the Mau Mau Society led by Charles X Kenyatta, many of them in jungle dress, the kids swinging bicycle chains, the whole band demanding entry to College Walk, while the jocks, a couple of hundred strong, demand their exclusion from campus, and Dean Coleman with the aid of the faculty patrol seeks to "cool it"—and finally does. Again, at about 10 p.m. on Thursday the 25th, it is the jocks again, this time moving on Fayerweather, determined to drag out the rebels who had earlier added this fourth building to their university-complex. No city police or campus police are on hand to intercede. So 301 Philosophy is largely emptied of Ad Hocs to serve as riot police. There is no bull-horn, but Seymour Melman (industrial engineering) has a voice (and spirit) of roughly equivalent carrying power. He uses it. The jocks hesitate, listen. An exchange of witticisms between Westin and a boy in the crowd relaxes things. Belknap—calm, sensible, teacherly—says, "I am Robert Belknap of the Russian Department, chairman of freshman humanities. You've read all those books by Plato and Aristotle and Thucydides. You know that violence is no good." The crowd attends, but one youth slips around the corner to climb unseen on to a windowsill. "If you go inside you'll have the blood on your mind for a lifetime," somebody quietly says. The youth climbs down. The jocks are invited to send a delegation to the AHFG meeting. They agree to do so and the crowd disperses—for the time being.

Actual violence does briefly erupt early Friday, this time from the city police. It is about 1 a.m. and I am just leaving Philosophy for some reason when I see David Truman striding into the building with a very grim face, and naturally I follow him back inside. Taking his stand at the rear of the crowd, he says, "Gentlemen, you're not going to like what I have to tell you. Five minutes ago President Kirk was on the phone to call for the police." Since the police call defies AHFG sentiment, Truman may have felt that he owed it to his old colleagues to at least warn them, at whatever cost to his dignity. If so, this is decent of him and the cost is great. He promptly leaves amid cries of "Shame," "Liar," and "I resign." The meeting is in an uproar. Most of us rush outdoors, I to patrol Hamilton with about fifty others. There on the steps we form lines three deep, locking arms for warmth as well as solidarity. Inside Hamilton, the blacks show no awareness of our presence. In front of us a crowd of student sympathizers masses, some of them passing us containers of coffee. Occasional hoots of derision and menace come out the windows of Hartley, the residence hall adjacent to Hamilton. The hooters are jocks, evidently. A cherry bomb explodes in the narrow court between the buildings, making loud reverberations. Out of the darkness, one by one, come several eminent visitors to pass along our line, reviewing the troops: City Hall men, an unidentified Harlemite, the sympathetic Paul O'Dwyer, shaking our hands as he passes. After a couple of hours somebody announces that the raid has been called off and work on the gym site suspended. The "abortive bust," as it came to be called, was over.

So at Hamilton our heroism went unrewarded that night, except that our presence there, and the presence of faculty lines at other occupied buildings, notably at Low, where plainclothesmen did attack the line and injure one man, made the Administration call off the raid. Meanwhile, several AHFG members had gone inside Low to join Mayor Lindsay's aides in urging restraint on the Administration. They report of finding Truman in a torment of indecision. One cause of his indecision may have been communicated to him by police officials: if the police were not used that night they would be unavailable in sufficient numbers until Sunday night at the earliest, because so many of them would be needed to control the Peace demonstrations and counter-demonstrations scheduled for the weekend (Saturday and Sunday the 27th and 28th) in several parts of the city.

The Administration seems to have tried to turn this delay to advantage. About noon on Friday a College dean remarked to me in a confidential tone, "We are educating the faculty." He meant, I think, that the Administration was granting us time to exhaust our mediation efforts, with the expectation that we would then become reconciled to police action. By Saturday, when Rudd made his historic cry of "bullshit," the attempts at mediation, conducted as they were without substantial support from the administration, *had* failed. A number of perfectly conscientious professors *were* reconciled to police action. But a good many others were *not* reconciled to it. Communication between the AHFG and the Administration became increasingly strained. There were intemperate public outbursts from high University officials and members of the Board of Trustees. These were taken by many to mean that the few conciliatory gestures made by the University authorities were bluff. A fifth domain was added to the rebel empire: Mathematics Hall, with a red flag flying from the roof, and the professional SDS organizer, Tom Hayden, more or less in charge. By Saturday some 600 police were on and around the campus, despite the Peace demonstrations.

The meetings in 301 Philosophy became wilder and stranger, especially at night, with the room's expanses taxed to capacity, the air dim with tobacco smoke. Outside, watchers pressed against the tall window in spectral masses. Along the north wall the row of windows was cut by a diagonal line made by the ramp leading up to Revlon Plaza outside. The watchers strung upward along the ramp diminished in size till, at the top, only their faces were visible, floating in air like disembodied cherubs or gargoyles. (The watchers at the top were seated on the ramp in order to see in.) Fingers slyly inserted themselves under the window frames to raise the frames so that our orations could be heard as well as seen. "Shut the windows, please," Westin the chairman repeatedly and patiently directed. As public figures we commanded vaster and more excited audiences than any of us could ever have had, or wanted, as mere teachers!

When we were outside on patrol the fantastic nature of our operations became unmistakable. Politically, this patrolling was a delicate business. We could be— and were—accused of, on the one hand protecting the demonstrators and, on the other hand, of sealing them off. In fact our platonic neutrality was almost impossible to maintain. Physical nearness to the rebels brought us closer to them in sympathy, hardship for hardship, danger for danger. And qualm for qualm, too (assuming *they* felt any), because their illegal acts were forcing us to engage in acts which if not illegal were certainly unconventional, turning teachers into cop watchers. Just as the demonstrators constantly improvised, so did we. Indeed certain of the Religious Counselors in our ranks excelled at improvisation, verbal and acrobatic, making some of us wish that God *hadn't* died. So, day and night, as violence threatened and the number of cops on campus steadily multiplied, and my block of West 116th Street filled up with squad cars, mobile information units, busloads of bored and waiting patrolmen, other busloads of hefty plainclothesmen in sweaters or sport coats, limousines bearing policewomen in chic uniforms, splendidly mounted police from (presumably) the theater district, our ambiguous patrolling went on.

v

Along the west wall of Low, on Sunday and Monday, real action threatened. Several hundred members of the Majority Coalition, their original ranks increased by the arrival of girl friends and of graduate recruits from the professional schools, moved in to block further deliveries of food to the demonstrators occupying the President's offices. The Ad Hoc patrol was strung along a narrow ledge (an architectural not a geological ledge) beneath the demonstrators' windows. A twelve-foot strip of turf separated us from a low-clipped privet hedge bordering a brick walk where the Coalitionists first gathered. On this accidental playground a heady three-cornered game commenced at close quarters. It got tougher when, after several impatient hours, the Coalitionists suddenly leaped the hedge *en masse* and gathered on the turf between ledge and hedge, within grabbing distance of the patrol—if either party, patrol or Coalitionists, had wished to do any grabbing. How the Ad Hoc group tried—and failed—to set up rules for this game may be seen from the following instructions, drafted and mimeographed at about 3 a.m. Sunday.

POLICY ON PATROLLING LOW LIBRARY

28 April, 1968

1. Faculty will not permit ingress of persons [i.e. demonstrators and sympathizers] except for specially designated couriers accompanied by a mediator or a member of the Steering Committee of the Ad Hoc Faculty Group.
2. If an individual reaches the ledge with food, he may hand it up; however, he may not approach the ledge via the steps.
3. Faculty will not assist individuals to run a blockade at the hedge.
4. Blockaders at the hedge will not be permitted on the ledge.
5. Faculty will aid the ingress of required medical supplies.

The hedge-ledge affair has become historic at Columbia. It epitomized, among other things, the eccentric uses to which our exuberant neo-Renaissance architecture (as full of inviting surfaces, ascents, and footholds as a jungle gym) and not so exuberant landscaping were being put, not to mention the eccentric roles now adopted by faculty members *vis-à-vis* the fiercely polarized bands of their students.

The game got still gamier as Sunday passed into Monday. Then rebels from the Math commune started tossing groceries to rebels in Low over the heads of the Coalitionists and the faculty patrol, while the athletic Coalitionists—barehanded or with bats, tennis rackets, and food trays from the dining hall—sought to intercept the groceries in their flight. Fights broke out—which members of the patrol or other peace-makers usually cooled. For a while on Monday afternoon my post was at one end of the ledge, adjoining a ground floor entrance to Low which some of the jocks were impatient to enter. From there I stared down into the leaders' imploring or defiant faces. "If they ever caught Rudd they'd tear him to pieces," another patrol member said in my ear. Though unbelieving, I knew that his remark was definitely in the bleaker mood of the moment.

Other moods were grotesquely orchestrated with that one. The weather—that weekend as throughout most of the crisis—was ideally the weather for a ball game, a sail, a picnic, a garden wedding—the sky deeply blue, the spring sunlight inexhaustibly benign. Below me the strip between hedge and ledge was full of sturdy pink tulips, and "Don't step on the tulips!" was one slogan everybody took up. The tulips stayed intact until two very little black boys, aged about ten, sneaked onto the ledge from somewhere. Could they pick some flowers? So they pulled several up by the bulbous roots, shouting, "Look, they got *onions* on them!" Just above me, a student I knew settled in an open window and began to thumb a guitar. In the other windows other rebels began to serenade us from above with "Solidarity Forever." Briefly, the yearning innocence of the oldtime

Labor song, and of the singers' voices, silenced the crowd below. For me, momentarily, hedge, ledge, jocks, rebels, faculty, tulips, little blacks, newsmen, and sunlight all resolved themselves into the constituents of a painted scene, unforgettable.

The scene inside the occupied buildings was, we knew, less idyllic during that weekend. The occupants were getting ready for the police raid that was generally thought imminent. Barricades were strengthened. Precautions were taken against possible assaults with chemical MACE. Individually each demonstrator pondered where he (or she) would take his stand and whether he would accept or resist arrest, or maybe "split" beforehand. A Fayerweather student writing in *Rat* (May 3–16) says, "each liberated area was different, ours being wracked with political debate, wrangling and tension. . . . Anyone who wanted could have left." The Fayerweather tensions came about because many occupants wanted, *primarily,* not a reformed world, but a reformed Columbia, one in which more self-determination would be possible for all, including workers in the University cafeterias.

In Fayerweather, too, a faction questioned the wisdom of the total amnesty demand and showed some willingness to consider an alternative—uniform, or collective, discipline—proposed by Ad Hoc mediators. Similar differences were possible, even in militant Math, where the commune spirit was especially exalted. But the several liberated areas finally stuck together, thanks chiefly to the persistence of the competitive militancy I have mentioned, with the supremely cohesive Hamilton blacks setting the pace for all the liberated areas, from Low to Math, to Avery, to Fayerweather.

At dawn on Sunday the 28th a Western Union operator waked me to read on the phone the text of a telegram from President Kirk that was sent to all members of the Morningside faculties. The convening of these traditionally separate entities in a joint meeting was unprecedented. President Kirk evidently wished to explore the sentiment and/or solicit the approval of faculties (Law, Business, Journalism, Engineering) whose members were not so likely to be found among the liberal arts activists who made up the Ad Hoc group's majority. There had been advanced knowledge of this joint meeting. For presentation to it, the Ad Hoc steering committee had drafted a document known formally as The April 28th Resolution and informally as the "bitter pill" because it proposed solutions to the crisis which exacted hard sacrifices from all parties, not excluding the Administration. The heart of the resolution was in the first and fourth of the clauses.

> I. . . . We believe that the dimensions and complexity of the current crisis demand that a new approach of collective responsibility be adopted, and in this light insist that uniform penalties be applied to all violators of the discipline of the University.

IV. These proposals being in our judgment a just solution to the crisis our University is presently undergoing, we pledge that
   a. If the President will not adopt these proposals, we shall take all measures within our several consciences to prevent the use of force to vacate these buildings.
   b. If the President does accept our proposals but the students in the buildings refuse to evacuate these buildings, we shall refuse further to interpose ourselves between the Administration and the students.

The resolution was accepted by a huge majority of the Ad Hoc membership meeting, at 9 a.m. on that same Sunday. It was then introduced into the Joint Faculties meeting at 10 a.m., with rhetorical skill and passion, by Allan Westin in conjunction with Immanuel Wallerstein (sociology) and Dankwart Rustow (international forces). The clause advocating collective punishment was debated pro and con on the floor. There appeared to be an increase in sentiment favorable to this promising compromise between, on the one hand, blanket amnesty, and on the other, a policy of graded individual punishments. The latter would require many separate trials for which acceptable evidence might be hard to produce. It would also thicken the punitive atmosphere on campus. Nonetheless Westin & Co. failed to bring our resolution to a vote. They decided, as I understand it, that a vote taken in this heterogeneous body might result in present cleavages which would lessen the chances of greater unity in the future. Instead, a substitute resolution was introduced by another group. Conciliatory toward all parties except the demonstrators, empty of any positive proposals, it was passed by a huge majority. I should add, the "greater unity" was never to materialize, the students eventually facing trials were to number some 900, and the punitive atmosphere on campus was to thicken and thicken.

The Ad Hoc resolution was not buried. It went to President Kirk with a request for a prompt reply. On Monday the 29th the reply came, in graciously phrased prose. Examined carefully, however, the phrasing was seen to be full of legal quibbles. There followed an agitated meeting of the Ad Hoc general membership that went on almost continuously until Monday midnight. One distinguished speaker urged us to trust in the President's good intentions. He seemed to be in the President's confidence. He suggested that the President's reply was as candid as possible under the circumstances. The President could not have said more without violating the University's statutes and exceeding the authority vested in him by the Trustees. In itself this appeal to trust was moving. But to go along with it meant trusting not only the President, whose conduct thus far was not reassuring. It also meant trusting the speaker's *impressions* of the President's mind. Finally it meant our asking the students to trust our impressions of the speaker's impressions of the President's mind. It all sounded like some improbable argument out of *Alice in Wonderland*. The President's reply was, in effect, rejected.

Later, as the evening of the 29th wore on to midnight, our immediate concern was with the probable imminence of a police raid. Nobody seemed to know for certain that a raid would or wouldn't occur that night. It *was* known that the President had appointed a three-man "notification committee" to act if and when the Administration decided to call the police—a decision which, it was also known, required giving Commissioner Leary at least five hours to collect and deploy his forces. But the notification committee's function was, evidently, to advise the Administration and not to notify us. We had to rely on news brought us by members of the patrol coming off duty. Some reported that the number of police on campus was increasing. One man rushed in to announce that they were already in the tunnels, Columbia's far-flung network of underground passages created for the innocent purpose of housing cables, heating pipes, and other utilities. The announcement was premature, but only by a couple of hours.

In the meeting we could only try to dream up last-ditch solutions. The room was more packed than ever, the air dimmer with smoke, the watchers outside the windows a spectral multitude. Should we immediately appeal to the Trustees to stop the raid? Yes, but did anybody *know* a trustee? Somebody knew Trustee Buttenwieser's *son*. How about Lindsay? No, he had probably washed his hands of the Columbia mess. Or Governor Rockefeller—for after all Columbia was chartered by the State of New York? A telegram to the Governor was actually drafted, offstage so to speak. But whether it was ever sent I don't know, and it didn't matter.

Around midnight many of us left 301 Philosophy to join various patrol lines or simply to wander and look around. The appearance of the night-bound campus differed little from its appearance the night before, when predictions of a bust had proved false. For an hour or so I managed to hold in suspension the certainty that tonight was the night and the certainty that tonight wasn't the night. This divided state probably registered some deeper tension in me between dread and desire—desire, I truly confess, that my suspicions of the Administration would be confirmed by a raid. But if they *were* confirmed, should I, aged sixty-three, really "interpose" myself between the students and the police, as, in a way, our patrol duties thus far, and clause III B of the Bitter Pill Resolution, prescribed that we should do? I wavered, and even when the decision came, it did so through a conjunction of impulse and accident.

As I see it now, the intervening hours intensified the impulse. Such a lot of things were going on everywhere. You felt quite lost, as when you go alone to a movie in the afternoon and emerge afterwards, blinking, confused, and anonymous in the glare and racket of the city. It was as if I were two distinct persons, one of them almost stifling in the blackout of his usual character, profession, identity; the other vaguely exulting in the strange feeling of freedom consequent upon the same feeling of loss.

This was a panic reaction and soon subsided. Joining the patrol on the crowded ledge at Low I found a couple of lively English instructors at the far end. They had got hold of a telephone connected to a long extension cord that snaked mysteriously through a half-open window into whatever dark office was inside. Neither of them knew how the phone got out there on the ledge, but one of them was calling his wife to tell her not to worry. We thought it amusing that the University's "facilities" were available to us in this outlandish situation. Below us were the milling jocks and their girls who, in the course of a couple of days and nights, had become fixtures on the scene. Farther off, in the dark gaps between Lewisohn and Earl, and Earl and Math, battalions of patrolmen moved in and took stands under the tall trees in that quarter of the campus. Perhaps, we said, they were only changing guard again. They too had become fixtures within the artificial eternity of the past few days. Above us, however, the windows of the presidential suite were completely black and there was no sign or sound from the demonstrators within. So one feature of the scene appeared to be absent. (I learned later that they had decided to wait for the police in darkness.) It was disturbing.

I was cold. The Low patrol was more than adequately staffed. I left to go home for a sweater. On College Walk, however, I stopped for a time. From there much of the whole campus spectacle could be seen in its sinister grandeur. It held me: the glare of floodlights coming from the television crews who were setting up their equipment in front of Low; the winking of flashlights at several points in the dark reaches of South Field; the fluttering of the little candles, sheltered in cups, among the sprawl of students who had come to be known as the Sundial People; the stars that spattered the high, cold New York sky. A police captain passed, unconcernedly checking with a pencil something attached to a clipboard—surely a map of the campus. I joined a couple of English department friends on the fringes of the Sundial crowd. Mostly, the Sundial People were neither for God nor for his enemies (the Kirkites or the Ruddites), only against the police. Boys and girls, they lay around on dormitory blankets making talk, and music. "It would be a good night to get laid," said one of my English department friends. Another reported the news from 301 Philosophy. There the band of faithful departmental secretaries, who for days had been supplying us with coffee and sandwiches, was about to set up an emergency First Aid station, since there was no sign that the University had itself made any provision for treating the injured. The secretaries were tearing up sheets for bandages—sheets commandeered, I believe, from one of the dormitories.

Something now occurred to me that had occurred earlier during the crisis but never before with such force. Just about everything on campus was being thoroughly *put to use* or would probably soon be put to use, although not for the purposes for which the things were intended. Blankets, sheets, ledges, window sills, lawns, walks, tunnels, the trees students perched in to see better, the roofs lined with watching students—or were they police? All were blithely liberated —the word was *true*—from their usual functions. What had been University or individual property was now almost anyone's property to make of what he liked in this charmed circle of pure improvisation. It was exhilarating.

I went home for a sweater. The warmth of the apartment was inviting. I hesitated whether to stay there or return to duty on campus. Suddenly the phone rang and my wife, calling from the country, said she had heard on the radio that the Bust was about to begin. I rushed out and, wearing a bulky ski sweater, was able to pass as one of fifty or so bulky plainclothesmen who were just then piling out of a bus and filing through the Amsterdam gate, which I heard banging shut behind me—or should I, considering my latest disguise, say "us"? The big bust of April 30 was started.

The following Friday (May 3) I met my Shakespeare students for the first time in ten days. About half of the class (forty) was present. Several wore bandages, one was on crutches, one had his arm in a sling, and the teacher had a black eye. A well organized student strike was strongly in force. There was great resentment of the police and still more resentment of an Administration which had been unable to solve the University's problems without resorting to force. The strike was supported—or in the prevailing euphemism—"respected" by large numbers of faculty members. Respecting the strike meant primarily holding class meetings in off-campus buildings, or on the lawn, or in the apartments of faculty members—anywhere except in regularly scheduled classrooms. This I, like many others, was delighted to do, and I asked the Shakespeare students to scribble down notes on what they wanted to do in class and where they wanted to do it. They were told that they could sign their notes or not as they pleased. All signed and with only two exceptions seemed to be pro-strike. Here are some representative responses:

> No formal classes, nothing under University auspices. Off-campus meetings.
>
> Classes: pure, unliberated Shakespeare.
>
> Shakespeare is relevant to nearly everything, even the past week. I feel we should meet in any way possible—but without opposing or violating the strike.
>
> Class should be kept as much as possible on Shakespeare. My saturation point for police and Trustee invective is very near.
>
> After six days in the liberated building, which seems like two years ago, I would like to re-connect with Western Civilization's past, after a rather exhausting vision of the future.
>
> The only studying I have been able to do in the past ten days has been to read *The Tempest* and *The Winter's Tale*. Classes *off-campus!*

Stephen Spender / Paris in the Spring

Mr. Spender had just observed at close hand the Columbia riots of April 1968 (described in Mr. Dupee's article) when he found himself in the midst of the greater disturbances that broke out shortly afterward in Paris. He speaks of the students with sympathy but always as an "old" man (for that is how they insisted on treating him) and always as a sensitive poetic observer. This last trait becomes evident at the outset, when he describes the building of barricades as "ritualistic." It is not enough that paving stones should be torn up; to do so is to re-enact the three great revolutionary outbursts Paris had previously witnessed. The cutting of the trees is a "dedicated desecration"; the smashed cars are not merely smashed cars, because the eye sees them as very modern sculpture.

But this concern with providing richer contexts (varying from the historically relevant to that mere richness of texture which, in poetry, obscures the structure of fact or idea) is not at all destructive of factual reporting. The lines of battle, the weapons of the students, the tactics of the police are all recorded. We learn what the Sorbonne looks like before we hear of the propaganda activities in the central courtyard and the slogans that emanate from it; the poet's eye selects one of these as the keynote of the uprising: Imagination is Revolution. And this judgment, which may seem abstract, does not prevent a detailed examination of the administrative, ideological, and defense programs of the students, or a cool evaluation of the claim that the student revolution was part of a much greater national uprising.

In the same way a philosophical discussion at a teach-in is described in detail—enhanced by the graphic figure of the boy who looks like a Raphael cartoon—and then dismissed as naïve. In such ways the mature and sensitive observer contrives both to be a part of, and yet a critic of, all that he sees, remembering no doubt his own youthful involvement in the revolutionary world of the 1930's, remembering also the subsequent disillusion; using these memories not to make gestures of irritated rejection but to understand in ways appropriate to his own life the peculiarity and the passion of this renewed concern for social justice. He records without rancor the insults brought on him by his white hair, and the absurd mistaking of him for Herbert Marcuse. The episodes of the Tunisian student and the German lady philosopher, the account of the bourgeois reaction to the rising, and the disillusion of the students when De Gaulle out-maneuvered them, set the tone of a conclusion in which a sixty-year-old man explains what he would like to say to the young "if it were possible to speak to them."

Wide World Photos

Although the writer, in the section called "Anti-climax," puts down his own piece by dwelling on the limitations of journalism, it is clear that in rather complex ways he has striven to avoid the narrowness of vision of which he complains. It is interesting, in considering this essay and Mr. Dupee's, to ask whether the richness of tone and breadth of reference they exhibit are part of what the young dislike about their elders, or the qualities which maturity can bring and that ought to be working in collaboration with the more extreme and single-minded perceptions of youth.

THE BARRICADES

The street battles which took place near the Sorbonne in mid-May between students and police were very ritualistic. In the late afternoon while it was still daylight, the students started building barricades. On Friday (May 24) these were particularly elaborate. First they tore up paving stones and piled them up as though they were rebuilding memories of 1789, 1848, 1870.* Then, in a mood of dedicated desecration, they axed down—so that they fell lengthwise across the street—a few of the sappy plane trees, spring-leafed, just awake from winter. Then they scattered over the paving stones and among the leaves, boxes, wood, trash from the uncollected strikebound garbage on the sidewalks. Lastly, as the night closed in, they tugged, pulled with much rumblings, neighboring parked cars, braked but dragged over the streets just the same, and placed them on their sides, like trophies of smashed automobiles by the sculptor César, on top of the paving stones, among the branches. In an arrangement of this kind on the Boulevard St. Germain, they had extended the contour of a burned-out car by adding to it the quarter section of one of those wrought-iron grills which encircle at the base the trunks of trees on the boulevards to protect their roots. After the night's fighting, this chassis had acquired a wonderful coral tint. On its pediment of bluish paving stones it looked like an enshrined museum object. It was left there for two or three days and much photographed by the tourists who poured into the Latin Quarter during the daytime.

There is not a sign of a policemen while the barricades are being built. Presumably the rules of what has become a war game are being observed; within a few days the police, after having attempted to occupy, have abandoned the territory of the Sorbonne. The Boulevard Saint-Michel is student territory, as witness the fact that students control the traffic. However the completion of the barricades is the sign that the territory may be invaded. The police are now to be let out of the long crate-like camions * with thick wire netting over the windows

* 1789, 1848, 1870: dates of the three French revolutions.
* camion: police wagon, paddy wagon.

behind which they wait like mastiffs. One sees them assembled at the end of the Boulevard near the bridge. Their massed forms in the shadows, solid, stirring, helmeted, some of them carrying shields, seem those of medieval knights. A few of the students also carry shields, the lids of dust-bins, and swords or spear-length sticks. Slowly the massed police advance up the street like a thick wedge of mercury up a glass tube. The students retreat to their barricades and set the trash and wood alight. The police now start firing tear gas shells and detonators which make heavy explosions. When they are within a few feet of the advancing black mass of police the students run away, occasionally picking up and hurling back shells which have not exploded.

The beatnik word "cat" suddenly occurs to me. The wild, quickly running, backward and sideways turning, yowling and scratching students are like cats, the police stolidly massively pursuing them are like dogs.

Terrible things happen to students who are caught and taken to the police cells.

Note that my friend, the painter Jean Hélion, told me of a couple seen weeping over the burned-out cadaver of their car on which they had spent their savings.

THE SORBONNE

The center of the Sorbonne is a courtyard enclosed by cliffs of buff-colored stucco walls. They don't shut out the sky but at the top they make an ugly edge against it. There are two tiers of rather grandiose steps across the whole width of one end of the courtyard leading up to the pillared chapel. Along the sides of the courtyard there are now tables piled with books, magazines, pamphlets, leaflets, etc., all of them "revolutionary." Behind the tables students sit, displaying these wares. Most of the slogans and posters appear to proclaim communism. But on closer inspection one finds that there is no variety of communism here to offer any comfort to Moscow or the French official Communist Party. Even a magazine called *La Nouvelle Humanité* turns out to be Trotskyist, abhorrent to the sellers of the old *Humanité* * who have been banished to the outer gates at the entrance of the Sorbonne. The brands of revolution offered by the students are Maoist, Castroite, Trotskyist. Pictures of Mao, Che Guevara, Trotsky, Lenin, Marx, are displayed on walls, hoardings, pamphlets, and leaflets. Stalin's portrait put in a brief appearance one day, but quickly disappeared.

One day there was a table for Kurds, Turks, Arabs, and Algerians; posters attacking Zionism were on the wall behind them. The Sorbonne is cosmopolitan French culture. I noticed among the bewildering assortment of advertisements —appeals, bulletins posted everywhere or leaflets thrust into your hand— directives to Greek, Spanish, Portuguese, and German students. And of course there were Americans. Two sat rather innocuously at a table collecting signa-

* *Humanité:* French Communist newspaper.

tures for a petition in support of Mendès-France.* A committee of American students hangs out at the sister offices of the Sorbonne in the Rue Censier, where there are also the American draft resisters, a bit left out of all this.

Entrances lead out of the Sorbonne courtyard onto passages and stairways, all of them plastered with notices. Almost every departmental office and classroom has been taken over by committees, organizers, planners, talkers: Committee of Action, Committee of Coordination, Committee of Occupation, Committee of Cultural Agitation, and the sinisterly named Committee of Rapid Intervention.

There seems a tendency for the movement to proliferate cells, activities, categories, subdivisions. I noticed that the Commando Poétique has its functions subdivided into *"Tracts poétiques—affiches poétiques—création collective—publications à bon marché—liaisons interartistiques—Recherches théoretiques—commandos poétique revolutionnaires—praxis poétique revolutionnaire."* *

The poems I saw (*Le Monde* published a selection from them) seemed unoriginal—a mixture of surrealism with the socially conscious leftist writing of the Thirties, and a return to the political style of Éluard.* The real poetry of the revolution is its slogans, politically revolutionary, but imaginative and witty. They are more revealing of the deepest impulses of the movement than most of the pamphlets and pronouncements. They all come together—as do all the finest impulses of the students—in the magnificently summary: "Imagination is Revolution." One understands from the slogans why the students cannot get on with the great trade unions, political parties, official communism:

> Prenez vos désirs pour des réalités.
> Monolithiquement bête, le Gaullisme est l'inversion de la vie.
> Ne changer pas d'employeurs changer l'emploi de la vie.
> Vive la communication à bas la télé-communication.
> Plus je fais l'amour plus je fais la révolution plus je fais la révolution plus je fais l'amour.
> Luttez dans la perspective d'une vie passionante.
> Toute vue des choses qui n'est pas étrange est fausse.*

---

* Pierre Mendès-France: (1907–), former French prime minister (1954–55); firmly anti-Gaullist, he was the figurehead behind whom many of the liberal-to-radical left were prepared to rally toward the end of May 1968, when a power vacuum seemed to be forming.
* *"Tracts poétiques . . ."* : poetical tracts—poetical posters—collective creation—cheap publications—interartistic liaisons—theoretical research—revolutionary poetic commandos—revolutionary poetic practice.
* Paul Éluard: (1895–1952), French poet and a leader of Surrealism.
* Prenez vos désirs . . . : Act in accordance with your desires. Monumentally stupid, Gaullism is the contrary of life. Don't change your directors, change the direction of your life. [Literally, Don't change your employers, change the way you spend your life.] Long live communication; down with tele-communication [i.e. the electronic media]. The more I make love the more I make revolution; the more I make revolution the more I make love. Fight in the prospect of an exciting life. Every picture of the world that isn't strange is false.

They equate revolution with spontaneity, participation, communication, imagination, love, youth. Relations between the students and young workers who share—or who are converted to—these values are of the first importance. They dramatize a struggle not between proletarian and capitalist interest so much as between forces of life and the dead oppressive weight of the bourgeoisie. They are against the consumer society, paternalism, bureaucracy, impersonal party programs, and static party hierarchies. Revolution must not become ossified. It is *la révolution permanente*.

One thing—perhaps the only one—which the Paris students have in common with the beatniks and hippies of the psychedelic generation is that they wish to live the life of the revolution even while they are taking action to bring it about. But they are opposed to drugs and other such eccentrically individualistic forms of self-realization: partly because their view of the revolution is of a community rather than of the individual, but still more because they have a sharp political awareness of the counter-revolutionary effects of drug-taking.

This May, for a few weeks at the Sorbonne, the students lived the communal life of sharing conditions, of arriving at all-important decisions by the method of "direct democracy"—that is to say by consulting the action committees of the movement (*les bases*) and not by imposing decisions from the top—of having meetings which are as far as possible spontaneous, with a different chairman for each meeting, resisting the "cult of personality."

However, by the end of May, under pressure from government and police, attacked by the Communists and without support from the *Confédération Générale* * of workers, the students had to reconsider their concept of organization. This they could not do without questioning "direct democracy." A press conference at the Sorbonne on the first of June developed into a disagreement between Cohn-Bendit * and the other student leaders as to whether organization for action and self-defense should arise spontaneously from discussions at *les bases* or should be imposed by the leaders. Cohn-Bendit thought that the dynamism of the movement should continue to come from the *bases*. His own words:

> The only chance of creating revolutionary forms that will not become ossified (*scelerosé*) lies in waiting until a common purpose has been discovered among all the committees of action from discussing matters at the *base*.

His colleagues agreed on "spontaneity" as a principle but did not think that the circumstances left them much time for discussion in action committees. They pointed out that they had to decide on measures for *"auto-défense"* * immediately. One of them, Weber, said that the committees were too disorganized and

---

* *Confédération Générale du Travail:* Communist led, the biggest labor union amalgamation in France.
* Daniel Cohn-Bendit: main leader of the student uprising.
* *auto-défense:* self-defense.

uncoordinated to be capable of *auto-défense* in the face of the very well organized Gaullist forces. The discussion about organization is crucial, because the danger inherent in too little organization is defeat by the Gaullist and communist forces outside the movement; while the danger of too much organization is defeat by loss of spontaneity from below. The demonstrations and marches, the barricades, were extraordinary examples of spontaneity with a minimum of organization. The undirected discussions at the Odéon Theatre, in which the chairman has to struggle with a tumultuous audience, succeed but do result in disorder and waste of energy. The same must be true, I suspect, of the committee of action. But I sympathize with Cohn-Bendit's view that organization should not be imposed from above.

During the first half of May a good many Parisian intellectuals, as well as many students, seemed to think of the student revolt as part of a larger revolution which had already happened in France. Of course it is not that, and the realization that the university revolt is threatened has added urgency to the debate about "organization" and "direct democracy." The students are reluctant to discuss the Bolsheviks and the anarchists of the Spanish Republic who also said they wanted direct democracy. Or, reminded of this, they take refuge in the idea that theirs is an unprecedented generation. To recall the failures of previous revolutions is to seem in their eyes patronizing, paternalistic. The London *Times* in an editorial pointed out as a weakness of the students that they did not appear to have read George Orwell's *Animal Farm*. But they would not want to read it and if they did read it would find there nothing which they thought applied to their case.

Perhaps because they are so insulated in the Sorbonne, without their being literary, they yet keep on reminding one of behavior and characters in literature. There is something about their movements which reminds one of *The Lord of the Flies*,* with a thuggish Katanga "Committee of Sudden Intervention" ready to emerge from the cellars to produce a final fall. And when one has stepped into the Sorbonne one often seems to be in the world of *Alice Through the Looking Glass* where all the values of the circumambient trafficking world outside are reversed.

THE EXPLOSION OF TALK

In a classroom there is a discussion going on about the nature of work in the consumer society. The room is crowded and contains older as well as young people. The discussion is dominated by two young men, one of whom, in the well of the classroom, is evidently a worker. He has a lean face with jutting features and bristly straw-colored hair emphasizing the line of the back of his head which seems almost continuous with his neck. He talks about work, which, he says, in

---

* *The Lord of the Flies:* novel by William Golding (1955).

all circumstances must be hard and boring. The opposite of work, he says, is pleasure, and he describes, quite exhibitionistically, his own holidays which are spent, it seems, in driving about the country on his motorcycle and laying as many girls as he can pick up. Obviously this is the opposite of what is meant by work.

He is confronted by a student standing a few feet above him. He is small and dark and vigorous and has in his eyes and on his lips an expression like that of the blind made miraculously to see in a cartoon of Raphael. He says that work is joy if you are one of a group, a collective (any backward echoes of that remark are suppressed by his smile). Joy is participation, it is release from the self. He describes holidays that he and his companions have made together where they have done a great deal of work. The individual must not be like the bourgeois intellectual, alienated and separate, existing in no "social context" but that of other intellectuals like himself; nor must he be a cog in a machine. He must be in society like a fish in the water.

The worker interrupts and says, You are not talking about work, you are talking about sport. Sport is not work, it is the free development of the individual. Work means taking orders from someone set above you. The student says that in the revolution, automation will replace the kind of work which is slavery. Work will then consist of participation. There will be no oppression of power because there will be a constant to-ing and fro-ing between those at the base of society and those at the top, a vital current. Machines will function but the goods and services they produce will be a means for leading a life of better value, and not ends which prove that the individual owns things or acquires status. He says the students and the workers combining together could achieve this kind of society: not the intellectuals who are void because they reflect problems peculiar to them, outside the context of society. To be truly revolutionary, you have to experience reality.

This discussion was naïve. Often at the Sorbonne and the Odéon one heard things worse than naïve, chaotic and stupid and dull, and one longed to hear a professor talk for half an hour about Racine. There was wisdom though perhaps in the relief of talking simply as an act, like action painting. Talk, uninhibited, crude, theoretical, confessional, has overtaken Paris, Lyons, Bordeaux, and other cities. It is the breaking out of forces long suppressed. Not just the Sorbonne and the Censier,* the Beaux Arts,* the Odéon, were filled with talk but also the streets themselves. Another part of the French revolutionary tradition had emerged—the idea of joining forces with others in the streets—*dans la rue!* In the Rue de Rennes I find myself standing in a group of shoppers and shop assistants outside a closed Monoprix.* A frustrated shopper is saying indignantly, "Where will all this end? In communism, universal poverty." "Not at all," says a

---

* the Censier: part of the University of Paris, mainly a student center.
* the Beaux Arts: the principal French art school.
* Monoprix: a chain store selling things cheaply.

natty black-coated worker, "Communism means *more* refrigerators, *more* television sets, *more* automobiles. *Le communisme, c'est le luxe pour tous.*" *

This definition shows how difficult it is for the students—conscious, many of them, of themselves as bourgeois, and seeking for a world in which material things are subservient to other human values, to get on with the workers, most of whom, of course, want consumer goods. The relation of the French students to *"les ouvriers"* * is not unlike that of the American students to the Negroes. It cannot be seen just politically, but as a love affair in which the guilt-conscious whites and bourgeois are trying to win the members of what they regard as a wronged class to their own ideas of what are real values.

Not that the students want altogether to dispense with washing machines and refrigerators. Their attitude is shown in a document of thirty theses drafted at the Censier by a group called *Les Yeux Crevés*.* It begins by defining the students as a privileged class, not so much economically as because "we alone have the time and possibility to become aware of our own conditions and the condition of society. Abolish this privilege and act so that everyone may become privileged." It goes on to say that students are workers like everyone else. They are not parasites, economic minors. They do not condemn *"en bloc"* the consumer society. "One has to consume, but let us consume what we have decided to produce. . . . We wish to control not only the means of production but also those of consumption—to have a real choice and not a theoretic one."

It is significant that the movement of the students at the Sorbonne—called the movement of the *22 Mars* *—started among sociologists at the newly built extension of the University in the desolate industrial suburb of Nanterre. A long declaration by Cohn-Bendit and some of his colleagues, in *Esprit* (the May number), depicts the sociology students as seeing sociology as a statistical account of existing society, the result of American influence. The very few sociology students who would get jobs after they left the university would be engaged in such activities as making consumer reports. They realized that sociology instead of being an instrument of bourgeois society, could be turned against it to make a revolution and construct a new society. Here the beginnings of an ideology of the students are implicit.

Inevitably perhaps, the students are unself-critical. They do not notice inconsistencies in their own attitudes, even when, to an outsider, it must seem that these could be disastrous. This struck me when I heard a student who had organized the revolt at Strasbourg University describe his experiences to a great

* *"Le communisme, c'est le luxe pour tous."*: "Communism means luxury for everyone."
* *"les ouvriers"*: the workers.
* *Les Yeux Crevés:* roughly, The Opened Eyes.
* *Mars:* March.

gathering in the Amphitheatre of the Sorbonne. He spoke about the professors with whom the students had to deal with that kind of contempt which is current among some students. He told how he had been asked by someone why he had not explained things adequately to the authorities at his university, and how he had answered: "because one does not enter into discussions with people who are non-existent." People you do not talk to because they are non-existent! Whatever justification there might be for adopting this attitude when confronted with the stuffed geese of Strasbourg, I could not help wondering as I listened how it would work out in the "direct democracy." Supposing—I thought—our student from Strasbourg goes to a factory or to a village where there are peasants, is it not likely that he will meet a few people with attitudes not altogether dissimilar from those he encountered at Strasbourg—people "who understand nothing," *(qui n' ont rien compris)*: that was another of his phrases for describing those who did not agree with him? And had not one heard all this before? Did not the Soviets start off very willing to talk to anyone and everyone who agreed with them, and then make the horrible discovery that there were still bourgeois elements floating around, and that there were very recalcitrant peasants, people who understand nothing, people finally whom one stops talking to—or just stops talking? At this point the phrase *"On ne parle pas avec des gens qui n'existent pas"* begins to acquire a sinister ring.

The students are, I emphasize, conscious of these dangers and do not wish to repeat them. I wonder what might happen if someone wrote on the walls of the Sorbonne: "The streets of Hell are paved with good intentions." If it were written there, I wonder how long it would last. I noticed that they are very good at deleting.

CRABBED AGE AND YOUTH CANNOT LIVE TOGETHER

As I left the Odéon Theatre one evening two youths looking more like Dickensian street urchins perhaps than students called to each other: "Why doesn't he cut his hair?" "Perhaps he should tear it out with his nails!" "Perhaps it's a wig!" Respect for white hairs is certainly not one of the dues paid in Paris this May.

Usually, though, the old just feel invisible as the blacks were supposed to do in America. "The young make love, the old obscene gestures," a slogan in the anarchist magazine *L'Enragé* runs. They have read *Romeo and Juliet* it seems, but not *Antony and Cleopatra*.

I observed to a contemporary that I enjoyed, on the whole, my invisibility. He said: "I thought that too until I went one day with my twenty-year-old son to the Sorbonne. I sat there quietly, and as I had to slip out early was specially grateful to be a ghost. But directly I had gone another student came up and said to my son: *'Qui était ce vieux con avec toi?'* " *

* *"Qui était ce vieux con avec toi?":* "Who was that old bastard with you?"

One night I am at the Odéon, Jean-Louis Barrault's old-style *avant garde* theater which the students have "liberated" and made open for completely unplanned marathon discussions which go on almost till daybreak. The scene is like the sixth act of some play in the Theater of Cruelty * in which the audience have rung down the curtain and taken over the house for their own performance. And they find themselves much more entertaining than Ionesco and Beckett,* I am afraid. The performance itself—the debates for which there are no subjects set —can be chaotic, and I am often sorry for the student chairmen who stand in the aisle yelling *"Silence! N'interrompez pas! Un peu de l'ordre! * Discipline!"*

Everyone calls everyone "comrade" and most of us here are in the world where the revolution has already happened, although there are also intruding misbelievers, generously admitted, howled at, but nevertheless, despite many interruptions, intermittently, fragmentarily, listened to, because whatever might happen later (and I have these fears), the students are most noble in their attempt to be open to all points of view—even that of Gaullists and of the Fascist members of the *"Occident."*

On a particular occasion I was suddenly struck with a thought—or a hysterical seizure—that I ought to communicate to the Sorbonne students the fact that when I spoke with the students at Columbia some of them had asked me whether the students at the Sorbonne had any thoughts about them. I was no emissary, I had not been told to say anything, and yet I felt I should transmit this. So comforting myself that with my white hair I would not be listened to anyway, I touched the arm of the particularly vigorous young man who was conducting the audience and, gradually acquiring some of the mannerisms of Leonard Bernstein, I mentioned, humbly, that I would like to say a word. There was only one disapprobating yell (which was silenced by the young chairman with a severe *"On a écouté même Jean-Louis Barrault"*) * and I started to speak my poor French to what seemed an electric silence. To my amazement they listened and then started asking questions. Could I compare the situation of students in American Universities with that in France? One student even offered the opinion that the American students were far more advanced than "ours." Then someone asked whether it was true that all American students were always under the influence of drugs. I struggled to answer these questions and then, at the first opportunity, left the theater and walked to a bar. I was followed there by three stu-

* The Theater of Cruelty: conceived by the French writer, actor, and theatrical producer Antonin Artaud (1895–1948), who believed that the theater should be a ritualistic and primitive experience, liberating our repressed, unconscious feelings into universal and haunting images created through gesture, rhythm, and sound rather than through language; see his book *The Theater and Its Double* (1938; Eng. trans., 1958).
* Eugène Ionesco and Samuel Beckett: avant-garde playwrights.
* *"N'interrompez pas! Un peu de l'ordre!":* "Don't interrupt! A little order!"
* *"On a écouté même . . .":* "We have listened even to Jean-Louis Barrault."

dents. Then one of them came up to me very shyly and said: *"Monsieur . . . Monsieur . . . Est ce que c'est vrai que vous êtes M. Marcuse?"* *

When the discussions at the Odéon happened to light on a "subject" they could be serious and very sympathetic. One night a young man got up in the gallery (people spoke from whatever part of the theater they happened to be sitting in) and (with his head, seen by me from below, seeming to butt against André Masson's multi-colored ceiling) he stated very simply that he had taken into his care some adolescent delinquents and that he felt he was having little success in helping them, and he would like to hear the views of the audience about delinquency. At this person after person got up and discussed the problem, seriously, sensibly, though without saying anything new.

It was surprising how many people there turned out to be social workers. The conditions in prisons and slums that they reported were deplorable. The discussion continued on a level of concern and without silliness for over an hour. After which I got up to leave, but was stopped at the exit by a Tunisian student who said to me: "They all talk about the harm prison does people—but to me it did good. I was sent to prison in Tunis, I cried, I cursed, I kicked them and I was beaten, and I prayed all day, but at the end of two years I started writing poems and stories, and for that reason here I am—thanks to prison—at the Sorbonne." "Go and tell them that," I said and followed him back into the theater where, a few minutes later, he made his speech, which, in the telling, turned out to be mostly an attack on President Bourguiba. Still he made his point and ended dramatically: "From prison, I learned that in order to achieve anything in this life you have to suffer. . . ." A remark which offered none of those present any handle to catch on to.

At this meeting there was a very distinguished German lady philosopher, with whom I went out afterward for a coffee. She punctured euphoria. What she noticed, she said, in all these discussions, was that they consisted of people saying things as though for the first time, and as though they had no continuity with anything said before or to be said after. Moreover what was said came out of ideas we had all read in books anyway, or were ideas snatched from the intellectual atmosphere. She said she thought the real problem was not that the young wanted to have no contact with the old but that, precisely, they lacked contact with truly adult minds. The teachers and older people with whom they had to deal were in fact mentally adolescent. She attributed a good many of the students' attitudes to a shallow nihilism which had been the fashion for a long while. She wondered whether the university had not already been destroyed, and whether it would recover. A university was to her mind not a place where there were only the best teachers but where there were values so pervasive that even an inferior teacher could fit in without letting the standard down.

* *"Est ce que vrai . . .":* "Is it true that you are Mr. Marcuse?"

ANTI-CLIMAX

Journalism inevitably falsifies by concentrating on the scene and the subject, in a situation where what is most significant may be not the scene and not the subject. More important probably than the happenings which I have been describing in Paris in the spring were the non-happenings. Walk a few hundred yards away from one area of the *Quartier Latin* and despite the strikes and the students there was a remarkably normal atmosphere. One way of describing it would be to say that it was like an over-long rather restrained holiday, with well-dressed people strolling on the sidewalks, the cafés crowded, the food in restaurants up to its usual standard, and many small shops open. Most foreign tourists, it is true, had gone away, but then Parisians, having nothing else to do, were touring their own city, including the Sorbonne in which the actors were inextricably mixed up with the spectators. The only people who seemed to be notably suffering from shortages (of their clientèle) were the male tarts. I asked one of them what he thought of *"les étudiants"* and he shrieked, with an extraordinary gesture—*"Scandaleux!"*

Dust and dirt from ungathered rubbish exhaled a vague smog, a halo over the streets like old varnish over a new green painting, but the presence of these odors was largely compensated for by the absence of petrol. One had to walk long distances but this was good for health and not much slower than going by car when there is traffic.

The spring itself reasserted what was so much more apparent than the revolutionary situation—the non-revolutionary one. In fact, if there were going to be a revolution, it would be—everyone I think agreed—against the evidence of one's senses which lay down certain external rules for revolutions. The weather, of course, can be contradictory, but it is difficult to think of a revolution taking place when—in daylight at all events—everyone looks particularly good humored. For the result of the explosion of talk in Paris this May was that most people looked more self-complacent—even friendly—than they have done in Paris for years.

Yet there was that ugly evening which happened after De Gaulle's second speech in which he adroitly substituted for the referendum he had so mistakenly offered in his first speech a referendum under a more resounding name—a General Election. He accompanied this gesture with the release of a flood of gasoline upon which came floating in their automobiles a flood of *Gaullistes*. They came joyously claxoning up the boulevards, hooting at one another, hooting to urge others to hoot, stopping their cars suddenly, getting out to embrace some fellow driver or passenger, in their chic clothes and their make-up, their tawdry elegance, the triumphant bacchanal of the Social World of Conspicuous Consumption, shameless, crowing, and vulgarer than any crowd I have seen on Broadway or in Chicago. It would have been agonizing at the best of times, but it was more so when one thought of the students, the self-condemned secular monastics of the Sorbonne.

The next day the students had a great parade on the Boulevard Montparnasse and it seemed like a farewell. I walked away from it down the Rue de Rennes and saw an extraordinary sight. In the hot sun, the whole road seemed covered with snow. Actually it was torn-up newspapers. I asked a bystander what had happened. "Nothing." she said, "except that France is mad." The students had seen announcements in *France Soir* of the end of the strikes, the end of their movement, and they had scattered hundreds of copies of the newspaper, in fury, all over the road. Oddly enough, with all the fighting and the barricades, it was the first sign I had seen of real anger.

If it were possible to speak to them, I would like to say two things. The first is that however much the university needs a revolution and the society needs a revolution, it would be disastrous for them not to keep the two revolutions apart in their minds and their acts. For the university, even if it does not conform to their wishes, is an arsenal from which they can draw the arms which can change society. To say, "I won't have a university until society has a revolution." is as though Karl Marx * were to say "I won't go to the reading room of the British Museum until it has a revolution."

The second thing is that although the young today do have reasons for distrusting the older generation, anything that is worth doing involves their having to get old. What they are now is not so important as what they will be ten years from now. And if ten years from now they have become their own idea of what it is to be old, then what they are fighting for now will have come to nothing.

Tom Wolfe / The Pump House Gang

Tom Wolfe is a pioneer-explorer on the social, it seems almost appropriate to say the anthropological, frontiers of American life. California summers, the Ken Kesey gang, rock and hippie manifestations, high society in its eccentric and pathetic efforts to escape boredom—nearly any emerging life style finds him on the scene. It is to be assumed that the sequence of his experiences there resembles the structure of his reports: of first joining in activities which are momentarily foreign to him, of learning the modes, the speech, the styles of the gang, and of then reporting these back to the more

---

* Karl Marx: it was in the reading room of the British Museum that Marx acquired the vast knowledge of economics on which his revolutionary work *Das Kapital* is based.

Surfer, *John Severson Publications*

settled and sedate readers who want to know what, if anything, they are missing.

Like other pioneer-explorers, he is of course proud of his knowledge of the exotic, and especially of having been accepted into tribes like the Pump House gang. Thus, he makes a point at the very start of showing off his special, initiated familiarity with their customs and language. For all the energy and bravado with which he usually comes on at the outset, however, Wolfe, as he progresses, shows a rather anxious respect for a gang quite unlike the Pump House gang, namely, his readers. He seems to imagine them, and the magazines where they read him, like *Esquire,* as secure but swinging, powerfully enough situated but tolerant of strangeness when it pleases them. By about the middle of a characteristic piece by Wolfe all the obscurities will have been translated into terms quite familiar to such readers. More than that, the implication is clear that the kids in this and in other instances are to have a destiny, as Wolfe sees it, that is economically, socially, and at last biologically, not unlike the destiny of the so-called ordinary people from whom they have tried to separate themselves.

Our boys never hair out. The black panther has black feet. Black feet on the crumbling black panther. Pan-thuh. Mee-dah. Pam Stacy, 16 years old, a cute girl here in La Jolla, California, with a pair of orange bell-bottom hip-huggers on, sits on a step about four steps down the stairway to the beach and she can see a pair of revolting black feet without lifting her head. So she says it out loud, "The black panther."

Somebody farther down the stairs, one of the boys with the *major* hair and khaki shorts, says, "The black feet of the black panther."

"Mee-dah," says another kid. This happens to be the cry of a, well, *underground* society known as the Mac Meda Destruction Company.

"The pan-thuh."

"The poon-thuh."

All these kids, seventeen of them, members of the Pump House crowd, are lollygagging around the stairs down to Windansea Beach, La Jolla, California, about 11 a.m., and they all look at the black feet, which are a woman's pair of black street shoes, out of which stick a pair of old veiny white ankles, which lead up like a senile cone to a fudge of tallowy, edematous flesh, her thighs, squeezing out of her bathing suit, with old faded yellow bruises on them, which she probably got from running eight feet to catch a bus or something. She is standing with her old work-a-hubby, who has on *san*dals: you know, a pair of navy-blue anklet socks and these sandals with big, wide, new-smelling tan straps going this way and that, *for keeps.* Man, they look like orthopedic sandals, if one can imagine that. Obviously, these people come from Tucson or Albuquerque or one of those hincty adobe towns. All these hincty, crumbling black feet come to La Jolla-by-the-sea from the adobe towns for the weekend. They even drive in cars all full of thermos bottles and mayonnaisey sandwiches and some kind of latticework wooden-back support for the old crock who drives and Venetian blinds on the back window.

"The black panther."

"Pan-thuh."

"Poon-thuh."

"Mee-dah."

Nobody says it to the two old crocks directly. God, they must be practically 50 years old. Naturally, they're carrying every piece of garbage imaginable: the folding aluminum chairs, the newspapers, the lending-library book with the clear plastic wrapper on it, the sunglasses, the sun ointment, about a vat of goo—

It is a Mexican standoff. In a Mexican standoff, both parties narrow their eyes and glare but nobody throws a punch. Of course, nobody in the Pump House crowd would ever even jostle these people or say anything right to them; they are too cool for that.

Everybody in the Pump House crowd looks over, even Tom Coman, who is a cool person. Tom Coman, 16 years old, got thrown out of his garage last night. He is sitting up on top of the railing, near the stairs, up over the beach, with his legs apart. Some nice long willowy girl in yellow slacks is standing on the sidewalk but leaning into him with her arms around his body, just resting. Neale Jones, 16, a boy with great lank perfect surfer's hair, is standing nearby with a Band-Aid on his upper lip, where the sun has burnt it raw. Little Vicki Ballard is up on the sidewalk. Her older sister, Liz, is down the stairs by the Pump House itself, a concrete block, 15 feet high, full of machinery for the La Jolla water system. Liz is wearing her great "Liz" styles, a hulking rabbit-fur vest and black-leather boots over her Levis, even though it is about 85 out here and the sun is plugged in up there like God's own dentist lamp and the Pacific is heaving in with some fair-to-middling surf. Kit Tilden is lollygagging around, and Tom Jones, Connie Carter, Roger Johnson, Sharon Sandquist, Mary Beth White, Rupert Fellows, Glenn Jackson, Dan Watson from San Diego, they are all out here, and everybody takes a look at the panthers.

The old guy, one means, you know, he must be practically 50 years old, he says to his wife, "Come on, let's go farther up," and he takes her by her fat upper arm as if to wheel her around and aim her away from here.

But she says, "No! We have just as much right to be here as they do."

"That's *not the point*—"

"Are you going to—"

"*Mrs. Roberts,*" the work-a-hubby says, calling his own wife by her official married name, as if to say she took a vow once and his word is law, even if he is not testing it with the blond kids here—"farther up, *Mrs. Roberts.*"

They start to walk up the sidewalk, but one kid won't move his feet, and, oh,

god, her work-a-hubby breaks into a terrible shaking Jello smile as she steps over them, as if to say, Excuse me, sir, I don't mean to make trouble, please, and don't you and your colleagues rise up and jump me, screaming *Gotcha—*
Mee-dah!

But exactly! This beach *is* verboten * for people practically 50 years old. This is a segregated beach. They can look down on Windansea Beach and see nothing but lean tan kids. It is posted "no swimming" (for safety reasons), meaning surfing only. In effect, it is segregated by age. From Los Angeles on down the California coast, this is an era of age segregation. People have always tended to segregate themselves by age, teenagers hanging around with teenagers, old people with old people, like the old men who sit on the benches up near the Bronx Zoo and smoke black cigars. But before, age segregation has gone on within a larger community. Sooner or later during the day everybody has melted back into the old community network that embraces practically everyone, all ages.

But in California today surfers, not to mention rock 'n' roll kids and the hot-rodders or Hair Boys, named for their fanciful pompadours—all sorts of sets of kids—they don't merely hang around together. They establish whole little societies for themselves. In some cases they live with one another for months at a time. The "Sunset Strip" on Sunset Boulevard used to be a kind of Times Square for Hollywood hot dogs of all ages, anyone who wanted to promenade in his version of the high life. Today "The Strip" is almost completely the preserve of kids from about 16 to 25. It is lined with go-go clubs. One of them, a place called It's Boss, is set up for people 16 to 25 and won't let in anybody over 25, and there are some terrible I'm-dying-a-thousand-deaths scenes when a girl comes up with her boyfriend and the guy at the door at It's Boss doesn't think she looks under 25 and tells her she will have to produce some identification proving she is young enough to come in here and live The Strip kind of life and—she's *had* it, because she can't get up the I.D. and nothing in the world is going to make a woman look stupider than to stand around trying to argue *I'm younger than I look, I'm younger than I look*. So she practically shrivels up like a Peruvian shrunken head in front of her boyfriend and he trundles her off, looking for some place you can get an old doll like this into. One of the few remaining clubs for "older people," curiously, is the Playboy Club. There are apartment houses for people 20 to 30 only, such as the Sheri Plaza in Hollywood and the E'Questre Inn in Burbank. There are whole suburban housing developments, mostly private developments, where only people over 45 or 50 can buy a house. Whole towns, meantime, have become identified as "young": Venice, Newport Beach, Balboa—or "old": Pasadena, Riverside, Coronado Island.

Behind much of it—especially something like a whole nightclub district of a major city, "The Strip," going teenage—is, simply, money. World War II and

* Verboten: forbidden.

the prosperity that followed pumped incredible amounts of money into the population, the white population at least, at every class level. All of a sudden here is an area with thousands of people from 16 to 25 who can get their hands on enough money to support a whole nightclub belt and to have the cars to get there and to set up autonomous worlds of their own in a fairly posh resort community like La Jolla—

—Tom Coman's garage. Some old bastard took Tom Coman's garage away from him, and that means eight or nine surfers are out of a place to stay.

"I went by there this morning, you ought to see the guy," Tom Coman says. Yellow Stretch Pants doesn't move. She has him around the waist. "He was out there painting and he had this brush and about a thousand gallons of ammonia. He was really going to scrub me out of there."

"What did he do with the furniture?"

"I don't know. He threw it out."

"What are you going to do?"

"I don't know."

"Where are you going to stay?"

"I don't know. I'll stay on the beach. It wouldn't be the first time. I haven't had a place to stay for three years, so I'm not going to start worrying now."

Everybody thinks that over awhile. Yellow Stretch just hangs on and smiles. Tom Coman, 16 years old, piping fate again. One of the girls says, "You can stay at my place, Tom."

"Um. Who's got a cigarette?"

Pam Stacy says, "You can have these."

Tom Coman lights a cigarette and says, "Let's have a destructo." A destructo is what can happen in a garage after eight or 10 surfers are kicked out of it.

"Mee-dah!"

"Wouldn't that be bitchen?" says Tom Coman. Bitchen is a surfer's term that means "great," usually.

"Bitchen!"

"Mee-dah!"

It's incredible—that old guy out there trying to scour the whole surfing life out of that garage. He's a pathetic figure. His shoulders are hunched over and he's dousing and scrubbing away and the sun doesn't give him a tan, it gives him these . . . *mottles* on the back of his neck. But never mind! The hell with destructo. One only has a destructo spontaneously, a Dionysian . . . *bursting out*, like those holes through the wall during the Mac Meda Destruction Company Convention at Manhattan Beach—Mee-dah!

Something will pan out. It's a magic economy—yes!—all up and down the coast from Los Angeles to Baja California kids can go to one of these beach towns and live the complete surfing life. They take off from home and get to the beach, and if they need a place to stay, well, somebody rents a garage for twenty bucks a month and everybody moves in, girls and boys. Furniture—it's like, one means, you know, one *appropriates* furniture from here and there. It's like the Volkswagen buses a lot of kids now use as beach wagons instead of woodies. Woodies are old station wagons, usually Fords, with wooden bodies, from back before 1953. One of the great things about a Volkswagen bus is that one can . . . *exchange* motors in about three minutes. A good VW motor exchanger can go up to a parked Volkswagen, and a few ratchets of the old wrench here and it's up and out and he has a new motor. There must be a few nice old black panthers around wondering why their nice hubby-mommy VWs don't run so good anymore—but—then—they—are—probably—puzzled—about—a—lot of things. Yes.

Cash—it's practically in the air. Around the beach in La Jolla a guy can walk right out in the street and stand there, stop cars and make the candid move. Mister, I've got a quarter, how about 50 cents so I can get a *large* draft. Or, I need some after-ski boots. And the panthers give one a Jello smile and hand it over. Or a guy who knows how to do it can get $40 from a single night digging clams, and it's nice out there. Or he can go around and take up a collection for a keg party, a keg of beer. Man, anybody who won't kick in a quarter for a keg is a jerk. A couple of good keg collections—that's a trip to Hawaii, which is the surfer's version of a trip to Europe: there is a great surf and great everything there. Neale spent three weeks in Hawaii last year. He got $30 from a girl friend, he scrounged a little here and there and got $70 more and he headed off for Hawaii with $100.02, that being the exact plane fare, and borrowed 25 cents when he got there to . . . blast the place up. He spent the 25 cents in a photo booth, showed the photos to the people on the set of *Hawaii* and got a job in the movie. What's the big orgy about money? It's warm, nobody even wears shoes, nobody is starving.

All right, Mother gets worried about all this, but it is limited worry, as John Shine says. Mainly, Mother says, *Sayonara,* you all, and you head off for the beach.

The thing is, everybody, practically everybody, comes from a good family. Everyone has been . . . *reared well,* as they say. Everybody is very upper-middle, if you want to bring it down to that. It's just that this is a new order. Why hang around in the hubby-mommy household with everybody getting neurotic hang-ups with each other and slamming doors and saying, Why can't they have some privacy? Or, it doesn't mean anything that I have to work for a living, does it? It doesn't mean a thing to you. All of you just lie around here sitting in the big orange easy chair smoking cigarettes. I'd hate for you to have to smoke standing up, you'd probably get phlebitis from it—Listen to me, Sarah—

—why go through all that? It's a good life out here. Nobody is mugging everybody for money and affection. There are a lot of bright people out here, and there are a lot of interesting things. One night there was a toga party in a garage, and everybody dressed in sheets, like togas, boys and girls and they put on the appropriated television set to an old Deanna Durbin movie and turned off the sound and put on Rolling Stones records, and you should have seen Deanna Durbin opening her puckered kumquat mouth with Mick Jagger's voice bawling out, *I ain't got no satisfaction.* Of course, finally everybody started pulling the togas off each other, but that is another thing. And one time they had a keg party down on the beach in Mission Bay and the lights from the amusement park were reflected all over the water and that, the whole design of the thing, those nutty lights, that was part of the party. Liz put out the fire throwing a "sand potion" or something on it. One can laugh at Liz and her potions, her necromancy and everything, but there is a lot of thought going into it, a lot of, well, mysticism.

You can even laugh at mysticism if you want to, but there is a kid like Larry Alderson, who spent two years with a monk, and he learned a lot of stuff, and Artie Nelander is going to spend next summer with some Outer Mongolian tribe; he really means to do that. Maybe the "mysterioso" stuff is a lot of garbage, but still, it is interesting. The surfers around the Pump House use that word, mysterioso, quite a lot. It refers to the mystery of the Oh Mighty Hulking Pacific Ocean and everything. Sometimes a guy will stare at the surf and say, "Mysterioso." They keep telling the story of Bob Simmons' wipeout, and somebody will say "mysterioso."

Simmons was a fantastic surfer. He was fantastic even though he had a bad leg. He rode the really big waves. One day he got wiped out at Windansea. When a big wave overtakes a surfer, it drives him right to the bottom. The board came in but he never came up and they never found his body. Very mysterioso. The black panthers all talked about what happened to "the Simmons boy." But the mysterioso thing was how he could have died at all. If he had been one of the old pan-thuhs, hell, sure he could have got killed. But Simmons was, well, one's own age, he was the kind of guy who could have been in the Pump House gang, he was . . . *immune,* he was plugged into the whole pattern, he could feel the whole Oh Mighty Hulking Sea, he didn't have to think it out step by step. But he got wiped out and killed. Very mysterioso.

Immune! If one is in the Pump House gang and really keyed in to this whole thing, it's—well, one is . . . *immune,* one is not full of black pan-thuh panic. Two kids, a 14-year-old girl and a 16-year-old boy, go out to Windansea at dawn, in the middle of winter, cold as hell, and take on 12-foot waves all by themselves. The girl, Jackie Haddad, daughter of a certified public accountant, wrote a composition about it, just for herself, called "My Ultimate Journey":

"It was six o'clock in the morning, damp, foggy and cold. We could feel the bitter air biting at our cheeks. The night before, my friend Tommy and I had seen one of the greatest surf films, *Surf Classics.* The film had excited us so much we made up our minds to go surfing the following morning. That is what brought us down on the cold, wet, soggy sand of Windansea early on a December morning.

"We were the first surfers on the beach. The sets were rolling in at eight to 10, filled with occasional 12-footers. We waxed up and waited for a break in the waves. The break came, neither of us said a word, but instantly grabbed our boards and ran into the water. The paddle out was difficult, not being used to the freezing water.

"We barely made it over the first wave of the set, a large set. Suddenly Tommy put on a burst of speed and shot past me. He cleared the biggest wave of the set. It didn't hit me hard as I rolled under it. It dragged me almost 20 yards before exhausting its strength. I climbed on my board gasping for air. I paddled out to where Tommy was resting. He laughed at me for being wet already. I almost hit him but I began laughing, too. We rested a few minutes and then lined up our position with a well known spot on the shore.

"I took off first. I bottom-turned hard and started climbing up the wave. A radical cut-back caught me off balance and I fell, barely hanging onto my board. I recovered in time to see Tommy go straight over the falls on a 10-footer. His board shot nearly 30 feet in the air. Luckily, I could get it before the next set came in, so Tommy didn't have to make the long swim in. I pushed it to him and then laughed. All of a sudden Tommy yelled, 'Outside!'

"Both of us paddled furiously. We barely made it up to the last wave, it was a monster. In precision timing we wheeled around and I took off. I cut left in reverse stance, then cut back, driving hard toward the famous Windansea bowl. As I crouched, a huge wall of energy came down over me, covering me up. I moved toward the nose to gain more speed and shot out of the fast-flowing suction just in time to kick out as the wave closed out.

"As I turned around I saw Tommy make a beautiful drop-in, then the wave peaked and fell all at once. Miraculously he beat the suction. He cut back and did a spinner, which followed with a reverse kick-up.

"Our last wave was the biggest. When we got to shore, we rested, neither of us saying a word, but each lost in his own private world of thoughts. After we had rested, we began to walk home. We were about half way and the rain came pouring down. That night we both had bad colds, but we agreed it was worth having them after the thrill and satisfaction of an extra good day of surfing."

John Shine and Artie Nelander are out there right now. They are just "outside," about one fifth of a mile out from the shore, beyond where the waves start breaking. They are straddling their surfboards with their backs to the shore, looking out toward the horizon, waiting for a good set. Their backs look like some kind of salmon-colored porcelain shells, a couple of tiny shells bobbing up and down as the swells roll under them, staring out to sea like Phrygian sacristans looking for a sign.

John and Artie! They are—they are what one means when one talks about the surfing life. It's like, you know, one means, they have this life all of their own; it's like a glass-bottom boat, and it floats over the "real" world, or the square world or whatever one wants to call it. They are not exactly off in a world of their own, they are and they aren't. What it is, they float right through the real world, but it can't touch them. They do these things, like the time they went to Malibu, and there was this party in some guy's apartment, and there wasn't enough *legal* parking space for everybody, and so somebody went out and painted the red curbs white and everybody parked. Then the cops came. Everybody ran out. Artie and John took an airport bus to the Los Angeles Airport, just like they were going to take a plane, in khaki shorts and T-shirts with Mac Meda Destruction Company stenciled on them. Then they took a helicopter to Disneyland. At Disneyland crazy Ditch had his big raincoat on and a lot of flasks strapped onto his body underneath, Scotch, bourbon, all kinds of stuff. He had plastic tubes from the flasks sticking out of the flyfront of his raincoat and everybody was sipping whiskey through the tubes—

—Ooooo-eeee—Mee-dah! They chant this chant, Mee-dah, in a real fakey deep voice, and it *really bugs people*. They don't know what the hell it is. It is the cry of the Mac Meda Destruction Company. The Mac Meda Destruction Company is . . . an *underground* society that started in La Jolla about three years ago. Nobody can remember exactly how; they have arguments about it. Anyhow, it is mainly something to *bug* people with and organize huge beer orgies with. They have their own complete, bogus phone number in La Jolla. They have Mac Meda Destruction Company decals. They stick them on phone booths, on cars, any place. Some mommy-hubby will come out of the shopping plaza and walk up to his Mustang, which is supposed to make him a hell of a tiger now, and he'll see a sticker on the side of it saying, "Mac Meda Destruction Company," and for about two days or something he'll think the sky is going to fall in.

But the big thing is the parties, the "conventions." Anybody can join, any kid, anybody can come, as long as they've heard about it, and they can only hear about it by word of mouth. One was in the Sorrento Valley, in the gulches and arroyos, and the fuzz came, and so the older guys put the young ones and the basket cases, the ones just too stoned out of their gourds, into the tule grass, and the cops shined their searchlights and all they saw was tule grass, while the basket cases moaned scarlet and oozed on their bellies like reptiles and everybody else ran down the arroyos, yelling Mee-dah.

The last one was at Manhattan Beach, inside somebody's poor hulking house. The party got *very Dionysian* that night and somebody put a hole through one wall, and everybody else decided to see if they could make it bigger. Everybody was stoned out of their hulking gourds, and it got to be about 3:30 a.m. and everybody decided to go see the riots. These were the riots in Watts. The Los Angeles *Times* and the San Diego *Union* were all saying, WATTS NO-MAN'S LAND and STAY WAY FROM WATTS YOU GET YO' SE'F KILLED, but naturally nobody believed that. Watts was a blast, and the Pump House gang was immune to the trembling gourd panic rattles of the L. A. *Times* black pan-thuhs. Immune!

So John Shine, Artie Nelander and Jerry Sterncorb got in John's VW bus, known as the Hog of Steel, and they went to Watts. Gary Wickham and some other guys ran into an old man at a bar who said he owned a house in Watts and had been driven out by the drunk niggers. So they drove in a car to save the old guy's house from the drunk niggers. Artie and John had a tape recorder and decided they were going to make a record called "Random Sounds from the Watts Riots." They drove right into Watts in the Hog of Steel and there was blood on the streets and roofs blowing off the stores and all these apricot flames and drunk Negroes falling through the busted plate glass of the liquor stores. Artie got a nice recording of a lot of Negroes chanting "Burn, baby, burn." They all got out and talked to some Negro kids in a gang going into a furniture store, and the Negro kids didn't say Kill Whitey or Geed'um or any of that. They just said, Come on, man, it's a party and it's free. After they had been in there for about three hours talking to Negroes and watching drunks collapse in the liquor stores, some cop with a helmet on came roaring up and said, "Get the hell out of here, you kids, we cannot and will not provide protection."

Meantime, Gary Wickham and his friends drove in in a car with the old guy, and a car full of Negroes *did* stop them and say, Whitey, Geed'um, and all that stuff, but one of the guys in Gary's car just draped a pistol he had out the window and the colored guys drove off. Gary and everybody drove the old guy to his house and they all walked in and had a great raunchy time drinking beer and raising hell. A couple of Negroes, the old guy's neighbors, came over and told the old guy to cut out the racket. There were flames in the sky and ashes coming down with little rims of fire on them, like apricot crescents. The old guy got very cocky about all his "protection" and went out on the front porch about dawn and started yelling at some Negroes across the street, telling them "No more drunk niggers in Watts" and a lot of other unwise slogans. So Gary Wickham got up and everybody left. They were there about four hours altogether and when they drove out, they had to go through a National Guard checkpoint, and a lieutenant from the San Fernando Valley told them he could not and would not provide protection.

But exactly! Watts just happened to be what was going on at the time, as far as the netherworld of La Jolla surfing was concerned, and so one goes there and sees what is happening and comes back and tells everybody about it and laughs at the L.A. *Times*. That is what makes it so weird when all these black pan-thuhs come around to pick up "surfing styles," like the clothing manufacturers. They don't know what any of it means. It's like archaeologists discovering hieroglyphics or something, and they say, god, that's neat—Egypt!—but they don't know what the hell it is. They don't know anything about . . . *The Life*. It's great to think of a lot of old emphysematous pan-thuhs in the Garment District in New York City struggling in off the street against a gummy 15-mile-an-hour wind full of soot and coffee-brown snow and gasping in the elevator to clear their old nicotine-phlegm tubes on the way upstairs to make out the invoices on a lot of surfer stuff for 1966, the big nylon windbreakers with the wide, white horizontal competition stripes, nylon swimming trunks with competition stripes, bell-bottom slacks for girls, the big hairy sleeveless jackets, vests, the blue "tennies," meaning tennis shoes, and the . . . *look,* the Major Hair, all this long lank blond hair, the plain face kind of tanned and bleached out at the same time, but with big eyes. It all starts in a few places, a few strategic groups, the Pump House gang being one of them, and then it moves up the beach, to places like Newport Beach and as far up as Malibu.

Well, actually there is a kind of back-and-forth thing with some of the older guys, the old heroes of surfing, like Bruce Brown, John Severson, Hobie Alter and Phil Edwards. Bruce Brown will do one of those incredible surfing movies and he is out in the surf himself filming Phil Edwards coming down a 20-footer in Hawaii, and Phil has on a pair of nylon swimming trunks, which he has had made in Hawaii, because they dry out fast—and it is like a grapevine. Everybody's got to have a pair of nylon swimming trunks, and then the manufacturers move in, and everybody's making nylon swimming trunks, boxer trunk style, and pretty soon every kid in Utica, N.Y., is buying a pair of them, with the competition stripe and the whole thing, and they never heard of Phil Edwards. So it works back and forth—but so what? Phil Edwards is part of it. He may be an old guy, he is 28 years old, but he and Bruce Brown, who is even older, 30, and John Severson, 32, and Hobie Alter, 29, never haired out to the square world even though they make thousands. Hair refers to courage. A guy who "has a lot of hair" is courageous; a guy who "hairs out" is yellow.

Bruce Brown and Severson and Alter are known as the "surfing millionaires." They are not millionaires, actually, but they must be among the top businessmen south of Los Angeles. Brown grossed something around $500,000 in 1965 even before his movie *Endless Summer* became a hit nationally; and he has only about three people working for him. He goes out on a surfboard with a camera encased in a plastic shell and takes his own movies and edits them himself and goes around showing them himself and narrating them at places like the Santa Monica Civic Auditorium, where 24,000 came in eight days once, at $1.50 a person, and all he has to pay is for developing the film and hiring the hall. John Severson has the big surfing magazine, *Surfer.* Hobie Alter is the biggest surfboard manufacturer, all hand-made boards. He made 5,000 boards in 1965 at $140 a board. He also designed the "Hobie" skate boards and gets 25 cents for every one sold. He grossed between $900,000 and $1 million in 1964.

God, if only everybody could grow up like these guys and know that crossing the horror dividing line, 25 years old, won't be the end of everything. One means, keep on living *The Life* and not get sucked into the ticky-tacky life with some insurance salesman sitting forward in your stuffed chair on your wall-to-wall telling you that life is like a football game and you sit there and take that stuff. The hell with that! Bruce Brown has the money and *The Life*. He has a great house on a cliff about 60 feet above the beach at Dana Point. He is married and has two children, but it is not that hubby-mommy you're-breaking-my-gourd scene. His office is only two blocks from his house and he doesn't even have to go on the streets to get there. He gets on his Triumph scrambling motorcycle and cuts straight across a couple of vacant lots and one can see him . . . *bounding* to work over the vacant lots. The Triumph hits ruts and hummocks and things and Bruce Brown bounces into the air with the motor—*thraggggh*—moaning away, and when he gets to the curbing in front of his office, he just leans back and pulls up the front wheel and hops it and gets off and walks into the office barefooted. *Barefooted;* why not? He wears the same things now that he did when he was doing nothing but surfing. He has on a faded gray sweatshirt with the sleeves cut off just above the elbows and a pair of faded corduroys. His hair is the lightest corn yellow imaginable, towheaded, practically white, from the sun. Even his eyes seem to be bleached. He has a rain-barrel old-apple-tree Tom-Sawyer little-boy roughneck look about him, like Bobby Kennedy.

Sometimes he carries on his business right there at the house. He has a dugout room built into the side of the cliff, about 15 feet down from the level of the house. It is like a big pale green box set into the side of the cliff, and inside is a kind of upholstered bench or settee you can lie down on if you want to and look out at the Pacific. The surf is crashing like a maniac on the rocks down below. He has a telephone in there. Sometimes it will ring, and Bruce Brown says hello, and the surf is crashing away down below, roaring like mad, and the guy on the other end, maybe one of the TV networks calling from New York or some movie hair-out from Los Angeles, says:

"What is all that noise? It sounds like you're sitting out in the surf."

"That's right," says Bruce Brown, "I have my desk out on the beach now. It's nice out here."

The guy on the other end doesn't know what to think. He is another Mr. Efficiency who just got back from bloating his colon up at a three-hour executive lunch somewhere and now he is Mr.-Big-Time-Let's-Get-This-Show-on-the-Road.

"On the beach?"

"Yeah. It's cooler down here. And it's good for you, but it's not so great for the desk. You know what I have now? A warped leg."

"A warped leg?"

"Yeah, and this is an $800 desk."

Those nutball California kids—and he will still be muttering that five days after Bruce Brown delivers his film, on time, and Mr. Efficiency is still going through memo thickets or heaving his way into the bar car to Darien—in the very moment that Bruce Brown and Hobie Alter are both on their motorcycles out on the vacant lot in Dana Point. Hobie Alter left his surfboard plant about two in the afternoon because the wind was up and it would be good catamaranning and he wanted to go out and see how far he could tip his new catamaran without going over, and he did tip it over, about half a mile out in high swells and it was hell getting the thing right side up again. But he did, and he got back in time to go scrambling on the lot with Bruce Brown. They are out there, roaring over the ruts, bouncing up in the air, and every now and then they roar up the embankment so they can . . . fly, going up in the air about six feet off the ground as they come up off the embankment—*thraaagggggh*—all these people in the houses around there come to the door and look out. These two . . . nuts are at it again. Well, they can only fool around there for 20 minutes, because that is about how long it takes the cops to get there if anybody gets burned up enough and calls, and what efficient business magnate wants to get hauled off by the Dana Point cops for scrambling on his motorcycle in a vacant lot.

Bruce Brown has it figured out so no one in the whole rubber-bloated black pan-thuh world can trap him, though. He bought a forest in the Sierras. There is nothing on it but trees. His own wilds: no house, no nothing, just Bruce Brown's forest. Beautiful things happen up there. One day, right after he bought it, he was on the edge of his forest, where the road comes into it, and one of these big rancher king motheroos with the broad belly and the $70 lisle Safari shirt comes tooling up in a Pontiac convertible with a funnel of dust pouring out behind. He gravels it to a great flashy stop and yells:

"Hey! You!"

Of course, what he sees is some towheaded barefooted kid in a torn-off sweatshirt fooling around the edge of the road.

"Hey! You!"

"Yeah?" says Bruce Brown.

"Don't you know this is private property?"

"Yeah," says Bruce Brown.

"Well, then, why don't you get your ass off it?"

"Because it's mine, it's my private property," says Bruce Brown. "Now you get *yours* off it."

And Safari gets a few rays from that old-apple-tree rain-barrel don't-cross-that-line look and doesn't say anything and roars off, slipping gravel, the dumb crumbling pan-thuh.

But . . . perfect! It is like, one means, you know, poetic justice for all the nights Bruce Brown slept out on the beach at San Onofre and such places in the old surfing days and would wake up with some old crock's black feet standing beside his head and some phlegmy black rubber voice saying:

"All right, kid, don't you know this is private property?"

And he would prop his head up and out there would be the Pacific Ocean, a kind of shadowy magenta-mauve, and one thing, *that* was nobody's private property—

But how many Bruce Browns can there be? There is a built-in trouble with age segregation. Eventually one *does* reach the horror age of 25, the horror dividing line. Surfing and the surfing life have been going big since 1958, and already there are kids who—well, who aren't kids anymore, they are pushing 30, and they are stagnating on the beach. Pretty soon the California littoral will be littered with these guys, stroked out on the beach like beached white whales, and girls, too, who can't give up the mystique, the mysterioso mystique, Oh Mighty Hulking Sea, who can't *conceive* of living any other life. It is pathetic when they are edged out of groups like the Pump House gang. Already there are some guys who hang around with the older crowd around the Shack who are stagnating on the beach. Some of the older guys, like Gary Wickham, who is 24, are still in *The Life,* they still have it, but even Gary Wickham will be 25 one day and then 26 and then. . . . and then even pan-thuh age. Is one really going to be pan-thuh age one day? Watch those black feet go. And Tom Coman still snuggles with Yellow Slacks, and Liz still roosts moodily in her rabbit fur at the bottom of the Pump House and Pam still sits on the steps contemplating the mysterioso mysteries of Pump House ascension and John and Artie still bob, tiny pink porcelain shells, way out there waiting for godsown bitchen *set,* and godsown sun is still turned on like a dentist's lamp and so far—

—the panthers scrape on up the sidewalk. They are at just about the point Leonard Anderson and Donna Blanchard got that day, December 6, 1964, when Leonard said, Pipe it, and fired two shots, one at her and one at himself. Leonard was 18 and Donna was 21—21!—god, for a girl in the Pump House gang that is almost the horror line right there. But it was all so mysterioso. Leonard was just lying down on the beach at the foot of the Pump House, near the stairs, just talking to John K. Weldon down there, and then Donna appeared at the top of the stairs and Leonard got up and went up the stairs to meet her, and they didn't say anything, they weren't *angry* over anything, they never had been, although the police said they had, they just turned and went a few feet down the sidewalk, away from the Pump House and—blam blam!—these two shots. Leonard fell dead on the sidewalk and Donna died that afternoon in Scripps Memorial Hospital. Nobody knew what to think. But one thing it seemed like—well, it seemed like Donna and Leonard thought they had lived *The Life* as far as it would go and now it was running out. All that was left to do was—but that is an *insane* idea. It can't be like that, *The Life* can't run out, people can't change all that much just because godsown chronometer runs on and the body packing starts deteriorating and the fudgy tallow shows up at the thighs where they squeeze out of the bathing suit—

Tom, boy! John, boy! Gary, boy! Neale, boy! Artie, boy! Pam, Liz, Vicki, Jackie Haddad! After all this—just a pair of bitchen black panther bunions inching down the sidewalk away from the old Pump House stairs?

IV   PERSONS

This section affords material for a study of the many ways in which writing can register personality and social circumstance. From Lillian Hellman's "Helen" to the weird and tortured life of the English-Jewish man of letters, Meyerstein, is a distance which is a measure of the varieties of existence possible within the over-all scope of Western culture; it is also a measure of the power of civilized prose to compass the gap. Jonathan Miller's cool but affectionate appraisal of a strange rebel within that culture is further evidence of the range and flexibility of easy traditional prose. The Manso and Terkel pieces go about their work quite differently and record the spoken word, though each for its own purposes. We have ended the section with a double play: Stein on Hemingway, Hemingway on Stein, or two of the greatest and most idiosyncratic of modern American writers commenting, without much charity, on the way they remembered their early association in Paris. These last are the work of artists; but the material upon which they work with their extreme refinement of means is still human nature, the great subject and the structuring force of all language.

Peter Manso / Interview with Jackie Stewart

This interview with racing-car champion Jackie Stewart can be compared to the other interviews of this collection—with McLuhan, Frost, and Stravinsky, for example. Any such comparison would necessarily measure the degree to which the interviewer begins to compete for our attention with the interviewee and the extent to which the subject of the interview becomes something other than what it was expected to be. Stewart is here prodded into talking not only about racing but about other sports, then about other kinds of performance, such as those by Sinatra or the Beatles, and then about politics, film stars, and the American Marine Corps.

Stewart is less sure than his interviewer, Peter Manso, "that all the material we've been discussing is relevant," but it has already become clear that Manso sees racing as a metaphor for the whole complex subject of "performance" and of what he calls "existential adventuresomeness." He succeeds in making the interview nearly as aggressively competitive as car racing. Thus he makes Stewart reveal in the process of interviewing some of the quite ambitious emotional and intellectual stakes for which he competes while on the track.

Topics occur here in response to challenge, and the reader might be led to speculate about this factor as an incentive to the writings found elsewhere in this collection. To what extent does writing, like conversation, involve the discovery of difficulties, analogues, extensions, complications that, if met and dealt with, propel the essay forward?

Scottish, born 1939. Married, two children, presently lives in Geneva. Probably the best Grand Prix driver today. He began racing in the usual way, with sports cars, in 1961. During this period he was regarded as among the world's best trap shooters. During 1964 he had eleven consecutive wins in Ken Tyrrell's Formula 3 Cooper, taking fourteen out of sixteen races. In 1965, his first Grand Prix season, he was third in the World Driver's championship at the wheel of a BRM, winning the Grand Prix of Italy, taking second at Spa, Zandvoort, and Clermont-Ferrand. In 1966 he beat Jim Clark's Lotus to win the Tasman series in a BRM. The same year he also won the Grand Prix of Monaco and, going to Indianapolis for the first time, was comfortably leading the "500" when forced out several laps from the finish. Still driving the BRM in Formula 1, he scored second at Spa in 1967 and, later, third at LeMans. In 1968 he was forced to miss

Richard Corson for Road and Track

three of the season's eleven Grand Prix races due to a wrist injury incurred early in the Spring, but nevertheless won the Dutch and German Grand Prix and managed to finish the season in second spot. The poignance of this second-place finish is even greater, as he'd probably have won the championship had he not been taxed his sure win at Spa when his Matra-Ford ran out of fuel on the last lap. [After this interview, Stewart went on to win the 1969 championship.]

PETER MANSO: You have the reputation of being one of the more safety-conscious drivers. You introduced shoulder harnesses into Formula 1 racing * and these days one sees you driving in an aluminized-asbestos suit. Have you always been concerned with this sort of thing?

JACKIE STEWART: I can remember my first couple of seasons in motor racing, when I drove in a nylon short-sleeve shirt, a pair of sandals and a pair of plain slacks, with a crash helmet that I thought looked very nice. At the time I didn't like the idea of wearing any of these dome cones that completely envelop things because they never looked very good. Stirling Moss used to wear a little one, so I thought maybe I should wear a little one too. In large part it was a question of not wanting to appear too much the racing driver because I knew I wasn't. I was an amateur driver and I didn't want to be kidding anyone on. For instance, I didn't want to be seen in Dunlop racing overalls because I thought only the boy racers used them and really I didn't want to pretend to be someone I wasn't.

P.M.: So you wore a costume in reverse?

J.S.: Exactly. Now in 1964, when I started driving single seaters for the first time, I started dealing with professional people. I started driving for Ken Tyrrell and I had the good fortune to have a very competitive car and we won most every race we entered in Formula 3. And of course I was driving in GT cars and prototype sport cars as well as in Formula 2. This meant that I was mixing with the big timers. In 1964 I met Graham Hill for the first time and came onto more racing terms with Jimmy Clark and all the people who were top, and of course I was picking up some things from them. From Jo Bonnier I learned that I should wear very heavy-duty Dunlop flame-proof overalls, much thicker than everyone else was wearing; so I got a set of these, along with an American crash helmet. At the time we were wearing a Herbert Johnson, a very well-known British helmet, but the Americans were so much more advanced than us in headgear that I got an American helmet. Now this was my first step towards looking after myself.

P.M.: Had you had any accidents at this time?

* Formula I racing: Grand Prix racing. Formulas I, II, and III are sets of specifications laid down by the FIA (Fédération Internationale de l'Automobile) governing the size, weight, and type of vehicle permitted in various classes of racing events.

J.S.: None at all. Then I found out from Graham Hill that he wore woolen, thermal underwear saturated with fire retardant in case of a fire. Therefore I started to wear flame-proof underwear as well as flame-proof heavy-duty overalls. This was in '64. In '65 the same pattern developed. I went to America and found out over there that they were doing quite a few other things, looking into new materials that were of benefit to us. So in a sense my concern for safety started early and has developed. Motor racing will always be a dangerous sport because one is always going much too fast for the things around you. But being professionals and racing as often as we do, we have to try and look out for ourselves in the best manner that we can. Now this means that each week we've got to look out for better things. I believe at the moment we're at the start of a new era in motor racing safety, not only in relation to the drivers but in the area of spectator protection as well.

P.M.: What you say is doubtless true but nonetheless difficult to accept in the face of the numerous accidents this past season.

J.S.: Well, I think these trends started before these accidents happened. I had an accident in '66 where I went off the road at Spa, Francorchamps, at some hundred-and-fifty-odd mph, aquaplaned, completely through no fault of my own. Eight or nine drivers went off on that same lap, and this is a very unusual thing to happen in Grand Prix racing. And it all happened because of the thunder and rain that we never knew was there, over on the far side of the circuit. Now, I went off the road and knocked down a couple of walls and part of a house and a few other things and luckily got off with very light injuries. But on that occasion I was trapped in the car for some thirty-five minutes, the petrol tanks were ruptured so that the monocoque, being like a bath, filled up with thirty-two gallons of petrol. The thing was just rolling around like a tub completely filled, with me lying in it. We couldn't get the electrics switched off because the dashboard had been destroyed. The electric pumps were going, the power was still on, so the fire risk was enormous. Now this is not a pleasant experience.

P.M.: Were you upside down?

J.S.: No, the car stayed upright but they couldn't get me out because the car had come round about me.

P.M.: You were conscious?

J.S.: Mainly, yes. The fumes were occasionally getting me unconscious and then I would come back again. Both Graham Hill and Bob Bondurant had accidents at the same corner and they both helped to get me out of the car. They had to remove the steering wheel. They had no tools so they had to borrow the tools from a spectator's car, as there were no marshals there. It was a bit of a problem to get everything collected and I was very keen to get out of it. But I couldn't get out. I had broken my collarbone and dislocated a shoulder, and I had some ribs cracked. I had a bit of a sore back and a little bit of concussion. But my main concern was that gasoline. I was getting gasoline burns because gasoline, as you know, takes your skin off if you're submerged in it for any length of time; so therefore this was extremely uncomfortable.

P.M.: Rumor had it that you couldn't sit down for weeks.

J.S.: Oh, Christ, all my skin came off from top to bottom. You know, the whole lot came off. It really wasn't all that painful, just nipping like hell. Anyway, I was very keen to get out but at the same time I wasn't completely conscious all of the time. I sort of drifted away from time to time. And I must say it didn't feel like thirty-five minutes; it might have felt fifteen minutes, you know, because of my unconsciousness. I'm sure I wasn't completely aware of what was happening.

P.M.: Were you conscious of people working around you?

J.S.: Oh, yes. I can remember a helicopter up above me, and I can remember speaking quite clearly to Graham Hill, asking him to get me the hell out of the car and get the chopper which I heard overhead. Also I thought there was something wrong with my back. I thought the chopper had come for me but, in fact, it was doing some filming for the movie *Grand Prix*. And this was a bit of a disappointment. But then they couldn't find an ambulance, that was another thing. That held me up a bit. I had to lie in a barn for some time before an ambulance came. But I can remember asking Graham to get me by chopper to the hospital. And I can remember telling him that I wanted to be flown back to London, that I didn't want to be treated in Belgium. You know, things like this were really way ahead of the fact of getting me out of the car but nevertheless at the time I was frightened that I shouldn't be treated in London because a few of my friends had been in accidents and sadly affected by not getting the right treatment in some overseas hospital. So I was terribly keen that I be taken back to London. Now as this happened I was in London, at St. Thomas' Hospital, six hours after my accident, which was a terrific effort. And it was following this accident that the Grand Prix medical unit was formed. There are things which you learn only as you go along, and since my accident I have a set of spanners that fit my steering wheel taped inside the cockpit of the car. These are painted in day-glo colors with a description of how to remove the car's steering wheel in the language of whatever country I happen to be racing in. This is a small but important point if you get trapped as I did. A safety harness, in my opinion, is a very safe thing to have, a good safety harness. But there's no good of having a safety harness if it's not mounted properly and if it's not a good one. I have a six-point one that holds my thighs and my waist as well as my shoulders. Now I think this is a good one. It's a question of always finding the best thing possible. Fortunately, we're in a sport where people are keen to help us. Aviation probably has the most experience in this area so therefore I had my seat belts done by a company which mainly makes parachutes and ejector seats for the British Air Force. We had an accident expert specializing in air traffic accidents come and tell us what we could use in the way of minimizing the dangers in case of an accident. You know, in a car you can be protected in what you think is the best way possible, but the car doesn't allow you to be protected in such an accident that you may have. We are developing all the time. I am particularly interested in this because, you know, I'm very concerned about my own well-being.

P.M.: Did this accident at all lead you to thoughts of quitting racing?

J.S.: No. When I was lying in the hospital I can remember thinking that perhaps I might be better doing something else. But it never gave me any serious thought of retiring from racing.

P.M.: How profound an impression did the accident make?

J.S.: I haven't consciously felt that it interferes with my driving. I really don't think it has.

P.M.: When you were driving the Masta straight * four weeks ago, were there any remnants of your accident floating around?

J.S.: No, it has had no effect at all. The year following my accident, in '67, I went back to Spa and led the race until three or four laps from the end, when the transmission packed up, and with the transmission not working I had to hold it in gear some of the time and drive with one hand. Now, you know the Masta didn't have anything for me, I mean it could have been classed as more of a challenge but I didn't grit my teeth and say, like the storybooks say, "Look, I'm going to show you." There was nothing of that. It was purely a case of its being another corner that has to be taken as quickly as possible, and it's one of the places in the circuit that is most satisfying. When you go around the Masta properly it's a tremendous achievement—you're flicking the car in and out at a hundred and seventy-five mph between two houses, and this is part of why we motor race.

P.M.: Can you tell me why it's enjoyable?

J.S.: It's a very difficult thing to explain because to drive a race car . . .

P.M.: Would you prefer to skip this question?

J.S.: No, I think it's an interesting question. Driving a race car is one of the most satisfying things that I've ever done because you're controlling something that as a machine should do things without irregularity. It should do things always the same because most machines do. But a racing car very much has a personality and sometimes it does things that are completely and utterly out of character. It reacts in a way that is just not expected. Now to completely master this machine, to be able to tell it exactly what you want it to do and to drive yourself along with the machine to the very limit that only you yourself can determine, why, this requires a tremendous amount of honesty.

P.M.: Honesty?

---

* the Masta straight: a three-mile section of road in the Belgian Grand Prix at Spa; it is not in fact straight but has one sharp bend which is extremely difficult to negotiate properly.

J.S.: Honesty in your own personality and your belief in who you are and what you are and how good you are. Because there's a very good saying, "When the flag drops, the bullshit stops." You can have a lot of chaps sitting in a bar egotistically saying they were doing such and such a thing around such and such a corner because they drive faster than anybody else. But when it actually comes to going around that corner, you must be extremely honest with yourself to say, "Now, this is the limit at which I can take this turn." Now it might be your limit, it might be the car's limit, but the two limits together, the combination of the two, the synchronizing of the human element with the mechanical element, is the difference between the top three or four racing drivers and all the others. This is the mark of what it's all about. When you synchronize your complete body and mind to this racing car at its best you're achieving something that you know is good and that you're doing well. You get a tremendous amount of satisfaction from this. Some days you go out in a race car and everything happens in a big rush. You don't seem to have time to change gears or brake and the corners are all coming up too quickly. You're not synchronized. And thus the most important thing is to synchronize yourself with the elements that you're competing against, the motor car and the track. Your mind must take these elements and completely digest them so as to bring the whole vision into slow motion. For instance, as you arrive at the Masta you're doing a hundred and ninety-five mph. The corner can be taken at a hundred and seventy-three mph. At a hundred and ninety-five mph you should still have a very clear vision, almost in slow motion, of going through that corner—so that you have time to brake, time to line the car up, time to recognize the amount of drift, and then you've hit the apex, given it a bit of a tweek, hit the exit and are out at a hundred and seventy-three mph. Now, the good driver will do this in a calculated way such that as he gets out the other side he'll say "Whew, I did that well." It wasn't a case of coming out and trying to catch the car and regain control. The driver who's fighting it, who doesn't have a mental picture in advance, will arrive at the corner to find that it's all happening very quickly. He's too heavy on the brake, the car is sliding too much, it's a big, deep breath in and a hope that I get around. Now this man doesn't have it. There's a real similarity here between Cassius Clay in the boxing ring and the good racing driver.

P.M.: Mohammed Ali!

J.S.: Mohammed Ali! He sees a punch coming from way down here, the punch comes up and it comes straight to him, he sees the punch coming and he's out of the way before the punch ever arrives because he's *seeing* it, seeing it in slow motion. He's the Fangio * of boxing, if you want to put a name to it. Because he *sees* these things; it's intuition and it's balance. And he's doing this in the best way that a man can.

* Juan Manuel Fangio: (1911–), famous Argentine racing driver.

P.M.: Is this to suggest a special analogy between racing and boxing?

J.S.: No, not really, I think it's the same in every sport. It's the same in playing tennis. As Rod Laver hits a ball over he already sees it coming back to him. In that situation I might not see it coming but he sees it coming. It's not a case of reaction time, it's a case of synchronizing. And I think this applies to other sports as well.

P.M.: Discipline and harmony come to mind—the discipline of self-understanding and self-control, and the harmony of your whole self—your imagination, your eyes and ears and even your butt, the whole of it—working in unison, as an organic, felt presence. Does the elation of flicking the car through the Masta, for example, depend on this feeling of unity?

J.S.: Yes, it's a feeling of satisfaction. It's a feeling of doing anything well. But in motor racing it's so different because you have a heightening of feeling, which I think you must also have in bullfighting. If Rod Laver misses that forehand smash it's simply bad luck, he's dropped a point. But if I miss that point in the Masta, I knock all the houses down. Therefore the feeling of doing it well must be exaggerated. The elation must be higher because we live in such a very narrow street. There's a big drop on this side and there's a big drop on that side. As racing drivers we're under the same pressures as other professional sportsmen, the strain of constant competition and constant travel and constant press. But we have this additional thing. There is no doubt that motor racing is dangerous. The consequences of our mistakes are so different from those in most other sports, thus we have more to consider, a greater responsibility. If Arnold Palmer doesn't fancy his chances in the New Orleans Open after he's sliced his tee shot on the ninth and he's down to a seventy-six or something, well, the Oklahoma Open's next week. The consequences of his mistakes simply don't carry the same weight. Therefore there is this difference when we speak of the pleasures of racing, and the difference is definitely related to the imminent dangers in racing. I think they heighten the pleasure or elation.

P.M.: You're living more intensely because you're coming that much closer to dying?

J.S.: Well, I don't think it's dying because I don't see it that way. I think of it in terms of coming that much closer to a mistake, a mistake which doesn't necessarily mean dying. But it does mean a pretty nasty experience.

P.M.: During the Middle Ages one of the more exciting heresies was a kind of devil worship, the belief that you cannot know goodness until you know evil; cannot know God until you know the devil. And thus there was a certain existential adventuresomeness there that argued for bringing the two, the white and the black, together. It's an attitude not entirely foreign to our own time.

J.S.: Well, I think you may be right because I feel that I enjoy my family more, perhaps, than you do yours.

P.M.: Oh?

J.S.: Yes, because I'm living to this high degree of brinkmanship, if you like, because I'm living at a level which is a little bit on its tiptoes. You know, I don't consider that I take any unnecessary risks at driving a racing car. I'm a professional so I don't take unnecessary risks. But there are times when I know that I've made a slight error of judgment and it's a "eeeeeehh." You know, it's a big deep breath in. So therefore I know that due to the hot competition in the sport that I'm involved in, I must take myself to the maximum all the time—whether I be testing tires or chassis or practicing for the French Grand Prix or actually racing in it. Every day I drive a racing car I've got to take it to the same limits. There's no good of testing tires to a lower lap speed than I'll have to do in the race because the tire might not go that fast, so I've got to take it to the limit all the time. Therefore every day I live to the same limit and every now and again I get myself a fright. I don't stop motor racing because that's got nothing to do with it; I get a fright driving in the street. But I don't think the street driver getting a fright goes home and cuddles his child because he thinks, you know, "that was a bad fright I had." When I do come home I enjoy my family more. And this may have a lot to do with the extremes that make up my life. I don't know.

P.M.: I'm quite sympathetic to your logic, at least in principle.

J.S.: Fine. But this may in fact have some relation because I am not the sort of person who I would immediately regard as a terribly strong family man. I'm very independent. I'm very selfish. I'm very difficult to live with in many respects I'm sure. And yet come my family, I think they have complete importance to me. I live in Geneva now because in Scotland I just couldn't spend enough time with my children. They weren't growing up with me. They had two fathers—one drove a racing car and one came home occasionally. Now I spend so much more time with them—and when I'm at home I do spend an enormous amount of time with them. I don't believe I would be this dedicated to them if I were working in a stockbroker's office.

P.M.: But how much of this is simple guilt? You spend most of your time racing cars, traveling all over the world, operating pretty much as an independent agent jeopardizing not only your own life but the security of your family as well. Many people, I'm sure, would regard what you've said as sentimental guilt.

J.S.: I think that is probably true, because of the recent past, when we have had a few very close friends taken by motor racing and have seen the grief that it brought to their immediate families. And grief personally to me. And because of this these hypothetical people you've mentioned might be correct in saying that I'm guilty or feel guilty. I would hate—very, very, very much hate—to see my family go through the grief that I have seen a few very close friends of mine go through. So this is perhaps true. But I enjoy my life so much that I think part of that enjoyment is heightened because of how I live.

P.M.: You have a son?

J.S.: Yes, two of them.

P.M.: How would you feel if they started racing cars?

J.S.: I'd hate it, just hate it. I would use most everything to make sure they didn't do it.

P.M.: Why?

J.S.: Because I think it must be one of the most difficult occupations to be a racing driver's father or a racing driver's mother. You know, I think sometimes it's a bloody stupid sport. I get so much pleasure out of doing it personally, and yet sometimes when things go wrong, I really do think it's stupid. Stupid. I say this assuming that you are writing a serious book, because I haven't said this to anyone before. I would much prefer that my son played professional golf.

P.M.: Professional golf?

J.S.: Yes, because then he could keep his father in comfort for the rest of his life and live a very safe existence.

P.M.: So why don't you stop racing automobiles and take up golf?

J.S.: Because I know I just don't have the ability to do it. You know, golf is something else. I enjoy playing golf, it's the sport that I enjoy doing more than anything else, but it's a sport that I don't do particularly well. I used to trap shoot a lot and I know that I could step into that again and immediately do it well. But golf I know I can't do well. I play a few times a year, when I can, and sometimes play to an eight handicap and sometimes to a sixteen handicap. But I enjoy it, and probably because I don't want to be successful at it. If I had to shoot, I know that I would feel that I had to be successful and therefore I wouldn't enjoy it. I feel the same way about squash. Do you know squash?

P.M.: Yes, it's one of the few games I've enjoyed.

J.S.: I get annoyed if I don't play squash well because it's an immensely competitive sport, which golf isn't. Golf to me is a social sport. I wouldn't go out and play golf with people that I don't know because I'd be frightened that I'd hold them up because I wasn't playing well. I would prefer to go out with a bunch of the boys and have a great foursome and a nice time, a great conversation, a social outing. Squash, on the other hand, is fiercely competitive. You're doing something against your opponent. You're outrunning him, you're outthinking him. You're trying to put him in an embarrassing position so that he can't get the ball back to you. And also you may be putting yourself in an embarrassing position if you can't retrieve it. I suppose it takes quick reactions but again, like driving, it's not so much reflexes as it is the intuition to think ahead, to know what your opponent is going to do, what's coming up.

P.M.: What interests me here is the three sports you've isolated—squash, shooting, racing cars—all put a premium on individual performance, on self-reliance. They're not "team sports."

J.S.: Yes, I'm not a particularly good team man. I don't see myself as sitting quietly in the background helping the team along. I feel as if the team should be helping me.

P.M.: Why?

J.S.: I don't know. I suppose it's the same as when I do anything. The fraternity of motor racing travels around the world maybe seven or eight times a year. We meet an enormous number of interesting people during our trips. But each year I think I meet only a handful of people whom I consider to be something special, whose ability I genuinely respect. The others I think must be quite good at their jobs but have got glaring weaknesses that put them down one step from being the top. And I suppose the demand that I put on myself to be the best, or the best that I can personally be, is reflected in my judgment of other people. In America I met a man who does the PR for a large clothing concern, and in my opinion he is one of the sharpest, most fast-thinking professionals I've met. He's a PR man and he's a really good PR man. He has the great ability to do his job well but also to understand people who don't understand his business. He covers people well. He takes them along with him. If somebody has got a weakness, he'll cover for that weakness, not allow a man to be embarrassed. You know, if there's a woman in the company who doesn't really know a hell of a lot about what is being said in the conversation, he'll always be the one to keep her right, keep her up with the conversation.

P.M.: Then it's his competence you respect?

J.S.: Yes, and this goes along with his top-grade position in his field. Yes, competence. Weakness really annoys me. People must be competent about their job. Now this man has got this. Another example in this respect is the Director-General of Matra,* and he's of the same nature. He's a top man at his job and that's a man I respect tremendously.

P.M.: And how do you feel about a guy who's quite well intentioned but is a loser?

J.S.: This comes into a different class. There are some people who you immediately take in and enjoy being with, and then there are the people who you completely respect and admire. I think there are two different classes. Those whom I respect are not narrow people. In America, for instance, you find many specialists who are simply not complete people. America is a very good country for this. Let's say you have a man who is top in electronics, really a top man. Take him out of his own environment, and in America you'll sometimes find him to be basically immature, childish, and really a bad person to be with. He's so incomplete and immature outside of his specialized unit. In cases like this I think to myself, "How does this man manage to be as good as he is?" He's concentrated in this very narrow band and he has managed to succeed in it. But life outside of that very narrow band has eluded him. He doesn't understand a sense of humor, for instance. He doesn't understand what

---

* Matra: French manufacturer of racing cars.

a woman wants to know. He doesn't understand anyone else's point of view. He doesn't understand how to play golf, or to dress, or to do the simple things in life. He's just not a man, he's a child. He hasn't matured because of having specialized on one avenue of life.

P.M.: By reputation Fangio is a very shy man, socially shy. . . .

J.S.: I know Fangio well now and he is one man I look at and get a tremendous amount of excitement from him. You know, when you walk into a room you notice Fangio straight away. I do. He has fantastic eyes. They show life. Some people have eyes that are alive and are either deep or sparkle or something. But they're *there,* you notice them. And Fangio is one of these men. But his whole personality goes with his eyes. He's just got a personality that projects. I still today get a great thrill out of speaking to the man and seeing him.

P.M.: What you're really talking about is a kind of aggressiveness.

J.S.: What I'm talking about is probably my difficulty in being concerned with other people. This is one of the things I mean when I say I'm difficult to live with because perhaps I'm more demanding than most people. Just demanding, let's say, of my wife, of how she conducts herself.

P.M.: You're a tyrant?

J.S.: No, I'm not a tyrant. I think I'm very sympathetic in that respect. But I feel that she should be able to recognize the things to do when they should be done, and therefore see how I operate and therefore see through me without having to ask me. She should recognize when not to speak to me, as when there are racing problems at moments of tension. Things like that. You know, I see through people usually quite quickly and I keep thinking that she should be parallel with me. The same applies to people in business: they've got the basic capabilities perhaps and they don't use them. This annoys me.

P.M.: There's certainly more than a touch of the romantic about you.

J.S.: That's interesting, because I don't really see myself that way. I'm a very calculated person in my attitude to my racing. You know, I have a complete spare helmet kit—overalls, underwear, socks, uniform, crash helmet, goggles, spare lenses—in my Formula 1 transporter. I have a similar spare kit in my Formula 2 transporter. And I carry my normal racing kit when I travel because I might otherwise lose it in some aircraft that's had four stopovers. I don't think the other drivers do that sort of thing. I perhaps think a little bit more about the safety thing. I'm serious about that sort of thing much more than they are. Also I happened to be the first that started using seat belts and face masks in Europe, and then started getting these proper suits made and so forth. And it's because I don't want to be hurt. Basically I'm a coward, so therefore maybe I am cautious in these ways. I look at my motor racing seriously but I get a tremendous amount of pleasure from it. I really enjoy my motor racing.

P.M.: Don't you feel that the other drivers enjoy it also?

J.S.: Oh, yes, they do enjoy it.

P.M.: In 1966, you went to Indianapolis for the first time, were leading the race and some twenty miles from the finish . . .

J.S.: Fifteen!

P.M.: Fifteen miles—so sorry—fifteen miles from the end the car fell apart. What happened to the car and what happened to you?

J.S.: Well, I was leading by two laps or something similar when the oil pressure fell away and the engine began to seize. I felt a slight tinge of disappointment, but I wasn't angry. You can never get annoyed with these things because there is nothing you can do about it. The deed is done and who are you going to get annoyed at?

P.M.: You dropped fifty, seventy-five thousand dollars?

J.S.: That was minimum. I must have dropped, personally, a hundred and thirty, a hundred and forty thousand dollars. That's a lot of money for an American but think of it from a Scotsman's point of view! But I had led Indianapolis, never having been there before. I had done something that I never thought I would do because I didn't expect to win Indianapolis the first year I went there. So, therefore, I had a certain amount of elation from having led the race and thinking, "Well, these bastards will at least know I've been here." And really I was personally satisfied by my own performance. So therefore the fact that I didn't win didn't immediately disappoint me. The day after the race, well, I can't say that it didn't disappoint me then.

P.M.: What do you do with your money?

J.S.: I buy a very nice house in Switzerland. I buy myself nice clothes because I enjoy buying nice clothes. I invest and I bank money because I'm basically, I think, an insecure person and like to think that someday I'm going to stop motor racing, and then I might need an income. I also have an auto business in Scotland. Because I had no money when I started motor racing, I've tried to accumulate a certain amount of capital and securities.

P.M.: Do your parents have money?

J.S.: No, not to any great extent. I wouldn't claim to be a poor kid. My father and mother gave me a great deal of luxuries that lots of other people never have. They had a small garage business that could afford to keep our family very well. But money which I've made in motor racing has supplied me with security which I would not normally have had, and it's also allowed me to live an extremely nice and comfortable life. Therefore money is not unimportant, but when it comes to winning a motor race or having a disappointment at Indianapolis, then I think it is unimportant. I had completely and utterly satisfied myself by the drive that I had made.

P.M.: But earlier you said that as you were driving two laps in the lead you were chuckling with satisfaction, saying "I'll show those bastards." Were you referring generically to the American drivers or simply to your competitors in general?

J.S.: To everybody. To the spectators as well as the drivers.

P.M.: What do you mean by calling them "bastards"?

J.S.: That was perhaps a very loose term.

P.M.: But it interests me.

J.S.: Well, all right then. It could be said that at that time . . . no, I think I was wrong when I said that.

P.M.: Why?

J.S.: Because I don't . . .

P.M.: Are you being polite?

J.S.: No, no, no. Because I don't think I meant it, really. I think I used it simply because it came into my head.

P.M.: Maybe it's an affectionate term.

J.S.: Under the circumstances it could be classed as affectionate because as it happened they treated me extremely well at Indianapolis, the drivers and the crowd alike. Everyone received me well. It wasn't a case of my having a bad, rough drive to get in number one position. It was a case of that when I had done it I rather felt that at least they've got me down here as having come and having done it successfully. They would know I had been there. I had proved to them I could win Indianapolis. I wasn't really saying that I had a mean touch towards them because this is not true. So therefore the phraseology I used was my error.

P.M.: This touches on something I've thought about while talking to racing people. On the one hand you evaluate your drive by a standard of personal satisfaction which is entirely private or subjective, and on the other you'll measure your performance more objectively. On the one hand you're happy because you've done it right and it just simply and plainly feels good, and on the other hand you'll get excited because everyone respects you and is impressed with what you've done. There seem to be two yardsticks, one internal, the other public.

J.S.: There are some races, lots of races, that I don't win that I get tremendous satisfaction out of. In 1965, I finished second to Jim Clark in three Grands Prix, and I was completely satisfied at finishing second. You know, that's a poor thing to say because I should have been winning and I should have wanted to win. Sure I wanted to win, but I was satisfied with finishing second because I was so much further ahead of everybody else.

P.M.: Fine, but didn't you feel moved to regard yourself as a better driver than Jim Clark and thus chafe at your second spot?

J.S.: I wasn't sure. I really wasn't sure because it was my first season in Formula I racing. I had a competitive car, the BRM, but no more competitive than anybody else's. I knew Jimmy had a competitive car and probably the best car, and I respected him as the best driver too. I wasn't sure that if put in a Lotus I could have kept up with him, I might not have been able to beat him.

P.M.: Did you often think about this?

J.S.: I think so, yes. It's always a thought because when somebody is beating you, you want to know why.

P.M.: When you drive nowadays, do you assume you're the best? What's the quality of your confidence?

J.S.: Confidence is very important, confidence in knowing how much you can do. You see, I don't know what anybody else can do. I'm extremely honest with myself, and I know my own weaknesses and I recognize them. I can't know the weaknesses in other people; I can see them, but I don't know how they feel.

P.M.: Don't you plan on their weaknesses in a race?

J.S.: Oh, yes, of course I do. Of course, you use every advantage you can. I know of their weaknesses but not sometimes their actual driving weaknesses. Sometimes it's a car weakness because it's a combination of the driver and the car, and some individual drivers, I know, tire after fifty or sixty laps or whatever it is, and I can think ahead and know who I'm competing against. But that's not the point. In sport, in all the things I've done, in my shooting, for instance, where I was almost as successful as I've been in motor racing, I never really thought I would ever win anything. I was always pleasantly surprised when I won because I never actually thought that I could beat this other bloke called Rossini who happened to be the world champion. But when I did beat him, it was a pleasure and surprise. This is almost a Scottish trait, really.

P.M.: Were you surprised two weeks ago when you won the Grand Prix of Holland at Zandvoort or did you accept the win as a matter of course?

J.S.: No, I accepted it as evidence of the fact that I drove a race which I considered to be a good race. In the rain I didn't make the mistakes that the other fellows made; I recognized the limitations of the road and the car. They weren't using the same piece of the road that I was using, they were using the road that they normally use. I was using a piece of road that wasn't being used so therefore there wasn't any oil on it. This was giving me an untold advantage. I was surprised and disappointed that they didn't recognize this and it was to my advantage, and I was very happy that it was to my advantage. But, you know, I also had an advantage in the tires that I was using and my car went well. So the combination of everything won the motor race. Now I would have been disappointed if I had made a mistake that had lost me the race, which was very easy to do. You don't get people like Graham Hill and Jack Brabham and Dan Gurney and John Surtees and Jochen Rindt all making mistakes without some very severe conditions. These people usually just don't make these mistakes, but they were making them, so I was very pleased that I didn't make them.

P.M.: Well, a number of the people you've mentioned, certainly one of them, aquaplaned his way off the circuit, and it's my understanding that there's little you can do about aquaplaning.

J.S.: Well, no, that's not quite true. You've got to avoid the big puddles. I had it too, we all aquaplaned. But mainly you're right, when you aquaplane there's nobody who can help you . . . not even God can get you out of it. You're on your own.

P.M.: All right, now, what has this to do with your self-confidence? Couldn't it be said that you simply didn't have the bad luck to slide off the road?

J.S.: Exactly.

P.M.: Doesn't this mitigate your satisfaction in winning the race?

J.S.: Not at all. In the early stages I thought that I was driving a fairly well-balanced race and therefore felt that I had a good chance of winning if I continued to drive properly. But you can't always do that.

P.M.: How do you pace yourself? It's obvious that there's an orderliness and discipline about your driving—how do you achieve that?

J.S.: Well, I think it has a great deal to do with your temperament. A fiery individual usually looks a bit fiery in a racing car. You know, a racing car is very much like a human being. Sometimes you could say it's very much like a woman, you know. This has been said before so it's no new material for you, but it is . . .

P.M.: Let me decide, please . . .

J.S.: . . . well, I don't want you to think that it's a new quote because it's been said before. But, you know, sometimes you have to be extremely sympathetic with a car. You have to caress it. You have to coax it into doing the things that you want it to do. You've got to tempt it into everything. You've got to be very gentle with it and be very careful with it.

P.M.: All cars?

J.S.: No, only some cars. With others, on some occasions, you've got to drive the hell out of them. You've got to give them a really good thrashing. And this is the way they've got to be driven. So they do have character. As you know, you can alter the car's personality somewhat. I set a car up, suspension-wise, to be treated nicely; other people prefer to set their cars to be treated more harshly.

P.M.: You know about the mechanics?

J.S.: Well, yes, we all know much the same thing. Some are more knowledgeable than others. I would say I was in a medium bracket here. I don't fetch to be a designer of racing cars so therefore I have a designer who works on it. I try to relate what the car is doing to him the best way that I can. I try to paint a picture to him as clear and as colorful as I can so that he can read back and see that picture as well as he can see a photograph. Now if I color it correctly, the chances are that he's going to bring out on paper and in mathematics the faults that I feel through my backside. So therefore, I don't profess to be the man who decides what is causing a particular weakness in my car. On the other hand, some of the drivers profess to know these things and some do, in fact, have this ability.

P.M.: Let's go back, though, to the question of discipline and pacing one's self. Presumably, before a race you decide on a strategy?

J.S.: No, I very seldom set up a strategy before a race. I never say that I'm going to hang back or something similar to that because I don't believe this can happen. I believe that "strategies," in most cases, are a lot of bullshit and sometimes mean that you can't keep up and must hang back through necessity rather than choice. In my case, I prefer not to have any strategy. If I happen to find that I can comfortably keep up the pace that the others are driving without endangering the motor car or my own limits, well and good. If I have to be in the lead or if I want to build up a sufficient lead to be comfortable, I'll simply drive as hard as I can.

P.M.: Tell me about this nine-tenths, ten-tenths business.

J.S.: Well, there comes a point when you drive very hard and you're right on the limit. You're occasionally locking a wheel into a corner, you're going into the corner really on the limit of adhesion, the car sliding out to the last piece of road, occasionally using up a piece of grass—all the things that bring you to the absolute that you can drive to. That is nine-tenths motoring, you know, or ten-tenths. If you use ten-tenths it usually means an accident because some of these times you make a slight error of judgment, and when you're driving to the very highest point any error is an accident.

P.M.: What do you mean by an accident?

J.S.: Well, a crash.

P.M.: But an accident is not bending the suspension?

J.S.: It depends on how hard you bend it. It depends on how big the crash is.

P.M.: Well, if you tweak it, if you break a casting or something?

J.S.: Yes, if you break a casting you might just be hitting a curb or something. That's not an accident, that's a mistake. But an accident is when you lose control of the car and you have a shunt. When you're driving at nine-tenths you're within that and this is usually the limit to win races at. At eight-tenths you fall off a little bit and you hold the pace of the race; at nine-tenths, on the other hand, you're drawing away from everyone else. At eight-tenths, you're fallen off a little bit and you hold the pace, and the pace has been determined by you if you're leading the race. And at seven-tenths you're feathering off and letting them catch you; you've decided that you've got ten laps to go and that you've got forty seconds at hand and they're only catching up a second a lap, so you play it cool and finish thirty seconds ahead instead of forty seconds ahead.

P.M.: What's most comfortable?

J.S.: About eight-tenths. But I'd love to be at nine-tenths and drawing away all the time. At that rate I'm taking advantage of everybody else and proving that

I'm the quickest that day. At eight-tenths, you know, I'm leaving a little bit of doubt in their minds.

P.M.: In their minds—but what about your mind?

J.S.: Well, in my mind if I've gone off to eight-tenths, I know that I've slackened off to eight-tenths as a matter of decision. It's like at Zandvoort—I had a lap ahead of Beltoise, there was no point in my setting better times than him when he passed me with fifteen laps to go. You know, there was no common sense in me trying to keep up with him, of pressing my car, or risking aquaplaning, or doing anything else. So I slackened off and this was my pace.

P.M.: But when you talk of "showing them" who are you showing—them or yourself?

J.S.: Well, them—because it's what you do to them that affects their performance. If you press on all the time at nine-tenths and keep advancing on them, you're demoralizing them. Because if I were in that same position and trying like hell and I'm lying second and they're still drawing away from me and I can't do anything about it, what am I going to do? Am I going to keep trying real hard or am I going to settle down and say now, "Well, I can't catch him anyway." This you've got to recognize. Now after you've had twenty or thirty seconds in the lead and you decide that that pace is fast enough and the fellow behind you says "Oh, you know, I'm holding him there." He thinks that he's going as quickly as you are, but in fact he's not. Let's say you go up a lap or a couple of cars and he catches you two seconds in that lap and he looks at his board and he sees minus eighteen seconds. He tries to go a little bit quicker. So the next lap you know you've gone two seconds slower so you go a little bit quicker again, and this knocks him back down again. He gets demoralized.

P.M.: Are you talking about winning races or putting someone down?

J.S.: Oh, entirely winning races because while you're out there winning a motor race, while you're actually doing it, your ego is not at stake at all. The only time your ego comes into play is when you've got lots and lots of time to think about it. Sometimes you then think about the fact that you are leading the motor race. All of a sudden you think, "Yes, I'm winning the motor race." This is a pleasure. When I'm leading the race, I think, "Well, I've done this, it's recognized as being done," you know, with me and with them satisfying my own . . . what is it? Satisfying my own . . . my . . . well, whatever I'm doing motor racing for. It's when I say I am satisfied at my performance. What is it I'm satisfying? Is it my ego I'm satisfying?

P.M.: I don't know.

J.S.: Well, I don't know either. I'm just satisfied. I know that I'm in control of it. I know that it's mine. I know that I've done it.

P.M.: Well, do you care that twenty years from now somewhere in a record book it'll say that you won at Zandvoort in 1968?

J.S.: Oh, hell, I don't know about that. I suppose in twenty years' time if I look at the Dutch Grand Prix trophy and I see my own name on it I'll get a slight tinge of pride, yes. I think I'd be a liar if I said no. Yes, I'm sure I will. You know, it's one of the things that I like to think that I've achieved. It's an achievement in life so therefore if you have achieved something it's no good without some kind of recognition. I don't care who you are, it's just not human nature to disregard success.

P.M.: But you care more for the fun of it than for the so-called achievement?

J.S.: Oh, yes, I think I do. Of course, if I weren't winning, hadn't a chance of winning, I think then perhaps I would lose a lot of the pleasure because I'm basically a competitive person. So therefore, if I had no chance of winning I'm sure I wouldn't have the same pleasure that I get now. You see, in motor racing, I've always been fortunate enough to be involved in winning, in whatever class of racing I've been coming through. I've always been in with a chance.

P.M.: Drunk or sober, haven't you asked yourself why?

J.S.: I've never been drunk.

P.M.: A Scotsman and never drunk?

J.S.: I've never been drunk. I don't like the taste of alcohol. From the primitive years of sixteen or seventeen or whenever it is that people start to take a wee dram, I've been driving a car and have been very responsible to that. Also at that age I was shooting competitively and probably put more effort into my shooting than my motor racing, because it was my first love and certainly my first success. I got a great deal of pleasure out of it and I put a lot into it. So therefore everything that I did at that time related to my competition and alcohol just didn't go along with it. It certainly wasn't as if I had anything against alcohol, rather that I didn't like either the taste or the effects. I tasted gin and I didn't like the taste. Somebody gave me a taste from their glass and I went "Ugh." There's only a few drinks that I've found to be palatable. I like champagne (I have rich tastes), I like Pims Cup #1, which is an English drink, and I sometimes take a Dubonnet with 7-Up. I also like a table wine that's not too dry, but then I seldom take wine; I won't take it, say, three days before a race. You see, I've been used to drinking soft drinks so if I do drink the effect is noticeable. I get a sore head. If we were having dinner and had a bottle of wine between us, the next morning I would know that I had wine even when I had been eating a full meal.

P.M.: All right. To go back, you've doubtlessly asked yourself why you've been successful. What do you tell yourself?

J.S.: I'm damned if I know and I mean that, I really mean it. It's not bullshit and it's not evading the question. I don't know. I don't know if it's the way I drive the racing car or whether everybody's slower or something. I honestly don't know. It's a very natural thing for me, driving a racing car. If you do something naturally, you don't know why you're better at that than somebody else.

P.M.: A rather interesting thing that has emerged in talking with a number of drivers is that most of them tend to be politically conservative. This comes as a rather disappointing surprise to me because I don't regard driving a race car as a conservative activity.

J.S.: Well, you've got to be a fairly conservative individual to control your emotions sufficiently to drive a racing car competitively and successfully. I don't know whether this emotional conservatism reflects politics or not, but I think politics is a very difficult subject to discuss in any case.

P.M.: Why?

J.S.: Because I think politicians are damned liars in most cases, very insincere people. There are very few of them that I have been in contact with, but I find them very difficult to digest because of their insincerity.

P.M.: What do you think of the Beatles?

J.S.: Fabulous. I admire the Beatles more than most people because they are true professionals who enjoy enormously what they do, and do it with such tremendous success. I think they themselves have been basically unprepared for the adulation that they've received. They are much like racing drivers in a sense because in becoming very successful they haven't had the time to enjoy their success—one success comes after another, what was last week's hit may today be out of the top ten or the number one spot. They've got to substitute another one, and thus the pleasure they had from doing an earlier song has now been destroyed or lessened. Therefore, they now have to look for something else, they have to keep ahead, moving all the time. And I'm not sure they know where they've gone. You see, this applies not only to their music, but to their leisure and pleasure as well. And I think that this side of their life, which has nothing whatsoever to do with me and therefore I shouldn't really be criticizing it, is unfortunate. I think it's unfortunate that they have gone so abstract.

P.M.: In their music?

J.S.: No, in their music I think this is nice. I'm referring to the abstraction in their life. All of a sudden they've found a certain emptiness through not having time to digest the pleasures that have come with their success.

P.M.: For better or worse, many people are taking acid.

J.S.: Well, this is unfortunate but not because of the Beatles. Now look, I don't take it. I've never known anyone directly who has. Frankly, I'm a person who can be very easily misled in many respects. I mean, if I get a sore head tonight I'll really want to take a couple of aspirins but I'll think about it because if I've got a sore head tomorrow night I'll take three, you know, instead of taking two. So therefore, because of the height of one's way of living one is more easily taken by anything that seems to be of advantage. So if you feel a bit down and you think taking a pill will liven you up, well, I can see that this has a derogatory effect at the end of the line. What I'm trying to say about the Beatles, and this is where I think it's sad but doesn't deter from my adulation of them, is that they've never sat down and properly understood themselves because they've never been allowed to take time off. The people surrounding them and dictating the pace of their lives have put them into this position. You know, I don't think that they would enjoy any less than I would staying in the very best hotel and having the best service, the best food, and the best weather. I don't think they've had a chance to do this at their leisure so therefore they've had to go to other things. Therefore, all the nice things I'm talking about are now stale, they mean nothing to them, they're square because they themselves have gone beyond this into heights that they're not really controlling.

P.M.: But then again, my dear grandmother would look at you and think you're leading an improper life because you haven't had a haircut in many, many weeks.

J.S.: Sure, but you're speaking of something which isn't the same.

P.M.: St. Paul regarded long hair on men as unnatural and as a sin against God. So who's to say?

J.S.: I'm a hell of a sinner.

P.M.: How do you feel about the Rolling Stones?

J.S.: They don't give me the same excitement at all. I think the Beatles are fantastic. They're the people who produce the sound and who have the beat and everything. To me they're everything. They're not simply what's happening today, they're ahead of it. At the same time, let me say, my adulation also goes out to Sinatra. He's a real pro.

P.M.: Oh, I know what you like about Frank Sinatra. . . .

J.S.: Well, tell me.

P.M.: All right. You like a number of things which we'll put under the category of his being a "pro." What this means is Frank Sinatra has Jack Kennedy sleeping in his Palm Springs house; he wears very expensive, if vulgar, clothes; he has a helicopter ferrying him back and forth between his Los Angeles home and his Palm Springs home; and finally he has, on his dining table, a huge crystal vase in which there's a package of every brand of cigarette for his guests of various and doubtlessly capricious tastes. In a word, the fact that Frank Sinatra is an elaborate and efficient operator.

J.S.: Bullshit!

P.M.: All right, then, you tell me!

J.S.: Frank Sinatra is a performer. I saw him in Las Vegas and I've listened to his records for years and I have most of them and I enjoy hearing Sinatra sing. He has the finesse, the class, to put a song over; he has the ability to make me feel it. He's got the same success or professionalism as the Beatles. But he's done it for how many years? In Las Vegas he had an audience eating out of his hand for an hour and a half. They were turning away a thousand people a night who'd come to see this man, not because he's got this crystal bowl with all of the cigarettes in it but because he is tremendous to listen to.

He excites me. I look at him and I feel, Jesus, that's Frank Sinatra. You know, he's a star. The fact is that he's an entertainer, a singer. I don't care anything else about him. When I see Frank Sinatra, I enjoy him. You know, when I met him I felt that I was meeting somebody of importance. He's a success. He's done better than anybody else. Ella Fitzgerald, what's wrong with her?

P.M.: Oh, not the least thing is wrong with her. And Billie Holliday?

J.S.: Okay, now I just happen to take Ella Fitzgerald. Again I adore her. I adore her as much as Sinatra and the Beatles. Right now I adore Petula Clarke because she's got the same ability.

P.M.: Perhaps, but she doesn't sound as good.

J.S.: Well, maybe not, but to me she is of the moment. I enjoy her, the way she puts it over, the numbers she does and everything else. So therefore I'm not taking Sinatra because he's a successful man. You know, I've met a lot of rich men. That doesn't make me admire them all. Look, Sinatra may have very bad taste in many respects. But this isn't the point. It is just that he's a top-class operator. He's a fabulous man to listen to.

P.M.: Did you go to school?

J.S.: Until I was fifteen, when I went to work in a garage. I didn't think that my future was in the academic heights of a university or college. Moreover, I didn't want to continue. I am a very slow learner when I'm not interested in the things that have been put forward.

P.M.: Do you do a lot of reading?

J.S.: Yes, light books.

P.M.: What's a "light book"?

J.S.: I've just finished *Topaz,* which I enjoyed tremendously. I read all of Harold Robbins' books. I read *The Prize,* which I enjoyed very much. I enjoy the Fleming books, Alistair McLean. I read a book by Lord Moran because it was interesting, because here was a different type of story which I enjoyed. Basically, they're all easy to read. They don't take a lot of concentration. When I get onto an airplane or when I lie in bed I want something that dictates me. You know, I'm reading the *Dirty Dozen* just now and . . .

P.M.: Did you see the movie?

J.S.: Fantastic!

P.M.: Do you like Lee Marvin?

J.S.: Yes, he got me feeling that he was the man controlling the Dirty Dozen and he is a bloody fine actor. As a matter of fact, when I saw Sinatra, Lee Marvin was at the next table with the sort of Mexican-looking chap that was in the movie, I forget his name.

P.M.: Oh, Telly Savalas.

J.S.: I'm very bad with names. He's a big star. He's another good chap. You see, I'm very easily taken in. I see all these actors in the roles that they played.

P.M.: What about Marlon Brando?

J.S.: Well, again, in the *Magnificent Seven* I thought he was terrific.

P.M.: He wasn't in the *Magnificent Seven*.

J.S.: Oh, sorry, I thought he had been.

P.M.: Did you see *Streetcar Named Desire?*

J.S.: No.

P.M.: All right. I'm getting tired, so let me ask you one final question—What's your reaction to this interview, to the material we've been discussing?

J.S.: Well, I'm sure that you mean well but I'm not sure that all the material we've been discussing is relevant. I hope it's a help to you, but I'm not sure that it necessarily will do. But I think anyone doing a serious effort, something of this kind, should obviously get the best information that is available. It would be wrong for me to give you twenty minutes instead of several hours and for you not to get the picture because . . .

P.M.: Of course, I appreciate your attitude . . .

J.S.: No, it's not a case of your appreciating it. It's a case of your coming out with the wrong picture because you're not going to get the picture in twenty minutes.

P.M.: Well, I'm not going to get it in two hours either, but this way I certainly stand a better chance.

J.S.: From that point of view, it's better for me to answer the questions you ask. None of the questions you've asked have been out of context, with the possible exception of the Beatles and these things.

P.M.: Well, that interests me.

J.S.: Well, that's fine, but you see I don't see it because you're looking for a different reason, from a different angle.

P.M.: Shall I tell you why? Both Frank Sinatra and Lee Marvin project a kind of personality which is quite different from the personality of Marlon Brando, for example. Brando, in most respects, is anti-establishment. Sinatra and Lee Marvin are anti-establishment but less sympathetic. What I mean by that is the quality of alienation, of being outside, lonely, isolated, frightened, if you will, which one sees in Brando is far more authentic and effective I think, than the kinds of things coming from a Sinatra or certainly a Lee Marvin. And I would say, too, that there is something infinitely more human, more sensitive about Brando than Marvin, whom I also find to my slight embarrassment and to my wife's continual annoyance, attractive in some devilish way. But I feel a touch uneasy in this because I strongly suspect he's a son of a bitch, a nasty, ruthless guy who doesn't take anything for real, save himself. Now I know that's not true with Brando.

J.S.: Well, I don't know. I think it's very difficult to tell with actors.

P.M.: But it's very interesting. The people that I've isolated are certainly by profession actors, but their personalities in life are more varied. I tend to see people like Lee Marvin and Marlon Brando in political terms because in the United States both are out in the open politically.

J.S.: This is something I can't really understand with people. American politics are so difficult. It's like everything else in America, there's much more specialization there than anywhere else. Having these actors and personalities involved in politics must be a tremendous advantage to the politicians.

P.M.: Oh, indeed it is. For instance, Lee Marvin is a Marine. He actually was a Marine and on several occasions he's made what amount to publicity statements for the Marines. I find this offensive because not only do the Marines scare me, they also offend me. I don't like the ideology of the Marines and, personally, I don't like most Marines as people; I think they're bullies.

J.S.: Oh, well, I haven't met many Marines. But you see this is inbred, part of their training.

P.M.: Yes, but one seeks the training, doesn't one?

J.S.: Well, I don't know. Let's say you're a timid little chap from . . .

P.M.: The Marines won't take you.

J.S.: Now hold on a second, I'm not so sure. Let's say you're basically an insecure individual who has got some sort of complex. You trade these complexes for something that you see as capable of removing them or making you . . .

P.M.: Burying them?

J.S.: Yes, burying them. And these people are put in, they go and sign up for the Marines and they just so happen to be big strong lads.

P.M.: Now you wait a second. You go and sign up to be a Marine, the Marines don't call you.

J.S.: All right, you call them. This is fine because our hypothetical person thinks that he's going in and maybe he's had a big brother who's always been bigger and stronger than he has . . .

P.M.: And thus we ought to be sympathetic with his needs?

J.S.: No, no, so therefore he wasn't sure that he was strong enough and wanted to be a big brother too, so therefore you say, how can I do that? I'm going to go and do it in the Marines.

P.M.: I don't think you give a gun and the option to kill people to such individuals. However, this doesn't really put our finger on the problem, which is a certain arrogance which informs the Marine Corps.

J.S.: Because it's necessary. I think it is. I really do think it is.

P.M.: At what price?

J.S.: Maybe not having you like them.

P.M.: But that's small potatoes in comparison with other things.

J.S.: Exactly, but how many other things affect their success?

P.M.: What do you mean by success? The fact that they first topped Iwo Jima or something like that?

J.S.: Just because if they are the boys to have, they are the best.

P.M.: Too simple, too simple . . .

J.S.: Well, I'm a very simple person. Unfortunately, this is the way my mind works.

P.M.: You're not all that simple.

J.S.: Oh, I am, I really am. You could say you don't like the Marines because there are some things you don't like people to do and that they themselves are nasty people. I could say that the press, generally, is made up of nasty people. They're unsympathetic. In the case of tragedy they can be so painfully callous that it's detestable. Unfortunately, however much as we detest them, they're merely doing their job. They are covering . . .

P.M.: Right, but there's such a thing as grace.

J.S.: Yes, but they're covering for a mass media who don't particularly accept grace.

P.M.: Come on, to use one of your own frequent words, bullshit. And I'll tell you what I mean by that. What you're saying is that the common denominator, the lowest sensibility establishes the heights to which society . . .

J.S.: Not at all, not at all, because they're selling. You know, this is being aimed at me. I'm accepting it because they are supplying news, the sensationalism, and they are selling their news and the only way that they're going to get anything better than anybody else is to come out with something that the other bloke doesn't get. Sometimes that requires digging that is unpalatable.

P.M.: All right. Let's say tomorrow you crash and die . . .

J.S.: That's not a very nice thing to say.

P.M.: No, it's not, it's not at all, and I don't say it easily; but what you're saying is serious and in its extreme form rather dangerous. Tomorrow you crash and die and your wife over there, right now sitting beside you . . .

J.S.: Let's take the Kennedy affair, if you don't mind.

P.M.: Okay, go ahead, take the Kennedy affair.

J.S.: Now in the Kennedy affair—the pictures of Kennedy I think were extremely distasteful and they were shown in the Swiss papers and in the English papers and in the French papers. It's unfortunate that this is the way they work, the way they've got to be, and this is the way they will always be and this is the way the Marines will always be.

P.M.: Look, what I'm really saying about the Marines is simple. The Marines for me are a kind of metaphor, a kind of symbol for major attitudes in America which distress me. And of course, I don't think these things are limited to the Marines. I think that you find them in many areas of society, but I think the Marines epitomize these things, a certain callousness, a certain kind of brutality, or worse, a certain kind of self-righteousness. And I don't appreciate those things.

J.S.: You don't appreciate them but, unfortunately, I think that they're necessary. I really do. I think perhaps you don't like the Marines because one of them punched you at one time.

P.M.: Maybe yes, maybe no. But friend, that's not the point; I only wish it were.

Studs Terkel / Bob Carter and Therese Carter

Tape recorders have had at least one enormously beneficial effect. They have made available the direct testimony of the many kinds of Americans —the average as well as the exceptional—who otherwise exist for study only in the various official mythologies created about them by poll takers, statisticians, sociologists, or literary mythologizers. Of course people not able or apt to write about themselves have before been the subject of transcription by stenographic means or by studio recorders. But tape recorders, portable and inconspicuous, have encouraged a much wider documentation of the complex, hidden lives that make up the society of this or any other country. In addition, they have caught the varieties of styles and tones that authentically belong to these lives.

Our whole concept of what constitutes society and history has been changed by the increased technical power to take account of vast numbers of people hitherto left mute. Most of what we think of the past is a result of what the privileged thought worth recording in written form. What would be our image of, say, sixteenth-century France if we knew as much about the peasantry as we now know about the economically underprivileged of our own time and country? Because of the freedom allowed them by Terkel as an interviewer and by his instruments, Bob and Therese Carter, residents of a lower-middle-class area near Chicago, are shown to be quite intricately involved in the very issues posed by these new demographic and technological realities: he, in his amiableness toward a black friend despite neighborhood disapproval; she, in her passion for reading, which she characterizes as peculiar in a neighborhood where people are bound to television and almost no one else reads books. The Carters feel rather special and the reader might tend to find them so, until he asks if that characterization isn't probably the result of one's having thought too long of such people as stereotypes. Indeed, in Terkel's books *Division Street: America* and *Hard Times: An Oral History of the Great Depression,* it is apparent that everybody can be called unique or even strange if measured against standard expectations. The Carters, like other people in Terkel's interviews, show a mixture of attitudes, many of them seemingly contradictory, that would, it's safe to guess, be sorted out and rationalized were any of these people given the task of writing about themselves rather than being allowed to speak. This blend or mixture of attitudes on social and political matters may be more confusing than are reports from poll takers, but it is probably a far truer portrait and certainly a more hopeful one.

BOB CARTER, 38

Downers Grove Estates, an unincorporated area west of Chicago. A lower-middle-class section. He is the foreman of an auto-body repair shop. He built his own house. He is still in the process of completing it to his satisfaction.

I leave the house at, let's say, ten after seven usually in the morning. And seven, seven-fifteen, I get home at night. And Tuesdays, that's firehouse. I'm available every time there's a fire, volunteer. Tuesday's our training night. I go down to the firehouse from about seven-thirty till . . . well, there are times when we play poker or something like that, you know. And it's usually around twelve o'clock at night when I get home from there. And the rest of the week, I'm just beat, actually. That's what it amounts to, and I just don't have time to do anything. It's just like a vicious circle, you just get started on something, and by the time you get started, it's time to go to bed.

I don't have much. What I have is my own. Nobody's gonna take it away from me. If I can't build it, I don't want it. I don't care what people think of my home. I fix it the way I see it, and I do things the way I see fit. And I don't want anybody telling me how I'm gonna do it.

That's the thing that's a sore spot with me, that status symbol. New car, boat, and all that, I can't see it. Who are you trying to impress? Why should I go into debt where every dime I make is going to some loan shark? I know a lot of people out here who do it. Everything is charge accounts, and I think if the economy was to bust in two today, every one of them would lose everything they got, everything, I would say, across the street there, the fancy homes and all, new cars and everything they want. If the husband lost his job and he couldn't get another job for a year, they'd lose everything. They'd be beggars on Madison Street. I guarantee it.

I could live that way without any trouble, because I think I make as much money as they do. But my problem is I do things myself. I can't see hiring somebody to do my work. I like to do my own. I like to work with my hands. I think if I was tied down behind a desk, I'd go crazy. I have to be moving, I gotta be doing something. Even before I went into service, I loved to pull things apart and put them back together, make them work, that's how I like to do things. Cars, I don't know, cars have always intrigued me.

He recounts his work experience after coming out of the Navy in 1946. He had worked fourteen years for a Packard dealer in Cicero, becoming foreman of the shop. His boss, a retired lieutenant colonel, decided to finish his college education, and "closed the doors" on one week's notice. "Sure it hurt, you work in a place fourteen years and there were times when the guy was like a father to me." He remembered his boss coming through when he, Bob, had TB. Though he lost out on the bonus due him, "the other things compensate a heck of a lot more." He's been at his present job four years, foreman for the last three.

I don't care what my neighbors think. My father, he didn't care what people thought. He figured if they were his friends, they didn't care what he lived in. But when they came to our house, they were treated like kings and queens whoever they may be. That's the thing that was in his mind, to treat people decently. I guess that's where I got it.

I'm an outcast down at work almost, because I can't see what's going on. That stuff really burns me up, just burns me up. Everybody you talk to is against the colored, and I've worked with colored people all my life. Every job I've had has been with colored people. I mean, I've never worked side by side with them, but they've been around me. And they're decent people, they're good people in my book.

I had this job in Cicero at this Packard agency. This one fella who musta been around fifty years old, a colored fella, Eddie François was his name. One day we got to talking and he said, "Boy, I'd like to come out and see your house." And I said, "Well, whenever you want to come out, you let me know." I said, "You could come out with me on a Saturday afternoon and have dinner with us." The rest a' the fellas in the shop looked at me kinda funny. I don't care. He's a friend of mine. I don't care what color his skin is or anything else. And he says, "Fine, I'll let you know." I guess he figured I was just pulling his leg. So I left it go for a couple of weeks and he never mentioned it, so I thought maybe he just doesn't want to come out.

So one day I says, we got to talking about something, I don't know how it come around, and I said, "Oh you lousy skunk, you. You'll never come out to my house. You think you're too good for me or something." And he says, "Can I come out to your house?" and I said, "You're doggone right you can come out to my house." So he said, "I don't want to cause you any trouble." And I said, "What do you mean, cause me trouble?" I says, "You want to come out?" He says, "Yeah." And I said, "What about this Saturday?" This was during the week. So he said, "Fine, okay, I'll come out." I said, "Okay, we'll leave here right after you're through scrubbing the floors." That was his job on Saturday. We got through working at twelve o'clock and he usually got through about one.

So I hung around till one o'clock, and I told Therese, "Make some fried chicken." 'Cause he loved fried chicken, he could eat that seven days a week. So she made some fried chicken and I come out with him. And the neighbors were out here and nobody said anything. But when I pulled in the yard with him, man, you could see them, looking all over, boy, their eyes were just about popped out of their heads. I guess they got the idea I was probably gonna sell to a colored man, see? But he came in here and had his dinner, and like I say, he was a friend of mine. I don't care, the color of his skin didn't make a damn bit of difference to me. The neighbors never said anything but you could see something was bothering them.

So one day we had a, you might say, picnic out here in the yard. And we got to talking about the colored, and they had to bring it up, "What was that colored guy doing here?" And I said he was a friend of mine: "I brought him out to dinner." You mean he ate in your house? "You're doggone right he ate in my house. What the hell, he was hungry." That's all that was ever said.

From that time on, that colored guy down at work, if I told him to dig me a ten-foot hole, he woulda dug it for me. Just to show his appreciation, I guess. I didn't want that. I mean that wasn't my idea of bringing him out. It wasn't my idea to show the neighbors that I can bring out colored or do anything like that. I did it because I liked the man, that's all.

He got fired from the job anyway, and that was the last time . . . I never seen him since.

Over here, at this shop, the boss, he's a year younger than me, and he owns the business, and he's always coming around with these stories about the niggers, what he calls them. The niggers are gonna have a march down 22nd Street and he's gonna be one of the ones in line to help them bust it up. And I said, "Well, the only thing I can hope for, Bob, is to have one of them so-called niggers bust a bottle over your head."

Oh yeah. I speak my piece. I figure this way: If he doesn't like what I say, that's too bad. I do my job. I make him money. If that isn't good enough, I'm sorry. I have my own feeling about certain things and I don't want anybody to tell me what I can do or what I can't do. I just can't see just for the sake of a job . . .

What he'll do is sort of needle me all the time. He'll bring up Martin Luther King, he shouldn't have got this Nobel Prize. And, oh, the different colored entertainers. You take Bill Cosby or Godfrey Cambridge, I tell ya, I could listen to those guys all day long. And this John Bubbles, I love him. There was a time I liked Sammy Davis, Jr. But it seems that he's pulled away from the rest of them, like he's maybe getting too good for them. Setting himself up on a pedestal. I don't like that type. Same with the white. I mean the class of people who want to set themselves up as better than anybody else.

I mean you've seen a lot of people that are poor that you wouldn't even give breathing space to. And I've got them right here in this area. But the class of people that think they're better just because they have money, I can't see that either.

I've got one brother, especially, I swear he's a communist. I mean, the way he talks. He works for the gas company and he says he was working in the colored district in Joliet and he saw those colored kids running around the truck, and he said, "If you colored kids don't stop running around that truck, I'll run you little bastards over." I said, "Ronnie, are you going out of your mind? Those are kids." "Ah," he said, "they should take them all and put 'em on a boat and drop them in the ocean. Ship 'em back to Africa where they belong." We go round and round every time.

With me, one instance in the Navy maybe had something to do with it. I was in Charleston, South Carolina, and a buddy and myself were gonna go to the show. We walked in the theater and they said standing room only. What the heck, we'll stand, we didn't care. The place downstairs and the mezzanine were jammed, you couldn't get a fly in there. So there was a balcony upstairs. So I said, "Let's take a walk up there, see if there's anything up there." We walked up there and there was all kinds of seats. So we sat down and watched the movie. I was comfortable up there, I mean the seats were nice.

When we came down after the movie was over, well, there must have been fifty, sixty people standing downstairs there, waiting to get in. When they saw us, they turned around and started laughing, you know. It still didn't dawn on me why they were laughing. I don't know what possessed me to turn around, but I turned around and there must have been about twenty-five colored people coming down the steps behind me. I was so mad at the time when I realized what was going on, I think if I probably had something on me, I'd a probably hit somebody. I was burning no end. I can't express it. But it was a feeling they were trying to say they were better. The whites were trying to say they were better than me and the colored 'cause I was sitting with them. See. I think that was the one thing that really set me off on this.

After we walked out there, when I went to the door, there was a colored man, and I waited, thinking he was gonna walk out, but he grabbed the door and opened it for me. I thought he was gonna go out. I'm standing there waiting for him to go out. You know how you see some body in front of you, you go to put your hand on 'em, to more or less guide them through. And the minute I put my hand on him, he looked like he was gonna drop, you know? I guess he thought I was gonna hit him or something. But he didn't flinch or anything, it was just that shyness, you know. I said, "No, go ahead." I guess then he realized I wasn't from that area. And he went ahead of us.

You see, he was older than I was, and my dad always taught me to respect my elders. To this day, I don't dare call any of my uncles by their first name. It's always Uncle Charlie or Uncle Elmer, and I'm thirty-eight years old. I've got cousins that will call my dad by his first name. He's never said anything, but you can see he doesn't like it. He wants the respect and that's something he's always wanted.

Are you respected out here?

Oh, yes. I've never heard anyone talk bad about me. Maybe they do behind my back, but I've never heard anything from anybody else. I'm a lieutenant at the firehouse. I could be higher, but I don't want to be any higher.

I'd like my kids to be better than I am in a way of working. They don't have to work with their hands. I mean, if they want that, fine. If Bobby wants to be a body man, fine. I'd welcome it, actually. But if he wants to be an engineer . . . I'm trying to get him into electronics, I think that's a good thing to get into. I'd just as soon have them have a white-collar job. Not where they're looked at, where you live in, say, the slum area of a town, which this is. That's what this amounts to. This is a low-class section here, and I don't want my kids to be where they think they're better than anybody else, but I'd like them to have something a little better than I have, that's all.

I like my work. I mean I couldn't do anything else. I could do carpentry work, but I've seen some carpentry work today and it's actually a sin. If things aren't just right, I guess I just don't want to do it. You can see it even in my line. How would you say it? There just isn't any pride in what they do. I think that's the biggest trouble today. No pride in what a person does. It's just slipshod, everything's slipshod.

I think personally myself that people are too interested in the money end of it than the actual skill. Just to get it out, just to produce. You have flat-rate shops, like in my line. You see the workmanship that goes on in them shops. There's no comparison to a shop that's on straight time. A man who's on straight time, he knows what he's gonna make at the end of the week, so if he takes ten hours to do a ten-hour job, he's not hurting himself, but he's gonna make sure the job is right. Because if the job isn't right, he's gonna get screamed at, and maybe even lose his job. So he's gonna make sure he's doing a decent job and he's getting a decent wage. That's why I can see the difference between your flat-rate shop and your straight-time shop.

I'll tell anybody the amount of money I make a week. I could ask the people here what they make and I could never get an honest answer. They would never tell me. But I don't care if they know mine. Money doesn't make that much difference to me. Like I told Therese, even before we got married: I want food on the table, I want a clean house, I want clean clothes for my kids, and I want bills paid. That's all I want with my paycheck.

If Christ came back to earth, what do you think would happen to Him?

In this day and age, I hope to God He doesn't. It'd be the same thing all over again. He'd be crucified. Because the temperament of the people today, you just can't describe it. They're your friend today and they're your enemy tomorrow. There's no friendship today. Like I say, it goes right back to the status symbol. If you don't have a new car or a new home, you don't belong. You may be invited; if you do show up, why there's a doubt in your mind whether you should have gone or not. It's not because you don't think you're as good. It's the idea that you can see they weren't expecting you. They give you the invitation because you're supposed to be a friend, but when you do show up, you get the impression you weren't welcome to begin with.

I have friends. I don't think any of them would ever let me down. But there are times when it seems like the friendship, it's not given willingly. Whatever the favor you do, or they do for you, isn't done willingly. It seems like, well, you're a friend of mine, so I have to do it. It isn't because I *want* to do it. I feel like I *have* to do it because you're a friend of mine.

If I were God, I would take this feeling of superiority out of people's minds and make everybody feel they weren't better than anybody else.

What would I like to do? Therese bought me a wood lathe for Christmas. I've had it now fourteen years and I've yet to use it. One of these days, I said, when I built the garage, I'm gonna put up a bench and I'm gonna start working with that wood lathe. And it's still setting in the corner. I still don't have the time, that's all. As much as I'd love to do it. One of these days I'm gonna get next to myself and start that thing going, 'cause I love to work with wood. If I could be a cabinetmaker, now that to me is the thing I'd like to do. . . . I'd love that.

THERESE CARTER, 35

The kitchen of the Carter home, Downers Grove Estates. The children, two boys and a girl, are asleep. Bob, her husband, is in another room. On the wall is a kitchen prayer:

> Bless the kitchen in which I cook
> Bless each moment within this nook
> Let joy and laughter share this room
> With spices, skillets and my broom.
> Bless me and mine with love and health
> And I'll ask not for greater wealth.

Sometimes I wish the neighbors weren't as friendly as they are. I would like to have friends that you don't have to feel that you've always got to be real happy and smiley and everything. When you feel like not talking, it's all right, too. Bob and I went on a vacation last year for the first time, for four days, and that's okay that you went, but what did you find to talk about? For four days? Well, you don't have to talk all the time. You talk when you feel like it, and when you don't, you don't say anything, that's all. I like to be alone most of the time. Be alone, just to think.

Oh, I think about everything. First of all, I keep changing my mind about things all the time. Oh, you know, maybe about Vietnam and things like that. But the more you read, the more confused I get until I really don't know. I couldn't say how I feel. Because when I hear about anybody being killed, hurt, I don't care who it is, it drives me wild, and yet I don't know what . . .

Not just Vietnam, not just big things like that. Even little things, just anything. There's always problems about something, and you'd just like to have a little peace and quiet and just like to have everybody happy, that's all. It sounds real corny, but it's the only thing I can say.

I mean, can you ever just pick up a newspaper and read it and not find about two million problems on the first couple of pages? It's with everything. Maybe it's because I haven't tried hard enough to even do anything. Just right here, I wouldn't even know where to start. Because it just seems that everything is just one-sided out here, and everybody who would even think a little bit different is . . . Well, for one thing, I'm not supposed to know how to read a book. If you do that it's just a waste of time, to read a book, *to do anything* even. To sew is even too much for some of the women out here, I don't know. And I don't think I'm that good, I'm so dumb and I've got so much to learn yet, but I would at least like to learn these things.

I can learn about the John Birch Society any time I want, just by calling up a friend of mine or something. But that's not really what I want. There's this one lady that was always passing me literature last year. I just kept ignoring her, but I'm sure if I encouraged her on, maybe she'd be friendly. I met her through the Girl Scouts.

I'll betcha there's three or four on the block that wouldn't know what I was talking about. I think there's very few, anybody that really tries to think for themselves. There's no way you can even talk to them. The things they hear, that's it, there's no way of swaying them at all. I argue back but it doesn't do any good. The thing they always say is: You don't know, because you don't have any colored living around here. I had one here for dinner years ago. And I made the biggest mistake in the world. He said he loved it out here so much, and I said, "Well, why don't you buy the lot next door?" And he said, "They wouldn't want me here." And I didn't know what to say then. That was the only colored I knew.

You say things like that here, they don't pay any attention to you. I mean, they don't stop talking to me or anything, they just think, well, maybe you're kooky or something. That's all. They leave you alone. (Laughs.) Well, maybe I am, I don't know. (Laughs.) I have more fun this way.

About the worst thing you can do is read a book. I've got a neighbor that's had a book three years and hasn't finished it yet. And I have only one neighbor that ever reads anything. This other neighbor, she has only one boy and he's fourteen years old. If she washes clothes on a Monday morning, she has had it for the day. Now I wash clothes in the morning, get rid of the clothes so I can do something else. They have no outside interests at all that I can see. They go visiting a lot, you know, back and forth.

They talk about what's gonna happen to somebody on the television tomorrow, or they had a big wash, or they had a big ironing. And those things are important. I'm a housewife, I enjoy even that. It's nice to see an empty ironing basket, it's nice to see an empty hamper. But that's just the end, I mean . . .

I wanted to be a teacher. Oh, yes, I'm going to be a teacher. I'll probably be the oldest one, but I'm gonna be one. Bob said it would be all right, and I thought maybe as soon as David goes to school all day in September, I wanted to start doing something.

You want to go back to school?
   Yes. Why? Don't laugh.
I'm not laughing.
   Everybody else would. I wouldn't even tell anybody.
Why wouldn't you?
   Because they would think it was the most ridiculous thing any woman would want to do. Because why would anybody do that when they're married and have kids? There just wouldn't be any sense to it, that's all. Why would anybody want to do anything that ridiculous? Maybe I wouldn't tell anybody I was going, but I would just go and come home and bar the doors and do my homework and that's all.
   I would as long as I could. I know that sounds terrible, but I really would. Because if I told anybody, they would just all go around and everybody would know, and then they'd all laugh. They're just not the kind to think those things are the things to bother with. Like I say, they would shop seven days a week if they could, and they're not even good cooks. I don't know. That's why I've tried to figure out, what do they do all day? 'Cause I never have enough hours in a day. If I could get by on four hours' sleep, I'd be real happy.
   Well, I get out of bed and make breakfast for Bob, I make his lunch. When he goes off to work I either usually have ironing to do before the kids get up. I'll wash, I read, I sew. I make almost all of Cathy's clothes, almost all of my own. I read . . . I won't read anywhere near what I would like to, I'd be the first to admit that.
What do you like to read?
   Anything, anything. Matchbook covers, if there's nothing else. Oh, I read everything. Because when I talk to anybody else they're almost all much smarter than I am. There's so much more I'd like to know. And I don't want anybody to tell me what I should or what I shouldn't know. I want to find out for myself.
   It's the same with this Vietnam deal. Why, I was all for Johnson throwing in everything he could throw in there, and yet the more I hear, the more I read, I get wishy-washy. And I still think he's good, but I can find things, faults with some of the things he's doing, and before that I couldn't. Everything he did, to me, was just perfect.
   I might question it, but I don't know how I could stop these situations or anything. I figure, does it do any good to write a letter to the editor? I don't know. What else can I do? Because most people, when you talk about Vietnam, they really don't know enough. I don't know all about it either. I just try to keep finding out more and more and more.
   You hear millions of dollars a day or a week or whatever, my God, it's just

. . . it seems to me it wouldn't take that much to make peace as it does to make war. I just keep hoping there won't be a nuclear war. I don't know if you can stop anybody from doing it if they want to. I would like to see everything stopped, but how? There's one thing I can't understand, is they've had this test-ban treaty and it's worked. We had to take the Russians at their word, and we did. I really think that they won't want anything to happen any more than we do. They're humans, they're not robots or anything, they're humans, too.

Bob and I argue about these things. Bob thought it was all right if they picket for civil rights. He just didn't like them laying in the streets. And I said: Well, what about on March 17 or whatever it was, St. Patrick's Day, when Mayor Daley held up traffic for three hours? (Laughs.) That was just the same. No, it doesn't bother me. Where else can they turn to? I don't know how else they can do it. I mean, even if you're against it, at least you're talking about it and maybe something will come about. I don't know what other way they can do it any more.

Suppose your neighbors heard you say this?

They would agree with me because I don't think they even know enough. All they ever talk about is getting a new car and going on a vacation. Oh, they talk about their jobs. All their kids play pony league and things, like that, that's all. Their husbands? All they do is drink beer and go play golf and bowl and that's it . . . and coach Little League. In this Little League, I don't know, I think maybe the parents are trying to show themselves through the kids or something. But it's just a game, they're kids. Does it matter if they win or lose?

Everybody's just really only interested in themselves. I've never really needed anything, really desperately, from any of them, but you get the feeling that maybe they would help you if they had to, but then everybody would have to know about it, too.

Do you have a friend you could trust, let's say, in a crisis?

No, I don't think so. No, I think they would all be good in a little pinch, like if you needed a ride or something, but no real big crisis, no. Mmmm-hmmm.

When I listen to Bob's dad talk sometimes, and he talks like people during the Depression years or something, like if they had something, it was shared. But I don't know. I just don't think people would be that way now.

I'm not saying they're not happy, 'cause sometimes I think they really are. And yet they spend their time being miserable. Because I see people who have a lot of things and they look at each other: oooh! like they can't stand each other; their kids, they're screaming at them all the time. I holler, too, but . . . It's just like they don't enjoy anything. They have furniture, they don't enjoy it. No matter what they have. I can't figure out why. Maybe it's something else they're looking for. But I mean, if it would be like paying off a mortgage or something, well, everybody would be happy with that. But I mean, they get a car, and you would think they would be so happy because they've got a car. But they don't get any enjoyment out of that. They buy things for their kids, and the first screw or nut or bolt that comes out of it, they're all . . . they just can't be happy. They buy a barbecue pit and they can't be happy with that. I just can't understand that.

From what I read and hear, I guess people will always be banging up their cars, and if Bob's happy fixing them, I guess we're all set for a while. I suppose there's always gonna be some people that will get a raw deal when automation takes over. But when you come right down to it, there's still nothing like a human being when it comes to certain things.

. . . I feel like the average man would be good, and they could be a lot better. You hear more about these days: I don't want to get involved. Maybe the same thing happened years ago, and we just didn't hear about them. Maybe I could be just the biggest coward in the world, if I was to face something like that, I don't know. But I think I would try to do something.

I don't know, maybe there's a bigger group of people that think the way you do. I think maybe it kind of stimulates you into doing something. But when I think that there's one here, like me, and there's maybe twenty miles away from something . . .

The greatest day of my life was the day I went to see a Pete Seeger concert. I think he's good. But to me the biggest thrill that I got was the fact that here were that many people together that felt a certain way. And I've never been in a crowd where everybody felt that way. And yet at the same time, how come . . . You could read in the paper that so many people felt like you do, yet you could never yourself meet anybody that feels the same way. That's what I told Bob, I said, that was one thing I thought he missed, that night, whether he likes him or not, the feeling that you're in with people that think the way you do. . . . I could just stand up and cheer. It makes you feel so good all over.

Lillian Hellman / Helen

The book from which this piece is taken is entitled *An Unfinished Woman,* and the style suggests what is meant, in a positive way, about being "unfinished." Everything that is recollected here—about Helen and Sophronia, the two Negro women who were important to the shaping of Lillian Hellman's life, about Martha's Vineyard, New York, and Washington—is kept alive and "unfinished" in the mind, the subject of a kind of musing soliloquy wherein the recollections fall into patterns at once unpremeditated and revealing, like the gathering of sea things washed up to the shore which, at the beginning of the piece, the writer admits liking to look at and study.

All the materials coalesce, that is, from a continuing debate within the writer and between her and people now dead or disappeared, a debate she never lets herself win. This is a writer who admits that "It takes me too long to know things" and who is told that "you never lose your temper at the right time," a writer who therefore keeps the past alive in herself, never becoming abstracted from it or from the Negroes who have meant so much, so intimately in her life. There is no political generalizing about them or about herself, though the politics of race is clearly among the subjects that concern her. She has a familial intimacy about everyone she chooses to remember, white or black, and can also show a familial anger.

One of the most attractive evidences of this closeness is the pride she feels, a good kind of pride in that it comes from understanding others and of letting others fully understand you, when she reports her conversations with the Negroes she has loved and liked. The piece is full of listening and remembered listening, and of the recollections in this volume it probably offers more conversation than does any other. Words are often the subject of the conversation, the cause of new friendships, as with Old George, and of the near fracture of old loves, as in the disagreements with Helen and Sophronia. Understandings and misunderstandings, that is, are the result always of that most difficult, most easily mismanaged, and afterward most haunting of human contacts which is speech.

In many places I have spent many days on small boats. Beginning with the gutters of New Orleans, I have been excited about what lives in water and lies along its edges. In the last twenty years, the waters have been the bays, ponds and ocean of Martha's Vineyard, and autumn, when most people have left the island, is the best time for beaching the boat on a long day's picnic by myself—other people on a boat often change the day into something strained, a trip with a purpose—when I fish, read, wade in and out, and save the afternoon for digging and mucking about on the edge of the shore. I have seldom found much: I like to look at periwinkles and mussels, driftwood, shells, horseshoe crabs, gull feathers, the small fry of bass and blues, the remarkable skin of a dead sand shark, the shining life in rockweed.

One night about six months ago, when I was teaching at Harvard, it occurred to me that these childish, aimless pleasures—my knowledge of the sea has grown very little with time, and what interested me as a child still does—which have sometimes shamed me and often caused self-mocking, might have something to do with the digging about that occasionally happens when I am asleep. It is then that I awake, feeling that my head is made of sand and that a pole has just been pulled from it with the end of the pole carrying a card on which there is an answer to a long-forgotten problem, clearly solved and set out as if it had been arranged for me on a night table.

On that night I was living in a rickety Cambridge house and went running down the steps at the sound of a crash. A heavy rainstorm had broken the cheap piece of modernity that had been lighting the ceiling and, as I stood looking at the pieces on the floor, I thought: Of course, one has been dead three years this month, one has been dead for over thirty, but they were one person to you, these two black women you loved more than you ever loved any other women, Sophronia from childhood, Helen so many years later, and it was all there for you to know two months ago when, poking about the beach, a long distance from the house Helen and I had lived in, I found a mangled watch, wondered where I had seen it, and knew a few hours later that it was the watch I had bought in the Zurich airport and that had disappeared a short time after I gave it to Helen. The answer now was easy. She never walked much because her legs hurt. Sam had brought it down to the beach and she didn't want to tell me that my dog, who loved her but didn't love me, could have done anything for which he could be blamed.

From the night of that rainstorm in Cambridge, for weeks later, and even now, once in a while, I have dreamed of Sophronia and Helen, waking up sometimes so pleased that I try to go on with a dream that denies their death, at other times saddened by the dream because it seems a deep time-warning of my own age and death. When that happens, in argument with myself, I feel guilty because I did not know about Sophronia's death for two years after it happened, and had not forced Helen into the hospital that might have saved her. In fact, I had only been angry at her stubborn refusal to go. How often Helen had made me angry, but with Sophronia nothing had ever been bad. . . . But the answer there is easy: Sophronia was the anchor for a little girl, the beloved of a young woman, but by the time I had met the other, years had brought acid to a nature that hadn't begun that way—or is that a lie?—and in any case, what excuse did that give for irritation with a woman almost twenty years older than I, swollen in the legs and feet, marrow-weary with the struggle to live, bewildered, resentful, sometimes irrational in a changing world where the old, real-pretend love for white people forced her now into open recognition of the hate and contempt she had brought with her from South Carolina. She had not, could not have, guessed this conflict would ever come to more than the sad talk of black people over collard greens and potlikker, but now here it was on Harlem streets, in newspapers and churches, and how did you handle what you didn't understand except with the same martyr discipline that made you work when you were sick, made you try to forgive what you really never forgave, made you take a harsh nature and force it into words of piety that, in time, became almost true piety. Why had these two women come together as one for me? Sophronia had not been like that.

I don't know what year Helen came to work for me. We never agreed about the time, although when we felt most affectionate or tired we would argue about it. But it was, certainly, a long time ago. The first months had been veiled and edgy: her severe face, her oppressive silences made me think she was angry, and my nature, alternating from vagueness to rigid demands, made her unhappy, she told me years later. (She did not say it that way: she said, "It takes a searching wind to find the tree you sit in.")

Then one day, at the end of the first uncomfortable months, she said she was grateful, most deeply. I didn't know what she meant, didn't pay much attention, except that I knew she had grown affectionate toward me, even indulgent. Shortly after, she brought me three hundred dollars done up in tissue paper with a weary former Christmas ribbon. I asked her what it was, she said please to count it, I asked her what it was, she said please to count it, I counted it, handed it back, she handed it back to me and said it was the return of the loan for her daughter. I said I didn't know what she was talking about. Her face changed to angry sternness as she said, "I want no charity. I pay my just debts, Miss Hellman. Mr. Hammett * must have told you I said that to him."

Hammett hadn't told me she said anything, but it turned out that one night when he had come from the country to have dinner with me, and found he was too tired to return to the country—it was the early period of emphysema—he decided to spend the night in the library. He had been reading at about three in the morning when the phone rang and a frightened voice said there was an emergency, was it possible to call Helen? He had climbed four flights of steps to fetch her, and when she had finished with the phone she said her niece or her daughter or somebody-or-other had had a terrible accident and she would have to go immediately. He asked her if she needed money and, after the long wait she always took when pride was involved, she asked him for taxi money.

Hammett had said, "What about money for the hospital?"

She had said, "Black people don't have it easy in a hospital."

He had said, "I know. So a check won't do you any good. You'd better have cash."

I said to Hammett, "But what's this got to do with me?"

He said, "It's your money she's returning. I took it out of the safe."

He told me how disturbed she had been when he had opened my safe and so he had said, "Don't worry. It's O.K. There's no sense waking Miss Hellman because she can't learn how to open the safe and that makes her angry."

For many years after, whenever I tried to open the safe, she would come as close to mirth as ever I saw her, saying always that I wasn't to get disturbed, she thought my fingers were too thin for such work, and then always reminding me of the night Hammett gave her the money, "before he even knew me, that is a Christian man."

* Dashiell Hammett: (1894–1961), American writer, originator of the "tough guy" school of detective fiction. Among his books are *The Maltese Falcon* (1930) and *The Thin Man* (1932). Miss Hellman was an intimate friend of Mr. Hammett's for many years.

I said to him, "Helen thinks you're a Christian man."

"Sure. She's a convert to my ex-church. We teach 'em to talk like that."

"I won't tell her that. She might not like you."

"I won't find that too tough."

"But I'm worried that she might think you don't like her."

"I don't like her."

He didn't like her and he was the only person I ever met who didn't. Sometimes he would say it was because she spoke rudely to me. (He was right: when she didn't feel well, she often did.) Sometimes he would say he couldn't stand Catholic converts, or overbig women, or he would complain that she was the only Negro in America who couldn't carry a tune. Even through the last four and a half years of his life, when he had come to live in the house and when she, a woman older than he by a number of years I never knew, would climb the steps with endless trays or mail or books or just to ask if there was anything he wanted, he never said anything more to her than "Good morning," or "Thank you," or, on special occasions, "It looks like a pleasant day." I think it is possible that the two of them, obsessed with pride and dignity, one of the more acceptable forms of self-love, but self-love nevertheless, had come face to face with a reflection and one of them didn't like what he saw in the mirror.

Other people always came, in time, to like her and admire her, although her first impression on them was not always pleasant. The enormous figure, the stern face, the few, crisp words did not seem welcoming as she opened a door or offered a drink, but the greatest clod among them came to understand the instinctive good taste, the high-bred manners that once they flowered gave off so much true courtesy. And, in this period of nobody grows older or fatter, your mummie looks like your girl, there may be a need in many of us for the large, strong woman who takes us back to what most of us always wanted and few of us ever had.

It is difficult to date anything between people when they have lived together long enough, and so I can't remember when I knew, forgot, knew, doubted, and finally understood that her feelings for white people and black people were too complex to follow, because what had been said on one day would be denied on the next. In the early years, when she told me of the white family in whose house she had been raised in Charleston, her mother having been the cook there, I would dislike the Uncle-Tomism of the memories, and often when the newspapers carried a new indignity from the South we would both cluck about it, but she would turn away from my anger with talk about good and bad among white people, and she had only known the good. During the University of Mississippi mess,* I asked her what she meant by good whites, good to her?

* the University of Mississippi mess: in September 1962, Negro student James Meredith sought enrollment at the University of Mississippi and was denied entry; when President Kennedy made it clear that the federal appeals court ruling in favor of Meredith would be enforced by government intervention, there was rioting on the Oxford, Mississippi, campus and federal troops were sent in to restore order; Meredith was finally enrolled.

She said, "There's too much hate in this world."

I said, "Depends on where you carry the hate, doesn't it, what it's made of, how you use it?"

She shrugged. "I ain't ever hated."

I said, too fast, "Yes, you have. You just don't know it—" and stopped right before I said, You often hate me, I've known it for years and let you have it as a debt I wouldn't pay anybody else but Sophronia.

Oh, Sophronia, it's you I want back always. It's by you I still so often measure, guess, transmute, translate and act. What strange process made a little girl strain so hard to hear the few words that ever came, made the image of you, true or false, last a lifetime? I think my father knew about that very early, because five or six years after I was separated from Sophronia by our move to New York, when I saw her only during our yearly visits to New Orleans, he shouted at me one night, "To hell with Sophronia. I don't want to hear about her anymore."

That night started in Montgomery, Alabama, although why or how we got to Montgomery I no longer remember. My father had, among other eccentricities, an inability to travel from one place to another in a conventional line; if it was possible to change trains or make a detour, he arranged it. And since we traveled a great deal between New York and New Orleans, stopping for business or for friends, we were often to be found in railroad stations waiting for a train that would take us out of our way.

I had been sleeping on a bench that night in Montgomery, Alabama, so I don't know when I first saw the three figures—a young, very thin Negro girl, and two white men. The men were drunk, my father said later, and maybe that accounted for the awkward, shaggy movements, their sudden twists and turns. The girl would move to a bench, sit, rise as the men came toward her, move to a wall, rest, slide along it as the men came near, try for another bench, circle it, and move fast when they moved fast. She was trying to stay within the station lights and, as the train came in, she ran down the platform toward it. But she miscalculated and ran outside the lights. I saw one of the men light matches and move in the darkness. When he caught the girl he put the lighted matches to her arm before he kissed her. The girl dropped her valise and there was the noise of glass breaking. I have no clear memory of the next few minutes until I heard my father say, "Let the girl alone." Then he hit the man and the other man hit my father, but he didn't seem hurt because he picked the girl up and shoved her up the steps of the train, came running back for me, shoved me up the steps of the train, got in himself and suddenly began to yell, "My God, where is your mother?" My mother was on the ground repacking the girl's valise. The two men were running toward her but she smiled and waved at my father and put up her hand in a gesture to quiet him. She had trouble with the lock of the valise but she seemed unhurried about fixing it. My father was halfway down the train steps when she rose, faced the two men and said, "Now you just step aside, boys, and take yourselves on home." I don't know whether it was the snobbery of the word "boys" or the accents of her native Alabama, but they made no motion as she came aboard the train.

The girl was invited to share our basket supper and she and my mother spent the next few hours speaking about the nature of men. I went into the corridor to find my bored father.

Like most other children, I had learned you usually got further by pretending innocence. "What did those men want to do with the girl?"

When he didn't answer, I said, "Rape, that's what. You're a hero. Sophronia will be pleased."

His voice was loud and angry. "To hell with Sophronia. I don't want to hear about her anymore."

A few days later, sitting on a bench in Audubon Park, while the two small boys she now nursed played near us, I told Sophronia the story. When she didn't speak, I said, "Papa was brave, wasn't he?"

"Yep."

"What's the matter?"

"Things not going to get themselves fixed by one white man being nice to one nigger girl."

I thought hard and long about that, as I thought about everything she said, and by the next year's visit to New Orleans I had decided on a course for myself. Sophronia and I had gone to the movies and were returning home on a streetcar. We had always moved back to sit in the Negro section of the car, but this time I sat in the front directly behind the driver and pulled her down next to me. She whispered to me, I whispered back, she half rose, I pulled her down, and she sat still for a minute waiting for me to grow quiet. The conductor had evidently been watching us, because he turned his head.

"Back."

I held so tight to her arm that she couldn't move.

He said, "Get back in the car. You know better than this."

I said, my voice high with fright, "We won't. We won't move. This lady is better than you are—"

And the car came to a sudden jolt in the middle of the street. People rose and an old woman moved toward us. The conductor opened the doors.

Sophronia got to her feet and I screamed, "Come back, Sophronia, don't you dare move. You're better than anybody, anybody—" and the old lady slapped me as the conductor took my arm. I was carrying a book bag and I threw it at him, turned to push the old lady, turned back to find Sophronia. She had moved between me and the conductor, who looked more surprised than angry. Now she grabbed my arm and pulled me into the street.

I said, "Let's run."

She said, "You run. I'm past the runnin' age."

So we stood together, staring up at the streetcar, waiting for what we did not know. Then the car started up and moved away from us. I was crying as we walked together toward my aunts' house.

After a while she said, "Crybaby."

"I did wrong?"

It was an old question and she had always had a song for it:

> Right is wrong and wrong is right
> And who can tell it all by sight?

I said, "Sophronia, I want to go away with you for always, right now. I've thought a lot about it all year and I've made up my mind. I want to live with you the rest of my life. I won't live with white people anymore—"

She put her hand over my mouth. When she took it away, I knew she was very angry. She said, "I got something to tell you, missy. There are too many niggers who like white people. Then there are too many white people think they like niggers. You just be careful."

She crossed the street and was gone before I could move. Sleepless that night and miserable the next day, I went on the second day to find her in Audubon Park.

I said, "Aren't you going to see me anymore?"

She said, "I got a no good daughter and a no good son."

I had heard this from my mother, but I didn't know then, and I don't know now, what no good meant to her, and so I waited. We sat without speaking on the park bench watching one little red-haired brother push the other off a tricycle.

She called out, "Stanley. Hugh," and the fight stopped immediately.

After a while, I said, "Aren't you going to see me anymore?"

"You're growing up, a few years away. Time's approachin' to straighten things out."

"You mean I'm no good, either?"

She turned her head and looked at me as if she were puzzled. "I mean you got to straighten things out in your own head. Then maybe you goin' to be some good and pleasure me. But if they keep on pilin' in silly and gushin' out worse, you goin' to be trouble, and you ain't goin' to pleasure me and nobody else."

Many years later, I came to understand that all she meant was that I might blow up my life with impulsiveness or anger or jealousy or all the other things that she thought made a mess, but that day, in my thirteenth year, I shivered at the contempt with which she spoke. (And there I was not wrong. I came to know as she grew older and I did, too, that she did feel a kind of contempt for the world she lived in and for almost everybody, black or white, she had ever met, but that day I thought it was only for me.)

I got up from the bench in maybe the kind of pain you feel when a lover has told you that not only does the love not exist anymore, but that it possibly never existed at all.

I said, "You mean I am no good and you don't want to see me anymore. Well, I won't hang around and bother you—"

She got slowly to her feet. "You all I got, baby, all I'm goin' to have."

Then she leaned down and kissed me. She hadn't kissed me, I think, since I was three or four years old. Certainly I have had happier minutes since, but not up to then. We shook hands and I went back to the park bench the next day.

There has always been a picture of Sophronia in my house, all of them taken with me as a young child. Some years after Helen came to work for me, I came into the library to find her with one of the pictures in her hand.

I said, "My nurse, my friend. Handsome woman, wasn't she?"

"You look like a nice little girl."

"Maybe I was, but nobody thought so. I was trouble."

"She didn't think so."

I took the picture from Helen and, for the first time in the forty years since it had been taken, saw the affection the woman had for the child she stood behind.

I said, "It takes me too long to know things."

"What?"

"Nothing. I hadn't seen her for two years before she died."

"You didn't go to the funeral?"

"I didn't know she died. Her daughter didn't tell me."

"She was a light-skinned woman?"

I know about that question, I've known about it all my life.

"Yes, very. But she didn't use it, if that's what you mean."

"How old was she?"

"In the picture? I don't know. I—my God. She couldn't have been thirty. I can't believe it, but—"

"Black women get old fast."

"Yes," I said, "watching white women stay young."

"White women never been bad to me."

I was in a sudden bad humor, maybe because she wasn't Sophronia. I said, "Colored women who cook as well as you do never had a bad time. Not even in slavery. You were the darlings of every house. What about the others who weren't?"

She said, "You mean the good house nigger is king boy."

I said, "I mean a house nigger pay no mind to a field hand."

She laughed at the words we had both grown up on. A half hour later I went down to the kitchen for a cup of coffee. She was using an electric beater and so neither of us tried to talk over the noise. Then she turned the beater off and, I think for the first time in her life, raised her voice in a shout.

"You ain't got no right to talk that way. No right at all. Down South, I cook. Nothing else, just cook. For you, I slave. You made a slave of me and you treat me like a slave."

I said, "Helen! Helen!"

"A slave. An old, broken slave."

"You're a liar," I said, "just a plain God-damned liar."

"God will punish you for those words."

"He is, right now."

She took a check from her apron pocket—her share of the royalties from *Toys in the Attic*—tore it up, and held out the pieces to me.

"There. Take it. You think money and presents can buy me, you're wrong."

I said, "I'm going up to Katonah. That will give you a few days to move out."

That night, sitting on a pile of books that had become the only place one could sit in the depressing little cottage filled with furniture broken by the weight of phonograph records and books, ashtrays toppling on the edges of manuscripts, a giant desk loaded with unopened mail that had arrived that day or five years ago, facing a window that had been splintered by the gun of somebody who didn't like his politics, I told Hammett about the afternoon.

He said, "Why do you talk to her about the South?"

"I didn't think she hated me."

"She doesn't. She likes you very much and that scares her, because she hates white people. Every morning some priest or other tells her that's not Christian charity, and she goes home more mixed up than ever."

"I guess so. But I don't care about what she hates or doesn't. I care about what I said to her. I'll wait until she has left and then I'll write and say I'm sorry I screamed liar."

He stared at me and went back to reading. After a while he said, "You should have screamed at her years ago. But of course you never lose your temper at the right time. Then you feel guilty and are sure to apologize. I've always counted on that, it's never failed."

I said, "All these years, waiting to catch me out."

"Yep. And shall I tell you something else that goes hand in hand, kind of?"

"I am, as you know, grateful for all high-class revelations."

"Well," he said, "when you start out being angry, you're almost always right. But anybody with a small amount of sense learns fast that if they let you go on talking you come around to being wrong. So after you've slammed the door, or taken a plane, or whatever caper you're up to, that fine, upright, liberal little old sense of justice begins to operate and you'll apologize not only for the nonsense part of what you've said but for the true and sensible part as well. It's an easy game—just a matter of patience."

I thanked him and went back to New York. It has long been my habit to enter the house on the bedroom floor, and on that day I did not wish to see the kitchen without Helen, did not wish to face a life without her, so it was four or five hours before I went downstairs. Helen was sitting in a chair, her Bible on the table.

She said, "Good evening. Your hair is wet."

"Yes," I said, "I'm trying to curl it."

We did learn something that day, maybe how much we needed each other, although knowing that often makes relations even more difficult. Our bad times came almost always on the theme of Negroes and whites. The white liberal attitude is, mostly, a well-intentioned fake, and black people should and do think it a sell. But mine was bred, literally, from Sophronia's milk, and thus I thought it exempt from such judgments except when I made the jokes about myself. But our bad times did not spring from such conclusions by Helen—they were too advanced, too unkind for her. They came, I think, because she did not think white people capable of dealing with trouble. I was, thus, an intruder, and in the autumn of 1963 she told me so.

I had gone down to Washington to write a magazine piece about the Washington March. Through Negro friends, through former Harvard students, through a disciple of Malcolm X, I had arranged to meet the delegations from Louisiana and Alabama. Sophronia's grandson, whom I had never seen, was to arrive with the Alabama delegation. Many years before, I had had letters from his older sister, a teacher at Tuskegee. Now, when I wrote to ask if they would like to come to Washington, she had written back that they could not make the trip. Immediately after, I had a letter from Orin saying that he wanted to come if I would send the bus fare, but please not to tell his sister, because she did not approve. I had sent the money and, as far as I knew, he was on his way.

At seven o'clock on the morning of the March, I was sitting on the steps of the Lincoln Memorial waiting for Orin, wondering if he looked like Sophronia, if he had brought me the photographs I had asked for, if his mother had ever told him much about her. At nine o'clock I went to look for the Alabama delegation. They had been in Washington for six hours, but nobody had heard of Orin and they were sure he had never been on the bus, never signed up to come.

It was, of course, a remarkable day. Two hundred thousand people come to ask only what they thought had been promised, still calm, pleasant and gay in the face of the one-hundred-year-old refusal. But as the day wore on, I felt as if a respectable Madison Avenue funeral had gone on too long. When Martin Luther King rose to speak—and there was no question of the pride the audience felt in the man, no question that he represented all that was gentle and kind in this kindest of people—I remembered too many Negro preachers from my childhood and grew impatient with "I have a dream."

I wandered off looking for something to eat. I dropped my pocketbook, spilled the contents, and was helped by a small colored boy who, when I thanked him, said "O.K., lady, courtesy of the Commonwealth." I laughed and found that his companion, a tall young Negro, was laughing, too.

I said, "What's that mean, courtesy of the Commonwealth?"

"Nothing," said the young man. "Old George tries to learn a new word every day. We were up around Boston last night so today it will be 'Commonwealth.' "

Old George turned out to be fourteen years old, small for his age, and the young man's name was Gene Carondelet.

I said, "That's the name of a street in New Orleans."

He said, "Yep. That's why I took it."

Old George weaved in and out of the crowd, bringing frankfurters and then coffee, while Carondelet told me he had been in jail seven times for trying to register Negroes in Greenwood, Mississippi, and for leading a march in Baton Rouge. He said he had never seen old George before McComb, Mississippi, where a policeman had hit George over the head and George's mother had hit the policeman. The next day George's mother said, "Take the boy with you. He's in danger here. Take him and teach him."

"He's been with me for eight months. That George can do, learn anything. Makes a mighty fine speech. Make a speech for the lady."

George rose. "You folks better take your black behinds down to vote your way to freedom. The first correlative to freedom—" At the word "correlative" George grinned at me and sat down, saying he didn't feel too well, he had his headache back again. Carondelet explained that in a few days they were coming to New York to see a doctor about the headaches George had been having since he got hit over the head by the policeman.

About a week later, I came in the house to find Carondelet, George, and a gangly popeyed man of about twenty-four sitting in the living room with Helen. Carondelet said they'd been waiting for an hour and now they had to go because George was on his way to the doctor's. As I took them to the elevator, I did notice that the strange man was still in the living room until George said, "You wanted him, you got him."

"Who?"

"That Orin something."

Carondelet said, "He's silly stuff."

Orin was, indeed, a dull young man, sleepy, over-polite, as anxious as I was to get the visit over with. He had been born long after Sophronia's death, had no memory of his mother's ever having talked about her. What about his uncle, Sophronia's son? Never heard of him. Where was his mother? She'd skipped long ago, maybe dead, maybe still turning a trick. Why hadn't he come to Washington with the Alabama delegation? They weren't his kind. He'd come to New York, been robbed, lost my address, hadn't eaten, where was the men's room? I pointed toward the kitchen, waited a long time, puzzled and sad that this man should be Sophronia's grandson. When he did come back, I said I had to go to work, and rose to shake his hand. He suddenly began to talk in a more animated way, although the words were now slurred. I had become Miss Hellmar or, more often, "man" in puzzling sentences like "Man, this is some town and they can take me to it any time they got enough, man," and "Man, where them two finkies I come here with, and where is here, just where is here at?" After a while I said I'd get him some money for the trip back home if he wanted to make it, and he began to laugh as I went into the hall to find Helen standing by the door.

She said, "He took a shot in the toilet."

"What do you mean?"

"A no good punkie-junkie. Maybe heroin."

The words were so modern, so unlike her, that I stared, amused and puzzled that there was a side of her I didn't know.

"I don't think so. He's just stupid, and uncomfortable with me."

When I came back down the steps, the phonograph was playing very loudly and Orin was moving around the room. I couldn't hear what Helen said, but his voice was very loud.

"Lady man, I'm stayin' right where I fall, see?"

Helen said, "You a sick boy. You going for a cure, or you going to hell."

"Lady man, hell's my place and you my girl, tired and old. Maybe even have to send you on a little errand soon—"

She crossed to him, pulled his arms behind his back, and stepped to one side as he tried to kick her. She held him easily, gracefully, as she pulled him toward a chair.

She said to me, "Go for a walk," and closed and locked the door.

The following morning she said, "You see, things happen to people."

I didn't answer her, and after an hour or so she appeared again—an old habit, conversation without prelude, in space, from hours or days or months before— "I locked the door 'cause I wanted you out of trouble."

"No," I said. "You just didn't think I'd be any good at it."

"Time I told you what I ain't told you. My daughter, same way, same thing."

After a while I said, "That shouldn't have happened to you."

"No good for colored people to come North, no good," she said. "Live like a slummy, die like one. South got its points, no matter what you think. Even if just trees."

I was never to see or hear from Orin again, but when George got out of the hospital he came to stay with us several times, appearing and disappearing without explanation. There was something odd about his relations with Helen, something teasing on his side, cautious on hers.

The next summer he came to stay with us for a few days on the Vineyard. He was romping with the poodle on the lawn outside her window, while I read on the porch above their heads.

He said to her, "Hey, Mrs. Jackson, your poodle got fleas."

"Lot of people got fleas," she said.

After a long pause, George called out, "I've been thinking about what you said, and I'm God-damned if I understand it."

"You been sleepin' here, Miss Hellman been sleepin' here. That's all I got to say."

George screamed with laughter. "You mean *we* give the dog the fleas? You some far-out lady, Mrs. Jackson." And a door slammed.

At dinner, a few weeks later, he said to Helen, "Could I have a piece of your cornbread?"

"Where you see cornbread?"

"Why you hide it where you do?"

It had long been her habit to hide any food that was fattening on the pretense that she ate very little and thus had inherited her "fat glands." Now she opened the stove, reached far back into the oven, and slammed down on the table a giant cornbread cake and a pot of greens and fatback.

"Can I have some," I said, knowing he had made a bad mistake—"nothing in the world like potlikker and corn—"

She said to George, "What you do all day, besides snoopin'? You know more about this island than we ever find out, or want to."

"Sure do," said George, "that my job. Got to find out before you organize. You, for example. Find out all about you being like crazy with your money. You got so much money, give it to SNCC instead of wasting it on that no good Almira family down in town."

Helen said, softly, "Eat your dinner, son."

George said to me, "Old man Almira leave his family for a fourteen-year-old girl, and Mrs. Jackson here, that makes her sad, so she send money all year round, *all year round,* to the wife and kiddies—"

Helen said, "No good men, that's what you all are."

George said, "And no good kiddies. You some fine picker, Mrs. Jackson. The Almira boy was the one set the fire last week and the girl whores all over the Cape."

"You lie, boy, and you a mighty dirty talker about your own people."

"First," said George, "they ain't my people 'cause they ain't all black, they part Portuguese. Two, bums is bums, forget the color. Three, a revolutionary got no right to defend the baddies even of his own color, kind or faith. Otherwise it comes about—"

I said, "Oh, shut up, George," and Helen hit me on the arm, an old sign of affectionate approval.

George came to visit us the next summer for a few days but I did not see him at all in 1965, until the cold autumn day of Helen's funeral. That night, quite late, he rang the bell, a small suitcase in his hand.

He said, "I wouldn't have come like this, but I'm going back to Atlanta, and I wanted to—Well, I don't know."

We talked for a while about what he'd been doing, where he'd been, and then he said, "You're worried, Miss Hellman."

"Yes," I said, "if that's the word."

"About the funeral. They didn't come to you?"

"I guess that's part of it, but not much. No, they didn't come to me, although they telephoned, the two nieces, and the daughter I'd never heard from before. They asked me what kind of funeral I wanted, but I didn't like to intrude, or maybe—I don't know."

"Stinking funeral."

I said, "It's hard to know what strong people would want. I've been there before. You think they're trying to tell you something, forbid you something, but you don't know—"

"Ah," he said, "the one thing they knew for sure was she didn't want that coffin, all done up for a bishop, with brass. Seventeen hundred dollars."

"My God, I didn't know that. What fools—Well, at least I talked them into burying her in South Carolina. That I know she wanted."

"It's my birthday," George said, so we had two drinks. When he got up to leave he said, "Don't worry about the funeral or the coffin. It's done, done."

"That's not what's worrying me. She got sick on Monday. I wanted her to go to the hospital. She wanted to go home. I was annoyed with her and went for a walk. When I came back she was gone. I phoned the next day and she said she was better, but might not be able to work for a while, and then as if she wanted to tell me something. The next morning she was dead."

"She did want to tell you something. She was getting ready to die."

I said, "You know too much, George, too much you're sure of. I don't believe she knew she was going to die. I won't believe it. And how do you know how much the coffin cost?"

"They told me," he said. "On Tuesday morning, Mrs. Jackson asked me to come round."

"She asked you, she didn't ask me. I'm jealous, George."

"She had things for me to do, errands."

I said, "She always had people doing secret errands. I didn't know you saw each other."

"Oh, sure, whenever I came up North, and then I always wrote to her. My second operation, I stayed in her place till I was better."

"You didn't tell me you had a second operation."

He smiled. "Anyway, there I am on Tuesday. She shows me two Savings Bank things and says they're for her grandchildren. Then she give me orders to pack her clothes and take 'em to the post office, all of them except one dress and shoes."

"Where did she send them?"

"Somebody in Augusta, Georgia. Then I take around the TV radio set and I sell that for her. When I come back, she asked me to make her a lemonade and said she wanted to sleep. I said I'd be back at night, but she said not to come, she wanted rest. Then she gave me one hundred dollars. Eighty-five for me, she said, or wherever I wanted to give it. Fifteen for Orin when I found him."

"Orin? Orin?"

"He's still hanging around. She always gave him a little money. But he ain't going to get his fifteen, 'cause I ain't going to find him. She was some far-out lady, Mrs. Jackson. Some far-out Christian lady."

"Sure was," I said.

"I hope you feel better," he said. "Next time I'm here, I'll come see you."

But he never has come to see me again.

Jonathan Miller / On Lenny Bruce (1926–1966)

As Miller explains, he came into contact with Bruce when he and his associates hired Bruce to perform in a satirical nightclub in London. Bruce's account of his earlier life as an entertainer may be studied in his own book *How To Talk Dirty and Influence People*. This essay is a kind of obituary. Miller blames the intellectuals for taking him up and making him fit their needs; but he also blames Bruce for complying too easily with their demands. Believing, however, that Bruce was a great talent and that his death had some social importance, he then tries to put on record a little of the entertainer's character, and something about the nature of his act. Note here the necessary blend of deft description and exemplification. The writer's own personal contact with Bruce, of which he does not make very much, is described at the point where there is a necessary transition from a general account of his art to a more particular account of his character. Here, as in the passages on Bruce's "thought," Miller is careful not to exaggerate the truth or importance of what Bruce said or believed; and this control of emphasis will be seen to provide an important contribution to the total effect. An obituary notice will usually overlook a man's failings, unless he is unusually important. The judicious tone of Miller's essay may therefore help to suggest that its subject is important.

It is hard to write fairly about Lenny Bruce now that he's dead. At least it is difficult to be just, in the way that he, in his more realistic moments, might have preferred. For Bruce became an issue in the last years of his life. He became the focus of controversy between opposing vested interests, neither of which really gave a damn for the man himself. The complementary roles of mascot and victim proved inevitably fatal, and through a strange mixture of simple-minded vanity and courageous generosity he lived up too thoroughly to a public personality partly supplied by his sponsors and tormentors. In the end it led quite inexorably to an ordeal which both sides, with different types of satisfaction, saw coming a long way off. The villains of the piece were all those thick-necked hypocritical authorities who hounded him down, in state after state, until he was finally too poor, too weak, and too confused to survive. All along he was up against a brutal, prejudiced society which somehow seemed unable to afford the easy conversational freedom that Bruce offered to his audiences. But we, his sponsors, his eager fluting publicists, must also bear some of the responsibility for the way things turned out. Bruce was in many ways a willing sucker for the sort of martyrdom upon which affluent, free-thinking liberals vicariously thrive. His dreadful ordeal through the courts, destitution, and ultimate death, provided a nice, flourishing proof of the liberals' conviction that the world is cruel, repressed, and indifferent. But Bruce was too ready to sacrifice *himself* on behalf of this demonstration. He was too accommodating, and those of us who supported him in print were sometimes too excited, or else too selfish, to notice that Bruce's uneducated simplicity often led him to yield without criticism to the flattery of over-elaborate interpretation. Underneath all that hipster cool, it is to be remembered that Bruce was rather an innocent bloke, badly read, and so keen to be accepted and admired by educated people that he was sometimes deceived by the over-complicated program which certain missionary intellectuals read into his act. It's possible that he suffered very badly from being taken up quite like this. As intellectual support for his act grew, he began to take seriously all that stuff about being the prophet of a new morality and would replace a lot of his regular material with sentientious sermons. He would quote from Doctor Albert Ellis, M.D.,* recite dubious pharmacological justifications for "pot," and generally became quite boring.

He was so generously open to intellectual flattery, so pleased to discover that he had authoritative support, that he sometimes failed to realize how much he was being used as a dispensable stalking horse for middle-class liberal dares. Strangely enough, by stepping up the dirt in the service of this mission he was to some extent being exploited by a mirror image of the very prejudice which finally hounded him to his death. I can still, with some shame, recall my own euphoric horror at hearing him come out with four-letter words in front of a solid middle-class audience at The Establishment in London. It seems contemptible now, the way in which we used him to do our dubious dirty work of evangelical sexual shock therapy. For the marvelous thing about Bruce was not the way in which he deliberately introduced obscenity into his act, though as time went on, with encouragement from us, he did do more and more of this, but the way in which he never held back obscenity if it was relevant to his subject. He spoke to his audience just as most of us speak to each other in private, without feeling that he had any need to button his lip when dealing with pelvic affairs. But we got too zealously worked up on behalf of this particular aspect of his act, and egged him on to fresh excesses of sexual radicalism. Left to himself, I sometimes doubt whether he would have pressed on this point quite so much. But as it is, he rose a bit too eagerly to the bait of our shady approval, and found himself assuming more and more the role of persecuted prophet of a slightly phony gospel. For as Christopher Lasch has pointed out, "by insisting that sex was the highest form of love, the highest form of human discourse, the modern prophets of sex

* Albert Ellis, M.D.: author of such books as *Sex Without Guilt* (1958) and *The Encyclopedia of Sexual Behavior* (with A. Abarbanel, 1961).

did not so much undermine the prudery against which they appeared to be in rebellion . . . as invert it."

It would be foolish, simply in the light of his painful death, to exonerate Bruce himself altogether from the comparative absurdity of this position. Intellectually underprivileged in several important respects, he was in every other way fully aware and even proud of his participation in the campaign for utopian sexual enlightenment. He did feel, I'm quite sure, that if only prudery would relax we could screw our way to peace and prosperity for all. That in some hypothetical millennium, bigotry and suffering would not be heard for the swishing of the pricks. Perhaps it's significant that it was *Playboy* magazine which serialized his autobiography. Commercially this publication also embodies the half-formed belief that sexual knots alone contort the body politic. Heffner's interminable editorial philosophy often reads like a transcript of one of Bruce's more didactic bits, and the rest of the magazine, too, reverberates with the idea that by being honestly sybaritic human beings will simply forget to be nasty and collapse instead into a voluptuous communion, peacefully noshing * on Plumrose Playmates, their savagery soothed by first-class hi-fi. It is sad that Bruce should have allowed himself to be hanged until he was dead from the yard-arm of this particular ship of fools. But he was encouraged to do so by people who were prepared to push a much more sophisticated version of the same argument. I doubt if Lionel Trilling's essay on "Freud and the Crisis of Our Culture" ever got to Bruce's immediate attention, but the general idea was familiar to intellectuals with whom Bruce came in contact. They believed, sincerely, though I think mistakenly, that the biological core of human nature, inaccessible to the repressive threats of culture, offered a life-saver for the individual who found himself drowning in modern life. Without fully wishing to understand the complex institutional history of this proposal, certain intellectuals leaped at its utopian possibilities and then found Bruce a conveniently self-sacrificing public spokesman on behalf of the doctrine.

But that's enough carping. I make it sound as if Bruce was no more than a gullible ass who went down in the name of something completely ludicrous, although even if that were the case there would be a certain pathetic honor in his death. But even if the cause, as fought, was riddled with absurdity, so, of course, were the brutal idiots who considered it important enough to oppose it to the death. Anyway, there was much more to Bruce than that. So that his life and death *are* significant and serious attention must be paid.

Bruce was a great stage artist, a soloist of unbelievable virtuosity. The thousands of people who filled two houses of an old movie theater in Greenwich Village in December 1963 are a witness of that. So were the audiences that came back night after night during his month in London. The people who followed

* noshing: eating.

him were charmed by the free conversational directness of the man. He liked his audiences and took great pains to feel his way towards the individual temperament of each one. And if he felt comfortable with a group there was no end to the effort he would make to entertain and delight them. It's not really true that he thrived on hostility, though he sometimes managed to put on a show of hard, glittering verve when the animals were in—people who talked loudly throughout his act, sounding "like tape played backwards." But generally an unfriendly audience made him stiff and defiant, and then he would sometimes become brutally dirty, just for the hell of it. He also had amazing resources of descriptive finesse with which he would reward friendly attention. He had an uncannily accurate ear and a novelist's eye for the sort of crucial visual detail which could suddenly delight spectators with a shock of recognition. Midgets with blue suits and brown boots, hands only visible on the steering wheel of a car, speeding along the Santa Ana freeway; or holidaymakers sunning themselves on a sward of green paper grass laid out in front of their trailer. He could reproduce the whole screenplay of old movies or daytime radio serials, twisting them here and there with touches of nutty invention—the Lone Ranger as a fag. And mad Catholic fantasies too—Christ at St. Patrick's Cathedral:

> "Don't look now, but you'll never guess who's in tonight."
> "Which one, which one?"
> "The one that's glowing, dummy."
> "Police! You've got to get me out of here. I'm up to my ass in wheel chairs and crutches."

Or an M.C.A. agent on the line to Pope John—"Sure we can get you the Sullivan show. But wear the big ring, Johnny. No. No one'll guess you're Jewish."

He did not actually create all this stuff on the stage as he went along. Anyone who saw him regularly began to realize that he had a vast repertoire of "bits" and that the improvisation consisted in the unexpected way he would weave it all together, sometimes only alluding to sketches which he might have played in full the night before.

This would often madden people who only managed to see him once or twice. But it was an indication of the affectionate trust he had in his audience. Without any arrogance, he expected people to come again and again, to join him in creating the rambling, show-biz-saturated saga of American life. He was not a conventional nightclub comic who could be guaranteed to deliver a self-contained package of laughing matter for a casual door trade. But like an old-time story teller he was always filling out familiar routines with unexpected additions of vivid new detail. It was impossible to judge him fairly on a single showing. It's a shame that we'll never have a chance of arriving at a just summary. Because apart from a few rather meager and slightly inaudible records, his creation dies with him. Unlike his conventional colleagues, most of whom held him in contempt, he was quite unfitted for mechanical reproduction, since his art and his personality were indistinguishable.

He came to London during the summer of 1961 and I met him for the first time about ten days before he was due to open. He was upstairs in the office of The Establishment, seated on the edge of a desk, bent over an electrical gadget which he was trying to fix with a bread knife. He had obviously been engaged in this for some time because a secretary was twiddling her thumbs at another desk, plainly rather at a loss. He was dressed in a black uniform with a high Nehru collar, open to show an orange T shirt. On his feet he had what looked like high-heeled white cricket boots. The secretary introduced me tentatively, and Bruce looked up, sweating from the exertion of his obscure task. "Hiya Jonathan. Hey, yah." He breathed with vague unfocused enthusiasm. And then he caught sight of a motorcycle helmet I was holding. "Hey man, what do you ride?" "A motor scooter," I said apologetically. After which it took nearly ten days to regain his interest and confidence. But then he never really displayed anything one could call direct personal interest. It was just a restless, incoherent curiosity which he would try to satisfy by quizzing more or less anyone with whom he came in contact. And he was always off at odd tangents—worrying about some gadget, or else running on about a doctor he had heard of who could get him prescriptions. Then there was endless trouble about his hotel accommodation. Largely because of girls, but also because hotel proprietors were badly jangled by his eccentric diurnal routines. Not that he was a night person, or anything straight-forwardly hippy like that. He followed no discernible rhythm whatever in his sleeping and waking. He might sleep for twenty-four hours, and then race around for another forty-eight, walking the streets of Soho, taking down notes about clothes in shop windows, or stopping passers-by to ask them about their jobs. Sometimes he would cat-nap in the office while the secretaries clattered on all round him. And as the opening drew nearer he became more and more noncommittal about what he was actually going to do on the stage; though he would spend hours panting and squawking over a grubby screed to which he kept adding and then crossing out. Or out of the blue he would dictate some dubious paragraph to one of the bewildered girls in the office who had by this time developed a distracted affection for the man. Then he held a press conference and baffled all the reporters, who had expected to find a ferocious slavering junkie, by mildly asking them so many questions about themselves that they never seemed able to get one in edgeways about him. He was always intrigued by their cameras and anyone unlucky enough to be sporting an unusual model had to suffer endless catechism while Bruce turned the machine over lovingly in his hands, breathing and crooning with a naive, savage wonder. Bruce had plenty of "character" but seemed to possess nothing that one could properly call a personality. There were so many epicycles of interest and activity that it was impossible to make out the central point around which they all moved. Perhaps there wasn't any. I often thought of him like Peter Pan, resolutely fickle and somehow in flight from his and everyone else's maturity. He was comparatively young when he died and yet it was hard to imagine him being any older. His special talent arose from a sort of daft, alienated infantilism which ruled out the possibility of his ever enjoying senior citizenship. Perhaps in some obscure vision of expediency he sought the ordeal which brought about his own annihilation. The horrible thing is that in willing his own execution Bruce actually found society only too willing to oblige him with cruel and extravagant fulfilment.

John Wain / E. H. W. Meyerstein

This is an account, written when the author was in his thirties and established as a writer, of a friendship, begun when he was an eighteen-year-old student at Oxford, with a man almost forty years older and wildly eccentric. Wain does not spare himself—his youthful defects and ignorance were as essential as his juvenile virtues to a relationship which was, "given the circumstances, extremely natural." Meyerstein was of course not the only older man who influenced the clever student; he speaks of others, especially C. S. Lewis and Charles Williams. But there was more to say of Meyerstein, and Wain's well-illustrated memoir fills a gap in literary history; Meyerstein, though weird and neglected, was by no means a nonentity, and there is more information, affectionate and yet critical, here than in any other source. The manner of the piece is appropriately unaffected; the self-criticism it contains is important to the tone and affects what we feel about Meyerstein. Since the work is part of an autobiography its ultimate purpose is to contribute to an understanding of Wain himself, but that could not have been achieved without, in this passage, focusing attention on Meyerstein, as well as on the peculiar conditions which enabled so unlikely a friendship to develop.

The case I refer to was that of E. H. W. Meyerstein, whose acquaintance I made in my third term and who was one of my closest companions for the rest of my undergraduate days. Meyerstein was such a fantastic figure that I doubt if I can make him credible to anyone who never met him: still, this being my story and he being one of the principal characters in it, I must see what I can do.

To begin with, let me fill in the public facts, so to speak, about Meyerstein. The son of a wealthy man (about whom I know nothing except that he seems to have been the caricaturist's ideal of the Edwardian Hampstead-Jewish Croesus) Edward Harry William, having duly got himself born and been equipped with three aggressively English Christian names, was launched into the pre-1914 world by way of Harrow * and Magdalen.* No expense was spared, and neither, if we are to believe the son's own posthumous narrative,[1] was any ordeal or humiliation. Not only was "Eddie" expected to hold his own in the harsh world of the Edwardian public school, with its Spartan discipline and its frank, overt snobberies; he had also to justify his existence in the eyes of a large, interfering family who seem to have achieved a rare blend of Jewish inquisitiveness with British arrogance. Dreamy, solitary, a passionate student, the boy was at home among books and music, awkward and troubled anywhere else; it is easy to imagine the ideal upbringing for such a child, one that would have brought out the latent sweetness of his character and developed his gifts, which were unquestionably very fine. What he actually got was an upbringing calculated to turn him into a raging neurotic by the time he was twenty-one, which it duly did.

Meyerstein was fifty-five when I first met him, and I don't want to waste time on speculation about things that happened twenty years before I was born; but this question of his upbringing really has some importance, since it accounts for a great many features of his behaviour, tastes, and attitudes which I, as a youth of eighteen, found utterly baffling. What I could see—what anyone could see, at first glance—was that this man had some sort of a place for himself in literature. He had studied deeply, and had the Greek and Latin classics more or less by heart, as well as a vast quantity of French and English literature; he had written hundreds of poems, publishing volume after volume at his own expense; he had translated the *Elegies* of Propertius, written a monumental life of Chatterton, contributed to scores of learned controversies in organs like *The Times Literary Supplement* and *Notes and Queries;* he had published immense novels, volumes of short stories, at least one play, and a mass of musical criticism in various papers. Day after day, year after year, he had guided his pen across the paper, or hammered away at one or other of his beaten-up old typewriters (that he, a rich man, should have used typewriters not only obsolete but worn-out, on which it was impossible to type a line without the letters jumping all over the paper, is a good pointer to his horror of spending money). What I didn't realize at the time, of course, was that it had all come to nothing. All I could see was that Meyerstein was a wonderfully learned man who lived in a rich confusion of books and manuscripts and was always reading and writing—just the sort of life I was hoping to lead myself—and that he had an imposing shelf-ful of books with his name on the spine. I don't believe I had heard, at that time, of private publication; no doubt I just thought that an author wrote a book and sent it to a publisher, and the publisher either published it or didn't. I was ready to admire anyone who had smelt printer's ink, and here was a man who had a couple of dozen books to his name. It is only when I look back that I see it all clearly—the

---

1. E. H. W. Meyerstein, *Of My Early Life* (London: Neville Spearman, 1958).
* Harrow: famous public (i.e. private preparatory) school near London.
* Magdalen: a college of Oxford University.

tragic disappointment, the sense of heaving away for years at a weight too heavy to lift, the deep frost that had settled on his hopes. By this time, Meyerstein's parents were both dead; even if he were to win recognition, it would be too late now to go and confront them with the visible signs of it. That particular series of early humiliations could not be wiped out. What remained? Well, there was Oxford; another of the great unhealed wounds in Meyerstein's soul was that he had failed to get his First, and had then worked desperately hard for a Magdalen fellowship, one of the kind that are awarded competitively, and had failed there too. The disappointment and overstrain had driven him into some kind of breakdown; he had fled from Oxford, taken rooms in Gray's Inn,* and lived the life of a secluded man of letters for twenty years. When the war came, he stayed in London until his chambers were smashed up by a bomb, and then went— significantly—first to Cambridge and finally to Oxford. The decision to go to Cambridge first seems to me to point to a preliminary hesitation, a kind of screwing up of his courage, before confronting Oxford—which must, in its corporate character, have loomed up in front of him very much in the way his parents had done. Coming back to Magdalen, he had obtained permission to live in College (since he had, during all the intervening years, "kept his name on the books" or performed some similar Oxford shibboleth) and set himself once more to the hopeless task of getting Oxford to accept him. Tragic folly! Oxford has worlds to offer, but not to those who ask. Furthermore, Meyerstein was approaching Oxford by the wrong avenue—through the dons; * and, as a general rule, it is true to say that the dons represent the worst side of Oxford—the excluding, sneering, ungenerous, unforgiving, parochial side. And so it came about that Meyerstein, for the second time in his life, broke his knuckles by beating them against the flinty sides of Magdalen Senior Common Room. It was no use; he made no headway with the dons; he was not admitted as a member of Common Room, and had to find his companionship in the less critical, more shifting world of the undergraduates.

In all this, I do not greatly blame the dons themselves. An Oxford college is a kind of club; if a man is elected to a fellowship, or to membership of the Common Room, those who have elected him have not only to work with him but to eat, drink, and spend many of their leisure hours in his company. And Meyerstein was not everyone's idea of an easy-going companion. He wrote to me once that at some dinner or other, where for once he had been admitted to the cabal, he had found himself sitting next to C. S. Lewis: * "He was extremely boastful of his knowledge of Milton, but did not seem to know that the name Lycidas,

---

* Gray's Inn: one of the four Inns of Court where English barristers study or practice law; its rooms are not confined to members of the legal profession, but are sometimes let to the right kind of bachelor tenant.
* don: university teacher (originally, a fellow of one of the colleges of Oxford or Cambridge).
* C. S. Lewis: famous medievalist and professor of English literature at Oxford and Cambridge.

for a soldier nearly drowned, occurs in Lucan." I think the whole tone of their conversation can be deduced from that one sentence, and my sympathies are with Lewis. After a hard day's work, you do not want to find yourself sitting next to a man who finds his chief pleasure in shooting you down over obscure points of literary scholarship. The Magdalen Common Room was protecting itself, and justifiably—though worse bores than Meyerstein, and men with none of his underlying sweetness of temperament and genuine love of art, have been tolerated for years in every Common Room in Oxford. What is harder to forgive is the general attitude towards Meyerstein that obtained among Oxford dons. Not to put too fine a point on it, they sneered at him. He was a figure of fun, for all sorts of reasons. He was a failure, and academics are, notoriously, success-worshippers; in any case, no one ever has any sympathy with a *rich* man who is a failure, whose failure, however painful, does not involve him in actual want. Again, they knew that he had vast learning, and their tidy minds were irritated by his clumsiness, his lack of control over what he knew, his inability to tie it up in neat little bundles and market it. The average don has climbed to his eminence as much by canniness as by hard work or flair; Meyerstein was not canny, and they despised him for it while they half-feared him for his huge random erudition. There were honourable exceptions, but in the main it has to be recorded that Oxford, to the extent that it was personified by the dons, treated Meyerstein shabbily, and that his attitude of half-crazy resentment had its crumb of justification.

However, the picture has its bright side. Exile among the undergraduates was by no means the hard fate for Meyerstein that it would have been for many another man; for, doubtless as another result of his pernicious upbringing, the slant of his emotions was distinctly homosexual. I do not say, and no one who knew him could ever say, that Meyerstein was a practising homosexual. He was simply homosexual in the way in which many schoolmasters are sadists—that is, the cast of his emotions was that way, but he managed to keep it from presenting itself to his conscious mind in any overtly sexual form. To put it bluntly, Meyerstein was completely without any sexual life, but if he had had any (which would have meant re-structuring the whole of his emotional system) it would have been of a homosexual character. Certainly he had one trait by which the pervert can usually be recognized—the hatred of women. Besides being repelled by their physiology, he was paranoid about their having designs on him. His few friendships with women usually came to an abrupt end when he took it into his head that marriage was being plotted; as, for instance, his fleeting spell of camaraderie with Dorothy L. Sayers, back in the 'twenties, which crashed in flames when someone told him that Miss Sayers, being shown over a house that was for sale, had been heard to remark, "This wouldn't do for Eddie."

I first met Meyerstein in the autumn of 1943, when I was hunting for guest speakers to come to an undergraduate club at St. John's called the Essay Society. He was living in a couple of rooms at the top floor of No. 12, Longwall Street, whose front windows looked across over Magdalen grove and whose back ones gave one of the best available views of the old City Wall. The house was desperately uncomfortable, with no bathroom and a lavatory out in the back yard, but Meyerstein was genuinely indifferent to physical comfort; he had a neurosis about getting enough to eat, which was related to his persecution mania—if he failed to keep his strength up, the hounds would overtake him and drag him down—but beyond that, his wishes were of the simplest. All he demanded of a house was that it should carry no suggestion of modernity, for the modern world had rejected him and he was its implacable enemy.

Early one afternoon in October, I climbed the stairs of No. 12 and found him sitting among his treasures. Old books, manuscripts, and pictures were everywhere; Meyerstein was famous as a collector, and he was certainly far removed from the kind of connoisseur who keeps his "items" under lock and key, or carefully tabulated behind glass. If he invited you to take a seat, you were quite likely to have to remove several hundred pounds' worth of books or manuscripts from the chair before you could get into it. (He once told me that he kept the manuscript of Wordsworth's 1807 poems, a very valuable item even for him, in a box *under his bed.*) I was enchanted; I should be staggered, even today, to walk into such a place; then, I felt like Aladdin. To cap it all, Meyerstein was in one of his benign, humorous moods. Except when his crazy fits of paranoia were on him, he could be very likeable; he had a childlike simplicity that was very touching. To use a term that has come into currency since those days, he had no Lifemanship. No one ever had less skill at putting up a front; he was what he was, and you saw immediately what was going on in his mind. The cause of his good humour, no doubt, was that he was happily at work on a task that was not too demanding, and which he had reason to hope would lead him a little nearer to recognition by the scholarly world. Briefly, he had seen an item in a bookseller's catalogue which engaged his interest, written off for it, and realized, when it arrived, that he was on to something remarkable. It was the manuscript life-story of a seventeenth-century Kentish seaman, Edward Coxere (pronounced "Coxery"), written in what was evidently the man's own hand and bound in coarse but strong parchment. Before I had been there two minutes, he was showing me the manuscript and talking animatedly about how interesting it was. I sat there, with waves of new impressions breaking over me, blinking and trying to cope with everything as it came. The manuscript seemed interesting, though not wildly so; I was unfamiliar with seventeenth-century hand, and could only make out a word here and there; still, the pictures of ships seemed well done, and I had the pleasant sense that someone long dead was speaking directly to me. But I was much more interested in my first impressions of Meyerstein himself. He was a big, thick-set man, dressed in the ruin of what had been a well-cut grey suit, augmented by a dark-blue jersey of which the sleeves poked out over his wrists. The first thing one noticed about him, inevitably, was that one side of his face was tightly screwed up by some kind of nervous seizure which had happened a few years previously—a pointer, I suppose, to the strokes which eventually killed him. His right eye—I think it was the right—was almost hidden, and I could never tell how much he was able to see with it. Even if the eye itself was undamaged, its usefulness must have been restricted by the fact that it could never fully open. His mouth, too, was drawn upwards on that side, which gave his speech an odd flavour: it was not that his articulation was affected, but rather that, if you watched his face while he was talking there was something impish or gnome-like about the way the words seemed to come out obliquely. He looked, in short, like a gargoyle: not one of the hideously ugly ones, but one of those in which the grotesquerie is tempered by a satiric good humour. He was given, as we are told Shelley was, to bursts of demoniac laughter, and as he shook and rocked back and forth in one of these fits, his half-closed eye would twinkle brightly out through its tiny slit with an unimaginably impish malice and glee. However, this afternoon he was in one of his quieter moods, and his face consequently suggested that of a gargoyle in repose.

The second thing that I, at any rate, noticed was that his hands were finely shaped and that he instinctively held them in graceful attitudes. The nails were unkempt, forming an odd contrast to the slight touch of *dandysme* provided by the signet-ring on one finger, but the hands, and their poise, were unmistakably graceful. That contrast, in a way, epitomizes Meyerstein. He was clumsy and awkward; his voice was hoarse in its deeper register, and rose to a grating shriek when he became excited; he never mastered the art of shaving, so that there were always tufts of stiff greyish hair sticking out from odd portions of his face —and even if he had succeeded in overcoming all these things, there was always the crazily twisted face to put him hopelessly beyond any possible definition of good looks. And yet it is also true, as anyone who knew him will testify, that Meyerstein's physical presence was not altogether unpleasing. There was a lightness and grace about some of his movements—particularly, as I have said, with the hands; intelligence and imagination flashed from his eyes; he would dart across the room for a book he wanted to consult, and back to his desk to make a note of what he had found, with the impulsive speed of a boy of fifteen. He was not one of those people who give the impression that they would be happier without bodies. Some intellectual men are like talking, thinking heads set on inert trunks; they move as if their clothes contained not limbs, but rolls of linoleum. Meyerstein was not like that; nor, even when he was dying, did he suggest decay, lifelessness, helpless weight. I could never see him as paralysed even when he was in fact paralysed, when he was in a wheel-chair and could not move his limbs. And in his active years, the force of the mind that pulsed through him seemed to animate his body with more than the energy one would have expected even in such a big, powerfully built man. He was, in a word, very much of the same physical type as Johnson, Beethoven, any of those large, clumsy, bear-like men of genius. Finally—and this is most important in trying to form a picture of him—he was no Bohemian. His clothes, however creased and soiled (for, like many solitary men, he was a messy feeder), were always of the correct style for the company he was in; he was equally free of the shirt-sleeve type of affectation, as represented at that time by people like C. E. M. Joad, and of the Chelsea beard-and-corduroy conceit. He dressed simply and quietly; the only licence he allowed himself was a taste for dark shirts, and even that was probably in the intersts of cutting down on laundry bills.

That was my first impression of Meyerstein. What was Meyerstein's first impression of me can never be known in so much detail. But I can easily guess at it: he liked my youth, my enthusiastic *naïveté,* my utter absorption in "art and song." We began to see each other often; indeed, for some weeks I went every day to his rooms, to help him in checking over a typescript he had made of Coxere's manuscript. For an hour or so each afternoon, we sat there, I following the typescript silently while he read out from the manuscript, his hoarse voice grating on and on through the short autumnal sunlight. "Coxere" is an old story now; the Clarendon Press published it in a neat little edition, which I treasured because it contained, among the acknowledgements, the first printed mention of my name: Meyerstein sounded a few people within the academic Establishment to see if there were any chance of his being given a doctorate for the editorial work he had done on it; they told him there wasn't, and one more light went out in his mind. That episode is closed, except for the occasional student of seventeenth-century *mores* who will read through Coxere's story and feel a flicker of gratitude to Meyerstein for having put it conveniently in his hands. But for me, looking back, the name of Coxere is a potent charm, recalling that first autumn and the beginning of my relationship with Meyerstein—which continued, with plenty of love and hate on both sides, during the nine years of life that remained to him.

It was an odd friendship, and yet, given the circumstances, very natural. Looking back, I realize that I wasn't fully aware of how extraordinary Meyerstein was. I was still young enough to accept the adult world as I found it; I couldn't pass judgement, because I knew nothing of mature life and had no normative background to refer things to. I was, for example, completely innocent about homosexual emotions. Not having been to a boarding school, I had very rarely given a thought to the subject. My schoolfellows and I had discussed "sex" a good deal (indeed, for about four years previously, we had seldom talked of anything else), but the mention of homosexuality had cropped up no more than two or three times perhaps, in all those years, and then only as a curiosity. I mention this fact not only as being significant in itself (in view of the guilt-ridden obsession about homosexuality that seems to build up in every boarding school without exception), but as helping to explain the whole nature of my relationship with Meyerstein. We quickly became familiar enough for his life, though not, of course, his psychology, to become an open book to me; I knew where he went, whom he saw, and what he did; and I knew, beyond question, that he had no dealings with women. I did not find this extraordinary. My attitude was simply, "If he's lucky enough to be able to do without it, all the better for him"; for I was in the process of being trained to think of man's natural sexuality, not as something God-given, a glorious bounty, but as "the flesh," something that had to be resisted, ignored, or, if it made itself too obtrusive, "mortified." Of course, if I had gone up to Oxford from a public school where homosexual emotions had been the chief focus of everyone's life, I should at once have jumped to the conclusion that Meyerstein was only waiting his opportunity to make a pass at me—and this would have imparted a defensiveness to my attitude towards him and ruined our relationship from the start. But such a thing never entered my head. It even puzzled me, so utterly was the whole subject strange to my mind, that he should get so wrapped up in his friendships and enmities with the undergraduates among whom he lived; he was for ever retailing stories about this or that piece of kindness, or selfishness, or malice, or aggressiveness, on the part of some whippersnapper who sat next to him in Hall. It amazed me; I had no suspicion of the extent to which his emotional capital was invested in these relationships.

There is no doubt, in fact, that the friendship between Meyerstein and myself was made possible by an extraordinary series of chances. There can hardly have been, anywhere in the world, an eighteen-year-old boy and fifty-five-year-old man who could have approached each other so directly. I had no suspicions, no defensiveness, no reservations about him; he was simply a fascinating companion, his mind crammed with miscellaneous learning, the eternal student living for his books and music. Sometimes, thinking it over, I regret that during the years I knew Meyerstein best, I was so utterly simple and youthful; after all, the man had real problems, and terrible ones, and I might have been able, had I been fifteen years older, to help him face them. On the other hand—the reflection quickly follows—if I, as I am now, were to meet Meyerstein as he was then, we would simply quarrel violently and never speak to each other again. The thing that drew us together was precisely that I didn't criticize him, didn't pass any kind of judgement on him either personal or literary. I even tried to like his poetry, and read a good deal of it, which I certainly couldn't do now.

And so we became constant companions, so much so that I can never think of my undergraduate years without pictures of Meyerstein flooding into my mind. Meyerstein sitting among his muddle of books and papers, or thumping on the piano in the downstairs front room; Meyerstein going for an afternoon constitutional, and stopping (invariably) at the fishmonger's for a pint of shrimps, which he would carry along in a paper bag and munch as he walked. (He always offered me a share, and I always refused; the things looked repulsive to me, and the impression wasn't helped by his habit of holding forth on some literary subject with a shrimp's head sticking out of his mouth.) Meyerstein feverishly hunting for his false teeth, which when alone he always took out and laid on the floor beside his chair—on hearing footsteps coming up the stairs, he would begin a frantic search for the teeth, always hoping, but rarely managing, to get them in place in time to call "Come in!" as the visitor knocked. After I got to know him well, he didn't bother to keep the teeth in for me, but this policy also had its complications; one day, pacing up and down the room as he talked, he crunched them underfoot, a grievous loss.

What annoyed him most about the teeth was having to pay for new ones. Anything, at any time, that required the spending of money always brought Meyerstein's paranoia straight to the surface. During the war years, of course, he extended his miserliness to food as well as money; food was scarce, and it was a patriotic duty to husband it—a respect in which Meyerstein was the world's greatest patriot. Once, while having tea in his lodgings, I felt something hard and sharp in my mouth, which investigation proved to be a piece of glass. Meyerstein, amid bursts of laughter, explained that while going across the road to College for his breakfast (he ate all his meals in Hall, though he lived outside) he had had the misfortune to drop his marmalade-jar and smash it; still, by carefully gathering it up, he had managed to save most of it, and what was a little internal bleeding from glass-wounds compared with the loss of half a pound of marmalade? I fled home and spent the rest of the afternoon alternately brushing my teeth, in case any splinters had lodged between them, and praying that I had not already swallowed any; Meyerstein laughed himself sick over the episode and referred to it for the rest of his life as one of his most amusing memories.

The thing that kept our friendship going, as I say, was that I never sized him up. I don't mean by that to imply that he hoodwinked me, that if I had "seen through him" it would have meant the end. What I mean is that if I had been adult, if I had any kind of mature, critical insight into the nature of his life and his ways, I could never have restrained myself from offering advice—and then, of course, he would have flown into one of his rages. In the summer of 1944, very proud that my college study should be the scene of a historic meeting, I introduced Meyerstein to that gentle and good man, J. B. Leishman; * I was puzzled when Meyerstein reacted violently against Leishman, so that to mention his name was to release a storm of invective, sneers and paranoid accusations. Only afterwards did I learn that Leishman, realizing how troubled and anguished Meyerstein was, had written him a letter in which he had made, in the kindness of his heart, a few practical suggestions for conquering his melancholia. The incident, which was repeated many times with different people, stays in my mind as an indication of what would have happened to me if I had been mature enough to see what was wrong with Meyerstein and try to help him. Because—and this is the point—no one could see a man suffer as he suffered, without wanting to help. However little of a do-gooder, however opposed to interference, one would have had to try to throw him a rope. His agonies were terrible to watch; he would have black days in which persecution mania and nameless

* J. B. Leishman: fellow of St. John's College, translator of Rilke, and author of many important critical works.

dread descended and sent him, to all practical purposes, insane. I could always tell when he had a black day on, as soon as I woke up in the morning. After moving out of College, I took lodgings at No. 13 Longwall and my bedroom window was within a few feet of Meyerstein's, though it was one floor lower down. Morning after morning, in 1944 and '45, I woke to hear Meyerstein "making his noises." There was no other word for it; it wasn't singing, or shouting, but an unearthly blend of the two; I can't hit on any formula that will describe it in words, though, if anyone is interested, I can reproduce it in a way that good judges have admitted to be uncannily perfect. It was a noise that had its origin in the kind of crooning and mumbling to himself that an author naturally produces as he sits at his typewriter; I know, for instance, that I make queer noises—mostly gibbering, interspersed with a hellish cackle and bursts of obscene language—and I expect it will get worse as I grow older and more eccentric. Meyerstein was aware of his noises, and his own explanation of them was that "it all began with Harrow football." Forced out on to the football field, it had been his one defence to run wildly up and down, giving as far as possible the appearance of keen activity but in reality dodging the ball whenever it came near him, and all the while, to keep his sanity, "singing the symphonies of Beethoven." The habit took hold, and in later years, when the football field was a distant though still festering memory, he transferred his semi-automatic singing to the typewriter keyboard. When in the throes of composition, he would give out with a terrifying "na-na-na-na-na-na-NAAA-NAAAA-NAAAAAAH!" which at one time nearly got him turned out of his chambers at Gray's Inn. On his good days, he would be silent except when actually writing; but when the bad fits were on him, he started to perform as soon as he opened his eyes in the morning. For eighteen months, I woke up several mornings a week to the sound of his sufferings, accompanied by an *obbligato* from my landlady, Mrs. Bashforth, who used to stand out in our yard, under my window, and wail in a thin, querulous soprano, "Oh, that dreadful noise! Oh, what a wretched noise!"

Those morning awakenings are not among my happiest memories; the room was chill and damp, and I had no appetite for the watery porridge and mysterious sausages that would be carried up and left in my sitting-room, to go cold if I did not get up; I used to read late at night, so that my eyes, always working under difficulties because of the retina detachment that had caused me to be rejected by the army, "purged thick amber and plum-tree gum"; * and on top of it, I would be woken by "na-na-na-na-NAAA-NAAA," "Oh, that dreadful noise," "na-NAA-na-NAAA-NAAAH-na-na," "Oh, dear, that dreadful wretched noise," "na-na-NAA." One morning, a woman's voice I had never heard before shouted from some neighbouring yard, "For Christ's sake stop that bloody row!" Meyerstein faltered, was silent for a moment, and then unleashed a fresh Niagara of yells and groans.

* "purged thick amber . . .": Shakespeare, *Hamlet,* II.2.200.

During 1944 and '45, the bad days were increasingly frequent, and the spells of calm and self-assurance more brief and uncertain. Oxford was not going to yield, and the fact was daily looking Meyerstein more squarely in the face. It was one of his last arrows, and it had fallen short of the target. Soon the war would be over, the young men would flood back, every inch of accommodation would be needed, and Oxford would no longer have any nooks and corners to spare for such as himself. And with this hope dying down in his breast, the various other passions, frustrations and bewilderments that racked him, and which for a time he had probably managed to calm, awoke into renewed obstinacy and cruelty. There were days when, as I climbed his stairs, the sound of his "noises" would be so loud, and have in it so much of madness and desperation, that I would pause on the final landing, hesitating whether to go on or to creep down again and visit him at some quieter moment. But I always went on: for anyone who knew Meyerstein, who had once been admitted to his confidence, the impulse to help him always outweighed every other.

So I would knock on the door, gently at first, more loudly if he did not hear me through the racket of his own groans and cries, till finally—after five minutes' hammering, it might be—he would suddenly realize that someone was there, fall silent, listen to see if one knocked again, and finally (after the usual flurry of looking for his teeth) call out sombrely, "Come in." And there, when I entered, he would be, sitting at his desk, working, always working, never slackening in his pursuit of the recognition that *must* come, if only he kept pounding away. Oxford, the world, his relatives, the ghosts of his parents—they would relent, one day, and let him in to sit at their fireside, if only he kept trying. And then waves of fatigue, of disgust, of unutterable despair, would break over him, and he would sit at his desk and groan—hour after hour, unable to do anything but stare at the muddle of books and papers, and groan. Usually, if a friend visited him, it would do him good, at least to the extent of getting him to launch into a passionate complaint as to how someone or other had slighted him, or some pundit had revealed a chink of ignorance ("He did not seem aware that the name Lycidas, for a soldier nearly drowned, occurs in Lucan"), and so substitute rage for despair, and feel more cheerful for a moment. But on his worst days, nothing would lighten his mind: he was tired, he was finished, the weight was too heavy to carry for another step. There was one day when I, having by this time arrived at the mature age of nineteen, and counting myself as one of Meyerstein's most solid friends, felt so shocked at his condition, so bristling with pity, that I tried to force him, by sheer nagging, to put his trouble into words. "But what *is* it?" I kept saying. "Why *do* you feel so awful?" For answer, he merely groaned, or fenced me away with, "All I know is that I can't see how to go on"; but finally, perhaps driven crazy by my insistence, he laid his head down on the desk, with a groan more terrible than any I had ever heard from him, then suddenly snapped upright, thrust his face into mine, and said with dreadful intensity, "It's like this, John Wain—*work* has to be *done!*" He brought this out with so much the air of a man saying something supremely meaningful that I fell silent, pondering the words, and could not afterwards go back to my questioning. But of course it was merely another of his formulae. The truth is that Meyerstein did not know what was wrong with his own mind. He must have been one of the last men in history to combine acute intelligence, imaginative insight, and the habit of constant introspection with complete *naïveté* about his own emotions.

When I hear people question the usefulness of psychoanalysis, or express doubts about the central position it occupies in modern life, I think of Meyerstein. For the tragic thing about him is that help *was* available, if he could only have stretched out his hand to take it. Beethoven's deafness, I believe, resulted from a condition which can nowadays be cured, and no doubt the same thing is true of Chekhov's tuberculosis and even Milton's blindness. Still, one cannot simple-mindedly wish that "they had lived today, and been spared the suffering and premature death." If they had, the pressures of modern life might have been harder on them than anything imposed by their physical ailments; the seventeenth century may have been lacking in good ophthalmic techniques, but it was the only century in which Milton could have written *Paradise Lost*. But in Meyerstein's case, the treatment was there—and yet, for one reason and another, it was as inaccessible to him as if it had not yet been invented. I don't believe Meyerstein's neuroses were particularly complicated; a competent analyst, if one had managed to win his confidence, could probably have straightened out the whole lot in twelve months; and when I remember his sufferings, I can only grieve that such a cure should have been impossible, inconceivable.

But impossible it was. Meyerstein could not have been dragged within a mile of a psycho-analyst. He had all the resistance that was normal in his generation (I can testify that even as late as the nineteen-thirties it was usual for English boys to grow up thinking of the whole range of psycho-therapeutic medicine as nothing but a dirty joke—what it must have been before 1914 can be imagined); and, in addition, he had the whole range of phobias which stemmed from his being "an artist." Even at his worst moments he comforted himself with the thought that he could write poetry and his academic detractors couldn't; it was his defence against the world, and he was terrified of any interference that might stop the flow. I think he would have died rather than submit to anything that seemed like outside interference with the mechanism of his imagination.

Nevertheless, unlike most of the people who need psycho-analysis and shy away from taking it, he never bothered to use the "I'm-perfectly-normal" defence. He recognized himself as a neurotic, and simply refused to take the next step and recognize neurosis as a condition both undesirable and curable. He had a deep interest in the work of any artist who had gone mad, or committed suicide, or been conventionally dismissed as a lunatic, and inasmuch as his own oddity made him a member of this fellowship, he even derived a certain comfort from it. Everyone, after all, has *some* club he can join. I don't think Meyerstein was ever afraid of going mad (his fear was always of "not being able to go on"), but he certainly recognized abnormal tendencies in himself. His homosexuality, as I said earlier, was pretty safely buried; but there were other things—the interest in flagellation, for instance, which led him to form a notable collection of whips. (He was thus gratifying two instincts at once when he wrote in his will that he bequeathed a whip to his father, that he might scourge himself with it.) His erotic fantasies often concerned the whipping of boys; I recall, suddenly, the first two lines of his "Ode to Lautréamont"—

> O thou who compared'st ocean to blue backs
> Of beaten cabin-boys, receive my prayer.

This quirk was largely responsible for his detailed acquaintance with the literature of old sailing-ship days (he was an authority on Marryat, for instance); so that, in a sense, even the editing of Coxere, which allowed our acquaintance to spring up so fast, grew from this soil. He was quite clear-sighted about the matter, and once remarked to me that if he had his time over again he would not attempt to put any respectable front over an interest of this kind; to study honest writers like Marryat in order to gratify a thirst for reading about whipped cabin-boys had come to seem to him tedious and artificial. As he put it, "if you must keep a brothel, don't try to make the whores domesticated!"

Altogether, Meyerstein's kinks followed a not unusual pattern. One sees it in Housman, for instance, of whom Auden so brilliantly wrote—

> Food was his public love; his private lust
> Something to do with violence and the poor.

The instincts, early turned aside from their proper course (the English public school system did a real job on Meyerstein), flowed into images of pain, violence, and death. Meyerstein loved a murder, especially if it was followed by an execution. He would walk miles—did, on occasion, make *me* walk miles—to examine the scene of a murder; and some of his favourite characters were hangmen. He used to speak with particular affection of one William Marwood, who he said had been the first to make the hangman's position a respected one in society, by such tradesmanly devices as having notepaper printed with the heading "William Marwood: Executioner: Boots Repaired." "If Pa killed Ma," ran a Victorian riddle, "who'd kill Pa?" The answer, of course, was "Marwood." Even I, who know little about murder and execution and would gladly know nothing, could not help being full of such scraps of information after a year or two of Meyerstein's company. As for murderers, he liked them even better than hangmen, if possible. I understand that one of his friends, whom I never met, was a man who, earlier in life, had been convicted of murder, and spared from execution because of his youth; he had long since served his sentence and taken his normal place in society, but to Meyerstein the unearthly gleam that irradiated the man was that he had murdered a fellow-creature. Towards the end of his stay in Oxford, he read me a poem he had just written, in which he declared his faith in his own superiority to the materialistic-minded:

> For these anatomise a murderer,
> Yet never feel the love-touch of his fur.

I think that was the moment when I first realized that Meyerstein was deranged; even I, with my extraordinary (and culpable) degree of innocence, couldn't take his word for it that an obsession with murder was a sign of spiritual health.[2]

I call my innocence "culpable," and so I am convinced it was. The Scriptures are in the right when they enjoin, "Be ye therefore as wise as serpents, and harmless as doves." Looking back on my whole relationship with Meyerstein, I see in it an early example of a tendency in me that has done real harm, to myself and others, and which it cost me a great effort to uproot: the tendency to see in others only what I was immediately interested in finding, to concentrate on what I enjoyed or admired and let the rest go. I don't mean what is called "seeing their good points"; I mean deliberately not taking into account the whole nature of the person I was dealing with. In Meyerstein's case, I loved his passion for art, his frankness, lack of defences, companionable ways; I ignored, even when it was forced on my attention, the fact that he was crazed with a consciousness of failure, eaten up with resentments and jealousies, his fine natural intelligence only half available for the work it should have found to do in the world.

One consequence of this was that I was always startled, always annoyed and self-pitying, whenever a chance remark or casually revealed attitude happened to draw down on me the hailstorm of Meyerstein's rage and venom. These outbursts never lasted long, but no one who was close to him could avoid them altogether.

For instance: we were walking, one afternoon, on the high plateau of Shotover, whose keen air was always a relief from Oxford's spongy breezes. Enjoying ourselves, we chatted amicably, until Meyerstein happened to mention some book of Thackeray's. Had I read it? "No," I replied, adding innocently, "I've never got on to Thackeray." Meyerstein's explosion was immediate and appalling. It was rage, genuine rage and hatred: if not actually hatred of me, certainly hatred of the attitude he took me to have revealed. By speaking in this fashion of "getting on to" Thackeray, I had, in his eyes, lined up with the people whose businesslike (not to say tradesmanlike) attitude to literature was responsible for so much of his own neglect. A true scholar and gentleman doesn't *get on to* Thackeray; he reads him. I tried to argue the point, but it was useless. Our excursion was in ruins. One moment he had been happy; the next, I had stumbled against his lightly sleeping paranoia and awoken it, and in a flash he was

---

2. The poem that contains this couplet will be found in Meyerstein's posthumous *Verse Letters to Five Friends* (Heinemann, 1954).

angry, miserable, tormented. So thin was the crust, so delicate the balance of his brief spells of contentment. In my own defence (and it is significant of the power of Meyerstein's personality that I can't help defending myself as if he were still here, still glowering at me), I thought then and I think now that my remark was a very natural one. To this day, it is my habit, on approaching an author who is new to me, not simply to pick up one of his books and dive in, but to wait until I have not too many other things to do, and then allow myself the time to read several of his books in succession; it seems the only way to give him a fair chance. But to Meyerstein, it was the language of the enemy—and to hear it from my mouth must have seemed like a betrayal.

Still, on the whole our relationship was very free of these jolts; in fact, as his Oxford period lengthened out, he began to recognize me as one of his chief allies against this businesslike, prudential spirit. For his distinction between dons (worldly, discouraging, hidebound) and undergraduates (young, fresh, spontaneous) could hardly be expected to survive a prolonged sojourn in Oxford. There is a certain kind of undergraduate who is a professor *in petto* *—ready to come forward as one at the appropriate time—and who already sees literature and art as teachable, examinable subjects at which he means to do well. Naturally Meyerstein attracted such types, industrious youths who realized that the companionship of so learned a man would put a fine gloss on their academic surface. Meyerstein never discouraged these people—he put all of them to his own kind of use—but he was sensitive to the delicate interplay of a relationship, and anyone who came to him in this acquisitive spirit would leave him fatigued and depressed, rather than revived as he usually was by young people. One such man in particular used to leave him almost suicidal; his only remedy was to run straight out of his own lodgings and into mine, bursting in to me with, "*Tell* me something! Tell me what you've just been reading! X has been with me, sucking at my brains!" Poor Meyerstein—those brains that everyone else wanted to use, but which somehow never seemed to do their owner any good!

But I see I am in danger of making the picture too monotonously dark. Because Meyerstein was a tragic figure, it does not follow that every day and hour of his life was tragic. He had a considerable streak of self-protective astuteness, not to say cunning, which he used with some success in fighting that lifelong battle against his environment. Indeed, from some points of view, his was a curiously successful life, given its demented premises. Many people have hated the age they lived in, but few can have been as methodical as he was in blotting it out. Although he lived fifty-two of his years in the twentieth century, the daily life of that century scarcely touched him. In his chambers at Gray's Inn, with the rumble of London filtered by quiet courtyards and whispering trees, he lived a life that would have seemed perfectly familiar to his Gray's Inn predecessors of centuries—to Bacon, for instance. Except for the telephone, there was noth-

---

* *in petto:* in his secret heart.

ing in his rooms that could possibly suggest the modern age. Even his love of music could not force him to compromise with modernity; his detailed knowledge of it was built up by a combination of concert-going and the playing over of piano arrangements, gramophone and radio being taboo. The internal combustion engine, naturally, was also taboo. He could sometimes be persuaded to travel by car, if it was to somewhere he wanted to go to, but he never lost his hatred of cars and the only motor vehicle I ever saw him willingly enter was a London bus. He had various rationalizations to offer ("I can't listen to music on the wireless. You're every minute expecting the wretched thing to break down"), but he must have realized, however intermittently, that his objection to modern apparatus was simply that it was modern.

The positive side to this, naturally, was his love of the antique. "That's old!" he would say, suddenly, on catching sight of a door, window, or chimney-stack, and immediately dart across the road to investigate. To walk round a strange town with Meyerstein was an extraordinary experience. His first action, on getting off the train, was to ask to be directed to the old parish church ("That always takes you straight to the old part of the town, you see"), and within a few minutes the cry would begin to go up: "That's old!" It was not that he had no aesthetic discrimination; as between one "old" thing and another, he preferred the more beautiful, and his taste was always fine. But age was the first important condition. He was like a man endlessly searching among the rubble of an earthquake, patiently trying to reconstruct the detail of a smashed city. That was, indeed, how he saw himself. He felt towards his "old" things the same sort of yearning pity that I had felt, as a child, for the wild creatures of the countryside: seeing them as the last survivors of a gentler world, doomed to be crushed and hounded by a brutal dispensation that grew daily more powerful. But where I, at seven years old, could do nothing except pity the wild animals and dramatize their desperation in my own imaginative life, Meyerstein, carrying his obsession onward through the years, built up more and more elaborate defences, till finally he enclosed himself so completely in the past that the twentieth century simply did not exist for him; he never, of course, read a newspaper and even during the war I doubt if he ever had much idea of what was going on.

Meyerstein died, from a succession of strokes, in 1952. After a spell in hospital at Highgate (with "Karl Marx buried just on the other side of that wall," as he pointed out to me with a ghost of his old manic cackle), he was sent home to his Gray's Inn chambers to die in peace. I remember thinking, for the first time, what a lot of money it costs to die. He had two nurses, who sat with him round the clock; I don't remember whether both were male, but certainly one of them was, and Meyerstein reported with great satisfaction that the fellow's literary education was going well: "I'm getting him to read Jane Austen to me. He's never read her before and he likes it."

He died bravely; and, as one always knew he would, he kept a pen in his hand as long as he could hold one. He failed to make his name stand out clearly in his own lifetime—so be it! He would keep on trying, still thinking, still writing, still chipping away at the rock-face, until the moment when he keeled over into the grave. For posterity *must* recognize him—he would force it to learn his name, by the sheer intensity of his struggle to be known, to be heard and recognized. Long before he died, the regard of future generations had come to be his chief ambition and the focus of his dreams. His own love of raising the dead, which was the driving force behind that huge random scholarship, had in it a self-regarding streak so obvious that even I could see it, little as I scrutinized his motives. The preoccupation with posterity was always active in his mind, and always near the surface. I remember one afternoon when he had come to tea, and was, as usual, turning over the books I had most recently bought. Among them was a pretty little set of Chaucer, three volumes in white imitation parchment, which had belonged to a man called "W. McQueen." I remember the elegant signature: "W. McQueen, Wadham, 1912," accompanied by a little drawing of a flower. Now (and I admit it with shame) I had, at that time, not yet shaken off the habit formed by my years of school life, where, if you inherited a book from another boy, you immediately crossed out his name and wrote your own, very plainly, because if you did not he would claim the book back and sell it over again. So, in writing my own name on the fly-leaf of the Chaucer, I had put a single, decisive pen-stroke through McQueen's. You could still read his name; I was not afraid that McQueen would come back from the grave, or wherever he was, and make me pay for the books again; it was simply the unconscious carrying-on of a habit.

I can see the whole scene so vividly now. Meyerstein, settling back with a cup of tea at his elbow, opened the Chaucer, staring at it fixedly, and turned pale. Laying it down, he looked up at me with an expression of deep inward suffering —too deep to issue in rage. *This is what I'm up against,* he must have been thinking: *even in a youth whose instincts are generally sound, I find this urge to obliterate the past.* The dialogue that followed was short. "May I say something to you?" "Yes." "Never cross anybody's name out of a book." Silence. Tea was drunk, poured out, stirred, drunk again. "You see," said Meyerstein gently, "you might pick up a book one day and find that some person had crossed out *S. T. Coleridge.*" Or *E. H. W. Meyerstein,* I thought. And I understood, for once, how deeply even I could wound him.

In all this, Meyerstein's instinct was sound enough. One of the reasons why his name is unlikely to be altogether forgotten is, undoubtedly, because of the great collection of books and manuscripts which was dispersed at his death; most of them went to libraries, where they are duly registered as bequests from him.

These bequests, in fact, were Meyerstein's last weapon against the indifference of the world, the one gun that would keep on firing after he was dead and at peace. The more's the pity that, even there, his judgement let him down. Some unlucky chain of reasoning led him to bequeath a colossal sum of money to "Oxford University." Not to this or that college, where there might be a chance that his memory would linger on, but to the abstraction, the heartless, mindless, gutless University. It was his last effort to write his name on the wall in letters so big that Oxford would *have* to see it. I suppose the University accountants used the money to pay the interest on an overdraft, after which the name of Meyerstein was forgotten by everyone concerned within forty-eight hours.[3] It all illustrates that wonderful line of Pope's—

> Die, and endow a college or a cat!

But then Meyerstein hated Pope, and never read him. He always persisted in the nineteenth-century belief that satire cannot be poetry. But there it is. If you want to see a memorial to Meyerstein anywhere in Oxford, forget about the bequest to the University and look instead at the handsome knocker on the door of No. 12 Longwall Street—Meyerstein's gift to the house that had sheltered him.

Why, finally, do I write about Meyerstein at such length? Is the literary world not full of neurotics, people knocked out of shape by disappointment and envy of one kind and another? Certainly—and in my occasional forays into that world I have met people who made Meyerstein seem a model of balance and contentment by comparison. No, it is not his oddity that engages my attention in retrospect, nor even the part he plays in my story, important as that is. His appeal is to the historian in me. His is such a perfect example of a life smashed by collision with an Establishment. I shall never see another such example, partly because I have more control over my own life than I had when I was eighteen, and choose to live it in places, and among people, not open to that kind of social pressure; and partly because Meyerstein belonged to the last generation to feel that pressure with really devastating force.

Why? What did it matter to him whether he was "accepted" or not? In the answer to that question lies the tragedy of his life. Here was a man with substantial private means, enamoured of the beautiful and significant in art, and with definite talent of his own. With no need to earn his living by hack-work, he might have spent a happy life, gently and industriously bringing to their full growth the plantings of his imagination. Instead of which, his life was hell, and his talent produced hardly a line worth the paper it was written on. What went wrong?

It is no answer to say, simply, "The Establishment." Many intelligent and useful people have been born within that particular enclosure, and lived out their lives in it, and still managed to do useful work and be reasonably happy. It was Meyerstein's peculiar misfortune to be born on the *fringe* of the Establishment, to grow up under an invisible question mark: *does he belong or doesn't he?* His father was wealthy, knighted, a lavish contributor to charities; the household was cultivated enough (his mother had studied music under Sir Julius Benedict, who

---

3. I am guessing here, and guessing quite wrongly. It seems that the University set up a Meyerstein Trust whose income continues to be spent (1) on buying books for the English Faculty Library and (2) on travelling and research expenses for young graduates.

had studied under Weber, who had known Beethoven); from some points of view, the record could not have been bettered. But it was the very goodness of the record that put the young Edward into such an exposed position. As the son of such parents, growing up at such a time, he could hardly avoid a direct confrontation with the Juggernaut, with what results we know. He could neither run nor fight. With that money and social position, he could not simply move out of range of the Establishment. But with Jewish blood and a German name, he could not win complete acceptance without more than usual charm and address. In other words, he had to *work*. It was his duty to get himself accepted, or answer to his family for it. And if he rejected his family, he still had to answer to the spiteful little demon that they had reared and trained to follow him about. That demon never left him alone. It was always there, to run a needle into him at the sight of anyone else's success, anyone else's recognition. He could find relief in mocking hatred of his family ("If Pa killed Ma, who'd kill Pa?"), but there was no hiding from the demon.

The other thing one has to realize, in order to grasp the full history of Meyerstein's desperation, is the extraordinarily frank brutality of English upper-class anti-Semitism in the early years of this century. I, having grown up in a region where the Jewish population was small and inconspicuous, was as green about this as about everything else; I didn't recognize a man as Jewish unless he looked like a caricature of a Jew in a comic paper, and even then I had no very easily aroused emotions on the subject. There was no reason for me to have; anti-Semitism is only felt by people who are clinging to an exclusive or secure position, who have some special enclosure of their own into which they are determined to keep the Jew from intruding. In the world of my boyhood, it was commonest among Nazis (self-conscious about the large Jewish element in the German population, and anxious to keep it from sullying the Wagnerian purity of Aryan blood) and Trade Unionists (anxious to keep the refugees from causing unemployment). In Meyerstein's boyhood, it was commonest among the business class and in "Society"—since it was they, and not the population at large, who had something they wished to avoid sharing. And again it was Meyerstein's particular misfortune to be flung headlong into the place where the brambles were thickest. Harrow! Could anyone imagine a worse place for a sensitive Jewish boy, already frightened into insecurity and given a terror of not belonging? Why could not some merciful fate have arranged for Meyerstein *père* to go smash and lose all his money, so that the whole family could have sunk into protective obscurity? If only Meyerstein could have been brought up in North Staffordshire! Provinciality, which is supposed to be the root of so many evils, would have done him far less harm than the cruel pressures of upper-class Middlesex.

Well, the story is over now. No kind fate intervened; "Eddie" was sent to Harrow; the damage was done, and it only remained for Oxford to torture him in more refined ways, as becomes the greater subtlety of the University mind. And if anyone feels that I am exaggerating the harm done to Meyerstein's na-scent intelligence at Harrow, the independent testimony will be found in Arnold Lunn's novel *The Harrovians* (1913)—a book that not only deals with the period when Meyerstein was at the school but actually introduces him as a character, "Brunstein," who on his first appearance in the story is described in so many words as "an unpopular Jew." Here are a few brush-strokes from the portrait:

> Brunstein . . . had come to the meeting expecting to be hissed. The unexpected intoxication of public applause went to his head like wine. He was quite overcome. They strolled into the music school together, Brunstein gesticulating wildly. "It was splendid, perfect in every detail. The whole setting was dramatic. The great crowd waiting in the yard like the mobs at Tyburn. And the way they cheered us! Magnificent! Harrovian! Worthy of our great traditions!"
> In his excitement he had not noticed the presence of a flannel who had strolled into the music school. "Oh, dry up, you ruddy Jew! I'll tell you what. You monitors are getting a damned side [*sic*] too lippy, let me tell you. Why the deuce should you wear bluers! I'd like to see the whole lot of you get a 'Phil' whopping."
> He went out growling. Brunstein collapsed like a pricked balloon.

Without bothering to annotate this passage, to explain what stage it represents in the plot or gloss such terms as "flannel," "bluers," and "a Phil whopping," one still feels safe in letting it stand as an indication of what happened, in the Harrow of 1907, to anyone who gave way to fits of emotional relief, who was voluble and gesticulated, who—in short—took insufficient pains to conceal the discreditable fact that the Creator had not made him an Englishman of the right social type. The point is hammered home in the book by the introduction of a sympathetic Jewish character named Solomon, whose function is to demonstrate that it is not, after all, impossible even for a Jew to win acceptance; all he has to do is, first, to develop a rhinoceros-skin about insults to his race, and secondly to batter his way into respectability with a horny pair of fists. Solomon does both these things. On his first appearance in the book, he is greeted with,

> "Hallo, Ikey! Any Jews among the new men? Hope not. What with old Ikey pawning our Sunday bags, one has about enough of the nimble Israelite."
> Solomon laughed heartily; the rest of the room tittered with forced joy.

Solomon is a thoroughly sound type—an Englishman under the skin, so to speak—and he shares the final curtain with the hero. The two of them are looking back, in classic fashion, on the long campaign they have survived: the hero remarks,

> "The wild animals at 'The Oaks' are all thoroughly domesticated nowadays."
> Solomon grunted his disapproval. "There was none of that bally

tameness about the House in our day. Gad, do you remember our mills? Fought like young demons, didn't we? Well, dash it all, there's nothing like fists to settle these things, eh? We didn't like each other any the worse for bashing each other's noses in, eh?"

"Yes," said Peter drily, "there's nothing like a good old English mill to get rid of the bad blood, is there, Solomon?"

And Solomon agreed with enthusiasm.

Whereupon, the book ends. Were it not for the all-pervading *naïveté* of tone and language, I should be tempted to read all sorts of ironies and nuances into these concluding sentences; but it seems fairly clear that the undertones are not conscious ones. Solomon's schoolfellows have done him the kindness of bashing his nose in, thus symbolically releasing him from his Jewish appearance and hence from his "bad blood." Ikey, the nimble Israelite, has slugged his way through to Harrovian manliness with all the other young demons. And no doubt, the date being what it was, he was presently in uniform and having his insides torn out by shrapnel in Flanders. After Harrow, it couldn't have seemed very different. But for Meyerstein, there was no such blessed release. Purgation by violence was not for him. He could no more be Ikey than he could be Lieutenant Henry.

When I think over this sad and wasted life, I feel glad that the meeting of Meyerstein and myself occurred when I was young enough to feel simple, unmixed admiration for him. What does it matter that I could offer him no sound advice on how to deal with his problems? I gave him—and it is no credit to myself, just a lucky accident—something he needed more: the admiration and encouragement of a younger person, someone with a stake in that future he so much dreaded. It was the most hopeful thing that could have happened to him. Inevitably, our intimacy lessened as I grew older. My life curved away from his, into its own morass of doubts, crises, and self-absorbed suffering. Had he lived another three or four years, I think we might have come together again, on a different level. As it is, he survives in my memory, undiminished as the years go by; I think of him often, with sorrow, exasperation, and affection. Even in death he is a vivid presence.

Gertrude Stein / Ernest Hemingway

Ernest Hemingway / Gertrude Stein

The Gertrude Stein passage is from *The Autobiography of Alice B. Toklas.* Miss Toklas was Miss Stein's companion, but it is generally believed that Gertrude Stein wrote the book, not Alice B. Toklas. Hemingway's version of the relationship is from his posthumously published *A Moveable Feast*. The point of bringing these two passages together is not merely the obvious one, namely, that it is fun to find out what these two writers had to say each about the other. There is also the relation of styles. Hemingway was at the time described very much a disciple of Stein's, and although her usual manner—full of hypnotic repetitions and flat exactitudes—is watered down in the *Toklas* piece, and his, at whatever date he wrote these words, had developed away from hers, there is still a family resemblance. This may be because in a sense Hemingway is answering this very passage of Stein's. She presents a somewhat pitying account of him, not without a note of gratitude for services rendered, but rather critical, in a more or less oblique way, of a softness in the hard young man. Hemingway, with a similar obliquity, explains the wrongness of Stein's judgments and the peculiarities of her life as the consequences of homosexuality and leaves little doubt that his hardness included a detestation of homosexuality. Here are two subtly written and spiteful intimate portraits, which are also complementary in that each writer proclaims, if only indirectly, a certain lingering respect for the achievement of the other.

STEIN ON HEMINGWAY

In the days when the friendship between Gertrude Stein and Picasso had become if possible closer than before, (it was for his little boy, born February fourth to her February third, that she wrote her birthday book with a line for each day in the year) in those days her intimacy with Juan Gris displeased him. Once after a show of Juan's pictures at the Gallérie Simon he said to her with violence, tell me why you stand up for his work, you know you do not like it; and she did not answer him.

Later when Juan died and Gertrude Stein was heart broken Picasso came to the house and spent all day there. I do not know what was said but I do know that at one time Gertrude Stein said to him bitterly, you have no right to mourn, and he said, you have no right to say that to me. You never realised his meaning because you did not have it, she said angrily. You know very well I did, he replied.

The most moving thing Gertrude Stein has ever written is The Life and Death of Juan Gris. It was printed in transition * and later on translated into german for his retrospective show in Berlin.

Picasso never wished Braque away. Picasso said once when he and Gertrude Stein was talking together, yes, Braque and James Joyce, they are the incompréhensibles whom anybody can understand. Les incompréhensibles que tout le monde peut comprendre.

* *transition:* an avant-garde journal published in Paris.

The first thing that happened when we were back in Paris was Hemingway with a letter of introduction from Sherwood Anderson.*

I remember very well the impression I had of Hemingway that first afternoon. He was an extraordinarily good-looking young man, twenty-three years old. It was not long after that that everybody was twenty-six. It became the period of being twenty-six. During the next two or three years all the young men were twenty-six years old. It was the right age apparently for that time and place. There were one or two under twenty, for example George Lynes but they did not count as Gertrude Stein carefully explained to them. If they were young men they were twenty-six. Later on, much later on they were twenty-one and twenty-two.

So Hemingway was twenty-three, rather foreign looking, with passionately interested, rather than interesting eyes. He sat in front of Gertrude Stein and listened and looked.

They talked then, and more and more, a great deal together. He asked her to come and spend an evening in their apartment and look at his work. Hemingway had then and has always a very good instinct for finding apartments in strange but pleasing localities and good femmes de ménage * and good food. This his first apartment was just off the place du Tertre. We spent the evening there and he and Gertrude Stein went over all the writing he had done up to that time. He had begun the novel that it was inevitable he would begin and there were the little poems afterwards printed by McAlmon in the Contact Edition. Gertrude Stein rather liked the poems, they were direct, Kiplingesque, but the novel she found wanting. There is a great deal of description in this, she said, and not particularly good description. Begin over again and concentrate, she said.

Hemingway was at this time Paris correspondent for a canadian newspaper. He was obliged there to express what he called the canadian viewpoint.

He and Gertrude Stein used to walk together and talk together a great deal. One day she said to him, look here, you say you and your wife have a little money between you. Is it enough to live on if you live quietly. Yes, he said. Well, she said, then do it. If you keep on doing newspaper work you will never see things, you will only see words and that will not do, that is of course if you intend to be a writer. Hemingway said he undoubtedly intended to be a writer. He and his wife went away on a trip and shortly after Hemingway turned up alone. He came to the house about ten o'clock in the morning and he stayed, he stayed for lunch, he stayed all afternoon, he stayed for dinner and he stayed until about ten o'clock at night and then all of a sudden he announced that his

* Sherwood Anderson: (1876–1941), American novelist and short-story writer, best remembered now for his book of stories about small-town people, *Winesburg, Ohio* (1919). On page 399 Miss Stein comments that "Hemingway had been formed" by Anderson and herself; add to this that Anderson acknowledged his own indebtedness to Miss Stein, especially apparent in his novel *Dark Laughter* (1925). Hemingway's parody of Anderson, *The Torrents of Spring*, appeared in 1926.
* femme de ménage: charwoman.

wife was enceinte * and then with great bitterness, and I, I am too young to be a father. We consoled him as best we could and sent him on his way.

When they came back Hemingway said that he had made up his mind. They would go back to America and he would work hard for a year and with what he would earn and what they had they would settle down and he would give up newspaper work and make himself a writer. They went away and well within the prescribed year they came back with a new born baby. Newspaper work was over.

The first thing to do when they came back was as they thought to get the baby baptised. They wanted Gertrude Stein and myself to be god-mothers and an english war comrade of Hemingway was to be god-father. We were all born of different religions and most of us were not practising any, so it was rather difficult to know in what church the baby could be baptised. We spent a great deal of time that winter, all of us, discussing the matter. Finally it was decided that it should be baptised episcopalian and episcopalian it was. Just how it was managed with the assortment of god-parents I am sure I do not know, but it was baptised in the episcopalian chapel.

Writer or painter god-parents are notoriously unreliable. That is, there is certain before long to be a cooling of friendship. I know several cases of this, poor Paulot Picasso's god-parents have wandered out of sight and just as naturally it is a long time since any of us have seen or heard of our Hemingway god-child.

However in the beginning we were active god-parents, I particularly. I embroidered a little chair and I knitted a gay coloured garment for the god-child. In the meantime the god-child's father was very earnestly at work making himself a writer.

Gertrude Stein never corrects any detail of anybody's writing, she sticks strictly to general principles, the way of seeing what the writer chooses to see, and the relation between that vision and the way it gets down. When the vision is not complete the words are flat, it is very simple, there can be no mistake about it, so she insists. It was at this time that Hemingway began the short things that afterwards were printed in a volume called In Our Time.

One day Hemingway came in very excited about Ford Madox Ford * and the Transatlantic. Ford Madox Ford had started the Transatlantic some months before. A good many years before, indeed before the war, we had met Ford Madox Ford who was at that time Ford Madox Hueffer. He was married to Violet Hunt and Violet Hunt and Gertrude Stein were next to each other at the tea table and talked a great deal together. I was next to Ford Madox Hueffer and I liked him very much and I liked his stories of Mistral and Tarascon and I liked his having been followed about in that land of the french royalist, on account of his re-

---

* enceinte: pregnant.
* Ford Madox Ford: (1873–1939), English writer, changed his name from Hueffer to Ford in 1919; he is best remembered for his experimental novel *The Good Soldier* (1915).

semblance to the Bourbon claimant. I had never seen the Bourbon claimant but Ford at that time undoubtedly might have been a Bourbon.

We had heard that Ford was in Paris, but we had not happened to meet. Gertrude Stein had seen copies of the Transatlantic and found it interesting but had thought nothing further about it.

Hemingway came in then very excited and said that Ford wanted something of Gertrude Stein's for the next number and he, Hemingway, wanted The Making of Americans * to be run in it as a serial and he had to have the first fifty pages at once. Gertrude Stein was of course quite overcome with her excitement at this idea, but there was no copy of the manuscript except the one that we had had bound. That makes no difference, said Hemingway, I will copy it. And he and I between us did copy it and it was printed in the next number of the Transatlantic. So for the first time a piece of the monumental work which was the beginning, really the beginning of modern writing, was printed, and we were very happy. Later on when things were difficult between Gertrude Stein and Hemingway, she always remembered with gratitude that after all it was Hemingway who first caused to be printed a piece of The Making of Americans. She always says, yes sure I have a weakness for Hemingway. After all he was the first of the young men to knock at my door and he did make Ford print the first piece of The Making of Americans.

I myself have not so much confidence that Hemingway did do this. I have never known what the story is but I have always been certain that there was some other story behind it all. That is the way I feel about it.

Gertrude Stein and Sherwood Anderson are very funny on the subject of Hemingway. The last time that Sherwood was in Paris they often talked about him. Hemingway had been formed by the two of them and they were both a little proud and a little ashamed of the work of their minds. Hemingway had at one moment, when he had repudiated Sherwood Anderson and all his works, written him a letter in the name of american literature which he, Hemingway, in company with his contemporaries was about to save, telling Sherwood just what he, Hemingway, thought about Sherwood's work, and that thinking was in no sense complimentary. When Sherwood came to Paris Hemingway naturally was afraid. Sherwood as naturally was not.

As I say he and Gertrude Stein were endlessly amusing on the subject. They admitted that Hemingway was yellow, he is, Gertrude Stein insisted, just like the flat-boat men on the Mississippi river as described by Mark Twain. But what a book, they both agreed, would be the real story of Hemingway, not those he writes but the confessions of the real Ernest Hemingway. It would be for another audience than the audience Hemingway now has but it would be very wonderful. And then they both agreed that they have a weakness for Hemingway

---

* *The Making of Americans:* Miss Stein's experimental family chronicle, written in 1906–8 and published in 1925.

because he is such a good pupil. He is a rotten pupil, I protested. You don't understand, they both said, it is so flattering to have a pupil who does it without understanding it, in other words he takes training and anybody who takes training is a favourite pupil. They both admit it to be a weakness. Gertrude Stein added further, you see he is like Derain.* You remember Monsieur de Tuille said, when I did not understand why Derain was having the success he was having that it was because he looks like a modern and he smells of the museums. And that is Hemingway, he looks like a modern and he smells of the museums. But what a story that of the real Hem, and one he should tell himself but alas he never will. After all, as he himself once murmured, there is the career, the career.

But to come back to the events that were happening.

Hemingway did it all. He copied the manuscript and corrected the proof. Correcting proofs is, as I said before, like dusting, you learn the values of the thing as no reading suffices to teach it to you. In correcting these proofs Hemingway learned a great deal and he admired all that he learned. It was at this time that he wrote to Gertrude Stein saying that it was she who had done the work in writing The Making of Americans and he and all his had but to devote their lives to seeing that it was published.

He had hopes of being able to accomplish this. Some one, I think by the name of Sterne, said that he could place it with a publisher. Gertrude Stein and Hemingway believed that he could, but soon Hemingway reported that Sterne had entered into his period of unreliability. That was the end of that.

In the meantime and sometime before this Mina Loy had brought McAlmon to the house and he came from time to time and he brought his wife and brought William Carlos Williams. And finally he wanted to print The Making of Americans in the Contact Edition and finally he did. I will come to that.

In the meantime McAlmon had printed the three poems and ten stories of Hemingway and William Bird had printed In Our Time and Hemingway was getting to be known. He was coming to know Dos Passos and Fitzgerald and Bromfield and George Antheil and everybody else and Harold Loeb was once more in Paris. Hemingway had become a writer. He was also a shadow-boxer, thanks to Sherwood, and he heard about bull-fighting from me. I have always loved spanish dancing and spanish bull-fighting and I loved to show the photographs of bull-fighters and bull-fighting. I also loved to show the photograph where Gertrude Stein and I were in the front row and had our picture taken there accidentally. In these days Hemingway was teaching some young chap how to box. The boy did not know how, but by accident he knocked Hemingway out. I believe this sometimes happens. At any rate in these days Hemingway al-

---

* André Derain: (1880–1954), French painter; early in this century he was associated with the modernist art movement called fauvism (*fauve:* wild beast); but it was not long before his more conservative tendencies began to emerge.

though a sportsman was easily tired. He used to get quite worn out walking from his house to ours. But then he had been worn by the war. . . .

HEMINGWAY ON STEIN

It was wonderful to walk down the long flights of stairs knowing that I'd had good luck working. I always worked until I had something done and I always stopped when I knew what was going to happen next. That way I could be sure of going on the next day. But sometimes when I was starting a new story and I could not get it going, I would sit in front of the fire and squeeze the peel of the little oranges into the edge of the flame and watch the sputter of blue that they made. I would stand and look out over the roofs of Paris and think, "Do not worry. You have always written before and you will write now. All you have to do is write one true sentence. Write the truest sentence that you know." So finally I would write one true sentence, and then go on from there. It was easy then because there was always one true sentence that I knew or had seen or had heard someone say. If I started to write elaborately, or like someone introducing or presenting something, I found that I could cut that scrollwork or ornament out and throw it away and start with the first true simple declarative sentence I had written. Up in that room I decided that I would write one story about each thing that I knew about. I was trying to do this all the time I was writing, and it was good and severe discipline.

It was in that room too that I learned not to think about anything that I was writing from the time I stopped writing until I started again the next day. That way my subconscious would be working on it and at the same time I would be listening to other people and noticing everything, I hoped; learning, I hoped; and I would read so that I would not think about my work and make myself impotent to do it. Going down the stairs when I had worked well, and that needed luck as well as discipline, was a wonderful feeling and I was free then to walk anywhere in Paris.

If I walked down by different streets to the Jardin du Luxembourg in the afternoon I could walk through the gardens and then go to the Musée du Luxembourg where the great paintings were that have now mostly been transferred to the Louvre and the Jeu de Paume. I went there nearly every day for the Cézannes and to see the Manets and the Monets and the other Impressionists that I had first come to know about in the Art Institute at Chicago. I was learning something from the painting of Cézanne that made writing simple true sentences far from enough to make the stories have the dimensions that I was trying to put in them. I was learning very much from him but I was not articulate enough to explain it to anyone. Besides it was a secret. But if the light was gone in the Luxembourg I would walk up through the gardens and stop in at the studio apartment where Gertrude Stein lived at 27 rue de Fleurus.

My wife and I had called on Miss Stein, and she and the friend who lived with her had been very cordial and friendly and we had loved the big studio with the great paintings. It was like one of the best rooms in the finest museum except there was a big fireplace and it was warm and comfortable and they gave you good things to eat and tea and natural distilled liqueurs made from purple plums, yellow plums or wild raspberries. These were fragrant, colorless alcohols served from cut-glass carafes in small glasses and whether they were *quetsche*, *mirabelle* or *framboise* they all tasted like the fruits they came from, converted into a controlled fire on your tongue that warmed you and loosened it.

Miss Stein was very big but not tall and was heavily built like a peasant woman. She had beautiful eyes and a strong German-Jewish face that also could have been Friulano * and she reminded me of a northern Italian peasant woman with her clothes, her mobile face and her lovely, thick, alive immigrant hair which she wore put up in the same way she had probably worn it in college. She talked all the time and at first it was about people and places.

Her companion had a very pleasant voice, was small, very dark, with her hair cut like Joan of Arc in the Boutet de Monvel illustrations and had a very hooked nose. She was working on a piece of needlepoint when we first met them and she worked on this and saw to the food and drink and talked to my wife. She made one conversation and listened to two and often interrupted the one she was not making. Afterwards she explained to me that she always talked to the wives. The wives, my wife and I felt, were tolerated. But we liked Miss Stein and her friend, although the friend was frightening. The paintings and the cakes and the *eau-de-vie* were truly wonderful. They seemed to like us too and treated us as though we were very good, well mannered and promising children and I felt that they forgave us for being in love and being married—time would fix that—and when my wife invited them to tea, they accepted.

When they came to our flat they seemed to like us even more; but perhaps that was because the place was so small and we were much closer together. Miss Stein sat on the bed that was on the floor and asked to see the stories I had written and she said that she liked them except one called "Up in Michigan."

"It's good," she said. "That's not the question at all. But it is *inaccrochable*. That means it is like a picture that a painter paints and then he cannot hang it when he has a show and nobody will buy it because they cannot hang it either."

"But what if it is not dirty but it is only that you are trying to use words that people would actually use? That are the only words that can make the story come true and that you must use them? You have to use them."

"But you don't get the point at all," she said. "You mustn't write anything that is *inaccrochable*. There is no point in it. It's wrong and it's silly."

She herself wanted to be published in the *Atlantic Monthly,* she told me, and she would be. She told me that I was not a good enough writer to be published there or in *The Saturday Evening Post* but that I might be some new sort of

---

* Fruilano: a person from the Northern Italian district of Friuli, whose inhabitants are descended from Celtic peoples.

writer in my own way but the first thing to remember was not to write stories that were *inaccrochable*. I did not argue about this nor try to explain again what I was trying to do about conversation. That was my own business and it was much more interesting to listen. That afternoon she told us, too, how to buy pictures.

"You can either buy clothes or buy pictures," she said. "It's that simple. No one who is not very rich can do both. Pay no attention to your clothes and no attention at all to the mode, and buy your clothes for comfort and durability, and you will have the clothes money to buy pictures."

"But even if I never bought any more clothing ever," I said, "I wouldn't have enough money to buy the Picassos that I want."

"No. He's out of your range. You have to buy the people of your own age— of your own military service group. You'll know them. You'll meet them around the quarter. There are always good new serious painters. But it's not you buying clothes so much. It's your wife always. It's women's clothes that are expensive."

I saw my wife trying not to look at the strange, steerage clothes that Miss Stein wore and she was successful. When they left we were still popular, I thought, and we were asked to come again to 27 rue de Fleurus.

It was later on that I was asked to come to the studio any time after five in the winter time. I had met Miss Stein in the Luxembourg. I cannot remember whether she was walking her dog or not, nor whether she had a dog then. I know that I was walking myself, since we could not afford a dog nor even a cat then, and the only cats I knew were in the cafés or small restaurants or the great cats that I admired in concierges' windows. Later I often met Miss Stein with her dog in the Luxembourg gardens; but I think this time was before she had one.

But I accepted her invitation, dog or no dog, and had taken to stopping in at the studio, and she always gave me the natural *eau-de-vie,* insisting on my refilling my glass, and I looked at the pictures and we talked. The pictures were exciting and the talk was very good. She talked, mostly, and she told me about modern pictures and about painters—more about them as people than as painters—and she talked about her work. She showed me the many volumes of manuscript that she had written and that her companion typed each day. Writing every day made her happy, but as I got to know her better I found that for her to keep happy it was necessary that this steady daily output, which varied with her energy, be published and that she receive recognition.

This had not become an acute situation when I first knew her, since she had published three stories that were intelligible to anyone. One of these stories, "Melanctha," was very good and good samples of her experimental writing had been published in book form and had been well praised by critics who had met her or known her. She had such a personality that when she wished to win anyone over to her side she would not be resisted, and critics who met her and saw her pictures took on trust writing of hers that they could not understand because of their enthusiasm for her as a person, and because of their confidence in her judgment. She had also discovered many truths about rhythms and the uses of words in repetition that were valid and valuable and she talked well about them.

But she disliked the drudgery of revision and the obligation to make her writing intelligible, although she needed to have publication and official acceptance, especially for the unbelievably long book called *The Making of Americans*.

This book began magnificently, went on very well for a long way with great stretches of great brilliance and then went on endlessly in repetitions that a more conscientious and less lazy writer would have put in the waste basket. I came to know it very well as I got—forced, perhaps would be the word—Ford Madox Ford to publish it in *The Transatlantic Review* serially, knowing that it would outrun the life of the review. For publication in the review I had to read Miss Stein's proof for her as this was a work which gave her no happiness.

On this cold afternoon when I had come past the concierge's lodge and the cold courtyard to the warmth of the studio, all that was years ahead. On this day Miss Stein was instructing me about sex. By that time we liked each other very much and I had already learned that everything I did not understand probably had something to it. Miss Stein thought that I was too uneducated about sex and I must admit that I had certain prejudices against homosexuality since I knew its more primitive aspects. I knew it was why you carried a knife and would use it when you were in the company of tramps when you were a boy in the days when wolves was not a slang term for men obsessed by the pursuit of women. I knew many *inaccrochable* terms and phrases from Kansas City days and the mores of different parts of that city, Chicago and the lake boats. Under questioning I tried to tell Miss Stein that when you were a boy and moved in the company of men, you had to be prepared to kill a man, know how to do it and really know that you would do it in order not to be interfered with. That term was *accrochable*. If you knew you would kill, other people sensed it very quickly and you were let alone; but there were certain situations you could not allow yourself to be forced into or trapped into. I could have expressed myself more vividly by using an *inaccrochable* phrase that wolves used on the lake boats, "Oh gash may be fine but one eye for mine." But I was always careful of my language with Miss Stein even when true phrases might have clarified or better expressed a prejudice.

"Yes, yes, Hemingway," she said. "But you were living in a milieu of criminals and perverts."

I did not want to argue that, although I thought that I had lived in a world as it was and there were all kinds of people in it and I tried to understand them, although some of them I could not like and some I still hated.

"But what about the old man with beautiful manners and a great name who came to the hospital in Italy and brought me a bottle of Marsala or Campari and behaved perfectly, and then one day I would have to tell the nurse never to let that man into the room again?" I asked.

"Those people are sick and cannot help themselves and you should pity them."

"Should I pity so and so?" I asked. I gave his name but he delights so in giving it himself that I feel there is no need to give it for him.

"No. He's vicious. He's a corrupter and he's truly vicious."

"But he's supposed to be a good writer."

"He's not," she said. "He's just a showman and he corrupts for the pleasure of corruption and he leads people into other vicious practices as well. Drugs, for example."

"And in Milan the man I'm to pity was not trying to corrupt me?"

"Don't be silly. How could he hope to corrupt you? Do you corrupt a boy like you, who drinks alcohol, with a bottle of Marsala? No, he was a pitiful old man who could not help what he was doing. He was sick and he could not help it and you should pity him."

"I did at the time," I said. "But I was disappointed because he had such beautiful manners."

I took another sip of the *eau-de-vie* and pitied the old man and looked at Picasso's nude of the girl with the basket of flowers. I had not started the conversation and thought it had become a little dangerous. There were almost never any pauses in a conversation with Miss Stein, but we had paused and there was something she wanted to tell me and I filled my glass.

"You know nothing about any of this really, Hemingway," she said. "You've met known criminals and sick people and vicious people. The main thing is that the act male homosexuals commit is ugly and repugnant and afterwards they are disgusted with themselves. They drink and take drugs, to palliate this, but they are disgusted with the act and they are always changing partners and cannot be really happy."

"I see."

"In women it is the opposite. They do nothing that they are disgusted by and nothing that is repulsive and afterwards they are happy and they can lead happy lives together."

"I see," I said. "But what about so and so?"

"She's vicious," Miss Stein said. "She's truly vicious, so she can never be happy except with new people. She corrupts people."

"I understand."

"You're sure you understand?"

There were so many things to understand in those days and I was glad when we talked about something else. The park was closed so I had to walk down along it to the rue de Vaugirard and around the lower end of the park. It was sad when the park was closed and locked and I was sad walking around it instead of through it and in a hurry to get home to the rue Cardinal Lemoine. The day had started out so brightly too. I would have to work hard tomorrow. Work could cure almost anything, I believed then, and I believe now. Then all I had to be cured of, I decided Miss Stein felt, was youth and loving my wife. I was not at all sad when I got home to the rue Cardinal Lemoine and told my newly acquired knowledge to my wife. In the night we were happy with our own knowledge we already had and other new knowledge we had acquired in the mountains.

V COMMUNITIES

Richard Hoggart leads off this section with his study of the roles of mother and father in the homes of the English industrial working class during the time of his youth; Robert Coles takes his psychiatrist's assumptions to an even poorer home and finds them confounded by the creative and organizing abilities of another mother, this one black. James McPherson's essay describes the painful evolution of a new community in a hostile environment; and the essays of Edmund Wilson and James Baldwin are also studies in white oppression. For the study of communities, which is the concern now of so many fine writers, is likely, if conscious of broad social and political implications, to concentrate on the underprivileged, the good and ill of their position, as the aspect of our society which most concerns everybody. The tone varies from the observant nostalgia of Hoggart to the emotionally involved rhetoric of Baldwin; the personalities of the writers, however objectively they handle their material, show through, and we realize that very rarely are we presented with information that is not colored by the professional and personal attributes of the reporter. But it is important to understand that this is not a disadvantage so much as a condition creating an imperative need for controlled writing and reading.

Richard Hoggart / Mother and Father

Hoggart is writing about working-class life in the north of England. He draws heavily on his own childhood memories and even includes descriptions of his mother's life, and his own. But his purpose is not autobiographical. Writing in 1956, he is trying to show that there are genuine continuities in working-class culture. The most important force for domestic coherence and stability being the mother, he gives her a good deal more space here than the "mester," the husband who is master only in a qualified way.

Writing of this sort presents the author with special difficulties. He values the degree to which he still understands the working class, but of course his ability to describe and analyze it could only have been acquired by leaving it. Note that Hoggart deals with this problem directly, not by compromise. He quotes working-class expressions freely, but his own prose is not "proletarian" and is occasionally rather markedly "middle-class." ("There are some who . . . make . . . their toil a badge of dreadful honour.") This clearly indicates an educated observer, not an active participant in the society he describes. But notice that he allows for this: for instance, the brief account of his own physique is strategically placed as a reminder of the writer's peculiar situation—a professional man indelibly marked, even in bodily appearance, by his origins in a different culture.

MOTHER

> *I know her scrubbed and sour humble hands*
> *. . . this monumental*
> *Argument of the hewn voice, gesture . . .**

To write of a working-class mother is to run peculiar risks. We know, if only from the profusion of novels published during the documentary 'thirties, that she has an honoured place in most accounts of working-class childhoods. Her own menfolk may appear careless of her for much of the time, but like to buy ornaments inscribed "What is home without a mother," and for years after she has "gone" will speak lovingly of "me mam."

* *I know her scrubbed* . . . : from Dylan Thomas, "After the Funeral (in memory of Ann Jones)."

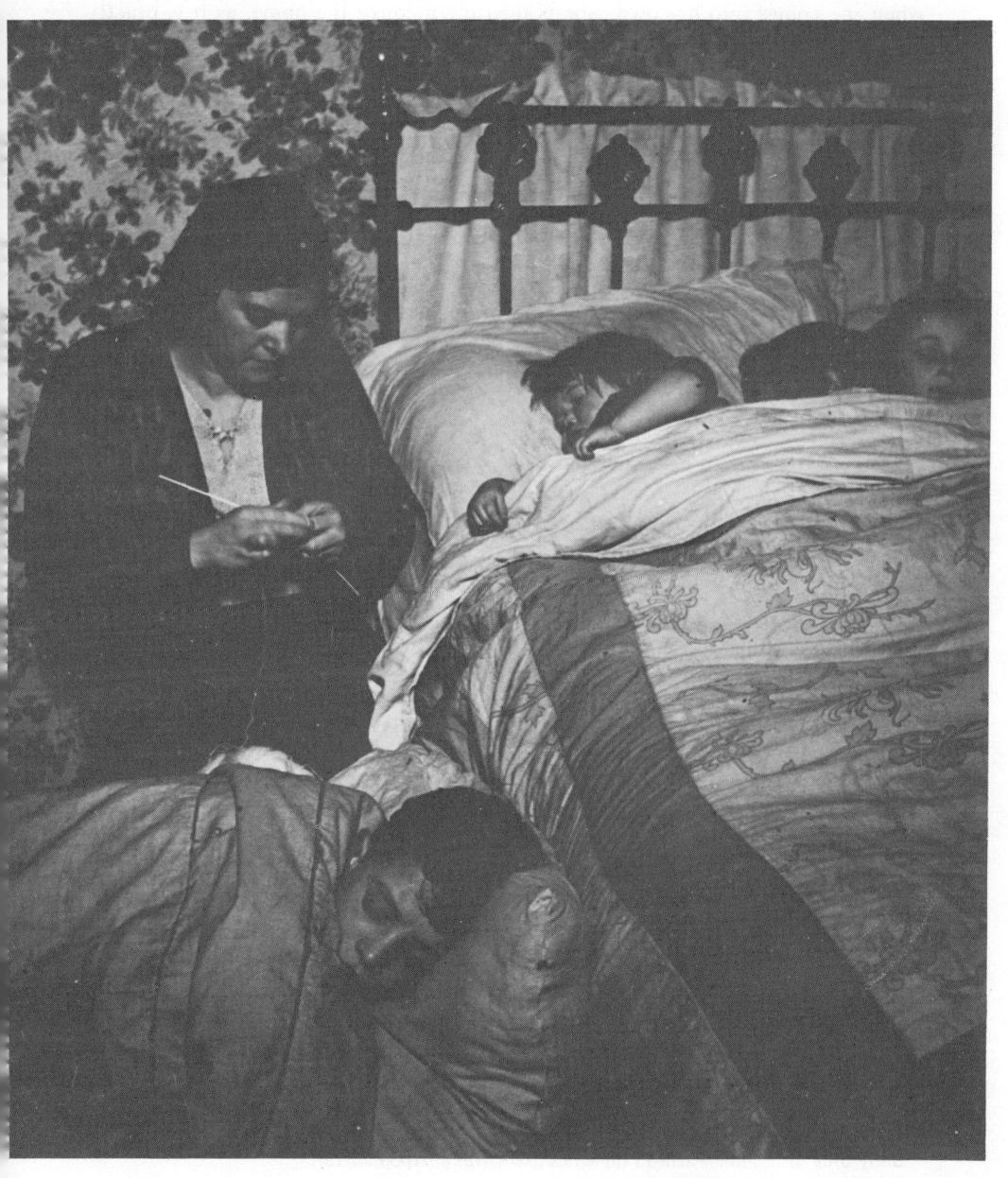

Bill Brandt from Rapho Guillumette

Yet one can have little but admiration for the position such a mother naturally assumes in her household. I am thinking of her chiefly in early-middle or middle age, when she has fully established herself as the mother of the family, when she comes into her own. She is then the pivot of the home, as it is practically the whole of her world. She, more than the father, holds it together; writes with difficulty to a son in the Services or to a daughter working away. She keeps close contact with those other members of the family who live near, with the grandparents, brothers, sisters and cousins; occasionally she may go to sit with one of them or with a neighbour for an hour. She leaves the outer world of politics and even of the "news" to her husband; she knows little about his job; such friends as she has from outside are usually his, since on marriage she drops her own.

So far this is too boldly drawn, but it is necessary to establish first the close, the myopic nature of the lives of most working-class mothers. The pressure is so strong that in those who have special troubles or are very poorly gifted imaginatively it can produce a turned-in-upon itself world into which nothing which does not concern the family penetrates.

It is a hard life, in which it is assumed that the mother will be "at it" from getting up to going to bed: she will cook, mend, scrub, wash, see to the children, shop and satisfy her husband's desires. Even today, it is often a life with few modern aids such as vacuum cleaners and electric washers, and yet with more dirt to fight than in the more prosperous districts. Curtains can hardly be kept "a good colour" even with frequent washing in dolly blue or cream; * the fireplace and range may need blackleading * and hard "nursing." Everywhere the smoke and soot from the nearby factories and railway lines creep in, and most women "can't abide the thought of dirt getting a hold."

Some free time can be occupied with darning and patching, rarely with making new clothing for the children. Not many mothers, even if they have worked in a clothing factory, are trained in the making of complete garments. In any case, sewing-machines are expensive and working-class people do not seem to buy them, even by hire-purchase, as readily as they buy articles which more obviously give pleasure to the whole family. Ready-made clothing is inexpensive and attractive. The husband's clothes are knocked about at work, and so the endless patching-up goes on, interspersed with the buying of new articles which, because they are cheap, are not economical and soon show wear.

Partly because the husband is at work but also because women are simply expected to look after such things, it will be the mother who has the long waits in public places, at the doctor's for "a bottle," at the clinic with a child who has eye-trouble, at the municipal offices to see about the instalment on the electricity bill.

---

* dolly blue or cream: washtub bleaches used with a tripod stirrer.
* blackleading: graphite used to polish ironwork.

All this is made more difficult because there is in most cases, or has been until the last few years, little room for manœuvre financially, only just enough to "wag on"; the housekeeping money is usually "mortgaged" to a penny or so. To manage on a tight string like this requires considerable skill, and that often comes hard, but come it must or the family is likely to be in trouble. A wife soon takes it for granted—indeed, assumes with marriage—that she will have to "fadge" to make ends meet. Rowntree * pointed out years ago that there is often a period between the growing-up of the children and going on to the old-age pension during which matters are easier. But, in the main, it is a life of "tightness" and "contriving." I often noticed that some of the happier wives were those whose husbands earned just a few shillings above the average for the street, but who in other respects lived in the same manner as the rest. If the husband were a decent sort and let his wife have an extra shilling or two, then she could be relieved of a deal of fine calculation; a sudden call for an electric-light bulb, shoe repairs or a boy's Scout outfit did not cause her serious worry. Partly because ready money in any substantial amount is hard to come by, partly because housewives often do not see just how awkward a position they are putting themselves into by the slow mounting of a debt, the most elaborate shifts and devices can be carried out with pathetic concentration. I know one housewife who now spends about eight pounds a week at the grocer's and could in these easier days pay it off weekly: but the habits of the 'thirties cannot be shaken off and she can never bring herself to clear it; she is happier on the "paying something off" system then she would be in paying outright. At my grandmother's we were not living "on relief" but, like many around us, we were "a bit short." For years during the early 'thirties, I queued on Friday evenings for the family groceries; each weekly bill was between fifteen and twenty shillings, and always we carried something over. In my self-conscious 'teens I had a regular sick envy of those who paid off cheerfully, a horrid shyness at going through the weekly form of words, "Grandma says she'll leave five shillings till next week." More recently, I know of one woman who slowly built up a debt of about one pound at the butcher's and then suddenly realised how large it was. She saw no way of finding a spare pound all at once, and simply stopped going for meat. But her family was still registered with him, so that she must have found it difficult to manage through the winter of 1952, when meat was none too plentiful. The butcher, meanwhile, would have been glad to see her and suggest an arrangement, but he knew she would not come. Any similar shopkeeper can give plenty of other examples. This is a situation which full employment and Welfare State arrangements have done a great deal to alter, but not as much as might be thought; the old habits persist.

Usually the wife has to operate on her own this narrow system of weekly

---

* B. Seebohm Rowntree: 1871–1954, Quaker philanthropist of a rich chocolate-making family; author of *Poverty, a Study of Town Life* (1910) and other books.

finance. That is why there is still strong competition between small shopkeepers over a penny off this or the willingness to make up small portions of that; these things may decide a sale. Twopence a pound on meat may seem negligible but can cause a bad wobble in the week's planning; so can the sudden call to "rig out" a boy for school camp or a girl for the Sunday-school concert, or for a present to a cousin who is getting married. There are always the clubs, or those drapers and fancy-goods shops which, whether they take agents' checks or not, are a shilling cheaper than the big shops in town and may let you take articles away on a small payment. Almost always their materials are by no means as good as those which do cost only a shilling more: presents are shoddy and break, chromium is thin and peels soon. The clubs, or check-trading, tend to become a habit and the house-to-house agents are adept at persuading clients to "keep the account open" continuously, so that in many cases more money is leaking away weekly in this way than really be spared. The cycle goes on: if the family is suddenly hard-up, then it is usually the mother who goes short, who "pinches herself" on food or clothes.

Life is very much a week-by-week affair, with little likelihood of saving a lump sum to "fall back upon." There may be a tin box on the mantelpiece in which savings for the holiday are put, but this is not usual. There is no bank account, no sick pay except that from the "National Health" and perhaps something from a club, and these come to little enough. You may still see housewives queueing at a quarter to nine each Tuesday outside the post-offices to claim their family allowances. If "the mester* is laid off" there may be real distress. The old habit of looking well after the wage-earners, particularly in food, is still alive; so is the stress on the need for all to "pull together": the boat is likely to founder quickly otherwise. A wife is happy if she can "manage" or "get along"; if she can find something left over for extras at the end of the week, she is very content.

Here, as in most aspects of domestic life, the wife is by tradition responsible; the husband is out, wage-earning. He wants food and his own sort of relaxation when he comes home. I suppose this explains why, as it seems to me, the wife is often expected to be responsible for contraceptive practice. Most non-Catholic working-class families accept contraception as an obvious convenience, but both husbands and wives are shy of clinics where advice is given, unless they are driven there by near-desperation. The husband's shyness and an assumption that this is really her affair often ensure that he expects her to take care of it, that he "can't be bothered with it." She has rarely been told anything before marriage, and the amount she has picked up from older girls or married women at work or nearby varies enormously. She must take what advice she can early unless there are to be more children than either she or her husband want. When she has done that her knowledge of the possibilities is likely to be limited to coitus interrup-

* mester: master (husband).

tus, the best-known type of pessary and the sheath. Husbands tend not to like sheaths—"they take away the pleasure"; she may be embarrassed in buying either those or pessaries, and both are dear; coitus interruptus is probably the commonest practice.

But to use any of these methods requires a rigid discipline, a degree of sustained competence many wives are hardly capable of. She forgets just once or "lets herself go," or a sheath is cheap and bursts or the husband demands awkwardly after a night at the club. How often, therefore, it is assumed that any children after the first one or two were "not intended." I am inclined to think that among, say, the lower middle-classes the child who was "not intended" is apt to arrive when the parents are about forty. They have had two or three children during their late twenties and early thirties and their contraceptive practice has thereafter been effective. Perhaps by the time they reach forty they feel safer and grow careless. With the working-classes the pattern seems to be different: unless a miscarriage is procured, the first unintended child is likely to arrive only a year or two after the others. It is usually accepted "philosophically"; after all, "what did yer get married for?" It is a "philosophic" acceptance but one without much sentimentality; "kids are a trouble"; they mean more work and less money to go round. But they receive the same indulgences and smothering attention.

It is evident that a working-class mother will age early, that at thirty, after having two or three children, she will have lost most of her sexual attraction: that between thirty-five and forty she rapidly becomes the shapeless figure the family know as "our mam." She went into the world earlier than girls of other classes, began going around with boys at sixteen and was probably "courting regular" at eighteen. At that time she was using freely a cheap and restricted range of cosmetics—lipstick, "rouge" and the cheaper perfumes, powders and creams. She may practise some of this simple cosmetic routine for a time after marriage, but it fairly soon ends, except for a rather heavy and crude "rouging" on special occasions—a "rouging" that gives to faces insufficiently prepared the faintly Grock-like * quality which some people take as evidence of the coarseness of the working-classes when they see them on holiday.

By forty-five or fifty, ailments begin: you hear during the poorer periods that she is "nobbut middling" just now. There may be rheumatism, or a regular back-ache from a twenty-year-old undetected prolapse. The big fear, one which recurs constantly in conversation, is of a growth, visualised as some huge and ramping cancerous organism; or of a "stone," imagined as a great hard pebble. I remember watching a middle-aged mother with a full shopping-basket passing through Hunslet Feast (fair) one Friday, obviously "ailing" and worried. She was attracted by the patter of a vast, screamingly and coarsely opulent woman in a herbalist stall. After a few moments of hesitation she went nearer and whispered her problem. She was sold for six shillings a packet of some sort of crystals . . .

* Grock: Adrien Wellach (1880–1959), famous Swiss clown.

"Never mind what the doctors tell you, me dear. Take these twice a day in a tumbler of warm water and they'll wash the stone away. You'll know no more about it. It'll all come away in the toilet, dear."

There is little time for "doctoring"; if things are bad she might get a bottle from the surgery, but usually the long wait there or a disinclination to keep on troubling the doctor (and something of a doubt that he can really do much to help) ensure that most times nothing is done. Now and again there will be trials of recommended patent medicines. Most doctors in working-class districts know that there is usually little they can do. Their middle-aged housewife patients look after themselves badly, work too long or hard, do not know how to relax, take insufficient sleep, have a badly balanced diet. They expect to have to go on all the time, "fadging," often muddling because the demands are complex and heavy and yet must be met somehow. Always at the back of the wife's mind, though probably not consciously, is the knowledge that if "anything happens" to the husband she will have to "turn to" and manage on her own, finding what "charring" she can to supplement her pension.

During the years in which my mother had the three of us on her own, she was never strong enough, since she had acute bronchial trouble, to do any outside work. She managed with surprising skill on a weekly twenty-odd shillings from "the Guardians" * (some of this was in the form of coupons exchangeable at specified grocers'). Surprising to a spectator, but not to her: she had been a gay young girl, I believe, but by this time had lost most of her high spirits. She was well past the striking of attitudes about her situation, and though she would gladly take a pair of old shoes or a coat, she thanked no one for their pity or their admiration; she was without sentimentality about her position and never pretended to do more than go through with it. It was too much an unrelieved struggle to be at all enjoyable, and three young children, always hungry for more food and pleasures than she could afford, were not—except occasionally—rewarding companions. She helped herself along by smoking Woodbines *—furtively, in case "They" found out: my brother was trained to put the twopenny packet in the drawer without a word if he came back from the shop to find a visitor at home. The tiny house was damp and swarming with cockroaches; the earth-closet was a stinking mire in bad weather. Food was unvaried but a lot more nourishing than it would have been with many mothers in that situation. My mother had firmness and intelligence enough to resist all our demands for fish-and-chips and tea, and we drank nothing but cocoa. We had a succession of cheap stews with vegetables throughout each week: I remember someone bringing (I must have been about six at the time) a small box of assorted biscuits to the house, and how dazzled we were by them. For a tea-time treat, we occasionally had sweetened condensed milk on bread. Pocket-money was one penny a week for the whole family, so our separate turns came up every three weeks. We were usually advised to buy something that could be shared, and we

---

* Guardians: citizens charged with the administration of the Poor Laws.
* Woodbines: cheapest brand of cigarette.

usually objected. We were always "well turned out," well darned throughout the year, and had new outfits at Whitsun; the last I remember were sailor-suits with whistles for the two boys.

On one occasion my mother, fresh from drawing her money, bought herself a small treat, something which must have been a reminder of earlier pleasures—a slice or two of boiled ham or a few shrimps. We watched her like sparrows and besieged her all through tea-time until she shocked us by bursting out in real rage. There was no compensation; she just did not want to give us this, and there could be no easy generosity in the giving. We got some, though we sensed that we had stumbled into something bigger than we understood.

This is an extreme case, though one in the true line of the tradition. We need to avoid any suggestion of a sense of heroism in the people (and there are men, as well as women) who actually live this kind of life. It is challenging, and the lines on the face of an old working-class woman are often magnificently expressive but they are hard earned. We should not try to add a glamour to such a face; it has its fineness without any artificial light. It is often a face with a scaly texture and the lines, looked at closely, have grime in them; the hands are bony claws covered with densely-lined skin, and again the dirt is well-ingrained there: years of snatched washes, usually in cold water, have caused that. The face has two marked lines of force—from the sides of the nose down to the compressed lips; they tell of years of "calculating." Or notice that many old working-class women have an habitual gesture which illuminates the years of their life behind. D. H. Lawrence remarked it in his mother: my grandmother's was a repeated tapping of her fingers on the arm of her chair, a tapping which accompanied an endless working out of something in her head; she had had years of making out for a large number on very little. In others you see a rhythmic smoothing of the hand down the chair-arm, as though to smooth everything out and make it workable; in others there is a working of the lips or a steady rocking. None of these could be called neurotic gestures, nor are they symptoms of acute fear; they help the constant calculation.

Today, if I hear someone using words like "sorrow" and "misery" freely, they usually sound slightly archaic; they are to be reserved for special events. To my grandmother they were regular words, together with "care" and "hardship," used as often and as meaningfully as "nuisance" and "awkward" among many of the people I know today. When my grandmother spoke of someone "taking the bread from her mouth" she was not being dramatic or merely figurative; she was speaking from an unbroken and still relevant tradition, and her speech at such times had something of the elemental quality of Anglo-Saxon poetry:

> I can utter a true song about myself . . . how in toilsome days I often suffered a time of hardship, how I have borne bitter sorrow in my breast.*

* "I can utter a true song . . ." : from the anonymous Anglo-Saxon poem "The Seafarer" (Everyman edition).

So a working-class mother carries on. She has her "treats" occasionally, as the men do. Her greatest pleasure, as Dr. Zweig notes, is to be "waited upon" in some way; it may be by the daughters and the father taking over the house for a day, it may be by going on a day trip, with large knife-and-fork meals laid on at intervals: it may be simply that she is taken to the pictures by the father. But in general she carries on with work until she becomes a grandmother, and then she has new calls for her help.

There are some who become bitten-in and make it all a harsh ritual and their toil a badge of dreadful honour; there are some who are shiftless: for most there is, in varying degrees, a steady and self-forgetful routine, one devoted to the family and beyond proud self-regard. Behind it, making any vague pity irrelevant, is pride in the knowledge that so much revolves around them. This can make the most unpromising and unprepossessing young woman arrive at a middle-age in which she is, when in the midst of her home and family, splendidly "there" and, under all the troubles, content. Her husband may be the "mester" in the household, but she is not a door-mat; she and he know her value and virtue if she is, in her way, a "good mother." The nagging wife is still one of the major villains in truly popular art.

But how far is all this being transmitted, it may be asked, to the teen-age girls who walk the streets in the evening? They seem to fill the space between leaving school and marriage with thrice-weekly visits to "musicals" and "romantic dramas" at the pictures, with fantasy love-stories, and with successive hops at the "Palais," the "Mecca," the "Locarno" or the Public Baths. Their jobs rarely engage more than a small portion of their personalities, they seem to have little interest as committed individuals in anything, they take no interest in Trade Union activities and little in the home. Surely they are most of them flighty, careless and inane?

. . . [But] matters are not always as bad as they at first appear. Girls like these have only a brief flowering period, only a few years during which they have no responsibilities and some spare money. A surprisingly high proportion of them, in view of the forces which discourage it, take up healthy outdoor activity. For most, what is so conveniently and insistently offered is sufficient, and these are indoor activities. These girls are often bored by their work; there are plenty of people who know the easier ways of winning from them the money in their pockets. They seem soon to be enveloped in the chrysalis of an adolescent daydream. Everything they choose to do seems urban and trivial; it would be difficult to hold their attention for long to anything not part of the dream.

Yet there is rarely any revolt against home, even though there may be little apparent positive response to it. Home's "alright" (the adjective is used to indicate something you accept but have no enthusiasm for); you live there; you do not usually leave it; nor do you think about it or stay in it if you can get out at nights. But it seems to me that this gay, and it is in many ways gay, life of the teens is not regarded as finally "real," as the real business of life. It is enjoyed and not regretted; it rarely affects the sense that, after all, the real business of life is getting married and having a family. It is certainly "life" in a sense that school never was; you learn a lot in this period about what life really is and means, through gossip and the talk at work; you enjoy yourself. But real life, questions of fun apart, is marriage: for both sexes the main dividing-line in a working-class life is this, not a change of job or town or going up to a university or qualifying in a profession. Marriage is the end of this temporary freedom for a woman and the beginning of a life in which "scraping" will be normal. With most this pattern is taken for granted; the free period is a kind of butterfly flight, giddy while it lasts but short. There is a wealth of meaning in the phrase used as soon as a girl has found a man she is going to marry, "I'm going steady now."

Once that happens, she begins to draw upon her older roots. She has some hard lessons to learn, and there are bound to be awkward periods before she finally settles. The more careless refuse to learn, go on smoking and "picture-going" while the kids knock around scruffily. Most pick up a rhythm which goes back beyond the dance-tunes and the cinema's lovers. Watch the way a girl who, in view of the extent to which her taste is assaulted by the flashy and trivial, should have an appalling sense of style can impose on even the individually ugly items she buys that sense of what it is important to re-create in a living-room. Watch the way she handles a baby; not the more obvious features, the carelessness of hygiene and the trivialities, but the acceptance of a child in the crook of the arm or in a bath by the fire.

She has usually had some training before leaving school, helping a little with the cleaning at home, looking after younger brothers, pushing out their own or the neighbour's baby. But this may not amount to a lot, and after six or seven years of determined trivialisation the surprising fact is that she takes up the threads so well. That is because they have never been broken, but only casually covered over. Those young wives who stay at work until the children come, or after, if grandma or a nursery will look after them, are not usually revolting against the demands of marriage but rather prolonging, for what they know must be a limited period, the time when they can have spare money for little luxuries —fairly frequent boiled ham at two shillings a quarter or fish-and-chips for supper two or three nights a week. When that goes, it goes: most working-class girls do not much pine for their lost freedom, they never regarded it as other than temporary.

They do mishandle their children by "educated" standards; I mean by the standards usually advocated in modern books on child-care. It is a working-class tradition of long standing to indulge not only children but young people all the way up to marriage. Babies are smothered with love and attention, not allowed to cry, stuffed till their little bellies ache and then given dubious remedies in sixpenny packets; even today many of them are rarely left without a "dummy" and that probably dipped in syrup, jogged continually in their magnificent prams, hardly ever left alone by mother, by father when he gets home from work, by grandparents, and kept up far too late. Later, though sometimes the girls may be expected to help a little in the house and the boys may take on a "newspaper-round," the remarkable feature, in view of how much the mother has to do and how short is spare money, is that they are asked to do so little and that spare-time money-making is so often regarded as for their own pockets. How often do the children wash up? How often are they bought disproportionately expensive presents—bikes of the most splendid kind and prams almost full-size? Parents expect and encourage the children, even in adolescence, to do little to support the house in labour or money. Most of what a working-class girl knows on marrying about the running of a home she has usually assimilated unconsciously. She may be "earning good money" and costing a lot to keep, but she is probably paying less than she costs to her mother. If this is a blind selfishness, it is a selfishness which the parents condone and support; there is all the rest of life to come and you cannot do much about that; you must let them " 'ave a good time while they can"; after all, "yer only young once."

FATHER

Like his wife, a working-class man often seems to me almost physically recognisable. He tends to be small and dark, lined and sallow about the face by the time he has passed thirty. The bone-structure of the face and neck then shows clearly, with a suggestion of the whippet about it. In general, these physical marks are observable early, and remain throughout life. Thus—though this is lightly put —if I or some of my professional acquaintance who were born into the working-classes put on the sort of flat cap and neckerchief which go with looking "county," * or if we leave our collars open, the sit of the cap and the neckerchief, or the structure of the bones round the neck make us look, not like the sporting middle-classes, but like working-men on a day off.

The point of departure for an understanding of the position of the working-class father in his home is that he is the boss there, the "master in his own house." This he is by tradition, and neither he nor his wife would want the tradition changed. She will often refer to him before others as "Mr. W." or "the mester." This does not mean that he is by any means an absolute ruler or that he gets or expects his own way in everything. It often accompanies a carefulness, a willingness to help and be "considerate," to be "a good husband." In the lazy or insensitive, it may support a considerable selfishness or near-brutality. In either case, there is likely to be a deference to him as the main breadwinner and heavy worker, even though these assumptions are not always correct today. He remains the chief contact with the outer world which puts the money into the house.

There is often a kind of roughness in his manner which a middle-class wife

---

* "county": having the appearance and manners of upper-class families associated with country houses, etc.

would find insupportable. A wife will say how worried she is because something is amiss, and "the mester will be mad" when he gets home; he may "tell yer off" harshly or in a few cases may even "bash" you, especially if he has had a couple of pints on the way from work. Or middle-aged wives will say to a younger one, " 'e's good to yer, i'n't 'e?" meaning that he is not likely to become violent in word or act, or that he does not leave his wife alone almost every night, or that he will "see 'er out" if she gets into difficulties with the housekeeping allowance. This is in part a heavy peasant crudeness in personal relations and expression, and clearly does not necessarily indicate a lack of affection, or a helplessness on the wife's part. The man who is able to growl is also able to defend; he has something of the cock about him. Hence, rough boys are often admired; the head-shaking over them is as proud as it is rueful—" 'e's a real *lad,*" people say.

A husband is therefore not really expected to help about the house. If he does, his wife is pleased; but she is unlikely to harbour a grudge if he does not. "When all's said and done," most things about a house are woman's work: "Oh, that's not a man's job," a woman will say, and would not want him to do too much of that kind of thing for fear he is thought womanish. Or the highest praise will take the form, " 'E's ever so good about the 'ouse. Just like a woman": if he does help much he is doing it in place of the woman whose job it should be; the household chores are not joint responsibilities.

So it is a positive act of helpfulness if he decides to help with washing up or the baby. In many cases a wife would not only "never dream" of having his help with the washing, but does not feel that she can "'ave the washing around" when he is at home. There are often difficulties of drying-space, especially on rainy days, that are aggravated by the need for a complicated system of putting the damp stuff round the fire on a clothes-horse and taking it off again into a basket or zinc bath at the times when the husband wants to "see t'fire."

There are many husbands who regard all the family's money affairs as a shared concern, who hand over their wage-packet on Friday night and leave its disposition to their wives. But an assumption just as characteristic, in my experience, is that the wage-packet is the husband's, and that he gives his wife a fixed amount for housekeeping each week. There are many households where the wife does not know how much her husband earns. This does not necessarily mean that she is poorly treated. "Oh, 'e sees me alright," or " 'e treats me alright," she will say, meaning that she is not left short but implying, in the phrasing itself, that the distribution of the wage lies with him. The wife is often responsible, out of this fixed amount, for any replacements—of crockery, furnishings and so on; the more thoughtful of these husbands will be open to suggestion, will promise something out of the next payment of overtime. Quite often the wife's share of any overtime money only arrives quixotically. Sometimes she feels unable to discuss family financial problems with her husband, and this may extend even to such a question as whether it is possible to send a child to the grammar-school. There will be discussion of a kind, and particularly if it has to be decided whether a child can be kept at a grammar-school after sixteen, but it is not usually a precise discussion of financial ways and means, of how this can be cut here or that pleasure reduced there.

If he is on the dole, and the same assumptions naturally apply whether he is in that position through ill health or ill luck or shiftlessness, both husband and wife assume that he must still have his pocket-money. Self-respect is involved; "a man can't be without money in 'is pocket"; he would then feel less than a man, feel "tied to" his wife and inferior to her, and such a situation is against nature. He must have money for cigarettes and beer, perhaps even for an occasional bet; the amount regularly spent each week, even by men out of work, would seem in many cases excessive to, say, the professional middle-classes. Fifteen cheap cigarettes a day seems normal, and those cost about thirteen shillings a week; for a man out of work and drawing the dole, one pound a week for pocket-money is the figure I most commonly hear nowadays. Such things as cigarettes and beer, it is felt, are part of life; without them, life would not be life; there are rarely any other major interests to make these pleasures less relevant and worth forgoing. It is, I suppose, the sense that such things are part of the minimum staple of life which makes many families, even where the husband is working well and has plenty of money in his pocket, maintain the old arrangement whereby the wife buys "with the groceries"—that is, out of the housekeeping money—a proportion of the husband's weekly cigarettes.

I noted that girls are usually indulged by parents, but that, especially before they leave school, they are expected to do more about the house than their brothers. A boy soon acquires something of the feeling that "it's different for men" which he will have in greater strength when he is grown-up. On leaving school the attitude quickly strengthens; he is, probably for the first time, close to his father and finds his father ready to be close to him: they now share the real world of work and men's pleasures.

All this is still largely true and must be put first, but has much too strongly implied that the husband is selfish and leaves all the troubles to his wife. The basic assumption is that the man is master of the house. Some of the expressions of this assumption, and these not the more unusual ones, might seem grossly unfair to the women. Yet there are a great many husbands who are thoughtful and helpful, who spend much of their free time at home, making and mending. Even so, there is the sense that the father occupies a special position. There are some things, difficult and men's things—such as chopping wood—which only he can do; there are others which he may do without undermining the order, such as getting himself off to work or bringing his wife a cup of tea in bed occasionally.

Among some younger husbands there are signs of a striking change in the basic attitude. Some wives press for it and find their husbands ready to modify the outlook they inherited from their fathers. Here as elsewhere, no doubt, educational improvements are quietly but pervasively promoting a different attitude among those who are ready to be affected. More particularly, a few husbands and wives may be influenced by the example of some young professional and lower middle-class husbands who have learned, especially since the war, to help their wives as partial substitute for the daily help their class can no longer always afford. Some working-class husbands will share the washing up if their wives go out to work, or will take turns with the baby if their job releases them early and not too tired. But many wives come home from work just as tired as their husbands and "set to" to do all the housework without help from them. And not many working-class husbands will help their wives by pushing the baby round the streets in its pram. That is still thought "soft," and most wives would sympathise with the view.

If a wife has a conscious wish, it is probably not for a husband who does such things, but rather for one who remains a husband in much the old sense, yet "a good one" in the old sense, for one who is "steady" and "a good worker," one who is not likely to land her suddenly in poverty, who is likely to be kept on if sackings begin, who brings home his money regularly, who is generous with his bonuses.

Emotionally, his best contribution is to be, without being soft or "womanish," ready to agree, to live according to the idea that happy married life is "a matter of give and take." A great many, perhaps most, husbands do this: working-class people have a host of jokes about marriage, but not against marriage. They are not harassed by the ambivalences of some more self-conscious people who are so shocked at the thought that they may end up in the bourgeois satisfaction of their parents that it takes them years to realise that they like being married, and even enjoy its ordinary duties and everyday necessities. Working-class men and women still accept marriage as normal and "right," and that in their early twenties. What a husband is earning at twenty-one, he is likely to be earning at fifty-one; he probably marries a girl from exactly his own class, and they set about "getting a home of their own together" and living their lives inside it.

James Alan McPherson / Chicago's Blackstone Rangers

Factional differences within the black community are often much the same as those in the white community. They have to do not only with economic and political power but with styles of life and manners. McPherson writes of a group of black young men who live in the Woodlawn area of Chicago's South Side ghetto. He gathers testimony from a wide range of informed persons, white and black, and what emerges is evidence that the confrontation between the Rangers and those opposed to them is probably only incidentally racial. Instead it involves the question of whether or not the community in which the Rangers live can be freed of the social and economic pressures coming as much from the black as from the white middle class.

The investigation is scrupulous, even wary. And this is as it should be, given the complications that need to be accounted for: the Police Gang Intelligence Unit that harasses the Rangers includes, for example, a substantial corps of black officers. McPherson is careful not to organize his impressions around any particular motif or political position. Note how reticently he treats the mystique of "energy" which dominates some of the Rangers's thinking and the decor of their headquarters. So, too, is he cautious lest his portrait of a community in formation turn into a portrait of its leaders, saving the latter, notably Jeff Fort, for attention only at the end. Indeed, McPherson, a talented young black writer of fiction, doesn't even project himself very forcefully into the piece. It's as if in the writing he displays some of the "cool" which made him, after four months of unobtrusive observation, someone who could be trusted by the Rangers and their friends.

The method of McPherson in this piece and that of Tom Wolfe in "The Pump House Gang" (in Section III) display an intimacy with the groups on which they are reporting; each is aware of the probable attitudes or prejudices of the reader. But unlike Wolfe, McPherson avoids eccentricities both in his style and in his characterizations of the people he describes.

Few uniformed policemen walk the streets in the Woodlawn area. Those who do are black. Most white policemen drive through the area in cars, usually accompanied by a black officer. Most of the policemen in the area seem to be young. They are, for the most part, polite, and a little cold. On occasion one notices a parked patrol car with two hard-faced white officers in the front seat and the barrel of a shotgun framed in the window between them. Only then does one remember the tension which is supposed to exist between the police and the black community. It is present, but it is not racial; at least not in the traditional—black-white—sense of the word.

Black people, if Blackstone Rangers can be called representative of black people, feel a tension between black policemen and themselves. It is a feeling of mistrust, of discomfort. Rangers do not seem to be under continual harassment from the police, but it is a fair assumption that they, or at least their leaders, are being watched by other blacks. If one sits too long in a restaurant with a Ranger of any status within the organization, he will eventually become aware of another black sitting in the next booth, sipping an eternal cup of coffee. Perhaps he is merely enjoying his coffee; perhaps he is a plainclothesman on the job. In any case, Rangers find it more relaxing to converse inside the Center or in one of their other meeting places.

"It shouldn't be called the Police Gang Intelligence Unit," says Mickey Cogwell, one of the Main 21 (the leadership of the Blackstone Rangers). "It should be called the Gang *Stupid* Unit because they are so stupid. If they really wanted to get us, they would wait until we commit crimes and then arrest us. Instead, they try to stop us from doing anything."

Mickey Cogwell is another busy man. Among the Main 21, he is recognized as the Ranger leader with the most business ability. For this reason Ranger president Jeff Fort put him in charge of West Side business operations of the Blackstone Nation. Cogwell is intelligent, and his directness suggests honesty and candor. He wears a black derby and a blue turtleneck sweater and talks very fast. He has had considerable experience with the Gang Intelligence Unit. He has been arrested more than sixty times.

"Every time people do things for us the G.I.U. tries to publicize it so that donators get bad publicity," Cogwell says. "It doesn't want the Rangers and Disciples to have a peace treaty because it threatens the security of their jobs. I feel that the G.I.U.—black men—use the Rangers and the rivalry between us and the D's to make their work more important to the system."

Cogwell believes that the members of the G.I.U. have extra-police powers. According to him, they can go into the Cook County Jail whenever they want; they have easy access to the press whenever they want to publicize stories about the Rangers; they have the help of the power structure in Chicago; and they can even influence judges. "Suppose one of the younger cats go out and does something and is put in the Cook County Jail. They will be offered a chance to get out if they swear that they were told to do something by one of the older Rangers, by one of the Main," he says. "The police have realized that they can't break up the Stones now. They might have done it four or five years ago, but now all they can do is arrest the Main. But Stone will still go on. In order to break us up, they will have to arrest everyone from the Main down to the peewees.

"If the police pick up a Stone, we take the number of the car, call a lawyer, and follow the car to the station," Cogwell states. "We wait in the halls until the lawyer comes. Then we try to find out what the bond is. If it's not too high, we try to raise it. But most bonds are set too high." He attributes the high bonds to intervention by members of the G.I.U. and the influence they seem to have over judges.

Cogwell denies that there was a payoff behind the November "Don't Vote" campaign. He says that it was an expression of the dissatisfaction of the Rangers with the local political structure. He observes that just after their campaign, G.I.U. chief Edward Buckney was promoted to captain and plans were made to increase the G.I.U. from 38 to 200 men. He believes that the campaign frightened the Chicago power structure. And the Rangers, he says, are now planning for 1971, the year of the next mayoralty election. Winston Moore, the black warden of the Cook County Jail and a critic of the Rangers, called the campaign "outright stupid," but whether or not the activity was politically naïve, it seems that the Chicago power structure is presently attempting to tighten up its control of the Blackstone Rangers.

Still, the Rangers appear to be growing, in both number and the scope of their business ventures. Besides the restaurant, they have obtained the use of a building from Humble Oil Company for $1 a year. The building, Cogwell says, will be used for Ranger businesses which will be operated by the eight Blackstone Rangers who are presently receiving training from the Chicago Small Businessmen's Association. Also, the Westinghouse Corporation has donated to the Rangers, through the University of Chicago's Firman House, fourteen washers and three dryers. The corporation will teach the Rangers how to operate them so they will be able to start their own laundromat. They have received two car-wash units from other sources, and have been given an interest in the Sammy Davis, Jr. Liquor Store, a pilot project owned by the famous entertainer and managed by the Rangers. The profits from the store go into a "slush fund" against the time when the Rangers are prepared to set up other businesses. Finally, an unnamed manufacturer has supplied them with 20,000 "All Mighty Black P. Stone" sweat shirts with the phrase "black is beautiful" printed on their backs in every major language. Lamar Bell, a Ranger leader, wears one with the phrase written in Greek.

"We want the Stones to be able to know something when they go into business," Mickey Cogwell says. He is not pleased with his attempts to run the West Side operation, he notes, because of what he calls attempts of the G.I.U. to stop Ranger business development by finding violations of the building and zoning codes, and reporting them to city agencies. At one point, he says, the Rangers had $800 worth of violations against them.

Mickey Cogwell claims that the Rangers made a genuine effort to keep the South Side cool during the April riots. "Jeff sent word out all over the Nation to keep peace," he says, "because King was killed and everybody was hurting. All the Main leaders went out into the streets to keep peace. Plus, the G.I.U. was out too, to provoke the Rangers into rioting. We feel that the city was out to get us to burn down our own community. But since we need the stores—our babies need milk—Jeff decided that all the stores in the area were part of the Ranger Nation."

I asked Mickey Cogwell if the Rangers would like to patrol their neighborhoods as a kind of community police force similar in some respects to the Black Panthers on the West Coast. "There is quite a difference between the power structure on the West Coast and the power structure in Chicago," he replied. "Mayor Daley is the most powerful man in America. He can tell the President what to do. On the Coast the Panthers can ride around in cars with guns, but not here. Mayor Daley is a powerful cat, very powerful. And dangerous, very dangerous."

While the Rangers can, in many instances, be considered a kind of spontaneous para-police force in their efforts to show the strength of their organization, there is another consideration to place in focus: are the police, specifically the members of the Gang Intelligence Unit, themselves a para-political force? This question is important in a very singular respect. It is evident that the Blackstone Ranger Nation is not interested in voluntarily *helping* the police: all of their activities which may be called helpful to the police seem to arise, unavoidably, from their efforts to keep the name of the Ranger organization safe from adverse publicity or else to demonstrate the tremendous power and community appeal, at least among the young, of the Blackstone Ranger Nation. In both of these areas the activities of the Gang Intelligence Unit seem to contribute the necessary pressure or motivation. The relative ease with which its members operate within the police department and the co-operation they receive from the State's Attorney's Office and the Cook County Jail, the influence they seem to have in the courts, and the easy willingness of the press to publicize incidents about the Rangers all suggest that members of the Unit have more than ordinary police powers.

For example, in December of 1968 after Jeff Fort was found guilty of contempt of Congress and released on $5000 bond, he was arrested by members of the G.I.U. on an old charge: failure to pay a $50 fine for a previous disorderly conduct arrest. The arrest warrant was issued on March 17, 1967. The eight G.I.U. officers who arrested Fort arrived at his home carrying axes, prepared to break down the door. They had no search warrant, but they searched his apartment and found a .22 caliber gun. Fort was charged with failure to register the gun.

Marshall Patner, the white Chicago lawyer who walked out of Senator McClellan's investigation of Poverty Program funding of a Ranger project with his client Jeff Fort last summer, has been in a position which enabled him to observe the activities of the Gang Intelligence Unit firsthand. "The question is," he says, "whether the police run the whole show. The G.I.U. can say 'no bond' to the judges, and no bond is given. Judges listen to them. State's attorneys listen to them."

Patner is paid by the Kettering Foundation to provide legal counsel for Rangers in general and Jeff Fort in particular. A 1956 University of Chicago Law School graduate, he quit his job as head of the appellate and test case division of the Legal Aid Bureau of Chicago to help William W. Brackett, who served as counsel for the Reverend John Fry before the McClellan Committee. Fry is a white clergyman whose church, the First Presbyterian, housed one of the Rangers' training centers funded by the Office of Economic Opportunity through a local grass roots group, The Woodlawn Organization (T.W.O.). The church thought Fort should have a black lawyer, but Fort preferred Marshall Patner.

"As a lawyer," Patner says, "I don't see my function as looking over a client to see what he's doing. I see these people as needing defense because they are being picked on for offenses which other people wouldn't be charged with, and subject to high bond just because they are Rangers." Since the McClellan hearings, Marshall Patner has received angry letters and telephone calls suggesting that he should be put into a concentration camp.

In Ranger cases, according to Patner, the judges set very high bonds. In one arrest for aggravated assault, the night judge set bond at $4000 and the morning judge reset bond at $5000. For a fight in the jail, Fort's bond was set at $10,000, and for a charge of resisting arrest, Jeff Fort's bond was again set at $10,000. He estimates that Fort has been picked up over one hundred and eighty times. Sometimes he will be arrested, processed, and released in a few minutes. Patner is bringing a suit in federal court for injunctive relief. The suit is against Mayor Daley, Captain Buckney, the State's Attorney, and certain judges, and is on behalf of Jeff Fort, Mickey Cogwell, and the Black P. Stone Nation.

Marshall Patner feels that the peacekeeping role of the Rangers is a "funny" one. "I would guess that as a matter of defiance and as a show of power the Rangers exert all the energy possible to see that police prophecies about them are not fulfilled. In contrast, they do this in areas where interests are common to their own. I believe that they keep a lot of ghetto kids out of trouble by giving them something with which they can identify."

"The police are definitely out to get the Stones," Carl Banks, a Ranger teacher, tells me at the Black P. Stone Youth Center, "especially since Nixon got in. Every time a black gets arrested, if he's from this neighborhood he's treated like a Stone. His bond is hiked up, he's harassed." Bank's voice changes to anger. "They don't want the Stones to have anything." He crushes a cigarette butt with his foot. "They want to keep us right down here on the ground."

"Why do you think they're out to get you?" I ask him.

Banks lights up another cigarette. "Some people in the area are still scared of us. This neighborhood used to be terrible, especially for strangers. Now all that's changed."

"How has it changed?"

"Stone run it," he says. "There's less fighting now. Stones are keeping dope and faggots out of the neighborhood. We even try to keep prostitutes out."

I follow Carl Banks over to the stage where the drums are assembled. It is time for his practice session. "We want to represent to the kids that this is our neighborhood," he continues; "we love it, it's all we got. We want the kids to feel the same way. We try to instill some dignity and pride in them. That's what the P. stands for."

"Are the kids forced to join?" I ask.

Carl considers this. He beats out a roll on one of the drums before answering. "It might have been that way in the old days," he admits. "But there's no pressure now. That's why we're going slow now. The older brothers aren't as active as they should be, some of them are drifting away. Having the peewees with us is OK, but we really need the adults to get our program going good."

"How do you get the kids to join?" I ask.

"They just come in," Banks says. "This is the only place open at night for kids to attend. There's nothing else in the area that's open except the Y.M.C.A. on Seventy-first Street."

Black children, at least those from the Woodlawn area, do come to the Center. They wander in and out of the broken door from the time it is unlocked in the morning until after ten every night. Except for the percussion class, there are few organized activities available for them. For the most part, they stand around the office, expectantly, waiting for something to develop; or else they wander back into the main room and sit in the metal chairs against the walls, under the painted faces of Marcus Garvey, Harriet Tubman, Malcom X, Muhammad Ali, Martin Luther King, and Frederick Douglas. All of the walls in the main room are painted black. And the historical faces are on the right wall. On the left wall, also against a black background, there is a skillfully drawn mural of cosmic forces, the universe in motion, flaming comets, and the overall suggestion of pure energy.

The wall has its symbolic significance, although the children seem to favor the right side of the room and the faces on its wall, behind the metal chairs where they sit. Young people are only barred from the back room when the older Rangers come in—Jeff Fort, Edward Bey, Mickey Cogwell, and other Main leaders—and secret meetings are held. At these times the children wait in the small office, under orders to remain silent, or else they go outside. And whenever they do leave the Center, many of them, especially the younger ones, are quick to call back to anyone still standing in the room: "Stone Run It!"

Congressman Abner Mikva, a white reformer who has fought the Daley machine, was elected to his first term in Congress last November from the Second Congressional District of Chicago, which encompasses the Woodlawn part of the South Side. He is considered by many people in Chicago to be something of an expert on Ranger affairs. Over coffee in his home on South Kenwood Avenue, Mikva offers some of his impressions of the group.

"I'm not a pro-Ranger. If someone commits a crime in the area and if he is a kid, the victim will assume that he's a Ranger, but if the Rangers had committed all the crimes they have been charged with, there would probably have to be at least 100,000 of them, or they would have to be some of the most energetic criminals who ever lived," he says. "I don't think they are civic-minded young reformers. I think that many of them are so alienated that it will be a hard job trying to bring them back into the mainstream. But even if you could bust up the gang structure, it would cost more to keep these kids apart than it would cost to help them do something constructive."

Unlike most groups of young, organized blacks, the Rangers do not seem to be primarily racially oriented. If they believe in any form of black power at all, it's the physical energy which they are attempting to harness in the black community and the economic power which, they believe, will come through constructive uses of that energy. If they hold any political philosophy at all, it is truly a grass roots one: they want to wrest control of their community not so much from the power structure as from the control of an older generation of blacks. They have a large number of the young people; now they are attempting to expand their source of energy by moving into the black, middle-class neighborhoods. And it is in such areas that the limitations of the Ranger appeal are tested. It is within these areas that class lines become more apparent.

Abner Mikva admits the reality of these class lines which contribute to polarization in the black community. "In other neighborhoods they really are recruiting, but these are different kinds of kids. They're middle-class, with two parents in the home—home-owning parents—not kids from broken families. The Rangers are scaring the day-lights out of them. And unfortunately, some of the white churchmen are helping them. I get violent mail, more from the black community than from the white, asking: 'What are you doing defending the Rangers?'

"Some people in the South Woodlawn and Oakland areas would say that the police are too easy on the Rangers," he observes. "Some parents believe that they should crack some skulls. They're scared to death. And these are *black* people. This shows that it's not so much a color thing between the police and the Rangers. I can't recall any time over the last two years when I saw two white policemen alone in a car in the community. They're mostly black and white teams now. Or, if there are two white policemen, they don't respond to street calls. A good part of the G.I.U. is black, and some of these men have done community work in Woodlawn or with Operation Breadbasket.* Some of them are militant, but they're against the Rangers because they're policemen and for obeying the law." Mikva feels, however, that the police do create a problem in the black community, in spite of the sameness of color. "The police insist on using direct, terrorist, violent methods and only succeed in polarizing people. They force people like myself to come out pro-Ranger because of their tactics. I come out saying more in defense of the Rangers than I would like to. Other people come out being more anti-Ranger than they would ordinarily be."

In spite of whatever constructive things they are attempting to do, Mikva says, the Rangers are unpredictable. He recognizes that the community has to deal with them, but, he says, "If they weren't here, I wouldn't invent them."

There was a birthday party given for Joyce Green at the Black P. Stone Youth Center one Saturday night in late November. The girls brought homemade cake

---

* Operation Breadbasket: economic program of S.C.L.C. (the Southern Christian Leadership Conference) whose purpose is to protect black consumers against economic exploitation (e.g. overpricing of goods in ghetto-area supermarkets) and to encourage the distribution and sale of goods produced by black manufacturers.

and potato chips, a bowl of punch, balloons, some cookies, and a few records. Fifteen or so boys, ranging in age from nine to fourteen, sat on the metal chairs against the wall, under the pictures of Marcus Garvey, Malcom X, Muhammad Ali, Martin Luther King, Du Bois, and the others, waiting for the party to start. They sat quietly, waiting for the girls to start the record player. And when the music finally began, the boys cut the lights out and proceeded to select dancing partners. Art Richardson, director of the Center, put the lights on. One of the boys cut them off again. "The lights have to stay on, little brother," Richardson told him.

"We want them out," some of the other boys said.

Richardson motioned for all the boys to come closer to him. "If it's not worth doing in the light," he said, "then it's not worth doing at all." Then he added: "That's what Stone is all about."

The boys considered this, and when Art left the room again one of them cut the lights off. Art came back into the room, put the lights on again, and stood next to the switch. All of the boys left the Center. And after gathering the cakes and the punch and the chips and records, and after breaking all the balloons, the girls followed them.

On Sunday morning before ten o'clock the boy who had made the last effort to darken the room leaned against the locked door of the Center, waiting for it to open. I waited with him.

"Art will be here in a while," I told him.

"I don't like Art," the boy said. "He's mean."

"Do you know what he was trying to tell you last night?" I asked him.

"Yeah," he said. "I know. But nobody wants to dance with girls with the lights on. If the other guys see it, they'll talk about you."

To get out of the wind, while we waited, we went across Sixty-seventh Street to a restaurant and played records and drank Cokes. The boy's name is Danny Jackson. He is in Carl Banks's percussion class. He is fourteen, an eighth-grader, has semi-processed hair, and he never smiles. He wants to be a musician because his father is a musician. He wants to finish high school and then work in a factory because his father works in a factory. He has never thought about college. He does not know much about what it means to be a Blackstone Ranger, but he knows that he is one because he is allowed to walk in and out of the Center whenever he wants. Asked why he likes being a Ranger and living in Woodlawn, he says, "Because Stone Run It!"

Youth Action, a Chicago youth organization funded by the Y.M.C.A. and the Chicago Boys' Club, opened the center on Sixty-seventh and Blackstone as an outpost early in 1968. There was a one-year lease taken on the building. Last September, according to Art Richardson, Youth Action abandoned the outpost. "In October," he says, "I just walked in the Center off the street, pulled the desks out of the basement, and got the Stones to clean up and paint the place. Then the kids started coming in."

Richardson believes that Youth Action abandoned the outpost because it could not reach the youth in the community. I asked Richardson why he thought the Center was more successful under his direction than it was under the administration of Youth Action.

"I'm a legitimate person from the community," he replied. "They were outsiders. The most important thing in this work is understanding the *needs* of the community. I don't profess to be able to *teach,* but I do come from the community. I know the needs. If I had the resources, I would be able to get peoples who are capable of carrying out my program. I'll always welcome agency peoples to come in, and I'll always welcome their ideas, but *we* have to run it."

"How do you know you *can* run it?" I asked him.

Art nodded toward the mural of the solar system on the left side of the main room. "That's energy," he said. "It only responds to the right vibrations. It's that way in nature. An outsider comes in projecting an outside vibration, communicating over the heads of the younger, grass roots brothers. That's wrong. You have to relate to young brothers simply, give off simple vibrations. Otherwise, the little brothers will not respond energetically."

I asked him if any black, and not just Rangers, could produce the right vibrations.

"No," he said. "A lot of Afro brothers don't know how to respond on the street level. So a lot of the little brothers here don't relate to and don't respect some of the outside brothers."

When Art Richardson speaks of "universal vibrations," he seems to imply that the Ranger Nation is not necessarily organized along racial lines; and the fact that many black residents of areas in which they operate condemn their activities serves to support this assumption. Subtle, almost imperceptible class lines are slowly being drawn. And the Rangers seem to be aware of this. "The Chief [Jeff Fort] wants to have white Stones and Mexican Stones and any other kind of person who has the ability to be a Stone," Richardson told me. "He's already extended the invitation."

The directors of the Center have worked out a "Performing Arts Program," with a selected schedule of classes running from Monday through Saturday. Among the classes listed are history, job training, dancing, speeches by interested religious leaders, businessmen, teachers, and entertainers, a class in percussion, boxing, current events, and a class in the importance of education. All these classes are still on paper. So far only one class, the percussion class taught by Lamar Bell and Carl Banks, has started. The others are waiting, like the children who come in every evening, perhaps for financial backing, perhaps for the trust and the enthusiasm of the adult community to grow.

In the middle of November Art Richardson and Lamar Bell began to make plans for the Ranger Thanksgiving show, to draw the interest of the Woodlawn community to the Black P. Stone Youth Center. The floors were cleaned, spotlights were rented or borrowed, posters were distributed over the Woodlawn, Hyde Park, Oakland, and Kenwood areas. Then they went out into the black community to recruit talent.

On the Friday evening just before Thanksgiving the Blackstone Rangers presented their show. It was well attended, but the young people in the audience far outnumbered the adults. A fair contingent of whites from the university areas came, and a TV newsman also came to film the first part of the show. Some of them, the whites, looked puzzled as they tried to comprehend the significance of the mural on the left wall of the auditorium room.

All of those who had volunteered to perform kept their promise. Darlene Blackburn even put on a small fashion show of female African clothing. And although Youth Action provided the microphone and helped the Rangers transport chairs from the Saint Ambrose Church, the show, for the most part, was an independent Ranger accomplishment. Visitors to the Center were asked, but not required, to make a contribution. Raffle tickets for a Thanksgiving turkey were given in exchange for the contributions. The Rangers collected almost seventy dollars.

During the late afternoon and evening there was a steady flow of people in and out of the Center. The Rangers estimate that they had between 300 and 400 people in the Center during the event. The whites who came in the early evening left, almost in a group, when the major part of the show was over. Jeff Fort, Edward Bey, Mickey Cogwell, all in leather jackets, came with some of the other older Rangers, some of them new faces in the Center. They walked, almost nervously, back and forth between the office and the auditorium during most of the show, watching. Occasionally they conferred together at the back of the auditorium, and occasionally they called Art Richardson aside and whispered to him.

Late into the evening, the real Ranger show began.

"We want to present now some Stones who have been on nationwide television," the M. C. said. "They've been on the Smothers Brothers. And they're here, back with us now: The *Blackstone Singers!*"

There were cries of Stone! Stone! from the young people in the audience. Most of the adults had already left.

"We haven't appeared much this year," the spokesman for the group began, "because of what went on in Washington, D.C., and because of what's going on with the Gang Intelligence Unit and with Uncle Toms and Aunt Sallys. And because of what Stones are like in the newspapers and radio and TV. We have not appeared."

The young people, who had been noisy all through the performance of a progressive jazz group some five or six minutes before, were silent as the spokesman finished his introduction. Then there were again cries of "Stone! Stone! Stone Run It!" And after the voices had subsided, the spokesman for the Blackstone Singers made the observation that: "*They're* in trouble, but we're together because Stone *is* going to run it!" Then he announced their first song, a variation of an old Temptations piece, rewritten by the Blackstone Singers. The song was called "You're In Trouble," and they asked everyone to sing along. Everyone did. The young people in the metal chairs, in the dark room, clapped their hands in time to the music and kept yelling "Stone! Stone!" or "Stone Run It!" during places in the song where they did not know the lyrics. The singing went on a long time.

When Jeff Fort moves around, people scatter to make connections with him. He is always moving. And when the word comes that he will eventually be at a certain place, a crowd of people—Rangers and non-Rangers alike—gather at that point to wait for him. He never arrives on time, but everyone waits. And when he does come, all activities and conversations and eyes stop moving and focus on him. Jeff Fort is a man completely aware of himself, and of what he represents. He is playful, full of laughter and good humor with his men. But there is a tenseness and a seriousness behind it all, and his men seem to guard their laughter and movements when he is about. It is obvious that each Ranger has great respect for him. Even the small boys, the "peewees," imitate his hair-style and the way he walks.

Fort may call a single man aside to converse in secret, but one is aware that, somehow, he is always conscious of the movements of everyone else in the room. He had been aware of me, of my movements in and out of the Center, for over four months. It was necessary to have his permission to talk with the Rangers. Then, when the talking was done and the Rangers who had spoken had read in type what they had said to me, I waited, patiently like the others in the Center, for Jeff to give me a few minutes of his time.

"What future plans have you made for the Nation?" I asked him when he walked close to me.

"Did you rap to him, Bop?" he said to Lamar Bell.

"Yeah, Chief," Bell said.

"How is it?"

"It's cool, Chief."

"You got everything I have to say," Jeff said to me.

Perhaps one of the few white men who can claim to have some close associations with the Blackstone Rangers is Charles Lapaglia, the youth worker whom McClellan called to testify to certain allegations made against him and the First Presbyterian Church where he is employed. He lives in Hyde Park and is planning to write a book about the Ranger Nation. Lapaglia is not an easy man to talk to because, like Reverend Fry, he has been subjected to adverse publicity and is suspicious of people who take notes of what he says. But when he begins to talk, he can relate a wealth of detail about the Rangers.

On Christmas Eve, in his home on Kimbark Street, Charles Lapaglia begins to talk. He is frequently interrupted by telephone calls from merchants who have unsold Christmas trees they want the Rangers to distribute in the area. He allows me to read something about the Gang Intelligence Unit he has written. "For both black militants and police," the paper states,

> the issue of who runs it [the black community] is both conscious and immediate. Traditionally, the black community has been controlled by white institutions who disguise the oppressive methods of control by their own institutional rhetoric. The black community has seen through the rhetoric and is attempting to escape oppression by those institutions by asserting their will to determine their own destiny. The order establishing the G.I.U. is the establishment's response to the black community's attempt to gain control of their own destiny. It gives the G.I.U. the direct authority to exercise political control in the black community. Its scope extends far beyond the generally accepted police functions of apprehending law violators. Nor is the intent primarily to control violence through aggressive police action. Its purpose is to maintain tight control over a potentially rebellious colony, and to eliminate all significant opposition. The order deals directly with who runs it. It gives the G.I.U. the power to determine what is good and bad for the community—what services should be subverted—what laws are to be enforced and what laws are to be ignored—what groups should exist and what groups should be destroyed.

Lapaglia claims that the alleged "raid" on the First Presbyterian Church and the firing of guns in the church vault by members of the G.I.U. were a publicity stunt. He maintains that the Treasury Department had asked the church to act as a repository for the Ranger weapons when it began its attempt, after the riots in the summer of 1966, to decrease the level of gun ownership in ghettos all over the country. "In that gun affair," he says, "we were actually a third party in gun-collection activities between the police and the Treasury Department and the Rangers."

A few of the older Rangers hang around the Black P. Stone Youth Center. There are no children. Lamar Bell is there. He is upset because, he says, since the first of December, just after the Thanksgiving show, policemen from the Gang Intelligence Unit have come into the Center at least six times. He says that they park in front of the building from time to time—four men in a car—or else they come in, searching for young boys or for certain of the Main leaders. Bell is worried about the new pop machine which the Center has acquired since the Thanksgiving show, and he says that the policemen have questioned him about it. Bell wants to go to Syracuse, New York, during the Christmas holidays to work with a band there and earn money, but he is reluctant to leave Carl Banks, who is not a union musician and who therefore cannot work with him. Jeff Fort is at home with his wife and two children on Christmas Eve. Some of the other Rangers are said to be out delivering baskets to the poor.

"They are quiet passing out Christmas baskets now," Marshall Patner told me.

"At one time it was a famous thing. They solicited funds last year with a card that said 'Please Give to the Christmas Fund: Blackstone Rangers.' Some of them were arrested on an 1890 ordinance saying you can't solicit funds without disclosing the name of the organization. Their lawyer argued that signing 'Blackstone Rangers' was sufficient. The case was dismissed.

"In some areas the Rangers don't even want to take credit for the good that they do," Patner said. "They worry that it may be turned back on them."

Perhaps James Houtsma, a white, former Gang Intelligence Unit detective who gave damaging testimony against the Blackstone Rangers in Washington, was close to accurate in his assessment of the present dilemma of the group. "A lot of confusion is in their minds," he observed, "because of pressures on them from their affiliation with other groups. Organizations use them as guinea pigs in experimental projects and just brought them along too fast. They started as kids, but with all the pressures, they don't even know themselves now."

But again, perhaps the Rangers are now beginning to understand what they are, or better, the potentially creative power which they represent. Early this year Jeff Fort was invited, it is said by certain Illinois politicians, to attend one of the Inaugural Balls given for President Nixon in Washington. Characteristically, Fort did not go himself, but sent two of the Main leaders to represent the Blackstone Ranger Nation. One of the two men who dressed in tails and who mingled with political dignitaries was Mickey Cogwell. While Cogwell was having "a lovely time" at the Ball (as he later told Chicago reporters), detectives from the G.I.U. came to his house in Chicago to arrest him. After returning to Chicago, Cogwell was asked why the Rangers had accepted an invitation to celebrate the election of Richard Nixon, a man, it has been said, who did not actively court the black voter.

"*We* elected Nixon," Cogwell stated.

"What do you mean?" he was asked. "Do you mean that your 'Don't Vote' campaign helped him to beat Humphrey in Illinois?"

"No," said Mickey Cogwell, who talks very fast. "*We* are the ones who put crime in the streets."

Robert Coles / Whose Strengths, Whose Weaknesses

Interviews, like those provided by Studs Terkel, and the kind of testimony reported here by Robert Coles, help loosen the grip of stereotypes and promote some fresh reality of perception. Coles offers more than that, however. He dramatizes in much of his work the great difficulty of escaping from the most sophisticated of stereotypes: the very tools by which the investigator hopes to produce clues and insights. The "strengths" to which he refers be-

Whose Strengths, Whose Weaknesses

long to the people, Ruth, a black cook in a prosperous house in the Mississippi Delta, her husband, and their seven children; the "weaknesses" belong, he discovers, to himself, an investigator into their lives who is also a child psychiatrist and a research psychiatrist at Harvard. It is the "weaknesses" in his way of thinking that have prevented him from recognizing their "strengths."

But long before he arrives at this admission it is possible to guess from his writing that he is the sort of man discomfited by the usual scholarly or clinical ways of knowing other people. He is, as it were, so well trained that the categories, methods, and predeterminations of his various fields of competence—in psychiatry, sociology, anthropology—precede him to the people or scene at which he is looking and can obscure as much as enlighten his vision. He is initially shy, not only in meeting Ruth and her family but equally so in addressing us: note how much of his vocabulary is put into quotation marks, as if he needs to cast off investigatory jargons before he can truly talk to the reader or to the people he is visiting.

They would be sitting or standing there in front of the cabin, or peering at me from the inside; and I would start slowing myself down. I always needed the extra seconds that a few more steps provide. I would hold my head bowed or pretend to notice something up there in the sky, or over toward the plantation proper. That way their eyes and mine didn't connect, and I didn't have to smile and start saying hello before they could really hear me. That way I could get my mind set for the purpose of my visit, the discovery of certain things, the unearthing of information I thought I ought to possess.

In the beginning ritual masked fear on both sides. I noticed how quiet they all were. My car's noise was a signal to them. They usually heard the car before they saw it because of a sudden turn in the road that made us visible to one another only at the very end of a milelong unpaved, dusty road. By the time I was in sight they had taken up their positions. They seemed rooted. They never looked at me. Or rather, they looked at me when I would not notice. At times I thought them wooden, impassive—and, of course, frightened. When the day came that *I* was not so frightened, their eyes caught mine. I remember being close to grateful that I had someone else's nervousness to observe. Fear has power; power seeks to affirm itself by exertion. And so the edgy, responsive dark irises and white eyeballs belied the calm, the silence. I looked on feet crossed, making still circles out of many legs, and knees crossed, enabling worn, mud-caked shoes to point, but not move an inch. Hungry for the truth, I found it in movement. The eyes did, after all, move and the eyes, my mother told me, were the "windows of the soul." What is more, I thought (or had to think) I saw dilated pupils, which every doctor knows to be a telltale sign that all is not well inside, below, underneath, wherever. (And haven't we learned in this century that any worthwhile truth has to be buried, concealed, and apparent only to the well-trained, in contrast to the well-educated or the desperately or necessarily or naturally sensitive?)

I now realize that my movements and postures underwent the same careful scrutiny that theirs did. Five years later we could reminisce: "I don't believe we knew what you were after. I thought maybe you was here to spy on us, or to sell something. But my sister, she said there was nothing around here to spy, that they didn't already know, the bossman and all. And we don't have the money to buy nothing, so one could be wasting his time every week for that, to sell. Well, we thought there was no harm just waiting to see. Before long you find out everything you ask about—that's what my daddy used to tell me, and he's right.

"Now, with you we figured you was too slow to be with the sheriff, and not sure of yourself, not enough. And my little boy, James it was, he said, 'Mama, the man doesn't always know what to say.' I think maybe that was the first time any of us, we'd seen a man in a suit be shy—I mean be shy himself and be shy with words, too. Then, when you switched to regular clothes, the summer pants, and no more of the tie and like that, well then we decided you might be from up there in Washington, and the government. You know, they're trying to be for us, on our side. I tried to tell people you are a doctor with a college, but they said doctors don't go around the country sitting and talking here and there.

"No, I can't say I ever have been to a doctor's office. They ask you to pay first, and we can't, not first or later. So, it's just as well. They'd give us medicine, if they agreed to see us, and then the next thing you knew there'd be the sheriff here, and we'd be hauled off to jail for not paying the doctor's bill."

But before we can to that kind of mutual confession—in which I replied in kind, about my thoughts about their thoughts, and finally, about my thoughts period—there had to be one long stretch of coming and going, of sly and bewildered talk, of muscles relaxed a bit, quickly tightened up, then once again allowed to slacken, now for a little more time. They began to realize that I was in fact an oddball—who belonged to no recognizable part of their world. And after much too long a period of time I began to realize—an important first step—that they were not the helpless, pitiable objects of study I have to admit I predominantly felt them to be. Oh, it was never necessary to be that blunt. Instead of calling them the wretched of the Southern earth, I could lash out at the South itself: the region's blacks are terribly poor people; they are mercilessly exploited by the individual bossmen, often "managers" or "foremen" who do the rough and tough work, the squeezing dry of lazy bodies, the extraction of ergs from machines that are running at a caloric loss. (But aren't millions of people in other countries and continents even worse off?) And finally, they are badly educated people, barely literate or for all practical purposes illiterate.

All that is true, I thought to myself in the beginning, but someone has to be hardheaded enough to document what oppression does to its victims, how degraded they actually become. Cannot relentless psychological scrutiny turn into the sharpest kind of social criticism? Romantics may speak of a "culture" that peasants have, or include them in some "agrarian tradition"; but I came to them armed with both Marx and Freud, and so in a way any desire to cover up their "condition" and my account of it with soft, understated, merely allusive or (worst of all) ambiguous language was doubly suspect. I knew to ask myself whether I was beholden to the "power structure"—perhaps one I simply don't care to recognize myself, let alone acknowledge to others. I knew to ask myself whether sharecroppers, simple sharecroppers, vulnerable sharecroppers, made me feel scared and to blame for something. And of course I knew that we are all afraid; we all feel at fault; everyone has "work" to do, fears and guilts to understand and "resolve."

So, it is better to be blunt, I decided as I started visiting them. They are "deprived" and "disadvantaged" and all the rest. They need "higher horizons." They should go North. They need "enrichment programs." They are eligible for every "title" in every federal law; and they need more laws with more "titles." *Headstart* is only a beginning. *Leap* is a drop in the bucket. *Upward Bound* * is not "relevant," not to people so badly off, so out of things, so firmly, almost intractably part of—what is it called?—the *lumpenproletariat*.* The only things that will help them, change them, make them part of America, are "massive programs," a "frontal assault" on their poverty, a "basic restructuring" of our society, a "planned attack" on—well, everything "socioeconomic" and "psychosocial" and "sociocultural" that amounts to their very bad lot.

And here are some of the things I found—in one family from the Mississippi Delta—that go to make up that bad lot. The cabin has no heat, no running water, although three miles away there is a faucet and "all the water you can tote." (Not every family in the "area" is that lucky.) And the children: none was born in hospitals; none was delivered by doctors; none has ever seen physicians; none has taken vitamin "supplements" as infants or vitamin pills as children; none is without evidence of illness; and none has any clothes that can be called his, his alone.

"The children, they're the most trouble when they're by their-selves. Most of the time they're together, though. And then I know it's okay." They are indeed together. They sleep together: four in one bed, three in another, all in one room. The other room belongs to their parents, and also serves as the kitchen—and living room and dining room. They share not only space and time but clothes and plates and forks. There are three pairs of shoes to go around, so only certain children can fight their way into them, or fight to fill them up—and then go to church, or, yes, to school. (And, naturally, it is the absence from school that bothers us secular, twentieth-century Americans, for whom education is sacred, a

---

* *Headstart, Leap,* and *Upward Bound:* federally funded education programs for the disadvantaged.
* the *lumpenproletariat:* the underprivileged laboring classes.

way to virtually everything, at least on this earth.) As for the children in that cabin, church wins over school hands down. They fight to go with their parents on Sunday, "to walk with them" as one boy put it, and to sit there and see and hear "everyone get to talking, and have a real good time." Those who stay at home are sad, but they turn happy on Monday if spared school because they still don't have those shoes, or because they feel tired and sick, or because they have to mind the younger ones and help around the house—which means in the fields or around "the place." (It is no mansion. It has no columns, not even a magnolia tree. It is a substantial house, nondescript in style, painted white with green shutters and a green door.)

I don't know what the United States Census Bureau did with the information they obtained from the parents of those seven children. (Such families are sometimes overlooked and not counted at all.) Are they classified sharecroppers or tenant farmers or field hands or employees or retainers or servants or just plain slaves? Are they listed as educated up to this grade or that one? Are they called citizens of this country, or aliens? The questions, the questions you and I answer every decade, can be very embarrassing, although not to "us." They weren't the questions I first had in mind when I started my "study," and they may seem a bit simpleminded to serious social scientists. But they are questions that I rather think no psychoanalytic study of sharecroppers ("in depth," of course) can quite afford to ignore.

"No sir, I can't say I've ever voted," said the father one day when I got around to that issue. "Yes sir, I think I know what you mean. [He knew damn well what I meant.] They have the law now, that says we can go vote. Some are trying it, and some aren't. I'm afraid I haven't got around to it, yet. But I hope to, before I die I hope to. Right now I guess I've some other things to do."

Well, what other things? (Those are the good moments, when the observer is practically invited to ask something.) "I don't know—things like where to live, you know. We're thinking of going North. My sister is up there, in Chicago, and she keeps telling us to leave. But we're afraid to. They don't need a lot of us here, but I hear they don't need us there, either. We don't know what to do. We work on the crops part of the time, but the machines do more and more. There's some cotton they can't get, and there's the cattle and a few vegetables we have. I've got the chores to do. And my wife helps out in The House."

His father "worked on shares." Put differently, his father produced cotton and gave it over to the present bossman's father, and in return they continued to live side by side, the sharecropper and the bossman—on the latter's land. The bossman gave the sharecropper a few hundred dollars to spend during the course of the year, and The House sent over some food and some outgrown and secondhand clothes. The man I know grew up and became a field hand. There was no point getting credit for seed and tools and living quarters and food, and then working the land and receiving a share of the crop's value, minus charges for all the credit advances, including the money required for drainage, for irrigation, for fencing: "The bossman, he came and told me that with my daddy it was one thing, but times are changing, and a lot of the sharecroppers, they're not needed, and he was switching. I could work for him and in return I could live in the house and he would make sure that I never starve to death. And even with the machines coming, we could stay, because my wife is such a good help and especially her cooking."

His wife's cooking: until then I thought I knew everything about her cooking. In the morning she makes breakfast. She fries up some grits and they are washed down with either a coke or some coffee. There is no such thing as lunch. The children have another coke, and some very cheap candy like licorice or sugar-coated gum, which they chew and chew, and chew dry, and take out of their mouths and stretch and tear into fragments and laugh over and play with and stick upon one another. The parents also have another coke and some candy, which they eat with greater reserve. Supper is the main meal. It is served early, about half past four or five, and includes without exception fried potatoes and more grits and greens; and bread with peanut butter sometimes, and fatback sometimes. Every once in a while a stew appears, made of potatoes and gravy and pork. Even more unusual is a soup, the product of boiled bones and potatoes and greens. For dessert there is another coke, and maybe more candy.

I asked about cooking and I heard this: "We have practically no money, so it's hard to get by. We grow a little, but we haven't much land to do it on, and the bossman wouldn't want us spending too much time on that. My kids grow some flowers, the zinnias. You can't eat zinnias, I know it, but you can like them—just like you can rest beside a sunflower. We get our greens from the yard, and some tomatoes, though they don't last long. We don't have the money to buy the foodstamps. We get the commodities, and that's how we live. We'd be dead right now without the lard and flour they give, the government. Yes sir, everyone of us would be dead. I try to fill my kids' stomachs up as best I can. I figure if they doesn't hurt them too much, their stomachs, well then, that's good. They gets their energy from the candy and the coke. They take a drink and bite on the licorice, and I know they've got their sugar in them and can keep going."

But her husband was talking about the cooking she did for the bossman. I asked her about that and she told me: "Oh, yes. I've been helping her out for years. I go up there and do what she tells me. I don't plan anything. She always says to me: 'Ruth, I've planned today's menus out.' Then she lists what I've got to do and I go ahead and get to work there."

She gets to work in a spacious, well-equipped kitchen. The sink is stainless steel. The stove is an electric range. The refrigerator is huge, and next to it stands a freezer, and next to *it* stands a washing machine and then a dishwasher. ("I do the dishes and some laundry, too.") Obviously, she has a few minutes to relax, because there is a small television set on one counter—and also a waffle iron, and a toaster, and a mixer for "working up" cakes, and an electric knife sharpener, which also takes care of pencils. I never would have seen all those electrically run gadgets had I not decided to compare her place of work with her place of residence. I knew her bossman well, and, in fact, once heard him say this about Ruth: "She's a fine woman, and so is her husband a fine man. They do an honest day's work, and we'll never let them go without a roof over their heads. I'm going to build them a new place, as a matter of fact. We're letting a lot go, though a lot of them don't want to. I tell them they may as well go North. We can't use them here. One by one they slip away; but you know, we have quite a few still here, right on our land. Eventually I suppose we'll only have maybe five families left here. Imagine that! It's hard for me to believe, after all these years with about a hundred or more. But I sure hope Ruth never leaves. I told my wife I think we'd near starve to death. She's the best cook in this county, easily."

I discovered what he meant. I had lunch with him and his wife. I had a big lunch, that started with a glass of tomato juice and a neatly cut piece of lemon. Then Ruth served us hot diced chicken and rice with raisins mixed in and peas and chutney on the side. And finally we had deep-dish apple pie and ice cream and coffee. It was all tasty, all neatly and attractively presented. The rice was fluffy and warm and covered with butter and seasoned just right. The chicken was cut perfectly, not too small and not too large. The peas were not overcooked; they were fresh, not frozen or canned, and like the rice, delicately salted. The pie had a light crust, and inside were warm tart apples, neither too syrupy nor dry. I was afraid I was going to be told that the ice cream was homemade, but no, it was store-bought: "It used to be we'd make our ice cream here, when I was a child. But you know it's too easy to buy it, and I think Ruth has enough to do as it is." I had commented on how good the ice cream was, and on how good the ice cream was at a nearby (and larger) plantation, where it was a bit ostentatiously, if generously, handed over with the hostess' advice from across the table that "Mary-Jean makes it, fresh every day." Ruth's mistress had been there many times—and clearly regretted the unfavorable comparison that I suppose I had unwittingly made.

When I left the house my stomach was filled with Ruth's food, and my mind was finally brought up short, the way it should have been months before. I kept on thinking of Ruth and that kitchen and of all the Ruths in America. I was there in that county to "study" her and her family, to get to know how they *really* live and think and feel. I had spent months visiting them and being observed by them and taking stock of all sorts of things they said and did. I was really rather proud of myself; and I was ashamed, too. I had made the effort to reach Ruth's family; and in so doing found out once again how awful their kind of American experience is—in contrast, say, to mine.

But guilt masks many things, one of which is pride. The guilt I easily knew about was the kind I easily notice in both myself and in patients. We have so much; others have so little. We feel ashamed of ourselves because we know the inadequacy of whatever good deeds we have done, whatever goodwill we feel.

The guilt I began to feel for the first time after that lunch was something else, though; it had to do with the recognition of a willful kind of ignorance and blindness—mine. For a long time I had known that Ruth worked for the bossman's wife—cooked and cleaned and dusted for her, looked after her clothes and her dishes and her bedroom and bathroom. I knew all that, but I never really allowed myself to go any further; in fact, to bridge the two worlds that Ruth did every day. It was all right, of course, for *me* to bridge those two worlds; but Ruth in my mind had to be a sharecropper's wife, pure and simple. (And don't thousands of them work in those big houses in one capacity or another?)

Perhaps—to be generous to myself—I was merely a pedantic, unimaginative, anxious "investigator," who was slightly overwhelmed by all he was meeting up with. The search for order and clarity can often help a case of the nerves, can help a person come to terms with his worries and fears as well as his "methodology." Somehow a confusing, ambiguous, irony-filled world becomes a little more manageable when this man is distinguished from that one; and if they both can be placed on a graph or two and made part of a few percentages and made to possess a few "attitudes" and "beliefs" and "habits" and "problems"—well then, all the better. Ruth and her mistress live worlds apart on that plantation. I was busy finding out precisely how far apart; and every liberal bone in my body, I assure you, was full of the proper mixture of outrage and pity and sadness. In my cool, farsighted, evenhanded moments I felt sorry not only for Ruth but for her mistress, a kind, soft-spoken woman who speaks ill of no one and at moments can challenge my stereotypes as significantly as Ruth eventually did: "I have a lot of respect for Ruth, and you know we have many like her in Mississippi. She is a good person, and we have never had cause to complain about her. I never made this world, but I'll admit there are times when I say to myself that there but for the grace of God go I. What I mean is that I do believe Ruth has the same intelligence we do, and if things were different—well, I think she could be, well, I think she could be just like me, more or less. She could run the house, I'm sure, and plan things and make sure everything goes according to schedule."

When I heard that, I was in danger of being a very smug listener. I felt like getting up and screaming at the polite and honorably frank speaker. I felt like telling her that Ruth already was running her house, that without Ruth the house would be messy and disorganized, and its occupants would find mealtimes a lot less pleasant. But I was really agitated because I was hearing from someone else a very familiar kind of condescension, one that I fear is all too much the property of people like me rather than of Southern white ladies who "favored" Barry Goldwater * and refer to themselves as "of conservative disposition." Neither she nor I—although I have to say, she at least a little better than I—seemed

---

* Barry Goldwater: U.S. Senator from Arizona (1953–); leader of the extreme conservative wing of the Republican party when he ran against President Johnson in the 1964 election.

able to talk about the extent of Ruth's social and cultural achievement. Yes, we know that she is a good cook; and her mistress *senses* (and perhaps does not dare let her mind become more explicit) that without such "nigra help" life would be far different; and all along I knew, prided myself on knowing, that Ruth is a fine, hardworking, reliable person who is exploited and only appreciated in ways that don't cost a cent. But in the last analysis (the commendably unsparing one) I had to conclude that Ruth lacked dignity, even as her mistress knows that Ruth is only potentially capable of being dignified. And, needless to say, I had set out to study the consequences of the indignity America has visited upon people like Ruth: what happens to a woman who is stripped of her legal rights, her rights as a citizen, and kept socially apart as well as miserably poor.

I think it was the array of electric appliances in the kitchen that first made me stop and think and realize how much had been escaping my notice. Ruth was the master of all those machines. She was a gracious hostess, who served fine meals. She knew better than I where on the table a lot of those extra forks or spoons go. She knew her spices. She knew how to take care of the finest, most expensive clothes. She knew which plants needed a lot of water, which very little. She knew how to care for flowers. I remember my mind latching on to that last fact. I remember deciding to ask Ruth about those flowers: "Well, she likes her flowers. She grows a lot of them, and there will be times when she has to send for them, from the store, you know. I fix them up. I know which vases to use for which flowers, and how she likes them. She used to say 'good'; but now she just expects it, I guess—that I'll do right. You see what I mean?"

Of course I hadn't been seeing; that is the point. I had been figuring out how Ruth lives, and how her mind deals with "reality" and what psychological "defenses" she used. I had been developing a very clear idea of the hardships she faces every day, and even the stubborn persistence she possesses. I had declared her in my mind a desperate but inventive woman who somehow, beyond all explanation, endured. I was not so sure that she would, as Faulkner predicted, prevail; but I was prepared to say it was possible. I had at least shaken off the simpleminded view that the poor and even persecuted people are *only* hurt, sad, beaten down in spirit, deracinated, and branded with the unforgettable "mark of oppression." I was not going to become a "romantic" about Ruth and her family, but I would no longer be a slobbering, so-called reformer who needs the people whose cause he espouses to be as down-and-out, wretched and shattered as possible. Life is hard and even brutal for Ruth, and to survive has cost her a lot. But she is shrewd and ingenious, I had gradually persuaded myself; in the words of contemporary psychoanalysis, her mind has learned to be "adaptive"—and so has her overworked, tired body.

For all that generosity, for all the evolution my mind had been going through before I ate Ruth's lunch in her mistress' home, I had failed miserably to realize that Ruth is a *cultured lady,* a woman who knows her cuisine and her horticulture. Her manners are impeccable; her sense of timing in polite company faultless. She knows what people want and need and deserve and she gives it all to them. She is intuitive and sensitive. Her sensibilities are refined; and she even is at ease with our reigning technology. Her hands deal with the racks of the dishwasher, the shelves of the freezer, the clocks and pointers of the stove—and that pencil sharpener. ("The mister, he taught me how, and now missus gives me the pencils every once in a while, from all over the house. She says the noise of the machine gets to her; it makes her nervous. So she has to leave the room before I start.")

I am not saying that suddenly my mind came to its senses and fought its way to a more accurate and honorable picture of Ruth and her family. But over time, starting with that lunch, I did come to see more and more of Ruth's life, and the more I saw the harder put I was to fit her into convenient categories I had brought with me when I first met her. She is still poor. She is still disenfranchised. She continues to speak ungrammatical English, and so I have to edit her remarks. To this day she needs a doctor, a lawyer, a teacher—as do her children and her husband. She has no more money now than she ever did. And *she* would like a different life—so who am I to wax ecstatic over the countryside of the lovely Delta, the trees and flowers near her cabin, the rich, productive land, the mighty and almost mythic river than she can see by taking a good long walk for herself. Yet, who am I to do something else, deny her life its achievements and its ironies and its ambiguities, refuse her mind the sense of style and the subtlety it surely demonstrates all the time?

At times I am pleased with my own ability to leave Cambridge, Massachusetts, and somehow come to a reasonably strong and valuable "relationship" with a family like Ruth's. I am not so pleased, however, when I remind myself how long it took me as an anthropologist or psychiatrist or whatever, to recognize *Ruth's* experience and competence. She, too, goes back and forth between two worlds; every day she does. She, too, watches others and tries to help them out. She, too, takes away burdens from people and makes them feel less harried, less at the mercy of this and that. Like a "trained mental health professional" (as they rather ponderously call themselves) she adjusts herself to the lives, the problems, the needs of others. She doesn't get "overinvolved," though. When she and they part company, she knows how to go back to her own life and live it. If she has any "fantasies" about life over there in The House, she controls them, buries them or, more likely, lets them quietly come and quickly go. ("Oh, every once in a while I ask myself why God did things the way he did, and made me me and her her; but pretty soon there's the next thing I have to tend to.") Ignorant and barely literate, she is sophisticated and worldly; and as the bossmen in my profession say about precious few of us, she has "very good ego-defenses." She has taught me a lot I rather expected to find out; but most of all she has taught me about the weaknesses in my way of thinking that prevented her various strengths from being immediately and properly obvious to me. The arrogant man wants to make his world the whole world. He pushes himself ahead of anyone in sight and blinds himself to all sorts of things that he might see in others. When he is safely up front he may mellow, and here or there grant a few favors; but without prodding, I fear, only a few.

Edmund Wilson / The Iroquois Resurgence

Mr. Wilson likes to find out about things, and when he discovered that he knew very little about the original inhabitants of America he proceeded to remedy his ignorance. His book, a collection of articles describing his new knowledge and how he got it, is called *Apologies to the Iroquois*—apologies, because he had throughout his life slighted them by neglect and ignorance, as, he feels, most Americans do. In this passage he deals discursively with several aspects of the American Indian and his life in a society dominated by the interests and ethics of the white invader. Writing in 1966 he refers to the world politics of that time (the Algerian war of liberation was still in progress) and to the exchange between Khrushchev and Dulles on Bertrand Russell's open letter of 1957. Khrushchev referred to a fact that was conveniently neglected in the U.S.: the dispossession by force and fraud of the Indian.

From this point Wilson goes on to consider the unreflecting way in which it is assumed (perhaps one should say *was* assumed, since there is evidence that the situation has altered and people are more conscious of the existence and values of the Indian) that the imported American way of life is so self-evidently a good one that the Indians would join it if they could. (In fact their own is not only very different but in many ways desirable.) Having no concept of private property and quite different notions of social pleasure and prestige, they were at the outset ill-adapted for the way of life forced onto them by legislators whose financial and moral interests so conveniently and convincingly coincided that they listened to no opposition. When Indians did intelligently adapt, they were ousted anyway, sometimes at gunpoint. And Wilson shows that they have, even now, maintained some of their ancient mores in a society which may use them as steelworkers rather than as hunters and which disposes of the whole notion of Indians in terms of a vulgarized commercial mythology.

Here Wilson, asserting that the Iroquois "resurgence" has been caused by further inroads on their property by state and federal governments, swings round into a general denunciation of similar interference in the private property of all modern Americans, including himself. The building of highways, dams, and so on, with a ruthless disregard for the natural scene and the quiet enjoyment of one's property he describes as a compulsive and unstoppable bureaucratic drive.

As it will be seen, this is a curiously constructed piece; the swing away from the ostensible subject is very marked and might be thought self-indulgent. It is true that the author is interested in himself, that he is not only apologizing to the Iroquois but explaining that he has had to put up with interference of much the same kind from a bureaucracy whose values he rarely approves. And this introduces a difficult consideration. For an author as important as Wilson seems to have a right, which almost at times becomes a duty, to give expression to his own personality as part of the interest of the situation described. In short, one ought to consider whether this study of the Indians, if by some lesser hand, would not be subject to the criticism that it had serious rhetorical and structural flaws. There are things an important writer can do that are not permissible to others. Or so it might be argued.

What are the causes, at the present time, of this reawakening of Indian nationalism?

For one thing, it is a part of the world-wide reaction on the part of the non-white races against the meddling and encroachments of the whites. The leaders of these Indian movements are well aware of what is going on in Asia and Africa. They know that they came from the Orient—many of them, as I have said, could be easily mistaken for Mongolians—and they know what has been happening in China. They also know that India has freed herself, that Ghana is now a free state, and that the Algerians are struggling to become one. They have sensed that the white man has been losing his hold, and, like the rest of the non-white races, they are sick of his complacency and arrogance. They find this a favorable moment for declaring their national identity because, in view of our righteous professions in relation to the Germans and Russians, they know that, for the first time in history, they are in a position to blackmail us into keeping our agreements and honoring their claims. When in November, 1957, Bertrand Russell * addressed, in the English *New Statesman,* an open letter to Khrushchyóv and Eisenhower, imploring them to drop their nonsense and forget about the possibility of annihilating one another, our Secretary of State Dulles, answering for the President, replied that "the creed of the United States" was "based on the tenets of moral law"—derived from "the religious convictions that guided our forefathers in writing the documents that marked the birth of America's independence"—and that this creed "rejected war except in self-defense." The

---

* Bertrand Russell: (1872–1970), British philosopher; after World War II, Russell became an outspoken pacifist and a powerful advocate of unilateral nuclear disarmament.

Soviets, on the other hand—quite unlike the American colonists—had "seized power by violence of an intensity and extent that shocked the civilized world. It has extended its power by violence, absorbing one nation after another by force or the threat of force." Khrushchyóv could not afford to let pass the marvellous opportunity offered him. He sent the *Statesman* a long rebuttal, in which, before getting on to the Mexican War, the Spanish colonies and Guatamala, he—or whoever does his history—retorted, "What about the Indians?" His description of our dealings with them is somewhat inaccurate, but he is near enough to the truth to be able to score a telling point in invoking their fate to support him in his statement that, "One must have a great belief in miracles to appeal to the memory of peoples and say that in the history of the United States there has not been any occasion 'when an effort has been made to spread its creed by force of arms.' " And this point has occurred to the Iroquois.* It has also troubled Mrs. Roosevelt, who has devoted at least two of her columns to the complaints of the Six Nations; and it may be that—though there has always been a certain oscillation in our policy in regard to the Indians—the decision in favor of the Tuscaroras * and the non-materialization of the Kinzua Dam have been due to a certain embarrassment vis-à-vis the rest of the world. For whatever the difference in scale, is there any real difference in principle between uprooting whole communities of well-to-do Russian farmers and shipping them off to the Urals, and depriving the Senecas of the use of their lands in such a way as to shatter their republican unit, and dismissing this intelligent and capable people to go and find homes where they can?

It is easy to ignore the Indians, and I am not, as I showed at the beginning of these articles, myself in any position to take a self-righteous tone about them, having assured my visitor from England that there were almost no Indians left in New York State and that the Mohawks were the same as the Mohicans—a people, once the enemies of the Mohawks, of whom, I believe, at the present time, only a few descendants survive in the neighborhood of Groton, Connecticut. I apologize to the Iroquois for this, and I want here to try to explain why it is possible thus to disregard the Indians and why it is difficult for people who care about them to get other people interested in them. The primary reason, of course, is that, having come here a long time before us—the ethnologists talk in terms of twenty or twenty-five thousand years—the Indians do not fit into, and for the most part do not want to fit into, the alien life we have brought here. It

---

* the Iroquois: a confederacy of Indian tribes in western New York which was formed in the sixteenth century and originally consisted of Five Nations: Mohawk, Oneida, Onondaga, Cayuga, and Seneca. When the Tuscaroras joined in 1715, the league became known as the Six Nations; during the seventeenth and eighteenth centuries, the Iroquois were an important political force.

* the decision in favor of the Tuscaroras: the New York State Power Commission wanted to construct a power plant in the Niagara Falls area; the reservoir connected with this plant would have flooded a large part of a Tuscarora reservation, and when the Tuscaroras protested, the Federal Power Commission ruled in their favor (1959).

seems quite self-evident to many of us that the "American Way of Life" is a wonderful thing and that everyone ought to want to share in it. Why can't they —like the Germans, the Italians, the Scandinavians and everybody else— become good American citizens, enjoying our privileges and luxuries? Wouldn't they, obviously, be much better off? Isn't it the trouble that they are not really up to it? This point of view has always been a popular one. But the nature of the obstacles it is bound to encounter is admirably shown in a recent book—the best possible short guide to the Indian situation—*Indians and Other Americans: Two Ways of Life Meet,* by Harold E. Fey and D'Arcy McNickle. One of the most serious of these obstacles is that the Indian's relation to the land he inhabits is entirely different from ours. The early Europeans imagined that the Indians of the East were rovers, who lived and hunted at random wherever they pleased. They were mistaken: the tribes had their separate tracts that were marked off by definite boundaries. See, for example, the Six Nations map in Morgan's *League of the Iroquois,** which shows how a strip of the Iroquois territory was assigned to each of these nations. But the fundamental difference between the European conception of property and that of the American Indians was that Indian property was held in common. The Indian had no idea of legal title, of the individual ownership of land, and the white man was incapable of thinking in any other terms. In 1879, a General Allotment Act was introduced in Congress. The object, or ostensible object, was to encourage the Indians to engage in farming by breaking up the reservations. The fragments were to be allotted, a hundred and sixty acres to heads of families and eighty to single persons. The remainder could be bought by the government, and the individual owners, after twenty-five years, were authorized to sell their land. A Sioux agent had reported to the Indian Commissioner that "as long as the Indians live in villages, they will retain many of their old and injurious habits. Frequent feasts, heathen ceremonies and dances, constant visiting—these will continue as long as people live together in close neighborhoods and villages. I trust that before another year is ended, they will generally be located upon individual land or farms. From that date will begin their real and permanent progress." Carl Schurz, then Secretary of the Interior, had recommended the allotment system. "The enjoyment and pride of the individual ownership of property is one of the most effective civilizing agencies." The bill encountered opposition. "If I stand alone in the Senate," said a senator from Colorado, "I want to put upon the record my prophecy in this matter, that when thirty or forty years will have passed and these Indians shall have parted with their title, they will curse the hand that was raised professedly in their defense to secure this kind of legislation, and if the people who are clamoring for it understood Indian character, and Indian laws, and Indian morals, and Indian religion, they would not be here clamoring for this at all." A minority of a Com-

---

* L. H. Morgan, *League of the Iroquois:* (1851), available in a paperback reprint (New York: Corinth Books).

mittee on Indian Affairs expressed a similar opinion: "However much we may differ with the humanitarians who are riding this hobby, we are certain that they will agree with us in the proposition that it does not make a farmer out of an Indian to give him a quarter section of land. There are hundreds of thousands of white men, rich with the experiences of Anglo-Saxon civilization, who cannot be transformed into cultivators of the land by any such gift. . . . The real aim of this bill is to get at the Indian lands and open them up to settlement. The provisions for the apparent benefit of the Indian are but the pretext to get at his lands and occupy them. . . . If this were done in the name of greed, it would be bad enough; but to do it in the name of humanity, and under the cloak of an ardent desire to promote the Indian's welfare by making him like ourselves, whether he will or not, is infinitely worse." But the act was passed in 1887, and had the effect, say Fey and McNickle, of depriving the Indians of ninety million of their hundred and forty million acres. Few of them had taken to farming. Even if they had been eager to farm, they had no money to invest in equipment or livestock, and since their allotments were held in trust, they were unable to get commercial credit. If they did not dispose of their property, and it was divided among their descendants, there was soon very little for anybody left. Nor had they been induced by the dominant race to abandon their "frequent feasts," their "heathen ceremonies and dances" and their "constant visiting." A new bill now before the legislature, against which, in September of '58, an Indian congress in Montana was held to protest, is a proposed further step in this same direction. It has been said of it by Mrs. La Verne Madigan, executive director of the Association on American Indian Affairs: "The question is whether the Indian tribes are communities of people or hills of ants. They should not have to live in perpetual fear that the federal foot is going to squash them to death. Yet this is the situation in which they exist under an on-again off-again application of federal pressures that would be considered intolerable by any white community."

It should be noted that the result of the first great attempt on the part of the Indians to assimilate themselves was not such as to encourage them further. Toward the end of the eighteenth century, the Iroquois's able cousins, the Cherokees, who inhabited the Alleghanies and other regions further south, set out to master European techniques and to live as the white men did. They exchanged their tribal lands for farm implements, spinning wheels, looms and other tools of civilization. In the twenties of the following century, the Cherokee leader Sequoya invented a syllabary for their language, and the Cherokees began getting out a newspaper called the *Cherokee Phoenix*. In 1826, the editor of this paper was able to report in Philadelphia to the First Presbyterian Church on the remarkable progress of his people in raising sheep, pigs and cattle, blacksmithing and milling, spinning and weaving, roadbuilding, ferrying and schooling. "In one district there were, last winter, upward of a thousand volumes of good books." The reward for this effort of adaptation was Andrew Jackson's Indian Removal Act of 1830—as a result of which the literate Cherokees, along with less adaptable tribes, were moved to the primitive wilderness beyond the Mississippi. Some of them took to their hills; but most of them—driven out at the point of the gun—made the journey in winter on foot, and a quarter of their number perished.

In a society of competing property-owners, it is easy to ignore or to underrate a people who do not care about this kind of prestige. To the white man who passes through a reservation—or through parts of certain reservations—it is likely to look like a slum. He will note that many houses are unpainted, and if he should happen to visit one, he might find that the rooms were littered, that the stuffing was protruding from old armchairs and that the paper was peeling off the walls. But this would give him no true index to the quality of the inhabitants, who might be people of much brains and fine character. It has, in fact, been a tradition of the *royaneh,* the families from which chiefs are chosen, that they should not be ostentatious. Indifference to money and belongings was a sign of superiority. Cadwallader Colden, in his history,* speaks of the contempt of the Indians for the traders with whom they dealt: they were far more at home with the officers of the monarchs across the sea; and the authors of *Indians and Other Americans* quote one of the early Indian agents as complaining that the colonies have "seldom if at all sent proper persons" to treat with the Indians. "But the management of them has often been left to traders, who have no skill in public affairs, are directed only by their own interests, and being generally the lowest kind of people, are despised and held in great contempt by the Indians as liars, and persons regarding nothing but their own gain." The Iroquois does not become a farmer, and he does not become a bourgeois. If he prospers, he lives "like a gentleman," as a white observer said to me—though this word belongs to our system, not theirs, and is likely to be misleading, for though it is accurate as applied to the Iroquois in suggesting dignity and leisure and a love of independence, it is less so in implying a place which is kept so far as possible in good repair and a pride in interior decorating.

The most curious feature of Iroquois life, as transposed into terms of the twentieth century, and one of those that are most difficult for the white man to grasp, is the substitution of iron and steel work for the ancient male pursuits of hunting and fighting. A good deal of light has been thrown on the relation between these two kinds of activity, the substitution in the modern age of one for the other, in a paper by Dr. Morris Freilich called *Cultural Persistence Among the Modern Iroquois.*[1] He shows that the steelworkers travel in bands as the hunters and warriors did, leaving their women at home, and that they amuse themselves on their return—as they did in the past—by sitting together and boasting about the feats they have performed in their travels and the dangers they have overcome. Mr. Freilich believes that the foreman, or "pusher," who bosses a band of young steelworkers corresponds to the head of a party of war-

1. *Anthropos,* Volume 53, 1958, published in Fribourg, Switzerland.

* Cadwallader Colden, *History of the Five Indian Nations:* (1727), available in reprint (Ithaca: Cornell University Press).

riors, and that the prizes, a new car or a well-stuffed wallet, that the adventurer brings back to the reservation, correspond to the captives or loot carried off from a raid on the enemy. The discrepancy between the new occupation and the old way of living and worshipping is thus largely in the eye of the white beholder; but unless one has studied the Indians, one is liable to the alternative errors of assuming, from their homes, that they are shiftless or, from their expert mechanical competence, that they ought to, and, therefore, that they must, desire to live as we do.

    I have shown in various ways the impingement of the white man's gimmicks on even the stoutest of the reservations; yet the Indians have never ceased to be critical of the alien civilization. Their recent interpretations of their prophecies tend to show that they are becoming skeptical as to the value of white inventions which negate human life itself. Are the Indians, they ask, really conscienceless savages and the white men enlightened Christians? I have heard some fine Bernard Shaw speeches delivered by eloquent Indians: Ray Fadden and William Rockwell (the latter a solitary Oneida, over ninety and incredibly vigorous, who possesses a one-man reservation, of which his family had been deprived by the foreclosure of a mortgage, after the rest of the Oneidas had been lured to Wisconsin, but which—by bringing suit on the valid grounds that such liens on Indian property are illegal—he finally recovered for himself). "The white man," Ray Fadden will say, "has invented an Indian in his own image: unforgiving, vindictive, treacherous. The Indian is none of these things and never was. The white man has foisted on the Indian all the worst of his own characteristics." "Does the Indian boy," demands Rockwell, "come home with a gun and shoot his father and mother and his little brothers and sisters? Did he ever amuse himself by sitting in a bar and watching a television show in which somebody else is sitting in a bar and another man comes in, and they look at one another like cats, and then 'Bang, bang, bang!—Bang, bang, bang!'?" And it is impossible not to be disgusted—when one has seen even a little of the real Indian world—by our surreptitious efforts, on the one hand, to despoil and disperse the Indians and, on the other, our loud exploitation of literary Indian romance: the Mohawk Airlines, the Pontiac cars, the Hotels Onondaga and Iroquois, and the Seneca Cocktail Lounges. This romance—from James Fenimore Cooper to the latest galloping Western—is at least as much a myth of the whites as the double-dealing fiend of Ray Fadden, also a creation of Cooper's, in whose novels the Iroquois are the horrible Mingoes bedevilling the noble Mohicans. A scene that sticks in my mind as a synthesis of incongruities is a Seneca living room, with a handsome boy, naked to the waist, working over an airplane model while his sister, somewhat younger, was studying a school textbook called *How We Became Americans,* in which the Indians got very little attention. The lively and handsome mother—having first made the boy put his shirt on—served us an excellent dinner in the style of upstate New York, but, unlike a New York State matron, did not sit with the men and the children but served us standing up and presided over the conversation. She did not give us the conventional invitation to eat. "All I say," she announced, "is ——," some word that made everybody laugh. I was told that it meant, "Beware!" She had with Fenton—through his standing as a member of a clan and some kinship which this implied—what I had read about in anthropological works as a "joking relationship" but had never seen illustrated before. This relationship was extended to me, and the evening became a contest of repartee. Had we all "become Americans"?

But what has set off the Iroquois resurgence and caused it to gather power is the gluttonous inroads on tribal property—such as have also been felt by the whites as an encroachment on personal property—by state and federal projects. The struggle to restrain these projects is undoubtedly at the present time one of the principle problems of American life. In a letter to his English publisher, the Russian Boris Pasternák has explained that he wanted, in *Doctor Zhivago,* to dramatize the conflict of the modern individual with the forces of the centralized state, which were becoming more formidable all over the world, and for reasons that were sometimes contradictory. Some years before these articles were written, the writer, who then lived on Cape Cod and who still spends a part of the year there, was informed that a new state highway was to run straight past his front porch in such a way as to shave off his whole front lawn. I made strong representations in Boston to the Department of Public Works and eventually averted this nuisance; but in the spring of 1958, it was suddenly announced to the inhabitants of the Cape that, at the cost of dispossession of some seven hundred families, many of whom had lived there for generations, almost the whole eastern part of Cape Cod was to be turned into a national park. The indifference or opposition to local zoning laws had partly led to this, and we had been quite prepared for the government to take steps to protect the beaches, but not, without any previous consultation, to be told we were to be turned wholesale out of our homes, whether located on beaches or not—for the park, at the Provincetown end, was to cover the whole breadth of the Cape. The resistance was prompt and determined, and a meeting at which questions were supposed to be answered but for the most part were simply evaded by Park Commissioner C. L. Wirth was anything but reassuring. We presently learned that a bill—apparently in counterattack to the local resistance—had just been presented to Congress on behalf of the Department of the Interior, of which the purpose, in the words of an editorial in the *Saturday Evening Post* of July 18, 1959, was "arbitrarily to take over sections of Cape Cod or any other area regarded by the National Park Service as suitable for a park, with scant regard to local interest. Instead of adhering to the usual practice of designating specific areas designed for park purposes, Senator [Richard] Neuberger's bill authorizes the Secretary of the Interior to take over not more than 100,000 acres distributed as he may decide among any three areas in the whole country. . . . There is no opportunity of a debate in Congress on the merits of the areas selected, because their identity would be the secret of the National Park Service until it elects to announce them. No reference is made to an effort to consult the owners of the desired property on how it would be 'procured.' " I have learned also while working on the Indians that Shrewsbury, New Jersey, the little crossroads community in which my father was born and where my grandfather preached for fifty years, which is still one of the most attractive of the old New Jersey towns—the Episcopal Church has a communion service donated by Queen Anne and a charter from George III—is to be gutted, unless the people find a device to prevent it, by another of these state highways at the expense of encroachment on the churchyard and the destruction of a seventeenth-century house; and, returning last summer to the village in New York State in which I am writing this, I found that—to the horror of many of the inhabitants—a planting of splendid elms that had made a majestic approach to Boonville on the road that leads from Utica was in process of being chopped down in order to transform this road into a four-lane highway for trucking. I should have said, when I first started out on my travels in Iroquoia, that I myself was almost as much a member of a half-obsolete minority as these even more old-fashioned Americans of twenty thousand years ago, but I have come to believe that there are many white Americans who now have something important in common with these recalcitrant Indians, that the condition of being an American, whether from A.D. or B.C., should imply a certain minimum security in the undisturbed enjoyment of our country. If it was true that one found, in Niagara Falls, a good deal of sympathy on the part of the whites for the fight of the Tuscaroras, this attitude, I was told, when they won their decision from the Federal Power Commission, turned soon into a kind of resentment: "If the Indians can stand up to the Power Authority, why can't we white voting Americans?" The Indians have actually a better case: they can appeal to the terms of their treaties. But by defending their rights as Indians, they remind us of our rights as citizens.

One cannot, of course, when one contemplates these great highways and seaways and dams, fail to be much impressed by the genius of engineering they represent, by the practical imagination, the delicate mechanical devices and the complicated computations that have gone to lay down and erect them, to start them going and to keep them running, to deepen and divert the great waterways, to light more lamps and to set more wheels turning, to enmesh all mankind, to girdle the earth. But it is well to remember the beavers. The beavers are engineers. A friend of mine in Massachusetts, who has recently retired to the country, imported a pair of beavers, which were furnished him by the State Division of Fisheries and Game, and put them to live in a little stream that runs through his rather wild place. These animals proceeded immediately to construct an enormous dam, and thus flooded a whole area of woodland. The trees are now broken-off sticks that prick dismally out of the beaver pond, in the middle of which humps an igloo bristling with gray dead twigs; the managerial offices are here, the housing for the personnel. All around this, the forest has been devastated. The stumps end in pyramidal spikes, produced by symmetrical chiselling; the trunks lie rotting on the ground, with the bark partly or wholly gnawed off.

The beavers are indifferent to landscape, to the convenience of human beings, whom they fearlessly swim up to and stare at, and whom they try to frighten away by insolently slapping their tails. They build burrows as well as lodges, to take refuge in if the lodge should be threatened. They plan and put through canals and they clear away the brush on the edges of these in order to transport the branches which they anchor underwater for their winter store. When anything goes wrong with the dam, they immediately swim out to repair it, each assigning itself a specific task. They are untiring and, if not interfered with, can go on with their operations along infinite networks of streams and through infinite generations. The descendants of my friend's beaver couple have now built a whole new series of dams and lodges. When they started on a stream in which he did not want them, he had to destroy one of their dams eleven times—taking a pickaxe to it: their mud construction is almost as tough as masonry—before its so expert builders, who had trusted their own calculations in regard to water level and current, were convinced that they had made an error. Lewis Morgan, who, following his book on *The League of the Iroquois*, wrote one on *The American Beaver and His Works*, believed that the activity of beavers was to some extent unnecessary, gratuitous. They compulsively keep on building and digging, cannot be happy if they are not doing this. Mr. Merle Deardorff of Warren, Pennsylvania, whose studies I have cited earlier and who has always, in the matter of the Kinzua Dam, been strongly sympathetic with the Indians, has told me that a colonel of Engineers who had been sent to look over the site once said to him: "You and I may never live to see that dam. But in the long run nothing under Heaven can prevent an engineer from building it. You can dam so much water for so little money!" This is the blind gift of building, the will to build. But my friend, when his beavers are going too far, is able to call a halt to their operations. He has twice summoned the Fisheries and Game people to take some of the beavers away. Unlike the Seneca Indians if the Kinzua project goes through, he can avoid having his whole property flooded. One is coming more and more to feel, as our bureaucrats and enginers seem to be getting more and more out of hand, that the problem for all the rest of us is to provide some reliable means of checking on the desirability of what they propose to do, and, if necessary, as in the case of the beavers, of having them removed from the premises.

James Baldwin / Letter from a Region of My Mind

James Baldwin has a vision of America in which the racial suffering of blacks is symptomatic of the larger plight of the whole nation: its fear of freedom and of loving. His argument is initiated in terms that are conspicuously more general than specifically racial:—"the fact," as he asserts in the opening paragraph, "that life is tragic"—and the generality continues in the rest of this selection from *The Fire Next Time*. Baldwin, like Mailer, wants desperately to believe in the possible achievement of some functional relationship of equality among the various factions, including racial ones, that make up this country. Surrender by the whites of a fear-ridden domination of blacks would release the energy, beauty, and consciousness of both and redirect it from its currently perverse and sometimes violent expression.

Personal urgency is apparent in the style of this piece, as if Baldwin were writing about a possible love affair gone bad, making an anguished appeal to principles beyond expediencies of power, politics, or economics. In this respect, his writing about racial and social problems is markedly different from McPherson's account of the Blackstone Rangers, even though both writers refuse to talk about issues in exclusively racial terms. The degree to which Baldwin's treatment of racial conflicts partakes of some more ambitious inquiry into the problems of freedom and love in American society will probably make those readers who want a guide to action respond with at least some degree of impatience. His essay can in no sense be translated into a program; indeed one might ask what possible actions anyone could take which would be equivalent to his rhetoric.

Behind what we think of as the Russian menace lies what we do not wish to face, and what white Americans do not face when they regard a Negro: reality —the fact that life is tragic. Life is tragic simply because the earth turns and the sun inexorably rises and sets, and one day, for each of us, the sun will go down for the last, last time. Perhaps the whole root of our trouble, the human trouble, is that we will sacrifice all the beauty of our lives, will imprison ourselves in totems, taboos, crosses, blood sacrifices, steeples, mosques, races, armies, flags, nations, in order to deny the fact of death, which is the only fact we have. It seems to me that one ought to rejoice in the *fact* of death—ought to decide, indeed, to *earn* one's death by confronting with passion the conundrum of life. One is responsible to life: It is the small beacon in that terrifying darkness from which we come and to which we shall return. One must negotiate this passage as nobly as possible, for the sake of those who are coming after us. But white Americans do not believe in death, and this is why the darkness of my skin so intimidates them. And this is also why the presence of the Negro in this country can bring about its destruction. It is the responsibility of free men to trust and to celebrate what is constant—birth, struggle, and death are constant, and so is love, though we may not always think so—and to apprehend the nature of change, to be able and willing to change. I speak of change not on the surface but in the depths— change in the sense of renewal. But renewal becomes impossible if one supposes things to be constant that are not—safety, for example, or money, or power.

One clings then to chimeras, by which one can only be betrayed, and the entire hope—the entire possibility—of freedom disappears. And by destruction I mean precisely the abdication by Americans of any effort really to be free. The Negro can precipitate this abdication because white Americans have never, in all their long history, been able to look on him as a man like themselves. This point need not be labored; it is proved over and over again by the Negro's continuing position here, and his indescribable struggle to defeat the stratagems that white Americans have used, and use, to deny him his humanity. America could have used in other ways the energy that both groups have expended in this conflict. America, of all the Western nations, has been best placed to prove the uselessness and the obsolescence of the concept of color. But it has not dared to accept this opportunity, or even to conceive of it as an opportunity. White Americans have thought of it as their shame, and have envied those more civilized and elegant European nations that were untroubled by the presence of black men on their shores. This is because white Americans have supposed "Europe" and "civilization" to be synonyms—which they are not—and have been distrustful of other standards and other sources of vitality, especially those produced in America itself, and have attempted to behave in all matters as though what was east for Europe was also east for them. What it comes to is that if we, who can scarcely be considered a white nation, persist in thinking of ourselves as one, we condemn ourselves, with the truly white nations, to sterility and decay, whereas if we could accept ourselves *as we are,* we might bring new life to the Western achievements, and transform them. The price of this transformation is the unconditional freedom of the Negro; it is not too much to say that he, who has been so long rejected, must now be embraced, and at no matter what psychic or social risk. He is *the* key figure in his country, and the American future is precisely as bright or as dark as his. And the Negro recognizes this, in a negative way. Hence the question: Do I really *want* to be integrated into a burning house?

White Americans find it as difficult as white people elsewhere do to divest themselves of the notion that they are in possession of some intrinsic value that black people need, or want. And this assumption—which, for example, makes the solution to the Negro problem depend on the speed with which Negroes accept and adopt white standards—is revealed in all kinds of striking ways, from Bobby Kennedy's assurance that a Negro can become President in forty years to the unfortunate tone of warm congratulation with which so many liberals address their Negro equals. It is the Negro, of course, who is presumed to have become equal—an achievement that not only proves the comforting fact that perseverance has no color but also overwhelmingly corroborates the white man's sense of his own value. Alas, this value can scarcely be corroborated in any other way; there is certainly little enough in the white man's public or private life that one should desire to imitate. White men, at the bottom of their hearts, know this. Therefore, a vast amount of the energy that goes into what we call the Negro problem is produced by the white man's profound desire not to be judged by those who are not white, not to be seen as he is, and at the same time a vast amount of the white anguish is rooted in the white man's equally profound need to be seen as he is, to be released from the tyranny of his mirror. All of us know, whether or not we are able to admit it, that mirrors can only lie, that death by drowning is all that awaits one there. It is for this reason that love is so desperately sought and so cunningly avoided. Love takes off the masks that we fear we cannot live without and know we cannot live within. I use the word "love" here not merely in the personal sense but as a state of being, or a state of grace—not in the infantile American sense of being made happy but in the tough and universal sense of quest and daring and growth. And I submit, then, that the racial tensions that menace Americans today have little to do with real antipathy—on the contrary, indeed—and are involved only symbolically with color. These tensions are rooted in the very same depths as those from which love springs, or murder. The white man's unadmitted—and apparently, to him, unspeakable—private fears and longings are projected onto the Negro. The only way he can be released from the Negro's tyrannical power over him is to consent, in effect, to become black himself, to become a part of that suffering and dancing country that he now watches wistfully from the heights of his lonely power and, armed with spiritual traveller's checks, visits surreptitiously after dark. How can one respect, let alone adopt, the values of a people who do not, on any level whatever, live the way they say they do, or the way they say they should? I cannot accept the proposition that the four-hundred-year travail of the American Negro should result merely in his attainment of the present level of the American civilization. I am far from convinced that being released from the African witch doctor was worthwhile if I am now—in order to support the moral contradictions and the spiritual aridity of my life—expected to become dependent on the American psychiatrist. It is a bargain I refuse. The only thing white people have that black people need, or should want, is power—and no one holds power forever. White people cannot, in the generality, be taken as models of how to live. Rather, the white man is himself in sore need of new standards, which will release him from his confusion and place him once again in fruitful communion with the depths of his own being. And I repeat: The price of the liberation of the white people is the liberation of the blacks—the total liberation, in the cities, in the towns, before the law, and in the mind. Why, for example—especially knowing the family as I do—I should *want* to marry your sister is a great mystery to me. But your sister and I have every right to marry if we wish to, and no one has the right to stop us. If she cannot raise me to her level, perhaps I can raise her to mine.

In short, we, the black and the white, deeply need each other here if we are really to become a nation—if we are really, that is, to achieve our identity, our maturity, as men and women. To create one nation has proved to be a hideously difficult task; there is certainly no need now to create two, one black and one white. But white men with far more political power than that possessed by the Nation of Islam movement * have been advocating exactly this, in effect, for generations. If this sentiment is honored when it falls from the lips of Senator Byrd, then there is no reason it should not be honored when it falls from the lips of Malcolm X. And any Congressional committee wishing to investigate the latter must also be willing to investigate the former. They are expressing exactly the same sentiments and represent exactly the same danger. There is absolutely no reason to suppose that white people are better equipped to frame the laws by which I am to be governed than I am. It is entirely unacceptable that I should have no voice in the political affairs of my own country, for I am not a ward of America; I am one of the first Americans to arrive on these shores.

This past, the Negro's past, of rope, fire, torture, castration, infanticide, rape; death and humiliation; fear by day and night, fear as deep as the marrow of the bone; doubt that he was worthy of life, since everyone around him denied it; sorrow for his women, for his kinfolk, for his children, who needed his protection, and whom he could not protect; rage, hatred, and murder, hatred for white men so deep that it often turned against him and his own, and made all love, all trust, all joy impossible—this past, this endless struggle to achieve and reveal and confirm a human identity, human authority, yet contains, for all its horror, something very beautiful. I do not mean to be sentimental about suffering—enough is certainly as good as a feast—but people who cannot suffer can never grow up, can never discover who they are. That man who is forced each day to snatch his manhood, his identity, out of the fire of human cruelty that rages to destroy it knows, if he survives his effort, and even if he does not survive it, something about himself and human life that no school on earth—and, indeed, no church—can teach. He achieves his own authority, and that is unshakable. This is because, in order to save his life, he is forced to look beneath appearances, to take nothing for granted, to hear the meaning behind the words. If one is continually surviving the worst that life can bring, one eventually ceases to be controlled by a fear of what life can bring; whatever it brings must be borne. And at this level of experience one's bitterness begins to be palatable, and hatred becomes too heavy a sack to carry. The apprehension of life here so briefly and inadequately sketched has been the experience of generations of Negroes, and it helps to explain how they have endured and how they have been able to produce children of kindergarten age who can walk through mobs to get to school. It demands great force and great cunning continually to assault the mighty and indifferent fortress of white supremacy, as Negroes in this country have done so long. It demands great spiritual resilience not to hate the hater whose foot is on your neck, and an even greater miracle of perception and charity not to teach your child to hate. The Negro boys and girls who are facing mobs today come out of

---

* Nation of Islam movement: The Muslim Black nationalist movement led by Elijah Muhammad and centered in Chicago.

a long line of improbable aristocrats—the only genuine aristocrats this country has produced. I say "this country" because their frame of reference was totally American. They were hewing out of the mountain of white supremacy the stone of their individuality. I have great respect for that unsung army of black men and women who trudged down back lanes and entered back doors, saying "Yes, sir" and "No, Ma'am" in order to aquire a new roof for the schoolhouse, new books, a new chemistry lab, more beds for the dormitories, more dormitories. They did not like saying "Yes, sir" and "No, Ma'am," but the country was in no hurry to educate Negroes, these black men and women knew that the job had to be done, and they put their pride in their pockets in order to do it. It is very hard to believe that they were in any way inferior to the white men and women who opened those back doors. It is very hard to believe that those men and women, raising their children, eating their greens, crying their curses, weeping their tears, singing their songs, making their love, as the sun rose, as the sun set, were in any way inferior to the white men and women who crept over to share these splendors after the sun went down. But we must avoid the European error; we must not suppose that, because the situation, the ways, the perceptions of black people so radically differed from those of whites, they were racially superior. I am proud of these people not because of their color but because of their intelligence and their spiritual force and their beauty. The country should be proud of them, too, but, alas, not many people in this country even know of their existence. And the reason for this ignorance is that a knowledge of the role these people played—and play—in American life would reveal more about America to Americans than Americans wish to know.

The American Negro has the great advantage of having never believed that collection of myths to which white Americans cling: that their ancestors were all freedom-loving heroes, that they were born in the greatest country the world has ever seen, or that Americans are invincible in battle and wise in peace, that Americans have always dealt honorably with Mexicans and Indians and all other neighbors or inferiors, that American men are the world's most direct and virile, that American women are pure. Negroes know far more about white Americans than that; it can almost be said, in fact, that they know about white Americans what parents—or, anyway, mothers—know about their children, and that they very often regard white Americans that way. And perhaps this attitude, held in spite of what they know and have endured, helps to explain why Negroes, on the whole, and until lately, have allowed themselves to feel so little hatred. The tendency has really been, insofar as this was possible, to dismiss white people as the slightly mad victims of their own brainwashing. One watched the lives they led. One could not be fooled about that; one watched the things they did and the excuses that they gave themselves, and if a white man was really in trouble, deep trouble, it was to the Negro's door that he came. And one felt that if one had had that white man's worldly advantages, one would never have become as bewildered and as joyless and as thoughtlessly cruel as he. The Negro came to the white man for a roof or for five dollars or for a letter to the judge; the white man came to the Negro for love. But he was not often able to give what he came seeking. The price was too high; he had too much to lose. And the Negro knew this, too. When one knows this about a man, it is impossible for one to hate him, but unless he becomes a man—becomes equal—it is also impossible for one to love him. Ultimately, one tends to avoid him, for the universal characteristic of children is to assume that they have a monopoly on trouble, and therefore a monopoly on *you*. (Ask any Negro what he knows about the white people with whom he works. And then ask the white people with whom he works what they know about *him*.)

How can the American Negro past be used? It is entirely possible that this dishonored past will rise up soon to smite all of us. There are some wars, for example (if anyone on the globe is still mad enough to go to war) that the American Negro will not support, however many of his people may be coerced—and there is a limit to the number of people any government can put in prison, and a rigid limit indeed to the practicality of such a course. A bill is coming in that I fear America is not prepared to pay. "The problem of the twentieth century," wrote W. E. B. Du Bois * around sixty years ago, "is the problem of the color line." A fearful and delicate problem, which compromises, when it does not corrupt, all the American efforts to build a better world—here, there, or anywhere. It is for this reason that everything white Americans think they believe in must now be reexamined. What one would not like to see again is the consolidation of peoples on the basis of their color. But as long as we in the West place on color the value that we do, we make it impossible for the great unwashed to consolidate themselves according to any other principle. Color is not a human or a personal reality; it is a political reality. But this is a distinction so extremely hard to make that the West has not been able to make it yet. And at the center of this dreadful storm, this vast confusion, stand the black people of this nation, who must now share the fate of a nation that has never accepted them, to which they were brought in chains. Well, if this is so, one has no choice but to do all in one's power to change that fate, and at no matter what risk—eviction, imprisonment, torture, death. For the sake of one's children, in order to minimize the bill that *they* must pay, one must be careful not to take refuge in any delusion—and the value placed on the color of the skin is always and everywhere and forever a delusion. I know that what I am asking is impossible. But in our time, as in every time, the impossible is the least that one can demand—and one is, after all, emboldened by the spectacle of human history in general, and American Negro history in particular, for it testifies to nothing less than the perpetual achievement of the impossible.

* W. E. B. Du Bois: (1868–1963), important Negro leader and writer, who fought for cultural unity and for a sense of racial identity among American Negroes. He was one of the founders of the National Association for the Advancement of Colored People and from 1910 to 1932 he edited *Crisis,* the magazine of the NAACP.

When I was very young, and was dealing with my buddies in those wine- and urine-stained hallways, something in me wondered, *What will happen to all that beauty?* For black people, though I am aware that some of us, black and white, do not know it yet, are very beautiful. And when I sat at Elijah's * table and watched the baby, the women, and the men, and we talked about God's—or Allah's—vengeance, I wondered, when that vengeance was achieved, *What will happen to all that beauty then?* I could also see that the intransigence and ignorance of the white world might make that vengeance inevitable—a vengeance that does not really depend on, and cannot really be executed by, any person or organization, and that cannot be prevented by any police force or army: historical vengeance, a cosmic vengeance, based on the law that we recognize when we say, "Whatever goes up must come down." And here we are, at the center of the arc, trapped in the gaudiest, most valuable, and most improbable water wheel the world has ever seen. Everything now, we must assume, is in our hands; we have no right to assume otherwise. If we—and now I mean the relatively conscious whites and the relatively conscious blacks, who must, like lovers, insist on, or create, the consciousness of the others—do not falter in our duty now, we may be able, handful that we are, to end the racial nightmare, and achieve our country, and change the history of the world. If we do not now dare everything, the fulfillment of that prophecy, re-created from the Bible in song by a slave, is upon us: *God gave Noah the rainbow sign, No more water, the fire next time!*

* Elijah: Elijah Muhammad.

VI LANGUAGE

This anthology emphasizes the creative power of language and its supreme importance as our principal means of communication and personal fulfillment; it is not the only one, but it is the most important by all counts. Views of language have changed greatly in recent years; it used to be assumed that there were recognizable standards from which good speakers or writers did not deviate, and indeed deviation was regarded as synonymous with degeneracy. But this opinion has been largely given up; the spoken language has taken priority over the written, not only among theoretical linguists but by writers, who range much more widely than ever before in those areas of language that used to be called colloquial.

We include an extremely brief account of the ideas of Noam Chomsky as representing best the modern attitude to language in general, and an older essay by Leonard Bloomfield which gives a careful and interesting account of the problems attaching to the issue of literate and illiterate speech. More familiar and more disputed ground is covered by Dwight Macdonald in his dictionary review; for whereas the modern linguist, almost without exception, regards usage and acceptability to native speakers as the only criteria of linguistic correctness, Macdonald takes issue with a major dictionary compiled according to those principles.

The Orwell essay, probably the most famous in this anthology, is based on the assumption that language can be corrupted for dishonest political purposes and that this results in the corruption of humanity itself. Tendencies of modern usage—the great growth in the employment of acronyms and euphemisms, for example—furnish him with examples, and they are treated by him as indications of what might be expected under a powerful police state. Again, the implications are of the utmost importance and should be considered together with the arguments of the "linguistic" scientists, who give little encouragement to the idea that language ought to be kept "clean" by the moral and intellectual efforts of those who care for an accuracy of statement based on traditional models.

Herbert Marcuse makes a similar point in a much more abstract manner

—the language of political discourse is tautological and designed to exclude contrary arguments, so that, in the Orwellian terms Marcuse himself employs, freedom is servitude, "peace is war," and so on. And this kind of linguistic corruption spreads through all our daily activities and through the whole public domain. The effect is authoritarian; the people are victimized.

Both Orwell and Marcuse are concerned that language can be, and is, manipulated in the interests of power structures, political or commercial. They give great importance to the preservation of linguistic purity as an essential precondition of full and honorable human expressiveness. We have included Philip French's piece because, in spite of its light essayistic style, it comments on the difficulties in achieving normal expression that are experienced by the vast number of people who have speech defects and alludes to the social and artistic trials and victories associated with their condition. In the final analysis his theme, we believe, joins the others. Language is not only the instrument—sometimes imperfect, always corruptible in some measure —of our social communication, but the most distinctive and irreplaceable of the creative attributes that make man different from the rest of the animal creation. This does not mean that its place in modern life may not be affected by new technologies and new demands; William Burroughs, in the piece we have chosen, tells about some of them.

Philip French / The Stammerer as Hero

This piece might seem to be quite close to an old-fashioned essay: On Being a Stammerer might have been its title. But in matching its actual title it turns out to be something more. It is concerned with a speech disorder and with the evidence that this disorder has for various reasons recently acquired a cultural significance different from any it formerly had. Although French is on occasion witty and never solemn his approach to the subject is fundamentally serious. He touches on explanations of this mysterious impediment, and shows it as it affects the sufferer in different social situations. He is interested in representations of it in the arts, even in opera. Autobiographical material is unassumingly, though authoritatively, used, and much of the effect of the essay comes from the deft deployment of illustrations. The result is quite remote from simple autobiography, and equally so from any formal article, whether medical or aesthetic in orientation, on stammering. Its contribution to the sociology of language may not be great, but it is genuine; and it should be obvious that it depends not only on the information conveyed but on the way it is assembled, and on the personality of the writer as his tone conveys it.

O Word, Word that I Lack.

"The avowal of such an imperfection in the Handsome Sailor should be evidence not alone that he is not presented as a conventional hero, but also that the story in which he is the main figure is no romance."

So wrote Herman Melville of the one flaw in the otherwise perfect Billy Budd —"his organic hesitancy—in fact, more or less of a stutter or even worse." This illiterate, illegitimate seaman, who is identified with Adam and with Christ, is perhaps the outstanding instance of what has recently become a fairly common dramatic character—the hero as stammerer. As such he has a good deal in common with later examples, though unfortunately it is only the range of his affliction—from a hesitation, through the stutter to total paralysis—that relates him to stammerers of everyday life. Melville's observations about the source of "the imperfection" that leads Billy to strike dead the devilish, swift-tongued Claggart and on to his untimely end on the yard-arm, would not however find much approval, at least not express approval, today:

> In this particular Billy was a striking instance that the arch-interpreter, the envious marplot of Eden, still has more or less to do with every human consignment to this planet of earth. In every case, one way or another, he is sure to slip in his little card, as much as to remind us—I too have a hand here.

Still, if we did believe this then we might well feel that "the envious marplot" had recently been having something of a field day, or garden party.

In December 1965 Somerset Maugham—since the deaths of King George VI and Aneurin Bevan * the best-known living stammerer—died in his ninety-second year. This event was, one might think, a fitting end to what could be called with some justice the Year of the Stammer. At Sir Laurence Olivier's National Theatre Albert Finney was stuttering in repertory as the hero of John Arden's *Armstrong's Last Goodnight*. At the National Film Theatre, and on TV, the late Charles Laughton provided an even more striking impediment in the title role of Josef von Sternberg's *I Claudius,* the salvaged rushes of which (contained in the documentary "The Epic that Never Was") proved the movie find of the year. At Covent Garden the tongue-tied Moses vied with the eloquent Aaron in Schoenberg's opera. On television Ian Carmichael affected the fashionable 'twenties hesitation in his successful impersonation of P. G. Wodehouse's Bertie Wooster. And also on TV—and the most extraordinary of these events, though only in this context—there was the bewildering success as a conversationalist of the Irish humorist and chronic stammerer Patrick Campbell in the satire show *Not So Much a Programme* and its sequel *BBC-3*.

The irony of it all might have amused Maugham, though I doubt if it would

---

* Aneurin Bevan: (1897–1960), ex-miner, British Labour politician and famous inflammatory orator; as Minister of Health in the first postwar Labour government, he introduced the revolutionary National Health Service (1948).

have brought much comfort to a man who could write at the age of sixty-four so vividly and with such bitterness:

> I had not been long at school before I discovered, through the ridicule to which I was exposed and the humiliations I suffered, how great a misfortune it was to me that I stammered: and I had read in the Bible that if you had faith you could move mountains. My uncle assured me that it was a literal fact. One night, when I was going back to school next day, I prayed to God with all my might that he would take away my impediment; and, such was my faith, I went to sleep quite certain that when I awoke next morning I should be able to speak like everyone else. I pictured to myself the surprise of the boys (I was still at preparatory school) when they found that I no longer stammered. I woke full of exultation, and it was a real, a terrible shock, when I discovered that I stammered as badly as ever.

And he recalled going on to King's School, Canterbury, where he was persecuted in much the same way that Aneurin Bevan was to be several decades later at a rather less celebrated academy, Sirhowy elementary school in South Wales. Of King's School, Maugham wrote:

> The masters were clergymen; they were stupid and irascible. They were impatient of my stammering, and if they did not ignore me completely, which I preferred, they bullied me. They seemed to think that it was my fault that I stammered.*

I doubt if any stammerer in the past twenty years or so has been made to suffer quite as harshly as Maugham was.

As a playwright Maugham might have been intrigued by the serious role that the stammerer has been accorded in *Moses and Aaron, Armstrong's Last Goodnight,* and *I Claudius* (we must remember, however, that Schoenberg's opera and Sternberg's film date from the 'thirties), as well as in John Osborne's television play *A Subject of Scandal and Concern* and Jules Dassin's *Celui Qui Doit Mourir,** a 1957 film version of Kazantzakis' *Christ Recrucified*. For Maugham, like other stammerers (*e.g.* Nevil Shute and Arnold Bennett), invariably created fluent, articulate characters. Even in the closely autobiographical *Of Human Bondage,* the stammer became Philip Carey's crippled leg. When Maugham wrote for the theatre the stutterer was entirely a figure of fun. Indeed the truly great comic stammerers occur in the golden age of pre-World War I French farce where the fundamental cruelty of the proceedings and the brilliant mechanics forced (and still force) the audience to dispense with any scruples of taste. The classic instances are the stuttering cuckold in Feydeau's *L'Hôtel du Libre-*

* W. Somerset Maugham, *The Summing Up* (1938).
* *Celui Qui Doit Mourir:* He Who Must Die.

Echange,* and, most especially, the lecherous clerk with the cleft palate in the same author's *La Puce à L'Oreille,** now working its old disarming magic on National Theatre audiences who would obviously be shocked at the slightest giggle that greeted such an affliction outside the Old Vic.

If, as I say, Maugham might have been intrigued by the plays I have mentioned, he would have been shocked by the bizarre headline of a popular newspaper's gossip column "STAMMERING IS IN," which of course referred to Patrick Campbell. And he would have been appalled by the title of the recent anthology *P-P-Penguin Patrick Campbell,* which must recall to any stammerer the playground and barrack-room taunts of his youth.

Yet many people have suggested to me this past year, apparently in all seriousness, that I should take some kind of pride or satisfaction in Patrick Campbell's achievement. Which is, I am inclined to think, only slightly less insensitive than commending the popularity of Stepin Fetchit to James Baldwin.

It should perhaps be explained here that I myself have stammered for as long as I can recall. Like all stammerers I am desperately conscious of the impediment though it is no longer as bad as Campbell's. Or at least so I am told, for whenever a fellow-stammerer's affliction comes up one is always hastily assured that "it's far worse than yours." Indeed nice people pretend that it does not exist ("How *sweet* of you to pretend not to notice," says the aunt of the cleft-palated clerk to her friend in *La Puce à L'Oreille*)—while supplying the word they think you are fighting to deliver, though it is invariably the wrong one. At the same time as they are informing you that you have not *really* got a stammer at all, they will tell you how much it has improved over the past couple of years— which is just what they told you two years ago. It is a touchy subject.

Until the coming of Campbell I had assumed that the stammering joke, like many less innocuous species of humour, was dying out. That it might be having a new lease of life is not something I find particularly disturbing. After all, jokes about stammerers are a good deal less offensive than, say, anti-semitic jokes— and a good deal funnier.

Now it might be said that Patrick Campbell's success on television is due to his ability as a *raconteur* and it is true that he has a reputation of some years' standing as a humorous writer. But it would seem to me that his sudden TV prominence is largely because of his stammer, not despite it. This is certainly borne out by the franker observers of current taste, and confirmed by the title of the Penguin book and the gossip column to which I have referred as well as by the recent Cossack Vodka advertisement which carries Campbell's endorsement and, presumably, was found up to its rigorous standards by the Institute of Practitioners in Advertising. The advertisement actually manages to have it both ways. "LORD OF THE STAMMER" it is headed, and the opening paragraph reads:

* *L'Hôtel du Libre-Echange: Hotel Paradiso* (1894), by Georges Feydeau.
* *La Puce à L'Oreille: A Flea in her Ear* (1907).

Most stammerers have the upper hand. People listen to them because they're embarrassed at the poor fellow's plight or because they're fascinated to hear what gibberish will ultimately emerge. But Patrick Campbell has more of a hold on them than that.[1]

It is naturally important to remember that Campbell is a comedian, an entertainer. A stammer if not funny in itself (which it probably is) can be a valuable piece of comic equipment. It is inconceivable that a stammerer—a bad stammerer, that is—would be acceptable as a regular contributor to a serious television discussion. (I recall with embarrassment being present some years ago after Maugham had received a literary award in London. He was persuaded to be interviewed for TV—being assured by his interviewer that the stammer was no problem. The recording went quite well, or so I thought, although Maugham got stuck a couple of times. After it was completed the interviewer thanked Maugham, but making his way through the throng of reporters and technicians who filled the room he turned to me and said: "Christ, we're going to have a job putting *that* straight!") If anything I should say that the situation is even less favourable than in the past for a stammerer wanting to enter public life. Aneurin Bevan, for instance, were he starting out in politics today might well be faced by a constituency selection committee reluctant to adopt a candidate so apparently ill-fitted for the requirements of mass media politics. I refer here not merely to the stammer, which is not the sort of thing that is going to attract a stream of invitations to participate in *Any Questions?, Panorama,* or a Party Political programme, but also to the personality that a stammer is likely to produce—spiky, aggressive, unpredictable, yet at the same time highly vulnerable. In short, the wrong kind of image. Nor must one forget the usual assumption, not always unjustified, that a stammer is a symptom of some inner disturbance or conflict.

It could be argued that a stammerer ought to keep out of public life, and the majority elect to do so. Nevertheless all these recent plays are precisely about stammerers in public life. It is a case, however, of greatness being thrust upon them. Moses, of course, is chosen by God. Arden's Johnny Armstrong has been born to lead his border clan. Osborne's George Holyoake is brought before the early 19th-century courts to defend himself for allegedly blasphemous writings. The previously mocked Claudius reluctantly assumes the Emperor's throne after Rome has been reduced to chaos. The Greek shepherd, Manolis, in *Celui Qui Doit Mourir,* unwillingly takes the part of Christ in a Passion Play and is drawn into leading an insurrection against the Turks. All of them retain their stammers to the end except for Manolis who is miraculously and unconvincingly transformed as he comes to identify himself with his appointed role. And all of them are confronted with an antagonist who speaks with rare fluency. There are the

1. This line of advertising opens up all sorts of new possibilities that others should not be slow to develop. "Epileptics have the upper hand—but Fyodor Dostoevsky . . . ." or "Most blind people—but John Milton. . . ." and so on.

magistrates and judges who humiliate Holyoake and the silver-tongued diplomat Sir David Lindsay who leads Armstrong into James V's noose; but the conflict is seen in its purest form in *Moses and Aaron*. In Schoenberg's opera, Moses does not actually stammer; he merely speaks (or to be precise is given a *Sprechstimme*) * while Aaron sings. As Egon Wellesz has written, it was Schoenberg's intention to portray Moses

> as the uncompromising representative of the *idea,* whereas from Aaron an unending flow of images emerges, exciting the people of Israel, so that by creating the Golden Calf he becomes a prey to the creation of his own mind.

An underlying theme of all these works is that a stammer is a sign of integrity, that in the country of the bland the tongue-tied man is, if not actually king, worthy of greatest respect. He is the man who has difficulty over words and, hence, despises the glib, facile, seductive phrase. In an age that has seen the wholesale corruption of language and in which the mass media place such an emphasis upon easy eloquence, he is an appealing figure. Or, at least, he is in the theatre, if not in everyday life. To be sure, one has to be careful just how the stammer is handled. Many people have complained of great difficulty in following what Albert Finney's "Armstrong" says, but this could be due to the thick Scots accent and the unfamiliar dialect words. Arden's stage direction says that Armstrong "has difficulty in talking coherently, a congenital defect like an exaggerated stammer that he is only able to overcome when excited or when he sings. . . ." John Osborne's *A Subject of Scandal and Concern* has a characteristically sensible stage direction to the effect that Holyoake's stammer "must be emphasised sufficiently to appear painful when it happens, but obviously it must be exploited sparingly, and its later dramatic effectiveness must depend upon the nicest discretion of the actor and the director." Richard Burton served Osborne well in the 1960 television production; he was especially moving in the penultimate scene where a grisly prison chaplain preaches a sermon directly at Holyoake who "makes an animal effort to speak but nothing will happen." There is a striking resemblance between this scene and the passage in *Billy Budd* where the tragic foretopman faces Claggart in the presence of Captain Vere and is paralysed, "bringing to the face an expression which was as a crucifixion to behold." It is worth noting that Holyoake is Osborne's only wholly sympathetic protagonist—and the only one not blessed by the gift of the gab.

I had always considered Burton's the finest stage stammer I had seen until I saw Laughton's Claudius. (I use the word "seen" advisedly.) In the documentary film that included the rushes of Alexander Korda's abandoned 1937 production,

---

* *Sprechstimme:* "speaking voice"; a special type of singing in which the tone of voice resembles that of speech, but is modulated according to the composer's notation; used especially by the Viennese 12-tone composers Schoenberg and Berg.

Korda's secretary recalled that Laughton eventually discovered his model in Edward VIII's abdication speech and "always listened to it before going on the set." This rather odd revelation seems to have been accepted without question by the critics, though it strikes me that the career of Claudius and the stammer so excruciatingly developed by Laughton have more obvious parallels with those of George VI. One can only imagine what the completed film would have been like. It certainly would have been the first picture in which the hero had the kind of really painful stammer that would have affected the audience with the same crawling embarrassment that a bad stammerer does in real life. This is very different from the aesthetic purity of Arnold Schoenberg's treatment where we are never made aware of anything except the spiritual problem involved for Moses. Still, Moses' anguished cry at the end of the Second Act, *"O Word, Word that I lack,"* is in a literal sense the stammerer's dilemma, just as the last words of Wittgenstein's *Tractatus,** "whereof one cannot speak, thereof one must be silent" (which George Steiner has suggested is the exact analogue of Moses' curtain line), should be the stammerer's motto.

Perhaps one should be grateful for this serious attention, though the present trend (if such it is) away from the comic or neurotic stammerer of tradition is taking us too far in the opposite direction. There are of course very few occasions when a stammerer appears without his impediment being the major issue, comic or tragic, just as there are not many films in which a Negro appears other than as a dramatic device for discussing colour prejudice. Only two instances in the cinema come readily to mind—the stammering cowboy in Howard Hawks' *Red River* (he gets trampled to death fairly early on in the cattle drive) and, more recently, the flight engineer (Richard Attenborough) who rallies the survivors of an air-crash in Robert Aldrich's *Flight of the Phoenix*.

The stammerer, however, must not be carried away by all this. He must resist the temptation of feeling that his essentially saintly character is at last being recognised, of endorsing the perspicacity of the artists discussed, of arguing that the stammerer's situation is gradually being changed by this sympathetic concern. Even if these plays *were* about the predicament of the stammerer, the result could be the same as our attitude to Arthur Miller's Willy Loman * who, as Tennessee Williams rightly pointed out, we can tolerate for an evening in the theatre but would quickly show to the door if he invaded our office during the day. But the dilemma of the stammerer though touched upon on the dramatic surface is not the theme of these plays—why should it be? His life is altogether more complicated and his problems less obviously universal. And they are not problems likely to be solved in the main by a change in social attitude brought about by Patrick Campbell's television popularity or by the coincidence of so many appearances of the stammerer-as-hero on the stage.

* *Tractatus Logico-philosophicus:* (1921), by the Austrian philosopher Ludwig Wittgenstein.
* Arthur Miller's Willy Loman: principal character in *Death of a Salesman* (1949).

Stammerers might be compared with members of an oppressed minority group or the physically disabled, and in certain respects they do resemble both. Like Jews, Negroes, and homosexuals they are the object of discrimination (real or imagined), are made the butt of jokes (often involving grotesque impersonation), are cast dramatically in symbolic roles, are the subject of much psychological investigation and theorising, and are faced with grave problems of social adjustment. They are like the physically disabled inasmuch as they have a personal handicap beyond their control and the most frequently used descriptions for speech impediments draw on the condition of the bodily disabled—"a crippling stammer," "a stumbling tongue," "speech paralysis." Yet stammerers differ from these other groups more than they resemble them, however much at times they may recognise a sense of kinship and act upon that recognition.[2] Of course there must be an overlap among these groups—no doubt the speech defect would be the least of the worries of a homosexual Jewish Negro stammerer going around Selma, Alabama, in a bath-chair, though it is the one that a change in social attitudes would do least for.

Most people stammer at some time during their lives. They stammer slightly between the ages of two and five when they learn to speak, and later in life when they are frightened, excited or embarrassed. And they are supposed to stammer when they are in love—as the old song has it:

> Your heart's a flutter
> And all day long you only stutter
> 'Cos your poor tongue just will not utter
> The words "I love you."

It is associated in effect with extremes of emotion. For the stammerer, however, the act of oral communication is for much of the time an extreme situation in itself. As Maugham wrote:

> When I was young and stammered badly, to talk for long singularly exhausted me, and even now that I have to some extent cured myself, it is a strain. It is a relief to me when I can get away and read a book.

But like most stammerers, and despite his shyness, Maugham was constantly engaging in conversation. There is even a drive towards it. Stammerers tend to be compulsive talkers; it is as if every stuttering Moses really wanted to be an Aaron. Few content themselves with developing a written style alone. Aneurin Bevan, for instance, became a clear, forceful journalist, but (as his biographer, Michael Foot, observes) he "could always talk better than he wrote" and was in fact among the finest public speakers of his time. He forced himself to confront audiences, preferably hostile:

2. As Michael Foot writes of Bevan: "He was driven back on his own resources . . . 'a lonely chap.' Any natural bent towards questioning the wisdom of authority was reinforced. Both his mind and his will were influenced by his stutter."

His own real remedy was to hurl himself into speeches or arguments. To the question—"How did you cure the stutter, Nye?"—he replied, "By torturing my audiences."

So when he speaks a stammerer can also be engaged in an act of therapy and demonstration. He is also likely to develop as a defence mechanism a bitter wit, a sharp abrasive technique. His words are gauged to bite rapidly like acid into an etching plate rather than like water flowing gently to smooth a stone; if his tongue will not do service as a lasso, it will at least function as a whip.

I am here generalising from the conduct of some well-known stammerers and from my own experience. And yet stammers are like finger-prints—no two are quite the same. One must at the same time distinguish stammers from other impediments. According to the *Encyclopaedia Britannica,* between five and ten per cent of the U.S. population over the age of six have some speech defect (which is more than the crippled, blind, and deaf together); I assume that such a rough calculation holds true for Britain as well. But this figure covers all kinds of defect from so-called baby talk to lisping. Only ten per cent of this group (or roughly one per cent of the total population) have an actual stammer —the inability to speak without stumbling over words or getting hung up over particular ones. In the trade the principal distinction is between the *clonic* (repeating) and the *tonic* (blocking) interruption of speech. A permanent stammer usually starts between the ages of two and five. It is without definable physical basis or at least none has been effectively established. There is a great deal of conflicting theory and I personally have nothing new to contribute. In general it is of multiple causation—the continuation of the normal beginner's speech hesitation through environmental and psychological factors. There are plenty of pat explanations, and at the drop of a consonant many people will tell a stammerer whom they scarcely know just how his impediment came about. Bevan's mother, for instance, denied that Nye had always stammered and a family myth developed to the effect that he acquired it by imitating a stuttering relative. Michael Foot rightly dismisses this, though the more orthodox origin he substitutes is not especially satisfactory:

> According to some modern psychologists, Aneurin must have been a shifted sinistral, having been born left-handed and forced to write with his right hand. His distaste for the physical act of writing lends strong support to the idea. But no one knows for certain the date when the consequent nervous disorder began.

The same explanation has been offered in my own case (I can see people whom I have just met watching me reach for my pen) though I have always been left-handed and no attempt was made to make me otherwise. And also in my own case, as in that of most other stammerers, no one in my family has been able to tell me exactly when the impediment began. One feels that it must have happened like Mike Campbell's bankruptcy in *The Sun Also Rises:* * "Two ways. Gradually and then suddenly." There is little evidence to indicate that it is hereditary, though according to Robin Maugham this was Somerset Maugham's belief. He reports his uncle recalling an encounter early in this century with a remote American relative who had an appalling stammer. This apparently convinced Maugham that

> we're the product of our genes and chromosomes. And there's nothing whatever we can do about it . . . no one can. Because we can't change the essential natures we're born with. . . . All we can do is to try and supplement our own deficiencies. Meeting that young man in the Ritz-Carlton made me certain of that.

This is of course, on the face of it, a scientific way of saying the same thing as Melville says of Billy Budd, or of expressing what we read in the Fourth chapter of Exodus:

> And Moses said unto the Lord, O my Lord, I am not eloquent, neither heretofore, nor since thou hast spoken to thy servant: but I am slow of speech and of a slow tongue.
> And the Lord said unto him, Who hath made man's mouth? or who maketh the dumb, or deaf, or the seeing, or the blind? have not I the Lord.

It is, I suppose, a bold man who would reject in the same sentence the medical opinion of Maugham, the literary interpretation of Melville, and the divine revelation of the authors of the Pentateuch.

Despite the claims of therapists who advertise their achievements in Underground stations, there are few cases of completely successful cures. (The case is different with other speech defects.) The principal aim of therapy is, firstly, to teach the stammerer to control his delivery somewhat and to lead towards a gradual alleviation of his condition, and, secondly, to have the stammerer adjust to his condition and to see it in proper perspective. Actually the stammer, once it has become a permanent fixture, is more the cause of nervous disorder than the other way around. It is one of the great chicken-and-egg territories.

As a child I never underwent any therapy though until my late 'teens I was scarcely able to get out the simplest sentence without stammering. This was probably due to my parents finding it an impossibly delicate subject to discuss with the family doctor who happened to have a genuinely paralysing stammer. He would sit there, his face locked in agony, his eyes shut; an audience could have vacated the Albert Hall before he got his next word out. A few years ago, a general practitioner, erroneously attributing the results of a period of overwork to my stammer, sent me to a speech clinic. This I attended weekly for a couple

* *The Sun Also Rises:* (1926), novel by Ernest Hemingway.

of months submitting myself to bouts of Cat-Mat exercises, free-association, and half-baked analysis before it all became too much. As I was at that time doing regular scripted broadcasts I felt like one of those resourceful lotharios in "sophisticated" Hollywood comedies who poses as a homosexual in order to seduce the comely psychiatrist. But what drove me away more than anything else was having to sit in the waiting-room with people to whom such phrases as "Have you finished with *Punch?*" were tongue-twisters of "The Leith police dismisseth us" proportions. The fact is, and it is a sad and important one, that stammerers cannot stand each other's company. For them there can be no equivalent of the invalid car rally, the homosexual bar, or B'nai B'rith. Stammerers do not need each other—on the contrary, as I have mentioned before, they seek out and admire the fluent, as Moses was told by God to use Aaron and as Somerset Maugham needed the smooth, personable Gerald Huxton, his indispensable companion for twenty-five years.

I remember with peculiar vividness a visit to my school by Sir William Emrys Williams to lecture on the function of the Arts Council of which he was then secretary-general. After he had spoken about state subsidies for the arts, it was expected of us by our headmaster that, as bright grammar school sixth-formers, we should get up and ask a few intelligent, probing questions. Suddenly and uncharacteristically I rose to ask a question, emboldened no doubt by the lecturer's own stammer—the first public speaker with a stammer (other than George VI) that I had ever heard. I asked him about state encouragement for the cinema and jazz which in 1950 was a rather more unfashionable thing to do than it would be today. Sir William, however, cut me down with an acerbity that seemed out of all proportion to the gravity of my offence. No doubt my memory of this humiliation is even more unreasonable. But even now I can recall the laughter of my peers when it was enquired of me whether I thought that the Arts Council should subsidise the marble players on "T-Tinsley Green," my rising to reply, finding myself speechless, and sinking down again among my heartless class-mates in that steeply raked auditorium. Maybe Sir William thought I was imitating him, maybe he was annoyed by what he took to be a flippant question, and he undoubtedly has long since forgotten the occasion. But I now know that I might well react in much the same way if faced by a stammering schoolboy.

My vivid recollection of this incident emphasises the extent to which an impediment becomes for the stammerer a central, if not *the* central, fact about his life. Rightly or wrongly, it is this which seems to provide the driving force, to determine what he can or cannot do, to colour all his relationships. He oscillates between the belief that it is something extrinsic, for which he has no responsibility, and the conviction that it is somehow all his own fault. There recurs, too, the suspicion that it is the symptom of an inner disturbance and it is, as I have said, useful for him to be aware of this for it is a constant preoccupation of many people he meets, however much the subject may be avoided. Yet as Maugham's story about praying for his stutter to disappear shows, there is a sense in which a stammerer feels at the mercy of the gods or of fate; the stammer *might* just go away or be whisked away. And indeed a stammer can vary from moment to moment often in the most unpredictable manner. Every time a stammerer speaks he thinks, usually in vain, that he might not stammer, and he tries not to—like a cripple thinking every time he walks that he might make it without his crutches or a political fugitive hoping that a frontier guard will not discover his false papers. The stammerer is thus constantly attempting to find for himself a *persona*, a role he can play in which he can pass himself off as other than what he is. In doing this his case is scarcely unique, though his state may be extreme.[3]

I have tended perhaps so far to dwell on the psychological and social disadvantages. What of the advantages? Well, first of all, a stammer is said to be a rather becoming characteristic—though, like drink, it must be in moderation. Patrick Campbell writes that "from my earliest days I have enjoyed an attractive impediment in my speech." William Randolph Hearst's biographer, W. A. Swanberg, says that Marion Davies "stuttered delightfully." Hazlitt said of Charles Lamb that "no one ever stammered out such fine, piquant, deep, eloquent things in half a dozen half-sentences as he does." Such praise is all very well but the stammer robbed Lamb of the chance of a university education and brought further misery to an already intolerably burdened life. Equally, had it not been for the influence of Hearst it is doubtful whether Marion Davies' film career would have survived the coming of sound (though without pressure from Hearst she probably would not have wanted it to do so). The idea of Miss Davies being a film star with a stammer is perhaps preposterous, but judging by the accounts of her friends she was a more accomplished comedian in private life with her stammer than she was on the screen (by dint of endless and painful retakes) without it. Many of her ad-libbed jokes (*e.g.*, "H-Hearst come, H-Hearst served") gained greatly from the tripping delivery.

There are, however, uses to which a stammer can be put if it is under control—as Bevan's became part of his oratorical style. There is, for instance, that marvellous opening to André Roussin's play *Figure of Fun*. A radio interviewer ar-

---

3. An amusing instance of the variable impediment occurs in a recent film, the comedy-thriller *Blindfold*. A chronic stammerer turns up at a psychiatrist's consulting room and then drops the stammer to proclaim himself a CIA agent. He is able to affect such a convincing impediment he says because once he really did have a stammer but has cured himself by "will power." The analyst warns him that under stress it will return. And indeed it does. For it transpires that this shifty fellow is actually the villain of the piece, an agent for Red China no less. (The producer has already signalled this punch by placing a Negro in the opposing group upon which suspicion initially falls.) After the stammer has several times broken through the smooth treacherous mask, it eventually floods back with a vengeance. The picture ends with the poor chap, pinioned by U.S. marines, speechless in the face of our smiling hero (Rock Hudson). Shades of Claggart!

rives to interrogate a cartoonist. As the broadcasting equipment is set up it is revealed that the interviewer has a terrible stammer while the prospective interviewee is relaxed and articulate. The red light goes on: the interviewer switches into an easy, fluent questioning style and the cartoonist collapses into incoherent stammering. This is the stammerer's dream come true. And it is one of the most inventive uses of stage stammering I have come across—quite different from the usual "K-K-Katie" yokel, the bumbling aesthete, or that old stage and screen device employed in the Boulting Brothers' *I'm All Right Jack* where a stammering union official is constantly getting hung up on *F*'s and *C*'s which, to the amusement though scarcely one should think the surprise of the audience, lead eventually into quite harmless words.

But most stammerers do not have that perfect control that would enable them to follow the good advice of John Osborne's stage direction quoted earlier. It would be idle to pretend, though, that stammerers do not at times take advantage of their impediment or play a little with the tension that it creates between themselves and their listeners. There is a distinction here, however, between the genuine stammerer and someone who adopts the device for effect—a distinction between the afflicted and the affected. The latter is rarely found today though he was quite common in the past and particularly in the 'twenties. Christopher Isherwood in *Lions and Shadows* recalls the skilfully-used stammer of a Repton schoolmaster who excelled as a *raconteur*. He so impressed his pupils that they emulated him and Isherwood remarks that "I sometimes catch myself trying the pseudo-stammer on strangers, even today." The best-known example is the "luxurious, self-taught stammer" of Anthony Blanche in *Brideshead Revisited*,* the Oxford "aesthete par excellence." [4] The stammer of Ian Carmichael's Bertie Wooster is, I take it, a milder version of this. Undoubtedly it is an effective attention-catching device that within limits seems to work well. Though only within limits; and it is quite divorced from the actual agony involved in real stammering. There is, too, a major distinction to be drawn between being articulate, in the sense of being able to express oneself clearly and precisely, and stammering. Many stammerers are highly articulate in this sense, while a high proportion of people who don't even have to pause for a word are pitifully inarticulate.

It is difficult for a stammerer to convey in print just how it feels to stammer, just as an author finds that a stammering character in a novel presents him with pretty intractable problems. You can say repeatedly that the character stammers, but it is impossible to embody this in the book itself and still make it readable. The stammerer has problems of communication and himself presents a problem

---

4. In reading George Scott's account of post-war Oxford in *Time and Place*, I am struck by the quite extraordinary resemblance between his description of a genuine stammerer of the time, Kenneth Tynan, and Evelyn Waugh's affected fictional stammerer of an earlier generation. At times Scott could almost have been writing about Blanche.

* *Brideshead Revisited:* (1945), novel by Evelyn Waugh.

in communication. Who can forget that dazzling line, an unconscious precursor of concrete poetry, in Cyril Connolly's parody of Aldous Huxley, "Told in Gath":

> "S-s-s-s-s-s-s-s-s-s-s-s-s-s-s-s-s-s-s-s-s-s-suppose," said Reggie Ringworm, who stammered.

It is quite otherwise on the stage. But if one could ideally represent the condition of the stammerer in artistic form it would be neither in a play nor a book but as a surrealist cartoon film drawn by Saul Steinberg from a scenario by Samuel Beckett. It would represent the journey of an alternately brave and timid man and his encounters with three-dimensional letters and words. Sometimes he would be juggling with them; sometimes he would be running across the room with them on a tray trying to serve them to his guests before he dropped them; sometimes he would be sitting alone in the desert with words lying all around him in the sand. Inevitably he would have a face like the late Buster Keaton, my own favourite comedian and a man whose voice no one ever wanted to hear.

Dwight Macdonald / The String Untuned

Everyone now and again goes to the dictionary, sometimes merely to find out how a word is correctly spelled, more often to find out what it means. After reading Mr. Macdonald's account of the difference between the third and, to him more satisfactory, second edition of Webster's New International Dictionary (Unabridged) few readers will turn again to any dictionary with complete confidence in its authority. Words get to mean what they are said to mean by their derivation, by the use to which they have been put in the literature of the past, and by common usage. To give the last of these criteria more weight than the other two is to say that a dictionary is a recording instrument, presumably a scientifically tested one, rather than an authority. Such is Macdonald's complaint about the principles at work in the third edition. In the process he bumptiously attacks the science of lexicography, inaccurately making villains of linguists and scholars who in putting together the second edition showed greater reverence for historical usage, as illustrated in a number of distinguished writers, than for current usage gleaned from researches into the vagaries of newspapers or daily conversation.

Needless to say, Macdonald's own command of the language is meant to be on display here in an exemplary and aggressive way. Indeed, arguments that could be quite dull are made zestful by the energy of Macdonald's own lexicographical playfulness. However great his stress on tradition, he is persuasive less because of arguments about linguistics, with which some readers will be able to find fault, than for the evidence that his own idiom is unusually alive, functional, in touch not merely with the past but with the liveliest kinds of contemporary writing and speaking.

The third edition of Webster's New International Dictionary (Unabridged), which was published last fall by the G. & C. Merriam Co., of Springfield, Massachusetts, tells us a good deal about the changes in our cultural climate since the second edition appeared, in 1934. The most important difference between Webster's Second (hereafter called 2) and Webster's Third (or 3) is that 3 has accepted as standard English a great many words and expressions to which 2 attached warning labels: *slang, colloquial, erroneous, incorrect, illiterate*. My impression is that most of the words so labelled in the 1934 edition are accepted in the 1961 edition as perfectly normal, honest, respectable citizens. Between these dates in this country a revolution has taken place in the study of English grammar and usage, a revolution that probably represents an advance in scientific method but that certainly has had an unfortunate effect on such nonscientific activities as the teaching of English and the making of dictionaries—at least on the making of this particular dictionary. This scientific revolution has meshed gears with a trend toward permissiveness, in the name of democracy, that is debasing our language by rendering it less precise and thus less effective as literature and less efficient as communication. It is felt that it is snobbish to insist on making discriminations—the very word has acquired a Jim Crow flavor—about usage. And it is assumed that true democracy means that the majority is right. This feeling seems to me sentimental and this assumption unfounded.

There have been other recent dictionaries calling themselves "unabridged," but they are to Webster's 3 as a welterweight is to a heavyweight. 3 is a massive folio volume (thirteen inches by nine and a half by four) that weighs thirteen and a half pounds, contains four hundred and fifty thousand entries—an "entry" is a word plus its definition—in 2,662 pages, cost three and a half million dollars to produce, and sells for $47.50 up, according to binding. The least comparable dictionary now in print is the New Webster's Vest Pocket Dictionary, which bears on its title page the charmingly frank notation, "This dictionary is not published by the original publishers of Webster's Dictionary or by their successors." It measures five and a half inches by two and a half by a half, weighs two and a quarter ounces, has two hundred and thirty-nine pages, and costs thirty-nine cents. The only English dictionary now in print that *is* comparable to 3 is the great Oxford English Dictionary, a unique masterpiece of historical research that is as important in the study of the language as the King James Bible has been in the use of the language. The O.E.D. is much bigger than 3, containing sixteen thousand four hundred pages in thirteen folio volumes. It is bigger because its purpose is historical as well as definitive; it traces the evolution of each word through the centuries, illustrating the changes in meaning with dated quotations. The latest revision of the O.E.D. appeared in 1933, a year before Webster's 2 appeared. For the language as it has developed in the last quarter of a century, there is no dictionary comparable in scope to 3.

The editor of 2, Dr. William A. Neilson, president of Smith College, followed lexical practice that had obtained since Dr. Johnson's day and assumed there was such a thing as correct English and that it was his job to decide what it was. When he felt he had to include a sub-standard word because of its common use, he put it in, but with a warning label: *Slang, Dial.,* or even bluntly *Illit.* His approach was normative and his dictionary was an authority that pronounced on which words were standard English and which were not. Bets were decided by "looking it up in the dictionary." It would be hard to decide bets by appealing to 3, whose editor of fifteen years' standing, Dr. Philip Gove, while as dedicated a scholar as Dr. Neilson, has a quite different approach. A dictionary, he writes, "should have no traffic with . . . artificial notions of correctness or superiority. It must be descriptive and not prescriptive." Dr. Gove and the other makers of 3 are sympathetic to the school of language study that has become dominant since 1934. It is sometimes called Structural Linguistics and sometimes, rather magnificently, just Modern Linguistic Science. Dr. Gove gives its basic concepts as:

1. Language changes constantly.
2. Change is normal.
3. Spoken language is the language.
4. Correctness rests upon usage.
5. All usage is relative.

While one must sympathize with the counterattack the Structural Linguists have led against the tyranny of the schoolmarms and the purists, who have caused unnecessary suffering to generations of schoolchildren over such matters as *shall* v. *will* and the *who-whom* syndrome—someone has observed that the chief result of the long crusade against "It's me" is that most Americans now say "Between you and I"—it is remarkable what strange effects have been produced in 3 by following Dr. Gove's five little precepts, reasonable as each seems taken separately. Dr. Gove conceives of his dictionary as a recording instrument rather than as an authority; in fact, the whole idea of authority or correctness is repulsive to him as a lexical scientist. The question is, however, whether a purely scientific approach to dictionary-making may not result in greater evils than those it seeks to cure.

When one compares 2 and 3, the first difference that strikes one is that 2 is a work of traditional scholarship and hence oriented toward the past, while 3—though in many ways more scholarly, or at least more academic, than 2—exhales the breezy air of the present. This is hardly surprising, since the new school of linguistics is non-historical, if not anti-historical. Henry Luce's *Time* rather than Joseph Addison's *Spectator* was the hunting ground for 3's illustrative quotations. There is a four-and-a-half-page list of consultants. Its sheer bulk is impressive—until one begins to investigate. One can see why James W. Perry had to be consulted on Non-numerical Computer Applications and Margaret Fulford on Mosses and Liverworts, but it seems overdoing it to have *two* consultants on both Hardware and Salvation Army, and some people might even question the one apiece on Soft Drinks, Boy Scouts, Camp Fire Girls, and Girl Guiding, as well as the enrolling of Mr. Arthur B. LaFar, formerly president of the Angostura-Wuppermann bitters company, as consultant on Cocktails. Such padding is all the more odd, considering that the editors of 3 have forgotten to appoint anybody in Philosophy, Political Theory, or Theatre. The old-fashioned 2 had six consultants on Catholic Church and Protestant Churches. 3 has only one, on Catholic Church. But it also has one on Christian Science, a more up-to-date religion.

• • •

Quantitative comparison between 2 and 3 must be approached cautiously. On the surface, it is considerably in 2's favor: 3,194 pages v. 2,662. But although 2 has six hundred thousand entries to 3's four hundred and fifty thousand, its entries are shorter; and because 3's typography is more compact and its type page larger, it gets in almost as much text as 2. The actual number of entries dropped since 2 is not a hundred and fifty thousand but two hundred and fifty thousand, since a hundred thousand new ones have been added. This incredible massacre —almost half the words in the English language seem to have disappeared between 1934 and 1961—is in fact incredible. For the most part, the dropped entries fall into very special categories that have less to do with the language than with methods of lexicography. They are: variants; "nonce words," like *Shakespearolatry* ("excessive reverence or devotion to Shakespeare"), which seemed a good idea at the time, or for the nonce, but haven't caught on; a vast number of proper names, including nearly every one in both the King James and the Douay Bibles; foreign terms; and obsolete or archaic words. This last category is a large one, since 2 includes "all the literary and most of the technical and scientific words and meanings in the period of Modern English beginning with the year 1500," plus all the words in Chaucer, while 3, in line with its modernization program, has advanced the cut-off date to 1755. A great many, perhaps most, of the entries dropped from 2 were in a section of small type at the foot of each page, a sort of linguistic ghetto, in which the editors simply listed "fringe words" —the definitions being limited to a synonym or often merely a symbol—which they thought not important enough to put into the main text. 3 has either promoted them to the text or, more frequently, junked them.

Some examples of the kinds of words that are in 2 but not in 3 are: *arrousement, aswowe* (in a swoon), *dethronize, devoration* (act of devouring), *disagreeance, mummianize* (mummify), *noyous* (annoying), *punquetto* (strumpet), *ridiculize,* and *subsign* (subscribe). Two foreign words that one might expect to find in 3 were left out because of insufficient "backing"; i.e., the compilers didn't find enough usages to justify inclusion. They were *Achtung* and *niet;* the researchers must have skipped spy movies and Molotovian diplomacy. *Pot holder* was left out, after considerable tergiversating, because (a) for some reason the compilers found little backing for it, and (b) it was held to be self-explanatory (though considering some of the words they put in . . .). If it had been considered to be a single word, it would have been admitted, since one rule they followed was: No word written solid is self-explanatory.

The hundred thousand new entries in 3 are partly scientific or technical terms, partly words that have come into general use since 1934. The sheer quantity of the latter is impressive. English is clearly a living, growing language, and in this portion of their task the compilers of 3 have done an excellent job. Merriam-Webster has compiled some interesting lists of words in 3 that are not in 2.

Some of the political ones are:

<table>
<tr><td>character assassination</td><td>loyalty oath</td></tr>
<tr><td>desegregation</td><td>McCarthyism</td></tr>
<tr><td>freedom of speech</td><td>segregated</td></tr>
<tr><td>globalize</td><td>red-baiting</td></tr>
<tr><td>hatemonger</td><td>shoo-in</td></tr>
<tr><td>integrationist</td><td>sit-in</td></tr>
<tr><td>welfare capitalism</td><td>subsistence economy</td></tr>
</table>

Among the new entries in the cocktail-party area are:

<table>
<tr><td>club soda</td><td>name-dropping</td></tr>
<tr><td>elbow bending</td><td>pub crawler</td></tr>
<tr><td>gate-crasher</td><td>quick one</td></tr>
<tr><td>glad-hander</td><td>rumpot</td></tr>
<tr><td>good-time Charlie</td><td>silent treatment</td></tr>
<tr><td>Irish coffee</td><td>table-hop</td></tr>
<tr><td>jungle juice</td><td>yakety-yak</td></tr>
</table>

The most important new aspect of 3, the rock on which it has been erected, is the hundred thousand illustrative quotations—known professionally as "citations" or "cites"—drawn from fourteen thousand writers and publications. (Another hundred thousand "usage examples" were made up by the compilers.) Most of the cites are from living writers or speakers, ranging from Winston Churchill, Edith Sitwell, Jacques Maritain, J. Robert Oppenheimer, and Albert Schweitzer to Billy Rose, Ethel Merman, James Cagney, Burl Ives, and Ted Williams. Many are from publications, extending from the Dictionary of American Biography down to college catalogues, fashion magazines, and the annual report of the J. C. Penney Company. The hundred thousand cites were chosen from a collection of over six million, of which a million and a half were already in the Merriam-Webster files; four and a half million were garnered by Dr. Gove and his staff. (The O.E.D. had about the same number of cites in its files—drawn mostly from

English literary classics—but used a much larger proportion of them, almost two million, which is why it is five or six times as long as 3.) For years everybody in the office did up to three hours of reading a day—the most, it was found, that was possible without attention lag. Dr. Gove presently discovered a curious defect in this method: the readers tended to overlook the main meanings of a word and concentrate on the peripheral ones; thus a hundred and fifty cite slips were turned in for *bump* as in burlesque stripping but not one for *bump* as in a road. To compensate for this, he created a humbler task force, whose job it was to go through the gutted carcasses of books and magazines after the first group had finished with them and arbitrarily enter on a slip one word—plus its context—in the first sentence in the fourth line from the top of each surviving page. The percentage of useful slips culled by this method approximated the percentage of useful slips made out by the readers who had used their brains. Unsettling.

The cites in 2 are almost all from standard authors. Its cite on *jocund* is from Shakespeare; 3's is from Elinor Wylie. Under *ghastly* 2 has cites from Gray (two), Milton (three), Poe, Wordsworth, Shakespeare, Shelley, Hawthorne, and —as a slight concession to modernity—Maurice Hewlett. 3 illustrates *ghastly* with cites from Louis Bromfield, Macaulay, Thackeray, Thomas Herbert, Aldous Huxley, H. J. Laski, D. B. Chidsey, and J. C. Powys. For *debonair,* 2 has Milton's "buxom, blithe and debonair," * while 3 has H. M. Reynolds' "gay, brisk and debonair." One may think, as I do, that 3 has dropped far too many of the old writers, that it has overemphasized its duty of recording the current state of the language and skimped its duty of recording the past that is still alive (Mr. Reynolds would hardly have arrived at his threesome had not Mr. Milton been there before). A decent compromise would have been to include both, but the editors of 3 don't go in for compromises. They seem imperfectly aware of the fact that the past of a language is part of its present, that tradition is as much a fact as the violation of tradition.

• • •

I notice no important omissions in 3. *Namby-pamby* is in. However, it was coined—to describe the eighteenth-century Ambrose Philips' insipid verses—not "by some satirists of his time" but by just one of them, Henry Carey, whose celebrated parody of Philips is entitled "Namby-Pamby." *Bromide* is in ("a conventional and commonplace or tiresome person"), but not the fact that Gelett Burgess invented it. Still, he gets credit for *blurb* and *goop*. *Abstract expressionism* is in, but *Tachism* and *action painting* are not. The entries on Marxist and Freudian terms are skimpy. *Id* is in, but without citations and with too brief a definition. *Ego* is defined as Fichte, Kant, and Hume used it but not as Freud did. The distinction between *unconscious* and *subconscious* is muffed; the first is adequately defined and the reader is referred to the latter; looking that up, he finds

---

* John Milton, *L'Allegro.*

"The mental activities just below the threshold of consciousness; *also*: the aspect of the mind concerned with such activities that is an entity or a part of the mental apparatus overlapping, equivalent to, or distinct from the unconscious." I can't grasp the nature of something that is overlapping, equivalent to, *or* distinct from something else. While *dialectical materialism* and *charisma* (which 2 treats only as a theological term, although Max Weber had made the word common sociological currency long before 1934) are in, there is no *mass culture,* and the full entry for the noun *masses* is "pl. of mass." There is no reference to Marx or even to Hegel under *reify,* and under *alienation* the closest 3 comes to this important concept of Marxist theory is "the state of being alienated or diverted from normal function," which is illustrated by "alienation of muscle." Marx is not mentioned in the very brief definition of *class struggle.*

The definitions seem admirably objective. I detected only one major lapse:

> McCarthyism—a political attitude of the mid-twentieth century closely allied to know-nothingism and characterized chiefly by opposition to elements held to be subversive and by the use of tactics involving personal attacks on individuals by means of widely publicized indiscriminate allegations esp. on the basis of unsubstantiated charges.

I fancy the formulator of this permitted himself a small, dry smile as he leaned back from his typewriter before trudging on to *McClellan saddle* and *McCoy* (the real). I'm not complaining, but I can't help remembering that the eponymous hero of *McCarthyism* wrote a little book with that title in which he gave a rather different definition. The tendentious treatment of *McCarthyism* contrasts with the objectivity of the definition of *Stalinism,* which some of us consider an even more reprehensible *ism:* "The political, economic and social principles and policies associated with Stalin; *esp:* the theory and practice of communism developed by Stalin from Marxism-Leninism." The first part seems to me inadequate and the second absurd, since Stalin never had a theory in his life. The definitions of *democratic* and *republican* seem fair: "policies of broad social reform and internationalism in foreign affairs" v. "usu. associated with business, financial, and some agricultural interests and with favoring a restricted governmental role in social and economic life." Though I wonder what the Republican National Committee thinks.

One of the most painful decisions unabridgers face is what to do about those obscene words that used to be wholly confined to informal discourse but that of late, after a series of favorable court decisions, have been cropping up in respectable print. The editors of 2, being gentlemen and scholars, simply omitted them. The editors of 3, being scientists, were more conscientious. All the chief four- and-five-letter words are here, with the exception of perhaps the most important one. They defend this omission not on lexical grounds but on the practical and, I think, reasonable ground that its inclusion would have stimulated denunciations and boycotts. There are, after all, almost half a million other words in their dictionary—not to mention an investment of three and a half million dollars—and they reluctantly decided not to imperil the whole enterprise by insisting on that word.

• • •

The editors of 3 have sneaked in many proper names by the back door; that is, by entering their adjectival forms. *Walpolian* means "1: of, relating to, or having the characteristics of Horace Walpole or his writings," and "2: of, relating to, or having the characteristics of Robert Walpole or his political policies," and we get the death dates of both men (but not the birth dates), plus the information that Horace was "Eng. man of letters" and Robert "Eng. statesman" (though it is not noted that Horace was Robert's son). This method of introducing proper names produces odd results. Raphael is in (*Raphaelesque, Raphaelism, Raphaelite*), as are Veronese (*Veronese green*) and Giotto and Giorgione and Michelangelo, but not Tintoretto and Piero della Francesca, because they had the wrong kind of names. Caravaggio had the right kind, but the editors missed him, though *Caravaggesque* is as frequently used in art criticism as *Giottesque*. All the great modern painters, from Cézanne on, are omitted, since none have appropriate adjectives. Yeats is in (*Yeatsian*) but not Eliot, Pound, or Frost (why not *Frosty?*). Sometimes one senses a certain desperation, as when *Smithian* is used to wedge in Adam Smith. *Menckenian* and *Menckenese* get an inch each, but there is no *Hawthornean,* no *Melvillesque,* no *Twainite.* All the twentieth-century presidents are in—Eisenhower by the skin of *Eisenhower jacket—* except Taft and Truman and Kennedy. Hoover has the most entries, all dispiriting: *Hoover apron* and *Hooverize,* because he was food administrator in the First World War; *Hooverville,* for the depression shanty towns; *Hoovercrat,* for a Southern Democrat who voted for him in 1928; and *Hooverism.*

This brings up the matter of capitalization. 2 capitalized proper names; 3 does not, with one exception. There may have been some esoteric reason of typographical consistency. Whatever their reasons, the result is that they must cumbersomely and forever add *usu. cap.* (Why *usu.* when it is *alw?*) The exception is *God,* which even these cautious linguisticians couldn't quite bring themselves to label *usu. cap. Jesus* is out because of adjectival deficiency, except for *Jesus bug,* a splendid slang term, new to me, for the waterbug ("fr. the allusion to his walking on water," the "his" being firmly lower case). He does get in via His second name, which, luckily, has given us a rather important adjective, *usu. cap.*

• • •

One of the problems of an unabridger is where completeness ends and madness begins. The compilers of 2 had a weakness for such fabrications as *philomuse, philomythia* ("devotion to legends . . . sometimes, loquaciousness"), *philonoist* ("a seeker of knowledge"), *philophilosophos* ("partial to philosophers"), *philopolemic, philopornist* ("a lover of harlots"), and *philosopheress* (which means not only a woman philosopher, like Hannah Arendt, but a philosopher's wife, like Xantippe). These are omitted by the compilers of 3, though they could not resist *philosophastering* ("philosophizing in a shallow or pretentious manner"). But why do we need *nooky* ("full of nooks") or *name-caller* ("one that habitually engages in name-calling") or all those "night" words, from *night clothes* —"garments worn in bed," with a citation from Jane Welsh Carlyle, of all people—through *nightdress, nightgear, nightgown, nightrobe, nightshirt,* and *nightwear?* What need of *sea boat* ("a boat adapted to the open sea") or *sea captain* or *swimming pool* ("a pool suitable for swimming," lest we imagine it is a pool that swims) or *sunbath* ("exposure to sunlight"—"or to a sun lamp," they add cautiously) or *sunbather* ("one that takes sunbaths")? Why *kittenless* ("having no kitten")? Why need we be told that *white-faced* is "having the face white in whole or in part"? Or that *whitehanded* is "having white hands"? (They missed *white-lipped.*)

Then there are those terrible negative prefixes, which the unwary unabridger gets started on and slides down with sickening momentum. 3 has left out many of 2's absurdities: *nonborrower, nonnervous, non-Mohammedan, non-Welsh, non-walking.* But it adds some of its own: *nonscientist, nonphilatelic, non-inbred, nondrying* (why no *nonwetting?*), *nonbank* ("not being or done by a bank"), and many other non-useful and nonsensical entries. It has thirty-four pages of words beginning with *un-,* and while it may seem carping to object to this abundance, since the O.E.D. has three hundred and eighty such pages, I think, given the difference in purpose, that many may be challenged. A reasonably bright child of ten will not have to run to Daddy's Unabridged to find the meaning of *unreelable* ("incapable of being wound on a reel"), *unlustrous* ("lacking luster"), or *unpowdered* ("not powdered"). And if it's for unreasonably dumb children, why omit *unspinnable, unshining,* and *unsanded?*

For a minor example of Gnostomania, or scholar's knee, see the treatment of numbers. Every number from *one* to *ninety-nine* is entered and defined, also every numerical adjective. Thus when the reader hits *sixty* he goes into a skid fifteen inches long. *Sixty* ("being one more than 59 in number") is followed by the pronoun ("60 countable persons or things not specified but under consideration and being enumerated") and the noun ("six tens: twice 30: 12 fives," etc.) Then comes *sixty-eight* ("being one more than 67 in number") and *sixty-eighth* ("being number 68 in a countable series"), followed by *sixty-fifth, sixty-first,* and so on. The compilers of 2 dealt with the *sixty* problem in a mere two entries totalling an inch and a half. But the art of lexicography has mutated into a "science" since then. (*"Quotation mark* . . . sometimes used to enclose . . . words . . . in an . . . ironical . . . sense . . . or words for which a writer offers a slight apology.") In reading 3 one sometimes feels like a subscriber who gets two hundred and thirty-eight copies of the May issue because the addressing machine got stuck, and it doesn't make it any better to know that the operators jammed it on purpose.

My complaint is not that 3 is all-inclusive—that is, unabridged—but that *pedantry* is not a synonym of *scholarship*. I have no objection to the inclusion of such pomposities, mostly direct translations from the Latin, as *viridity* (greenness), *presbyopic* (farsighted because of old age), *vellication* (twitching), *pudency* (modesty), and *vulnerary* (wound-healing). These are necessary if only so that one can read James Gould Cozzens' "By Love Possessed," in which they all occur, along with many siblings. And in my rambles through these 2,662 pages I have come across many a splendid word that has not enjoyed the popularity it deserves. I think my favorites are *pilpul,* from the Hebrew *to search,* which means "critical analysis and hair-splitting; casuistic argumentation"; *dysphemism,* which is the antonym of *euphemism* (as, *axle grease* for *butter* or *old man* for *father), subfusc,* from the Latin *subfuscus,* meaning brownish, which is illustrated with a beautiful citation from Osbert Sitwell ("the moment when the word Austerity was to take to itself a new subfusc and squalid twist of meaning")—cf. the more familiar *subacid,* also well illustrated with "a little subacid kind of . . . impatience," from Laurence Sterne; *nanism,* which is the antonym of *gigantism; mesocracy,* which is the form of government we increasingly have in this country; and *lib-lab,* which means a Liberal who sympathizes with Labor—I wish the lexicographers had not restored the hyphen I deleted when I imported it from England twenty years ago. One might say, and in fact I will say, that H. L. Mencken,* whose prose was dysphemistic but never subfusc, eschewed pilpul in expressing his nanitic esteem for lib-lab mesocracy. Unfortunately, 3 omits 2's *thob* ("to think according to one's wishes"), which someone made up from *think-opinion-believe,* or else I could also have noted Mencken's distaste for thobbery.

Dr. Gove met the problem of *ain't* head on in the best traditions of Structural Linguistics, labelling it—reluctantly, one imagines—*substandard* for *have not* and *has not,* but giving it, unlabelled, as a contraction of *am not, are not,* and *is not,* adding "though disapproved by many and more common in less educated speech, used orally in most parts of the U.S. by many cultivated speakers esp. in the phrase ain't I." This was courageous indeed; when Dr. C. C. Fries, the dean of Structural Linguists today, said, at a meeting of the Modern Language Association several years ago, that *ain't* was not wholly disreputable, a teapot tempest boiled up in the press. When Dr. Gove included a reference to the entry on *ain't* in the press announcement of 3, the newspapers seethed again, from the Houston *Press* ("It Ain't Uncouth To Say Ain't Now") to the San Francisco *Examiner* ("Ain't Bad at All—In Newest Revised Dictionary") and the *World-Telegram* ("It Just Ain't True That Ain't Ain't in the Dictionary"). But moral courage is not the only quality a good lexicographer needs. Once the matter of education and culture is raised, we are right back at the non-scientific business of deciding

* H. L. Mencken: (1880–1956), American journalist, essayist, satirist; author of *The American Language* (1st ed., 1919), a discussion of the development of the English language in the U.S.

what is correct—*standard* is the modern euphemism—and this is more a matter of a feeling for language (what the trade calls *Sprachgefühl*) than of the statistics on which Dr. Gove and his colleagues seem to have chiefly relied. For what Geiger counter will decide who is in fact educated or cultivated? And what adding machine will discriminate between *ain't* used because the speaker thinks it is standard English and *ain't* used because he wants to get a special effect? "Survival must have quality, or it ain't worth a bean," Thornton Wilder recently observed. It doesn't take much *Sprachgefühl* to recognize that Mr. Wilder is here being a mite folksy and that his effect would be lost if *ain't* were indeed "used orally in most parts of the U.S. by many cultivated speakers." Though I regret that the nineteenth-century schoolteachers without justification deprived us of *ain't* for *am not,* the deed was done, and I think the *Dial. or Illit.* with which 2 labels all uses of the word comes closer to linguistic fact today.

The pejorative labels in 2 are forthright: *colloquial, erroneous, incorrect, illiterate.* 3 replaces these self-explanatory terms with two that are both fuzzier and more scientific-sounding: *substandard* and *nonstandard.* The first "indicates status conforming to a pattern of linguistic usage that exists throughout the American language community but differs in choice of word or form from that of the prestige group in that community," which is academese for "Not used by educated people." *Hisself* and *drownded* are labelled *substand.,* which sounds better than *erron.*—more democratic. *Nonstandard* "is used for a very small number of words that can hardly stand without some status label but are too widely current in reputable context to be labelled *substand.*" *Irregardless* is given as an example, which for me again raises doubts about the compilers' notion of a reputable context. I think 2's label for the word, *erron. or humorous,* more accurate.

The argument has now shifted from whether a dictionary should be an authority as against a reporter (in Dr. Gove's terms, prescriptive v. descriptive) to the validity of the prescriptive guidance that 3 does in fact give. For Dr. Gove and his colleagues have not ventured to omit all qualitative discriminations; they have cut them down drastically from 2, but they have felt obliged to include many. Perhaps by 1988, if the Structural Linguists remain dominant, there will be a fourth edition, which will simply record, without labels or warnings, all words and non-words that are used widely in "the American language community," including such favorites of a former President as *nucular* (warfare), *invidous,* and *mischievious.* But it is still 1962, and 3 often does discriminate. The trouble is that its willingness to do so has been weakened by its scientific conscience, so that it palters and equivocates; this is often more misleading than would be the omission of all discriminations.

One drawback to the permissive approach of the Structural Linguists is that it impoverishes the language by not objecting to errors if they are common enough. ("And how should I presume?"—*T. S. Eliot.*) * There is a natural ten-

---

* "The Love Song of J. Alfred Prufrock," 1917.

dency among human beings, who are *by def.* fallible, to confuse similar-sounding words. "One look at him would turn you nauseous," Phil Silvers said on television one night, as better stylists have written before. Up to now, dictionaries have distinguished *nauseous* (causing nausea) from *nauseated* (experiencing nausea); 2 labels *nauseous* in the sense of experiencing nausea *obs.*, but it is no longer *obs.* It is simply *erron.*, a fact you will not learn from 3, which gives as its first definition, without label, "affected with or inclining to nausea." So the language is *balled up* and *nauseous* is telescoped into *nauseated* and nobody knows who means which exactly. The magisterial Fowler *—magisterial, that is, until the Structural Linguists got to work—has an entry on Pairs & Snares that makes sad reading now. He calls *deprecate* and *depreciate* "one of the altogether false pairs," but 3 gives the latter as a synonym of the first. It similarly blurs the distinction between Fowler's *forcible* ("effected by force") and *forceful* ("full of force"), *unexceptional* ("constituting no exception to the general rule") and *unexceptionable* ("not open or liable to objection," which is quite a different thing). A Pair & Snare Fowler doesn't give is *disinterested* (impartial) and *uninterested* (not interested); 2 lists the *uninterested* sense of *disinterested* but adds, *"now rare;"* even such permissive lexicographers as Bergen and Cornelia Evans, in their "Dictionary of Contemporary American Usage," state firmly, "Though *disinterested* was formerly a synonym for *uninterested,* it is not now so used." But 3 gives *disinterested* as a synonym of *uninterested.*

Each such confusion makes the language less efficient, and it is a dictionary's job to *define* words, which means, literally, to set limits to them. 3 still distinguishes *capital* from *capitol* and *principle* from *principal,* but how many more language-community members must join the present sizable band that habitually confuses these words before they go down the drain with the others? Perhaps nothing much is lost if almost everybody calls Frankenstein the monster rather than the man who made the monster, even though Mrs. Shelley wrote it the other way, but how is one to deal with the *bimonthly* problem? 2 defines it as "once in two months," which is correct. 3 gives this as the first meaning and then adds, gritting its teeth, *"sometimes:* twice a month." (It defines *biweekly* as "every two weeks" and adds "2: twice a week.") It does seem a little awkward to have a word that can mean every two weeks *or* every eight weeks, and it would have been convenient if 3 had compromised with scientific integrity enough to replace its perfectly accurate *sometimes* with a firm *erroneous.* But this would have implied authority, and authority is the last thing 3's modest recorders want. ("Let this cup pass from me."—*New Testament.*)

The objection is not to recording the facts of actual usage. It is to failing to give the information that would enable the reader to decide which usage he wants to adopt. If he prefers to use *deprecate* and *depreciate* interchangeably, no dictionary can prevent him, but at least he should be warned. Thus 3 has under

---

* H. W. Fowler: English lexicographer and grammarian; the entry on Pairs & Snares is in his *Dictionary of Modern English Usage* (1926).

transpire—"4: to come to pass; happen, occur." 2 has the same entry, but it is followed by a monitory pointing hand: *"transpire* in this sense has been disapproved by most authorities on usage, although the meaning occurs in the writings of many authors of good standing." Fair enough. I also prefer 2's handling of the common misuse of *infer* to mean *imply*—"5: loosely and erroneously, to imply." 3 sounds no warning, and twice under *infer* it advises "compare imply." Similarly, 2 labels the conjunctive *like* "illiterate" and "incorrect," which it is, adding that "in the works of careful writers [it] is replaced by *as."* 3 accepts it as standard, giving such unprepossessing citations as "impromptu programs where they ask questions much like I do on the air—Art Linkletter" and "wore his clothes like he was . . . afraid of getting dirt on them—*St. Petersburg (Fla.) Independent."* Enthuse is labelled *colloq.* in 2 but not in 3. It still sounds *colloq.* if not *godawf.* to me, nor am I impressed by 3's citations, from writers named L. G. Pine and Lawrence Constable and from a trade paper called *Fashion Accessories.* Or consider the common misuse of *too* when *very* is meant, as "I was not too interested in the lecture." 2 gives this use but labels it *colloq.* 3 gives it straight and cites Irving Kolodin: "an episodic work without too consistent a texture;" Mr. Kolodin probably means "without a very consistent texture," but how does one know he doesn't mean "without an excessively consistent [or monotonous] texture"? In music criticism such ambiguities are not too helpful.

In dealing with words that might be considered slang, 2 uses the label wherever there is doubt, while 3 leans the other way. The first procedure seems to me more sensible, since no great harm is done if a word is labelled slang until its pretensions to being standard have been thoroughly tested (as long as it is admitted into the dictionary), while damage may be done if it is prematurely accepted as standard. Thus both 2 and 3 list such women's-magazine locutions as *galore, scads, scrumptious,* and *too-too,* but only 2 labels them slang. (Fowler's note on *galore* applies to them all: "Chiefly resorted to by those who are reduced to relieving the dullness of matter by oddity of expression.") Thus *rummy, spang* (in the middle of), and *nobby* are in both, but only 2 calls them slang.

Admittedly, the question is most difficult. Many words begin as slang and then rise in the world. Dean Swift,* a great purist, objected to *mob* (from the Latin *mobile vulgus), banter, bully,* and *sham;* he also objected to *hyp,* which has disappeared as slang for *hypochondriac,* and *rep,* which persists for *reputation* but is still labelled slang even in 3. Some slang words have survived for centuries without bettering themselves, like the Jukes * and the Kallikaks.* *Dukes* (fists)

* Dean Swift: Jonathan Swift (1667–1745), Irish satirist and political writer.
* the Jukes: "fictitious name of a family that was the subject of a study of hereditary tendencies to crime, immorality, disease and poverty by Richard L. Dugdale, 1883, American sociologist: a stupid person . . . compare Kallikak" (*Webster's Third International Dictionary*).
* the Kallikaks: "fictitious name of a family having one branch consisting mainly of intelligent and successful persons and another branch containing a large proportion of mentally deficient and immoral persons that was studied by H. H. Goddard, 1957, American psychologist: . . . a stupid person . . .' compare Jukes" (*Webster's Third International Dictionary*).

and *duds* (clothes) are still slang, although they go back to the eighteenth and the sixteenth century, respectively.

The definition of *slang* in 3 is "characterized primarily by connotations of extreme informality . . . coinages or arbitrarily changed words, clipped or shortened forms, extravagant, forced, or facetious figures of speech or verbal novelties usu. experiencing quick popularity and relatively rapid decline into disuse." A good definition (Dr. Gove has added that slang is "linguistically self-conscious"), but it seems to have been forgotten in making up 3, most of whose discriminations about slang strike me as arbitrary. According to 3, *scram* is not slang, but *vamoose* is. *"Goof 1"* ("to make a mistake or blunder") is not slang, but *"goof 2"* ("to spend time idly or foolishly") is, and the confusion is compounded when one finds that Ethel Merman is cited for the non-slang *goof* and James T. Farrell for the slang *goof*. *"Floozy 1"* ("an attractive young woman of loose morals") is standard, but *"floozy 2"* ("a dissolute and sometimes slovenly woman") is slang. Can even a Structural Linguist make such fine distinctions about such a word? The many synonyms for *drunk* raise the same question. Why are *oiled, pickled,* and *boiled* labelled slang if *soused* and *spiflicated* are not? Perhaps cooking terms for *drunk* are automatically slang, but why?

I don't mean to *imply* (see *infer*) that the compilers of 3 didn't give much thought to the problem. When they came to a doubtful word, they took a staff poll, asking everybody to check it, after reviewing the accumulated cites, as either slang or standard. This resulted in *cornball's* being entered as slang and *corny's* being entered as standard. Such scientific, or quantitative, efforts to separate the goats from the sheep produced the absurdities noted above. Professor Austin C. Dobbins raised this point in *College English* for October, 1956:

> But what of such words as *boondoggle, corny, frisk, liquidate, pinched, bonehead, carpetbagger, pleb, slush fund,* and *snide*? Which of these words ordinarily would be considered appropriate in themes written by cultivated people? According to the editors of the ACD [the American College Dictionary, the 1953 edition, published by Random House] the first five of these words are slang; the second five are established usage. To the editors of WNCD [Webster's New Collegiate Dictionary, published by Merriam-Webster in the same year] the first five of these words represent established usage; the second five are slang. Which authority is the student to follow?

Mr. Dobbins is by no means hostile to Structural Linguistics, and his essay appears in a recent anthology edited by Dr. Harold B. Allen, of the University of Minnesota, an energetic proponent of the new school. "Perhaps the answer," Mr. Dobbins concludes, "is to advise students to study only one handbook, consult one dictionary, listen to one instructor. An alternate suggestion, of course, is for our textbooks more accurately to base their labels upon studies of usage." Assuming the first alternative is ironical, I would say the second is impractical unless the resources of a dozen Ford Foundations are devoted to trying to decide the matter scientifically—that is, statistically.

Short of this Land of Cockaigne, where partridges appear in the fields ready-roasted, I see only two logical alternatives: to label all doubtful words slang, as 2 does, or to drop the label entirely, as I suspect Dr. Gove would have liked to do. Using the label sparingly, if it is not to produce bizarre effects, takes a lot more *Sprachgefühl* than the editors of 3 seem to have possessed. Thus *horse* as a verb ("to engage in horseplay") they accept as standard. The citations are from Norman Mailer ("I never horse around much with the women") and J. D. Salinger ("I horse around quite a lot, just to keep from getting bored"). I doubt whether either Mr. Mailer or Mr. Salinger would use *horse* straight; in these cites, I venture, it is either put in the mouth of a first-person narrator or used deliberately to get a colloquial effect. Slang is concise and vivid—*jalopy* has advantages over *dilapidated automobile*—and a few slang terms salted in a formal paragraph bring out the flavor. But the user must know he *is* using slang, he must be aware of having introduced a slight discord into his harmonics, or else he coarsens and blurs his expression. This information he will not, for the most part, get from 3. I hate to think what monstrosities of prose foreigners and high-school students will produce if they take 3 seriously as a guide to what is and what is not standard English.

Whenever the compilers of 3 come up against a locution that some (me, or I) might consider simply wrong, they do their best, as Modern Linguists and democrats, to be good fellows. The softening-up process begins with substituting the euphemistic *substandard* for 2's blunt *erroneous* and *illiterate*. From there it expands into several forms. *Complected* (for *complexioned*) is *dialect* in 2, *not often in formal use* in 3. *Learn* (for teach) is *now a vulgarism* in 2, *now chiefly substand.* in 3. (*Chiefly* is the thin end of the wedge, implying that users of standard English on occasion exclaim, "I'll learn you to use bad English!") *Knowed* is listed as the past of *know* though *broke* is labelled substandard for *broken*—another of those odd discriminations. Doubtless they counted noses, or citation slips, and concluded that "Had I but knowed!" is standard while "My heart is broke" is substandard.

(To be entirely fair, perhaps compulsively so: If one reads carefully the five closely printed pages of Explanatory Notes in 3, and especially paragraphs 16.0 through 16.6 (twelve inches of impenetrable lexical jargon), one finds that light-face small capitals mean a cross-reference, and if one looks up know—which is given after *knowed* in light-face small capitals—one does find that *knowed* is dialect. This is not a very practical or sensible dictionary, one concludes after such scholarly labors, and one wonders why Dr. Gove and his editors did not think of labeling *knowed* as substandard right where it occurs, and one suspects that they wanted to slightly conceal the fact or at any rate to put off its exposure as long as decently possible.)

The systematic softening or omitting of pejorative labels in 3 could mean: (1)

we have come to use English more loosely, to say the least, than we did in 1934; or (2) usage hasn't changed, but 3 has simply recorded The Facts more accurately; or (3) the notion of what is a relevant Fact has changed between 2 and 3. I suspect it is mostly (3), but in any case I cannot see *complected* as anything but *dialected*.

In 1947 the G. & C. Merriam Co. published a little book entitled "Noah's Ark"—in reference to Noah Webster, who began it all—celebrating its first hundred years as the publisher of Webster dictionaries. Toward the end, the author, Robert Keith Leavitt, rises to heights of eloquence which have a tinny sound now that "Webster" means not 2 but 3:

> This responsibility to the user is no light matter. It has, indeed, grown heavier with every year of increasing acceptance of Webster. Courts, from the United States Supreme Court down, rely on the *New International's* definitions as a sort of common law: many a costly suit has hinged on a Webster definition, and many a citizen has gone behind prison bars or walked out onto the streets a free man, according to the light Webster put upon his doings. The statute law itself is not infrequently phrased by legislators in terms straight out of Webster. Most daily newspapers and magazines, and nearly all the books that come off the press, are edited and printed in accordance with Websterian usage. Colleges and schools make the *New International* their standard, and, for nearly half a century, students have dug their way through pedantic obscurity with the aid of the *Collegiate*. In business offices the secretary corrects her boss out of Webster and the boss holds customers and contractors alike in line by citing how Webster says it shall be done. In thousands upon thousands of homes, youngsters lying sprawled under the table happily absorb from Webster information which teachers have striven in vain to teach them from textbooks. Clear through, indeed, to the everyday American's most trivial and jocose of doings, Webster is the unquestioned authority.

While this picture is a bit idyllic—Clarence Barnhart's American College Dictionary, put out by Random House, is considered by many to be at least as good as the Webster Collegiate—it had some reality up to 1961. But as of today, courts that Look It Up In Webster will often find themselves little the wiser, since 3 claims no authority and merely records, mostly deadpan, what in fact every Tom, Dick, and Harry is now doing—in all innocence—to the language. That freedom or imprisonment should depend on 3 is an alarming idea. The secretary correcting her boss, if he is a magazine publisher, will collide with the unresolved *bimonthly* and *biweekly* problem, and the youngsters sprawled under the table will happily absorb from 3 the information that *jerk* is standard for "a stupid, foolish, naïve, or unconventional person." One imagines the themes: "Dr. Johnson admired Goldsmith's literary talent although he considered him a jerk." The editors of the New Webster's Vest Pocket Dictionary, thirty-nine cents at any cigar store, label *jerk* as *coll*. But then they aren't Structural Linguists.

The reviews of 3 in the lay press have not been enthusiastic. *Life* and the *Times* have both attacked it editorially as a "say-as-you-go" dictionary that reflects "the permissive school" in language study. The usually solemn editorialists of the *Times* were goaded to unprecedented wit:

> A passel of double-domes at the G. & C. Merriam Company joint in Springfield, Mass. [the editorial began], have been confabbing and yakking for twenty-seven years—which is not intended to infer that they have not been doing plenty work—and now they have finalized Webster's Third New International Dictionary, Unabridged, a new edition of that swell and esteemed word book.
>
> Those who regard the foregoing paragraph as acceptable English prose will find that the new Webster's is just the dictionary for them.

But the lay press doesn't always prevail. The irreverent may call 3 "Gove's Goof," but Dr. Gove and his editors are part of the dominant movement in the professional study of language—one that has in the last few years established strong beachheads in the National Council of Teachers of English and the College English Association. One may grant that for the scientific study of language the Structural Linguistic approach is superior to that of the old grammarians, who overestimated the importance of logic and Latin, but one may still object to its transfer directly to the teaching of English and the making of dictionaries. As a scientific discipline, Structural Linguistics can have no truck with values or standards. Its job is to deal only with The Facts. But in matters of usage, the evaluation of The Facts is important, too, and this requires a certain amount of general culture, not to mention common sense—commodities that many scientists have done brilliantly without but that teachers and lexicographers need in their work.

The kind of thinking responsible for 3 is illustrated by Dr. Gove's riposte, last week, to the many unfavorable reviews of his dictionary: "The criticisms involve less than one per cent of the words in the dictionary." This quantitative approach might be useful to novelists who get bad reviews. It is foolproof here; a reviewer who tried to meet Dr. Gove's criterion and deal with a sizable proportion of 3's words—say, ten per cent—would need forty-five thousand words just to list them, and if his own comments averaged ten words apiece he would have to publish his five-hundred-thousand-word review in two large volumes. Some odd thinking gets done up at the old Merriam-Webster place in Springfield.

Dr. Gove's letter to the *Times* objecting to its editorial was also interesting. "The editors of *Webster's Third New International Dictionary* are not amused by the ingenuity of the first paragraph of your editorial," it began loftily, and continued, "Your paragraph obscures, or attempts to obscure, the fact that there are so many different degrees of standard usage that dictionary definitions cannot hope to distinguish one from another by status labelling." (But the *Times*' point was precisely that the editors did make such distinctions by status labelling, only they were the wrong distinctions; i.e., by omitting pejorative labels they accepted as standard words that, in the opinion of the *Times,* are not standard.) There followed several pages of citations in which Dr. Gove showed that the *Times* itself had often used the very words it objected to 3's including as standard language. "If we are ever inclined to the linguistic pedantry that easily fails to distinguish moribund traditions from genuine living usage [the adjectives here are perhaps more revealing than Dr. Gove intended] we have only to turn to the columns of the *Times,"* Dr. Gove concluded. The *Times* is the best newspaper in the world in the gathering and printing of news, but it has never been noted for stylistic distinction. And even if it were, the exigencies of printing a small book every day might be expected to drive the writers and editors of a newspaper into usages as convenient as they are sloppy—usages that people with more time on their hands, such as the editors of an unabridged dictionary, might distinguish from standard English.

There are several reasons that it is important to maintain standards in the use of a language. English, like other languages, is beautiful when properly used, and beauty can be achieved only by attention to form, which means setting limits, or de-fining, or dis-criminating. Language expresses the special, dis-tinctive quality of a people, and a people, like an individual, is to a large extent defined by its past—its traditions—whether it is conscious of this or not. If the language is allowed to shift too rapidly, without challenge from teachers and lexicographers, then the special character of the American people is blurred, since it tends to lose its past. In the same way a city loses its character if too much of it is torn down and rebuilt too quickly. "Languages are the pedigrees of nations," said Dr. Johnson.*

The effect on the individual is also unfortunate. The kind of permissiveness that permeates 3 (the kind that a decade or two ago was more common in progressive schools than it is now) results, oddly, in less rather than more individuality, since the only way an individual can "express himself" is in relation to a social norm—in the case of language, to standard usage. James Joyce's creative distortions of words were possible only because he had a perfect ear for orthodox English. But if the very idea of form, or standards, is lacking, then how can one violate it? It's no fun to use *knowed* for *known* if everybody thinks you're just trying to be standard.

Counting cite slips is simply not the way to go about the delicate business of deciding these matters. If nine-tenths of the citizens of the United States, including a recent President, were to use *inviduous,* the one-tenth who clung to *invidious* would still be right, and they would be doing a favor to the majority if they continued to maintain the point. It is perhaps not democratic, according to some recent users, or abusers, of the word, to insist on this, and the question comes up

* Dr. Johnson: Samuel Johnson (1709–81), published his great *Dictionary of the English Language* in 1755; he strongly resisted linguistic change, though he admitted that it was inevitable.

of who is to decide at what point change—for language does indeed change, as the Structural Linguists insist—has evolved from *slang, dial., erron.,* or *substand.* to *standard.* The decision, I think, must be left to the teachers, the professional writers, and the lexicographers, and they might look up Ulysses' famous defense of conservatism in Shakespeare's "Troilus and Cressida":

> The heavens themselves, the planets and this centre
> Observe degree, priority and place,
> Insisture, course, proportion, season, form,
> Office and custom in all line of order. . . .
> Take but degree away, untune that string,
> And, hark, what discord follows! Each thing meets
> In mere oppugnancy. The bounded waters
> Should lift their bosoms higher than the shores
> And make a sop of all this solid globe.
> Strength should be lord of imbecility
> And the rude son should strike his father dead.
> Force should be right, or rather right and wrong
> (Between whose endless jar justice resides)
> Should lose their names, and so should justice too.
> Then every thing includes itself in power,
> Power into will, will into appetite
> And appetite, a universal wolf,
> So doubly seconded with will and power,
> Must make perforce a universal prey
> And, last, eat up himself. . . .

Dr. Johnson, a dictionary-maker of the old school, defined *lexicographer* as "a harmless drudge." Things have changed. Lexicographers may still be drudges, but they are certainly not harmless. They have untuned the string, made a sop of the solid structure of English, and encouraged the language to eat up himself.

George Orwell / Newspeak

This is the Appendix to Orwell's novel *Nineteen Eighty-four,* published in 1949. The novel is about the life of an intelligent man who lives under absolute totalitarian control. The Party regulates the life of everybody, alters history, and above all corrupts language in its pursuit of power. Winston Smith himself is employed in altering old newspapers to make Party statements therein conform to what happened rather than allow them to stand as incorrect predictions. He destroys historical persons for the Party, has power to make anyone, alive or dead, an unperson; and he invents others who never really existed.

Smith hates the squalor of life in his society and constantly commits "thoughtcrime." Newspeak is a means of abolishing thoughtcrime. A colleague tells him: "It's a beautiful thing, the destruction of words. . . . If you have a word like 'good,' what need is there for a word like 'bad'? 'Ungood' will do just as well. . . . It was B.B.'s [Big Brother's] idea originally, of course. . . . Do you know that Newspeak is the only language in the world whose vocabulary gets smaller every year? . . . Don't you see that the whole aim of Newspeak is to narrow the range of thought? In the end we shall make thoughtcrime literally impossible, because there will be no words in which to express it. . . . Every year fewer and fewer words, and the range of consciousness always a little smaller. . . . The Revolution will be complete when the language is perfect."

The book says that the Party is interested only in power, and that power can be asserted only by making people suffer. Smith becomes its victim; the last representative of the human spirit, he ends as a physical and mental wreck, loving Big Brother.

Orwell, like any other writer about the future, was thinking about tendencies he took to be already present. One of these was the undermining of language, notably by politicians. Newspeak is an extension of this on an appropriately totalitarian scale. It is the instrument of Ingsoc (English Socialism) and of tyranny. In the Appendix he works out its structure in considerable grammatical and lexical detail. The corruption of society by allowing or causing language to degenerate to the point where it is the instrument of lies is not a new idea; it was familiar to Ben Jonson and Swift. But Orwell was writing at the height of Stalinism; such concepts as "unperson" and thoughtcrime were being expressed in everyday practice, and they seemed, perhaps more terribly than anything had before, to threaten the civilized concepts of truth, freedom, and the value of the personality. It is the more remarkable that he was able coolly to work out this fantasy of a new and totally corrupt language. The value of his work survives the historical moment that produced it. It is easy enough to see in the modern world the same processes in motion, whether in political speeches or in advertisements.

Newspeak was the official language of Oceania and had been devised to meet the ideological needs of Ingsoc, or English Socialism. In the year 1984 there was not as yet anyone who used Newspeak as his sole means of communication, either in speech or writing. The leading articles in the *Times* were written in it, but this was a tour de force which could only be carried out by a specialist. It was expected that Newspeak would have finally superseded Oldspeak (or Standard English, as we should call it) by about the year 2050. Meanwhile it gained ground steadily, all Party members tending to use Newspeak words and grammatical constructions more and more in their everyday speech. The version in use in 1984, and embodied in the Ninth and Tenth Editions of the Newspeak dictionary, was a provisional one, and contained many superfluous words and archaic formations which were due to be suppressed later. It is with the final, perfected version, as embodied in the Eleventh Edition of the dictionary, that we are concerned here.

The purpose of Newspeak was not only to provide a medium of expression for the world-view and mental habits proper to the devotees of Ingsoc, but to make all other modes of thought impossible. It was intended that when Newspeak had been adopted once and for all and Oldspeak forgotten, a heretical thought—that is, a thought diverging from the principles of Ingsoc—should be literally unthinkable, at least so far as thought is dependent on words. Its vocabulary was so constructed as to give exact and often very subtle expression to every meaning that a Party member could properly wish to express, while excluding all other meanings and also the possibility of arriving at them by indirect methods. This was done partly by the invention of new words, but chiefly by eliminating undesirable words and by stripping such words as remained of unorthodox meanings, and so far as possible of all secondary meanings whatever. To give a single example. The word *free* still existed in Newspeak, but it could only be used in such statements as "This dog is free from lice" or "This field is free from weeds." It could not be used in its old sense of "politically free" or "intellectually free," since political and intellectual freedom no longer existed even as concepts, and were therefore of necessity nameless. Quite apart from the suppression of definitely heretical words, reduction of vocabulary was regarded as an end in itself, and no word that could be dispensed with was allowed to survive. Newspeak was designed not to extend but to *diminish* the range of thought, and this purpose was indirectly assisted by cutting the choice of words down to a minimum.

Newspeak was founded on the English language as we now know it, though many Newspeak sentences, even when not containing newly created words, would be barely intelligible to an English-speaker of our own day. Newspeak words were divided into three distinct classes, known as the *A* vocabulary, the *B* vocabulary (also called compound words), and the *C* vocabulary. It will be simpler to discuss each class separately, but the grammatical peculiarities of the language can be dealt with in the section devoted to the *A* vocabulary, since the same rules held good for all three categories.

THE A VOCABULARY

The A vocabulary consisted of the words needed for the business of everyday life—for such things as eating, drinking, working, putting on one's clothes, going up and down stairs, riding in vehicles, gardening, cooking, and the like. It was composed almost entirely of words that we already possess—words like *hit*, *run, dog, tree, sugar, house, field*—but in comparison with the present-day English vocabulary, their number was extremely small, while their meanings were far more rigidly defined. All ambiguities and shades of meaning had been purged out of them. So far as it could be achieved, a Newspeak word of this class was simply a staccato sound expressing *one* clearly understood concept. It would have been quite impossible to use the A vocabulary for literary purposes or for political or philosophical discussion. It was intended only to express simple, purposive thoughts, usually involving concrete objects or physical actions.

The grammar of Newspeak had two outstanding peculiarities. The first of these was an almost complete interchangeability between different parts of speech. Any word in the language (in principle this applied even to very abstract words such as *if* or *when*) could be used either as verb, noun, adjective, or adverb. Between the verb and the noun form, when they were of the same root, there was never any variation, this rule of itself involving the destruction of many archaic forms. The word *thought*, for example, did not exist in Newspeak. Its place was taken by *think*, which did duty for both noun and verb. No etymological principle was followed here; in some cases it was the original noun that was chosen for retention, in other cases the verb. Even where a noun and verb of kindred meaning were not etymologically connected, one or other of them was frequently suppressed. There was, for example, no such word as *cut*, its meaning being sufficiently covered by the noun-verb *knife*. Adjectives were formed by adding the suffix *-ful* to the noun-verb, and adverbs by adding *-wise*. Thus, for example, *speedful* meant "rapid" and *speedwise* meant "quickly." Certain of our present-day adjectives, such as *good, strong, big, black, soft*, were retained, but their total number was very small. There was little need for them, since almost any adjectival meaning could be arrived at by adding *-ful* to a noun-verb. None of the now-existing adverbs was retained, except for a very few already ending in *-wise;* the *-wise* termination was invariable. The word *well,* for example, was replaced by *goodwise.*

In addition, any word—this again applied in principle to every word in the language—could be negatived by adding the affix *un-,* or could be strengthened by the affix *plus-,* or, for still greater emphasis, *doubleplus-.* Thus, for example, *uncold* meant *"warm,"* while *pluscold* and *doublepluscold* meant, respectively, "very cold" and "superlatively cold." It was also possible, as in present-day English, to modify the meaning of almost any word by prepositional affixes such as *ante-, post-, down-,* etc. By such methods it was found possible to bring about an enormous diminution of vocabulary. Given, for instance, the word *good,* there was no need for such a word as *bad,* since the required meaning was equally well—indeed, better—expressed by *un-good.* All that was necessary, in any case where two words formed a natural pair of opposites, was to decide which of them to suppress. *Dark,* for example, could be replaced by *unlight,* or *light* by *undark,* according to preference.

The second distinguishing mark of Newspeak grammar was its regularity. Subject to a few exceptions which are mentioned below, all inflections followed the same rules. Thus, in all verbs the preterite and the past participle were the same and ended in *-ed*. The preterite of *steal* was *stealed,* the preterite of *think* was *thinked,* and so on throughout the language, all such forms as *swam, gave, brought, spoke, taken,* etc., being abolished. All plurals were made by adding *-s* or *-es* as the case might be. The plurals of *man, ox, life* were *mans, oxes, lifes.* Comparison of adjectives was invariably made by adding *-er, -est* (*good, gooder, goodest*), irregular forms and the *more, most* formation being suppressed.

The only classes of words that were still allowed to inflect irregularly were the pronouns, the relatives, the demonstrative adjectives, and the auxiliary verbs. All of these followed their ancient usage, except that *whom* had been scrapped as unnecessary, and the *shall, should* tenses had been dropped, all their uses being covered by *will* and *would.* There were also certain irregularities in word-formation arising out of the need for rapid and easy speech. A word which was difficult to utter, or was liable to be incorrectly heard, was held to be ipso facto a bad word; occasionally therefore, for the sake of euphony, extra letters were inserted into a word or an archaic formation was retained. But this need made itself felt chiefly in connection with the B vocabulary. *Why* so great an importance was attached to ease of pronunciation will be made clear later in this essay.

THE B VOCABULARY

The B vocabulary consisted of words which had been deliberately constructed for political purposes: words, that is to say, which not only had in every case a political implication, but were intended to impose a desirable mental attitude upon the person using them. Without a full understanding of the principles of Ingsoc it was difficult to use these words correctly. In some cases they could be translated into Oldspeak, or even into words taken from the A vocabulary, but this usually demanded a long paraphrase and always involved the loss of certain overtones. The B words were a sort of verbal shorthand, often packing whole ranges of ideas into a few syllables, and at the same time more accurate and forcible than ordinary language.

The B words were in all cases compound words.[1] They consisted of two or more words, or portions of words, welded together in an easily pronounceable form. The resulting amalgam was always a noun-verb, and inflected according to the ordinary rules. To take a single example: the word *goodthink,* meaning, very roughly, "orthodoxy," or, if one chose to regard it as a verb, "to think in an orthodox manner." This inflected as follows: noun-verb, *goodthink;* past tense and past participle, *goodthinked;* present participle, *goodthinking;* adjective, *goodthinkful;* adverb, *goodthinkwise;* verbal noun, *goodthinker.*

1. Compound words, such as *speakwrite,* were of course to be found in the A vocabulary, but these were merely convenient abbreviations and had no special ideological color.

The B words were not constructed on any etymological plan. The words of which they were made up could be any parts of speech, and could be placed in any order and mutilated in any way which made them easy to pronounce while indicating their derivation. In the word *crimethink* (thoughtcrime), for instance, the *think* came second, whereas in *thinkpol* (Thought Police) it came first, and in the latter word *police* had lost its second syllable. Because of the greater difficulty in securing euphony, irregular formations were commoner in the B vocabulary than in the A vocabulary. For example, the adjectival forms of *Minitrue, Minipax,* and *Miniluv* were, respectively, *Minitruthful, Minipeaceful,* and *Minilovely,* simply because *-trueful, -paxful,* and *-loveful* were slightly awkward to pronounce. In principle, however, all B words could inflect, and all inflected in exactly the same way.

Some of the B words had highly subtilized meanings, barely intelligible to anyone who had not mastered the language as a whole. Consider, for example, such a typical sentence from a *Times* leading article as *Oldthinkers unbellyfeel Ingsoc.* The shortest rendering that one could make of this in Oldspeak would be: "Those whose ideas were formed before the Revolution cannot have a full emotional understanding of the principles of English Socialism." But this is not an adequate translation. To begin with, in order to grasp the full meaning of the Newspeak sentence quoted above, one would have to have a clear idea of what is meant by *Ingsoc.* And, in addition, only a person thoroughly grounded in Ingsoc could appreciate the full force of the word *bellyfeel,* which implied a blind, enthusiastic acceptance difficult to imagine today; or of the word *oldthink,* which was inextricably mixed up with the idea of wickedness and decadence. But the special function of certain Newspeak words, of which *oldthink* was one, was not so much to express meanings as to destroy them. These words, necessarily few in number, had had their meanings extended until they contained within themselves whole batteries of words which, as they were sufficiently covered by a single comprehensive term, could now be scrapped and forgotten. The greatest difficulty facing the compilers of the Newspeak dictionary was not to invent new words, but, having invented them, to make sure what they meant: to make sure, that is to say, what ranges of words they canceled by their existence.

As we have already seen in the case of the word *free,* words which had once borne a heretical meaning were sometimes retained for the sake of convenience, but only with the undesirable meanings purged out of them. Countless other words such as *honor, justice, morality, internationalism, democracy, science,* and *religion* had simply ceased to exist. A few blanket words covered them, and, in covering them, abolished them. All words grouping themselves round the concepts of liberty and equality, for instance, were contained in the single word *crimethink,* while all words grouping themselves round the concepts of objectivity and rationalism were contained in the single word *oldthink.* Greater precision would have been dangerous. What was required in a Party member was an outlook similar to that of the ancient Hebrew who knew, without knowing much else, that all nations other than his own worshiped "false gods." He did not need to know that these gods were called Baal, Osiris, Moloch, Ashtaroth, and the like; probably the less he knew about them the better for his orthodoxy. He knew Jehovah and the commandments of Jehovah; he knew, therefore, that all gods with other names or other attributes were false gods. In somewhat the same way, the Party member knew what constituted right conduct, and in exceedingly vague, generalized terms he knew what kinds of departure from it were possible. His sexual life, for example, was entirely regulated by the two Newspeak words *sexcrime* (sexual immorality) and *goodsex* (chastity). *Sexcrime* covered all sexual misdeeds whatever. It covered fornication, adultery, homosexuality, and other perversions, and, in addition, normal intercourse practiced for its own sake. There was no need to enumerate them separately, since they were all equally culpable, and, in principle, all punishable by death. In the C vocabulary, which consisted of scientific and technical words, it might be necessary to give specialized names to certain sexual aberrations, but the ordinary citizen had no need of them. He knew what was meant by *goodsex*—that is to say, normal intercourse between man and wife, for the sole purpose of begetting children, and without physical pleasure on the part of the woman; all else was *sexcrime*. In Newspeak it was seldom possible to follow a heretical thought further than the perception that it *was* heretical; beyond that point the necessary words were nonexistent.

No word in the B vocabulary was ideologically neutral. A great many were euphemisms. Such words, for instance, as *joycamp* (forced-labor camp) or *Minipax* (Ministry of Peace, i.e., Ministry of War) meant almost the exact opposite of what they appeared to mean. Some words, on the other hand, displayed a frank and contemptuous understanding of the real nature of Oceanic society. An example was *prolefeed,* meaning the rubbishy entertainment and spurious news which the Party handed out to the masses. Other words, again, were ambivalent, having the connotation "good" when applied to the Party and "bad" when applied to its enemies. But in addition there were great numbers of words which at first sight appeared to be mere abbreviations and which derived their ideological color not from their meaning but from their structure.

So far as it could be contrived, everything that had or might have political significance of any kind was fitted into the B vocabulary. The name of every organization, or body of people, or doctrine, or country, or institution, or public building, was invariably cut down into the familiar shape; that is, a single easily pronounced word with the smallest number of syllables that would preserve the original derivation. In the Ministry of Truth, for example, the Records Department, in which Winston Smith worked, was called *Recdep,* the Fiction Department was called *Ficdep,* the Teleprograms Department was called *Teledep,* and so on. This was not done solely with the object of saving time. Even in the early decades of the twentieth century, telescoped words and phrases had been one of the characteristic features of political language; and it had been noticed that the tendency to use abbreviations of this kind was most marked in totalitarian countries and totalitarian organizations. Examples were such words as *Nazi, Gestapo, Comintern, Inprecorr, Agitprop*. In the beginning the practice had been adopted as it were instinctively, but in Newspeak it was used with a conscious purpose. It was perceived that in thus abbreviating a name one narrowed and subtly altered its meaning, by cutting out most of the associations that would otherwise cling to it. The words *Communist International,* for instance, call up a composite picture of universal human brotherhood, red flags, barricades, Karl Marx, and the Paris Commune. The word Comintern, on the other hand, suggests merely a tightly knit organization and a well-defined body of doctrine. It refers to something almost as easily recognized, and as limited in purpose, as a chair or a table. *Comintern* is a word that can be uttered almost without taking thought, whereas *Communist International* is a phrase over which one is obliged to linger at least momentarily. In the same way, the associations called up by a word like *Minitrue* are fewer and more controllable than those called up by *Ministry of Truth*. This accounted not only for the habit of abbreviating whenever possible, but also for the almost exaggerated care that was taken to make every word easily pronounceable.

In Newspeak, euphony outweighed every consideration other than exactitude of meaning. Regularity of grammar was always sacrificed to it when it seemed necessary. And rightly so, since what was required, above all for political purposes, were short clipped words of unmistakable meaning which could be uttered rapidly and which roused the minimum of echoes in the speaker's mind. The words of the B vocabulary even gained in force from the fact that nearly all of them were very much alike. Almost invariably these words—*goodthink, Minipax, prolefeed, sexcrime, joycamp, Ingsoc, bellyfeel, thinkpol*, and countless others—were words of two or three syllables, with the stress distributed equally between the first syllable and the last. The use of them encouraged a gabbling style of speech, at once staccato and monotonous. And this was exactly what was aimed at. The intention was to make speech, and especially speech on any subject not ideologically neutral, as nearly as possible independent of consciousness. For the purposes of everyday life it was no doubt necessary, or sometimes necessary, to reflect before speaking, but a Party member called upon to make a political or ethical judgment should be able to spray forth the correct opinions as automatically as a machine gun spraying forth bullets. His training fitted him to do this, the language gave him an almost foolproof instrument, and the texture of the words, with their harsh sound and a certain willful ugliness which was in accord with the spirit of Ingsoc, assisted the process still further.

So did the fact of having very few words to choose from. Relative to our own, the Newspeak vocabulary was tiny, and new ways of reducing it were constantly being devised. Newspeak, indeed, differed from almost all other languages in that its vocabulary grew smaller instead of larger every year. Each reduction was a gain, since the smaller the area of choice, the smaller the temptation to take thought. Ultimately it was hoped to make articulate speech issue from the larynx without involving the higher brain centers at all. This aim was frankly admitted in the Newspeak word *duckspeak,* meaning "to quack like a duck." Like various other words in the B vocabulary, *duckspeak* was ambivalent in meaning. Provided that the opinions which were quacked out were orthodox ones, it implied nothing but praise, and when the *Times* referred to one of the orators of the Party as a *doubleplusgood duckspeaker* it was paying a warm and valued compliment.

THE C VOCABULARY

The C vocabulary was supplementary to the others and consisted entirely of scientific and technical terms. These resembled the scientific terms in use today, and were constructed from the same roots, but the usual care was taken to define them rigidly and strip them of undesirable meanings. They followed the same grammatical rules as the words in the other two vocabularies. Very few of the C words had any currency either in everyday speech or in political speech. Any scientific worker or technician could find all the words he needed in the list devoted to his own speciality, but he seldom had more than a smattering of the words occurring in the other lists. Only a very few words were common to all lists, and there was no vocabulary expressing the function of Science as a habit of mind, or a method of thought, irrespective of its particular branches. There was, indeed, no word for "Science," any meaning that it could possibly bear being already sufficiently covered by the word *Ingsoc.*

From the foregoing account it will be seen that in Newspeak the expression of unorthodox opinions, above a very low level, was well-nigh impossible. It was of course possible to utter heresies of a very crude kind, a species of blasphemy. It would have been possible, for example, to say *Big Brother is ungood.* But this statement, which to an orthodox ear merely conveyed a self-evident absurdity, could not have been sustained by reasoned argument, because the necessary words were not available. Ideas inimical to Ingsoc could only be entertained in a vague wordless form, and could only be named in very broad terms which lumped together and condemned whole groups of heresies without defining them in doing so. One could, in fact, only use Newspeak for unorthodox purposes by illegitimately translating some of the words back into Oldspeak. For example, *All mans are equal* was a possible Newspeak sentence, but only in the same sense in which *All men are redhaired* is a possible Oldspeak sentence. It did not contain a grammatical error, but it expressed a palpable untruth, i.e., that all men are of equal size, weight, or strength. The concept of political equality no longer existed, and this secondary meaning had accordingly been purged out of the word *equal.* In 1984, when Oldspeak was still the normal means of communication, the danger theoretically existed that in using Newspeak words one might remember their original meanings. In practice it was not difficult for any person well grounded in *doublethink* to avoid doing this, but within a couple of generations even the possibility of such a lapse would have vanished. A person growing up with Newspeak as his sole language would no more know that *equal* had once had the secondary meaning of "politically equal," or that *free* had once meant "intellectually free," than, for instance, a person who had never heard of chess would be aware of the secondary meanings attaching to *queen* and *rook*. There would be many crimes and errors which it would be beyond his power to commit, simply because they were nameless and therefore unimaginable. And it was to be foreseeen that with the passage of time the distinguishing characteristics of Newspeak would become more and more pronounced—its words growing fewer and fewer, their meanings more and more rigid, and the chance of putting them to improper uses always diminishing.

When Oldspeak had been once and for all superseded, the last link with the past would have been severed. History had already been rewritten, but fragments of the literature of the past survived here and there, imperfectly censored, and so long as one retained one's knowledge of Oldspeak it was possible to read them. In the future such fragments, even if they chanced to survive, would be unintelligible and untranslatable. It was impossible to translate any passage of Oldspeak into Newspeak unless it either referred to some technical process or some very simple everyday action, or was already orthodox (*goodthinkful* would be the Newspeak expression) in tendency. In practice this meant that no book written before approximately 1960 could be translated as a whole. Prerevolutionary literature could only be subjected to ideological translation—that is, alteration in sense as well as language. Take for example the well-known passage from the Declaration of Independence:

> We hold these truths to be self-evident, that all men are created equal, that they are endowed by their Creator with certain inalienable rights, that among these are life, liberty and the pursuit of happiness. That to secure these rights, Governments are instituted among men, deriving their powers from the consent of the governed. That whenever any form of Government becomes destructive of those ends, it is the right of the People to alter or abolish it, and to institute new Government . . .

It would have been quite impossible to render this into Newspeak while keeping to the sense of the original. The nearest one could come to doing so would be to swallow the whole passage up in the single word *crimethink*. A full translation could only be an ideological translation, whereby Jefferson's words would be changed into a panegyric on absolute government.

A good deal of the literature of the past was, indeed, already being transformed in this way. Considerations of prestige made it desirable to preserve the memory of certain historical figures, while at the same time bringing their achievements into line with the philosophy of Ingsoc. Various writers, such as Shakespeare, Milton, Swift, Byron, Dickens, and some others were therefore in process of translation; when the task had been completed, their original writings, with all else that survived of the literature of the past, would be destroyed. These translations were a slow and difficult business, and it was not expected that they would be finished before the first or second decade of the twenty-first century. There were also large quantities of merely utilitarian literature—indispensable technical manuals and the like—that had to be treated in the same way. It was chiefly in order to allow time for the preliminary work of translation that the final adoption of Newspeak had been fixed for so late a date as 2050.

John Lyons / Chomsky

The study of language nowadays assumes a general importance probably greater than ever before, and it is a view held by more than one school of thought that linguistics can provide the model for other human sciences, notably anthropology. Thus in modern France the structuralist movement, best known from the work of Claude Lévi-Strauss in anthropology but extending far beyond that discipline, depends upon the linguistics of de Saussure and Jakobson. Outside France, however, there is no doubt that the dominant linguistics is that of Noam Chomsky, whose theories have very great implications for psychology, philosophy, and other subjects.

In detail these theories, scientifically presented, contain a good deal of very technical matter, hard for the uninstructed layman to understand. In his short book *Language and Mind* Chomsky himself draws out the implications of his work in a fashion more adapted to the lay public, but even so it is not an easy book. John Lyons has written a brief book which offers a critical exposition of Chomsky's doctrines, and here we reprint the first and last chapters of that book. Lyons can make connections between various aspects of Chomsky's activities which the subject himself could do much less easily; and he can present Chomsky in the context of other modern linguists. His exposition, as we have it here, is of course not full or detailed, but it gives, probably, a clearer notion of the importance of its subject than can be found anywhere else in such brief compass. The lucidity of Lyons's explanations and commentary is such that it requires no further comment than that it is a model of how these things should be done. The importance of acquiring some grasp of these far-reaching theories of language is equally self-evident.

Chomsky's position is not only unique within linguistics at the present time, but is probably unprecedented in the whole history of the subject. His first book, published in 1957, short and relatively non-technical though it was, revolutionized the scientific study of language; and now, at the age of 42, he speaks with unrivalled authority on all aspects of grammatical theory. This is not to say, of course, that all linguists, or even the majority of them, have accepted the theory of transformational grammar that Chomsky put forward some thirteen years ago in *Syntactic Structures*. They have not. There are at least as many recognizably different "schools" of linguistics throughout the world as there were before the "Chomskyan revolution." But the "transformationalist," or "Chomskyan," school is not just one among many. Right or wrong, Chomsky's theory of grammar is undoubtedly the most dynamic and influential; and no linguist who wishes to keep abreast of current developments in his subject can afford to ignore Chomsky's theoretical pronouncements. Every other "school" of linguistics at the present time tends to define its position in relation to Chomsky's views on particular issues.

However, it is not so much Chomsky's status and reputation among linguists that has made him a "master of modern thought." After all, theoretical linguistics is a rather esoteric subject, which few people had even heard of and still fewer knew anything about until very recently. If it is now more widely recognized as a branch of science which is worthwhile pursuing, not only for its own sake but also for the contributions it can make to other disciplines, this is very largely due to Chomsky. More than a thousand university students and teachers are said to have attended his lectures on the philosophy of language and mind in the University of Oxford in the spring of 1969. Few of these could have had any previous contact with linguistics, but all of them presumably were convinced, or prepared to be convinced, that it was worth making the intellectual effort required to follow Chomsky's at times quite technical argument; and the lectures were widely reported in the national press.

Readers who are not already familiar with Chomsky's work may well be wondering at this point what possible connexion there might be between a field of study as specialized as transformational grammar and such better known and obviously important disciplines as psychology and philosophy. This is a question we shall be discussing in some detail in the later chapters of this book. But it may be worth while attempting a more general answer here.

It has often been suggested that man is most clearly distinguished from other animal species, not by the faculty of thought or intelligence, as the standard zoological label "homo sapiens" might indicate, but by his capacity for language. Indeed, philosophers and psychologists have long debated whether thought in the proper sense of the term is conceivable except as "embodied" in speech or writing. Whether or not this is so, it is obvious that language is of vital importance in every aspect of human activity and that, without language, all but the most rudimentary kind of communication would be impossible. Granted that language is essential to human life as we know it, it is only natural to ask what contribution the study of language can make to our understanding of human nature.

But what is language? This is a question that few people even think of asking. In one sense of course we all know what we mean by "language"; and our use of the word in everyday conversation depends upon the fact that we all interpret it, as we interpret the other words we use, in the same or in a very similar way. There is, however, a difference between this kind of unreflecting and practical knowledge of what language is and the deeper or more systematic understanding that we should want to call "scientific." As we shall see in the following chapters, it is the aim of theoretical linguistics to give a scientific answer to the question "What is language?" and, in doing so, to provide the evidence that philosophers and psychologists can draw upon in their discussion of the relationship that holds between language and thought.

Chomsky's system of transformational grammar was developed, as we shall see, in order to give a mathematically precise description of some of the most striking features of language. Of particular importance in this connexion is the ability that children have to derive the structural regularities of their native language—its grammatical rules—from the utterances of their parents and others around them, and then to make use of the same regularities in the construction of utterances they have never heard before. Chomsky has argued, in his most recent publications, that the general principles which determine the form of grammatical rules in particular languages, such as English, Turkish or Chinese, are to some considerable degree common to all human languages. Furthermore, he has claimed that the principles underlying the structure of language are so specific and so highly articulated that they must be regarded as being biologically determined; that is to say, as constituting part of what we call "human nature" and as being genetically transmitted from parents to their children. If this is so, and if it is also the case, as Chomsky maintains, that transformational grammar is the best theory so far developed for the systematic description and explanation of the structure of human language, it is clear that an understanding of transformational grammar is essential for any philosopher, psychologist or biologist who wishes to take account of man's capacity for language.

The significance of Chomsky's work for disciplines other than linguistics derives primarily, then, from the acknowledged importance of language in all areas of human activity and from the peculiarly intimate relationship that is said to hold between the structure of language and the innate properties or operations of the mind. But language is not the only kind of complex "behaviour" that human beings engage in; and there is at least a possibility that other forms of typically human activity (including perhaps certain aspects of what we call "artistic creation") will also prove amenable to description within the framework of specially constructed mathematical systems analogous to, or even based upon, transformational grammar. There are many scholars working now in the social sciences and the humanities who believe that this is so. For them, Chomsky's formalization of grammatical theory serves as a model and a standard.

From what has been said in the last few paragraphs it will be clear that

Chomsky's influence is now being felt in many different disciplines. So far, however, it is the study of language that has been most profoundly affected by the "Chomskyan revolution"; and it is from current research on the grammatical structure of English and other languages that Chomsky draws most of his more general philosophical and psychological views. It is for this reason that we shall give so much attention in the present volume to the linguistic background of Chomsky's thought.

Chomsky's current fame and popularity is not due solely, or even mainly, to his work in linguistics and the effect that this is having on other disciplines. In the last few years, he has become known as one of the most outspoken and most articulate critics of American politics in Vietnam *—a "hero of the New Left," who has risked imprisonment by refusing to pay half his taxes and has given support and encouragement to young men refusing to undertake military service in Vietnam. It is undoubtedly for his political writings and his political activity that Chomsky is now most famous, especially in the United States. Relatively few people may have read the lengthy and scholarly essays he contributed to *Liberation, Ramparts* and *The New York Review of Books* (now collected together with other material and republished as *American Power and the New Mandarins*). But the general theme of these essays will be familiar to many—his condemnation of American "imperialism" and of those academic advisers to the American Government who, posing as "experts" in a field where there is no such thing as scientific expertise and where consideration of common morality should have prevailed, have been guilty of deceiving the public about the character of the War in Vietnam, American involvement in Cuba and other issues.

Although this book is mainly about Chomsky's views on language, it should perhaps be emphasized here that his theory of language and his political philosophy are by no means unconnected, as they might appear to be at first sight. As we shall see . . . Chomsky has long been an opponent of at least the more extreme form of behaviourist psychology—"radical behaviourism," according to which all human knowledge and belief, and all the "patterns" of thought and action characteristic of man, can be explained as "habits" built up by a process of "conditioning," lengthier and more complex no doubt in its details, but not qualitatively different from the process by which rats in a psychological laboratory "learn" to obtain food by pressing a bar in the cage in which they are housed. Chomsky's attack on radical behaviourism was first made in a long and well-documented review of B. F. Skinner's *Verbal Behaviour* in 1959, in which he claimed that the behaviourists' impressive panoply of scientific terminology and statistics was no more than camouflage, covering up their inability to account for the fact that language simply is not a set of "habits" and is radically different from animal communication. It is the same charge that Chomsky now makes in his political writings against the sociologists, psychologists and other social scien-

* See his article "The Responsibility of Intellectuals" on p. 723.

tists whose "expert" advice is sought by governments: that they "desperately attempt . . . to imitate the surface features of sciences that really have significant intellectual content," neglecting in this attempt all the fundamental problems with which they should be concerned and taking refuge in pragmatic and methodological trivialities. It is Chomsky's conviction that human beings are different from animals or machines and that this difference should be respected both in science and in government; and it is this conviction which underlies and unifies his politics, his linguistics and his philosophy.

Chomsky's message is familiar enough, and it will find an immediate response in all those who subscribe to a belief in the brotherhood of man and the dignity of human life. Only too often, however, the defence of these traditional values is left to scholars who by academic training are unfitted for the kind of argument which appeals to hard-headed "pragmatists." Chomsky cannot be written off quite so easily as a "woolly-minded liberal." He is as well read in the philosophy of science as his opponents are, and he can manipulate the conceptual and mathematical apparatus of the social sciences with equal ease. His arguments may be accepted or rejected: they cannot be ignored. And anyone who wishes to follow and evaluate these arguments must be prepared to meet Chomsky on his home ground: linguistics, or the scientific investigation of language. For Chomsky believes (as I said earlier) that the structure of language is determined by the structure of the human mind and that the universality of certain properties characteristic of language is evidence that at least this part of human nature is common to all members of the species, regardless of their race or class and their undoubted differences in intellect, personality and physical attributes. This belief is quite traditional (and Chomsky himself, we shall see, explicitly relates his views to those of the rationalist philosophers of the seventeenth and eighteenth centuries). What is new is the way in which Chomsky argues his case and the kind of evidence that he adduces in support of it.

It is appropriate, and symbolic of his position and influence, that the institution in which Chomsky carries out his research into the structure of language and the properties of the human mind should be that citadel of modern science, the Massachusetts Institute of Technology, but that the views he expresses in summarizing his research should be those more characteristic of the humanities departments of a traditional university. The contradiction is only apparent. For Chomsky's work suggests that the conventional boundary that exists between "arts" and "science" can, and should, be abolished.

● ● ●

. . . I must not leave the reader with the impression that Chomsky's position is impregnable and his critics simply misguided or malevolent. I will redress the balance somewhat by giving a more personal assessment of the significance of Chomsky's work. Although my own views are very similar to Chomsky's on most issues, there are some points on which I think he has overstated his case.

I have already said that it was Chomsky's research on the formalization of syntactic theory that constitutes his most original and probably his most enduring contribution to the scientific investigation of language; and there can be little doubt about this. He has greatly extended the scope of what is called "mathematical linguistics" and opened up a whole field of research, which is of interest not only to linguists, but also to logicians and mathematicians. Even if it were decided eventually that none of Chomsky's work on generative grammar was of any direct relevance to the description of natural languages, it would still be judged valuable by logicians and mathematicians, who are concerned with the construction and study of formal systems independently of their empirical application. I will say no more about this point.

It is of course the fact that Chomsky's model of transformational grammar was designed for the analysis of natural languages and has been employed with considerable success for that purpose over the last ten or fifteen years that has attracted the attention of psychologists and philosophers. Chomsky himself has argued . . . that the findings of transformational grammar have certain very definite implications for psychology and philosophy. He has made a strong, and to my mind convincing, case against behaviourism (in its extreme form at least); and he has argued, again cogently, that the gap between human language and systems of animal communication is such that it cannot be bridged by any obvious extension of current psychological theories of "learning" based on laboratory experiments with animals. This follows from the principle of "creativity" manifest in the use of language and does not depend, it should be observed, upon the validity of any particular model of generative grammar, or indeed even upon the possibility of constructing one. I should perhaps repeat that, although Chomsky has given good reason to believe that the model of "stimulus-and-response" is incapable of accounting for *all* the facts of language behaviour, he has not shown that it cannot explain *any* of them. It might well be that some of the words referring to objects in the child's environment and certain utterances that occur frequently in the repetitive situations in which he finds himself in early life are learned by him in a way that is quite reasonably described in behaviourist terms (by saying that the words and utterances are "responses" and the objects and situations are "stimuli"); and it could also be true that this part of language not only can, but must, be learned and related to the external world and the world of social activity in this way. As far as I know, there is no evidence to suggest that this view is wrong or even implausible. What Chomsky has demonstrated is that the behaviourist account of language acquisition, if it is not entirely abandoned, must be supplemented with something more substantial than rather empty appeals to "analogy."

But what of the wider philosophical issues that he has raised in his later work? Here I think that the only verdict that can be returned, on the evidence available, is that Chomsky's case for rationalism is not quite as strong as he suggests. It rests, as we have seen, upon the alleged universality of certain formal principles of sentence construction in natural languages; and he is committed to the view "that if an artificial language were constructed which violated some of these general principles, then it would not be learned at all, or at least not learned with the ease and efficiency with which a normal child will learn human language" (*The Listener,* 30 May, 1968, p. 688). But this hypothesis, as Chomsky's critics have pointed out, is not subject to direct empirical verification. For it is obviously impracticable to bring up a child from birth with no knowledge of any natural language, exposing him only to utterances in an artificial language spoken in a full range of "normal" situations. Nor is it at all clear how one would go about designing an acceptable psychological experiment bearing less directly upon the issues involved. (Chomsky has referred to "preliminary experiments" being carried out at Harvard by George Miller: but the subjects in these experiments are apparently adults, and we cannot assume that the results would be valid for the acquisition of languages by children.)

Even if we grant for the sake of argument that the formal principles to which Chomsky appeals are universal in the sense that they do indeed hold in all languages actually spoken by human beings, are we justified in maintaining that they are peculiarly congenial to the human mind, so that any *conceivable* human language *must* conform to them? Since we cannot prove, as yet, that languages violating these principles could not be learned or used by human beings, we are entitled to withhold our assent to Chomsky's hypothesis that these formal universals are innate. An alternative explanation of their universality might be that all languages have a common origin in the remote past and have preserved the formal principles of their source.[1] Whether all existing languages do in fact derive from one source is not known—and, once again, we are faced with what seems to be an unverifiable hypothesis—but it is a possibility that should be allowed for.

In so far as linguistics is an empirical science, whose purpose it is to construct a theory of the structure of human language, it is of course important that linguists should incorporate within the theory all the substantive and formal universals that can be established in the investigation of particular languages. Chomsky is right, I believe, when he says that the diversity of structure found throughout

1. This point has been explicitly discussed by Chomsky in *Language and Mind* (pp. 74–5), where he argues that it "involves a serious misunderstanding of the problem at issue." It is true, as he says, that the hypothesis of common origin "contributes nothing to explaining" how "the grammar of a language must be discovered by the child from the data presented to him." But this is not the problem for which the hypothesis of common origin is being proposed here as an explanation. Chomsky's assumption that certain formal principles of grammar are innate is intended to account for two problems simultaneously: (i) the universality of the principles (on the assumption that they are in fact found to be universal) and (ii) the child's success in constructing the grammar of his language on the basis of the utterances he hears around him. It is the second of these questions that Chomsky regards as the more important ("the language is 'reinvented' each time it is learned, and the empirical problem to be faced by the theory of learning is how this invention of grammar can take place").

the languages of the world is less striking than the "structuralists" have claimed. On the other hand, it should be emphasized that relatively few languages have yet been described in any great depth. Syntactic research of the last few years, much of it inspired directly by Chomsky's work, seems to me to lend a fair amount of support to the adherents of "universal grammar." But the results that have been obtained so far must be regarded as very tentative; and this fact should be borne in mind when linguistic evidence is being used in philosophical arguments.

It is in any case arguable that some of the old philosophical and psychological oppositions, like rationalism *vs.* empiricism, instinct *vs.* learning, mind *vs.* body, heredity *vs.* environment, and so on, have lost much of their force. Current work in the comparative study of animal and human behaviour would suggest that behaviour which is normally described as "instinctual" requires very particular environmental conditions during the period of "maturation." Whether one says that such behaviour is "innate" or "learned by experience" is a matter of emphasis: both "instinct" and "environment" are necessary, and neither is sufficient without the other. . . . Chomsky, though he calls himself a "mentalist," does not wish to be committed to the traditional opposition of "body" and "mind." His position would seem to be consistent with the view that the "knowledge" and "predispositions" for language, though "innate," require rather definite environmental conditions during the period of "maturation." One might go on to suggest, as an alternative to Chomsky's hypothesis, that it is not a "knowledge" of the formal principles of language as such that is innate, but a more general "faculty," which, given the right environmental conditions, will interact with these to produce linguistic competence.[2] This could still be called a "rationalist" hypothesis in the sense that it contradicts the more extreme form of empiricism. But then there are probably very few extreme empiricists. Most philosophers and psychologists would no doubt accept that some "mental faculties" are specific to human beings (although they might prefer not to use the words "mental faculty") and are both biologically and environmentally determined. Once again, it must be admitted that there is no evidence to show that this alternative hypothesis (which many scholars who call themselves "empiricists" might favour) is correct.

2. Chomsky says that he is not convinced that this is a true "alternative": he accepts that the proper environmental conditions are necessary for the maturation of innate structures (cf. *Aspects of the Theory of Syntax*, pp. 33–34). He believes that "no more is at stake than a decision as to how to apply the term 'knowledge' in a rather obscure area." He further suggests that I should point out that "even the most narrow empiricist would not regard a hypothesis as devoid of empirical content because it is not directly testable in practice," that it is generally accepted by modern empiricists "that meaningful hypotheses, in general, must only meet the condition that some possible evidence have some bearing on them—that they not be entirely neutral with respect to all conceivable evidence." I did not intend to give the impression in my criticism of Chomsky's hypothesis that I regard it as meaningless or vacuous, but it may be as well to make this point explicit.

But I am not claiming that Chomsky is wrong. What I am saying is that the evidence, so far at least, is inconclusive.

The fact that we have delivered a verdict of "not proven" on Chomsky's particularly strong form of the rationalist thesis does not mean that it is without importance. He has shown that there is nothing inherently unscientific about the assumption, or hypothesis, that competence in speaking a language implies that the speaker has in his "mind" (whether they are "innate" or "learned") a number of generative rules of a highly restricted kind and is capable of "storing" and operating upon abstract "mental structures" in the course of producing or analysing utterances. This in itself is a considerable achievement, given the strong prejudice that existed not long ago among psychologists and linguists, and perhaps also philosophers of science, against any theory that went beyond the observable data. Chomsky was surely right to challenge "the belief that the mind must be simpler in its structure than any known physical organ and that the most primitive of assumptions must be adequate to explain whatever phenomena can be observed" (*Language and Mind*, p. 22).

It would be inappropriate in a book of this nature, and impossible in the space available, to give a detailed criticism of Chomsky's theory of generative grammar from a purely linguistic point of view.[3] I must be content with two general points. The first has to do with the distinction he draws between "competence" and "performance," which was mentioned in Chapters 4 and 8. Although a distinction of this kind is undoubtedly both a theoretical and a methodological necessity in linguistics, it is by no means certain that Chomsky himself draws it in the right place. It can be argued that he describes as matters of "performance" (and, therefore, as irrelevant) a number of factors that should be handled in terms of "competence." The second point is that, on questions of detail, any linguist's judgement of what is a more "natural" or more "revealing" way of describing the data will tend to be somewhat arbitrary. Furthermore, it is not always clear when the differences between two alternative descriptions of the same data are differences of substance and when they are merely differences of terminology and notation. Chomsky himself has said, of current work in generative grammar, that "at present the field is in considerable ferment, and it will probably be some time before the dust begins to settle and a number of outstanding issues are even tentatively resolved" (*Language and Mind*, p. 54, fn. 6). He has claimed elsewhere (in more recent and more technical publications) that the differences between his own position and that of other linguists on many of these issues is purely "notational." Many will disagree with him.

I will not try to justify the two points I have just made. They have been mentioned simply to indicate that even those linguists who are generally sympathetic

---

3. For a critical discussion of the more technical points in Chomsky's theory the reader is referred to P. H. Matthews's review of *Aspects of the Theory of Syntax*. [See also *Journal of Linguistics*, vol. 3 (1967), pp. 119–52.]

to Chomsky's views may differ from him on various issues. Other linguists of course have more fundamental objections to his theory of generative grammar. Any reader who wishes to weigh Chomsky's arguments against those of his critics and to come to his own conclusions is advised to read *The State of the Art* by C. F. Hockett.

Earlier in this chapter I said that we must at least envisage the possibility that Chomsky's theory of generative grammar will be dismissed one day, by the consensus of linguists, as irrelevant to the description of natural languages. I should add that I personally believe, and very many linguists will share this belief, that even if the attempt he has made to formalize the concepts employed in the analysis of languages should fail, the attempt itself will have immeasurably increased our understanding of these concepts and that in this respect the "Chomskyan revolution" cannot but be successful.

Leonard Bloomfield / Literate and Illiterate Speech

Bloomfield was the leader of the American "behavioristic" school of linguistics, now in part, at any rate, superseded by the "rationalist" school of Chomsky. He was interested in nonliterate Indian languages, and this enabled him to consider the criteria of "correct linguistic behavior in a culture where literacy affects spoken language." These criteria seemed to him to be upheld by considerations that in themselves have nothing to do with language, but are rather of social origin.

He begins, therefore, by contesting the popular view of correctness, which derives from the written rather than from the primary spoken language. He explains how this comes about and distinguishes the situation that prevails in England from that which obtains in the United States. However, it does not follow as it ought from this explanation that where a community is uniform as to language there exist no distinctions between "good" and "bad" usage. The Menomini Indians, who constitute such a community, prove to have criteria of good and bad; and Bloomfield concludes that authority of a kind not necessarily linguistic—it may be founded on character or social standing—determines standards of linguistic correctness.

This paper, which is of course itself written in "good" English, is an excellent model for certain kinds of speculative work in prose. Behind it lies a theoretical structure worked out, but not obtruded, by a master of his subject; and although the subject is of general interest, the decisive illustrations are derived from fieldwork and display information available to no one but the author. Note that apart from a few expressions which are neatly explained in the text—*obviative, quotative*—the piece is free of jargon, something one can rarely say of the writings of linguists.

I

Literate and illiterate speech in a language like English are plainly different. We find it easy, aside from occasional points of detail, to judge of "incorrect" or "faulty" locutions, "bad grammar," "mispronunciation," and the like. This, in fact, is the layman's chief interest in linguistics.

When we try, however, to define what we mean by these judgments, to state the causes of "mistakes," or to set up a standard, we run into great difficulties. The popular explanation of these matters is certainly wrong; scientific students of language have dealt little with them explicitly, somewhat more by implication, and never in a satisfactory way. In this paper I shall give some facts from a speech-community where conditions differ from ours to so great an extent as to provide a kind of check, and shall try to draw conclusions; I may say at the outset that these conclusions are neither decisive nor complete enough to be satisfactory.

II

The popular explanation of "correct" and "incorrect" speech reduces the matter to one of knowledge versus ignorance. There is such a thing as correct English. An ignorant person does not know the correct forms; therefore he cannot help using incorrect ones. In the process of education one learns the correct forms and, by practice and an effort of will ("careful speaking"), acquires the habit of using them. If one associates with ignorant speakers, or relaxes the effort of will ("careless speaking"), one will lapse into the incorrect forms.

It would be easy, but would require much space, to show that these notions do not correspond to the facts. There is no fixed standard of "correct" English; one need only recall that no two persons speak alike, and that, take it as a whole, every language is constantly changing. At the time when we learn to speak we are all ignorant babies, yet many children of five or six years speak "correct" English. Even some ignorant adults speak "good" English; on the other hand, there are highly educated people, even teachers and professors, who speak "bad" English. All speaking, good or bad, is careless; only for a few minutes at a time can one speak "carefully" and when one does so, the result is by no means pleasing. In fatiguing effect and in ungracefulness, "careful" speaking is like walking a chalk-line or a tight-rope.

If we leave aside all this, there is one error in the popular view which is of special interest. The incorrect forms cannot be the result of ignorance or carelessness, for they are by no means haphazard, but, on the contrary, very stable. For instance, if a person is so ignorant as not to know how to say *I see it* in past time, we might expect him to use all kinds of chance forms, and, especially, to resort to easily formed locutions, such as *I did see it,* or to the addition of the regular past-time suffix: *I seed it.* But instead, these ignorant people quite consistently say *I seen it.* Now it is evident that one fixed and consistent form will be no more difficult than another: a person who has learned *I seen* as the past of *I see* has learned just as much as one who says *I saw.* He has simply learned something different. Although most of the people who say *I seen* are ignorant, their ignorance does not account for this form of speech. On the other hand, I once knew a school-teacher who, when she spoke carefully, sometimes said *I have saw it;* in normal speech she said *I have seen it.* In short, what we find is not well-informed and regulated activity opposed to ignorant and careless, but rather a conflict of definite, fixed locutions, one of which, for some reason, is "good," while the others are "bad."

Mistaken as are the popular notions on this subject, they are interesting because they throw some light on our attitude to language. The popular explanation of incorrect language is simply the explanation of incorrect *writing,* taken over, part and parcel, to serve as an explanation of incorrect speech. It is the writing of every word for which a single form is fixed and all others are obviously wrong. It is the spelling of words that ignorant people, or better, unlettered people, do not know. It is writing that may be done carefully or carelessly, with evident results as to correctness. With all this it accords that popular comment on a wrong form of speech is often given in terms that properly apply to writing, not to speech; for instance, he who says *git* instead of *get,* or ketch instead of catch, is popularly said to be substituting one *letter* for another, to be mistaking the *spelling* of the word. In sum, the popular ideas about language apply very well to writing, but are irrelevant to speech.

Now, writing, of course, is merely a record of speech. Making this record is an activity very different from the activity of speaking. This is especially striking among us, since our writing is not entirely parallel with speech, but contains numbers of such spellings as *go: throw: sew: beau: though,* where different spellings represent one sound-type, and such as *though: through: bough: cough: rough,* where one spelling represents different sound-types. Writing, like telegraphy or short-hand, is an activity that deals with language, but it is quite different, far less practised and ingrained, far more superficial in our make-up, than speech. Until quite recently only very few people knew how to read and write; even today many peoples do not write their language. Writing is based on speech, not speech on writing.

The fact that almost anyone except a professed student of language explains matters of speech by statements which really apply only to writing, is of great psychologic interest. In infancy, when we learn to speak, we necessarily had no words with which to describe what we were doing. After we had learned to speak, we had no occasion to acquire such words or to make such a description. Consequently, as adults, we cannot state what we do when we talk: we are unconscious of the movements we make with our tongue or vocal chords, of the sound-pattern or the grammatical structure of our speech. (This appears in the difficulty with which school-children learn the few and fairly superficial facts of English grammar that have found a place in the school curriculum. To give anything like a full description of even his native language is a difficult undertaking for any linguist.) Writing, on the other hand, we learned after we knew how to speak; in fact, we learned it through the medium of speech. The teacher told us, in words, what to do, and trained us to state it; we learned the names of the letters, and to spell words, that is, to state which letters we use for a given word. Consequently, ever after, we are able to describe what we do when we write: we are conscious of our movements in writing, and of the forms and succession of the letters. It is on the basis of such contrasts that some psychologists make out a very good case for the view that a "conscious" action is simply one which we are able to describe in words. Whether one accepts this view or not, it is easy to see why a normal person, when asked to explain something about language, really talks about writing; to see why it took generations of students to develop a set of technical terms about speech, and why it now takes a long time to learn the use of these terms, in case one wants to enter upon the scientific study of language.

III

The popular view of "good" and "bad" English has led us a good way round and has shown us some interesting outlooks, but it has brought us back to where we started. The scientific view, though not satisfactory, will bring us farther. It has the advantage of being based on a more extensive survey of various languages and of their history than any one person could make; also it has the advantage of a methodical approach. This last means that we shall not operate with the terms "good" and "bad" language, or their equivalents, since it is precisely these which we are trying to define.

We observe, to begin with, that in every group of people, savage or civilized, ignorant or educated, the infants learn, by imitation, the speech-habits of the older people round them. Even the child learning to speak does not use haphazard forms: he approaches more and more closely the forms used by his elders, and finally talks just like them. Speech defects after early childhood are individual abnormalities; aside from these, the individual's peculiarities of speech are minute. Through the rest of his life he seems to speak uniformly, so far as an observer could note.

History, however, shows that there is a constant and gradual, imperceptibly slow, change in the language of every community. This change is uniform within a group of people who are constantly talking with one another, say, within a single village. But where communication is less frequent, the changes are sure to be different. For instance, if people of the same speech settle so as to form two mountain villages, with a big valley between, then, in a few generations, different changes will have taken place in the two groups. In time they may find it hard to understand each other when they meet; if they stay apart long enough, they may finally be speaking mutually unintelligible languages. When some of the Angles and Saxons left the Continent in the fifth century A.D., they spoke the same language as the less enterprising members of their tribes who stayed at home. Since then, however, both the language of the emigrants and that of the stay-at-homes have changed, and, since there has necessarily been little communication across the North Sea, they have changed in different ways, until today an Englishman and a Dutchman or a North German do not understand each other's speech. In this way, wherever there are lines across which communication is hampered—water, mountains, deserts, political boundaries, and the like—we find differences of speech, even though history may tell us that once upon a time, say, at the original settlement, there was uniformity.

Now, as civilization progresses, the population grows denser, means of communication improve, and petty political boundaries lose their importance. More and more often people from different parts of the country, speaking different local dialects, have occasion to converse with each other. They soon learn, on these occasions, to avoid forms of speech that are misleading or unintelligible to the other fellow. Usually, too, there is some city which serves as a center for the larger activities of the nation. The contact of persons from different regions occurs more in this city than elsewhere; the provincial has more occasion to speak with natives of this city than with speakers of any one other dialect. In the history of English, London played this part. Thus there arises a *Standard Language* of more or less definite form. Finally, civilization leads to the widespread use of writing. Since writing is a very deliberate activity, it is easy to adapt one's writing to the requirements of wide communication: one avoids provincialisms and, if there is a metropolis, imitates the writing of the city. Thus it happens that the *Standard Language* is most definite and best observed in its written form, the *Literary Language*. The next step is popular education: children are taught in schools to write and, if possible, to speak in the forms of the Standard Language.

It is at this point that the science of language gives its explanation, if I understand it aright, of "good" and "bad" language. The child, growing up in the province, say, in some mountain village, learns to speak in the local dialect. In time, to be sure, this local dialect will take in more and more forms from the standard language, but so far in the history of mankind complete standardization seems nowhere to have taken place. The child, then, does not speak the standard language as its native tongue. It is only when he reaches school, long after his speech-habits are formed, that he is taught the standard language. No language is like the native speech that one learned at one's mother's knee; no one is ever perfectly sure in a language afterward acquired. "Mistakes" in language are simply dialect forms carried into the standard language. The "bad" English for *I saw it* is not any haphazard error, but the perfectly fixed and definite form, *I seen it,* the form used in most American dialects of English. So far as age is concerned, *Do you want out?* is more respectable than *Do you want to go out?*—but the latter happens to be the form of Standard English: questions of age, of logical or esthetic value, or even of consistency within the system of the language are irrelevant. Dialect forms in the standard language are "bad."

Since only part of the population lives in the metropolis (when there is one, as in England), and since, even there, different social classes communicate little, and since the standard language, closely tied up with the literary language, tends to become archaic (that is, to ignore the changes of the last generations), it results that only relatively few children speak Standard Language as their real mother tongue. Almost everybody's standard speech will show dialect coloring and occasional lapses into dialect.

Sometimes a large dialect group will re-assert itself; thus an Englishman will say that all Americans speak bad Standard English (that is, dialectally colored Standard), but we, finding the British standard too unlike our native forms, have developed a standard of our own, which deviates decidedly in pronunciation and to some extent in word-forms and constructions. The situation is all the more complicated in that we have no one center, like London. But, with the literary language in its usual function as a kind of guide to the standard speech, we have worked out in practice a fairly definite American standard, and are able, except for small details, to agree on what is and what is not "good"—that is, Standard—American English.

Beside mixing dialect into standard speech, we are likely to distort the latter in some other ways. Native speakers of dialect are prone, once in a while, to speak carefully, that is, to worry about their speech, and go too far in substituting school forms for native forms. A person whose native speech says *I see: I seen: I have seen,* after learning in school to say *I saw,* may occasionally go too far in substituting *saw's* for *seen's* and say *I have saw it*—a "hyper-urban" form. Knowing that the standard language is close to the written form, we are likely to go too far in guiding ourselves by the latter, for instance, to pronounce a t-sound in *often*—"spelling-pronunication." Or again, many words common in writing are rare in speech; when, for once, we speak them, we may violate the habit of those who know the spoken form. Sometimes the spoken tradition of a fairly rare word in this way dies out: *author, Gothic* used to be pronounced *autor, Gotic;* the th-sound is due to lapse of the oral tradition.

These details could be elaborated, but in the main the scientific diagnosis of "bad" language seems to be: standard language with dialect features. In the local dialect one native speaker would thus be as good as another, and "mistakes" or "bad" forms impossible.

IV

According to the scientists' view of the matter, then, a small community of people speaking a uniform language, and above all, a community without schools or writing, would not distinguish "good" and "bad" language. When I first studied such a community, I found, to my great surprise, that these distinctions were made, if perhaps less frequently among us.

The Menomini Indians of Wisconsin, a compact tribe of some 1700 people, speak a language without dialectal differences and have no writing. Yet the Menomini will say that one person speaks well and another badly, that such-and-such a form of speech is incorrect and sounds bad, and another too much like a shaman's preaching or archaic ("the way the old, old people talked").

To a surprisingly large extent, considering how slight my acquaintance with their language, I was able to share in these judgments of the Menomini. A foreigner who recorded English as though it were an unwritten language, might obtain several forms of a locution, as, for instance,

> You'd better do that,
> You had better do that,
> You would better do that,
> You ought better do that.

His written record would probably fail to give him any distinction between the value of these forms. But if he listened to us long enough, and if fortune favored him, he might learn that the normal good form is the first; that the second is more deliberate and elevated; that the other two strike us as unidiomatic, vulgar, pedantic, or what you will—in short, as incorrect. So in Menomini we have, for "What are you laughing at?"

> wǽkiʔ wǽh-ayǽniyan?
> wǽkiʔ aya:yó:sinaman?
> tá:niʔ wǽtǽ:hpiyan?

The first form is illiterate, childish, stupid; the second is normal; the third elevated, poetic, archaizing.

Some people say *tsí:pin* instead of *kí:spin* for "if"; this sounds as bad as *git* and *ketch* in English.

Here is a sketch of the linguistic position of some of the speakers whom I knew best:

Red-Cloud-Woman, a woman in the sixties, speaks a beautiful and highly idiomatic Menomini. She knows only a few words of English, but speaks Ojibwa and Potawatomi fluently, and, I believe, a little Winnebago. Linguistically, she would correspond to a highly educated American woman who spoke, say, French and Italian in addition to the very best type of cultivated, idiomatic English.

Her husband, Storms-At-It, a shaman, is half Potawatomi, and speaks both languages. Of English he knows not even the cuss-words. In Menomini he often uses unapproved—let us say, ungrammatical—forms which are current among bad speakers; on the other hand, slight provocation sets him off into elevated speech, in which he uses what I shall describe as spelling-pronunciations, together with long ritualistic compound words and occasional archaisms. He corresponds, perhaps, to a minister who does not put on much "dog," speaks very colloquially in ordinary life, but is at the same time very intelligent and able to preach or exhort in the most approved semi-biblical language.

Stands-Close, a man in the fifties, speaks only Menomini. His speech, though less supple and perfect than Red-Cloud-Woman's, is well up to standard. It is interlarded with words and constructions that are felt to be archaic, and are doubtless in part really so, for his father was known as an oracle of old traditions.

Bird-Hawk, a very old man, who has since died, spoke only Menomini, possibly also a little Ojibwa. As soon as he departed from ordinary conversation, he spoke with bad syntax and meagre, often inept vocabulary, yet with occasional archaisms.

White-Thunder, a man round forty, speaks less English than Menomini, and that is a strong indictment, for his Menomini is atrocious. His vocabulary is small; his inflections are often barbarous; he constructs sentences of a few threadbare models. He may be said to speak no language tolerably. His case is not uncommon among younger men, even when they speak but little English. Perhaps it is due, in some indirect way, to the impact of the conquering language.

Little-Doctor, a half-breed, who died recently in his sixties, spoke English with some Menomini faults, but with a huge vocabulary and a passion for piling up synonyms. In Menomini, too, his vocabulary was vast; often he would explain rare words to his fellow-speakers. In both languages his love of words sometimes upset his syntax, and in both languages he was given to over-emphatic diction, of the type of spelling pronunciation.

Little-Jerome, a half-breed, now in the fifties, is a true bilingual. He speaks both English (the dialectal type of the region) and Menomini with racy idiom, which he does not lose even when translating in either direction. He contrasts strikingly with the men (usually somewhat younger) who speak little English and yet bad Menomini.

To recite the features of good and bad Menomini would be to annotate almost every item of the grammar, and many of the lexicon.

In the pronunciation of good speakers, Menomini has, of course, its typical cadence and glide-sounds. Young people who speak English often diverge in Anglicizing the pronunciation. Older bad speakers exaggerate certain glide-sounds and miss some of the cadences, confusing short and long vowels. Over-elegant speech, on the other hand—as from the lips of shamans or of the well-educated Little-Doctor—displaces the stress-accent toward the end of the word, and gives full long quantity to vowels which in good, idiomatic speech are not entitled to it. This last feature is a fairly close parallel to our "spelling-pronunciations," such as the full form *fore-head* for *forrid* and the now perhaps accepted *waist-coat* and *seam-stress,* for *weskit* and *semstress.* Only, there is no writing in Menomini, hence no spelling to explain "spelling-pronunciations." Sometimes there is a clear analogic basis. Thus the word *niná:tumik* "he calls me" may be distorted to *niná:tomik* or even to *nina:tó:mik,* the *o:* being the long vowel that corresponds in Menomini to the short *u*. Now, these distorted forms are probably due to the influence of other inflectional forms which properly have the long *o:*, such as *nina-nató:mik* "he will call me." But in other cases this explanation seems not to hold, as when *atǽhimin* "strawberry" is in spelling-pronunciation *atǽhe:me:n* where the long *e:* corresponds to short *i*.

As a whole, this phenomenon is due to the fact that Menomini has a living morphologic alternation of long and short vowels; in emphatic or rhetorical speech the long vowels are carried into forms where normally they do not belong.

In inflection, Menomini, like the other Algonquian languages, has an *obviative* form for subsidiary third persons. Thus, if our story is of a man meeting another man and of the ensuing occurrences, our first man will be spoken of in the normal third person form, and the other man in the obviative form. The good Menomini speaker has no such difficulty as we have with our single pronoun *he*. But bad Menomini speakers profit not at all from this distinction, but get as tangled in their two forms as a bad speaker of English with his one ambiguous *he*.

Whatever is hearsay and not the speaker's own experience has the predicate verb or particle in a special *quotative* form. Hence in traditional narrative all predicates are in this form, unless they be actual thoughts or speeches of the actors in the story, or parenthetic insertions of the narrator; these exceptions, indeed, make possible some nice shadings of sense and style. In ordinary speech even the bad speaker will use his quotatives correctly, but as soon as he embarks on a longer story, he may lapse into non-quotatives for whole sentences at a time, which make the story sound as though he had been present when it took place.

Many archaisms of the medicine-man's language are pinchbeck—distortions in the direction of Ojibwa, or of Triballian. Others are genuine, as comparison with related languages will show. Still others are circumlocutions. No doubt the starting-point for these was in cases where the normal word was tabu during ritual. The Algonquian word for "bear" is lost in Menomini, and is replaced by a word which used to mean "little animal"; in ritual other terms are used, such as "ant-eater," "berry-gatherer," "Bruin." But the habit has been extended to words where there is no tabu; the shaman uses long compounds or derivatives, such as "extensive woman" or "grandmother-expanse" for "earth," and "standing-men" for "trees," or "eternal men" for "stones."

V

It would be useless to seek the criterion of good and bad Menomini by gauging the alternative forms as to consistency with the general system of the language, for Menomini, like English, contains many irregularities. It is often the irregular form that is the proper one, just as in English *You had better do it* is preferred to *You ought better (to) do it,* although the latter accords with the general forms of our syntax. Similarly, *forrid* is preferred to the logically more explicable *fore-head*. On the other hand, the irregular form may be less acceptable than a regular one: *I dove* is not so good as *I dived, I ain't* not so good as *I'm not*. A good Menomini speaker will say for "medicine-man" *maski:hkí:wineniw,* a form which has the accent on a syllable that in almost any other word would be incapable of stress, and has vowel-shortening in the last element; yet only a bad speaker will use the logical combination of the words "medicine" and "man," and speak horrid-sounding *maskí:hkiw-inǽniw*.

The nearest approach to an explanation of "good" and "bad" language seems to be this, then, that, by a cumulation of obvious superiorities, both of character and standing, as well as of language, some persons are felt to be better models of conduct and speech than others. Therefore, even in matters where the preference is not obvious, the forms which these same persons use are felt to have the better flavor. This may be a generally human state of affairs, true in every group and applicable to all languages, and the factor of Standard and Literary Language versus dialect may be a superadded secondary one.

Herbert Marcuse / The Closing of the Universe of Discourse

Herbert Marcuse has had enormous influence on the radical student movement, but no one who reads this essay or any of his other numerous writings will consider him a spokesman for that movement. In their complexity, even at times their opaqueness, his writings do not lend themselves to the sloganeering characteristic of much of the rhetoric of youthful activists. Instead, Marcuse provides a rather weighty, intellectual resource, a complicated lesson in analysis, a philosophical and academically accredited reference for those who want to substantiate their interpretation of the repressive guile of contemporary social systems. He offers, too, at least the prospect of linking contemporary critical analysis of those systems with some of the modes of analysis developed by others: Hegel and Marx, about both of whom Marcuse has written at length, and such contemporary theorists of the relation of language to politics as the French critic Roland Barthes.

Marcuse was born in Germany in 1898 and taught there before coming to the United States in 1934, so it is not surprising that he should be more revered by European youth, who tend to find their revolutionary heroes where they find their revolutionary thought, than by American youth who gravitate more to romantic revolutionaries like Che Guevara. Nonetheless, nearly all Marcuse's illustrations of "one dimensional" language are distinctly American. He is protesting the loss of dialectical tension in the language of daily and political life, the merely grammatical "reconciliation of opposites by welding them together in a firm and familiar structure." Language is being deprived of its capacity to register anything except communal complacencies even while there is increasing evidence that every aspect of contemporary life is fraught with contradictions which need to be accounted for. Marcuse's analysis extends the earlier analysis of language and its relation to twentieth-century totalitarianism made in the essay by George Orwell.

> *Dans l'état présent de l'Histoire, tout écriture politique ne peut que confirmer un univers policier, de même toute écriture intellectuelle ne peut qu'instituer une para-littérature, qui n'ose plus dire son nom.*
>
> *In the present state of history, all political writing can only confirm a police-universe, just as all intellectual writing can only produce para-literature which does not dare any longer to tell its name.*
>
> Roland Barthes

The Happy Consciousness—the belief that the real is rational and that the system delivers the goods—reflects the new conformism which is a facet of technological rationality translated into social behavior. It is new because it is rational to an unprecedented degree. It sustains a society which has reduced—and in its most advanced areas eliminated—the more primitive irrationality of the preceding stages, which prolongs and improves life more regularly than before. The war of annihilation has not yet occurred; the Nazi extermination camps have been abolished. The Happy Consciousness repels the connection. Torture has been reintroduced as a normal affair, but in a colonial war which takes place at the margin of the civilized world. And there it is practiced with good conscience for war is war. And this war, too, is at the margin—it ravages only the "underdeveloped" countries. Otherwise, peace reigns.

The power over man which this society has acquired is daily absolved by its efficacy and productiveness. If it assimilates everything it touches, if it absorbs the opposition, if it plays with the contradiction, it demonstrates its cultural superiority. And in the same way the destruction of resources and the proliferation of waste demonstrate its opulence and the "high levels of well-being"; "the Community is too well off to care!" [1]

THE LANGUAGE OF TOTAL ADMINISTRATION

This sort of well-being, the productive superstructure over the unhappy base of society, permeates the "media" which mediate between the masters and their dependents. Its publicity agents shape the universe of communication in which the one-dimensional behavior expresses itself. Its language testifies to identification and unification, to the systematic promotion of positive thinking and doing, to the concerted attack on transcendent, critical notions. In the prevailing

---

1. John K. Galbraith, *American Capitalism* (Boston, Houghton Mifflin, 1956), p. 96.

modes of speech, the contrast appears between two-dimensional, dialectical modes of thought and technological behavior or social "habits of thought."

In the expression of these habits of thought, the tension between appearance and reality, fact and factor, substance and attribute tend to disappear. The elements of autonomy, discovery, demonstration, and critique recede before designation, assertion, and imitation. Magical, authoritarian and ritual elements permeate speech and language. Discourse is deprived of the mediations which are the stages of the process of cognition and cognitive evaluation. The concepts which comprehend the facts and thereby transcend the facts are losing their authentic linguistic representation. Without these mediations, language tends to express and promote the immediate identification of reason and fact, truth and established truth, essence and existence, the thing and its function.

These identifications, which appeared as a feature of operationalism, reappear as features of discourse in social behavior. Here functionalization of language helps to repel non-conformist elements from the structure and movement of speech. Vocabulary and syntax are equally affected. Society expresses its requirements directly in the linguistic material but not without opposition; the popular language strikes with spiteful and defiant humor at the official and semi-official discourse. Slang and colloquial speech have rarely been so creative. It is as if the common man (or his anonymous spokesman) would in his speech assert his humanity against the powers that be, as if the rejection and revolt, subdued in the political sphere, would burst out in the vocabulary that calls things by their names: "head-shrinker" and "egghead," "boob tube," "think tank," "beat it" and "dig it," and "gone, man, gone."

However, the defense laboratories and the executive offices, the governments and the machines, the time-keepers and managers, the efficiency experts and the political beauty parlors (which provide the leaders with the appropriate make-up) speak a different language and, for the time being, they seem to have the last word. It is the word that orders and organizes, that induces people to do, to buy, and to accept. It is transmitted in a style which is a veritable linguistic creation; a syntax in which the structure of the sentence is abridged and condensed in such a way that no tension, no "space" is left between the parts of the sentence. This linguistic form militates against a development of meaning. I shall presently try to illustrate this style.

The feature of operationalism—to make the concept synonymous with the corresponding set of operations—recurs in the linguistic tendency "to consider the names of things as being indicative at the same time of their manner of functioning, and the names of properties and processes as symbolical of the apparatus used to detect or produce them." [2] This is technological reasoning, which tends "to identify things and their functions." [3]

2. Stanley Gerr, "Language and Science," in: *Philosophy of Science,* April 1942, p. 156.
3. *Ibid.*

As a habit of thought outside the scientific and technical language, such reasoning shapes the expression of a specific social and political behaviorism. In this behavioral universe, words and concepts tend to coincide, or rather the concept tends to be absorbed by the word. The former has no other content than that designated by the word in the publicized and standardized usage, and the word is expected to have no other response than the publicized and standardized behavior (reaction). The word becomes *cliché* and, as cliché, governs the speech or the writing; the communication thus precludes genuine development of meaning.

To be sure, any language contains innumerable terms which do not require development of their meaning, such as the terms designating the objects and implements of daily life, visible nature, vital needs and wants. These terms are generally understood so that their mere appearance produces a response (linguistic or operational) adequate to the pragmatic context in which they are spoken.

The situation is very different with respect to terms which denote things or occurrences beyond this noncontroversial context. Here, the functionalization of language expresses an abridgement of meaning which has a political connotation. The names of things are not only "indicative of their manner of functioning," but their (actual) manner of functioning also defines and "closes" the meaning of the thing, excluding other manners of functioning. The noun governs the sentence in an authoritarian and totalitarian fashion, and the sentence becomes a declaration to be accepted—it repels demonstration, qualification, negation of its codified and declared meaning.

At the nodal points of the universe of public discourse, self-validating, analytical propositions appear which function like magic-ritual formulas. Hammered and re-hammered into the recipient's mind, they produce the effect of enclosing it within the circle of the conditions prescribed by the formula.

. . . Such nouns as "freedom," "equality," "democracy," and "peace" imply, analytically, a specific set of attributes which occur invariably when the noun is spoken or written. In the West, the analytic predication is in such terms as free enterprise, initiative, elections, individual; in the East in terms of workers and peasants, building communism or socialism, abolition of hostile classes. On either side, transgression of the discourse beyond the closed analytical structure is incorrect or propaganda, although the means of enforcing the truth and the degree of punishment are very different. In this universe of public discourse, speech moves in synonyms and tautologies; actually, it never moves toward the qualitative difference. The analytic structure insulates the governing noun from those of its contents which would invalidate or at least disturb the accepted use of the noun in statements of policy and public opinion. The ritualized concept is made immune against contradiction.

Thus, the fact that the prevailing mode of freedom is servitude, and that the prevailing mode of equality is superimposed inequality is barred from expression by the closed definition of these concepts in terms of the powers which shape the respective universe of discourse. The result is the familiar Orwellian language ("peace is war" and "war is peace," etc.), which is by no means that of terroristic totalitarianism only. Nor is it any less Orwellian if the contradiction is not made explicit in the sentence but is enclosed in the noun. That a political party which works for the defense and growth of capitalism is called "Socialist," and a despotic government "democratic," and a rigged election "free" are familiar linguistic—and political—features which long pre-date Orwell.

Relatively new is the general acceptance of these lies by public and private opinion, the suppression of their monstrous content. The spread and the effectiveness of this language testify to the triumph of society over the contradictions which it contains; they are reproduced without exploding the social system. And it is the outspoken, blatant contradiction which is made into a device of speech and publicity. The syntax of abridgment proclaims the reconciliation of opposites by welding them together in a firm and familiar structure. I shall attempt to show that the "clean bomb" and the "harmless fall-out" are only the extreme creations of a normal style. Once considered the principal offense against logic, the contradiction now appears as a principle of the logic of manipulation— realistic caricature of dialectics. It is the logic of a society which can afford to dispense with logic and play with destruction, a society with technological mastery of mind and matter.

The universe of discourse in which the opposites are reconciled has a firm basis for such unification—its beneficial destructiveness. Total commercialization joins formerly antagonistic spheres of life, and this union expresses itself in the smooth linguistic conjunction of conflicting parts of speech. To a mind not yet sufficiently conditioned, much of the public speaking and printing appears utterly surrealistic. Captions such as "Labor is Seeking Missile Harmony," [4] and advertisements such as a "Luxury Fall-Out Shelter" [5] may still evoke the naïve reaction that "Labor," "Missile," and "Harmony" are irreconcilable contradictions, and that no logic and no language should be capable of correctly joining luxury and fall-out. However, the logic and the language become perfectly rational when we learn that a "nuclear-powered, ballistic-missile-firing submarine" "carries a price tag of $120,000,000" and that "carpeting, scrabble and TV" are provided in the $1,000 model of the shelter. The validation is not primarily in the fact that this language sells (it seems that the fall-out business was not so good) but rather that it promotes the immediate identification of the particular with the general interest, Business with National Power, prosperity with the annihilation potential. It is only a slip of the truth if a theater announces as a "Special Election Eve Perf., Strindberg's *Dance of Death*." [6] The announcement reveals the connection in a less ideological form than is normally admitted.

4. *New York Times*, December 1, 1960.
5. *Ibid.*, November 2, 1960.
6. *Ibid.*, November 7, 1960.

The unification of opposites which characterizes the commercial and political style is one of the many ways in which discourse and communication make themselves immune against the expression of protest and refusal. How can such protest and refusal find the right word when the organs of the established order admit and advertise that peace is really the brink of war, that the ultimate weapons carry their profitable price tags, and that the bomb shelter may spell coziness? In exhibiting its contradictions as the token of its truth, this universe of discourse closes itself against any other discourse which is not on its own terms. And, by its capacity to assimilate all other terms to its own, it offers the prospect of combining the greatest possible tolerance with the greatest possible unity. Nevertheless its language testifies to the repressive character of this unity. This language speaks in constructions which impose upon the recipient the slanted and abridged meaning, the blocked development of content, the acceptance of that which is offered in the form in which it is offered.

The analytic predication is such a repressive construction. The fact that a specific noun is almost always coupled with the same "explicatory" adjectives and attributes makes the sentence into a hypnotic formula which, endlessly repeated, fixes the meaning in the recipient's mind. He does not think of essentially different (and possibly true) explications of the noun. Later we shall examine other constructions in which the authoritarian character of this language reveals itself. They have in common a telescoping and abridgment of syntax which cuts off development of meaning by creating fixed images which impose themselves with an overwhelming and petrified concreteness. It is the well-known technique of the advertisement industry, where it is methodically used for "establishing an image" which sticks to the mind and to the product, and helps to sell the men and the goods. Speech and writing are grouped around "impact lines" and "audience rousers" which convey the image. This image may be "freedom" or "peace," or the "nice guy" or the "communist" or "Miss Rheingold." The reader or listener is expected to associate (and does associate) with them a fixated structure of institutions, attitudes, aspirations, and he is expected to react in a fixated, specific manner.

Beyond the relatively harmless sphere of merchandising, the consequences are rather serious, for such language is at one and the same time "intimidation and glorification." [7] Propositions assume the form of suggestive commands—they are evocative rather than demonstrative. Predication becomes prescription; the whole communication has a hypnotic character. At the same time it is tinged with a false familiarity—the result of constant repetition, and of the skillfully managed popular directness of the communication. This relates itself to the recipient immediately—without distance of status, education, and office—and hits him or her in the informal atmosphere of the living room, kitchen, and bedroom.

7. Roland Barthes, *Le Degré zéro de l'écriture* (Paris, Editions du Seuil, 1953), p. 33.

The same familiarity is established through personalized language, which plays a considerable role in advanced communication.[8] It is "your" congressman, "your" highway, "your" favorite drugstore, "your" newspaper; it is brought "to you," it invites "you," etc. In this manner, superimposed, standardized, and general things and functions are presented as "especially for you." It makes little difference whether or not the individuals thus addressed believe it. Its success indicates that it promotes the self-identification of the individuals with the functions which they and the others perform.

In the most advanced sectors of functional and manipulated communication, language imposes in truly striking constructions the authoritarian identification of person and function. *Time* magazine may serve as an extreme example of this trend. Its use of the inflectional genitive makes individuals appear to be mere appendices or properties of their place, their job, their employer, or enterprise. They are introduced as Virginia's Byrd, U. S. Steel's Blough, Egypt's Nasser. A hyphenated attributive construction creates a fixed syndrome:

> "Georgia's high-handed, low-browed governor . . . had the stage all set for one of his wild political rallies last week."

The governor,[9] his function, his physical features, and his political practices are fused together into one indivisible and immutable structure which, in its natural innocence and immediacy, overwhelms the reader's mind. The structure leaves no space for distinction, development, differentiation of meaning: it moves and lives only as a whole. Dominated by such personalized and hypnotic images, the article can then proceed to give even essential information. The narrative remains safely within the well-edited framework of a more or less human interest story as defined by the publisher's policy.

Use of the hyphenized abridgment is widespread. For example, "brush-browed" Teller, the "father of the H-bomb," "bull-shouldered missileman von Braun," "science-military dinner" [10] and the "nuclear-powered, ballistic-missile-firing" submarine. Such constructions are, perhaps not accidentally, particularly frequent in phrases joining technology, politics, and the military. Terms designating quite different spheres or qualities are forced together into a solid, overpowering whole.

The effect is again a magical and hypnotic one—the projection of images which convey irresistible unity, harmony of contradictions. Thus the loved and feared Father, the spender of life, generates the H-bomb for the annihilation of life; "science-military" joins the efforts to reduce anxiety and suffering with the job of creating anxiety and suffering. Or, without the hyphen, the Freedom

---

8. See Leo Lowenthal, *Literature, Popular Culture, and Society* (Prentice-Hall, 1961), pp. 109 ff. and Richard Hoggart, *The Uses of Literacy* (Boston, Beacon Press, 1961), pp. 161 ff.
9. The statement refers, not to the present Governor, but to Mr. Talmadge.
10. The last three items quoted in *The Nation*, Feb. 22, 1958.

Academy of cold war specialists,[11] and the "clean bomb"—attributing to destruction moral and physical integrity. People who speak and accept such language seem to be immune to everything—and susceptible to everything. Hyphenation (explicit or not) does not always reconcile the irreconcilable; frequently, the combine is quite gentle—as in the case of the "bull-shouldered missileman"—or it conveys a threat, or an inspiring dynamic. But the effect is similar. The imposing structure unites the actors and actions of violence, power, protection, and propaganda in one lightning flash. We see the man or the thing in operation and only in operation—it cannot be otherwise.

Note on abridgment. NATO, SEATO, UN, AFL-CIO, AEC, but also USSR, DDR, etc. Most of these abbreviations are perfectly reasonable and justified by the length of the unabbreviated designata. However, one might venture to see in some of them a "cunning of Reason"—the abbreviation may help to repress undesired questions. NATO does not suggest what North Atlantic Treaty Organization says, namely, a treaty among the nations on the North-Atlantic—in which case one might ask questions about the membership of Greece and Turkey. USSR abbreviates Socialism and Soviet; DDR: democratic. UN dispenses with undue emphasis on "united"; SEATO with those Southeast-Asian countries which do not belong to it. AFL-CIO entombs the radical political differences which once separated the two organizations, and AEC is just one administrative agency among many others. The abbreviations denote that and only that which is institutionalized in such a way that the transcending connotation is cut off. The meaning is fixed, doctored, loaded. Once it has become an official vocable, constantly repeated in general usage, "sanctioned" by the intellectuals, it has lost all cognitive value and serves merely for recognition of an unquestionable fact.

This style is of an overwhelming *concreteness*. The "thing identified with its function" is more real than the thing distinguished from its function, and the linguistic expression of this identification (in the functional noun, and in the many forms of syntactical abridgment) creates a basic vocabulary and syntax which stand in the way of differentiation, separation, and distinction. This language, which constantly imposes *images,* militates against the development and expression of *concepts*. In its immediacy and directness, it impedes conceptual thinking; thus, it impedes thinking. For the concept does *not* identify the thing and its function. Such identification may well be the legitimate and perhaps even the only meaning of the operational and technological concept, but operational and technological definitions are specific usages of concepts for specific purposes.

---

11. A suggestion of *Life* magazine, quoted in *The Nation,* August 20, 1960. According to David Sarnoff, a bill to establish such an Academy is before Congress. See John K. Jessup, Adlai Stevenson, and others, *The National Purpose* (produced under the supervision and with the help of the editorial staff of *Life* magazine, New York, Holt, Rinehart and Winston, 1960), p. 58.

Moreover, they dissolve concepts in operations and exclude the conceptual intent which is opposed to such dissolution. Prior to its operational usage, the concept *denies* the identification of the thing with its function; it distinguishes that which the thing *is* from the contingent functions of the thing in the established reality.

The prevalent tendencies of speech, which repulse these distinctions, are expressive of the changes in the modes of thought discussed in the earlier chapters [of Marcuse's book *One-Dimensional Man*]—the functionalized, abridged and unified language is the language of one-dimensional thought. In order to illustrate its novelty, I shall contrast it briefly with a classical philosophy of grammar which transcends the behavioral universe and relates linguistic to ontological categories.

According to this philosophy, the grammatical subject of a sentence is first a "substance" and remains such in the various states, functions, and qualities which the sentence predicates of the subject. It is actively or passively related to its predicates but remains different from them. If it is not a proper noun, the subject is more than a noun: it names the *concept* of a thing, a universal which the sentence defines as in a particular state or function. The grammatical subject thus carries a meaning in *excess* of that expressed in the sentence.

In the words of Wilhelm von Humboldt: the noun as grammatical subject denotes something that "can enter into certain relationships," [12] but is not identical with these relationships. Moreover, it remains what it is in and "against" these relationships; it is their "universal" and substantive core. The propositional synthesis links the action (or state) with the subject in such a manner that the subject is designated as the actor (or bearer) and thus is distinguished from the state or function in which it happens to be. In saying: "lightning strikes," one "thinks not merely of the striking lightning, but of the lightning itself which strikes," of a subject which "passed into action." And if a sentence gives a definition of its subject, it does not dissolve the subject in its states and functions, but defines it as being in this state, or exercising this function. Neither disappearing in its predicates nor existing as an entity before and outside its predicates, the subject constitutes itself in its predicates—the result of a process of mediation which is expressed in the sentence.[13]

I have alluded to the philosophy of grammar in order to illuminate the extent to which the linguistic abridgments indicate an abridgment of thought which they in turn fortify and promote. Insistence on the philosophical elements in grammar, on the link between the grammatical, logical, and ontological "subject," points up the contents which are suppressed in the functional language,

---

12. W. v. Humboldt, *Über die Verschiedenheit des menschlichen Sprachbaues*, reprint Berlin 1936, p. 254.
13. See for this philosophy of grammar in dialectical logic Hegel's concept of the "substance as subject" and of the "speculative sentence" in the Preface to the *Phaenomenology of the Spirit*.

barred from expression and communication. Abridgment of the concept in fixed images; arrested development in self-validating, hypnotic formulas; immunity against contradiction; identification of the thing (and of the person) with its function—these tendencies reveal the one-dimensional mind in the language it speaks.

If the linguistic behavior blocks conceptual development, if it militates against abstraction and mediation, if it surrenders to the immediate facts, it repels recognition of the factors behind the facts, and thus repels recognition of the facts, and of their historical content. In and for the society, this organization of functional discourse is of vital importance; it serves as a vehicle of coordination and subordination. The unified, functional language is an irreconcilably anti-critical and anti-dialectical language. In it, operational and behavioral rationality absorbs the transcendent, negative, oppositional elements of Reason.

I shall discuss these elements in terms of the tension between the "is" and the "ought," between essence and appearance, potentiality and actuality—ingression of the negative in the positive determinations of logic.* This sustained tension permeates the two-dimensional universe of discourse which is the universe of critical, abstract thought. The two dimensions are antagonistic to each other; the reality partakes of both of them, and the dialectical concepts develop the real contradictions. In its own development, dialectical thought came to comprehend the historical character of the contradictions and the process of their mediation as historical process. Thus the "other" dimension of thought appeared to be *historical* dimension—the potentiality as historical possibility, its realization as historical event.

The suppression of this dimension in the societal universe of operational rationality is a *suppression of history,* and this is not an academic but a political affair. It is suppression of the society's own past—and of its future, inasmuch as this future invokes the qualitative change, the negation of the present. A universe of discourse in which the categories of freedom have become interchangeable and even identical with their opposites is not only practicing Orwellian or Aesopian language but is repulsing and forgetting the historical reality—the horror of fascism; the idea of socialism; the preconditions of democracy; the content of freedom. If a bureaucratic dictatorship rules and defines communist society, if fascist regimes are functioning as partners of the Free World, if the welfare program of enlightened capitalism is successfully defeated by labeling it "socialism," if the foundations of democracy are harmoniously abrogated in democracy, then the old historical concepts are invalidated by up-to-date operational redefinitions. The redefinitions are falsifications which, imposed by the powers that be and the powers of fact, serve to transform falsehood into truth.

The functional language is a radically anti-historical language: operational ra-

* *One-Dimensional Man,* Chapter 5.

tionality has little room and little use for historical reason.[14] Is this fight against history part of the fight against a dimension of the mind in which centrifugal faculties and forces might develop—faculties and forces that might hinder the total coordination of the individual with the society? Remembrance of the past may give rise to dangerous insights, and the established society seems to be apprehensive of the subversive contents of memory. Remembrance is a mode of dissociation from the given facts, a mode of "mediation" which breaks, for short moments, the omnipresent power of the given facts. Memory recalls the terror and the hope that passed. Both come to life again, but whereas in reality, the former recurs in ever new forms, the latter remains hope. And in the personal events which reappear in the individual memory, the fears and aspirations of mankind assert themselves—the universal in the particular. It is history which memory preserves. It succumbs to the totalitarian power of the behavioral universe:

> Das "Schreckbild einer Menschheit ohne Erinnerung . . . ist kein blosses Verfallsprodukt . . . sondern es ist mit der Fortschrittlichkeit des bürgerlichen Prinzips notwendig verknüpft." "Oekonomen und Soziologen wie Werner Sombart und Max Weber haben das Prinzip des Traditionalismus den feudalen Gesellschaftsformen zugeordnet und das der Rationalität den bürgerlichen. Das sagt aber nicht weniger, als dass Erinnerung, Zeit, Gedächtnis von der fortschreitenden bürgerlichen Gesellschaft selber als eine Art irrationaler Rest liquidiert wird. . . ."[15]

If the progressing rationality of advanced industrial society tends to liquidate, as an "irrational rest," the disturbing elements of Time and Memory, it also tends to liquidate the disturbing rationality contained in this irrational rest. Recognition and relation to the past as present counteracts the functionalization of thought by and in the established reality. It militates against the closing of the universe of discourse and behavior; it renders possible the development of concepts which de-stabilize and transcend the closed universe by comprehending it

---

14. This does not mean that history, private or general, disappears from the universe of discourse. The past is evoked often enough: be it as the Founding Fathers, or Marx-Engels-Lenin, or as the humble origins of a presidential candidate. However these too, are ritualized invocations which do not allow development of the content recalled; frequently, the mere invocation serves to block such development, which would show its historical impropriety.

15. "The spectre of man without memory . . . is more than an aspect of decline—it is necessarily linked with the principle of progress in bourgeois society." "Economists and sociologists such as Werner Sombart and Max Weber correlated the principle of tradition to feudal, and that of rationality to bourgeois, forms of society. This means no less than that the advancing bourgeois society liquidates Memory, Time, Recollection as irrational leftovers of the past. . . ." Th. W. Adorno, "Wes bedeutet Aufarbeitung der Vergangenheit?", in: Bericht über die Erzieherkonferenz am 6 und 7. November in Wiesbaden; Frankfurt 1960, p. 14.

as historical universe. Confronted with the given society as object of its reflection, critical thought becomes historical consciousness; as such, it is essentially judgment. Far from necessitating an indifferent relativism, it searches in the real history of man for the criteria of truth and falsehood, progress and regression. The mediation of the past with the present discovers the factors which made the facts, which determined the way of life, which established the masters and the servants; it projects the limits and the alternatives. When this critical consciousness speaks, it speaks "le langage de la connaissance" * (Roland Barthes) which breaks open a closed universe of discourse and its petrified structure. The key terms of this language are not hypnotic nouns which evoke endlessly the same frozen predicates. They rather allow of an open development; they even unfold their content in contradictory predicates.

The Communist Manifesto provides a classical example. Here the two key terms, Bourgeoisie and Proletariat, each "govern" contrary predicates. The "bourgeoisie" is the subject of technical progress, liberation, conquest of nature, creation of social wealth, *and* of the perversion and destruction of these achievements. Similarly, the "proletariat" carries the attributes of total oppression *and* of the total defeat of oppression.

Such dialectical relation of opposites in and by the proposition is rendered possible by the recognition of the subject as an historical agent whose identity constitutes itself in *and against* its historical practice, in *and against* its social reality. The discourse develops and states the conflict between the thing and its function, and this conflict finds linguistic expression in sentences which join contradictory predicates in a logical unit—conceptual counterpart of the objective reality. In contrast to all Orwellian language, the contradiction is demonstrated, made explicit, explained, and denounced.

I have illustrated the contrast between the two languages by referring to the style of Marxian theory, but the critical, cognitive qualities are not the exclusive characteristics of the Marxian style. They can also be found (though in different modes) in the style of the great conservative and liberal critique of the unfolding bourgeois society. For example, the language of Burke * and Tocqueville * on the one side, of John Stuart Mill * on the other is a highly demonstrative, conceptual, "open" language, which has not yet succumbed to the hypnotic-ritual formulas of present-day neo-conservatism and neo-liberalism.

However, the authoritarian ritualization of discourse is more striking where it affects the dialectical language itself. The requirements of competitive industrial-

---

* "le langage de la connaissance": the language of the understanding.
* Edmund Burke: (1729–97), British statesman and philosopher, best known for his writings in opposition to the French Revolution, e.g. his *Reflections on the Revolution in France* (1790).
* Alexis de Tocqueville: (1805–59), French traveler and historian of conservative views; see his *Democracy in America* (1835).
* John Stuart Mill: (1806–73), English philosopher, political and economic theorist, and radical reformer, best remembered for his essay *On Liberty* (1859).

ization, and the total subjection of man to the productive apparatus appears in the authoritarian transformation of the Marxist into the Stalinist and post-Stalinist language. These requirements, as interpreted by the leadership which controls the apparatus, define what is right and wrong, true and false. They leave no time and no space for a discussion which would project disruptive alternatives. This language no longer lends itself to "discourse" at all. It pronounces and, by virtue of the power of the apparatus, establishes facts—it is self-validating enunciation. Here,[16] it must suffice to quote and paraphrase the passage in which Roland Barthes describes its magic-authoritarian features: "il n'y a plus aucun sursis entre la dénomination et le jugement, et la clôture du langage est parfaite. . . ."[17]

The closed language does not demonstrate and explain—it communicates decision, dictum, command. Where it defines, the definition becomes "separation of good from evil"; it establishes unquestionable rights and wrongs, and one value as justification of another value. It moves in tautologies, but the tautologies are terribly effective "sentences." They pass judgment in a "prejudged form"; they pronounce condemnation. For example, the "objective content," that is, the definition of such terms as "deviationist," "revisionist," is that of the penal code, and this sort of validation promotes a consciousness for which the language of the powers that be is the language of truth.[18]

Unfortunately, this is not all. The productive growth of the established communist society also condemns the libertarian communist opposition; the language which tries to recall and preserve the original truth succumbs to its ritualization. The orientation of discourse (and action) on terms such as "the proletariat," "workers' councils," the "dictatorship of the Stalinist apparatus," becomes orientation on ritual formulas where the "proletariat" no longer or not yet exists, where direct control "from below" would interfere with the progress of mass production, and where the fight against the bureaucracy would weaken the efficacy of the only real force that can be mobilized against capitalism on an international scale. Here the past is rigidly retained but not mediated with the present. One opposes the concepts which comprehended a historical situation without developing them into the present situation—one blocks their dialectic.

The ritual-authoritarian language spreads over the contemporary world, through democratic and non-democratic, capitalist and non-capitalist countries.[19] According to Roland Barthes, it is the language "propre à tous les régimes

16. See my *Soviet Marxism, loc. cit.,* pp. 87 ff.
17. "there is no longer any delay between the naming and the judgment, and the closing of the language is complete."
18. Roland Barthes, *loc. cit.,* pp. 37–40.
19. For West Germany see the intensive studies undertaken by the Institut für Sozialforschung, Frankfurt am Main, in 1950–1951: *Gruppen Experiment,* ed. F. Pollock (Frankfurt, Europaeische Verlagsanstalt, 1955), esp. pp. 545 f. Also Karl Korn, *Sprache in der verwalteten Welt* (Frankfurt, Heinrich Scheffler, 1958), for both parts of Germany.

d'autorité," * and is there today, in the orbit of advanced industrial civilization, a society which is not under an authoritarian regime? As the substance of the various regimes no longer appears in alternative modes of life, it comes to rest in alternative techniques of manipulation and control. Language not only reflects these controls but becomes itself an instrument of control even where it does not transmit orders but information; where it demands, not obedience but choice, not submission but freedom.

This language controls by reducing the linguistic forms and symbols of reflection, abstraction, development, contradiction; by substituting images for concepts. It denies or absorbs the transcendent vocabulary; it does not search for but establishes and imposes truth and falsehood. But this kind of discourse is not terroristic. It seems unwarranted to assume that the recipients believe, or are made to believe, what they are being told. The new touch of the magic-ritual language rather is that people don't believe it, or don't care, and yet act accordingly. One does not "believe" the statement of an operational concept but it justifies itself in action—in getting the job done, in selling and buying, in refusal to listen to others, etc.

If the language of politics tends to become that of advertising, thereby bridging the gap between two formerly very different realms of society, then this tendency seems to express the degree to which domination and administration have ceased to be a separate and independent function in the technological society. This does not mean that the power of the professional politicians has decreased. The contrary is the case. The more global the challenge they build up in order to meet it, the more normal the vicinity of total destruction, the greater their freedom from effective popular sovereignty. But their domination has been incorporated into the daily performances and relaxation of the citizens, and the "symbols" of politics are also those of business, commerce, and fun.

The vicissitudes of the language have their parallel in the vicissitudes of political behavior. In the sale of equipment for relaxing entertainment in bomb shelters, in the television show of competing candidates for national leadership, the juncture between politics, business, and fun is complete. But the juncture is fraudulent and fatally premature—business and fun are still the politics of domination. This is not the satire-play after the tragedy; it is not *finis tragoediae*—the tragedy may just begin. And again, it will not be the hero but the people who will be the ritual victims.

* "propre à tous les régimes d'autorité": proper to all authoritarian regimes.

William Burroughs / The Invisible Generation

Since a substantial amount of the writing in this book is transcribed speech: interviews, recorded conversations, even, in Murray Kempton's piece (Section VIII), a bit of some phone taps made by the F.B.I., it seems suitable that an essay should be devoted to the subject of taped sound, especially taped language. As treated by the novelist William Burroughs the subject of taped language is really the subject of minds. There is a degree to which all of us, or so it is suggested, are electrified, our minds reproducing the sounds implanted there by a nearly continuous exposure to the various media. Much that we say is probably, and without our knowing it, what we have pre-recorded, just as what we see, as Burroughs illustrates in the opening paragraph, can be determined (and transformed) by the sounds that accompany it.

Burroughs's style is meant to illustrate these propositions. Though he manages to render the accents of voice, his writing is cleansed of those punctuational signs, such as capitalization, commas, etc., that cannot be recorded on tape; he will quite unexpectedly switch from a relatively formal mode of address to a familiarly casual or slangy one; and interjected throughout are phrases that suggest, with a usually comic self-posturing, that Burroughs's mind and speech have been momentarily taken over by the worst aspects of law-and-order jingoism or the roles provided by television serials.

The social and political implications of this essay are made somewhat less disturbing by the element of play which Burroughs introduces into the uses of tapes. It is possible, as he shows, to experiment with them in ways that reveal how meaninglessly arbitrary many of the forms of expression are that pass for necessary or "real." This is at least some form of resistance against forces that would occupy and control the mind.

---

what we see is determined to a large extent by what we hear you can verify this proposition by a simple experiment turn off the sound track on your television set and substitute an arbitrary sound track prerecorded on your tape recorder street sounds music conversation recordings of other television programs you will find that the arbitrary sound track seems to be appropriate and is in fact determining your interpretation of the film track on screen people running for a bus in piccadilly with a sound track of machine-gun fire looks like

1917 petrograd   you can extend the experiment by using recorded material more or less appropriate to the film track for example take a political speech on television shut off sound track and substitute another speech you have prerecorded   hardly tell the difference isn't much record sound track of one danger man from uncle spy program run it in place of another and see if your friends can't tell the difference   it's all done with tape recorders   consider this machine and what it can do   it can record and play back activating a past time set by precise association a recording can be played back any number of times you can study and analyze every pause and inflection of a recorded conversation why did so and so say just that or this just here play back so and so's recordings and you will find out what cues so and so in you can edit a recorded conversation retaining material which is incisive witty and pertinent   you can edit a recorded conversation retaining remarks which are boring flat and silly   a tape recorder can play back fast   slow or backwards   you can learn to do these things   record a sentence and speed up   now try imitating your accelerated voice   play a sentence backwards and learn to unsay what you just said . . . such exercises bring you a liberation from old association locks   try inching tape   this sound is produced by taking a recorded text for best results a text spoken in a loud clear voice and rubbing the tape back and forth across the head   the same sound can be produced on a philips compact cassette recorder by playing a tape back and switching the mike control stop start on and off at short intervals which gives an effect of stuttering   take any text speed it up slow it down run it backwards inch it and you will hear words that were not in the original recording new words made by the machine   different people will scan out different words of course but some of the words are quite clearly there and anyone can hear them words which were not in the original tape but which are in many cases relevant to the original text as if the words themselves had been interrogated and forced to reveal their hidden meanings   it is interesting to record these words words literally made by the machine itself   you can carry this experiment further using   as your original recording material that contains no words animal noises for instance record a trough of slopping hogs the barking of dogs   go to the zoo and record the bellowings of Guy the gorilla the big cats growling over their meat goats and monkeys   now run the animals backwards speed up slow down and inch the animals and see if any clear words emerge   see what the animals have to say see how the animals react to playback of processed tape

the simplest variety of cut up on tape can be carried out with one machine like this record any text rewind to the beginning   now run forward at arbitrary intervals stop the machine and record a short text wind forward stop record where you have recorded over the original text the words are wiped out and replaced with new words   do this several times creating arbitrary juxtapositions you will notice that the arbitrary cuts in are appropriate in many cases and your cut up tape makes surprising sense   cut up tapes can be hilariously funny twenty years ago i heard a tape called the drunken newscaster prepared by jerry newman of new york cutting up news broadcasts i can not remember the words at this distance but i do remember laughing until i fell out of a chair paul bowles calls the tape recorder god's little toy maybe his last toy fading into the cold spring air poses a colorless question

  any number can play

  yes any number can play anyone with a tape recorder controlling the sound track can influence and create events the tape recorder experiments described here will show you how this influence can be extended and correlated into the precise operation this is the invisible generation he looks like an advertising executive a college student an american tourist doesn't matter what your cover story is so long as it covers you and leaves you free to act you need a philips compact cassette recorder handy machine for street recording and playback you can carry it under your coat for recording looks like a transistor radio for playback playback in the street will show the influence of your sound track in operation of course the most undetectable playback is street recordings people don't notice yesterday voices phantom car holes in time accidents of past time played back in present time screech of brakes loud honk of an absent horn can occasion an accident here old fires still catch old buildings still fall or take a prerecorded sound track into the street anything you want to put out on the sublim eire play back two minutes record two minutes mixing your message with the street waft your message right into a worthy ear some carriers are much better than others you know the ones lips moving muttering away carry my message all over london in our yellow submarine working with street playback you will see your playback find the appropriate context for example i am playing back some of my dutch schultz * last word tapes in the street five alarm fire and a fire truck passes right on cue you will learn to give the cues you will learn to plant events and concepts after analyzing recorded conversations you will learn to steer a conversation where you want it to go the physiological liberation achieved as word lines of controlled association are cut will make you more efficient in reaching your objectives whatever you do you will do it better record your boss and co-workers analyze their associational patterns learn to imitate their voices oh you'll be a popular man around the office but not easy to compete with the usual procedure record their body sounds from concealed mikes the rhythm of breathing the movements of after-lunch intestines the beating of hearts now impose your own body sounds and become the breathing word and the beating heart of that organization become that organization the invisible brothers are invading present time the more people we can get working with tape recorders the more useful experiments and extensions will turn up why not give tape recorder parties every guest arrives with his recorder and tapes of what he intends to say at the party recording what other recorders say to him it

---

* Dutch Schultz: famous gangster of the 1930's.

is the height of rudeness not to record when addressed directly by another tape recorder and you can't say anything directly have to record it first the coolest old tape worms never talk direct

    what was the party like   switch on playback
    what happened at lunch   switch on playback

eyes old unbluffed unreadable he hasn't said a direct word in ten years and as you hear what the party was like and what happened at lunch you will begin to see sharp and clear   there was a grey veil between you and what you saw or more often did not see   that grey veil was the prerecorded words of a control machine once that veil is removed you will see clearer and sharper than those who are behind the veil whatever you do you will do it better than those behind the veil this is the invisible generation   it is the efficient generation   hands work and go see some interesting results when several hundred tape recorders turn up at a political rally or a freedom march   suppose you record the ugliest snarling southern law men several hundred tape recorders spitting it back and forth and chewing it around like a cow with the aftosa you now have a sound that could make any neighborhood unattractive   several hundred tape recorders echoing the readers could touch a poetry reading with unpredictable magic and think what fifty thousand beatle fans armed with tape recorders could do to shea stadium   several hundred people recording and playing back in the street is quite a happening right there   conservative m.p. spoke about the growing menace posed by bands of irresponsible youths with tape recorders playing back traffic sounds that confuse motorists carrying the insults recorded in some low underground club into mayfair and piccadilly   this growing menace to public order   put a thousand young recorders with riot recordings into the street   that mutter gets louder and louder   remember this is a technical operation one step at a time here is an experiment that can be performed by anyone equipped with two machines connected by extension lead so he can record directly from one machine to the other   since the experiment may give rise to a marked erotic reaction it is more interesting to select as your partner some one with whom you are on intimate terms we have two subjects b. and j.   b. records on tape recorder 1   j. records on tape recorder 2   now we alternate the two voice tracks   tape recorder 1 playback two seconds tape recorder 2 records   tape recorder 2 playback two seconds tape recorder 1 records alternating the voice of b. with the voice of j.   in order to attain any degree of precision the two tapes should be cut with scissors and alternate pieces spliced together   this is a long process which can be appreciably expedited if you have access to a cutting room and use film tape which is much larger and easier to handle   you can carry this experiment further by taking a talking film of b. and talking film of j. splicing sound and image track twenty four alternations per second   as i have intimated it is advisable to exercise some care in choosing your partner for such experiments since the results can be quite drastic b. finds himself talking and thinking just like j.   j. sees b's image in his own face   who's face   b. and j. are continually aware of each other   when separated invisible and persistent presence they are in fact becoming each other   you see b. retroactively was j. by the fact of being recorded on j.'s sound and image track experiments with spliced tape can give rise to explosive relationships properly handled of course to a high degree of efficient cooperation you will begin to see the advantage conveyed on j. if he carried out such experiments without the awareness of b. and so many applications of the spliced tape principle will suggest themselves to the alert reader suppose you are some creep in a grey flannel suit you want to present a new concept of advertising to the old man it is creative advertising so before you goes up against the old man you record the old man's voice and splices your own voice in expounding your new concept and put it out on the office air-conditioning system splice yourself in with your favorite pop singers   splice yourself in with newscasters prime ministers presidents

why stop there

why stop anywhere

everybody splice himself in with everybody else yes boys that's me there by the cement mixer   the next step and i warn you it will be expensive is programmed tape recorders   a fully programmed machine would be set to record and play back at selected intervals to rewind and start over after a selected interval automatically remaining in continuous operation   suppose you have three programmed machines tape recorder 1 programmed to play back five seconds while tape recorder 2 records   tape recorder 2 play back three seconds while tape recorder 1 records now say you are arguing with your boy friend or girl friend remembering what was said last time and thinking of things to say next time round and round you just can't shut up   put all your arguments and complaints on tape recorder 1 and call tape recorder 1 by your own name   on tape recorder 2 put all the things he or she said to you or might say when occasion arises out of the tape recorders   now make the machines talk   tape recorder 1 play back five seconds tape recorder 2 record   tape recorder 2 play back three seconds tape recorder 1 record   run it through fifteen minutes half an hour now switch intervals running the interval switch you used on tape recorder 1 back on tape recorder 2   the interval switch may be as important as the context   listen to the two machines mix it around   now on tape recorder 3 you can introduce the factor of irrelevant response so put just anything on tape recorder 3 old joke old tune piece of the street television radio and program tape recorder 3 into the argument

tape recorder 1   i waited up for you until two o'clock last night

tape recorder 3   what we want to know is who put the sand in the spinach

the use of irrelevant response will be found effective in breaking obsessional association tracks   all association tracks are obsessional   get it out of your head and into the machines   stop arguing stop complaining stop talking let the machines argue complain and talk   a tape recorder is an externalized section of the human nervous system   you can find out more about the nervous system and gain more control over your reactions by using the tape recorder than you could find out sitting twenty years in the lotus posture or wasting your time on the analytic couch

   listen to your present time tapes and you will begin to see who you are and what you are doing here   mix yesterday in with today and hear tomorrow your future rising out of old recordings   you are a programmed tape recorder set to record and play back

   who programs you

   who decides what tapes play back in present time

   who plays back your old humiliations and defeats holding you in prerecorded preset time

   you don't have to listen to that sound   you can program your own playback   you can decide what tapes you want played back in present time   study your associational patterns and find out what cases in what prerecordings for playback   program those old tapes out it's all done with tape recorders there are many things you can do with programmed tape recorders stage performances programmed at arbitrary intervals so each performance is unpredictable and unique allowing any degree of audience participation readings concerts programmed tape recorders can create a happening anywhere programmed tape recorders are of course essential to any party and no modern host would bore his guests with a straight present time party   in a modern house every room is bugged recorders record and play back from hidden mikes and loudspeakers phantom voices mutter through corridors and rooms words visible as a haze tape recorders in the gardens answer each other like barking dogs sound track brings the studio on set you can change the look of a city by putting your own sound track into the streets here are some experiments filming a sound track operations on set find a neighborhood with slate roofs and red brick chimneys cool grey sound track fog horns distant train whistles frogs croaking music across the golf course cool blue recordings in a cobblestone market with blue shutters all the sad old showmen stand there in blue twilight a rustle of darkness and wires when several thousand people working with tape recorders and filming subsequent action select their best sound tracks and film footage and splice together you will see something interesting now consider the harm that can be done and has been done when recording and playback is expertly carried out in such a way that the people affected do not know what is happening thought feeling and apparent sensory impressions can be precisely manipulated and controlled riots and demonstrations to order for example they use old anti-semitic records against the chinese in indonesia run shop and get rich and always give the business to another tiddly wink pretty familiar   suppose you want to bring down the area   go in and record all the ugliest stupidest dialogue the most discordant sound track you can find and keep playing it back which will occasion more ugly stupid dialogue recorded and played back on and on always selecting the ugliest material possibilities are unlimited   you want to start a riot put your machines in the street with riot recordings move fast enough you can stay just ahead of the riot surf boarding we call it no margin for error recollect poor old burns caught out in a persian market riot recordings hid under his jellaba and they skinned him alive raw peeled thing writhing there in the noon sun and we got the picture

do you get the picture

the techniques and experiments described here have been used and are being used by agencies official and non official without your awareness and very much to your disadvantage   any number can play   wittgenstein * said no proposition can contain itself as an argument   the only thing not prerecorded on a prerecorded set is the prerecording itself that is any recording in which a random factor operates any street recording you can prerecord your future   you can hear and see what you want to hear and see   the experiments described here were explained and demonstrated to me by ian sommerville of london in this article i am writing as his ghost

look around you   look at a control machine programmed to select the ugliest stupidest most vulgar and degraded sounds for recording and playback which provokes uglier stupider more vulgar and degraded sounds to be recorded and play back inexorable degradation   look forward to dead end   look forward to ugly vulgar playback tomorrow and tomorrow and tomorrow what are newspapers doing but selecting the ugliest sounds for playback by and large if its ugly its news and if that isn't enough i quote from the editorial page of the new york daily news   we can take care of china and if russia intervenes we can take care of that nation too the only good communist is a dead communist lets take care of slave driver castro next what are we waiting for let's bomb china now and let's stay armed to the teeth for centuries this ugly vulgar bray put out for mass playback you want to spread hysteria record and play back the most stupid and hysterical reactions

marijuana   marijuana   why that's deadlier than cocaine

it will turn a man into a homicidal maniac he said steadily his eyes cold as he thought of the vampires who suck riches from the vile traffic in pot quite literally swollen with human blood   he reflected grimly and his jaw set pushers should be pushed into the electric chair

strip the bastards naked

all right let's see your arms

or in the mortal words of harry j anslinger   the laws must reflect society's disapproval of the addict

an uglier reflection than society's disapproval would be hard to find the mean cold eyes of decent american women tight lips and no thank you from the shop keeper snarling cops pale nigger killing eyes reflecting society's disapproval fuck-

---

* Ludwig Wittgenstein: (1889–1951), Austrian philosopher whose major concern was linguistic analysis and semantics.

ing queers i say shoot them   if on the other hand you select calm sensible reactions for recordings and playback you will spread calmness and good sense

   is this being done

   obviously it is not   only way to break the inexorable down spiral of ugly uglier ugliest recording and playback is with counterrecording and playback   the first step is to isolate and cut association lines of the control machine carry a tape recorder with you and record all the ugliest stupidest things cut your ugly tapes in together speed up slow down play backwards inch the tape   you will hear one ugly voice and see one ugly spirit is made of ugly old prerecordings   the more you run the tapes through and cut them up the less power they will have   cut the prerecordings into air into thin air

VII   PERFORMANCES

Good writing is valuable for the record of physical as well as intellectual performances, and the selections from A. Alvarez, T. H. White, and George Plimpton are intended to illustrate this. Performance in a more usual sense is discussed by Eric Bentley (the actor-playwright relation) and Edwin Denby, who talks about the situation of watching a performance, and its relation to everyday feelings and modes of seeing. Robert Frost, in an interview in which he discusses a theory of performance, is himself offering one: an extraordinary, controlled display of character and a concomitant mastery of language, under the special conditions of the taped interview. Steinberg is an artist of great distinction, but in the piece included here he is performing a sort of free interpretative dance before the masterpieces to which Pierre Schneider leads him. And in the final selection Stravinsky, who has proved himself to be not only the greatest of living composers but also, in his old age, probably the greatest master of the interview form, provides us with a culminating conversational dance, a performance depending on the intellectual development of a witty lifetime.

Josef Muench

A. Alvarez / Shiprock

Mr. Alvarez is a poet who likes fast cars and difficult climbs. This piece was written for a climbers' journal, and has a few technical terms, mostly about grades of climb and equipment, but Alvarez communicates more than a problem in technique. He tries to give the reader the whole feel of a climb, including the reluctance that may be felt at the outset, the mixed beauty and terror of the mountain, the strangeness of inhospitable landscapes; the vastness of the desert night and the heat of the day. There is a climax to the sense of nightmare which underlies much of the piece in the description of the rottenness of the rock. But this is surmounted, matter of factly, by the use of pitons; and fear itself, except for a residue necessary to the climber's safety, is burned away by the arduous exercise of body and mind that a climb of this difficulty imposes.

Possibly an inarticulate man feels much as Alvarez does on a mountain. What the command of language enables him to do is to examine and structure his own feelings, and so to express them without losing close contact with fact, with human technique, and with the substance of the world.

I suppose the first sight of a mountain is always the best. Later, when you are waiting to start, you may grow to hate the brute, because you are afraid. And when, finally, you are climbing, you are never aware of the mountain as a mountain: it is merely so many little areas of rock to be worked out in terms of hand-holds, foot-holds and effort, like so many chess problems. But when you first see it in the distance, remote and beautiful and unknown, then there seems some reason for climbing. That, perhaps, is what Mallory meant by his "Because it's there." *

I first saw Shiprock on a midsummer day. I was exhausted, having driven the two-and-a-half-thousand miles from New Jersey to New Mexico in relatively few days. Moreover, I was unfit; I had not climbed for several weeks and I looked forward without much pleasure to what would probably be thirty-six hours on a vertical face. Finally, I had that morning left my wife and baby son in Taos; and going off for a big climb is always a wretched business; it leaves you tense and sick at heart. I think now that serious climbs are for bachelors; they become so much more difficult when you leave anything behind.

I was feeling, in short, just a bit sorry for myself as I drove across the rolling Apache country and into the wastes of the Navajo reservation. The area set aside by the U.S. Government for the Navajo Indians is the most desolate land in the world, flat, dried-up, harsh, stony. But, recently, oil and uranium have been found and a little wealth is beginning to creep in. In places the desolation seems almost busy—though no less desolate. It was a few miles south of one of these little centres, a new boom town called Farmington, that I first saw Shiprock. I had come out, imperceptibly, on top of a huge flat hill. To the north and west the desert dropped away to a lower level. A long way north rose the blue tiers of the Mesa Verde, where the prehistoric cave cities are. Sweeping round to the south, the desert was ringed with smaller mesas, the queer, flat-topped hills, looking like bits of plain set up on vertical cliffs. But in the west, about fifty miles away, below the sinking sun, where the desert seemed blank and endless, was Shiprock. Its bluish, hazy mass swam sheer out of the desert, rising

---

* "Because it's there": George Leigh Mallory's famous reply to the question, "Why do you want to climb Everest?" In 1924 Mallory lost his life while attempting to climb the summit of Mt. Everest.

eighteen hundred feet to the huge twin east and south towers. Between them peered the north tower, farther away and seeming smaller: then the bulk of the mountain bending a little towards the western desert.

I had never even seen a photograph of it before. Perhaps that is why I had agreed to join the climbing party. But in the late afternoon sun it looked very beautiful. No wonder it is the sacred mountain of the Navajos. It dominates the whole landscape continuously and effortlessly. As I drove towards it, it was hidden at times by corners and edges of sandstone, but it controlled, always, my whole sense of direction. According to the picture post-cards, Shiprock got its name because at sunset it looks like a great ship floating forward across the desert. Perhaps it does. But in Navajo myth it stretches towards heaven and the souls of men descend to earth from it. It dominates their cosmology as it dominates the landscape.

There is a tiny Indian town of Shiprock, about twenty miles from the mountain. I had arranged to meet my Princeton climbing companions there. "O, we'll meet at the main restaurant," we had said. "If we're not there, we'll be camping under the climb." It was vague, of course, but then none of us knew what the town—or the mountain, for that matter—would be like. Mercifully, there were only a couple of restaurants, a couple of gas stations, a school and a couple of trading posts. There were mule carts in the street, which made it look more like Mexico than I had ever seen before in the States, and Indians were cramming into the usual pick-up trucks to return to their villages for the night. The men, small, thickish and rather saturnine, wore the regulation denims, except for a few wrapped in their blankets like dark, heavy Della Robbia * infants. But the women were splendid, skirted to their feet and shawled in vivid reds, purples and oranges. In the huge golden sunset they looked oddly unreal—or at least, unexpected—as if I'd walked into the middle of some vast play, and didn't know the plot.

There is a big motel and restaurant run by the Navajos. One of the Princeton cars was outside it, but there was no sign of my friends in the café. They had left half an hour before, the proprietress told me. They would be under the mountain. It was almost dark now, so, with nothing to lose, I ordered a meal. If we were to climb the next day, heaven knew when I'd next eat properly.

Then I set about finding my way out to the rock. The directions were simple enough: go south on the main road until the gravelled turn-off to Lukachukai. Follow that for eight miles over the desert. When you come to the ridge, go right on a track straight towards the mountain. It was quite dark by the time I started, but the full moon was up, my headlights were good and the others would probably have lit a fire. I wasn't worried.

At first, the driving was easy enough. But it was darker than I thought and the

---

* Andrea Della Robbia: (1435–1525), Florentine worker in bas-relief, known especially for his bambini medallions.

eight miles bumping along the gravel road across the desert seemed long and slow. Finally, a great black wall of rock loomed up on either side of the road: the ridge. My headlights made strange, impertinent shadows on it. There was a track off to the right just before the ridge, but it seemed improbably vague. So I went past the thing and saw another. There seemed nothing to do but take it. As I swung the car off the road, it was like walking unexpectedly into the deep-end of a swimming pool. The car jerked and heaved and wallowed. The track was hardish sand, full of pot-holes and strewn with rocks. Sometimes it would go round the little dunes, sometimes it went over them. Then I usually had to back the car and take a run at the rise, careering over the top, headlights flailing in the air, not knowing if the track went straight on over or turned on the top.

It took me about an hour to drive two miles. Finally, of course, I went wrong. I found myself with the car stuck in the sand on the top of a dune, the track entirely vanished and what appeared to be a vertical drop on three sides. The only way off was to back down the steep slope I had just come up. Without a reversing light, it seemed impossible. The great black ridge rose sheer above me, its darkness jagged and menacing against the sky. I could just make out the peak of Shiprock heaving up darkly behind it. There was no sign of the others' fire, only that great black, menacing ridge looming up in front, and the desert, eerie and shimmering and vague under the moon. The wind blew soft but insistent sand into my eyes and mouth. I began to shout in the hope that the others were just the far side of the ridge. My yells echoed back to me and faded away. So I gave up and went back to the car. Being outside in the moonlit desert made me feel terribly exposed and isolated. The place is too vast and indifferent to be bearable at night. I stretched out in the back of the car, drank some whisky and settled down to sleep. A huge grasshopper which had settled on the ledge of the rear window creaked heavily from time to time, like a pair of ancient corsets. The moon shone in on me and all around was the vast, rustling silence of the desert. Oddly enough, I slept very well.

At dawn, I climbed the ridge, one of three thin, curving tentacles spreading out from Shiprock. The path I should have taken ran, quite distinct, along the other side. At the end of it, tiny against the desert, was the other car and my friends lying around it in their sleeping-bags.

The rest of that day was like a bad dream. We had three things to do: find the start of the route; get some more food and liquid from the town; wait for the fifth member of the party to arrive. We were to be in all four Englishmen and an American, all from Princeton. One Englishman was still missing. Simple enough. But what happened in fact was that we were systematically demoralized. First, there was the rock itself: the bulk of the mountain is sheer sandstone, whilst the back is shattered basalt. All of it is utterly rotten. It came away as you touched it, hardly waiting to be pulled. Most of the ordinary holds were useless; the only safe ones were cracks to jam your toes and fingers into. Second, there was the thirst. All day the wind blew steadily; our mouths and eyes and ears were full of sand; we were parched whenever we were not actually drinking. It was a permanent condition, like the beating of your blood, or the pain of someone with cancer. It seemed impossible that we should ever have enough to drink again. Third, was the heat. Shiprock had never been climbed later than May. This was the end of June. To move into the sun was like swinging open some great furnace door. The whole landscape shimmered and swayed and faded in the heat. The rocks became almost too hot to touch. In the village the temperature was about 110° F. in the shade. Heaven alone knows what it was out in the desert. Fourth, was the Accident. On the last ascent a man had been killed. When we went to get our stores in the village, we heard of nothing else. "He was a young guy, just like you-all. Say," one would turn to the other, "he looked just like this guy, didn't he?" "Sure. And he bought the same candies. You should have seen him when they brought him in. Gee." And so on. We fled from the place as soon as we could. But by the time we drove back across the desert we were sick to death of the whole miserable business: the rotten rock, the thirst, the heat, the shopkeepers' gloating over that poor wretch's death, and the mountain looming there impassively against another unbelievable sunset. It seemed a silly, pointless way of getting oneself killed.

Dick Sykes, the missing Englishman, had still not arrived, so we decided to go up without him. We had our excuses, of course: I had to get back to my family; the others were expected in the Tetons in two days; and so on. But the truth was none of us could bear the thought of another day of tension, heat and waiting like this one. If we didn't climb the mountain the next day, we wouldn't climb it at all. So we loaded ourselves up, like so many mules, with climbing equipment, food, drink and sleeping-bags, and groped in the fading light painfully up to the start of the climb.

The west wall of Shiprock is basalt. It drops down to a huge, curving overhang. The climb begins on the left side of this, where the lip of the rock sticks out less angrily. Underneath the overhang is a shallow, level, sandy cave shaped like a scimitar. We built a fire, heated some of the precious water for tea and lay down to sleep in the cave. Again I slept surprisingly well, but I was woken a couple of times by faint rustlings. For such a dead lunar landscape, the place seemed strangely unquiet.

I suppose it goes without saying that the climb, after all the horrors of thinking about it, was perfectly straightforward. We were up before the sun, had a miserable breakfast of cornflakes and tepid baked beans, and were off. It is a violent beginning. You go straight from the ground on to stirrups * on the overhang. But this is mercifully short; four heaves, a little awkward straddling with the feet and we were up. And most important, once we began to climb all the worries and fears and tensions left us. Fear is always a matter of the future tense; the present is too blessedly factual.

You come over the overhang into a vast amphitheatre of shattered basalt. At

---

* stirrups: short rope ladders.

the back of it the head-wall goes up a thousand feet in four giant steps. At the bottom, facing you as you pull over the lip, is a plaque to mark the spot where the poor devil had landed last year. He had fallen on the way back from the second ascent of the north tower. Still, we had our own work to do. We started to climb the head-wall.

It was surprisingly easy, just another rock climb, most of it not more than about grade IV.* And provided you jammed in the cracks instead of pulling on the crumbling face, it was quite safe. Towards the top of the head-wall the climbing was harder for a little; but climbing, doing something, was such a blessed relief from thinking about it, that we were going well and quickly. John Wharton, the young leader of the climb, and I were at the top of the head-wall in a couple of hours.

The others were still two hundred feet down when there was a shout from below. It was Dick Sykes. He had arrived late in the night, and like me, had got stuck in the desert. Now he was angry, roaring at us from far below because we hadn't waited for him. Urged by his annoyance, he climbed the overhang and the first eight hundred feet of the head-wall on his own and unroped. But he had said his say and tied on to a rope before the real difficulties began.

Once we got to the top of the head-wall we lost the route. There were two ways on: the ordinary route and the north tower which went up vertically in front of us. The latter had been climbed only twice before and was technically harder than the ordinary route, but also much shorter. As for the ordinary: according to the description we had unearthed, we were supposed to rope down a smooth, vertical hundred-and-twenty-foot wall to a ledge, leaving the rope in position for the return. From the ledge the crux of the climb began: a hundred-and-twenty-foot friction traverse.* Wharton had seen some horrifying photographs of it at the American Alpine Club. Mercifully, he had not shown the rest of us. After the traverse, there were only two small overhangs between you and the summit of the south tower. From where we perched we could see plenty of smooth vertical walls, but no ledges at the bottom of them. It took a long time to find the right one. It was far below and strewn with cans, as though too many people had waited there far too long a time. But there was no way of fixing a rope to get down there. The walls were quite smooth, without the smallest crack for a piton.* Finally, we found two little holes drilled in the rock, where the bolts, of which the Americans are so fond, had been screwed. But being four Englishmen to one American, it had never occurred to us to bring bolts. Only Wharton, in fact, had ever used them. So there we were. It was the north tower or nothing.

It was, of course, the north tower. The route goes straight up from the plat-

---
* grade IV: in the classification system for assessing the technical standard of individual rock pitches, grade IV is "severe"; VI is the most difficult grade.
* friction traverse: way of moving across a smooth rock face that has no foot or hand holds.
* piton: a peg for sticking into a rock face.

form at the top of the head-wall in two pitches of VI. It is not strenuous, but very thin and very rotten. It took a great deal of juggling with stirrups and pitons. But Wharton and Sykes led it beautifully between them. There was never any question but that we would get up. Only in the last fifty feet did the rottenness of the rock reach a point of lunacy. You could stick your fingers into the stuff, almost like mud. But the Colorado guide who had first climbed it must have known a great deal about rock structure; there was a string of pitons going straight up this putty, and they were as solid as the rock should have been. We had to climb from one to the other, ignoring the face itself contemptuously.

We sat on the summit and took the usual photographs. We opened the little steel canister bolted to the top and added our names to the list; we were the third party to get there. Then, since we knew we wouldn't be spending the night on the mountain after all, we passed our water-bottles round with wanton generosity. But the sun was high and the wind still blew parchingly. We could see trees and the San Juan River glinting twenty miles away in the town of Shiprock. Way to the north the Mesa Verde rose cool and blue. So we didn't stay long on the summit. We began to rope down the rotten vertical face at four p.m. By six-thirty we were back at our camp under the overhang, thirteen hours after we left it.

And that was that. The climb had been hard and was a brilliant lead by Wharton, who was, incidentally, only eighteen. But it was just a climb. It was not, oddly enough, the climbing that made the ascent of Shiprock so difficult. It was the place itself; the eerie, untouched lunar desert, the almost unbearable thirst and heat, the strange sense of threat in its continual rustling sounds. I understood better now why to the Navajos the mountain is sacred. You are often scared climbing, but scare is local: a move out of balance, a loose hold, too much exposure. You climb better when you are scared. But fear is generalized, like superstition. It clings to a place like its shadow. It is when you have to sit still under the shadow, wait and do nothing, that fear goes over you.

But it could have been worse. The following day I was in one of the trading posts buying a Navajo rug. The shopkeeper had asked me about the climb. Then, just as I was leaving, he added casually: "Say, how many rattlers did you see?" "Rattlers?" I asked. "Sure, rattlers. Rattlesnakes. The place is full of them." And I thought of that rustling, empty cave where we had slept and the deep cracks in the rocks we had so carefully climbed in. Full of rattlesnakes. But, mercifully, we had never known.

T. H. White / The Goshawk

White's book is a remarkable account of how, using an old manual of falconry, he trained a goshawk. He did not know of more modern methods of training and undertook the whole agonizing Elizabethan treatment, which involved among other things "watching" the hawk—that is, staying awake to make it stay awake—starving it, "manning" it (letting it grow slowly accustomed to the human world), and training it on a creance. These last two are described in the present extract. In the course of his exhausting, exhilarating task, White discovered that he was doing what Petruchio did to Katherine in *The Taming of the Shrew* (watching, starving, calling her on a creance, asserting mastery) and a number of words and lines in Shakespeare suddenly acquired new life.

White was a literary writer, hence the range of reference; he was also a man capable of fanatic dedication to such an end as the training of a hawk. His book is admirable for its practical detail as well as for more lyrical writing—its minute accounts of training and diet as well as its expert descriptions of the hawk, and the eery account of it flying, through the twilight, at the head of the falconer.

It might be interesting to compare this kind of eccentric solo achievement by a novelist with that of Alvarez, a poet, challenging a crumbling mountain; or with George Plimpton's briefer and qualitatively different, yet still in its way literary, experience in pro football. All three, be it noted, are writers. Normally the deeds of sportsmen are recorded by their "ghosts" or through the eyes of journalists. But writers handle this kind of experience with greater depth; perhaps they might argue that there is a similarity between their two kinds of performance—their daily job and the exceptional physical challenges they accept, for one reason or another, in sport.

Deluded and imaginative recluse, I was beginning to feel that I could talk about the training of short-winged hawks with experience. It had before been a fumbling among conjectures, with only the printed word to help; but now, inside, there seemed to have begun to grow the personal flower of knowledge. Secretly and not quickly enough to be visible as motion, the roots had begun to push their filigree net through the loam of the unconscious mind. Gently and tenderly the smallest buds of intrinsic certainty had begun to nose out of the stalk, fed with the sap of life rather than theory.

Goshawks were Hamlet, were Ludwig of Bavaria.* Frantic heritors of frenetic sires, they were in full health more than half insane. When the red rhenish wine of their blood pulsed at full spate through their arteries, when the airy bird bones were gas-filled with little bubbles of unbiddable warm virility, no merely human being could bend them to his will. They would break before they would bend. "A fat hawk," said the old austringer's * adage, "maketh a lean horse, a

* Ludwig of Bavaria: Ludwig II (1845–86), the "Mad King of Bavaria," fanatic castle builder and patron of Richard Wagner.
* austringer: a keeper of short-winged or "true" hawks, the largest of which is the goshawk; a falconer is a keeper of long-winged hawks.

weary falconer, and an empty purse." A week of full, bloody crops would send the best reclaimed goshawk in Europe bating * from the best hawk-master in the world. Now, at last, I had learned this from the inside of my heart, the first commandment of the austringer's decalogue, a saw of three words which were the beginning and the end of falconry: Regulate the crop. Terrified by the horrible hunger trace * which he already possessed, I had spent the weeks of my novitiate in over-feeding him, to guard against a repetition of the ill. No wonder he had refused to come to me, had been intemperate and intransigent, while his small body burned with high living and lack of exercise. He had exercised himself by rage.

I saw now that I must learn to feed him with diligent and minute observation. Suddenly I realized that this was the secret of all training. I had thought before, without understanding the thought, that the way to the heart lay through the belly. The way to government lay through the deprivation of the belly. Every great overlord had known this about my companions in the lower classes. On £90 a year those who lived in workmen's cottages were just on that happy borderland of being sharp-set which kept us out of presumptuous courses. We were in perfectly good health, but not in a surplus state, not riotous, not fierce with surfeit. They kept us efficient and well-manned.

So with good mastery. The trainer of horses had to look first to their oats. I wondered that schoolmasters had not discarded the ferula for washed meat. Perhaps, when I recollected the food at schools, they had: or preferred to run them both together, because of the pleasures of flagellation.

Gos was to be trained now as Napoleon's army had marched.* It was this that must be called the fundamental of the trainer's eye in every branch of training for the blood sports. Those checked and gaitered men at Newmarket,* with their lean faces and bow legs, ultimately they were assessing the amount of food given. The lines of the blood horse on which I should lay my money next point-to-point season would not be artistic lines, not lines of force or beauty or bone or muscle: they would be lines of judicious deprivation. Of course they would not be lines of starvation, but they would be lines whose axis was the belly. This was the first law of mastery.

MONDAY

Gos was hungry enough to make enormous strides, and at last I was determined to keep him so. It was a strain and a problem at first, a strain because to reward him with food was a great pleasure and temptation, a problem because it had yet

* bating: "the headlong dive of rage and terror, by which a leashed hawk leaps from the fist in a wild bid for freedom and hangs upside down by his jesses in a flurry of pinions like a chicken being decapitated, revolving, struggling, in danger of damaging his primaries" (*The Goshawk,* p. 15).
* hunger trace: if a growing hawk is stinted in its food, a line appears across its tail feathers; the feathers are weak at this hunger trace and are liable to break off.
* "as Napoleon's army had marched": i.e. "on its stomach"; Napoleon believed that careful attention to food supplies was essential in maintaining an efficient army.
* Newmarket: famous horse-racing center in England.

to be found out how much food was necessary to keep him healthy. He had been fed low for two days now, so that this day I allowed him a foreleg, a hindleg, two kidneys and half the liver of a rabbit, feeling that I was being over-generous [1] and that he would go back next day. A third of a pound of raw beef was laid down as the daily ration for a peregrine, and I reckoned that Gos, being a tiercel,* must be about the size of a female peregrine * and should merit the equivalent of the same weight. It was evidently a matter of exquisite assessment which could only be judged by the austringer who knew his hawk (it would vary with different hawks of the same species)—by the austringer whose subconscious mind was in minutely contact with the subconscious mind of the bird. Every alteration in its mental behaviour, every feel of its weight on the wrist, every premonition of greater acuity in the breastbone when stroked: these and all other manifestations must tell the austringer of the fitness of his mate. Too hungry: too flourishing: the exact equipoise was the whole secret of falconry.

The morning was spent in making Gos come quickly to the fist, off the bow perch, a distance up to two yards. He was fed with small scraps at each flight, and he behaved well. In the afternoon he was carried from one o'clock until six, and taken to the main road at Lillingstone Lovell in order to re-introduce him to the motor cars. It was a blazing day (which had its effect in raising his temperature) but on the whole the visit was successful. I sat down with him on tree-stumps, first one hundred yards, then fifty yards, then not more than one yard from the main road: and he bated from nothing except two brightly dressed country lassies who glided by on bicycles. He bated at, not from, a brood of pheasants, and took deep interest in jays and a kestrel which put out of a hedge beside the oats. Home, he came obediently the whole length of a double leash immediately for his evening meal, and ate the rabbit's hind leg in its entirety, finishing bones, claws and all. It gave him something very like hiccups.

Sitting on the night perch of his mews he looked up at the ceiling, wriggled his head and neck like an eel or snake dancer from Ind, attempted to thrust down those three enormous bones into his interior with a kind of shimmy, regarded me, hiccupping, with glassy eye.

Reluctant to say good night I stood at the door, observing this astonishing and vaguely disquieting spectacle (would he be able to digest such a mouthful?) and thought about the morrow. It had been a splendid day. He would go back. He was sure to. Goshawks, and this was the second thing I had learned from experience, went back two paces every time they went forward one. "There is no short cut," said the good book, "to the training of a Gos."

TUESDAY

I supposed that what I was going to write eventually would be the kind of book which would madden every accomplished falconer, and I was sorry that it should

1. One hindleg would have been enough.
* tiercel: the male hawk, about a third smaller in size than the female.
* peregrine: a (long-winged) falcon.

be so. I could imagine an aged austringer sitting at the very top of the tree which I was now so laboriously climbing. He had a pettish and know-all expression, soured by years of contact with intractable goshawks. So much of his patience had been absorbed by these creatures that he had none left for his fellow mortals. In appearance slightly crochetty—he would be wearing a twa-snooted-bonnet, and his long white moustachios would be waxed at the ends—he sat at the top of the ladder and proclaimed that he had been manning hawks for sixty years. What right had a cowardly recluse who fled from his fellow men, said he, to write about these almost fabulous creatures? Fools, he remarked in a very pouncy way, rushed in where angels feared to tread.

But I was sure of one thing that I still loved, and that was learning. I had learned always, insatiably, looking for something which I wanted to know. Of all things which I had begun to learn or thrown aside almost at once, the most wildly yet tranquilly and enduringly happy had been the mystery of the divine salmon and his exquisite fly. Perhaps, in the end, giving up all other attempts, I should grow middle-aged and acquiesce in my second-hand destiny, which would be to lie beside a highland ripple in which my monster dwelled. Meanwhile the search continued, and with it the necessity of earning a living. It was easier to combine the two: to learn and then to write about it, thus making money out of what one loved. I determined to tell my aged austringer to come down out of his tree (an American idiom) because mine was not a falconer's book at all. It would be a learner's book only: in the last resort, a writer's book, by one who might have tried in vain to be a falconer.

I was proud of Gos. He flew to the fist quickly, though not far, for a small tit-bit, when taken up in the morning. He ate, coming a yard or two, much of the flesh off a large rabbit's leg, given in small repeated offerings before noon. He was carried without unusual scenes from one o'clock till six, except for a small interval when I had to go off and shoot a rabbit, and then I decided to try him on the creance.

A creance is a long length of twine, strong string or fishing line, not too heavy for the hawk to carry in flight. Usually, I believed, some assistant would carry the hawk while the master called it, tied by the creance, from the assistant's fist to his own. But I had no assistant, and preferred not to have one.

I set Gos down on a quiet railing and tied the creance to his leash. As a fisherman I was fond of knots, could indeed occasionally entertain myself by tying the blood knot, which Chaytor * made romantic and famous as well as beautiful (which it had been all along), on odd bits of string. But now the knot had be-

---

* Chaytor: the "blood knot" (a complex knot for tying together strands of gut) was kept a secret for years, until its formula was discovered and made public by A. H. Chaytor, a salmon angler; he discusses this knot and its history at length in *Letters to a Salmon Fisher's Son* (1910).

come a thing to fear as well as to love. At the other end of it there was a bird momently more valuable than anything one had ever possessed, and one of the few things left that one did possess. Ceaselessly, day and night, the neat and ingenious knots of his jesses,* the falconer's knot by which his leash was attached to the ring on the perch, the slip of the jesses on to the swivel, and of the leash through the swivel, these became critical and not untouched with fear. The suspicion with which the salmon fisherman makes all sure became a part of falconry, and one never tied a knot without the anxiety of a turnkey and a faint dubiety at heart.

My creance, which was made of brand-new tarred twine, was twenty-four yards long. At the end remote from the hawk—that is the end which was tied to the railing—there were bound in two yards of strong catapult elastic so that he should have no chance of snapping it by a sudden jerk. I stood twenty yards away from him—with the result that he would in any case have a surplus of four yards slack—and began to whistle the accursed hymn.* He had previously shown himself much fascinated by the rabbit.

I must have gone on at this for an hour, sometimes giving up for a moment and lying down among the cows (who had just come out from being milked and caused some anxiety by sauntering over the creance, as it lay stretched in a double line from the railing outwards for ten yards and back to the hawk), sometimes standing up to redouble my efforts. The problem was to make Gos understand that though he was still tied he was now free to come those extra nineteen yards.

I tried coming nearer, up to six yards, but he was still bemused. Taunted by the feeding hymn, whistled from a distance which he had never before been free to fly, the unfortunate tyrant blew out his feathers to their full extent, paced up and down his railing, glared about in all directions and practically bit his finger nails with indecision. I tried tweaking at the length of the creance between him and me, holding the twine in the hand which flourished the rabbit as a lure and jerking it in time to the "Lord's my Shepherd."

After more than an hour of failure I decided upon what I took to be drastic measures. Standing ten yards away, I pulled Gos off his railing by means of the creance. He fluttered to the ground and flew back. After more tweaking I pulled him off again. Again the same, and again and again.

At the fourth attempt he remained on the ground. Picking his way between thistles he hopped to and fro, finally in my direction. I retreated before him as you do when training a retriever. Skipping and leaping, fluffed full, a terrible toad, he bounded in my train. The last two yards of the twenty-four were flown

---

* jesses: leather thongs permanently attached to the legs of the hawk and fastened to a swivel.
* the accursed hymn: hawks must be taught to come to a particular call; White felt that "Gos was too beautiful to be shrilled at" with an ordinary metal whistle, and so used the old Scottish hymn-tune, "The Lord's my Shepherd."

to the fist: and the reward was, before he went to bed, a good two-thirds of a crop of fresh young rabbit.

WEDNESDAY

At this time two interests were going on simultaneously. There was the excitement of hoping to accomplish the fourth or penultimate great step of his education—the moment at which I wanted to see him fly one hundred yards on his creance—and there was the bother of getting him properly manned to the surrounding world. Living as we did in a wood, so far even from a road, his had been a sequestered life with few novelties. Seeing so few strangers, meeting no motors unless carried a couple of miles to do so, he was at present unaccustomed by habitat as well as by instinct to the bustle of the modern world. Yet he had to learn to stand that bustle, as we all have to do, however little we visit it.

On that Wednesday, determining for the first time to hazard him against the gentle traffic of a country town, I walked to Buckingham and back, in order to introduce him slowly. He stood it well, except for two bad bates, one on entering the market square and one on leaving. His bates at the people were less annoying than the people's reaction to him. Nervous mothers wheeled their children's perambulators to the opposite pavements, exclaiming women stepped out on the road in front of motors, rather than pass us within a yard, while troops of children followed us about. To evade this nuisance he was left in a back room of the Swan and Castle for half an hour, while I did my shopping.

It was a great joy to shop in Buckingham, especially when you had a shopping list which began with "bit of ribbon for kitchen curtain" and went on through "leather for lure, two big staples and bit of strawberry netting, scales, stronger string, rabbit nets, blue paint for door, screws and nails, seccotine, good penknife, darning wool, cotton, needles," until it reached "Bert's *Treatise of Hawks and Hawking,* For the First Time Reprinted from the Original of 1619, with an Introduction by J. E. Harting, Librarian to the Linnaean Society of London." For you were more likely to come across a copy of Bert, of which there are only about 102 in existence, in the ironmonger's or the saddler's at Buckingham than you were to find it at Bumpus or the Bodleian. There was a kind of glory about the backward parts of the better shops in Buckingham, in which you might find anything. If I had wanted a battle axe, or a quiver with some arrows, or a pair of skis, I should have found at least two of them at Herring's: while I was sure that Mr. Evenson could have found for me, somewhere about the premises (if only he could put his hand upon it), an eighteenth-century coach or a billiard table.

Sated with these excitements, and with the walk of twelve miles, we got home at eight o'clock. The hawk did not like cars or cyclists or numbers of people, but if he were in a good temper he could be persuaded not to bate from them. It was perhaps in this side of manning that he was most backward of all, and I could not really assert that he was at ease with my own right hand. All the way home I had been boresomely jerking it about at varying intervals to accustom him to its movements.

We got home at eight and he was put at once on the creance. Immediately, or at any rate after less than five minutes of hymnody and hesitation, the great bird was sailing owl-like through the twilight. I cowered as my master stooped upon my shrinking shoulder, and then gave him gleefully five ounces of beef steak—previously weighed out on the scales—deciding that on the morrow the ration should be increased to seven.

THURSDAY

I lay in the long grass at Silston cross roads with Gos on the fist. The cars came past pretty regularly there. It was shady where we lay, with a good breeze keeping the trees alive, two men making hay in the fields opposite. Gos himself stood with full fluffed feathers and semi-contented eye, meditating standing on one leg. When he was in a good humour he would rouse his feathers, and this would leave them ruffled. Before he had done this, while the feathers lay close and sleek, you might be sure that he was not content. But if he had done it, and if he began further to stand on one leg, then you knew that you were in for peace.

It was a lovely day, and Gos was being as good as gold. He stood there, lifting the spare leg with clenched talons in tentative thrusts: a monocular or uhlan-officer * expression his face, as the eye remoter from the sun dilated more than the nearer one.

It was a scene perfectly idyllic—until another of the cars came by. Then down would go the rising claw, the erect posture would be lost, the hawk would flinch upon the fist with mad round-questing eye that meditated a bate, the feathers lying flat to his body.

I lay in the warm afternoon and thought about Gos. If one were to give him a proper name, what should it be? Hamlet would be suitable, or Macbeth (as he was subject to illusions): then there was Strindberg, or Van Gogh, or Astur, like the giant warrior in Macaulay (the hawk's Latin name was Astur Palombarius): there was Baal, as in the poem by Kipling, or Tom (he who had the host of furious fancies), or Medici or Roderick Dhu ("fierce lightning flashed from Roderick's eye"), or Lord George Gordon of the lunatic riots, or Byron, or Odin, or Death, or Edgar Allen Poe, or Caligula, or Tarquin, or, for his happier moments, Gos: a cross between a gosling and a goose. Reflecting upon this problem I decided that the best solution would be to call him all of these. The last Duke of Buckingham had been called Richard Plantagenet Temple Nugent Brydges Chandos Grenville, and I could derive my goshawk's lineage no lower than his.

On the way home Gos had a proper bath in a roadside ditch, ducked his head, toppled over, flapped his wings, splashed, paused to meditate and scratch his chin in the middle of it: all in the lovely sun and ripple.

* uhlan-officer: a lancer in a light-cavalry outfit, especially prominent in the old Prussian armies.

At six o'clock we went out to the well and he was set down on the railing which enclosed it. While at Silston, half a pound of beef steak had been bought, and this had been divided into two equal parts. (The hawk had been given a rabbit's hind leg that morning.) I had been out previously to the well and measured a piece of twine fifty yards long. One end of this was attached to the rail of the well, the other end extended down the ridings to its full extent. It had been doubled then back to the place where it was attached, so that at the well head there were two ends of twine, one tied and the other free, while a double string stretched twenty-five yards to its bend which lay in the grass.

I put Gos on the railing and retreated to a distance of forty yards, giving ten yards law in order to prevent his being checked in flight, and began to call and whistle. The pursed lips repeatedly proclaimed the Lord their Shepherd, urgently, caressingly, madly, nobly, slowly, rapidly, continuously, with pauses. "Dinner!" they blew, commandingly, pleadingly, majestically, rapaciously. "Come along, Gos," they panderingly, whiningly, peremptorily, softly articulated. "Now, now," they remonstrated, feeling rather thankful that this could be done without an audience, "don't be silly, come-along, be-a-good-Gos, Gossy-gossy-gos." And Tiddly-tum, tiddly-tum, Tiddly Tum Tum repeated echo to whistle, whistle to echo.

For nearly ten minutes the extraordinary uproar went on in the still ridings. So far away that even his flaming eye could no longer be distinguished, the loved goshawk stood with his back to me, turning his head this way and that. At last he turned upon the perch, roused his feathers into a greedy puff, began to hop upon the railing. The pleas, the tuneless whistling, the staccato notes rose to an orgasm of lust for beef: in vain. They relapsed into the majestic, the quiet, the filled-with-silence pauses. Suddenly, after ten minutes during which he had cocked his head at the creance and visibly pondered its reliability as he moved about, suddenly, and without relation to the pathos of my music, sweet Gos began to fly.

To fly: the horrible aerial toad, the silent-feathered owl, the hump-backed aviating Richard III, he made toward me close to the ground. His wings beat with a measured purpose, the two eyes of his low-held head fixed me with a ghoulish concentration: but like head-lamps, like the forward-fixed eyes of a rower through the air who knew his quay. The French called him *rameur* * as well as *cuisinier*.* Too frighteningly for words (when I had taken him up to bring him to the well—and given him the shred of beef with which he was always rewarded for a voluntary jump—he had flown to my shoulder and fixed his talons in the unprotected flesh, taking me by the scruff of the neck), too menacingly he flew, not toward the at-right-angles-held-out beef, but directly toward

---
* *rameur:* rower.
* *cuisinier:* the caterer for the mess (White remarks upon this term earlier in his book while speculating on the hawk's potential usefulness as a hunter, should we be devastated by another world war).

my face. At five paces nerve broke. I ducked, still holding the beef at the stretch of my arm, and stayed coweringly for two beats of the heart.

But the sudden movement, or the sudden discovery of the red setter fooling about in the long grass at my side, had put him off. Before I could see where he had gone, while I was still bunching together for the strike, Gos slewed off on a miss-stoop, flew to the nearest tree of the riding, missed his grip of it because the creance caught him short (very luckily), hung inverted for a moment, dropped into the hedge.

I called him for another few seconds, and then, going to disentangle him, took him back to the well-head. For letting me pick him up without protest (he jumped to the fist) he was rewarded with another shred of beef.

We started again. This time, after only five minutes, the attack was launched again. I stood to my guns. Imminently confronted with death, stared in the face by those two Athene-noctua * eyes which were coming at my head rather than at the beef a full arm's length away from it, I braced the breast muscles not to flinch. It was too much. At two yards humanity became again the inherent coward, and cringed away to the right, averting face from the eyes of slaughter, humping shoulder, powerless to remain erect. But Gos bound to the shoulder with a decisive blow, stepped quickly down the arm, was feeding on two ounces of beef.

When he had eaten it (and tried to eat the paper—which had been kept as a visible lure) I took him back to the rail. He left me for the rail reluctantly and avariciously, insisting upon taking the paper with him. After I had returned to the distance of forty yards, which had increased by five, he dropped the paper and, showing more interest in it than in me, jumped down to make a final test of its edibility. I waited till he had jumped back to the rail.

Now, for the third time, the calls were reiterated: and then, with less than a minute's pause, the brooding death was launched at the face. I stood, and scarcely more than an inch or two flinched: for the second two ounces of beef steak Gos came quickly on a creance nearly fifty yards.

George Plimpton / Paper Lion

Plimpton has managed in the past decade to enact what for most people would have remained day dreams. In his late thirties and early forties, having been no more than an amateur athlete at best, he realized the boyish and boyhood ambition of being allowed to pitch in a professional baseball game, go three rounds with a light-heavy-weight champion of the world (Archie

* Athene-noctua: also called the Little Owl.

Moore), and call the signals as quarterback for five plays (against the first-string Detroit defense).

Because Plimpton begins his account of this last experience with an allusion to Jack Benny, the would-be concert violinist, the reader might expect that what follows will be a merely comic account of clownish floundering. The fumblings and confusions are comic enough, but somehow the writing doesn't commit itself only to that aspect of what happened on the football field. Knowing full well that he cannot match the professionals with whom he is playing, Plimpton still wants to carry himself sufficiently well for the brief time he is allowed to play with them. So that while his experiences may be funny, his reporting of them, the way he writes about them, carries a measure of frustration and embarrassment. This piece offers a good opportunity for discriminating between the performance being written about and the performance which is the writing itself.

Jack Benny used to say that when he stood on the stage in white tie and tails for his violin concerts and raised his bow to begin his routine—scraping through "Love in Bloom"—that he *felt* like a great violinist. He reasoned that, if he wasn't a great violinist, what was he doing dressed in tails, and about to play before a large audience?

At Pontiac I *felt* myself a football quarterback, not an interloper. My game plan was organized, and I knew what I was supposed to do. My nerves seemed steady, much steadier than they had been as I waited on the bench. I trotted along easily. I was keenly aware of what was going on around me.

I could hear Bud Erickson's voice over the loudspeaker system, a dim murmur, telling the crowd what was going on. He was telling them that number zero, coming out across the sidelines, was not actually a rookie, but an amateur, a writer, who had been training with the team for three weeks and had learned five plays, which he was now going to run against the first-string Detroit defense. It was like a nightmare come true, he told them, as if one of *them*, rocking a beer around in a paper cup, with a pretty girl leaning past him to ask the hot-dog vendor in the aisle for mustard, were suddenly carried down underneath the stands by a sinister clutch of ushers. He would protest, but he would be encased in the accoutrements, the silver helmet, with the two protruding bars of the cage, jammed down over his ears, and sent out to take over the team—that was the substance of Erickson's words, drifting across the field, swayed and shredded by the steady breeze coming up across the open end of Wisner Stadium from the vanished sunset. The crowd was interested, and I was conscious, just vaguely, of a steady roar of encouragement.

The team was waiting for me, grouped in the huddle watching me come. I went in among them. Their heads came down for the signal. I called out,

"Twenty-six!" forcefully, to inspire them, and a voice from one of the helmets said, "Down, down, the whole stadium can hear you."

"Twenty-six," I hissed at them. "Twenty-six near oh pinch; on three. *Break!*" Their hands cracked as one, and I wheeled and started for the line behind them.

My confidence was extreme. I ambled slowly behind Whitlow, poised down over the ball, and I had sufficient presence to pause, resting a hand at the base of his spine, as if on a window-sill—a nonchalant gesture I had admired in certain quarterbacks—and I looked out over the length of his back to fix in my mind what I saw.

Everything fine about being a quarterback—the embodiment of his power—was encompassed in those dozen seconds or so: giving the instructions to ten attentive men, breaking out of the huddle, walking for the line, and then pausing behind the center, dawdling amidst men poised and waiting under the trigger of his voice, cataleptic, until the deliverance of himself and them to the future. The pleasure of sport was so often the chance to indulge the cessation of time itself —the pitcher dawdling on the mound, the skier poised at the top of a mountain trail, the basketball player with the rough skin of the ball against his palm preparing for a foul shot, the tennis player at set point over his opponent—all of them savoring a moment before committing themselves to action.

I had the sense of a portcullis down. On the other side of the imaginary bars the linemen were poised, the lights glistening off their helmets, and close in behind them were the linebackers, with Joe Schmidt just opposite me, the big number 56 shining on his white jersey, jumpjacking back and forth with quick choppy steps, his hands poised in front of him, and he was calling out defensive code words in a stream. I could sense the rage in his voice, and the tension in those rows of bodies waiting, as if coils had been wound overtight, which my voice, calling a signal, like a lever would trip to spring them all loose. "Blue! Blue! Blue!" I heard Schmidt shout.

Within my helmet, the schoolmaster's voice murmured at me: "Son, nothing to it, nothing at all. . . ."

I bent over the center. Quickly, I went over what was supposed to happen—I would receive the snap and take two steps straight back, and hand the ball to the number two back coming laterally across from right to left, who would then cut into the number six hole. That was what was designated by 26—the two back into the six hole. The mysterious code words "near oh pinch" referred to blocking assignments in the line, and I was never sure exactly what was meant by them. The important thing was to hang on to the ball, turn, and get the ball into the grasp of the back coming across laterally.

I cleared my throat. "Set!" I called out—my voice loud and astonishing to hear, as if it belonged to someone shouting into the earholes of my helmet. "Sixteen, sixty-five, forty-four, *hut* one, *hut* two, *hut* three," and at three the ball slapped back into my palm, and Whitlow's rump bucked up hard as he went for the defensemen opposite.

The lines cracked together with a yawp and smack of pads and gear. I had the sense of quick, heavy movement, and as I turned for the backfield, not a second having passed, I was hit hard from the side, and as I gasped the ball was jarred loose. It sailed away, and bounced once, and I stumbled after it, hauling it under me five yards back, hearing the rush of feet, and the heavy jarring and wheezing of the blockers fending off the defense, a great roar up from the crowd, and above it, a relief to hear, the shrilling of the referee's whistle. My first thought was that at the snap of the ball the right side of the line had collapsed just at the second of the handoff, and one of the tacklers, Brown or Floyd Peters, had cracked through to make me fumble. Someone, I assumed, had messed up on the assignments designated by the mysterious code words "near oh pinch." In fact, as I discovered later, my *own man* bowled me over—John Gordy, whose assignment as offensive guard was to pull from his position and join the interference on the far side of the center. He was required to pull back and travel at a great clip parallel to the line of scrimmage to get out in front of the runner, his route theoretically passing between me and the center. But the extra second it took me to control the ball, and the creaking execution of my turn, put me in his path, a rare sight for Gordy to see, his own quarterback blocking the way, like coming around a corner in a high-speed car to find a moose ambling across the center line, and he caromed off me, jarring the ball loose.

It was not new for me to be hit down by my own people. At Cranbrook I was knocked down all the time by players on the offense—the play patterns run with such speed along routes so carefully defined that if everything wasn't done right and at the proper speed, the play would break down in its making. I was often reminded of film clips in which the process of a porcelain pitcher, say, being dropped by a butler and smashed, is shown in reverse, so that the pieces pick up off the floor and soar up to the butler's hand, each piece on a predestined route, sudden perfection out of chaos. Often, it did not take more than an inch or so off line to throw a play out of kilter. On one occasion at the training camp, practicing handoff plays to the fullback, I had my chin hanging out just a bit too far, something wrong with my posture, and Pietrosante's shoulder pad caught it like a punch as he went by, and I spun slowly to the ground, grabbing at my jaw. Brettschneider had said that afternoon: "The defense is going to rack you up one of these days, if your own team'd let you *stand* long enough for us defense guys to get *at* you. It's aggravating to bust through and find that you've already been laid flat by your own offense guys."

My confidence had not gone. I stood up. The referee took the ball from me. He had to tug to get it away, a faint look of surprise on his face. My inner voice was assuring me that the fault in the tumble had not been mine. "They let you down," it was saying. "The blocking failed." But the main reason for my confidence was the next play on my list—the 93 pass, a play which I had worked successfully in the Cranbrook scrimmages. I walked into the huddle and I said with considerable enthusiasm, "All right! All *right!* Here we go!"

"Keep the voice down," said a voice. "You'll be tipping them the play."

I leaned in on them and said: "Green right" ("Green" designated a pass play, "right" put the flanker to the right side), "three right" (which put the three back to the right), "ninety-three" (indicating the two primary receivers: nine, the right end, and three, the three back) "on *three* . . . *Break!*"—the clap of the hands again in unison, the team streamed past me up to the line, and I walked briskly up behind Whitlow.

Again, I knew exactly how the play was going to develop—back those seven yards into the defensive pocket for the three to four seconds it was supposed to hold, and Pietrosante, the three back, would go down in his pattern, ten yards straight, then cut over the middle, and I would hit him.

"Set! . . . sixteen! . . . eighty-eight . . . fifty-five . . . *hut* one . . . *hut* two . . . *hut* three. . . ."

The ball slapped into my palm at "three." I turned and started back. I could feel my balance going, and two yards behind the line of scrimmage I *fell down* —absolutely flat, as if my feet had been pinned under a trip wire stretched across the field, not a hand laid on me. I heard a great roar go up from the crowd. Suffused as I had been with confidence, I could scarcely believe what had happened. Mud cleats catching in the grass? Slipped in the dew? I felt my jaw go ajar in my helmet. "Wha'? Wha'?"—the mortification beginning to come fast. I rose hurriedly to my knees at the referee's whistle, and I could see my teammates' big silver helmets with the blue Lion decals turn toward me, some of the players rising from blocks they'd thrown to protect me, their faces masked, automaton, prognathous with the helmet bars protruding toward me, characterless, yet the dismay was in the set of their bodies as they loped back for the huddle. The schoolmaster's voice flailed at me inside my helmet. "Ox!" it cried. "Clumsy oaf."

I joined the huddle. "Sorry, sorry," I said.

"Call the play, man," came a voice from one of the helmets.

"I don't know what happened," I said.

"Call it, man."

The third play on my list was the 42, another running play, one of the simplest in football, in which the quarterback receives the snap, makes a full spin, and shoves the ball into the four back's stomach—the fullback's. He has come straight forward from his position as if off starting blocks, his knees high, and he disappears with the ball into the number two hole just to the left of the center —a straight power play, and one which seen from the stands seems to offer no difficulty.

I got into an awful jam with it. Once again, the jackrabbit-speed of the professional backfield was too much for me. The fullback—Danny Lewis—was past me and into the line before I could complete my spin and set the ball in his belly. And so I did what was required: I tucked the ball into my own belly and followed Lewis into the line, hoping that he might have budged open a small hole.

I tried, grimacing, my eyes squinted almost shut, and waiting for the impact, which came before I'd taken two steps—I was grabbed up by Roger Brown.

He tackled me high, and straightened me with his power, so that I churned against his three-hundred-pound girth like a comic bicyclist. He began to shake me. I remained upright to my surprise, flailed back and forth, and I realized that he was struggling for the ball. His arms were around it, trying to tug it free. The bars of our helmets were nearly locked, and I could look through and see him inside—the first helmeted face I recognized that evening—the small, brown eyes surprisingly peaceful, but he was grunting hard, the sweat shining, and I had time to think, "It's Brown, it's *Brown!*" before I lost the ball to him, and flung to one knee on the ground I watched him lumber ten yards into the end zone behind us for a touchdown.

The referee wouldn't allow it. He said he'd blown the ball dead while we were struggling for it. Brown was furious. "You taking that away from *me,*" he said, his voice high and squeaky. "Man, I took that ball in there good."

The referee turned and put the ball on the ten yard line. I had lost twenty yards in three attempts, and I had yet, in fact, to run off a complete play.

The veterans walked back very slowly to the next huddle.

I stood off to one side, listening to Brown rail at the referee. "I never scored like that befo'. You takin' that away from me?" His voice was peeved. He looked off toward the stands, into the heavy tumult of sound, spreading the big palms of his hands in grief.

I watched him, detached, not even moved by his insistence that I suffer the humiliation of having the ball stolen for a touchdown. If the referee had allowed him his score, I would not have protested. The shock of having the three plays go as badly as they had left me dispirited and numb, the purpose of the exercise forgotten. Even the schoolmaster's voice seemed to have gone—a bleak despair having set in so that as I stood shifting uneasily, watching Brown jawing at the referee, I was perfectly willing to trot in to the bench at that point and be done with it.

Then, by chance, I happened to see Brettschneider standing at his corner linebacker position, watching me, and beyond the bars of his cage I could see a grin working. That set my energies ticking over once again—the notion that some small measure of recompense would be mine if I could complete a pass in the Badger's territory and embarrass him. I had such a play in my series—a slant pass to the strong-side end, Jim Gibbons.

I walked back to the huddle. It was slow in forming. I said, "The Badger's asleep. He's fat and he's asleep."

No one said anything. Everyone stared down. In the silence I became suddenly aware of the feet. There are twenty-two of them in the huddle, after all, most of them very large, in a small area, and while the quarterback ruminates and the others await his instruction, there's nothing else to catch the attention. The sight pricked at my mind, the oval of twenty-two football shoes, and it may have been responsible for my error in announcing the play. I forgot to give the signal on which the ball was to be snapped back by the center. I said: "Green right nine slant *break!*" One or two of the players clapped their hands, and as the huddle broke, some of them automatically heading for the line of scrimmage, someone hissed: "Well, the *signal,* what's the signal, for Chrissake."

I had forgotten to say "on two."

I should have kept my head and formed the huddle again. Instead, I called out "Two!" in a loud stage whisper, directing my call first to one side, then the other, *"two! two!"* as we walked up to the line. For those that might have been beyond earshot, who might have missed the signal, I held out two fingers spread like a V, which I showed around furtively, trying to hide it from the defense, and hoping that my people would see.

The pass was incomplete. I took two steps back (the play was a quick pass, thrown without a protective pocket) and I saw Gibbons break from his position, then stop, buttonhooking, his hand, which I used as a target, came up, but I threw the ball over him. A yell came up from the crowd seeing the ball in the air (it was the first play of the evening which hadn't been "blown"—to use the player's expression for a missed play), but then a groan went up when the ball was overshot and bounced across the sidelines.

"Last play," George Wilson was calling. He had walked over with a clipboard in his hand and was standing by the referee. "The ball's on the ten. Let's see you take it all the way," he called out cheerfully.

One of the players asked: "Which end zone is he talking about?"

The last play of the series was a pitchout—called a flip on some teams—a long lateral to the number four back running parallel to the line and cutting for the eight hole at left end. The lateral, though long, was easy for me to do. What I had to remember was to keep on running out after the flight of the ball. The hole behind me as I lateraled was left unguarded by an offensive lineman pulling out from his position and the defensive tackle could bull through and take me from behind in his rush, not knowing I'd got rid of the ball, if I didn't clear out of the area.

I was able to get the lateral off and avoid the tackler behind me, but unfortunately the defense was keyed for the play. They knew my repertoire, which was only five plays or so, and they doubted I'd call the same play twice. One of my linemen told me later that the defensive man opposite him in the line, Floyd Peters, had said, "Well, here comes the forty-eight pitchout," and it *had* come, and they were able to throw the number four back, Pietrosante, who had received the lateral, back on the one yard line—just a yard away from the mortification of having moved a team backward from the thirty yard line into one's own end zone for a safety.

As soon as I saw Pietrosante go down, I left for the bench on the sidelines at midfield, a long run from where I'd brought my team, and I felt utterly weary, shuffling along through the grass.

Applause began to sound from the stands, and I looked up, startled, and saw people standing, and the hands going. It made no sense at the time. It was not derisive; it seemed solid and respectful. "Wha'? Wha'?" I thought, and I wondered if the applause wasn't meant for someone else—if the mayor had come into the stadium behind me and was waving from an open-topped car. But as I came up to the bench I could see the people in the stands looking at me, and the hands going.

I thought about the applause afterward. Some of it was, perhaps, in appreciation of the lunacy of my participation, and for the fortitude it took to do it; but most of it, even if subconscious, I decided was in *relief* that I had done as badly as I had: it verified the assumption that the average fan would have about an amateur blundering into the brutal world of professional football. He would get slaughtered. If by some chance I had uncorked a touchdown pass, there would have been wild acknowledgment—because I heard the groans go up at each successive disaster—but afterward the spectators would have felt uncomfortable. Their concept of things would have been upset. The outsider did not belong, and there was comfort in that being proved.

Some of the applause, as it turned out, came from people who had enjoyed the comic aspects of my stint. More than a few thought that they were being entertained by a professional comic in the tradition of baseball's Al Schacht, or the Charlie Chaplins, the clowns, of the bullfights. Bud Erickson told me that a friend of his had come up to him later: "Bud, that's one of funniest goddamn . . . I mean that guy's *got* it," this man said, barely able to control himself.

I did not take my helmet off when I reached the bench. It was tiring to do and there was security in having it on. I was conscious of the big zero on my back facing the crowd when I sat down. Some players came by and tapped me on the top of the helmet. Brettschneider leaned down and said, "Well, you stuck it . . . that's the big thing."

The scrimmage began. I watched it for a while, but my mind returned to my own performance. The pawky inner voice was at hand again. "You didn't stick it," it said testily. "You funked it."

At half time Wilson took the players down to the band shell at one end of the stadium. I stayed on the bench. He had his clipboards with him, and I could see him pointing and explaining, a big semicircle of players around him, sitting on the band chairs. Fireworks soared up into the sky from the other end of the field, the shells puffing out clusters of light that lit the upturned faces on the crowd in silver, then red, and then the reports would go off, reverberating sharply, and in the stands across the field I could see the children's hands flap up over their ears. Through the noise I heard someone yelling my name. I turned and saw a girl leaning over the rail of the grandstand behind me. I recognized her from the Gay Haven in Dearborn. She was wearing a mohair Italian sweater, the color of spun pink sugar, and tight pants, and she was holding a thick folding wallet in one hand along with a pair of dark glasses, and in the other a Lion banner, which she waved, her face alive with excitement, very pretty in a perishable, childlike way, and she was calling, "Beautiful; it was beautiful."

The fireworks lit her, and she looked up, her face chalk white in the swift aluminum glare.

I looked at her out of my helmet. Then I lifted a hand, just tentatively.

Edwin Denby / Dancers, Buildings, and People in the Street

This lecture by Edwin Denby, one of America's most distinguished dance critics and, at one time, a dancer himself, has the extemporized, even random charm of a lecture to a class of young professional dancers. Denby asks them to consider the problem of "seeing" performances in art and in life as non-professionals do. How does one "look at daily life or at art, especially dancing, for the mere pleasure of seeing . . . without meaning to do anything about it"? This is an especially challenging question for anyone trained, as is a professional artist, to look at performances from the special point of view of craft or technique and to look at life, very often, from that same perspective. Denby wants to induce a vividly open and exploratory way of seeing certain aspects of daily life that are related to dance movement: walking or lolling or the way objects occupy space. Looking intensely at these things reveals their exciting strangeness and thereby makes related aspects of art, where planning and intention are involved, seem even more interestingly peculiar than they ordinarily seem.

Denby's relation to his audience is full of affectionate and teasing and yet diffident inquiry. Do you get my jokes? isn't it silly to be listening to a lecture anyway? wouldn't we all be better off merely wandering the streets and looking at things?—such interrogations condition the style throughout. "I have to go on with this nonsense," he says at one point, "and I have to go on logically, which we both realize is nonsense." The meandering movement of the piece is its message, a confirmation of Denby's own commitment to what he recommends and a device of persuasion that seems genuinely without guile. Fuzziness may sometimes be the price for such an indulgence in freedom of mind and spirit, as at the outset of the third paragraph from the end, but most readers will consider this a small price for the liberating effect of the whole piece.

Elaine Mayes

On the subject of dance criticism, I should like to make clear a distinction that I believe is very valuable, to keep the question from getting confused. And that is that there are two quite different aspects to it. One part of dance criticism is seeing what is happening on stage. The other is describing clearly what it is you saw. Seeing something happen is always fun for everybody, until they get exhausted. It is very exhausting to keep looking, of course, just as it is to keep doing anything else; and from an instinct of self-preservation many people look only a little. One can get along in life perfectly well without looking much. You all know how very little one is likely to see happening on the street—a familiar street at a familiar time of day while one is using the street to get somewhere. So much is happening inside one, one's private excitements and responsibilities, one can't find the energy to watch the strangers passing by, or the architecture or the weather around; one feels there is a use in getting to the place one is headed for and doing something or other there, getting a book or succeeding in a job or discussing a situation with a friend, all that has a use, but what use is there in looking at the momentary look of the street, of 106th and Broadway. No use at all. Looking at a dance performance has some use, presumably. And certainly it is a great deal less exhausting than looking at the disjointed fragments of impression that one can see in traffic. Not only that the performance is arranged so that it is convenient to look at, easy to pay continuous attention to, and attractive, but also that the excitement in it seems to have points of contact with the excitement of one's own personal life, with the curiosity that makes one want to go get a special book, or the exciting self-importance that makes one want to succeed, or even the absorbing drama of talking and listening to someone of one's own age with whom one is on the verge of being in love. When you feel that the emotion that is coming toward you from the performance is like a part of your own at some moment when you were very excited, it is easy to be interested. And of course if you feel the audience thrilled all around you just when you are thrilled too, that is very peculiar and agreeable. Instead of those people and houses on the street that are only vaguely related to you in the sense that they are Americans and contemporary, here in the theatre, you are almost like in some imaginary family, where everybody is talking about something that concerns you intimately and everybody is interested and to a certain extent understands your own viewpoint and the irrational convictions you have that are even more urgent than your viewpoint. The amplitude that you feel you see with at your most intelligent moments, this amplitude seems in the theatre to be naturally understood on stage and in the audience, in a way it isn't often appreciated while you are with the people you know outside the theatre. At a show you can tell perfectly well when it is happening to you, this experience of an enlarged view of what is really so and true, or when it isn't happening to you. When you talk to your friends about it after the curtain goes down, they sometimes agree, and sometimes they don't. And it is strange how whether they do or don't, it is very hard usually to specify what the excitement was about, or the precise point at which it gave you the feeling of being really beautiful. Brilliant, magnificent, stupendous, no doubt all these things are true of the performance, but even if you and your friends agree that it was all those things, it is likely that there was some particular moment that made a special impression which you are not talking about. Maybe you are afraid that that particular moment wasn't really the most important, that it didn't express the idea or that it didn't get special applause or wasn't the climax. You were really excited by the performance and now you are afraid you can't show you understand it. Meanwhile while you hesitate to talk about it, a friend in the crowd who talks more readily is delivering a brilliant criticism specifying technical dance details, moral implications, musicological or iconographic finesses; or else maybe he is sailing off into a wild nonsensical camp that has nothing to do with the piece but which is fun to listen to, even though it's a familiar trick of his. So the evening slips out of your awareness like many others. Did you really see anything? Did you see any more than you saw in the morning on the street? Was it a real excitement you felt? What is left over of the wonderful moment you had, or didn't you really have any wonderful moment at all, where you actually saw on stage a real person moving and you felt the relation to your real private life with a sudden poignancy as if for that second you were drunk. Dance criticism has two different aspects: one is being made drunk for a second by seeing something happen; the other is expressing lucidly what you saw when you were drunk. I suppose I should add quite stuffily that it is the performance you should get drunk on, not anything else. But I am sure you have understood me anyway.

Now the second part of criticism, that of expressing lucidly what happened, is of course what makes criticism criticism. If you are going in for criticism you must have the gift in the first place, and in the second place you must cultivate it, you must practice and try. Writing criticism is a subject of interest to those who do it, but it is a separate process from that of seeing what happens. And seeing what happens is of course of much more general interest. This is what you presumably have a gift for, since you have chosen dancing as a subject of special study, and no doubt you have already cultivated this gift. I am sure you would all of you have something interesting and personal to say about what one can see and perhaps too about what one can't see.

Seeing is at any rate the subject I would like to talk about today, I can well imagine that for some of you this is not a subject of prime interest. Some of you are much more occupied with creating or inventing dances, than with seeing them; when you look at them you look at them from the point of view of an artist who is concerned with his own, with her own, creating. Creating, of course, is very exciting, and it is very exciting whether you are good at it or not; you must have noticed that already in watching other people create, whose work looks silly to you, but whose excitement, even if you think it ought not to be, is just as serious to them as that of a creator whose creating isn't silly. But creating dancing and seeing dancing are not the same excitement. And it is not about creating that I mean to speak; I am telling you this, so you won't sit here unless you can spare the time for considering in a disinterested way what seeing is like; please don't feel embarrassed about leaving now, though I agree it would be rude of you to leave later. And it is not very likely either that I shall tell you any facts that you had better write down. I rather think you know all the same facts I do about dancing, and certainly you know some I don't; I have forgotten some I used to know. About facts, too, what interests me just now is how differently they can look, one sees them one way and one sees them another way another time, and yet one is still seeing the same fact. Facts have a way of dancing about, now performing a solo then reappearing in the chorus, linking themselves now with facts of one kind, now with facts of another, and quite changing their style as they do. Of course you have to know the facts so you can recognize them, or you can't appreciate how they move, how they keep dancing. We are supposed to discuss dance history sometime in this seminar and I hope we will. But not today.

At the beginning of what I said today I talked about one sort of seeing, namely a kind that leads to recognizing on stage and inside yourself an echo of some personal, original excitement you already know. I call it an echo because I am supposing that the event which originally caused the excitement in one's self is not literally the same as the event you see happen on stage. I myself, for instance, have never been a Prince or fallen in love with a creature that was half girl and half swan, nor have I myself been an enchanted Swan Princess, but I have been really moved, and transported by some performances of *Swan Lake*,* and by both sides of that story. In fact, it is much more exciting if I can feel both sides happening to me, and not just one. But I am sure you have already jumped ahead of me to the next step of the argument, and you can see that not only have I never been such people or been in their situation, but besides that I don't look like either of them, nor could I, even if I were inspired, dance the steps the way they do. Nor even the steps of the other dancers, the soloists or the chorus.

You don't seem to have taken these remarks of mine as a joke. But I hope you realized that I was pointing out that the kind of identification one feels at a dance performance with the performers is not a literal kind. On the other hand, it is very probable that you yourselves watch a dance performance with a certain professional awareness of what is going on.

A professional sees quite clearly "I could do that better, I couldn't do that nearly so well." A professional sees the finesse or the awkwardness of a performer very distinctly, at least in a field of dance execution he or she is accustomed to working in; and a choreographer sees similarly how a piece is put together, or as the phrase is, how the material has been handled. But this is evidently a very special way of looking at a performance. One may go further

---

* *Swan Lake:* the ballet by Tchaikovsky.

and say that a theatre performance is not intended to be seen from this special viewpoint. Craftsmanship is a matter of professional ethics; a surgeon is not bound to explain to you what he is doing while he is operating on you, and similarly no art form, no theatre form is meant to succeed in creating its magic with the professionals scattered in the audience. Other doctors, seeing a cure, may say, your doctor was a quack but he was lucky; and similarly professionals may say after a performance, Yes, the ballerina was stupendous, she didn't fake a thing —or else say, she may not have thrilled you, but there aren't four girls in the world who can do a something or other the way she did—and this is all to the good, it is honorable and it is real seeing. But I am interested just now to bring to your attention or recall to your experience not that professional way of seeing, but a more general way. I am interested at the moment in recalling to you how it looks when one sees dancing as non-professionals do, in the way you yourselves I suppose look at pictures, at buildings, at political history or at landscapes or at strangers you pass on the street. Or as you read poetry.

In other words the way you look at daily life or at art for the mere pleasure of seeing, without trying to put yourself actively in it, without meaning to do anything about it. I am talking about seeing what happens when people are dancing, seeing how they look. Watching them and appreciating the beauty they show. Appreciating the ugliness they show if that's what you see. Seeing this is beautiful, this ugly, this is nothing as far as I can see. As long as you pay attention there is always something going on, either attractive or unattractive, but nobody can always pay attention, so sometimes there is nothing as far as you can see, because you have really had enough of seeing; and quite often there is very little, but anyway you are looking at people dancing, and you are seeing them while they dance.

Speaking personally, I think there is quite a difference between seeing people dance as part of daily life, and seeing them dance in a theatre performance. Seeing them dance as part of daily life is seeing people dance in a living room or a ballroom or a nightclub, or seeing them dance folk dances either naturally or artificially in a folk dance group. For that matter classroom dancing and even rehearsal dancing seems to me a part of daily life, though it is as special as seeing a surgeon operate, or hearing the boss blow up in his office. Dancing in daily life is also seeing the pretty movements and gestures people make. In the Caribbean, for instance, the walk of Negroes is often, well, miraculous. Both the feminine stroll and the masculine one, each entirely different. In Italy you see another beautiful way of strolling, that of shorter muscles, more complex in their plasticity, with girls deliciously turning their breast very slightly, deliciously pointing their feet. You should see how harmoniously the young men can loll. American young men loll quite differently, resting on a peripheral point, Italians loll resting on a more central one. Italians on the street, boys and girls, both have an extraordinary sense of the space they really occupy, and of filling that space harmoniously as they rest or move; Americans occupy a much larger space than their actual bodies do; I mean, to follow the harmony of their movement or of their lolling you have to include a much larger area in space than they are actually occupying. This annoys many Europeans; it annoys their instinct of modesty. But it has a beauty of its own, that a few of them appreciate. It has so to speak an intellectual appeal; it has because it refers to an imaginary space, an imaginary volume, not to a real and visible one. Europeans sense the intellectual volume but they fail to see how it is filled by intellectual concepts—so they suppose that the American they see lolling and assuming to himself too much space, more space than he actually needs, is a kind of a conqueror, is a kind of non-intellectual or merely material occupying power. In Italy I have watched American sailors, soldiers and tourists, all with the same expansive instinct in their movements and their repose, looking like people from another planet among Italians with their self-contained and traditionally centered movements. To me these Americans looked quite uncomfortable, and embarrassed, quite willing to look smaller if they only knew how. Here in New York where everybody expects them to look the way they do, Americans look unselfconscious and modest despite their traditional expansivity of movement. There is room enough. Not because there is actually more—there isn't in New York—but because people expect it, they like it if people move that way. Europeans who arrive here look peculiarly circumspect and tight to us. Foreign sailors in Times Square look completely swamped in the big imaginary masses surging around and over them.

Well, this is what I mean by dancing in daily life. For myself I think the walk of New Yorkers is amazingly beautiful, so large and clear. But when I go inland, or out West, it is much sweeter. On the other hand, it has very little either of Caribbean lusciousness or of Italian *contrapposto*.* It hasn't much savor, to roll on your tongue, that it hasn't. Or at least you have to be quite subtle, or very much in love to distinguish so delicate a perfume.

That, of course, is supposed to be another joke, but naturally you would rather travel yourself than hear about it. I can't expect you to see my point without having been to countries where the way of walking is quite different from what ours is here. However, if you were observant, and you ought to be as dance majors, you would have long ago enjoyed the many kinds of walking you can see right in this city, boys and girls, Negro and white, Puerto Rican and Western American and Eastern, foreigners, professors and dancers, mechanics and businessmen, ladies entering a theatre with half a drink too much, and shoppers at Macy's. You can see everything in the world here in isolated examples at least, peculiar characters or people who are for the moment you see them peculiar. And everybody is quite peculiar now and then. Not to mention how peculiar anybody can be at home.

Daily life is wonderfully full of things to see. Not only people's movements, but the objects around them, the shape of the rooms they live in, the ornaments

---

* *contrapposto:* in art criticism, the opposition of contrasted masses.

architects make around windows and doors, the peculiar ways buildings end in the air, the watertanks, the fantastic differences in their street façades on the first floor. A French composer who was here said to me, "I had expected the streets of New York to be monotonous, after looking at a map of all those rectangles; but now I see the differences in height between buildings, I find I have never seen streets so diverse one from another." But if you start looking at New York architecture, you will notice not only the sometimes extraordinary delicacy of the window framings, but also the standpipes, the grandiose plaques of granite and marble on ground floors of office buildings, the windowless side walls, the careful, though senseless, marble ornaments. And then the masses, the way the office and factory buildings pile up together in perspective. And under them the drive of traffic, those brilliantly colored trucks with their fanciful lettering, the violent paint on cars, signs, houses, as well as lips. Sunsets turn the red-painted houses in the cross-streets to the flush of live rose petals. And the summer sky of New York for that matter is as magnificent as the sky of Venice. Do you see all this? Do you see what a forty- or sixty-story building looks like from straight below? And do you see how it comes up from the sidewalk as if it intended to go up no more than five stories? Do you see the bluish haze on the city as if you were in a forest? As for myself, I wouldn't have seen such things if I hadn't seen them first in the photographs of Rudolph Burckhardt. But after seeing them in his photographs, I went out to look if it were true. And it was. There is no excuse for you as dance majors not to discover them for yourselves. Go and see them. There is no point in living here, if you don't see the city you are living in. And after you have seen Manhattan, you can discover other grandeurs out in Queens, in Brooklyn, and in those stinking marshes of Jersey.

All that is here. And it is worth seeing. When you get to Rome, or to Fez in Morocco, or to Paris, or to Constantinople, or to Peking, I hope you will get there, I have always wanted to, you will see other things beautiful in another way, but meanwhile since you are dance majors and are interested and gifted in seeing, look around here. If you cut my talks and bring me instead a report of what you saw in the city, I will certainly mark you present, and if you can report something interesting I will give you a good mark. It is absurd to sit here in four walls while all that extraordinary interest is going on around us. But then education is a lazy, a dull way of learning, and you seem to have chosen it; forget it.

However, if you will insist on listening to me instead of going out and looking for yourselves, I will have to go on with this nonsense. Since you are here I have to go on talking and you listening, instead of you and me walking around and seeing things. And I have to go on logically, which we both realize is nonsense. Logically having talked about what you can see in daily life, I have to go on that very different way of seeing, which you use in seeing art.

For myself, I make a distinction between seeing daily life and seeing art. Not that seeing is different. Seeing is the same. But seeing art is seeing an ordered and imaginary world, subjective, and concentrated. Seeing in the theatre is seeing what you don't see quite that way in life. In fact, it's nothing like that way. You sit all evening in one place and look at an illuminated stage, and music is going on, and people are performing who have been trained in some peculiar way for years, and since we are talking about a dance performance, nobody is expected to say a word, either on stage or in the house. It is all very peculiar. But there are quite a lot of people, ordinary enough citizens watching the stage along with you. All these people in the audience are used to having information conveyed to them by words spoken or written, but here they are just looking at young people dancing to music. And they expect to have something interesting conveyed to them. It is certainly peculiar.

But then, art is peculiar. I won't speak of concert music, which is obviously peculiar, and which thousands every evening listen to, and evidently get satisfaction out of. But even painting is a strange thing. That people will look at some dirt on a canvas, just a little rectangle on a wall, and get all sorts of exalted feelings and ideas from it is not at all natural, it is not at all obvious. Why do they prefer one picture so much to another one? They will tell you and get very eloquent, but it does seem unreasonable. It seems unreasonable if you don't see it. And for all the other arts it's the same. The difference between the "Ode on a Grecian Urn" * and a letter on the editorial page of the *Daily News* isn't so great if you look at both of them without reading them. Art is certainly even more mysterious and nonsensical than daily life. But what a pleasure it can be. A pleasure much more extraordinary than a hydrogen bomb is extraordinary.

There is nothing everyday about art. There is nothing everyday about dancing as an art. And that is the extraordinary pleasure of seeing it. I think that is enough for today.

Susanne Langer / A Note on the Film

This brief excursion into the theory of film appeared in Mrs. Langer's *Feeling and Form,* an important study in aesthetics which appeared in 1953. It should be remembered that the note was written before the occurrence of those changes which have made the movie medium—even in films of wide circulation—the very different thing it is today. Nevertheless, it was possible for the author, as she considered the theoretical implications of the form, to distinguish it sharply from theater, and to touch on its closer relationship with dreams.

Mrs. Langer, following and modifying the work of Ernst Cassirer, argued

* "Ode on a Grecian Urn": poem by John Keats.

that man is distinguished from other animals in that he is the only one that uses symbols; this is true not only of his mathematically based activities, but also of his language and his arts. She suggests that film is not merely the application of new techniques to the familiar symbolic mode of fiction, but rather stands in the same kind of relation to dream as fiction does to memory. It swallows up other media, and there seems hardly any limit to its adaptation of technical resources in the interest of its "poetic" purposes. These are to present its own version of "virtual" history. "Virtual" is a difficult word in Mrs. Langer's thought; perhaps it could be rendered here simply as "fictive." A novel or a play contains not a "real" past, but one that by virtue of its representing in a shared symbolism a significant human past offers an experience more humanly satisfying than memory can. A film does something similar, but the argument is that in creating a "virtual" present, as dream does, film offers an experience not only resembling but also, presumably, transcending dream.

Mrs. Langer develops the comparison with dream—the special treatment of space and time in movies, the role of the audience in the creation of the experience of film. Her note is a highly original and suggestive performance. It is not easy, because of the need for a special terminology in handling a subject so new and relating it to what may be said of the other arts. We include it as a very civilized example of how an enterprising and learned mind copes with the problem of describing both the newness of a situation and its relationship with older situations which, presumably, we understand better.

Cinema is "like" dream in the mode of its presentation; it creates a virtual present, an order of direct apparition.

In her book, *Philosophy in a New Key,* Susanne Langer put forward the proposition that man differs from other creatures primarily because he uses symbolic means of communication. It is natural, therefore, that this Columbia University professor of philosophy would be interested in the film and would find it "not only a new technique, but a new poetic mode." This mode is not the mode of fiction, which is "like" memory, or of drama, which is "like" action. It is the mode of dream, with the dreamer "always at the center of it."

Because of its unique character, this new art "seems to be omnivorous, able to assimilate the most diverse materials." She finds film more closely related to the epic and the novel than to the drama. The stage has a framework of fixed space; dream events are "often intensely concerned with space—intervals, endless roads, bottomless canyons, things too high, too near, too far—but they are not oriented in any total space." Film is free of temporal restrictions, too, because "the dream mode is an endless Now."

Here is a new art. For a few decades it seemed like nothing more than a new technical device in the sphere of drama, a new way of preserving and retailing dramatic performances. But today its development has already belied this assumption. The screen is not a stage, and what is created in the conception and realization of a film is not a play. It is too early to systematize any theory of this new art, but even in its present pristine state it exhibits—quite beyond any doubt, I think—not only a new technique, but a new poetic mode. . . .

The moving camera divorced the screen from the stage. The straightforward photographing of stage action, formerly viewed as the only artistic possibility of the film, henceforth appeared as a special technique. The screen actor is not governed by the stage, nor by the conventions of the theatre, he has his own realm and conventions; indeed, there may be no "actor" at all. The documentary film is a pregnant invention. The cartoon does not even involve persons merely "behaving."

The fact that the moving picture could develop to a fairly high degree as a silent art, in which speech had to be reduced and concentrated into brief, well-spaced captions, was another indication that it was not simply drama. It used pantomime, and the first aestheticians of the film considered it as essentially pantomime. But it is not pantomime; it swallowed that ancient popular art as it swallowed the photograph.

One of the most striking characteristics of this new art is that it seems to be omnivorous, able to assimilate the most diverse materials and turn them into elements of its own. With every new invention—montage, the sound track, Technicolor—its devotees have raised a cry of fear that now its "art" must be lost. Since every such novelty is, of course, promptly exploited before it is even technically perfected, and flaunted in its rawest state, as a popular sensation, in the flood of meaningless compositions that steadily supplies the show business, there is usually a tidal wave of particularly bad rubbish in association with every important advance. But the art goes on. It swallows everything: dancing, skating, drama, panorama, cartooning, music (it almost always requires music).

Therewithal it remains a poetic art. But it is not any poetic art we have known before; it makes the primary illusion—virtual history—in its own mode.

This is essentially, *the dream mode*. I do not mean that it copies dream, or puts one into a daydream. Not at all; no more than literature invokes memory, or makes us believe that *we* are remembering. An art mode is *a mode of appearance*. Fiction is "like" memory in that it is projected to compose a finished experiential form, a "past"—not the reader's past, nor the writer's, though the latter may make a claim to it (that, as well as the use of actual memory as a model, is a literary device). Drama is "like" action in being causal, creating a total imminent experience, a personal "future" or Destiny. Cinema is "like" dream in the mode of its presentation; it creates a virtual present, an order of direct apparition. That is the mode of dream.

The most noteworthy formal characteristic of dream is that the dreamer is always at the center of it. Places shift, persons act and speak, or change or fade—facts emerge, situations grow, objects come into view with strange importance, ordinary things become infinitely valuable or horrible, and they may be superseded by others that are related to them essentially by feeling, not by natural proximity. But the dreamer is always "there," his relation is, so to speak, equidistant from all events. Things may occur around him or unroll before his eyes; he may act or want to act, or suffer or contemplate; but the *immediacy* of everything in a dream is the same for him.

This aesthetic peculiarity, this relation to things perceived, characterizes the *dream mode:* it is this that the moving picture takes over, and thereby it creates a virtual present. In its relation to the images, actions, events that constitute the story, the camera is in the place of the dreamer.

But the camera *is* not a dreamer. We are usually agents in a dream. The camera (and its complement, the microphone) is not itself "in" the picture. It is the mind's eye and nothing more. Neither is the picture (if it is art) likely to be dreamlike in its structure. It is a poetic composition, coherent, organic, governed by a definitely conceived feeling, not dictated by actual emotional pressures.

The basic abstraction whereby virtual history is created in the dream mode is immediacy of experience, "givenness," or "authenticity." This is what the art of the film abstracts from actuality, from our actual dreaming.

The percipient of a moving picture sees with the camera; his standpoint moves with it, his mind is pervasively present. The camera is his eye (as the microphone is his ear—and there is no reason why a mind's eye and a mind's ear must always stay together). *He takes the place of the dreamer,* but in a perfectly objectified dream—that is, he is not in the story. The work is the appearance of a dream, a unified, continuously passing, significant *apparition.*

Conceived in this way, a good moving picture is a work of art by all the standards that apply to art as such. Sergei Eisenstein * speaks of good and bad films as, respectively, "vital" and "lifeless";[1] speaks of photographic shots as "elements,"[2] which combine into "images," which are "objectively unpresentable" (I would call them poetic impressions), but are greater elements compounded of "representations," whether by montage or symbolic acting or any other means.[3] The whole is governed by the "initial general image which originally hovered before the creative artist"[4]—the matrix, the commanding form;

1. *The Film Sense,* p. 17.
2. *Ibid.,* p. 4.
3. *Ibid.,* p. 8.
4. *Ibid.,* p. 31.

* Sergei Eisenstein: (1898–1948), Russian film maker and important theorist of cinema as a new and revolutionary art form; the quotations here are from *The Film Sense,* trans. and ed. Jay Leyda (New York: Harcourt, Brace, 1942).

and it is this (not, be it remarked, the artist's emotion) that is to be evoked in the mind of the spectator.

Yet Eisenstein believed that the beholder of a film was somewhat specially called on to use his imagination, to create his own experience of the story.[5] Here we have, I think, an indication of the powerful illusion the film makes not of things going on, but of the dimension in which they go on—a *virtual* creative imagination; for it *seems* one's own creation, direct visionary experience, a "dreamed reality." Like most artists, he took the virtual experience for the most obvious fact.[6]

The fact that a motion picture is not a plastic work but a poetic presentation accounts for its power to assimilate the most diverse materials and transform them into nonpictorial elements. Like dream, it enthralls and commingles all senses; its basic abstraction—direct apparition—is made not only by visual means, though these are paramount, but by words, which punctuate vision, and music that supports the unity of its shifting "world." It needs many, often convergent, means to create the continuity of emotion which holds it together while its visions roam through space and time.

It is noteworthy that Eisenstein draws his materials for discussion from epic rather than dramatic poetry; from Pushkin rather than Chekhov, Milton rather than Shakespeare. That brings us back to the point that the novel lends itself more readily to screen dramatization than the drama. The fact is, I think, that a story narrated does not require as much "breaking down" to become screen apparition, because it has no framework itself of fixed *space,* as the stage has; and one of the aesthetic peculiarities of dream, which the moving picture takes over, is the nature of its space. Dream events are spatial, often intensely concerned with space—intervals, endless roads, bottomless canyons, things too high, too near, too far—but they are not oriented in any total space. The same is true of the moving picture and distinguishes it—despite its visual character—from plastic art; *its space comes and goes.* It is always a secondary illusion.

The fact that the film is somehow related to dream, and is in fact in a similar mode, has been remarked by several people, sometimes for reasons artistic, sometimes nonartistic. R. E. Jones noted its freedom not only from spatial restriction, but from temporal as well. "Motion pictures," he said, "are our thoughts made visible and audible. They flow in a swift succession of images, precisely as our thoughts do, and their speed, with their flashbacks—like sudden

---

5. *Ibid.,* p. 33: ". . . the spectator is drawn into a creative act in which his individuality is not subordinated to the author's individuality, but is opened up throughout the process of fusion with the author's intention, just as the individuality of a great actor is fused with the individuality of a great playwright in the creation of a classic scenic image. In fact, every spectator . . . creates an image in accordance with the representational guidance, suggested by the author, leading him to understanding and experience of the author's theme. This is the same image that was planned and created by the author, but this image is at the same time created also by the spectator himself."
6. Compare the statement in Ernest Lindgren's *The Art of the Film,* p. 92, apropos of the moving camera: "It is the spectator's own mind that moves."

uprushes of memory—and their abrupt transition from one subject to another, approximates very closely the speed of our thinking. They have the rhythm of the thought-stream and the same uncanny ability to move forward or backward in space or time. . . . They project pure thought, pure dream, pure inner life." [7]

The "dreamed reality" on the screen can move forward and backward because it is really an eternal and ubiquitous virtual present. The action of drama goes inexorably forward because it creates a future, a Destiny; the dream mode is an endless Now.

Donald Barthelme / And Now Let's Hear It for the Ed Sullivan Show!

Donald Barthelme, best known as a fiction writer, uses in his work almost all the styles of contemporary expression that the media produce. He is here writing about the show run by Ed Sullivan, which has for some years dominated a key hour of early Sunday evening television. It isn't wholly accurate, however, to say that he is writing about it. Rather he is rendering it as it passes before him on the screen. He tries to catch fleeting images, misses some, makes mistakes, corrects them, and, as he goes along, notes his responses. His writing is meant to register his anxiety over matching the fast pace of the show as it moves, and he is barely able to find time to record his own impressions. In a way the piece is about the obliteration of critical response by the profusion of images which pass into his mind. Even when his attention wanders during a song he doesn't much like, its wandering is triggered by the words of another television program he is sorry to have missed. He and his language are an extension of the television set, and we witness how, as a medium, it almost entirely determines the pace and the vocabulary of that other medium which is writing.

The Ed Sullivan Show. Sunday night. Church of the unchurched. Ed stands there. He looks great. Not unlike an older, heavier Paul Newman. Sways a little from side to side. Gary Lewis and the Playboys have just got off. Very strong act. Ed clasps hands together. He's introducing somebody in the audience. Who is it? Ed points with his left arm. "Broken every house record at the Copa," Ed says of the man he's introducing. Who is it? Its . . . Don Rickles! Rickles stands up. Eyes glint. Applause. "I'm gonna make a big man outa you!" Ed says. Rickles hunches a shoulder combatively. Eyes glint. Applause. Jerry Vale intro-

---

7. R. E. Jones: in *The Dramatic Imagination: Reflections and Speculations on the Art of the Theatre* (New York: Duell, Sloan, and Pearce, 1941), pp. 17–18.

Wide World Photos

duced. Wives introduced. Applause. "When Mrs. Sullivan and I were in Monte Carlo" (pause, neatly suppressed belch), "we saw them" (pause, he's talking about the next act), "for the first time and signed them instantly! The Kuban Cossacks! Named after the River Kuban!"

Three dancers appear in white fur hats, fur boots, what appear to be velvet jump suits. They're great. Terrific Cossack stuff in front of onion-dome flats. Kuban not the U.S.S.R.'s most imposing river (512 miles, shorter than the Ob, shorter than the Bug) but the dancers are remarkable. Sword dance of some sort with the band playing galops. Front dancer balancing on one hand and doing things with his feet. Great, terrific. Dancers support selves with one hand, don and doff hats with other hand. хорошо! (Non-Cyrillic approximation of Russian for "neat.") Double-хорошо! Ed enters from left. Makes enthusiastic gesture with hand. Triple-хорошо! Applause dies. Camera on Ed who has hands knit before him. "Highlighting this past week in New York. . . ." Something at the Garden. Can't make it out, a fight probably. Ed introduces somebody in audience. Can't see who, he's standing up behind a fat lady who's also standing up for purposes of her own. Applause.

Pigmeat Markham comes on with cap and gown and gavel. His tag line, "Here come de jedge," is pronounced and the crowd roars but not so great a roar as you might expect. The line's wearing out. Still, Pigmeat looks good, working with two or three stooges. Stooge asks Pigmeat why, if he's honest, he's acquired two Cadillacs, etc. Pigmeat says: "Because I'm very *frugal,"* and whacks stooge on head with bladder. Lots of bladder work in sketch, old-timey comedy. Stooge says: "Jedge, you got to know me." Pigmeat: "Who are you?" Stooge: "I'm the man that introduced you to your wife." Pigmeat shouts, *"Life!"* and whacks the stooge on the head with the bladder. Very funny stuff, audience roars. Then a fast commercial with Jo Anne Worley from Rowan and Martin singing about Bold. Funny girl. Good commercial.

Ed brings on Doodletown Pipers, singing group. Great-looking girls in tiny skirts. Great-looking legs on girls. They sing something about "I hear the laughter" and "the sound of the future." Phrasing is excellent, attack excellent. Camera goes to atmospheric shots of a park, kids playing, mothers and fathers lounging about, a Sunday feeling. Shot of boys throwing the ball around. Shot of black baby in swing. Shot of young mother's ass, very nice. Shot of blonde mother cuddling kid. Shot of black father swinging kid. Shot of a guy who looks like Rod McKuen lounging against a . . . . a what?? A play sculpture. But it's not Rod McKuen. The Doodletown Pipers segue into another song. Something about hate and fear, "You've got to be taught . . . hate and fear." They sound great. Shot of integrated group sitting on play equipment. Shot of young bespectacled father. Shot of young black man with young white child. He looks into camera. Thoughtful gaze. Young mother with daughter, absorbed. Nice-looking mother. Camera in tight on mother and daughter. One more mother, a medium shot. Out on shot of the tiny black child asleep in swing. Wow!

And Now Let's Hear It for the Ed Sullivan Show! 583

Sullivan enters from left applauding. Makes gesture toward Pipers, toward audience, toward Pipers. Applause. Everybody's having a good time! "I want you to welcome . . . George Carlin!" Carlin is a comic. Carlin says he hates to look at the news. News is depressing. Sample headlines: "Welcome Wagon Runs Over Newcomer." Audience roars. "Pediatrician Dies of Childhood Disease." Audience roars but a weaker roar. Carlin is wearing a white turtleneck, dark sideburns. Joke about youth asking father if he can use the car. Youth says he's got a heavy date. Pa says, then why don't you take the pickup? Joke about the difference between organized crime and unorganized crime. Unorganized crime is when a guy holds you up on the street. Organized crime is when two guys hold you up on the street. Carlin is great, terrific, but his material is not so funny. A Central Park joke. Cops going into the park dressed as women to provoke molesters. Three hundred molesters arrested and two cops got engaged. More cop jokes. Carlin holds hands clasped together at waist. Says people wonder why the cops don't catch the Mafia. Says have you ever tried to catch a guy in a silk suit? Weak roar from audience. Carlin says do you suffer from nagging crime? Try the Police Department with new improved GL-70. No roar at all. A whicker, rather. Ed facing camera. "Coming up next . . . right after this important word." Commercial for Royal Electric Jetstar Typewriter. "She's typing faster and neater now." Capable-looking woman says to camera, "I have a Jetstar now that helps me at home where I have a business raising St. Bernard's." Behind her a St. Bernard looks admiringly at Jetstar.

Ed's back. "England's famous Beatles" (pause, neatly capped belch) "first appeared on our shew . . . Mary Hopkin . . . Paul McCartney told her she must appear on our shew . . . the world-famous . . . Mary Hopkin!" Mary enters holding guitar. Sings something about "the morning of my life . . . ceiling of my room. . . ." Camera in tight on Mary. Pretty blonde, slightly plump face. Heavy applause for Mary. Camera goes to black, then Mary walking away in very short skirt, fine legs, a little heavy maybe. Mary in some sort of nightclub set for her big song, "Those Were the Days." Song is ersatz Kurt Weill but nevertheless a very nice song, very nostalgic, days gone by, tears rush into eyes (mine). In the background, period stills. Shot of some sort of Edwardian group activity, possible lawn party, possible egg roll. Shot of biplane. Shot of racecourse. Camera on Mary's face. "Those were the days, my friends. . . ." Shot of fox hunting, shot of tea dance. Mary is bouncing a little with the song, just barely bouncing. Shot of what appears to be a French 75 firing. Shot of lady kissing dog on nose. Shot of horse. Camera in tight on Mary's mouth. Looks like huge wad of chewing gum in her mouth but that can't be right, must be her tongue. Still of balloon ascension in background. Live girl sitting in left foreground gazing up at Mary, rapt. Mary in chaste high-collar dress with that short skirt. Effective. Mary finishes song. A real roar. Ed appears in three-quarter view turned toward the right, toward Mary. "Terrific!" Ed says. "Terrific!" Mary adjusts her breasts. "Terrific. And now, sitting out in the audience is the famous

... Perle Mesta!" Perle stands, a contented-looking middle-aged lady. Perle bows. Applause.

Ed stares (enthralled) into camera. "Before we introduce singing Ed Ames and the first lady of the American theatre, Helen Hayes. . . ." A Pizza Spins commercial fades into a Tareyton Charcoal Filter commercial. Then Ed comes back to plug Helen Hayes's new book, *On Reflection*. Miss Hayes is the first lady of the American theatre, he says. "We're very honored to. . . ." Miss Hayes sitting at a desk, Louis-something. She looks marvelous. Begins reading from the book. Great voice. Tons of dignity. "My dear Grandchildren. At this writing, it is no longer fashionable to have Faith; but your grandmother has never been famous for her chic, so she isn't bothered by the intellectual hemlines. I have always been concerned with the whole, not the fragments; the positive, not the negative; the words, not the spaces between them. . . ." Miss Hayes pauses. Hand on what appears to be a small silver teapot. "What can a grandmother offer. . . ." *She speaks very well!* "With the feast of millennia set before you, the saga of all mankind on your bookself . . . what could I give you? And then I knew. Of course. My own small footnote. The homemade bread at the banquet. The private joke in the divine comedy. Your roots." Head and shoulders shot of Miss Hayes. She looks up into the lighting grid. Music up softly on, "So my grandchildren . . . in highlights and shadows . . . bits and pieces . . . in recalled moments, mad scenes and acts of folly. . . ." Miss Hayes removes glasses, looks misty. "What are little grandchildren made of . . . some good and some bad from Mother and Dad . . . and laughs and wails from Grandmother's tales . . . I love you." She gazes down at book. Holds it. Camera pulls back. Music up. Applause.

Ed puts arm around Miss Hayes. Squeezes Miss Hayes. Applause. *Heavy* applause. Ed pats hands together joining applause. Waves hands toward Miss Hayes. More applause. It's a triumph! Ed seizes Miss Hayes's hands in his hands. Applause dies, reluctantly. Ed says ". . . but first, listen to this." Shot of building, cathedral of some kind. Organ music. Camera pans down facade past stained-glass windows, etc. Down a winding staircase. Music changes to rock. Shot of organ keyboard. Close shot of maker's nameplate, HAMMOND. Shot of grinning organist. Shot of hands on keyboard. "The sound of Hammond starts at $599.95." Ed introduces singer Ed Ames. Ames is wearing a long-skirted coat, holding hand mike. Good eyes, good eyebrows, muttonchop side-burns. Lace at his cuffs. Real riverboat-looking. He strolls about the set singing a Tom Jones-Harvey Schmidt number, something about the morning, sometimes in the morning, something. Then another song, "it takes my breath away," "how long have I waited," something something. Chorus comes in under him. Good song. Ames blinks in a sincere way. Introduces a song from the upcoming show *Dear World*. "A lovely new song," he says. "Kiss her now, while she's young. Kiss her now, while she's yours." Set behind him looks like one-by-two's nailed vertically four inches on centers. The song is sub-lovely but Ames's delivery is very comfortable, easy. Chorus comes in. Ah, ah ah ah ah. Ames closes his eyes, sings something something something something; the song is sub-memorable. (Something memorable: early on Sunday morning a pornographic exhibition appeared mysteriously for eight minutes on television-station KPLM, Palm Springs, California. A naked man and woman did vile and imaginative things to each other for that length of time, then disappeared into the history of electricity. Unfortunately, the exhibition wasn't on a network. What we really want in this world, we can't have.)

Ed enters from left (what's over there? a bar? a Barcalounger? a book? stock ticker? model railroad?), shakes hands with Ames. Ames is much taller, but amiable. Both back out of shot, in different directions. Camera straight ahead on Ed. "Before I tell you about next week's . . . show . . . please listen to this." Commercial for Silva Thins. Then a shot of old man with ship model, commercial for Total, the vitamin cereal. Then Ed. "Next week . . . a segment from . . . the new Beatles film . . . The Beatles were brought over here by us . . . in the beginning. . . . Good night!" Chopping gesture with hands to the left, to the right.

Music comes up. The crawl containing the credits is rolled over shot of Russian dancers dancing (хорошо́!). Produced by Bob Precht. Directed by Tim Kiley. Music by Ray Bloch. Associate Producer Jack McGeehan. Settings Designed by Bill Bohnert. Production Manager Tony Jordan. Associate Director Bob Schwarz. Assistant to the Producer Ken Campbell. Program Coordinator Russ Petranto. Technical Director Charles Grenier. Audio Art Shine. Lighting Director Bill Greenfield. Production Supervisor Herb Benton. Stage Managers Ed Brinkman, Don Mayo. Set Director Ed Pasternak. Costumes Leslie Renfield. Graphic Arts Sam Cecere. Talent Coordinator Vince Calandra. Music Coordinator Bob Arthur. The Ed Sullivan Show is over. It has stopped.

Richard Poirier / Robert Frost Interviewed

Robert Frost was one of the great conversationalists of this century, as well as one of its greatest poets. His material is almost never sensational or fashionable or scandalous, and he seldom uses, in any philosophical excursions, a vocabulary that identifies his thinking as important to any school or tradition. Instead, he holds his listeners by bringing to his talk some of the extraordinary suppleness of tone and timing that can be found in his poetry. His intention almost always is, as he says, to "score." Perhaps the best clue to his unique personal and poetic power is to be found in his discussion here of "performance." Therein we can see why if it is a mistake to think of him as a poet of New England folk wisdom, it is also a mistake, in counter-

Yousef Karsh from Rapho Guillumette

ing that impression, to think of him as a poet of "terror" or "darkness." He cared as much as any poet of this century about the way, in the face of obstacles, he composed himself, both in poetry and in the give and take of conversation.

A regional poet who has achieved international stature, Robert Frost was born in San Francisco on March 26, 1874. His father, an editor, politician, and Democrat, had gone there to escape the Republican atmosphere of New England. Sympathizing with the Southern cause, he christened his son Robert Lee Frost. When the senior Frost died, young Robert returned with his mother to New England to live with his paternal grandfather in Lawrence, Massachusetts. Here he soon began, but with little encouragement, his life-long commitment to poetry. He attended Dartmouth but could not abide the academic routine. At twenty-two he entered Harvard, specializing in Latin and Greek during his two years there. He then went to live on a farm in Derry, New Hampshire, teaching, doing occasional work for a local newspaper, and continuing to write his poems. It was a trip to England, however, in 1912, which gave his literary career its decisive push forward. There his first two books were published—*A Boy's Will* and *North of Boston*. When he returned to America in 1915, he was already well known, and his future as a poet and teacher was secure.

Mr. Frost received the Pulitzer Prize for poetry four times—in 1924, for *New Hampshire;* in 1931, for *Collected Poems;* in 1937, for *A Further Range;* and in 1943, for *A Witness Tree*. His latest collection, *In the Clearing*, was published in 1962.

More than any other quality in Frost, his individualism stood out. He spurned what he called "the necessary group." As in other areas of life, he believed "there are too many gangs, cliques, or coteries in poetry. Maybe that's one of the ways they have to manage it. But I'm a lone wolf."

Robert Frost died on January 29, 1963.

Mr. Frost came into the front room of his house in Cambridge, Massachusetts, casually dressed, wearing high plaid slippers, offering greetings with a quiet, even diffident friendliness. But there was no mistaking the evidence of the enormous power of his personality. It makes you at once aware of the thick, compacted strength of his body, even now at eighty-six; it is apparent in his face, actually too alive and spontaneously expressive to be as ruggedly heroic as in his photographs.

The impression of massiveness, far exceeding his physical size, isn't separable from the public image he creates and preserves. That this image is invariably associated with popular conceptions of New England is no simple matter of his own geographical preferences. New England is of course evoked in the scenes and titles of many of his poems and, more importantly, in his Emersonian tendencies, including his habit of contradicting himself, his capacity to "unsay" through the sound of his voice what his words seem to assert. His special resemblance to New England, however, is that he, like it, had managed to impose upon the world a wholly self-created image. It is not the critics who have defined him, it is Frost himself. He stood talking for a few minutes in the middle of the room, his remarkably ample, tousled white hair catching the late afternoon sun reflected off the snow in the road outside, and one wondered for a moment how he had managed over so long a life never to let his self-portrait be altered despite countless exposures to light less familiar and unintimidating. In the public world he has resisted countless chances to lose himself in some particular fashion, some movement, like the Georgians, or even in an area of his own work which, to certain critics or readers, happens for the moment to appear more exotically colorful than the whole. In one of the most revealing parts of this interview, he says of certain of his poems that he doesn't "want them out," the phrase itself, since all the poems involved have been published, offering an astonishing, even peculiar, evidence of the degree to which he feels in control of his poetic character. It indicates, too, his awareness that attempts to define him as a tragic philosophical poet of man and nature can be more constricting, because more painfully meaningful to him, than the simpler definitions they are designed to correct.

More specifically, he seemed at various points to find the most immediate threat to his freedom in the tape recorder. Naturally, for a man both voluble and often mischievous in his recollections, Frost did not like the idea of being stuck, as he necessarily would be, with attitudes expressed in two hours of conversation. As an aggravation of this, he knew that no transcript taken from the tape could catch the subtleties of voice which give life and point to many of his statements. At a pause in the interview, Mr. Robert O'Clair, a friend and colleague at Harvard who had agreed to sit in as a sort of witness, admitted that we knew very little about running a tape recorder. Frost, who'd moved from his chair to see its workings, readily agreed. "Yes, I noticed that," he laughed, "and I respect you for it," adding at once—and this is the point of the story—that "they," presumably the people "outside," "like to hear me say nasty things about machines." A thoroughly supple knowledge of the ways in which the world tries to take him and a confidence that his own ways are more just and liberating was apparent here and everywhere in the conversation.

Frost was seated most of the time in a blue overstuffed chair which he had bought to write in. It had no arms, he began, and this left him the room he needed.

ROBERT FROST: I never write except with a writing board. I've never had a table in my life. And I use all sorts of things. Write on the sole of my shoe.

RICHARD POIRIER: Why have you never liked a desk? Is it because you've moved around so much and lived in so many places?

R.F.: Even when I was younger I never had a desk. I've never had a writing room.

R.P.: Is Cambridge your home base now pretty much?

R.F.: In the winter. But I'm nearly five months in Ripton, Vermont. I make a long summer up there. But this is my office and business place.

R.P.: Your place in Vermont is near the Bread Loaf School of Writing, isn't it?

R.F.: Three miles away. Not so near I know it's there. I'm a way off from it, down the mountain and up a side road. They connect me with it a good deal more than I'm there. I give a lecture at the school and a lecture at the conference. That's about all.

R.P.: You were a co-founder of the school, weren't you?

R.F.: They say that. I think I had more to do with the starting of the conference. In a very casual way, I said to the president [of Middlebury], "Why don't you use the place for a little sociability after the school is over?" I thought of no regular business—no pay, no nothing, just inviting literary people, a few, for a week or two. The kitchen staff was still there. But then they started a regular business of it.

R.P.: When you were in England from 1912 to 1915, did you ever think you might possibly stay there?

R.F.: No. No, I went over there to be poor for a while, nothing else. I didn't think of printing a book over there. I'd never offered a book to anyone here. I was thirty-eight years old, wasn't I? Something like that. And I thought the way to a book was the magazines. I hadn't too much luck with them, and nobody ever noticed me except to send me a check now and then. So I didn't think I was ready for a book. But I had written three books when I went over, the amount of three books—*A Boy's Will, North of Boston,* and part of the next [*Mountain Interval*] in a loose-leaf heap.

R.P.: What were the circumstances of your meeting Pound * when you were in England?

R.F.:That was through Frank Flint. The early Imagist and translator. He was a friend of Pound and belonged in that little group there. He met me in a bookstore, said, "American?" And I said, "Yes. How'd you know?" He said, "Shoes." It was the Poetry Book Shop, Harold Monro's, just being organized.

---

* Ezra Pound: (1885–), American poet; for a time, leader of the Imagist movement. His energetic advice and criticism had an important effect on the work of other modern poets, notably on that of W. B. Yeats and T. S. Eliot. His belief in the radical evils of "usura" or credit capitalism led him to support Mussolini's social programs, and during World War II he broadcast Fascist propaganda over the Rome radio; returned to the U.S. to face trial for treason but then adjudged to be of unsound mind, he was committed, in 1946, to St. Elizabeth's Hospital in Washington; after his release in 1958 (obtained through the help of Frost and others), he went back to Italy, where he now lives.

He said, "Poetry?" And I said, "I accept the omen." Then he said, "You should know your fellow countryman, Ezra Pound." And I said, "I've never heard of him." And I hadn't. I'd been skipping literary magazines—I don't ever read them very much—and the gossip, you know, I never paid much attention to. So he said, "I'm going to tell him you're here." And I had a card from Pound afterwards. I didn't use it for two or three months after that.

R.P.: He saw your book—*A Boy's Will*—just before publication, didn't he? How did that come about?

R.F.: The book was already in the publisher's hands, but it hadn't come out when I met Pound, three or four months after he sent me his card. I didn't like the card very well.

R.P.: What did he say on it?

R.F.: Just said, "At home, sometimes." Just like Pound. So I didn't feel that that was a very warm invitation. Then one day walking past Church Walk in Kensington, I took his card out and went in to look for him. I found him there, a little put out that I hadn't come sooner, in his Poundian way. And then he said, "Flint tells me you have a book." And I said, "Well, I ought to have." He said, "You haven't seen it?" And I said, "No." He said, "What do you say we go and get a copy?" He was eager about being the first one to talk. That's one of the best things you can say about Pound: he wanted to be the first to jump. Didn't call people up on the telephone to see how they were going to jump. He was all silent with eagerness. We walked over to my publisher; he got the book. Didn't show it to me—put it in his pocket. We went back to his room. He said, "You don't mind our liking this?" in his British accent, slightly. And I said, "Oh, go ahead and like it." Pretty soon he laughed at something, and I said I knew where that was in the book, what Pound would laugh at. And then pretty soon he said, "You better run along home, I'm going to review it." And I never touched it. I went home without my book and he kept it. I'd barely seen it in his hands.

R.P.: He wrote perhaps the first important favorable review, didn't he?

R.F.: Yes. It was printed in the States, in Chicago, but it didn't help me much in England. The reviewing of the book there began right away, as soon as it was out. I guess most of those who reviewed it in England didn't know it had already been reviewed in Chicago. It didn't sound as though they did. But his review had something to do with the beginning of my reputation. I've always felt a little romantic about all that—that queer adventure he gave me. You know he had a mixed, a really curious position over there. He was friends with Yeats, Hueffer,* and a very few others.

R.P.: Did you know Hueffer?

R.F.: Yes, with him. And Yeats, with him.

R.P.: How much did you see of Yeats when you were in England?

* Hueffer: see note p. 398.

R.F.: Oh, quite a little, with him nearly always—I guess always.

R.P.: Did you feel when you left London to go live on a farm in Gloucestershire that you were making a choice against the kind of literary society you'd found in the city?

R.F.: No, my choices had been not connected with my going to England even. My choice was almost unconscious in those days. I didn't know whether I had any position in the world at all, and I wasn't choosing positions. You see, my instinct was not to belong to any gang, and my instinct was against being confused with the—what do you call them?—they called themselves Georgians, Edwardians, something like that, the people Edward Marsh * was interested in. I understand that he speaks of me in his book, but I never saw him.

R.P.: Was there much of a gang feeling among the literary people you knew in London?

R.F.: Yes. Oh, yes. Funny over there. I suppose it's the same over here. I don't know. I don't "belong" here. But they'd say, "Oh, he's that fellow that writes about homely things for that crowd, for those people. Have you anybody like that in America?" As if it were set, you know. Like Masefield *—they didn't know Masefield in this gang, but, "Oh, he's that fellow that does this thing, I believe, for that crowd."

R.P.: Your best friend in those years was Edward Thomas? *

R.F.: Yes—quite separate again from everybody his age. He was as isolated as I was. Nobody knew he wrote poetry. He didn't write poetry until he started to war, and that had something to do with my life with him. We got to be great friends. No, I had an instinct against belonging to any of those crowds. I've had friends, but very scattering, a scattering over there. You know, I could have . . . Pound had an afternoon meeting once a week with Flint and Aldington * and H. D.* and at one time Hulme.* I think. Hulme started with them. They met every week to rewrite each other's poems.

R.P.: You saw Hulme occasionally? Was it at these rewriting sessions, or didn't you bother with them?

---

* Edward Marsh: (1872–1953), editor of the anthology of contemporary verse, *Georgian Poets* (5 vols., 1912–22); his book of reminiscences, *A Number of People,* appeared in 1939.
* John Masefield: (1878–1967), poet, novelist, playwright; considered a "popular" writer on "homely" subjects; he was appointed England's poet laureate in 1930.
* Edward Thomas: (1878–1917), English writer of biographies until he was over thirty, when he began writing poetry at Frost's suggestion; he was killed in Flanders in World War I.
* Richard Aldington: (1892–1962), English poet and novelist; in 1913, editor of the Imagist periodical *The Egoist*.
* H. D.: Hilda Doolittle (1886–1961), American Imagist poet; married Aldington in 1913.
* T. E. Hulme: (1883–1917), English critic; an anti-romantic, he championed modern abstract formalism; his advocacy of "clear outlines," of "dry hardness" strongly influenced the Imagist movement; "the great aim," he said, "is accurate, precise and definite description."

R.F.: Yes, I knew Hulme, knew him quite well. But I never went to one of those meetings. I said to Pound, "What do you do?" He said, "Rewrite each other's poems." And I said, "Why?" He said, "To squeeze the water out of them." "That sounds like a parlor game to me," I said, "and I'm a serious artist"—kidding, you know. And he laughed and he didn't invite me any more.

R.P.: These personal associations that you had in England with Pound and Edward Thomas and what you call the Georgians—these had nothing to do with your establishing a sense of your own style, did they? You'd already written what were to be nearly the first three volumes of your poetry.

R.F.: Two and a half books, you might say. There are some poems out in Huntington Library that I must have written in the nineties. The first one of mine that's still in print was in '90. It's in print still, kicking round.

R.P.: Not in *A Boy's Will*—the earliest poem published in there was written in '94, I think.

R.F.: No, it's not in there. First one I ever *sold* is in there. The first one I ever had printed was the first one I wrote. I never wrote prose or verse till 1890. Before that I wrote Latin and Greek sentences.

R.P.: Some of the early critics like Garnett and Pound talk a lot about Latin and Greek poetry with reference to yours. You'd read a lot in the classics?

R.F.: Probably more Latin and Greek than Pound ever did.

R.P.: Didn't you teach Latin at one time?

R.F.: Yes. When I came back to college after running away, I thought I could stand it if I stuck to Greek and Latin and philosophy. That's all I did those years.

R.P.: Did you read much in the Romantic poets? Wordsworth, in particular?

R.F.: No, you couldn't pin me there. Oh, I read all sorts of things. I said to some Catholic priests the other day when they asked me about reading, I said, "If you understand the word 'catholic,' I was very catholic in my taste."

R.P.: What sort of things did your mother read to you?

R.F.: That I wouldn't be able to tell you. All sorts of things, not too much, but some. She was a very hard-worked person—she supported us. Born in Scotland, but grew up in Columbus, Ohio. She was a teacher in Columbus for seven years—in mathematics. She taught with my father one year after he left Harvard and before he went to California. You know they began to teach in high schools in those days right after coming out of high school themselves. I had teachers like that who didn't go to college. I had two noted teachers in Latin and Greek who weren't college women at all. They taught Fred Robinson.[1] I had the same teachers he had. Fritz Robinson, the old scholar. My mother was just like that. Began teaching at eighteen in the high school, then married along about twenty-five. I'm putting all this together rather lately, finding out

---

1. Editor of Chaucer, and formerly a professor of English at Harvard.

strolling around like I do. Just dug up in Pennsylvania the date of her marriage and all that, in Lewistown, Pennsylvania.

R.P.: Your mother ran a private school in Lawrence, Massachusetts, didn't she?

R.F.: Yes, she did, round Lawrence. She had a private school. And I taught in that some, as well as taking some other schools. I'd go out and teach in district schools whenever I felt like springtime.

R.P.: How old were you then?

R.F.: Oh, just after I'd run away from Dartmouth, along there in '93, '4, twenty years old. Every time I'd get sick of the city I'd go out for the springtime and take school for one term. I did that I think two or three times, that same school. Little school with twelve children, about a dozen children, all barefooted. I did newspaper work in Lawrence, too. I followed my father and mother in that, you know. I didn't know what I wanted to do with myself to earn a living. Taught a little, worked on a paper a little, worked on farms a little, that was my own departure. But I just followed my parents in newspaper work. I edited a paper a while—a weekly paper—and then I was on a regular paper. I see its name still up there in Lawrence.

R.P.: When you started to write poetry, was there any poet that you admired very much?

R.F.: I was the enemy of that theory, that idea of Stevenson's * that you should play the sedulous ape to anybody. That did more harm to American education than anything ever got out.

R.P.: Did you ever feel any affinity between your work and any other poet's?

R.F.: I'll leave that for somebody else to tell me. I wouldn't know.

R.P.: But when you read Robinson * or Stevens,* for example, do you find anything that is familiar to you from your own poetry?

R.F.: Wallace Stevens? He was years after me.

R.P.: I mean in your reading of him, whether or not you felt any—

R.F.: Any affinity, you mean? Oh, you couldn't say that. No. Once he said to me, "You write on subjects." And I said, "You write on bric-a-brac." And when he sent me his next book he'd written "S'more bric-a-brac" in it. Just took it good-naturedly. No, I had no affinity with him. We were friends. Oh, gee, miles away. I don't know who you'd connect me with.

R.P.: Well, you once said in my hearing that Robert Lowell * had tried to connect you with Faulkner, told you you were a lot like Faulkner.

* Robert Louis Stevenson: (1850–94), who, speaking of the formation of his own style, remarked, "I have thus played the sedulous ape to Hazlitt, to Lamb, to Wordsworth, to Sir Thomas Browne, to DeFoe, to Hawthorne, to Montaigne, to Baudelaire, and to Obermann." *(Memories and Portraits,* Chapter 4)
* E. A. Robinson: (1869–1935), American poet in the traditional line, mostly read now for his dryly ironic character studies, e.g. "Miniver Cheevy" and "Richard Cory."
* Wallace Stevens: (1879–1955), American poet; his first book, *Harmonium,* did not appear until 1923, ten years after Frost's first book, *A Boy's Will,* was published.
* Robert Lowell: see pp. 137–65, Section II.

R.F.: Did I say that?

R.P.: No, you said that Robert Lowell told you that you were a lot like Faulkner.

R.F.: Well, you know what Robert Lowell said once? He said, "My uncle's dialect—the New England dialect, *The Biglow Papers*—was just the same as Burns's wasn't it?" I said, "Robert! Burns's was not a dialect, Scotch is not a dialect. It's a language." But he'd say anything, Robert, for the hell of it.

R.P.: You've never, I take it then, been aware of any particular line of preference in your reading?

R.F.: Oh, I read 'em all. One of my points of departure is an anthology. I find a poet I admire, and I think, well, there must be a lot to that. Some old one—Shirley,* for instance, "The glories of our blood and state"—that sort of splendid poem. I go looking for more. Nothing. Just a couple like that and that's all. I remember certain boys took an interest in certain poems with me in old times. I remember Brower one day in somebody else's class when he was a student at Amherst—Reuben Brower, afterwards the Master of Adams House at Harvard. I remember I said, "Anyone want to read that poem to me?" It was "In going to my naked bed as one that would have slept," Edwards's * old poem. He read it so well I said, "I give you A for life." And that's the way we joke with each other. I never had him regularly in a class of mine. I visited other classes up at Amherst and noticed him very early. Goodness sake, the way his voice fell into those lines, the natural way he did that very difficult poem with that old quotation—"The falling out of faithful friends is the renewing of love." I'm very catholic, that's about all you can say. I've hunted. I'm not thorough like the people educated in Germany in the old days. I've none of that. I hate the idea that you ought to read the whole of anybody. But I've done a lot of looking sometimes, read quite a lot.

R.P.: When you were in England did you find yourself reading the kind of poetry Pound was reading?

R.F.: No. Pound was reading the troubadours.

R.P.: Did you talk to one another about any particular poets?

R.F.: He admired at that time, when I first met him, Robinson and de la Mare. He got over admiring de la Mare anyway, and I think he threw out Robinson too. We'd just bring up a couple of little poems. I was around with him quite a little for a few weeks. I was charmed with his ways. He cultivated a certain rudeness to people that he didn't like, just like Willy Whistler.* I thought he'd

---

* James Shirley: (1596–1666), English poet and playwright; his dramatic entertainment *The Contention of Ajax and Ulysses* ends with the dirge "The glories of our blood and state / Are shadows, not substantial things . . . ," a poem reported to have struck fear into Oliver Cromwell.
* Richard Edwards: (1523?–1566), English poet and playwright; both lines quoted are from "Amantium Irae Amoris Redintegratio."
* James McNeill Whistler: (1834–1903), American painter who settled in England; his acid wit may be sampled in *The Gentle Art of Making Enemies* (1890), a collection of his letters and comments on criticisms of his work.

come under the influence of Whistler. They cultivated the French style of boxing. They used to kick you in the teeth.

R.P.: With grace.

R.F.: Yes. You know the song, the nasty song: "They fight with their feet—" * Among other things, what Pound did was show me Bohemia.

R.P.: Was there much Bohemia to see at that time?

R.F.: More than I had ever seen. I'd never had any. He'd take me to restaurants and things. Showed me jiu jitsu in a restaurant. Threw me over his head.

R.P.: Did he do that?

R.F.: Wasn't ready for him at all. I was just as strong as he was. He said, "I'll show you, I'll show you. Stand up. Stand up." So I stood up, gave him my hand. He grabbed my wrist, tipped over backwards and threw me over his head.

R.P.: How did you like that?

R.F.: Oh, it was all right. Everybody in the restaurant stood up. He used to talk about himself as a tennis player. I never played tennis with him. And then he'd show you all these places with these people that specialized in poets that dropped their aitches and things like that. Not like the "beatniks," quite. I remember one occasion they had a poet in who had a poem in the *English Review* on Aphrodite, how he met Aphrodite at Leatherhead.[2] He was coming in and he was a navvy.* I don't remember his name, never heard of him again—may have gone on and had books. But he was a real navvy. Came in with his bicycle clips on. Tea party. Everybody horrified in a delighted way, you know. Horror, social horror. Red-necked, thick, heavy-built fellow, strong fellow, you know, like John L. Lewis or somebody. But he was a poet. And then I saw poets made out of whole cloth by Ezra. Ezra thought he did that. Take a fellow that had never written anything and think he could make a poet out of him. We won't go into that.

R.P.: I wonder about your reaction to such articles as the recent lead article by Karl Shapiro in the *New York Times Book Review* which praised you because presumably you're not guilty of "Modernism" as Pound and Eliot * are. [*Telephone rings.*]

---

2. Frost is thinking of a poet named John Helston, author of "Aphrodite at Leatherhead," which took up fourteen pages of the *English Review* for March 1913. Frost's recollection gives a special flavor, if one is needed, to the note appended to the poem by the editors of the magazine: "Without presuming to 'present' Mr. Helston after the manner of fashionable actors, we think it will interest the public to know that he was for years a working mechanic—turner, fitter, etc.—in electrical, locomotive, motor-car, and other workshops."

* "They fight with their feet, they fuck with their faces": English animadversion on French soldiers.
* navvy: a laborer working on heavy jobs such as excavation.
* T. S. Eliot: (1888–1965). With the publication (1922–23) of his poem *The Waste Land,* dedicated to Pound, he became the major voice of literary modernism.

R.R.: Is that my telephone? Just wait a second. Halt! [*Interruption. Frost leaves for phone call.*]

R.F.: Where were we? Oh yes, you were trying to trace me.

R.P.: I wasn't trying to trace you. I was—

R.F.: Oh, this thing about Karl Shapiro. Yeah, isn't it funny? So often they ask me—I just been all around, you know, been out West, been all around—and so often they ask me, "What is a modern poet?" I dodge it often, but I said the other night, "A modern poet must be one that speaks to modern people no matter when he lived in the world. That would be one way of describing it. And it would make him more modern, perhaps, if he were *alive* and speaking to modern people."

R.P.: Yes, but in their way of speaking, Eliot and Pound seem to many people to be writing in a tradition that is very different from yours.

R.F.: Yes. I suppose Eliot's isn't as far away as Pound's. Pound seems to me very like a troubadour, more like the troubadours or a blend of several of them, Bertrand de Born and Arnault Daniel. I never touched that. I don't know Old French. I don't like foreign languages that I haven't had. I don't read translations of things. I like to say dreadful, unpleasant things about Dante. Pound, though, he's supposed to know Old French.

R.P.: Pound was a good linguist, wasn't he?

R.F.: I don't know that. There's a teacher of his down in Florida that taught him at the University of Pennsylvania. He once said to me. "Pound? I had him in Latin, and Pound never knew the difference between a declension and a conjugation." He's death on him. Old man, still death on Ezra. [*Breaks into laughter.*] Pound's gentle art of making enemies.

R.P.: Do you ever hear from Pound? Do you correspond with him now?

R.F.: No. He wrote me a couple of letters when I got him out of jail last year. Very funny little letters, but they were all right.

R.P.: Whom did you speak to in Washington about that?

R.F.: Just the Attorney General. Just settled it with him. I went down twice with Archie [MacLeish] and we didn't get anything done because they were of opposite parties, I think. And I don't belong to any party.

R.P.: Yes, but weren't you named Robert Lee because your father was a stanch Democrat around the time of the Civil War? That makes you a Democrat of sorts, doesn't it?

R.F.: Yeah, I'm a Democrat. I was born a Democrat—and been unhappy ever since 1896. Somebody said to me, "What's the difference between that and being a Republican?" Well, I went down after we'd failed, and after Archie thought we'd failed, I just went down alone, walked into the Attorney General's office and said, "I come down here to see what your mood is about Ezra Pound." And two of them spoke up at once. "Our mood's your mood; let's get him out." Just like that, that's all. And I said, "This week?" They said, "This week if you say so. You go get a lawyer, and we'll raise no objection." So, since they were

Republicans, I went over and made friends with Thurman Arnold, that good leftish person, for my lawyer. I sat up that night and wrote an appeal to the court that I threw away, and, in the morning, just before I left town, I wrote another one, a shorter one. And that's all there was to it. Ezra thanked me in a very short note that read. "Thanks for what you're doing. A little conversation would be in order." Then signed, in large letters. And then he wrote me another one, a nicer one.

R.P.: Did you see him before he left for Italy?

R.F.: No, no, I didn't want to high-hat him. I wanted him to feel kind of free from me. But he feels, evidently, a little gratitude of some kind. He's not very well, you know. Some of them didn't want . . . [*What Frost was about to say here, it turned out later in the interview, not recorded, was that some friends of Pound—he mentioned Merrill Moore—felt Pound would be better off staying in St. Elizabeth's Hospital. Moore said Pound had a room to himself and a cabana!*] Well, it's a sad business. And he's a poet. I never, I never questioned that. We've been friends all the way along, but I didn't like what he did in wartime. I only heard it second-hand, so I didn't judge it too closely. But it sounded pretty bad. He was very foolish in what he bet on and whenever anybody really loses that way, I don't want to rub it into him.

R.P.: I've been asking a lot of questions about the relationship of your poetry to other poetry, but of course there are many other non-literary things that have been equally important. You've been very much interested in science, for example.

R.F.: Yes, you're influenced by the science of your time, aren't you? Somebody noticed that all through my book there's astronomy.

R.P.: Like "The Literate Farmer and the Planet Venus"?

R.F.: Yes, but it's all through the book, all through the book. Many poems—I can name twenty that have astronomy in them. Somebody noticed that the other day: "Why has nobody ever seen how much you're interested in astronomy?" That's a bias, you could say. One of the earliest books I hovered over, hung around, was called *Our Place among the Infinities,* by an astronomer in England named Proctor, noted astronomer. It's a noted old book. I mention that in one of the poems: I use that expression "our place among the infinities" from that book that I must have read as soon as I read any book, thirteen or fourteen, right in there I began to read. That along with *Scottish Chiefs*.* I remember that year when I first began to read a book through. I had a little sister who read everything through, lots of books, everybody's books—very young, precocious. Me, I was—they turned me out of doors for my health.

R.P.: While we're thinking about science and literature, I wonder if you have any reaction to the fact that Massachusetts Institute of Technology is beginning to offer a number of courses in literature?

---

* *The Scottish Chiefs:* (1810), popular historical romance by Jane Parker, based on events in the career of the thirteenth-century Scottish patriot William Wallace.

R.F.: I think they'd better tend to their higher mathematics and higher science. Pure science. They know I think that. I don't mean to criticize them too much. But you see it's like this: the greatest adventure of man is science, the adventure of penetrating into matter, into the material universe. But the adventure is our property, a human property, and the best description of us is the humanities. Maybe the scientists wanted to remind their students that the humanities describe you who are adventuring into science, and science adds very little to that description of you, a little tiny bit. Maybe in psychology, or in something like that, but it's awful little. And so, the scientists to remind their students of all this give them half their time over there in the humanities now. And that seems a little unnecessary. They're worried about us and the pure sciences all the time. They'd better get as far as they can into their own subject. I was over there at the beginning of this and expressed my little doubts about it. I was there with Compton * one night—he was sitting on the platform beside me. "We've been short"—I turned to him before the audience—"we've been a little short in pure science, haven't we?" He said, "Perhaps—I'm afraid we may have been." I said, "I think that better be tended to." That's years ago.

R.P.: You just mentioned psychology. You once taught pscyhology, didn't you?

R.F.: That was entirely a joke. I could teach psychology. I've been asked to join a firm of psychiatrists, you know [by Merrill Moore], and that's more serious. But I went up there to disabuse the Teacher's College of the idea that there is any immediate connection between any psychology and their classroom work, disabuse them of the notion that they could mersmerize a class if they knew enough psychology. That's what they thought.

R.P.: Weren't you interested at one time in William James? *

R.F.: Yes, that was partly what drew me back to Harvard. But he was away all the time I was around here. I had Santayana,* Royce, and all that philosophy crowd, Munsterberg, George Herbert Palmer, the old poetical one. I had 'em all. But I was there waiting for James, and I lost interest.

R.P.: Did Santayana interest you very much at that time?

R.F.: No, not particularly. Well, yes, I always wondered what he really meant, where he was headed, what it all came to. Followed that for years. I never knew him personally. I never knew anybody personally in college. I was a kind of—went my own way. But I admired him. It was a golden utterance—he was something to listen to, just like his written style. But I wondered what he really meant. I found years afterward somewhere in his words that all was illusion, of two kinds, true and false. And I decided false illusion would be the truth: two negatives make an affirmative.

---

* Arthur Holly Compton: (1892–1962), educator, Nobel Prize winner in Physics.
* William James: (1842–1910), American psychologist and "radical empiricist" who developed the philosophy of pragmatism.
* George Santayana: (1863–1952), Spanish-born American skeptical philosopher and man of letters, celebrated for his prose style.

R.P.: While we're on things other than poetry that you were and are interested in, we might get onto politics for a moment. I remember one evening your mentioning that Henry Wallace became somehow associated with your poem, "Provide, Provide."

R.F.: People exaggerate such things. Henry Wallace * was in Washington when I read the poem. Sat right down there in the first row. And when I got to the end of it where it says, "Better to go down dignified—With boughten friendship at your side—Than none at all. Provide, Provide!" I added, "Or somebody else will provide for ya." He smiled; his wife smiled. They were right down there where I could see them.

R.P.: Well, you don't have a reputation for being a New Dealer.

R.F.: They think I'm no New Dealer. But really and truly I'm not, you know, all that clear on it. In "The Death of the Hired Man" that I wrote long, long ago, long before the New Deal, I put it two ways about home. One would be the manly way: "Home is the place where, when you have to go there, They have to take you in." That's the man's feeling about it. And then the wife says, "I should have called it/Something you somehow hadn't to deserve." That's the New Deal, the feminine way of it, the mother way. You don't have to deserve your mother's love. You have to deserve your father's. He's more particular. One's a Republican, one's a Democrat. The father is always a Republican toward his son, and his mother's always a Democrat. Very few have noticed that second thing; they've always noticed the sarcasm, the hardness of the male one.

R.P.: That poem is often anthologized, and I wonder if you feel that the poems of yours that appear most often in the anthologies represent you very well.

R.F.: I'm always pleased when somebody digs up a new one. I don't know. I leave that in the lap of the gods, as they say.

R.P.: There are some I seldom see; for example, "A Servant to Servants" or "The Most of It" or "The Subverted Flower." All of these I noticed the other day are omitted, for instance, from Untermeyer's anthology of your poems. Strange, isn't it?

R.F.: Well, he was making his own choice. I never said a word to him, never urged him. I remember he said [Edward Arlington] Robinson only did once. Robinson told him, "If you want to please an old man you won't overlook my 'Mr. Flood's Party.' " That is a beautiful poem.

R.P.: Do you feel that any particular area of your work hasn't been anthologized?

R.F.: I wouldn't know that. "The Subverted Flower," for instance, nobody's ever touched. No—I guess it is; it's in Matty's [F. O. Matthiessen's] anthology. That's the one he made for the Oxford people.

---

* Henry Wallace: (1888–1965), Cabinet member and vice president under Franklin D. Roosevelt; in 1946 dismissed from the Cabinet by President Truman because of his denunciation of U.S. foreign policy in maintaining the Cold War; in 1948, unsuccessful Progressive party candidate for the Presidency.

R.P.: Yes, but its appearance is extremely rare in any selection of your work. It doesn't seem to fit some people's preconceptions about you. Another neglected poem, and an especially good one, is "Putting in the Seed."

R.F.: That's—sure. They leave that sort of thing out; they overlook that sort of thing with me. The only person ever noticed that was a hearty old friend of mine down at the University of Pennsylvania, Cornelius Weygandt.[3] He said, "I know what *that's* about."

R.P.: Do you ever read that poem in public?

R.F.: No, I don't bother with those. No, there are certain ones. I wouldn't read "The Subverted Flower" to anybody outside. It isn't that I'm afraid of them, but I don't want them out. I'm shy about certain things in my books, they're more—I'd rather they'd be read. A woman asked me, "What do you mean by that 'subverted flower'?" I said, "Frigidity in women." She left.

R.P.: Do you think that it was to correct the public assumption that your poetry is represented by the most anthologized pieces such as "Birches" that Lionel Trilling in his speech at your eighty-fifth birthday emphasized poems of a darker mood?

R.F.: I don't know—I might run my eye over my book after Trilling, and wonder why he hadn't seen it sooner: that there's plenty to be dark about, you know. It's full of darkness.

R.P.: Do you suppose he imagined he was correcting some sort of public ignorance —some general mistake about your work?

R.F.: He made the mistake himself. He was admitting he made it himself, wasn't he? He was telling what trouble he'd had to get at me. Sort of a confession, but very pleasant.

R.P.: That's true, but many admirers of yours did object to his emphasis on the "darkness" or "terror" in your poems.

R.F.: Yes, well, he took me a little by suprise that night. He was standing right beside me and I had to get up right after him. Birthday party. And it took me —it didn't hurt me, but I thought at first he was attacking me. Then when he began comparing me to Sophocles and D. H. Lawrence I was completely at sea. What the two of them had to do with me, you know. Might be I might like it about Sophocles, but I'd be puzzled, oh, utterly at sea about D. H. Lawrence. It's all right, though. I had to get up and recite soon after that, and so I was a little puzzled what to recite to illustrate what he was talking about. And right there—new to me: I hadn't read his paper. I'd never read him much. I don't read criticism. You see no magazines in the house.

R.P.: Did you feel better about his talk when you read his substantiation of it in the *Partisan Review*?

R.F.: I read his defense of it. Very clever, very—very interesting. Admired him. He's a very—intellectual man. But I read very little, generally, in the

---

3. Author of historical and descriptive studies of New Hampshire.

magazines. Hadn't read that Shapiro thing you mentioned. That's new to me what he said. Is he a friend of mine?

R.P.: Oh, yes. He's a friend of yours, but he's like many friends of yours: he chooses to see in you something more simple than your best friends see. It's a bit like J. Donald Adams, also in the *Times,* angrily defending you against Trilling, only J. Donald Adams doesn't understand you very well either.

R.F.: What was Shapiro saying?

R.P.: He was saying that most modern poetry is obscure and overdifficult, that this is particularly true of Pound and Eliot, but that it isn't true of you.

R.F.: Well, I don't want to be difficult. I like to fool—oh, you know, you like to be mischievous. But not in that dull way of just being dogged and doggedly obscure.

R.P.: The difficulty of your poetry is perhaps in your emphasis on variety in tones of voice. You once said that consciously or unconsciously it was tones of voice that you counted on to double the meaning of every one of your statements.

R.F.: Yes, you could do that. Could unsay everything I said, nearly. Talking contraries—it's in one of the poems. Talk by contraries with people you're very close to. They know what you're talking about. This whole thing of suggestiveness and *double entendre* and hinting—comes down to the word "hinting." With people you can trust you can talk in hints and suggestiveness. Families break up when people take hints you don't intend and miss hints you do intend. You can watch that going on, as a psychologist. I don't know. No, don't . . . no don't you . . . don't think of me . . . See, I haven't led a literary life. These fellows, they *really* work away with their prose trying to describe themselves and understand themselves, and so on. I don't do that. I don't want to know too much about myself. It interests me to know that Shapiro thinks I'm not difficult. That's all right. I never wrote a review in my life, never wrote articles. I'm constantly refusing to write articles. These fellows are all literary men. I don't have hours; I don't work at it, you know. I'm not a farmer, that's no pose of mine. But I have farmed some, and I putter around. And I walk and I live with other people. Like to talk a lot. But I haven't had a very literary life, and I'm never very much with the gang. I'm vice-president, no, I'm Honorary President of the Poetry Society of America. Once in a great while I go. And I wish them well. I wish the foundations would take them all, take care of them all.

R.P.: Speaking of foundations, why do you think big business, so long the object of literary ridicule for being philistine, should now be supporting so much literary effort?

R.F.: It's funny they haven't sooner, because most of them have been to college and had poetry pushed into them. About half the reading they do in all languages will be in verse. Just think of it. And so they have a kind of respect for it all and they probably don't mind the abuse they've had from our quarter. They're people who're worried that we just don't have enough imagination—

it's the lack of imagination they're afraid of in our system. If we had enough imagination we could lick the Russians. I feel like saying, "Probably we won the Civil War with Emily Dickinson." We didn't even know she was there. Poor little thing.

R.P.: Would you agree that there are probably more good prizes for poetry today than there are good poets?

R.P.: I don't know. I hate to judge that. It's nice for them—it's so nice for them to be interested in us, with their foundations. You don't know what'll come of it. You know the real thing is that the sense of sacrifice and risk is one of the greatest stimuli in the world. And you take that all out of it—take that away from it so that there's no risk in being a poet, I bet you'd lose a lot of the pious spirits. They're in it for the—hell of it. Just the same as these fellows breaking through the sound barrier up there, just the same. I was once asked in public, in front of four or five hundred women, just how I found leisure to write. I said, "Confidentially—since there's only five hundred of you here, and all women—like a sneak I stole some of it, like a man I seized some of it—and I had a little in my tin cup." Sounds as if I'd been a beggar, but I've never been consciously a beggar. I've been at the mercy of . . . I've been a beneficiary around colleges and all. And this is one of the advantages to the American way: I've never had to write a word of thanks to anybody I had a cent from. The colleges came between. Poetry has always been a beggar. Scholars have also been beggars, but they delegate their begging to the president of the college to do for them.

R.P.: I was suggesting just now that perhaps the number of emoluments for poets greatly exceeds the number of people whose work deserves to be honored. Isn't this a situation in which mediocrity will necessarily be exalted? And won't this make it more rather than less difficult for people to recognize really good achievement when it does occur?

R.F.: You know, I was once asked that, and I said I never knew how many disadvantages anyone needed to get anywhere in the world. And you don't know how to measure that. No psychology will ever tell you who needs a whip and who needs a spur to win races. I think the greatest thing about it with me has been this, and I wonder if others think it. I look at a poem as a performance. I look on the poet as a man of prowess, just like an athlete. He's a performer. And the things you can do in a poem are very various. You speak of figures, tones of voice varying all the time. I'm always interested, you know, when I have three or four stanzas, in the way I *lay* the sentences in them. I'd hate to have the sentences all lie the same in the stanzas. Every poem is like that: some sort of achievement in performance. Somebody has said that poetry among other things is the marrow of wit. That's probably way back somewhere —marrow of wit. There's got to be wit. And that's very, very much left out of a lot of this labored stuff. It doesn't sparkle at all. Another thing to say is that every thought, poetical or otherwise, every thought is a feat of association. They tell of old Gibbon *—as he was dying he was the same Gibbon at his historical parallels. All thought is a feat of association: having what's in front of you bring up something in your mind that you almost didn't know you knew. Putting this and that together. That click.

R.P.: Can you give an example of how this feat of association—as you call it —works?

R.F.: Well, one of my masques * turns on one association like that. God says, "I was just showing off to the Devil, Job." Job looks puzzled about it, distressed a little. God says, "Do you mind?" And, "No, no," he says, "No," in that tone, you know, "No," and so on. That tone is everything, the way you say that "no." I noticed that—that's what made me write that. Just that one thing made that.

R.P.: Did your other masque—*Masque of Mercy*—have a similar impetus?

R.F.: I noticed that the first time in the world's history when mercy is entirely the subject is in Jonah. It does say somewhere earlier in the Bible, "If ten can be found in the city, will you spare it? Ten good people?" But in Jonah there is something worse than that. Jonah is told to go and prophesy against the city—and he *knows* God will let him down. He can't trust God to be unmerciful. You can trust God to be anything but unmerciful. So he ran away and—and got into a whale. That's the point of that and nobody notices it. They miss it.

R.P.: Why do you suppose, Mr. Frost, that among religious groups the masques had their best reception among Jesuits and rabbis?

R.F.: Amusing you say that—that's true. The other, the lesser sects without the law, you see, they don't get it. They're too apt to think there's rebellion in them —what they go through with their parents when they're growing up. But that isn't in them at all, you know. They're not rebellious. They're very doctrinal, very orthodox, both of them. But how'd you notice that? It's amusing to me too. You see, the rabbis have been fine to me and so have the SJ's particularly, all over the country. I've just been in Kansas City staying with them. See, the masques are full of good orthodox doctrine. One of them turns on the thought that evil shows off to good and good shows off to evil. I made a couplet out of that for them in Kansas City, just the way I often do, offhand: "It's from their having stood contrasted/That good and bad so long have lasted."

R.P.: Making couplets "offhand" is something like writing on schedule, isn't it? I know a young poet who claims he can write every morning from six to nine, presumably before class.

R.F.: Well, there's more than one way to skin a cat. I don't know what that would be like, myself. When I get going on something, I don't want to just—you know . . . Very first one I wrote I was walking home from school and I began

* Edward Gibbon: (1737–94), English historian, author of *The Decline and Fall of the Roman Empire*.
* *A Masque of Reason* (1945).

to make it—a March day—and I was making it all afternoon and making it so I was late at my grandmother's for dinner. I finished it, but it burned right up, just burned right up, you know. And what started that? What burned it? So many talk, I wonder how falsely, about what it costs them, what agony it is to write. I've often been quoted: "No tears in the writer, no tears in the reader. No surprise for the writer, no surprise for the reader." But another distinction I made is: however sad, no grievance, grief without grievance. How could I, how could anyone have a good time with what cost me too much agony, how could they? What do I want to communicate but what a *hell* of a good time I had writing it? The whole thing is performance and prowess and feats of association. Why don't critics talk about those things—what a feat it was to turn that that way, and what a feat it was to remember that, to be reminded of that by this? Why don't they talk about that? Scoring. You've got to *score*. They say not, but you've got to score, in all the realms—theology, politics, astronomy, history, and the country life around you.

R.P.: What do you think of the performances of the poets who have made your birthplace, San Francisco, into their headquarters? *

R.F.: Have they? Somebody said I saw a lot of them in Kansas City at the end of my audience. They said, "See that blur over there? That's whiskers." No, I don't know much about that. I'm waiting for them to say something that I can get hold of. The worse the better. I like it anyway, you know. Like you say to somebody, "Say something. Say something." And he says, "I burn."

R.P.: Do young poets send you things?

R.F.: Yes, some—not much, because I don't respond. I don't write letters and all that. But I get a little, and I meet them, talk with them. I get some books. I wonder what they're at. There's one book that sounded as if it might be good, "Aw, hell." The book was called "Aw, hell." Because "aw," the way you say "aw," you know, "Aw, hell!" That might be something.

R.P.: Most of the titles are funny. One is called *Howl* * and another *Gasoline*.*

R.F.: *Gasoline*, eh? I've seen a little of it, kicking around. I saw a bunch of nine of them in a magazine in Chicago when I was through there. They were all San Franciscans. Nothing I could talk about afterwards, though, either way. I'm always glad of anybody that says anything awful. I can use it. We're all like that. You've got to learn to enjoy a lot of things you don't like. And I'm always ready for somebody to say some outrageous thing. I feel like saying, "Hold that now, long enough for me to go away and tell on you, won't you? Don't go back on it tomorrow." Funny world.

R.P.: When you look at a new poem that might be sent to you, what is it usually that makes you want to read it all or not want to read it?

R.F.: This thing of performance and prowess and feats of association—that's

---

* the poets . . . : i.e. the Beats.
* *Howl*: (1956), by Allen Ginsberg.
* *Gasoline*: (1958), by Gregory Corso.

where it all lies. One of my ways of looking at a poem right away it's sent to me, right off, is to see if it's rhymed. Then I know just when to look at it. The rhymes come in pairs, don't they? And nine times out of ten with an ordinary writer, one of two of the terms is better than the other. One makeshift will do, and then they get another that's good, and then another makeshift, and then another one that's good. That is in the realm of performance, that's the deadly test with me. I want to be unable to tell which of those he thought of first. If there's any trick about it, putting the better one first so as to deceive me, I can tell pretty soon. That's all in the performance realm. They can belong to any school of thought they want to, Spinoza or Schopenhauer, it doesn't matter to me. A Cartesian I heard Poe called, a Cartesian philosopher, the other day . . . tsssssss . . .

R.P.: You once saw a manuscript of Dylan Thomas's where he'd put all the rhymes down first and then backed into them. That's clearly not what you mean by performance, is it?

R.F.: See, that's very dreadful. It ought to be that you're thinking forward, with the feeling of strength that you're getting them good all the way, carrying out some intention more felt than thought. It begins. And what it is that guides us —what is it? Young people wonder about that, don't they? But I tell them it's just the same as when you feel a joke coming. You see somebody coming down the street that you're accustomed to abuse, and you feel it rising in you, something to say as you pass each other. Coming over him the same way. And where do these thoughts come from? Where does a thought? Something does it to you. It's him coming toward you that gives you the animus, you know. When they want to know about inspiration, I tell them it's mostly animus.

Eric Bentley / Actor and Playwright

This is a brief extract from a long and highly original book, *The Life of the Drama,* which provides a whole new theory of theater. We hope that these pages will demonstrate the originality and modernity of the work. That Western acting is organized round the eyes of the performer, that "we are led by the eyes," is an observation which produces many insights into the nature of our traditional theater, in which performance intensifies a text. This intensification is of two kinds, appropriate to the modes of tragedy and comedy; but it is related to our conduct in real life, as, in Bentley's view, the theater always is. In discussing the contribution of the writer to the actor's art, Bentley establishes a distinction between character and role which is equally illuminating. A little later he discusses the role and the mask as we use them in everyday life, and the union between that life and theatricality as it is demonstrated in the psycho-dramatic technique of certain analysts. Observe that this quite difficult material is here presented in very untechnical language, a silent reproach to those who believe that original ideas can be expressed only in a terminology invented to accommodate them.

WHAT THE ACTOR GIVES THE PLAYWRIGHT

Should a novelist turn to playwriting, he might well feel that he has made certain sacrifices, even if he does not go all the way with Henry James, who envisaged the novelist-turned-playwright as throwing out the cargo to save the ship. However, if his plays were very well acted, such a writer might conclude that his losses had been recouped.

What does acting add to a play? Many things. Let me mention, first, one of the simplest but not least interesting: that the actors' eyes meet. This is probably not true of some of the older theatres, and some of the Oriental ones, but in our modern Western theatre it is a well-established, if not essential, feature. Though some today may think of it as a product of the Stanislavsky Method,* or even of the movies, one can in fact trace it much further back. There is, for example, an eighteenth-century comment on the actress Mrs. Clive, which reads:

> Mr. Garrick complained that she disconcerted him, by not looking at him in the time of action; and neglecting to watch the motion of the eye; a practice he was sure to observe to others. I am afraid this accusation is partly true; for Mrs. Clive would suffer her eyes to wander. . . .

Watch the acting of any intimate scene between a man and a woman—say, the last scene of *Pygmalion*.* One can imagine an ancient Greek or a more recent devotee of classical Chinese theatre or Kabuki * finding in our acting of *Pygmalion* a lack of formality and pattern, no special significance in where the feet are going, no special beauty in the way the body moves or stands. "Why, they're not doing anything," any of these visitors might say, "but alternately looking at each other and looking away." And this is essentially true. Acting, in such an instance, has come to concentrate itself in the eyes. And the eyes are subject to this physiological paradox: that to go on looking cancels out a look. To keep a look going, one has to interrupt it, and then look again; hence, in the various interruptions, all the looking away. A look is more dynamic as it is beginning to

---

* The Stanislavsky method: Constantin Stanislavsky (1863–1938), Russian theatrical director, actor, and teacher, co-founder of the Moscow Art Theater. His "method," stressing the empathic identification of the actor with his role, aimed at getting rid of artificial and mechanical acting techniques.
* *Pygmalion:* play by George Bernard Shaw.
* Kabuki: Japanese theatrical genre developed in the seventeenth century.

happen than when it actually happens; and having happened, it slows down into stony stare or sentimental gaze. As between persons, a look has its consummation when it is returned. The meeting of eyes constitutes a kind of center of human communication. The contact established is more personal than touch. What is communicated may be in doubt, but what is not in doubt is the aliveness of the lines of communication. On stage this is an aliveness of the actors, which they add to the much less directly physical life of the script. Spectators who might have difficulty with the written script have none responding physically, by empathy, to the actors' looking at each other. The stage, which renders things physically, neurologically, sensuously, is a great instrument of legitimate popularization. Conversely, the overliterary spectator who has seized Bernard Shaw's ideas all too readily, may not have lived through the drama of a Shavian scene until he, too, receives it from the actors' lips, through the actors' bodies, and especially through the actors' eyes. Usually, when we speak of seeing something through another's eyes, we are speaking only of the mind's eye. In the theatre, the actors' eyes guide us through the labyrinthine ways of the scenes; and all that joins us to the actors' eyes is the magnetics of looking. In the theatre, we may not be led by the nose: we *are* led by the eyes.

If a play in the theatre should prove hallucinatory in its vividness, it is the actor who finally has brought it to that pitch, adding to the play, one might put it, the crowning touch. Again, if a role is skeletal—and this I shall go into later—it may be possible for the actor to put some flesh on the bones. Some actors spend a lifetime filling in for inadequate playwrights. If they are stars, one often hears them disparagingly spoken of as mere personalities. The disparagement is misplaced, as "mere personality," in the sense here suggested, is exactly what the circumstances require.

And as we have seen in the chapter on Character, a good play may also have what novel-readers consider thin characterizations. If they do not need filling in, it is because the play survives by its plot or by a combination of plot, style, and theme. What the actor can contribute to a good play is not to fill up gaps—there may not be any he could fill—but *to intensify its effects*. Stanislavsky is right: it is fundamentally a matter of being able to "live" on stage. And Stanislavsky correctly assumed that what most people do on stage is not alive. Projection is lacking, and on stage not to project is not to live.

Pirandello points up this contrast wittily in *Six Characters* when two of the Characters speak without projecting their voices because people in real life do not project their voices. The result is that these Characters are not alive in the theatre. Now projection of the voice is a comparatively mechanical matter, and it does not follow that, if the voice is projected, the whole performance has "projection." We must take it that Pirandello here offers the part for the whole. To "live" on stage means to do more than live offstage, it means to give off life, to make it audible, and visible, to make of it a projectile which is thrown out into the auditorium and reaches the back row of the balcony.

"The point," says Jean Cocteau, "is not to put life onto the stage but to make the stage live."

What the actor has intensified when we out front have an "hallucination" is the illusion. Such is the acting of the tragic tradition, which in this century found its spokesman in Stanislavsky. What comic actors intensify is not the illusion but the aggression. (The comic tradition has recently been renewed by that most aggressive of playwrights—Brecht.) The comic aggression may take the form of satire and be called realistic, or it may take the form of high spirits and celebration and earn the description of fantastic. In either case the actor's fundamental contribution is not mimicry but vitality.

What indeed is that limited kind of acting which is so effectively practiced by friends of ours at parties in the way of malicious mimicry? The degree of likeness to what they mimic is a minor matter compared to the degree of wickedness with which they do it. A very little observation will suffice, provided very much fantasy and malice are superadded. Fantasy and malice are in this case the vehicles of vitality.

What acting testifies to in dramatic art is not in the first place its imitative character but its exaggerative character. The dramatist is immoderate. He likes to push his effects to the limit. The actor aids and abets him, adding powder to the bomb. The great actor resembles the great plays in that, beneath the formal calm which must be his normal aspect, he makes an immense violence felt. The impression given is that of living at great speed. And perhaps that, as Hebbel said, is just what the actor does—he lives "at speed, at unimaginable speed." Hebbel's idea is helpful for the understanding of all dramatic art. Rather than describe drama as an abridged, abbreviated form, as if something were missing from it, we should speak of it as an art in which more ground is covered in less time.

WHAT THE PLAYWRIGHT GIVES THE ACTOR

If the actor helps the playwright by adding his presence and his vitality (not to mention his craft), the playwright helps the actor by writing, not just a character, but a role. This is perhaps the most overlooked of all the playwright's tasks, at least among students of literature. It is understood only to the extent that the differences between playwright and novelist are understood. The novelist uses artifice, but in a setting of nature—natural scenery and natural characters. The playwright uses artifice in a setting of artifice—stage roles amid stage scenery. Such are the rules of the game, the controlling conditions of this art. While the novelist has the illusion of seeing actual characters in actual settings, the playwright has to learn to visualize the actor of the character and visualize him in that most unnatural of all settings: a theatre.

A character is not a role until, to begin with, it can be put across in a few acted scenes. Any idea for a character which cannot be put across at that velocity and by that method is unsuited to dramatic art. Conversely, an idea for a character which suggests opportunities for several self-explaining and violent stage encounters can prove effective even though it be lacking in depth and complexity. This second proposition begins to explain the success of certain roles, such as that of Marguerite Gautier,* which are by no means great characters. To create *dramatis personae* which are great both as roles and characters is to be, in this department at least, a great dramatist.

The matter is a subtle one and has not been sufficiently studied, partly because the full possibilities of a role are only revealed by first-rate acting, and partly because histrionic phenomena have not traditionally been found worthy of the detailed study that is lavished on many lesser subjects. Anyone can see, for example, that Goethe was a greater genius than Schiller, yet Schiller was able to write characters that were also great roles. Goethe only managed it occasionally—as with his Mephisto who saved *Faust* for the theatre.

There is a moment when we might all feel, with Etienne Souriau, that the dramatist's heroic deed is to give existence to characters. This is the moment when these characters go out on the stage and demonstrate that existence—it is *the moment when the characters show themselves to be roles.* That is the eating which is the proof of the pudding. It is as if, in the theatre, the physical existence of the actor were necessary to complete the sense of the verb *to exist.* This moving, speaking incarnation of character which is an acted role is an instrument of such unique power that, for the time being at any rate, we cease to long for the vaunted advantages of other forms and arts.

Which comes first, the character or the role? We tend to think of a writer starting with a character and, if he is playwright enough, going on to make sure it is a role as well. That is because we live in a literary age. In a theatrical age, it was the other way around. The actor was there and needed lines. One handed him a role. Only when he was lucky did he get anything that deserved the name of a character. Inquiring further back in history, we find a repertoire of fixed roles which actor-writers would refurbish as effective characters. Such was the *commedia dell'arte.**

Pierre Schneider / At the Louvre with Steinberg

This is an unusual dialogue, conducted before the works of art which form its principal topics and illustrated, in the original, by examples of Stein-

---

* Marguerite Gautier: heroine of *La Dame aux camélias* (1852) by Alexandre Dumas *fils.*
* *commedia dell'arte:* a form of Italian popular comedy which flourished from the sixteenth to the eighteenth centuries; based on a fixed set of characters who improvise dialogue for a given scenario.

berg's own work. These we reproduce, and add to them reproductions of three of the paintings discussed.

The part of Pierre Schneider is to provide a characterization of Steinberg and to bring out the degree of seriousness implicit in his comments, which are in the nature of the case random and impromptu. When Steinberg remarks that he regards a work of art as "to some extent a matter of graphology" we are helped in our understanding not only by Steinberg's own drawings, where the graphological interest is very evident, but also by Schneider's comments on the subject, and on the propriety of Steinberg's use of the word "script."

To some readers it may appear that the comments of the artist on the Louvre pictures are rather sophisticated and difficult, but all will feel their authority, which derives from the artist's own mastery and from his command of the theoretical problems that arise in considerations of fictive representations of reality. A good illustration of this is the discussion of Uccello's *Battle,* a painting famous in the history of perspective. Schneider's final paragraph relates this kind of comment to Steinberg's own obsession with graphology and with the making of such drawings as we reproduce, drawings which contain the artist who draws them and which therefore cannot be "read" in conventional fashion. They rather force us to attend to the human skills in perceiving and rendering which condition our ways of "matching" the world as we see it. This point is converted into a little joke at the end.

Schneider's purpose is here obvious. He takes a distinguished and original artist to the Louvre and records his comments on some of the masterpieces of Western art. Then he compiles a report in a manner intended to teach us not only about the paintings but about the mind and hand which made possible Steinberg's drawings and his insights into the older works. The traditional and the modern are brought into confrontation in an instructive but unpedantic way. The dialogue is one of a series in which Schneider gives other great modern artists the same treatment.

I was preparing to face, not without feelings of guilt, the usual objections: "I am an artist, you know. Talk isn't my forte. Besides, what can you say about it? Like mystic experience, aesthetic experience cannot be explained. . . ." In no time, Steinberg reassures me:

"I am wary of people who remain dazzled, exalted, silent in front of a painting. They believe in miracles. But it is we who must make our paradises. The true mystics have always been talkative. To honour a picture, you must tell it to yourself with every possible detail. When you freeze up, you know that you are standing before a boss."

Silence is the consequence of fear, and Steinberg hates tyranny.

[*Mr. Saul Steinberg's drawings are reproduced with his kind permission.*]

"Art is a sphinx. The beauty of the sphinx is that you yourself must do the interpreting. When you have found an interpretation, you are already cured. The mistake people make is to believe that the sphinx can give only one answer. Actually, it gives hundreds of answers, or maybe none at all. Interpretation probably does not give us the truth, but the act of interpretation saves us."

The word brings salvation. And, no doubt, it is to the essential role of the word that we may attribute Steinberg's avocation:

"I am a writer. I draw because the essence of a good piece of writing is precision. Drawing is a precise mode of expression."

Indeed, caricature is not a purely visual medium but rather the most visual form that thought, language, are capable of assuming. What distinguishes the draftsmanship of Goya * from that of Daumier * is function rather than talent. One looks at Goya; one reads Daumier. The taunt of literature does not frighten Steinberg.

"In art everything has a literary origin—except abstract expressionism, which pretended to grow out of the activity of the body, not out of thought. However, even action painting is the intelligence of the body. Anything that implies some sort of intelligence, of whatever kind, belongs at least partly to the realm of literature. The body's intelligence is the metaphysics of the nose."

Besides, all things speak.

"Everything has a message: even the smell of museums. In Europe, museums smell of town halls and grade schools; in America they smell like banks."

If in most cases we do not perceive these messages, it is because their richness is drowned out by a thunderous vacuousness, as the noise of traffic drowns conversation in sidewalk cafés.

"We spend almost our whole lives reading boisterous, ready-made messages (the mail, the newspapers, traffic lights). To decipher the other kind of messages requires an effort which we prefer to avoid making. Yet it is this effort that renders life rich, gay and so to say, inexhaustible."

Therefore, people must be encouraged to decipher these deeper messages. But how? Laziness, sloth, routine, impel them to read only the language that is familiar to them. One must use tricks. Let them proceed along the track, but tamper with the switches.

"One must build attractive traps."

Steinberg's drawings are like traffic lights signalling "You may cross now" on all sides at once: you confidently step off the curb—and are run over.

"Humour is a very good trap. Laughter disarms and opens the way for instinct. It is like hiccups, yawns. When you try to repress a yawn, it comes out of your ears. Yawning is animal criticism—dogs yawn. Laughter is mental or maybe mineral. Let's drop this subject. Trying to define humour is one of the definitions of humour."

This is particularly true when Steinberg manipulates the language used in the definition. The language is the same, all right, but it has been placed in a different context. Caricature, as practised by most humourists, fits the definition implicit in its etymology: it is loaded. As practised by Steinberg, caricature *unloads;* it frees language from its customary obligations. Its burden removed, language flies out the window and into the world of things. All that is needed is

* Francisco de Goya y Lucientes: (1746–1828), Spanish artist, fresco and portrait painter; executed two famous series of satirical etchings—*The Caprices* (1796–98), which attacks contemporary manners, morals, and ecclesiastical corruption, and *The Disasters of War* (1810–20).
* Honoré Daumier: (1808–97), French realist painter, lithographer, and caricaturist; he did a number of satirical political cartoons on themes of corruption and incompetence in the government.

to mix up the established circuits between sign and sense. This man, whose drawings so often seek to upset communication, confesses:

"Without wanting to, I have become a moralist."

At first sight, he has the modest and just a trifle doctoral air of a chemistry professor: yet there is something disquieting in the eyes, the smile, the cap. But after all, the chemistry professor might be on holiday in Europe. Such is obviously the opinion of the four schoolgirls who come to us as we are chatting in a room filled with Roman sculpture. At once, we are plunged into a typically Steinbergian predicament: faced with sounds that possess the obvious earmarks of language yet are impossible to understand. They are speaking Spanish. Little by little, we manage to reconstruct the question that they are absolutely convinced my companion will answer. Why are the eyesockets in the colossal head of Antinous, Emperor Hadrian's favourite page, empty? Without hesitation, Steinberg explains that the eyes had been made of precious stones and that when the barbarians came. . . . There follows a gesture of legerdemain so precise and so swift that one would swear this innocent-looking gentleman had learned the pickpocket trade in the Trastevere.*

We begin our visit to the Louvre with the Roman mosaics. *"The Battle of the Amazons,"* found at Daphne, near Antioch, dates from the third or fourth cen-

* the Trastevere: low-life district in Rome.

tury A.D. Steinberg points to the central part, which is lost and has been filled in with cement:

"This empty space in the middle transforms the whole work into a geographical business. One can see how abstract art derives from the museum. It is there that one sees vertical floors. These gaps—how restful. That is why there are dull pages in all good novels. After this gap, the head of the dying soldier is much more moving: like an action taking place behind a bush. It is interesting to show only a little part of things: female eroticism. . . ."

He turns his glance to the horsemen on the left:

"How elegant these warriors are! In them, the artist is the passive instrument of a period style, of decadence, rococo.* . . . But when he got to the horse's teeth, the resemblance between the marble cubes and the teeth made him into a dentist making a denture for a horse. Here the mosaic became a collage and a pun. The artist also realised that the whole mosaic was made of horse's teeth. Look: everything is abstract, derivative—the horse's nostrils, for instance—except those teeth. They are real teeth."

And now it looks as if some monstrous Pegasus had spat out, by the millions, the little cubes that compose the pavement on which we tread.

"Those horse's teeth, they are everywhere. . . . Once you see something, you can no longer get rid of it, you are contaminated, you see it everywhere. Right now you, I, everything is made of horse's teeth. Of course, it is my eye that is contaminated."

And this contamination is hailed as a symptom of life: by its contagiousness the microbe proves itself alive.

A bit later, in front of a mediocre Roman high-relief:

"I am very fond of high-reliefs. They lead to such absurdities! To make the sculpture from a rock, which already is a sculpture! It is absurd, amusing, moving. Sculptors are primarily idol makers. To translate flesh into stone, for instance, is to deify man. For a stone to be admitted into the temple—the museum—it has to have been translated into bronze. Bronze is the sublimation of stone, wood is the sublimation of iron, and so on. That, by the way, is the secret of pop art."

What fascinates Steinberg in Wayne Thiebaud's * pop paintings, as in the horse's teeth of the Roman mosaic, is the coincidence, perfect to the point of coalescence, of "nature" and "art" by way of a simple, basic form. Here, the cube; there, the cuisine of creamy pigment. We can no longer tell whether the artist

---

* rococo: eighteenth-century European art style which flourished principally in architecture and interior decoration; rococo ornament is characteristically distinguished by its asymmetric arrangements of curves and foliage and by an air of refined gaiety, of light and playful elegance.
* Wayne Thiebaud: (1920–), American artist; has done, for example, paintings of popsicles and of slices of pie.

has caught nature or whether nature has caught up with him. Later, in front of Sellajo's * *"Saint Jerome Penitent"*:

"Marvellous! See how the trees are trimmed. Architecture first imitated trees, then the trees imitated architecture. Campaniles and minarets were invented by cypress trees."

The theme of a large number of Steinberg's own drawings is the unforeseen, upsetting, comic abolition of the distance between the artist and the world: the

person drawing a table turns, without knowing it, into part of the table itself. The instrument of this trespass is the virulence of line, its ability to proliferate. Line is the common bond between man and things; the modulations of line constitute a language. And here it is necessary to take the word "literally" literally: the identity of human language and the language of things occurs at the level of the alphabet. The combination of letters draws them away from their origin and reality, turns them into envelopes of purely human sounds, into vehicles of abstract meanings. They no longer designate the world, they signify what the tyranny of man wishes them to signify. All's well, the words of a friend's letter tell

* Jacopo del Sellajo: (1441?–93), Italian painter of the Florentine school, imitator of Botticelli; his subjects were religious and mythological.

you; but if you have the slightest knowledge of, or feeling for, graphology, you can easily detect the anxiety that lies behind his optimistic affirmations. Steinberg says:

"For me, seeing a work of art is, to some extent, a matter of graphology."

The man who hates all forms of despotism will seek to free the alphabet from its master, to deliver it from its semantic chains and turn it loose again in nature. When man and nature are analogous and continuous, writing means what it says. Writing is simply script: not so much signs as signatures (Steinberg's passion for signatures is well known), not an object of cognition but rather of recognition. The world is one—if we decipher the correspondences of which its unity is woven. It is a task that requires punctilious, almost paranoiac attention. Such an attitude of mind characterised the late Middle Ages and the early Renaissance, which saw the universe as a body tattooed with messages whose hermeticism was precisely the clue to their presence and to their importance. "Herbs communicate with the curious physician through their signature," wrote Crollius in his *Treatise on Signatures,* * "thereby revealing to him their inner virtues, hidden under nature's veil of silence."

There's something that doesn't quite fit in with the appearance of a chemistry professor: perhaps more like a professor of alchemy.

More numerous than Deucalion's teeth, the little cubes of the Louvre. . . . We stand before the *"Phoenix,"* that great stone rug brought back from Tunisia:

"Amazing! Upside down, the goats' heads turn into coat hangers. And those wings, they are there to finish off the goat. That is what those wings are for, those pun butterflies. A flourish of the pen, a script. These goats with their horns and wings are the fathers of topographic ornaments."

The word "script" is uttered seemingly at random, or like a tic. Yet it is the right word. For when a goat's head becomes a coat hanger, when eagle's wings suddenly readjust themselves into giant butterflies, our attention is attracted—as long as we do not perceive exclusively either one or the other of the two terms —to the common form, to the line that binds them. The visual pun is the moment of levitation between two equally loaded messages, the moment when script, usually hidden behind meanings, is unburdened, freed from the gravitational pull of significant sound, and stands for itself.

"The phoenix looks rather like a duck in a phoenix outfit—like Shriners * dressed as Turks. You can see how the children of the house, on traversing this room, invented and rigorously followed the tradition of jumping over the goats, setting one foot on the rock and another on the duck."

---

* *Treatise on Signatures of Internal Things* (1669), book by the English scientist Oswaldus Crollius.
* Shriners: members of a secret fraternal society, The Ancient Arabic Order of Nobles of the Mystic Shrine, which has adopted the fez (formerly the national Turkish headdress) as its special garb.

We enter the Room of Augustus, certainly one of the ugliest in the Louvre.

"This, for me, is the real museum. At once you feel yourself surrounded by thousands of butterflies. The ceiling, the frescos, the gilt reliefs, the marble pavement, the busts—everything clamours to be looked at. It's too much. All those butterflies staring at us."

Indeed, nothing is more dead, more hypnotic than a butterfly pinned to the bottom of a box—unless it is a perfect glass imitation of a butterfly. Steinberg contemplates the ceiling, covered with a hideous fresco in the distinguished manner of Puvis de Chavannes.*

"To get rid of those too noble things that he painted on the walls of public buildings, Puvis did grotesque erotic drawings at home."

The ceiling of the next room is no less conspicuous.

"A nightmare! It is an octagon, which is very tiring shape. And it is filled to the brim! It is the nineteenth century saying: 'Me too!' It competes with the works on exhibit, like Frank Lloyd Wright's Guggenheim." *

What in *your* opinion is the best solution for a museum?

"There is no solution. A good museum is a dead museum."

Fayum portraits,* imperial busts . . . In front of that representing Annius Verus, who died in 169:

"The broken nose, the missing nose makes the beauty of the sphinx. Death takes the noses. A fleshy nose is a sign of life. The death's head, that is the secret of Greta Garbo's fascination. It is also Brigitte Bardot's: a gay death's-head, with a baby's mouth, sensual fish-lips."

Further on, a Fayum portrait, crude, beautiful:

"It is never possible to imitate primitives. You can imitate geniuses, discoverers, inventors. You can explore what they discovered—Cézanne,* for instance. But a primitive is the pinnacle of a pyramid. After him, there is nothing. Rousseau,* for example. . . . No offence meant, but who are the primitives today?"

Bust of a young woman, in marble:

"A real baby, with the real, suction-cup little mouth that babies have. It's the portrait of a Marine, the baby-faced killer. The face is broad as a pizza and the mouth tiny. Small-scale sensuality is what horrifies."

We walk towards the grand staircase. At its foot, a colossal head, that of Lucilla, Lucius Verus' wife:

---

* Puvis de Chavannes: (1824–98), eminent French mural painter who tried to re-create and modernize the monumental Italian fresco style.
* The Guggenheim Museum in New York (built 1952–59), designed around a dramatic spiralling ramp.
* Fayum portraits: second-century mummy portraits from the Fayum, a province of upper Egypt.
* Paul Cézanne: (1839–1906), the great French Impressionist painter.
* Henri Rousseau (1844–1910), an amateur French painter of great talent whose fanciful, vivid, dream-like pictures are sometimes called "modern primitives."

"That enormous thing, it's a bibelot.* Its scale doesn't fit it. Out-of-scaleness is the symbol of tyranny. Slaves created the fussy arts of Indochina (microphilia) and bank architecture (macrophilia). Actually both are forms of necrophilia."

Lucilla, or an introduction to dictatorship: we have reached the first floor and are running the gauntlet of the mammoth Salon * canvases. David * to the right, David to the left. . . .

"He didn't have faith. The monster. The people of David's sort are sculptor-architects. They regard painting as a form of polychrome sculpture. They translate, transpose. The contrast of the robes in 'The Lictors' is borrowed from the engraver's grisaille.* The blue is the stencil blue one finds in popular prints. How proud he was of his high-relief whites!"

At *"The Coronation of Napoleon"*:

"What an incredible thing to do! Those huge candlesticks, for example, painted again and again in perspective, what a nightmare! It is the opposite of painting, it is physical labour. Only in sculpture are art and work connected. The sculptor needs to exercise his body. I distrust skinny sculptors."

* bibelot: a small ornamental object, a trinket.
* Salon: at first, the name given to what became an annual exhibition of works by members of the French Royal Academy, held in the Salon d'Appollon in the Louvre; after the Revolution, it was thrown open to all artists, but the jury who selected the paintings to be exhibited notoriously used its power to exclude artists of whom it disapproved; thus the term "Salon painting" is associated with academic and "official" styles.
* Jacques Louis David: (1748–1825), member of the Academy; painted, in the neo-classic style, large pictures on historical or mythological themes; his success at the Salon of 1784 established his reputation.
* grisaille: monochrome painting in shades of gray, often resembling sculptured relief.

Fatigue is death's fifth column, sneaked into life by dictatorship. Death sticks to David. In front of the *"The Portrait of Madame Récamier":*

"It's funereal. He has rediscovered, perhaps unconsciously, the attitude of the deceased on Etruscan tombs."

Deeper and deeper into fatigue's kingdom. Ingres' * *"The Apotheosis of Homer":*

"Professor's art. Homework! How could such a marvellous artist fall in this trap! You can see how he tired himself painting it. Dante changed into a caryatid by the ram's horns of the column behind him—that's the pedant's pun."

About Picot's * *"Love and Psyche":*

"Classical painters, educated by statues, endow their male figures with undersized phalluses, and this causes confusion in girls educated by museums. The academic artists starts to copy plaster folds from childhood. They will remain his great love. Trees, clouds, faces—he would like to translate everything into coloured plaster folds. Folds fascinate, they are the sensuality of children. Van Gogh * was obsessed by the ear because it contained all folds: sheets, a woman's shape. It was a form of eroticism. Folds tell everything—too much, in fact. One of the painter's great worries is to make sure that no involuntary symbols hide in his folds. Then, too, folds are connected with the oldest of all the arts: embalming. Folds embalm reality and thereby deify or sublimate it. The best folds I have seen are in a portrait of Lenin. The draped chairs in it are the clouds in the apotheoses—those levitations and ascensions—in the Virgins by Raphael * or Rubens.* The history of art as viewed by the historians is an embalming concern. One likes relics, not living people. The living disturb. Churches like administrators, not martyrs. Any museum is essentially a wax museum."

Fortunately, *"The Death of Sardanapalus"** cheers us up.

Dictatorship, terror, fatigue, silence, or (it amounts to the same thing) imposed speech make up the constellation whose evil influence manifests itself by the disappearance of script.

"All good pictures are based on a script, a handwriting. If we don't see this signature, this handwriting, we enter into something frightening (with Puvis' or

---

* Jean Auguste Dominique Ingres: (1780–1867), dominant figure in the nineteenth-century French neoclassic school; fiercely antagonistic to Romantic art, especially to the work of Delacroix.
* François Edouard Picot: (1786–1868), minor French neoclassic painter, a pupil of David.
* Vincent Van Gogh (1853–90), Dutch post-impressionist painter.
* Raphael: (1483–1520) great Italian painter of the High Renaissance.
* Peter Paul Rubens (1577–1640): Flemish painter, deeply influenced by the Renaissance painting he had studied on a visit to Italy.
* "The Death of Sardanapalus": by Eugène Delacroix (1798–1863), major painter of the French Romantic movement; when this painting was exhibited at the Salon in 1829, Delacroix was violently attacked for his brilliant colors and free handling of his material.

Ingres' *'The Apotheosis of Homer'*), in which it's no longer the artist but society that paints."

We stand before Giotto's * *"Saint Francis Receiving the Stigmata"*:

"To represent the house, the tree, is a little like writing 'tree,' 'house.' It's like executing beautiful hieroglyphs. What renders pictures like 'The Apotheosis of Homer' frightening is the fact that their creators have been eliminated: there is no longer any writing in them, only a projection of images, of clichés. Whereas in the 'Sardanapalus,' you can always see the personal writing."

Still, since there is a message in Ingres, there must also be some writing. . . .

"Put it this way then," Steinberg explains, "Delacroix's work is handwriting, Ingres' is typography."

Is the hand that essential?

"Yes. There is no writing without the hand and everything that lies behind the hand, all the architecture that weighs on it, moves it—biology, geology, man's history. Writing is the tip of an enormous inverted pyramid."

So all writing is automatically good?

"No, there are bad kinds. In bad writing, you see society's pathological side —like those calligraphic devices they teach girls in finishing schools. Bad writing is artistic bureaucracy—it's an offence against nature. If man expresses himself only through society's means, he has wasted his life; and that is what society wants him to do."

Saint Francis, in brown serge, is kneeling at the foot of the mountain:

"Triangles, circles, rectangles: the composition (a pentagon) is very rigid but not visible. It is a tightrope-walking act. The rays emanating from the saint's hands sustain the angel's heavy image in the air. It is like a very solid mechanical toy. It is a miracle in which all the ingredients are visible. That is the beauty of miracles: they are normal, natural. The transmission of stigmata through gear-shifting or geometry delighted the art historian who saw it as the invention of didactic composition."

Is it not madness to hope that an abstract, arbitrary construction such as the alphabet will correspond to the make-up of reality? However, is the distance between a picture painted around 1450 and someone who looks at it today not just as great? And yet, it would seem as if Uccello's * *"Battle"* is the visual concretisation of Steinberg's most personal preoccupations.

"Magnificent! It is a philosophic conception of painting. The most interesting thing is the monster formed by the three figures, one behind the other, on the

---

* Giotto: (1267?–1331), Florentine painter; in his naturalism, his dramatic sense for emotional values, the new solidity of his figures, he broke away from the abstract medieval conventions, and is often regarded as the founder of modern painting.

* Paolo Uccello: (1396–1475), Florentine painter, noted for his severe experiments in perspective and foreshortening; although his later work (especially the three famous "Battle" paintings) is more decorative in character.

left. The centre part is the least interesting [it shows the victorious condottiere].* It is writing on orders, dictated. There must always be a feebler part.

"The only clear elements in the Uccello are the condottiere, the heads and the rumps of the horses. Everywhere else there are monsters, still lifes. Those flags, those plumes. . . . People have tried to imitate this picture to show war's horrors. But Uccello was frightened, fascinated, by the horror of armour, of hooves. It was his nature. This metaphor of terror holds only for him. Extended to others, generalised, it becomes an allegory, hypocrisy. Strangely, the only bare thing in this picture is the condottiere's face—because he is shown frontally rather than in profile. A profile is already a mechanism, a mask. Everything else in the painting is masked, even the soldiers' legs, which are masked by those vivid colours. These are no longer feet, toes, as in the Giotto. And the breastplates, the caparisoned horses: everything here is a masquerade. Uccello is a master of camouflage. The ground, the horizon, are masked by blackness, as well as by the cage formed by the spears. The entire scene takes place in a void. It is a battle between crocodiles, tortoises and crabs locked in a cage. On the ground, only a few tufts of the old nature remain. By losing their green colour (which was suppressed by the painter himself, or by time?), these tufts of grass are bones and beards—relics in a battlefield. And the flag! A flag is always a collage, a mask. But here the flag is even more masked by its undulation, which turns it into a truly indecipherable piece of writing. But what attracts me above all is the left-hand corner: every figure wears a mask. The result is an incredible tricephalous monster.

"It reminds me of something I saw when I was living in Santo Domingo, in 1941. One night I woke up in terror. I sensed that there was something horrible near me. I switched on the light and saw ants, by the thousands, transporting a fat cockroach up the wall. The swarming mass was constantly changing shape—but the centrepiece and the logic of the labour gave it the sinister symmetry of the coat-of-arms, the accumulation of visas in my passport, the political demonstrations seen from a balcony. Grouping makes monsters."

A little farther along, Perugino's * *"Virgin and Child Between Saint Catherine and Saint John the Baptist"*:

"How marvellous! That deep green and that red! I like it because of the oleographs I used to see as a child. They lent exactly the same qualities to colours. It is something one likes not as painting but almost as pastry. One looks at it with one's tongue, not with the eyes. It is angelically simple, perfectly natural. Like Braque.* However, monsters have always interested us more than angels."

* *condottiere:* leader of a band of professional mercenary soldiers, common in Europe from the fourteenth to sixteenth centuries.
* Pietro Perugino: (1446?–1523), one of the masters of the Umbrian school of Italian painting, distinguished by a quiet, pietistic style.
* Georges Braque: (1882–1963), French painter; a founder, with Picasso, of Cubism; later he developed a non-geometric, semiabstract style, and especially liked doing still-life compositions.

St. Francis Receiving the Stigmata by Giotto

Battle by Uccello

Virgin and Child Between Saint Catherine and Saint John the Baptist by Perugino

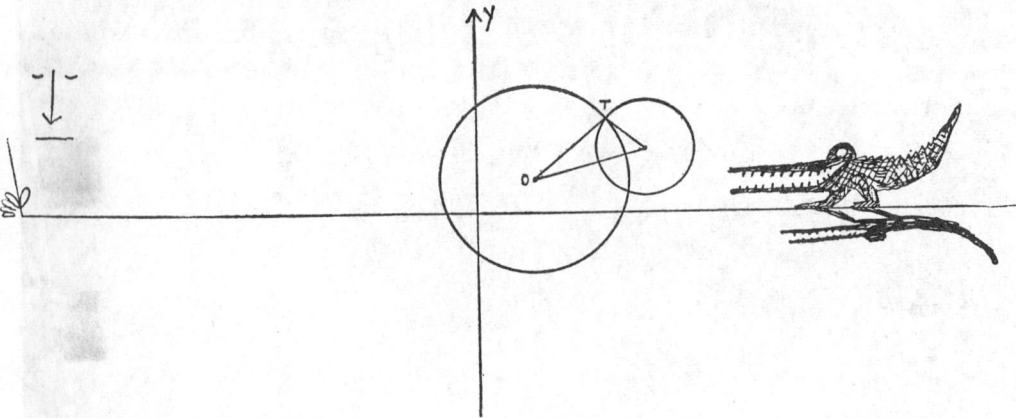

This cult of the monstrous derives from Steinberg's view of monstrosity as nature's revenge on the tyranny of the noble, the conventional, the mediocre. We are walking towards the exit when Steinberg stops short in front of Gérard's * "*Madame Visconti.*" White flesh, a dress whiter yet, stand out against the greens, blues and dark grays of garden and sky:

"From a distance it is a magnificent sight, this banana springing out of the shade. All the clichés of art are there. I would love to own something like that. A civilisation which slowly created this as its image of what the work of art should be! It contains all the battles between Saint George and the dragon, all the Madonnas, as well as quotations from Zurbarán,* Velázquez,* the Venetians. . . . The background is by a great theatre specialist. In the sky, on the other hand, he has used the watercolour technique. And in the landscape, the technique of tapestry. Top and bottom have the same intensity. That man invented the photographer's backdrop. He has a special brushstroke for grass, and he has gold following exactly the meanders of the dress. . . . It's horrible. But this is a picture of Uccello's monster—or Melville's Moby Dick, the white whale."

Monstrosity is the absence of writing. But for us to be saved, it is not enough that the writing appear; it must also persist. Yet writing disappears in the process of reading; it dissolves into the meanings that have used it as their vehicle. It must therefore exist as writing, but as indecipherable writing (or as writing that no interpretation will exhaust), like those handwritten messages with which Steinberg fills page upon page. All writing finds its fulfilment in illegibility: such

---

* Baron François Gérard: (1770–1837), pupil of David and fashionable portrait painter who turned out his showy pictures with the help of a large studio of assistants.
* Francisco de Zurbarán: (1598–1664), Spanish painter of religious scenes, especially of saints for altarpieces.
* Diego de Silva y Velázquez: (1599–1660), one of the great Spanish masters.

is the law he proclaims. There must be a good deal of truth in it if I am to judge by the difficulties (even greater than usual, no doubt because I was contaminated) which I experienced in decoding the pad on which I noted Steinberg's remarks at the Louvre.

Igor Stravinsky / Interview: Side Effects

The translated epigraph for the first part of this interview is a reminder that Stravinsky's native tongue is Russian. As a mere biographical fact the reminder isn't necessary; but it does serve to turn admiration into something like awe for his command, at age eighty-five, of English styles and of the vocabularies of the several special matters—hospitals and illness, Los Angeles, smog, television news, the contemporary fashions of dress and of undress, literature—to which he addresses himself. Stravinsky obviously loves to show off his command of idioms and information; he relishes his capacity to have fun not only in but with the English language, and he enjoys, too, lending some theatrical extravagance to his encounters with the customs and hazards of his adopted country. He likes to seem the embattled near-victim of various circumstances, but the fact that he has prevailed and will prevail is implicit in the alert, self-exhilarating wit of his talk and, perhaps even more, in that remarkable familiarity with his environment which lets him see in one feature of it some comic aspect of another. In moving through a range of topics Stravinsky reveals extraordinary intellectual energy and momentum, and they are almost entirely self-generated. The interviewer here has, or is allowed, less to do than in any other interview in this collection. In any comparisons carried out along those lines Stravinsky's interviewer would be nearly the extreme opposite of the interviewer of the racing-car driver Jackie Stewart, for example.

I

> "To avenge the wrongs of our time . . . the wounds of Igor."
> The Song of Igor's Campaign (*Nabokov translation*)

HARPER'S: Your New York appearances have become rare, Mr. Stravinsky. The cancellation of the recent Carnegie Hall concerts was a great disappointment to us.

IGOR STRAVINSKY: The city itself is hazardous for me now. I started out on a walk one afternoon during my last visit, in May, but the wind was so strong I

Yousef Karsh from Rapho Guillumette

had to lean against walls and hold on to No Parking signs. A Meter Maid was soon watching me censoriously, probably thinking I was drunk. Then a young man approached, not to offer help, but to ask for an autograph. To oblige him I inched my way like a mountain climber out of the Sixty-first Street wind tunnel and back into the hotel lobby, where I duly signed my name. But the absence of a sense of the absurd in this collector, or dealer in disguise, left me so out of spirits I did not try to resume my wind-blown promenade.

HARPER'S: Newspaper accounts of the cancellation said you had been in the hospital.

I.S.: True. I was in for two weeks because of a gastric ulcer, a "benign" one, in medicalese, but if it isn't "benign" you are as good as dead. The doctors blamed the lesion on too much alcoholic vasodilation, but of course their report mentioned only the alcohol part and omitted the virtuous intentions. I was not worried at first, and my presentiments that the real trouble might lie further upstream and that I might be headed for the rapids, were aroused only by the sudden bedside manner of certain music critics. But it *was* only an ulcer. And I recovered more quickly from it than from the hospital for ailing philanthropists to which I was sent. There the meters started to tick when I broke the electric beam of the front door, the pills came with my name on them, and the bill may still have to be paid by a charity ball.

But seriously, penitential orders—Desert Fathers * and such—seeking to update their mortifications could hardly find more ingenious exemplars than in a modern hospital. My day began at *ca.* 5 a.m. with an urgent and for some reason unpostponable mopping of the cell, and once it began even earlier, when the television started by itself. From then until "lights out," when I was regularly awakened and told it was time to sleep. I remained constantly, ulceratingly vigilant to avoid being injected with someone else's medicines, nearly having been fatally so injected during another hospital siege some years before. As it was, not many fakirs can have been so often stuck, jabbed, poked, punctured, perforated, and considering that loss of blood was the reason for my incarceration in the first place, the further withdrawals seemed remarkably copious and frequent. I also swallowed, was pumped with, breathed, absorbed through the pores, an impressive variety and volume of medications; and was between-times tourniquetted for blood pressure, radiologically sensitized, laxitized, squeezed, thumped, and subjected to much "laying on of hands."

The hospital was partly audio-tactile; the patient addresses his pleas to wall tubes sieve-ended like the speaking grills in confessional boxes, then waits for the answers to boom back at him, like flight announcements, from the ceiling. This ceiling voice reminding me to drink my milk was a torture worse than the milk itself, I might add, my tongue becoming ermine-coated, as it might

---

* Desert Fathers: fourth-century Christians who became hermits in the Egyptian desert.

have done with one of Pavlov's hounds,* at the first crackle of the sound system. Some of the humans, moreover, were as automated as the automata. One of them brought Jello three times a day and another yogurt, but so far as I could discover, neither did anything else. At first I thought this arrangement had been devised to safeguard easily overtaxed brains, but now I suspect that there weren't any (brains) and that all cerebral zones except those controlling Jello and yogurt deliveries had been surgically removed. I now wonder, since these automata had been programmed to clear away empty but not unconsumed dishes, how long it took to discover the forty or so uneaten jars of Jello in my closet.

My own nurses were not yet automated, and in fact one of them was so old-fashioned that she drew a curtain around my bed before giving me B_{12} shots *in the arm!* Her sense of delicacy was less exacting in keeping me informed on the new diseases caused by the new medicines, but she *did* teach me an effective sleep-inducing formula: gamma globulin, hemoglobin, the threshold of pain, the front door of pain, pain itself . . . zzzzzz.

My love of painkillers has now been confirmed, incidentally, and if I had been a "terminal" patient I would have opposed the anti-drug lobbyists who claim to be "entitled" to their deaths. A mere three doses of morphine were enough to "hook" me, and to raise my allowance of Demerol I began to "put" the doctors "on." I have been able to "kick" the colchicine habit—shared by gophers, incidentally—only because of the disquieting knowledge that it splits chromosomes in plant cells; but Darvon is still prescribed, and I am still, therefore, at least temporarily, a legal addict.

I still feel like Amfortas,* too, and still feel giddy at moments, as if I had stepped from a Ferris wheel. I have become a milk dipsomaniac, too, and pharmacology continues to be my "life style." Worst of all, the retreating ulcer left a booby trap of digital gout. The pains are both erratic and pedantic, hence difficult to accustom to. They are so strong at times, too—I do not believe Aubrey's * account of Milton singing in his "gout fits": he was more likely howling—that I am no longer certain of being "an artist to my fingertips." It is almost impossible to hatch any new music for the moment, as you see, and absolutely impossible to do so at the piano, the gout having deprived me of my dexterity.

HARPER'S: Only "almost," Mr. Stravinsky?

I.S.: I am composing a set of pieces provisionally titled *Etudes, Inventions, and a Sonata.* Only two selections, both ante-ulcer, are completed. I hope the plural is not over-optimistic.

---

* I. P. Pavlov: (1849–1936) physiologist who experimented with dogs and established the theory of the conditioned reflex; as the dogs salivated at the sound of a bell meaning food was ready for serving, so Stravinsky's tongue is conditioned to react in advance to the idea of milk.
* Amfortas: the sick king in Wagner's opera *Parsifal* (1882).
* John Aubrey: (1629–1697), whose *Brief Lives* (pub. 1813) has an account of Milton in his old age.

II

> *Of Paradys ne can I not speken propurly for I was not there.*
> Sir John Mandeville

> *. . . for months together, vast, wet, melancholy fogs arise and come shoreward from the ocean . . . it is always sad.*
> R. L. Stevenson on California, 1880.

HARPER'S: Why do you live in Los Angeles, Mr. Stravinsky?

I.S.: I came there for my health, originally, or in other words for the same reason I am now advised to leave, the effects of smog, and the phlegm in this interview is among them, currently being estimated as the equivalent damage from two packs of cigarettes a day; the poet's "Fear death?—to feel the fog in my throat" * has a literal meaning in Los Angeles. I had been considering La Paz as the next step, not because I had a message for Guevara,* or anyone, but because gastric ulcers are almost unknown there, owing to what is thought to be the "benign" influence of altitude on the gastric enzymes.

HARPER'S: But is Los Angeles really so different, or is it merely that certain forms of social behavior are developing there a few steps ahead of the rest of the world?

I.S.: The latter, unless by ahead you mean in the *real* sense, *i.e.*, retrogressing faster. Los Angeles is well ahead (meaning behind) in, for example, such relatively minor developments as the cinematizing of politics, and in such fads as, currently, decal tattooing and silicon rejuvenating (with which, to adapt Eliot,* most over-forty faces that you meet have been prepared). But the city is undeniably ahead also in such fairly important developments as the changeover—men to women, women to men—and in the elimination of death.

Dying in Los Angeles is only remotely connected with death. According to notices of burial bargains all over the city, the question is merely one of tidying up a few problems (namely your remains) which, thanks to certain altruistic business services, can be arranged by a telephone call and then put out of mind. In the past these advertisements struck me as merely ribald, except in the center page of Philharmonic program books where they were usually quite fitting and on bus-stop benches where, buses being the transportation of elderly poor people, they are cruel. But I see them now as the logical end of the local philosophy of life (meaning death). By taking the funereal out of funerals, and with it the nonsense about bereavement, as well as the sense of a "supreme irony" and any lingering superstitions about a "victory over the grave"; by substituting the movie-style fade-out for the baroque-style celebration with trumpets, elegies, and marble tombs; in short, by connecting the transaction to ne-

---

* Robert Browning, "Prospice."
* La Paz . . . Guevara: La Paz, capital of Bolivia, where Guevara went to begin an abortive revolution.
* to adapt Eliot: see T. S. Eliot, "The Lovesong of Alfred J. Prufrock," 1917.

gotiables, and reducing it to a supermarket service, death itself is made in some measure less unknowable. This, I think, is the reason why the moribund take such a lively interest in ascertaining the relative advantages of cremation *versus* Pharaonic preservation ("keeping up appearances") and in securing the most favorable installment ("pay now, go later") terms.

A late-lamented friend of mine, shortly before her own final collapse, told me that a salesman in the mortuary "studio" she first visited had tried to persuade her that satin was the most becoming material for her casket lining. This so annoyed my friend that she had to remind him who was dying, that it was *her* funeral and not *his*. She also said that the musical resources of this atelier included, in addition to the usual assortment of Japanese electronic canaries, a choice of "cremation blues," one of which really did make her flesh creep. Next year's advertisements will no doubt offer to present our corpses not only in their daily habiliments (Polaroid glasses are *de rigueur* * in Los Angeles) but in "not quite living color" as well.

The transsexual trend, or switching of sexual roles, is hardly less interesting but more difficult to follow because the sociological point of view is switching as well. At first the new *Nacktkultur* * was classified, by unvested interests, as merely the latest manifestation of the visual-tactile revolution. But now, under pressure from the Garment Industry, the same experts tend to see it as a reactive phenomenon. The nude waitress is a sexual suffragette, the new argument runs, a diehard demonstrator in the cause of the old-style binary design of the sexes.

However that issue is decided, the sexual acculturation of the rest of the country sags far behind Los Angeles in the free exposure of the American former-male's mammary fixations. And by this I mean not only the topless restaurant, but the ice cream parlor as well, for at the time of day when the Gaul is downing his *marc* or his Pernod the adult male Angeleno, a parent, it may be, of consenting daughters majoring in sun-tanning or surfing at UCLA, is himself ensconced in a milk pub sucking an ice cream soda. (Let me remind you that my own present incontinencies in the matter of milk do not stem from the same cause, which is that of not being properly "fed-up" as an infant.) But what of the mammalogical future? After a few centuries of natural selection, what will the Supergirl foldout of A.D. 2500 look like, taking as outside measurements of progresś the Eves of a Cranach * or Clouet * and *Playboy?*

---

* *de rigueur:* obligatory.
* *Nacktkultur:* nudism.
* Lucas Cranach: (1472–1553), court painter to the Elector Frederick; the reference is to his small-breasted nudes.
* Clouet: probably François Clouet (c. 1516–1572), son of Jean Clouet, Dutch painter at court of François I of France. François painted some mythological subjects; the reference is again to small-breasted nudes.

(Is *au naturel** restaurant service beneficial to digestion, or does simultaneous emotional involvement have a disturbing effect on the digestive juices? Does anyone ever inadvertently order a tomato or a fig leaf? Music appears to have entered the bottomless era, too, incidentally, not in the sense of profundity, of course, but, as in the film *Night Games,** in the actual use of the anatomical surfaces for musical notations.)

III

> . . . *a few are riding but the rest have been run over.*
>
> Thoreau

> *A personal God . . . who loves us dearly with some exceptions for reasons unknown.*
>
> Waiting for Godot

> *Is it possible that Shakespeare should be forced to accuse himself of ignorance of the 'ism?*
> *Is it possible that Stravinsky should be dragged through screaming streets with a pail of garbage on his white hair?*
>
> Voznesensky, March 1967

HARPER'S: Are you aware of a "gap" between yourself and the young, Mr. Stravinsky?

I.S.: Judging from a news program that I happened to watch for a moment last night, an Arizona-size canyon divides me from practically *everyone* else. The telecast began with an announcement about overpopulation that included statistics like "7.2 people"; by the end of the century the expression "joined the majority" will mean born rather than died. Then in that alternately serious and facetious man-to-man and man-to-woman (and denture-setting-on-edge) tone, the newscaster read the latest toll from "anti-personnel" (*i.e.,* people) bombs. This count included some non-Communists killed by mistake, though happily, in their case, their families are to be reimbursed, the announcer promised, at the $34 going price *per* non-Communist corpse. And so far from any trace of doubt underlying this specious recital, the price-fixing on lives and the paying for them as hunters are paid for pelts was made to sound like a matter for handshakes all around. I switched off at this point for the sake of my ulcer, though in truth the promise of a "round-up" of cultural events, meaning a movie closing and a prediction concerning tomorrow's smog, did not tempt me.

The gap between myself and the protesting young, to return to your question, is only as deep as my furrows compared to the chasm separating me from the people who can be so mendaciously mouthed to. In fact, as the Sunset Strip, that dry Ganges for hippie holies (immersions in water not being in their line)

---

* *au naturel:* i.e. in its natural state, often used of food without sauces; here applied to nude girls.
* *Night Games:* Swedish film directed by Mai Zetterling.

is only a few steps from me, I shall probably apply for membership among the young Hindus myself. As for their elders, it hardly seems to be worth asking whether they know what became of humanity. (*P.S.:* Voznesensky must have been thinking of Stokowski.* I am bald.)

IV

To occupy the sense of hearing . . . with many noises.
                                     The Imperfections of Modern Music (*1600*)

HARPER'S: Is there a talent famine, Mr. Stravinsky?

I.S.: Not of small talent, if sheer volume means anything. But I must hold my tongue. I am a dropout myself, no longer being able to attend the picnics of those small, ingrown, and not very saturnalian new-music groups through whose efforts, nevertheless, a talent of any size would most likely *have* to appear. My opinions are formed from the tapes and scores I receive in the mail. (The scores, by the way, are for the most part verbal descriptions and diagrams, some of which I suspect of being fashion-market research charts in the literal as well as graphic sense.) The yield has included nothing enticing of late, though I *have* learned something about certain operations of chance,* namely, that it is not so much that it doesn't make any difference, but that in not making any difference it still sounds very much the same. In other words, the infinite range of possibilities between those *à la mode* * landslides of noise which neither man nor beast can unscramble (I say nothing about machines), and those equally *à la mode* silences is in practice a small and patented area of cliché. And I say this not forgetting that the harvest of my mailbox is also an aleatory. But do I hear that way merely because I still require music, not just sounds, and because "open-ended" art does nothing for me, or "minimal" art (already leaning indistinguishably flatly on "no" art), or that glare of publicity and high commerce which calls itself the "Underground"?

What, may I ask, has become of the idea of universality—of a character of expression not necessarily popular but compelling to the highest imaginations of a decade or so beyond its own time—and which artist in any medium born in the last fifty years has come within a Mars shot of it?

• • •

V

Everything must be learned, from talking to dying.
                                                                              Flaubert

HARPER'S: Apart from your new composition, what has most occupied your thoughts recently, Mr. Stravinsky?

---

* Leopold Stokowski (1882–), orchestral conductor; he has a shock of white hair.
* operations of chance: alluding to the random or "aleatory" techniques developed by some avant-garde musicians, John Cage and Karlheinz Stockhausen, for instance.
* *à la mode:* fashionable.

I.S.: The ultimate *force majeure,** naturally, for in spite of all those little capsules, "mood raisers," to shoo away the truth, a hospital bed provides an abundance of both time and "motivation." The darkest thoughts have been dispelled since then, and I feel as if I had been reprieved from, say, one minute before twelve to eleven thirty (I hope it is no later than that!). But I look and feel like the Seventh Age of Man.* Stiff, creaky, slow, I am hardly certain at times of being "in possession of all of my facilities." *

The chief mental problem in being eighty-five, though intelligent people are afflicted with it already at twenty-five, is the realization that one may be powerless to change the *quality* of one's work. The quantity can be increased, even at eighty-five, but can one change the whole? I, at any rate, am absolutely certain that my *Variations* and *Requiem Canticles* * have altered the picture of my whole work, and I seek the strength now to change that completed picture just one more time.

By some unlucky circumstance I happened to reread *The Death of Ivan Ilytch* * a few months ago, and, as every reader of the story must, I have been seeing myself in it ever since. (For similar reasons Groddeck's *Das Buch vom Es* * should be avoided by anyone with an overactive auto-suggestivity.) While identifying with Ivan Ilytch, however, I admired the skill with which Tolstoy projects his hero's consciousness of growing separateness, and of the irrelevance of himself and his condition in the lives of younger people. As for Ivan Ilytch's awareness of the transparency of doctors' professionalism, of the diplomatic dishonesty of his family, and of such subtleties as the feeling that a goodnight kiss must be under-expressed to avoid a collision of unsaid thoughts —of these things my recent experience has equipped me to be an ideal literary critic. No less brilliant, as my experience has also taught me, is Tolstoy's delineation of the awareness of transitional stages; of the alternation of struggle and acceptance; of the need for sympathy and the rejection of sympathy; of the onslaughts of childhood memories; of the attacks of philosophy in endless interior dialogues about the meaning of life; and, above all, of the sick man's acute sense both of the nature of his destiny and of the terrifyingly accidental aspect of life (and how much of it *is* accident if, as Rank * claims, our birth history—instrument landings and so forth—is the all-important event in it).

But thank Heaven it is Ivan Ilytch I am talking about! As for myself, let me say: "To be continued, I hope."

---

* the ultimate *force majeure:* i.e. death.
* Seventh Age of Man: Shakespeare, *As You Like It,* II.vii.
* facilities: facetious for "faculties."
* *Variations* and *Requiem Canticles:* late works of the composer.
* *The Death of Ivan Ilytch:* (1886), novella of Leo Tolstoy (1828–1910).
* *Das Buch vom Es: The Book of the It* (1926) by the German psychiatrist Georg Groddeck (1886–1934), who held that all our diseases are expressions of unconscious conflicts.
* Otto Rank, (1884–1939): famous Austrian psychologist and psychotherapist; the reference is to his theory of birth trauma.

VIII INVESTIGATIONS

Smoking, Stonehenge, the Mafia, the financial market, the circumstances of Hitler's death, are some of the subjects investigated. The blend of researched information, opinion, and prejudice varies from case to case; the conclusions are more or less surprising; each depends upon the firm ordering of material and a strong communicable intelligence developed by the habitual use of language in contemplation, action, and comment. (Hollander is a poet, Galbraith an economist-diplomat, Kempton a political commentator of great experience, and Trevor-Roper an elegantly prolific history professor.) The McLuhan interview was an attempt to investigate the thinking of McLuhan before television cameras and for a wide audience (a modern, perhaps not very efficient way of finding things out). Chomsky's magisterial essay is an investigation of the relations between the American academy and the politico-military "establishment," and it strongly implies the need for radical action to correct the errors and nullify the dangers inherent in these relations. Cohen's work is a more abstract consideration of a related subject, namely, civil disobedience in a democratic state; it is easy for people who are aware of the urgency of such issues to be impatient with what may seem to be the rather relaxed and disengaged speculations of philosophers and academic lawyers; but it is traditional in our culture that such meditations should proceed without undue pressure from contemporaneous events, in order that their disinterested conclusions may have a chance to affect future thinking.

Courtesy of the American Cancer Society

John Hollander / From Beyond the Cigarette: Notes of a Redeemed Smoker

There is no reason to assume that the study of high arts, like literature or chamber music, reveals more of the lines of force and gravity in a culture than does the study of popular arts, like cooking and smoking—smoking, that is, not as a process for preserving and flavoring certain kinds of meat but as an activity carried out with cigarettes, cigars, and pipes by all kinds of people. For example, the French anthropologist Claude Lévi-Strauss has done an exhaustive investigation of the way modes of cooking, whether boiling, broiling, poaching, or roasting, reveal the structure of the culture within which any one of them may be predominant. Similarly, John Hollander's investigation of cigarette smoking properly concerns itself with much more than the thing itself; or perhaps one should say that cigarettes *are* much more than what any literalist would call a cigarette. A cigarette is, after all, what Humphrey Bogart made of it by his way of lighting it in one movie and inhaling it in another, or flicking it, still burning, into a gutter. Hollander's concern with the folklore of smoking and with what, to use his phrase, might be called the "mythology of tobacco dependency," is wide ranging—extending into literature, history, philosophy, daily routines, advertising, as well as film—but it has little of the anthropologist's scientific detachment. Within the first four paragraphs Hollander moves from a historical to a more intimate perspective having to do with the sexual atmosphere of smoking with a girl in a car, then to some gossipy illustrations of how one responds to friends who do not or did not smoke, and hence to some rather in-group joking about smoking and Jean Paul Sartre's "viscosity." Cigarettes and smoking are, as this investigation suggests, intimately bound up with the entire range of one's interests and needs, and Hollander's brilliant modulations from one subject to another are determined not by pedantry but by personal fascinations.

> LADY BRACKNELL: *Do you smoke?*
> JACK: *Well, yes, I must admit I smoke.*
> LADY BRACKNELL: *I am glad to hear it. A man should always have an occupation of some kind. There are far too many idle men in London as it is.*
>
> The Importance of Being Earnest

This has been the century of the cigarette. It was just about one hundred years ago that the so-called "double cigarette," using good tobacco (instead of the glorified floor sweepings called cut canister) and better paper than had previously been employed, came into being. A century is a well-rounded, symbolic time span. In actuality, the century of the cigarette starts when the real twentieth century does: in 1914. Our culture has about fifty years of really heavy cigarette smoking behind it, fifty years during which cigarettes became gradually civilized into a state of being actually prosaic.

Cigarettes were for a whole generation the very atom of the universe of lovers: the shared cigarette. This is the only equivalent in the American language for *tutoiement*.* Or the other opening gesture: they are both in a car, he driving, and she lights a cigarette for him and passes it over. The sexually charged atmosphere of the car tends to mold the significance of this one. These are both times, though, when the unending *ordinariness* of the cigarette for the real smoker can become important, for that very ordinariness gives way significantly when the cigarette becomes something very special.

Wasn't there a whole historical moment during which not to smoke was eccentric, if not actually perverse? Certainly from about 1945 to 1962 everyone I knew who didn't smoke or had stopped in the distant past seemed to be making some kind of social and moral production out of it. In some cases it was obviously just a big camp. In others, a tolerable eccentricity. In still others, a self-indulgence. Thus, *"Oh yes, I forgot. You don't smoke,"* was always more like, *"I forgot. You're a vegetarian"* (or, in some cases, *"That's right. The only card game you play is cribbage"*) than it was ever like, *"I forgot. You don't take sugar."* But it was never really like, *"Oh, you don't drink,"* notwithstanding the minim of naughtiness that there always was about it. Abstention from nicotine couldn't help smacking of the self-righteous somehow. Also, even then, it was unquestionably better for one's health not to smoke, but only in the mildly problematic way that made the risk a moral virtue. But other questions were far more important. How could one understand not only the psyche but the physique and the daily life of a nonsmoker, especially a friend, someone who was otherwise a real person, and not just another human being?

And even now, one can't imagine what it would have been like not to smoke in 1952, for example. . . . Then, when all phenomena, all manners, all conventions and even language of the heart conspired to give cigarette smoke a *substance,* a moral and spiritual *density,* that it has now lost—not to smoke was to lack an organ, somehow. Was this quality like what Sartre * calls viscosity?

The great exhaled lungful of smoke was for decades the only deep sigh to which a grown man could give vent without embarrassment. The cigarette permitted it, and that permission has now been withdrawn. What does this mean? May a man again learn to cry? For "Laughing and Grief" are, as the Mock Turtle in *Alice in Wonderland* implies, the classical languages. In our time, smoking was also taught, first to the men, then to the girls, the way undifferentiated infants are taught to laugh and cry. The inhalation of *something* (love? spiritual food? fresh air? energy? courage? anodyne? nothing?) against hurt or against fear

---

* *tutoiement:* in French, the familiar form of addressing another person: *tu* = thou.
* Jean-Paul Sartre: (1905–), French philosopher, novelist, playwright; in Sartre, the absolute contingency of the world manifests itself as viscosity, stickiness.

was being counseled in the late Thirties and thereafter. Counseled, of course, by visions, images, live gestures, myths; actual cigarette advertising was often at odds with the very nature of its product. Real smokers always knew that cigarette advertising was a kind of joke. Particular brands were always a matter of a private mystique far more elaborate than the kinds of patterns of consumption that any advertiser could anticipate. Smoking Camels was not like: rooting (say) for the Yankees, not liking broccoli, preferring to play second base . . . but it was certainly one of just such a group of preferences that can easily be changed, but that are clung to like one's name.

Why was it, incidentally, that the proliferation of so many brands of filtered crap in the late Fifties and after should have produced so much mentholation, and so many images of nautical relaxation. (Formerly, the mentholated brands, Kools and Spuds, were really *hors choix,** as far as *brands* were concerned.) Were these all just an excuse to have blue-green packages? The coincidential intersection of all this with the naval theme in British cigarettes may someday puzzle Martian sociologists.

On cigars: How fascinatingly irrelevant they are! It is very hard to remember that for most of the nineteenth century, the cigar and the pipe are Smoking, the Real Thing. All of the mythology of tobacco dependency before our own age is attached to these. Kipling: "And a woman is only a woman, but a good cigar is a Smoke" *—how innocent all that seems now. But again, all those cigars! The great and fabled ones, like Freud's, and the basic repertory in twentieth-century literature: the cigars in *The Magic Mountain;* * Eliot's Bleistein * with *his* cigar; the last, crucial memory that the singer of the Brecht-Weill *"Bills Ballhaus in Bilbao"* * can muster up—even though she forgets, in the last chorus, the very words of the song itself, and must hum along, she does finally remember the line about her lover's cigar . . . *"Er war Brasil gewohnt."* * These are all examples of the great German cigar, by far the most common numerically since the 1840s, and far more prominent phenomenally than they might be expected to be for the American imagination. The contrasting American cigar: the disgusting butt of Moon Mullins. . . .*

Pipes are, again, another matter. They were, if possible, even more irrelevant than cigars. In one's adolescence, anyone who really became committed to pipes was bogus, while a cigar was merely a pardonable affectation. Pipe smoking in our time is really much more like inland fishing than it has ever been like *smoking;* there is far too much lore equipment and general ideology, too much prattle about breaking-in and caking, too much immaterial aesthetics about grain and

---

* *hors choix:* outside the range of choice.
* "And a woman . . .": from Rudyard Kipling's poem "The Betrothed."
* *The Magic Mountain:* (1924), by the German novelist Thomas Mann.
* Bleistein: in T. S. Eliot's poem "Burbank with a Baedecker, Bleistein with a Cigar."
* *"Bills Ballhaus in Bilbao":* song from the Brecht-Weill opera *Happy End* (1929).
* *"Er war Brasil gewohnt":* "He used to smoke Brazilian cigars."
* Moon Mullins: popular comic-strip character.

the like, for pipes to be part of the smoking experience. All the more remarkable, then, to come across a passage like the following:

> Some years ago I brought myself to the decision not to smoke anymore. The struggle was hard, and in truth, I did not care so much for the *taste* of the tobacco which I was going to lose, as for the *meaning* of the act of smoking. A complete crystallization had been formed. I used to smoke at the theater, in the morning while working, in the evening after dinner; it seemed to me that in giving up smoking I was going to strip the theater of its interest, the evening meal of its savor, the morning work of its fresh animation. Whatever unexpected happening was going to meet my eye, it seemed to me that it was fundamentally impoverished from the moment that I could not welcome it while smoking. To-be-capable-of-being-met-by-me-smoking: such was the concrete quality which had been spread over everything. It seemed to me that I was going to snatch it away from everything and that in the midst of its universal impoverishment, life was scarcely worth the effort.

(Surely, so far, this is about as authentic an account of a familiar condition as has been written down. But let it continue now:)

> But to smoke is an appropriative, destructive action. Tobacco is a symbol of "appropriated" being, since it is destroyed in the rhythm of my breathing in a mode of "continuous destruction," since it passes into me and its change in myself is manifested symbolically by the transformation of the consumed solid into smoke. The connection between the landscape seen while I was smoking and this little crematory sacrifice was such that as we have just seen, the tobacco symbolized the landscape. This means then that the act of destructively appropriating the tobacco was the symbolic equivalent of destructively appropriating the entire world. Across the tobacco which I was smoking was the world which was burning, which was going up in smoke, which was being reabsorbed into vapor so as to enter into me. In order to maintain my decision not to smoke, I had to realize a sort of decrystallization; that is, without exactly accounting to myself for what I was doing, I reduced the tobacco to being nothing but itself—an herb which burns. I cut its symbolic ties with the world. . . .

This is still fine. The reader cannot help responding with the thought that he has obviously been talking prose all his life. But then the strange part:

> I persuaded myself that I was not taking anything away from the play at the theater, from the landscape, from the book which I was reading, if I considered them without my pipe; that is, I rebuilt my possession of these objects in modes other than that sacrificial ceremony. As soon as I was persuaded of this, my regret was reduced to a very small matter; I deplored the thought of not perceiving the odor of the smoke, the warmth of the bowl between my fingers and so forth. But suddenly my regret was disarmed and quite bearable.
> —J. P. Sartre, *Being and Nothingness*, trans. Hazel E. Barnes (Philosophical Library, 1956).

How could this be about a pipe? Well, it is very easy to see, after all. A cigarette smoker would have to expand the quality of to-be-capable-of-being-met-by-me-smoking into something that would cover *acts* like breathing, awakening, resting, pausing, deciding, avoiding, soothing, even, one is tempted to add, *being,* instead of mere *activities* like going to the theater or reading or having a meal. It is precisely the condition of the cigarette smoker that his "possession" of these acts cannot be rebuilt like the mere ownership of objects and activities, that he feels he must rebuild the self, the subject of the possession. This of course is nonsense. But no one can ever believe it until he has, indeed, stopped.

Starting to Stop . . . again the great fear that this will mean only and always Stopping Starting, a constant series of switching-off movements occurring more frequently than any smoking itself. The fear that the whole process will be this unendingly. No. Absolutely impossible: how could I manage this when I can't even stop starting once or twice, let alone continually? The answer, of course, is that this never has been known to happen in actuality. It's one of those deceptive models of what really happens, like Zeno's arrow * which, since at any point of time may be said to be at a particular point, certainly can't ever be in motion. So with the discrete series of switch-offs—this is merely a way of describing what one does when stopping, rather than what one actually does.

Some of the how-to-stop books may recommend more sophisticated routines like this one: *Pretend that you don't smoke.* It sounds plausible, but you and I know that it isn't. For example, I say to Jean, "Why not start right now by pretending for the rest of the evening that you don't smoke and never have?" Jean: "But how can I do that? It's no easier than not smoking." I: "No, sweetie, you don't understand the dialectic. If you pretend that you don't smoke you'll never be reaching for cigarettes or thinking about having one or the like." But what looks like feminine logical crudity is merely a grasp of the whole picture. One can't pretend that he doesn't smoke without not smoking! It's easy for someone who has stopped to pretend that he never has—all he needs do is lie. It's easy to pretend for an evening that one can't talk—one simply says nothing, knowing that one really can. But this is not the same thing as walking around, not smoking, and really being a smoker, all the time. It's more like saying to an amputee, "Pretend you have both legs." The trouble is that if it were enough like it, people would have the good taste not to recommend it.

Remember this, if it's any consolation. The books about how to stop smoking are all odious and contemptible; they are Job's comforters, in whose sincerity lay their vileness. You are sitting on your dungheap probably quietly suffering, when the comforter tells you that there is indeed an order and a justice in the Universe and all you must do is listen to them—"Do X and Y and Z," whether that means taking deep breaths every time you want a cigarette or beating your

---

* Zeno's arrow: one of the four arguments against motion proposed by the Greek philosopher Zeno of Elea (fifth century B.C.) in his attempt to defend Parmenidian monism against Pythagorean pluralism.

breast and saying, "It must have been something naughty I did," every time a boil ruptures. Fine. We agree on this. The only trouble is that you then are driven into Job's corner. Your moral superiority over the Recommenders is unquestioned—they either don't know what it's really like, or they talk as if they don't. Which, as with Job's comforters, is much the same thing. But, just as Job is driven by their total lack of moral imagination to dismiss them with, "Go Away! I've done nothing. It's just that He's perverse," you fall back on, "It's too hard to stop. I can't. I really enjoy it too much," or the like.

Writers one may have used to start smoking with in the first place: Hemingway, John O'Hara (particularly his pillow-talk, always occurring between puffs), Raymond Chandler, Dashiell Hammett, Graham Greene (despite everything: for some Christians he may contribute to the texts for use in refusing to stop). This partially comprises, for a whole American generation, the literature of initiation, sexual, aesthetic, moral, and even political. There lurks about this list a common image—a man in a trench coat, leaning against a wall in the rain, relaxed yet with narrowed eyes, a hat brim shading all but those eyes, lighting up.

He is Humphrey Bogart, of course. What he seems to have meant to a whole generation of imaginative boys was only gradually unveiled to that generation itself. One not only followed the shape of his career with one's own developing sensibility, but a revision of all the old images of him was constantly going on. Thus, the progression of identities from Duke Mantee in *The Petrified Forest* (callow, not really him yet) through various silly thug parts to *High Sierra* (the doomed man; Ida Lupino loves him because he's doomed), to Sam Spade * and then the series of textbook allegories of engagement suspended until the possibility of bad faith is obviated (*Casablanca, To Have and Have Not,* etc.), to the crisis in *The Treasure of Sierra Madre,* where the old images were blasted to pieces, and to the final ripeness of *The African Queen,* for example. And thus, at the same time, the re-visions: seeing a film with five years' perspective, having learned something about history and about oneself in the meanwhile. Not only did *The Maltese Falcon* get funnier each time, but the reasons for the undiscriminating adulation of the Parisian intellectuals, in the Forties, of so many of the films became, in retrospect, almost predictable. But through all this there was the emblem of the cigarette, its smoke helping to diffuse light in a particular way, it seemed; its lending or giving or sharing becoming a tremendous act, moral and intimate beyond any conversation; the lighting of one signaling the moment of self-awareness; the putting-out of one signaling the moment of decision. The juvenile iconography of one generation—Bulldog Drummond,* in the great moment of crisis, surrounded by evil types who will Stop at Nothing, calmly produces a gold case, flips it open, and, in answer to the menacing question

---

* Sam Spade: character played by Humphrey Bogart in *The Maltese Falcon.*
* Bulldog Drummond: British ex-army officer and gentleman sleuth; hero of a popular series of books by Sapper, the pen name of H. C. McNeile (1888–1937); Drummond later figured in radio and film dramas.

(whatever it is)—"Turkish on the left, domestic on the right." This is replaced by the infinitely more complex Bogart-smoking, which, unlike the earlier crude version of Twenties "grace under pressure" seems to be taking place in history instead of merely in dream. Its badge is not the opening of a costly cigarette case, but the flicking away of the still burning butt in a low, flat arc, into the roaring, rain-filled gutter seven feet away. Whether one actually ever saw him do it or not, this was the Bogart gesture.

All that one knew of his private life, as one got older, made the series of movie images more precious. His marriage looked good, which was more hip than Hollywood serials, he never embarrassed when quoted. He contracted, as if to show us something, throat cancer. So died Humphrey Bogart, with whom we delighted to identify.

There was Bogart, then. What were the complementary images for girls? The trench coat and berets again: Dietrich,[1] Ingrid Bergman (these were both refugee personas). Then Lauren Bacall, who became, in a way, a refugee too. All these smoking women had been kicked around a lot but had not lost their capacities for feeling. Their smoking was of a different order from that of previous generations of cigarette initiates—the long jade holder, for example, of the exotic, or the briskly lit, delicately held, frank, cross-legged smoking of the straightforward, mid-Thirties girl in comedies. No—Lauren Bacall's "Anybody got a match?" (her opening line in *To Have and Have Not*) is her confession, password, self-betrayal, and plea all at once. It shows tokens of authenticity and, without completely dropping her guard, asks for love. The girls we were taking out while starting were thinking of some of these things as they started to smoke.

Other women, of course, used cigarettes in the movies. Bette Davis' great gesture of putting out a cigarette in *Dark Victory*, for example; but I dare say that one must perhaps be homosexual to feel anything for Bette Davis in the way that we and our girls, even that we through our girls, loved the ladies in trench coats. These all reeked of men, and of the men we would like to have imagined ourselves as being. And the men around them knew what style was, too: Paul Henried in *Now, Voyager* makes the culminating gesture in a whole tradition of movie-smoking by lighting two cigarettes at once, for himself and Bette Davis; the two white cylinders fork out from his lips, not like the twin braying cones of some Dionysian *aulos* * on a Greek vase, but like two tiny, important bits of light which must be caressed, lovingly and skillfully, into health.

Mythologies; folklore; routines . . . —The nine-year-olds wait on line for noon recess; they shuffle and fuss, and toward the front of the line, one, briefcase on the corridor floor between his legs, stares out through leaded glass doors, half in dream. Then another nudges him: "Look there!" One looks around, star-

---

1. As when, in *Morocco,* "There is a Foreign Legion of women, too."

* *aulos:* wind instrument (like a double oboe) of Greek antiquity.

tled, sees nothing, hears Other's laugh: "OK, you looked." And then starts the staccato rapping of Other's knuckle, from exactly a span away, on his upper arm, while the formula is delivered in a mumbled, barely enunciated rapidity: "Name ten brands of cigarettes and whistle, go on!" The only elegant response, the only good move is to name the most recherché brands conceivable, still hardly hesitating lest the pounding raise a black-and-blue mark. Once I tried Melachrino and ended up near tears and beautifully discolored when they were not believed and I refused to revise ("Go on, say 'Old Gold' and I'll stop"). That's what names were good for.

Other games: Hits and Cracks—a Camels package lying empty in the gutter, opened at the still-closed end, revealed frequently either the block letter "H" or "C," followed by one or two digits. When we found the packages, One would cry for Hits or Cracks, the package end would be opened, and One or the Other would claim the reward in the universal coin of the rap in the triceps. That's what Camels were good for. Raleighs had coupons and, one day we discovered, were preferred by leftish parental friends because Union Made. That's what Raleighs were good for. Herbert Tareyton: the parents smoked those. They had premium cards in their packages—wild fowl, then Kings of England, then *Henry*.* Filial query: "Why don't you smoke Lucky Strike or Chesterfield?" (there was something deviant about these: they didn't advertise heavily). Parental answer: "These taste nice enough and besides, the people who make them are decent about their advertising. Have you ever noticed, dear, what it says on the package? Only, 'There's something about them you'll like.' They don't make any extravagant claims. . . ." That's what Tareytons were good for.

Other visions: Green Lucky Strike packages. Flat tins of fifty and round tins of more. The Philip Morris midget. I'd walk a mile for a. First Pall Mall ads with long and short cigarettes, King-size and Regular, being compared against the backdrop of soon-to-be-antiquated artillery. All the other visions and sounds. All the other mythologies and games. This is not superflux.

More folklore: To strike a match away from you was considered effeminate; masculinity could strut about by brandishing cigarettes! What about the unlit, white stick, waggling about in a closed mouth, say, behind the wheel of a car halted at a light? What a gesture of justified, barely contained impatience? And how bogus. . . . The incredible poignancy of the whole cigarette swagger was caught so beautifully at the end of *Breathless* when Belmondo, still inextricably involved with his image of Humphrey Bogart, blows out his dying lungful of smoke in an exaggerated imitation of his favorite movie star. And then, too, there was the crumbled swagger stick as a badge of a shattered ego. James Gleason, in *Here Comes Mr. Jordan:* we know that he is maudlin drunk before we hear him talk because of his crumpled, unlit cigarette.

* *Henry:* a mute comic-strip character.

From Beyond the Cigarette: Notes of a Redeemed Smoker

All of these mythologies, then, were teaching us how to use cigarettes in the process of becoming ourselves. Some expanse of shadows on a screen in the shape of a man, blowing even more shadowy smoke across the fictive scene before us, was showing us how to decide: one stared at something, moved awkwardly as if on camera, then lit a cigarette. With the first exhaled lungful of smoke, one had decided it, whatever it was. This was always so much a part of the language of introspection that a good director had only to show his man in this sequence for the audience to know that, indeed, some decision had been made. And indeed, they knew. . . .

More and more of our time had been taken up, since smoking happened, in institutionalized waiting, whether nominally part of work, play, devotion, giving and receiving of benefits, or even love: "Mr. Quangle will see you in a moment," "I'm sovvy but they'll be a short wait fa vawl seats," "Visiting hours are from—" "My God! It's bumper to bumper like this for three miles!" "PLEASE ARRIVE A FULL HOUR BEFORE FLIGHT TIME." The only traditional training for waiting was orthodox Christianity in its more medieval aspects, teaching that even the most energetic and concentrated activities, the highest leaps of human enterprise, the most blinding flashes of practical dream were all merely waiting for Something in any case. But if one cannot despise, or at least neglect, human time, then one must fall back on manners, as always. The only secular teaching about how to wait that we had was the use of the cigarette. It covered all the dreadfully ordinary intervals, and the great gulfs of silence before the Showdowns as well. Thus: Beau Geste * and his narrator brother John, *ein reiner Narr,** taking one of the most splendid coffee breaks in the history of Western trash—on the roof of the fort at Zinderneuf, the entire remainder of the garrison save for themselves and the dirty dog, Lejaune, dead and propped up with their rifles in the embrasures of the wall, the great Michael Geste, soon to be killed, looks around and says, "Last lap. Last swig of coffee, last cigarette. . . ." The rest is unimportant. This last cigarette contributes to the same great cloud of cigarette smoke with which our past has been filled. It is no less real than the smoke of the yet another one we light in the peculiarly sick illumination in waiting rooms at three in the morning. Or of the one we light at the window, waiting for morning to declare itself, looking out at a rare bus proceeding rapidly up the avenue far below us . . .

How can I stop smoking? How will I know whether I'm breathing or not?—
You will, Oscar. You will.

* *Beau Geste:* (1924), novel by P. C. Wren who wrote stories about the Foreign Legion.
* *ein reiner Narr:* a pure fool (Wagner's characterization of Parsifal, the hero of one of his operas).

Gerald S. Hawkins / Stonehenge and the Computer

This essay, originally in *Stonehenge Decoded,* by Gerald Hawkins and John B. White, appears in the collection of historical investigations entitled *The Historian as Detective: Essays on Evidence,* edited by Robin W. Winks. Hawkins is a professor of astronomy at Boston University. He decoded Stonehenge by feeding data on it into a computer; his conclusion, that the ancient circle of stones was an early astronomical observatory, has been attacked by some astronomers, defended by others.

In this piece Hawkins gives a popular account of what computers can do in general, and of what he asked his to do in the particular case of Stonehenge. His reduction of a highly technical matter of astronomy and computer technique to such simple language raises the larger question of popularization in general. That it is necessary there is no doubt, and we have included several examples of it, from Dubos to Chase. It is very difficult to popularize well, and the reader might like to consider this and the other examples with a view to determining the nature of the difficulties, and the degree of success achieved in these extracts.

Hawkins was writing, with the help of John B. White, for a lay audience, for he had presented his scientific findings to specialists in earlier journal articles. Such popular writing is not unlike a translation, in that it forces the scientist to use terms and comparisons which distort, however slightly. The late Anthony Boucher, who reviewed crime fiction for the *New York Times Book Review,* used to take his authors to task for their mangled efforts at putting Spanish or French into the mouths of their actors (revealing, incidentally, as if his own *The Case of the Seven of Cavalry* had not already done so, that he was a student of Romance languages at the University of California in Berkeley), and he was quick to scourge a bad translation of Simenon or Dürrenmatt. Boucher commented less frequently in his latter days, a sign that the standard of spoken Spanish had come up phenomenally among detectives or that the reviewer had given up the battle. (He reviewed favorably a book in which a feminine Sancho Panza is permitted that masculine name.) Scientists do care about how they are translated, and time and again they comment on how a popularized version of an important piece of scientific research has lost one or more of its points. C. P. Snow, scientist, humanist, and author of detective novels himself, has shown us the obvious dangers arising from the gap between the two cultures.

Bill Brandt from Rapho Guillumette

648   Investigations

We would be closer to historical truth if we read the scientific papers used by the scientists themselves as the basis for their discussion, but obviously few historians—excepting those historians of science who have taken advanced training in both disciplines—can do so. The historian, in his determination to avoid jargon and thus to be read, may have been too successful, for in the very readability of much that he has done, he has given many careless minds the impression that his discipline is less rigorous than the natural or even the social sciences. The next essay shows what may be done by a scholar from another discipline who recognizes the complexity of history and who does not conclude that it is simpler than his own area of knowledge.

As a boy in England I took little enough interest in my country's most famous ancient monument. I knew that it somehow pointed to midsummer sunrise, and I thought that the druids had built it, probably for human sacrifice, and beyond that my curiosity did not go. Actually, I grew up in Great Yarmouth, home of David Copperfield's Peggotty, and was much more curious about the mechanics of how the Peggotty family lived in that upturned boat.

Then I became an astronomer, and began to wonder about the midsummer sunrise alignment.

In 1953 I worked at the Larkhill Missile-testing Base just a mile north of Stonehenge. The idea of a missile-firing base so close to the stones naturally worried many people, but the missiles were always fired safely to the north. There is a story that during World War I a British airstrip commander had complained that the megaliths constituted a hazard to his planes, and formally requested that they be flattened, but I think that story is apocryphal.

From Larkhill I went often to Stonehenge, and soon became so interested that I took to reading about it. I quickly found that there is an immense amount of literature on the subject—so much that I would not presume to add to it now if I did not have new light to throw on the old mystery. Mythologists and sociologists and historians and other specialists as well as archaeologists—and poets—have written about the unique place, in many different ways. However, my attention quickly focused on that one astronomical aspect, the fact, first noted by W. Stukeley in 1740, that the main axis of the monument was aligned to the midsummer sunrise. That seemed to me by far the most remarkable thing about the whole structure.

I was not alone, of course, in my interest in that alignment. The sad fact is that the fame, or notoriety, of viewing midsummer sunrise over the heel stone has grown to such proportions that thousands of people come each year to watch, and to carouse. Each June an increasingly carnival-like air pervades the site, beginning the night before the sunrise itself. So many merrymakers gather that occasionally the great event is marred by near-riot. . . .

The sunrise alignment has interested other astronomers. Since the line from the center over the heel stone does not *exactly* point to midsummer sunrise today, earlier astronomers assumed that the error had been caused by time—that is, by the slow drift of the horizon point of midsummer sunrise during the centuries since Stonehenge was built. Because the angle, or "tilt," of the earth's axis with respect to its orbit plane changes with time, the point on the horizon at which the sun rises on midsummer morning moves, very slowly. For the last 9000 years this movement has been to the right along the horizon at a rate of about 2/100 of a degree per century. Since this motion can be calculated very accurately, and since it seemed reasonable to suppose that the Stonehenge builders had aligned the monument to point exactly to midsummer sunrise, it was thought that the date of building might be deduced by determining when the axis had pointed to midsummer sunrise.

In 1901 the brilliant British astronomer Sir [Joseph] Norman Lockyer made such a determination, and arrived at an estimated Stonehenge construction date of between 1880 and 1480 B.C. . . . [T]hat estimated date was quite close to the actual date (circa 1850)—but Lockyer's result was discredited when it was announced, because two of his basic assumptions were not accepted as unique or even compellingly probable by archaeologists:

1. He assumed that "sunrise" was the first flash as the top of the sun appears over the horizon, but, the archaeologists pointed out, modern man does not know whether ancient man regarded sunrise as first flash; or midpoint, when the disc's center appears; or "last flash," as the whole sun lifts clear of the horizon. The differences between the three positions are large—at Stonehenge, on midsummer day, the angular distance between the horizon points of first flash and final disc clearance, four minutes later, is almost a full degree.

2. Lockyer assumed that the Stonehenge builders had aligned the line from the center to the Avenue midpoint to point to the sunrise; if he had made the equally plausible assumption that they had intended the center-heel stone line to point to the first flash of the solstice sunrise, he would have produced an estimated construction date of about 6000 A.D.! . . .

Since Lockyer's time there had been little direct astronomical investigation of Stonehenge, although the problem of the solstice sunrise alignment continued to be of concern to those astronomers who interested themselves in the monument.

In 1960, I was writing a book on astronomy, *Splendor in the Sky*. In a discussion of eclipses, and the ancients' attitudes toward them (terror, mostly—even after the cause was understood), I wrote, "There must be a great deal of magic that has been forgotten in the course of time. . . . Stonehenge probably was built to mark midsummer, for if the axis of the temple had been chosen at random the probability of selecting this point by accident would be less than one in five hundred. Now if the builders of Stonehenge had wished simply to mark the sunrise they needed no more than two stones. Yet hundreds of tons of volcanic rock were carved and placed in position. . . . Stonehenge is therefore much more than a whim of a few people. It must have been the focal point for ancient Britons. . . . The stone blocks are mute, but perhaps some day, by a chance discovery, we will learn their secrets."

As I wrote those words I suddenly thought, "some day" perhaps is now—what better time for that "chance discovery"? I felt that the astronomic aspect of Stonehenge should be thoroughly explored.

By then I had gone from England to Cambridge, Massachusetts, to continue research and teaching. My wife and I made our plans, and the following summer we returned to England, like hunters stalking Stonehenge's celestial secret.

Like proper hunters, or explorers, we set up our base camp in a hotel in Amesbury, close by, and checked our equipment: cameras, campass, watch, binoculars, astronomical tables. Many people came that year to see the sunrise, but few could have prepared for it so meticulously. We had deliberately planned our visit for June 12, nine days before the solstice, because we feared that on the day itself the crowd would make it impossible to set up a camera on the correct alignment and have an unobstructed view, and from previous calculations I knew that the sun would then rise just one diameter to the east of its solstice position.

Dawn was to be about 4:30, daylight time. Among all our welter of preparations the night before we forgot two things: to pay our hotel bill, and to tell the manager that we would be going out so abnormally early. So feeling and looking like the archcriminals the authorities certainly would have branded us had they seen us . . . we furtively tiptoed down the long dark hall, no sound disturbing the silence except the soft ticking of the grandfather clock. . . .

Stonehenge stood black and massive against the lightening sky. From a distance it was most imposing. As we looked across the downs we saw not much evidence of dilapidation, and except for the modern road the time could have been June, 1600 B.C. A few hares were scampering around, starlings were chirping loudly, and it was quite cool. . . .

I set up my eight-millimeter movie camera with telephoto lens trained down the axis line so as to include in its field the sarsen circle archway through which the distant heel stone showed darker than the dark ground. We waited. Purple-tinged mist drifted across the valley, and we were apprehensive lest it creep up Larkhill and obscure the sun. Then suddenly, in the band of brightness to the northeast, we saw it—the first red flash of the sun, rising just over the tip of the heel stone!

It was a tremendous experience. The camera's whirring was the only reminder that we were not in the Stone Age; we experienced primitive emotions of awe and wonder.

Then, as I returned to the twentieth century and began to walk around, my astronomical sense reasserted itself. I felt strongly that the sunrise line had certainly been carefully planned, and that many other stones had also probably been laid out with alignment intended. Indeed, as I peered over and between the stones, I came to feel that *all* of them might have been placed according to some master plan; their relative positions seemed so carefully arranged. It was as if the stones were posing questions which called out for answers, like these:

1. On midsummer morning the full disc of the sun would rise over the heel stone so precisely that if I had been a Stone Age man I would have been delighted or frightened or comforted or awestruck or whatever the priest-astronomers wanted me to be—that alignment had been beautifully established.

Why?

2. The trilithon archways are astonishingly narrow. The space between the gigantic pillars is so small that you can hardly poke your head through (I tried). The average width of the three standing archways is 12 inches, and the average thickness of the bordering uprights is 2 feet, so that when you look through two aligned archways your view is restricted to a very small angle. I felt that my field of observation was being tightly controlled, as by sighting instruments, so that I couldn't avoid seeing something.

What was I supposed to see?

3. The sighting-lines through the trilithon archways extend on through corresponding wider archways of the surrounding sarsen circle. But as I walked along the axis I noticed that those three sighting-lines flashed into view one after the other, and, as rapidly, out of view again. At no one spot could I stand and look down all of those double-archway-framed vistas. Viewing had to be from well-separated points. Such an arrangement is unusual. It violates customary architectural design which radiates vistas from a central single focus, and it somehow seems not "natural." I felt again that the placement had been deliberate, to stress the importance of the viewing.

Why was the viewing important?

4. The only two outer stones now standing, number 93 and the heel stone, are both of such a height that an average-sized man looks across their tops to the line of the horizon.

Why was there such precise arrangement of height?

5. The line joining corners 91–94 of the station stone rectangle lies just a few feet outside the stones of the sarsen circle.

Did they form a sighting-line which had been preserved?

Most of those questions, I felt, might somehow be answered by astronomy. Those precise alignments and controlled vistas, so carefully directing the eye to nothing now visible, might well have been sighting-lines for celestial events such as special rise or set points of those godlike forces of prehistory, the sun, moon, planets, and stars. Primitive men observed with apprehension the places where the great rulers of day and night entered and emerged from the dark earth. It would have been natural that the Stonehengers should mark those points by various means.

I thought immediately of the most obvious "God," the sun. As most schoolboys and all sailors, farmers, navigators and astronomers know, the sun moves from north to south as June moves to December. Only two days in the year—

the spring and fall equinoxes—does it rise and set due east and west. Because of heavenly complexities involving factors like the obliquity of the ecliptic, . . . the sun swings annually from a summer declination (or celestial sphere latitude) of $+23.5°$ (north) to a corresponding winter declination of $-23.5°$ (south). That declination shift is a sizable 47°, but because of the facts of spherical geometry the angular variation in earthly viewing can be much larger. At the latitude of Stonehenge sunrise goes from a compass direction of 51°, almost northeast, at midsummer, down to 129°, almost southeast, at midwinter. That is an angular distance of 78° along the horizon, an average motion of more than 12° per month. If you have the habit of watching sunrises or sunsets, you will have noticed the astonishing rapidity with which the sun seesaws up and down the sky. And if it seems odd that in summer the sun, which everybody knows is always south of Florida and far south of England, rises to the north of an English viewer, remember that it seems to move in a small circle around the polestar once every 24 hours, and as one moves north on the earth the polestar is higher overhead. When the path of the sun is raised, it cuts the horizon closer to due north. . . . Therefore, the farther north you are, the more northerly is summer sunrise. Residents of Alaska see the June sun rise practically due north; within the Arctic Circle the sun rises and doesn't set for several days, and at the North Pole itself there is only one "day" a year, with sunrise in March, noon in June, and sunset in September.

By means of this north-south swing of the sun earthlings can follow the course of the year. If you are a sophisticated modern earthling, with knowledge of latitudes and declinations and great circles—and if you have some rather expensive equipment—you can use the sun as a cosmic calendar and tell the date to the nearest day. But if you were only a simple Stone Age man, you might regard yourself as fortunate if you could be sure of marking one special day every year, and you might well take great pains to mark it, because from such a known day you could reckon forward to the times for plantings and harvests, hunting, and other vital concerns for the whole year, until that day came again and the cycle was complete.

The Stonehenge builders had done that. Their axis pointed to the place of sunrise at midsummer. They had given themselves an accurate marker for midsummer day. What else had they done?

I thought of the sun, as its red disc moved rapidly away from the heel stone. Could Stonehenge have more solar alignments?

The noted archaeologist R. S. Newall once suggested that the axis reversed might point over some landmark, now lost, to midwinter sunset. There has even been a theory that the most important direction of Stonehenge was intended to be southwest, toward that midwinter sunset, rather than northeast, toward midsummer sunrise, because the Avenue entrance is from the northeast and most structures, like cathedrals, have the most important direction opposite the entrance. But that theory has not been proved. Nor has evidence ever been found that there was a marker on the axis extended toward the southwest.

Could there be alignments to celestial bodies other than the sun—to the stars or planets or moon?

The sun was moving eastward at such an angle that it was a full degree to the right of its first flash position when it finally lifted clear of the horizon. I marveled once more at the precision of placement of the axis and the heel stone, and at the whole precision of Stonehenge. I kept looking at those alignments formed by the ancient stones, and thinking of the many objects in the sky, and suddenly I felt defeated.

"It's no use just wondering," I said to myself. "To answer these questions—to find if these alignments have any celestial significance—we need precise measurement and comparison, a great volume of trial-and-error work—much more work than I can find time to do.

"We need the machine."

Computers are indeed wonderful things.

They are, of course, not new. For about as many ages as he has been Homo sapiens, perhaps for *exactly* as many ages, man has used things as tools to help him count. First there were fingers. Then, sticks, stones, scratches, any units which could be grouped and tallied. Then more elaborate devices like the sandglass, the running-water clock, the 2500-year-old abacus (which, in the hands of a good operator, is still faster than an electric desk calculator). The ancient Chinese also used small "counting rods," and the Romans made simple computations with little pebbles, or "calculi." The tenth-century Pope Sylvester II was credited with magical powers of divination, possibly because he mastered the abacus which the Saracens were then using. Three hundred years later the learned Roger Bacon developed many ingenious engines, some of them perhaps capable of performing calculations—he was popularly supposed to have obtained prophecies by means of a brazen head. In the sixteenth century Lord Napier, inventor of logarithms, apparently performed arithmetical and geometrical calculations with "certain pieces of wood or ivory with numbers on them, and these were called Napier's Bones." And in the seventeenth century the art of mechanical computing began to become a science.

In that century England's William Oughtred invented the slide rule. (Oughtred was the gentle cleric who taught Christopher Wren mathematics. . . .) France's Blaise Pascal designed a set of wheels "for the execution of all sorts of arithmetical processes in a manner no less novel than convenient." And Germany's Leibnitz made a crude device that could multiply.

At the end of the next century the French tried to make a monstrous calculating machine out of about a hundred human beings, but even Napoleon couldn't order that. In the nineteenth century the extraordinary Englishman Charles Babbage, responsible for dozens of innovations including flat-rate postage, skeleton keys and the cowcatcher, put together a "Difference Engine" which managed to compute simple mathematics tables. Then he dreamed, publicly, of an improved "Analytical Engine," capable of performing at the then alarming rate of sixty arithmetic operations a minute. . . . But the "Analytical Engine" never got off the drawing board. After Babbage, there was little improvement in the machine calculation field; Victorian computers were turned by hand, at a suitably stately pace.

The really great advance took place in the 1940s. Howard Aiken of Harvard, employing some of the principles of the old "Analytical Engine," devised an automatic sequence controlled electromechanical computer. His "Mark 1" was completed in 1944. The next year John von Neumann proposed internal storage, and the race was fairly on. Now, a scant twenty years later, those early collections of vacuum tubes, switches and flashing neon bulbs have metamorphosed into transistorized magnetic tape giants, which shape the world of our time, and beyond.

A modern electronic digital computer like the IBM 7090 has 50,000 transistors, 125,000 resistors and 500,000 connectors, joined by some twenty miles of wire. Its successor, the 7094, has about 10 per cent more of those components, and is about a third faster in operation. The next generation of machines will be faster in operation. The next generation of machines will be faster still. (And, oddly enough, the machines are growing smaller—because of increased use of transistors and other miniature parts, and more efficient circuitry.) . . .

[A computer] can perform 250,000 simple operations—additions, subtractions, trigonometric functions, etc.—per second, producing its answers in lines containing 26 5-unit "words" in figures or in alphabet letters or in any other code you choose, at the rate of 600 printed lines per minute. At those rates it could "read" the whole Bible in a minute, print it in some seven hours. It is uncomplaining, untemperamental, tireless—like that of mercy, its quality is not strained, nor is its capacity. Furthermore, it does not make mistakes.

In the early days of the model called "650" we were told that certain slight errors in a numerical check were caused by the machine's "warming up." We believed that. And we were wrong. The machine was trying to tell us that there was a significant error in the program that we had put into it; ultimately we had to recalculate the entire program. Nowadays if there is an error in the input program the computer not only detects it but gives the approximate description and location of the error and recommends procedure for correction. I am told that for new programmers this can be rather unnerving.

Computers are now being used for a wide range of tasks including such not obviously mathematical jobs as weather forecasting, diagnosis of illness, invention, literary composition and translation. In our space effort they are of course indispensable; without them there could hardly be a space effort. . . . Now there are some 500 man-made objects moving through space—all of them being tracked comfortably enough by the improved machines. The so-called Space Age might just as well be termed the Computer Age. . . .

Ours is becoming a computer world. University students are nudged into the computer room in their freshman year. To them, the machine is a way of life. Recently I asked a student to do a mathematical job worth about three pencil-hours. A week later she gave me the result. She had referred the problem to the 7090, which meant that for days she had to wait her turn for the use of a fraction of a second of the machine's time. In honest puzzlement I asked her, "Why didn't you use a desk calculator?" "I don't know how." "Then what about a pencil and graph paper?" "What's graph paper?" The moral, I suppose, is that one should keep one's problems hard.

Presently it is a popular occupation among the computer fraternity to compare their mechanism to the human brain. The conclusions are not disheartening —marvelous as the machines are, the brain seems still a good deal more marvelous. Like the mills of the gods, it grinds slow compared to the machines, but it grinds exceeding fine—it is original, imaginative, resourceful, free in will and choice. The machine operates at a speed approaching that of light, 186,000 mi. per sec., whereas the brain operates at the speed at which impulses move along nerve fiber, perhaps a million times slower—but the machine operates linearly, that is, it sends an impulse or "thought" along one path, so that if that path proves to be a dead end the "thought" must back up to the last fork in the road and try again, and if the "thought" is derailed the whole process must be begun again; the brain operates in some mysterious multipath fashion whereby a thought apparently splits and moves along several different paths simultaneously so that no matter what happens to any one of its branches there are others groping along. And whereas even a transistorized computer has a fairly modest number of components, the brain, it seems, has literally billions of neurons, or memory-and-operation cells. To rival an average human brain a computer built by present techniques would have to be about as big as an ocean liner, or a skyscraper. And even then it would lack the capacity for originality and free will. To initiate free choice in a machine the operator would have to insert into its program random numbers, which would make the machine "free" but uncoordinated—an idiot. . . .

In 1961, after I had decided that the problem at Stonehenge was worthy of a computer's attention, I had to fit that problem to the machine: feed it information it could digest, and ask it a question it could understand and answer. The machine requires definiteness. . . .

In this century there has been a great deal of conjecture, some of it very acute, about possible astronomic significance at Stonehenge. After Lockyer's 1901 attempt to date the monument by astronomic methods several qualified scholars have speculated about celestial orientations and significances. But their speculations lacked one thing—the calculation. Such theories should be tested mathematically. Figures alone put teeth into any astronomical theory—or, if the theorizer is unfortunate, take the teeth out.

For the machine, I needed something concrete; a well-defined problem, the best data available on Stonehenge, and a clearly stated question. Only with such input could there be effective output, and the question answered.

My question was definite enough: "Do significant Stonehenge alignments point to significant celestial positions?" The requirement of *significance,* on the ground and in the sky, was obvious. There are so many possible Stonehenge alignments —27,060 between 165 positions—that one could be found to point to practically anything in the sky, and, vice versa, there are so many objects in the sky —perhaps literally an infinite number—that hardly any line extended from earth could fail to hit at least one.

To answer that question, the machine needed pertinent information about Stonehenge and the sky.

We proceeded to give it that information.

First the programmers, Shoshana Rosenthal and Julie Cole (Judy Copeland joined us later), took a chart showing the 165 recognized Stonehenge positions —stones, stone holes, other holes, mounds—and placed it in "Oscar," an automatic plotting machine. Then they placed the cross hairs over each position and singular geometric point like the center and the archway midpoints, pressed the button, and "Oscar" punched each point's X and Y coordinates on a card. The X-Y intersection or origin was arbitrarily set well outside the charted area, in the southwest quadrant, so that all coordinates would be positive.

Then they went to the computer. They primed it with the geographic information—the latitude and longitude of "Oscar's" origin point, the compass orientation of the axes, and the scale—and they instructed it to do three things:

1. extend lines through 120 pairs of the charted points (some pairs, such as neighboring points, were judged valueless as alignment indicators),

2. determine the compass directions or azimuths of those lines,

3. determine the declinations at which those lines going out from Stonehenge would hit the sky. (If the heavenly bodies are regarded as lying in a hollow sphere enclosing the earth then the circles on that sphere corresponding to latitude circles on earth are called declinations.)

I hope this is clear. Perhaps it would help to put it this way: it was as if they told the machine to stand at each of the selected points, look across each of the other points to the horizon, and each time report what spot of the sky—the declination only—it saw.

This priming process, the programming of the machine, took about one day.

Then they gave the "Oscar" cards to a computer operator, who fed them into the machine. In a few seconds it transferred the card information to magnetic tape, scanned the tape, processed the information according to the programmed instructions, and shot forth its result—some 240 Stonehenge alignments translated into celestial declinations. (The 120 pairs yielded twice as many alignments because each line was considered as pointing in both directions.)

That task took the machine less than a minute. It would have kept a human calculator busy for perhaps four months. (To check the machine, Mrs. Rosenthal did one of the computations by hand. It took her four hours.)

And so we had half of the answer to our question. We knew where the important Stonehenge alignments met the sky, the declinations. The next part of the question was, "Were those declinations celestially significant? Did they mark special rise or set points of special heavenly bodies?"

We noticed at once that among the declinations which the machine had produced there was a large number of duplications. Figures approximating + (north) 29°, +24° and +19°, and their southern counterparts, −29°, −24° and −19°, occurred frequently. We decided to see what celestial bodies were close to those declinations.

Quickly we checked the planets. The closest one was Venus, but its maximum declination, ±32°, was not close enough. . . .

Then we ran through (nice phrase!) the stars. The six brightest stars are, in order, Sirius, Canopus, α Centauri, Vega, Capella and Arcturus. Of those, only Sirius, the brightest, was near. Sirius is at declination −16°39′ now, but in 1500 B.C. was at about −18°, according to Lockyer—the stars change declination at different rates, their positions as seen from earth being affected by their own actual motion, called "proper motion," as well as the motion of the earth's axis relative to the celestial sphere. . . . There seemed no probable significance to the possible star alignments; even if further calculation showed that Sirius worked exactly at some date in the past and one or two more alignments of fainter stars turned up, this is just what one would expect from pure chance. Furthermore even a bright star like Sirius can only be seen at rising under extremely favorable weather conditions. Fainter stars are totally invisible on the horizon. We decided to try the most obvious celestial bodies, those prehistoric deities, the sun and the moon.

This time the result was astonishing. Repeatedly and closely those declinations which the machine had computed seemed to fit extreme positions of the sun—which I had suspected that they might—and also—which I had *not* suspected—the moon. Pair after pair of those significant Stonehenge positions seemed to point to the maximum declinations of the two most significant objects in the sky.

I say "seemed" because at that stage we were using a preliminary search program of no great celestial accuracy. The stone alignments and resulting declinations as produced by the machine were as exact as the original chart allowed, but we did not then have correspondingly precise positions for the sun and moon as of the time of Stonehenge. We were using only rough approximations, gotten by mentally chasing those objects backward 4000 years in time. To verify the apparent correlations we needed precise sun-moon extreme positions as of 1500 B.C.

Back, of course, to the machine.

We gave it the present solar-lunar extreme declinations and the rate of change, and instructed it to determine what the extreme declinations had been in 1500 B.C. At the same time we programmed the machine to calculate the direction of rise and set of the sun and moon. Not knowing what the Stonehengers might have chosen we allowed three definitions: (a) sun just showing, (b) sun's disc cut in half by horizon, and (c) disc standing tangent on the horizon. There is about 1° difference between the direction of (a) and (c), which of course is not very great, but I wanted to determine if possible what the Stonehengers had chosen as their definition.

And now I must try the reader's patience with some more basic astronomy. I must explain a little about the moon.

I have explained that the sun moves from a northernmost maximum position of $+23°.5$ declination in summer to a corresponding $-23°.5$ extreme southern declination in winter. Just the reverse motion is true of the full moon. It goes north in winter, south in summer. And it has a more complicated relative motion than the sun; it has two northern and two southern maxima. In an 18.61-year cycle it swings so that its far north and south declinations move from 29° to 19° and back to 29°. Thus it has two extremes, 29° and 19°, north and south. This pendulum like relative motion is caused by the combined effects of tilt and precession of the orbit and it is much too difficult to clarify quickly; even an astronomer has trouble visualizing the processes involved. Here it is only necessary to understand that the moon *does* have two extreme positions for every one of the sun.

To position the sun and moon as of 1500 B.C. took the machine a few more seconds. The declinations it reported were $\pm 23°.9$ for the sun and $\pm 29°.0$ and $\pm 18°.7$ for the moon. The most cursory glance showed us that those declinations were close, very close, to the ones determined by the Stonehenge alignments.

We compared the figures carefully. There was no doubt. Those important and often-duplicated Stonehenge alignments were oriented to the sun and moon. And the orientation was all but complete.

As I have said, I was prepared for *some* Stonehenge-sun correlation. I was not prepared for total sun correlation—and I had not at all suspected that there might be almost total moon correlation as well. For what the machine's figures showed was this:

To a mean accuracy of less than one degree, 12 of the significant Stonehenge alignments pointed to an extreme position of the sun. And to a mean accuracy of about a degree and a half, 12 of the alignments pointed to an extreme of the moon.

. . . [N]ot one of the most significant Stonehenge positions failed to line up with another to point to some unique sun or moon position. Often the same Stonehenge position was paired with more than one other to make additional alignments. And of the 12 unique sun-moon rise-set points, only two—the midsummer moonsets at $-29°$ and $-19°$—were not thus marked.[1] . . .

It was an extraordinary correspondence.

And the precision of the alignments was noteworthy. The best fit was with the assumption of the sun or moon tangent on the horizon. . . . [T]he average accuracy of the sun lines was $0°.8$ and the moon lines $1°.5$. These average errors are caused to a large extent by two "bad" archways with errors of $3°.2$ and $5°.4$ on the western side. . . . Because of the slanting direction of sunrise, an error of $1°$ in the vertical direction corresponds to about $1°.6$ in the horizontal, at $24°$.

Usually a scientist does not discuss errors. When all precautions have been taken, an error is recorded without comment because a second attempt might reduce the error and a third attempt cause it to be larger again. An error is an error is an error.

But at Stonehenge we might learn something by such discussion.

Firstly, . . . when I wrote [my] *Nature* article I had no information about actual skyline—afterwards I obtained a chart showing actual skyline altitude variations around the site. . . . However, neither the theoretical uniform skyline nor the actual skyline as of today would necessarily correspond to the skyline that circled Stonehenge in 1500 B.C. Trees growing then where now there are none could have elevated that ancient skyline by some $0°.2$—which would mean that an error presently recorded at $+°.2$ might actually then have been 0.

Secondly, we found disagreement between one plan and another, and from the data available we were uncertain which plan was more correct. This gives an uncertainty in each figure of about $±0°.2$. . . . This is annoying but not serious. Bear in mind that $0°.5$ is a small angle for a naked-eye observer.

Thirdly, some of the trouble may have occurred when the priests were laying down the lines. The sun is easy to see during the several critical days at midsummer and midwinter, and sighting errors would be small. But the full moon had to be observed on *the* night of full moon at *the* particular year of a 19-year cycle. If it was cloudy, and the lines were set the night before or the night after full moon, the moon would not have been exactly at its extreme. When this happened, the error would have been positive when the moon's declination was positive and negative when the declination was negative. . . .

Fourthly, Stonehenge is not what it used to be. Stones have tumbled over to lie broken or to be re-erected by modern cranes. The worst errors involve stones that have disappeared long ago—24, 15 and 20. For these, I could only make an estimate of the original positions. Perhaps the errors for these three alignments should be left blank until the archeologists can provide more information. Is there a hole beneath the turf near the expected position, is the hole a foot or two displaced from the estimates that I made? Furthermore, it is just possible that

1. The stones which would complete these two alignments should by symmetry be near Aubrey hole 28, but this area beyond the ditch has not been thoroughly excavated.

construction was deliberately halted at some stage of the work, because the builders realized that the design problem they had set themselves was insoluble. A completely symmetrical structure could not have exactly fitted the asymmetrical sky positions.

Finally, the most serious displacement of all may be due to modern man. . . . [T]he moonset archways 57-58, 21-22 . . . fell in 1797. . . . The Ministry of Public Buildings and Works pulled them up straight in 1958, but the stones were originally in shallow holes and it was difficult to reset them exactly. My calculations show . . . there is a horizontal displacement of 16 inches in one or the other of the archways; perhaps that shift has been caused by the re-positioning of these massive blocks.

Then again the sunset trilithons are presently in a sorry state. The great trilithon is broken, having fallen hundreds of years ago. Although 56 was re-erected in 1901, several authors have questioned the accuracy of the restoration; the stone is not perpendicular to the Stonehenge axis but is turned counterclockwise by several degrees. The summer sunset trilithon is half fallen and the corresponding arch marked by 23 is unreliable. Stone 23 fell, and was finally set in cement in 1964.

To support my suggestion that some of the errors are modern, note that the trilithons and archways which have never fallen are more accurately aligned.

The error for the most famous alignment of all, the midsummer sunrise as seen from the center over the heel stone, deserves particular discussion. At present a six-foot man looking from the center sees the top of the heel stone level with the distant skyline. In 1800 B.C. the first flash of the sun appeared about ¾ of a degree to the north, or left, and so the six-foot man standing in the center would have seen its lower edge pass just one-half of a degree above the top of the heel stone—*if* that stone had then been leaning at the angle it stands at today. But if the stone was upright in 1800 B.C., as I believe it was, it stood some 20 inches higher then, and the $0°.5$ error registered by the machine for its present position would have been practically zero. I have calculated . . . on the assumption that the heel stone was upright, and the Stone Age viewer saw the solstice rising sun just graze the tip of the heel stone as it moved upward and over. Here there seems no doubt that the builders intended the disc of the sun to stand exactly on the marker.

Such precision of placement is, or was, astounding. To erect a boulder as irregularly shaped and ponderous as the 35-ton heel stone so that it was horizontally aligned to an accuracy of a foot was a task difficult enough; to sink that great block into the ground just so far and no further, so that its tip was also aligned vertically to an accuracy of inches, was an achievement requiring another whole dimension of skill. How in fact, was it done? If, after erection, the stone had settled too deeply it would have been out of alignment—and how could it have been lifted? Of course, if it had not settled far enough its top could have been bashed away to lower it to the proper height—but the top was *not* bashed. Perhaps the heel stone was erected first, and the viewing point laid out afterwards?

So much for the errors.

Finally, in a consideration of these sun-moon alignments, it should be remarked how carefully those alignments were preserved, added to, and made more spectacular down through the successive waves of building. During the 300-year period of construction many people of many different thoughts and cultures came to Stonehenge. Different rulers, designers, priests and workmen set their brains and hands to the vast work of alteration, adaptation, change and creation. The great monument grew from a simple circle open toward the midsummer sunrise to a rectangle-within-a-circle to a massive and complex cathedral of stones standing in arched circles and horseshoes. Yet the oldest orientation of all, the axis alignment to summer solstice sunrise, was never lost; rather was it maintained, duplicated, emphasized. . . .

What the original builders had done was remarkable enough; to arrange a circle and a rectangle and six outlying stones so that between them, paired, they form 16 alignments on 10 of the 12 unique sun or moon points is very difficult. What the last builders did was even more remarkable; they duplicated 8 of those earlier, two-position alignments in archwayed vistas. Where the Stonehenge I and II people obtained their sighting directions by standing at one place and looking over another, the men of Stonehenge III saw 8 unique sun and moon risings and settings *through* tall stone arches. And the last builders, like the first, used one position for more than one sighting line. . . .

That final megalithic temple to the sun and moon required of its creators an absolutely extraordinary blending of theoretical, planning abilities with practical building skills. Consider the problem they set for themselves: to design and erect a circle enclosing a horseshoe in such a way that the units of both figures were regularly spaced and yet so arranged that the 5 narrow archways of the horseshoe aligned with 7 narrow archways of the circle to point to 7 of the 12 unique sun and moon horizon positions while the axis of the whole structure pointed through another circle archway to an eighth celestial position—all this to be managed with primitive tools, using "units" of stone, gigantic blocks weighing 30 tons or more. How well they solved that problem we see today.

The first builders—or rather we should say single designers with their groups of builders, because obviously there was directed planning before the construction gangs started work—needed intelligence, purpose and patience as well as physical skill and strength to create Stonehenge I. For Stonehenge II, more intelligence, and continuing purpose were required. To complete the great structure, incorporating the earlier works into a unified whole, a monumental temple with intricate celestial alignments concealed in apparent simplicity and symmetry of design—that required intelligence of a still higher order, a single purpose steadfastly maintained during three hundred years of changing populations, customs, and cultures, and varied skills beyond those possessed by many twentieth-century men. . . .

Once the machine had established that the Stonehenge builders had aligned their monument-temple to the sun and moon with such skill and persistence and impressiveness, the question of course arose, Why? Why had they gone to all that trouble? . . .

Only the archaeologists and other students of the past can ever answer that question. We astronomers with our computing machines can only provide facts for the trained fancies of those ancient-man specialists to play over.

But I would like to put forward this opinion.

The Stonehenge sun-moon alignments were created and elaborated for two, possibly three, reasons: they made a calendar, particularly useful to tell the time for planting crops; they helped to create and maintain priestly power, by enabling the priest to call out the multitude to see the spectacular risings and settings of the sun and moon, most especially the midsummer sunrise over the heel stone and midwinter sunset through the great trilithon, and possibly they served as an intellectual game.

To amplify a little on those three supposed reasons, let me state that it is well known that methods for determining the times of planting were of most vital concern to primitive men. Those times are hard to detect. One can't count backwards from the fine warm days, one must use some other means. And what better means could there be for following the seasons than observation of those most regular and predictable recurring objects, the heavenly bodies? Even in classic times there were still elaborate sets of instructions to help farmers to time their planting by celestial phenomena. Discussing the "deepe question" of the "fit time and season of sowing corne," Pliny * declared, "this would bee handled and considered upon with exceeding great care and regard; as depending for the most part of Astronomie. . . ." Doubtless there are today many farmers who time their planting by the sky.

As for the value of Stonehenge as a priestly power-enhancer, it seems quite possible that the man who could call the people to see the god of day or night appear or disappear between those mighty arches and over that distant horizon would attract to himself some of the aura of deity. Indeed, the whole people who possessed such a monument and temple must have felt lifted up.

The other possible reason for the astronomical ingenuity and contrivance of Stonehenge is, I must admit, my own invention. I think that those Stonehengers were true ancestors of ours. I think that the men who designed its various parts, and perhaps even some of the men who helped to build those parts, enjoyed the mental exercise above and beyond the call of duty. I think that when they had

---

* Pliny the Elder: (A.D. 23–79), in his *Natural History of the World* (trans. Philemon Holland, 1601).

solved the problem of the alignments efficiently but unspectacularly, as they had in Stonehenge I, they couldn't let the matter rest. They had to set themselves more challenges, and try for more difficult, rewarding, and spectacular solutions, partly for the greater glory of God, but partly for the joy of man, the thinking animal. I wonder if some day some authority will establish a connection between the spirit which animated the Stonehenge builders and that which inspired the creators of the Parthenon, and the Gothic cathedrals, and the first space craft to go to Mars.

In any case, for whatever reasons those Stonehenge builders built as they did, their final, completed creation was a marvel. As intricately aligned as an interlocking series of astronomical observing instruments (which indeed it was) and yet architecturally perfectly simple, in function subtle and elaborate, in appearance stark, imposing, awesome, Stonehenge was a thing of surpassing ingenuity of design, variety of usefulness and grandeur—in concept and construction an eighth wonder of the ancient world. . . .

Murray Kempton / Crime Does Not Pay

Of the many taped conversations in this collection this is the only piece that includes conversations from wire taps, conversations recorded without the knowledge or consent of the participants. The result is that certain aspects of the American mafioso that have been exaggerated by scholars as well as by journalists are humanized and miniaturized. Kempton makes his points effectively by juxtapositions of the taped conversations of suspected mafioso (some of it having the quality of comic, if pathetically comic, dialogue) with the often pompous, inside-dopesterism of "experts" in the field of crime. Both the authority of the experts and the power and wealth of the criminals is thereby called into question. Small wonder, then, that in writing about crime Kempton should himself be more sardonic than moralistic, more skeptical than awed, and wary at all times of the myths and counter-myths that invest any writing or thinking about crime in a society whose authorized, seemingly lawful processes are themselves so often exploitive. Perhaps for that very reason, organized crime is difficult to isolate as an object for investigation and especially elusive of statistical summary.

> "Gregory the Great tells us how the nun of a convent, walking in the garden, ate a lettuce-leaf without making the cautionary sign of the cross, and was immediately possessed by a demon. St. Equitius tor-

> *tured the spirit with his exorcisms till the unhappy imp exclaimed: 'What have I done? I was sitting on the leaf and she ate me.' But Equitius would listen to no excuse and forced him to depart."*
>
> Henry Charles Lea,
> A History of the Inquisition in the Middle Ages

The Federal Bureau of Investigation has yielded up to us the transcripts of its long eavesdropping upon the office hours of Simone Rizzo (Sam) DeCavalcante, boss of a Cosa Nostra Family seated in Union County, New Jersey. DeCavalcante was facing trial for conspiracy to extort; his counsel demanded that the Justice Department produce any wire taps that might have assisted it toward the indictment; and to his surprise, and probable chagrin, he was granted the public release of his client's conversation, the private as well as the professional, all of it faithfully and indiscriminately recorded by the special agents of the FBI, and none of it, by the way, bearing upon the particular crime charged. This mass of intimacies, disjointed and expensive though it is, carries the sizeable reward of providing us with more that we can trust than we have ever before been told about an American *mafioso* of executive stature.

Donald R. Cressey is Professor of Sociology at the University of California, Santa Barbara, and though we may think that *Theft of the Nation* is a title that might have better served the Sierra Club, the work itself comes to us with academic credentials more elaborate than any before offered in Mafia studies. Ed Reid began as a reporter in Brooklyn, which is to organized crime what Rome is to the Church. He won a Pulitzer Prize for investigating police corruption more than twenty years ago. *The Grim Reapers* is at least his fifth book in the field. Yet read alongside the real life of Sam DeCavalcante, the reports of these two authorities seem astoundingly credulous, the journalist and the academic being our chief sources of social misinformation. One of the few knowledgeable persons I can imagine believing them is Sam DeCavalcante himself; the faith of witches survives the failure of witchcraft.

The gap between such authority and the world itself begins when we set down first Dr. Cressey's notion of our general condition and then DeCavalcante's description of his particular circumstance. For example:

> The $6 or $7 billion going into the hands of ordinary criminals each year is not all profit. . . . Neither can it be assumed that the amount is divided equally among the five thousand or so members of Cosa Nostra. But the profits are huge enough that any given member of Cosa Nostra is more likely to be a millionaire than not.
>
> (Dr. Cressey)
>
> We got 31 or 32 soldiers. Most of them are old people who ain't making much. Those making money give me one third. Say one makes $600, then he gives me $200 and I don't split with anyone else.
>
> (Sam DeCavalcante, June 4, 1964)

DeCavalcante was describing his province, of course, a little while after his elevation to command of a Family of such modest dimensions as to be unlisted in most Cosa Nostra public registers. Then too he was talking to Gene Catena, whose brother Jerry was a rather more substantial figure; and DeCavalcante may have thought it wise to undervalue his estate in conversation with imperialists. For a more respectful view of the property, we have the estimate of Anthony Russo, Cosa Nostra's man in Long Branch, New Jersey: "I wish I had Elizabeth [New Jersey] locked up like you have. . . . There's a lot of money in Elizabeth."

But it is clearly not an environment productive of millionaires. Any given DeCavalcante soldier can hardly sit in his presence without giving way to confessions of indigence:

> Frank Cocchiaro told DeCavalcante that he has money problems, as he gives his wife $50 a week, pays $125 a month rent in N.J. and $115 rent per month for his wife.

In December, 1964, DeCavalcante and Frank Majuri, his underboss, meet to arbitrate a protocol dispute between Joe Riggi and Joe Sferra, two *capiregime*. "Sam, I came to you yesterday," Riggi says, "because I felt that, as an *amico nos* and a *caporegima*, I'm not getting the respect I should from Joe Sferra." Sferra's *regime* was the Elizabeth Hod Carriers local; his affront was in not relieving Riggi's father from carrying brick and finding him a lighter assignment.

"Sam, I had the understanding that our people came first," Riggi went on. "I think we went in and asked for the job before anybody else. I didn't get the cooperation or the respect from Joe. I have to answer for my father. . . . First I feel offended as an *amico nos*—that I can't go to my friend and get a favor for one of my soldiers. Second, even as a *caporegima*, I can't do nothing. I did what I did only because of my father who has lived a dog's life for three years."

These are not the problems of affluence. This penury, of course, may not be typical; the legendary metropolitan Families (the Luccheses, the Gambinos, and the Profacis) could have a dividend picture closer to Dr. Cressey's gaudy colors. DeCavalcante certainly shares that impression. In January of 1965, he tells underboss Majuri: "Listen, if we don't join these big outfits and try to make a buck, we're dead. They got the money."

Still, there are overtones in DeCavalcante's long courtship of the Gambino Family which raise doubts even about *its* majesty. His control over the Elizabeth hod carriers union was mainly useful to DeCavalcante for providing jobs for unemployed soldiers; and Carlo Gambino seems to have felt more gratitude at having its courtesies extended to his Family than comports with one's image of a great prince of unlimited resources.

In September of 1964, Joseph Zoppo, a Gambino soldier, is laid off his job as a hod carrier; and DeCavalcante taxes the local's *caporegima* with having caused this embarrassment. "What did he run to you for?" Sferra asks. "He's got a lot of nerve."

"Joe, nerve or no nerve," his Boss replies. "You know I promised Carl Gambino that we'd treat their men better than our own people. And I want it that way. . . . You see, Joe, over here, I'm trying to build a good relationship with everybody on the Commission. Our *brigata* is small, but we could do things as good as anybody else. And I told you—as long as they are *amico nostro,* I want to keep them working before anyone else."

In the end Sferra was deposed from his *regime.* One culminating offense was his loss of dignity in a traffic dispute: "The [other driver] went after him like a tiger and put Joe off his feet. When he fell he broke his foot. Now is that any way for an *amico nos* and a *caporegima* to act?" But Sferra's worse sin was in neglecting his duty to provide Cosa Nostra soldiers what special favors we can imagine as available to persons seeking common labor: "I told Sferra I was saving his life by removing him; he was defying Carl Gambino." Over who gets to carry brick?

There is indeed very little evidence in these conversations that even the major Families have attained that security beyond worry about the basic necessities. "Joe Notaro [underboss of the Bonnano Family] owes me money," Joe Bayonne says, "He owes Mike Coppola money—he can't pay. He hasn't got a quarter." Joe Columbo, who inherited the Profaci Family, steals dresses from factories, two out of each lot. These are hardly either the circumstances or enterprises of captains who rule over millionaires.

The true case is rather more like the scene described in one talk between DeCavalcante and Anthony Russo, his colleague in Long Branch:

> DECAVALCANTE: Do you know Frank [Cocchiaro] is a rough guy I have to watch. Frank would do heist jobs [armed robberies] if I'd let him.
> RUSSO: Sammy, do you know how many friends of ours are on heists.
> DECAVALCANTE: They can't support themselves.
> RUSSO: Do you know how many guys are safe-cracking? What they gonna do? Half these guys are handling junk [narcotics]. Now there's a [Cosa Nostra] law out that they can't touch it. They have no other way of making a living, so what can they do? All right, we're fortunate enough that we didn't have to move around and didn't have to resort to that stuff. What are the other poor suckers going to do? Pretty soon we'll have all the mob here [in New Jersey]. Guys are coming here asking to be put on [work gambling games], and they're friends of ours, so I put them on because I can't let them starve to death. Sam, pretty soon I may have to say no to them because I got to look out for myself. I'll help your boys when I can.
> DECAVALCANTE: My people won't starve to death. I'll feed them.

> Criminal organizations dealing only in illicit goods and services are no great threat to the nation. The danger of organized crime arises because the vast profits acquired from the sale of illicit goods and services are being invested in licit enterprises in both the economic sphere and the political sphere. It is when criminal syndicates start to undermine basic economic and political traditions and institutions that the real trouble begins.
>
> (Dr. Cressey)

> No, Bob, we're doing real good here. I don't know how long it's going to last, but we're doing okay. If I can continue for two or three years, I will be able to show $40,000 or $50,000 legitimately and can walk out. Then my family situation will be resolved.
>
> (Sam DeCavalcante)

Experts on the Mafia conceive of its legitimate businesses as disguises; Sam DeCavalcante thinks of his as an escape from the instabilities of illegitimacy. His chief licit enterprise is the Kenworth Corporation, a plumbing and heating supply house in Kenilworth, N.J. It is very much a Family business, having been bequeathed to him by Nick Delmore, the deceased head of what is now called the DeCavalcante Family. His partner is Lawrence Wolfson, who, if he cannot with full assurance be described as a legitimate business man, is certainly a licensed one. DeCavalcante seems to have brought little wealth to the partnership except the weight of his name as a Cosa Nostra boss; building contractors use Wolfson and DeCavalcante to bribe construction trades labor leaders for exemption from union conditions, and reward this service by buying their plumbing from Kenworth.

Wolfson appears to have indulged this special sales technique with so much more enthusiasm than DeCavalcante ever did that these even arose complaints that he was damaging DeCavalcante's good name.

"You are known as a shakedown artist, Sam," his cousin Bobby Basile tells him. "You are shaking the contractors down! Do you think anybody would come in here and tell you this, Sam? Do you know that to the outside world your reputation is unbelievable? They dread the thought of coming in and talking to you. How come Larry Wolfson can get $150-a-unit more than anyone else?"

"Our equipment and jobs are much superior," DeCavalcante answers, to which Basile gives reply, "Don't you believe it."

A few days afterward DeCavalcante feels compelled to bring up the peril of greed with his partner. The FBI summarizes:

> Subject criticized Lawrence Wolfson for his aggressiveness in "grabbing people" on union matters. Subject pointed out the dangers of

being charged with extortion if they continue this activity. He noted that he feels very strongly about jeopardizing their legitimate business. He is willing to finish whatever arrangements are now pending but has strictly forbidden Larry to start any more deals between contractors and labor officials.

Speaking in confidence, subject told Larry that his purpose in bringing Frank Cocchiaro into his business (Imperial Refrigeration and Air Conditioning) was to keep an eye on him. He described Frank as a "professional thief" who was heading for disaster as he got older.

Stealing seems to DeCavalcante an altogether less fruitful occupation than it does to Dr. Cressey, because DeCavalcante has been there. The advantage of the illicit over the licit is finally described in a conversation between Wolfson and Joseph Ippolito, a DeCavalcante soldier:

Ippolito told Wolfson that he is making $700–$800 a week in his mason business. Ippolito claims that he is doing better at the mason business than with the numbers business he has. Ippolito claimed he lost $1300 a day and $1200 the next in paying off hits and believes that his numbers business is on the decline. . . . He would give up his numbers in a minute if DeCavalcante would let him. Ippolito says he owes $50,000 to various people and DeCavalcante will not let him give up the numbers until he repays all the money he owes. Ippolito says he sweats out all day to 6:00 p.m. when he finds out what the day's number is.

Dr. Cressey accepts that canon of Mafia studies that a numbers bank is all but guaranteed a profit. We have plainly been pursuing the wrong witches; DeCavalcante's experience indicates that when an old gypsy woman in East Harlem dreams a number, it comes up alarmingly often enough to wreck the bank. The DeCavalcante Family introduces the Twin Double Lottery to Northern New Jersey; in December, 1964, Lou Larasso reports the total business down to $100 a day; in January, Whitey Danzo, as soldier-in-charge, has to confess a $6000 loss on just one number.

"DeCavalcante," the FBI reports, "apparently intends to relinquish his one-third interest in the operation to Frank Cocchiaro as soon as he returns to Florida."

The men holding knives at the throats of American businessmen. . . .

(Dr. Cressey)

Larry explains that "we" want to sue Pako (phonetic) for selling Kenworth inferior valves and pumps. Larry mentioned that in addition to Pako the following firms are involved: Essex Plumbing Supply, Jani-

> trol and Federal Boilers. . . . Larry feels that Pako will settle rather than go to court. . . . Sam disagrees with Larry.
>
> (Special Agent Brudnicki, summarizing DeCavalcante transcripts, September, 1964)

The foreign relations of Cosa Nostra—its attitude toward outside institutions like the businessman and the politician—constitute the heart of the mystery and the one least reducible to the simplicities. That is the way with international matters; when two sovereign entities come to negotiate, it is a rare observer who can resist dividing the sides into a wrong one and a right one. Foreign policy is invariably mythic. Dr. Cressey's errors are those of a patriot; to him, the Mafia is foreign and legitimate business is native. His work falls quite naturally into the spirit of Cold War studies.

Still the changeless key of nationalism wears out all but the deafest or hardiest ear after a while; one expatriate in Paris, after being hammered upon by the Gaullist myth for ten years, said that his mind felt like a tired piano. We commence to cry out for the opposite, particularly in moments of distaste for ourselves. The more dreadful we know Saigon to be, the lovelier we conceive Hanoi. It would otherwise be curious that the most popular of all examples of literature about the Mafia should be Mario Puzo's *The Godfather,* a novel celebrating the counter-myth of a Don, just, omnipotent, and in every way the moral better of the respectable Americans with whom he deals. We want, I suppose, in times of self-disgust to believe in Uncle Vito Corleone as we already do in Uncle Ho.

But long immersion in the affairs of Sam DeCavalcante does not carry with it quite enough such consolation when we surface. We can fairly compare his ethical sense to the norms prevailing in honest trade only in small snatches of his conversations with Joseph Wilf and Samuel Halpern, two builders who made him their broker with corruptible labor unions. There is here no intimation of terror on DeCavalcante's side, but considerable indication of chicanery by both:

> DeCavalcante claimed that he does not make a nickel on arranging these payoffs and that he and Wolfson are paid only by being allowed to do the heating-plumbing work on those contracts on which he arranged the labor peace.

That statement is, of course, false; it seems to be the Family custom to take half of all packages assembled for distribution to union officials. But, on their side, Wilf and Halpern are so slow to pay that DeCavalcante complains continually that he has had to lay out his own money, and is finally driven to say that he will make no payoffs "before receiving the money aforehand":

> DeCavalcante told them that he wants payoff money from them in the future and when he asks for it and does not expect to be kept waiting.

DeCavalcante told them that, any time they feel they can do better with someone else to arrange their payoffs, they are welcome to stop seeing him.

His dealings with businessmen seem to have the soundly based tenor of mutual distrust familiar to the construction industry with no distinct moral advantage for either party.

In his own Family, DeCavalcante appears altogether a better master than the character of his servants deserves. Dr. Cressey expatiates at length on the Cosa Nostra code with its emphasis on "(1) *extreme loyalty* to the organization and its governing elite; (2) *honesty* in relationships with members; (3) *secrecy* . . .; and (4) *honorable behavior* which sets members off as morally superior to those outsiders who would govern them." Dr. Cressey sounds very much the way Louis Budenz * and Whittaker Chambers * used to sound when they were describing the iron moral fiber of the enemy, and he sustains some of the same contradictions by the facts.

Indeed, we draw that same impression of general Family delinquency which common sense ought to have led us to expect from the conduct of persons who have led the life these have. DeCavalcante's day is a fairly continuous and seldom effectual engagement with lethargic soldiers, wandering husbands, and insufficiently trustworthy lieutenants: "Louis Larasso is a cockroach." . . . "Corky can't seem to settle down. He sent me a message that he's going to start stealing again" . . . "I have to keep Danny Noto in the Family because he is a moneymaker."

In addition to his own troops, policemen and labor officials constitute the two categories of citizens beside whom DeCavalcante seems assured of his own moral superiority. The Family assumes that, in cases of arrest, the police steal your watch unless advance precautions are taken. When Angelo Bruno complains that one DeCavalcante soldier had once confessed himself a numbers banker ("No friend of ours is supposed to sign a statement with the police") De Cavalcante offers the sovereign excuse that Joe's poor wife had been caught with the numbers and that the police had threatened to take her in unless he confessed himself solely responsible.

"We're all married, Ange," DeCavalcante explains. "What man will let his wife go through an embarrassment *standing alone with detectives* being questioned?" In his youth, Bruno severely replies, the police had caught him and his

---

* Louis Budenz: American journalist, labor organizer, professor of economics; witness for the Government in numerous Communist trials; author of *The Bolshevik Invasion of the West* (1965).
* Whittaker Chambers: (1901–61) former agent of a Communist spy ring who left the Party in 1938; in 1948 he named Alger Hiss as a fellow spy in the prewar years; Hiss was finally indited for perjury; the case made a great stir and began what is known as the McCarthy Era.

wife in the same situation. *"I gave them $700 to take me alone.* I didn't sign no statement."

The unredeemed dishonor of the labor skate * is taken as much for granted, although it occasionally surprises:

> Bernie noted that Joe Perucci [a construction union delegate] claimed only to have received $250 all last year. Sam was astounded that he would say this because he recalled giving him $225 on one occasion at Ned's Ranch House and another $225 three months later.

But duplicity in the building trades is a habit about which nothing can be done. Sam Halpern discovers that he and DeCavalcante have each made a separate payment to an officer of the painters union for the same favor: "DeCavalcante was angered at the man for accepting a double payoff, but told Halpern not to say anything to this man, as it would be bad for Halpern to embarrass him."

"It would be bad to embarrass this man . . ."—that, you finally decide, is one of the two dominant thoughts in the night mind of the *mafioso,* the other being Angelo Bruno's reminder: "Sam, you are a man who is watched."

So all confrontations with persons whose morals are too much better or too much worse than one's own seem to end with the recognition that one is helpless. Sam DeCavalcante's only struggle with a force of unmixed purity comes when he intervenes in the strike of Local 1199 of the Drug and Hospital Workers against the Northfield Nursing Home in Plainfield: "This is a slap in the face to me. . . . I got money in there. . . . You better watch your step where you put your feet. . . . Tell [the union president] he better not threaten people or I will wash every street with him. . . . Cars overturned . . . fights in the streets . . . police beaten up . . . this sort of thing stopped in the 20's. . . . We're more educated now. . . . I wouldn't want to take you to court."

After such fulminations, the union continues its effronteries as though there were no Sam DeCavalcante; and, after two days, he can only press his clients to compromise: "Everybody is trying to save face. They don't want to embarrass me and I don't want to embarrass them because we may need them again."

Indeed there runs throughout his life that same ritual pattern of threat ("Make him holler until he hears the name Sam"), followed by the revelation that the threat is without force and the weary acceptance of reality ("Remember there are situations where it is best to walk away").

Still the myth of the Mafia must be watered and cultivated, myth being the Family's main asset. Larry Wolfson flourishes it as the firm's chief article of sale: "Sam's the biggest man in the country." He is visited by Robert Rapp, a state plumbing inspector tired of petty larceny—"Five dollars a unit; that's like stealing a ham sandwich"—and wondering if they cannot all join together to "establish strong prices."

* skate: someone who evades a creditor.

"Everybody in this area has to go through Sam," Wolfson grandly explains to him. "We can break their backs union-wise." This, of course, is just commercial puffery; in private moments, DeCavalcante is all too aware of how small a mete his rule really runs. It seems to him a signal honor to be trusted with the *private* telephone number of Tony Provenzano, Jimmy Hoffa's New Jersey delegate. Even on one week's notice, he cannot get his nephew a reservation at the Copacabana, which belongs to the Gambino Family; reservations at the Copa turn out indeed to be matters of high strategy for the agenda of Family conferences: DeCavalcante instructs Larasso that "if he goes to the Copa again and has trouble obtaining a table, he should see CARMINE and tell him he's a friend of Dr. Joe."

And, as a man who is watched, he does not seem able to expect even those routine courtesies which society accords any property-holder. He needs a pistol permit to protect his payroll and calls the Kenilworth Chief of Police:

> Hello, Chief, how are you. Sam DeCavalcante—remember me? Kenworth Corporation . . . Listen, Chief, I need a favor . . . my cousin takes care of the payroll. We'd like to get him a gun permit for this area. . . . We're trying to stop crime. This is for protection . . . We have forty men working and we pay in cash. . . . A lot of people know he's carrying money and if they know he's got a pistol they might change their minds . . . He's a clean-cut kid—never had a pinch in his life. . . . I'll send him down for an application. . . .

(It appeared that SAM was getting noplace.)

> Okay, Buddy, take care of yourself . . . I just got 25 tickets from you people. When are you going to stop coming here with tickets. . . . Listen, it's a pleasure; it's for a good cause—anytime. Goodbye.

Now a man who cannot get this small favor from the chief of police of Kenilworth, N.J. hardly seems capable of getting large favors anywhere; and, after so many examples of futility, it becomes difficult not to wonder whether the Mafia is quite the majestic instrument which prevailing popular and scholarly opinion conceives it to be.

Can organized crime be described as a success in America? One great problem in assaying that question is that the existing research provides no really useful statistics. For example, Dr. Cressey says, "Estimates of the amount bet illegally each year range from $7 billion to $50 billion." Calculations of the sort that fail to fix a figure within $43 billion are hard to trust, and so are calculators innocent enough to entertain the possibility that every man, woman, and child in the United States is to invest $250 a year in illegal gaming.

Still there is the testimony of the *Wall Street Journal,* which in other cases has given us every reason to respect its hard-headedness:

> [The Mafia's] yearly revenues from gambling, narcotics, usorious loans, prostitution and the numbers game has been estimated at as much as $50 billion. [*WSJ*, August 12, 1969.]

But then the notion of the Mafia's infinite resource seems to be an article of faith among persons who otherwise make their living casting a very cold eye on any customer's statement of his net worth. One reason why Tino DeAngelis was able to swindle himself and other businessmen in his salad oil speculations for so long was the assumption in Wall Street that he had Mafia backing. "We figured afterwards that Tino DeAngelis must have planted the rumor that he was in Cosa Nostra," a broker who was his victim has said. "If he was backed by that kind of money, we would have known that he was good for all he owed us."

It is curious that an institution of resources reputed to be so boundless would surface in enterprises as petty as those illuminated by its investigators. As an instance of underworld penetration of legitimate enterprise, the *Wall Street Journal* picks out the attempt of the Gambino Family to capture control of the knife-sharpening concession in the Brooklyn meat industry. This raid was important enough to be directed by Paul Gambino, brother of the boss and a certified *capo-regima;* at the height of his dominance of the market he had attained a *gross business of $1600 a week* and was dividing its profits among *four* sons-in-law.

The disparity between the wealth the *mafioso* is supposed to command and the risks he will sometimes take for the smallest profits is a source of puzzlement to Ed Reid. He cites the case of Nick Nuccio, one of Carlo Marcello's New Orleans lieutenants, "with a $4-million a year bookie business," which by prevailing calculations should yield him more than $1 million annual profit. "Like others of the Mafia hierarchy, Nuccio could not keep his hand out of relatively minor matters," Reid says, "and thereby he provided one more look at that baffling facet of the Mafia character. Nuccio was caught in the act of burglarizing the safe of a large dairy in Baton Rouge in 1963."

"Why risk such punishment," Reid asks, "when you are already a chief lieutenant to a boss of bosses? Perhaps because most Mafiosi have a fatally flawed character. They always want more." But perhaps they want more because the revenues of "a lieutenant of a boss of bosses" are so much more paltry than we think them as to make such shifts as safecracking necessities to him.

Eight years ago, Daniel Bell [1] argued uniquely and persuasively that organized crime's share of the economy was shrinking rather than growing: "as an *organized* business, functioning as a chain operation across the country, with police protection, prostitution has disappeared from American life. . . . Gambling, which in the forties was the major source of illegal revenue, has declined considerably." Policy is a good case in Bell's point.

1. "The Myth of Crime Waves," in *The End of Ideology* by Daniel Bell.

"I'll tell you something about the numbers," says Joseph Valachi, a remarkable witness to the insecurity of criminal enterprise.[2] "The numbers are good only when times are bad. It's poor people that play the numbers, and, if you want the truth, most of them play because they are desperate for money, and they don't have no other way to get it."

Narcotics is the only criminal staple which appears to be enjoying an increase in demand; and here, even though we can hardly believe the repeated disclaimers of the Cosa Nostra captains that they reject such traffic as immoral, there is considerable evidence that they do think it dangerous enough to be resorted to only in moments of desperation.

"Strapped for money, Valachi followed the fashion of other Cosa Nostra soldiers in the same fix," says Maas. "He went back into narcotics for a quick buck. . . . He knew a number of members who were still in heroin, took a percentage of their shipments, and made his own distribution deals with a 'couple of colored fellows'. . . . Valachi is reluctant to talk about his narcotics period. He says he only dealt in 'small amounts to get on my feet.'" Heroin, then, remains an enterprise for freebooters, inside or outside the Family, and subject to enough ambivalence to deny that central place in its distribution which we accord the Mafia when we discuss other illegal enterprises.

Finally, even Ed Reid, after more than twenty years of turning over and over the pages of the Mafia myth, begins to wonder whether these studies may not present a lifetime of missing the point:

> Are the men of the Mafia in the thumbscrews of a power that overwhelms them. . . . Who are the suckers? The suckers themselves or the men born to bleed the suckers white? Perhaps the answer lies in a simple concept: the mob boys have reduced their lives to such common concepts of eating and drinking and sleeping that they go on each day, doing the accepted job, but really serving as slave to bigger people about whom they know nothing, like so many ears of corn in a willing windrow ready to be chopped down at the first sign of insurrection or ripeness.
>
> Who really bosses the crime syndicate?

Slaves they certainly are of our credulous imagination; and we go on picking over them. They are, after all, that precious asset to journalism, men who have crossed the shadow line beyond which they can no longer sue for libel and where they can thus be blamed, with impunity, for *everything*.

2. *The Valachi Papers* by Peter Maas. Putnam.

John Kenneth Galbraith / Financial Genius Is Before the Fall: How Fools and Their Money Are Still Being Parted

The first paragraph of this essay is worth careful attention. It explains the theme of the article (a crash is certain, but the date cannot be predicted), and it also explains the qualifications of the writer. If you did not know already that Galbraith is a famous economist you at least know now that he wrote a well-known book on the 1929 stock-market collapse. The light, anecdotal manner is not achieved at the expense of the material. A more technical, but still not heavy-footed, manner is used in the second paragraph. The third describes the strategy of the article that follows. Galbraith can make his points about the market today mostly by describing, with some picturesque detail, the course of events in 1929. The situation is somewhat different now (less marginal trading, a better understanding of proper government action) but essentially it is the same. Hence the firmness of his prediction, and the clarity of his reasons for making it.

This essay illustrates once again the importance of being well informed, but it demonstrates with equal force the kinds of skill required to make a technical subject available to a large audience: clarity, lightness of tone, well-chosen illustration.

One day in the winter of 1969 I was in Los Angeles on a political errand that called for a press conference. With an air of obvious thoughtfulness, a reporter asked me if I expected another stock market crash. I replied, as I had a hundred times since I wrote a book on the 1929 experience, that of course there would be. The only difficulty was telling when. Because of some unnatural shortage of news, this was a headline the next morning without, of course, the qualification. The following summer, when the market was falling by large coarse steps, I got a number of calls congratulating me on my foresight and one from a Pittsburgh businessman telling me that I had made him, or anyhow saved him, a great deal of money. He offered a contribution to some good cause. I felt a little guilty about these compliments, though I accepted them gracefully, for I did not want to say whether market weakness in 1969 portended a new collapse.[1] The only thing certain forty-odd years after the 1929 debacle was that *some* day, without fail, there would be another such disaster.

The reason is that the stock market is inherently unstable, the instability being

1. As, a year later, in the summer of 1970, it became clear that it did.

Cornell Capa, Magnum

related to its superbly orchestrated ability to attract people with a promise of effortless riches, give them a taste of such gains, give them the promise of a great deal more gain, persuade them that it is rewarding their financial acuity (of which they have none) or that of the people who are managing their money (which may be less) and then, usually after overcoming some preliminary setbacks which greatly add to the general state of confidence, destroy these illusions in one mortal thud. What is necessary for a new disaster is only for memories of the last one to fade, and no one knows how long that takes. This essay has primarily to do with what happened in the autumn of 1929 and it draws shamelessly on my earlier book on the subject.[2] But first I must say a word as to the way the stock market, in combination with the avarice so celebrated as an incentive of the free enterprise system, contributes to mass illusion, even insanity, and of some of the evidence of fading memory which encourages the conviction that, sooner or later, we will have another debacle.

II

The anatomy of the self-destroying speculative boom is simple. Over time with advancing technology, an increasing national product and a reliable tendency in the economy to inflation, most common stocks will rise in value. As this happens, people are attracted to the market and this causes the stocks to rise more. This further gain attracts yet more people and gradually, perhaps over a period of some years, the purchases of people looking for this increase in value come to determine what stocks are worth. Prospective earnings are still mentioned but as an afterthought—or to show that there is still some tie to reality. The knowledgeable man, as he unwisely considers himself, is now concerned with the way a stock is attracting buyer interest. That, rightly for the moment, determines its value.

Then, at some stage, the supply of buyers runs out—or dries up. Or there may be public action, e.g., a drastic tightening of bank lending, to dry up the spring. The increase falters. This causes the more nervous to get out. This in turn causes the market to falter still more. More decide to get out and the slow upward climb is replaced by a precipitate drop. As I have previously noted, there usually will be some preliminary episodes of nervousness before the climactic fright arrives. The greater the preceding buildup, the more stocks have come to depend on a continuing influx of buyers attracted by the prospect of capital gains, the more violent will be the eventual collapse.

III

This simple design is, on the whole, less interesting than the secondary insanity which it induces. Because the market is going up, almost everyone associated with the market makes money. Almost anyone can thus look like a financial genius and with little qualification or none at all. In the late twenties the nation

2. *The Great Crash,* 1929 (Boston, Houghton Mifflin Company, 1955).

was replete with instant Rothschilds. There have been even more in these last years. Then as now they were not engaged in a put-on. Most of them were perfectly sincere men who first fooled themselves as to their financial genius and then proceeded to fool other people.

The most common vehicle for manifesting this genius in the twenties was the investment trust of which there was an explosion. Instead of buying shares in the ultimate companies, the investor bought shares in a company managed by a man of genius who in turn did the investing. If these investment trusts in the late twenties sound suspiciously like a mutual fund, of which in these last years there has been an even more spectacular explosion, that suspicion is well founded. There is a technical difference between the closed-end trusts of those days and the modern fund. The former had an authorized capital which it sold and used to purchase common stocks. The investor who wanted out did not cash in his stock for its share *pro rata* * in the current value of the stock held by the company, as in the case of a mutual fund. Up until the time of the Crash, he simply sold the stock on the open market. After the Crash, he practiced Christian (or some equivalent) forbearance, for the stock in most of the investment trusts became unsaleable.[3]

One of the breathtaking discoveries of the late twenties was leverage. Nothing so marked a man of financial genius as his bold and knowledgeable use of this device. It meant that an individual or firm in one fashion or another bought common stocks with borrowed money or preferred stock. In consequence, the individual or firm could own much stock for a little investment and when the stock went up in value, since the debt (or its equivalent) remained the same, all the gain accrued to that small stake. Margin buying, which means, of course, that the individual borrows money to buy stocks, is a manifestation of leverage. The big utility and railroad promoters, whom I will mention in a moment,

---

3. One of the greatest investment trust promotions of the twenties was by Goldman, Sachs and Company, since become more austere, under the auspices of Waddill Catchings, the most notable of the contemporary financial geniuses until the Crash. In 1929 Goldman, Sachs sold nearly half a billion dollars worth of securities in its investment trusts. In 1932, the following colloquy took place before a Senate Committee in Washington:

> SENATOR COUZENS: Did Goldman, Sachs and Company organize the Goldman, Sachs Trading Corporation? [One of the investment trusts.]
> MR. SACHS: Yes, sir.
> SENATOR COUZENS: And it sold its stock to the public?
> MR. SACHS: A portion of it. The firms invested originally in 10 per cent of the entire issue for the sum of $10,000,000.
> SENATOR COUZENS: And the other 90 percent was sold to the public?
> MR. SACHS: Yes, sir.
> SENATOR COUZENS: At what price?
> MR. SACHS: At 104. That is the old stock . . . the stock was split two for one.
> SENATOR COUZENS: And what is the price of the stock now?
> MR. SACHS: Approximately 1¾.

* *pro rata:* in proportion.

bought control of their numerous companies with borrowed money. And the investment trusts sold bonds and preferred stock in large volume in order to buy common stocks and thus win the advantages of leverage for their own stockholders.

It was also learned, in the very late twenties, although no one had much thought of it before, that when stocks go down, leverage goes brutally into reverse. For now, since the claims of the bonds (or preferred stock) are undiminished, all of the fall is taken by the stock. For those who own the stock, it is a formula for becoming poor with remarkable celerity. Leverage has a similar reverse effect on reputations for financial genius.

In recent years leverage has been rediscovered. The gamier of the funds, the hedge funds in particular, have been operating on borrowed money in order to concentrate all of the gains on the stock. Heavy borrowing with resulting leverage has also been important in agglomerating the conglomerates, an outrage to which I will return. One lesson has, however, been learned. Margin trading, which was the most damaging way of getting leverage before 1929, has been circumscribed.

In 1928 and 1929, the investment trusts invested extensively in each other's securities. (If a leverage trust invested in a leverage trust, it got a terrific leverage.) Here again legislation enacted since then has been inconvenient; such financial incest is forbidden by the Securities Exchange Commission. Fortunately for genius, if not for the investors involved, the SEC's jurisdiction stops at the water's edge. So this manifestation of genius has reappeared among American entrepreneurs (notably Mr. Bernie Cornfeld) operating in Europe, and causing great hopes for enrichment among the deserving people there.

In the twenties there was particular interest in glamor stocks, among which an electronics firm, RCA, was far and away the speculative favorite. On September 3, 1929, it reached 505, up from 94.5 in the preceding year and a half. It had never paid a dividend. Glamor stocks have been greatly celebrated in these last years. Electronics have been among the favorites.

The late twenties were a period of Napoleonic mergers. These led in turn to much exchanging and reshuffling of securities, the rumors of which led to great action on the exchanges. Principally involved were the utilities and railroads—Samuel Insull, the Van Sweringen brothers and Howard C. Hopson then enjoyed an eminence that would be the envy more recently of James Ling or Charles Bludhorn. The basic technique was to issue bonds or preferred stocks with which to buy the common stocks of the companies being merged. Interest payments were then paid out of dividends. Some of the new creators were conglomerates, though not so called. Only days after the 1929 Crash, and adding appreciably to the gloom, one of these folded up. It was the Foshay enterprises of Minneapolis, owners of hotels, flour mills, banks and manufacturing and retail establishments at random sites in the United States and Canada. Its 32-story obelisk in downtown Minneapolis had been dedicated only a few weeks before by Secretary of

War James Wood at a time when the firm was already at least technically insolvent. Secretary Wood had called the tower "The Washington Monument of the Northwest." Nothing has been so admired in these last years as the rediscovery of the conglomerates. Most of them, as noted, have been built by issuing debentures or other fixed income obligations. In the case of Ling-Temco-Vought the common stock equity in 1969 was estimated at around seven per cent, the rest of the capital being long-term debt or the minority interest in the constituent firms. There was also a small amount of preferred stock. Around half of all net earnings were absorbed by fixed charges. Several other of the more admired conglomerates—Bangor Punta, General Host, Rapid-American—had a common stock equity of 12 per cent or less. Some had even larger proportions of their earnings absorbed by fixed charges than L-T-V.

In the 1920's the combines and conglomerates did well as long as they could acquire new companies—such expansion brings growth without going through the slow and tedious process of acquiring new customers. But such expansion proved to be possible only when the market was rising. That too has been the recent experience. When the market fell in 1929, reverse leverage went into effect. All earnings and more were needed to support the debt. No more money could be borrowed. A company that was busted itself was in no position to buy others, however Napoleonic its management. At this writing (1969) reverse leverage has again been operating and if the slide in the market continues and is combined with a reduction in earnings, a number of the new agglomerators will go the way of Foshay, Insull, the Van Sweringen brothers, Howard Hopson and the other men of earlier genius. Some of this earlier genius consisted less in earning money than in so keeping the books as to give this impression. That manifestation of genius has also been extensively rediscovered.

In 1929 money to borrow was scarce and interest rates were painfully high. That meant that a banker with his privileged access to funds could do a great deal for himself and his friends. The Chase National Bank was shortly to suffer painfully for the conflicting private operations of its president, the redoubtable Albert H. Wiggin. In 1929 he borrowed from the bank to sell the stock of the bank short and subsequently claimed that such operations heightened a man's interest in his business. The president of the National City, Charles E. Mitchell, gave his bank an even worse name. In the last months of 1969 an officer of the Chase was explaining how he happened to give a loan to one of the sportier of the conglomerates, Gulf & Western, just before departing to join that firm.

In 1929 the brokerage houses had trouble keeping their paper work abreast of the volume of trading. Back office problems were particularly oppressive at the time of the Crash. The paper work problem has again become very serious in recent times.

In 1929, as I have observed, margin trading was far more important than of late. In contemplating a security, there may have been more of a tendency to lose sight entirely of the firm that had issued it. (One 1929 favorite was Seaboard Air Line, a railroad. Many thought it was an aviation firm with growth prospects.) But at a homier level the parallel between the two eras is sustained. In April of 1929 an article in *The North American Review* told how women had become players of "man's most exciting capitalistic game." It explained that the modern housewife now reads that, "Wright Aero is going up [sic] . . . just as she does that fresh fish is now on the market. . . ." In August of 1969 the *New York Times Book Review* carried an advertisement for a *Teenager's Guide to the Stock Market*. "Absolutely the first book to give young people who show the slightest interest in finance. Only $5.25. Worth millions. . . ."

In the months before the 1929 Crash men of academic reputation and substance looked at the market and the mergers and put their blessing on everything that was going on. This was very reassuring. Professor Irving Fisher of Yale, a few days before the Crash, told an audience that stocks had reached a new high plateau from which they could only go on up. Even more eloquent was Professor Charles Amos Dice of Ohio State University. Looking at the financial geniuses in 1929 (some of whom were soon to be broke and a few in bad trouble with the law), he was struck by their "vision for the future and boundless hope and optimism." He noted that "they did not come into the market hampered by the heavy armor of tradition." He described their market impact in a splendid sentence: "Led by these mighty knights of the automobile industry, the steel industry, the radio industry . . . and finally joined, in despair, by many professional traders who, after much sack cloth and ashes, had caught the vision of progress, the Coolidge market had gone forward like the phalanxes of Cyrus, parasang upon parasang and again parasang upon parasang. . . ."

No academic figure in this prosaic age has matched Professor Dice's parasangs. But one, Dr. Neil H. Jacoby, on detached service from being Dean of Business Administration at UCLA to the Center for the Study of Democratic Institutions, recently held in an article of intolerable length, that the modern conglomerates, including the outrageous ones, attest, "in a broader perspective . . . to the flexibility and adaptability of the U.S. economy in response to underlying structural changes." Of their assaults on other corporate managements, he said encouragingly, "No institution of a democratic society should be above challenge." Such thoughts make one yearn for Professor Dice and his parasangs.

In 1929 any suggestion that anything was wrong was badly received. The principal offender was Paul M. Warburg, the banker and a founder of the Federal Reserve System. In March of 1929 he attacked the orgy of "unrestrained speculation" and said he feared it would "bring about a general depression involving the whole country." He was accused of "sandbagging" American prosperity. Some implied that he was short in the market. He described the experience as the most difficult of his life. It remains to be seen whether those who compare the present generation of geniuses with those of the earlier age can escape reproach.[4]

But my concern is not to find or even to suggest precise parallels between now and then any more than it is to predict when the present enthusiasm will have run its course. I am concerned with reminding everyone that financial genius consists almost entirely of avarice and a rising market. And I would like to do anything possible to keep bright the memory of the events of that first great crash. To the latter end, let me now turn back to the chronology of those days.

IV

The speculative market which ended in the Crash of October 1929 was some five to six years in the making. For a long while the movement was far from violent. At the beginning of 1924 the *New York Times* averages of the prices of twenty-five representative industrial stocks stood at 110. They had eased up to 135 at the beginning of 1925. At the close of trading on January 2, 1929, they were at 338.35. Apart from mild setbacks, notably in early 1926 and early 1928, the advance was steady. By the beginning of 1929, the speculative phase to which I adverted in the early pages of this essay had fully arrived. People were wholly preoccupied with capital gains; this being so, stocks were being bought extensively on margin. This was also an added source of market instability. If the value of the stock dropped, there were calls for more margin, i.e., for more cash, or collateral security. If the owner of the stock could not provide these, he was of course forced to sell his shares. Forced sales of this kind could greatly accelerate any downward movement of the market, and did.

There was nervousness in the early months of 1929 caused by some highly diffident warnings about speculation from the Federal Reserve. The Federal Reserve was made even more nervous by its own warnings and soon became silent. In June, stock prices started on their last great surge. Almost every day that summer the market went on to new highs. By the end of August, the *Times* averages were at 449, up 110 points since the beginning of the year. Margin accounts expanded enormously, and from all over the country—indeed, from all over the world—money poured into New York to finance these transactions. During the summer, brokers' loans to carry the margined stocks increased at the rate of $400,000,000 a month.

Not everyone was playing the market as legend holds—the great majority of Americans were then as innocent of knowledge of how to buy stocks as they are today. Subsequent estimates have suggested that as many as a million people

---

4. Actually, from some personal experience, I think the financial community and the country in general has become more tolerant of criticism. In this connection, modesty barely allows the mention of another parallel. On his death, Paul Warburg's family endowed a chair in economics at Harvard in his honor and for many years I have been the Paul M. Warburg Professor of Economics.

were involved in the speculation. During that summer, almost all of them made money—at least on paper.

V

In September of 1929 the market faltered. The first break was blamed on Roger Babson, a notable economic prophet who in early September said with stunning accuracy, "Sooner or later a crash is coming, and it may be terrific." In consequence, he added, "factories will shut down . . . men will be thrown out of work . . . the vicious circle will get in full swing and the result will be a serious business depression." Babson, like Warburg, was roundly denounced. His reputation was damaged by this premature pessimism. And for a while the market was steady. Then things went bad again. On October 18 there were heavy declines on late trading and the *New York Times* industrial averages dropped about seven points. And on the nineteenth things were worse. In the second heaviest Saturday's trading in history, 3,488,100 shares changed hands. At the close of the day the *Times* industrial index was down twelve points.

On Sunday, October 20, the break was front-page news—the *New York Times* headline read: "Stocks driven down as wave of selling engulfs market." Its financial editor, who along with the editor of the *Commercial and Financial Chronicle* was one of the few financial journalists who had never wavered in his conviction that people had gone mad, said that for the moment at least, "Wall Street seemed to see the reality of things." The news stories also made two points which the papers were to make wonderfully familiar in the next fortnight. They reported that, at the end of Saturday's trading, an exceptionally large number of margin calls went out. And they said that if the decline continued, the men of genius would do something about it. The market would have "organized support."

Things got worse on Monday, October 21. Sales totalled 6,091,870, the third greatest volume in history. There was a further and disturbing phenomenon. The anxious men and women who were watching the market throughout the country had no way of telling what was happening. Previously on big days of the bull market * the ticker had often fallen behind, and one didn't discover until well after the market closed how much richer one had become. That, however, was information for which one could wait with safety if not with patience. Now with a falling market one might be totally ruined, and not know it. Such information one needed to have. Also, even if one were not going to be ruined, there was a strong tendency to imagine it so a late ticker added to the rush to sell. From the opening on October 21, the ticker lagged and by noon it was an hour late. Not until an hour and forty minutes after the close of the market did it record the last transaction. Every ten minutes

---

* bull market: rising market, opposite of bear market.

prices of selected stocks were printed on the bond ticker, but the wide divergence between these and the prices on the tape only added to the uneasiness —and to the conviction that it might be best to sell.

However, this was not yet disaster. The Monday market closed well above its low for the day—the net loss on the *Times* industrial averages was about six points—and on Tuesday there was a rather shaky gain. Some credit for this improvement goes to Wall Street's academic prophets. Thus on Monday in New York, Professor Fisher said that the declines had represented only a "shaking out of the lunatic fringe." He went on to argue that the prices of stocks during the boom had not yet caught up with their real value. Among other things, the market had not yet reflected the beneficent effects of Prohibition, which had made the America worker "more productive and dependable." Others echoed his optimism.

By Wednesday, October 23, the effect of this cheer had been dissipated. Instead of further gains, there were now heavy losses. The opening was quiet enough, but toward mid-morning automobile accessory stocks were sold heavily, and volume began to increase throughout the list. The last hour was quite phenomenal—2,600,000 shares changed hands at rapidly declining prices. The *Times* industrials for the day dropped from 415 to 384, giving up all of their gains since the end of the previous June. Again the ticker was far behind, and to add to the uncertainty an ice storm in the Middle West caused widespread disruption of communications. That afternoon and evening thousands of speculators decided to get out while—as they mistakenly supposed—the getting was good. For many, it was too late. Other thousands were told they would have no choice but to get out unless they provided more collateral for, as the day's business came to an end, a flood of margin calls went out.

Speaking in Washington, even Professor Fisher was somewhat less optimistic. He told a meeting of bankers that "security values in *most instances* were not inflated." Almost desperately it was predicted that, on the morrow, the market would receive "organized support."

VI

Thursday, October 24, is the day history designates as the beginning of the Crash of 1929. The designation is deserved. On that day 12,894,650 shares changed hands, most of them at prices which shattered the dreams and the hopes of those who had owned them. Of all the mysteries of the stock exchange, there is none so impenetrable as why there should be a buyer for everyone who seeks to sell. October 24, 1929, showed that what is mysterious is not inevitable. Often there were no buyers, and only after wide vertical declines could anyone be induced to bid.

The morning was the bad time. The opening was unspectacular, and for a little while prices were firm. Volume, however, was large and soon prices began to sag. Once again the ticker dropped behind the market. Prices fell faster and farther, and the ticker lagged more and more. By eleven o'clock what had been a market was only a wild scramble to sell. In the crowded board rooms across the country the ticker told of a frightful collapse. But the selected quotations coming in over the bond ticker also showed that current values were far below the ancient history of the tape. The uncertainty led more and more people to try to sell. Others, no longer able to respond to margin calls, were sold out. By 11:30 a.m., panic, pure and unqualified, had taken over.

Outside the New York Stock Exchange on Broad Street a weird roar could be heard. A crowd gathered. Police Commissioner Grover Whalen, though a man of limited perception, sensed that something might be wrong and dispatched a special police detail to Wall Street to protect the peace. A workman appeared to accomplish some routine repairs atop one of the high buildings. The multitude, assuming he was a would-be suicide, waited impatiently for him to jump. At 12:30 p.m. the visitors' gallery of the Exchange was closed on the wild scenes below. One of the visitors, oddly enough, was the former British Chancellor of the Exchequer, Winston Churchill. He had never better revealed his instinct for being on hand for history.

At noon, however, things had taken a turn for the better. The long-awaited organized support materialized. The heads of the National City Bank, Chase, Guaranty Trust and Bankers Trust met with Thomas W. Lamont, the senior Morgan partner, at 23 Wall Street, the Morgan citadel. Bankers in those days were men of prestige—indeed, they were the folk heroes of the age. These were the greatest bankers of all. They quickly agreed to come to the support of the market and to pool resources for this purpose. Lamont then met with reporters to offer what achieved fame as one of the more remarkable understatements of history. He said, "There has been a little distress selling on the Stock Exchange." He added that this passing inconvenience was "due to a technical situation rather than any fundamental cause," and he told the newsmen the situation was "susceptible to betterment."

Meanwhile, word had reached the Exchange floor that the bankers were meeting and salvation was in sight. Prices promptly firmed and rose. Then at 1:30 p.m., Richard Whitney, known to be a floor broker for Morgan's, walked to the post where Steel was traded and left with the specialist an order for 10,000 shares at several points above the current bids. He continued the rounds with this largesse. Confidence was wonderfully revived, and the market now boomed upward. In the last hour the selling orders which were still flooding in from afar turned it soft again. But the net loss for the day—about twelve points on the *New York Times* industrial averages—was far less than the day before. Some issues, Steel among them, were actually higher on the day's trading.

However, this recovery was of distant interest to the tens of thousands who had sold or been sold out during the decline and whose dreams of affluence had gone glimmering. It was eight and a half minutes past seven that night before the ticker finished recording the day's terrible misfortunes. In the board rooms, speculators who had been sold out since early morning sat silently watching the tape. The habit of months or years, however idle it had now become, could not be broken at once. Then the final trades were registered and they made their way out into the gathering darkness.

In Wall Street itself lights blazed from every office as clerks struggled to come abreast of the day's business. Messengers and boardroom boys, caught up in the excitement and untroubled by losses, went skylarking through the streets until the police arrived to quell them. Representatives of thirty-five of the largest stock market houses assembled at the offices of Hornblower and Weeks and told the press on departing that the market was "fundamentally sound," adding, by way of emphasis, that it was "technically in better condition than it has been in months." The host firm dispatched a market letter which stated that "commencing with today's trading the market should start laying the foundation for the constructive advance which we believe will characterize 1930." In a small corner of heaven those financial men who are saved are required nonetheless to assemble each morning and read aloud these predictions.

VII

On Friday and Saturday following the Thursday debacle, trading continued heavy—just under six million on Friday and over two million at the short session on Saturday. Prices, on the whole, were steady—the averages were a trifle up on Friday but slid off on Saturday. Not only were things better but everyone knew it was the bankers who had made them so. They had shown their courage and their power, and the people applauded—warmly and generously. The *Times* observed that the financial community was "secure in the knowledge that the most powerful banks in the country stood ready to prevent a recurrence."

But security in knowledge notwithstanding, nothing was left to chance. Not only were financial resources mobilized, so were those of public bamboozlement. Colonel Leonard Ayres of Cleveland, another well-regarded prophet of the time, assured people that no other country could have survived such a crash so well. Eugene M. Stevens, the president of the Continental Illinois Bank, said: "There is nothing in the business situation to justify any nervousness"; Walter Teagle, the oil magnate, said there had been no "fundamental change" in the oil business to justify concern; Charles M. Schwab, the steel tycoon, said that the steel business had been making "fundamental progress" toward stability and added that this "fundamentally sound condition" was responsible for the prosperity of the industry; Samuel Vauclain, chairman of the Baldwin Locomotive Works, declared that "fundamentals are sound"; President Hoover said that "the fundamental business of the country, that is production and distribution of commodities, is on a sound and prosperous basis." A Boston investment trust took space in the *Wall Street Journal* to say, "s-t-e-a-d-y Everybody! Calm thinking is in order. Heed the words of America's greatest bankers." Only Governor Franklin

D. Roosevelt, one day to become the scourge of Wall Street and the bankers (as they saw it) criticized the "fever of speculation." No one paid any attention to *him*.

On Sunday in the New York churches there were sermons suggesting that a certain measure of divine retribution had been visited on the Republic, and there were hints that it had not been entirely unmerited. It was evident, however, that almost everyone believed that this heavenly knuckle-rapping was over and that speculation could now be resumed in earnest. The newspapers on the Sabbath were full of the prospects for next week's market. Stocks, it was agreed, were again cheap and, accordingly, there would be a heavy rush to buy. Stories from the brokerage houses told of a fabulous volume of buying orders piling up in anticipation of the opening of the next day's market. In a concerted advertising campaign in Monday's papers, stock market firms urged the wisdom of buying stocks promptly. On Monday, October 28, the real disaster began.

Trading on Monday, though in great volume, was smaller than on the previous Thursday—9,212,800 as compared with the nearly thirteen million. But the sustained drop in prices was far more severe. The *Times* industrials were down forty-nine points for the day. General Electric was off 47½; Westinghouse, 34½; Tel. & Tel., 34. Indeed, the decline on this one day was greater than that of all the preceding week of panic. Once again a late ticker left everyone in ignorance of what was happening save that it was very bad.

At 1:10 p.m., there was a momentary respite; Charles E. Mitchell of the National City Bank—with the Chase National Bank, then one of the two largest—was detected going into Morgan's and the news ticker carried the magic word. Steel rallied and went from 193½ to 198. But this time Richard Whitney did not appear; "organized support" was not forthcoming. Mitchell, on the strength of later evidence, was almost certainly negotiating a much-needed personal loan. He too had been caught by the market, and for the next ten years he would be defending himself in various courts in consequence. The market weakened again and in the last hour three million shares changed hands at rapidly declining prices.

The bankers also assembled that day at Morgan's and remained in session from 4:30 p.m. to 6:30 p.m. They were described only as having a "philosophical attitude," and they told the press that the situation "retained hopeful features." But, alas, it was also explained at the conclusion that it was no part of the bankers' purpose to maintain any particular level of prices on the market. Their operations were confined to seeing that the market was orderly—that offers would be met by bids at some price, and that "air holes", as Mr. Lamont dubbed them, would not be allowed to appear in the market. In other words, the bankers had decided to go short on promises and this was chilling news. To the man who held stock on margin, disaster wore only one face and that was falling prices. He wanted to be saved from disaster. It was poor comfort that his ruin would be accomplished in an orderly and becoming manner.

VIII

Tuesday, October 29, was the most devastating day in the history of the New York Stock market, and it may have been the most devastating in the history of markets. Selling began at once and in huge volume. The air holes, which the bankers had promised to close, opened wide. Repeatedly and in many issues there was a plethora of selling orders and no buyers at all. Once again, of course, the ticker lagged—at the close it was two and a half hours behind. By then 16,410,030 shares had been known to have been traded—more than three times the number that had once been considered a fabulously big day. Despite a closing rally on dividend news, the losses were again appalling. The *Times* industrials were down forty-three points, thus finally cancelling all of the huge gains of the preceding twelve months. Losses on individual issues were far greater. By the end of the trading, members were near collapse from strain and fatigue. Office staffs, already near the breaking point, now had to tackle the greatest volume of paper work yet. By now, also, there was no longer any certainty that things would get better. Perhaps they would go on getting worse.

During the first week of the Crash, it seems likely, the slaughter had been of the innocents. Now the well-to-do and the wealthy—the men of affairs—were suffering. During the first week the board rooms were crowded; now they were nearly empty for the new victims had facilities for suffering in private. On this day at noon the bankers met again and they met once more in the evening but there was no suggestion that they were even philosophical. In truth, their prestige had been falling even more disconcertingly than the market. During the day the rumor had swept the Exchange that, of all things, the "organized support" was busy selling stocks. Lamont met the press after the evening session with the trying assignment of denying that this was so. Nor for the moment was there much effort at reassurance from other quarters. James J. Walker, then the remarkably indolent Mayor of New York, offered the only constructive proposal of the day. Addressing an audience of motion picture exhibitors, he asked them to "show pictures that will reinstate courage and hope in the hearts of the people."

On the Exchange itself it was felt that courage and hope might best be reinstated if the market were simply closed and everyone given a breathing spell. This forthright thought derived impressive further support from the fact that everyone was badly in need of sleep. The difficulty was that the announcement of the closing of the Exchange might simply worsen the panic. At noon on October 29 the issue came to a head. So as not to attract attention and add to the panic, the members of the governing committee left the floor in twos and threes to attend a meeting; for reasons of secrecy the meeting itself was held not in the regular room but in the office of the Stock Clearing Corporation below the trading floor. The panic roared on a few feet above. Richard Whitney, who besides being the instrument of salvation the previous Thursday was also Vice-President of the Exchange, later described the session. (Later still, and no longer a financial genius, Whitney would go to jail for covering his losses in applejack, peat and other products with stolen money.) Nervous brokers lit cigarettes, stubbed them out and lit fresh ones. The air soon became blue. Everyone wanted a respite from the agony. Quite a few firms needed a few hours to ascertain whether they were still solvent. But caution was on the side of keeping the market open until it could be closed on some note of strength and optimism. So the reluctant decision was to carry on. Again in the financial district the lights glowed all night. In one brokerage house an employee fainted from exhaustion, was revived, and promptly put back to work again.

Next day, just when salvation seemed impossible, salvation came. Volume was still enormous, but prices were much better—the *Times* industrials rose thirty-one points. No one knew why; maybe it was because all the available prophets had again gone all out with optimism. On the evening of the twenty-ninth, Julius Klein, a leading figure in the national administration, took to the radio to remind the country that President Hoover had said that the "fundamental business of the country" was sound and prosperous. To be certain that no one missed the fundamental point, he added: "The main point I want to make is the fundamental soundness of [the] great mass of economic activities." On Wednesday, Waddill Catchings, the financial genius hitherto mentioned, announced on returning from a western trip that general business conditions were "unquestionably fundamentally sound." (The same could not be said for the stock of the great investment trusts he had launched—Blue Ridge, Shenandoah, Goldman, Sachs Trading Corporation. Reverse leverage was reducing their value to next to nothing.) Of more importance, perhaps, from Pocantico Hills the aged John D. Rockefeller issued his first public statement in many years: "Believing that fundamental conditions of the country are sound . . . my son and I have for some days been purchasing sound common stock." Eddie Cantor, describing himself as Comedian, Author, Statistician, and Victim, said later, "Sure, who else had any money left?"

Just before the Rockefeller statement arrived, things looked good enough on the Exchange so that Richard Whitney felt safe in announcing that the market would not open until noon the following day (Thursday) and that on Friday and Saturday it would stay shut. The announcement was greeted by cheers. Nerves were everywhere past the breaking point. On LaSalle Street in Chicago, a boy exploded a firecracker. The rumor spread that gangsters whose margin accounts had been closed out were shooting up the street. Several squads of police arrived to make them take their losses like honest men. In New York the body of a commission merchant was fished out of the Hudson River. His pockets contained $9.40 in change and some margin calls.

IX

No feature of the Great Crash was more remarkable than the way it passed from climax to anticlimax to destroy again and again the hope that the worst had passed. Even on the thirtieth when the Crash was over the worst was still to come. It was only that it came more slowly. Day after day during the next two weeks prices fell with monotonous regularity. At the close of trading on October 29, the *Times* industrials stood at 275. In the rally of the next two days they gained more than fifty points. By November 13 they were down to 224 for a further net loss of fifty points. By then the stock of investment trusts was largely unsaleable. Their creators had, by now, ceased to be men of genius. A similar demotion will come one day to the men of genius who now command the mutual funds—or to some of them. So also to the men who made the conglomerates—or some of them.

The levels of late 1929 were wonderful compared with what were to follow. On July 8, 1932, the average of the closing levels of the *Times* industrials was 58.46. This was not much more than the amount by which they dropped on the single day of October 28, and considerably less than a quarter of the closing values on October 29. But by then, of course, business conditions were no longer sound, fundamentally or otherwise. The United States, indeed the industrial world, was in a terrible depression.

X

In later years when considering the causes of the Great Depression, economists were inclined to exculpate the market. Looking back at the summer before the Crash, evidence was found that production of consumers' goods was outrunning demand. Business investment was thus due for curtailment. The stock market, it was held, was only reflecting this change in underlying factors, i.e., in those fundamentals. None of this is so. If the economy was in recession in the late summer of 1929, it had certainly gone unnoticed. Unnoticed it couldn't have affected the market. And if there was weakness, the current doctrine and view held that it would be self-correcting. The stock market crash was the consequence of the preceding speculation. And the collapse itself had an immediate, powerful and unmistakable effect on the economy.

In the weeks following the Crash, spending for automobiles, radios and other durable goods fell off sharply as people reacted to their own misfortunes or those of their neighbors. Business investment plans were scaled down as firms found themselves pressed for cash, worried about existing debt and unable to raise new money. As security values fell, business and bank failures increased, forcing further contraction of spending and investment by those affected. The Crash of 1929, along with the speculation that preceded it, was, in short, a prime cause of the depression that ensued. My own guess is that the further consequences of the next speculative episode will be less alarming. There is a better knowledge now of what the government might do to offset the deflation in consumer and investment spending that would follow such a collapse. The danger could thus be contained. But it would be better not to have the speculation and crash in the first place.

Hugh Trevor-Roper / The Last Days of Hitler

This is the climax of a very unusual historical investigation. Professor Trevor-Roper, an Oxford historian before and after World War II, served in Germany as a British Army Intelligence officer during the last months of the war. In September 1945, some four months after Hitler's death, Trevor-Roper's superior officer invited him to investigate that event, of which almost nothing was known at that time. He had access to captured documents, and also the survivors from Hitler's bunker. Piecing together the reports of eye-witnesses, doctors, generals, and the evidence of Goering and other high party officials, Trevor-Roper gave what is basically the definitive account of the conduct and policies of Hitler in the last days of his life. He himself states its purpose: "to establish the facts of Hitler's end, and thereby to prevent the growth of a myth." Of the success of the book, considered as a means to that end, he was not over-sanguine, but he placed his confidence in the power of hard fact to inhibit the growth of a Hitler myth. At least he had shown beyond cavil that Hitler was dead. Insofar as this fact is generally held to have been established, the investigation was one of quite exceptional importance, although Russian evidence released much later throws some doubt on the details of Hitler's suicide.

The author's professional accomplishments were essential to the enterprise; the historical problem under examination was of the very recent past, but the method employed—the collation of all available information, the cross-checking of variant versions, the decision, after a careful weighing of the probabilities, in favor of one against another—this is the method of all good history writing. There must be evidence for every statement (note the provision of authority for the description of Hitler's corpse on the stretcher and the lapse of time in the burning of his body) and yet there must be reasonable inferences as to the character of individuals and the behavior of people under great stress (the dancing in the bunker). Another historian would have made a different job of this, for history is a discipline which makes the same demands on every historian but allows him his own style. Trevor-Roper happens to be a conscious stylist, and anybody who has read Gibbon will hear a faint imitative note of that writer. But it will be agreed that this personal quality adds to the value and authority of the work.

When von Below * left the Bunker,* Hitler was already preparing for the end. During the day the last news from the outside world had been brought in. Mussolini was dead. Hitler's partner in crime, the herald of Fascism, who had first shown to Hitler the possibilities of dictatorship in modern Europe, and had preceded him in the stages of disillusion and defeat, had now illustrated in a signal manner the fate which fallen tyrants must expect. Captured by partisans during the general uprising of northern Italy, Mussolini and his mistress Clara Petacci had been executed, and their bodies suspended by the feet in the market place of Milan to be beaten and pelted by the vindictive crowd. If the full details were ever known to them, Hitler and Eva Braun * could only have repeated the orders they had already given: their bodies were to be destroyed "so that nothing remains"; "I will not fall into the hands of an enemy who requires a new spectacle to divert his hysterical masses." In fact it is improbable that these details were reported, or could have strengthened an already firm decision. The fate of defeated despots has generally been the same; and Hitler, who had himself exhibited the body of a field-marshal on a meathook, had no need of remote historical examples or of a new and dramatic instance, to know the probable fate of his own corpse, if it should be found.[1]

In the afternoon, Hitler had had his favourite Alsatian dog, Blondi, destroyed. Professor Haase, his former surgeon, who was now tending the wounded in his clinic in Berlin, had come round to the Bunker and killed it with poison. The two other dogs belonging to the household had been shot by the sergeant who looked after them. After this, Hitler had given poison capsules to his two secretaries, for use in extremity. He was sorry, he said, to give them no better parting

---

1. It has often been stated, by those whose imagination is stronger than their memory, that Hitler's decision was affected by the fate of Mussolini. An account of the table-talk of the prisoners at Nuremberg, ascribed to the chief psychiatrist at the Trial and printed in the *Sunday Express,* August 25th, 1946, even quotes Goering as saying, "You remember the Mussolini incident? We had pictures of Mussolini dead in the gutter with his mistress, and hanging in the air upside-down. They were awful! Hitler went into a frenzy, shouting: 'This will never happen to me!' " A glance at the dates disposes of this romance. Goering saw Hitler for the last time eight days before Mussolini's death. Goering may have seen pictures of Mussolini's body in captivity; Hitler never. Such is the value of unchecked human testimony, on which, however, much of written history is based.

* Lieutenant-Colonel Nicolaus von Below: Hitler's air-force adjutant and the last person to leave the Bunker before Hitler's death.
* The Bunker: built underneath Hitler's original headquarters, the old Reich Chancellery, which had been bombed out and burned; the Fuehrerbunker was that part of the Bunker reserved for Hitler's own use and consisting of eighteen rooms, "all of them small, cramped, and uncomfortable" (*The Last Days of Hitler,* Chapter 4).
* Eva Braun: Hitler's close and loyal friend for at least twelve years, although during his lifetime, knowledge of this friendship was confined to their immediate circle, and nothing, according to Trevor-Roper, is known of their more intimate relations. On the day before he died Hitler married Eva Braun, apparently in order to gratify her wish to share in the Fuehrer's death.

gift; and praising them for their courage, he had added, characteristically, that he wished his generals were as reliable as they.²

In the evening, while the inhabitants of the two outer bunkers were dining in the general dining-passage of the Fuehrerbunker, they were visited by one of the SS guard, who informed them that the Fuehrer wished to say goodbye to the ladies and that no one was to go to bed till orders had been received. At about half past two in the morning the orders came. They were summoned by telephone to the Bunker, and gathered again in the same general dining-passage, officers and women, about twenty persons in all. When they were assembled, Hitler came in from the private part of the Bunker, accompanied by Bormann.* His look was abstracted, his eyes glazed over with that film of moisture which Hanna Reitsch * had noticed. Some of those who saw him even suggested that he had been drugged; but no such explanation is needed of a condition upon which more familiar observers had often commented. He walked in silence down the passage and shook hands with all the women in turn. Some spoke to him, but he said nothing, or mumbled inaudibly. Ceremonies of silent handshaking had become quite customary in the course of that day.³

When he had left, the participants in this strange scene remained for a while to discuss its significance. They agreed that it could have one meaning only. The suicide of the Fuehrer was about to take place. Thereupon an unexpected thing happened. A great and heavy cloud seemed to roll away from the spirits of the Bunker-dwellers. The terrible sorcerer, the tyrant who had charged their days with intolerable melodramatic tension, would soon be gone, and for a brief twilight moment they could play. In the canteen of the Chancellery, where the soldiers and orderlies took their meals, there was a dance. The news was brought; but no one allowed that to interfere with the business of pleasure. A message from the Fuehrerbunker told them to be quieter; but the dance went on. A tailor ⁴ who had been employed in the Fuehrer's headquarters, and who was now immured with the rest in the Chancellery, was surprised when Brigadefuehrer Rattenhuber, the head of the police guard and a general in the SS, slapped him cordially on the back and greeted him with democratic familiarity. In the strict heirarchy of the Bunker the tailor felt bewildered. It was as if he had been a high officer. "It was the first time I had ever heard a high officer say 'good evening,'" he said; "so I noticed that the mood had completely changed." Then,

2. Frau Junge.
3. Von Varo.
4. W. O. Mueller.

* Martin Bormann: rose to the position of head of the Party Chancery; nominally second in power to Hermann Goering, who had been appointed Hitler's successor, he was in fact the most powerful member of Hitler's entourage, entrusted with all his secrets and allowed total access to the Fuehrer.
* Hanna Reitsch: the celebrated test pilot, whose account of her last visit to the Bunker Trevor-Roper discusses in Chapter 5.

from one of his equals, he learned the reason of this sudden and irregular affability. Hitler had said goodbye, and was going to commit suicide. There are few forces so solvent of class distinctions as common danger, and common relief.

Though Hitler might already be preparing for death, there was still one man at least in the Bunker who was thinking of life: Martin Bormann. If Bormann could not persuade the German armies to come and rescue Hitler and himself, at least he would insist on revenge. Shortly after the farewell ceremony, at a quarter past three in the morning of April 30th, he sent another of those telegrams in which the neurosis of the Bunker is so vividly preserved. It was addressed to Doenitz* at Ploen; but Bormann no longer trusted the ordinary communications, and sent it through the Gauleiter of Mecklenburg. It ran:

> DOENITZ!—Our impression grows daily stronger that the divisions in the Berlin theatre have been standing idle for several days. All the reports we receive are controlled, suppressed, or distorted by Keitel.* In general we can only communicate through Keitel. The Fuehrer orders you to proceed at once, and mercilessly, against all traitors.— BORMANN.[5]

A postscript contained the words: "The Fuehrer is alive, and is conducting the defence of Berlin." These words, containing no hint of the approaching end—indeed seeming to deny its imminence—suggest that Bormann was reluctant even now to admit that his power would soon be over, or must be renewed from another, less calculable, source.

Later in the same morning, when the new day's work had begun, the generals came as usual to the Bunker with their military reports. Brigadefuehrer Mohnke, the commandant of the Chancellery, announced a slight improvement: the Schlesischer railway station had been recaptured from the Russians; but in other respects the military situation was unchanged. By noon the news was worse again. The underground railway tunnel in the Friedrichstrasse was reported in Russian hands; the tunnel in the Vossstrasse, close to the Chancellery, was partly occupied; the whole area of the Tiergarten had been taken; and Russian forces had reached the Potsdamer Platz and the Weidendammer Bridge over the river Spree. Hitler received these reports without emotion. At about two o'clock he took lunch. Eva Braun was not there; evidently she did not feel hungry, or ate alone in her room; and Hitler shared his meal, as usually in her absence, with his two secretaries and the cook. The conversation indicated nothing unusual. Hitler remained quiet, and did not speak of his intentions. Nevertheless, preparations were already being made for the approaching ceremony.

---

5. In the German text the name of Keitel is represented by his codename "Teilhaus."

* Grand Admiral Karl Doenitz: Supreme Commander in the Northern Sector of the Reich; named as Hitler's successor (replacing Goering) in the political testament the Fuehrer wrote on his last day.

* Field Marshal Wilhelm Keitel: one of Hitler's sycophants.

In the morning, the guards had been ordered to collect all their rations for the day, since they would not be allowed to pass through the corridor of the Bunker again; and about lunchtime Hitler's SS adjutant, Sturmbannfuehrer Guensche, sent an order to the transport officer and chauffeur, Sturmbannfuehrer Erich Kempka, to send 200 litres of petrol to the Chancellery garden. Kempka protested that it would be difficult to find so large a quantity at once, but he was told that it must be found. Ultimately he found about 180 litres and sent it round to the garden. Four men carried it in jerricans [6] and placed it at the emergency exit of the Bunker. There they met one of the police guards, who demanded an explanation. They told him that it was for the ventilating plant. The guard told them not to be silly, for the plant was oil-driven. At this moment Hitler's personal servant, Heinz Linge, appeared. He reassured the guard, terminated the argument, and dismissed the men. Soon afterwards all the guards except those on duty were ordered to leave the Chancellery, and to stay away. It was not intended that any casual observer should witness the final scene.

Meanwhile Hitler had finished lunch, and his guests had been dismissed. For a time he remained behind; then he emerged from his suite, accompanied by Eva Braun, and another farewell ceremony took place. Bormann and Goebbels * were there, with Burgdorf, Krebs, Hewel, Naumann, Voss, Rattenhuber, Hoegl, Guensche, Linge, and the four women, Frau Christian, Frau Junge, Fraeulein Krueger, and Fraeulein Manzialy. Frau Goebbels was not present; unnerved by the approaching death of her children, she remained all day in her own room. Hitler and Eva Braun shook hands with them all, and then returned to their suite. The others were dismissed, all but the high-priests and those few others whose services would be necessary. These waited in the passage. A single shot was heard. After an interval they entered the suite. Hitler was lying on the sofa, which was soaked with blood. He had shot himself through the mouth. Eva Braun was also on the sofa, also dead. A revolver was by her side, but she had not used it; she had swallowed poison. The time was half past three.[7]

Shortly afterwards, Artur Axmann, head of the Hitler Youth, arrived at the Bunker. He was too late for the farewell ceremony, but he was admitted to the private suite to see the dead bodies. He examined them, and stayed in the room for some minutes, talking with Goebbels. Then Goebbels left, and Axmann remained for a short while alone with the dead bodies. Outside, in the Bunker, another ceremony was being prepared: the Viking funeral.

After sending the petrol to the garden, Kempka had walked across to the

---

6. A jerrican is a German petrol can containing 4½ gallons.
7. The method of death chosen by Hitler and Eva Braun has been reported identically by Fraeulein Krueger and Frau Junge (who had it from Guensche) and Frau Christian (from Linge), and by others who heard it from the same sources. It is also described by Axmann, who personally inspected the bodies. Kempka, who carried out the body of Eva Braun, unblanketed, observed no signs of blood.

* Joseph Goebbels: "the intellectual of the Nazi Party" and its propaganda minister; appointed Reich Chancellor in Hitler's testament.

Bunker by the subterranean passage which connected his office in the Hermann Goering Strasse with the Chancellery buildings. He was greeted by Guensche with the words, "The Chief is dead." [8] At that moment the door of Hitler's suite was opened, and Kempka too became a participant in the funeral scene.

While Axmann was meditating among the corpses, two SS men, one of them Hitler's servant Linge, entered the room. They wrapped Hitler's body in a blanket, concealing the bloodstained and shattered head, and carried it out into the passage, where the other observers easily recognized it by the familiar black trousers. Then two other SS officers carried the body up the four flights of stairs to the emergency exit, and so out into the garden. After this, Bormann entered the room and took up the body of Eva Braun. Her death had been tidier, and no blanket was needed to conceal the evidence of it. Bormann carried the body into the passage, and then handed it to Kempka, who took it to the foot of the stairs. There it was taken from him by Guensche; and Guensche in turn gave it to a third SS officer, who carried it too upstairs to the garden. As an additional precaution, the other door of the Bunker, which led into the Chancellery, and some of the doors leading from the Chancellery to the garden, had been hastily locked against possible intruders.

Unfortunately, the most careful precautions are sometimes unavailing; and it was as a direct result of this precaution that two unauthorized persons in fact witnessed the scene from which it was intended to exclude them. One of the police guards, one Erich Mansfeld, happened to be on duty in the concrete observation tower at the corner of the Bunker, and noticing through the opaque, sulphurous air a sudden, suspicious scurrying of men and shutting of doors, he felt it his duty to investigate. He climbed down from his tower into the garden and walked round to the emergency exit to see what was afoot. In the porch he collided with the emerging funeral procession. First there were two SS officers carrying a body wrapped in a blanket, with black-trousered legs protruding from it. Then there was another SS officer carrying the unmistakable corpse of Eva Braun. Behind them were the mourners—Bormann, Burgdorf, Goebbels, Guensche, Linge, and Kempka. Guensche shouted at Mansfeld to get out of the way quickly; and Mansfeld, having seen the forbidden but interesting spectacle, returned to his tower.[9]

After this interruption, the ritual was continued. The two corpses were placed side by side, a few feet from the porch, and petrol from the can was poured over them. A Russian bombardment added to the strangeness and danger of the ceremony, and the mourners withdrew for some protection under the shelter of the porch. There Guensche dipped a rag in petrol, set it alight, and flung it out

---

8. "Der Chef ist tot." Hitler's personal servants referred to him as "der Chef."
9. This account is given independently by Kempka and Mansfeld, who agree. Kempka mentions the incident when a guard (*ie* Mansfeld) collided with the procession in the porch and was dismissed by Guensche. Some of the details were accidentally noticed by Schwaegermann.

upon the corpses. They were at once enveloped in a sheet of flame. The mourners stood to attention, gave the Hitler salute, and withdrew again into the Bunker, where they dispersed. Guensche afterwards described the spectacle to those who had missed it. The burning of Hitler's body, he said, was the most terrible experience in his life.[10]

Meanwhile yet another witness had observed the spectacle. He was another of the police guards, and he too came accidentally upon the scene in consequence of the precautions which should have excluded him. His name was Hermann Karnau. Karnau, like others of the guard who were not on duty, had been ordered away from the bunker by an officer of the SS Escort, and had gone to the Chancellery canteen; but after a while, in spite of his orders, he had decided to return to the Bunker. On arrival at the door of the Bunker, he had found it locked. He had therefore made his way out into the garden, in order to enter the Bunker by the emergency exit. As he turned the corner by the tower where Mansfeld was on duty, he was surprised to see two bodies lying side by side, close to the door of the Bunker. Almost at the same instant they burst, spontaneously it seemed, into flame. Karnau could not explain this sudden combustion. He saw no one, and yet it could not be the result of enemy fire, for he was only three feet away. "Possibly someone threw a match from the doorway," he suggested; and his suggestion is essentially correct.

Karnau watched the burning corpses for a moment. They were easily recognizable, though Hitler's head was smashed. The sight, he says, was "repulsive in the extreme." Then he went down into the Bunker by the emergency exit. In the Bunker, he met Sturmbannfuehrer Franz Schedle, the officer commanding the SS Escort. Schedle had recently been injured in the foot by a bomb. He was distracted with grief. "The Fuehrer is dead," he said; "he is burning outside"; and Karnau helped him to limp away.

Mansfeld, on duty in the tower, also watched the burning of the bodies. As he had climbed the tower, after Guensche had ordered him away, he had seen through a loophole a great column of black smoke rising from the garden. As the smoke diminished, he saw the same two bodies which he had seen being brought up the stairs. They were burning. After the mourners had withdrawn, he continued to watch. At intervals he saw SS men come out of the Bunker and pour more petrol on the bodies to keep them alight. Some time afterwards he was relieved by Karnau, and when Karnau had helped him to climb out of the tower, the two went together to look at the bodies again. By now the lower parts of both bodies had been burned away and the shinbones of Hitler's legs were visible. An hour later, Mansfeld visited the bodies again. They were still burning but the flame was low.

In the course of the afternoon a third member of the police guard sought to watch the spectacle of the burning bodies. His name was Hans Hofbeck. He

10. Fraeulein Krueger, Frau Junge.

went up the stairs from the Bunker and stood in the porch; but he did not stay there. The stench of burning flesh was intolerable and drove him away.

Late that night Brigadefuehrer Rattenhuber, the head of the police guard, entered the Dog-bunker where the guards were spending their leisure, and spoke to a sergeant of the SS Escort. He told him to report to his commanding officer, Schedle, and to pick three trustworthy men to bury the corpses. Soon afterwards Rattenhuber returned to the Dog-bunker and addressed the men there. He made them promise to keep the events of the day a holy secret. Anyone talking about them would be shot. Shortly before midnight Mansfeld returned to duty in the tower. Russian shells were still falling, and the sky was illuminated by flares. He noticed that a bomb crater in front of the emergency exit had been newly worked upon, and that the bodies had disappeared. He did not doubt that the crater had been converted into a grave for them; for no shell could have piled the earth around it in so neat a rectangle. About the same time, Karnau was on parade with the other guards in the Vossstrasse, and one of his comrades said to him: "It is sad that none of the officers seems to worry about the Fuehrer's body. I am proud that I alone know where he is." [11]

That is all that is known about the disposal of the remnants of Hitler's and Eva Braun's bodies. Linge afterwards told one of the secretaries that they had been burned as Hitler had ordered, "till nothing remained"; but it is doubtful whether such total combustion could have taken place; 180 litres of petrol, burning slowly on a sandy bed, would char the flesh and dissipate the moisture of the bodies, leaving only an unrecognizable and fragile remainder; but the bones would withstand the heat. These bones have never been found. Perhaps they were broken up and mixed with the other bodies, the bodies of soldiers killed in the defence of the Chancellery, and the body of Fegelein, which were also buried in the garden. The Russians have occasionally dug in that garden, and many such bodies have been unearthed there. Perhaps, as Guensche is said to have stated, the ashes were collected in a box and conveyed out of the Chancellery. Or perhaps no elaborate explanation is necessary. Perhaps such investigations as have been made have been somewhat perfunctory. Investigators who left Hitler's engagement diary unobserved in his chair for five months may easily have overlooked other relics which were more deliberately concealed. Whatever the explanation, Hitler achieved his last ambition. Like Alaric, buried secretly under the riverbed of Busento, the modern destroyer of mankind is now immune from discovery.

While these last rites and pieties were being observed by guards and sentries, the regents of the Bunker were busy with more practical matters. Having set the

---

11. In their narratives of the burning of the bodies, Karnau and Mansfeld agree on facts, but differ on dates and times. Both mistake the date. Mansfeld's times are correct where they can be checked, while Karnau's are hopelessly erratic. If Mansfeld is reliable throughout, the bodies were set alight at about 4 p.m. (this is almost certainly correct), and were still burning at 6.30; Rattenhuber's orders for burial were given "late at night"; and the bodies had been buried by 11 p.m.

bodies alight and paid their last summary respects, they had returned to safety underground, there to contemplate the future. Once again, as after Hitler's first leavetaking, a great cloud seemed to have been lifted from their spirits. The nightmare of ideological repression was over, and if the prospect before them remained dark and dubious, at least they were now free to consider it in a businesslike manner. From this moment nobody seems to have bothered about the past or the two corpses still sizzling in the garden. That episode was over, and in the short space of time remaining they had their own problems to face. As the tragically-minded guard observed, it was sad to see everyone so indifferent to the Fuehrer's body.

The first evidence of the changed atmosphere in the Bunker was noticed by the secretaries, who had been dismissed during the ceremony, but who now returned to their stations. On arrival they learned the details from Guensche and Linge; but it was not from such secondhand information only that they knew that Hitler was dead. Everyone, they observed, was smoking in the Bunker. During Hitler's lifetime that had been absolutely forbidden; but now the headmaster had gone and the boys could break the rules. Under the soothing influence of nicotine, whose absence must have increased the nervous tension of the past week, they were able to consider the administrative problems which the Fuehrer had left them to face.

Marshall Cohen / Civil Disobedience in a Constitutional Democracy

The work of Gandhi and of Martin Luther King, challenges to racially biased legislation and to the legality of the war in Indochina—all of these and related matters considered in this essay have had the effect of making arguments about the legitimacies of dissent a subject not merely of law schools and newspaper editorials but of the household and the classroom. Readers may therefore find Mr. Cohen's careful discriminations of some practical value during those inevitable and usually agitated political arguments in which they become engaged. He encourages us, for example, to ponder the differences between rebellious or revolutionary or merely disobedient acts, with the implicit hope that such distinctions will make our assessments of public protest more just than they might otherwise be.

Emphasizing the political value of civil disobedience, Cohen is anxious to keep his own tone markedly civil. Yet his vocabulary when describing what he considers a badly managed argument is notably sharp precisely because he is defending here the effort to keep issues within the range of moral and rational persuasion. Beyond that range is not only the violence of rebellion but also the violence of inflammatory rhetoric and of the retaliation by officers of the law who interpret statutes inflexibly or institute them without due regard for justice. In defending civil disobedience Cohen adopts a position which is essentially conservative. Ultimately, he is defending the best possibilities, as he sees them, of the judicial and social systems against which disobedience is often directed, and while pointing to the fallibility of the workings of the courts he depends heavily on the evocation of traditional moral principles.

In traditional democratic theory revolution provides the only alternative to normal politics. If conditions do not justify overthrowing the government a dissenter must confine himself to protesting against them. He may protest by speaking against the government, or by voting against it, but this meager list exhausts the possibilities. Due to the very great originality of Gandhi * we can now envisage, and many people have in fact begun to practice, a third type of protest—civil disobedience. If it does not qualify as normal politics it is not a kind of revolutionary activity, either.

Unfortunately, the term "civil disobedience," which always suffered from a certain ambiguity, has now been utterly debased in the vulgar national debate on "law and order." It has been used to describe everything from bringing a test-case in the federal courts to taking aim at a federal official. Indeed, for Vice President Agnew it has become a code-word describing the activities of muggers, arsonists, draft evaders, campaign hecklers, campus militants, anti-war demonstrators, juvenile delinquents and political assassins. Anyone who wishes to defend the practice of civil disobedience must therefore explain just what it is that he wishes to defend. And in doing so I shall not hestitate to free Gandhi's conception from its religious bias and from those political emphases peculiarly appropriate to the fundamentally undemocratic circumstances in which he worked. Only then will it be possible to reject Ambassador Kennan's * confident assertion that civil disobedience "has no place" in a democratic society, or Justice Fortas' * apparently more liberal view that "indirect" disobedience, at least has no such place.

The civil disobedient is often described as a man who defies the law out of conscience or moral belief. But this description is imprecise, and it fails to distinguish him from the moral innovator on the one hand, or the conscientious re-

---

* Mahatma Gandhi: (1869–1948), the Indian reformer and "nonviolent resistance" leader whose civil disobedience campaigns for Home Rule in India made him an international hero (or villain, to some).

* George F. Kennan: Former Ambassador to Soviet Union, and the author of many works on American foreign policy. Mr. Cohen hopes to refute Kennan's short book, *Democracy and the Student Left* (1968).

* Abe Fortas: former associate justice, U.S. Supreme Court; his ideas on dissent were set forth in a book entitled *Concerning Dissent and Civil Disobedience* (1968).

fuser on the other. Unlike the moral innovator, the civil disobedient does not invoke the standards of a higher morality or of a special religious dispensation. He is no Zarathustra * proposing a transvaluation of all values, and he does not ask the public to act on principles that it plainly rejects. If he acts out of conscience it is important to remember that he appeals to it as well, and the principles he invokes are principles that he takes to be generally acknowledged. It is to protest the fact that the majority has violated these principles that the disobedient undertakes his disobedience, and it is this element of protest that distinguishes his actions from those of the conscientious refuser. For the doctor who performs a clandestine abortion, or the youth who surreptitiously evades the draft, may be acting out of moral motives—the doctor to fulfill his obligations to a patient, the youth to avoid complicity in an evil undertaking—but they are not defying the law in order to protest the course of public conduct. They can achieve their purposes in private, and their defiance of the law need never come to light. The civil disobedient's actions are political by their very nature, however, and it is essential that they be performed in public, or called to the public's attention.

It is for this reason that the civil disobedient characteristically notifies government officials of the time and place of his actions and attempts to make clear the point of his protest. Obviously, one of the problems of a modern democracy is that many immoral actions taken in the people's name are only dimly known to them, if they are known at all. In such cases, the main difficulty in touching the public's conscience may well be the difficulty in making the public conscious. The civil disobedient may therefore find that in addition to making his actions public it is necessary to gain for them a wide publicity as well. Indeed, Bertrand Russell * has suggested that making propaganda, and bringing the facts of political life to the attention of an ignorant, and often bemused, electorate constitutes the main function of disobedience at the present time. It is certainly true that nothing attracts the attention of the masses, and of the mass media, like flamboyant violations of the law, and it would be unrealistic of those who have political grievances not to exploit this fact. But it is important—especially in this connection—to recall Gandhi's warning that the technique of law violation ought to be used sparingly—like the surgeon's knife. For, in the end, the public will lose its will, and indeed its ability, to distinguish between those who employ these techniques whenever they wish to advertise their political opinions and those, the true dissenters, who use them only to protest deep violations of political principle. The techniques will then be of little use to anybody.

After openly breaking the law, the traditional disobedient willingly pays the penalty. This is one of the characteristics that serve to distinguish him from the typical criminal (his appeal to conscience is another) and it helps to establish the

---

* Zarathustra: a reference to *Thus Spake Zarathustra* (1883) by Friedrich Nietzsche, in which the German philosopher develops his idea of the superman.
* Bertrand Russell: (1872–1970), English philosopher and social agitator; strong advocate of unilateral nuclear disarmament.

seriousness of his views and the depth of his commitment as well. Unfortunately, paying the penalty will not always demonstrate that his actions are in fact disinterested. For the youth protesting the draft, or the welfare recipient protesting poverty, has an obvious and substantial interest in the success of his cause. If the majority suspects that these interests color the disobedient's perception of the issues involved, its suspicions may prove fatal to his ultimate success. This is one reason why the practice of civil disobedience should not be limited to those who are directly injured by the government's immoral or lawless course (as Judge Wyzanski * and others have suggested). A show of support by those who have no substantial interest in the matter may carry special weight with a confused, and even with an actively sceptical, majority. The majority simply cannot dismiss those over thirty-five as draft-dodgers or those who earn over $35,000 a year as boondogglers. It may therefore consider the issues at stake, and this is the first objective of the civil disobedient.

It is in misinterpreting the role of punishment in the theory of civil disobedience that Ambassador Kennan makes one of his most conspicuous errors. For the theory of civil disobedience does not suggest (although such exponents as James Farmer and Harris Wofford have sometimes argued) that the disobedient's actions are justified by his willingness to pay the penalty that the law prescribes. The idea that paying the penalty justifies breaking the law derives, not from Gandhi and the tradition of civil disobedience, but from Oliver Wendell Holmes * and the tradition of legal realism. According to Holmes and the legal realists the law characteristically presents us with an option—either to obey, or to suffer the consequences that attach to disobedience. This doctrine is indefensible even in the area of contract law where it arose, and where it has a fragile plausibility, but it is plainly absurd to suppose that the citizen has such an option in the area of criminal law. Criminal punishments are not a simple tax on criminal misconduct, and the citizen is not given the option of engaging in such conduct on the condition that he pay the tax. It is mindless to suppose that murder, rape or arson would be justified if only one were willing to pay the penalty, and the civil disobedient is committed to no such mindlessness. Holmes was looking at the law from the point of view of a bad man for whom paying the penalty is always an option and often a source of advantage. Gandhi considered it from the point of view of a good man for whom paying the penalty is often a necessity and always a source of pain. This punishment does not justify the act of civil disobedience, but it helps to establish the disobedient's seriousness and his fidelity to law in the eyes of the majority whose actions have, in his opinion, justified it.

* Charles Wyzanski: Federal judge in Boston. In 1969 he gained national attention by declaring unconstitutional the section of the draft law which requires a conscientious objector to be religiously motivated.
* Oliver Wendell Holmes: (1841–1935), Supreme Court justice; the greatest judicial figure of his time.

The disobedient's willingness to suffer punishment has another purpose as well. It is meant to weaken the will of the transgressors and to dissuade them from a course of action that the dissenters consider immoral. For, if the transgressors do not draw back, they may be forced to punish some of the most scrupulous and dedicated members of the community. The fact that this is so will often persuade those who heedlessly supported the original measures, not to mention those who supported them with a dim sense of their injustice, to withdraw their support or even to join the opposition. Forcing others to suffer for their moral beliefs is a high price to pay for pursuing a questionable course of conduct and many will prefer not to pay it.

The disobedient's willingness to face suffering and punishment may be seen, then, as a useful way of reinforcing the effects of his protest and appeal. It constitutes a use of pressure, to be sure, but this pressure does not amount to coercion. If the majority remains unconvinced, it will consider itself free to act as it wishes and to impose legal sanctions if these should be required. On occasion, however, the dissenters may actually attempt to coerce the majority. They may attempt to create a situation in which the majority cannot pursue its purposes unless it acts in ways that it believes to be morally impermissible. The actions of the captain and the crew of The Golden Rule provide a case in point. For, when they sailed into the government's nuclear testing grounds in the Central Pacific these men were not simply registering a protest against its testing program and hoping that their arrest would give the public painful second thoughts. Rather, they were telling the government that it would have to incinerate them if it wished to proceed as planned and this, they hoped, the government would find it impossible to do. In cases like this the dissenters cross the line that separates civil disobedience from those forms of political action that actually attempt to paralyze the majority's will or the government's operations. As such, they may be compared to public strikes and acts of sabotage (although such acts normally employ quite different methods) and they constitute a form of incipient rebellion. Certainly, they issue a more radical challenge to governmental authority than the civil disobedient wishes to pose.

The disobedient's interest in establishing that his actions are neither rebellious nor revolutionary provides him with a final reason for accepting punishment. For, by accepting the punishment prescribed by law the disobedient is able to emphasize his commitment to law, and it is especially important for him to do so in a democratic society. The values that the disobedient wishes to defend are, after all, precisely the values that are best served by a democracy under law, if only these laws remain within bounds. Should it come to a choice, the disobedient's ultimate commitment is certainly to justice, and not to the will of the majority. But his present purpose is to persuade the majority not to force this choice upon him and his present intention is to make the established system viable. It must not be supposed, incidentally, that the civil disobedient's position implies that he will never submit to the requirements of an unjust law. In fact, the citizen in a democracy often has a moral obligation to do just that. But there are limits to the injustice he will endure as there are limits to the injustice he will perpetuate. It is the civil disobedient's conviction that these limits have been reached.

Of course, it does not follow from the fact that the disobedient is willing to pay the penalty that the government ought to exact it. The disobedient has been placed in an acute moral dilemma and he may have acted with good will toward the community. Certainly, his punishment may cause profound ruptures in the community. All these facts, and others, ought to be considered by the government in deciding whether to prosecute, and the judiciary in deciding the terms of sentence. It will often be in the government's and, indeed, in the community's best interests to act with flexibility and discretion in these matters and it is a particularly barbarous fallacy to suppose that the government owes the disobedient his just portion of punishment. That it may owe him a day in court when he wishes to raise constitutional issues, perhaps even a day free from the threat of punishment, is another, insufficiently canvassed question, that cannot be pursued here.

The dissenter may commit illegal actions, but in the view of Gandhi and of Martin Luther King such actions ought to be non-violent in nature. Gandhi and King were, of course, committed to non-violence quite generally and as a matter of religious principle. Their views in this matter are therefore unconvincing to those who are willing to contemplate the use of violence in certain circumstances. Thoreau, for one, was not opposed to its occasional use. In the famous essay that gave currency to the very term "civil disobedience" he remarked that when conscience is wounded a little blood is shed, and the suggestion that on occasion a little blood ought to be shed in return was not far to seek.* In later life Thoreau did, in fact, endorse the violence of John Brown * and his associates without scruple. It is possible to share Thoreau's general attitudes rather than Gandhi's or King's, and to hold, nevertheless, that violence, or at least certain forms of it, are incompatible with the distinctive purposes of civil disobedience. Thus, John Rawls,* to whom these remarks are very much indebted, argues that violent actions are incompatible with the nature of civil disobedience because they will be understood as threats, not as appeals. And it is possible to add that the fear of violence (or of sudden death) puts men beyond the reach of rational

---

* Henry Thoreau's essay "Civil Disobedience" (1849) was originally a lecture protesting U.S. prosecution of the Mexican War, U.S. treatment of its native Indian population, and the institution of slavery; Thoreau urged our duty to renounce cooperation (e.g. in the form of tax payments) with a government that was pursuing criminal courses.
* John Brown: (1800–1859), abolitionist leader who deliberately had murdered five pro-slavery settlers in Kansas and who in 1859, with twenty-one others, captured the U.S. armory at Harpers Ferry, Virginia, which they planned to use as a base from which to free slaves by forcible intervention; the attempt failing, he was subsequently convicted and hanged.
* John Rawls: professor of philosophy at Harvard.

and moral persuasion. There is a time for violence in human affairs, but, when it arrives, civil disobedience is no longer an appropriate form of political activity.

Rawls' suggestion is persuasive and especially so when it restricts the prohibition on violence to a prohibition on violence against other persons. It is less convincing when violence against property is in question. For the violation of symbolically important public property may be a dramatic, and not very dangerous, way of lodging effective protests, and the razing of the slums has been understood as a cry of despair as often as it has been perceived as a declaration of war. The argument against violence is at its weakest in the case of violence against the self. A sacrifice like Norman Morrison's,* far from frustrating the purposes of civil disobedience, realized them in a peculiarly impressive and moving way. If it inspired fear it was not the fear of sudden death but the fear of eternal wrath, and that is a fear that often brings men to their moral senses.

Civil disobedience is, then, an appeal to the public to alter certain laws or policies that the minority takes to be incompatible with the fundamental principles of morality, principles to which it believes the majority is committed. If the minority is mistaken and the majority is not in fact committed to them civil disobedience will undoubtedly prove a pointless form of political activity, but it will not, for that reason, be an unjustifiable one.

The moral duty to obey particular laws derives from the moral duty to support constitutional arrangements on which others have relied, so long as it is reasonable to believe that these arrangements are intended to implement, and are capable of implementing, the principles of freedom and justice. But one's moral obligation to obey particular laws lapses when one solemnly believes that such laws constitute deep violations of those arrangements, or of the principles on which they rest. (It goes without saying that discharging one's moral duty is not the only legitimate ground for obeying the law.) These principles of political morality normally find expression in the public morality of the state and, given the circumstances of the modern democracies, they guarantee to citizens the basic freedoms (including freedom to participate in the political life) and also a minimum of justice (by which I understand not only the disinterested administration of justice, but also a fair share of the benefits of the common life). In addition, they prohibit inflicting pain and suffering on innocent persons and they require fidelity to the idea of justice between nations. These principles are adumbrated, and often find remarkably full expression, in the constitutions of modern states, although the constitution, especially the constitution as interpreted by the courts, may be an imperfect expression of them. Thus, our own public morality, as articulated in the Constitution, makes very broad guarantees of freedom and justice in the First, the Fifth, and the Fourteenth Amendments, and Article VI makes treaties part of the supreme law of the land. The treaties to which we are

---

* Norman Morrison: a young man who burned himself to death in front of the Pentagon to protest U.S. policy in Vietnam (November 1965).

in fact a party define the rights of foreign peoples in considerable detail and they enumerate the legitimate grounds, and acceptable methods, of war.

I have little doubt that, at the present time, the government of the United States is violating these principles of political morality and providing dissenters with legitimate grounds for civil disobedience. It is important to recall, however, that the public morality of our society, especially as it is articulated in the federal constitution, gives voice to these very principles, and we must now examine the consequences of this fact for the traditional theory of civil disobedience. For, on the traditional view a man who commits civil disobedience believes that he is, in fact, violating a legally valid (if morally insupportable) law or order. But in a constitutional democracy like our own those who are asked to conform to laws that they think immoral will normally be in a position to claim, and if they are legally well-advised they will claim, that the laws in question are unconstitutional nullities, not laws at all.[1]

The altered position I have described was, of course, the position of Martin Luther King and his disciples in the civil rights movement. As one would expect, they rarely, if ever, pleaded guilty to violating the laws under which they were charged. Rather, they argued that the laws were themselves in violation of the federal constitution and that they were, in consequence, invalid and without legal effect. In a remarkable number of cases (when federal legislation had not already rendered the issues moot) the courts agreed with them.

Despite the fact that they did not believe themselves to be violating the law, Martin Luther King and his followers continued to refer to themselves as civil disobedients. Justice Fortas has fallen in with their usage and this fact has, I believe, contributed to his wholly undeserved reputation for having a liberal, and even a concessive position on the issue of civil disobedience. For it is one thing to endorse "civil disobedience" of the type practiced by King and quite another thing to endorse civil disobedience in the stricter, traditional and more serious sense. Certainly, Justice Fortas has not endorsed civil disobedience in this more traditional sense. In fact, his liberalism comes to nothing more than this: the dissenter is granted a moral right to test, or to try to test, the validity of a law that he considers immoral and believes to be unconstitutional. It finds its consummation in a proposition that Vice-President Agnew would hardly contest: if the courts agree that the law is invalid, the dissenter was within his legal rights in refusing to obey it.

The fact that Justice Fortas has not endorsed anything like the classical conception of civil disobedience becomes apparent when we consider his attitude toward the "disobedient" who does not win, but who loses in the courts. For on

1. Irving Kristol is, therefore, either being obtuse or supercilious when he writes that "those who are morally committed to civil disobedience can properly claim that the law which arrests them, or the law that punishes them is so perverse as to be without authority. What they may not do in good conscience is to practice civil disobedience and then hire a clever lawyer to argue that it wasn't a violation of the law at all, but rather the exercise of a right."

Justice Fortas' view the man who loses in court is under a moral, as well as a legal obligation to refrain from any further disobedience (he has had his day in court) and he is morally, as well as legally, obliged to suffer the punishment prescribed by law (that is the way we play the game). Surely, this is a rigid and untenable view; indeed, Justice Fortas implies on occasion that even he does not really accept it. If Congress passed a law requiring Negroes to observe a discriminatory curfew, to confine themselves to certain restricted geographical areas (as Ambassador Kennan has now hinted might be a good idea) and to go naked through the streets if they wished to apply for welfare few would suppose that they had a moral obligation to do so. The fact that the courts ultimately sustained such a law would not alter the situation in any serious way. But it is hardly necessary to seek examples that may seem fantastic or purely theoretical. After all, the Court on which Judge Fortas sat once decided the Dred Scott case and it is hard to believe that Justice Fortas, or anyone else, is going to say (at least at this late date) that in the period following the Fugitive Slave Law and the Dred Scott decision abolitionists had a moral obligation to return slaves to their owners or that slaves had an obligation to return of their own free will.

Even if we were to assume that the Court's interpretation of the Constitution in the Dred Scott case was a defensible one it would not follow that one had a moral obligation to acquiesce in its decision. For the constitution itself would then have been in violation of the fundamental principles of political morality and one simply does not have a moral obligation to abide by such a constitution. Of course, there is very good reason to doubt that the constitution did in fact mean what the Court said it meant and it is important, now, to challenge the view that the constitution, or that the law, is inevitably what the courts say it is. For the doctrine gives a false view of the nature of law and of what it means to obey it.

The English school of Hobbes and Austin held that the law is to be identified with the command of the sovereign and, insofar as he delegates authority to them, with the decisions and orders of his courts. The American legal realists have associated the law and the courts even more closely. For Holmes the law is "nothing more pretentious" than a prophecy of what the courts will do; for Fortas "the rule of law" requires nothing more ignoble than acquiescing in whatever they may have commanded. The objections to such views are powerful, indeed, and a far more persuasive and commonsense tradition holds that the law is to be identified, not with the holdings of courts, but with the authorized rules and principles that the courts interpret and apply. Of course, the interpretations and holdings of courts must be considered in determining the state of the law (the doctrine of precedent has an important place in our jurisprudence), but these interpretations and decisions must not be identified with the law. For one thing, the courts can misinterpret the law, and their decisions are often mistaken. When this is so it would be foolish and harmful to identify these dubious interpretations and questionable decisions with the law itself. Certainly the courts do not do so. It may have taken the Union Armies to "reverse" the Dred Scott case, but the courts often admit that they have been in error and agree to reverse themselves. Indeed, the Supreme Court has reversed itself in such momentous cases as *Erie R.R. v. Tomkins*, *Brown v. Board of Education*, and *West Virginia State Board of Education v. Barnette*.

This fact is of importance to the dissenter for a number of reasons. In the first place, it may strengthen the case for disobedience on purely moral grounds. For, as Ronald Dworkin has observed, it is one thing for a man to sacrifice his principles (or to violate his conscience) when it is plain that the law requires him to do so. But it is quite another thing for him to do so when the law, or the court's view of it, is of questionable validity. In addition to making a moral difference the fact that the courts may be wrong makes a practical difference as well. One of the disobedient's aims is to change the existing law and the most effective way of doing so in a constitutional democracy will often be to persuade the courts that the obnoxious legislation is unconstitutional. Continued defiance of the law may be the only practical way for the dissenter to obtain a rehearing of the questions at issue and even when other methods are available the disobedient's willingness to face criminal punishment in defense of his beliefs may help the court to see that it had misjudged the strength, and perhaps even the nature, of his interests in the first place.

For this reason it is possible to agree with Dworkin's claim that the Jehovah's Witnesses behaved properly in refusing to observe Justice Fortas' canons of correct behavior after the Court found against them in the first "flag-salute" case. As they saw it, the law denied them a basic religious freedom and they were being asked to violate their fundamental religious convictions on the basis of dubious constitutional doctrine. Continued defiance did not require them to injure the interests, or abridge the rights, of others in any serious way and, in the end, it probably helped to convince the Court that its original decision had been mistaken. In any event, the Court did reverse itself in the well-known case of *West Virginia State Board of Education v. Barnette* only a few years later. As it now viewed the matter the intransigent Witnesses had only been exercising their constitutional rights all along. The moral is plain. It is often those who insist on their legal rights, rather than those who acquiesce in the fallible (and occasionally supine and even corrupt) opinions of courts, who strengthen the "rule of law" that Justice Fortas is so anxious to defend.

If the argument for civil disobedience is strengthened when there is reason to believe that the courts are in error it is strengthened still more when there is reason to believe that the courts will refuse to adjudicate the issues at all. This is, of course, precisely what they have refused to do in the crucial cases arising out of the war in Vietnam. In the "Spock" case the trial court invoked the "political question" doctrine and denied its jurisdiction to hear any issues concerning the legality of the war or of its conduct. And in the cases of David Mitchell (who refused to report for induction) and of the "Fort Hood" three (who refused to report for service in Vietnam) the Supreme Court simply denied *certiorari*.* It has been suggested that when the courts invoke the "political question" doctrine and refuse to adjudicate the crucial issues they in fact endorse the actions of the executive or of the legislative branches. But it is far more plausible to argue that when they invoke this doctrine they assume a wholly agnostic position on the issues involved and simply enforce as law the determinations of the "political" branches. In the case of the "Fort Hood" three this agnostic attitude is assumed toward questions that Justice Stewart * and Justice Douglas consider, and that plainly are, "of great magnitude." In his dissent to the Court's decision denying *certiorari* in the case of the "Fort Hood" three Justice Stewart indicates that these questions include, among others, these:

> I. Is the present United States military activity in Vietnam a "war" within the meaning of Article I, Section 8, Clause 11 of the Constitution?
> II. If so, may the Executive constitutionally order the petitioners to participate in that military activity, when no war has been declared by the Congress?
> III. Of what relevance to Question II are the present treaty obligations of the United States?
> IV. Of what relevance to Question II is the joint Congressional ("Tonkin Bay") Resolution of August 10, 1964?
>   a. Do present United States military operations fall within the terms of the Joint Resolution?
>   b. If the Joint Resolution purports to give the Chief Executive authority to commit United States forces to armed conflict limited in scope only by his own absolute discretion, is the Resolution a constitutionally impermissible delegation of all or part of Congress' power to declare war?

"These are," he continues, "large and deeply troubling questions. Whether the Court would ultimately reach them depends, of course, upon the resolution of serious preliminary issues of justiciability. We cannot make these problems go away simply by refusing to hear the case of three obscure Army privates. I intimate not even tentative views upon any of these matters, but I think the Court should squarely face them by granting certiorari and setting this case for oral argument."

In turn, I do not wish to intimate any views on the "political question" doctrine or on the Court's unwillingness to review the actions of the executive and legislative branches in these sensitive areas. But it is important to recognize that

---

* *certiorari:* A writ issuing from a superior court upon the complaint of a party that he has not received justice in an inferior court, or cannot have an impartial trial, by which the records are called up for trial in the superior court.
* Justice Potter Stewart and Justice William O. Douglas: associate justices of the U.S. Supreme Court.

the Court's refusal to consider these matters can only increase the weight that the three obscure Army privates, and others like them, must give to their own appraisal of the issues.[2] Certainly, a very formidable body of opinion supports the view that the government's behavior is in many particulars both illegal and unconstitutional. And there is little doubt, I believe, that it has frequently violated the principles of international law and morality. The case for disobedience in these circumstances is very strong.

The discussion has focussed, so far, on what Gandhi called "defensive," and others have called "direct," disobedience. In cases of this type the law the dissenter violates is the very law that he regards as immoral. It will be worth commenting, briefly and in conclusion, on what Gandhi called "offensive," and others have called "indirect," disobedience. For in this type of disobedience the dissenter violates laws (usually traffic laws or the laws of trespass) that he finds unobjectionable in themselves in order to protest still other laws, policies or orders that he thinks immoral and even wicked. While Justice Fortas displays some sympathy for those who engage in "direct" disobedience (the courts may, after all, vindicate them) his hostility to those who practice indirect disobedience is unremitting (there is no doubt that they are disobedients in the strict sense). In his view their behavior is unnecessary and unjustifiable; it is, in fact, nothing less than a form of "warfare" against society.

I would argue, to the contrary, that "indirect" disobedience is both justifiable and necessary. It is justified, as all civil disobedience is justified, as a solemn protest against important violations of moral principle. And it is necessary, because there is often no alternative form of protest at a comparable level of depth. In particular, it must not be supposed that whenever the government violates the principles of political morality it does so by enacting a positively wicked law that the dissenters can protest "directly." For instance, the object of protest may well be the government's failure to pass a law, or to enforce one. Thus, Ralph Abernathy's violation of the law of trespass was meant to protest the government's failure to enact an adequate poverty program, and the obstruction of segregated construction sites is a familiar technique for protesting the government's failure to enforce fair employment practices statutes that have long been part of the law.[3] Then, too, the object of protest may be a governmental policy or order,

---

2. Professor Michael Katz has objected to this contention as it was formulated in the original version of this essay and I have replied to his objection in *The Massachusetts Review,* Vol. XI, No. 1, Winter 1970, pp. 172–75.

3. It is worth noting the view of the present Solicitor General (and former Dean of the Harvard Law School) on a related point. Mr. Griswold writes that he "cannot distinguish in principle the legal quality of the determination . . . to block a workman from entering a segregated job site from the determination to fire shots into a civil rights leader's home to protest integration." If all Mr. Griswold means by his fine periphrastic phrase ("cannot distinguish in principle the legal quality") is that both actions are illegal few will dispute his point. If he means anything else—-perhaps that they are equally serious violations of the law—it is all to his credit that he couldn't quite bring himself to say so.

rather than a law, strictly speaking. It makes no sense to speak of violating the government's policy of intervening in the affairs of foreign states and the ordinary citizen is in no position to defy orders issued to military personnel. It is for this reason that such "indirect" methods of protest as sit-ins at draft boards and demonstrations at the Pentagon have been employed to protest the government's violent intervention in Vietnam, and this is why men have even endured self-immolation to protest the military's use of fire-bombs against a defenseless civilian population. It is unfortunate that these are the acts of "warfare" that Justice Fortas finds it most important to protest. In fact, the government's various failures and transgressions constitute a far greater threat to "the rule of law" that he is so concerned to defend. It is one of the great merits of those who practice civil disobedience to have seen this and to have acted on their painful knowledge.

Frank Kermode / Marshall McLuhan Interviewed

Here, untreated except for minor clarifications—the elimination of a few false starts, obscurities and repetitions—is the report of an interview made by BBC Television in 1965. The interview, which was made for an arts program, was in the end suppressed as being too difficult even for the rather special audience of that program. Now it is all reasonably familiar. In the course of the discussion McLuhan gives fairly clear expression to his most central and innovating doctrines. Both McLuhan and the interviewer were conscious of the television camera, and a long section of the program turns on a crucial disagreement about the nature of the camera and the images it provides. They arrived at no conclusion. Note also the curious discussion of "cool" (compare Fiedler's "The New Mutants"), and McLuhan's apparent self-contradictions on the subject of "nationalism" later. A conversation of this sort is not free; its first purpose is to make plain and interesting the opinions of one man by having another ask the right questions and make the right objections. In cases such as this, it would not do for the interviewer to claim an equal share of the dogmatic output. There is a curious variety of collaboration, with the object, as McLuhan put it, of "establishing a beachhead." The television viewer, or in this instance the reader, is the judge of whether McLuhan was right to say that this had been done.

FRANK KERMODE: Marshall, we're going to be using the word "technology" probably rather a lot in this conversation, so could we start by asking you exactly what you mean in the context of your argument by this word.

Yousef Karsh from Rapho Guillumette

MARSHALL MCLUHAN: I try not to have any private meanings, Frank. But I think of technologies as extensions of our own bodies, of our own faculties, whether clothing, housing, and the more familiar kinds of technologies like wheels, stirrups and such, as extensions of various parts of the body. The need to amplify the human powers in order to cope with various environments brings on these extensions whether of tools or furniture. These amplifications of our powers, sorts of deifications of man, I think of as technologies.

F.K.: Yes, and you argue that by developing them we alter the whole pattern of our senses.

M.M.: They create environments. Every technology at once rearranges patterns of human association, and in effect really creates a new environment which is perhaps most felt, although not most noticed, in changing sensory ratios and sensory patterns.

F.K.: Well, can I put this to you—in a sense you've been a historian as you've gone about your work, and let's talk first a little, if we may, about your book, *The Gutenberg Galaxy,* where you argue that for a long time, without actually understanding it, we've been living in a culture in which our whole way of looking at the world has been determined by typography, by the successiveness of print and so on. Would you like to enlarge on that a bit?

M.M.: Well, I remember I decided to write that book when I came across a piece by J. C. Carruthers, the psychiatrist, on *The African Mind in Health and Disease*, describing the effects of the printed word on the African populations. It startled me and decided me to plunge in, but we have a better opportunity of seeing our whole technologies when they confront other populations elsewhere in the world. The effects they have on those people are so startling and so sudden that we have an opportunity to see what happened to us over many centuries.

F.K.: Yes, which we couldn't see because we're inside the system. You say what happened was that we got used to having our information processed as it is in print, that is to say, set out successively; whereas at the root of your thought there's the view that we can see the world as an image, instantaneously, but that we've chosen under the pressure of a technology to set it out successively like a block of print.

M.M.: Well, every technology has its own laws. It decides all sorts of arrangements in other spheres. The fact of script and the ability to make inventories and collect and store data changed many social habits and processes back as early as three thousand B.C. The effects of rearranging one's experience, organising one's experience by these new extensions of our powers are quite unexpected. One of the very definite effects of scripting was the rise of what we call architecture. Instead of just scooped out cave spaces or wrap-around wigwams and igloos, it made possible enclosed space.

F.M.: Now, you're talking about script rather than—

M.M.: The effect of writing as a way of organising experience stepped up the visual factor until things like architecture became possible.

F.K.: You mean that sight has become the pre-eminent sense as it was for Plato, and it went on being so in so-called civilised, as opposed to primitive societies.

M.M.: Increasingly so.

F.K.: We supplied a match with the invention of printing.

M.M.: Printing stepped it up to a considerable pitch, yes.

F.K.: Now, how would you describe the impact of the invention of the printing press? Give me some instances of what happened as a consequence of this.

M.M.: It created almost overnight what we call nationalism—what, in fact, was a public. The older manuscript forms were not sufficiently powerful instruments of technology to create publics in the sense that print was able to do, unified, homogeneous reading publics.

F.K.: Yet somehow private because they could read alone.

M.M.: Yes, or very highly fragmented. The fragmented, private outlook of the literate man is very much related to typography and tends to disappear with changes in technology such as the electronic. We can come round to that later.

F.K.: We can come to that in a minute. What about the Reformation? You argue in your book, *The Gutenberg Galaxy,* that the Reformation is a kind of consequence of our moving into a typographical phase of history.

M.M.: I don't, I think, stress that. I left that more or less to be implied perhaps. Everything that we prize in our Western world in matters of individualism and separatism is highly favoured by the printed word and not really favoured by other forms of culture like radio, or, earlier, even by manuscript. But this stepping up of the fragmented, the private, the individual, the private judgment, the point of view—all in fact, our whole vocabularies—underwent huge change with the arrival of such technology.

F.K.: Would it be fair to say that the concept of liberty of the individual, of freedom of speech if you like, is essentially a typographical matter which could well disappear in the other kind of culture that we're now moving into?

M.M.: It could indeed, if it hasn't already. The whole stress on "point of view" also creates the image of importance of expression, instead of the importance of belonging and being involved in a deep role in society; the need for private expression comes in with the technical possibility of extending one's voice or one's outlook into the community.

F.K.: So a whole phase of art, in fact, and of poetry belongs to this typographically determined culture and may end with it. We've now, I think, got some idea of what you've meant by Gutenberg technology, by a phase of history which is determined by the invention of printing. I think we might emphasise that it does involve to a marked extent the treatment of information as sequential, as not coming instantaneously but as set out in the stereotypes of phonetic alphabet.

Well, now could I ask you about the technology which on your view is superseding it and which is having its own effect on our lives comparable with, but of course entirely different in kind to the Gutenberg technology?

M.M.: Well, the Gutenberg technology was mechanical to an extreme degree. In fact it originated a good deal of the later mechanical revolution, assembly line style, and the fragmentation of operations and functions as the very rationale of industrialisation. This fragmentation had begun much earlier, after the hunter and the food gatherers, with Neolithic man. I suppose in an extreme way one might say that Gutenberg was the last phase of the Neolithic revolution. Gutenberg plus the Industrial Revolution that followed was a pushing of specialism that came in with the Neolithic man and the agrarian revolution;—a pushing of specialism all the way, and then, suddenly, we encounter the electric or electro-magnetism which seems to have a totally different principle. Some people feel it is an extension of our nervous system, not an extension merely of our bodies. If the wheel is an extension of feet, and tools of back, hands, arms, the electro-magnetism seems to be an extension of our nerves, and becomes mainly an information system. It is above all a feedback or looped system.

F.K.: Yes. Now this is something that began to move in on us with the invention of the telegraph, and we are now quite far advanced into what you call the electric galaxy.

M.M.: A century—over a century advanced. But: the peculiarity!—after the age of the wheel, you suddenly encounter the age of the circuit. A wheel, pushed to an extreme, suddenly acquires opposite characteristics. This seems to happen with a good many technologies: if they get pushed to a very distant point they reverse their characteristics. The wheel reversed its characteristics when it became an electric circuit or loop, and the feed-back in that loop system has a completely different set of effects on psyche and society from any effects that the old mechanical technologies had.

F.K.: What difference is the electric technology making to our interest in content, in what the medium actually says?

M.M.: This is a very complex business, but one of the effects of switching over to circuitry from mechanical and moving parts and wheels is an enormous increase in the amount of information that is moving. You tend to go looking for mythic and structural forms in order to manage such complex data moving at very high speeds, so that the electric engineers often speak of "pattern recognitions"—a normal need of people processing data electrically and by computers and so on. It's a need which the poets foresaw a century ago in their drive back to mythic forms of organising experience.

F.K.: Yes. What you're saying is that there's a kind of built-in primitivism in this antithetical technological system that we've got.

M.M.: Yes. In the midst of complaining about our superficiality, our lack of integral qualities, we suddenly found ourselves in a super primitive swamp of integral involved mankind.

F.K.: I wonder if we could try and get down crudely to the principal differences between what you call typographical, and what you call electric culture. The first is visual, and the second oral? What do these terms mean?

M.M.: Well, we haven't got on to that visual one. The visual sense has properties that are quite unique to the visual sense, and not characteristic of the other senses. I think it was Alec Layton who said, "To the blind all things are sudden." Without the sense of sight there is an absence of continuity and uniformity and connectiveness in the ordinary data of experience, in this kind of expectation of living in a space such as we sit in or as most people live in, in which we believe all parts of it are uniform and homogeneous, and that one space is very much like another space.

F.K.: But how would this come about as a result of typography—perhaps you could tell us that.

M.M.: Well, as a result of literacy. As early as Euclid the expectation that space is uniform and continuous and connected became the very basis of Greek science. But to relativity and nuclear physics and electronic man there is no such space available. Similarly, time takes on many of the characteristics of a literate culture, of a uniformly homogenised and connected visual culture, as well of space. We extend the culture pattern to all facts of our experience.

F.K.: Yes. But it would be very hard to show that there is another culture, I think, in which time was not thought of roughly as we think of it, otherwise there'd be no way of our communicating with—

M.M.: You are probably familiar with the ancient Chinese efforts to measure time by the sense of smell.

F.K.: I'm not, no.

M.M.: The scent of time—there is a fascinating recent study on that subject. But the idea of time as a continuum, as a uniform and connected continuum is not at all present to the oral societies. This is a peculiar illusion of visual and literate man.

F.K.: Well, we have this in our own traditions, the distinction between merely successive time and time thought of as seasons. You know the difference between the Greek *Chronos* * and the Greek *Kairos,** and I suppose this is always being brought back to us by accounts of mystical experiences and so on. The sense of intemporality in certain experiences is something we know about.

M.M.: Yes, the experience of time has always been discontinuous. The ways of measuring it took on this visual character—clockwise, with literacy; and yet no longer satisfactory for many scientific purposes.

F.K.: How would the arrival of the electric technology modify our views of time?

M.M.: I think it's well enough manifested in Lewis Carroll, where both time and

---

* *Chronos:* "merely successive time," time as continuum.
* *Kairos:* "time thought of as seasons"; a moment when conditions are ripe for the accomplishment of some crucial action.

space are suddenly subjected to total discontinuity and nonconformities and disconnections.

F.K.: We've always been aware of this in dreams, of course, haven't we?

M.M.: Yes, but Lewis Carroll—or Charles Dodgson *—was a mathematician who had become quite fascinated by Lobachevsky * and non-Euclidian spaces and non-Euclidian geometries and he transferred those to the nursery world, but in effect, he wrote a very avant-garde symbolist treatise by so doing. So our world, beginning as early in fact as Rimbaud,* our whole environmental world electromagnetically moved into a world of discontinuity and disconnection and of unique spaces rather than homogeneous spaces.

F.K.: This way of talking really depends, doesn't it, on what you said before, namely that these changes occur without people recognising them, until we reach a certain point. Now, a lot of people, presumably, don't know that these changes are happening to them. How will they recognise them? How, in their ordinary use of the media—the newspaper, the radio, television and so on—will they recognise these changes?

M.M.: They frequently encounter one medium bumping into another medium—when the sound track is put on movies, when the radio goes around the picture, all sorts of strange things happen to make them aware. At the present time, movies have become the content of T.V. We're totally unaware of T.V. as a form, tremendously aware of the content, which is the movie—much more so than when the movie was an environment. When the movie was environmental it was relatively imperceptible. Now that it has become the content of T.V. we can see it clearly.

F.K.: Well, here we are a couple of archaic literate men, Gutenberg men, talking on the television. What is the audience getting from this? Is it listening to what we're saying or is it feeling the impact of a new electric medium?

M.M.: There is a book called *Is Anybody Listening?* It's what worries the advertising man a great deal. The idea of feed-back, of being involved in one's—participating in one's—own audience participation is a natural product of this circuitry. Everything under electric conditions is looped. You become folded over into yourself, the image of yourself changes completely.

F.K.: In your other book, the more recent one, *Understanding Media* where you go into all this, you use as a kind of slogan, I think, the expression, "the medium is the message"; would you like to illuminate that?

M.M.: Well I think it is more satisfactory to say that any medium, be it radio or be it wheel, tends to create a completely new human environment. The human

* Lewis Carroll, Charles Dodgson: (1832–98): author of *Alice's Adventures in Wonderland* and *Through the Looking Glass.*
* N. I. Lobachevsky: Russian pioneer in non-Euclidean geometry.
* Arthur Rimbaud: (1854–91), precocious French poet, much admired by the Symbolists, who sought techniques for "expressing the inexpressible" and tried to realize the purely evocative, sensational qualities in words by liberating them from ordinary contexts and from syntactical relationships with other words.

environment as such tends to have a kind of invisible character about it. The unawareness of the environmental is compensated for by some attention to the content of the environment. The environment as merely a set of ground rules —as a kind of overall enveloping force—gets very little recognition as a form, except from the artist.

I think that our arts, if you look at them in this connection, do throw quite a lot of light on environments. The artist is usually engaged in somewhat excitedly explaining to people the character of new environments and new strategies of culture necessary to cope with them. Blake * is an extreme case, a man who was absolutely panicked by the kind of new environment that he saw forming around him under the auspices of Newton and Locke and industrialism. He thought it was going to smash the unity of the imaginative and sensory life all to bits. But what the artist was insisting upon in his own lifetime became quite a popular and widespread movement later on.

F.K.: Can I return to television?—because here we are: whoever's listening to us is also undergoing the impact of television at the moment. On your view they're all deceiving themselves insofar as they're paying attention to what we're saying, because what's going on is a medium which is in itself the image that they ought to be concerning themselves with.

M.M.: The medium of television has many characteristics which have been unheeded. Mostly it is seen under the aspect of movie form; the T.V. camera doesn't have its shutter, does not take pictures. As radio picks up, the T.V. camera picks up its environment, handles it, scans it, and the effect of the T.V. image is iconic in the sense that it shapes things by contours rather than by little snapshots.

F.K.: Now this is one of the words that you use a good deal, "iconic"—I think we'd better be clear what you mean by it.

M.M.: Yes, well I think of it again to tie in with Blake and his whole insistence upon the engraved, the highly patterned and highly sculptured forms and images. The "iconic" in that sense is very low in visual quality, very high in tactual quality—active touch, not cutaneous, but active touch as the psychologists insist.

F.K.: So you call television a tactile medium in fact.

M.M.: "Iconic" medium; having much in common with the cartoon for which it is ideally suited—much more well suited than for pictures.

F.K.: Let me put a couple of possible objections to that. In a sense, when you look at a picture, whatever kind of a picture it is, a temporal process is involved because you scan this picture, don't you? It doesn't matter whether it's Mantegna * or Coronation Street,* you scan it, and the television camera also

---

* William Blake: (1757–1827), English Romantic poet and artist, author of "Songs of Innocence," "Songs of Experience," and a number of long "Prophetic" poems.
* Andrea Mantegna: (1431–1506), Italian painter.
* Coronation Street: popular British soap-opera.

does this, as I understand it (not that I do understand it!)—proceeding by means of a moving point scanning very quickly. It's not selective, whereas your cartoon is something which makes its effect by exclusions.

M.M.: The T.V. camera is very much more selective and abstract than the picture camera. The picture camera—in fact, what makes the pictorial as opposed to the iconic—is the inclusion of a vast amount of detail. The filling in of space with great quantities of detail is what the Renaissance painters learned to do in the third dimension. They discovered that you could take space and fill it with objects. The iconic man doesn't fill space with objects; he makes space. The icon form tends not to be three-dimensional space so much as a made, shaped, moulded, modulated, resonating space.

F.K.: This would be true I think of a cartoon, truer than of a television picture.

M.M.: You think of a T.V. picture as much filled in with detail?

F.K.: Well, it's not selective, that's to say that if the microphone drops down into the picture the camera records it.

M.M.: Compared to a photograph of similar size it is enormously selective and abstract.

F.K.: Yes. Now the next point: the camera is working with its dots, and out of these dots we by our collaboration make a picture.

M.M.: There's much to fill in.

F.K.: There's a good deal to fill in, but this is something that we've got a lot of practice at doing and so it comes—it's a natural physiological movement by which we do it, isn't it? This doesn't seem to me to be the same thing as the way in which we supply the missing elements of a cartoon, for example.

M.M.: There's more to fill in.

F.K.: There's more to fill in, but it's also a different kind of filling in. What the television camera's trying to do because it's working on material which retains images—like a retina, as it were—is give us something rather like the kind of picture we're accustomed to and the cartoon is deliberately not doing so.

M.M.: This is very tricky terrain because many people are disturbed when they learn that natives and preliterates cannot see pictures; that in fact they do not use their eyes in the way that a literate man has learned to use his eyes. They can't recognise—an Arab has great difficulty in recognising—a postcard or a statue of a camel or any other object of everyday familiarity. John Wilson of the African Institute here said that after twenty years of teaching writing by film in Africa, he decided to teach writing so that they could see movies. They have to be taught to see movies the way we're taught to read and write. It is not something that people are naturally able to do. Now what we call the picture, well filled in, naturalistically and realistically filled in on a picture, is by no means visible to the non-literate man.

F.K.: No, but when they do learn it, they learn to scan it, in other words, there is a sequential element, a successive element involved in both this kind of image and in the typographical image.

M.M.: The picture has a great deal in common with the printed word, which is in effect a series of little black and white pictures, images, which you scan in sequence. On the other hand, the picture, because it gives you a vast amount of data in a single flash tends to be very much of a *Gestalt*,* and you can't spell out all the data that you perceive in a single instance.

F.K.: But to talk about "in a flash," the *Gestalt*, is really to beg the question of simultaneity, isn't it? Is there any such thing?

M.M.: There tends to be a great deal that is simultaneous in such a form of experience.

F.K.: You feel that we're going to have to come to terms, or we are coming to terms much more than the typographical man, with this kind of instantaneous image, and I'd like now just to ask you about the distinction which you draw between different kinds of media within the electric technology. You call some, such as television, "cool," and some such as radio, "hot." Now what does this mean?

M.M.: It has to do with the slang phrase, the "hot" and the "cool," which puzzles many people. The way it's used in slang reverses the meaning of cool. "Cool" in the slang form has come to mean involved, deeply participated, deeply engaged. Everything that we had formerly meant by heated argument is now called "cool" in slang. The idea that "cool" has reversed its meaning has, I think, some bearing on the fact that our culture has shifted a good deal of its stress into a demand that we be more committed, more involved in the situations in which we ordinarily work.

F.K.: A cool medium is one in which the definition is low and the audience has to work and supply the gaps.

M.M.: Like the cartoon, you see. This is real cool, whereas jazz as compared with classical music has many of these aspects of discontinuity and very much room for fill in; but where the information or data level is low, the fill in or participation is high. If you fill the situation with a complex of data the opportunity for completion fill in is less and participation is less.

F.K.: There's a kind of paradox, many paradoxes! But the one that I'm thinking of at the moment here is that a lot of people would suppose that television is something before which you slump—

M.M.: No, they're paying attention only to the programming, to the content, which has nothing to do with T.V.

F.K.: That's right. So you would say that the fact that some people may still be struggling to follow our conversation—that's not what we mean by, it's not our conversation that's—cool. Our conversation is hot, presumably, is it?

M.M.: Well, insofar as we're managing to be relatively detached, and are obeying—

---

* *Gestalt:* a unified whole, a configuration or structure so integrally organized that the nature and properties of the whole cannot be derived from the sum of its individual parts.

F.K.: We're cool—

M.M.: No, we're square.

F.K.: Ah, that's another concept altogether.

M.M.: Oh yes, we're a couple of squares all right as far as any "cool" audience is concerned. That is very complicated matter though. It's a new syndrome, as it were, in our culture, this cool business, and it isn't easy to unravel. Jack Paar on his show a few weeks ago asked some young chap "Why do you use the word 'cool' in the sense that we mean by 'hot?' " "Well," the youngster said, "you old folk had used up the word 'hot' before we came along!" This whole drive towards role playing and depth participation, the need for commitment and involvement began though with our poets and artists a hundred years ago. They began to devise opaque and difficult forms that were real cool— Rimbaud, and Baudelaire * and onward. They began to create these forms that required that you did—that you do—a great deal to complete the meaning. Remember Edgar Allen Poe's invention of the detective story at the time of the symbolist poem also. He devised this form in which the reader in effect made the story by filling in all sorts of clues and gaps. The reader became part of the creative process. The discovery that you could really involve the reader or viewer in the creative process by leaving out a great deal began over a century ago.

F.K.: And, incidentally, this is presumably now on the way out, isn't it?

M.M.: Well, the connected story line as a means of organising data, yes, is dropping out, even in film, with Fellini or Bergman.

F.K.: It depends on a different notion of what a logical or intelligible sequence of events is. We're passing out of that into electric, which as you repeatedly say, is an oral kind of culture. This reminds me to ask you, what I think is pretty important about your work, that if you've got phases like this which are determined technologically, one can not only speak about the kind of—the state of —affairs which we now have; one can also to some degree do some prediction. Now, I think in *Understanding Media* you sometimes write as if we'd pushed on deeper into electric technology than we actually have; but you do venture some predictions about the kind of life, the kind of quality of feeling that we're going to have with the new alteration in our senses. Could you say something about that?

M.M.: Well, I remember when I was here two years ago after a long absence I was quite startled at the upsurge of regional dialects in England, as compared with twenty years earlier, and the relative decline of standard and homogeneous English, and the quite proud display of dialects that I'd hardly heard before when I lived here. This driving depth—toward regional depth of culture—is a normal feature of electronic forms because of this circuitry that

---

* Charles Baudelaire: (1821–67), French poet, often thought of as the first "modern" poet, who had a strong influence on Rimbaud; author of *Les Fleurs du mal* (*Flowers of Evil*).

involves us deeper and deeper in ourselves. The French separatists, for example, at the present time, are very much related to this new image they have of themselves since television—a depth image.

F.K.: This is something you get in the typographical heartland of the nineteenth century—Matthew Arnold; there is a good deal of this emphasis on regionalism.

M.M.: I was thinking, though, more of the so-called nationalist movements of the Irish, the Scots, the Welsh, and now the French-Canadians and many other areas—this sudden insistence upon ancient folk ways, depth, roots of culture.

F.K.: On the other hand nationalism in itself is typographical, you say.

M.M.: Yes, well you see the term is used loosely like the "hot" and the "cool" to fit quite contrasting situations. Nationalism originated in a highly visual unity when people could for the first time see themselves as a single public or a single social group.

F.K.: Well, when shall we come to live in the global village, as you call it? When shall we have lost these—the sense that we have now—of being individuals and of being nations, which I think you say, is going to be one of the effects of the electric?

M.M.: I think an amazing amount of it is dissipated right now. Look at the sort of disturbance that is felt in the United States in recent years—the difficulty they now have in focusing their own image, quite strangely and powerfully represented by the Goldwater mood as it is called, in an attempt to rediscover the old blueprint of culture that they started out with in the eighteenth century, to get back to the old ground rules of culture. At present, the United States is undergoing a depth movement into itself, this teenagerism being only one aspect of it. The attempt to rediscover itself in a much greater depth than it was ever founded in, is disturbing the whole image of the American.

F.K.: The vision of the future that your book could leave one with is a big brother image, in a sense. You speak of "programming" cultures. For instance, you say that if the South African scene looks like getting too hot because of an overdose of radio, we programme a lot of television to cool them off. This kind of interference with what the typographical literate man calls human rights—

M.M.: We have never stopped interfering drastically with ourselves by every technology we could latch on to. We have absolutely disrupted our lives over and over again.

F.K.: And you think this can lead us into an electric totalitarianism?

M.M.: No, I think the logic if unimpeded—the logic of this sort of the electric world—is stasis.

F.K.: Out of this, where do you see—is there?—a terminus? Or shall we always go from the thesis of typography to the antithesis of electricity?

M.M.: If the natural play of circuitry is depth and ever-increasing involvement and responsibility, it would seem that it does demand a great increase of human autonomy, and human awareness. I think if there is a logic—and a hopeful one—in this, it is the dispelling of all unconscious aspects of our lives altogether; that we—in order to live with ourselves in such depth in such instant feed-back situations—have to understand everything, so that our easygoing lolling about in the lap of the unconscious cannot endure; that we will have to take over the total human environment as an artefact.

F.K.: So that the print-made split between head and heart that you speak of in one of your books, will be healed.

M.M.: Completely.

F.K.: By a return to—almost to—a pre-palaeotechnic state.

M.M.: Well, if we have used the arts at their very best, as a means of heightening our awareness of the otherwise unconscious environment, then the turning that whole skill to the making of the environment itself into a work of art, namely, of transcendent awareness, would seem to be the logic of this form. And the programming of environments as artefacts, as works of art, is something that people have been moving towards on many hands, even town planners—a familiar example of this attempt to fashion the total environment as if it were artefact instead of just introducing artefacts into environments. I think until now mankind has been content to introduce artefacts into environments that are otherwise beyond control—to use the arts as a control. The possibility of using the total environment as a work of art, as an artefact, is a quite startling and perhaps exhilarating image, but it seems to be forced upon us—the need to become completely autonomous and aware of all the consequences of everything we're doing before the consequences occur. That's where we're heading.

F.K.: Well, Marshall, I hope the people out there have got a clearer notion now of the difference between a medium and a message.

M.M.: I hope so too, but I don't think that clarity is necessarily the thing to discover in the beachhead—we've really established a beachhead.

Noam Chomsky / The Responsibility of the Intellectuals

Chomsky first emphasizes the relative freedom of the intellectual in the West, a freedom which leave no doubt of his responsibility "to speak the truth and expose lies." Examples of the failure of intellectuals to do so follow. The deceptions, he argues, are all made in the interests of American imperialism. He insists that American motives are as subject to disinterested analysis as those of any other power and that analysis by experts in human values are not to be excluded in favor of those by "value-free" technicians of various kinds. In illustrating this, Chomsky embarks on a wide-ranging critique of U.S. foreign policy, though his central interest is Vietnam. The essay is necessarily a blend of political and historical analysis with polemic, and of minutely detailed inquiry with rhetorical expansiveness. The author's personal authority is an invisible support for his argument; he is the greatest of living linguists and a master of various value-free skills.

It should be added that this and other, similar performances of Chomsky's have provoked responses from people he attacks, or who think differently. Our immediate purpose in including the essay is to illustrate the point that scholarly detail and ordered exposition are consistent with a passionate expression of political and ethical positions.

Twenty years ago, Dwight Macdonald published a series of articles in *Politics* on the responsibilities of peoples, and specifically, the responsibility of intellectuals. I read them as an undergraduate, in the years just after the war, and had occasion to read them again a few months ago. They seem to me to have lost none of their power or persuasiveness. Macdonald is concerned with the question of war guilt. He asks the question: To what extent were the German or Japanese people responsible for the atrocities committed by their governments? And, quite properly, he turns the question back to us: To what extent are the British or American people responsible for the vicious terror bombings of civilians, perfected as a technique of warfare by the Western democracies and reaching their culmination in Hiroshima and Nagasaki, surely among the most unspeakable crimes in history? To an undergraduate in 1945–1946—to anyone whose political and moral consciousness had been formed by the horrors of the 1930s, by the war in Ethiopia, the Russian purge, the "China Incident," the Spanish Civil War, the Nazi atrocities, the Western reaction to these events and, in part, complicity in them—these questions had particular significance and poignancy.

With respect to the responsibility of intellectuals, there are still other, equally disturbing questions. Intellectuals are in a position to expose the lies of governments, to analyze actions according to their causes and motives and often hidden intentions. In the Western world, at least, they have the power that comes from political liberty, from access to information and freedom of expression. For a privileged minority, Western democracy provides the leisure, the facilities, and the training to seek the truth lying hidden behind the veil of distortion and misrepresentation, ideology and class interest, through which the events of current history are presented to us. The responsibilities of intellectuals, then, are much deeper than what Macdonald calls the "responsibility of peoples," given the unique privileges that intellectuals enjoy.

The issues that Macdonald raised are as pertinent today as they were twenty years ago. We can hardly avoid asking ourselves to what extent the American people bear responsibility for the savage American assault on a largely helpless rural population in Vietnam, still another atrocity in what Asians see as the "Vasco da Gama era" * of world history. As for those of us who stood by in silence and apathy as this catastrophe slowly took shape over the past dozen years, on what page of history do we find our proper place? Only the most insensible can escape these questions. I want to return to them, later on, after a few scattered remarks about the responsibility of intellectuals and how, in practice, they go about meeting this responsibility in the mid-1960s.

It is the responsibility of intellectuals to speak the truth and to expose lies. This, at least, may seem enough of a truism to pass without comment. Not so, however. For the modern intellectual, it is not at all obvious. Thus we have Martin Heidegger * writing, in a pro-Hitler declaration of 1933, that "truth is the revelation of that which makes a people certain, clear, and strong in its action and knowledge"; it is only this kind of "truth" that one has a responsibility to speak. Americans tend to be more forthright. When Arthur Schlesinger * was asked by the *New York Times,* in November 1965, to explain the contradiction between his published account of the Bay of Pigs incident * and the story he had given the press at the time of the attack, he simply remarked that he had lied; and a few days later, he went on to compliment the *Times* for also having suppressed information on the planned invasion, in "the national interest," as this was defined by the group of arrogant and deluded men of whom Schlesinger gives such a flattering portrait in his recent account of the Kennedy administration. It is of no particular interest that one man is quite happy to lie in behalf of a cause which he knows to be unjust; but it is significant that such events provoke so little response in the intellectual community—no feeling, for example, that there is something strange in the offer of a major chair in humanities to a historian who feels it to be his duty to persuade the world that an American-sponsored invasion of a nearby country is nothing of the sort. And what of the incredible sequence of lies on the part of our government and its spokesmen concerning such matters as negotiations in Vietnam? The facts are known to all who care to know. The press, foreign and domestic, has presented documentation to refute each falsehood as it appears. But the power of the government

---

* Vasco da Gama: (c. 1469–1524), Portuguese navigator and the first European to reach India by sea; on his second voyage he founded colonies at Mozambique and Sofala, extending the range of the Portuguese Empire and making possible European exploitation of the wealth of the Indies.
* Martin Heidegger: (1889–), German philosopher; author of *Sein und Zeit* (*Being and Time,* 1927); was retired in 1945 from his post at Freiburg University because of his connection with the Nazi regime.
* Arthur Schlesinger: historian; former Harvard professor; special assistant to the President, 1961–64; author of *A Thousand Days: John F. Kennedy in the White House* (1965).
* Bay of Pigs incident: on 17 April 1961 some 1500 Cuban exiles, recruited, trained, and supplied by the U.S. Central Intelligence Agency, landed on the coast of Cuba intending to overthrow the regime of Fidel Castro; within three days the attempt was crushed.

propaganda apparatus is such that the citizen who does not undertake a research project on the subject can hardly hope to confront government pronouncements with fact.[1]

The deceit and distortion surrounding the American invasion of Vietnam is by now so familiar that it has lost its power to shock. It is therefore well to recall that although new levels of cynicism are constantly being reached, their clear antecedents were accepted at home with quiet toleration. It is a useful exercise to compare government statements at the time of the invasion of Guatemala in 1954 with Eisenhower's admission—to be more accurate, his boast—a decade later that American planes were sent "to help the invaders."[2] Nor is it only in moments of crisis that duplicity is considered perfectly in order. "New Frontiersmen,"* for example, have scarcely distinguished themselves by a passionate concern for historical accuracy, even when they are not being called upon to provide a "propaganda cover" for ongoing actions. For example, Arthur Schlesinger describes the bombing of North Vietnam and the massive escalation of military commitment in early 1965 as based on a "perfectly rational argument": "so long as the Vietcong thought they were going to win the war, they obviously would not be interested in any kind of negotiated settlement."[3] The date is important. Had the statement been made six months earlier, one could attribute it to ignorance. But this statement appeared after months of front-page

---

1. Such a research project has now been undertaken and published as a "Citizens' White Paper": F. Schurmann, P. D. Scott, R. Zelnik, *The Politics of Escalation in Vietnam* (New York, Fawcett World Library, and Boston, Beacon Press, 1966). For further evidence of American rejection of UN initiatives for diplomatic settlement, just prior to the major escalation of February 1965, see Mario Rossi, "The US Rebuff to U Thant," *New York Review of Books,* November 17, 1966. See also Theodore Draper, "How Not to Negotiate," *New York Review of Books,* May 4, 1967. There is further documentary evidence of NLF attempts to establish a coalition government and to neutralize the area, all rejected by the United States and its Saigon ally, in Douglas Pike, *Viet Cong* (Cambridge, The M.I.T. Press, 1966). In reading material of this latter sort one must be especially careful to distinguish between the evidence presented and the "conclusions" that are asserted, for reasons noted briefly below (see note 33).

It is interesting to see the first, somewhat oblique published reactions to *The Politics of Escalation,* by those who defend our right to conquer South Vietnam and institute a government of our choice. For example, Robert Scalapino (*New York Times Magazine,* December 11, 1966) argues that the thesis of the book implies that our leaders are "diabolical." Since no right-thinking person can believe this, the thesis is refuted. To assume otherwise would betray "irresponsibility," in a unique sense of this term—a sense that gives an ironic twist to the title of this chapter. He goes on to point out the alleged central weakness in the argument of the book, namely, the failure to perceive that a serious attempt on our part to pursue the possibilities for a diplomatic settlement would have been interpreted by our adversaries as a sign of weakness.

2. *New York Times,* October 14, 1965.
3. *New York Times,* February 6, 1966.

* "New Frontiersmen": those officials brought into the government by President Kennedy, largely from American colleges and universities. "New Frontier" was used to characterize the aims of the Kennedy administration.

news reports detailing the UN, North Vietnamese, and Soviet initiatives that preceded the February 1965 escalation and that, in fact, continued for several weeks after the bombing began, after months of soul-searching by Washington correspondents who were trying desperately to find some mitigating circumstances for the startling deception that had been revealed (Chalmers Roberts, for example, wrote with unconscious irony that late February 1965 "hardly seemed to Washington to be a propitious moment for negotiations [since] Mr. Johnson . . . had just ordered the first bombing of North Vietnam in an effort to bring Hanoi to a conference table where bargaining chips on both sides would be more closely matched" [4]). Coming at this moment, Schlesinger's statement is less an example of deceit than of contempt—contempt for an audience that can be expected to tolerate such behavior with silence, if not approval.[5]

To turn to someone closer to the actual formation and implementation of policy, consider some of the reflections of Walt Rostow,* a man who, according to Schlesinger, brought a "spacious historical view" to the conduct of foreign affairs in the Kennedy administration.[6] According to his analysis, the guerrilla warfare in Indochina in 1946 was launched by Stalin,[7] and Hanoi initiated the guerrilla war against South Vietnam in 1958 (*The View from the Seventh Floor,* pp. 39 and 152). Similarly, the Communist planners probed the "free world spec-

4. *Boston Globe,* November 19, 1965.
5. At other times, Schlesinger does indeed display admirable scholarly caution. For example, in his Introduction to *The Politics of Escalation* he admits that there may have been "flickers of interest in negotiations" on the part of Hanoi. As to the administration's lies about negotiations and its repeated actions undercutting tentative initiatives towards negotiations, he comments only that the authors may have underestimated military necessity and that future historians may prove them wrong. This caution and detachment must be compared with Schlesinger's attitude toward renewed study of the origins of the Cold War: in a letter to the *New York Review of Books,* October 20, 1966, he remarks that it is time to "blow the whistle" on revisionist attempts to show that the Cold War may have been the consequence of something more than mere Communist belligerence. We are to believe, then, that the relatively straightforward matter of the origins of the Cold War is settled beyond discussion, whereas the much more complex issue of why the United States shies away from a negotiated settlement in Vietnam must be left to future historians to ponder.

It is useful to bear in mind that the United States government itself is on occasion much less diffident in explaining why it refuses to contemplate a meaningful negotiated settlement. As is freely admitted, this solution would leave it without power to control the situation. See, for example, note 37.
6. Arthur M. Schlesinger, Jr., *A Thousand Days: John F. Kennedy in the White House* (Boston, Houghton Mifflin Company, 1965), p. 421.
7. Walt W. Rostow, *The View from the Seventh Floor* (New York, Harper & Row, Publishers, 1964), p. 149. See also his *United States in the World Arena* (New York, Harper & Row, Publishers, 1960), p. 244: "Stalin, exploiting the disruption and weakness of the postwar world, pressed out from the expanded base he had won during the Second World War in an effort to gain the balance of power in Eurasia . . . turning to the East, to back Mao and to enflame the North Korean and Indochinese Communists. . . ."

* Walt Rostow: economist; formerly professor at Massachusetts Institute of Technology; chairman of the State Department's policy planning council, 1961–66; special assistant to President Johnson, 1966–68.

trum of defense" in Northern Azerbaijan and Greece (where Stalin "supported substantial guerrilla warfare"—*ibid.*, pp. 36 and 148), operating from plans carefully laid in 1945. And in Central Europe, the Soviet Union was not "prepared to accept a solution which would remove the dangerous tensions from Central Europe at the risk of even slowly staged corrosion of communism in East Germany" (*ibid.*, p. 156).

It is interesting to compare these observations with studies by scholars actually concerned with historical events. The remark about Stalin's initiating the first Vietnamese war in 1946 does not even merit refutation. As to Hanoi's purported initiative in 1958, the situation is more clouded. But even government sources [8] concede that in 1959 Hanoi received the first direct reports of what Diem * referred to [9] as his own Algerian war and that only after this did they lay their plans to involve themselves in this struggle. In fact, in December 1958 Hanoi made another of its many attempts—rebuffed once again by Saigon and the United States—to establish diplomatic and commercial relations with the Saigon government on the basis of the status quo.[10] Rostow offers no evidence of Stalin's support for the Greek guerrillas; in fact, though the historical record is far from clear, it seems that Stalin was by no means pleased with the adventurism of the Greek guerrillas, who, from his point of view, were upsetting the satisfactory postwar imperialist settlement.[11]

Rostow's remarks about Germany are more interesting still. He does not see fit to mention, for example, the Russian notes of March–April 1952, which proposed unification of Germany under internationally supervised elections, with withdrawal of all troops within a year, *if* there was a guarantee that a reunified

8. For example, the article by CIA analyst George Carver in *Foreign Affairs,* April 1966. See also note 33.
9. Cf. Jean Lacouture, *Vietnam: Between Two Truces* (New York, Random House, 1966), p. 21. Diem's analysis of the situation was shared by Western observers at the time. See, for example, the comments of William Henderson, Far Eastern specialist and executive, Council on Foreign Relations, in R. W. Lindholm, ed., *Vietnam: The First Five Years* (East Lansing, Michigan State University Press, 1959). He notes "the growing alienation of the intelligentsia," "the renewal of armed dissidence in the South," the fact that "security has noticeably deteriorated in the last two years," all as a result of Diem's "grim dictatorship," and predicts "a steady worsening of the political climate in free Vietnam, culminating in unforeseen disasters."
10. See Bernard Fall, "Vietnam in the Balance," *Foreign Affairs,* Vol. 45 (October 1966), pp. 1–18.
11. Stalin was neither pleased by the Titoist tendencies inside the Greek Communist party, nor by the possibility that a Balkan federation might develop under Titoist leadership. It is nevertheless conceivable that Stalin supported the Greek guerrillas at some stage of the rebellion, in spite of the difficulty in obtaining firm documentary evidence. Needless to say, no elaborate study is necessary to document the British or American role in this civil conflict, from late 1944. See D. G. Kousoulas, *The Price of Freedom* (Syracuse, Syracuse University Press, 1953), *Revolution and Defeat* (New York, Oxford University Press, 1965), for serious study of these events from a strongly anti-Communist point of view.

* Ngo Dinh Diem: president of the Republic of Vietnam, 1955–63; overthrown by a military coup, November 1963.

Germany would not be permitted to join a Western military alliance.[12] And he has also momentarily forgotten his own characterization of the strategy of the Truman and Eisenhower administrations: "to avoid any serious negotiation with the Soviet Union until the West could confront Moscow with German rearmament within an organized European framework, as a *fait accompli*" [13]—to be sure, in defiance of the Potsdam agreements.

But most interesting of all is Rostow's reference to Iran. The facts are that there was a Russian attempt to impose by force a pro-Soviet government in Northern Azerbaijan that would grant the Soviet Union access to Iranian oil. This was rebuffed by superior Anglo-American force in 1946, at which point the more powerful imperialism obtained full rights to Iranian oil for itself, with the installation of a pro-Western government. We recall what happened when, for a brief period in the early 1950s, the only Iranian government with something of a popular base experimented with the curious idea that Iranian oil should belong to the Iranians. What is interesting, however, is the description of Northern Azerbaijan as part of "the free world spectrum of defense." It is pointless, by now, to comment on the debasement of the phrase "free world." But by what law of nature does Iran, with its resources, fall within Western dominion? The bland assumption that it does is most revealing of deep-seated attitudes toward the conduct of foreign affairs.

In addition to this growing lack of concern for truth, we find, in recent statements, a real or feigned naïveté with regard to American actions that reaches

12. For a detailed account, see James Warburg, *Germany: Key to Peace* (Cambridge, Harvard University Press, 1953), pp. 189f. Warburg concludes that apparently "the Kremlin was now prepared to accept the creation of an All-German democracy in the Western sense of that word," whereas the Western powers, in their response, "frankly admitted their plan 'to secure the participation of Germany in a purely defensive European community' " (i.e. NATO).

13. *The United States in the World Arena,* pp. 344–45. Incidentally, those who quite rightly deplore the brutal suppression of the East German and Hungarian revolutions would do well to remember that these scandalous events might have been avoided had the United States been willing to consider proposals for neutralization of Central Europe. Some of George Kennan's recent statements provide interesting commentary on this matter, for example, his comments on the falsity, from the outset, of the assumption that the USSR intended to attack or intimidate by force the Western half of the continent and that it was deterred by American force, and his remarks on the sterility and general absurdity of the demand for unilateral Soviet withdrawal from Eastern Germany together with "the inclusion of a united Germany as a major component in a Western defense system based primarily on nuclear weaponry" (Edward Reed, ed., *Peace on Earth* [New York, Pocket Books, 1965]).

It is worth noting that historical fantasy of the sort illustrated in Rostow's remarks has become a regular State Department specialty. Thus we have Thomas Mann justifying our Dominican intervention as a response to actions of the "Sino-Soviet military bloc." Or, to take a more considered statement, we have William Bundy's analysis of stages of development of Communist ideology in his Pomona College address, February 12, 1966, in which he characterizes the Soviet Union in the 1920s and early 1930s as "in a highly militant and aggressive phase." What is frightening about fantasy, as distinct from outright falsification, is the possibility that it may be sincere and may actually serve as the basis for formation of policy.

startling proportions. For example, Arthur Schlesinger has recently characterized our Vietnamese policies of 1954 as "part of our general program of international goodwill." [14] Unless intended as irony, this remark shows either a colossal cynicism or an inability, on a scale that defies comment, to comprehend elementary phenomena of contemporary history. Similarly, what is one to make of the testimony of Thomas Schelling * before the House Foreign Affairs Committee, January 27, 1966, in which he discusses the two great dangers if all Asia "goes Communist"? [15] First, this would exclude "the United States and what we call Western civilization from a large part of the world that is poor and colored and potentially hostile." Second, "a country like the United States probably cannot maintain self-confidence if just about the greatest thing it ever attempted, namely to create the basis for decency and prosperity and democratic government in the underdeveloped world, had to be acknowledged as a failure or as an attempt that we wouldn't try again." It surpasses belief that a person with even minimal acquaintance with the record of American foreign policy could produce such statements.

It surpasses belief, that is, unless we look at the matter from a more historical point of view, and place such statements in the context of the hypocritical moralism of the past; for example, of Woodrow Wilson, who was going to teach the Latin Americans the art of good government, and who wrote (1902) that it is "our peculiar duty" to teach colonial peoples "order and self-control . . . [and] . . . the drill and habit of law and obedience." Or of the missionaries of the 1840s, who described the hideous and degrading opium wars as "the result of a great design of Providence to make the wickedness of men subserve his purposes of mercy toward China, in breaking through her wall of exclusion, and bringing the empire into more immediate contact with western and Christian nations." Or, to approach the present, of A. A. Berle, who, in commenting on the Dominican intervention, has the impertinence to attribute the problems of the Caribbean countries to imperialism—*Russian* imperialism.[16]

As a final example of this failure of skepticism, consider the remarks of Henry Kissinger * in concluding his presentation in a Harvard-Oxford television debate

14. *New York Times,* February 6, 1966.
15. *United States Policy Toward Asia,* Hearings before the Subcommittee on the Far East and the Pacific of the Committee on Foreign Affairs, House of Representatives (Washington, D.C., U.S. Government Printing Office, 1966), p. 89.
16. *New York Times Book Review,* November 20, 1966. Such comments call to mind the remarkable spectacle of President Kennedy counseling Cheddi Jagan on the dangers of entering into a trading relationship "which brought a country into a condition of economic dependence." The reference, of course, is to the dangers in commercial relations with the Soviet Union. See Schlesinger, *A Thousand Days,* p. 776.

* Thomas Schelling: economist and university professor; served on the U.S. Air Force's science advisory board, 1960–64; on the Defense Department's science board, 1966–; adviser to the State Department's Bureau of European Affairs, 1966–.
* Henry Kissinger: former Harvard professor of government; consultant to the Department of State, 1965–; adviser to President Nixon on foreign policy and national security matters.

on American Vietnam policies. He observed, rather sadly, that what disturbs him most is that others question not our judgment but our motives—a remarkable comment on the part of one whose professional concern is political analysis, that is, analysis of the actions of governments in terms of motives that are unexpressed in official propaganda and perhaps only dimly perceived by those whose acts they govern. No one would be disturbed by an analysis of the political behavior of Russians, French, or Tanzanians, questioning their motives and interpreting their actions in terms of long-range interests, perhaps well concealed behind official rhetoric. But it is an article of faith that American motives are pure and not subject to analysis (see note 1). Although it is nothing new in American intellectual history—or, for that matter, in the general history of imperialist apologia—this innocence becomes increasingly distasteful as the power it serves grows more dominant in world affairs and more capable, therefore, of the unconstrained viciousness that the mass media present to us each day. We are hardly the first power in history to combine material interests, great technological capacity, and an utter disregard for the suffering and misery of the lower orders. The long tradition of naïveté and self-righteousness that disfigures our intellectual history, however, must serve as a warning to the Third World, if such a warning is needed, as to how our protestations of sincerity and benign intent are to be interpreted.

The basic assumptions of the "New Frontiersmen" should be pondered carefully by those who look forward to the involvement of academic intellectuals in politics. For example, I have referred to Arthur Schlesinger's objections to the Bay of Pigs invasion, but the reference was imprecise. True, he felt that it was a "terrible idea," but "not because the notion of sponsoring an exile attempt to overthrow Castro seemed intolerable in itself." Such a reaction would be the merest sentimentality, unthinkable to a tough-minded realist. The difficulty, rather, was that it seemed unlikely that the deception could succeed. The operation, in his view, was ill-conceived but not otherwise objectionable.[17] In a similar vein, Schlesinger quotes with approval Kennedy's "realistic" assessment of the situation resulting from Trujillo's assassination: "There are three possibilities in descending order of preference: a decent democratic regime, a continuation of the Trujillo regime or a Castro regime. We ought to aim at the first, but we really can't renounce the second until we are sure that we can avoid the third."[18] The reason why the third possibility is so intolerable is explained a few pages later: "Communist success in Latin America would deal a much harder blow to the power and influence of the United States." Of course, we can never really be sure of avoiding the third possibility; therefore, in practice, we will always settle for the second, as we are now doing in Brazil and Argentina, for example.[19]

17. *A Thousand Days*, p. 252.
18. *Ibid.*, p. 769.
19. Though this too is imprecise. One must recall the real character of the Trujillo regime to appreciate the full cynicism of Kennedy's "realistic" analysis.

Or consider Walt Rostow's views on American policy in Asia.[20] The basis on which we must build this policy is that "we are openly threatened and we feel menaced by Communist China." To prove that we are menaced is of course unnecessary, and the matter receives no attention; it is enough that we feel menaced. Our policy must be based on our national heritage and our national interests. Our national heritage is briefly outlined in the following terms: "Throughout the nineteenth century, in good conscience Americans could devote themselves to the extension of both their principles and their power on this continent," making use of "the somewhat elastic concept of the Monroe doctrine" and, of course, extending "the American interest to Alaska and the mid-Pacific islands. . . . Both our insistence on unconditional surrender and the idea of post-war occupation . . . represented the formulation of American security interests in Europe and Asia." So much for our heritage. As to our interests, the matter is equally simple. Fundamental is our "profound interest that societies abroad develop and strengthen those elements in their respective cultures that elevate and protect the dignity of the individual against the state." At the same time, we must counter the "ideological threat," namely "the possibility that the Chinese Communists can prove to Asians by progress in China that Communist methods are better and faster than democratic methods." Nothing is said about those people in Asian cultures to whom our "conception of the proper relation of the individual to the state" may not be the uniquely important value, people who might, for example, be concerned with preserving the "dignity of the individual" against concentrations of foreign or domestic capital, or against semifeudal structures (such as Trujillo-type dictatorships) introduced or kept in power by American arms. All of this is flavored with allusions to "our religious and ethical value systems" and to our "diffuse and complex concepts" which are to the Asian mind "so much more difficult to grasp" than Marxist dogma, and are so "disturbing to some Asians" because of "their very lack of dogmatism."

Such intellectual contributions as these suggest the need for a correction to De Gaulle's remark, in his *Memoirs,* about the American "will to power, cloaking itself in idealism." By now, this will to power is not so much cloaked in idealism as it is drowned in fatuity. And academic intellectuals have made their unique contribution to this sorry picture.

Let us, however, return to the war in Vietnam and the response that it has aroused among American intellectuals. A striking feature of the recent debate on Southeast Asian policy has been the distinction that is commonly drawn between "responsible criticism," on the one hand, and "sentimental," or "emotional," or "hysterical" criticism, on the other. There is much to be learned from a careful study of the terms in which this distinction is drawn. The "hysterical critics" are to be identified, apparently, by their irrational refusal to accept one fundamental

20. W. W. Rostow and R. W. Hatch, *An American Policy in Asia* (New York, Technology Press and John Wiley & Sons, Inc., 1955).

political axiom, namely, that the United States has the right to extend its power and control without limit, insofar as is feasible. Responsible criticism does not challenge this assumption, but argues, rather, that we probably can't "get away with it" at this particular time and place.

A distinction of this sort seems to be what Irving Kristol * has in mind, for example, in his analysis of the protest over Vietnam policy, in *Encounter,* August 1965. He contrasts the responsible critics, such as Walter Lippmann, the *New York Times,* and Senator Fulbright, with the "teach-in movement." "Unlike the university protesters," he maintains, "Mr. Lippmann engages in no presumptuous suppositions as to 'what the Vietnamese people really want'—he obviously doesn't much care—or in legalistic exegesis as to whether, or to what extent, there is 'aggression' or 'revolution' in South Vietnam. His is a *Realpolitik* * point of view; and he will apparently even contemplate the possibility of a *nuclear* war against China in extreme circumstances." This is commendable, and contrasts favorably, for Kristol, with the talk of the "unreasonable, ideological types" in the teach-in movement, who often seem to be motivated by such absurdities as "simple, virtuous 'anti-imperialism,' " who deliver "harangues on 'the power structure,' " and who even sometimes stoop so low as to read "articles and reports from the foreign press on the American presence in Vietnam." Furthermore, these nasty types are often psychologists, mathematicians, chemists, or philosophers (just as, incidentally, those most vocal in protest in the Soviet Union are generally physicists, literary intellectuals, and others remote from the exercise of power), rather than people with Washington contacts, who, of course, realize that "had they a new, good idea about Vietnam, they would get a prompt and respectful hearing" in Washington.

I am not interested here in whether Kristol's characterization of protest and dissent is accurate, but rather in the assumptions that it expresses with respect to such questions as these: Is the purity of American motives a matter that is beyond discussion, or that is irrelevant to discussion? Should decisions be left to "experts" with Washington contacts—that is, even if we assume that they command the necessary knowledge and principles to make the "best" decision, will they invariably do so? And, a logically prior question, is "expertise" applicable —that is, is there a body of theory and of relevant information, not in the public domain, that can be applied to the analysis of foreign policy or that demonstrates the correctness of present actions in some way that the psychologists, mathematicians, chemists, and philosophers are incapable of comprehending? Although Kristol does not examine these questions directly, his attitudes presuppose answers, answers which are wrong in all cases. American aggressiveness, however it may be masked in pious rhetoric, is a dominant force in world affairs

---

* Irving Kristol: former editor of *Encounter;* editor, with Daniel Bell, of *The Public Voice;* adviser on student affairs to President Nixon.
* *Realpolitik:* political realism; especially, policy based on power rather than on ideals or ideologies.

and must be analyzed in terms of its causes and motives. There is no body of theory or significant body of relevant information, beyond the comprehension of the layman, which makes policy immune from criticism. To the extent that "expert knowledge" is applied to world affairs, it is surely appropriate—for a person of any integrity, quite necessary—to question its quality and the goals that it serves. These facts seem too obvious to require extended discussion.

A corrective to Kristol's curious belief in the administration's openness to new thinking about Vietnam is provided by McGeorge Bundy * in a recent article.[21] As Bundy correctly observes, "on the main stage . . . the argument on Viet Nam turns on tactics, not fundamentals," although, he adds, "there are wild men in the wings." On stage center are, of course, the President (who in his recent trip to Asia had just "magisterially reaffirmed" our interest "in the progress of the people across the Pacific") and his advisers, who deserve "the understanding support of those who want restraint." It is these men who deserve the credit for the fact that "the bombing of the North has been the most accurate and the most restrained in modern warfare"—a solicitude which will be appreciated by the inhabitants, or former inhabitants, of Nam Dinh and Phu Ly and Vinh. It is these men, too, who deserve the credit for what was reported by Malcolm Browne as long ago as May 1965: "In the South, huge sectors of the nation have been declared 'free bombing zones,' in which anything that moves is a legitimate target. Tens of thousands of tons of bombs, rockets, napalm and cannon fire are poured into these vast areas each week. If only by the laws of chance, bloodshed is believed to be heavy in these raids."

Fortunately for the developing countries, Bundy assures us, "American democracy has no enduring taste for imperialism," and "taken as a whole, the stock of American experience, understanding, sympathy and simple knowledge is now much the most impressive in the world." It is true that "four-fifths of all the foreign investing in the world is now done by Americans" and that "the most admired plans and policies . . . are no better than their demonstrable relation to the American interest"—just as it is true, so we read in the same issue of *Foreign Affairs*, that the plans for armed action against Cuba were put into motion a few weeks after Mikoyan * visited Havana, "invading what had so long been an almost exclusively American sphere of influence." Unfortunately, such facts as these are often taken by unsophisticated Asian intellectuals as indicating a "taste for imperialism." For example, a number of Indians have expressed their "near exasperation" at the fact that "we have done everything we can to attract foreign capital for fertilizer plants, but the American and the other Western pri-

---

21. "End of Either/Or," *Foreign Affairs,* Vol. 45 (January 1967), pp. 189–201.

* McGeorge Bundy: former university professor of government; Dean of Arts and Sciences at Harvard, 1953–61; special assistant to the President for national security, 1961–66; president of the Ford Foundation, 1966–.
* Mikoyan: a top Soviet government official.

vate companies know we are over a barrel, so they demand stringent terms which we just cannot meet," [22] while "Washington . . . doggedly insists that deals be made in the private sector with private enterprise." [23] But this reaction, no doubt, simply reveals once again how the Asian mind fails to comprehend the "diffuse and complex concepts" of Western thought.

It may be useful to study carefully the "new, good ideas about Vietnam" that are receiving a "prompt and respectful hearing" in Washington these days. The United States Government Printing Office is an endless source of insight into the moral and intellectual level of this expert advise. In its publications one can read, for example, the testimony of Professor David N. Rowe, Director of Graduate Studies in International Relations at Yale University, before the House Committee on Foreign Affairs (see note 15). Professor Rowe proposes (p. 266) that the United States buy all surplus Canadian and Australian wheat, so that there will be mass starvation in China. These are his words: "Mind you, I am not talking about this as a weapon against the Chinese people. It will be. But that is only incidental. The weapon will be a weapon against the Government because the internal stability of that country cannot be sustained by an unfriendly Government in the face of general starvation." Professor Rowe will have none of the sentimental moralism that might lead one to compare this suggestion with, say, the *Ostpolitik* * of Hitler's Germany.[24] Nor does he fear the impact of such policies on other Asian nations, for example Japan. He assures us, from his "very long acquaintance with Japanese questions," that "the Japanese above all are people who respect power and determination." Hence "they will not be so much alarmed by American policy in Vietnam that takes off from a position of power and intends to seek a solution based upon the imposition of our power upon local people that we are in opposition to." What would disturb the Japanese is "a policy of indecision, a policy of refusal to face up to the problems [in China and Vietnam] and to meet our responsibilities there in a positive way," such as the way just cited. A conviction that we were "unwilling to use the power that they know we have" might "alarm the Japanese people very intensely and shake the degree of their friendly relations with us." In fact, a full use of American power would be particularly reassuring to the Japanese, because they have had a demonstration "of the tremendous power in action of the United States . . . because they have felt our power directly." This is surely a

22. *Christian Science Monitor,* November 26, 1966.
23. *Ibid.,* December 5, 1966.
24. Although, to maintain perspective, we should recall that in his wildest moments, Alfred Rosenberg spoke of the elimination of thirty million Slavs, not the imposition of mass starvation on a quarter of the human race. Incidentally, the analogy drawn here is highly "irresponsible," in the technical sense of this neologism discussed earlier. That is, it is based on the assumption that statements and actions of Americans are subject to the same standards and open to the same interpretations as those of anyone else.

* *Ostpolitik:* Hitler's policy in respect to eastern Europe.

prime example of the healthy *"Realpolitik* point of view" that Irving Kristol so much admires.

But, one may ask, why restrict ourselves to such indirect means as mass starvation? Why not bombing? No doubt this message is implicit in the remarks to the same committee of the Reverend R. J. de Jaegher, Regent of the Institute of Far Eastern Studies, Seton Hall University, who explains that like all people who have lived under Communism, the North Vietnamese "would be perfectly happy to be bombed to be free" (p. 345).

Of course, there must be those who support the Communists. But this is really a matter of small concern, as the Honorable Walter Robertson, Assistant Secretary of State for Far Eastern Affairs from 1953 to 1959, points out in his testimony before the same committee. He assures us that "The Peiping regime . . . represents something less than 3 percent of the population" (p. 402).

Consider, then, how fortunate the Chinese Communist leaders are, compared to the leaders of the Vietcong, who, according to Arthur Goldberg,* represent about "one-half of one percent of the population of South Vietnam," that is, about one half the number of new Southern recruits for the Vietcong during 1965, if we can credit Pentagon statistics.[25]

In the face of such experts as these, the scientists and philosophers of whom Kristol speaks would clearly do well to continue to draw their circles in the sand.

Having settled the issue of the political irrelevance of the protest movement, Kristol turns to the question of what motivates it—more generally, what has made students and junior faculty "go left," as he sees it, amid general prosperity and under liberal, Welfare State administrations. This, he notes, "is a riddle to which no sociologist has as yet come up with an answer." Since these young people are well-off, have good futures, etc., their protest must be irrational. It must be the result of boredom, of too much security, or something of this sort.

Other possibilities come to mind. It might be, for example, that as honest men the students and junior faculty are attempting to find out the truth for themselves rather than ceding the responsibility to "experts" or to government; and it might be that they react with indignation to what they discover. These possibilities Kristol does not reject. They are simply unthinkable, unworthy of consideration. More accurately, these possibilities are inexpressible; the categories in which they are formulated (honesty, indignation) simply do not exist for the tough-minded social scientist.

---

25. *New York Times,* February 6, 1966. What is more, Goldberg continues, the United States is not certain that all of these are voluntary adherents. That is not the first such demonstration of Communist duplicity. Another example was seen in the year 1962, when according to United States government sources 15,000 guerrillas suffered 30,000 casualties. See Arthur Schlesinger, *A Thousand Days,* p. 982.

* Arthur Goldberg: U.S. Supreme Court justice, 1962–65; U.S. representative to the United Nations, 1965–68.

In this implicit disparagement of traditional intellectual values, Kristol reflects attitudes that are fairly widespread in academic circles. I do not doubt that these attitudes are in part a consequence of the desperate attempt of the social and behavioral sciences to imitate the surface features of sciences that really have significant intellectual content. But they have other sources as well. Anyone can be a moral individual, concerned with human rights and problems; but only a college professor, a trained expert, can solve technical problems by "sophisticated" methods. Ergo, it is only problems of the latter sort that are important or real. Responsible, nonideological experts will give advice on tactical questions; irresponsible "ideological types" will "harangue" about principle and trouble themselves over moral issues and human rights, or over the traditional problems of man and society, concerning which "social and behavioral science" have nothing to offer beyond trivialities. Obviously, these emotional, ideological types are irrational, since, being well-off and having power in their grasp, they shouldn't worry about such matters.

At times this pseudoscientific posing reaches levels that are almost pathological. Consider the phenomenon of Herman Kahn,* for example. Kahn has been both denounced as immoral and lauded for his courage. By people who should know better, his *On Thermonuclear War* has been described "without qualification . . . [as] . . . one of the great works of our time" (Stuart Hughes). The fact of the matter is that this is surely one of the emptiest works of our time, as can be seen by applying to it the intellectual standards of any existing discipline, by tracing some of its "well-documented conclusions" to the "objective studies" from which they derive, and by following the line of argument, where detectable. Kahn proposes no theories, no explanations, no factual assumptions that can be tested against their consequences, as do the sciences he is attempting to mimic. He simply suggests a terminology and provides a façade of rationality. When particular policy conclusions are drawn, they are supported only by *ex cathedra* remarks for which no support is even suggested (e.g., "The civil defense line probably should be drawn somewhere below $5 billion annually" to keep from provoking the Russians—why not $50 billion, or $5.00?). What is more, Kahn is quite aware of this vacuity; in his more judicious moments he claims only that "there is no reason to believe that relatively sophisticated models are more likely to be misleading than the simpler models and analogies frequently used as an aid to judgment." For those whose humor tends towards the macabre, it is easy to play the game of "strategic thinking" à la Kahn, and to prove what one wishes.

* Herman Kahn: defense analyst and consultant on military strategy; in *On Thermonuclear War* (1960), he considers the probability of another world war and criticizes those who refuse to think realistically about the nature and consequences of such a war; a firm advocate of preparedness, he believes that the effects of a nuclear war could be alleviated by an adequate civil defense program. His book was attacked by some as "bloodthirsty" and as a tract on how to commit mass murder. His other books include *Thinking about the Unthinkable* (1962) and *On Escalation: Metaphors and Scenarios* (1965).

For example, one of Kahn's basic assumptions is that "an all-out surprise attack in which all resources are devoted to counter-value targets would be so irrational that, barring an incredible lack of sophistication or actual insanity among Soviet decision makers, such an attack is highly unlikely." A simple argument proves the opposite. Premise 1: American decision makers think along the lines outlined by Herman Kahn. Premise 2: Kahn thinks it would be better for everyone to be red than for everyone to be dead. Premise 3: If the Americans were to respond to an all-out countervalue attack, then everyone would be dead. Conclusion: The Americans will not respond to an all-out countervalue attack, and therefore it should be launched without delay. Of course, one can carry the argument a step further. Fact: The Russians have not carried out an all-out countervalue attack. It follows that they are not rational. If they are not rational, there is no point in "strategic thinking." Therefore . . .

Of course this is all nonsense, but nonsense that differs from Kahn's only in the respect that the argument is of slightly greater complexity than anything to be discovered in his work. What is remarkable is that serious people actually pay attention to these absurdities, no doubt because of the façade of tough-mindedness and pseudo-science.

It is a curious and depressing fact that the "antiwar movement" falls prey all too often to similar confusions. In the fall of 1965, for example, there was an International Conference on Alternative Perspectives on Vietnam, which circulated a pamphlet to potential participants stating its assumptions. The plan was to set up study groups in which three "types of intellectual tradition" will be represented: (1) area specialists; (2) "social theory, with special emphasis on theories of the international system, of social change and development, of conflict and conflict resolution, or of revolution"; (3) "the analysis of public policy in terms of basic human values, rooted in various theological, philosophical and humanist traditions." The second intellectual tradition will provide "general propositions, derived from social theory and tested against historical, comparative, or experimental data"; the third "will provide the framework out of which fundamental value questions can be raised and in terms of which the moral implications of societal actions can be analyzed." The hope was that "by approaching the questions [of Vietnam policy] from the moral perspectives of all great religions and philosophical systems, we may find solutions that are more consistent with fundamental human values than current American policy in Vietnam has turned out to be."

In short, the experts on values (i.e., spokesmen for the great religions and philosophical systems) will provide fundamental insights on moral perspectives, and the experts on social theory will provide general empirically validated propositions and "general models of conflict." From this interplay, new policies will emerge, presumably from application of the canons of scientific method. The only debatable issue, it seems to me, is whether it is more ridiculous to turn to experts in social theory for general well-confirmed propositions, or to the specialists in the great religions and philosophical systems for insights into fundamental human values.

There is much more that can be said about this topic, but without continuing, I would simply like to emphasize that, as is no doubt obvious, the cult of the expert is both self-serving, for those who propound it, and fraudulent. Obviously, one must learn from social and behavioral science whatever one can; obviously, these fields should be pursued in as serious a way as is possible. But it will be quite unfortunate, and highly dangerous, if they are not accepted and judged on their merits and according to their actual, not pretended, accomplishments. In particular, if there is a body of theory, well tested and verified, that applies to the conduct of foreign affairs or the resolution of domestic or international conflict, its existence has been kept a well-guarded secret. In the case of Vietnam, if those who feel themselves to be experts have access to principles or information that would justify what the American government is doing in that unfortunate country, they have been singularly ineffective in making this fact known. To anyone who has any familiarity with the social and behavioral sciences (or the "policy sciences"), the claim that there are certain considerations and principles too deep for the outsider to comprehend is simply an absurdity, unworthy of comment.

When we consider the responsibility of intellectuals, our basic concern must be their role in the creation and analysis of ideology. And, in fact, Kristol's contrast between the unreasonable ideological types and the responsible experts is formulated in terms that immediately bring to mind Daniel Bell's interesting and influential essay on the "end of ideology," [26] an essay which is as important for what it leaves unsaid as for its actual content. Bell presents and discusses the Marxist analysis of ideology as a mask for class interest, in particular, quoting Marx's well-known description of the belief of the bourgeoisie "that the *special* conditions of its emancipation are the *general* conditions through which alone modern society can be saved and the class struggle avoided." He then argues that the age of ideology is ended, supplanted, at least in the West, by a general agreement that each issue must be settled on its own individual terms, within the

---

26. Reprinted in a collection of essays with the title *The End of Ideology: On the Exhaustion of Political Ideas in the Fifties* (New York, The Free Press, 1960). I have no intention here of entering into the full range of issues that have been raised in the discussion of the "end of ideology" for the past dozen years. It is difficult to see how a rational person could quarrel with many of the theses that have been put forth, e.g., that at a certain historical moment the "politics of civility" is appropriate, and perhaps efficacious; that one who advocates action (or inaction—a matter less frequently noted) has a responsibility to assess its social cost; that dogmatic fanaticism and "secular religions" should be combated (or if possible, ignored); that technical solutions to problems should be implemented, where possible; that *"le dogmatisme idéologique devait disparaître pour que les idées reprissent vie"* (Aron); and so on. Since this is sometimes taken to be an expression of an "anti-Marxist" position, it is worth keeping in mind that such sentiments as these have no bearing on non-Bolshevik Marxism, as represented, for example, by such figures as Luxemburg, Pannekoek, Korsch, Arthur Rosenberg, and many others.

framework of a welfare state in which, presumably, experts in the conduct of public affairs will have a prominent role. Bell is quite careful, however, to characterize the precise sense of "ideology" in which "ideologies are exhausted." He is referring only to ideology as "the conversion of ideas into social levers," to ideology as "a set of beliefs, infused with passion, . . . [which] . . . seeks to transform the whole of a way of life." The crucial words are "transform" and "convert into social levers." Intellectuals in the West, he argues, have lost interest in converting ideas into social levers for the radical transformation of society. Now that we have achieved the pluralistic society of the Welfare State, they see no further need for a radical transformation of society; we may tinker with our way of life here and there, but it would be wrong to try to modify it in any significant way. With this consensus of intellectuals, ideology is dead.

There are several striking facts about Bell's essay. First, he does not point out the extent to which this consensus of the intellectuals is self-serving. He does not relate his observation that, by and large, intellectuals have lost interest in "transforming the whole of a way of life" to the fact that they play an increasingly prominent role in running the Welfare State; he does not relate their general satisfaction with the Welfare State to the fact that, as he observes elsewhere, "America has become an affluent society, offering place . . . and prestige . . . to the onetime radicals." Secondly, he offers no serious argument to show that intellectuals are somehow "right" or "objectively justified" in reaching the consensus to which he alludes, with its rejection of the notion that society should be transformed. Indeed, although Bell is fairly sharp about the empty rhetoric of the "New Left," he seems to have a quite utopian faith that technical experts will be able to come to grips with the few problems that still remain; for example, the fact that labor is treated as a commodity, and the problems of "alienation."

It seems fairly obvious that the classical problems are very much with us; one might plausibly argue that they have even been enhanced in severity and scale. For example, the classical paradox of poverty in the midst of plenty is now an ever increasing problem on an international scale. Whereas one might conceive, at least in principle, of a solution within national boundaries, a sensible idea as to how to transform international society in such a way as to cope with the vast and perhaps increasing human misery is hardly likely to develop within the framework of the intellectual consensus that Bell describes.

Thus it would seem natural to describe the consensus of Bell's intellectuals in somewhat different terms than his. Using the terminology of the first part of his essay, we might say that the Welfare State technician finds justification for his special and prominent social status in his "science," specifically, in the claim that social science can support a technology of social tinkering on a domestic or international scale. He then takes a further step, proceeding, in a familiar way, to claim universal validity for what is in fact a class interest: he argues that the special conditions on which his claims to power and authority are based are, in fact, the general conditions through which alone modern society can be saved; that social tinkering within a Welfare State framework must replace the commitment to the "total ideologies" of the past, ideologies which were concerned with a transformation of society. Having found his position of power, having achieved security and affluence, he has no further need for ideologies that look to radical change. The scholar-expert replaces the "free-floating intellectual" who "felt that the wrong values were being honored, and rejected the society," and who has now lost his political role (now, that is, that the right values are being honored).

Conceivably, it is correct that the technical experts who will (or hope to) manage the "postindustrial society" will be able to cope with the classical problems without a radical transformation of society. Just so, it is conceivably true that the bourgeoisie was right in regarding the special conditions of its emancipation as the general conditions through which alone modern society would be saved. In either case, an argument is in order, and skepticism is justified where none appears.

Within the same framework of general utopianism, Bell goes on to pose the issue between Welfare State scholar-experts and Third World ideologists in a rather curious way. He points out, quite correctly, that there is no issue of communism, the content of that doctrine having been "long forgotten by friends and foes alike." Rather, he says, "the question is an older one: whether new societies can grow by building democratic institutions and allowing people to make choices—and sacrifices—voluntarily, or whether the new elites, heady with power, will impose totalitarian means to transform their countries." The question is an interesting one; it is odd, however, to see it referred to as "an older one." Surely he cannot be suggesting that the West chose the democratic way—for example, that in England during the industrial revolution, the farmers voluntarily made the choice of leaving the land, giving up cottage industry, becoming an industrial proletariat, and voluntarily decided, within the framework of the existing democratic institutions, to make the sacrifices that are graphically described in the classic literature on nineteenth-century industrial society. One may debate the question whether authoritarian control is necessary to permit capital accumulation in the underdeveloped world, but the Western model of development is hardly one that we can point to with any pride. It is perhaps not surprising to find a Walt Rostow referring to "the more humane processes [of industrialization] that Western values would suggest." [27] Those who have a serious concern for the problems that face backward countries and for the role that advanced industrial societies might, in principle, play in development and modernization, must use somewhat more care in interpreting the significance of the Western experience.

Returning to the quite appropriate question, whether "new societies can grow by building democratic institutions" or only by totalitarian means, I think that

27. Rostow and Hatch, *An American Policy in Asia,* p. 10.

honesty requires us to recognize that this question must be directed more to American intellectuals than to Third World ideologists. The backward countries have incredible, perhaps insurmountable problems, and few available options; the United States has a wide range of options, and has the economic and technological resources, though evidently neither the intellectual nor moral resources, to confront at least some of these problems. It is easy for an American intellectual to deliver homilies on the virtues of freedom and liberty, but if he is really concerned about, say, Chinese totalitarianism or the burdens imposed on the Chinese peasantry in forced industrialization, then he should face a task that is infinitely more significant and challenging—the task of creating, in the United States, the intellectual and moral climate, as well as the social and economic conditions, that would permit this country to participate in modernization and development in a way commensurate with its material wealth and technical capacity. Massive capital gifts to Cuba and China might not succeed in alleviating the authoritarianism and terror that tend to accompany early stages of capital accumulation, but they are far more likely to have this effect than lectures on democratic values. It is possible that even without "capitalist encirclement" in its varying manifestations, the truly democratic elements in revolutionary movements—in some instances, soviets and collectives, for example—might be undetermined by an "elite" of bureaucrats and technical intelligentsia; but it is a near certainty that the fact of capitalist encirclement, which all revolutionary movements now have to face, will guarantee this result. The lesson, for those who are concerned to strengthen the democratic, spontaneous, and popular elements in developing societies, is quite clear. Lectures on the two-party system, or even the really substantial democratic values that have been in part realized in Western society, are a monstrous irrelevance in the face of the effort that is required to raise the level of culture in Western society to the point where it can provide a "social lever" for both economic development and the development of true democratic institutions in the Third World—and for that matter, at home as well.

A good case can be made for the conclusion that there is indeed something of a consensus among intellectuals who have already achieved power and affluence, or who sense that they can achieve them by "accepting society" as it is and promoting the values that are "being honored" in this society. And it is also true that this consensus is most noticeable among the scholar-experts who are replacing the free-floating intellectuals of the past. In the university, these scholar-experts construct a "value-free technology" for the solution of technical problems that arise in contemporary society,[28] taking a "responsible stance" towards these

28. The extent to which this "technology" is value-free is hardly very important, given the clear commitments of those who apply it. The problems with which research is concerned are those posed by the Pentagon or the great corporations, not, say, by the revolutionaries of Northeast Brazil or by SNCC. Nor am I aware of a research project devoted to the problem of how poorly-armed guerrillas might more effectively resist a brutal and devastating military technology—surely the kind of problem that would have interested the free-floating intellectual who is now hopelessly out of date.

problems, in the sense noted earlier. This consensus among the responsible scholar-experts is the domestic analogue to that proposed, in the international arena, by those who justify the application of American power in Asia, whatever the human cost, on the grounds that it is necessary to contain the "expansion of China" (an "expansion" which is, to be sure, hypothetical for the time being) [29] —to translate from State Department Newspeak,* on the grounds that it is essential to reverse the Asian nationalist revolutions, or at least to prevent them from spreading. The analogy becomes clear when we look carefully at the ways in which this proposal is formulated. With his usual lucidity, Churchill outlined the general position in a remark to his colleague of the moment, Joseph Stalin, at Teheran in 1943: ". . . the government of the world must be entrusted to satisfied nations, who wished nothing more for themselves than what they had. If

29. In view of the unremitting propaganda barrage on "Chinese expansionism," perhaps a word of comment is in order. Typical of American propaganda on this subject is Adlai Stevenson's assessment, shortly before his death (cf. *New York Times Magazine,* March 13, 1966): "So far, the new Communist 'dynasty' has been very aggressive. Tibet was swallowed, India attacked, the Malays had to fight 12 years to resist a 'national liberation' they could receive from the British by a more peaceful route. Today, the apparatus of infiltration and aggression is already at work in North Thailand."

As to Malaya, Stevenson is probably confusing ethnic Chinese with the government of China. Those concerned with the actual events would agree with Harry Miller, in *Communist Menace in Malaya* (New York, Frederick A. Praeger, Publishers, 1954), that "Communist China continues to show little interest in the Malayan affair beyond its usual fulminations via Peking Radio." There are various harsh things that one might say about Chinese behavior in what the Sino-Indian Treaty of 1954 refers to as "the Tibet region of China," but it is no more proof of a tendency towards expansionism than is the behavior of the Indian government with regard to the Naga and Mizo tribesmen. As to North Thailand, "the apparatus of infiltration" may well be at work, though there is little reason to suppose it to be Chinese—and it is surely not unrelated to the American use of Thailand as a base for its attack on Vietnam. This reference is the sheerest hypocrisy.

The "attack on India" grew out of a border dispute that began several years after the Chinese had completed a road from Tibet to Sinkiang in an area so remote from Indian control that the Indians learned about this operation only from the Chinese press. According to American Air Force maps, the disputed area is in Chinese territory. Cf. Alastair Lamb, *China Quarterly,* July–September, 1965. To this distinguished authority, "it seems unlikely that the Chinese have been working out some master plan . . . to take over the Indian sub-continent lock, stock and overpopulated barrel." Rather, he thinks it likely that the Chinese were probably unaware that India even claimed the territory through which the road passed. After the Chinese military victory, Chinese troops were, in most areas, withdrawn beyond the McMahon Line, a border which the British had attempted to impose on China in 1914 but which has never been recognized by China (Nationalist or Communist), the United States, or any other government.

It is remarkable that a person in a responsible position could describe all of this as Chinese expansionism. In fact, it is absurd to debate the hypothetical aggressiveness of a China surrounded by American missiles and a still expanding network of military bases backed by an enormous American expeditionary force in Southeast Asia. It is conceivable that at some future time a powerful China may be expansionist. We may speculate about such possibilities if we wish, but it is American aggressiveness that is the central fact of current politics.

* Newspeak: see piece by George Orwell (p. 494).

the world-government were in the hand of hungry nations, there would always be danger. But none of us had any reason to seek for anything more. The peace would be kept by peoples who lived in their own way and were not ambitious. Our power placed us above the rest. We were like rich men dwelling at peace within their habitations." [30]

For a translation of Churchill's biblical rhetoric into the jargon of contemporary social science, one may turn to the testimony of Charles Wolf, Senior Economist of the RAND Corporation, at the congressional committee hearings cited earlier:

> I am dubious that China's fears of encirclement are going to be abated, eased, relaxed in the long-term future. But I would hope that what we do in Southeast Asia would help to develop within the Chinese body politic more of a realism and willingness to live with this fear than to indulge it by support for liberation movements, which admittedly depend on a great deal more than external support . . . the operational question for American foreign-policy is not whether that fear can be eliminated or substantially alleviated, but whether China can be faced with a structure of incentives, of penalties and rewards, of inducements that will make it willing to live with this fear.[31]

The point is further clarified by Thomas Schelling: "There is growing experience which the Chinese can profit from, that although the United States may be interested in encircling them, may be interested in defending nearby areas from them, it is, nevertheless, prepared to behave peaceably if they are." [32]

In short, we are prepared to live peaceably within our—to be sure, rather extensive—habitations. And quite naturally, we are offended by the undignified noises from the servants' quarters. If, let us say, a peasant-based revolutionary movement tries to achieve independence from foreign domination or to overthrow semifeudal structures supported by foreign powers, or if the Chinese irrationally refuse to respond properly to the schedule of reinforcement that we have prepared for them, if they object to being encircled by the benign and peace-loving "rich men" who control the territories on their borders as a natural right, then, evidently, we must respond to this belligerence with appropriate force.

It is this mentality that explains the frankness with which the United States government and its academic apologists defend the American refusal to permit a political settlement in Vietnam at a local level, a settlement based on the actual distribution of political forces. Even government experts freely admit that the

---

30. W. S. Churchill, *Closing the Ring,* Vol. 5 of *The Second World War* (Boston, Houghton Mifflin Company, 1951), p. 382.
31. *United States Policy Toward Asia,* p. 104. See note 15.
32. *Ibid.,* p. 105.

NLF * is the only "truly mass-based political party in South Vietnam"; [33] that the NLF had "made a conscious and massive effort to extend political participation, even if it was manipulated, on the local level so as to involve the people in a self-contained, self-supporting revolution" (p. 374); and that this effort had been so successful that no political groups, "with the possible exception of the Buddhists, thought themselves equal in size and power to risk entering into a coalition, fearing that if they did the whale would swallow the minnow" (p. 362). Moreover, they concede that until the introduction of overwhelming American force, the NLF had insisted that the struggle "should be fought out at the political level and that the use of massed military might was in itself illegitimate. . . . The battleground was to be the minds and loyalties of the rural Vietnamese, the weapons were to be ideas" (pp. 91–92; cf. also pp. 93, 99–108, 155f.); and correspondingly, that until mid-1964, aid from Hanoi "was largely confined to two areas—doctrinal know-how and leadership personnel" (p. 321). Captured NLF documents contrast the enemy's "military superiority" with their own "political superiority" (p. 106), thus fully confirming the analysis of American military spokesmen who define our problem as how, "with considerable armed force but

33. Douglas Pike, *op. cit.*, p. 110. This book, written by a foreign service officer working at the Center for International Studies, MIT, poses a contrast between our side, which sympathizes with "the usual revolutionary stirrings . . . around the world because they reflect inadequate living standards or oppressive and corrupt governments," and the backers of "revolutionary guerrilla warfare," which "opposes the aspirations of people while apparently furthering them, manipulates the individual by persuading him to manipulate himself." Revolutionary guerrilla warfare is "an imported product, revolution from the outside" (other examples, besides the Vietcong, are "Stalin's exportation of armed revolution," the Haganah in Palestine, and the Irish Republican Army—see pp. 32–33). The Vietcong could not be an indigenous movement since it has "a social construction program of such scope and ambition that of necessity it must have been created in Hanoi" (p. 76—but on pp. 77–79 we read that "organizational activity had gone on intensively and systematically for several years" before the Lao Dong party in Hanoi had made its decision "to begin building an organization"). On page 80 we find that "such an effort had to be the child of the North," even though elsewhere we read of the prominent role of the Cao Dai (p. 74), "the first major social group to begin actively opposing the Diem government" (p. 222), and of the Hoa Hao sect, "another early and major participant in the NLF" (p. 69). He takes it as proof of Communist duplicity that in the South, the party insisted it was "Marxist-Leninist," thus "indicating philosophic but not political allegiance," whereas in the North it described itself as a "Marxist-Leninist organization" thus "indicating that it was in the main-stream of the world-wide Communist movement" (p. 150). And so on. Also revealing is the contempt for "Cinderella and all the other fools [who] could still believe there was magic in the mature world if one mumbled the secret incantation: solidarity, union, concord"; for the "gullible, misled people" who were "turning the countryside into a bedlam, toppling one Saigon government after another, confounding the Americans"; for the "mighty force of people" who in their mindless innocence thought that "the meek, at last, were to inherit the earth," that "riches would be theirs and all in the name of justice and virtue." One can appreciate the chagrin with which a sophisticated Western political scientist must view this "sad and awesome spectacle."

* NLF: the National Liberation Front, a political organization formed in 1960 by the Vietcong in South Vietnam to carry out an insurgent policy.

little political power, [to] contain an adversary who has enormous political force but only modest military power." [34]

Similarly, the most striking outcome of both the Honolulu conference in February and the Manila conference in October was the frank admission by high officials of the Saigon government that "they could not survive a 'peaceful settlement' that left the Vietcong *political* structure in place even if the Vietcong guerilla units were disbanded," that "they are not able to compete *politically* with the Vietnamese Communists." [35] Thus, Mohr continues, the Vietnamese demand a "pacification program" which will have as "its core . . . the destruction of the clandestine Vietcong political structure and the creation of an iron-like system of government political control over the population." And from Manila, the same correspondent, on October 23, quotes a high South Vietnamese official as saying: "Frankly, we are not strong enough now to compete with the Communists on a purely political basis. They are organized and disciplined. The non-Communist nationalists are not—we do not have any large, well-organized political parties and we do not yet have unity. We cannot leave the Vietcong in existence." Officials in Washington understand the situation very well. Thus Secretary Rusk has pointed out that "if the Vietcong come to the conference table as full partners they will, in a sense, have been victorious in the very aims that South Vietnam and the United States are pledged to prevent" (January 28, 1966). Similarly, Max Frankel reported from Washington: "Compromise has had no appeal here because the Administration concluded long ago that the non-Communist forces of South Vietnam could not long survive in a Saigon coalition with Communists. It is for that reason—and not because of an excessively rigid sense of protocol—that Washington has steadfastly refused to deal with the Vietcong or recognize them as an independent political force." [36]

In short, we will—magnanimously—permit Vietcong representatives to attend negotiations only if they will agree to identify themselves as agents of a foreign power and thus forfeit the right to participate in a coalition government, a right which they have now been demanding for a half-dozen years. We know well that in any representative coalition, our chosen delegates could not last a day without the support of American arms. Therefore, we must increase American force and resist meaningful negotiations, until the day when a client government can exert both military and political control over its own population—a day which may never dawn, for as William Bundy has pointed out, we could never be sure of the security of a Southeast Asia "from which the Western presence was effectively withdrawn." Thus if we were to "negotiate in the direction of solutions that are put under the label of neutralization," this would amount to

---

34. Lacouture, *op. cit.*, p. 188. The same military spokesman goes on, ominously, to say that this is the problem confronting us throughout Asia, Africa, and Latin America, and that we must find the "proper response" to it.
35. Charles Mohr, *New York Times,* February 11, 1966. Italics mine.
36. *New York Times,* February 18, 1966.

capitulation to the Communists.³⁷ According to this reasoning, then, South Vietnam must remain, permanently, an American military base.

All of this is of course reasonable, so long as we accept the fundamental political axiom that the United States, with its traditional concern for the rights of the weak and downtrodden, and with its unique insight into the proper mode of development for backward countries, must have the courage and the persistence to impose its will by force until such time as other nations are prepared to accept these truths—or simply to abandon hope.

If it is the responsibility of the intellectual to insist upon the truth, it is also his duty to see events in their historical perspective. Thus one must applaud the insistence of the Secretary of State on the importance of historical analogies, the Munich * analogy, for example. As Munich showed, a powerful and aggressive nation with a fanatic belief in its manifest destiny will regard each victory, each extension of its power and authority, as a prelude to the next step. The matter was very well put by Adlai Stevenson, when he spoke of "the old, old route whereby expansive powers push at more and more doors, believing they will open, until, at the ultimate door, resistance is unavoidable and major war breaks out." Herein lies the danger of appeasement, as the Chinese tirelessly point out to the Soviet Union, which they claim is playing Chamberlain to our Hitler in Vietnam. Of course, the aggressiveness of liberal imperialism is not that of Nazi Germany, though the distinction may seem rather academic to a Vietnamese peasant who is being gassed or incinerated. We do not want to occupy Asia; we merely wish, to return to Mr. Wolf, "to help the Asian countries progress toward economic modernization, as relatively 'open' and stable societies, to which our access, as a country and as individual citizens, is free and comfortable." ³⁸ The formulation is appropriate. Recent history shows that it makes little difference to us what form of government a country has as long as it remains an "open society," in our peculiar sense of this term—a society, that is, that remains open to American economic penetration or political control. If it is necessary to approach genocide in Vietnam to achieve this objective, then this is the price we must pay in defense of freedom and the rights of man.

It is, no doubt, superfluous to discuss at length the ways in which we assist other countries to progress towards open societies "to which our access is free and comfortable." One enlightening example is discussed in the recent congressional hearings from which I have now quoted several times, in the testimony of

---

37. William Bundy, in A. Buchan, ed., *China and the Peace of Asia* (New York, Frederick A. Praeger, Publishers, 1965).
38. *Op. cit.,* p. 80.
* Munich: the Munich Conference (September 1938) between Germany, Great Britain (Chamberlain), France, and Italy led to the Munich Pact, permitting immediate occupation by Germany of certain Czechoslovakian territories claimed by Hitler; this pact, resulting in the dismemberment of Czechoslovakia, marked the pinnacle of Anglo-French appeasement policy toward Nazi Germany.

Willem Holst and Robert Meagher, representing the Standing Committee on India of the Business Council for International Understanding.[39] As Mr. Meagher points out: "If it was possible, India would probably prefer to import technicians and know-how rather than foreign corporations. Such is not possible; therefore India accepts foreign capital as a necessary evil." Of course, "the question of private capital investment in India . . . would be no more than a theoretical exercise" had the groundwork for such investment not been laid by foreign aid, and were it not that "necessity has forced a modification in India's approach to private foreign capital." But now, "India's attitude toward private foreign investment is undergoing a substantial change. From a position of resentment and ambivalence, it is evolving toward an acceptance of its necessity. As the necessity becomes more and more evident, the ambivalence will probably be replaced by a more accommodating attitude." Mr. Holst contributes what is "perhaps a typical case history," namely, "the plan under which it was proposed that the Indian Government in partnership with a United States private consortium was to have increased fertilizer production by a million tons per year, which is just double presently installed capacity in all of India. The unfortunate demise of this ambitious plan may be attributed in large part to the failure of both Government and business to find a workable and mutually acceptable solution within the framework of the well-publicized 10 business incentives." The difficulty here was in connection with the percentage of equity ownership. Obviously, "fertilizers are desperately needed in India." Equally obviously, the consortium "insisted that to get the proper kind of control majority ownership was in fact needed." But "the Indian Government officially insisted that they shall have majority ownership," and "in something so complex it was felt that it would be a self-defeating thing."

Fortunately, this particular story has a happy ending. The remarks just quoted were made in February 1966, and within a few weeks, the Indian government had seen the light, as we read in a series of reports in the *New York Times*. The criticism, inside India, that "the American Government and the World Bank would like to arrogate to themselves the right to lay down the framework in which our economy must function," was stilled (April 24); and the Indian government accepted the conditions for resumed economic aid, namely, "that India provide easier terms for foreign private investment in fertilizer plants" and that the American investors "have substantial management rights" (May 14). The development is summarized in a dispatch datelined April 28, from New Delhi, in these terms:

> There are signs of change. The Government has granted easy terms to private foreign investors in the fertilizer industry, is thinking about decontrolling several more industries and is ready to liberalize import policy if it gets sufficient foreign aid. . . . Much of

---

39. *United States Policy Toward Asia*, pp. 191–201, passim.

what is happening now is a result of steady pressure from the United States and the International Bank for Reconstruction and Development, which for the last year have been urging a substantial freeing of the Indian economy and a greater scope for private enterprise. The United States pressure, in particular, has been highly effective here because the United States provides by far the largest part of the foreign exchange needed to finance India's development and keep the wheels of industry turning. Call them "strings," call them "conditions" or whatever one likes, India has little choice now but to agree to many of the terms that the United States, through the World Bank, is putting on its aid. For India simply has nowhere else to turn.

The heading of the article refers to this development as India's "drift from socialism to pragmatism."

Even this was not enough, however. Thus we read a few months later, in the *Christian Science Monitor* (December 5), that American entrepreneurs insist "on importing all equipment and machinery when India has a tested capacity to meet some of their requirements. They have insisted on importing liquid ammonia, a basic raw material, rather than using indigenous naphtha which is abundantly available. They have laid down restrictions about pricing, distribution, profits, and management control." The Indian reaction I have already cited (see p. 268).

In such ways as these, we help India develop towards an open society, one which, in Walt Rostow's words, has a proper understanding of "the core of the American ideology," namely, "the sanctity of the individual in relation to the state." And in this way, too, we refute the simple-minded view of those Asians who, to continue with Rostow's phrasing, "believe or half-believe that the West has been driven to create and then to cling to its imperial holdings by the inevitable workings of capitalist economies." [40]

In fact, a major postwar scandal is developing in India as the United States, cynically capitalizing on India's current torture, applies its economic power to implement India's "drift from socialism to pragmatism."

In pursuing the aim of helping other countries to progress towards open societies, with no thought of territorial aggrandizement, we are breaking no new ground. Hans Morgenthau has aptly described our traditional policy towards China as one of favoring "what you might call freedom of competition with regard to the exploitation of China." [41] In fact, few imperialist powers have had explicit territorial ambitions. Thus in 1784, the British Parliament announced that: "to pursue schemes of conquest and extension of dominion in India are measures repugnant to the wish, honor, and policy of this nation." Shortly after, the conquest of India was in full swing. A century later, Britain announced its intentions in Egypt under the slogan "intervention, reform, withdrawal." It is un-

40. *An American Policy in Asia*, p. 10.
41. *United States Policy Toward Asia*, p. 128.

necessary to comment on which parts of this promise were fulfilled, within the next half-century. In 1936, on the eve of hostilities in North China, the Japanese stated their Basic Principles of National Policy. These included the use of moderate and peaceful means to extend her strength, to promote social and economic development, to eradicate the menace of Communism, to correct the aggressive policies of the great powers, and to secure her position as the stabilizing power in East Asia. Even in 1937, the Japanese government had "no territorial designs upon China." In short, we follow a well-trodden path.

It is useful to remember, incidentally, that the United States was apparently quite willing, as late as 1939, to negotiate a commercial treaty with Japan and arrive at a *modus vivendi* if Japan would "change her attitude and practice towards our rights and interests in China," as Secretary Hull put it. The bombing of Chungking and the rape of Nanking were rather unpleasant, it is true, but what was really important was our rights and interests in China, as the responsible, unhysterical men of the day saw quite clearly. It was the closing of the open door by Japan that led inevitably to the Pacific war, just as it is the closing of the open door by "Communist" China itself that may very well lead to the next, and no doubt last, Pacific war.

Quite often, the statements of sincere and devoted technical experts give surprising insight into the intellectual attitudes that lie in the background of the latest savagery. Consider, for example, the following comment by economist Richard Lindholm, in 1959, expressing his frustration over the failure of economic development in "free Vietnam": "the use of American aid is determined by how the Vietnamese use their incomes and their savings. The fact that a large portion of the Vietnamese imports financed with American aid are either consumer goods or raw materials used rather directly to meet consumer demands is an indication that the Vietnamese people desire these goods, for they have shown their desire by their willingness to use their piasters to purchase them." [42]

In short, the Vietnamese *people* desire Buicks and air conditioners, rather than sugar-refining equipment or road-building machinery, as they have shown by their behavior in a free market. And however much we may deplore their free choice, we must allow the people to have their way. Of course, there are also those two-legged beasts of burden that one stumbles on in the countryside, but as any graduate student of political science can explain, they are not part of a responsible modernizing elite, and therefore have only a superficial biological resemblance to the human race.

In no small measure, it is attitudes like this that lie behind the butchery in Vietnam, and we had better face up to them with candor, or we will find our government leading us towards a "final solution" in Vietnam, and in the many Vietnams that inevitably lie ahead.

Let me finally return to Macdonald and the responsibility of intellectuals.

---

42. Lindholm, *op. cit.*, p. 322.

Macdonald quotes an interview with a death-camp paymaster who bursts into tears when told that the Russians would hang him. "Why should they? What have I done?" he asked. Macdonald concludes: "Only those who are willing to resist authority themselves when it conflicts too intolerably with their personal moral code, only they have the right to condemn the death-camp paymaster." The question "What have I done?" is one that we may well ask ourselves, as we read, each day, of fresh atrocities in Vietnam—as we create, or mouth, or tolerate the deceptions that will be used to justify the next defense of freedom.

IX SCIENCE AND TECHNOLOGY

Technology and ecology are two of our deepest concerns; one depends on the physical, the other on the biological sciences. That these branches of science occasionally overlap—or borrow one another's ways of speaking—is clear enough from the title of G. Rattray Taylor's essay, which therefore serves as a bridge between the two departments. Lewis Mumford speaks of very ancient technology, Norbert Wiener, the inventor of "cybernetics," of the capacities of the computer, upon which the latest technologies depend. In either case there are human consequences of the highest importance.

So it is, of course, with "genetic engineering"—which could revolutionize our very sense of what it means to belong to a human community, even of what it means to be human; and so it is with the great problems of man's use of his space, and the space he arrogates to himself to do as he likes with —on an earth which he shares with many other forms of life, and which, as Dubos observes, he is tied to by the most powerful bonds.

Behind the new sciences which handle such problems there remain basic disciplines. These attract intelligent students, and Robert Oppenheimer's humane commentary on physics as such a discipline explains why. At the other end of the process we have to consider the ethical problems that arise when the sciences impinge on the lives of human beings. This impingement can be a matter of life and death, and the issues raised by Sir Peter Medawar are of this gravity. Miss Langer's essay is a study of the effect of the necessary involvement of women in the operation of a vast public communications system; it cannot live by technology alone. And the effect of commercial technology on the people who minister to it can be disquieting. The service of the machine, in our society, involves something like a loss of humanity.

For obvious reasons we have selected, for this section, essays by writers who may or may not be distinguished scientists—some are and some are not—but who are in any case good popularizers. The role of the popularizer has been important ever since we've had an educated public incapable, for lack of special training, of understanding advanced work in the sciences (and, for that matter, in the arts). But the need for the popularizer is now much greater than ever before; the work of modern science is so refined and technical as to be beyond the scope even of scientists who do not work in the same or in an adjacent field. Yet modern physics and modern genetics —to mention only two sciences—have an enormous effect on the present state of humanity, and they will have shortly an even greater one. So too with technology; the computer is already changing our lives, and perhaps it will threaten our liberties. Technological society has its special pressures on us, as on the telephone girls, and it is hardly necessary now to remind readers that the technologies of affluence are, as Dr. Dubos remarks, the technologies of effluence also. There is the further problem that technology is breeding distrust in the young, whose "protestantism" in respect of the "religion" of science seems to Paul Goodman to be of very great cultural importance. The situation evidently abounds in dangers; and lest they assume irreversible forms we need to be able to think clearly about many problems to which our only access is provided by popularizers. The onus on such writers to be accurate, clear, and unsensational is very great. The reader who has some scientific knowledge might care to judge by those standards the pieces reprinted here.

Lewis Mumford / The First Megamachine

Efforts to expand human energies, to overcome human limitations, to exert control over time, space, and the life process have throughout history been accompanied by destructive illusions of ultimate power. Kings and nations would assume the attributes of God. For that reason, Mumford considers most great human exercises of power, even when they are remote in time from one another, as the building of the pyramids and the harnessing of atomic energy, fit subjects for the same kind of skeptical inquiry.

Mumford has always been concerned in his writing, whether it be about Herman Melville or technology, to find ways of transforming power into an instrument of humanity. He finds here that the invention and use of the so-called human machine, without which the pyramids would never have been built, involved all the unfortunate accompaniments, such as bureaucratic regimentation, that are conspicuous in our present technological system. Power that creates superhuman structures tends by that very success to diminish the importance of the merely human components that contributed in the effort. Such is one of the paradoxes of civilization. But while Mumford ends his piece with eloquently negative criticisms of the way a Stalin or a

Elliott Erwitt, Magnum

Hitler are later versions of "the divinely appointed founders of the first machine civilisation," readers should remember passages earlier in the piece where his writing is enkindled with wonder and enthusiasm as he describes how the fantastic achievement of the pyramids represented an "extension of magnitude in every direction," a "raising of the ceiling of human effort."

THE DESIGN OF THE HUMAN MACHINE

Until the nineteenth century, history was largely a chronicle of the deeds and misdeeds of kings, nobles, and armies. In revolt against a general obliviousness to the daily life and affairs of ordinary people, democratic historians swung to the opposite extreme: so the part actually played by kings has, during the last half century, been grossly under-rated, even though most of the attributes of kingship are now exercized, on a larger scale than ever before, by the all-powerful sovereign state.

From the earliest records, we know that the king incarnated the whole community and by divine right arrogated to himself the functions and offices of communal life. Only one aspect of kingship has been left out of this traditional account: strangely, the king's greatest and most lasting achievement has passed unnoticed, despite the fact that all his other public activities rested upon it. For though the myth of royal power claimed divine sanction, its rise and spread would have been impossible without the invention of the human machine. That was the supreme feat of kingship: a technological exploit that was transmitted in one form or another through purely human agents for some five thousand years before it was finally embodied in an equally totalitarian but impersonal form in modern technology.

To understand the point of origin and the line of descent is to have a fresh insight into the fate and destiny of modern man: for unless our own civilization learns to control the processes and the purposes that have so long been automatically—that is unconsciously—at work, the social aberrations that have accompanied the perfection of a machine technology, threaten even worse consequences than they did in the Pyramid Age.

Though the collective human machine came into existence roughly during the same period as the first industrial use of copper, it was an independent innovation, and did not at first utilize any new mechanical aids. But the royal machine, once conceived, was assembled within a short period; and it spread rapidly, not by being imitated, but by being forcefully imposed by kings, acting as only gods or the anointed representatives of gods could act. Wherever it was successfully put together the new machine commanded power and performed labor on a scale that was never even conceivable before. With this ability to concentrate immense mechanical forces, a new dynamism came into play, which overcame, by the magic of success, the sluggish routines, the petty inhibitions, the dull repetitive routines of the basic neolithic village culture, once the scene of so many fresh experiments in horticulture and breeding.

With the energies available through the royal machine—let us call it the megamachine—the very dimensions of space and time were enlarged. Operations that once could hardly be finished in centuries were now accomplished in less than a generation. If whole mountains were not moved, large portions of them were, sometimes in blocks far bigger than any ordinary motor truck could now handle; while, on the level plains, man-made mountains of stone or baked clay, pyramids and ziggurats, arose in response to royal command. No power machines at all comparable to this mechanism were utilized on any scale until watermills and windmills swept over Western Europe from the fourteenth century of our era.

Why did this new mechanism remain invisible to the archaeologist and the historian? Because it was composed solely of human parts; and it possessed a definite functional structure only as long as the magical abracadabra and the royal command that put it together were accepted as beyond human challenge by all the members of society. Once the polarizing force of kingship was weakened, whether by death or defeat, by skepticism or by brute resistance, the whole machine would collapse and its parts would either regroup in smaller units (feudal or urban) or completely disappear, much in the way that a routed army does when the chain of command is broken. These first collective machines were as frail, as vulnerable, as the theological and magical conceptions that were essential to their performance.

From the beginning, this human machine presented two aspects: one negative and coercive, the other positive and constructive. In fact, the second factors could not function unless the first were present. Though the military machine probably came before the labor machine, it was the latter that first achieved an incomparable perfection of performance, not alone in quantity of work done, but in quality. To call these collective entities machines is no idle play on words If a machine be defined more or less in accord with the classic definition of Reuleaux,* as a combination of resistant parts, each specialized in function, operating under human control, to transmit motion and to perform work, then the labor machine was a real machine: all the more because its component parts, though composed of human bone, nerve, and muscle, were reduced to their bare mechanical elements and rigidly restricted to the performance of their mechanical tasks.

Such machines, of immense power and practical utility, had already been invented by kings in the early part of the Pyramid Age, from the end of the fourth millennium on. Just because of their detachment from any external structure, they had paradoxically much fuller capacities for change and adaptation than the

---

* Franz Reuleaux: German mechanical engineer, author of *The Kinematiks of Machinery* (1875).

more rigid metallic counterparts of a modern assembly line. In fact, it is in the building of the pyramids that we find the first indubitable evidence of the machine's existence, and the first proof of its astonishing efficiency. Wherever kingship spread, the human machine, in its destructive if not its constructive form, always went with it. This holds as true for Mesopotamia, India, China, or Peru, as for Egypt.

THE ARCHETYPAL MACHINE

Let us examine the human machine in its archetypal original form. As so often happens, there was a certain clarity in this first demonstration that was lost when the machine was diffused and worked into the more complex patterns of later societies, mingling with more familiar but humbler forms. And if it never achieved a higher peak of performance, this is perhaps not only because of the singular human talents that designed and operated these early machines, but also perhaps because the myth that held the human part of the machine together could never again exert such a massive attractive power, unstained as it was in Egypt, until the sixth dynasty, by letdowns and failures, its inherent perversities still unexposed.

The pyramid took form as a tomb to hold the embalmed body of the Pharaoh and secure his safe passage into the after-life: though he alone, at first, had the prospect of such a godlike extension of his existence, the very idea of being able to fabricate personal immortality shows an alteration in all the dimensions of existence.

Between the first small pyramid, built in the step form we find later in Central America, and the mighty pyramid of Cheops at Giza, the first and the most enduring of the Seven Wonders of the Ancient World, lies the short span of three hundred years. On the ancient time-scale for inventions the most primitive form and the final one, never again to be equalled, were practically contemporary. The swiftness of this development indicates a concentration of physical power and technical imagination: for it took far more than faith to move the mountain of stone that composed this ultimate monument. That transformation is all the more striking because the Pharaohs' tombs did not stand alone: they were part of a whole city of the dead, with buildings that housed the priests who conducted the elaborate rituals deemed necessary to ensure a happy fate for the departed divinity.

The Great Pyramid is one of the most colossal and perfect examples of the engineer's art at any period or in any culture. Considering the state of all the other arts in the third millennium, no construction of our own day surpasses this in either technical virtuosity or human audacity. This great enterprise was undertaken by a culture that was just emerging from the Stone Age, and was long to continue using stone tools, though copper was available for the chisels and saws that shaped building stones for the new monuments.

The actual operations were performed by specialized handicraft workers, aided by an army of unskilled or semi-skilled laborers, drafted at quarterly intervals from agriculture. The whole job was done with no other material aids than the "simple machines" of classical mechanics: the inclined plane and the lever, for neither wheel nor pulley nor screw had yet been invented. We know from graphic representations that large stones were hauled on sledges, by battalions of men, across the desert sands. Yet the single stone slab that covers the inner chamber of the Great Pyramid where the pharaoh lies weighed fifty tons. An architect today would think twice before calling for such a mechanical exploit.

Now the Great Pyramid is more than a formidable mountain of stone, 755 feet square at the base, rising to a height of 481.4 feet. It is a structure with a complex interior, consisting of a series of passages at different levels that lead into the final burial chamber. Yet every part of it was built with a kind of precision that, as J. H. Breasted * emphasized, belongs to the optician's art rather than that of the modern bridge builder or skyscraper constructor. Blocks of stone were set together with seams of considerable length, showing joints of one-ten-thousandth of an inch; while the dimensions of the sides at the base differ by only 7.9 inches, in a structure that covers acres. In short, what we now characterize as flawless machine precision and machine perfection first manifested itself in the building of this great tomb: at once a symbol of the mountain of creation that emerged out of the primeval waters and a visible effort, so far remarkably successful, by purely human measure, to solidify both time and the human body in an eternal form. No ordinary human hands, no ordinary human effort, no ordinary kind of human collaboration such as was available in the building of village huts and the planting of fields, could muster such a superhuman force, or achieve an almost supernatural result. Only a divine king could accomplish such an act of the human will and such a large-scale material transformation.

Was it possible to create such a structure without the aid of a machine? Emphatically not. I repeat, the product itself showed that it was not only the work of a machine, but of an instrument of precision. Though the technological equipment of dynastic Egypt was still crude, the patient workmanship and disciplined method made good these shortcomings. The social organization had leaped ahead five thousand years to create the first large-scale power machine: a machine of a hundred thousand manpower, that is, the equivalent, roughly, of 10,-000 horsepower: a machine composed of a multitude of uniform, specialized, interchangeable, but functionally differentiated parts, rigorously marshalled together and co-ordinated in a process centrally organized and centrally directed: each part behaving as a mechanical component of the mechanized whole: unmoved by any internal impulse that would interfere with the working of the mechanism.

In less than three centuries, this collective human machine was perfected.

* J. H. Breasted: American Egyptologist and archaeologist; his works include *The Development of Religion and Thought in Ancient Egypt* (1912) and *The Dawn of Conscience* (1933).

Once organized and set in motion by the Pharaoh through his chief architect, *the technical competence* and imagination that envisaged the entire design was passed on, by word of mouth, and written instruction, to the component parts: the skilled workers, the overseers and taskmasters, the dumb hands. The kind of mind that designed the Pyramid was a new human type, capable of abstraction of a high order, using astronomical observations for the siting of the structure, so that each side was oriented exactly in line with true points of the compass: since at inundation the Pyramid site is only one quarter of a mile from the river, a rock foundation—which demanded the removal of sand—was needed. In the Great Pyramid the perimeter of that bed deviates from true level by little more than one-half an inch.

But the workers who carried out the design also had minds of a new order: trained in obedience to the letter, limited in response to the word of command descending from the king through a bureaucratic hierarchy, forfeiting during the period of service any trace of autonomy or initiative; slavishly undeviating in performance. Their leaders could read written orders; for the men employed left their names in red ochre, Edwards * tells us, on the blocks of the Medium Pyramid: "Boat Gang," "Vigorous Gang." They themselves would have felt at home today on an assembly line. Only the naked pin-up girl was lacking.

Alike in organization, in mode of work, and in product, there is no doubt that the machines that built the pyramids, and that performed all the other great constructive works of "civilization" in other provinces and cultures, were true machines. In their basic operations, they collectively performed the equivalent of a whole corps of power shovels, bulldozers, tractors, mechanical saws, and pneumatic drills, with an exactitude of measurement, a refinement of skill, and even an output of work that would still be a theme for boasting today.

This extension of magnitude in every direction, this raising of the ceiling of human effort, this subordination of individual aptitudes and interests to the mechanical job in hand, and this unification of a multitude of subordinates to a single end that derived from the divine power exercized by the king, in turn, by the success of the result, confirmed that power.

For note: it was the king who uttered the original commands: it was the king who demanded absolute obedience and punished disobedience with torture, mutilation or death: it was the king who alone had the godlike power of turning live men into dead mechanical objects: and finally it was the king who assembled the parts to form the machine and imposed the new discipline of mechanical organization, with the same regularity that moved the heavenly bodies on their undeviating course.

No vegetation god, no fertility myth, could produce this kind of cold abstract order, this detachment of power from life. Only one empowered by the Sun God could remove all hitherto respected norms or limits of human endeavour. The

---

* I. E. S. Edwards, *The Pyramids of Egypt* (1947).

king figures, in early accounts, as being of heroic mold: he alone slays lions singlehanded, builds great city walls, or like Menes* turns the course of rivers. That straining ambition, that defiant effort belongs only to the king and the machine that he set in motion.

THE TRANSMISSION GEAR

To understand the structure or the performance of the human machine, one must do more than center attention upon the point where it materializes. Even our present technology, with its vast reticulation of visible machines, cannot be understood on those terms alone. In order to put together a collective machine composed solely of human parts, one needed a complex transmission mechanism, to ensure that commands issued at the top would be swiftly and accurately conveyed to every member of the unit, so that the parts would interlock to form a single operating whole.

Two collective devices were essential, to make the machine work: a reliable organization of knowledge, natural and supernatural: and an elaborate structure for giving and carrying out orders. The first was incorporated in the priesthood, without whose active aid divine kingship could not have come into existence; the second in a bureaucracy: both hierarchical organizations at whose apex stood the temple and the palace. Without them the power complex could not operate. This condition remains true today, even though the existence of automated factories and computer-regulated units conceals the human components essential even to automation.

What would now be called science was an integral part of the new machine system from the beginning. This science, based on cosmic regularities, flourished with the cult of the sun: record-keeping, time-keeping, star-watching, calendar-making, coincide with and support the institution of kingship, even though no small part of the efforts of the priesthood were, in addition, devoted to interpreting the meaning of singular events, such as the appearance of comets or eclipses of the sun or moon, or natural irregularities, such as the flight of birds or the state of a sacrificed animal's entrails.

No king could move safely or effectively without the support of such organized higher knowledge, any more than the Pentagon can move today without consulting scientists, "games theorists," and computers, a new hierarchy supposedly less fallible than entrail-diviners, but to judge by their repeated miscalculations, not notably so. To be effective, this kind of knowledge must remain a priestly monopoly: if everyone had equal access to the sources of knowledge and to the system of interpretation, no one would believe in infallibility, since its errors could not be concealed. Hence the shocked protest of Ipu-wer against the revolutionaries who overthrew the Old Kingdom was that the "secrets of the

---

* Menes: the first king of the first Egyptian dynasty, supposed to have founded Memphis on ground recovered from the Nile by deflecting its course.

temple lay unbared;" that is, they had made "classified information" public. Secret knowledge belongs to any system of total control. Until printing was invented, this remained a class monopoly.

Not the least affiliation of kingship with the worship of the sun is the fact that the king, like the sun, exerts force at a distance. For the first time in history, power became effective outside the immediate range of hearing and vision and the arm's reach. No military weapon by itself sufficed to convey such power: what was needed was a special form of transmission gear: an army of scribes, messengers, stewards, super-intendents, gang bosses, and major and minor executives, whose very existence depended upon their carrying out the king's orders, or those of his powerful ministers and generals, to the letter. In other words, a bureaucracy: a group of men, capable of transmitting and executing a command, with the ritualistic punctilio of a priest, the mindless obedience of a soldier.

To fancy that bureaucracy is a relatively recent institution is to ignore the annals of ancient history. The first documents that attest the existence of bureaucracy belong to the Pyramid Age. In a cenotaph description at Abydos, a career official under Pepi I, in the Sixth Dynasty, c. 2375 B.C., reported "His majesty sent me at the head of this army, while the counts, while the Seal-bearers of the King of Lower Egypt, while the sole companions of the Palace, while the nomarchs (governors) and *mayors* of Upper and Lower Egypt, the companions and chief dragomans, the chief prophets of Upper and Lower Egypt, and the Chief bureaucrats were (each) at the head of a troop of Upper or Lower Egypt, or of the villages and towns which they might rule."

Not merely does this text establish a bureaucracy: it shows that the division of labor and specialization of functions necessary for efficient mechanical operation, had already taken place in the organization that, as executors of the sovereign's will, already controlled the operations of both the military and the labor machine. This development had begun at least three dynasties before: not by accident, with the building of the great stone pyramid of Djoser at Sakkara. Wilson * observes, in *City Invincible,* that "we credit Djoser, not only with the beginnings of monumental architecture in stone in Egypt, but also with the setting up of a new monster, the bureaucracy." This was no mere coincidence. And W. F. Albright, commenting upon this, pointed out that "the greater number of titles found in sealings of the First Dynasty . . . certainly pre-supposes an elaborate officialdom of some kind."

Once the hierarchic structure of the human machine was established, there was no limit to the number of hands it might control or the power it might exert. The removal of human dimensions and organic limits is indeed the chief boast of the authoritarian machine. Part of its productivity is due to its use of unstinted physical coercion to overcome human laziness or bodily fatigue. Occu-

* John A. Wilson: in *City Invincible: A Symposium on Urbanization and Cultural Development in the Ancient Near East,* ed. C. H. Kraeling and R. M. Adams (1960).

pational specialization was a necessary step in the assemblage of the human machine: only by intense specialization at every part of the process could the super-human accuracy and perfection of the product have been achieved. The large scale division of labor throughout industrial society begins at this point.

The Roman maxim, that the law does not concern itself with trifles, applies likewise to the human machine. The great forces that were set in motion by the king demanded collective enterprises of a commensurate order. These human machines were by nature impersonal, if not deliberately dehumanized; they had to operate on a big scale or they could not work at all; for no bureaucracy, however well organized, could govern a thousand little workshops, each with its own traditions, its own craft skills, its own wilful personal pride and sense of responsibility. So the form of control imposed by kingship was confined to great collective enterprises.

The importance of this bureaucratic link between the source of power, the divine king, and the actual human machines that performed the works of construction or destruction can hardly be exaggerated: all the more because it was the bureaucracy that collected the annual taxes and tributes that supported the new social pyramid and forcibly assembled the manpower that formed the new mechanical fabric. The bureaucracy was, in fact, the third type of "invisible machine," co-existing with the military and labor machines, and an integral part of the total structure.

Now the important part about the functioning of a classic bureaucracy is that it originates nothing: its function is to transmit, without alteration or deviation, the orders that come from above. No merely local information or human considerations must alter this inflexible transmission process—except by corruption. This administrative method ideally requires a studious repression of all the autonomous functions of the personality, and a readiness to perform the daily task with ritual exactitude. Not for the first time does such ritual exactitude enter into the process of work: indeed, it is highly unlikely that submission to colorless repetition would have been possible without the millennial discipline of religious ritual.

Bureaucratic regimentation was in fact part of the larger regimentation of life, introduced by this power-centered culture. Nothing emerges more clearly from the Pyramid texts themselves, with their wearisome repetitions of formulae, than a colossal capacity for enduring monotony: a capacity that anticipates the universal boredom achieved in our own day. Even the poetry of both early Egypt and Babylonia reveal this iterative hypnosis: the same words, in the same order, with no gain in meaning, repeated a dozen times—or a hundred times. This verbal compulsiveness is the psychical side of the systematic compulsion that brought the labor machine into existence. Only those who were sufficiently docile to endure this regimen at every stage from command to execution could become an effective unit in the human machine.

THE MAGNIFICATION OF POWER

Though the human machine was powerful, it was likewise extremely fragile: once the royal power was switched off, it "went dead." The royal machine reached the limit of its capabilities, without doubt, in the construction of the Great Pyramids. Soon after this came a revolt so shattering, so profound, that centuries passed before the severed regions of Egypt could be assembled once more under a single divine ruler. Never was power to be raised to such heights of absolute command again until our own day. But the institutional forces set in motion by this first effort continued to operate. Wherever the army, the bureaucracy, and the priesthood worked together under unified royal command, the technics of unqualified power would resume operation.

The marks of this new mechanical order can be easily recognized: and first, there is a change of scale. The habit of "thinking big" was introduced with the first human machines: a superhuman scale in the individual structure magnifies the sovereign authority and reduces the size and importance of all the necessary human components, except the central figure, the king himself. Both in practice and even more in fantasy, this magnification applied to time and to space. Kramer * notes that in the early dynasties reigns of incredible length are attributed to legendary kings: a total of close to a quarter of a million years for the eight kings before the flood and a total of twenty-five thousand years for the first two dynasties after the flood: this tallies with similar periods that Egyptian priests were still assigning to ancient history when Herodotus and Plato visited them.

But this multiplication of years was only the secular side of the new conception of immortality: at first, in Egypt, solely the attribute of the divine king, though there, as one notes in Sumer where a whole court was massacred in the Royal Tomb at Ur to accompany the ruler to the next world, the king's servants and ministers might also participate in this imputed extension of life. In the Sumerian deluge myth Ziusudra the king (Noah's counterpart) is rewarded by the gods An and Enlil, not by a symbolic rainbow, but by being given "life like a god." The desire for life without limits was part of the general lifting of limits which the first great assemblage of power, by means of the machine, brought about.

But if death mocks at the infantile fantasy of absolute power, which the human machine promised to actualize, life mocks at it even more. The notion of eternal life, with neither conception, growth, fruition, or decay—an existence as fixed, as sterilized, as unchanging as that of the royal mummy—is only death in another form: a return to the state of arrest and fixation exhibited by the stable chemical elements that have not yet combined in sufficiently complex molecules to promote novelty and continued creativity. The old fertility gods did not shrink from the fact of death: they sought no infantile evasion, but promised re-

* S. N. Kramer, *The Sumerians: Their History, Culture, and Character* (1963).

birth and renewal, by prolongation of power. If the gods of power had not triumphed, if kingship had not found a negative mode of increasing the scope of the human machine and therewith bolstering up the royal claim to absolute obedience, the whole further course of civilization might have been radically different.

But along with the desire for eternal life, kings and their gods nourished other ambitions that have become part of the mythology of our own age. Etana, in the Sumerian fable, mounts an eagle to go in search of a curative herb for his sheep when they are stricken with sterility. At this moment, the dream of human flight was born, or at least became visible, though that dream still seemed so presumptuous that Etana, like Daedalus, was hurled to death as he neared his goal. Soon, however, kings were represented as winged bulls; and they had at their command heavenly messengers who conquered space and time in order to bring commands to their earthly subjects. Rockets and television sets were already beginning to germinate in this royal myth. The Genii of the *Arabian Nights* are only popular continuations of these earlier forms of power-magic.

Within the span of early civilization, 3000 to 1000 B.C., the formative impulse to exercize absolute control over both nature and man shifted back and forth between gods and kings. Joshua commanded the sun to stand still and destroyed the walls of Jericho by martial music: but Yahweh himself, at an earlier moment, anticipated the Nuclear Age by destroying Sodom and Gomorrah with a single visitation of fire and brimstone; and a while later He even resorted to germ warfare in order to demoralize the Egyptians and aid in the escape of the Jews.

In short, none of the destructive fantasies that have taken possession of leaders in our own age, from Hitler to Stalin, from the khans of the Kremlin to the khans of the Pentagon, were foreign to the souls of the divinely appointed founders of the first machine civilization. With every increase of effective power, extravagantly sadistic and murderous impulses emerged out of the unconscious: not radically different from those sanctioned, not only by Hitler's extermination of six million Jews and uncounted millions of other people, but the extermination by the United States Air Force of 200,000 civilians in Tokyo in a single night by roasting alive. When a distinguished Mesopotamian scholar proclaimed that "civilization begins at Sumer" he innocently overlooked how much be forgotten before this can be looked upon as a laudable achievement. Mass production and mass destruction are the positive and negative poles, historically, of the myth of the mega-machine.

The other great prerogative of this royal technic is speed; for speed itself, in any operation, is a function of power and in turn becomes one of the chief means of displaying it. So deeply has this part of the myth of the machine become one of the uncriticized basic assumptions of our own technology that most of us have lost sight of its point of origin. But royal commands, like urgent commands in the army, are performed "on the double."

Nothing better illustrates this acceleration of pace than the fact that in Egypt, and later in Persia, each new monarch in the Pyramid Age built a new capital for use in his own lifetime. (Compare this with the centuries needed to build a medieval cathedral without royal resources for assembling power). On the practical side, road-building and canal-building, which were the chief means for hastening transportation, have been all through history the favored form of royal public works: a form that reached its technological consummation in the Iron Age, with the building of the Corinth Canal through eighty feet or so of solid rock.

Only an economy of abundance, at a time when there were at most four or five million people in the Nile Valley, could have afforded to drain off the labor of a hundred thousand men annually, and provide them with sufficient food to perform their colossal task; for on the scale these works were executed, that was the most sterile possible use of man power. Though many Egyptologists cannot bring themselves to accept the implications, John Maynard Keynes' notion of Pyramid Building, as a necessary device for coping with the surplus labor force in an affluent society without resorting to social equalization, was not an inept metaphor.* This was an archetypal example of stimulated productivity. Rocket-building is our modern equivalent.

But the most lasting economic contribution of the first myth of the machine was the separation between those that worked and those that lived in idleness on the surplus extracted from the worker by reducing his standard of living to penury. According to Akkadian and Babylonian scriptures, no less than those of Sumer, the gods created men in order to free themselves from the hard necessity of work. Here, as in so many other places, the gods prefigure in fantasy what kings actually do. In times of peace, kings and nobles live by the pleasure principle; eating, drinking, hunting, playing games, and copulating endlessly. So at the very period when the myth of the machine was taking place, the problems of an economy of abundance first became visible in the behavior and the fantasies of the ruling classes.

If we watch the aberrations of the ruling classes throughout history, we shall see how far most of them were from understanding the limitations of power, or of a life that centered upon an effortless consumption: the reduced life of the parasite on a tolerant host. The boredom of satiety dogged this economy of surplus power and surplus food from the very beginning: it led to insensate personal luxury and even more insensate acts of collective delinquency and destruction.

One early example of this dilemma of affluence must suffice. An Egyptian story, translated by Flinders Petrie, reveals the emptiness of a Pharaoh's life, in which every desire was too easily satisfied, and time hung with unbearable heaviness on his hands. Desperate, he appeals to his counsellors for some relief from

---

*See Chapter 9, Section VI, of Keynes's *The General Theory of Employment, Interest and Money* (1936).

his boredom; and one of them has a classic suggestion: that he fill a boat with thinly veiled, almost naked girls, who will paddle over the water and sing songs for him. For the hour, tedium, to the Pharaoh's great delight, was overcome; for, as Petrie aptly remarks, the vizier had invented the first Musical Revue: that solace of the "tired business man."

In short, at its earliest point of development under the myth of divine kingship, the amorality and the purposelessness of unlimited power were revealed in both religious legend and recorded history. Though the whole panoply of modern inventions lay beyond the scope of the collective machine, which could provide only partial and clumsy substitutes, the fundamental animus behind these inventions—the effort to conquer space and time, to expand human energy through the use of cosmic forces and to establish absolute human control over both nature and man, all had been planted and nurtured in the soil of fantasy.

Some of these seeds sprouted immediately: others which needed for their execution a far higher degree of technical skill, a higher capacity for logical and mathematical abstractions, required five thousand years before they were ready to sprout. When that happened, the divine king would appear again in a new form.

Norbert Wiener / Cybernetics

Professor Wiener was largely responsible for developing the theoretical positions and the practical application he describes. In the chapter included here, which is not simple but is nonetheless reasonably clear, he tells something of the history of cybernetics (he also invented, or resurrected, that word) and sketches some of its philosophical implications. The leading ideas of the chapter are: a study of the ways in which information is communicated is essential to the understanding of man's inner as well as his outer world; this was apparent to Leibnitz, who invented not only a universal language but a primitive computer; modern physics enables one to understand that a message is such that, like the world, it is subject to a tendency to move from order to disorder (entropy); the more probable a message, the less information it gives—for order implies redundancy; animals, and especially men, are capable of reacting subtly to very complicated messages; some reactions, by the application of cybernetics, can now be simulated in machines and weapons, especially in computers; the terms *input, output, feedback,* and others, which have passed into common currency, arise from the applications of cybernetics to machines and also men.

Inherent in Wiener's view is the conviction that in the functioning of human beings, and of sophisticated communication machines, there is an

Constantine Manos, Magnum

attempt to control entropy (the move to disorder) by feedback. The implications are great for sociology, and even for ethics; Wiener suggests that the fall from and disciplined restoration of order represented by entropy and feedback are "Augustinian," that is, they presuppose a system of depravity and regeneration.

The importance of such thinking to the present and future of the world is obvious; perhaps the generalizations at the end cancel out the impression, disliked by some people, that Wiener treats human beings too much as if they were the most sophisticated of automata and subject to the same rules as "communication machines."

Since the end of World War II, I have been working on the many ramifications of the theory of messages. Besides the electrical engineering theory of the transmission of messages, there is a larger field which includes not only the study of language but the study of messages as a means of controlling machinery and society, the development of computing machines and other such automata, certain reflections upon psychology and the nervous system, and a tentative new theory of scientific method. This larger theory of messages is a probabilistic theory, an intrinsic part of the movement that owes its origin to Willard Gibbs. . . .*

Until recently, there was no existing word for this complex of ideas, and in order to embrace the whole field by a single term, I felt constrained to invent one. Hence "Cybernetics," which I derived from the Greek word *kubernētēs,* or "steersman," the same Greek word from which we eventually derive our word "governor." Incidentally, I found later that the word had already been used by Ampère with reference to political science, and had been introduced in another context by a Polish scientist, both uses dating from the earlier part of the nineteenth century.

I wrote a more or less technical book entitled *Cybernetics* which was published in 1948. In response to a certain demand for me to make its ideas acceptable to the lay public, I published the first edition of *The Human Use of Human Beings* in 1950. Since then the subject has grown from a few ideas shared by Drs. Claude Shannon, Warren Weaver, and myself, into an established region of research. Therefore, I take this opportunity occasioned by the reprinting of my

---

* Willard Gibbs: (1839–1903), American mathematician who, according to Wiener, initiated "the first great revolution of 20th century physics" by introducing statistics and probability into physics: "Gibbs's innovation was to consider not one world, but all the worlds which are possible answers to a limited set of questions concerning our environment, his central notion concerned the extent to which answers that we may give to questions about one set of worlds are possible among a larger set of worlds. Beyond this. Gibbs had a theory that this probability tends naturally to increase as the universe grows older. The measure of this probability is called entropy, and the characteristic tendency of entropy is to increase." *Introduction,* p. 15.

book to bring it up to date, and to remove certain defects and inconsequentialities in its original structure.

In giving the definition of Cybernetics in the original book, I classed communication and control together. Why did I do this? When I communicate with another person, I impart a message to him, and when he communicates back with me he returns a related message which contains information primarily accessible to him and not to me. When I control the actions of another person, I communicate a message to him, and although this message is in the imperative mood, the technique of communication does not differ from that of a message of fact. Furthermore, if my control is to be effective I must take cognizance of any messages from him which may indicate that the order is understood and has been obeyed.

It is the thesis of this book that society can only be understood through a study of the messages and the communication facilities which belong to it; and that in the future development of these messages and communication facilities, messages between man and machines, between machines and man, and between machine and machine, are destined to play an ever-increasing part.

When I give an order to a machine, the situation is not essentially different from that which arises when I give an order to a person. In other words, as far as my consciousness goes I am aware of the order that has gone out and of the signal of compliance that has come back. To me, personally, the fact that the signal in its intermediate stages has gone through a machine rather than through a person is irrelevant and does not in any case greatly change my relation to the signal. Thus the theory of control in engineering, whether human or animal or mechanical, is a chapter in the theory of messages.

Naturally there are detailed differences in messages and in problems of control, not only between a living organism and a machine, but within each narrower class of beings. It is the purpose of Cybernetics to develop a language and techniques that will enable us indeed to attack the problem of control and communication in general, but also to find the proper repertory of ideas and techniques to classify their particular manifestations under certain concepts.

The commands through which we exercise our control over our environment are a kind of information which we impart to it. Like any form of information, these commands are subject to disorganization in transit. They generally come through in less coherent fashion and certainly not more coherently than they were sent. In control and communication we are always fighting nature's tendency to degrade the organized and to destroy the meaningful; the tendency, as Gibbs has shown us, for entropy to increase.

Much of this book concerns the limits of communication within and among individuals. Man is immersed in a world which he perceives through his sense organs. Information that he receives is co-ordinated through his brain and nervous system until, after the proper process of storage, collation, and selection, it emerges through effector organs, generally his muscles. These in turn act on the external world, and also react on the central nervous system through receptor organs such as the end organs of kinaesthesia; and the information received by the kinaesthetic organs is combined with his already accumulated store of information to influence future action.

Information is a name for the content of what is exchanged with the outer world as we adjust to it, and make our adjustment felt upon it. The process of receiving and of using information is the process of our adjusting to the contingencies of the outer environment, and of our living effectively within that environment. The needs and the complexity of modern life make greater demands on this process of information than ever before, and our press, our museums, our scientific laboratories, our universities, our libraries and textbooks, are obliged to meet the needs of this process or fail in their purpose. To live effectively is to live with adequate information. Thus, communication and control belong to the essence of man's inner life, even as they belong to his life in society.

The place of the study of communication in the history of science is neither trivial, fortuitous, nor new. Even before Newton such problems were current in physics, especially in the work of Fermat, Huygens, and Leibnitz, each of whom shared an interest in physics whose focus was not mechanics but optics, the communication of visual images.

Fermat furthered the study of optics with his principle of minimization which says that over any sufficiently short part of its course, light follows the path which it takes the least time to traverse. Huygens developed the primitive form of what is now known as "Huygens' Principle" by saying that light spreads from a source by forming around that source something like a small sphere consisting of secondary sources which in turn propagate light just as the primary sources do. Leibnitz, in the meantime, saw the whole world as a collection of beings called "monads" whose activity consisted in the perception of one another on the basis of a pre-established harmony laid down by God, and it is fairly clear that he thought of this interaction largely in optical terms. Apart from this perception, the monads had no "windows," so that in his view all mechanical interaction really becomes nothing more than a subtle consequence of optical interaction.

A preoccupation with optics and with message, which is apparent in this part of Leibnitz's philosophy, runs through its whole texture. It plays a large part in two of his most original ideas: that of the *Characteristica Universalis,* or universal scientific language, and that of the *Calculus Ratiocinator,* or calculus of logic. This Calculus Ratiocinator, imperfect as it was, was the direct ancestor of modern mathematical logic.

Leibnitz, dominated by ideas of communication, is, in more than one way, the intellectual ancestor of the ideas of this book, for he was also interested in machine computation and in automata. My views in this book are very far from being Leibnitzian, but the problems with which I am concerned are most certainly Leibnitzian. Leibnitz's computing machines were only an offshoot of his interest in a computing language, a reasoning calculus which again was in his mind, merely an extension of his idea of a complete artificial language. Thus, even in his computing machine, Leibnitz's preoccupations were mostly linguistic and communicational.

Toward the middle of the last century, the work of Clerk Maxwell and of his precursor, Faraday, had attracted the attention of physicists once more to optics, the science of light, which was now regarded as a form of electricity that could be reduced to the mechanics of a curious, rigid, but invisible medium known as the ether, which, at the time, was supposed to permeate the atmosphere, interstellar space and all transparent materials. Clerk Maxwell's work on optics consisted in the mathematical development of ideas which had been previously expressed in a cogent but non-mathematical form by Faraday. The study of ether raised certain questions whose answers were obscure, as, for example, that of the motion of matter through the ether. The famous experiment of Michelson and Morley, in the nineties, was undertaken to resolve this problem, and it gave the entirely unexpected answer that there simply was no way to determine the motion of matter through the ether.

The first satisfactory solution to the problems aroused by this experiment was that of Lorentz, who pointed out that if the forces holding matter together were conceived as being themselves electrical or optical in nature, we should expect a negative result from the Michelson-Morley experiment. However, Einstein in 1905 translated these ideas of Lorentz into a form in which the unobservability of absolute motion was rather a postulate of physics than the result of any particular structure of matter. For our purposes, the important thing is that in Einstein's work, light and matter are on an equal basis, as they had been in the writings before Newton; without the Newtonian subordination of everything else to matter and mechanics.

In explaining his views, Einstein makes abundant use of the observer who may be at rest or may be moving. In his theory of relativity it is impossible to introduce the observer without also introducing the idea of message, and without, in fact, returning the emphasis of physics to a quasi-Leibnitzian state, whose tendency is once again optical. Einstein's theory of relativity and Gibbs' statistical mechanics are in sharp contrast, in that Einstein, like Newton, is still talking primarily in terms of an absolutely rigid dynamics not introducing the idea of probability. Gibbs' work, on the other hand, is probabilistic from the very start, yet both directions of work represent a shift in the point of view of physics in which the world as it actually exists is replaced in some sense or other by the world as it happens to be observed, and the old naïve realism of physics gives way to something on which Bishop Berkeley * might have smiled with pleasure.

At this point it is appropriate for us to review certain notions pertaining to

---

* George Berkeley: (1685–1753), the Irish Anglican divine and philosopher, a determined opponent of "naive realism"; *esse est percipi* ("to be is to be perceived") is the tag popularly associated with him.

entropy which have already been presented in the introduction. As we have said, the idea of entropy represents several of the most important departures of Gibbsian mechanics from Newtonian mechanics. In Gibbs' view we have a physical quantity which belongs not to the outside world as such, but to certain sets of possible outside worlds, and therefore to the answer to certain specific questions which we can ask concerning the outside world. Physics now becomes not the discussion of an outside universe which may be regarded as the total answer to all the questions concerning it, but an account of the answers to much more limited questions. In fact, we are now no longer concerned with the study of all possible outgoing and incoming messages which we may send and receive, but with the theory of much more specific outgoing and incoming messages; and it involves a measurement of the no-longer infinite amount of information that they yield us.

Messages are themselves a form of pattern and organization. Indeed, it is possible to treat sets of messages as having an entropy like sets of states of the external world. Just as entropy is a measure of disorganization, the information carried by a set of messages is a measure of organization. In fact, it is possible to interpret the information carried by a message as essentially the negative of its entropy, and the negative logarithm of its probability. That is, the more probable the message, the less information it gives. Clichés, for example, are less illuminating than great poems.

I have already referred to Leibnitz's interest in automata, an interest incidentally shared by his contemporary, Pascal, who made real contributions to the development of what we now know as the desk adding-machine. Leibnitz saw in the concordance of the time given by clocks set at the same time, the model for the pre-established harmony of his monads. For the technique embodied in the automata of his time was that of the clockmaker. Let us consider the activity of the little figures which dance on the top of a music box. They move in accordance with a pattern, but it is a pattern which is set in advance, and in which the past activity of the figures has practically nothing to do with the pattern of their future activity. The probability that they will diverge from this pattern is nil. There is a message, indeed; but it goes from the machinery of the music box to the figures, and stops there. The figures themselves have no trace of communication with the outer world, except this one-way stage of communication with the pre-established mechanism of the music box. They are blind, deaf, and dumb, and cannot vary their activity in the least from the conventionalized pattern.

Contrast with them the behavior of man, or indeed of any moderately intelligent animal such as a kitten. I call to the kitten and it looks up. I have sent it a message which it has received by its sensory organs, and which it registers in action. The kitten is hungry and lets out a pitiful wail. This time it is the sender of a message. The kitten bats at a swinging spool. The spool swings to its left, and the kitten catches it with its left paw. This time messages of a very complicated nature are both sent and received within the kitten's own nervous system through certain nerve end-bodies in its joints, muscles, and tendons; and by means of nervous messages sent by these organs, the animal is aware of the actual position and tensions of its tissues. It is only through these organs that anything like a manual skill is possible.

I have contrasted the prearranged behavior of the little figures on the music box on the one hand, and the contingent behavior of human beings and animals on the other. But we must not suppose that the music box is typical of all machine behavior.

The older machines, and in particular the older attempts to produce automata, did in fact function on a closed clockwork basis. But modern automatic machines such as the controlled missile, the proximity fuse, the automatic door opener, the control apparatus for a chemical factory, and the rest of the modern armory of automatic machines which perform military or industrial functions, possess sense organs; that is, receptors for messages coming from the outside. These may be as simple as photoelectric cells which change electrically when a light falls on them, and which can tell light from dark, or as complicated as a television set. They may measure a tension by the change it produces in the conductivity of a wire exposed to it, or they may measure temperature by means of a thermocouple, which is an instrument consisting of two distinct metals in contact with one another through which a current flows when one of the points of contact is heated. Every instrument in the repertory of the scientific-instrument maker is a possible sense organ, and may be made to record its reading remotely through the intervention of appropriate electrical apparatus. Thus the machine which is conditioned by its relation to the external world, and by the things happening in the external world, is with us and has been with us for some time.

The machine which acts on the external world by means of messages is also familiar. The automatic photoelectric door opener is known to every person who has passed through the Pennsylvania Station in New York, and is used in many other buildings as well. When a message consisting of the interception of a beam of light is sent to the apparatus, this message actuates the door, and opens it so that the passenger may go through.

The steps between the actuation of a machine of this type by sense organs and its performance of a task may be as simple as in the case of the electric door; or it may be in fact of any desired degree of complexity within the limits of our engineering techniques. A complex action is one in which the data introduced, which we call the *input,* to obtain an effect on the outer world, which we call the *output,* may involve a large number of combinations. These are combinations, both of the data put in at the moment and of the records taken from the past stored data which we call the *memory*. These are recorded in the machine. The most complicated machines yet made which transform input data into output data are the high-speed electrical computing machines, of which I shall speak later in more detail. The determination of the mode of conduct of these machines is given through a special sort of input, which frequently consists of punched cards or tapes or of magnetized wires, and which determines the way in which the machine is going to act in one operation, as distinct from the way in which it might have acted in another. Because of the frequent use of punched or magnetic tape in the control, the data which are fed in, and which indicate the mode of operation of one of these machines for combining information, are called the *taping*.

I have said that man and the animal have a kinaesthetic sense, by which they keep a record of the position and tensions of their muscles. For any machine subject to a varied external environment to act effectively it is necessary that information concerning the results of its own action be furnished to it as part of the information on which it must continue to act. For example, if we are running an elevator, it is not enough to open the outside door because the orders we have given should make the elevator be at that door at the time we open it. It is important that the release for opening the door be dependent on the fact that the elevator is actually at the door; otherwise something might have detained it, and the passenger might step into the empty shaft. This control of a machine on the basis of its *actual* performance rather than its *expected* performance is known as *feedback*, and involves sensory members which are actuated by motor members and perform the function of *tell-tales* or *monitors*—that is, of elements which indicate a performance. It is the function of these mechanisms to control the mechanical tendency toward disorganization; in other words, to produce a temporary and local reversal of the normal direction of entropy.

I have just mentioned the elevator as an example of feedback. There are other cases where the importance of feedback is even more apparent. For example, a gun-pointer takes information from his instruments of observation, and conveys it to the gun, so that the latter will point in such a direction that the missile will pass through the moving target at a certain time. Now, the gun itself must be used under all conditions of weather. In some of these the grease is warm, and the gun swings easily and rapidly. Under other conditions the grease is frozen or mixed with sand, and the gun is slow to answer the orders given to it. If these orders are reinforced by an extra push given when the gun fails to respond easily to the orders and lags behind them, then the error of the gun-pointer will be decreased. To obtain a performance as uniform as possible, it is customary to put into the gun a control feedback element which reads the lag of the gun behind the position it should have according to the orders given it, and which uses this difference to give the gun an extra push.

It is true that precautions must be taken so that the push is not too hard, for if it is, the gun will swing past its proper position, and will have to be pulled back in a series of oscillations, which may well become wider and wider, and lead to a disastrous instability. If the feedback system is itself controlled—if, in other words, its own entropic tendencies are checked by still other controlling mechanisms—and kept within limits sufficiently stringent, this will not occur, and the existence of the feedback will increase the stability of performance of the gun. In other words, the performance will become less dependent on the frictional load; or what is the same thing, on the drag created by the stiffness of the grease.

Something very similar to this occurs in human action. If I pick up my cigar, I do not will to move any specific muscles. Indeed in many cases, I do not know what those muscles are. What I do is to turn into action a certain feedback mechanism; namely, a reflex in which the amount by which I have yet failed to pick up the cigar is turned into a new and increased order to the lagging muscles, whichever they may be. In this way, a fairly uniform voluntary command will enable the same task to be performed from widely varying initial positions, and irrespective of the decrease of contraction due to fatigue of the muscles. Similarly, when I drive a car, I do not follow out a series of commands dependent simply on a mental image of the road and the task I am doing. If I find the car swerving too much to the right, that causes me to pull it to the left. This depends on the actual performance of the car, and not simply on the road; and it allows me to drive with nearly equal efficiency a light Austin or a heavy truck, without having formed separate habits for the driving of the two. I shall have more to say about this in the chapter in this book on special machines, where we shall discuss the service that can be done to neuropathology by the study of machines with defects in performance similar to those occurring in the human mechanism.

It is my thesis that the physical functioning of the living individual and the operation of some of the newer communication machines are precisely parallel in their analogous attempts to control entropy through feedback. Both of them have sensory receptors as one stage in their cycle of operation: that is, in both of them there exists a special apparatus for collecting information from the outer world at low energy levels, and for making it available in the operation of the individual or of the machine. In both cases these external messages are not taken *neat*, but through the internal transforming powers of the apparatus, whether it be alive or dead. The information is then turned into a new form available for the further stages of performance. In both the animal and the machine this performance is made to be effective on the outer world. In both of them, their *performed* action on the outer world, and not merely their *intended* action, is reported back to the central regulatory apparatus. This complex of behavior is ignored by the average man, and in particular does not play the role that it should in our habitual analysis of society; for just as individual physical responses may be seen from this point of view, so may the organic responses of society itself. I do not mean that the sociologist is unaware of the existence and complex nature of communications in society, but until recently he has tended to overlook the extent to which they are the cement which binds its fabric together.

We have seen in this chapter the fundamental unity of a complex of ideas which until recently had not been sufficiently associated with one another, namely, the contingent view of physics that Gibbs introduced as a modification of the traditional, Newtonian conventions, the Augustinian attitude toward order and conduct which is demanded by this view, and the theory of the message among men, machines, and in society as a sequence of events in time which, though it itself has a certain contingency, strives to hold back nature's tendency toward disorder by adjusting its parts to various purposive ends.

P. B. Medawar / Science and the Sanctity of Life

The author of this essay is a distinguished medical scientist and Nobel Prize winner. The fact is not without importance, since it confers its own authority on what he says. But of course this does not release him from the need to present his argument with cogency. Medawar is in fact known to be one of the most elegant and forceful writers among modern scientists, and he often ventures into discussions where there are strong humanistic elements, and which therefore call for skills other than those possessed by the average scientific worker, without, in his view, being removed from the scope of genuine scientific inquiry.

He offers a commonsense gloss on the idea of sanctity and allows that science, as well as many other weapons, may be used against it. Narrowing the approach in his third section, he seeks to isolate what can be called "distinctively medical"—as opposed, for example, to social or political—threats to human life. One is the use of medical science to keep people alive when to do so offends our sense (which is not inalterable) of what is fitting. Thus he argues for their preservation on the ground that they are each "intended" to be unique and privileged. Though he does not condone all or any eugenic interference with humans he thinks that action is desirable in cases where a disease arises in the children of two parents each carrying the same recessive gene. In such instances identification of the carriers can abolish the disease. The carriers themselves do not suffer, are otherwise healthy, and may marry anyone who is not a carrier—almost anybody else, in fact. And in defending this view against the charge of "medical officiousness" he launches into a concluding passage on the ways in which science has, in three centuries, altered our world and our expectations.

You may disagree with much or all of the argument; in doing so you should be sure you have answered all Medawar's points and examined all his assumptions. Whether or not you agree with him, consider carefully the skill with which he uses medical fact in relation to a social problem; how for instance, his technical terms—the names of rare diseases and of various genetic characteristics—are explained sufficiently to prevent confusion, yet

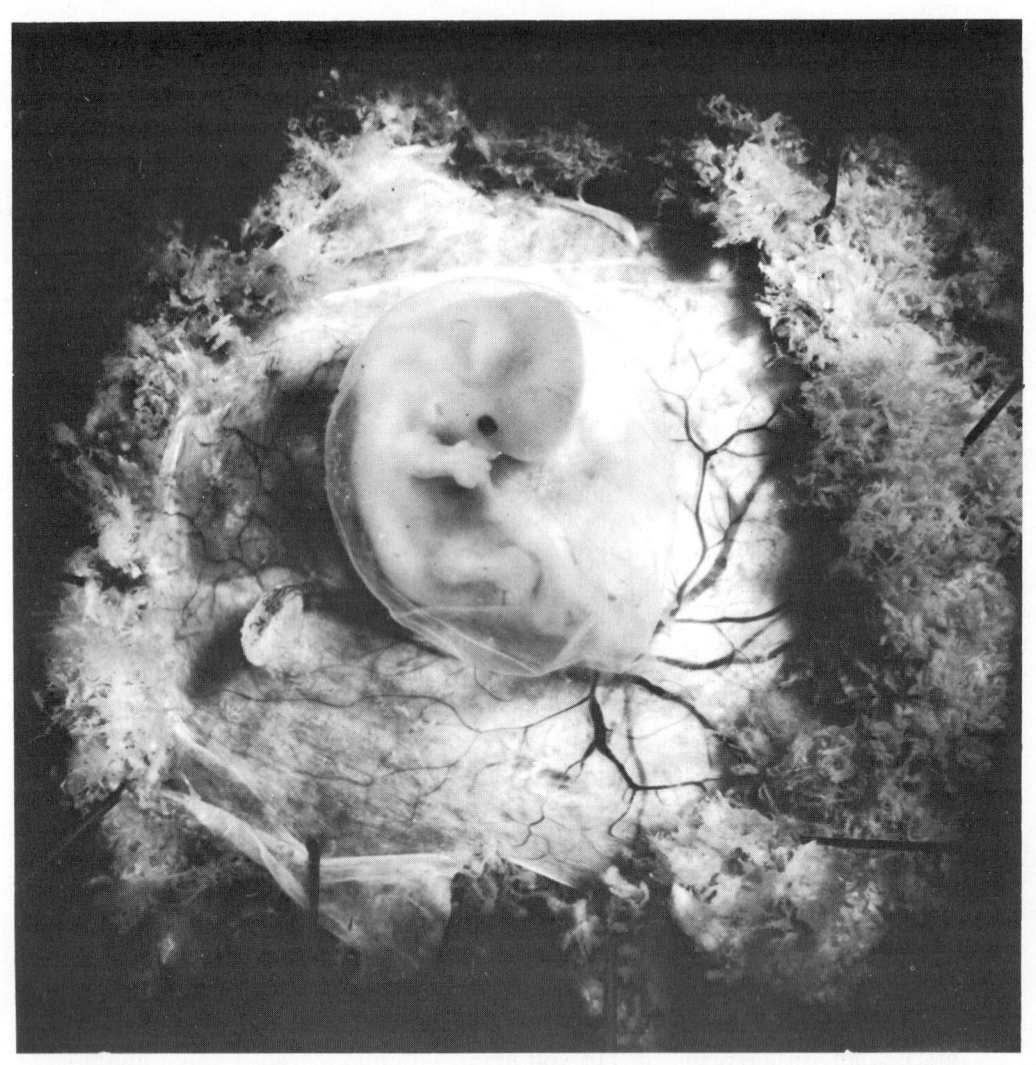

Courtesy of the Carnegie Institution of Washington

without interrupting the flow of the argument. Observe also the device of "funnelling" the whole argument into a single and limited channel, the question of preventable diseases of genetic origin.

I do not intend to deny that the advances of science may sometimes have consequences that endanger, if not life itself, then the quality of life or our self-respect as human beings (for it is in this wider sense that I think "sanctity" should be construed). Nor shall I waste time by defending science as a whole or scientists generally against a change of inner or essential malevolence. The Wicked Scientist is not to be taken seriously: Dr. Strangelove, Dr. Moreau, Dr. Moriarty, Dr. Mabuse, Dr. Frankenstein (an honorary degree, this), and the rest of them are puppets of Gothick fiction. Scientists, on the whole, are amiable and well-meaning creatures. There must be very few wicked scientists. There are, however, plenty of wicked philosophers, wicked priests, and wicked politicians.

One of the gravest charges ever made against science is that biology has now put it into our power to corrupt both the body and the mind of man. By scientific means (the charge runs) we can now breed different kinds and different races—different models, almost—of human beings, degrading some, making aristocrats of others, adapting others still to special purposes: treating them in fact like dogs, for this is how we *have* treated dogs. Or again: science now makes it possible to dominate and control the thought of human beings—to improve them, perhaps, if that should be our purpose, but more often to enslave or to corrupt with evil teaching.

But these things have always been possible. At any time in the past 5,000 years it would have been within our power to embark on a programme of selecting and culling human beings and raising breeds as different from one another as toy poodles and Pekinese are from St. Bernards and Great Danes. In a genetic sense the empirical arts of the breeder are just as applicable to human beings as to horses—more easily applicable, in fact, for human beings are highly *evolvable* animals, a property they owe partly to an open and uncomplicated breeding system, which allows them a glorious range of inborn diversity and therefore a tremendous evolutionary potential; and partly to their lack of physical specialisations (in the sense in which ant-eaters and woodpeckers and indeed dogs are specialised), a property which gives human beings a sort of amateur status among animals. And it has always been possible to pervert or corrupt human beings by coercion, propaganda, or evil indoctrination. Science has not yet improved these methods, nor have scientists used them. They have, however, been used to great effect by politicians, philosophers, and priests.

The mischief that science may do grows just as often out of trying to do good —as, for example, improving the yield of soil is intended to do good—as out of actions intended to be destructive. The reason is simple enough: however hard we try, we do not and sometimes cannot foresee all the distant consequences of scientific innovation. No one clearly foresaw that the widespread use of antibiotics might bring about an evolution of organisms resistant to their action. No one could have predicted that X-irradiation was a possible cause of cancer. No one could have foreseen the speed and scale with which advances in medicine and public health would create a problem of overpopulation that threatens to undo much of what medical science has worked for. (Thirty years ago the talk was all of how the people of the Western world were reproducing themselves too slowly to make good the wastage of mortality; we heard tell of a "Twilight of Parenthood," and wondered rather fearfully where it all would end.) But somehow or other we shall get round all these problems, for every one of them is soluble, even the population problem, and even though its solution is obstructed above all else by the bigotry of some of our fellow men.

I choose from medicine and medical biology one or two concrete examples of how advances in science threaten or seem to threaten the sanctity of human life. Many of these threats, of course, are in no sense distinctively medical, though they are often loosely classified as such. They are merely medical contexts for far more pervasive dangers. One of them is our increasing state of dependence on medical services and the medical industries. What would become of the diabetic if the supplies of insulin dried up, or of the victims of Addison's disease deprived of synthetic steroids? Questions of this kind might be asked of every service society provides. In a complex society we all depend upon and sustain each other, for transport, communications, food, goods, shelter, protection and a hundred other things. The medical industries will not break down all by themselves, and if they do break down it will be only one episode of a far greater disaster.

The same goes for the economic burden imposed by illness in any community that takes some collective responsibility for the health of its citizens. All shared burdens have a cost which is to a greater or lesser degree shared between us: education, pensions, social welfare, legal aid and every other social service, including government.

We are getting nearer what is distinctively medical when we ask ourselves about the economics, logistics, and morality of keeping people alive by medical intervention and medical devices. At present it is the cost and complexity of the operation, and the shortage of machines and organs, that denies a kidney graft or an artificial kidney to anyone mortally in need of it. The limiting factors are thus still economic and logistic. But what about the morality of keeping people alive by these heroic medical contrivances? I do not think it is possible to give any answer that is universally valid or that, if it were valid, would remain so for more than a very few years. Medical contrivances extend all the way from pills and plasters and bottles of tonic to complex mechanical prostheses, which will one day include mechanical hearts. At what point shall we say we are wantonly interfering with Nature and prolonging life beyond what is proper and humane?

In practice the answer we give is founded not upon abstract moralising but upon a certain natural sense of the fitness of things, a feeling that is shared by most kind and reasonable people even if we cannot define it in philosophically defensible or legally accountable terms. It is only at international conferences that we tend to adopt the convention that people behave like idiots unless acting upon clear and well turned instructions to behave sensibly. There is in fact no general formula or smooth form of words we can appeal to when in perplexity.

Moreover, our sense of what is fit and proper is not something fixed, as if it were inborn and instinctual. It changes as our experience grows, as our understanding deepens and as we enlarge our grasp of possibilities—just as living religions and laws change, and social structures and family relationships.

I feel that our sense of what is right and just is already beginning to be offended by the idea of taking great exertions to keep alive grossly deformed or monstrous new-born children, particularly if their deformities of body or mind arise from major defects of the genetic apparatus. There are in fact scientific reasons for changing an opinion that might have seemed just and reasonable a hundred years ago.

Everybody takes it for granted, because it is so obviously true, that a married couple will have children of very different kinds and constitutions on different occasions. But the traditional opinion, which most of us are still unconsciously guided by, is that the child conceived on any one occasion is the unique and necessary product of that occasion: *that* child would have been conceived, we tend to think, or no child at all. This interpretation is quite false, but human dignity and security clamour for it. A child sometimes wonderingly acknowledges that he would never have been born at all if his mother and father had not chanced to meet and fall in love and marry. He does not realise that, instead of conceiving him, his parents might have conceived any one of a hundred thousand other children, all unlike each other and unlike himself. Only over the past 100 years has it come to be realised that the child conceived on any one occasion belongs to a vast cohort of Possible Children, any one of whom might have been conceived and born if a different spermatozoon had chanced to fertilise the mother's egg cell—and the egg cell itself is only one of very many. It is a matter of luck then, a sort of genetic lottery. And sometimes it is cruelly bad luck—some terrible genetic conjunction, perhaps, which once in ten or twenty thousand times will bring together a matching pair of damaging recessive genes. Such a misfortune, being the outcome of a random process, is, considered in isolation, completely and essentially pointless. It is not even strictly true to say that a particular inborn abnormality must have lain within the genetic potentiality of the parents, for the malignant gene may have arisen *de novo* by mutation. The whole process is unhallowed—is, in the older sense of that word, profane.

I am saying that if we feel ourselves under a moral obligation to make every possible exertion to keep a monstrous embryo or new-born child alive *because* it is in some sense the naturally intended—and therefore the unique and privileged—product of its parents' union at the moment of its conception, then we are making an elementary and cruel blunder: for it is *luck* that determines which one child is in fact conceived out of the cohort of Possible Children that might have been conceived by those two parents on that occasion. I am not using the word "luck" of conception as such, nor of the processes of embryonic and foetal growth, nor indeed in any sense that derogates from the wonder and awe in which we hold processes of great complexity and natural beauty which we do not fully understand; I am simply using it in its proper sense and proper place.[1]

This train of thought leads me directly to Eugenics—"the science," to quote its founder, Francis Galton, "which deals with all the influences that improve the inborn qualities of a race; also with those that develop them to the utmost advantage." Because the upper and lower boundaries of an individual's capability and performance are set by his genetic make-up, it is clear that if eugenic policies were to be ill-founded or mistakenly applied they could offer a most terrible threat to the sanctity and dignity of human life. This threat I shall now examine.

Eugenics is traditionally subdivided into Positive and Negative Eugenics. Positive Eugenics has to do with attempts to improve human beings by genetic policies, particularly policies founded upon selective or directed breeding. Negative Eugenics has the lesser ambition of attempting to eradicate as many as possible of our inborn imperfections. The distinction is useful and pragmatically valid for the following reasons.[2] Defects of the genetic constitution (such as those which manifest themselves as mongolism, haemophilia, galactosaemia, phenylketonuria, and a hundred other hereditary abnormalities) have a much simpler genetic basis than desirable characteristics like beauty, high physical performance, intelligence or fertility. This is almost self-evident. All geneticists believe that "fitness" in its most general sense depends on a nicely balanced co-ordination and interaction of genetic factors, itself the product of laborious and long drawn out evolutionary adjustment. It is inconceivable, indeed self-contradictory, that an animal should evolve into the possession of some complex pattern of interaction between genes that made it inefficient, undesirable, or unfit—*i.e., less* well adapted to the prevailing circumstances. Likewise a motor car will run badly for any one of a multitude of particular and special reasons, but runs well because of the harmonious mechanical interactions made possible by a sound and economically viable design.

Negative eugenics is a more manageable and understandable enterprise than positive eugenics. Nevertheless, many well-meaning people believe that, with the

1. There are, perhaps, very weighty legal and social reasons why even tragically deformed children should be kept alive (for who is to decide? and where do we draw the line?), but these are outside my terms of reference.
2. See my book *The Future of Man* (Methuen, 1960).

knowledge and skills already available to us, and within the framework of a society that upholds the rights of individuals, it is possible in principle to raise a superior kind of human being by a controlled or "recommended" scheme of mating and by regulating the number of children each couple should be allowed or encouraged to have. If stock-breeders can do it, the argument runs, why should not we?—for who can deny that domesticated animals have been improved by deliberate human intervention?

I think this argument is unsound for a lesser and for a more important reason.

1. Domesticated animals have not been "improved" in the sense in which we should use that word of human beings. They have not enjoyed an all-round improvement, for some special characteristics or faculties have been so far as possible "fixed" without special regard to and sometimes at the expense of others. Tameness and docility are most easily achieved at the expense of intelligence, but that does not matter if what we are interested in is, say, the quality and yield of wool.

2. The ambition of the stock-breeder in the past, though he did not realise it, was two-fold: not merely to achieve a predictably uniform product by artificial selection, but also to establish an internal genetic uniformity (homozygosity) in respect of the characters under selection to make sure that the stock would "breed true"—for it would be a disaster if characters selected over many generations were to be irrecoverably lost or mixed up in a hybrid progeny. The older stock-breeder believed that uniformity and breeding true were characteristics that necessarily went together, whereas we now know that they can be separately achieved. And he expected his product to fulfil two quite distinct functions which we now know to be separable, and often better separated: on the one hand, to be in themselves the favoured stock and the top performers—the Super-sheep or Super-mice—and, on the other hand, to be the parents of the next generation of that stock. It is rather as if Rolls-Royces, in addition to being an end product of manufacture, had to be so designed as to give rise to Rolls-Royce progeny.

It is just as well these older views are mistaken, for with naturally outbreeding populations such as our own, genetic uniformity, arrived at and maintained by selective inbreeding, is a highly artificial state of affairs with many inherent and ineradicable disadvantages.

Stock-breeders, under genetic guidance, are now therefore inclining more and more towards a policy of deliberate and nicely calculated cross-breeding. In the simplest case, two partially inbred and internally uniform stocks are raised and perpetuated to provide two uniform lineages of parents, but the eugenic goal, the marketable end-product or high performer, is the progeny of a cross between members of the two parental stocks. Being of hybrid make-up, the progeny do not breed true, and are not in fact bred from; they can be likened to a manufactured end-product; but they can be uniformly reproduced at will by crossing the two parental stocks. Many more sophisticated regimens of cross-breeding have been adopted or attempted, but the innovation of principle is the same. (1) The end products are all like each other and are faithfully reproducible, but are not bred from because they do not breed true: the organisms that represent the eugenic goal have been relieved of the responsibility of reproducing themselves. And (2) the end products, though uniform in the sense of being like each other, are to a large extent hybrid—heterozygous as opposed to homozygous—in genetic composition.

The practices of stock-breeders can therefore no longer be used to support the argument that a policy of positive eugenics is applicable in principle to human beings in a society respecting the rights of individuals. The genetical manufacture of super-men by a policy of cross-breeding between two or more parental stocks is unacceptable today, and the idea that it might one day become acceptable is unacceptable also.

A deep fallacy does in fact eat into the theoretical foundations of positive eugenics and that older conception of stock-breeding out of which it grew.[3] The fallacy was to suppose that the *product* of evolution, *i.e.*, the outcome of an episode of evolutionary change, was a new and improved genetic formula (genotype) which conferred a higher degree of adaptedness on the individuals that possessed it. This improved formula, representing a new and more successful solution of the problems of remaining alive in a hostile environment, was thought to be shared by nearly all members of the newly evolved population, and to be stable except in so far as further evolution might cause it to change again. Moreover, the population would have to be predominantly homozygous in respect of the genetic factors entering into the new formula, for otherwise the individuals possessing it would not breed true to type, and everything natural selection had won would be squandered in succeeding generations.

Most geneticists think this view mistaken. It is *populations* that evolve, not the lineages and pedigrees of old-fashioned evolutionary "family trees," and the end product of an evolutionary episode is not a new genetic formula enjoyed by a group of similar individuals, but a new spectrum of genotypes, a new pattern of genetic inequality, definable only in terms of the population as a whole. Naturally out-breeding populations are not genetically uniform, even to a first approximation. They are persistently and obstinately diverse in respect of nearly all constitutional characters which have been studied deeply enough to say for certain whether they are uniform or not. It is the *population* that breeds true, not its individual members. The progeny of a given population are themselves a population with the same pattern of genetic make-up as their parents—except in so

---

3. See my article "A Biological Retrospect," *Nature* (London, 25 September, 1965) vol. 207, p. 1327.

far as evolutionary or selective forces may have altered it. Nor should we think of uniformity as a desirable state of affairs which *we* can achieve even if nature, unaided, cannot. It is inherently undesirable, for a great many reasons.

The goal of positive eugenics, in its older form, cannot be achieved, and I feel that eugenic policy must be confined (paraphrasing Karl Popper) * to *piecemeal genetic engineering*. That is just what Negative Eugenics amounts to; and now, rather than to deal in generalities, I should like to consider a concrete eugenic problem and discuss the morality of one of its possible solutions.

Some "inborn" defects—some defects that are the direct consequence of an individual's genetic make-up as it was fixed at the moment of conception—are said to be of *recessive* determination. By a recessive defect is meant one that is caused by, to put it crudely, a "bad" gene that must be present in both the gametes that unite to form a fertilised egg, *i.e.*, in both spermatozoon and egg cell, not just in one or the other. If the bad gene *is* present in only one of the gametes, the individual that grows out of its fusion with the other is said to be a *carrier* (technically, a heterozygote).

Recessive defects are individually rather rare—their frequency is of the order of one in ten thousand—but collectively they are most important. Among them are, for example, phenylketonuria, a congenital inability to handle a certain dietary constituent, the amino acid phenylalanine, a constituent of many proteins; galactosaemia, another inborn biochemical deficiency, the victims of which cannot cope metabolically with galactose, an immediate derivative of milk sugar; and, more common than either, fibrocystic disease of the pancreas, believed to by the symptom of a generalised disorder of mucus-secreting cells. All three are caused by particular single genetic defects; but their secondary consequences are manifold and deep-seated. The phenylketonuric baby is on the way to becoming an imbecile. The victim of galactosaemia may become blind through cataract and be mentally retarded.

Contrary to popular superstition, many congenital ailments can be prevented or, if not prevented, cured. But in this context prevention and cure have very special meanings.

The phenylketonuric or galactosaemic child may be protected from the consequences of his genetic lesion by keeping him on a diet free from phenylalanine in the one case or lactose in the other. This is a most unnatural proceeding, and much easier said than done, but I take it no one would be prepared to argue that it was an unwarrantable interference with the workings of providence. It is not a cure in the usual medical sense because it neither removes nor repairs the underlying congenital deficiency. What it does is to create around the patient a special

* Karl Popper, in his book *The Open Society and Its Enemies* (1945), argued that social reform must depend not on large-scale Utopian planning but on piecemeal engineering, which seeks out and fights the great social evils rather than aspiring toward some ultimate social good.

little world, a microcosm free from phenylalanine or galactose as the case may be, in which the genetic deficiency cannot express itself outwardly.

Now consider the underlying morality of prevention.

We can prevent phenylketonuria by preventing the genetic conjunction responsible for it in the first instance, *i.e.,* by preventing the coming together of an egg cell and a sperm each carrying that same one harmful recessive gene. All but a very small proportion of overt phenylketonurics are the children of parents who are both carriers—carriers, you remember, being the people who inherited the gene from one only of the two gametes that fused at their conception. Carriers greatly outnumber the overtly afflicted. When two carriers of the same gene marry and bear children, one quarter of their children (on the average) will be normal, one quarter will be afflicted, and one half will be carriers like themselves. We shall accomplish our purpose, therefore, if, having identified the carriers—another thing easier said than done, but it *can* be done, and in an increasing number of recessive disorders—we try to discourage them *from marrying each other* by pointing out the likely consequences if they do so. The arithmetic of this is not very alarming. In a typical recessive disease, about one marriage in every five or ten thousand would be discouraged or warned against, and each disappointed party would have between fifty and a hundred other mates to choose from.

If this policy were to carried out, the overt incidence of disease like phenylketonuria, in which carriers can be identified, would fall almost to zero between one generation and the next.

Nevertheless the first reaction to such a proposal may be one of outrage. Here is medical officiousness planning yet another insult to human dignity, yet another deprivation of the rights of man. First it was vaccination and then fluoride; if now people are not to be allowed to marry whom they please, why not make a clean job of it and overthrow the Crown or the U.S. Constitution?

But reflect for a moment. What is being suggested is that a certain small proportion of marriages should be discouraged for genetic reasons, to do our best to avoid bringing into the world children who are biochemically crippled. In all cultures marriages are already prohibited for genetic reasons—the prohibition, for example, of certain degrees of inbreeding (the exact degree varies from one culture or religion to another). It is difficult to see why the prohibition should have arisen to some extent independently in different cultures unless it grew out of the common observation that abnormalities are more common in the children of marriages between close relatives than in children generally. Thus the prohibition of marriage for genetic reasons has an immemorial authority behind it. As to the violation of human dignity entailed by performing tests on engaged couples that are no more complex or offensive than blood tests, let me say only this: if anyone thinks or has ever thought that religion, wealth, or colour are matters that may properly be taken into account when deciding whether or not a certain marriage is a suitable one, then let him not dare to suggest that the genetic welfare of human beings should not be given equal weight.

I think myself that engaged couples should themselves decide, and I am pretty certain they would guided by the thought of the welfare of their future children. When it came to be learned about twenty years ago that marriages between Rhesus-positive men and Rhesus-negative women might lead to the birth of children afflicted by haemolytic disease, a number of young couples are said to have ended their engagements—needlessly, in most cases, because the dangers were over-estimated through not being understood. But that is evidence enough that young people marrying today are not likely to take stand upon some hypothetical right to give birth to defective children if, by taking thought, they can do otherwise.

The problems I have been discussing illustrate very clearly the way in which scientific evidence bears upon decisions that are not, of course, in themselves scientific. If the termination of a pregnancy is now in question, scientific evidence may tell us that the chances of a defective birth are 100 per cent, 50 per cent, 25 per cent, or perhaps unascertainable. The evidence is highly relevant to the decision, but the decision itself is not a scientific one, and I see no reason why scientists as such should be specially qualified to make it. The contribution of science is to have enlarged beyond all former bounds the evidence we must take account of before forming our opinions. Today's opinions may not be the same as yesterday's, because they are based on fuller or better evidence. We should quite often have occasion to say "I used to think that once, but now I have come to hold a rather different opinion." People who never say as much are either ineffectual or dangerous.

We all nowadays give too much thought to the material blessings or evils that science has brought with it, and too little to its power to liberate us from the confinements of ignorance and superstition.

It may be that the greatest liberation of thought ever achieved by the scientific revolution was to have given mankind the expectation of a future in this world. The idea that the world has a virtually indeterminate future is comparatively new. Much of the philosophic speculation of three hundred years ago was oppressed by the thought that the world had run its course and was coming shortly to an end.[4] "I was borne in the last age of the World," said John Donne,[*] giving it as the "ordinarily received" opinion that the world had thrice two thousand years to run between its creation and the Second Coming. According to Arch-

---

4. See *The Discovery of Time,* by June Goodfield and Stephen Toulmin (Macmillan, 1965).

[*] John Donne: from a sermon delivered in Whitehall, 24 February 1625.

bishop Ussher's * chronology more than five-and-a-half of those six thousand years had gone by already.

No empirical evidence challenged this dark opinion. There were no new worlds to conquer, for the world was known to be spherical and therefore finite; certainly it was not all known, but the full extent of what was *not* known was known. Outer space did not put into people's minds then, as it does into ours now, the idea of a tremendous endeavour just beginning.

Moreover, life itself seemed changeless. The world a man saw about him in adult life was much the same as it had been in his own childhood, and he had no reason to think it would change in his own or his children's lifetime. We need not wonder that the promise of the next world was held out to believers as an inducement to put up with the incompleteness and inner pointlessness of this one: the present world was only a staging post on the way to better things. There was a certain awful topicality about Thomas Burnet's * description of the world in flames at the end of its long journey from "a dark chaos to a bright star," for the end of the world might indeed come at any time. And Thomas Browne * warned us against the folly and extravagance of raising monuments and tombs intended to last for many centuries. We are living in The Setting Part of Time, he told us: *the Great Mutations of the World are acted: it is too late to be ambitious.*

Science has now made it the ordinarily received opinion that the world has a future reaching beyond the most distant frontiers of the imagination—and that is perhaps why, in spite of all his faults, so many scientists still count Francis Bacon * their first and greatest spokesman: we may yet build a New Atlantis. The point is that when Thomas Burnet exhorted us to become Adventurers for Another World, *he* meant the next world—but we mean this one.

G. Rattray Taylor / Genetic Surgery: The New Eugenics

The discovery of DNA and the understanding of its structure are the great achievements of modern biology. The genetic transmission of information is now well enough understood to make it possible to speak of "genetic engineering" and "genetic surgery," techniques involving interference by man in

* James Ussher: (1581–1656), Irish divine and author of the *Annales Veteris et Novi Testamenti* which provided a chronology of Scripture (fixing the Creation at 4004 B.C.) that was accepted for two centuries.
* Thomas Burnet: (1635–1715), English clergyman, author of *The Sacred Theory of the Earth.*
* Thomas Browne: (1605–82), English writer; the quotation is from *Hydriotaphia: Urn Burial.*
* Francis Bacon: (1561–1626), English philosopher and statesman; his *New Atlantis* envisages a future rational society which includes a philosophic academy devoted to the scientific study of God's creation.

the microgenetic realm. This extract is concerned with the prospects for genetic surgery, which would involve physical intervention in the genetic process for the purpose of curing defects, or in order to control the characteristics of subsequent generations.

Here lie terrible difficulties and dangers; considered as mere "biomass," most of the world's men are redundant. And Dr. Taylor goes on to consider the new twist this gives to the old and vexed subject of eugenics (see the essay in this section by P. B. Medawar). The place of genetic control in some possible and acceptable eugenic system is a matter that will be more and more fiercely debated in the future. This extract gives some of the information necessary to a preliminary understanding of the problems and provides useful and pointed examples.

GENETIC SURGERY

Whether current techniques will lead first to methods of deleting unwanted genes, to methods of supplying missing genes, or whether the stage where whole blocks of characters can be altered simultaneously will be reached first, cannot yet be foreseen. Professor Edward Tatum has termed these possibilities gene deletion, gene insertion and gene surgery.

The microsurgery of DNA * may possibly be achieved by physical methods: fine beams of radiation (probably laser light or pulsed X-rays) may be used to slice through the DNA molecule at desired points, or to knock out small sections, so as to eliminate specific defects. Alternately, "repressor molecules" may be found which can be introduced to block the expression of particular characteristics in a precise manner. It is already clear that certain molecules are so shaped that they can embed themselves between the projections on the DNA chain and it may be that this is how repressor molecules work.

Some scientists place more hope in the idea of using viruses to carry information into the cell. But it may be that the copying of desired DNA's or even the synthesis of DNA to a desired pattern will eliminate the need for such detailed tinkering. It will be enough to insert the required DNA molecule as a whole, perhaps by some development of Dr. Teh's technique. Already molecules of the nucleic acid type, capable of assembling amino acids into protein-like structures, have been constructed in the laboratory. At present the message cannot be controlled in any real sense. The molecular biologist is like a telegraphist who cannot yet send messages: he can only send one letter repeatedly—AAAAAA or GGGGGG—or send random sequences such as AGCTCTAG. The step to being able to send actual "words" cannot be far off: it could be taken tomorrow.

* DNA: the genetic substance of all living cells; the structures of DNA molecules encode the hereditary information that is transmitted from one generation to the next.

Thus Professor Tatum, at a gathering in 1966, spoke of tailoring genes by obtaining the desired genetic material and using enzymes to copy it, in unlimited quantities. He also envisaged the use of suppressor substances to delete unwanted genes, and touched on the development of "gene insertion"—using nuclear grafts from healthy cells. Though there would be minor technical differences in treating germinal cells in this way, such experiments, he disclosed, were already being conducted in mammalian cells.

As the *New Scientist* commented at the time: he thus hinted "at the culture of embryos in the laboratory, destined to develop into adults whose physical, and possibly intellectual, characteristics have been chosen in advance by the genetic engineers."

One startling variation on this theme must be mentioned before we can discuss the wider implications of these developments. There seems to be no basic reason why one should not take the DNA from an egg and use it to fertilize another egg, whether by inserting it first into a spermatozoon or whether by direct injection. There are some technical problems to overcome: the entry of the sperm into the egg sets off a number of processes, before ever the nucleic acid contents fuse with that of the egg. But these could be started, in all probability, by the outer cases of spermatozoa, deprived of their DNA. In this way, a woman could be enabled to fertilize herself, a process christened by Professor Rostand "auto-adultery." Such a woman would bear a child which was genetically entirely her own, and her husband, if any, might well object that the child was not his and should, therefore, not be allowed to inherit his property. Indeed, he might justifiably refuse to support it.

The logical extension of this proposition is the complete elimination of men and the creation of a race of Amazons. While things will hardly go so far, on earth, it might be convenient to colonize another planet in this way.

Of course, it is already the case that men are present in far larger numbers than is genetically necessary. The semen from a single man would be more than sufficient to fertilize all the women in the country. Probably a single man could, by means of AID * and storage, in a single lifetime fertilize every fertile woman in the world, although it is true that, for fertilization to be achieved, considerable numbers of sperm must be present. As the British physiologist Professor A. S. Parkes has observed: "Women are beginning to have the scarcity value previously held by men. Biologically . . . . there are something like a million tons of unnecessary male biomass in this country alone." This is extremely inefficient, at least in the language of productivity, and unless men genuinely have something the others haven't got, outside sex, some shifting of the ratio between the sexes, by methods discussed in the previous chapter, could become a matter of policy.

Some scientists, it is true, are sceptical of the practicability of such develop-

* AID: Artificial Insemination by Donor.

ments. For instance, Dr. Max Perutz, who shared a Nobel award for his work at Cambridge on the structure of proteins, told a reporter: "I fail to visualize how you are going to perform surgery on the genetic apparatus of man. . . . The number of nucleotide base-pairs in a single human germ cell is of the order of 1000 million, distributed over 46 chromosomes. How could we delete a specific gene from a single chromosome, or add specific genes to it, or repair a mistake consisting of a single nucleotide pair in one gene? It hardly seems possible." But, as we have seen, the problem need not present itself in such uncompromising terms, and Perutz himself makes the qualification that "conceivably methods of transduction will become feasible; we may find harmless viruses which can be introduced into man and used to transduce desirable genes into people who lack them."

But Marshall W. Nirenberg, a leading biochemical geneticist who was one of the first to achieve the assembly of a simple nucleic acid in the test-tube, is still more confident. Pointing out that "genetic surgery, applied to micro-organisms, is a reality," he declares: "I have little doubt that the obstacles will eventually be overcome. The only question is when. My guess is that cells will be programmed with synthesized messages within 25 years. If efforts along these lines were intensified, bacteria might be programmed within five years." And he adds: "The point which deserves special emphasis is that man may be able to program his own cells with synthesized information long before he will be able to assess adequately the long-term consequences of such alterations, long before he will be able to formulate goals, and long before he can resolve the ethical and moral problems which will be raised."

Professor Tatum, likewise, considers that "We can be optimistic about long-range possibilities of therapy by the design and synthesis and introduction of new genes or gene products into cells of defective organs," while Joshua Lederberg of California Institute of Technology, in a broadcast, gave it as his opinion that "with a fairly strenuous effort" we might manage such tinkering with heredity in ten or twenty years.

That seems soon enough, and the question of how we should handle such powers—indeed whether we dare use them at all—is one we should begin to consider.

Such work opens up practical prospects at which the imagination boggles. While cloning methods could duplicate Derby winners indefinitely, genetic surgery could push up their speeds until they no longer looked like horses.

From making nonsense of sporting events in the animal world, it would be but a short step to making nonsense of human sporting events. Athletics could become a battle between geneticists, each seeking to endow his DNA with outstanding athletic properties. Given cloning as well, we may expect to see races in which every competitor crosses the finishing line at the same moment. And this is merely the physical aspect. The personnel selection boards of the future will work with a gene-map of the candidates, and a box of dice.

Professor Lederberg believes that the first step may be to implant human cell nuclei into animals, perhaps apes, and thus to produce hybrids; the next step will be to push this process further, incorporating organs and limbs of human origin in animals. These animal experiments, he believes, will be "pushed in steps as far as biology will allow" because of the "touchiness of experimentation on obviously human material." He makes clear that he does not advocate such experiments; indeed he fears that they may be tried without "even an adequate understanding of human values, not to mention vast gaps in human genetics." This makes it essential to think out the implications beforehand, otherwise policies may be adopted under the influence of the first publicly known results. Opinion may be unduly influenced by such factors as whether these first para-humans look attractive or gruesome, in popular terms. It is perhaps at this point that the layman may begin to say with Sir Macfarlane Burnet, "there are dangers in knowing what should not be known." As the *New Scientist* observed in a similar context, "Rules, perhaps laws, will be needed to allow for, say, treatment of congenitally malformed children, while excluding the temptation to 'improve' nature in socially undesirable ways."

The "man-farming biologist," in Professor Rostand's phrase, may be the most controversial figure of the immediate future.

But if all this seems too much to take seriously, we should at least face the fact that a very considerable power of intervention in heredity lies at our disposal right now, following the recent discoveries of germ-cell storage and inovulation, and the imminent achievement of *in vitro* * fertilization. . . . Eugenics has suddenly become a realistic issue.

THE NEW EUGENICS

Some scientists feel strongly that we should employ these new techniques without delay. As the late Herman J. Muller, of Indiana University, one of the earliest workers in the field of genetics, has emphatically said:

> The means exist right now of achieving a much greater, speedier and more significant genetic improvement of the population, by the use of selection, than could be effected by the most sophisticated methods of treatment of the genetic material that might be available in the twenty-first century.

Eugenics is sometimes regarded as divided into "negative eugenics" and "positive eugenics." Negative eugenics consists of the elimination of undesirable features, and especially the biochemical defects which are known to be propagated by a single damaged or defective gene. In addition to hemophilia, there are several severe diseases—many of them so handicapping that they tend to eliminate themselves. Thus some children are born without the ability to manufacture the substance gamma-globulin, from which the antibodies of the immune system

---

* *in vitro*: within an artificial environment, such as a test tube.

are made. Such children are wholly unable to resist infection and, until the discovery of antibiotics, died in the first weeks of life from one infection or another. Other children are unable to break up a substance known as phenylalanine, present in many varieties of food. If untreated, they become idiots, unable to feed or clean themselves, and are unlikely ever to reach the point of having children. Today, the condition can be detected and such children can be placed on a special diet, devoid of phenylalanine, when they develop normally and may even develop some ability to tolerate phenylalanine. Similarly, there are children who cannot tolerate certain natural sugars.

Though such children now survive, they may transmit the defective gene to their offspring, if they have any. Such a defect can rather rapidly spread through a population, as is shown by the case of the way in which the disease known as Huntington's chorea was introduced into the North American continent. This disease usually does not strike until after the reproductive age, so it does not tend to be bred out. It leads to progressive muscular and mental deterioration over a period of ten or twenty years, ending in a gruesome death. In the seventeenth century, six people with this condition arrived in America. When a survey was made in 1916, 962 cases could be identified, including those no longer alive, and the way in which the gene had spread across the country from east to west, with steps of one or more generations on the way, could be traced. None of these 962 people need have suffered if the original half dozen could have been persuaded not to procreate.

To discourage people carrying a known defect from transmitting it is clearly desirable. Moreover, if this can be done consistently, the defective gene will, at the end of one generation, vanish from the gene-pool. Thereafter the problem ceases to exist: perhaps, very occasionally a new case may crop up, as a result of mutation, and will have to be dealt with in the same way. Substantially, however, the defect has been eliminated.

Today sensitive tests for most of these conditions exist, so marriage counselling is feasible. Advice of this kind is no doubt already given by some doctors in civilized countries: but there is no compulsion to take it, and some cases may not come to the doctors' attention.

The case is simple when the defect is so clear-cut and there are no obviously desirable "good" genes in the same heredity. It would be harder to know whether one should discourage an Einstein or a Bach from procreating simply because he suffered from hemophilia or phenylketonuria. It is yet harder when we consider more generalized defects, let us say low intelligence, which are probably the outcome of many genes, some of which may well be associated with desirable characteristics. Should we discourage a poet like Rimbaud * from procreating because we disapprove of his moral character?

* Arthur Rimbaud: French poet of the late nineteenth century; Rimbaud was notorious for violence and dissipation, regarding a "disorder of all the senses" as necessary to his poetic program.

In asking this question, we have really moved into the area of positive eugenics, since to discourage the propagation of low intelligence is the same as to encourage the propagation of high intelligence.

The difficulty in making use of the new techniques is that we have no methods of measuring mental characteristics, other than intelligence (in the narrow sense), and it is precisely these in which we are most interested. Nor do we know how they are connected genetically, so that we run the risk of breeding out one characteristic in our attempts to breed in another. According to the doubtless apocryphal story, when the dancer Isadora Duncan proposed to George Bernard Shaw that they should have a baby, arguing, "Think of a child with my body and your mind," he declined, saying, "Ah, but suppose it had *my* body and *your* mind!" The animal or plant breeder can throw away his poor results, but human beings cannot so easily do so.

Until the day of gene surgery, therefore, eugenics must be a hit-and-miss business. Even so, it might be advantageous to a country, or any large group of people, to encourage selection, since subjective judgments are not without value and on the whole the genetic standard would tend to rise. Indeed, there are some who believe that it is currently deteriorating and that the people with poorer heredity are procreating more numerously than those with good heredity. Dr. William Shockley, famous as the inventor of the transistor, believes that this deterioration can be coupled with war and famine as the third great world problem. As we have no means of measuring total heredity, or of comparing the value of one trait with another, such a contention is impossible to prove. But if it is true it certainly makes the case for some kind of eugenic policy even stronger.

But it is unlikely that any western country will introduce compulsion. They are not even likely to move with any speed towards a permissive situation. On a matter which could arouse strong feeings, no democratic government is going to risk loss of votes until it becomes clear that a substantial section of the electorate is firmly in favour of such a move. They have already shown themselves reluctant to encourage or discourage procreation differentially in various social groups.

The most plausible solution, which has been hotly advocated by Herman Muller, is one sometimes known as "germinal choice." It is proposed that germ-cell banks be established containing a variety of types of semen, to which people can apply, stating what characteristics they personally would hope to see in their offspring. They would then be supplied with semen derived from donors having such characteristics. "As an aid in making these choices there would be provided as full documentation as possible concerning the donors of the germinal material, the lives they had led, and their relatives. The couples concerned would also have advice available from geneticists, physicians, psychologists, experts in the fields of activity of the donors being considered, and other relevant specialists, as well as generalizers." The donors would of course be anonymous and preferably no longer living, so that personality cultism and personal complications would be prevented.

It seems reasonable to suppose that a number of progressive people would take advantage of such a facility, at least in the case of some of their children, even where they were themselves perfectly fertile, and for infertile persons it would be an obvious course. They would be motivated as much by the desire of having above-average children (and this is a strong motivation) as by public spirit. Such a trend would develop slowly at first, no doubt, but if, after a generation, it became clear that such "pre-adopted" children—to use Sir Julian Huxley's term for it—were really above average, the practice might develop very rapidly.

The idea of germinal choice now dates back thirty years or more—at one time it was called by the highly discouraging name of eutelegenesis—and various people have attempted to draw up lists of desirable qualities. Muller, for instance, named such desirable qualities as moral courage and co-operative disposition, appreciation of nature and aptness of expression. But there is much evidence that these are the product at least as much of environment as of heredity.

Today the note is changing from one of advice to one of warning. Lederberg, for instance, fears that decisions may be taken hastily, on the basis of popular approval or disapproval of particular individuals who lend themselves to eugenic or other biological experiments.

However, Dr. Bronowski has pointed out that "multiplication of what we choose to call the fit can really have very little effect on the presence of recessives"—that is, of those genes which only show up when both parents carry them. Long ago, J. B. S. Haldane used the same argument to show that sterilization of the unfit, which was then being advocated, would not in fact eliminate the qualities objected to.

Professor Luria, while discounting the notion that genetics promises either a millennium or enslavement, told fellow biologists at a meeting two years ago: "What we, in anticipation of the remarkable advances that may soon be forthcoming, can do is to attempt to create some machinery by which the social implications of our work can be debated rationally and openly, so that any important decision as to its application can be arrived at by an informed and well-advised public. I would not think it premature, for example, for the United Nations as well as the National Academy of Sciences of the United States to establish committees on the genetic direction of human heredity."

So far, neither organization has shown any signs of taking the hint.

But the simple plan of germinal selection does not really come to grips with the issues, as Dr. Lederberg has pointed out. Changing the genetic constitution of man is a slow business and the question is, what will he need in the future, rather than what does he need now. To take a crude instance, evolution has developed in man elaborate defences against invasion by germs but has provided almost no defences against chemical attack. But in the modern world, with its growing range of antiseptics, antibiotics and so on, infection is decreasingly important. On the other hand, chemical pollution of the environment is increasing rapidly. The genetic engineer needs to consider whether he could not introduce quite new capacities to meet this hazard.

Again, evolution depends upon procreation and selects people so that they have a maximum chance of surviving to procreative age; with minor exceptions, it is unable to influence, or be influenced by, what they do after production of offspring ceases—and this is why we are so poor at resisting the ravages of age. But in the modern world, in which half the life span may be spent after bringing up one's offspring, this is no longer good enough. We therefore need to equip man with genes which will serve him in later life, and as life span is extended, the need will grow.

Lederberg thus offers us a glimpse of a future in which man will control his own evolution in a far more radical way than was even dreamed of until genetic engineering became, anyway, a theoretical possibility. Remote as it may seem now, when even conventional eugenics is still viewed askance, it needs only successful demonstration of such techniques in animal breeding for the question of their application to man to begin to be raised in earnest.

FAMILY PLAN

The proposition that we should inaugurate genetic policies right away raises a host of social questions which geneticists like Muller skate quickly over or ignore, but a number of them have been pinpointed by Professor Kingsley Davis of the University of California at Berkeley.

A state or national pedigree board would be required to decide who were to be donors. The natural desire of most people to bear their own children would lead to bootlegging of spermatozoa and possibly eggs, and, to make the programme work, non-donors—the bulk of the population—would probably have to be sterilized. But perhaps women of good hormonal constitution would be needed to serve as hosts or adoptive mothers to implanted, fertilized eggs. Whether people would learn to accept non-biological children as their own, as fully as they do their biological children, is an unanswered question.

Donors, presumably, would be free to produce biological children and this would make them an élite group. It would be a matter of status to belong and bribery, evasion and sperm-substitution would occur. The question of whether all couples are equally fit to bring up children would also arise, since the adult (as the psychologists and anthropologists have so forcibly argued) is the product of environment as well as of heredity.

René Dubos / The Pursuit of Significance

Several of the essays selected for this volume touch on the problems of a polluted environment. This one, by a writer who is at once a distinguished medical professor and a successful popularizer of biological science, steps back and takes a long view of the relation of man to his environment—to what is sometimes now called "the biosphere." He emphasizes the strictness of the limits within which human life is possible, and also the remarkable adaptability of man within those limits. This is a benefit deriving from his lack, relative to the other animals, of physiological specialization. The limits are strict; man belongs to the earth. There, admittedly, he can adapt to conditions which seem inimical to his life—undernourishment, pollution, ugliness. Yet in doing that he risks his future, for adaptation does not secure immunity from ill effects. What is to be made of the remarkable fact that in very prosperous countries, such as the U.S., life expectancy after the age of forty-five is not increasing and may even be falling? Such considerations launch Dr. Dubos on a study of the harmful characteristics of a typically overcrowded and polluted modern city environment, including the severance of our lives from natural stimuli and rhythms. The contrast between those who have lost contact with those rhythms except on country weekends and those who live in direct touch with them is pointed up by the story of Chief Seattle in the opening paragraphs, and by the allusion, at the end, to the myth of Antaeus.

The language of this essay is never difficult, yet it is never less difficult than the occasion requires. The author has in mind an educated non-specialist audience. He can talk about evolutionary theory or pulmonary disease with some certainty that there is still an overlap between the vocabularies of educated people and specialists. The importance of maintaining this overlap is obvious if there is to be that general understanding of our technological civilization which, as other writers such as Goodman insist, is necessary to the preservation of humane and rational ideas of human society.

SURROUNDINGS AND EVENTS

Western man tends to consider himself apart from and above the rest of creation. He has accepted to the letter the Biblical teaching that man was given by God "dominion over the fish of the sea, and over the fowl of the air, and over the cattle, and over all the earth" (Genesis 1:26).

In contrast, most primitive people identify themselves with the environment in which they are born and live. They worship the sky and the clouds, trees and animals, mountains, rocks, springs, and rivers as the living expressions of the cosmic order from which they derive their own being. Man's feeling of identity with Nature was beautifully expressed by the Indian chief Seattle in an address to Governor Isaac Stevens, Commissioner of Indian Affairs for the Territory of Washington. The occasion was a ceremony in 1853 or 1854 during which the Governor presented to the Indians the terms of a treaty for the surrender of the land on which the city of Seattle is now located. A few years later Dr. Henry A. Smith, who had witnessed the ceremony, reported it in the following words:

"Old Chief Seattle was the largest Indian I ever saw, and by far the noblest-looking. He stood nearly six feet in his moccasins, and was broad-shouldered, deep-chested, and finely proportioned. His eyes were large, intelligent, expressive and friendly when in repose, and faithfully mirrored the varying moods of the great soul that looked through them. . . .

"When rising to speak in council or tendering advice, all eyes were turned upon him, and deep-toned, sonorous and eloquent sentences rolled from his lips like the ceaseless thunder of cataracts." [1]

After being presented with the text of the settlement, Chief Seattle placed one hand upon General Stevens' head, slowly pointed the index finger of the other hand heavenward, and solemnly made his reply. His words were later translated by Dr. Smith as follows:

"There was a time when our people covered the whole land as the waves of a wind-ruffled sea covers its shell-paved floor, but that time has long since passed away with the greatness of tribes now almost forgotten. I will not dwell on nor mourn over our untimely decay, nor reproach my paleface brothers with hastening it, for we, too, may have been somewhat to blame. . . .

"We are two distinct races, and must ever remain so, with separate origins and separate destinies. There is little in common between us.

"To us the ashes of our ancestors are sacred and their final resting place is hallowed ground, while you wander far from the graves of your ancestors and, seemingly, without regret. . . .

"Our dead never forget this beautiful world that gave them being. They still love its winding rivers, its great mountains, and its sequestered vales. . . .

"Every part of this country is sacred to my people. Every hillside, every valley, every plain and grove has been hallowed by some fond memory or some sad experience of my tribe. Even the rocks, which seem to lie dumb as they swelter in the sun along the silent seashore in solemn grandeur, thrill with memories of past events connected with the lives of my people.

"The very dust under your feet responds more lovingly to our footsteps than to yours, because it is the ashes of our ancestors, and our bare feet are conscious

1. Quoted in John M. Rich, *Chief Seattle's Unanswered Challenge* (Seattle: John M. Rich, 1932), 30–31.

of the sympathetic touch, for the soil is rich with the life of our kindred" [2] [italics mine—R.D.].

Indians of other tribes have similarly expressed a feeling of organic unity with their ancestral lands. A few decades ago, the Navajos, protesting against new federal regulations which limited (for very good reasons) their grazing practices, reminded the government officials that ". . . before we were born, the white people and our old folks made a treaty. The treaty was made to the end that these encircling Mountains would always be ours, so that we could live according to them. The right to these was given to us, so that all the Navajos might live in accord with that which is called Mountain Soil, and the pollen of all plants. All Navajos live in accord with them." [3]

The Southwest is so different from the Northwest in climate, topography, and natural resources that there is little in common between the ways of life and traditions of the Navajos and those of Chief Seattle's tribe. But both tribes shared a mystic sense of relationship with the natural forces of their ancestral surroundings. Their lives derived significance from an emotional identification with Nature.

Before the industrial age, people had everywhere achieved some measure of integration with the physical and social environment in which they lived and on which they depended. When he first reached Europe from India, the philosopher Sir Rabindranath Tagore (1861–1941) marveled at the extent to which the quality of the European countryside was a loving creation of the peasantry, the result of an active wooing of the earth.[4] One of the reasons for the emotional impoverishment in countries were industry and technology have taken over is the loss of identification with the natural world. Increasingly we tend to deal with nature as if it were of value only as a source of raw material and entertainment.

Chief Seattle had good reasons for believing that the spirit of Western civilization was antithetical to the Red Man's ways of life and feeling for Nature. He was also right in stating to Governor Stevens, still according to Dr. Smith's account:

"Your religion was written on tablets of stone by the iron finger of an angry God. . . .

"Our religion is the traditions of our ancestors—the dreams of our old men given to them in the solemn hours of night by the Great Spirit . . . and is written in the hearts of our people." [5]

However, the great difference in attitude of the red man and the white man was not caused by their belonging to "two distinct races . . . with separate origins and separate destinies." Whether man considers himself part of nature, or

2. *Ibid.*, 33, 36, 40.
3. Robert W. Young and William Morgan, *Navajo Historical Selections,* Navajo Historical Series No. 3, Bureau of Indian Affairs, 1954.
4. Rabindranath Tagore, *Towards Universal Man* (New York: Asia Publishing House, 1961), 294.
5. Rich, *op. cit.,* 36.

outside of it and its master, is determined not by racial origins, but by cultural forces. Racial differences have little relevance to mental or emotional characteristics, and do not necessarily imply separate destinies. Within the past few decades, many Indians whose racial purity has not been diluted by mixed marriage have nevertheless become completely westernized and thereby lost the sense of identification with their ancestral lands and ways of life. In fact, this is particularly true of the Indians of the Northwest, in whose name Chief Seattle made his memorable address. Likewise, many Europeans who have migrated to the Americas, North and South, have now renounced their allegiance to the lands and civilizations of their origin.

All men are migrants from a common origin. For all of them life can be sustained only within extremely narrow physical limits defined by the physiological exigencies of the species *Homo sapiens*. But men of all races can learn to live in a wide variety of natural environments by adopting the proper ways of life. While man's physiologic adaptations are rather limited in range, he has learned to supplement them with sociocultural adaptations which are becoming increasingly effective and diversified.

Whatever their races and social origins, human beings have established their abodes under every possible type of physical condition; they have also developed emotional ties to all manifestations of nature on earth. *Homo sapiens* probably originated in a temperate climate, but human beings of all racial types have now made themselves at home under the sun of the Sahara and the fogs of Newfoundland, in the lowlands of the African rain forest and in the high Peruvian Andes. Human social life started in small isolated bands, but it is now happily carried out in huge crowded cities as well as in cozy villages. Home is that environment to which a particular person becomes adapted through biological and sociocultural mechanisms, and to which he becomes emotionally attached through the traditions of his group and his own personal experiences. Home is less a physical place than a locus with which past experiences are identified.

Throughout history, in all parts of the world, populations have been compelled to abandon their homes and to resettle in other lands, as a result either of wars or of natural disasters, or for economic or ideological reasons. But human adaptability is so great that displaced populations have usually succeeded in re-creating a home with all the connotations of the word even when the move had taken them to entirely different physical and human surroundings. Although most of the highland populations in Britain are Celtic in descent, they did not originate in the areas to which they now seem so well adapted; they were natives of the lowlands and were driven out by Saxon invaders.[6] Similarly, the northeast coast of the United States has become within a few generations the home of Irish, Italians, Jews, and Central Africans who were forced out of their original homelands for a variety of economic and social causes.

6. George Homans, *English Villagers of the Thirteenth Century* (New York: Russell & Russell, 1960).

Daily life in all the large cities of Western civilization provides endless examples of man's ability to function in physical and social surroundings totally different from those of his origins. Most human beings are potentially able to integrate their biological and social past with that of their neighbors and contemporaries. In the Old World as far north as London, and in the New World as far south as Buenos Aires, one can see—working at the same tasks, playing at the same games, acquiring the same habits—blond blue-eyed Scandinavians or Celts born in misty lands; Arabs and Indians originating from sandy deserts; dark-skinned Africans or yellow-skinned Asians whose parents lived in tropical rain forests. All these people eventually eat the same food, listen to the same music, watch the same spectacles, pledge allegiance to the same flag, worship the same God, or become equally indifferent to any form of traditional religion. They tend to forget their ancestral heritages, commonly suffer in much the same way from loss of traditional values, and together clumsily search for a new significance in life.

Irrespective of race and color, most human beings can also develop tolerance to a large variety of conditions that are certainly undesirable and may indeed appear at first sight almost unbearable. The Office of Civilian Defense recently made an exhaustive review of what is known concerning the effects on health of extreme physical crowding, such as occurred, for example, in slave ships, concentration camps, prisons, and bomb shelters.[7] Many people survived these horrible experiences and recovered rapidly from them because they controlled tension and reserved their energy during the ordeal; they allowed their systems to adjust by submitting to the stresses almost passively!

Two contemporary examples also illustrate the surprising range of conditions which human beings can learn to tolerate and even to enjoy. At the Valley Forge Interchange in Pennsylvania there is emerging a huge development accommodating 25,000 industrial employees, 1 million square feet of retail space, 1,000 acres of parking lots, expressways, and thoroughfares—but not a single family dwelling! Another instance of modern man's ability and willingness to let his life be mechanized for the sake of professional activities is the fact that the Los Angeles airport is becoming the largest office and hotel district on the West Coast. Many persons regard such a peculiar environment as a most satisfactory place for business and other meetings. How remote seem the palatial mansions in which government officials and business tycoons used to gather for state and business transactions!

History shows that cultures of a sort can emerge from the most improbable ways of life, provided these last long enough to become integrated into an organic whole. The emergence of a new culture is rarely if ever the result of a conscious choice with a definite goal in mind. What happens rather is that the

---

7. W. C. Loring, comments on "City Planning and the Treasury of Science" by John W. Dyckman, in William R. Ewald, Jr. (ed.), *Environment for Man* (Bloomington, Ind.: Indiana University Press, 1967), 52–56.

social customs for mating and raising children, providing shelter and means of subsistence, developing natural resources, protecting the land against enemies, enjoying life, or worshiping God interact and become organized into unique patterns. Societies of all types, from the simplest to the most complex, have achieved such integration of behavioral activities and thus have given rise to the marvelous diversity of human cultures.

The Australian aborigines, primitive as they are, have developed extremely sophisticated customs that enable them to survive under the harsh conditions of the bush.[8] These customs can hardly be traced to a systematic and entirely conscious exercise of human intelligence; they must have emerged progressively in the course of continued interactions between the people and their environment. The aborigines' responses to the conditions of their lives and the tribal memories of their past experiences have become incorporated in their social wisdom. Similarly, it is most improbable that any group of Englishmen, however intelligent and foresighted, could have devised in the abstract and then imposed on their fellowmen a scheme as complex as that of the British type of parliamentary government. Its formulation was the product of many successive pragmatic adjustments rather than of a complete plan thought out in its entirety and in all its details.

Biologically, man is still the great amateur of the animal kingdom; he is unique in his lack of anatomical and physiological specialization. The range of his adaptive potentialities has been greatly enlarged by sociocultural mechanisms that have enabled him to colonize most of the earth. His adventurous spirit now tempts him to conquer other worlds. But despite the success of launchings into space, his colonizing days are over.

Science-fiction writers and a few scientists notwithstanding, man will never be able actually to settle anywhere in the cosmos other than on or near the surface of the earth. At most, he will make hit-and-run raids on the moon, Mars, and perhaps other planets; he may also establish some stations for specialized purposes under the ocean waters. But he is earthbound forever because his life is completely dependent on fresh water and especially on the earth's atmosphere. While it is possible to re-create and maintain the earth's atmosphere out in space or on the bottom of the ocean, this technological enterprise is so formidable that it will be done only for very special missions.

The fact that modern man is constantly moving into new environments gives the impression that he is enlarging the range of his biological adaptabilities and thus escaping from the bondage of his past. This is only an appearance. Wher-

---

8. Quoted in Stanley M. Garn, *Culture and the Direction of Human Evolution* (Detroit, Mich.: Wayne State University Press, 1964), 16; see also Charles P. Mountford, *Ayers Rock: Its People, Their Beliefs, and Their Art* (Honolulu: East-West Center Press, 1965).

ever he goes, and whatever he does, man is successful only to the extent that he functions in a microenvironment not drastically different from the one under which he evolved. He can climb Mount Everest and fly at high altitudes only if he carries an adequate oxygen supply and is equipped to protect himself against cold. He moves in outer space and at the bottom of the sea only if he remains within enclosures that almost duplicate the terrestrial environment or links himself to the earth by an umbilical cord. Even the Eskimos, who appear so well adapted to the Arctic climate, in reality cannot long resist intense cold. Sheltered in their snow houses or clothed in their parkas, they live an almost tropical life! [9]

There is no hope whatever that man's biological nature can be changed enough to enable him to survive without the earth's atmosphere; in fact, the very statement of this possibility is meaningless. *Homo sapiens* achieved his characteristics as a biological species more than 100,000 years ago, and his fundamental biological characteristics could not be drastically altered without destroying his very being. He developed his human attributes in the very act of responding to the environment in which he evolved. The earth has been his cradle and will remain his home.

The experiences of the present century show that mankind has not lost the biological adaptability that enabled *Homo sapiens* to become established over most of the earth. Countless human beings have survived the frightful ordeal of combat during war, and many managed to function even in the worst concentration camps. In our own communities today, human life is adjusting itself to the multifarious physiological and mental stresses of urban and industrial environments. All over the world, indeed, the most polluted, crowded, and brutal cities are also the ones that have the greatest appeal. Some of the most spectacular increases in population are occurring in areas where living conditions are detestable from all points of view.

Modern man can adjust to environmental pollution, intense crowding, deficient or excessive diet, as well as to monotonous and ugly surroundings. Furthermore, biologically undesirable conditions do not necessarily constitute a handicap for economic growth. Great wealth is being produced by men working under extreme nervous tension amidst the infernal noise of high-power equipment, telephones, and typewriters, in atmospheres contaminated with chemical fumes or in crowded offices clouded with tobacco smoke.

Such adaptability is obviously an asset for survival and seems to assure the continued biological success of the human race. Paradoxically, however, the very fact that man readily achieves biological and sociocultural adjustments to so many different kinds of stresses and undesirable conditions is dangerous for his welfare and his future. But before justifying this statement, I must point out that the classical meanings of the term adaptation do not properly apply to the ad-

9. Vilhjalmur Stefansson, *The Friendly Arctic* (New York: Macmillan, 1953).

justments that human beings have to make under the conditions of modern life.[10]

For the general biologist, Darwinian adaptation implies a state of fitness to a given environment, enabling the species to survive and multiply. In this light, man is remarkably adapted to life in highly urbanized and industrialized societies; his populations continuously increase and he spreads urbanization and industrialization over more and more of the earth. Even if it is true that the modern ways of life do not contribute significantly to real happiness and may even increase the frequency of certain chronic disorders, these failures are of little importance from the purely biological point of view. The chronic disorders characteristic of modern civilization affect man chiefly during late adulthood after he has fulfilled his reproductive functions and contributed his share to social and economic development. The problem of happiness becomes important only when attention is shifted from the purely biological aspects of life to the far different problems of human values. In applying to man the concept of adaptation, we must therefore use criteria different from those used in general biology.

Physiologists or psychologists give the word adaptation a broader meaning than that associated with Darwinian population theory, but they, too, seem to underestimate the rich complexity of human life. To them, a response is adaptive when it promotes homeostasis—in other words, when it brings into action the metabolic, hormonal, or mental processes that tend to correct the disturbing effects of environmental forces on the body and mind. Such adaptive responses obviously contribute to the welfare of the organism at the time they occur, but unfortunately they commonly have secondary effects that may become deleterious.

Scar tissue heals wounds and helps in checking the spread of infection; it represents a successful homeostatic process at the time it is formed in response to a wound or a lesion. But scar tissue in the liver or in the kidney is responsible for serious diseases such as cirrhosis or glomerular nephritis; in the lungs it may seriously impede breathing; in the joints it generates the frozen immobility of rheumatoid arthritis. Similarly, many other medical problems have their origin in biological and mental adaptive responses that allowed man to cope with environmental threats earlier in life. All too often the wisdom of the body is a short-sighted wisdom.[11]

Man's physiological and psychological endowments thus give him a wide range of adaptive potentialities and enable him to survive and function even under extremely unfavorable conditions; however, the fact that all subsequent aspects of his life are affected by his past makes such adaptability a double-edged sword. Evaluated over the entire life span, the homeostatic mechanisms through

10. René Dubos, *Man Adapting, op. cit.,* Chapter 10.
11. Dickinson W. Richards, "Homeostasis: Its Dislocations and Perturbations," *Perspectives in Biology and Medicine,* 3 (1960), 238–251.

which adaptation is achieved often fail in the long run because they result in delayed pathological effects.

Countless incidents in the life of urban-dwellers illustrate how we overlook the dangers that result from our temporary adjustments to undesirable situations.

On a hot and humid Friday during midsummer, I landed at Kennedy Airport early in the afternoon. The taxicab that was taking me home was soon caught in a traffic jam, which gave the driver an opportunity to express his views on the state of the world. Noting my foreign accent, he assumed that I was unacquainted with the United States and proceeded to enlighten me on the superiorities of American life. "You probably are surprised by this heavy traffic so early on Friday afternoon," he remarked, as the cab stood still in the sultry air saturated with gasoline fumes. "The reason there are so many people on the road at this hour is that we have plenty of leisure in this country and all of us can afford an automobile." As we removed our coats and mopped our brows, he added forcefully, "In the United States we all live like kings."

Since I was irritated by the delay, the driver's statement that we lived like kings appeared to me completely irrational, as if coming from a deranged person. But he looked like a reasonable man, similar in outward appearance and behavior to the thousands of other automobile occupants who were spending the afternoon on the congested and ill-smelling road still called by poetic license an expressway.

Like millions of other persons breathing gasoline fumes and struggling with crowds all over the country on that midsummer Friday afternoon, my taxi driver had made some sort of adjustment to air pollution, to competition with countless anonymous motorists, and to the dismal monotony and ugliness of the suburban scenery. In fact, he was so well adjusted that he could carry out his professional activities with great effectiveness and thus contribute to the growth of the national economy. The pollution and other stresses that he experienced daily on the crowded highways increased the likelihood that he would eventually suffer from some physical and behavioral disturbances. But degenerative disorders would become manifest only in his late adulthood, after he had produced a family and played his role in the economic enterprise. He would not trace them to the nonsensical ways of life that he had come to accept as part of living like a king.

For some two centuries, Western man has believed that he would find his salvation in technology. Unquestionably technological innovations have increased his economic wealth and improved his physical health—although they have not necessarily brought him the kinds of wealth and health that generate happiness. Technology provided my taxi driver with all the raw materials required for building a large body and a reasonably equipped mind but it also imposed on him ways of life almost incompatible with the maintenance of physical and mental sanity. In this regard, his plight was symbolic of life in highly technicized societies. The precise causes of the diseases of civilization are difficult to identify, but there is no doubt that many originate directly or indirectly from deleterious environmental influences to which human beings *seem* to become adjusted.

Life expectancy at birth has increased enormously in all industrialized countries and is now 70 years or more in the prosperous social groups. However, life expectancy past the age of 45 has not significantly increased anywhere in the world, and especially *not* among the social groups that enjoy great comfort and can afford elaborate medical care; it may even be somewhat lower in very prosperous countries such as the United States or Sweden than in economically less-favored countries such as Spain or Ireland.[12]

The control of mortality during the early years of life accounts for the increase in life expectancy at birth all over the world, but the failure to control vascular disorders, malignancies, and other degenerative diseases has prevented so far any significant increase in true longevity. Relative to the total adult population, the percentage of nonagenarians and centenarians is probably no greater today than it was in the past. Adults have to pay in the form of chronic and degenerative diseases for the unrecognized insults they have received from the environment in their earlier years.

Many of the health problems of modern man, in the present and for the future, have their origin in slowly developing injurious effects of the technological environment and the new ways of life. It has long been known for example that radiation damage may not become apparent for one or two decades; the consequences of cigarette smoking and of environmental pollution likewise develop very slowly; certain medical and psychic problems of adult life have their origin in malnutrition and other forms of deprivation experienced during infancy. The biological remembrance of the past is thus of particular relevance to the understanding of the diseases that affect adult life and old age.

Atmospheric pollution in the industrial areas of northern Europe provides striking examples both of man's ability to function in a biologically undesirable environment and of the remote dangers inherent in this adaptability. Ever since the beginning of the Industrial Revolution, the inhabitants of northern Europe have been heavily exposed to many types of air pollutants, some produced by incomplete combustion of coal and others released in the fumes from chemical plants; these pollutants are rendered even more objectionable by the inclemency of the Atlantic climate. However, through long experience with pollution and with bad weather a variety of adaptive physiological reactions and living habits have progressively developed. Northern Europeans accept their dismal environment almost cheerfully, even though such conditions appear unbearable to outsiders who experience them for the first time.

Adaptive responses to environmental pollution occur in heavily industrialized areas all over the world. Since people can function effectively despite the almost

---

12. René Dubos, *Man Adapting, op. cit.,* Chapter 9.

constant presence of irritating substances in the air they breathe, one might assume that human beings can make adequate adjustments to massive air pollution. These adjustments are inadequate in the long run, however, because air pollution eventually causes suffering and economic loss. Even among persons who are almost unaware of the air pollutants surrounding them, the respiratory tract continuously registers the insult. After periods of time that differ from one case to another and commonly extend to several decades, the cumulative effects of irritation become manifest in the form of chronic bronchitis and other types of pulmonary disease. Since these pathological consequences do not occur until long after initial exposure, it is always difficult to relate them to the primary physiological insult, which may have been so mild as to have remained unnoticed.

Chronic pulmonary disease now constitutes the greatest single medical problem in northern Europe, as well as the most costly. It is increasing in prevalence at an alarming rate also in North America and will spread to all areas undergoing industrialization. Furthermore, air pollution probably increases the prevalence of various types of cancers and of fatalities among persons suffering from vascular diseases. Here again, the long time span between cause and effect makes it difficult to establish the causal relationships convincingly.

The delayed effects of air pollutants constitute models for the kind of medical problems likely to arise in the future from other forms of environmental pollution, such as the pollution of water and food by products of industry. Granted differences in detail, the course of events can be predicted in its general trends.

Wherever convenient, chemical pollution of air, water, and food will be sufficiently controlled to prevent immediately disabling or obviously unpleasant toxic effects. Human beings will then tolerate, without complaint, concentrations of pollutants that do not interfere seriously with social and economic life. This continued exposure to low levels of toxic agents will eventually result in a great variety of delayed pathological manifestations, creating physiological misery, increasing the medical burden, and lowering the quality of life. The point of importance here is that the most significant effects of environmental pollutants will not be detected at the time of exposure to them; indeed, they may not become evident until several decades later. In other words, society will become adjusted to levels of pollution sufficiently low not to have an immediate nuisance value, but this adjustment will eventually interfere with the enjoyment of later life and also with the full expression of its potentialities. Malnutrition or overnutrition, minor infections, and the indiscriminate use of drugs are other aspects of life which are likely to have long-range consequences far more dangerous than their immediate effects.

In view of the increase in the world population, the problems posed by adaptation to crowding will certainly change in character and become more important in the near future. Man is a gregarious animal; he generally tends to accept crowded environments and even to seek them. While this attitude unquestionably has social advantages, these may not be unmixed blessings. Physiological tests have revealed that crowding commonly results in an increased secretion of various hormones which affect the whole human physiology. An adequate hormonal activity is essential for well-being but any excess has a variety of harmful effects.

As the world becomes more and more urbanized and industrialized, constant and intimate contact with hordes of human beings has come to constitute the "normal" way of life, and men have eagerly adjusted to it. This change has certainly brought about all kinds of behavioral adaptations to social environments that appear normal to us even though they would have been shocking and possibly disastrous in the past. Crowding is a relative term; the past experience of the group conditions the manner in which each of its members interacts. Population density, in other words, is probably less important in the long run than the intensity of social conflicts it brings about, conflicts which usually become less intense after social adjustments have been made. Granted that the consequences of crowding are not yet well understood, there is little doubt that they will be found in most cases to have an insidious course. The worst effects will not be the initial ones, but the complex secondary responses called forth later in individual persons and in society as a whole.

During evolutionary development the human species probably functioned in small groups, each member knowing the others personally. Man may have need for larger gatherings now and then, but certainly not as a constant diet. When oversocialized, he is likely to react with frustrations, repressions, or aggressions that may evolve into neuroses.

Admittedly, children can be reared and trained in an environment so oversocialized that they no longer feel happy or safe outside a crowd of their own kind. This situation only illustrates once more that human beings can become habituated to conditions that are undesirable in the long run. Like adults, children can be habituated to search for happiness in overeating, unbalanced food, unsuitable amusements, perverted addictions. Such habituations provide temporary relief or even satisfaction, but they are of course dangerous. This is probably true of habituation to overcrowding. Architects have shown that more ingenious design of human settlements can compensate to some extent for insufficient space, but there are limits to what can be achieved by architectural ingenuity.[13] Beyond these limits, overcrowding is likely to cause psychological damage. To some overcrowded populations violence or even the bomb may one day no longer seem a threat but rather become a release.

Complete surrender to overcrowding in a highly technicized society is not likely to destroy mankind, but it will mean an increasingly organized world. The

---

13. See Richard Neutra, *Survival Through Design* (New York: Oxford University Press, 1954); Christopher Alexander, "The City as a Mechanism for Sustaining Human Contact" (60–102), and Moshe Safdie, "Habitat '67" (253–260), in Ewald, *op. cit.*

environment will favor the selective reproduction of people best suited to a regimented life. Many people today are maladjusted to crowded life, but as long as there are uncrowded places and social control remains ineffective, those who really want to enjoy a free life can still find a world of their own choosing. If crowding and regimentation continue to increase, however, the descendants of such maladjusted people will be progressively eliminated. When they disappear, many of our present human values will become meaningless and will eventually be forgotten. There will be no place for sensitive literature, intensely personal art, or unorthodox science in the human ant hill of the future; not even room for primitive Christianity. What meaning can the parables and poetry of the past retain if there are no lilies in the field? We must hope that there will still be rebels to champion freedom.

High levels of prosperity can thus create a whole range of undesirable situations accumulating throughout the whole life span. Environmental pollution, excessive food intake, lack of physical exercise, the constant bombardment of stimuli, the inescapable estrangement of civilized life from the natural biological rhythms are but a few among the many manifestations of these. An inevitable result of urbanization, of population growth, and, paradoxically, of higher living standards is that the affluent society is also, as some wags have called it, the "effluent" society.

It should be possible to identify the environmental factors responsible for the chronic and degenerative disorders of our societies. But even when this has been done, it may prove extremely difficult to control these factors because all aspects of the urban and industrial environment are intimately interwoven in the social fabric. Furthermore, the biological and social environment can hardly be dissociated from individual behavior.

Keeping streets and houses clear of refuse, filtering and chlorinating the water supplies, watching over the purity of food products, assuring a safe minimum of fresh air in public places constitute measures that can be applied by the collectivity without interfering seriously with individual freedom. These measures are readily accepted because they do not demand personal effort from their beneficiaries. In contrast, any measure that requires individual discipline is more likely to be neglected. Almost everybody is aware of the dangers associated with overeating, lack of physical exercise, chain-cigarette smoking, excessive consumption of alcohol or drugs, or exposure to polluted environments. But few are the persons willing to make the individual efforts required to avoid these dangers. Furthermore, the consequences of environmental threats are so often indirect and delayed that the public is hardly aware of them. Many effects of the environment become inscribed in the body and the mind without the affected person's realizing that he is being changed irreversibly by influences that do not enter his consciousness.

The adjustments to environmental threats mentioned in the preceding paragraphs are relevant to the pursuit of life's higher significance for several reasons.

One is simply that the state of health conditions human response to any situation. Another reason is that adjustments to environmental threats are often achieved through a blunting of awareness and can thereby interfere with the recognition of human values. Most persons come to be almost unaware of conditions which they know to be undesirable but to which they have become tolerant through continued exposure. Smogs, unpleasant odors, and other forms of environmental pollution, noise from street and air traffic, crowding and excessive stimuli are but a few among the common manifestations of modern life that are extremely objectionable when first experienced, then progressively escape conscious awareness. Few are the urban dwellers, even among the sensitive, who realize that they hardly ever experience fragrant air or a starry night. Most of us become oblivious to the filth, visual confusion, dirt, and outright ugliness that we encounter morning and night on our way to and from the office.

Similarly, when changes occur progressively in social life, the quality of human contacts can degenerate without the persons involved being conscious of the loss this entails. As one's social world enlarges, the number of acquaintances increases, but the depth of relationships usually decreases. Urban dwellers may have many friends, but the nature of the friendship is commonly superficial and rarely corresponds to the quality of Martin Buber's "I-Thou" encounter.* In its present form, urban life makes it difficult to maintain the intimate face-to-face association and cooperation experienced in the small groups of people that some psychologists designate as "primary groups." The widespread nostalgia for school or army days probably constitutes in many cases an unconscious acknowledgment of emotional hunger. Ordinary adult life rarely provides the enriching experience of close comradeship and mutual dependence which was possible when youthful generosity and constant associations gave a chance for really meaningful social encounters.

One of the worst consequences of modern life, according to the American urban planner Christopher Alexander, is the "autonomy-withdrawal" syndrome. Most people, he claims, use their homes to escape from the stresses of the outside world and practice social withdrawal as a form of self-protection. Eventually withdrawal becomes a habit; people reach a point where they become unable or unwilling to let others penetrate their own private world.[14]

Extreme individualism and autonomy commonly develop unconsciously as a consequence of the self-protective withdrawal from stress. Persons who have achieved such autonomy remain dependent on the social groups of which they are a part, but this dependence manifests itself almost exclusively through the medium of money. Money in turn tends to create a world reinforcing individualism and withdrawal. According to Alexander, the fact that the song "People who

---

14. Alexander, *op. cit.*, 74–86.

* Martin Buber: (1878–1965), Jewish philosopher and theologian, born in Vienna; see his book *I and Thou* (1923).

need people are the luckiest people in the world" made the top of the United States hit parade in 1964 indicates that this pathological individualism is very widespread. Unfortunately, few people are aware of the impoverishment of life resulting from the autonomy-withdrawal syndrome; even fewer seem to realize that the pursuit of significance is bound to fail unless man learns once more to speak to man.

History confirms present-day observations in demonstrating that man can become adjusted, socially and biologically, to ways of life and environments that have hardly anything in common with those in which civilization emerged and evolved. He can survive, multiply, and create material wealth in an overcrowded, monotonous, and completely polluted environment, provided he surrenders his individual rights, accepts certain forms of physical degradation, and does not mind emotional atrophy.

The threats to human needs and susceptibilities that are easiest to identify and control are those resulting directly from physicochemical and biological factors of the environment—such as unhealthful climate, pollution, disease germs, crowding, various forms of excessive stimuli. But the influences that affect human life most profoundly are not always the direct ones measured in such objective values as temperatures, chemicals, decibels, kinds of germs, or numbers of people. Man converts all the things that happen to him into symbols, then commonly responds to the symbols as if they were actual external stimuli. All perceptions and interpretations of the mind become so profoundly translated into organic processes that the actual biological and mental effect of a stimulus commonly bears little resemblance to the direct effects which could have been expected from its physicochemical nature.

Since each stimulus has a symbolic quality often more important than its objective characteristics, the effective environment does not consist only of the external forces and substances that impinge on the organism at a given time, but includes also the genetic, social, and individual memories of related past experiences. Mankind's responses to the environment always involve the biological remembrances of the past which in turn condition aspirations for the future. What man becomes is thus largely determined by the adjustments he has made to the stimuli he has experienced.

Man can learn to tolerate treeless avenues, starless skies, tasteless food, a monotonous succession of holidays which have become spiritless and meaningless because they are no longer holy days, a life without the fragrance of flowers, the song of birds, the joyous intoxication of spring, or the melancholy of autumn. Loss of the amenities of life may have no obvious detrimental effect on man's physical well-being or on his ability to perform effectively as part of the economic or technological machine. Increasingly, in fact, most professional activities are carried on in denatured dwellings, offices, and industrial plants. The popularity of the Los Angeles airport for important meetings has already been mentioned. Schools for young children are being built underground to facilitate the upkeep of rooms and lessen distractions for the pupils!

Little if anything is known, however, of the ultimate effect on man of such drastic elimination of the natural stimuli under which he has evolved as a biological being. Air, water, soil, and fire, the rhythms of nature and the variety of living things, are not of interest only as chemical mixtures, physical forces, or biological phenomena; they are the very influences that have shaped human life and thereby created deep human needs that will not change in the foreseeable future. The pathetic weekend exodus to the country or beaches, the fireplaces in overheated city apartments, testify to the persistence in man of biological and emotional hungers that developed during his evolutionary past, and that he cannot outgrow.

Man will continue searching for significance by relating himself to other men, and to the totality of the universe that he may identify with God. But while pursuing significance outside of himself he should not forget that he is still of the earth. Like Antaeus of the Greek legend, he loses his strength when both his feet are off the ground.

Stuart Chase / Our Shrinking Living Space

This selection comes from Mr. Chase's recent book, *The Most Probable Future,* and is an account of the situation caused by human domination and pollution of the planet. It is good expository prose, adequately but not overpoweringly provided with illustrations, concerned but without hysterical indignation. It offers scientific data of all kinds—from physics to ecology—with economy and without condescension. From time to time one hears a personal note, as in the description of the changes wrought over the years in the author's rural environment in Connecticut, but there is no attempt to put the author in the middle of the picture. Chase aims in his prose only at a workaday transparency. The subject requires to be understood in some detail by everybody; so this is the right style to choose for it.

We have observed the population curve, which seems to be leading to crisis. In this chapter we will observe the environment in which people must live for a long time to come. Many years ago I wrote a book about the American land. After presenting a good deal of evidence about forests, grasslands, soils, silting, water pollution, erosion, and wild life, I said:

Jim Kappes

> A continent is . . . a place to live and so more than a bread factory. People do not make continents, continents make people. The age-long strength of Russia is due to her latitude, climate, resources and sweep . . . the strength of our nation is due to the continent of North America. It has molded us, nourished us, fed its abundant vitality into our veins. We are its children, lost and homeless without its strong arms about us. Shall we destroy it? [1]

If I try to answer that question today after years of close attention, I must say yes and no, with rather more emphasis on the "yes"; we are destroying it. True, the conservation measures sponsored by Franklin Roosevelt, who loved the land, and before him by Theodore Roosevelt and Gifford Pinchot, have won some victories. The galloping destruction of American forests has been checked as perpetual-yield forestry replaces the slash and burn of the old lumber barons. Soil erosion has been checked with the skillful methods of the U.S. Soil Conservation Service, and replaced over great areas by plowing on the contours—as any cross-country flight will quickly make evident. The Tennessee Valley Authority has brought better patterns of land use to a great river basin.

Some of these gains, however, have been more than offset by the country's growth and prosperity. Bulldozers carving out superhighways and subdivisions are eating away topsoil and vegetation, and so increasing floods. The pollution of American waters is worse than ever, and so is open-pit mining, which produces a veritable lunar landscape. The correlation between high prosperity and mountains of refuse is not only direct, but ascends at an accelerating rate. In addition, some startling new techniques for destroying North America as a habitable environment have recently appeared, such as sonic boom.

Although the United States has undisputed leadership in laying waste its natural resources, all high-energy societies tend to follow the pattern. Even the careful Germans have not stopped the gross pollution of the Rhine. One fears that the poor countries will tend to do likewise, if and when they achieve affluence.

ONE-EIGHTH ONLY

It is sobering to remember that only about 12 percent of the surface of the earth is fit for human habitation. That surface has been called a "thin lamination." We live between an ocean of air above and a rocky crust beneath. The air must be reasonably pure if we are to breathe, the soil must be arable if we are to eat, the water must be clean if we are to drink. Two-thirds of the globe's surface is salt water, while polar ice, tundra, high mountains, deserts, swamps, and rain forests reduce the land on which we can live with any comfort to not more than one-eighth of the earth's surface.

How many of us in affluent societies have any conception of the meaning of

1. *Rich Land, Poor Land.*

these limitations? If we do not like where we are, we get in the car and go somewhere else. Yet living space is only a small part of the planet's surface, and now a series of technologies on the loose are squeezing it smaller. The man-land density is increasing, not only because land is limited and population is going up, but because more and more of the land is becoming unfit for human living. We have sturdily refused to accept our place in nature. "If any biological system," observed Dr. Dickerman Richards of Columbia, "were to have the kind of chaos our social system has, it would not survive five minutes."

Every once in a while, amid the stupendous chaos of ramming a new superhighway across the continent, the motorist sees a lonely frame house surrounded by great mounds of uprooted earth and blasted rock. It has been abandoned by its owner, but the bulldozers have not got around to pulling it down. This may be a fair analogy for what is happening to all our homes: the bulldozers have not got around to pulling them down. Day by day the roar grows louder. When they do get around, where shall we live?

EIGHT ASSAULTS ON LIVING SPACE

That modern dinosaur, the bulldozer, went into mass production during World War II, which it helped to win. Today it is a familiar sight, driven by an impetuous young man in a state of high exhilaration, leveling hills, obliterating brooks, toppling large trees. No forest, meadow, or shore is safe, as it roots out the habitat of plants and animals, including, in the last analysis, man. The bulldozer, indeed, can be taken as a symbol of a shrinking environment. It represents a technological trend only less menacing than the growth of population and the arms race.

We could begin the analysis far up in space, even at the moon. The military have splendid plans for burning up a continent with missiles fired from the moon. Then we could descend to the stratosphere and find more trouble, especially radioactive fallout. Descend again to normal atmosphere and note what is perhaps the most acute threat of all at present, air pollution. Then down to earth for disturbances in the balance of nature, governing land and water. But it may be better to arrange the assaults by their current urgency. There are at least eight of them, as follows:

1. *Pollutants of the air.* Water can be channeled in aqueducts and mains, but not so air. New York City is now discovering that any real control of smog is hopeless if it can roll across the bay from New Jersey on prevailing west winds. It bloweth where it listeth, to be sure, but it must carry whatever cargo presents itself. A raw mixture of carbon, sulphur, nitrogen compounds, water vapor, and stockyard odors hangs constantly over the Jersey meadows, awaiting transport.

The word "smog," coined as a combination of "smoke" and "fog," has lost its original meaning. Los Angeles, the most publicized producer, has little smoke today and almost no fog. The term, however, is apparently here to stay and the definition must be expanded. It now refers to any condition of the air we breathe that offers a danger to health—from a slight headache to a fatal coma.

Smog seldom becomes serious without the condition known as "temperature inversion," where hot air does *not* rise and blow away as it normally should. The inversion sits like a lid over the landscape. In certain geographic areas the warm air, by causes not yet well understood, is prevented at times from rising, and any impurities stay in it, keeping foul air at nose level.[2]

The inversion is not caused by a city as such. The Los Angeles area undoubtedly suffered from it long before people settled there. Some cities have spells of inversion, others do not. Dublin does not, thanks to much wind and rain. Inversion has been noted in Tokyo, Paris, Leningrad, New York, Buenos Aires, Mexico City, Sydney, San Francisco, among others. It can even be found in the middle of the Kansas prairie. Inversion plus pollution killed 12,000 Londoners in 1952—the estimate of excess deaths due to a smog in which visibility was reduced to three feet. Inversion killed 20 and made 6,000 very sick in Donora, Pennsylvania, in 1948. London had another attack in 1956, and again in 1962. New York had excess deaths from inversion in 1953, 1963, and, with enormous publicity, and no little irony, on Thanksgiving Day, 1966. In the Japanese town of Yokkaichi, children play in the school yards equipped with gas masks.[3] Scientists suspect, says *Time,* that thousands of deaths in cities around the world can be linked to air pollution. It is particularly hard on lung patients. It is hard, too, on plants and trees. Certain nursery crops can no longer be grown where air pollution is heavy.

When inversion clamps down its lid, trouble comes for everyone who breathes. It comes in two forms, and from two major sources. One form is the visible particles of carbon dirt, coating the windowsill, which are known to all city-dwellers. The other form, and far more serious, is invisible gas; it accounts for some 90 percent of all air pollution. The major source for a hundred years has been smoke and gas from factory chimneys, where coal and oil are burned. Now, an even great producer is the rear end of an automobile. Los Angeles, the prize example of inversion because of the city's encircling mountains, has long since compelled industry to use fuels with low sulphur content, but "smog" is worse than ever. Why? Because there are more cars than ever.

Stop-start driving in congested areas releases, along with carbon monoxide (a favorite compound for suicides), various hydrocarbons and nitrogen oxides, and the higher the engine compression, the more perverse they become. No gadget so far designed is able to do more than somewhat reduce the exhaust danger, and Dr. Carr doubts if an effective gadget can be designed.

Meanwhile Dr. Philip A. Leighton, professor emeritus of chemistry at Stan-

---

2. Following Dr. Donald E. Carr. [*The Breath of Life: The Problem of Poisoned Air,* 1965—Eds.]
3. *Time* has a picture of them in its issue of January 27, 1967, together with full-page color photographs of many cities wreathed in sulphur dioxide.

ford, concentrating on the nitrogen oxides (which seem to be the most insidious of the lot), has made the following calculation: A full-sized American car cruising at 60 miles an hour emits about three liters of nitrogen oxides per minute. To dilute this blast to safe breathing limits requires more than 60 million liters of fresh air per minute, "a rate which is enough to supply the average breathing requirements, over the same period, of five to 10 million people." This causes Dr. Leighton to wonder if the resource which will really force the control of population, will be not land, food or water, but *air* . . . sixty million liters of fresh air per car per minute.[4]

Here is a dilemma indeed. We have been quite unable to prevent bigger and better traffic jams, which produce bigger doses of nitrogen oxides. We managed to ban the testing of nuclear bombs in the atmosphere because of fallout, but to ban the burning of gasoline promises to be a much more serious business. It would not only bring Detroit and the petroleum industry in on the double-quick, but create a great outcry from the public, in defense of its most cherished artifact. John W. Gardner, Secretary of Health, Education, and Welfare, showed real courage when he declared at a 1966 conference that the gasoline automobile and the welfare of the American people are on a collision course: "None of us would wish to sacrifice the convenience of private passenger automobiles, but the day may come when we may have to trade convenience for survival."

The following figures furnish eloquent proof of the dilemma:

ANNUAL AIR POLLUTANTS IN THE UNITED STATES [5]

	Millions of Tons
From transportation engines, cars, trucks, etc.	85
manufacturing plants	22
electric power plants	15
space heating	8
refuse burning	3
Total	133

That means more than half a ton descending on every man, woman, and child in the country, every year.

2. *Fallout.* High above the exhaust fumes, fallout from nuclear explosions circles the globe in the stratosphere, gradually sifting down. It does not confine its donations to Los Angeles, New York, or London, but distributes them impartially to all mankind. True, the atmosphere of the planet, extending about 30 miles up, has been assailed with substances harmful to human beings ever since volcanoes erupted, or large forest fires were set by lightning, or certain rock formations gave off radiation. Such emissions were "Acts of God," assaults on living things by nature. In the last few years, however, man himself has led the radioactive assault.

4. *Geographic Review*, April, 1966.
5. United States Department of the Interior *Year Book*, 1966.

Following the Test Ban Treaty of 1963, nuclear explosions have been conducted underground by the United States, Russia, and Britain, but the other members of the "Nuclear Club," France and China, have continued to throw poisons into the air we breathe, and to coat with poison some of the plants we eat. The danger is certainly not building up at the rate that prevailed before the test ban, but there is plenty of toxic matter still aloft. Dr. Linus Pauling, Nobel laureate in chemistry, has predicted that millions of defective babies will be born over the years as a result of fallout which descended before 1963.

3. *Controlling the weather.* Contrails from the proposed supersonic airliners may upset weather by accident, but both the military and the rainmakers have larger designs. The former want to make weather very unpleasant for an enemy, while the latter want, for example, to alleviate such droughts as afflicted the New York area in the 1960's, and hopefully to dissolve hurricanes with silver iodide.

The National Science Foundation at Washington, however, considers tampering with the climate about on a par with a nuclear explosion. The Foundation calls for a good deal more research before swinging into action. This should include a study of the biological, social, economic, political, and legal effects of changing the established climate in a given area. The last promises to occupy platoons of lawyers and judges, both national and international. What if Canada wants rain for its wheat crop, while the state of Washington, on the other side of the boundary, is inundated by floods? Who wins when skiers and resort owners want snow and motorists want clear roads?

4. *Noise.* Sound waves traverse the air, and when they have unpleasant effects on eardrums, can be called a kind of air pollution. A whisper is rated by the sound engineers at 20 decibels, ordinary conversation is rated at 60, factory operations and cocktail parties compete at 85 to 90.[6] If you are subjected to 120 decibels for any length of time, you are likely to suffer permanent damage to your hearing.

It is estimated that average sound levels in the U.S. have increased by some 30 decibels in recent years. Indeed, why not? It seems a modest estimate. A few decades ago one might lie in his hammock in once-rural Connecticut, where I now live, and hear the croaking of frogs, the singing of birds, the lowing of cattle, the barking of dogs over the hill, perhaps a neighbor pounding nails, the occasional clatter of hooves on the dirt road, the complaint of a heavily loaded wagon, punctuated by the crack of a whip and a cry of "Giddap, you Dobbin!" That is about all he would hear.

Now, sitting on an aluminum garden chair where the hammock used to be, what does one hear? Some of the old sounds to be sure—birds and dogs—but no horses, no creaking wagons, no lowing cattle. You hear the woosh of car after car on the blacktop, the laboring gears of a 20-ton truck hauling sand and

6. Harland Manchester in the *National Civic Review,* September, 1964. Traffic noise on New York sidewalks is rated at 103 decibels; subway coaches at 100.

gravel to the new superhighway, the roar of motorcycles, a loudspeaker dispensing *Pagliacci* from a neighbor's house, a power lawn mower chattering, the rhythmic thump of a well driller, the screech of power saws clearing the telephone line, the grunt of bulldozers as they tear out a new subdivision, the wailing of an ambulance siren en route to the Danbury Hospital. These are not simultaneous decibels, to be sure, but they are all sounds I have entered in my notebook as occurring within a few hours.

In the troubled air, meanwhile, mingled with the alarms of crows, you can hear trainer planes from the Danbury Airport, helicopters from Sikorsky's, big four-engine props heading for La Guardia, and mammoth jets from across the Atlantic coming down in thunder to Kennedy Airport 50 miles away. This is what you hear in my rustic retreat today—with the bright promise of a "sonic carpet" descending tomorrow.

The sonic carpet is a truly uproarious item in the curve of technology. The term has been used by a Swedish engineer, after a study of sonic boom was made in Oklahoma in 1965.[7] The "carpet" delimits the broad swath of living space made momentarily uninhabitable by sonic boom. When a plane goes faster than the speed of sound (640 miles an hour), it may enter a less turbulent area in the sky, but the turbulence below becomes fantastic. It generates a minor earthquake, breaking windows, dishes, and nervous systems from coast to coast.

Dr. Lundberg reports that the Oklahoma effects were worse than expected. The boom carpet, he says, is between 50 and 80 miles wide, so that cities, suburbs, and countryside alike are blasted. Furthermore, he says, the boom is intensified by certain atmospheric conditions and can be more than doubled by reflection from walls; it seems that the decibels bounce. There will be intolerable insomnia for all in the boom carpet, much physical damage, and many serious accidents. "The comfort and safety of millions of people will be sacrificed to the convenience of a few travelers."

5. *The pollution of waters.* There is no major river in the United States which is not grossly polluted. People still drink the water after heavy chlorination, though many buy expensive bottled water, even for tea and coffee. The alarm some of us raised a generation ago has had very little effect.

The despoliation of American rivers is an old and dishonorable story, but lately the fate of Lake Erie has held the headlines. President Johnson made a special journey in 1966 to inspect the desolation. In the same week came a story from Russia that Lake Baikal in Siberia was threatened with the chemical wastes of a vast new pulp mill complex. Russian conservationists promptly moved to head off the disaster.

Lake Erie is a large inland sea, covering 2,600 square miles, large enough, one would expect, to be proof against any trash men might throw into it. Not so. From Detroit on the west to Buffalo on the east, city sewage and the offscour-

7. Dr. B. K. O. Lundberg in *Bulletin of the Atomic Scientists,* February, 1965.

ings of industry flush filth into waters which millions of American have long depended upon for drinking, swimming, fishing, and boating. The bathing beaches are now closed, and the boat liveries bankrupt. *Newsweek* in April, 1965, tells the sad story:

> Lake Erie is dying. Called *eutrophication,* this death comes ironically from too much nutrition, as when an obese man eats until his heart quits. Nitrogen, phosphorus and filth in the lake feed immense blooms of green algae that burn up oxygen at the lake's bottom needed by higher forms of life . . . useful water life has already been smothered. . . . Revitalization will require more than elaborate pollution-control schemes, for *eutrophication,* once started, feeds on itself.

At the other end of New York State, to the east, lies the Hudson River, in almost as sad a plight. Sixteen cities, from Troy southward to New York Harbor, contribute raw sewage, while other towns give it only a sketchy treatment. The U.S. Public Health Service estimates that the Hudson gets the waste of 10 million people. "That is what one would expect if, for these 158 miles, both banks of the river were lined solidly with outhouses." [8]

Additional wastes pour into the Hudson from scores of factories: fibers from paper mills, grease and flesh from slaughterhouses, dyes from chemical plants, chemicals from drug makers, acids from metal-processing, oils from automobile paint shops . . . a long way from the year 1609 when Henry Hudson found the river "clear, blue and wonderful to taste."

The Mississippi River, down which Huck Finn and Jim floated on their immortal raft in the old steamboat days, has been equally despoiled. Huck and Jim would not relish going overboard for a swim today. Meanwhile pesticides have been killing the few types of fish which can survive the standard load of pollution. A serious difficulty is that sewer mains and storm drains are combined in most American cities. A big rain is often too much for the sewage treatment plant, if there is one, and the excess overflows into the river along with the storm water.

When the rivers with their heavy burdens come down to the coast, bathing beaches, oyster beds, and lobster pots are abandoned as the bacteria count goes up. Nor are the rivers alone the source of coastal grief. Oil dumped from oceangoing tankers comes washing ashore, ruining the beaches for bathers, preventing shellfish from breeding, and killing gulls and terns. When a bird's feathers are coated with oil, the poor creature can neither swim nor fly, and must die of starvation.

6. *Water supply.* As in the case of air, the world's water supply is strictly limited. Only 3 percent of the total is fresh water, and most of this is locked in polar ice caps and mountain glaciers. Modern cities want more water for air-conditioning units; farmers want more for irrigation. Arizona, for instance, now

---

8. Peter T. White in the *New York Times Magazine,* July 17, 1966.

depends on underground waters for cities and farms and the water table is steadily falling—some 300,000 acres of cropland have been abandoned. Unless nuclear desalting of sea water becomes practical within a decade, a lot of people may have to move out of Arizona. Meanwhile California, Arizona, and Mexico are in a chronic legal battle as to which gets how much water from the Colorado River. A more sanguinary battle goes on between Jordan and Israel as to who controls the waters of the Jordan River.

There is, of course, a hopeful note in the coming desalting of sea water by nuclear energy. Intensive R & D is bringing costs per gallon down so rapidly that some coastal areas will surely receive a new and permanent supply of fresh water within a decade. How far inland desalted water can economically be pumped is another question. A further optimistic note from R & D is the recycling of used and dirty water. It is not particularly pleasant to contemplate, but the engineers say that it will taste all right. Foul water is recycled by nature too, but in a larger and slower operation.

7. *Pollution of the land.*

> Beside the road day-lilies grow
> Amid the beer cans, row on row.

There are worse pollutants than empty beer cans, but in America, at least, few things are more visible as one drives along the roads, except, of course, billboards. I pick up the cans, flung gaily from cars which pass in the night, every morning around my front gate. They are a symbol of the stupendous piles of junk and refuse which our affluent society throws off.

In *God's Own Junkyard,* Peter Blake superbly documents the trend—with the most dreadful photographs. One reason why junk grows faster than people is the up-and-coming merchandising of the container—the idea being to sell the package rather than what is in it. A comfortable 60 percent of Americans are now in the affluent class, with access to all the good things of life. This does not impress Marya Mannes: "Americans had better be told," she says, "that the more people attain the good things of life, the less good resides in these things." The American Academy of Sciences adds a statistical note. In 1920 the average American threw away 2.75 pounds of refuse a day. In 1965 he threw away eight pounds. "As the earth becomes more crowded, there is no longer any 'away.' One person's trash basket is another's living space."

The junk yards, the roadsides, and the beaches can someday hopefully be cleaned up—perhaps by using manpower made obsolete by automation—*if* enough people are sufficiently revolted by the "effluent age." Soil erosion, however, will take longer to heal. It is not so much the up-and-down plowing which causes it now as the runoff from blacktop highways. Soil, as well as air and water, can be so poisoned as to render it unfit for growing food. This condition results, says the U.S. Department of Agriculture, from adding waste products to the soil faster than they decompose. Pesticides also contribute to soil pollution, and so does fallout. A kind of somber cooperation exists where, says the Department, "air pollutants—such as automobile exhausts, industrial smoke and radioactive fallout—ultimately become soil pollutants as well."

The most spectacular destruction of the good earth is, of course, open-pit mining for coal and other minerals. Without careful and expensive replacement of the soil when the operation is over, nothing may ever grow there again. By contrast, in Germany a mine cannot be opened unless plans are first filed to heal the wound, with severe penalties for their neglect.

The United States lags far behind Europe in protecting its land, but the President's Advisory Committee on Environmental Pollution makes the sound point that *there should be no right to pollute.* Antipollution measures should take their place along with public schools as a mandatory public service. In due course industry must include the costs of pollution control together with materials and labor.

8. *Outer space.* Above the land, the waters, and the air lies outer space, safe from all human interference until a certain day in 1945 when the first nuclear bomb was exploded in a New Mexico desert. Its ancient peace is now violated so frequently that someone has proposed, not entirely humorously, that the United Nations send up a platoon of space policemen to control the traffic.

If space is ever used in thermonuclear war, it will be quite possible, scientists say, to incinerate a substantial fraction of a continent by firestorm. We remember Mr. Khrushchev's threat when he was head of the Russian state: "Germany will burn like a candle." Germany can be burned even more efficiently now, with the latest nuclear hardware.

Real damage, rather than speculative, occurred when the U.S. exploded a device in outer space a few years ago. It broke up the so-called Van Allen belt, which guards the earth from too much radiation. Scientists, including Dr. Van Allen himself, were shocked by this reckless act.

THE SPIRIT OF ST. FRANCIS

From the beer can tossers to the open-pit miners to the disrupters of the Van Allen belt, the trend continues almost unabated. Not only in North America but all over the world, living space is under concentrated attack.

No creature purposely destroys its home, and the only excuse for Homo sapiens is that most of us are still unaware of what we are doing. In our ignorance we suppose that air, water, and land are unlimited. We have in fact become, as the great ecologist Paul Sears once said, a kind of geologic force, more destructive in the long run than hurricanes or earthquakes.

This behavior is deep-rooted, and some students, such as Professor Lynn T. White, trace it back down the centuries to the very foundations of our Judeo-Christian culture. Though Copernicus demonstrated the fallacy of the Ptolemaic system, which had made man the center of the universe, with sun, planets, and the stars revolving deferentially around him, the theologians of the time were far from being defeated. They continued to regard man as the sole possessor of the planet, with dominion over the fish of the sea, the fowl of the air, and over every living thing that moveth upon the earth, and, to make it final, dominion over all the earth. Only St. Francis of Assisi seriously challenged this doctrine; he was bold enough to believe that other living creatures had some rights.

One might add, in all deference, that our children's children have some rights too.

The pollutants now at large—in space, in the air and water, and on land—are not confined to any one city or state or nation. The Van Allen belt fiasco affected the whole world. The "air shed" of New York City includes at least four states and may drift into Canada. Remedial measures and laws which apply to a single political division will be mostly unavailing. The protection of living space is a matter for the federal government in Washington, on one level; for all the countries of North America, or of Europe, on another level; for the United Nations on a planetary level. It is evident that we must make our peace with nature herself, as well as with the fact of thermonuclear bombs.

Robert Oppenheimer / Physics

It would have been easy to select for this anthology a more formal example of Oppenheimer's prose, but we have preferred to seek an instance of the variety of good modern prose by including this, and some other, examples of oral communication. Obviously a man who talks well, illustrates his arguments clearly, and, without losing informality, achieves coherence, is likely to be a very literate person to begin with. Oppenheimer certainly was that.

One should not look for anything like the careful structure Oppenheimer would have given to a more formal discourse. As the editors explain, he answered some questions, not all on closely related subjects, and then talked and reminisced as he felt inclined. Many of the questions he answers will have been settled in his mind long before the present occasion; his views on chemistry, for example, were not invented then and there. But they are expressed with the spontaneity of educated talk, and they are illustrated with examples not all of which are likely to have been prefabricated. His definition of physics at the outset is an example of something he must have had worked out long before, but in answering such questions as "what does physics do?" and "what kind of people are physicists?" he draws on his knowledge of his colleagues, and of the history of science, in a perfectly lucid yet impromptu way. Soon he finds himself describing a recent experiment and calling it beautiful and saying why. He recalls his own youth, and speaks of the kind of education a man needs to face the challenge of physics. He distinguishes subtly between the kinds of question each branch of science asks, without drawing firm boundaries between them. The language is occasionally technical; he is not talking down, especially when he discussed recent developments and current theoretical puzzles. In the end he describes his own satisfaction in the subject as deriving from one fact: "I love to understand". And he ends, after speaking of the beauty of physics, with some remarks on the role of physicists in the modern world; a matter upon which, given his leading role in the development of the A-bomb and the troubles this subsequently brought on him, he speaks with almost unrivaled authority.

It will be noted that prose of this kind is invested with the authority of its producer; Oppenheimer does not have to spell out his meanings and his sources as a popularizing writer might, needing to show that he is talking sense. He takes for granted not only an intelligent and educated listener, but the obviousness of the fact that, on this subject, he is worth listening to.

Dr. Oppenheimer has written many papers on many subjects and as a writer he is well known and rightly honored; but this time he was asked if he would sit in his office in Princeton, with the quiet and wooded land stretching away outside his window, and just talk about physics. He was asked some questions about physics and physicists. He was asked about young men preparing for a life in this science and about their possible future. He answered all these questions, and others too; but perhaps the most interesting and memorable part of the chapter is that in which he, unintentionally, let us see something of his own experiences and wonderment in physics. His talk was taken down on tape and edited very little. This is very much the way he himself said it.

Trying to say what physics is can be very learned, but I would say that physics is the study of matter. It is the study of order, of regularity, of what makes matter harmonious, and what makes it work.

Now what do physicists *do?* One of the very good things about physics is the great variety of things that physicists do. This is determined in part by the tradition of physics, in part by the techniques that it has available, in part by the interest and curiosity of physicists in some aspect of nature. Some physicists invent instruments; this has been a great part of physics: they work with their hands as well as figuring. Some work with the instruments to find out in more detail how things behave, so that the general wealth of our knowledge, its availability both for interpretation and for application, is richer. Some try to understand what has been discovered in the laboratory or even what has been discovered on paper. Many do many of these things.

Some physicists are very bright, some are very hard working, some are very dedicated; but one of the things about physics—and I think this is true of all sciences—is that it is really a house of many people, of many different kinds of people. There is a wonderful sense of gratitude even for work which is not particularly ingenious, particularly brilliant, or particularly deep, because it all helps. I would not know of any quality that I could predicate of all good physicists, except one. They all give a lot for physics; they care about it; they live it; they breathe it; they respect it; they respect its practitioners, and they are willing to work. This complex of things is important, for the temperament and taste of two men can have little in common, yet both can be successful physicists. It would really be hard to find very much that the three greatest men of our century in physics—Einstein, Rutherford, and Bohr—had in common except that, in this case, greatness gives something special. Because of the quality of living and breathing physics, if anyone were to ask, "Should I be a physicist or should I be something else," I am not sure but that he should be something else.

One often hears a distinction between the experimental and the theoretical physicists, but the distinction is far from absolute. Newton did some experiments —the refraction of light in the prism is a famous example. Still when we think of his work, what we mostly honor him for is the discovery of the laws of mechanics and the law of gravitation. He did this when he was very young, when he was about twenty-five, at the time of the Great Plague in London, 1664–1666; but the laws of mechanics had deep roots in twelfth- and thirteenth-century philosophy. There was no observation then, no experiment; but there was a serious challenge to the view of Aristotle, a challenge which itself went back to Greek times and then was rediscovered—with the really enormous discovery that we did not need to explain motion, but we needed to explain acceleration. This was the theory of impetus. And this was theoretical physics. It was nourished by checking with everyday experience, but it was mostly by thinking of the consistency of things that Buridan * and Oresme * and others came to this conclusion. The attempt to understand things, to see the order and simplicity of things by whatever means, is very old. It is not something that was invented in the twentieth century.

I do not think it is possible to be a theoretical physicist without a curiosity about nature. That is what distinguishes us from mathematicians, who may have that curiosity but need not, and often today do not. I think that the good theorist needs to have not only a lively curiosity but also a tremendous respect for nature, and a respect for those who investigate nature and tell what they find. I think, too, that the good experimental physicist must have some sense of theory. It may be almost free of mathematics, as it was with Faraday,* but it must be an imaginative vision of what makes some aspect of the world and nature go.

* Jean Buridan: fourteenth-century French scholastic philosopher and adherent of Nominalism.
* Nicole Oresme: fourteenth-century French prelate whose translations of various classical works helped to popularize science.
* Michael Faraday: (1791–1867), English chemist and physicist who made important discoveries relating to electricity.

While perhaps the healthiest thing is to be both a theorist and an experimentalist, the demands of the two techniques, the two sets of techniques, are elaborate and formidable for each. It is not astonishing that if a man has a talent for one, he will exercise that talent, and he will think it is a waste, not only of his time but of his colleagues' time, for him to do something that he does badly. When some men attempt even the most simple mechanical operation, you may hear them say, "I am all thumbs." Some people mechanically are all thumbs, and yet they may very well be able to advance our understanding of what is going on in nature.

Fermi * started out as a theorist and became an experimentalist. He never lost his interest in theory, but he was not in later years a great theorist. Einstein could not have done anything in the laboratory if his life had depended on it. Bohr * started out working in the laboratory of J. J. Thompson and later in Rutherford's laboratory, but then he had the great idea that the quantum "governed" the nuclear atom, that he could understand the atom, and he became just too busy to do experiments. His first scientific publication, which won him a prize, was the study of the oscillations of jets of water from which you can determine surface tension; but as time passed he fell in with his destiny—and so it goes for physicists, as for all men.

It is true that much of today's research is performed by teams, yet I would not have this discourage the individual who looks out at nature and asks questions. One very recent discovery was made, I think, by one or two people. I have no doubt that they used equipment which other people built, but they designed the experiment—even though they did not thoroughly expect the result. The result was completely odd and beautiful.

They used liquid helium II, which is a quantum liquid. It has no analogs in familiar liquids. It is superfluid; that is, it does not have any resistance to flow, and it shows many quite bizarre properties. They bombarded liquid helium with alpha particles. The alpha particles, which are helium nuclei, were stopped in the helium. Then they applied electric voltages and saw what happened to the ions. In the earlier work at very low voltages they found a behavior which was not particularly remarkable; but in another set of experiments they used accelerating voltages of tens of volts and noticed that the ions were accelerated very early, passing through the helium. Then it essentially did not matter how much helium there was; the ions came through without resistance.

They measured the velocity of the ions as a function of energy. Normally we think that the energy is proportional to the square of the velocity—or, at least, that it will increase with it. In this case, the energy and the velocity were in-

---

* Enrico Fermi: (1901–54), Italian nuclear physicist; demonstrated how artificial radioactive substances could be produced when he split uranium nuclei by bombarding them with neutrons.
* Niels Bohr: (1885–1962), Danish physicist who adapted the quantum theory to atomic structure.

versely proportional to each other. This is a property of smoke rings; and from this they could determine the vorticity with which the ions were associated, and from that they could get a good measurement of Planck's constant, because the vorticity is quantized.

This is clearly a beautiful discovery, and, in my thinking, it *is* a discovery. We knew something about the quantization of vorticity, but we did not know very much, and now it was made known to us by one or two persons. They worked in Berkeley, but not as a part of the radiation laboratory, not as a part of any great outfit. A person can indeed do experiments using the great accelerators, and both the machine he uses and the equipment he uses will probably involve the work of many physicists; but, here and there, one man will decide what to do with it. He will be indebted to other people, and, in the custom of the day, he will typically write their names on his paper. But despite all the vast experiments, and the multiple efforts of teams, there is room for a man.

Each person must decide for himself when he first glimpsed the world of physics, and when, later, he first became really excited about it. I first became interested in something related to physics when my grandfather gave me a small, purely conventional collection of minerals, when I was five or seven. I then became a collector of minerals and a student of their structure. I was not a learned fellow, but I was an active member of the New York Mineralogical Club, and I did some elementary explorations of crystal structure and birefringence and polarization.

I had a wonderfully good science teacher in high school. He has just died. Augustus Klock was his name. I had a course in physics from him which I liked, and I spent the next summer preparing laboratories in chemistry, and then that year took the course in chemistry. By then I was clear that I liked physical science. When I went to Harvard I had some doubt about whether to study mineralogy, because I liked the open mountains and the mines, or to study chemistry, which I loved. Elementary chemistry was, is, and should be the most beautiful subject; and I certainly was excited to learn about atomic theory, the periodic system, the existence of atoms, and valence, and all the rest of it.

I had a friend, a year older, a biologist, who said: "After all, there are vacations. You had better study chemistry here at the University. You can go to the mines in the summer." So I did, but chemistry in those days at Harvard was a very pedestrian affair. I took my degree in chemistry, but in my second year I petitioned the physics department to take graduate courses. I had never taken an undergraduate course. So the excitement grew; I think that the lectures of Bridgman on thermodynamics and electrodynamics are probably some of the high points of that excitement. And then, of course, I came just a minute after the birth of quantum theory and quantum mechanics—and the excitement has not stopped since.

Occasionally one is asked about the level of college or university training that is required for a lifetime in physics. There is, of course, no universal answer. I am sure that we can find physicists who never went to any school, and who are good. But with the American graduate schools what they are today in science, in physics and all natural science, it certainly is an immense help to have the apprenticeship, the training, the companionship, the standards, if you will, the conversation and the community of an American doctoral education. It is just too good to pass up.

One is asked, too, about specialization. When should specialization start? Here again there is no universal answer. It will depend on the man. In a certain sense I specialized fairly early, and, in a certain sense, not at all. My intellectual interests are wide and I have never found it necessary completely to abandon them, or even to compromise them, because I was interested in physics. On the other hand, my interest in physics—which I think is regarded today as very broad—is, in fact, somewhat specialized.

I would say that in the universities of this country, probably even more than in those of Europe, specialization is rather futile for the undergraduate. He will be frustrated by the university itself, and he might as well use his time to enlarge his curiosity even if, in part, it may only convince him that he does not want to know anything more about some subjects. He will find that when he goes into graduate work, specialization is inevitable, almost mandatory. Whatever he does will be engulfed by it, and it will take the form of trying to answer a question. Not everything in the world is relevant to that question, not every technique, not all knowledge; but some things are, and he is going to find himself compelled to deepen his knowledge because specialization means just that. If he is worried by this, I would think he might take readings in French literature, or learn Greek, or learn something else, whatever it may be, to make sure that he has a stern anchor out.

He can maintain his excitement in physics, however, and still want to study something that, along with physics, will tend to span man's intellectual and cultural enterprise. A blanket answer as to what he should study is meaningless, because just as physicists do physics differently, they do other things differently. It is very common for physicists to have a great love for and some talent in music. It is not uncommon for them to be painters and sculptors. It is less common, but by no means unheard of, for them to be writers. In this variety of men and interests I should think that the additional studies, whatever may be chosen, should not be something immediately contiguous to physics. I, for instance, did not take an interest in history until I got involved in it; but history would be a fine subject. Law would be a fine subject, with its very different sort of order from physics; but you will find very few physicists who think, as young men, that history and law are worth studying. They might think that literature is worth studying. They might think, perhaps, that anthropology or psychology are worth studying, just because they are so vividly removed in their certitudes, in their troubles, from physics.

Whatever the details of his studies, if a man continues in physics, he will come in time to face its challenges. And what are they? The challenge of physics is to understand what is going on in nature; and there is plenty that we do not understand at all. I happen to think that in some ways the description of sub-nuclear particles and interactions is the deepest challenge, because really we have only a rudimentary, partial, incomplete, qualified knowledge of what there is, and why there is, in that field. I would be glad, too, if someone would explain to me the smoke rings in liquid helium, or those apparently enormous sources of energy that appear perhaps a few billion light years away and that seem so very large that it is not clear what is going in. In very simple things, too, in very familiar things, there are always beautiful puzzles if you have the wit and the sense of taste to look for them. We do not explain everything, but the challenge to physicists is physics. All the rest is a way to make out somehow.

In discussing physics, or any science, one needs to take into account the old tradition and the partially continuing habit of separating the sciences. One should be careful about this demarcation. I could not, for example, give a valid, substantive separation of physics from chemistry. Chemistry and physics started with very different preoccupations, but with the clarification of atomic theory in 1925 it became clear that, in principle, atomic theory could describe all chemical phenomena. Still chemists do things that physicists do not do, particularly when they get interested in the chemistry of life. Nor is there a sharp line of separation between physics and astronomy. We think—though we may be wrong—that we have learned, and can learn, the physical laws that govern stars, galaxies, clusters of galaxies. This is the subject of astronomy, but the astronomer uses instruments which are his own yet which he has learned from the physicists, as the physicists, in turn, have borrowed instruments from him.

The boundaries between physics and other sciences are necessarily undefined: life is impossible without matter; matter is impossible without mathematical order, and there it is. The earth behaves in accordance with the laws of physics; the skies behave in accordance with the laws of physics; life behaves in accordance with the laws of physics, and physics itself reflects certain of the mathematically open, logically consistent possibilities. So I do not see how you could have sharp boundaries, or why it is desirable. Physical tools are used in all the natural sciences, and mathematical tools are used in physics and many of the natural sciences. You have interpenetration and ambiguity in these definitions, which I think are not completely natural, which are not completely in the nature of things.

The question is rather whether each science carries with it a certain style which is not convertible into the style of another. I think the relations between physics and biology are rather striking in this. A biologist simply does not ask the questions that a physicist would ask. The biologist asks the right questions about biology. Those physicists who have become good biologists, and there are many, have done so by having some moderate training in physics, which they did not forget, and then really learning to look at nature, living nature, through the eyes of the biologist. I think that the physicists who, without the knowledge of the biologists, think that they know the questions the biologists should be asking, and there are some of them, too, are really quite pitiable people.

In one area, teaching, the old boundaries I think are still desirable. I rather believe that since teaching is in part a shortcut to familiarity with, to an awareness of, to an ability to use, the historical tradition, teaching may be broken down into these historically separate developments.

I know a girl who in college took a course in chemistry from a chemist who was ashamed that he was not a physicist, who, instead of teaching elementary chemistry, ruined elementary chemistry. Instead of saying the beautiful things that chemists know, he said, inaccurately and with misgiving and uncertainty and ignorance, what physicists might have said about those same things. I don't believe in that.

I do believe in the chemist teaching chemistry, and I believe in the importance of what most physicists have traditionally done, that even today probably occupies more than half of them, which is to teach physics. This teaching is related to discovering truth, but it is also a separate activity because for the most part the truth you teach is not something that you have just discovered, and yet it is a very great contribution, I believe, to the vigor and beauty of the society in which we live.

One sometimes hears talk about the participation of physicists in other activities of society, particularly outside their own immediate scientific undertakings. Such talk is often vague, often misleading, and needs to be taken apart a little.

Physics is a demanding profession. Most professions are. But almost no professional is just a professional, and there is a lot of room in men, and in their lives, for that which does not derive from the profession itself. The fact that a man is a competent physicist may have associated with it the fact that he is politically very incompetent, politically inexperienced, so that the most he can do is vote; and he may not be entirely certain about even that. On the other hand, it may be accompanied by the fact that he is very astute and profound in politics. He may not want to perform in politics because he may not have the time for it, but circumstances may make him feel that he should perform for at least a limited time.

This is only to say that being a physicist is not all of a man. It is a lot, but not all. I think that being a physicist, a professional physicist, carries with it two duties. One is to seek the truth, and the other is to explain it. And those are ineluctable. But beyond that, whether you want to apply physics to practical things that seem to you, in themselves, good for men, or whether you want to apply practical things that seem profitable to somebody, or whether you want to apply them for what appear to you great human goals, these are all open questions; they are no more answered by the fact that you are a physicist than the color of your eyes is so determined. But I would say that if you do not have the sense of finding out about nature—and here I have in mind *homo sapiens* and *homo faber,* of man thinking and man doing—if you do not have that, then the rest of it is not relevant to physics.

In talking with physicists, particularly younger physicists, students perhaps, I have been asked occasionally what are the paramount problems currently at the forefront in physics and what are the promises of their solution.

I would not want to say for all physics because it ranges, really, from galaxies to nucleic acids. But if I think of those things that occupy physicists particularly, rather than astronomers and biologists, I believe that I would give as my own answer that the behavior of sub-nuclear particles and interactions is what puzzles me most and what seems to me least likely to follow from anything we know. There are strong forces that act between most of these particles, which involve energies of the order of the energy of the particle itself; electromagnetic forces about which we know a good deal, not perhaps everything, and which are a thousand times reduced; weak forces that manifest themselves in the decay of many of these particles and which are energy dependent, but normally about 10^{14} times weaker; and gravitation which is enormously weaker again than that. It is very odd that there should be forces of such radically different magnitude. It is still more odd that the selection rules—that is, the symmetries involved in the forces—are very different. The strong forces, for instance, do respect the equivalence of right handed and left handed. The weak forces, as Lee and Yang * suggested some years ago, do not. It is very odd that this should be so. There are many things that are unchanged when nucleons and mesons interact, except when they interact very slowly, and which have no analog in electrons and other light particles. So we have disparities that are very, very puzzling. In the past decade many more particles have been discovered, and there has been an attempt to see whether they did not represent some symmetry. The most promising efforts in this direction are fairly recent. They were made first by an Israeli, Nee'man, and by Gell-Mann who was at Caltech. They identified a certain eight-dimensional representation of a three-dimensional unitary group; they thought that this might have something to do with the eight quasi-stable baryons and the eight pseudo-scalar mesons.

This has had some success. It is puzzling because the things that are supposed to be equivalent have rather different masses and because the interactions that are supposed to be similar cannot really be very similar, but it is suggestive; it may be that one has to go beyond this and look for the three objects which are the fundamental representation of this group out of which all the others are built. Perhaps this symmetry would be more impressive than the symmetry we are seeing in the octets. This is, of course, still just talk, but it is very helpful to see relations between processes involving different particles which relate them to each other; and even more remarkable is the fact that often the difference of

---

* Tsung-Dao Lee, Chen Ning Yang: Chinese physicists awarded a Nobel Prize in 1957 for disproving the established physical principle known as the Parity Law.

mass between the particles can be described by really quite elementary formulae which are not fully understood. This is one hopeful thing.

Another hopeful thing, still in the domain of strong interactions and heavy particles, and again not fully understood, is that one can make models—crude and uncontrollable perhaps—in which the different particles bind each other to make each other.

None of this seems to bear any visible resemblance to the theory of the electron, which is an extraordinarily accurate theory, not beautiful but successful. None of it seems to have any special place for the mu mesons and the neutrinos. Yet I would say that these are the places where things look too good, as elements of progress, to be laughed off.

Now and then, a person will ask if there is any possible "ultimate reality," any objective truth which, in principle at least, is knowable, or is nature so infinitely complex that ultimately it is beyond the comprehension of man.

I think that all that we know is what we can tell each other, in science anyway. Of course I am not speaking here of revelation, only of objectivity. I think that objectivity has to do with communication and verifiability. We certainly won't ever know everything, but we can know something objectively. Nobody will ever know, I can say with some confidence, the times at which the waves of the Atlantic broke on the third of July, 1712. It is a fact of nature, but I do not worry about it. It probably is not absolutely out of the question to find out, but it is so relatively uninteresting that it probably would not be worth knowing, and so tangled that I cannot think how anyone would go about answering it. To a certain extent we decide what is worth knowing by knowing it. Yet here we are confronted with the fact that we do not know ahead of time what will be worth knowing. That is where luck comes in, and genius.

I think that quite different science, not contradictory to ours but complementary, could perfectly well exist, and may very well exist, if there are any other forms of people some other place. They may be talking about other subjects, and they may be concentrating on other questions, because history, tradition, humanity, accident all play a great part in what science is. But they play no part in whether it is true or not. That is its objectivity, its communicability, its verifiability.

In regard to knowing, Einstein expressed a very earnest hope. It was that the probabilistic considerations, in which prediction took the form of statements of probability and not of certainty, would be eliminated with the further progress of physics. In this sense, I think it will not happen. I think that the great breaks with the past that relativity and quantum theory have made are irrevocable breaks, and that what we have learned is that we had been led into error, and that into that error we will never go back.

But I think that the proper thing to look forward to is that just as Newtonian physics became a common, everyday part of knowledge, of thought, so some of the discoveries of this century will really be in our schooling; once they are in our schooling they are then everyday experiences. So, in this sense, I have a hopeful feeling; though I must say that the evidence gives no support for it. But then, the time has been short, the mood has been frivolous. I know that Bohr's great hope was that schoolboys should learn quantum theory.

I have spoken of the young men, particularly of students, who ask an older man their questions. One that they ask me occasionally is what satisfaction do I, after some years in physics, still realize in being a physicist.

For this question the answer is easy—I love to understand. And that *is* the answer. There are many ways that this comes about. I listen, and I read, and I think, and I talk. I love to understand, and only a little less I love to share understanding. Every day one hopes for something more in understanding. I hope, in particular, that I will understand the sub-nuclear puzzle before I am dead, or so old that I will not believe it. But on that, I am not taking bets.

A young man asked me the other day what is there for me beyond the facts of physics? What is there in its poetry and philosophy? Its esthetics and spiritual meaning?

Well, I would not want to understand it unless it had a really deep and breath-taking order. And those parts we look hard at, have turned out in the past to have such an order. The excitement today comes from the tension between this belief in order, and the apparent arbitrariness and cussedness of what we see, and our confidence that if we looked at it from the right angle, it would look in order. And order is, perhaps, the best word—regularity is a word that Bohr liked to use. Saying more than this is to grope, because beauty is beauty, and I never heard anyone say anything meaningful about the beauty of the B-minor Mass,* or the beauty of the *gezicht op Delft;* * I don't think that anybody can say anything meaningful about the beauty of physics either; but it is there.

When I was a student in the Twenties, the expectation of a man's devoting his life to physics was that he probably would be a teacher and if, as most people, he were only of moderate vigor, he would probably derive more and more joy from teaching physics as his powers to do original things declined. This has changed very much. There is now an extraordinarily avid market for physicists in industrial laboratories, some of which are really of superlatively high quality. Yet I think that even for people in institutes and industrial laboratories, they should keep their hand in at teaching, because very often what they are teaching is more beautiful than what they are doing, and because exercising the ability to explain will help them in their own work.

Physicists also have become involved in advisory activities, and therefore, inevitably, involved in political problems. This, I think, is the result of the Second World War. I can only say that I am not sorry for it. It is a distraction, and I think there are many physicists who might be doing physics more and better if

---

* the B-minor mass: by Johann Sebastian Bach (1685–1750).
* the *gezicht op Delft:* "View of Delft," painting by Jan Vermeer (1632–75).

they were not distracted; but I think that they contribute something to the level of reasonableness and the level of openmindedness in the political process, which is quite beyond the specific competence that they have. I think we should not deplore too much that some physicists now really bear a very great responsibility; other scientists do also, but it started with physicists. I think that if we are going to find, make, stumble, brave our way into a world in which war does not play its traditional part, the physicist will have had something to do with it.

Paul Goodman / Can Technology Be Humane?

Much of the present discontent of American students has its origin in a new understanding of the dominance of technology and technologists in the universities and in the society generally. This dominance is not new, but its effects—on the environment, on the relations between nations, and on the quality and content of teaching in the schools—are much more publicized, and also much more acute, than they have been in the past. Noam Chomsky's essay provides some of the background (Section VIII). Mr. Goodman undertakes to place the whole issue in a much wider context, seeing the new dissent as an indication not only of disillusionment about misdirected scientific research, but of "a new protestant Reformation." Such a reformation will of course have a political as well as a religious dimension.

Goodman describes first the broadening and deepening of protest; the corruption of scientific knowledge is, in the end, the corruption of humanity, but this does not mean the whole problem can be understood in relation to science alone. It can be agreed that technologists must, with newly acquired prudence and responsibility, have much more to say about social effects arising from their work, technology must in some respects be decentralized, and people must be educated enough to understand the problems; then we might have a truly scientific way of life. But as it is, people have lost confidence in such possibilities, and there is a revolt against the "religion" of science, and this is the protestantism Goodman has in mind. It is not an organized movement. He sees it as a symptom of "a transformation of conscience" rather than the thing itself.

On such subjects anybody, and especially students in the universities, can have an informed opinion. They arise from the morning newspaper, where the cost of the latest moonshot, the daily increasing problems of pollution, deteriorating slum housing, and starvation in the Third World, may all appear together on the first page. But the problems are indeed formidable, affecting as they must the decisions of men at all levels from the President and his Generals and Cabinet officers down to the school teacher and the counselor. The whole structure of scientific education and practice is in question; so, in the last resort, are the loyalties of the ordinary citizen. The questions Goodman asks have become sharp and urgent in the past few years and they will probably become more so. An essay of this length has to leave out many considerations of relevance and keep down the display of evidence, and yet it must reflect the urgency of the questions and it must impress its readers with the need to consider, and indeed to act. When writers take on responsibilities of this order, the corresponding duty of the reader is serious critical attention.

On March 4, 1969 there was a "work stoppage" and teach-in initiated by dissenting professors at the Massachusetts Institute of Technology, and followed at thirty other major universities and technical schools across the country, against misdirected scientific research and the abuse of scientific technology. Here I want to consider this event in a broader context than the professors did, indeed as part of a religious crisis. For an attack on the American scientific establishment is an attack on the world-wide system of belief. I think we are on the eve of a new protestant Reformation, and no institution or status will go unaffected.

March 4 was, of course, only the latest of a series of protests in the twenty-five years since the Manhattan Project to build the atom bomb, during which time the central funding of research and innovation has grown so enormously and its purposes have become so unpalatable. In 1940 the Federal budget for research and development was less than 100 million dollars, in 1967 17 billion. Hitler's war was a watershed of modern times. We are accustomed, as H. R. Trevor-Roper has pointed out, to write Hitler off as an aberration, of little political significance. But, in fact, the military emergency that he and his Japanese allies created confirmed the worst tendencies of the giant states, till now they are probably irreversible by ordinary political means.

After Hiroshima, there was the conscience-stricken movement of the Atomic Scientists and the founding of their Bulletin. The American Association for the Advancement of Science pledged itself to keep the public informed about the dangerous bearings of new developments. There was the Oppenheimer incident.* Ads of the East Coast scientists successfully stopped the bomb shelters, warned about the fall-out, and helped produce the test ban. There was a scandal about the bombardment of the Van Allen belt.* Scientists and technologists formed a powerful (and misguided) *ad hoc* group for Johnson in the 1964 election. In

---

* the Oppenheimer incident: in 1954 the nuclear physicist Robert Oppenheimer was suspended from nuclear research by a security review board who considered him a "security risk" apparently because he had objected to the building of the hydrogen bomb and because in the 1930's he had associated with people who belonged to various left-wing political groups, including the Communist Party.
* Van Allen belt: see Chase, p. 822.

some universities, sometimes with bitter struggle, classified contracts have been excluded. There is a Society for Social Responsibility in Science. Rachel Carson's book on the pesticides * caused a stir, until the Department of Agriculture rescued the manufacturers and plantation-owners. Ralph Nader * has been on his rampage. Thanks to spectacular abuses like smog, strip-mining, asphalting, pesticides, and oil pollution, even ecologists and conservationists have been getting a hearing. Protest against the boom has slowed up the development of the supersonic transport. Most recent has been the concerted outcry against the anti-ballistic missiles.

The target of protest has become broader and the grounds of complaint deeper. The target is now not merely the military, but the universities, commercial corporations, and government. It is said that money is being given by the wrong sponsors to the wrong people for the wrong purposes. In some of the great schools, such funding is the main support, e.g., at MIT, 90 percent of the research budget is from the government, and 65 percent of that is military.

Inevitably, such funding channels the brainpower of most of the brightest science students, who go where the action is, and this predetermines the course of American science and technology for the foreseeable future. At present nearly 200,000 American engineers and scientists spend all their time making weapons, which is a comment on, and perhaps explanation for, the usual statement that more scientists are now alive than since Adam and Eve. And the style of such research and development is not good. It is dominated by producing hardware, figuring logistics, and devising salable novelties. Often there is secrecy, always nationalism. Since the grants go overwhelmingly through a very few corporations and universities, they favor a limited number of scientific attitudes and preconceptions, with incestuous staffing. There is a premium on "positive results"; surprising "failures" cannot be pursued, so that science ceases to be a wandering dialogue with the unknown.

The policy is economically wasteful. A vast amount of brains and money is spent on crash programs to solve often essentially petty problems, and the claim that there is a spin-off of useful discoveries is derisory, if we consider the sums involved. The claim that research is neutral, and it doesn't matter what one works on, is shabby, if we consider the heavy funding in certain directions. Social priorities are scandalous: money is spent on overkill, supersonic planes, brand-name identical drugs, annual model changes of cars, new detergents, and color television, whereas water, air, space, food, health, and foreign aid are neglected. And much research is morally so repugnant, e.g., chemical and biological weapons, that one dares not humanly continue it.

* Rachel Carson's book on the pesticides: *Silent Spring* (1962).
* Ralph Nader: lawyer and crusader for consumer protection and improved working conditions; author of *Unsafe at Any Speed: The Designed-in Dangers of the Automobile* (1965); prime mover of the 1967 Wholesome Meat Act.

The state of the behavioral sciences is, if anything, worse. Their claim to moral and political neutrality becomes, in effect, a means of diverting attention from glaring social evils, and they are in fact used—or would be if they worked—for warfare and social engineering, manipulation of people for the political and economic purposes of the powers that be. This is an especially sad betrayal since, in the not-too-distant past, the objective social sciences were developed largely to dissolve orthodoxy, irrational authority, and taboo. They were heretical and intellectually revolutionary, as the physical sciences had been in their own Heroic Age, and they weren't getting government grants.

This is a grim indictment. Even so, I do not think the dissenting scientists understand how deep their trouble is. They still take themselves too much for granted. Indeed, a repeated theme of the March 4 complaints was that the science budget was being cut back, especially in basic research. The assumption was that though the sciences are abused, Science would rightly maintain and increase its expensive pre-eminence among social institutions. Only Science could find the answers.

But underlying the growing dissent there is an historical crisis. There has been a profound change in popular feeling, more than among the professors. Put it this way: Modern societies have been operating as if religion were a minor and moribund part of the scheme of things. But this is unlikely. Men do not do without a system of "meanings" that everybody believes and puts his hope in even if, or especially if, he doesn't know anything about it; what Freud called a "shared psychosis," meaningful because shared, and with the power that resides in dream and longing. In fact, in advanced countries it is science and technology themselves that have gradually and finally triumphantly become the system of mass faith, not disputed by various political ideologies and nationalisms that have also been mass religions. Marxism called itself "scientific socialism" as against moral and utopian socialisms; and movements of national liberation have especially promised to open the benefits of industrialization and technological progress when once they have gotten rid of the imperialists.

For three hundred years, science and scientific technology had an unblemished and justified reputation as a wonderful adventure, pouring out practical benefits, and liberating the spirit from the errors of superstition and traditional faith. During this century they have finally been the only generally credited system of explanation and problem-solving. Yet in our generation they have come to seem to many, and to very many of the best of the young, as essentially inhuman, abstract, regimenting, hand-in-glove with Power, and even diabolical. Young people say that science is anti-life, it is a Calvinist obsession, it has been a weapon of white Europe to subjugate colored races, and manifestly—in view of recent scientific technology—people who think that way become insane. With science, the other professions are discredited; and the academic "disciplines" are discredited.

The immediate reasons for this shattering reversal of values are fairly obvious. Hitler's ovens and his other experiments in eugenics, the first atom bombs and their frenzied subsequent developments, the deterioration of the physical environment and the destruction of the biosphere, the catastrophes impending over the cities because of technological failures and psychological stress, the prospect of a brainwashed and drugged 1984. Innovations yield diminishing returns in enhancing life. And instead of rejoicing, there is now widespread conviction that beautiful advances in genetics, surgery, computers, rocketry, or atomic energy will surely only increase human woe.

In such a crisis, in my opinion, it will not be sufficient to ban the military from the universities; and it will not even be sufficient, as liberal statesmen and many of the big corporations envisage, to beat the swords into ploughshares and turn to solving problems of transportation, desalinization, urban renewal, garbage disposal, and cleaning up the air and water. If the present difficulty is religious and historical, it is necessary to alter the entire relationship of science, technology, and social needs both in men's minds and in fact. This involves changes in the organization of science, in scientific education, and in the kinds of men who make scientific decisions.

In spite of the fantasies of hippies, we are certainly going to continue to live in a technological world. The question is a different one: is that workable?

PRUDENCE

Whether or not it draws on new scientific research, technology is a branch of moral philosophy, not of science. It aims at prudent goods for the commonweal and to provide efficient means for these goods. At present, however, "scientific technology" occupies a bastard position in the universities, in funding, and in the public mind. It is half tied to the theoretical sciences and half treated as mere know-how for political and commercial purposes. It has no principles of its own. To remedy this—so Karl Jaspers in Europe and Robert Hutchins in America have urged—technology must have its proper place on the faculty as a learned profession important in modern society, along with medicine, law, the humanities, and natural philosophy, learning from them and having something to teach them. As a moral philosopher, a technician should be able to criticize the programs given him to implement. As a professional in a community of learned professionals, a technologist must have a different kind of training and develop a different character than we see at present among technicians and engineers. He should know something of the social sciences, law, the fine arts, and medicine, as well as relevant natural sciences.

Prudence is foresight, caution, utility. Thus it is up to the technologists, not to regulatory agencies of the government, to provide for safety and to think about remote effects. This is what Ralph Nader is saying and Rachel Carson used to ask. An important aspect of caution is flexibility, to avoid the pyramiding catastrophe that occurs when something goes wrong in interlocking technologies, as in urban power failures. Naturally, to take responsibility for such things often requires standing up to the front office and urban politicians, and technologists must organize themselves in order to have power to do it.

Often it is clear that a technology has been oversold, like the cars. Then even though the public, seduced by advertising, wants more, technologists must balk, as any professional does when his client wants what isn't good for him. We are now repeating the same self-defeating congestion with the planes and airports: the more the technology is oversold, the less immediate utility it provides, the greater the costs, and the more damaging the remote effects. As this becomes evident, it is time for technologists to confer with sociologists and economists and ask deeper questions. Is so much travel necessary? Are there ways to diminish it? Instead, the recent history of technology has consisted largely of a desperate effort to remedy situations caused by previous over-application of technology.

Technologists should certainly have a say about simple waste, for even in an affluent society there are priorities—consider the supersonic transport, which has little to recommend it. But the moon shot has presented the more usual dilemma of authentic conflicting claims. I myself believe that space exploration is a great human adventure, with immense aesthetic and moral benefits, whatever the scientific or utilitarian uses. Yet it is amazing to me that the scientists and technologists involved have not spoken more insistently for international cooperation instead of a puerile race. But I have heard some say that except for this chauvinist competition, Congress would not vote any money at all.

Currently, perhaps the chief moral criterion of a philosophic technology is modesty, having a sense of the whole and not obtruding more than a particular function warrants. Immodesty is always a danger of free enterprise, but when the same disposition is financed by big corporations, technologists rush into production with neat solutions that swamp the environment. This applies to packaging products and disposing of garbage, to freeways that bulldoze neighborhoods, high-rises that destroy landscape, wiping out a species for a passing fashion, strip mining, scrapping an expensive machine rather than making a minor repair, draining a watershed for irrigation because (as in Southern California) the cultivable land has been covered by asphalt. Given this disposition, it is not surprising that we defoliate a forest in order to expose a guerrilla and spray teargas from a helicopter on a crowded campus.

Since we are technologically over-committed, a good general maxim in advanced countries at present is to innovate in order to simplify the technical system, but otherwise to innovate as sparingly as possible. Every advanced country is over-technologized; past a certain point, the quality of life diminishes with new "improvements." Yet no country is rightly technologized, making efficient use of available techniques. There are ingenious devices for unimportant functions, stressful mazes for essential functions, and drastic dislocation when anything goes wrong, which happens with increasing frequency. To add to the complexity, the mass of people tend to become incompetent and dependent on repairmen—indeed, unrepairability except by experts has become a desideratum of industrial design.

When I speak of slowing down or cutting back, the issue is not whether research and making working models should be encouraged or not. They should be, in every direction, and given a blank check. The point is to resist the temptation to apply every new device without a second thought. But the big corporate organization of research and development makes prudence and modesty very difficult; it is necessary to get big contracts and rush into production in order to pay the salaries of the big team. Like other bureaucracies, technological organizations are run to maintain themselves but they are more dangerous because, in capitalist countries, they are in a competitive arena.

I mean simplification quite strictly, to simplify the *technical* system. I am unimpressed by the argument that what is technically more complicated is really economically or politically simpler, e.g., by complicating the packaging we improve the supermarkets; by throwing away the machine rather than repairing it, we give cheaper and faster service all around; or even by expanding the economy with trivial innovations, we increase employment, allay discontent, save on welfare. Such ideas may be profitable for private companies or political parties, but for society they have proved to be an accelerating rat race. The technical structure of the environment is too important to be a political or economic pawn; the effect on the quality of life is too disastrous; and the hidden social costs are not calculated, the auto graveyards, the torn-up streets, the longer miles of commuting, the advertising, the inflation, etc. As I pointed out in *People or Personnel,* a country with a fourth of our per capita income, like Ireland, is not necessarily less well off; in some respects it is much richer, in some respects a little poorer. If possible, it is better to solve political problems by political means. For instance, if teaching machines and audio-visual aids are indeed educative, well and good; but if they are used just to save money on teachers, then not good at all—nor do they save money.

Of course, the goals of right technology must come to terms with other values of society. I am not a technocrat. But the advantage of raising technology to be a responsible learned profession with its own principles is that it can have a voice in the debate and argue for *its* proper contribution to the community. Consider the important case of modular sizes in building, or prefabrication of a unit bathroom: these conflict with the short-run interests of manufacturers and craft-unions, yet to deny them is technically an abomination. The usual recourse is for a government agency to set standards; such agencies accommodate to interests that have a strong voice, and at present technologists have no voice.

The crucial need for technological simplification, however, is not in the advanced countries—which can afford their clutter and probably deserve it—but in underdeveloped countries which must rapidly innovate in order to diminish disease, drudgery, and deepening starvation. They cannot afford to make mistakes. It is now widely conceded that the technological aid we have given to such areas according to our own high style—a style usually demanded by the native ruling groups—has done more harm than good. Even when, as frequently if not usually, aid has been benevolent, without strings attached, not military, and not dumping, it has nevertheless disrupted ways of life, fomented tribal wars, accelerated urbanization, decreased the food supply, gone wasted for lack of skills to use it, developed a do-nothing élite.

By contrast, a group of international scientists called Intermediate Technology argue that what is needed is techniques that use only native labor, resources, traditional customs, and teachable know-how, with the simple aim of remedying drudgery, disease, and hunger, so that people can then develop further in their own style. This avoids cultural imperialism. Such intermediate techniques may be quite primitive, on a level unknown among us for a couple of centuries, and yet they may pose extremely subtle problems, requiring exquisite scientific research and political and human understanding, to devise a very simple technology. Here is a reported case (which I trust I remember accurately): In Botswana, a very poor country, pasture was over-grazed, but the economy could be salvaged if the land were fenced. There was no local material for fencing, and imported fencing was prohibitively expensive. The solution was to find the formula and technique to make posts out of mud, and a pedagogic method to teach people how to do it.

In *The Two Cultures,* C. P. Snow berated the humanists for their irrelevance when two-thirds of mankind are starving and what is needed is science and technology. They have perhaps been irrelevant; but unless technology is itself more humanistic and philosophical, it is of no use. There is only one culture.

Finally, let me make a remark about amenity as a technical criterion. It is discouraging to see the concern about beautifying a highway and banning billboards, and about the cosmetic appearance of the cars, when there is no regard for the ugliness of bumper-to-bumper traffic and the suffering of the drivers. Or the concern for preserving an historical landmark while the neighborhood is torn up and the city has no shape. Without moral philosophy, people have nothing but sentiments.

ECOLOGY

The complement to prudent technology is the ecological approach to science. To simplify the technical system and modestly pinpoint our artificial intervention in the environment makes it possible for the environment to survive in its complexity evolved for a billion years, whereas the overwhelming instant intervention of tightly interlocked and bulldozing technology has already disrupted many of the delicate sequences and balances. The calculable consequences are already frightening, but of course we don't know enough, and won't in the foreseeable future, to predict the remote effects of much of what we have done. The only possible conclusion is to be prudent; when there is serious doubt, to do nothing.

Cyberneticists—I am thinking of Gregory Bateson—come to the same cautious conclusion. The use of computers has enabled us to carry out crashingly inept programs on the bases of willful analyses. But we have also become increasingly alert to the fact that things respond, systematically, continually, cumulatively; they cannot simply be manipulated or pushed around. Whether bacteria or weeds or bugs or the technologically unemployed or unpleasant thoughts, they cannot be eliminated and forgotten; repressed, the nuisances return in new forms. A complicated system works most efficiently if its parts readjust themselves decentrally, with a minimum of central intervention or control, except in case of breakdown. Usually there is an advantage in a central clearing house of information about the gross total situation, but decision and execution require more minute local information. The fantastically simulated moon landing hung on a last split-second correction on the spot. In social organization, deciding in headquarters means relying on information that is cumulatively abstract and irrelevant, and chain-of-command execution applies standards that cumulatively do not fit the concrete situation. By and large it is better, given a sense of the whole picture, for those in the field to decide what to do and do it (cf. *People or Personnel,* Chapter III).

But with organisms too, this has long been the bias of psychosomatic medicine, the Wisdom of the Body, as Cannon called it. To cite a classical experiment of Ralph Hefferline of Columbia: a subject is wired to suffer an annoying regular buzz, which can be delayed and finally eliminated if he makes a precise but unlikely gesture, say by twisting his ankle in a certain way; then it is found that he adjusts quicker if he is *not* told the method and it is left to his spontaneous twitching than if he is told and tries deliberately to help himself. He adjusts better without conscious control, his own or the experimenter's.

Technological modesty, fittingness, is not negative. It is the ecological wisdom of cooperating with Nature rather than trying to master her. (The personification of "Nature" is linguistic wisdom.) A well-known example is the long-run superiority of partial pest-control in farming by using biological deterrents rather than chemical ones. The living defenders work harder, at the right moment, and with more pin-pointed targets. But let me give another example because it is so lovely —though I have forgotten the name of my informant: A tribe in Yucatan educates its children to identify and pull up all weeds in the region; then what is left is a garden of useful plants that have chosen to be there and now thrive.

In the life sciences there is at present a suggestive bifurcation in methodology. The rule is still to increase experimental intervention, but there is also a considerable revival of old-fashioned naturalism, mainly watching and thinking, with very modest intervention. Thus, in medicine, there is new diagnostic machinery, new drugs, spectacular surgery; but there is also a new respect for family practice with a psychosomatic background, and a strong push, among young doctors and students, for a social-psychological and sociological approach, aimed at preventing disease and building up resistance. In psychology, the operant conditioners multiply and refine their machinery to give maximum control of the organism and the environment (I have not heard of any dramatic discoveries, but perhaps they have escaped me). On the other hand, the most interesting psychology in recent years has certainly come from animal naturalists, e.g., pecking order, territoriality, learning to control aggression, language of the bees, overcrowding among rats, trying to talk to dolphins.

On a fair judgment, both contrasting approaches give positive results. The logical scientific problem that arises is, What is there in the nature of things that makes a certain method, or even moral attitude, work well or poorly in a given case? This question is not much studied. Every scientist seems to know what "the" scientific method is.

Another contrast of style, extremely relevant at present, is that between Big Science and old-fashioned shoe-string science. There is plenty of research, with corresponding technology, that can be done only by Big Science; yet much, and perhaps most, of science will always be shoe-string science, for which it is absurd to use the fancy and expensive equipment that has gotten to be the fashion.

Consider urban medicine. The problem, given a shortage of doctors and facilities, is how to improve the level of mass health, the vital statistics, and yet to practice medicine, which aims at the maximum possible health for each person. Perhaps the most efficient use of Big Science technology for the general health would be compulsory biennial checkups, as we inspect cars, for early diagnosis and to forestall chronic conditions with accumulating costs. Then an excellent machine would be a total diagnostic bus to visit the neighborhoods, as we do chest X-rays. On the other hand, for actual treatment and especially for convalescence, the evidence seems to be that small personalized hospitals are best. And to revive family practice, maybe the right idea is to offer a doctor a splendid suite in a public housing project.

Our contemporary practice makes little sense. We have expensive technology stored in specialists' offices and big hospitals, really unavailable for mass use in the neighborhoods; yet every individual, even if he is quite rich, finds it almost impossible to get attention to himself as an individual whole organism in his setting. He is sent from specialist to specialist and exists as a bag of symptoms and a file of test scores.

In automating there is an analogous dilemma of how to cope with masses of people and get economies of scale, without losing the individual at great consequent human and economic cost. A question of immense importance for the immediate future is, Which functions should be automated or organized to use business machines, and which should not? This question also is not getting asked, and the present disposition is that the sky is the limit for extraction, refining, manufacturing, processing, packaging, transportation, clerical work, ticketing, transactions, information retrieval, recruitment, middle management, evaluation, diagnosis, instruction, and even research and invention. Whether the machines can do all these kinds of jobs and more is partly an empirical question, but it also partly depends on what is meant by doing a job. Very often, e.g., in college admissions, machines are acquired for putative economies (which do not eventuate); but the true reason is that an overgrown and overcentralized organization cannot be administered without them. The technology conceals the essential trouble, e.g., that there is no community of scholars and students are treated like things. The function is badly performed, and finally the system breaks down anyway. I doubt that enterprises in which interpersonal relations are important are suited to much programming.

But worse, what can happen is that the real function of the enterprise is subtly altered so that it is suitable for the mechanical system. (E.g., "information retrieval" is taken as an adequate replacement for critical scholarship.) Incommensurable factors, individual differences, the local context, the weighting of evidence are quietly overlooked though they may be of the essence. The system, with its subtly transformed purposes, seems to run very smoothly; it is productive, and it is more and more out of line with the nature of things and the real problems. Meantime it is geared in with other enterprises of society, e.g., major public policy may depend on welfare or unemployment statistics which, as they are tabulated, are blind to the actual lives of poor families. In such a case, the particular system may not break down, the whole society may explode.

I need hardly point out that American society is peculiarly liable to the corruption of inauthenticity, busily producing phony products. It lives by public relations, abstract ideals, front politics, show-business communications, mandarin credentials. It is preeminently overtechnologized. And computer technologists especially suffer the euphoria of being in a new and rapidly expanding field. It is so astonishing that the robot can do the job at all or seem to do it, that it is easy to blink at the fact that he is doing it badly or isn't really doing quite that job.

DECENTRALIZATION

The current political assumption is that scientists and inventors, and even social scientists, are "value-neutral," but their discoveries are "applied" by those who make decisions for the nation. Counter to this, I have been insinuating a kind of Jeffersonian democracy or guild socialism, that scientists and inventors and other workmen are responsible for the uses of the work they do, and ought to be competent to judge these uses and have a say in deciding them. They usually are competent. To give a striking example, Ford assembly line workers, according to Harvey Swados, who worked with them, are accurately critical of the glut of cars, but they have no way to vent their dissatisfactions with their useless occupation except to leave nuts and bolts to rattle in the body.

My bias is also pluralistic. Instead of the few national goals of a few decision-makers, I propose that there are many goods of many activities of life, and many professions and other interest groups each with its own criteria and goals that must be taken into account. A society that distributes power widely is superficially conflictful but fundamentally stable.

Research and development ought to be widely decentralized, the national fund for them being distributed through thousands of centers of initiative and decision. This would not be chaotic. We seem to have forgotten that for four hundred years Western science majestically progressed with no central direction whatever, yet with exquisite international coordination, little duplication, almost nothing getting lost, in constant communication despite slow facilities. The reason was simply that all scientists wanted to get on with the same enterprise of testing the boundaries of knowledge, and they relied on one another.

What is as noteworthy is that something similar holds also in invention and innovation, even in recent decades when there has been such a concentration of funding and apparent concentration of opportunity. The majority of big advances have still come from independents, partnerships, and tiny companies. (Evidence published by the Senate Sub-Committee on Antitrust and Monopoly, May 1965.) To name a few, jet engines, xerography, automatic transmission, cellophane, air-conditioning, quick freeze, antibiotics, and tranquilizers. The big technological teams must have disadvantages that outweigh their advantages, like lack of single-mindedness, poor communications, awkward scheduling. Naturally, big corporations have taken over the innovations, but the Senate evidence is that 90 percent of the government subsidy has gone for last-stage development for production, which they ought to have paid out of their own pockets.

We now have a theory that we have learned to learn, and that we can program technical progress, directed by a central planning board. But this doesn't make it so. The essence of the new still seems to be that nobody has thought of it, and the ones who get ideas are those in direct contact with the work. *Too precise* a preconception of what is wanted discourages creativity more than it channels it; and bureaucratic memoranda from distant directors don't help. This is especially true when, as at present, so much of the preconception of what is wanted comes from desperate political anxiety in emergencies. Solutions that emerge from such an attitude rarely strike out on new paths, but rather repeat traditional thinking with new gimmicks; they tend to compound the problem. A priceless advantage of widespread decentralization is that it engages more minds, and more mind, instead of a few panicky (or greedy) corporate minds.

A homespun advantage of small groups, according to the Senate testimony, is that co-workers can talk to one another, without schedules, reports, clock-watching, and face-saving.

An important hope from decentralizing science is to develop knowledgeable citizens, and provide not only a bigger pool of scientists and inventors but also a public better able to protect itself and know how to judge the enormous budgets asked for. The safety of the environment is too important to be left to scientists, even ecologists. During the last decades of the nineteenth century and the first decade of the twentieth, the heyday of public faith in the beneficent religion of science and invention, say from Pasteur and Huxley * to Edison and the Wright Brothers, philosophers of science had a vision of a "scientific way of life," one in which people would be objective, respectful of evidence, accurate, free of superstition and taboo, immune to irrational authority, experimental. All would be well, is the impression one gets from Thomas Huxley, if everybody knew the splendid Ninth Edition of the *Encyclopaedia Britannica* with its articles by Darwin * and Clerk Maxwell.* Veblen * put his faith in the modesty and matter-of-factness of engineers to govern. Sullivan * and Frank Lloyd Wright * spoke for an austere functionalism and respect for the nature of materials and industrial processes. Patrick Geddes * thought that new technology would finally get us out of the horrors of the Industrial Revolution and produce good communities. John Dewey * devised a system of education to rear pragmatic and experimental citizens to be at home in the new technological world rather than estranged from it. Now fifty years later, we are in the swamp of a scientific and technological environment and there are more scientists alive, etc., etc. But the mention of the "scientific way of life" seems like black humor.

Many of those who have grown up since 1945 and have never seen any other state of science and technology assume that rationalism itself is totally evil and dehumanizing. It is probably more significant than we like to think that they go in for astrology and the Book of Changes, as well as inducing psychedelic dreams by technological means. Jacques Ellul, a more philosophic critic, tries to show that technology is necessarily over-controlling, standardizing, and voraciously inclusive, so that there is no place for freedom. But I doubt that any of this is intrinsic to science and technology. The crude history has been, rather, that they have fallen willingly under the dominion of money and power. Like Christianity or communism, the scientific way of life has never been tried.

* Thomas H. Huxley: (1825–95), English biologist; leading advocate of Darwin's theory of evolution; religious "agnostic" (a term he introduced).
* Charles Darwin: (1809–82), English botanist; author of the epoch-making *Origin of Species by Means of Natural Selection* (1859).
* James Clerk Maxwell: (1831–79), Scottish physicist whose theory of electromagnetic radiation was his most important work.
* Thorstein Veblen: (1857–1929), American sociologist who made famous the phrase "conspicuous consumption"; among his books are *The Theory of the Leisure Class* (1899) and *Engineers and the Price System* (1921).
* Louis Henry Sullivan: (1856–1924), American architect, often regarded as the father of architectural modernism.
* Frank Lloyd Wright: (1869–1959), American architect, much influenced by Sullivan, whose work made a profound impression on modern European architecture.
* Patrick Geddes: (1854–1932), Scottish botanist, sociologist, city planner, and social reformer.
* John Dewey: (1859–1952), American philosopher and educator; adherent of William James's philosophy of pragmatism; a believer in "learning by doing"; author of *The School and Society* (1899) and *Democracy and Education* (1916).

To satisfy the March 4 dissenters, to break the military-industrial corporations and alter the priorities of the budget, would be to restructure the American economy almost to a revolutionary extent. But to meet the historical crisis of science at present, for science and technology to become prudent, ecological, and decentralized requires a change that is even more profound, a kind of religious transformation. Yet there is nothing untraditional in what I have proposed; prudence, ecology, and decentralization are indeed the high tradition of science and technology. Thus the closest analogy I can think of is the Protestant Reformation, a change of moral allegiance, liberation from the Whore of Babylon, return to the pure faith.

Science has long been the chief orthodoxy of modern times and has certainly been badly corrupted, but the deepest flaw of the affluent societies that has alienated the young is not, finally, their imperialism, economic injustice, or racism, bad as these are, but their nauseating phoniness, triviality, and wastefulness, the cultural and moral scandal that Luther found when he went to Rome in 1510. And precisely science, which should have been the wind of truth to clear the air, has polluted the air, helped to brainwash, and provided weapons for war. I doubt that most young people today have even heard of the ideal of the dedicated researcher, truculent and incorruptible, and unrewarded, for instance the "German scientist" that Sinclair Lewis described in *Arrowsmith*. Such a figure is no longer believable. I don't mean, of course, that he doesn't exist; there must be thousands of him, just as there were good priests in 1510.

The analogy to the Reformation is even more exact if we consider the school system, from educational toys and Head Start up through the universities. This system is manned by the biggest horde of monks since the time of Henry VIII. It is the biggest industry in the country. I have heard the estimate that 40 percent of the national product is in the Knowledge Business. It is mostly hocus-pocus. Yet the belief of parents in this institution is quite delusional and school diplomas are in fact the only entry to licensing and hiring in every kind of job. The abbots of this system are the chiefs of science, e.g., the National Science Foundation, who talk about reform but work to expand the school budgets, step up the curriculum, and inspire the endless catechism of tests.

These abuses are international, as the faith is. For instance, there is no essential difference between the military-industrial or the school system, of the Soviet Union and the United States. There are important differences in way of life and standard of living, but the abuses of technology are very similar: pollution, excessive urbanization, destruction of the biosphere, weaponry, and disastrous foreign aid. Our protesters naturally single out our own country, and the United States is the most powerful country, but the corruption we are speaking of is not specifically American nor even capitalist; it is a disease of modern times.

But the analogy is to the Reformation, it is not to primitive Christianity or some other primitivism, the abandonment of technological civilization. There is indeed much talk about the doom of Western civilization, and a few Adamites actually do retire into the hills; but for the great mass of mankind, and myself, that's not where it's at. There is not the slightest interruption to the universalizing of Western civilization, including most of its delusions, into the so-called Third World. (If the atom bombs go off, however?)

Naturally the exquisitely interesting question is whether or not this Reformation will occur, how to make it occur, against the entrenched worldwide system of corrupt power that is continually aggrandizing itself. I don't know. In my analogy I have deliberately been choosing the date 1510, Luther in Rome, rather than 1517 when, in the popular story, he nailed his Theses on the cathedral door. There are everywhere contradictory signs and dilemmas. The new professional and technological class is more and more entangled in the work, statuses, and rewards of the system, and yet this same class, often the very same people, are more and more protestant. On the other hand, the dissident young, who are unequivocally for radical change, are so alienated from occupation, function, knowledge, or even concern, that they often seem to be simply irrelevant to the underlying issues of modern times. The monks keep "improving" the schools and getting bigger budgets to do so, yet it is clear that high schools will be burned down, twelve-year-olds will play truant in droves, and the taxpayers are already asking what goes on and voting down the bonds.

The interlocking of technologies and all other institutions makes it almost impossible to reform policy in any part; yet this very interlocking that renders people powerless, including the decision-makers, creates a remarkable resonance and chain-reaction if any determined group, or even determined individual, exerts force. In the face of overwhelmingly collective operations like the space exploration, the average man must feel that local or grassroots efforts are worthless; there is no science but Big Science, and no administration but the State. And yet there is a powerful surge of localism, populism, and community action, as if people were determined to be free even if it makes no sense. A mighty empire is stood off by a band of peasants, and *neither* can win—this is even more remarkable than if David beats Goliath; it means that neither principle is historically adequate. In my opinion, these dilemmas and impasses show that we are on the eve of a transformation of conscience.

Elinor Langer / The Women of the Telephone Company

This is the second part of a long article. It is a story about the daily lives of women who work in a branch of the communications industry. The author, who is of a higher educational level than the other women, has infiltrated herself into the telephone company in order to do a first-hand report. She shares their work, but not their conceptions of it, since she brings in with her certain preformed opinions on social and economic issues. Her first object is to give the reader the "feel" of the work; hence the early description of the sense of panic that overtakes the girls at certain moments. Her second is to explain what this kind of work does to the lives of the workers. Obviously one can most easily be very detailed about work habits, clothes, attitudes to possessions, and the like, if one in no way identifies with the people discussed. The writer establishes her distance and is thus enabled to argue that the company exploits the "consumerism" which the women's jobs induce in them. The women fall in with this, losing an elementary decency (for example, about poor people) that they might originally have had, because they identify with the company and its interests. Against this background Miss Langer is able to discuss the inefficiency of their union, and to state her conclusion: "to free them (the women) to live more human lives . . . would require a total transformation of the way they think about the world and themselves." But the end of the article is again a necessary statement of the difference between the writer and her co-workers.

The writer of such a piece as this should be an accurate observer who understands her own position fully. She cannot explain that position in detail, but she must indirectly make it very clear what she thinks. Elinor Langer is asking the reader to accept her diagnosis of certain social ills made evident by the behavior of the women of the telephone company in relation to their jobs, their bosses, and their leisure. The inquiry is limited. The success of the enterprise depends upon her ability to suggest its larger implications.

Daily life on the job at the New York Telephone Company, where I recently worked as a Customer's Service Representative, consists largely of pressure. To a casual observer it might appear that much of the activity on the floor is random, but in fact it is not. The women moving from desk to desk are on missions of retrieving and refiling customers' records; the tête-à-têtes that look so sociable are anxious conferences with a Supervisor in which a Representative is Thinking and Planning What to Do Next. Of course the more experienced women know how to use the empty moments that do occur for social purposes. But the basic working unit is one girl: one telephone, and the basic requirement of the job is to answer it, perhaps more than fifty times a day.

For every contact with a customer, the amount of paperwork is huge: a single contact can require the completion of three, four, or even five separate forms. No problems can be dispensed with handily. Even if, for example, you merely

Courtesy of American Telephone and Telegraph

transfer a customer to Traffic or Repair you must still fill out and file a CF-1. At the end of the day you must tally up and categorize all the services you have performed on a little slip of paper and hand it in to the Supervisor, who completes a tally for the unit: it is part of the process of "taking credit" for services rendered by one unit vis-à-vis the others.

A Representative's time is divided into "open" and "closed" portions, according to a recent scientific innovation called FADS (for Force Administration Data System), of which the company is particularly proud; the innovation consists in establishing how many Representatives have to be available at any one moment to handle the volume of business anticipated for that month, that day, and that hour. Under this arrangement the contact with the customer and the processing of his request are carried out simultaneously: that is, the Representative does the paperwork needed to take care of a request while she is still on the line. For more complex cases, however, this is not possible and the processing is left for "closed" time: a time when no further calls are coming in.

This arrangement tends to create a constant low-level panic. There is a kind of act which it is natural to carry to its logical conclusion: brushing one's teeth, washing a dish, or filling out a form are things one does not leave half done. But the company's system stifles this natural urge to completion. Instead, during "open" time, the phone keeps ringing and the work piles up. You look at the schedule and know that you have only one hour of "closed" time to complete the work, and twenty minutes of that hour is a break.

The situation produces desperation: How am I to get it done? How can I call back all those customers, finish all that mail, write all those complicated orders, within forty minutes? Occasionally, during my brief time at the job, I would accidentally press the wrong button on my phone and it would become "open" again. Once, when I was feeling particularly desperate about time, I did that twice in a row and both times the callers were ordering new telephone service —a process which takes between eight and ten minutes to complete.

My feeling that time was slipping away, that I would never be able to "complete my commitments" on time was intense and hateful. Of course it was worse for me than for the experienced women—but not much worse. Another situation in which the pressure of time is universally felt is in the minutes before lunch and before five o'clock. At those times, if your phone is open, you sit hoping that a complex call will not arrive. A "new line" order at five minutes to five is a source of both resentment and frustration.

Given the pressure, it becomes natural to welcome the boring and routine— the simple suspensions or disconnections of service—and dread the unusual or complex. The women deal with the pressure by quietly getting rid of as many calls as they can, transferring them to another department although the proper jurisdiction may be a borderline matter. This transferring, the lightening of the load, is the bureaucratic equivalent of the "soldiering" * that Taylor * and the early scientific managers were striving to defeat. It is a subtle kind of slowdown, never discussed, but quickly transmitted to the new Representative as legitimate. Unfortunately, it does not slow things down very much.

As Daniel Bell points out in his extraordinary essay, "Work and Its Discontents," * the rhythm of the job controls the time spent off the job as well: the breaks, the lunches, the holidays; even the weekends are scarcely long enough to reestablish a more congenial or natural path. The work rhythm controls human relationships and attitudes as well. For instance: there was a Puerto Rican worker in the Schraffts downstairs whose job was to sell coffee-to-go to the customers: he spent his day doing nothing but filling paper cups with coffee, fitting on the lids, and writing out the checks. He was very surly and very slow and it looked to me as if the thoughts swirling in his head were those of an incipient murderer, not an incipient revolutionary. His slowness was very inconvenient to the thousands of workers in the building who had to get their coffee, take it upstairs, and drink it according to a precise timetable. We never had more than fifteen minutes to get there and back, and buying coffee generally took longer. The women resented him and called him "Speedy Gonzales," in tones of snobbery and hate. I know he hated us.

II

The women of the phone company are middle class or lower middle class, come from a variety of ethnic backgrounds (Polish, Jewish, Italian, Irish, Black, Puerto Rican), mainly high-school graduates or with a limited college education. They live just about everywhere except in Manhattan: the Bronx, Brooklyn, Staten Island, or Queens. Their leisure time is filled, first of all, with the discussion of objects. Talk of shopping is endless, as is the pursuit of it in lunch hours, after work, and on days off. The women have a fixation on brand names, and describe every object that way: it is always a London Fog, a Buxton, a White Stag. This fixation does not preclude bargain-hunting: but the purpose of hunting a bargain is to get the brand name at a lower price. Packaging is also important: the women will describe not only the thing but also the box or wrapper it comes in. They are especially fascinated by wigs. Most women have several wigs and are in some cases unrecognizable from day to day, creating the effect of a continually changing work force. The essence of wiggery is escapism: the kaleidoscopic transformation of oneself while everything else remains the same. Anyone who has ever worn a wig knows the embarrassing truth: it *is* transforming.

* "soldiering": malingering, loafing while pretending to work.
* Frederick W. Taylor: (1856–1915), American efficiency engineer whose idea of "scientific management" was based on the systematic analysis of each job into its smallest mechanical component; these elements were then reorganized to achieve the most efficient combination possible.
* Daniel Bell, *The End of Ideology* (1960).

Consumerism is one of the major reasons why these women work. Their salaries are low in relation to the costs of necessities in American life, ranging from $95.00 to $132.50 *before* taxes: barely enough, if one is self-supporting, to pay for essentials. In fact, however, many of the women are not self-supporting, but live with their families or with husbands who also work, sometimes at more than one job. Many of the women work overtime more than five hours a week (only for more than five extra hours do they get paid time and a half) and it seems from their visible spending that it is simply to pay for their clothes, which are expensive, their wigs, their color TVs, their dishes, silver, and so forth.

What the pressures of food, shelter, education, or medical costs contribute to their need to work I cannot tell, but it seems to me the women are largely trapped by their love of objects. What they think they need in order to survive and what they endure in order to attain it is astonishing. Why this is so is another matter. I think that the household appliances play a real role in the women's family lives: helping them to run their homes smoothly and in keeping with a (to them) necessary image of efficiency and elegance. As for the clothes and the wigs, I think they are a kind of tax, a tribute exacted by the social pressures of the work-place. For the preservation of their own egos against each other and against the system, they had to feel confident of their appearance on each and every day. Outside work they needed it to: to keep up, to keep their men, not to fall behind.

The atmosphere of passionate consuming was immeasurably heightened by Christmas, which also had the dismal effect of increasing the amount of stealing from the locker room. For a period of about three weeks nothing was safe: hats, boots, gloves. The women told me that the same happens every year: an overwhelming craving, a need for material goods that has to find an outlet even in thievery from one another.

The women define themselves by their consumerism far more than by their work, as if they were compensating for their exploitation as workers by a desperate attempt to express their individuality as consumers. Much of the consuming pressure is generated by the women themselves: not only in shopping but in constant raffles, contests, and so forth in which the prize is always a commodity— usually liquor. The women are asked to participate in these raffles at least two or three times a week.

But the atmosphere is also deliberately fostered by the company itself. The company gave every woman a Christmas present: a little wooden doll, about four inches tall, with the sick-humor look that was popular a few years ago and still appears on greeting cards. On the outside the doll says "Joy is . . ." and when you press down the springs a little stick pops up that says "Extensions in Color" (referring to the telephone extensions we were trying to sell). Under that label is another sticker, the original one, which says "Knowing I wuv you." The doll is typical of the presents the company distributes periodically: a plastic shopping bag inscribed with the motto "Colorful Extensions Lighten the Load"; a keychain with a plastic Princess telephone saying "It's Little, It's Lovely, It Lights"; plastic rain bonnets with the telephone company emblem, and so forth.

There were also free chocolates at Thanksgiving and, when the vending machine companies were on strike, free coffee for a while in the cafeteria. The women are disgusted by the company's gift-giving policies. Last year, I was told, the Christmas present was a little gold-plated basket filled with velour fruit and adorned with a flag containing a company motto of the "Extensions in Color" type. They think it is a cheap truck—better not done at all—and cite instances of other companies which give money bonuses at Christmas.

It is obvious that the gifts are all programmed, down to the last cherry-filled chocolate, in some manual of Personnel Administration that is the source of all wisdom and policy; it is clear from their frequency that a whole agency of the company is devoted to devising these gimmicks and passing them out. In fact, apart from a standard assortment of insurance and pension plans, the only company policy I could discover which offers genuine advantage to the employees and which is not an attempt at manipulation is a tuition support program in which the company pays $1000 out of $1400 of the costs of continuing education.

Going still further, the company, for example, sponsors a recruiting game among employees, a campaign entitled "People Make the Difference." Employees who recruit other employees are rewarded with points: 200 for a recommendation, an additional thousand if the candidate is hired. Employees are stimulated to participate by the circulation of an S&H-type catalogue, a kind of encyclopedia of the post-scarcity society. There you can see pictured a GE Portable Color Television with a walnut-grained polystyrene cabinet (46,000 points) a Silver-Plated Hors d'Oeuvres Dish By Wallace (3,900 points), and a staggering assortment of mass-produced candelabra, linens, china, fountain pens, watches, clothing, luggage, and—for the hardy—pup tents, power tools, air mattresses.

Similarly, though perhaps less crudely, the company has institutionalized its practice of rewarding employees for longevity. After every two years with the company, the women receive a small gold charm, the men a "tie-tac." These grow larger with the years and after a certain period jewels begin to be added: rubies, emeralds, sapphires, and eventually diamonds and bigger diamonds. The tie-tac evolves over the years into a tie-clasp. After twenty-five years you may have either a ceremonial luncheon or an inscribed watch: the watches are pre-fixed, pre-selected, and pictured in a catalogue.

The company has "scientifically structured" its rewards just as it has "scientifically structured" its work. But the real point is that the system gets the women as consumers in two ways. If consumption were less central to them, they would be less likely to be there in the first place. Then, the company attempts to en-snare them still further in the mesh by offering as incentives goods and images of goods which are only further way stations of the same endless quest.

III

Another characteristic of the telephone company is a kind of programmed "niceness" which starts from the top down but which the women internalize and mimic. For management the strategy is clear (the Hawthorne experiments,* after all, were carried out at Western Electric): it is, simply, make the employees feel important. For trainees this was accomplished by a generous induction ceremony complete with flowers, films, a fancy buffet, and addresses by top division representatives, all of which stressed the theme: the company cares about you.

The ceremonies had another purpose and effect: to instill in the minds of new employees the image the company would like the public to have of it, that it is a goodhearted service organization with modest and regulated profits. A deliberate effort was made to fend off any free-floating negative ideas by explaining carefully, for instance, why AT&T's monopolistic relationship with Western Electric was a good thing. The ideology of Service, embraced without much cynicism by the low-level managers who are so abundant, is in that way—and others— passed along.

The paternalism, the "niceness," filters down and is real. Employees are on a first-name basis, even the women with the managers. The women are very close to one another, sharing endless gossip, going on excursions together, and continually engaging in ceremonial celebration of one another's births, engagements, promotions. The generosity even extends to difficult situations on the job. I have, for example, seen women voluntarily sharing their precious closed time when one of them was overcommitted and the other slightly more free. Their attitude toward new employees was uniformly friendly and helpful. When I first went out on the floor my presence was a constant harassment to the other women in my unit: I didn't know what to do, had to ask a lot of questions, filed incorrectly. As a newcomer, I made their already tense lives far more difficult. Nonetheless I was made to feel welcome, encouraged. "Don't feel bad," one or another would say at a particularly stupid error. "We were all new once. We've all been through it. Don't worry. You'll catch on." In the same way I found them invariably trying to be helpful in modest personal crises: solicitous about

* the Hawthorne experiments: (1924–33), a series of studies conducted at one of the manufacturing plants of the Western Electric Co. by Elton Mayo and the Harvard Department of Industrial Research; seeking to determine the effect of external environmental factors on the output of workers, the experimenters came to realize that the workers were responding favorably to social forces, to the interest centered on them by the experiment itself; this led to a shift from the study of physical conditions to a study of the factory as a social system in which "teamwork" was important to productivity.

my health when I faked a few days of illness, comforting in my depression when a pair of gloves was stolen, always friendly, cheering me (and each other) on.

This "niceness" is carefully preserved by the women as a protection against the stress of the work and the hostility of customers. "We have to be nice to each other," Sally * told me once. "If we yelled at each other the way the customers yell at us, we'd go crazy." At the same time it is a triumph of their spirit as well. There is some level on which they are too proud to let the dehumanization overtake them; too decent to let the rat race get them down.

On the job, at least, the women's sense of identification with the company is absolute. On several occasions I tried to bring up issues on which their interests —and the public's—diverged from that of the company, and always I failed to make my point. It happened, for example, on the issue of selling, where I told my class frankly that I couldn't oversell, thought it was wrong, and that people needed far fewer telephones than we were giving them. Instead of noticing that I was advocating a position of principle, my class thought that, because I was so poor myself (as measured by having only one black telephone) I just somehow couldn't grasp the concept of the "well-telephoned home," but that I would catch on when I became convinced that the goods and services in question were truly valuable and desirable.

It happened again during a discussion of credit ratings when, because welfare women are always put in the lowest category, I said I thought credit rested on racist assumptions. The class explained to me that "if you worked in Billing and knew how hard it is to collect from those people" I wouldn't feel that way. And it happened another time during a particularly macabre discussion over coffee when the women were trading horror stories about tragic cases where telephone service had to be cut off because people weren't paying their bills: they were grotesque tales about armless veterans and blind old ladies of eighty-five.

I kept saying that terminating those services was intolerable, that some way should be found for people to have services free. Instead of thinking that was an odd position, the women reported that "every new representative feels that way," that they used to feel that way themselves, but they'd gotten over it. In other words they began their jobs with all the feelings any decent (never mind radical) person would have, and gradually learned to overcome them, because of the creeping identification with the company produced by their having to act out daily a company-defined role. Their basic belief in the legitimacy of the "make a buck" system established in their minds a link between company revenue and their own paychecks. "That's where your money comes from" was a common conclusion to these discussions.

The women have a strangely dissociated attitude toward company operations that aren't working well. What company *policy* is—that is the way they learn

---

* Sally: Elinor Langer's instructor in the training class for service representatives.

things are supposed to be—gets pressed into their heads so much that they get a little confused by their simultaneous understanding that it isn't really working that way at all. I pointed that out a lot to see what would happen. For instance our lesson books say: "Customers always get Manhattan directories delivered with their regular installations." I said, in class: "Gee, that's funny, Sally, I had a telephone installed recently and I didn't get any phone books at all." Sally would make sure not to lose control and merely repeat: "Phone books are delivered with the regular installations."

It was the same with installation dates, which, in the company's time of troubles, are lagging behind. Company *policy* is that installations are made two days from the date they are requested. In reality we were making appointments for two, three, or even four weeks in advance. There are explanations for these lapses—everyone knows that things go wrong all the time—but there are no reasonable explanations which do not undermine the basic assumption that the company has everything "scientifically" under control. Thus the "policy" is that they are not happening at all.

The effect of the pressure of work and the ethos of niceness is to defuse political controversy. There is a kind of compact about tolerance, a governing attitude which says, "Let's not talk about religion or politics." During the time I was there I heard virtually no discussion of Vietnam, the city elections, or race. There was a single exception—an argument between Betty and myself over Songmy *—after which I had the feeling that something had been breached, that she would take particular care not to let it happen again.

This is not characteristic of the men's departments of the company where political discussion is commonplace, and I believe the women think that such heavy topics are properly the domain of men: they are not about to let foolish "politics" interfere with the commonsensical and harmonious adjustments they have made to their working lives. Race relations were governed by the same kind of neutrality and "common sense." The black women of the Commercial Department were of the same type as the whites: lower middle class and upwardly mobile. Among the Representatives, not an Afro was in sight. There were good and close relationships between the blacks and the whites—close enough for jokes about hair and the word "nigger"—and, as far as I could tell, the undercurrents of strain that existed were no greater (though certainly no less intense) than are characteristic of such relations in the more educated and "liberal" middle classes.

IV

Normally the question of unions is far from the interests of the women in the Commercial Department. The women do not see themselves as "workers" in

* Songmy: South Vietnamese village where, in March 1968, U.S. troops allegedly massacred scores of South Vietnamese civilians; the incident did not come to public attention for nearly two years.

anything like the classical sense. The absence of this consciousness—deliberately stunted by management personnel strategies—is a natural and realistic response to the conditions of their work. Customer's Service Representative is the position from which lower (female) management is recruited, and promotions are frequent. Supervisors are always former Representatives and their relations with the women they supervise are close and friendly. The absence of rigid job definitions is an economic boon to the company as well as a psychic advantage to the employees. When a Supervisor is ill, for example, a "rep" will take over and handle her functions, and reps as well as Supervisors are occasionally asked to teach classes, coach new employees, or take "acting" titles: a natural managerial flow which is unthinkable under most union rules.

This is not to say that the women think their working conditions are good: they object to the salaries; they hate the pressure; they dislike Observation; and they resent the internalized time clocks which control their lunches and breaks. But the women's trust remains with the company and their hopes for escape are mainly fixed on the individual's upward mobility into managerial ranks. "Worker solidarity"—the consciousness that all workers advance through collective action —is weak.

The Union of Telephone Workers, which "represents" the Commercial Department, reflects this condition. It is an "independent" union lineally descended from the company-sponsored employee organizations that existed in the Bell System before the Wagner Act.* It belongs to an Alliance of Independent Telephone Unions composed of similar unions in Bell companies along the Eastern Seaboard. The UTW explicitly rejects the philosophy of "international" or "big" unionism in favor of a company-oriented approach "close to the problems" of workers and management. Its successes are precisely those modest concessions and policy changes which any remotely modern management would have had to make in recent years to maintain its work force.

The UTW's role is to stamp those concessions into the language and mold of "negotiated" agreements. It swings into action readily enough when it is attacked —a large part of the machinery of the Alliance exists for precisely this purpose —but it is generally a sleepy beast content to nuzzle in the bosom of Ma Bell. Numbers are irrelevant to its strength—only about 40 percent of the women belong—and it does not seem interested in recruiting. As a new employee, I had to seek it out. Similar company unions represent the telephone operators in the Traffic Department (the serfs of the system) and the Accounting Department. The only AFL-CIO Union in New York Telephone is the Communications Workers of America, which represents the Plant bargaining unit—installers, repairmen, switchmen, and so forth. CWA has a reputation for company-minded-

* the Wagner Act: the National Labor Relations Act (1935), the most important labor legislation of Franklin D. Roosevelt's administration; avowedly intended to diminish the causes of strikes upsetting interstate commerce, its effect was to strengthen unions by protecting their rights to free self-organization and collective bargaining.

ness elsewhere in the labor movement, but despite recent challenges it has long been the only "real" union with which New York Tel's management has had to deal.

This divided labor force (in addition to the four unions there are seven contracts, no two of which expire simultaneously) is crucial to management for three reasons. First of all, the work rules and sensitivities of the CWA would drive any rational management crazy. In the Plant department, a clerk will not answer a Foreman's telephone unless she is reclassified as a secretary; the men will not work "alongside" management even when—as now—a manpower shortage has created acute emergencies. And the men in the union not only obstruct a "rational" flow of work: they have interfered with management's efforts to expand its work force by hiring new employees at more generous starting salaries than those of the old employees. That—in addition to an undercurrent of racism—was a key issue in the telephone strike last fall. If that mentality were transferred to other departments, the company would be in far greater difficulty than it is now.

Second, it is precisely the absence of solidarity between departments that gives management the leverage to break or control the frequent strikes the men provoke. When CWA strikes occur, they are usually ignored by the other unions, and lower-level management from the other departments is sent around to Plant to help with repairs, handle complaints, and so forth. If their departments were also on strike, these junior executives would have to attend to their own jobs: they could not be used as scabs * against the CWA.

Third, though more remote, is a larger threat: the possibility of a single militant union of telephone workers, perhaps nationwide, actually stopping, or more fancifully, seizing, the network of telephone communications. For all these reasons, it is clear, management prefers the present arrangement to a more unified one.

In any event, the union question, normally static, uncharacteristically sprang to life during my stay at the telephone company because at the end of November the CWA opened a raid on the UTW. Its ultimate intention was to begin to assemble all company employees into a unified body. In this plan was a measure of wishful thinking, if not deception. CWA is not so popular within the company and though it recently won an election in the city Plant department (over a teamster-inspired challenge) it has also lost several others (against company unions) in upstate New York and in New England. Nevertheless, consolidation was its chief arguing point: in unity there will be strength.

CWA's problem was that members of the Commercial bargaining unit were spread out in small clusters in dozens of locations throughout New York. Their efforts, however, seemed particularly lackluster and should make New Left organizers take heart: the old dogs have no new tricks to teach.

* scabs: strike breakers, workers who cross picket lines to assume the jobs of other striking workers.

They began their campaign in my area by calling an after-work meeting of Commercial Department women in a small working-class bar close by several of the Commercial offices downtown, attempting to lure people there by desultory leafleting the same morning. From my office—that is from among the one hundred Representatives who worked with me—no one came but me, though there was a handful of women from other Commercial units in the same building.

From another office, however, whose function was identical to mine, about forty women came, and in exploring why I discovered subtle differences between offices in the relations between managers and women. It seems that a manager at the other office had just held a meeting with his women in which he complained that they were stretching their breaks too long and cheating on their closed time. They found his remarks threatening and reacted with hostility. I later learned that this office is particularly understaffed and has an intracompany reputation of being one of the more tense places to work. I believe that the ethers of solidarity that float between our manager, Y, and the women in my office would have prevented such an exchange from taking place there.

At the meeting the CWA was represented chiefly by shop stewards who had jobs as installers, switchmen, repairmen, and by one somewhat puffy and intellectualized bureaucrat from the International. The men were plain, decent, and serious, and had an intelligent point to make: if we stood together we would be the stronger for it. CWA dues were higher than UTW's, they admitted, but they paid for real union services: hard bargaining by trained negotiators, grievance procedures, fringe benefits, and so forth; most of the gains made by Commercial employees were the results of CWA pressures elsewhere in the Bell System.

The women's reaction to the sales pitch was pure Gomperism:* what about free dental care, medical checkups, low cost car-purchasing programs? Some issues were raised that were more basic. They were women and they were being raided by men. They would be asked to walk out to support the men. Would the men walk out to support them? Why were there no women in top positions in the union when 45 percent of the members were women? Why did women's salaries in the company start at $79.50 when the lowest amount paid to a man was $95.00?

Back at my office it developed that the women were not nearly so uninterested as their nonattendance had made it seem. Nor were they as anti-union as their lack of interest in the UTW suggested. It was more that they were not meeting-goers, on the one hand, and that they were disgusted by the UTW on the other. A group of women I talked to in the cafeteria one day told me that every time a

---

* Gomperism: Samuel Gompers (1850–1924), conservative labor leader, president of the American Federation of Labor, with one brief intermission, from 1886–1924; Gompers believed that unions should strictly avoid political involvements and organize for practical, "bread and butter" objectives—higher wages, shorter hours, better working conditions.

UTW contract came up for approval, they and others they knew voted "no" but that somehow their votes didn't get counted. They were seriously interested in the CWA alternative, discussed it a great deal among themselves, and began filling out the cards required to petition the NLRB for an election.

The union issue stirred up the most serious conversation I had heard at the company, and, for a time, I had private fantasies about the possibilities involved in a CWA takeover: could the women be made to see their women's interests in some opposition to a male-dominated union, once they were in it, more clearly than they could see them opposed to the company, which was always holding out the carrot of personal advancement? Would the union, simply because it was in motion and in some way organized, because consciousness in it was more free-floating, be the right forum in which to raise war-related issues such as AT&T's involvement with the ABM? Could the racism inherent in the union's opposition to the company's new policies of hiring what it always referred to as the "hard core" possibly be overcome? For a time, these things seemed possible to me. Then management began its counterattack.

By early December management was calling private meetings of Supervisors to feed them anti-CWA propaganda, which they in turn would feed back to the women. Sally came back from such a meeting filled with grisly facts: "The President of CWA makes $35,000 a year," she said; the top officials recently voted themselves a $4–6000 salary raise; top pay in New York is higher than top pay in places represented by CWA; it's true there's a dental plan but you have to use CWA dentists.

The main point of management's message was, if you're dissatisfied, reform the UTW. Is the President too old? Throw her out and get a more modern President. But don't throw away the union that has gotten you eleven paid holidays and all your other gains; don't throw out the baby with the bath. Later these arguments were repeated (almost word for word) in a similar chat which my floor supervisor, Laura, had with the women in her unit. The company also began to engage in all sorts of other activities, turning over the payroll lists to the UTW at an early date for propaganda mailings to the employees' homes, and at one point even circulating a UTW phone number which we were advised to call for "unbiased" information on what the raid was all about. The recorded message went like this:

> This is a message to all Commercial Department employees. Your independent union and all of you are being raided by CWA. They are trying to mislead you into believing that the raid is for the sake of unity. Nothing could be farther from the truth. They want you only for your money. CWA dues run from $5.50 to $10.50 a month to support their Washington fat cat. The dues you pay to your independent union, the Union of Telephone Workers, are not wasted for Washington offices and fat cats. CWA claims to represent a lot of telephone

workers in the United States but not a single contract for Commercial workers can meet your contract for wages. Your independent union, the UTW, has negotiated the highest wage rates for Commercial Department employees, anywhere in the United States.

Your intelligence will caution you not to become a tool of CWA's misleading tactics.

Your desire for effective and orderly representation will caution you against buying CWA's walkout, wildcat strike sellout policies, and the constant loss of wages over ridiculous disputes.

Your experience and knowledge of human nature will keep you from getting fouled up in foolish frustrations and the hopeless fury of CWA's ineffective puppets.

A step toward CWA is a costly step downward: more dues, frequent assessments, loss of autonomy and less take-home pay.

This does not make good sense, does it?

Stay with your independent union, the Union of Telephone Workers.

This propaganda was later multiplied in individual mailings, and I believed it was likely to be effective, particularly when communicated to the women by Supervisors whom they trust. At least in my department (a small fraction of the overall bargaining unit) the women did not have enough class consciousness to suspect it merely because it was coming from the company. In addition, the CWA's rebuttal campaign—conducted through mailings—did not deal solidly with these concrete objections. In the election, held in mid-February, the CWA lost by about seven to two.

My ultimate conclusion about the CWA-UTW issue as I watched it struggling to its finale was that it simply did not matter. Images were left in my head: Dan, a fat CWA chief steward, driving me to an appointment uptown in a car decorated with American flags and an antique Veterans Poppy; a later meeting with him in which he described the company's new employees exclusively as tramps, pushers, and smelly apes; an interview with a union official after I quit in which he sighed and remarked, "The trouble with people today is that they want change for the sake of change." I thought: CWA does inspire something more closely akin to true "consciousness" than the company unions, but the consciousness it inspires is not close enough to what is needed. In view of the top-down control and inflexible ways of the CWA, and the marginal role of any union in the women's lives, the women's immediate interests probably are better represented by the UTW; and the CWA does not offer the compensation of initiating fights for larger political objectives, or even for objectives that have to do with the quality of life within the company. Thus the issues of dues, strike pay, and socialized dentistry become real.

V

Perhaps the best way to think about the women of the telephone company is to ask the question: what reinforces company-minded behavior and what works against it? It is a difficult question. The reinforcement comes not from the work but from the externals of the job: the warmth of friendships, the mutual support, the opportunities for sharing and for gossip, the general atmosphere of company benevolence and paternalism; not to mention the need for money and the very human desire to do a good job.

I never heard any of the women mouth the company rhetoric about "service to the customer" but it was obvious to me that a well-handled contact could be satisfying in some way. You are the only person who has access to what the customer needs—namely, telephones—and if you can provide him with what he wants, on time and efficiently, you might reasonably feel satisfied about it. The mutual support—the sharing of closed time, helping one another out on commitments—is also very real. The continual raffles, sales contests, gimmicks, and parties are part of it, too. They simply make you feel part of a natural stream.

Working in that job one does not see oneself as a victim of "Capitalism." One is simply part of a busy little world which has its own pleasures and satisfactions as well as its own frustrations but, most important, it is a world, with a shape and an integrity all its own. The pattern of co-optation, in other words, rests on details: hundreds of trivial, but human, details.

What is on the other side? Everyone's consciousness of the iron fist, though what they usually see is the velvet glove; the deadening nature of the work; the low pay; what is going on in the outside world (to the extent that they are aware of it); the malfunctioning of the company; the pressure of supervision and observation. There was a sign that sat on the desk of one of the women while I was there, a Coney Island joke-machine sign: "Due to Lack of Interest, Tomorrow Will be Postponed." For a time I took it as an emblem and believed that was how the woman really felt. But now I am not sure.

I think that for these women to move they would have to have a sense of the possibility of change—not even to mention the desirability of change—which I am certain they do not feel. They are more satisfied with their lives than not, and to the extent that they are not, they cannot see even the dimmest possibility of remedial action through collective political effort. The reason they do not have "class consciousness"—the magic ingredient—is that in fact they are middle class. If they feel oppressed by their situation, and I think many of them do, they certainly see it only as an individual problem, not as something which it is their human right to avoid or overcome.

How one would begin to change that, to free them to live more human lives, is very hard to know. Clearly it would require a total transformation of the way they think about the world and about themselves. What is impossible to know is whether the seeds of that transformation lie close beneath the surface and are accessible, or whether they are impossibly buried beyond rescue short of general social convulsion. It is hard to believe that the women are as untouched as they seem by the social pressures which seem so tangible to radicals. Yet I saw little evidence that would make any other conclusion possible.

I have a strong feeling of bad faith to have written this at all. I know the women will not recognize themselves in my account, but will nonetheless be hurt by it. They were, after all, warm and friendly: sympathetic about my troubles, my frustrations; helpful in the work; cheerful in a businesslike way. Betty, at least, was a friend. It is almost as if a breach of the paternalism of the company is involved. I fear a phone call asking "Was that a nice thing to do?" and I would say, perhaps not, perhaps the intellectual and political values of my life by which I was judging yours make equally little sense. Perhaps the skills which give me leverage to do it allow me only to express alienation and not to overcome it; perhaps I should merely be thankful that I was raised as an alpha and not a beta. Sometimes I am not sure. But I know that however it will seem to them, this piece is meant to be for the women of the telephone company, and that it is written for them with both love and hope.

Epilogue

It is fitting that the Epilogue to this collection should be in substance a prologue to future history. The main divisions of the book, beginning with "Images of Childhood" and ending with "Science and Technology," are in a sequence designed to suggest how the interest of human beings, beginning in their earliest, formative stages, expands gradually outward to a concern for their fellows, to the learning of skills by which they can together make sense of the world, to a study of their capacities, their customs, their modes of communication, and the larger dimensions of the universe. Moving ever beyond the self as it is bound by exigencies of time and space, men and women inevitably become inquisitive about that future time and space which they may not themselves inhabit but which is even now being shaped for their distant offspring. In our imaginations, at least, we accept responsibility for the evolutionary success of our species and of the world it continues to help create.

In the statement by Buckminster Fuller and in John Donat's interview with him, there is a bumptious and irresistible excitement about the measures which might transform the imagination of the future into a course of present action. The question of whether man will or will not prove a success on "spaceship earth" is an environmental one which will out of necessity be answered fairly soon. Indeed, it might be decided before the year 2000, toward which Erik Erikson looks in asking some cultural and psychological questions about what youth might be like at the beginning of the next millennium. While by no means pessimistic, Erikson has measurably less zestful optimism than Fuller. Understandably so. Redesigning the world, as Fuller himself suggests, is perhaps easier than reforming man, and the results may even remove some of the pressures that make men behave as they now do. Being themselves men of great distinction and of an age nearly equivalent to the span of this century, Fuller and Erikson show, as we hope this book has also shown, that finally no questions are too large or too basic for those who want to create a better future, and that the surest bridge to it is in learning how to ask and answer such questions.

Buckminster Fuller / What I Am Trying To Do

Buckminster Fuller, when asked by "Who's Who" last year to write a one-sentence statement of his life objectives on the model of Tocqueville's 152-word "aphoristic declaration," in characteristic fashion wrote the following declaration about himself:

Acutely aware of our beings' limitations and acknowledging the infinite mystery of the a priori universe into which we are born but nevertheless searching for a conscious means of hopefully competent participation by humanity in its own evolutionary trending while employing only the unique advantages inhering exclusively to the individual who takes and maintains the economic initiative in the face of the formidable physical capital and credit advantages of the massive corporations and political states and deliberately avoiding political ties and tactics while endeavoring by experiments and explorations to excite individuals' awareness and realization of humanity's higher potentials I seek through comprehensive anticipatory design science and its reductions to physical practices to reform the environment instead of trying to reform men being intent thereby to accomplish prototyped capabilities of doing more with less whereby in turn the wealth augmenting prospects of such design science regenerations will induce their spontaneous and economically successful industrial proliferation by world around services' managements all of which chain reaction provoking events will both permit and induce all humanity to realize full lasting economic and physical success plus enjoyment of all the Earth without one individual interfering with or being advantaged at the expense of another.

Buckminster Fuller,
Aboard our 1,000-miles-per-minute speeding
spaceship Earth within the outer reaches of the cosmically
spiraling and expanding Milky Way,
the Galactic Nebula.

Modified from 152 to 200 words at the
location on spaceship Earth where the first man-made
atomic explosion occurred: Alamogordo.

John Donat / Buckminster Fuller

Buckminster Fuller is a sort of mystical engineer, and his theory and practice depend on a full understanding of the resources of the modern world and mind. He is a tireless propagandist for his own doctrines, and most people think of him in terms of what he says rather than in terms of what he writes. That is why we have chosen to represent him by this radio script, in which the British architect John Donat pieces together various recorded statements by Fuller with his own explanatory paragraphs. The peculiar rather folksy manner, the startling paradoxes and slogans, belong to an oral and not a literary style. Fuller, in the opinion of a growing number of people, is our most original and practical thinker. He presents a great paradox in that he sees the salvation of man in rational technology and takes a highly optimistic view of the possibilities of future human life on earth. That his inventions, all related to a basic uniform theory, actually work and that many of his predictions have already been fulfilled lends credibility to what he says and also justifies the confidence and individuality of the rhetoric. (The summary statement reprinted above is a highly characteristic Fuller device.) His physics and metaphysics are clearly expounded in Donat's article. Donat complains that Fuller is occasionally obscure or gnomic, but to have found for ideas so radical and unfamiliar a means of expression so intelligible and so engaging is no mean achievement in communication. The world Fuller so hopefully projects may have a new rhetoric to match its technology, and it is not impossible that he will have contributed to its development.

BUCKMINSTER FULLER: I just say to all of you: "Hullo, astronauts." You're all astronauts. I'm sure you are not thinking of yourselves as astronauts or you wouldn't have the word for somebody else. But you're all astronauts, you never have been anything else. You've just got to catch on that *you're all astronauts*. It's a very small little ship we've got here; it's superbly equipped and every part of it is reciprocal; there are no labels on it which say any thing belongs to anybody. Everything that's there is to regenerate all of life.

That was Richard Buckminster Fuller in full flight during one of his legendary discourses, which last on average about three hours. His subject-matter can cover anything from the colour question to student unrest—world resources, the geometry of thought, the ecology of man, politics, design, or whatever

Elliott Erwitt, Magnum

happens to be coursing through his mind at the time. Buckminster Fuller, known universally as "Bucky," defies categorisation. The list of his achievements is almost as endless as are his discourses. Part scientist, engineer, mathematician, philosopher, cartographer, he is not formally qualified as anything. He describes himself as a comprehensive designer and has only one idea at the back of his mind—to make the world work. He's a short, compact little man. *Time* magazine described him as having the shape of a milk bottle and a mind like a roll-top desk. His domed head is polished and brown, his eyes are magnified through powerful glasses. When he begins to speak he clasps his hands together as though in prayer, closes his eyes and tentatively seeks out a point of contact with his audience. After the slow beginning his words gather an irresistible momentum, throwing out ideas expressed in torrents of homemade technical jargon, like sparks from a Catherine-wheel. You feel a bit like a proton being bombarded in an electron accelerating chamber. The only thing to do is to let the verbal Niagara wash over you. After two or three hours there's generally a punch-line of truly cosmic proportions.

B.F.: Man, within the next 30 years, will become a total physical success on earth or he'll blow himself to bits. There will be no more men. That's how abrupt the future is. And if he blows himself to bits there'll be none of us here to mark the record. But if he is successful within the 30 years, you may begin to remember this kind of pattern: how do we get from here to making man really a physical success as a sort of a total world man? Sir, should I stop?

But no one has ever stopped him. Bucky is unstoppable. The keystone of his philosophy is to make man a success—at least physically—by doing more with less: a principle he seems to be incapable of applying to his legendary verbal outpourings. He was born in 1895 in Milton, Massachusetts, and spent boyhood summers on a family island, surrounded by the rational and inventive technology of the sea. Experience was his teacher where orthodox education failed. He was sent down from Harvard twice for general irresponsibility and lack of sustained interest. After various jobs he joined the Navy in 1917 and became one of the few midshipmen to qualify for training in comprehensive naval strategy. In an era of intense specialisation he found himself a student of a vast co-ordinated enterprise, commanding the latest scientific discoveries, backed up by massive industry, and exquisitely organised to get the highest possible performance out of its resources. This experience had a profound effect on his future thinking, particularly when after the war he went into the building business with his father-in-law and had five years' experience of what he has described as "the most ignorant and most prodigious of men's fumbling activities." He said: "It made me realise that craft-building was an art that belonged to the Middle Ages." Then, in 1922, his daughter died of three epidemic illnesses in succession. This acute personal tragedy, coupled with his disillusionment with the building business, led to a crisis. He resolved to stop earning a living. He wanted to explore and harvest his industrial, scientific and social experience, convinced through the work he did in the Navy that comprehensive design science, applying total scientific and industrial potential to the art of living, could make man a success instead of an inherent failure.

B.F.: In 1927 I gave up for ever what I felt was a fallacy of most of my contemporaries—in fact, it seemed to me of all my contemporaries. They all said: "I have to earn a living." And that had highest priority in what they were studying at school. The phrase "earning a living" I thought was wrong. The words really meant you had to prove your right to live; you had to prove that you were worth living; in the face of Darwin and Malthus,* there was nowhere near enough to go round, and survival only of the fittest. And I felt that all this was wrong, so I said in 1927: I'm going to give up for ever this concept of proving my right to live. I'm going to find out what it is that I've experienced, that I see needs to be done, that nobody else is attending to and that my experience tells me I know how to solve. Most people were attending to very narrow things; therefore it forced me to concentrate on big things, and employ the biggest pattern-comprehending capability with which we are all born.

Fuller is a product of that American anarchy that maintains the myth of individualism in an admass society, and selects for its heroes men who stand alone. Bucky has spent his whole life proving to an unreceptive world that his ideas will work: a Lone Ranger dispensing justice where the law has failed. He blamed substandard wartime housing for the influenza, polio and spinal meningitis that killed his daughter and were epidemic during the war. And this focused his mind on the problem of shelter. A house to Bucky is an environment control, whether the environment be Arctic or tropical. Houses, he wrote, "haven't changed in any fundamental way for thousands of years. Modern architecture is just so many fancy nozzles on the invisible sewer system." Design, like preventive medicine, had to anticipate future needs. Anything based on the needs of today was doomed to immediate obsolescence. It takes society at least 25 years to take advantage of any significant new idea. This prediction was absolutely right. He patiently endured massive inertia and resistance during nearly three decades of thinking, planning and designing. He lived on the knife-edge of poverty in a wilderness of rejection.

This was the era of his blind date with principle—an era in which he was prolifically inventive. He coined a word, *dymaxion*—a contraction of *dynamic, maximum* and *ion*—denoting maximum gain from minimum energy input. Or, as he now puts it more simply, "more-with-lessing." World housing could not be solved by an obsolete craft industry. It needed an industrial po-

* T. R. Malthus: (1766–1834), English economist; his *Essay on the Principle of Population* (1798 and 1803) argues that population naturally tends to increase faster than the means of subsistence.

tential comparable with ship-building and aircraft and motor manufacture. He designed his dymaxion house with this mass-production potential in mind. The floors were suspended from a central mast which contained all plumbing, lighting and air-conditioning. The interior was enclosed in vacuum double-glazing and the house was supplied fully equipped with household mechanisms that were then thought to be wildly impractical but have since come into general use, like automatic laundry and dish-washing, compressed air, and vacuum points for cleaning and dusting, and so on. The study was equipped for radio (and anticipated TV), typewriter, calculating machine and mimeograph, all housed in revolving book-shelves. The whole house was packaged for air-delivery anywhere in the world. It could be erected on site in one day and weighed only 1 per cent of traditional construction.

This was in 1927—the same year that Le Corbusier, Mies van der Rohe and Walter Gropius * were building the Weissenhof Siedlung in Stuttgart, modern architecture emerging in its new orthodox uniform. They were talking about machines for living in and the great new industrialisation. But the dymaxion house really was a machine for living in. It was also an indictment of modern architecture's technical obsolescence. There was one rather nice touch. In Bucky's model of the dymaxion house was a nude girl. Well, presumably clothes are an environment control and if you live in a perfect environment control there's no need to wear any clothes. The dymaxion house was followed by his experimental dymaxion car, then an industrialised dymaxion bathroom, and a brilliant new projection of a world map.

Bucky's own self-education through experience made him severely critical of orthodox education, which, he says, shuts off the valves a child is born with—an artist is a child who has refused to have his valves shut off.

B.F.: It is my conviction, from having watched a great many babies grow up, that all of humanity is born a genius and then becomes de-geniused very rapidly by unfavourable circumstances and by the frustration of all their extraordinary built-in capabilities. Everybody's specialised now. We couldn't be getting ourselves into worse trouble since we also learn that all the biological species became extinct because they over-specialised. So over-specialisation's the way to extinction, and society's all tied up with specialisation. Everybody's born to be a comprehensivist. If nature wants to develop a specialist, she does, and if nature wanted you to be a specialist, she'd have you born with one eye and a microscope fastened onto it.

Experience taught him that nature always works in the quickest, most direct

---

* Le Corbusier, Mies van der Rohe, Gropius: developed the so-called International Modern style of architecture and were members of the German Werkbund, a group of architects, artists, industrialists, and workmen collaborating in order to produce high-quality goods of aesthetic value; the Weissenhof settlement, an international and cooperative building enterprise, was fostered by the Werkbund.

and most economical way. In school, he was taught as though nature was divided into different departments—maths, physics, chemistry and so forth—but he strenuously questioned everything he was taught.

His own researches convinced him that nature might employ a system that was universal—and led to his discovery of what he calls "energetic geometry" and his confident assertion that he has discovered "nature's co-ordinate system for all her fundamental formulations." The key invention that emerged from these speculations was the geodesic dome—simply described as a sphere, or part of a sphere, made up of a triangulated web of short struts. He developed the geodesic principle with countless experimental structures designed with the enthusiastic support of students at American and other universities: structures that were exceptionally light but incredibly strong, and had an intrinsic natural beauty in place of designed aesthetics. The break-through came in the Fifties: Bucky's patient years of waiting for a reluctant world to catch up with him were coming to an end. In 1953, Ford, Mr. Industry himself, commissioned the first geodesic dome. Its immediate success, despite the reluctance of Ford executives from the start, led to a series of industrial applications, and within six years 1,000 Bucky domes had been made for government and industry: domes for emergency shelter for the US Marines, domes for warehouses, domes for the early-warning radar installations on the Dew Line. These were big enough to contain a three-storey house, strong enough to withstand hurricanes. They were erected under Arctic conditions by unskilled Eskimo labour in 14 hours. One was brought for exhibition in the Museum of Modern Art in New York. It took skilled union labour a month to put up. There were domes for the US Information Trade Fairs that were flown by air from Kabul to Bangkok, Tokyo, Osaka and round the world. Kaiser Aluminium commissioned a concert-hall that was manufactured in California and shipped to Hawaii, where it was erected in 20 hours. Kaiser himself flew out to watch it go up, but by the time he got there, the first concert was already over. A cardboard dome (nicknamed Kleenex by the Marines) won the *grande première* award at the Milan Triennale in 1954. By now, 4,000 domes have been built in 40 countries. It looks as if Bucky has just turned himself into a super dome salesman, but he insists that his dome was simply one consequence of his philosophy and not an end in itself.

B.F.: Quite clearly I am, to myself, not a dome salesman. In fact I don't want to be a salesman of anything. I don't want to persuade anybody to do anything that is illogical and anti-evolutionary. I'm identified with the dome only because, back in 1927, in trying to seek out how I might be able to affect and help man most, I said: if I could only protect younger life while it still has its comprehensive interest in the total universe and give it a chance to develop its faculties for comprehending the whole—it would be a way in which we might most rapidly arrive at a condition where all of humanity might be a success. So, I said, this means a controlled environment, and I kept searching for ways not only of controlling it, but of using the chemistry around us in our environment so effectively that there would be enough to go round to take care of everybody and not just a few. All this brought me into very deep study of all that science was doing and all forms of industrialisation, and how we could produce the most with the least. This meant then that I went into a series of experiments in how to control the environment, and it was the geodesic dome that was the practical break-through. The geodesic domes were the beginning of the public's realisation of what I'm talking about; therefore I became identified as the dome man. But I think I've made it quite clear that this was simply the inadvertent consequence of my concern with young life and protecting that young life.

One of Bucky's catch-phrases is "emergence through emergency." His structures were first employed when orthodox solutions had failed—he had anticipated a need and provided a solution ready and waiting for society to pick up when the time was ripe. During the Thirties he wrote a book called *Nine Chains to the Moon* which contained everything fundamental to his philosophy. As a young man he was tremendously excited by Einstein's Theory of Relativity and he devoted three chapters of his book to Einstein. The first chapter dealt with his philosophic conceptions, the second with the way he translated them into mathematical formulations. For the third chapter Bucky argued as follows: Einstein as an individual thinker paces the rest of science; science paces technology; technology paces economics; economics paces everyday affairs. So if Einstein is right, he must eventually affect our everyday lives. He called his third chapter "$E = MC^2 = $ Mrs. Murphy's Horsepower."

B.F.: When my manuscript went to the publishers, they sent it back to me and they said: "We're very sorry but you're not on the list of the men who understand Einstein. You must be an imposter." I felt stung. I didn't know too much but I was very earnest in my attempts. I didn't feel like an imposter, and so I had a happy idea and I sent it back and said: "Why don't you send the typescript to Dr. Einstein? See what he says." A great deal of time went by, and I'd really forgotten about it, when suddenly I received a telephone call from a doctor in New York who said Dr. Einstein was coming in from Princeton to spend a weekend with him, and he said: "He has your typescript and he would like to talk with you about it." So I was very excited and I went in and met him and he took me off to a side-room and he opened the manuscript and was thumbing it through. He said: "I approve of your interpretation of my thinking, my philosophy, and I approve of your explanation of how it's translated into mathematical formulations; but, young man, this next chapter," he said, "you amaze me. I cannot conceive of anything I have ever done having the slightest practical application." Really, it burned in my mind. Then out of that came the atomic bomb, and can you imagine the feelings of Einstein, a man who had said: "I have never thought of anything I've ever done having the slightest practical application."

The chilling accuracy of Bucky's prediction about relativity is paralleled by other predictions, validated by time. He indicated the great circle air routes on his One Town World plan of 1927, five years before they appeared on any map, many more before they became the regular flight-paths of international airlines. He predicted a new system of wealth-accounting that can already be seen developing in an infantile form in America's credit-card society. Not an accredited scientist himself, he found that scientists, working in nuclear physics, molecular biology, microscopic organisms, cell and virus behaviour, were coming to him with a whole family of related structures in remarkable congruence to his own experimental ideas. Someone has even suggested that in his geodesic principle, Bucky has taken out a patent on nature! After spending more than half his life earning what he ruefully describes as "negative income," his patents have earned something like two million dollars during the past ten years—and most of it has vanished into the coffers of the US tax collector.

B.F.: I'm just going to throw in some figures I find very startling. Have any of you any idea about the weight of air? Do you have any feelings about the weight of air? I have a 100-foot sphere full of air, ten storeys high. Somebody tell me quickly the weight of air in a 100-foot-diameter sphere. Everybody averages about three pounds of food a day; some way overdo that. We take on also about eight pounds of water and every one of you breathes and combines with that food and water 84 pounds of air a day. This is your really big food. I think it's simply astonishing. The sphere full of air—there's seven tons of air in it. Air weighs plenty.

Bucky observed that man's success depended on his ability, as he put it, to externalise his functions. He saw externalised tools, in the McLuhan sense, as extensions of man.

B.F.: More than a third of a century ago I became intuitively excited by the idea that, whereas I had been brought up in a world in which humanity spoke about the tools it used and the machinery of the new industrialisation as *artificial,* these artefacts and tools, if seen from far enough away in time, might be realised to be an actual and integral part of the pattern Man. So I began to feel that the word "artificial," which I'd heard so much of, was a word that was obsolete and could be discarded. I saw that everything I was experiencing couldn't be experienced unless nature permitted it, and it was all part of the extraordinary pattern of the universe, and therefore every bit of it was, I might say, not artificial but natural. As soon as I began to look at man in that way, I began to realise that men were really very large and I made some research as to how much our various tools were being employed relative to the total population. In America in 1936 I found that every American weighed nine tons of steel and 22 tons of concrete and 140 pounds of copper and so forth. This is the relative amount of externalised tooling, *per capita*. Man is really larger than the dinosaur, larger than the mammoth, but the dinosaur and the mammoth became obsolete simply because they tried to run all their tools around integrally: the dinosaur was pulling a great big one-ton tail along, with the idea that once in a while it could knock down a banana with it. So that man was uniquely successful, by virtue of this grand strategy of differentiating out his functions, and developing interchangeable functions.

Another observation was that man was the only species to have altered his own ecological patterning. Man was born as a walking invention, but his ships, railways, automobiles, aeroplanes and space capsules enormously increased the range of individual mobility. Society, in all its official undertakings, still assumes that the good citizen stays at home, but Bucky points out that the more responsibility you have, the more mobility you begin to demonstrate.

B.F.: I find that our society hasn't really caught up with this at all. In America today, the politicians representing the people in the democracy represent them on a fixed geographical basis, on the assumption that a responsible man stays put. However, in the last two censuses taken, the first showed that every year 20 per cent of America moves out of town: this is to say, every five years America moves out of town. The last census figures, which are just really getting analysed in America, show that America is now moving out of town every three years. This means that between these last two censuses something very important happened, because if you have to be represented on a geographical basis, practically nobody's going to be at home any more. In our last general election, 10 per cent of those who were entitled to vote could not vote because they'd not had residence in a new place long enough. And the rate of this change is such that within two more elections, nobody in America is going to be able to vote.

One of the things Fuller learned in his training as a midshipman in the Navy was to stretch his mind by asking larger and larger questions—like a weightlifter stretching his muscles by lifting larger and larger weights. What is the difference between mind and brain? What do you mean by thinking? And, ultimately, what do you mean by universe? He can persuade you that thought is spherical, or that the minimum subdivision of the universe is a tetrahedron; that brain is physical, mind metaphysical. He says, man is a conceptual machine, not a muscle machine, and therefore—in a typically outrageous Bucky generalisation—Marx's concept of the worker is obsolete. Here he is on a typical mind-stretching exercise.

B.F.: I've been asking some large questions—when you are a generalist you learn to look towards big patterns—and I ask myself the question, "Does man have a function in the universe?" and I am now confident that we can discover that man does have a function in the universe. And we discover his function in the universe in the following manner. Our nuclear physicists have now disclosed to us that every fundamental patterning in relation to the atom and its nucleus, every energy behaviour, has its opposite. The electron has its positron, the neutron its proton, and so forth. But having discovered in our physical experiments several centuries ago regarding energy, that every local system loses energy, we have the scientists in our own era discovering that the energies are always accountable. The energies do not get out of the universe. Energy is finite. We have, however, all the local systems that are continually giving off energies: as they give them off all in continual transformation and all in great motions, the giving off is in a very diffuse way, so that it's considered disorderly, and it's called by the mathematicians Law of Increase of the Random Element. So we have a physical universe which is locally everywhere becoming more and more disorderly. There must, by my inference of what scientists have found out about fundamental structure, be some kind of complementarity to this coming apart in a disorderly way. Because, by coming apart in this disorderly way, it of course takes up more room. Therefore it's an expanding universe and it becomes inferred that there must be some phase of the universe where phenomena are contracting and becoming increasingly orderly. And if we look for that, we see that all the stars which are observable are light objects, and therefore they represent that energy being given off in a diffuse and disorderly way. And we look for some black body where energy may be collected. We only find one that we know anything about and that's our spaceship, Earth. Our spaceship Earth we discovered in the Geophysical Year is receiving approximately 100,000 tons of star-dust daily. We're very much increasing our avoirdupois: the universe is collecting here. And we find, then, life being regenerated on our earth. In order to have life regenerated, more energy must be taken on than is given off. And the energies are impounded by the green vegetation on the dry land, which is a quarter of the earth, and by the algae in the sea—this is done by photosynthesis, and photosynthesis is an extraordinary process where beautiful molecules are built; and these beautiful molecules become orderly structures. This is the first transition from this increasing disorderliness, where the disorderliness has been picked up as random radiation and suddenly put into orderly form. In fact all the biologicals are developing beautiful orderly structures. And amongst all the biologicals we find by far the most interesting to us is the human being. We find in the human being, with this drive to apprehend and comprehend and order and sort out and rearrange in more favourable ways, the same fundamental drive towards what we call anti-entropy. And we find the human being to have this capability of the mind over the brain, and find that the brain then is physical and it's weighable, and it dies with the man. But what is unique to each of those lives is its weightless mind. We find that weightless mind, then, metaphysical, and the metaphysical's function apparently is to apprehend, comprehend, the physical disorder and to bring it back towards order.

We have it manifested at this little tiny point in our space travel in the great heavens. And we have Einstein, as intellect, metaphysically taking the measure of the physical and writing the most extraordinarily economical equation that has ever been written, making the most economic statement that has ever been made. I think in 100 years Einstein will be called a great poet of the 20th century. He said the most important things in the most simple way when he wrote his equation $E = MC^2$. We have here, then, intellect as metaphysical taking the measure and mastering the physical. We have nothing in any of our experience to suggest that this is reversible—that energy will ever write equations of intellect. I'm very confident that human beings have this very extraordinary metaphysical function in the universe, and we find that if this is their function, then they are absolutely essential to the universe.

As far as I can see, there's an absolute division between Fuller's worshippers and his detractors. It seems you're either an addict or an allergic. I really can't stand the po-faced * acceptance of every word from the lips of the master which is typical of the Bucky addict, any more than I can stand the critics who accuse him of being a megalomaniac whose naive views won't stand up to a moment's serious consideration. You don't have to swallow it all, hook, line and sinker. I've heard engineers who are scornful of his belief in the uniqueness of his principles—"there's nothing magic about a dome"—and many people are understandably suspicious of the frequently incomprehensible jargon. A favourite phrase of mine, which I still can't understand, is: "The degree of self-deception is proportional to the width of the angle of disagreement."

Undoubtedly he has scored his most resounding success with students. In 1965 he inaugurated the World Design Science Decade. It's no good sitting down on the pavement in negative protest against the way things are run—you must get up and do something about it, he says. What he's hoping to find in the student generation is what he calls Comprehensive Designers, and he looks for them among the architectural students—perhaps the last breed not to fall foul of the cult of specialisation. Comprehensive Designer should in no way be confused with industrial design, which merely replaces invention with superficial fashion. The Comprehensive Designer will be a paragon: a synthesis of artist, inventor, mechanic, economist and strategist. He will undertake a programme to integrate world resources, employing total science and total industry. This, says Bucky, is the Design Revolution.

B.F.: The revolutionaries are the young generation. We might say that they're the generation I often call the Berkeley generation, because they made world news by being in protest. We find that the Berkeley generation were born in the year of Hiroshima. But, most important, they're the first generation of humanity to grow up with television. We find that this generation has listened to television 1,000 hours a year. They hear television more than they do their own parents; their own parents come home and say, we had an awful time in the shoe store today, let's have a beer; and the children go back to the third

---

* po-faced: solemn.

parent, which is television, which tells them about the whole world, not about the shoe store. And the third parent tells them not only about the whole world but about all the inventions that are going on that are infinite. You can go around under the polar ice in a nuclear submarine, and you can get all the way to the other side of the Moon. The third parent has convinced the young world of all of humanity and not just the local family, and the compassion of young life is for all humanity. So they're the first generation to grow up without a bias, and the first generation to grow up with a conviction that man can do anything he needs to do, that he could make his world work.

Making the world work is a design problem, not a political problem, Bucky insists. All political systems arise because there is not enough to go round. They are predicated on the idea that it's You *or* Me. Politicians can only re-deal the unequal cards between the underfed and the overfed.

B.F.: The way we're now using our resources is so inadequate as to make it impossible for any politician really to do anything but take it away from the other guy and give it to this man. Now all the resources of the earth, particularly the metals which give high performance, are engaged in structures and machinery which are operating at full capacity, and can only take care of 46 per cent of humanity. The rate at which we find more metals is not as rapid as the population is growing: therefore the metals for each world-man are continually decreasing. Now I find that this young Berkeley generation is catching on to the fact that you can do more with less. What do you mean by that? You go, in communication, from wire to wire*less*. One communication satellite today, weighing one quarter of a ton, is out-performing the transatlantic cable built with 175,000 tons of copper. This is the more-with-lessing. So I have to count on that young generation to employ the design revolution of doing more with less, by virtue of which you make the resources which are now taking care of the 46 per cent take care of the 100 per cent. And this cannot be commanded by politics: a politician doesn't know about such a thing.

Bucky is convinced that there's enough to go round, and that in spite of the population explosion there's plenty of room: "Everyone in the world could be on Long Island and it would be less crowded than a cocktail party." To those who are frightened of automation, who see in mass-production a future world of appalling monotony created through some ultra-scientific fascism, Bucky is benignly reassuring: "The game is as wide open as the game of universe played by the Almighty. Nature uses simple aggregates such as cells, made with magnificent economy and mechanical efficiency, and she can put them together to come out as rock, tree or Twiggy. Why should we be afraid to emulate her example?" The idea of ardent young world-designing artist technocrats may now raise a smile, but within a generation, with 15 billion people to feed, clothe and shelter, we may be laughing on the other side of our faces—if we're still around to appreciate it. Bucky offers a typically extreme alternative between Utopia and Oblivion.

B.F.: If man is going to stay on board our spaceship Earth, it's going to be decided within the next decade. We're so close to the point of no return, to that pollution where there's no way that you can ever clean up the sky. But most of the young world is beginning to be convinced that this thing we've been talking about now for about ten years—the design revolution—is the only way out. If you really want to make your world work and you don't want to be a hypocrite, if you don't just like the idea of being a political leader, if you're really convinced you don't want war, the only way you're going to have no war is by having enough to go round, and that can only be accomplished by the design revolution. I find an increasing number of the young people suddenly discovering this is so, and this is the great new commitment.

Bucky's infectious optimism is welcome in a cynical world. I remember once he said that when Huxley started to write *Brave New World* there were two books he could have written—and he wrote the wrong one!

B.F.: I think we're in a moment of an extraordinary transfer of man from being a subconscious game-playing success on that little spaceship into man now discovering it really is a spaceship and having to behave appropriately. That is, for the first time in the history of man, man is about to have to take intellectual responsibility in the evolutionary success of man in the universe.

Erik H. Erikson / Youth Today and the Year 2000

One of the difficulties of prediction is that it has to be carried out in a terminology which the future will invalidate. Thus, any question of what "youth" will be like in the next century can't even be considered until other questions having to do with our language have been answered: Will the term "youth" refer in the year 2000 even to the same age group now designated by it? Will the "youth" of that era be conditioned by the same environmental pressures that help shape the identity of what is now called "youth"? Only when we face such knotty questions can we begin to know of what we are speaking when we get to bigger ones.

In dealing with the subject of his essay, Erikson finds it necessary to clear up some of the linguistic confusions that beset it and him. His answers to the questions posed by *Daedalus* magazine are therefore only implicitly a defense of today's youth. In fact, they are sometimes a criticism. More precisely, Erikson's answers are meant to correct certain misapprehensions that invest the whole issue of generational differences, generational changes, and the emergence of new patterns among the various age groups. The special contribution of youth now is that they manifest an impatience, felt also by many older people and notably by Erikson, with the use of outdated terms for new or emerging phenomena. These phenomena are by no means the exclusive property or problem of any particular generation. They have to do rather with new forms of energy, new modes of communication, the evolution of new social or learned hierarchies, and a changed conception of the aging process and of maturity. All of these are a consequence of technological and historical developments for which no one generation is responsible and to which all of them are, to different degrees, susceptible.

Erikson predicts some polarizations within the group called "youth" which are similar to those already separating "youth" from older groups. It is hoped that these tensions will be energizing and creative. They could be destructive unless each side—Erikson speaks of "technological and humanist identities"—helps bring the other to a more imaginative self-consciousness. Erikson's own humane scrupulousness of inquiry and his attempt to set the matter of generations into the perspective of a semantic as well as a historical problem is an example of the kind of effort necessary to make possible a liveable future for people of all ages.

"Hedonistic" perversity will soon
lose much of its attractiveness. . . . but
there may . . . be no predictable society to
"come back to."

I

ERIK H. ERIKSON: In responding to the inquiry of the Commission on the Year 2000, I will take the liberty of quoting the statements put to me in order to reflect on some of the stereotyped thinking about youth that has become representative of us, the older generation. This . . . is prognostically as important as the behavior of the young people themselves; for youth is, after all, a *generational phenomenon,* even though its problems are now treated as those of an outlandish tribe descended on us from Mars. The actions of young people are always in part and by necessity reactions to the stereotypes held up to them by their elders. To understand this becomes especially important in our time when the so-called communications media, far from merely mediating, interpose themselves between the generations as manufacturers of stereotypes, often forcing youth to live out the caricatures of the images that at first they had only "projected" in experimental fashion. Much will depend on what we do about this. In spite of our pretensions of being able to study the youth of today with the eyes of detached naturalists, we are helping to make youth in the year 2000 what it will be by the kinds of questions we now ask. So I will point out the ideological beams in our eyes as I attempt to put into words what I see ahead. . . .

DAEDALUS: I would assume that adolescents today and tomorrow are struggling to define new modes of conduct which are relevant to their lives.

E.H.E.: Young people of a questioning bent have always done this. But more than any young generation before and with less reliance on a meaningful choice of traditional world images, the youth of today is forced to ask what is *universally relevant* in human life in this technological age at this junction of history. Even some of the most faddish, neurotic, delinquent preoccupation with "their" lives is a symptom of this fact.

DAEDALUS: Yet, this is within the context of two culture factors which seem to be extraordinary in the history of moral temper. One is the scepticism of all authority, the refusal to define natural authority (perhaps even that of paternal authority) and a cast of mind which is essentially anti-institutional and even antinomian.

E.H.E.: I do not believe that even in the minority of youths to whom this statement is at all applicable there is a scepticism of *all* authority. There is an abiding mistrust of people who act authoritatively without authentic authority or refuse to assume the authority that is theirs by right and necessity. Paternal authority? Oh, yes—pompous fathers have been exposed everywhere by the world wars and the revolutions. It is interesting, though, that the word *paternal* is used rather than *parental;* for authority, while less paternal, may not slip altogether from the parent generation, insofar as a better balance of maternal and paternal authority may evolve from a changing position of women.

As a teacher, I am more impressed with our varying incapacity to own up to the almost oppressive authority we really do have in the minds of the young than in the alleged scepticism of *all* authority in the young. Their scepticism, even in its most cynical and violent forms, often seems to express a good sense for what true authority is, or should be, or yet could be. If they refuse "to define natural authority," are they not right if they indicate by all the overt, mocking, and challenging kinds of "alienation" that it is up to *us* to help them define it, or rather redefine it, since we have undermined it—and feel mighty guilty?

As to the essentially anti-institutional cast of mind, one must ask what alternative is here rejected. It appears that the majority of young people are, in fact, all too needy for, trusting in, and conforming to present institutions, organizations, parties, industrial complexes, super-machineries—and this because true personal authority is waning. Even the anti-institutional minority (whom we know better and who are apt to know our writings) seem to me to plead with existing institutions for permission to rebel—just as in private they often seem to plead with their parents to love them doubly for [being rejected by] them. And are they not remarkably eager for old and new uniforms (a kind of uniformity of nonconformity), for public rituals, and for a collective style of individual isolation? Within this minority, however, as well as in the majority, there are great numbers who are deeply interested in and responsive to a more concerted critique of institutions from a newer and more adequate ethical point of view than we can offer them.

DAEDALUS: The second factor is an extraordinary hedonism—using the word in the broadest sense—in that there is a desacralization of life and an attitude that all experience is permissible and even desirable.

E.H.E.: Again, the word *hedonism* illustrates the way in which we use outdated terms for entirely new phenomena. Although many young people entertain a greater variety of sensual and sexual experiences than their parents did, I see in their pleasure seeking relatively little relaxed joy and often compulsive and addictive search for *relevant* experience. And here we should admit that our generation and our heritage made "all" experience relative by opening it to ruthless inquiry and by assuming that one could pursue radical enlightenment without changing radically or, indeed, changing the coming generations radically. The young have no choice but to experiment with what is left of the "enlightened," "analyzed," and standardized world that we have bequeathed to them.

Yet their search is not for all-permissibility, but for new logical and ethical boundaries. Now only direct experience can offer correctives that our traditional mixture of radical enlightenment and middle-class moralism has failed to provide. I suspect that "hedonistic" perversity will soon lose much of its attractiveness in deed and in print when the available inventory has been experimented with and found only moderately satisfying, once it is permitted. New boundaries will then emerge from new ways of finding out what really counts, for there is much latent affirmation and much overt solidarity in all this search. All you have to do is to see some of these nihilists with babies, and you are less sure of what one of the statements, as yet to be quoted, terms the "Hegelian" certainty that the next generation will be even more alienated.

As for the desacralization of life by the young, it must be obvious that our generation desacralized their lives by (to mention only the intellectual side) naïve scientism, thoughtless scepticism, dilettante political opposition, and irresponsible technical expansion. I find, in fact, more of a search for resacralization in the younger than in the older generation.

DAEDALUS: At the same time society imposes new forms of specialization, of extended training, of new hierarchies and organizations. Thus, one finds an unprecedented divorce between the culture and the society. And, from all indications, such a separation will increase.

E.H.E.: Here, much depends on what one means by the word *imposes*. As I have already indicated, in much of youth new hierarchies and organizations are accepted and welcome. We are apt to forget that young people (if not burdened with their parents' conflicts) have no reason to feel that radical change as such is an imposition. The unprecedented divorce we perceive is between *our* traditional culture . . . and the tasks of *their* society. A new generation growing up with technological and scientific progress may well experience technology and its new modes of thought as the link between a new culture and new forms of society.

DAEDALUS: In this respect, assuming this hypothesis is true, the greatest strains will be on the youth. This particular generation, like its predecessors, may come back to some form of accommodation with the society as it grows older and accepts positions within the society. But the experiences also leave a "cultural deposit" which is cumulative consciousness and—to this extent I am a Hegelian—is irreversible, and the next generation therefore starts from a more advanced position of alienation and detachment.

E.H.E.: Does it make sense that a generation involved in such unprecedented change should "come back to some form of accommodation with the society"? This was the fate of certain rebels and romantics in the past; but there may soon be no predictable society to "come back to," even if coming back were a viable term or image in the minds of youth. Rather, I would expect the majority to be only too willing to overaccommodate to the exploiters of change, and the minority we speak of to feel cast off until their function becomes clearer —with whatever help we can give.

II

E.H.E.: Having somewhat summarily disavowed the statements formulated by others, I would now like to ask a question more in line with my own thinking, and thereby not necessarily more free from sterotypy: Where *are* some of the principal contemporary sources of identity strength? This question leads us from diagnosis to prognosis, for to me a sense of identity (and here the widest connotation of the term will do) includes a sense of anticipated future. The traditional sources of identity strength—economic, racial, national, religious, occupational—are all in the process of allying themselves with a new world-image in which the vision of an anticipated future and, in fact, of a future in a permanent state of planning will take over much of the power of tradition. If I call such sources of identity strength *ideological,* I am using the word again most generally to denote a system of ideas providing a convincing world-image. Such a system each new generation needs—so much so that it cannot wait for it to be tested in advance. I will call the two principal ideological orientations basic to future identities the *technological* and the *humanist* orientations, and I will assume that even the great politico-economic alternatives will be subordinated to them.

I will assume, then, that especially in this country, but increasingly also abroad, masses of young people feel attuned, both by giftedness and by opportunity, to the technological and scientific promises of indefinite progress; and that these promises, if sustained by schooling, imply a new ideological world-image and a new kind of identity for many. As in every past technology and each historical period, there are vast numbers of individuals who can combine the dominant techniques of mastery and domination with their identity development, and *become* what they *do*. They can settle on that *cultural consolidation* that follows shifts in technology and secures what mutual verification and what transitory familiarity lie in doing things together and in doing them right—a rightness proved by the bountiful response of "nature," whether in the form of the prey bagged, the food harvested, the goods produced, the money made, the ideas substantiated, or the technological problems solved.

Each such consolidation, of course, also makes for new kinds of entrenched privileges, enforced sacrifices, institutionalized inequalities, and built-in contradictions that become glaringly obvious to outsiders—those who lack the appropriate gifts and opportunities or have a surplus of not quite appropriate talents. Yet it would be intellectual vindictiveness to overlook the sense of embeddedness and natural flux that each age provides in the midst of the artifacts of organization; how it helps to bring to ascendance some particular type of man and style of perfection; how it permits those thus consolidated to limit their horizon effectively so as *not* to see what might destroy their newly won unity with time and space or expose them to the fear of death—and of killing. Such a consolidation along technological and scientific lines is . . . now taking place. Those young people who feel at home in it can, in fact, go along with their parents and teachers—not too respectfully, to be sure—in a kind of *fraternal identification,* because parents and children can jointly leave it to technology and science to provide a self-perpetuating and self-accelerating way of life. No need is felt to limit expansionist ideals so long as certain old-fashioned rationalizations continue to provide the hope (a hope that has long been an intrinsic part of an American ideology) that in regard to any possible built-in evil in the very nature of super-organizations, appropriate brakes, corrections, and amendments will be invented in the nick of time and without any undue investment of strenuously new principles. While they "work," these super-machineries, organizations, and associations provide a sufficiently adjustable identity for all those who feel actively engaged in and by them.

All of us sense the danger of overaccommodation in this, as in any other consolidation of a new world-image, and maybe the danger *is* greater today. It is the danger that a willful and playful testing of the now limitless range of the technically possible will replace the search for the criteria for the optimal and the ethically permissible, which includes what can be given on from generation to generation. This can only cause subliminal panic, especially where the old decencies will prove glaringly inadequate, and where the threat or the mere possibility of overkill can be denied only with increasing mental strain—a strain, incidentally, which will match the sexual repression of the passing era in unconscious pathogenic power.

It is against this danger, I think, that the nonaccommodators put their very existence "on the line," often in a thoroughly confounding way because the manifestations of alienation and commitment are sometimes indistinguishable. The insistence on the question "to be or not to be" always looks gratuitously strange to the consolidated. If the question of being oneself and of dying one's own death in a world of overkill seems to appear in a more confused and confusing form, it is the ruthless heritage of radical enlightenment that forces some intelligent young people into a seemingly cynical pride, demanding that they be human without illusion, naked without narcissism, loving without idealization, ethical without moral passion, restless without being classifiably neurotic, and political without lying: truly a utopia to end all utopias. What should we call this youth? *Humanist* would seem right if by this we mean a recovery, with new implications, of man as the measure, a man far grimmer and with much less temptation to congratulate himself on his exalted position in the universe, a self-congratulation that has in the past always encouraged more cruel and more thoughtless consolidations. The new humanism ranges from an *existential* insistence that every man *is* an island unto himself to a new kind of humaneness that is more than compassion for stray animals and savages, and a decidedly *humanitarian* activism ready to meet concrete dangers and hardships in the service of assisting the underprivileged anywhere. Maybe *universalist* would cover all this better, if we mean by it an insistence on the widest range of human possibilities—beyond the technological.

But whatever you call it, the universalist orientation, no less than the technological one, is a *cluster* of ideas, images, and aspirations, of hopes, fears, and hates; otherwise, neither could lay claim to the identity development of the young. *Somewhat* like the "hawks" and the "doves," the technologists and the universalists seem almost to belong to different species, living in separate ecologies. "Technological" youth, for example, expects the dominant forces in foreign as well as in domestic matters to work themselves out into some new form of balance of power (or is it an old-fashioned balance of entirely new powers?). It is willing, for the sake of such an expectation, to do a reasonable amount of killing—and of dying. "Humanist" youth, on the other hand, not only opposes unlimited mechanization and regimentation, but also cultivates a sensitive awareness of the humanness of any individual in gunsight range. The two orientations must obviously oppose and repel each other totally; the acceptance of even a part of one could cause an ideological slide in the whole configuration of images and, it follows, in the kind of courage to be—and to die. These two views, therefore, face each other as if the other were *the* enemy, although he may be brother or friend—and, indeed, oneself at a different stage of one's own life, or even in a different mood of the same stage.

Each side, of course, is overly aware of the dangers inherent in the other. In fact, it makes out of the other, in my jargon, a negative identity. I have sketched the danger felt to exist in the technological orientation. On the "humanist" side, there is the danger of a starry-eyed faith in the certainty that if you "mean it," you can move quite monolithic mountains, and of a subsequent total inertia when the mountain moves only a bit at a time or slides right back. This segment of youth lacks as yet the leadership that would replace the loss of revolutionary tradition, or any other tradition of discipline. Then there is the danger of a retreat into all kinds of Beat snobbishness or into parallel private worlds, each with its own artificially expanded consciousness.

III

E.H.E.: As one is apt to do in arguing over diagnosis, I have now overdrawn two "ideal" syndromes so as to consider the prognosis suggested in a further question presented to me:

DAEDALUS: Is it possible that the fabric of traditional authority has been torn so severely in the last decades that the re-establishment of certain earlier forms of convention is all but unlikely?

E.H.E.: . . . I would not expect a future accommodation to be characterized by a "coming back" either to conventions or to old-fashioned movements. Has not every major era in history been characterized by a division into a new class of *power-specialists* (who "know what they are doing") and an intense new group of *universalists* (who "mean what they are saying")? And do not these two poles determine an era's character? The specialists ruthlessly test the limits of power, while the universalists always in remembering man's soul also remember the "poor"—those cut off from the resources of power. What is as yet dormant in that third group, the truly under-privileged, is hard to say, especially if an all-colored anticolonial solidarity that would include our Negro youth should emerge. But it would seem probable that all new revolutionary identities will be drawn into the struggle of the two ideological orientations sketched here, and that nothing could preclude a fruitful [polarization] between these two orientations—provided we survive.

But is not the fact that we are still here already a result of [this] polarization? . . . If our super-technicians had not been able to put warning signals and brakes into the very machinery of armament, certainly our universalists would not have known how to save or how to govern the world. It also seems reasonable to assume that without the apocalyptic warnings of the universalists, the new technocrats might not have been shocked into restraining the power they wield.

What speaks for a fruitful polarization is the probability that a new generation growing up with and in technological and scientific progress as a matter of course will be forced by the daily confrontation with unheard-of practical and theoretical possibilities to entertain radically new modes of thought that may suggest daring innovations in both culture and society. "Humanist" youth, in turn, will find some accommodation with the machine age in which they, of course, already participate in their daily needs and habits. Thus, each group may reach in the other what imagination, sensitivity, or commitment may be ready for activation. I do not mean, however, even to wish that the clarity of opposition of the technological and the humanist identity be blurred, for dynamic interplay needs clear poles.

What, finally, is apt to bring youth of different persuasions together is a change in the generational process itself—an awareness that they share a common fate. Already today the mere division into an older—parent—generation and a younger—adolescing—one is becoming superannuated. Technological change makes it impossible for any traditional way of being older (an age difference suggested by the questions quoted) ever to become again so institutionalized that the younger generation could "accommodate" to it or, indeed, resist it in good old revolutionary fashion. Aging, it is already widely noted, will be (or already is) a quite different experience for those who find themselves rather early occupationally outdated and for those who may have something more lasting to offer. By the same token, young adulthood will be divided into older and younger young adults. The not-too-young and not-too-old specialist will probably move into the position of principal arbiter, that is, for the limited period of the ascendance of his specialty. His power, in many ways, will replace the sanction of tradition or, indeed, of parents.

But the "younger generation," too, will be (or already is) divided more clearly into the older- and the younger-young generation, where the older young will have to take over (and are eager to take over) much of the direction of the conduct of the younger young. Thus, the relative waning of the parents and the emergence of the young adult specialist as the permanent and permanently changing authority are bringing about a shift by which older youth will have to take increasing responsibility for the conduct of younger youth—and older people for the orientation of the specialists and of older youth. By the same token, future religious ethics would be grounded less in the emotions and the imagery of infantile guilt, than in that of mutual responsibility in the fleeting present.

In such change we on our part can orient ourselves and offer orientation only by recognizing and cultivating an age-specific *ethical* capacity in *older* youth, for there are age-specific factors that speak for a differentiation between morality and ethics. The child's conscience tends to be impressed with a moralism which says "no" without giving reasons; in this sense, the infantile super-ego has become a danger to human survival, for suppression in childhood leads to the exploitation of others in adulthood, and moralistic self-denial ends up in the wish to annihilate others. There is also an age-specific ethical capacity in older youth that we should learn to foster. That we, instead, consistently neglect this ethical potential and, in fact, deny it with the moralistic reaction that we traditionally employ toward and against youth (*anti-institutional, hedonistic, desacralizing*) is probably resented much more by young people than our dutiful attempts to keep them in order by prohibition.

At any rate, the ethical questions of the future will be less determined by the influence of the older generation on the younger one than by the interplay of subdivisions in a life scheme in which the whole life span is extended; in which the life stages will be further subdivided; in which new roles for both sexes will emerge in all life stages; and in which a certain margin of free choice and individualized identity will come to be considered the reward for technical inventiveness. In the next decade, youth will force us to help them to develop ethical, affirmative, resacralizing rules of conduct that remain flexibly adjustable to the promises and the dangers of world-wide technology and communication. These developments, of course, include two "things"—one gigantic, one tiny—the irreversible presence of which will have to find acknowledgment in daily life: the Bomb and the Loop. They together will call for everyday decisions involving the sanctity of life and death. Once man has decided not to kill needlessly and not to give birth carelessly, he must try to establish what capacity for living, and for letting live, each generation owes to every child planned to be born—anywhere. . . .